Check out the animations, videos, and activities on your FREE CD-ROM

Chapter 1
- Animation: The Motor Cortex
- Animation: The Sensory Cortex
- Bottom-Up versus Top-Down Approaches
  - Animation: The Object Reversal Task
  - Animation: The Concurrent Discrimination Task

Chapter 2
- The Neuron Structure
  - Animation: The Parts of a Neuron
  - Virtual Reality: The Structure of the Neuron
  - Interactive Puzzle: The Neuron
- Conduction of Information within Neurons
  - Animation: The Action Potential
  - Animation: Na+ Ions
  - Animation: The Resting Potential
  - Animation: Post-Synaptic Potentials

Chapter 3
- Communicating between Neurons
  - Animation: Cholinergic
  - Animation: Release of ACh
  - Animation: AChE Inactivates ACh
  - Animation: AChE Inhibitors
- Psychoactive Drugs
  - Animation: Opiate Narcotics
  - Animation: CNS Depressants
  - Animation: CNS Stimulants
  - Animation: Hallucinogenics

Chapter 4
- Viewing the Brain: Planes of Section
  - Virtual Reality: Head Planes
  - Virtual Reality: Body Planes
  - Interactive Puzzle: The Planes
- Viewing the Brain: Structure and Function
  - Sagittal Section: Right Hemisphere 1
  - Sagittal Section: Right Hemisphere 2
  - Sagittal Section: Right Hemisphere 3

- Virtual Reality: The Brain
- Interactive Puzzle: The Brain
- Viewing the Brain: Cerebral Cortex
  - Left Hemisphere Function 1
  - Left Hemisphere Function 2
  - Sagittal Plane
  - Virtual Reality: The Brain
  - Interactive Puzzle: The Cortex

Chapter 5
- Animation: Josephine Wilson's Brain Scans

Chapter 6
- Animation: The Withdrawal Reflex
- Animation: The Crossed Extensor Reflex
- Video: The Brain Pacemaker

Chapter 7
- Anatomy of the Eye
  - Animation: The Retina
  - Animation: Inverted Vision
  - Virtual Reality: The Eye
  - Interactive Puzzle: The Hearing Process
  - Interactive Somesthetic Experiment

Chapter 8
- Animation: Visual Pathways
- Video: Hearing Loss

Chapter 9
- Video: Classic Conditioning
- Video: Alzheimer's Patient
- Video: Amnesiac Patient
- Video: Attention Deficit Disorder

Chapter 10
- Video: Sleep Cycle
- Stages of Sleep on an EEG
  - Simulation: EEG
  - Animation: Awake

- Animation: Stage 1
- Animation: Stage 2
- Animation: Stage 3
- Animation: Stage 4
- Animation: REM

Chapter 11
- Video: Anorexia Patient—Susan
- Video: Stress and Fat

Chapter 12
- Animation: Menstruation Cycle
- Video: Erectile Dysfunction
- Video: Sex Dysfunction in Women

Chapter 13
- Multiple Choice Quiz: Facial Expressions of Emotion
- Video: Sources of Phobias

Chapter 14
- Simulation: Stress and Health
- Video: Stress and the Brain

Chapter 15
- Major Depressive Disorder
  - Video: Barbara 1
  - Video: Barbara 2
- Bipolar Disorder
  - Video: Mary 1
  - Video: Mary 2
  - Video: Mary 3
- Schizophrenia
  - Video: Common Symptoms of Schizophrenia
  - Video: Etta 1
  - Video: Etta 2

Chapter 16
- Video: Child with Autism
- Video: Brains on Ice

In addition to the above elements, you can review and test yourself using the chapter-specific interactive Recaps, quizzing, and the Interactive Biological Psychology Glossary.

Biological Foundations of Human Behavior

Biological Foundations of Human Behavior

Josephine F. Wilson
Wittenberg University

THOMSON

WADSWORTH

Australia • Canada • Mexico • Singapore • Spain
United Kingdom • United States

THOMSON

WADSWORTH

Psychology Editor: *Vicki Knight*
Developmental Editors: *Kate Barnes and Jim Strandberg*
Assistant Editor: *Dan Moneypenny*
Editorial Assistant: *Monica Sarmiento and Lucy Faridany*
Technology Project Manager: *Darin Derstine*
Marketing Manager: *Lori Grebe*
Director, Marketing Communications: *Margaret Parks*
Marketing Assistant: *Laurel Anderson*
Advertising Project Manager: *Shemika Britt*
Project Manager, Editorial Production: *Kirk Bomont*
Print Buyer: *Jessica Reed*

Permissions Editor: *Marcy Lunetta*
Production Service: *Nancy Shammas*
Text Designer: *Cloyce Wall*
Art Editor: *Kathy Joneson*
Photo Researcher: *Lilli Weiner and Kathleen Olson*
Illustrator: *Precision Graphics*
Cover Designer: *Cheryl Carrington*
Cover Image: *"Condition of Man" by Larisa Fuchs*
Cover Printer: *Transcontinental-Interglobe*
Compositor: *Parkwood Composition*
Printer: *Transcontinental-Interglobe*

Wadsworth/Thomson Learning
10 Davis Drive
Belmont, CA 94002-3098
USA

Asia
Thomson Learning
5 Shenton Way #01-01
UIC Building
Singapore 068808

Australia
Nelson Thomson Learning
102 Dodds Street
South Melbourne, Victoria 3205
Australia

Canada
Nelson Thomson Learning
1120 Birchmount Road
Toronto, Ontario M1K 5G4
Canada

Europe/Middle East/Africa
Thomson Learning
High Holborn House
50/51 Bedford Row
London WC1R 4LR
United Kingdom

Latin America
Thomson Learning
Seneca, 53
Colonia Polanco
11560 Mexico D.F.
Mexico

Spain
Paraninfo Thomson Learning
Calle/Magallanes, 25
28015 Madrid, Spain

For more information about our products, contact us at:
Thomson Learning Academic Resource Center
1-800-423-0563

For permission to use material from this text, contact us by:
Phone: 1-800-730-2214 **Fax:** 1-800-730-2215
Web: http://www.thomsonrights.com

Library of Congress Control Number: 2002106175

ISBN 0-15-507486-5

In gratitude to my mentors,

Mike Cantor,

Stan Schachter,

John Wing,

and Ken Wood,

for their wisdom and support.

About the Author

Josephine F. Wilson was born and raised in upstate New York. At her undergraduate college (SUNY Fredonia), Wilson's professors encouraged and supported her interest in psychology and biology. She pursued graduate study in psychology at Columbia University, where she studied brain stimulation reinforcement, and obesity and eating behavior. She received her Ph.D. in physiological psychology from Columbia University and joined the faculty at Wittenberg University in 1985, receiving the Omicron Delta Kappa Distinguished Teaching Award for New Faculty in 1988 and the Wittenberg University Alumni Association Distinguished Teaching Award in 1993. In 2001, Wilson was appointed to the Paul Luther Keil Chair in Psychology, a newly endowed faculty chair position at Wittenberg. Her ongoing research interests include food intake, eating disorders, alcohol intake, dental anxiety, and sex differences in route learning. Professor Wilson is married to David Wishart and has two sons, Tony and Jacob.

Brief Contents

Chapter 1
Studying the Biological Bases of Behavior 2

Chapter 2
The Building Blocks of the Nervous System 22

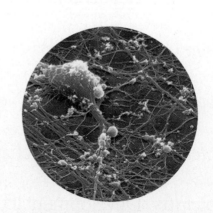

Chapter 3
Chemical Synapses, Neurotransmitters, and Drugs 54

Chapter 4
The Organization of the Nervous System 88

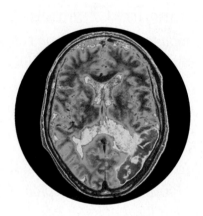

Chapter 5
Neuroscientific Research Methods 118

Chapter 6
Control of Movement 144

Chapter 7
Sensory Processes 172

Chapter 8
Perceptual Processes 212

Chapter 9
Cognitive Processes 248

Chapter 10
Consciousness and Sleep 278

Chapter 11
The Regulation of Motivated Behaviors 308

Chapter 12
Regulation of Sexual Behavior 348

Chapter 13
Biological Bases of Emotion and Addiction 376

Chapter 14
Stress and the Nervous System 408

Chapter 15
Disordered Behavior 442

Chapter 16
Developmental Disorders and Brain Damage 478

Preface

To the student

I have been teaching about the brain and behavior (in classes variously called Physiological Psychology, Biological Psychology, or Behavioral Neuroscience) for over two decades. Most of the students in my classes have been psychology majors or premed students who plan to "work with people" when they graduate from college. That is, most of my students do not become physiological psychologists or neuroscientists, but instead they use the knowledge gained in my course to inform their understanding of the psychological and physical states of the people they work with. I have written a textbook with those students in mind.

If you are one of those students whose career goal involves working with people, you need to know about the organization and function of the nervous system. You probably are not interested in learning about experiments with rats and invertebrates. However, research with nonhuman animals has given us a tremendous amount of information about the basic mechanisms in the brain and other parts of the nervous system. Here we will discuss classic and current studies involving nonhuman animals, with the goal of relating the findings of these studies to human behavior.

Throughout this book, I will relate known brain functions to disease states. We will start by looking at the structure and function of brain cells called neurons. Then we will consider the function of brain structures and groups of neurons. In every instance, I will introduce disorders related to dysfunction of the nervous system. Dysfunctions provide us with a lot of insight into normal brain functioning. You will learn quite a lot about the workings of the brain, based on the behavioral dysfunctions that are evident following damage to particular neurons in the central nervous system. Each chapter has a featured *Case Study* that examines the symptoms of a particular disorder and relates them to underlying biological pathology. Because I conduct research in a hospital setting, I see a lot of patients with intriguing disorders. In the case studies presented in this textbook, I have focused on some of the most interesting and educational cases I've encountered.

In this book, we will consider the wide range of human behaviors and experience. We will examine the role of the nervous system in movement, sensation, and perception. Next we will review research concerning memory, attention, learning, and consciousness, focusing on important new findings in cognitive neuroscience. Behaviors associated with motivational states, such as sleep, temperature, eating, drinking, and sex, will also be discussed. We will conclude our study of the brain and behavior with a focus on emotion, stress, and psychopathology. In every chapter, we will move from a discussion of the normal to a consideration of the abnormal. Although the last chapter focuses almost entirely on brain damage and dysfunction, every chapter in this textbook presents behavioral disorders associated with known neurochemical or brain pathology. Each chapter presents a special box called *For Further Thought* that elaborates a topic or concept of high interest.

I hope as you read this book you will gain a deep appreciation for the research that has contributed to our knowledge of the brain and behavior. I believe you will also come to see that we still have so much to learn about the nervous system and how it affects behavior. This is what I find most exciting about the discipline of biological psychology: every discovery that is made leads to new questions and new discoveries.

If you have questions as you read this book, you should raise them with your course instructor. You can also contact me at my email address (jwilson@ wittenberg.edu). I welcome all questions and comments about this book.

Pedagogical Features

The goal of this textbook is to provide an inviting and accessible introduction to the study of the brain and behavior. The intended audience is the student of behavior who plans to work with people in the near future. The most important pedagogical feature of this book is its clear, inviting prose that students should find engaging and accessible. The topics discussed include classic subjects normally encountered in biological psychology textbooks, as well as cutting-edge topics involving the most current research in brain pathology and psychological disorders.

To enhance learning, each chapter includes the following features:

▶ **Opening Vignette**—an introduction to each chapter designed to stimulate thought and interest in the topics covered in the chapter

▶ **Case Study**—a box that examines the symptoms of a particular disorder and relates them to underlying biological pathology

▶ **For Further Thought**—a box that elaborates a topic or concept of high interest for students

▶ **Margin Glossary**—a list of definitions of key terms in each chapter, found in the margin adjacent to the introduction of each key term

▶ **Recaps**—a chance for the student to review text material and check retention, in fill-in-the-blank format

▶ **Chapter Summary**—an in-depth summary of the important concepts presented in the chapter

▶ **Questions for Thought**—a series of questions posed to the student that encourage the student to think about issues and make connections beyond the scope of the text material

▶ **Questions for Review**—a series of questions that invite the student to think about and review important concepts covered in the text

▶ **Suggested Readings**—readings of high interest for students, written at a level that students can understand

▶ **Web Resources**—addresses for Web sites that provide additional information about topics covered in each chapter

▶ **Connections to the CD-ROM**—chapter-by-chapter connections to the interactive Exploring Biological Psychology CD

Additional Instructional Aids for Students

Exploring Biological Psychology This free supplement reviews important concepts covered in each chapter, provides multiple choice quizzes for each chapter, and presents animations and video clips that explain or demonstrate difficult concepts (Multiple Choice Quizzes: prepared by Linda Lockwood, Metropolitan State College; Multimedia Manager: Fred Shaffer, Truman State University)

Study Guide This is an extremely useful tool for students who want to get the most out of the textbook. For each chapter, learning objectives, activities for further learning, and practice tests in different formats are provided. (Study Guide author: Carol Pandey, Pierce College) ISBN: 0-15-507485-7

Instructional Aids for Instructors

Instructor's Manual This helpful guide for instructors provides lecture outlines, learning objectives, discussion questions, supplementary lecture suggestions, Internet Web sites with supplementary information and student exercises, video and software suggestions, and creative ideas for classroom and laboratory activities. (Instructor's Manual author: William Meil, Indiana University of Pennsylvania)

Test Bank   Test questions for each chapter are provided in a variety of formats. (Test Bank author: Timothy Barth, Texas Christian University)

Multimedia Manager   This book-specific resource uses Microsoft® PowerPoint presentations, pre-built graphics, simulations, and CNN® video clips, which you can use as-is or modify with your own materials

CNN Biological Psychology Video   A video with compelling footage from CNN® will help launch lectures and show how course topics are integrated in students' everyday lives

Acknowledgments

The publication of this book would not have been possible without the assistance of many individuals from Harcourt Brace and Wadsworth. My developmental editors at Harcourt Brace, especially Christine Abshire and Tracy Napper, gave me a great deal of useful advice about the organization of this book. At Wadsworth, I discovered a wonderful group of people who had a vision for my book. I want to thank Vicki Knight for her wonderful vision and critical ability to get things done right, Jim Strandberg for his great sense of humor and helpful advice, Dan Moneypenny for adroitly keeping many balls in the air at once, Kirk Bomont for smoothing the rough edges as the book went into production, Nancy Shammas for her infinite patience and willingness to incorporate many last minute changes, and Darin Derstine for his courteous, pleasant, yet skillful help with the production of the CD that accompanies this textbook. My most special thanks goes to my Wadsworth developmental editor, Kate Barnes, who very intelligently and diligently attended to all the final details of getting this book ready for print. I am extremely fortunate to have had the opportunity to work with all of these talented, caring people.

My thanks also to the many reviewers who provided helpful comments and suggestions as this book was written: Michael Babcock, Montana State University; Jay Bean, Vassar College; Carl D. Cheney, Utah State University; Ivy Dunn, Chicago State University; Steve Falkenberg, Eastern Kentucky University; Charlotte M. Farkas, ENMU and Clovis Community College; Thomas Fischer, Wayne State University; Sally Foster, MiraCosta College; Perry Fuchs, University of Texas at Arlington; John Garofalo, University of Pittsburgh; Thomas J. Gerstenberger, SUNY Potsdam; Arnold M. Golub, California State University-Sacramento; Greg Goodwin, Skidmore College; Susan Heidenreich, University of San Francisco; Robert Hoff, Mercyhurst College; Pamela S. Hunt, College of William and Mary; Maria Lavooy, University of Central Florida; Leslie MacGregor, Kennesaw University; William Meil, Indiana University of Pennsylvania; Carol Pandey, Los Angeles Pierce College; Cindy Miller-Perrin, Pepperdine University; Dean Murakami, American River College; Jack A. Palmer, University of LA at Monroe; Kim Purdy, University of South Carolina Spartanburg; Fred Shaffer, Truman State University; and Roy Smith, Mary Washington College.

In addition, I want to thank the creative faculty members who worked on the ancillaries for my book: Timothy Barth, Texas Christian University; Linda Lockwood, Metropolitan State College; William Meil, Indiana University of Pennsylvania; Carol Pandey, Pierce College; and Fred Shaffer, Truman State University.

I must also thank my beloved husband and partner, David Wishart, and sons, Jacob and Tony, for taking up the slack around the house for several years as I worked on this book.

Josephine F. Wilson

Biological Foundations of Human Behavior

1

Studying the Biological Bases of Behavior

Tyrone was riding in the front passenger seat of his roommate's car when the driver lost control of the car on an icy road. The car slid off the shoulder of the road and collided with a guardrail. Because he was not wearing a seat belt, Tyrone was thrown forward in the impact, and his head struck the dashboard with intense force. For several minutes, Tyrone was unconscious, although he was able to respond to rescue workers when they arrived to transport him to the hospital. He was released from the hospital in seemingly good health, but he began to develop some troubling symptoms within a couple of days. For example, he began to accuse his roommate of stealing his clothes and money. Then he became convinced that his girlfriend was cheating on him. When he attacked a stranger at a local shopping center because the stranger nodded and smiled at Tyrone's girlfriend, Tyrone was placed in the care of a neurologist (a physician who specializes in the treatment of brain disorders).

The neurologist ordered scans of Tyrone's brain, which indicated an accumulation of fluid within his brain, a condition known as *hydrocephalus*. In rare cases like Tyrone's, hydrocephalus can produce paranoia, delusions, and violent behavior (Bloom & Kraft, 1998). He was referred to a neurosurgeon who inserted a very thin tube into Tyrone's brain to allow the excess fluid to drain out of the brain. The reduction in fluid within his brain eliminated Tyrone's symptoms, and Tyrone was able to go back to a normal life.

An accidental bump to his head caused fluid to build up within Tyrone's brain, changing his behavior in a disturbing manner. Modern brain-imaging and surgical techniques helped restore Tyrone to health. An impressive body of research involving the brain and behavior, which you will learn about in this book, has enabled scientists and practitioners to develop techniques that permit diagnosis and treatment of a wide variety of disorders that affect the brain. However, since the dawn of humankind, people have sustained head injuries or developed brain diseases, and there is amazing evidence that the earliest humans tried to treat those unfortunate victims of accident and disease.

Take a close look at Figure 1.1. This is a skull of one of the native people from South America, estimated to be thousands of years old. You will notice that the skull has been punctured with a large hole. This hole was not made by some enormous, carnivorous animal. Rather, upon close inspection, it is obvious that this hole was deliberately drilled using sharpened stones. What's more, there is evidence that many of the "patients" who received this crude, prehistoric surgery lived weeks, months, or even years following the **craniotomy,** or skull incision.

It is not known why these craniotomies were performed. These crude surgeries were conducted before the advent of written history, so the story behind them has disappeared. Anthropologists have speculated that these craniotomies were performed to permit the escape of evil spirits. Perhaps the person was depressed, psychotic, or physically ill, and the local medical practitioner performed the craniotomy in a ritual meant to draw out the evil spirit that was causing the distress (Stewart, 1958). That's the leading **hypothesis,** or educated guess, held by scientific experts at the present time.

Certainly, practitioners of Western medicine no longer believe that evil spirits produce disordered behavior. As a result of careful research and observation, our understanding of the biological foundations of behavior has become quite sophisticated. In Chapter 1, we will examine how our knowledge of the workings of the brain developed. We will discuss opposing views about the brain and the mind. In addition, we will compare different scientific disciplines that study the brain and behavior, contrasting their methods and explanatory approaches. ●

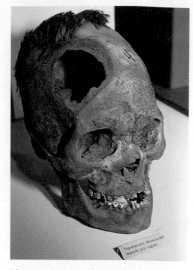

Figure 1.1 Ancient skull with craniotomy

craniotomy: an incision in the skull

hypothesis: proposal, supposition

The History of Brain Research

The concept of a brain did not figure prominently in the recorded histories of most early societies. In ancient China, more than 40 centuries ago, medical personnel, such as Shun Nung (circa 3000 BCE) and Huang Ti (circa 2700 BCE), treated mental afflictions with acupuncture and herbal remedies aimed at balancing the Yin and Yang and freeing the life energy known as Ch'i. The distinguished scholars Hua T'o (100 AD) and Chang Chung-Ching (200 AD), who perfected the art of Chinese medicine, prescribed treatment for the 12 major organs, which did not include the brain (Figure 1.2).

Cardiocentric explanations of behavior were popular in the great ancient civilizations of Western history, including those in Egypt and Greece. According to a cardiocentric explanation, the heart produces and regulates all behaviors, including thoughts and emotions. The brain was not considered a "vital" organ by the early Egyptians and was removed through the nose and discarded before mummification of a corpse, whereas the heart was preserved for use by the departed in the afterlife.

cardiocentric: heart-centered

Figure 1.2 The twelve major organs, according to Chinese medicine

According to ancient Chinese medicine, the body is controlled by 12 major organs. Each organ is most active at a particular time of the day, as shown in this drawing. Notice that some of the organs (for example, the triple heater) do not have a counterpart in the Western medical tradition.

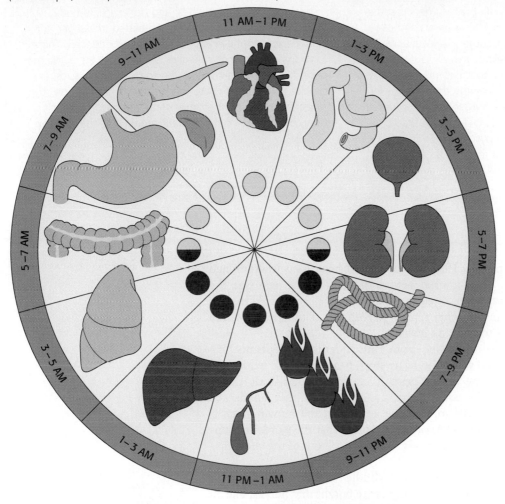

1–3 AM —Liver	1–3 PM —Small intestine
3–5 AM —Lung	3–5 PM —Bladder
5–7 AM —Large intestine	5–7 PM —Kidney
7–9 AM —Stomach	7–9 PM —Constrictor
9–11 AM —Spleen-pancreas	9–11 PM —Triple heater
11 AM–1 PM —Heart	11 PM–1 AM —Gallbladder

Brain-Centered Explanations of Behavior

Encephalocentric explanations of behavior came about as a result of dissection studies of human and other animal cadavers. Known as "the father of scientific medicine," Hippocrates (460–377 BCE), for whom the Hippocratic oath taken by doctors is named, supervised dozens of human dissections on the island of Cos. These dissections led to the discovery of nerves and nerve function. Only one discourse by Hippocrates on brain function is known:

encephalocentric: brain-centered

> Some people say that the heart is the organ with which we think and that it feels pain and anxiety. But it is not so. Men ought to know that from the brain and from the brain only arise our pleasures, joys, laughter, and tears. (Penfield, 1975, pp. 7–8)

The great philosopher Plato agreed with Hippocrates's encephalocentric view. But, Plato's most famous student, Aristotle (384–322 BCE), considered the heart to

Why Doesn't Poking the Brain Produce Pain?

As you will learn later in this book, brain surgery is sometimes performed on people who are conscious and can respond to questions during the surgery. A local *anesthetic* [*an-* = without; *-esthesia* = feeling], similar to the drug that your dentist uses to numb a tooth, is injected into the scalp and the connective tissue covering the skull to eliminate the sensation of pain as the surgeon cuts through the scalp and skull to reach the brain. Once inside the skull, however, no painkillers are necessary.

In order to feel pain, special nerve cells called pain receptors are needed. These pain receptors are located throughout the skin, muscles, and bones in the body. When these pain receptors are stimulated, messages about pain are sent to the brain, and pain is experienced. Therefore, an anesthesia or painkiller is needed to block the messages from pain receptors in the scalp, head muscles, and skull as the surgeon makes an incision through these structures. The brain, on the other hand, contains no pain receptors. Thus, no anesthesia is required as the surgeon removes or stimulates tissue in the brain. ●

be the organ of intelligence (Spillane, 1981). In his own observations, Aristotle had noticed that poking the brain of an injured person did not induce pain (see the *For Further Thought* box). Aristotle reasoned that the brain is not involved in pain perception nor, he concluded, in any other type of perception. The function of the brain, according to Aristotle, is to cool the heart.

Aristotle studied all manner of beasts, from tiny rodents to elephants. He observed that the body grows cold when the heart stops beating, which led him to believe that the heart produces the body's heat. It occurred to Aristotle that a mechanism is needed to cool the incessant heart, and he assigned this function to the brain. In addition, scholars in Aristotle's time knew that the human voice is produced by air exhaled from the lungs. Aristotle reasoned that the words are supplied by the heart and, therefore, that the words and voice roll out of the chest cavity together.

Aristotle's cardiocentric view survived into the Middle Ages. As late as the 16th century, medical students and students of anatomy were taught that nerves, like all veins and arteries, originate from the heart. Anatomical dissection studies demonstrated that arteries, veins, and nerves course through the body bundled together in sheaves. Tracing the veins and arteries back to the heart led to the obvious, but erroneous, conclusion that the nerves also come from the heart.

Galen (130–200 AD), often called "the father of experimental physiology," disagreed with Aristotle's cardiocentric view. He reasoned that, if indeed the function of the brain is to cool the heart, it would be located closer to the heart. His own work indicated that the brain is of paramount importance. In one experiment, Galen cut through the medulla, right above the spinal cord in the brain, and observed that breathing ceases, which led him to conclude that the brain controls respiration (Spillane, 1981).

However, Galen had a lot of wrong ideas, too. First of all, he believed that nerves are hollow. He proposed that *spiritus animalis* (or animal spirit) flows in these hollow nerves from the brain to other parts of the body, supplying sensation and motion. According to Galen, damage to the brain allows the animal spirit to escape, impairing sensory and motor functions. As absurd as Galen's hollow nerve theory seems to us today, it survived until the 19th century, when microscopic examination demonstrated that nerves are not hollow.

Galen firmly established the brain's central role in human behavior. Since Galen's time, over many centuries, scientists studied the anatomy of the brain, cataloguing its many structures, cavities, fissures, and bulges. But, descriptions of the brain's functioning were pure fantasy until the 19th century. For example, one popular notion that was taught in most medieval European medical schools was "cell doctrine," which originated in the 4th century (Finger, 1994). According to this doctrine, the brain is composed of three cells. It is important to remember that the compound microscope was not invented until the mid-17th century and that medieval scholars were not familiar with the modern-day concept of a cell as the basic unit of body tissues. In medieval times, the term *cell* was used to mean "room" or "chamber," as in "jail cell." Cell doctrine's notion of "cell" came from the observation that the brain contains a number of large, fluid-filled spaces, known as *ventricles*. Students were taught that the first cell regulates sensation, the second regulates reasoning and judgment, and the third regulates memories and movement (Figure 1.3). This doctrine, which was taught for over a thousand years, emphasized (wrongly) the importance of the brain's ventricles and ignored the brain proper.

Controlled experiments involving the brain were rare until the 19th century. Before 1800, most knowledge about the brain came from observations of people who suffered head injuries, such as a kick in the head from a horse or a gunshot wound to the head. It was observed that people who received injuries to the back of the head invariably had visual or motor impairments afterward. Those who incurred head wounds to the front of the brain often showed memory or personality disturbances. However, there was much disagreement over the extent to which specific behaviors could be localized to discrete brain areas (Sarter, Berntson, & Cacioppo, 1996).

Figure 1.3 Cell theory
Until the 17th century, medical students were taught that the three ventricles (or cells) of the brain controlled emotions, thoughts, and behavior.

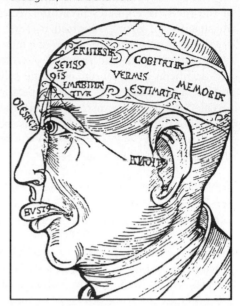

Holism Versus Localization

Vicious scientific debates ensued over whether the brain divides its labors or not. Those who supported the concept of **holism** claimed that every area of the brain is capable of controlling all human functions. The proponents of **localization** argued that human functions are regulated by distinct, specific areas of the brain. Most of the credit for popularizing the concept of localization goes to a highly regarded neuroanatomist, Franz Gall, who is best remembered today for developing the field of **phrenology** (Zola-Morgan, 1995).

From an early age, Gall was fascinated by the shapes of people's heads. Young Franz, at the age of 9, was quite impressed by his observation that his classmates with bulging eyes had excellent verbal memories. As an adult, he took time out from a successful neuroanatomy career to study hundreds of human skulls. Gall scoured hospitals, prisons, asylums, and schools, looking for odd-shaped heads and people with notable talents or dispositions. He took copious notes on his findings and ordered hundreds of head casts made (Spillane, 1981).

Gall was convinced that protuberances on the outside surface, or **cortex,** of the brain correspond to human capacities, such as thrift, courage, love, or jealousy (Figure. 1.4). Furthermore, he theorized that the shape of the skull reflects the shape of the lumpy, bumpy brain beneath and that a person's psychic endowments could be measured by cranioscopy, or examination of the skull's shape. So popular was Gall's phrenology by the beginning of the 19th century that the ancient Egyptian practice of head shaping, or applying pressure to the supple skulls of babies with cloth wrappings, returned. Whereas the Egyptians used head shaping to produce a more flattened, elongated skull, which was considered quite beautiful and desirable in their time, 19th-century Europeans used head shaping to encourage the development of such qualities as intelligence and moral character in their children (Fishman, 1988).

Head shaping aside, Gall's theory of localization, although not based on experimental evidence, changed the way many scientists began to think about the organization of the human brain. It appeared that the brain divides its labor, one part specializing in vision, for example, and another part specializing in speech. Scientific investigations conducted in the 19th century provided evidence to support the notion of localization.

holism: a theory that the brain works as a whole to produce behavior
localization: a theory that specific structures in the brain control specific behaviors
phrenology: study of the skull to understand the mind

cortex: the outermost surface of the brain

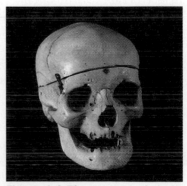

Figure 1.4 The preserved skull of Franz Gall

The Development of Brain Science

Julien Jean Cesar Legallois is credited with providing the first evidence in support of localization of function in 1812 (Finger, 1994). He was able to demonstrate that a specific, discrete area of the medulla regulates breathing. Another Frenchman, the physician Paul Broca, reported in 1861 the results of a *post-mortem* examination of the brain of a man, nicknamed "Tan" by other patients. Tan had suffered a stroke two decades earlier and had been able to utter only one syllable, "tan," since the stroke. The autopsy that Broca performed on Tan's brain revealed damage to a distinct area in the front portion of the left half of the brain (Figure 1.5). This area, today called *Broca's area* after the French doctor who discovered it, is known to control the production of speech.

Two German investigators, Gustav Fritsch and Edouard Hitzig, demonstrated in 1870 that specific areas of the motor cortex in dogs control particular movements of the body. When they electrically stimulated the motor cortex near the top of the brain, a dog's hind legs would wiggle. Stimulation of the motor cortex toward the bottom of the brain produced jaw movements. (The cortex was a favorite place to stimulate because it is located directly under the skull.) A Scottish physician, David Ferrier, documented the same findings in monkeys in 1876 (Figure 1.6) (Ferrier, 1876, 1886). In a much less rigorous fashion in 1874, an American physician, Roberts Bartholow from Cincinnati, Ohio, stimulated the cortex of a female patient who had an extensive skull fracture. Bartholow was able to produce movements of specific muscles depending on the placement of the stimulating probe on the woman's exposed motor cortex (Valenstein, 1973).

This precise mapping of the body onto an area of the brain is called **topographical organization.** Figure 1.7 illustrates the topographical organization of the motor cortex in humans. The motor cortex is organized in such a way that specific cells in the motor cortex control certain muscles in the body. Areas of the motor cortex near the top of the head command muscles in the feet and legs, whereas lower areas of the motor cortex command muscles in upper regions of the body. Ferrier's research also showed that the somatosensory cortex, which is located adjacent to the motor cortex, is topographically organized. Stimulation of different parts of the somatosensory cortex produces sensations in specific areas of the body (Figure 1.8). You will discover as you read this book that several areas of the brain display topographical organization.

Soon after David Ferrier reported his research on monkeys, scientific journals began to publish dozens of papers linking particular brain areas to specific behaviors. Despite the mounting evidence in support of localization, a number of highly regarded scholars refused to view the brain as anything more than an undifferentiated mass, much like the liver. Even in the 20th century, a prominent American psychologist, Karl Lashley, conducted a number of experiments on rat learning and intelligence that he claimed demonstrated support for the concept of holism (Lashley, 1929).

In one set of experiments, Lashley burned away discrete regions of the cerebral cortex of rats, destroying between 14 and 50% of each rat's cortex. Next, Lashley trained the rats to open a box by pressing down on two platforms located at opposite sides

Figure 1.5 Broca's area
Damage to Broca's area typically results in disordered speech production.

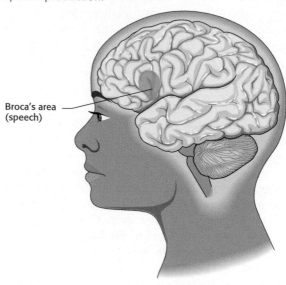

Broca's area (speech)

topographical organization: organization of receptive fields in the cerebral cortex, in which specific areas of the cortex receive information from specific regions of the body

Figure 1.6 Ferrier's findings on the motor cortex of the monkey brain
In 1876, David Ferrier stimulated the motor cortex of monkeys and demonstrated that each area indicated in this drawing of the monkey brain controls movement of a specific body part. Areas 1 and 2 control the hind limbs; 3 controls the tail; 4, 5, 6, the arm; a, b, c, d, hands and fingers; 7–11, face and mouth; 12, 13, eyes, head; 14, ear.

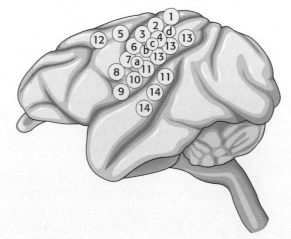

Figure 1.7 Topographical organization of the motor cortex
Specific regions of the motor cortex of the human brain control particular muscles in the body. A homunculus (little person) as shown can be drawn over the motor cortex based on the areas of the body controlled by specific regions of the motor cortex.

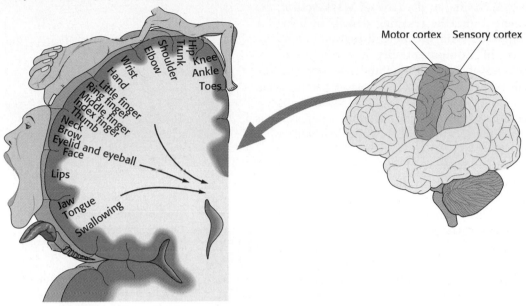

of the box (Figure 1.9). The lesioned rats all learned to open the box, although they required 75% more time than did intact (unlesioned) rats. In another series of studies, normal and cortex-lesioned rats were trained to locate food in four different mazes of increasing complexity. Lashley found that the lesioned rats required twice as much practice as the normal rats to learn the simplest maze and 65% more practice to learn the most complicated maze. However, all rats learned the maze discriminations, regardless of the amount of cortex that had been destroyed.

Figure 1.8 Topographical organization of the somatosensory cortex
Stimulation of specific regions of the sensory cortex of the human brain produces sensations in specific areas of the body. A homunculus can also be drawn over the sensory cortex.

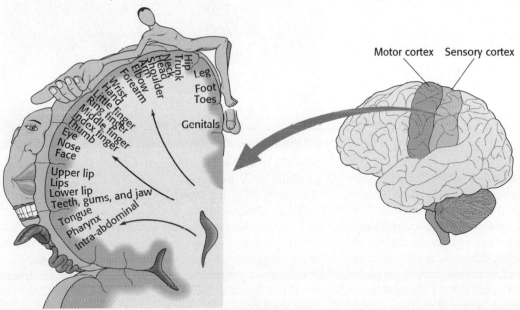

As a result of these studies, Lashley concluded that cortical brain damage in rats interferes with their learning and memory. However, it is not the location of the damage that matters, according to Lashley; rather, it is the size of the lesion. He postulated two laws, the Law of Mass Action and the Law of Equipotentiality. According to the **Law of Mass Action,** the amount of brain damage determines the resulting deficits in behavior. That is, the larger the lesion in the brain, the more disruption in function will be observed. The **Law of Equipotentiality** is a restatement of holism: The entire cortex is capable of learning and memory, and the same behavioral deficit will be produced regardless of the part of brain that is damaged.

Wilder Penfield, a Canadian neurosurgeon, conducted experiments on the exposed brains of awake but sedated patients while their skulls were open during surgery in the 1940s and 1950s (Penfield, 1977). Using a 3-volt battery, he stimulated different areas of the cortex with a probe. Memories were elicited when some areas of the cortex were stimulated. For example, patients would describe a childhood sweetheart or a room in an old home when areas toward the back of cortex were excited. Stimulation in the somatosensory cortex produced sensations in various parts of the body, depending on the location of the electrical probe. In fact, it was this research by Penfield that inspired the drawings of the homunculi in Figures 1.7 and 1.8. Penfield's work left no doubt that the brain is composed of a multitude of discrete regions that have specialized functions.

Modern brain-imaging techniques permit investigators to pinpoint active regions of the brain associated with particular behaviors (Figure 1.10). (You will learn more about these techniques in Chapter 5.) Brain-imaging studies have fueled the imaginations of scientists, journalists, and dreamers alike. Some authors believe that modern imaging techniques will eventually permit us to locate happiness, sadness, and moral centers in the brain, or pinpoint chess moves, compare brain activity in a mathematician with that of an architect, or determine which brain regions attorneys use when presenting or preparing a case (Gur & Gur, 1991).

However, most investigators are cautious about attributing mentalistic concepts, like happiness, wisdom, consciousness, and morality, to particular brain structures (Goldberg, 2001; Sarter et al., 1996). These cognitive factors result from simultaneous processing in many areas of the brain, including sensory and perceptual processing, learning, and memory. It may be that mental states, such as happiness or consciousness, are the product of several areas of the brain working at the same time. The highly respected Russian neuropsychologist Alexandr Luria theorized that all behaviors are produced by specific brain areas interacting and working together as a whole (Luria, 1973).

Locating the Mind

The location of the mind has been the subject of debate for thousands of years. As in any debate, there are at least two sides. And, in the debate over the mind's relationship to the brain, the two sides have been dubbed "dualism" and "monism." **Dualism** is the philosophy that the mind and body are separate entities. Those who subscribe to dualism believe that the mind is independent of the body and exerts control over it. Dualists believe that the body operates according to physical laws and that the mind

Figure 1.9 Lashley's test box
In Lashley's experiments, rats were trained to open the door (c) by pressing first platform a and then platform b.

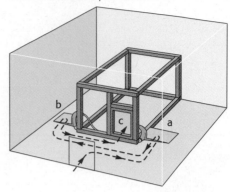

Law of Mass Action: Lashley's finding that the amount of brain damage determines the extent of the behavioral deficit observed

Law of Equipotentiality: Lashley's finding that the entire cortex is capable of learning and memory

dualism: a theory that the body and the mind are two separate entities

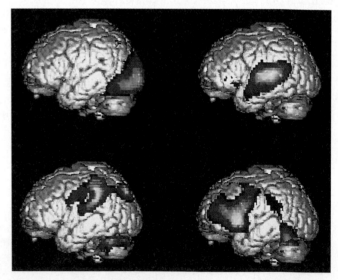

Figure 1.10 PET scans of person opening eyes, listening, touching, and speaking
In image at upper left, sight activates the visual area in the occipital cortex in the back of the brain. In image at upper right, hearing activates the auditory area in the temporal cortex. In image at lower left, touching Braille script activates the tactile area in the parietal cortex and an area of cognition (lower right of the brain scan). In image at lower right, activation of the frontal cortex occurs during word generation while speaking.

does not. Throughout much of Western history, most scholars were dualists who taught that the mind is a spiritual entity and separate from the brain. Plato (428–347 BCE) has been called the "father of Western dualism" (Maranto, 1984). During the Middle Ages, the mind was believed to hover above the head, where it received messages from God. The French philosopher Rene Descartes framed dualism in its modern form in the late 17th century. According to Descartes, the world consists of two substances, matter and spirit. Furthermore, Descartes postulated, the body is made of matter, and the mind is spiritual or immaterial.

Monism, or the view that the mind is a result of brain functioning and thus follows physical laws, had very few proponents until modern investigations of brain function were conducted beginning in the 19th century. One famous monist, the Renaissance scholar Leonardo da Vinci, shocked his peers by proclaiming that the mind is a product of the brain. Today many, if not most, brain scientists would agree with da Vinci. They have witnessed that damage to the brain can alter all aspects of a person's mind: personality, thinking, moral reasoning, memory, intellect, and even consciousness. Hence, it appears that these processes of the mind are produced by brain activity.

monism: a theory that the mind is not separable from the body

However, not all modern scholars are convinced that the monist view is correct. Two of the most outspoken proponents of dualism were the philosopher Sir Karl Popper and the Nobel-winning neuroscientist Sir John Eccles (Popper & Eccles, 1977). They preferred to regard the mind as a self-conscious entity that acts upon the brain. In *The Self and Its Brain*, they wrote:

> There is displayed or portrayed before [the mind] from instant to instant the whole of the complex neural processes, and according to attention and choice and interest or drive, it can select from this ensemble of performances in the liaison brain, searching now this now that and blending together the readouts of many different areas in the liaison brain. In that way the self-conscious mind achieves a unity of experience. (Popper & Eccles, 1977, p. 472)

According to Popper and Eccles, the mind *selects* what is to be perceived, what is to receive attention, what is to be done next. They did not believe that these activities are merely the by-products of electrical-chemical processes in our brains. Another Nobel Prize laureate, Sir Francis Crick, who has spent the past 30 years studying perception and conscious awareness, accused Eccles and Popper of committing the "Fallacy of the Homunculus," believing that there is a little person inside the brain who watches everything that happens (Crick, 1988). Crick maintains that "what we call our minds is simply a way of talking about the functions of our brains" (Crick, 1966, p. 87). This view of the mind is a fine statement of modern monism.

Psychologists like Benjamin Libet (1993) have attempted to study the mind experimentally. While monitoring the brain activity of healthy subjects using recordings of the electrical activity of the brain, Libet asked the subjects to bend one finger at any moment of their choosing and to note the exact time that they decided to bend the finger. Libet found that finger bending occurred 0.2 second after the decision was made to bend the finger. However, electrical brain recordings indicated that brain activity occurred 0.3 second before the subjects consciously made the decision to act. Monists believe that this finding demonstrates that the brain made the decision to bend the finger before the mind became aware of the decision. Dualists might argue that it took the subjects 0.3 second to read the digital clock in front of them.

The brain plays a central role in the expression of behavior according to both modern explanations of the mind-body relationship—monism and dualism. We've come a long way since Aristotle first concluded that the brain's function is to cool the heart.

Hippocrates, Plato, and Galen proposed (a)_____ explanations of behavior that focus on the brain as the chief source of behaviors, thoughts, and feelings. Scientific debates have taken place between proponents of (b)_____, who claim that every area of the brain is capable of controlling all human functions, and proponents of (c)_____, who claim that specific human functions are regulated by distinct areas of the brain. Research on (d)_____ _____ in dogs, monkeys, and people supports the concept of localization by showing that it is topographically organized in such a way that specific cells in the motor cortex control certain muscles in the body. (e) _____ _____'s studies of brain-damaged rats that learned to open a box or navigate a maze support the concept of holism. The location of the mind has been the subject of another scientific debate in which proponents of (f)_____ argue that the mind and brain are separate entities and proponents of (g)_____ argue that the mind is produced by brain activity.

Studying the Brain and Behavior

Disciplines Concerned with the Study of the Brain and Behavior

So far, we've covered the history of brain science and the relationship of the mind to the brain. These topics are relevant to a variety of fields of study, including: neuroscience, behavioral neuroscience, cognitive neuroscience, physiological psychology, biological psychology, biopsychology, and neuropsychology. Let's take a brief look at each of these fields.

Neuroscience is a multidisciplinary approach to studying the brain. Biologists, chemists, physicists, anatomists, physiologists, psychologists, mathematicians, and engineers work together to unlock the mysteries of the brain. Undergraduate or graduate students majoring in neuroscience are expected to have a strong background in the natural sciences and mathematics.

Behavioral neuroscience and **cognitive neuroscience** are specialized branches of both neuroscience and psychology. In general, psychologists who study the brain and behavior are usually classified as behavioral neuroscientists or cognitive neuroscientists, depending on their method of study. Behavioral neuroscience involves **bottom-up** research strategies in which cellular function is manipulated and the effect on behavior measured. Bottom-up research strategies begin by studying the basic unit of behavior, the **neuron**, and its interactions with other neurons, Behavioral neuroscientists strive to learn about the elementary levels of brain function in order to understand higher level functions like perception, attention, and motivation.

In contrast, cognitive neuroscience is characterized as a **top-down** approach in which the highest levels of functioning, cognitive events like thinking or problem solving, are manipulated in order to observe the effect on neural functioning (Farah, 1994). Top-down research strategies involve studying high-level cognitive functions in order to draw conclusions about functions at the cellular levels.

Physiological psychology and **biological psychology** are terms that have been in use longer than behavioral neuroscience, but there is considerable confusion over the difference among the three terms (Wilson, 1991). Like behavioral neuroscience, physiological psychology and biological psychology use a bottom-up approach to studying the brain and behavior. All three disciplines involve the study

neuroscience: a multi disciplinary approach to studying the brain

behavioral neuroscience: a field of neuroscience in which brain function is manipulated and the effect on behavior measured

cognitive neuroscience: a field of neuroscience in which cognitive events are manipulated in order to observe the effect on brain functioning

bottom-up: research strategies that involve studying the basic levels of brain function in order to understand higher level behavioral functions

neuron: a specialized cell that is the fundamental unit of the nervous system

top-down: research strategies that involve studying higher level cognitive function in order to draw conclusions about brain functions at the cellular level

physiological psychology: a discipline that involves the study of brain mechanisms underlying behavior

biological psychology: a discipline that involves the study of brain mechanisms underlying behavior

of brain mechanisms underlying behavior. Two other disciplines in psychology that are concerned with the brain and behavior are biopsychology and neuropsychology. Often the term biopsychology is used interchangeably with biological or physiological psychology. Similarly, *psychobiology* is another term frequently confused with physiological psychology and behavioral neuroscience.

Neuropsychology is usually defined as the study of higher functions and their disorders following brain injury or disease. Karl Lashley, the American psychologist introduced earlier in this chapter, is credited with coining the term and first using it in a 1936 lecture on behavior following brain damage (Finger, 1994). Most neuropsychologists assess and treat human patients with brain damage, in clinical settings; hence, they are called *clinical neuropsychologists*. Many neuropsychologists, however, work in research laboratories, conducting studies of brain dysfunction with animal subjects; these are *experimental neuropsychologists*.

neuropsychology: the study of higher functions and their disorders following brain injury or disease

In this textbook, we will examine a wide range of factors that affect behavior, including physiological, biochemical, cellular, pharmacological, genetic, and hormonal. But, we will not restrict our discussion to bottom-up approaches. We will also consider important findings of cognitive neuroscience, neuropsychology, and psychobiology, and we will integrate these findings with mechanisms studied by behavioral neuroscientists. Although we will focus primarily on human behavior, we will discuss bottom-up research strategies based on animal models as well as top-down strategies that use human subjects.

We will also include a few models from **computational neuroscience** in our discussion of the brain. Computational neuroscience attempts to relate electrical and chemical signals of brain cells to the processing of information in the brain, with the aid of computer-generated models of neural circuits (Mallot, 2000; Sejnowski, Koch, & Churchland, 1988). This new field has contributed especially to our understanding of sensory, perceptual, learning, and memory processes.

computational neuroscience: a field that relates the activity of brain cells to the processing of information in the brain, with the aid of computer-generated models of brain circuits

In this textbook, we will look at emotions and cognitive functions, which are typically studied in top-down experiments with human subjects. We will also look at movement, sensory processes, motivation, and homeostatic regulation, behavioral processes that have traditionally been examined using bottom-up approaches and laboratory animal subjects. It is my hope that you will come to appreciate the wealth of knowledge that both approaches have generated and that you will see that these approaches are complementary, rather than antagonistic.

Bottom-Up Versus Top-Down Approaches: An Example

One example of the complementary nature of bottom-up and top-down approaches involves studies of gender differences in young children and rhesus monkeys. In one series of top-down experiments (Overman, Bachevalier, Schuhmann, & Ryan, 1996), boys and girls between the ages of 15 and 55 months were tested in two nonverbal tasks: an object reversal task and a concurrent discrimination task (Figure 1.11). Boys younger than 30 months performed significantly better on the object reversal task than did girls who were the same age, whereas girls younger than 30 months of age outperformed age-matched boys on the concurrent discrimination task. No gender differences were detected for older children and adults who were tested on these tasks.

The investigators (Overman et al., 1996) speculated that these gender differences are due to the influence of sex hormones on the maturation of specific brain regions. To understand how Overman and his colleagues reached this conclusion, we must refer to a series of bottom-up experiments conducted by behavioral neuroscientists working with rhesus monkeys. Patricia Goldman-Rakic and her colleagues have studied object reversal in adult and infant rhesus monkeys. As with very young humans, 3-month-old male rhesus monkeys are better than females of the same age at that task. However, when Clark and Goldman-Rakic (1989) administered male sex hormones, called *androgens*, to female monkeys shortly after birth, these androgenized females performed the object reversal task as well as normal, age-matched males.

Figure 1.11 Object reversal and concurrent discrimination tasks

In the object reversal test, children learn to discriminate between a positive stimulus that always conceals a food reward and a negative stimulus. For example, a baby learns that a piece of candy can be found under the block marked with a triangle and that no candy will be found under the block marked with a star. After the young subjects learn this discrimination, the reward contingencies are switched so that the formerly positive stimulus no longer conceals food. A baby who learned that the block marked with a triangle was associated with candy is next presented with the same two blocks, except that candy is now found under the block marked with a star.

In the concurrent discrimination task, the children simultaneously learn eight discriminations. They are presented with eight pairs of stimuli, in the same order, once a day for several days. One stimulus in each pair always conceals a food reward, and one does not, although the positions of the two stimuli vary randomly. For example, the baby learns to find candy under the block marked with a star *and* under the block marked with a circle *and* under the block marked with an "X," and so forth, for eight different pairs of blocks.

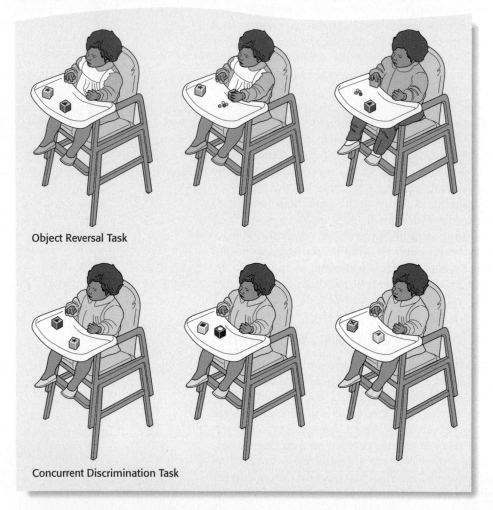

Object Reversal Task

Concurrent Discrimination Task

Clark and Goldman-Rakic's findings are clear evidence that male sex hormones speed up the maturation of the area of the cerebral cortex that is involved in the object reversal task. When we integrate Overman et al.'s (1996) findings with Clark and Goldman-Rakic's (1989) findings, we can speculate that male sex hormones also increase the maturation rate of this cortical area in humans. Girls do become proficient at the object reversal task, but it takes a little bit longer for this part of their brains to develop.

We can make the same case for the concurrent discrimination task. Infant female rhesus monkeys perform significantly better at this task than do age-matched males (Bachevalier, Hagger, & Bercu, 1989). However, when infant males are castrated, which removes the main source of their bodies' sex hormones, these castrated males perform as well as infant females. Putting all these findings together, we can conclude that observed gender differences in very young primates are due to the influences of sex hormones. We can also speculate that androgens play a role in brain development, speeding up the maturation rate in some areas of the brain and slowing down maturation in other areas. It is important to recognize that these conclusions are based on the results of several studies, some that used a top-down approach and others that used a bottom-up approach.

Why Use Animals as Research Subjects?

At this point you might be thinking, "Monkey babies are so cute. Why in the world would anyone want to experiment with them? That sounds cruel." If you feel this way, you are not alone. Many people, including some scientists, are opposed to the use of nonhuman animals as research subjects (Barnard & Kaufman, 1997; Morrison, 2001). A number of authors believe that the usefulness of animal models is especially limited when studying behavior, particularly higher functions like thinking and language. But, these objections to animal research are not new. David Ferrier, whose historic experiments with monkey brains are described earlier, was arrested under the Cruelty to Animals Act of 1876 in Great Britain. (He was later acquitted of these charges.)

Some authors argue that not only is experimentation on animal subjects cruel, but also it produces misleading findings (Barnard & Kaufman, 1997). There is no denying that all species are unique in some respects and that the unnatural environment of the laboratory can bias results. However, the judicious use of nonhuman subjects can provide important findings that can be used to improve the lives of humans and other animals and add to our understanding of brain organization and function (Figure 1.12) (Botting & Morrison, 1997). Examples of important medical developments that required animal research are listed in Table 1.1. Although species might differ in some aspects of their physiology, cellular and biochemical mechanisms are generally the same for all animals. For that reason, we can generalize from the activity in a squid neuron to that in a human brain cell.

All research involving nonhuman animals is strictly regulated by the U.S. government, under the Animal Welfare Act of 1966, and by the institution in which the research in conducted. Today, close monitoring and regulation of research involving vertebrate animals go on in all research institutions. The Animal Welfare Act requires that all experiments with nonhuman subjects be approved by a committee composed of scientists and nonscientists, called an **institutional animal care and use committee** (IACUC), before they are conducted. An IACUC is also charged with the responsibility of regularly inspecting the animal living quarters and other research areas.

institutional animal care and use committee (IACUC): a committee, composed of scientists and nonscientists, that approves all experimentation with nonhuman animals at a particular institution

Figure 1.12 The debate about animal research

Table 1.1

Benefits of animal research: Medical advances that required animal research for their development

Benefits to Humans

Immunization against polio, diphtheria, mumps, measles, rubella, smallpox
Antibiotics
Anesthetics and other painkillers
Blood transfusions
Radiation and chemotherapy for cancer treatment
Open-heart surgery for coronary bypass and correction of birth defects
Insulin treatment for diabetes
Asthma medication
Medication for epileptic seizures
Organ transplantation and drugs to prevent organ rejection
Medications to treat depression, anxiety, and psychosis
Microsurgery to reattach severed limbs
Rehabilitation of stroke and brain-damaged accident victims

Benefits to Animals

Vaccination against rabies, distemper, tetanus, and other infections
Corrective surgery for hip dysplasia in dogs
Orthopedic surgery and rehabilitation for horses
Treatment for leukemia and other cancers in pets
Improved nutrition for pets

Source: Foundation for Biomedical Research, 1988

When designing an experiment, the behavioral scientist must decide which species is going to be used as subjects. There is now widespread recognition that nonhuman subjects are never as good a choice as human subjects in studies of human behavior. In fact, the number of animals used as subjects in laboratory experiments has fallen by at least 50% for most species since the 1970s (Madhusree, 1997). All scientists who use nonhuman subjects in their laboratory experiments must balance the need for valid scientific data with the demand for the humane treatment of animals. However, when a "bottom-up" approach is used to study brain processes, nonhuman subjects are the best and sometimes the only choice (Gill, Smith, Wissler, & Kunz, 1989).

In the final section of this chapter, we will examine how psychologists attempt to explain behavior. Those psychologists who use animal subjects in their research typically use biological explanations to describe the underlying causes of behavior.

 Recap 1.2: Studying the Brain and Behavior

(a)_____ is a multidisciplinary approach to studying the brain. Behavioral neuroscience involves (b)_____-_____ research strategies that begin by studying the neuron and its interaction with other neurons. Cognitive neuroscience involves (c)_____-_____ research strategies that manipulate cognitive events like problem solving to produce an effect on neural functioning. Physiological psychology, biological psychology, and (d)_____ are often used interchangeably. (e)_____ involves the study of higher brain functions and their disorders following brain damage. Studies comparing the problem-solving abilities of very young boys and girls are examples of (f)_____-_____ experiments. Studies of the effects of androgen injections on problem solving in female monkeys are examples of (g)_____-_____ experiments.

Biological Explanations of Behavior

All psychologists are concerned with behavior. Some study behavior, and others treat disordered behavior. Some try to explain why particular behaviors occur, and others try to predict or control behavior. When it comes to explaining behavior, there are probably as many explanations as there are branches of psychology. Social, developmental, and personality psychologists may explain behaviors in terms of family history, societal influences, or unconscious conflicts. In this textbook, we will focus on biological explanations of behavior.

Biological explanations of behavior come in many varieties. **Natural selection** was one early biological explanation of behavior proposed by Charles Darwin in the late 19th century. According to Darwin's theory, specific traits (including behavioral traits) selectively develop because animals that survive to reproduce have those traits and pass them on to their offspring. For example, bats are animals that sleep during the day and hunt at night for food. Because vision is limited at night, bats have evolved with extremely sophisticated auditory systems that allow them to locate prey in the dark using echoes (Figure 1.13). Darwin's theory of natural selection predicts that those bats that are best able to survive and feed themselves are the individuals that will reproduce most successfully, producing offspring with their echolocation abilities.

The American psychologist William James (1842–1910) was extremely influenced by Darwin's writings. As a result, he introduced the concept of **functionalism** to explain behavior based on its selective advantage. A functionalist explanation of behavior attempts to identify the survival benefit of a specific behavior to a particular species. For example, investigators who study eating behavior are faced with the perplexing observation that we humans have a large number of neural controls that initiate eating but have few controls that make us stop eating, which encourages obesity. The functionalist explanation for obesity is that humans have survived in environmental niches in which starvation was a way of life (Pinel, Assanand, & Lehman, 2000). To survive starvation, it is necessary to have controls in place to stimulate eating behaviors, but controls to stop eating are not needed. Therefore, controls to initiate eating developed, and controls to stop eating did not.

Other biological explanations of behavior focus on biological properties of an individual, including the individual's genetic background, structural damage in the brain, or the role of various chemicals in the nervous system. In later chapters, we will examine the genetic bases of behavior and behavior disorders. For example, bipolar affective disorder (Chapter 15), also known as manic-depressive disorder, has been demonstrated to be related to an abnormality on several different chromosomes. Alzheimer's disease (Chapter 10), a particularly devastating disorder that robs an older person of memory, intellect, and personality, has been linked to defects on several chromosomes, including 1, 14, 19, and 21. Another progressive disorder, Huntington's disease (Chapter 6), which destroys motor and intellectual function, has been linked to an altered gene on chromosome 4 (see *Case Study*). Other authors claim that a variety of widespread disorders, including alcoholism, gambling, drug abuse, binge eating, and attention-deficit disorder, may have a genetic basis (Blum, Cull, Braverman, & Comings, 1996; Sullivan & Rudnik-Levin, 2001).

In this textbook, we will discuss how the organization of the nervous system is related to behavior. We will also look at the effects of physical damage to the nervous system, whether caused by trauma, disease processes, or environmental factors.

natural selection: Darwin's theory that proposes that specific traits selectively develop because animals that survive pass them on to their offspring

Figure 1.13 Echolocation in bats
A bat emits a series of high-pitched sounds too high for people to hear. These sounds produce echoes as they bounce off objects in the bat's environment. Echoes from objects located close to the bat (for example, the moth in this drawing) return to the bat more quickly than do echoes bouncing off distant objects, like the tree. Thus, the bat locates objects based on the time it takes echoes to return.

functionalism: William James's explanation of behavior that identifies the survival benefit of a specific behavior to a particular species

Genetic Alterations in Huntington's Disease

Samuel is a 5-year-old boy who comes into the hospital clinic with his mother. His symptoms are quite noticeable: involuntary jerking movements of his jaw and eyes and speech difficulties that include articulation errors caused by uncontrolled mouth movements. Although Samuel's abnormal movements are classic symptoms of Huntington's disease, his case is quite unusual because most cases of Huntington's disease are first detected in people in their 40s.

Phyllis is 47 years old and has symptoms similar to Samuel's. Like most patients with Huntington's disease, she and Samuel both presented initially with motor symptoms. In addition to involuntary movements of her head, neck, and shoulders, Phyllis sometimes experiences rigidity of the muscles in her face, arms, and legs, which makes it impossible for her to move smoothly. Most recently, her physicians have noted that Phyllis appears depressed and uninterested in her activities and surroundings.

Karen, age 13, has Huntington's disease, too. However, her symptoms include an abrupt change in her personality, delusions, and increased anxiety and irritability. She also engages in repetitive behaviors, such as compulsive hand-washing and smoothing wrinkles from her blankets and clothes. Motor symptoms, which frustrate Samuel and Phyllis, are totally absent in Karen.

All three of these patients have an altered gene on chromosome 4 that causes Huntington's disease. As you will learn in Chapter 2, genetic differences occur because the normal sequence of bases in the chromosome can vary. These bases (symbolized as A, C, G, and T) form the genetic code of each chromosome. In Huntington's disease, the triplet CAG is repeated over and over in a particular region of chromosome 4. In healthy people without Huntington's disease, this triplet is normally repeated 7 to 30 times in chromosome 4. In individuals with Huntington's disease, CAG is repeated from 36 to over 120 times. A higher number of CAG repeats is associated with faster progression of the disease. For example, Samuel has 96 repeats of CAG on chromosome 4; Karen has 72 CAG repeats; and Phyllis has 46 CAG repeats.

For more information on Huntington's disease, refer to Chapter 6.

One example of an environmental factor that affects the brain and, therefore, behavior is exposure to lead. There is ample experimental evidence that lead ingestion is associated with an increase in aggressiveness (Needleman, Riess, Tobin, Biesecker, & Greenhouse, 1996). We will devote an entire chapter to the effects of brain damage and developmental disorders (Chapter 16).

Most importantly, we will concern ourselves with biochemical bases of behavior. We will discuss the roles of many chemical substances in the brain, and we will consider what happens when a person has too much or too little of particular chemicals. These chemicals may be substances manufactured by neurons themselves, or they may be chemicals that a person consumes. For example, cigarette smoking has the effect of decreasing the brain's supply of a particular enzyme. A decrease in this enzyme will produce an increase in the activity of another brain chemical, dopamine. However, increased dopamine activity is associated with addictive behaviors. This may mean that cigarette smoking becomes addictive because it indirectly increases dopamine activity in the brain (Fowler et al., 1996).

In this book you will discover that there are all sorts of biological explanations for particular behaviors. These biological factors no doubt interact with social factors, although we will give brief consideration to social factors in this textbook. Our understanding of the relationship between the brain and behavior is growing every day, thanks to the research of behavioral and cognitive neuroscientists. Even as you read this book, important discoveries are being made that will alter the way we view biological influences on behavior in the future.

Let's begin our study of the biological influences on behavior by examining the organization of the nervous system. In Chapter 2, we will examine the nature of *neurons* and *glial cells*, the building blocks of the nervous system. To appreciate how the nervous system controls behavior, you must first understand the functions of neurons and glial cells.

(a)_____ _____ was proposed by Charles Darwin to explain how specific traits selectively develop in individual species. William James introduced the concept of (b)_____ to explain behavior based on its selective advantage or survival benefit to a particular species. Other biological explanations focus on the (c)_____ basis of behavior, the organization of the (d)_____ system, or the biochemical basis of behavior.

Chapter Summary

The History of Brain Research

▶ Hippocrates, Plato, and Galen proposed encephalo-centric explanations of behavior that focused on the brain as the chief source of behaviors, thoughts, and feelings. Aristotle supported a cardiocentric theory that regarded the heart as the source of all behavior.

▶ In the Western world, cardiocentric theories did not give way to encephalocentric explanations of behavior until the time of Galen in the second century.

▶ The modern concept of the brain and brain function did not develop until controlled experiments were conducted in the early nineteenth century.

▶ The earliest investigators of the brain disagreed about whether specific behaviors could be localized to discrete brain structures (localization) or whether the entire brain contributes to any given behavior (holism). Research on the motor cortex in dogs, monkeys, and people supports the concept of localization by showing that the motor cortex is topographically organized in such a way that specific cells in the motor cortex control certain muscles in the body. Karl Lashley's studies of brain-damaged rats that learned to open a box or navigate a maze supported the concept of holism.

▶ The location of the mind has been the subject of another scientific debate in which proponents of dualism argue that the mind and brain are separate entities and proponents of monism argue that the mind is produced by brain activity.

Studying the Brain and Behavior

▶ Many fields of inquiry are concerned with studying the relationship between the brain and behavior, including behavioral and cognitive neuroscience, physiological psychology, biological psychology, psychobiology, and neuropsychology.

▶ Neuroscience is a multi-disciplinary approach to studying the brain. Behavioral neuroscience involves bottom-up research strategies that begin by studying the neuron and its interaction with other neurons. Cognitive neuroscience involves top-down research strategies that manipulate cognitive events like problem solving to produce an effect on neural functioning. Physiological psychology, biological psychology, and biopsychology are often used interchangeably. Neuropsychology involves the study of higher brain functions and their disorders following brain damage.

▶ Some disciplines, like behavioral neuroscience, use bottom-up research strategies. Other disciplines, such as cognitive neuroscience, use a top-down approach.

▶ Bottom-up scientific approaches often require the use of non-human research subjects.

▶ Studies comparing the problem-solving abilities of very young boys and girls are examples of top-down experiments. Studies of the effects of androgen injections on problem solving in female monkeys are examples of bottom-up experiments.

Biological Explanations of Behavior

▶ Natural selection was one early biological explanation of behavior proposed by Charles Darwin in the late 19th century. According to Darwin, specific traits selectively develop in individual species due to a process called natural selection in which animals that survive to reproduce have traits that ensure survival and pass these traits on to their offspring.

▶ The American psychologist William James (1842–1910) introduced the concept of functionalism to explain behavior based on its selective advantage (that is, its survival benefit to a particular species).

▶ Other biological explanations of behavior focus on biological properties of an individual, including the individual's genetic background, structural damage in the brain, or the role of various chemicals in the nervous system.

Key Terms

behavioral neuroscience (p. 12)
biological psychology (p. 12)
bottom-up (p. 12)
cardiocentric (p. 4)
cognitive neuroscience (p. 12)
computational neuroscience (p. 13)
cortex (p. 7)
craniotomy (p. 4)
dualism (p. 10)

encephalocentric (p. 5)
functionalism (p. 17)
holism (p. 7)
hypothesis (p. 4)
institutional animal care and use
   committee (p. 15)
Law of Equipotentiality (p. 10)
Law of Mass Action (p. 10)
localization (p. 7)

monism (p. 11)
natural selection (p. 17)
neuron (p. 12)
neuropsychology (p. 13)
neuroscience (p. 12)
phrenology (p. 7)
physiological psychology (p. 12)
top-down (p. 12)
topographical organization (p. 8)

Questions for Thought

1. Descartes used the word *soul* when referring to the mind. What is the soul? What do you think is the relationship between the soul and the brain?

2. Design a top-down study and a bottom-up study that would help us to understand the relationship between handedness and verbal ability.

3. Under what circumstances should an investigator choose to use nonhuman participants in a study?

Questions for Review

1. What is topographical organization, and how was it discovered?
2. Who were the earliest proponents of localization and holism?
3. What is the difference between monism and dualism?

Suggested Readings

Crick, F. (1988). *What mad pursuit*. New York: Basic Books.

Dewsbury, D. A. (1991). Psychobiology. *American Psychologist, 46*, 198–205.

Finger, S. (1994). History of neuropsychology. In D. W. Zaidel (Ed.), *Neuropsychology* (pp. 1–28). San Diego: Academic Press.

Fishman, S. (1988). *A bomb in the brain*. New York: Charles Scribner's Sons.

Kandel, E. R., & Squire, L. R. (2000). Neuroscience: Breaking down scientific barriers to the study of brain and mind. *Science, 290*, 1113–1120.

Madhusree, M. (1997, February). Trends in animal research. *Scientific American, 2*, 86–93.

Web Resources

For a chapter tutorial quiz, direct links to the Internet sites listed below, and other features, visit the book-specific website at **www.wadsworth.com/product/ 0155074865**. You may also connect directly to the following annotated websites:

www.scienceexpress.org
Provides up-to-the-minute science news, including news on the latest neuroscience research. This is an excellent site to bookmark and search as you continue through the course.

http://www.neurosurgery.org/cybermuseum/pre20th/treph/trephination.html
This site contains a fascinating article about craniotomies and includes a discussion of ancient surgical tools as well as photos of ancient skulls on which craniotomies were performed.

http://faculty.washington/edu/chudler/hist.html
You will find a detailed timeline about the history of neuroscience at this site.

http://serendip.brynmawr.edu/Mind/Table.html
This site is a large resource for information on dualism and monism as well as information on many major figures in neuroscience history.

http://www.pbs.org/wgbh/aso/tryit/brain/
Try the interactive exercise that enables you to manipulate an electrode and produce movement in different parts of the body. See also the information regarding motor cortex mapping.

http://www.apa.org/science/anguide.html
This site contains the American Psychological Association guidelines for ethical conduct in the care and use of animals.

 For additional readings and information, check out InfoTrac College Edition at **http://www.infotrac-college.com/wadsworth**. Choose a search term yourself or enter the following search terms: Animal Research, Behaviorism, Broca's Area, Hydrocephalus (in opening vignette), Psychological Evolution.

CD-ROM: Exploring Biological Psychology

Animation: The Motor Cortex
Animation: The Sensory Cortex
Bottom-Up Versus Top-Down Approaches
    Animation: The Object Reversal Task
    Animation: The Concurrent Discrimination Task

Interactive Recaps
Chapter 1 Quiz
Connect to the Interactive Biological
    Psychology Glossary

2

The Building Blocks of the Nervous System

Camille was a junior psychology major when she began to experience some troubling symptoms. Sometimes she had trouble lifting her legs when climbing stairs, and sometimes her hands and arms stiffened when she was typing on the computer keyboard. Most troubling was the double vision that Camille experienced when she tried to read for long periods of time. The words on the pages of her textbook would swim around when she studied, making it difficult for her to focus on her reading.

During winter break, Camille made an appointment to see her doctor in her hometown. She told her physician about her symptoms, including the intermittent weakness in her arms and legs and her double vision. Camille's physician ordered a number of tests for her. Before she returned to spring semester classes, Camille learned that she had developed multiple sclerosis, a disorder in which the covering on her nerves progressively deteriorates. When the nerves lose their protective covering, information cannot be transmitted effectively from the brain to muscles. Thus, Camille was slowly losing control of the muscles in her arms, legs, and head.

In this chapter, we will examine the nervous system and the important cells, called neurons and glial cells, that comprise the nervous system. We will look at the function of neurons and glial cells, and we will discuss how information is transmitted within a neuron. Later in the chapter, we will come back to the topic of multiple sclerosis and examine the cause of this devastating disorder. First, let's focus on the organization of the nervous system. ●

The Organization of the Nervous System

My son, Tony, came home from school one day and shared with me a tidbit that he had learned in his fourth grade science class. "Systems are made of organs, organs are made of tissue, and tissues are made of cells." A bit simplistic perhaps, but it's a good place to begin our study of the nervous system. As you probably learned in fourth grade, or sometime in elementary school, our bodies are composed of systems that have particular functions that serve to keep us alive; for example, the digestive system, the respiratory system, the immune system, the urinary system, the skeletomuscular system, the cardiovascular system. The nervous system, which is the major focus of this textbook, is just another of the body's many systems.

Some systems are confined to particular regions of our bodies. For example, the respiratory system is located in the chest (the lungs), the neck (the trachea), and the head (throat, mouth, and nasal passages). The nervous system, however, is more similar to the cardiovascular system, which is spread from head to toe, fingertip to fingertip, in our bodies. Like the cardiovascular system, the nervous system courses throughout the entire body, sending messages to all parts of the body except for the epidermis (the dead layers of skin), the finger- and toenails, and hair.

The brain is the major organ of the nervous system, but many other structures comprise the nervous system as well. The **nervous system** consists of the brain, the spinal cord, and the extensive pathways of nervous tissue located throughout the body. It is divided into the **central nervous system** and the **peripheral nervous system**. The brain and the spinal cord compose the central nervous system, whereas all the nervous tissue located outside the brain and spinal cord comprise what is known as the peripheral nervous system (Figure 2.1). We will examine the organization of the central nervous system in Chapter 4.

Organization of the Peripheral Nervous System

The peripheral nervous system has two divisions, the **somatic nervous system** and the **autonomic nervous system.** The somatic nervous system controls *striated muscles,* which get their name from their striated or striped appearance under the microscope. Striated muscles are attached to the bones of the skeleton and are sometimes referred to as *skeletal muscles.* In addition, sensory information arising from the skeletal muscles and the skin is relayed to the brain and spinal cord by the somatic nervous system. Think about how you move about: Skeletal muscles, which are attached to your bones, contract, pulling the bones in one direction or another. Furthermore, these muscles are under your voluntary control. If you decide to

nervous system: one the body's major system, composed of neurons and glia
central nervous system: the nervous system, composed of the brain and spinal cord
peripheral nervous system: all nervous tissue located outside the brain and spinal cord
somatic nervous system: a division of the peripheral nervous system that controls skeletal muscles
autonomic nervous system: a division of the peripheral nervous system, controls smooth muscles

Figure 2.1 The nervous system
The nervous system has two divisions: the central nervous system (composed of the brain and spinal cord) and the peripheral nervous system (all of the nervous tissue located outside the brain and spinal cord).

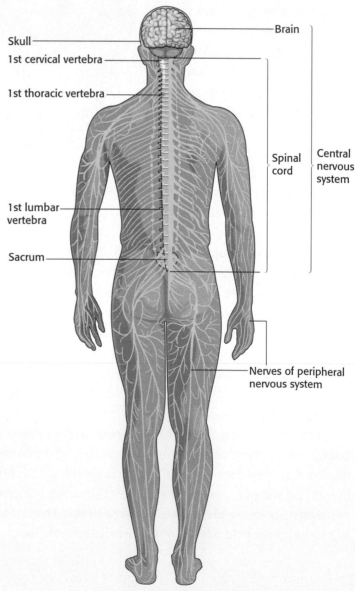

Skull
1st cervical vertebra
1st thoracic vertebra
1st lumbar vertebra
Sacrum

Brain
Spinal cord
Central nervous system
Nerves of peripheral nervous system

sit cross-legged on your chair, you do—thanks to your somatic nervous system. The same is true with raising your hand in class, jotting down notes, or asking a question. The somatic nervous system allows you to move your skeleton about voluntarily.

In contrast, the autonomic nervous system is not ordinarily under your conscious control. It acts automatically, in response to signals from the central nervous system. *Smooth muscles* are controlled by the autonomic nervous system. They have a characteristically smooth appearance under the microscope and are found throughout your body. For example, smooth muscles control the dilation and constriction of the pupils in your eyes. They also regulate the dilation and constriction of blood vessels. One of the reasons why blushing is so embarrassing for people who blush very noticeably is that they can't control it. That is, blushers turn quite red in the face due to activation of the autonomic nervous system, and there is nothing they can do to stop it.

Another example of smooth muscles are the muscles that open and close the ducts in certain glands in the body, like the sweat glands or salivary glands. You cannot will yourself to stop sweating. It is under the control of the autonomic nervous system. Mammary glands, too, are regulated by the autonomic nervous system, which makes it impossible to stop the flow of milk from the nipples, if you are a nursing mother.

Many organs, too, are lined with smooth muscles; for example, the stomach, the small and large intestines, the uterus, and the bladder. This means that you cannot consciously make your stomach digest your dinner faster, or you cannot will the uterus to stop contracting, if you are giving birth. The heart is composed of a special type of muscle, called *cardiac muscle*, that closely resembles smooth muscle. Cardiac muscle is also under the control of the autonomic nervous system.

With special training, people can gain some control over the autonomic nervous system. Yogi masters, who are trained in meditation and body exercises, can control autonomic functions such as heart rate, brain waves, and body metabolism. However, you don't have to be a yogi master to control the autonomic nervous system. Anyone can learn control over smooth muscles through *biofeedback* training. Biofeedback involves giving the trainee information, or feedback, about the state of a particular autonomic function, in an operant conditioning paradigm. This feedback acts as a reward that reinforces changes in autonomic function. For example, individuals can learn to lower their blood pressure through biofeedback (Di Cara & Miller, 1968; Nakao et al., 2000; Norris, Lee, Burshteyn, & Lea-Aravena, 2001). Information about a decrease in blood pressure is given to the trainee in the form of an auditory stimulus, such as a tone. That is, a tone is heard whenever the trainee has a decrease in blood pressure. The trainee then tries to keep the tone on for as long as possible, thereby lowering blood pressure.

Organization of the Autonomic Nervous System

The autonomic nervous system is composed of two divisions, the **sympathetic nervous system** and the **parasympathetic nervous system.** The sympathetic nervous system becomes activated when a person is excited, aroused, or in another highly emotional state. It functions to prepare the body for an emergency, channeling resources in order that a person can react quickly and effectively. Activation of the sympathetic nervous system causes the heart to beat faster and breathing to speed up. It also shunts blood from the organs in the gut to the skeletal muscles, readying an individual to respond to a stressful situation. In 1927, Walter Cannon, an eminent American physiologist, referred to the responses of the sympathetic nervous system as *fight-or-flight* reactions. In the face of a stressful stimulus, such as a verbal threat, we typically make one of two responses: We attack, or we retreat. The sympathetic nervous system organizes the body's reaction to fight or flee.

Think about what happens when a person tries to eat when upset. Imagine that, on your way to lunch, you stop at your mailbox and find a letter from your sweetheart, who goes to school at another campus. You read the letter as you walk to the cafeteria. In it, your sweetie tells you that he (or she) has developed a

sympathetic nervous system: a division of the autonomic nervous system, producing fight-or-flight responses

parasympathetic nervous system: a division of the autonomic nervous system, concerned with energy conservation

romantic interest in another person and never wants to see you again. Immediately, your heart begins to pound, you break into a sweat, and your breathing becomes more rapid—all sympathetic responses. You sit down with friends and try to eat, but the food is tasteless, hard to swallow, and sits like a rock in your stomach after you choke it down. This is because your saliva becomes thick and scant when the sympathetic nervous system is activated, making it difficult to taste and swallow food. The food in your stomach doesn't digest readily because the stomach has been turned off and blood has been diverted from your stomach to your skeletal muscles.

In contrast, the parasympathetic nervous system plays an energy-conserving role. Picture yourself lounging on the sofa after a quiet, filling meal. You are in a parasympathetic state, totally relaxed, almost falling asleep. Your breathing is slow and regular. Your heart rate is decreased, too. Your stomach and intestines are engorged with blood, and these organs contract rhythmically in a process called *peristalsis* as your dinner is digested and absorbed. The functions of the autonomic nervous system are summarized in Figure 2.2.

Figure 2.2 Functions of the sympathetic and parasympathetic nervous systems
The two divisions of the autonomic nervous system, the sympathetic and parasympathetic nervous systems, produce opposite effects throughout the body.

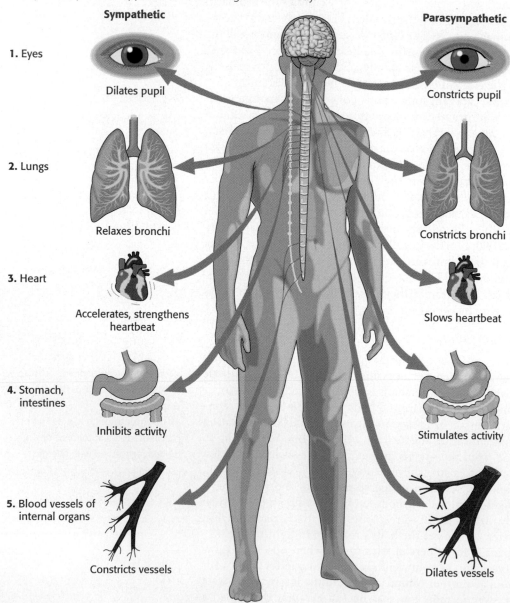

Sympathetic   **Parasympathetic**

1. Eyes — Dilates pupil / Constricts pupil
2. Lungs — Relaxes bronchi / Constricts bronchi
3. Heart — Accelerates, strengthens heartbeat / Slows heartbeat
4. Stomach, intestines — Inhibits activity / Stimulates activity
5. Blood vessels of internal organs — Constricts vessels / Dilates vessels

As you will learn, the nervous system is quite complex. Information is processed in the central nervous system. In response to this information, the central nervous system sends out orders to the peripheral nervous system, directing the action of muscles and glands. We can identify the nervous system anywhere in the body because of the presence of nervous tissue, which consists of two different types of cells, **neurons** and **glia.**

Originally, scientists believed that nervous tissue, unlike other tissue, was not made of cells. In 1840, when Jacob Schleiden and Theodor Schwann declared that cells were the basic units of bodily tissues, the leading scientists of the day agreed that this principle did not apply to the nervous system, which was viewed as a continuous network of strands of nervous tissue. The microscopes and stains available back then were not useful as far as the study of brain and other nervous tissue was concerned. When examined under the microscope, neurons are typically bunched together in tight clumps, making it difficult to discern where one cell ends and another begins, especially given their irregular shapes. Throughout the 19th century, most authorities believed that the brain, unlike other organs of the body, was not made up of cells.

It was another 50 years or so before Santiago Ramon y Cajal, using a silver impregnation staining technique developed by Camillo Golgi, was able to demonstrate that the brain is composed of a large number of cells, which he called "neurones" (Ramon y Cajal, 1933). Thus, Ramon y Cajal introduced a totally new view of the nervous system, called the *Neuron Doctrine.* According to the Neuron Doctrine, the nervous system is composed of millions of individual cells, rather than interconnecting strands of noncellular tissue. Ramon y Cajal and Golgi were jointly awarded the Nobel Prize for their discovery of neurons in 1906. The glia, or glial cells, were identified shortly after neurons were discovered, at the end of the 19th century.

In this chapter, we will examine in great detail the structure and function of the neuron and the glial cell. These two types of cells are considered to be the building blocks of the central and peripheral nervous systems. Let's consider neurons first.

neuron: major cell in the nervous system

glia: supporting cell in the nervous system

✏ Recap 2.1: The Organization of the Nervous System

The nervous system has two divisions, the (a)_____ nervous system, which is composed of the brain and the spinal cord, and the (b)_____ nervous system, which is composed of all the other nervous tissue outside the brain and spinal cord. The peripheral nervous system is composed of two divisions, the (c)_____ nervous system, which controls striated or skeletal muscles, and the (d)_____ nervous system, which controls smooth muscles. The autonomic nervous system is also composed of two divisions, the (e)_____ nervous system, which is activated when a person becomes excited or aroused, and the (f)_____ nervous system, which is activated when a person relaxes. Two types of cells are found in the nervous system, (g)_____ and (h)_____.

Neurons and Glial Cells

The Structure of Neurons

Neurons are very much like other cells in the body. Each has a cell body, or **soma** (plural is *somata*), that is filled with a watery liquid called **cytoplasm** and is bounded by a **cell membrane** (Figure 2.3). Inside the soma, various tiny structures, called **organelles,** are found: the nucleus, nucleolus, endoplasmic reticulum, Golgi complex,

soma: cell body
cytoplasm: fluid found within a cell
cell membrane: outer surface of any animal cell
organelle: specialized structure within a cell

microsomes, mitochondria, and ribosomes. You probably learned about organelles sometime ago in a science class, but let's review the functions of the most important organelles in the neuron now.

The **nucleus** of a cell is one of the most prominent structures in the cell. Under the microscope, even the most inexperienced eye can pick out this rather large, roundish structure. The nucleus is important because it contains the genetic information of the cell. This information is coded in the form of strings of nucleic acid that are located in **chromosomes.** The human cell typically contains 23 pairs of chromosomes, except for ova and sperm cells, which contain 23 unpaired chromo-

Figure 2.3 The parts of a cell

The cell body, or soma, is bounded by a cell membrane and contains numerous structures, including the nucleus, robosomes, and mitochondria.

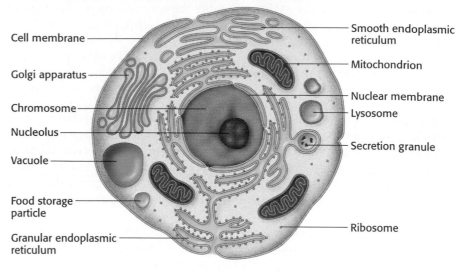

Cell membrane — Smooth endoplasmic reticulum — Golgi apparatus — Mitochondrion — Chromosome — Nuclear membrane — Lysosome — Nucleolus — Vacuole — Secretion granule — Food storage particle — Granular endoplasmic reticulum — Ribosome

somes, as we will discuss in Chapter 12. Of these 23 pairs of chromosomes, 22 are called *autosomes*, and the final pair is referred to as the *sex chromosomes*, designated X and Y chromosomes. Altogether, approximately 200,000 genes are encoded in 23 pairs of chromosomes in each human cell. The sum total of these genes is called the **genome,** and the same genome is found in every cell in an individual's body.

Nucleic acids are specialized phosphoric acids that are found in abundance in the nucleus of all cells. There are two types of nucleic acids: deoxyribonucleic acid, or **DNA,** and ribonucleic acid, or **RNA.** Besides having different chemical structures, DNA and RNA differ in a number of other respects. For example, DNA is found in chromosomes in the nucleus of the cell, whereas RNA is generally located in ribosomes. In addition, DNA is composed of four nucleotide bases, known as adenine (A), guanine (G), cytosine (C), and thymine (T). The building blocks of RNA, on the other hand, are adenine (A), guanine (G), cytosine (C), and uracil (U).

Genetic variations are produced when the normal sequence of nucleotide bases in DNA is disrupted. One example of a genetic alteration, fragile-X syndrome, which produces mental impairment in afflicted individuals. People with fragile X mental retardation possess X chromosomes that are so fragile that they often break when handled by researchers in the laboratory. The problem has been associated with a repeat of three bases (CGG) on the X chromosome. Normally, the CGG triad is repeated 10 to 30 times on the X chromosome. In individuals with fragile X mental retardation, however, this triad is repeated hundreds of times, producing a weakened, fragile arm of the affected X chromosome (Plomin, 1995). It is important to remember that fragile X is only one form of mental retardation and that not all mental retardation is associated with the X chromosome. For example, mental retardation that results from untreated phenylketonuria (PKU) has been linked to an altered gene on chromosome 12.

Genetic alterations are also produced when chromosomes are missing or when extra chromosomes are present in the cell nucleus. For example, in Down's syndrome, three copies of chromosome 21 are found, instead of the usual pair of chromosomes (Figure 2.4). This chromosomal abnormality contributes to faulty development of the brain, which leads to impairment of cognition. Thus, an individual with Down's syndrome will present with mental retardation, as well as a number of other skeletal and soft tissue abnormalities.

Ribosomes are tiny cellular structures responsible for the production of protein in the cell. RNA translation, which involves decoding strings of nucleotide bases into sequences of amino acids, occurs in the ribosomes (Tjian, 1995). Each sequence of amino acids is a particular protein that has a specific function in the cell.

nucleus: cluster of neuronal soma (cell bodies) in the central nervous system

chromosome: structure found in the cell nucleus that contain strings of nucleic acids that code for various genes

genome: the complete collection of genes that is encoded in the cell's chromosomes

DNA: deoxyribonucleic acid, the type of nucleic acid found in chromosomes

RNA: ribonucleic acid, the type of nucleic acid found in ribosomes

ribosomes: special cellular structures that direct the production of protein in the cell

Some proteins are enzymes, others are cellular building blocks, and still others are important chemicals required for cell function. Enzymes and other chemicals are used by neurons to synthesize special substances called *neurotransmitters*, which are unique to neurons. Neurotransmitters permit the neuron to carry out its most important function, which is communicating with other cells in the body. In Chapter 3, we will examine the many different neurotransmitters and their functions.

The final organelle that I would like to bring to your attention is the **mitochondrion** (plural is *mitochondria*). Mitochondria have a very important function: to produce the fuel, or energy source, of the cell. For all cells, this energy source is **adenosine triphosphate,** abbreviated as ATP. ATP is used by cells to fuel most metabolic reactions that keep us alive. Because of the special work that they do, neurons require a lot of ATP. Therefore, mitochondria are found in large numbers throughout the neuron, especially near the cell membrane, where most of the communicating functions of neurons take place.

Mitochondria are also of extreme interest to behavioral geneticists, who study the role that genes play in the development of certain behaviors. This interest is due to the fact that mitochondria contain DNA. A number of disorders have been associated with mutations in mitochondrial DNA, including migraine headaches, movement disorders, mental depression, diabetes accompanied by blindness and deafness, and neurodegenerative brain disorders that produce seizures, blindness, deafness, and severe headaches (Graf et al., 2000; Hanna & Bhatia, 1997; Hofmann et al., 1997; Kato, 2001; Katz et al., 1997; Kerrison et al., 1995; Montine et al., 1995; Onishi et al., 1997; Russell, Diamant, & Narby, 1997; Santorelli et al., 1997; Suomalainen, 1997; Uncini et al., 1995). Mitochondrial DNA is always inherited from the mother, whereas nuclear DNA is inherited from both parents. This is because ova contain mitochondria, whereas sperm do not. When an egg and sperm are united during fertilization, only the egg brings mitochondria to the newly created individual, and thus only the mother provides mitochondrial DNA.

Dendrites and Axons

The neuron is a cell and contains cytoplasm and the organelles found in other kinds of cells. But, it is no ordinary cell. First, the neuron has a special function: gathering, processing, and sending information to other cells and communicating with the outside world. Second, as you've just learned, neurons manufacture neurotransmitters, which are used to signal other cells.

The neuron also differs from other types of cells in its appearance. Look closely at Figure 2.5. Can you spot any differences between neurons and other cells? You may notice that neurons have many projections, whereas most other cells have a smooth appearance. These projections have names: **dendrites** and **axons.**

A neuron typically has many dendrites and one axon. Each dendrite is multibranched, and some are covered with **dendritic spines.** Most signals reaching the neuron are received by the dendrites, which have special proteins on their surface to process the signal. There is evidence that dendritic spines can change shape and, thus, alter the messages that are received (Koch, Zador, & Brown, 1992). The axon is a tube-shaped projection that arises from a thickened area on the soma known as the **axon hillock.** Unlike the dendrites, the axon is usually unbranched except at its end, where it branches into numerous button-shaped endings called **terminal buttons** in English or, more commonly, *terminal boutons*, as they were named by their French discoverers. The structure of both the axon and the dendrites is formed by a protein scaffolding known as the *cytoskeleton*. As you will learn in Chapter 16, this cytoskeleton plays an important role in the development of certain disorders, such as Alzheimer's disease.

Figure 2.4 Down's syndrome and trisomy of chromosome 21

The individual with Down's syndrome will present with mental retardation and a number of soft tissue abnormalities. This disorder is associated with the presence of three copies of chromosome 21 (bottom photograph).

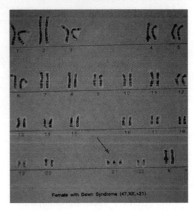

Female with Down Syndrome (47,XX,+21)

mitochondrion: organelle that produces ATP, the energy source for the cell

adenosine triphosphate: the principal fuel of the cell

dendrite: multibranched neuronal process that receives messages from other neurons

axon: single, long process that conducts information away from the cell body of the neuron

dendritic spines: tiny projections on dendrites that contain special proteins that process signals from other neurons

axon hillock: a thickened area on the soma that gives rise to the axon

terminal buttons: button-shaped endings on axons where neurotransmitters are stored

Figure 2.5 Different types of cells

Neurons have a distinctly different appearance, compared to other cells.

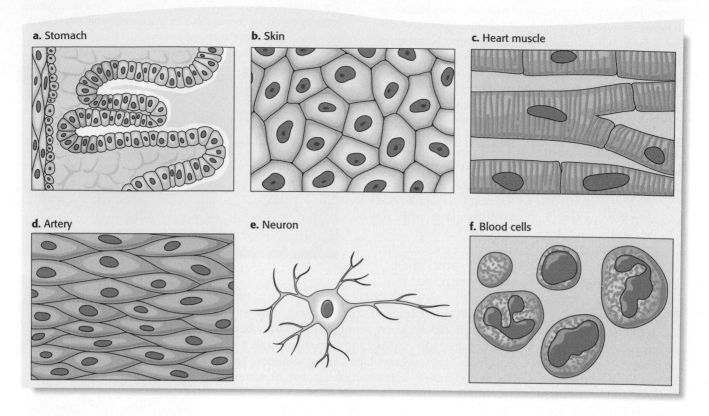

a. Stomach

b. Skin

c. Heart muscle

d. Artery

e. Neuron

f. Blood cells

Figure 2.6 is an illustration of a typical neuron. You can see that dendrites are much shorter than the axon. In fact, in some neurons, they can be more than 1,000 times shorter than an axon, given that axons can be 1 meter (m) or more long and that most dendrites are less than 1 millimeter (mm, or 10^{-3} m) long. By contrast, the soma of a neuron is usually measured in micrometers (10^{-6} m).

The enormous length of the axon, relatively speaking, gives us a clue as to its function. Why would a neuron possess a long projection that is a million times longer than the diameter of its soma? The axon obviously stretches far away from the cell body, which means that it is capable of taking signals from the soma to cells in other parts of the body. For example, thousands of axons from neurons in your spinal cord extend down your leg to communicate with muscles in your foot.

Figure 2.6 A typical neuron

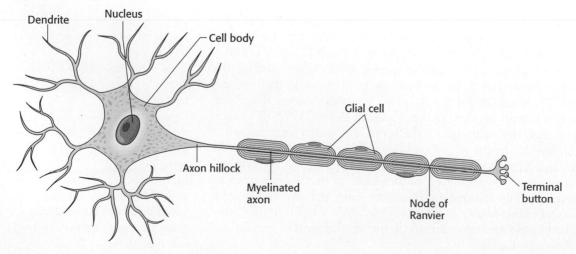

Dendrite

Nucleus

Cell body

Glial cell

Axon hillock

Myelinated axon

Node of Ranvier

Terminal button

Not all neurons have extremely long axons, however. In fact, most neurons, over 90%, are **interneurons** whose axons and dendrites are very short and do not extend beyond their cell cluster. These neurons are also called *intrinsic* or *local* neurons because they exchange messages with neighboring neurons and do not transmit information over long distances. Interneurons are found in both the peripheral and central nervous systems.

Figure 2.7 illustrates the wide range of shapes and sizes of neurons. Authorities have attempted to group these different types of neurons but have been unable to settle on one classification scheme. Hence, numerous classification systems for neurons are in use. Let's take a look at two such classification systems.

Classifying Neurons

Ramon y Cajal's Classification System

Probably the best-known classification system for neurons is based on the shape of the neuron. Ramon y Cajal, the investigator who discovered neurons, classified all neurons into one of three groups, based on the number of processes possessed by the neuron: (1) monopolar neurons, (2) bipolar neurons, and (3) multipolar neurons (Ramon y Cajal, 1933). A **monopolar neuron** (Figure 2.7a) has only one process that typically branches a short distance from the soma. This type of neuron is often found in the spinal cord and in the peripheral nervous system, for example, in the retina of the eye. As its name implies, a **bipolar neuron** possesses two processes, one dendrite and one axon (Figure 2.7b). These cells are usually located in the peripheral nervous system. The third type of neuron, the **multipolar neuron,** has three or more processes, typically many dendrites and only one axon (Figure 2.7c). Multipolar neurons, which make up the majority of all neurons, are found throughout the central and peripheral nervous systems.

At the time that Ramon y Cajal first discovered neurons, the tiny interneurons were not recognized as neurons. For many years, investigators assumed that these minuscule cells (some with very short, almost imperceptible dendrites and axons) were immature neurons that had no function. Therefore, Ramon y Cajal's classification did not include interneurons.

Classification System for Neurons Based on Function

The system that is widely used to classify neurons in the spinal cord is based on the function of the neuron. There are three types of neurons in this classification system: (1) motor neurons, (2) sensory neurons, and (3) interneurons.

Motor neurons carry information from the central nervous system to muscles and glands. Their soma are located in the central nervous system, and the terminal buttons of their axons are found interspersed among muscle fibers. When a motor neuron is excited, it produces contraction of muscle fibers.

A cross-section of the spinal cord is illustrated in Figure 2.8. Examine this diagram closely. You will notice that the spinal cord, when cut in cross-section, looks like a gray butterfly surrounded by a white border. The gray area, known as *gray matter*, contains the soma of neurons located in the spinal cord. The white area, or *white matter*, is comprised of axons. The axons appear white because most axons are covered with a white, fatty substance called *myelin*.

In addition, the spinal cord can be divided into two portions: the ventral aspect and the dorsal aspect. The **ventral** aspect of the spinal cord is the part of the spinal cord that is closest to your belly, whereas the **dorsal** aspect is closest to your back. The important point to remember here is that we are all "wired" alike: Motor neurons are always found in the ventral portion of the spinal cord. In Figure 2.8, you can see that

Figure 2.7 Different shapes of neurons
Neurons differ in form and function. Typical forms include: (a) unipolar, (b) bipolar, and (c) multipolar.

a.

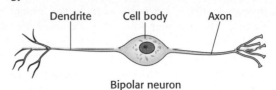

Unipolar neuron

b.

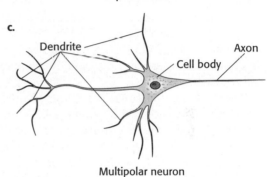

Bipolar neuron

c.

Multipolar neuron

interneuron: an intrinsic neuron that receives information from one neuron and passes it on to another
monopolar neuron: a neuron with only one process
bipolar neuron: a neuron with two processes
multipolar neuron: a neuron with many processes

motor neuron: a neuron in the central nervous that stimulates muscle contractions

ventral: toward the belly
dorsal: toward the back

the soma of motor neurons are located in the gray matter in the ventral horns of the spinal cord. Their axons leave the spinal cord and course through the peripheral nervous system to reach the muscle fibers that each stimulates.

Motor neurons are also located in the brain. Generally, in the brain, the soma of motor neurons are grouped together in little nests of gray matter called *nuclei*. (Throughout the central nervous system, the soma of neurons are clustered in functional groups called **nuclei**. In the peripheral nervous system, these clusters of neuronal cell bodies are called **ganglia**.) These motor nuclei are situated throughout the lower regions of the brain. Axons from the motor neurons leave the brainstem nuclei and course through the peripheral nervous system to stimulate muscles in the head and neck. A good rule of thumb is that the motor neurons located in the brain control muscles in the head and neck, whereas motor neurons in the spinal cord control muscles from the shoulders on down to the toes.

Sensory neurons are located in the peripheral nervous system and carry information to the central nervous system. Typically, the cell bodies of sensory neurons are found in ganglia in the peripheral nervous system. Their axons enter the brain or spinal cord, where they transmit information about the outside world to the central nervous system.

Sensory neurons situated anywhere in the body below the neck normally have axons that terminate in the spinal cord. In Figure 2.8, you can see that the axons of sensory neurons enter the spinal cord on its dorsal side. Located next to the dorsal aspect of the spinal cord are the *dorsal root ganglia*, where the soma of many sensory neurons are found. Axons leave the dorsal root ganglion and enter the dorsal root of the spinal cord, along with all the other axons that enter the spinal cord.

Take a moment to think about the organization of the spinal cord. The ventral portion contains motor neurons, and its dorsal aspect processes information from sensory neurons. According to the **Bell-Magendie law,** motor nerves exit from the ventral horns of the spinal cord, and sensory information enters the dorsal horns. What can you surmise about damage to the spinal cord? Damage to the ventral part of the spinal cord will produce motor dysfunction, whereas damage to the dorsal part will impair sensation. Obviously, damage to the entire spinal cord, as when the spinal cord is totally transected or torn apart, will affect both sensory and motor functions.

Sensory neurons in the head and neck send their axons directly to the brain, via *cranial nerves*, which we will examine in Chapter 4. Therefore, damage to the spinal cord does not affect sensory or motor functions of the head. Damage to a cranial nerve will impair the specific sense associated with that nerve. For example, damage to the olfactory nerve, or cranial nerve I, will impair the sense of smell, and injury to the optic nerve, also known as cranial nerve II, will impair vision.

In the spinal cord, an interneuron is an intrinsic neuron that receives information from one neuron and passes it on to another neuron. That is, as its name implies, an interneuron is situated between two other neurons. The axons and dendrites of interneurons do not extend beyond their cell clusters in the gray matter of the spinal cord. See Figure 2.8 for their location in the spinal cord.

Special Features of Neurons

As you've learned, neurons are a unique type of cell. They have many special features that set them apart from other cells in the body. Before we launch into a discussion of the function of neurons, consider a number of their distinctive characteristics because these will help you understand better the peculiar nature of neurons.

You've already learned about two special features of neurons. Neurons have unusual shapes, with dendrites and long processes called axons. In addition, neurons produce unique substances called neurotransmitters, which they use to transmit signals.

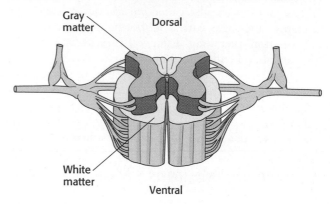

Figure 2.8 Cross-section of the spinal cord
Sensory information enters the dorsal aspect of the spinal cord, and motor information exits via the ventral root.

Gray matter

Dorsal

White matter

Ventral

nuclei: clusters of soma of neurons found in the central nervous system

ganglia: clusters of soma of neurons found in the peripheral nervous system

sensory neuron: a neuron that responds to stimuli in the periphery and sends information about the stimuli to the central nervous system

Bell-Magendie law: the rule that motor nerves exit from the ventral horns of the spinal cord and sensory nerves enter the dorsal horns

Another special feature of neurons is their enormous and constant need for oxygen, more than any other cell in the body. Neurons require large amounts of oxygen, even when they are inactive or "resting." Remember that neurons have large numbers of mitochondria throughout their cell bodies, dendrites, and axons. These mitochondria are miniature factories that use huge quantities of oxygen to produce ATP, the principal fuel of the cell. Neurons that don't get enough oxygen cannot make ATP, which supports the cell's vital functions. Think about it for a moment. Neurons keep us alive: They keep us awake and conscious, they allow us to see and hear, they make us breathe. If your brain does not get the oxygen it needs, if it is deprived of oxygen for more than 10–15 seconds, then you lose consciousness. If oxygen deprivation continues for longer than that, coma and, finally, death ensue. The *Case Study* (on page 34) illustrates the effects of oxygen deprivation of the brain.

Another unusual characteristic of neurons is that they are picky eaters. You see, other cells in the body can metabolize almost any nutrient. For example, muscles prefer fat but can also metabolize protein and carbohydrates. But, the only nutrient that neurons can metabolize is glucose, a simple sugar. This means that any shortage in glucose supplies will affect neuron function and that any disorder that affects glucose availability will affect the brain and, ultimately, behavior. Perhaps the best-known glucose-related disorder is diabetes, which afflicts over 15 million North American men, women, and children. People with diabetes lack adequate amounts of insulin, which is needed to transport glucose out of the blood and into cells. Without insulin, diabetic individuals cannot get glucose into their neurons, and, hence, neurons cannot function properly. Diabetic coma, a state of unconsciousness in which the individual does not respond to any stimulation, occurs when people with diabetes do not take their prescribed insulin and their neurons become starved for glucose.

Still another unique feature of neurons is their inability to regenerate. Other cells in the body, except for fat cells, will regenerate to replace dead cells. For example, skin cells are replaced every few days. On the other hand, when neurons in the central nervous system are damaged or die, they generally are not replaced, although there is some evidence that cells in some parts of the brain do regenerate (Barinaga, 1998; Gould & McEwen, 1993). What does this mean for brain function? Obviously, if enough brain cells are destroyed, the affected person's behavior could be severely disrupted, as happens in chronic alcoholism. A large percentage of chronic alcoholics show evidence of brain damage and develop symptoms of mental confusion and memory loss (Sugawara, Namura, & Hishikawa, 1997).

Finally, unlike other cells in the body, neurons have helper-companion cells called glia, or glial cells. In the next section, we will examine the structure and function of glial cells. Without these special cells, neurons could not carry out their important functions.

astrocytes: astroglia, star-shaped glial cells

The Role of Glia

Glial cells are the "glue" that hold the nervous system together. It is estimated that there are 10 times as many glial cells as neurons in the nervous system and that they comprise over 50% of the brain's volume (Travis, 1994). Therefore, because there are over 200 billion neurons in the human body, this means that our bodies contain at least 2 trillion glia!

In addition to being more plentiful than neurons, glia are much smaller. The soma of most glial cells range from 6 to 10 micrometers in diameter (Hammond, 1996). Like neurons, glia come in many shapes and sizes (Figure 2.9). **Astrocytes,** also called *astroglia*, are star-shaped and

Figure 2.9 Two common types of glia

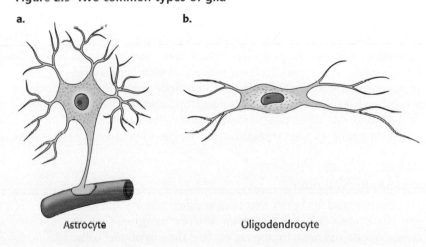

a. Astrocyte

b. Oligodendrocyte

Baby Trapped in a Recliner

Baby Amanda was nearly 15 months old when she was admitted to a metropolitan hospital in a coma. Shortly before the ambulance brought her to the hospital, Amanda had been toddling happily around the living room of her home, where she lived with her mother and father. Unfortunately, someone had left a recliner in its laid-back position, with its back down and its footstool up. Amanda threw herself down on the footstool, laughing. The weight of her body pushed the footstool down, causing the chair to automatically assume its upright position. Amanda's neck was trapped in the space between the footstool and the chair, and, when the chair folded upright, the footstool squeezed against her neck, obstructing the flow of blood to her brain.

Amanda's mother was in the living room at the time of this incident, and she raced over to the chair when she realized what had happened. It took her nearly 20 seconds to get Amanda free from the chair. However, by that time, Amanda was purple in the face and unconscious. Unable to revive her baby, Amanda's mother dialed 911 and summoned an ambulance.

When Amanda arrived at the hospital, she was breathing on her own but did not respond to any stimulation whatsoever. She was examined by a team of neurologists who determined that she was in a coma. The anoxia [*an-* = without; *-oxia* = oxygen] caused by the compression of the chair on her neck, which stopped the flow of blood to her brain, damaged Amanda's brain to such an extent that she was not expected to regain consciousness. Amanda remained in a vegetative state until her death three months later.

---

relatively large. **Microglia,** as you would guess from their name, are the tiniest of glial cells. **Radial glia** have long appendages that radiate out from the soma. Two other common types of glia, the **Schwann cells** and **oligodendrocytes,** have flattened shapes.

Glia play a number of important roles in the smooth running of the nervous system: (1) They provide nourishment to neurons; (2) they remove waste products and dead neurons; (3) they form scar tissue in the nervous system; (4) they direct the development of the nervous system in the embryo; (5) they provide insulation for axons; (6) they contribute to the blood-brain barrier; (7) they communicate information to each other and to neurons; and (8) they function as the brain's immune system (Hammond, 1996; Streit & Kincaid-Colton, 1995; Laming et al., 2000; Pfrieger & Barres, 1997). Let's examine each of these functions separately.

microglia: tiny glial cells

radial glia; glial cells that have long appendages that radiate out from the soma and direct the development of the nervous system

Providing Nourishment for Neurons

Glial cells, particularly astrocytes, are responsible for making sure that the neurons get the nutrients that they need, such as glucose, water, amino acids, and oxygen. Figure 2.10 is an illustration from Ramon y Cajal (1933), who conducted some of the earliest modern neuroanatomical studies of the brain. In this drawing, you can see exactly what Ramon y Cajal found when he studied certain astroglial cells. These astrocytes surround blood vessels, as in Figure 2.10, with several of their appendages actually penetrating the outer lining of the blood vessel. Ramon y Cajal called these appendages "sucking apparatuses" because he surmised that astrocytes remove nutrients from the blood. These nutrients are then transferred by the glia to neurons.

Removing Waste Products and Dead Neurons

You can imagine that a cell that uses as much glucose and oxygen as a neuron does will have a lot of waste products, such as *carbon dioxide* and *urea*, to dispose of. It is the job of glial cells,

Figure 2.10 Astrocytes surrounding a blood vessel
The foot processes of astrocytes completely surround the walls of capillaries in the brain. Using a microscope, Ramon y Cajal observed that some of these foot processes actually penetrate the outer lining of the capillaries, and he called them "sucking apparatuses."

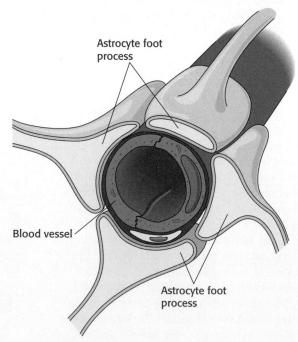

Astrocyte foot process

Blood vessel

Astrocyte foot process

especially microglia and astrocytes, to gather up waste and package it properly for transport in blood vessels back to the lungs and kidneys. Likewise, when there are dead neurons lying about, as might happen after an injury to the nervous system or, to a lesser extent, after a night of heavy alcohol consumption, glia package up these dead cells for transport in the blood. Microglia also function as *macrophages*, gobbling up dead neurons and foreign substances (Graeberg, Kreutzberg, & Streit, 1993).

Forming Scar Tissue in the Nervous System

When neurons die, new neurons are not generated to replace them. Glial cells are there to pick up the debris, as you just learned. But what about the empty space that the dead neurons used to occupy? Is it left empty? No, glial cells, typically astrocytes, migrate into the empty space, forming scar tissue. **Gliosis,** or the accumulation of glia in brain tissue, is a prominent feature in a number of neurodegenerative illnesses that occur in old age (reviewed in Chapter 16). In these illnesses, brain cells die in large numbers in particular regions of the brain, producing mental confusion, memory loss, seizures, speech impairment, and motor dysfunction in the afflicted individual (Andreasen et al., 2001; Jellinger, 2001; Lescaudron et al., 2001). These patches of dead neurons are replaced by glial cells, which multiply and take over large areas in the brain, disrupting brain function.

Directing the Development of the Nervous System in the Embryo

Early in embryonic development, the cells of the embryo fold in on themselves, creating a tubelike structure called the *neural tube* (Figure 2.11). The walls of the neural tube contain germinal cells, which give rise to all the neurons in the body. That is, all of the neurons in an individual's body are formed along the neural tube and then migrate out to their proper destination in the body. Each neuron is created as a particular type of neuron with a particular address. It is the responsibility of the radial glial cells to make sure that neurons arrive at their correct destination. Newly created neurons move along the hairlike processes of the *radial glia* to their proper position in the body (Cowan, 1979). Think about what a complicated process this must be: Over 200 billion neurons must migrate to their rightful place in the nervous system. During the development of the human embryo, neurons are created at a rate of 250,000 per minute, which means that radioglia must orchestrate the movements of a large number of neurons very quickly over relatively long distances. Astrocytes also play an important role linking neurons together, during maturation of the nervous system, to promote communication between neurons (Ullian, Sapperstein, Christopherson, & Barres, 2001). In Chapter 16, we will examine in greater detail the development of the nervous system and the problems that can arise from faulty brain development.

Figure 2.11 Neural tube development in the embryo
Neurons arise from germinal, or stem, cells located around the neural tube.

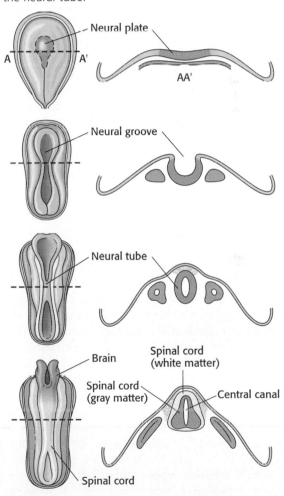

Providing Insulation for Axons

Most axons in the nervous system are surrounded by a special type of insulation composed of specialized glial cells, which are wrapped around selected axons dozens of times and form a fatty substance called **myelin** (Figure 2.12). There are breaks in the insulation, about 1 micron in length, known as **nodes of Ranvier,** in places where one glial cell ends and another begins. In the central nervous system, the glial cells forming the myelin sheaths are called oligodendrocytes; whereas in the peripheral nervous system, they are called Schwann cells.

An oligodendrocyte consists of a cell body with up to 70 long processes. Each process of the oligodendrocyte forms a myelin segment and wraps itself around a short distance (about 1 mm) of an axon (Hammond, 1996). Therefore, one oligodendrocyte can provide myelin segments for as many as 70 different axons. This means that damage to one oligodendrocyte can have a devastating effect on the functioning of large numbers of neurons. In contrast, the entire Schwann cell is wrapped around one axon, each Schwann cell forming only one myelin segment.

Another important difference between oligodendrocytes and Schwann cells accounts for why axonal regeneration and repair are possible in the peripheral nervous system but not in the central nervous system. When an axon is severed in the peripheral nervous system, the axon grows back and its function is often restored. This regrowth does not happen in the central nervous system. For example, when the spinal cord is damaged, the axons do not regenerate, leaving the injured person permanently disabled. In the central nervous system, when an axon is damaged, the myelin segments provided by oligodendrocytes collapse, and astrocytes fill in the empty space left by the degenerated axon, making it impossible for the regenerating axon to find its way back to the neurons with which it formerly communicated. However, Schwann cells do not collapse when an axon is damaged. Instead, they maintain their shape and provide an open tunnel through which the regenerating axon can grow (Figure 2.13). They also excrete a growth factor that stimulates the regrowth of the degenerated axon. Investigators are working to unlock the secret of the Schwann cell. If oligodendrocytes can be made to act like Schwann cells, spinal cord injuries and other damage to the central nervous system may be reversed. One promising treatment of injuries to the central nervous system involves implanting a peripheral nerve graft at the site of injury. The Schwann cells in the graft promote the regeneration and regrowth of central nervous system axons over relatively long distances (Berry, Carlisle, & Hunter, 1996; Brecknell & Fawcett, 1996).

Multiple sclerosis is a disorder caused by degeneration of the myelin covering of axons. Although there is disagreement as to what causes this degeneration, multiple sclerosis appears to be an auto-immune illness in which the body's immune system targets myelin as a foreign substance and attempts to destroy it. When the myelin insulation is stripped from the axon, communication of information down the axon becomes disrupted, and the neuron cannot function properly. This is especially devastating for motor neurons, which send their information via relatively long axons to muscles. Therefore, multiple sclerosis begins as a motor disorder, in which movement becomes slow, weak, and uncontrolled. Symptoms typically begin in early adulthood. For example, television talk show host Montel Williams was first diagnosed with multiple sclerosis when he was 43, but he experienced symptoms of the disorder for at least 10 years before the diagnosis (Figure 2.14). Most people with multiple sclerosis experience periods of poor motor function interspersed with periods of remission, in which symptoms disappear or diminish. Over time, however, symptoms usually get worse, leaving the victim unable to control movement.

In addition to providing a covering for axons, oligodendrocytes and Schwann cells lend structural support to the cell bodies of neurons (Hammond, 1996). In other organs of the body, connective tissue holds cells together and provides a structural framework for the organ. Glial cells perform this function in the nervous system, surrounding and encapsulating the cell bodies in the gray matter of the nervous system. They also segregate groups of neurons from each other, thus forming a structural framework in the nervous system. Many authors refer to these encapsulating glia as *satellite cells.*

Figure 2.12 A myelinated axon

Most axons are covered with a myelin sheath, composed of glial cells called oligodendrocytes in the central nervous system and Schwann cells in the peripheral nervous system.

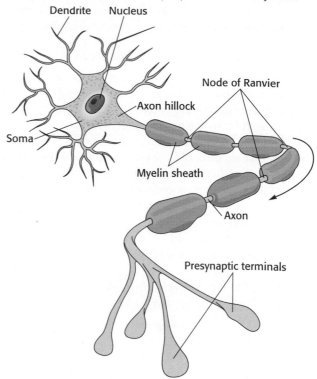

Contributing to the Blood-Brain Barrier

Neurons get their nourishment from the blood, which carries oxygen, glucose, water, amino acids, and needed vitamins and minerals to the brain and all other parts of the nervous system. The blood, however, carries other chemicals and microorganisms, such as bacteria and viruses, that are harmful to the cells of the brain. Glial cells, especially astrocytes, help form a barrier between the blood and the brain by causing the cells in the walls of blood capillaries to form tight, overlapping junctions that keep out harmful substances that could interfere with the smooth functioning of the brain. In other parts of the body, blood vessels are not connected to each other with tight junctions but instead have little gaps, called *fenestrations*, that allow substances to flow freely from the blood to body tissues (Figure 2.15). Janzer and Raff (1987) have demonstrated that blood vessels from intestinal muscles lose their fenestrations and develop tight junctions when implanted in the central nervous system. Astrocytes are suspected of promoting the development of these tight junctions because, when astrocytes are removed, even brain capillaries become fenestrated and do not develop tight junctions.

Bacteria are one example of a harmful agent that the blood-brain barrier tries to keep out of the brain. These microorganisms cause infection when they invade body tissues, producing swelling and inflammation. Obviously, swelling is not desirable in the brain because it is surrounded by a bony skull that does not expand. A bacterial infection in the brain would produce swelling, tissue damage, and neuronal death. Antibiotics are used to treat bacterial infections in the body. However, antibiotics cannot easily cross the blood-brain barrier, so attempts to stop the bacterial infection are quite limited.

Viruses, on the other hand, are very tiny, about 1,000 times smaller than bacteria. Because of their small size, some viruses are capable of sneaking through the blood-brain barrier. These viruses cause a brain infection called *encephalitis*. You've probably heard of encephalitis because outbreaks of this illness are very disturbing and often publicized. For example, during the fall of 1997, an outbreak of encephalitis in Florida prompted Disney World and other amusement parks in Orlando to close before dusk to reduce human contact with mosquitoes, which are believed to carry the encephalitis virus. When the virus enters the brain, it begins to reproduce, causing inflammation and swelling. Infected individuals at first feel like they have the flu, with a fever and achiness. But, delirium and then a coma-like state soon follow. Because we have no drugs available to treat viruses (and even if we did, they probably couldn't get through the blood-brain barrier), there is not much we can do to treat a person with encephalitis. About half die, and the other half who survive often show lingering signs of neurological damage.

Only substances that are fat soluble can easily cross the blood-brain barrier. This is because the cells that form the blood vessel walls are composed of lipid, or fat, molecules. Most psychoactive drugs, such as heroin, nicotine, and cocaine, are fat soluble and rapidly cross the blood-brain barrier. The same is true for oxygen. However, water-soluble substances have to be carried across the blood-brain barrier. Many important nutrients, including glucose, amino acids, iron, and many vitamins, are water soluble and require special carriers to enter the brain (Goldstein & Betz, 1986; Lewis, 1999).

Figure 2.13 Regeneration of a damaged axon
When an axon is injured, it degenerates back to the soma (cell body). Over time, the axon will begin to regrow, and the myelin sheath will be regenerated. This process of axonal regeneration can be successfully accomplished in the peripheral nervous system, but it is not possible in the central nervous system.

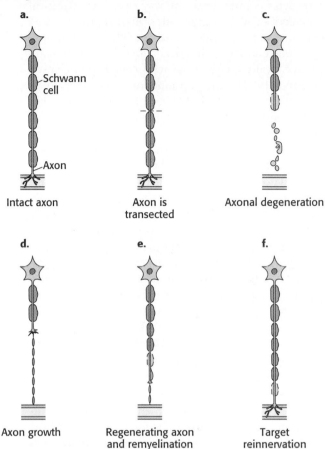

Figure 2.14 Montel Williams
Talk show host Montel Williams was first diagnosed with multiple sclerosis at the age of 43.

Communicating Information to Each Other and to Neurons

Scientists have learned only recently that some glia have receptors that are capable of receiving messages from neurons and other glia (Gallo & Chittajallu, 2001; Pfreiger & Barres, 1997). Most astrocytes communicate by way of special electrical connections, called **gap junctions** (Figure 2.16). A gap junction is a place where the cell membranes of two cells come together and allow the transmission of electrically charged particles called **ions** (Jensen & Chiu, 1993). The gap junction, then, is nothing more than a pore or opening in the cell membranes of two adjoining cells through which positively or negatively charged particles enter and leave the cell, producing an electrical signal. Gap junctions are found between astrocytes, between astrocytes and other types of glia, between astrocytes and neurons, and even between neurons. In addition, there is evidence that some glial cells have receptors on their surfaces that respond to neurotransmitters released by neurons and, hence, are capable of responding to messages from neurons (Iino, et al., 2001; Oliet, Piet, & Poulain, 2001; Travis, 1994). Other investigators have demonstrated that astrocytes even manufacture substances that regulate brain activity (Shinoda, Marini, Cosi, & Schwartz, 1989; Stornetta, Hawelu-Johnson, Guyenet, & Lynch, 1988).

Functioning as the Brain's Immune System

The immune system's major form of protection in the body is white blood cells, which provide surveillance and defense against infection and cancer. However, the blood-brain barrier keeps white blood cells from passing into the brain because these cells secrete substances that can kill neurons as well as invading microorganisms. For many years, scientists believed that the brain lacks immune protection. But, recent research has confirmed that the central nervous system does indeed possess an immunological defense system, microglia. Microglia provide immune protection in a variety of ways. They act as macrophages, devouring foreign substances and disabled microorganisms. They induce and organize attacks against invaders by behaving as antigen presenters, displaying pieces of protein from foreign invaders, which stimulates a larger immune response. They also secrete chemicals, just like the ones released by white blood cells outside the central nervous system, that are capable of killing microbe invaders. Unfortunately, although these chemicals do a great job killing or disabling foreign invaders, they also damage cell membranes, proteins, or DNA in neurons. Microglia are suspected of participating in the development of a number of nervous system diseases, including Alzheimer's disease, multiple sclerosis, Parkinson's disease, and amyotrophic lateral sclerosis, also known as Lou Gehrig's disease (Streit & Kincaid-Colton, 1995).

By now, you should have a good understanding of the many important functions of glial cells. They feed and clean up after neurons, they protect neurons and assist them in the communication of information, and they direct their migration in the body during embryonic development. The role of glia is to maintain the integrity and support the function of the nervous system.

Glial cells can sometimes go awry and cause problems in the nervous system. For example, brain tumors are often caused by disordered glial cells multiplying

Figure 2.15 Fenestrated and nonfenestrated blood vessels
A fenestrated blood vessel permits ready passage of molecules through the walls of the blood vessel. Most blood vessels are fenestrated. A nonfenestrated blood vessel, such as those that are found along the blood-brain barrier, have overlapping, tight junctions between cells of the capillary wall and do not permit passage of molecules across the capillary wall.

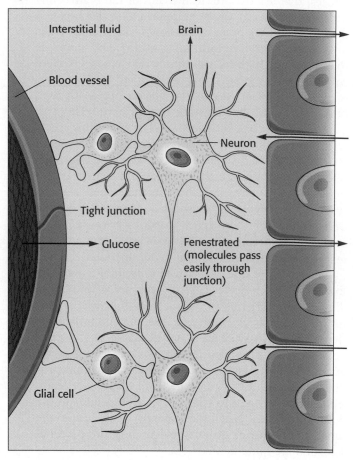

gap junctions: special electrical connections between cells

ion: an electrically charged molecule

uncontrollably. Tumors are abnormal growths of tissue that contain aberrant cells that reproduce faster than ordinary cells. There are two types of tumors generally found in the brain: primary tumors and metastatic tumors. Primary tumors occurring in the brain are typically the result of uncontrolled proliferation of abnormal glial cells and not neurons because neuron production ceases before birth. Metastatic tumors are due to metastasis, the migration of tumor cells from their primary site of origin in the body to another site. When examined microscopically, a metastatic tumor found in the brain will contain cells from the primary site, for example, from the lungs in a person with lung cancer or from the breast in a person with breast cancer.

Brain tumors composed of glial cells, especially astrocytes, are typically rapidly growing, aggressive tumors that often recur following surgery to remove them (Figure 2.17). Depending on where these tumors are situated, different symptoms occur. One patient with a tumor growing in the motor cortex will experience difficulty in walking or moving a limb, whereas a patient with a tumor in Broca's area will have impaired speech. Tumors differ from gliosis in that gliosis is due to the accumulation of normal glial cells in response to neuron damage, and tumors are growing masses of abnormal cells that destroy healthy brain tissue (McKeever, 1993).

Figure 2.16 Gap junction between two cells

A gap junction allows the transmission of ions from one cell to another. In a gap junction, the current flows from the more positive cell to the more negative cell. In (a), cell 1 is more positive, so the current flows from cell 1 to cell 2. In (b), cell 2 is more positive, so the current flows from cell 2 to cell 1.

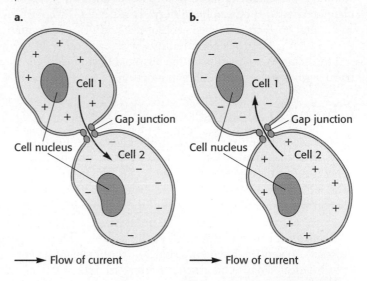

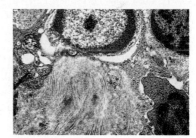

Figure 2.17 Astrocytoma, an astroglial-based tumor

As a tumor grows in the brain, it displaces and destroys healthy brain tissue.

Recap 2.2: Neurons and Glial Cells

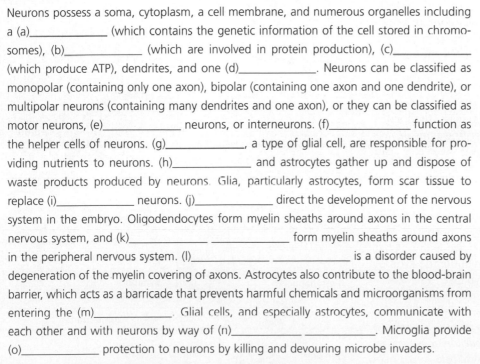

Neurons possess a soma, cytoplasm, a cell membrane, and numerous organelles including a (a)_____ (which contains the genetic information of the cell stored in chromosomes), (b)_____ (which are involved in protein production), (c)_____ (which produce ATP), dendrites, and one (d)_____. Neurons can be classified as monopolar (containing only one axon), bipolar (containing one axon and one dendrite), or multipolar neurons (containing many dendrites and one axon), or they can be classified as motor neurons, (e)_____ neurons, or interneurons. (f)_____ function as the helper cells of neurons. (g)_____, a type of glial cell, are responsible for providing nutrients to neurons. (h)_____ and astrocytes gather up and dispose of waste products produced by neurons. Glia, particularly astrocytes, form scar tissue to replace (i)_____ neurons. (j)_____ direct the development of the nervous system in the embryo. Oligodendocytes form myelin sheaths around axons in the central nervous system, and (k)_____ _____ form myelin sheaths around axons in the peripheral nervous system. (l)_____ _____ is a disorder caused by degeneration of the myelin covering of axons. Astrocytes also contribute to the blood-brain barrier, which acts as a barricade that prevents harmful chemicals and microorganisms from entering the (m)_____. Glial cells, and especially astrocytes, communicate with each other and with neurons by way of (n)_____ _____. Microglia provide (o)_____ protection to neurons by killing and devouring microbe invaders.

The Function of Neurons

Neurons have important work to do. They provide a communication network throughout the body linking the central nervous system and the peripheral nervous system: (1) to enable rapid responses, (2) to allow the central nervous system to regulate activity in the peripheral nervous system, (3) to permit cells within the brain and spinal cord to influence each other, and (4) to communicate with the outside environment. Neurons communicate with each other in two ways: through chemical messengers released from the terminal buttons of their axons and through electrical signals passed through gap junctions. Let's examine how this happens.

Chemical Synapses

Neurons communicate with each other across a junction called a **synapse.** Typically, in a **chemical synapse,** an axon from one neuron communicates with the dendrites of other neurons (Figure 2.18). The narrow space between the two neurons, a distance of less than 300 angstroms, is referred to as the **synaptic cleft.** The neuron whose axon makes up half of the synapse is called the **presynaptic neuron.** It comes before the synapse. The **postsynaptic neuron** comes after the synapse; its dendrite forms the other half of the synapse. Thus, a synapse is composed of a presynaptic neuron, a synaptic cleft, and a postsynaptic neuron. As a rule of thumb, at a chemical synapse, neurotransmitters are released from the terminal buttons of the presynaptic neurons, diffuse across the synaptic cleft, and are taken up by special proteins called receptors that are located on the dendrites of the postsynaptic neurons. In a chemical synapse, information is transmitted in the form of chemical substances called neurotransmitters.

Figure 2.19 is a photograph of an image of a chemical synapse, produced by a scanning electron microscope. Note in Figure 2.18 that the terminal button of the axon contains a multitude of little round sacs, or **vesicles.** These vesicles contain a neurotransmitter substance that has been produced in the soma and then transported to the terminal button. You can see that many of the vesicles are lined up along the terminal wall of the axon next to the synapse. When the presynaptic neuron becomes activated, some of these vesicles release their contents into the synaptic cleft, discharging neurotransmitter into the extracellular fluid, where it can diffuse to the receptors on nearby neurons.

The type of synapse illustrated in Figure 2.18 is an *axodendritic synapse*, in which the axon terminates on a dendrite. Other types of synapses are shown in Figure 2.20. In an *axoaxonic synapse*, both the presynaptic and postsynaptic elements are axons. That is, the terminal button of one axon abuts the axon of another neuron in an axoaxonic synapse. The *axosomatic synapse* is composed of a presynaptic terminal button of an axon terminating on a cell body of a neuron. Recently, investigators have identified another type of synapse, the *dendrodendritic synapse,* in which dendrites act as both presynaptic and postsynaptic elements. Some neurons terminate on muscles or glands, rather than another neuron, forming neuromuscular (neuron to muscle) and neuroglandular (neuron to gland) synapses.

synapse: a junction between two neurons

chemical synapse: a junction between two neurons that communicate using neurotransmitters

synaptic cleft: the narrow space between two communicating neurons

presynaptic neuron: the neuron sending a message across a synapse

postsynaptic neuron: the neuron receiving communication across a synapse

vesicle: a tiny sac in which neurotransmitters are stored

Figure 2.18 Synapse between an axon and dendrite
Neurotransmitter is released from the terminal button of the presynaptic axon, crosses the synaptic cleft, and binds with receptor sites on the postsynaptic dendrite.

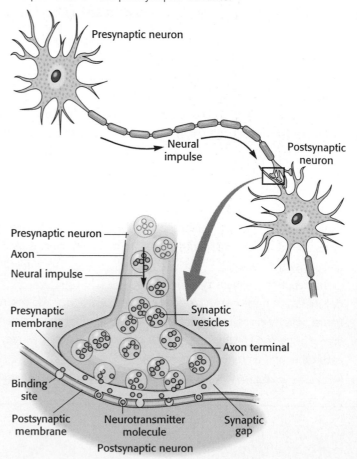

Please note that, in a chemical synapse, information flows from the presynaptic element to the postsynaptic element. Information flow is unidirectional, compared to the electrical synapse, in which information flow is bidirectional. Let's take a closer look at electrical synapses.

Electrical Synapses

In an **electrical synapse,** neurons transmit information across a synapse by means of electrically charged molecules, or ions. This type of synapse is often referred to as a gap junction, which you learned about earlier in this chapter. When one cell is more negative than its adjacent cell, the current flows from the more positive cell through the gap junction to the more negative cell, but only while the gap junction is open (Burt & Spray, 1988). It is not known, however, what causes a gap junction to open.

In the preceding section, you learned that chemical synapses are asymmetrical in structure and function. Structural asymmetry means that the presynaptic element, as you can see in Figure 2.18, contains transmitter vesicles and the postsynaptic element does not. *Functional asymmetry* refers to the fact that the presynaptic terminal button transmits information via the chemical transmitter substance, whereas the postsynaptic receptor receives information. The electrical synapse, on the other hand, is symmetrical in structure and function. Because ions can flow in both directions through a gap junction, either cell can be the presynaptic or the postsynaptic element at different times, depending on its electrical charge (see Figure 2.16).

Another difference between electrical synapses and chemical synapses is that messages travel much more quickly across electrical synapses than across chemical synapses. In an electrical synapse, there is no delay between the movement of ions through the gap junction and signal transmission to the second neuron. However, in the chemical synapse, a delay of 10 milliseconds or more takes place between the release of the neurotransmitter by the presynaptic element and the transfer of information to the postsynaptic cell. In order for information to be transmitted across a chemical synapse, a series of steps must occur: (1) The presynaptic vesicles containing transmitter substance must be opened, (2) the neurotransmitter is discharged into the synaptic cleft, (3) the neurotransmitter diffuses across the synaptic cleft, (4) the neurotransmitter binds with the receptors on the postsynaptic membrane, and (5) the postsynaptic receptors respond to the neurotransmitter binding. In the electrical synapse, the transfer of information is instantaneous: Ions flow from one neuron to the next and have an immediate effect on the activity of the postsynaptic neuron.

Electrical synapses play an important role in the excitation of large groups of neurons (Levitan & Kaczmarek, 1997). When a large number of neurons are required to fire at the same time (for example, neurons that release hormones), they must be activated simultaneously. The instantaneous spread of electrical activation through gap junctions between these hormone-secreting neurons enables these neurons to release their important transmitter substance at the same time. Gap junctions also appear to play an important role in the developing brain. Neurons in the brains of newborn rats communicate through gap junctions, but these

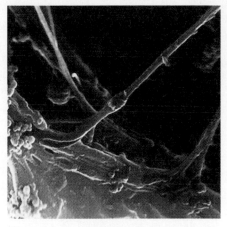

Figure 2.19 Electron micrograph of a synapse
The terminal buttons of the axon are located immediately adjacent to the postsynaptic membrane of the dendrite.

electrical synapse: a gap junction between two neurons across which ions pass

Figure 2.20 Different types of synapses

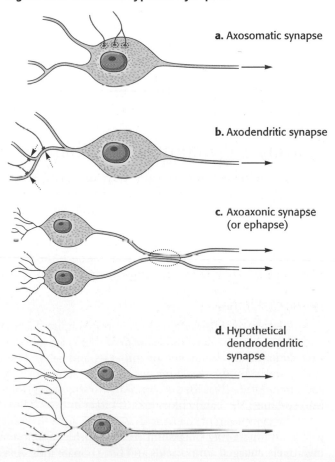

a. Axosomatic synapse

b. Axodendritic synapse

c. Axoaxonic synapse (or ephapse)

d. Hypothetical dendrodendritic synapse

same neurons do not use electrical synapses in the adult brain. Scientists theorize that gap junctions are important in neonatal neurons because they allow a number of neurons to become electrically active at the same time. Research has demonstrated that developing neurons that are electrically active at the same time establish chemical synaptic connections among themselves. Therefore, gap junctions in neonatal neurons direct the development of chemical synapses between these neurons (Lustig, 1994; Yuste, Peinado, & Katz, 1992).

Communication through gap junctions is the simplest form of intercellular communication and occurs in many types of cells, including heart cells and cells of the digestive tract, wherever activity must be synchronized. You learned earlier in this chapter that electrical synapses are found between glia and between glia and neurons. The truth is that relatively little is known about the functioning of electrical synapses. Although experimental models of chemical synapses have been with us since the time of Sir Charles Sherrington at the beginning of the 20th century, only recently have scientists begun identifying and studying electrical synapses. For the most part, the synapses discussed in this textbook will be chemical synapses, not because they are more important than electrical synapses, but because we know more about chemical synapses.

Recap 2.3: Synapses

(a)_____ provide a communication network linking the central nervous system and the peripheral nervous system. They communicate with each other across (b)_____ synapses, which involve neurotransmitters released by presynaptic terminals, and across (c)_____ synapses, which involve ions passed through gap junctions. Information flow across a chemical synapse is (d)_____ directional (flows in one direction from the presynaptic neuron to the postsynaptic neuron), whereas information flow across the synapse is (e)_____ directional (flows in both directions depending on the charge of the neurons). In an electrical synapse, information flows from the more (f)_____ neuron through the gap junction to the more (g)_____ neuron.

Transmitting Information Within a Neuron

We have examined the two major ways in which neurons transmit information to other cells: (1) via chemical synapses and (2) via electrical synapses. In this section, we will look at how a neuron transmits information from its dendrites and soma to the terminal buttons of its axon. *Intracellular* communication (the communication of information within a cell) is an important process in neurons because neurons receive many disparate messages from numerous other neurons and must sort out these messages before sending information on to other cells.

Resting Potential

First, it's best to consider a neuron at rest (Figure 2.21). A neuron at rest is bathed, like all neurons, in an *extracellular fluid* that is an aqueous (or water-based) solution that contains an abundance of minerals and salts. The salts are dissolved in the extracellular fluid, which means that the solution is full of ions. For example, sodium chloride (NaCl), the common salt that we sprinkle on our food, is dissolved into sodium (Na^+) and chloride (Cl^-) ions in extracellular fluid.

The cytoplasm of the neuron is also an aqueous solution that contains charged molecules, including potassium (K^+), chloride, ammonium ($NH4^+$), and a host of negatively charged amino acids and bicarbonate ions. As you can see in Figure 2.21, the negatively charged molecules far outnumber the positively charged ions in the cytoplasm of a resting neuron. It is possible to measure the voltage difference between the extracellular fluid and the cytoplasm by inserting a silver wire, which is connected to a voltmeter, into the extracellular fluid and another wire, connected to the same voltmeter, into the neuron. In a resting neuron, the voltmeter will show a voltage difference of 40–90 millivolts (mV) across the cell membrane, between the extracellular fluid and the inside of the neuron. By convention, negative potentials indicate that the inside of the cell is negative relative to the extracellular fluid. This means that the electric charge, or potential, inside the resting neuron is somewhere between –40 and –90 mV. For most neurons, it is typically around –70 mV. That is, most neurons have a **negative resting potential** of –70 mV.

Let's look at the resting neuron more closely. When a neuron is at rest, it maintains a negative potential across its cell membrane, with the inside of the membrane being more negative than the outside. This negative resting potential is due to an unequal distribution of ions across the cell membrane. You might be wondering: Why don't the negative ions just leave the inside of the neuron, or why don't some of those positive sodium ions flow into the cell, just to even things up a bit? Certainly, that's what you would expect, given that opposite charges attract and like charges repel.

But, you must remember that the cell membrane of the neuron is *semipermeable.* This means that some substances can cross the cell membrane easily, whereas others cannot. In the case of neurons, uncharged molecules, such as oxygen (O_2) and carbon dioxide (CO_2), diffuse readily across the cell membrane. Charged substances, such as ions, cannot cross the membrane at all except through special pores known as **ion channels.**

Ion Channels   The cell membrane is composed of a double layer of a fatty substance, known as phospholipid (Figure 2.22). The phospholipid molecule has two ends: a *hydrophilic* end and a *hydrophobic* end [*hydro-* = water; *-philic* = loving; *-phobic* = avoiding, Greek]. Because the cytoplasm and the extracellular fluid are water-based solutions, the two hydrophobic ends are tucked in the center of the double-walled, or *bilipid*, membrane, whereas the hydrophilic ends are exposed to the watery environments of the extracellular fluid and the cytoplasm. This double-walled membrane will readily allow the passage of uncharged molecules. However, ions cannot pass the hydrophobic layers of the cell membrane.

Ion channels are specialized proteins in the cell membrane that permit the passage of ions into and out of the neuron (Figure 2.22). These proteins form pores in the membrane that can be opened and closed. When the pores are opened, ions pass freely; when the pores are closed, ions cannot move in or out of the cell. Most ion channels are specialized passageways that permit only one particular ion to pass through the cell membrane. For example, ion channels have been identified for sodium, potassium, calcium, and chloride. Other ion channels appear to be more general purpose, allowing all positively charged ions, for example, to enter and leave the cell.

Ion Distribution and the Negative Resting Potential
In the resting neuron, the unequal distribution of ions, especially **potassium,** across the cell membrane contributes to the negative resting potential. The concentration of potassium is 20 times greater on the inside of the neuron than it is on the outside. This means that potassium is approximately 20 times more likely to leave the cell than to enter it. Because

Figure 2.21 A neuron at rest
A neuron at rest has a negative membrane potential, due to the uneven distribution of ion molecules across the cell membrane.

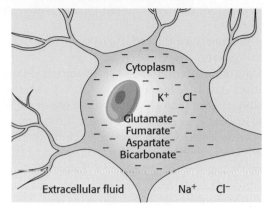

negative resting potential: the electrical charge across the cell membrane when a neuron is at rest

ion channel: special pores in the cell membrane that permit passage of ions into and out of the cell

potassium: a positively charged ion that is found in high concentrations in the inside of neurons

Figure 2.22 The bilipid cell membrane
The cell membrane of a neuron is composed of a double layer of a fatty substance called a phospholipid. Embedded in the bilipid cell membrane are ion channels that permit the passage of ions across the cell membrane.

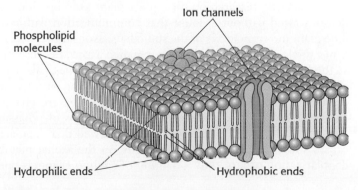

potassium channels are constantly open, potassium continually flows out of a neuron when that neuron is at rest. As potassium leaves the neuron, the cytoplasm loses some of its positive charge, becoming more negative than the extracellular fluid. Thus, there is a negative potential or charge across the neuronal cell membrane due to the movement of positively charged potassium ions out of a neuron at rest.

Outside of the cell, there is an abundance of sodium ions, compared to inside the neuron, where potassium ions and negatively charged molecules abound. In fact, the concentration of **sodium** outside the neuron is 10 times greater than that inside the cell (Fischbach, 1992). This creates two types of gradients: a concentration gradient and an electrostatic gradient. The term *gradient* refers to an unequal distribution of some attribute or property. For example, a concentration gradient is an unequal distribution of a chemical substance, whereas an electrostatic gradient is an unequal distribution of electrical charges. Sodium is attracted to the inside of the neuron because of the favorable concentration and electrostatic gradients across the cell membrane. That is, there a relatively few sodium ions or positively charged ions inside the neuron, so positively charged sodium ions slip into the cell every chance they get.

Unfortunately for sodium ions, sodium channels are closed most of the time, which means they cannot get into the neuron readily. In contrast, potassium channels are open most of the time, allowing potassium to enter and leave the cell as its concentration and electrostatic gradients dictate. The neuron's internal negative charge attracts and holds a substantial number of positively charged potassium ions inside the cell. Sodium can get inside the neuron only when the sodium channels open, and whenever these channels do open, however briefly, sodium ions rush into the neuron.

Depolarization   When positively charged sodium ions enter a neuron, they bring their positive charge with them, which makes the inside of the cell more positive (Figure 2.23). Whenever a neuron becomes more positive, we say that the cell has become *depolarized*. Remember that, in its resting state, a neuron has a negative resting potential of approximately −70 mV and, thus, is *polarized*. (A polarized neuron is a neuron that carries a positive or negative electrical charge.) Any positive movement away from this polarized state toward 0 mV is called **depolarization.**

Depolarization of the cell membrane causes sodium channels to open, which means more sodium ions can rush into the cell, further depolarizing the membrane and opening still more sodium channels. However, the cell has a built-in mechanism, a membrane protein called the *sodium-potassium pump*, to keep this process from getting out of control. The sodium-potassium pump has the duty of pumping sodium out of the neuron every time the ion slips in. This pump is constructed in a such a way that, for every three sodium ions it pumps out, it pumps in two potassium ions, thus maintaining the resting neuron's electrostatic and chemical gradients. The sodium-potassium pump maintains the neuron's negative resting potential at a great cost to the neuron. In order to actively pump sodium out of the cell against its concentration gradient, a lot of ATP is needed. Therefore, even when the neuron is "resting," it is burning up huge quantities of fuel. To make this fuel requires large amounts of glucose, oxygen, and water.

Pioneering research on the squid's giant axon by Hodgkin and Huxley (1952) demonstrated without a doubt that communication within a neuron is electrical. The giant motor neurons of the squid have axons that are relatively large, up to 500 times thicker in diameter than mammalian axons. Because the giant motor axon is so thick, tiny glass electrodes, called microelectrodes, can be inserted safely into the axon without damaging its structure or interfering with its function. These microelectrodes allowed Hodgkin and Huxley to measure changes in the membrane potential as they manipulated the concentrations of potassium and sodium both intracellularly and extracellularly. They showed that depolarization of the neuron causes sodium channels to open briefly on the axonal membrane. When a small depolarization occurs, only a handful of sodium channels open, and very few ions

sodium: a positively charged ion that is found in high concentrations on the outside of neurons

depolarization: a state in which a neuron loses its negative charge

Figure 2.23 Depolarization of a neuron
A neuron at rest (a) has a negative resting potential. Depolarization (b) occurs when positively charged sodium ions enter a neuron, which makes the inside of the cell more positive.

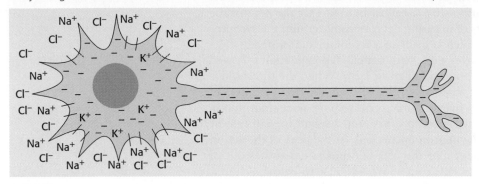

a. At rest

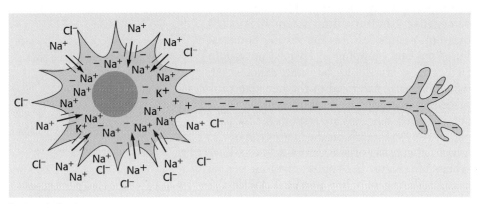

b. Depolarization

diffuse into the neuron. A large depolarization, on the other hand, causes many more ion channels to open, which permits an abundance of sodium ions to enter the cell, resulting in further depolarization, which in turn opens more sodium channels. Thus, Hodgkin and Huxley were able to show that depolarization causes the neuron to go from a resting state to a state of activation in which a wave of depolarization sweeps down the axon. For this research, Hodgkin and Huxley were awarded the Nobel Prize in 1963.

To get information down the axon with the least amount of time and effort, a neuron begins in a polarized state and shifts to a depolarized state. This means that the neuron expends no energy when it becomes depolarized. For a neuron, depolarization means allowing ions to flow naturally down their concentration and electrical gradients, that is, allowing positively charged ions, like sodium, to enter a negatively charged site. However, to get back into a polarized state, the cell has to expend energy. This process favors depolarization, which makes sense, given that depolarization activates a neuron and permits it to communicate with other cells.

Action Potential

The resting potential is the negative voltage measured across the cell membrane of a neuron that is in an "off" state. When an axon turns "on" or fires, an **action potential** is recorded. The action potential begins in one part of the neuron and travels down the axon all the way to its terminal buttons. Because neurons vary so much, it is difficult to specify exactly where the action potential begins. In some neurons, the action potential has been recorded in the dendrites (Barinaga, 1995). In others, it begins in the soma. But, in most neurons, the action potential is recorded only in the axon (Levitan & Kaczmarek, 1997).

In order for a neuron to turn "on," a threshold must be reached. This threshold is usually between 10 and 20 mV above (more positive than) the resting potential.

action potential: the voltage change recorded across the cell membrane in an excited neuron

This means that, in a typical neuron with a resting potential of −70 mV, the threshold is at about −55 mV. When the neuron's internal voltage depolarizes to −55 mV, the neuron turns "on," and an action potential is generated. The purpose of the action potential, remember, is to inform the terminal buttons that the neuron has been excited and to start the process of releasing neurotransmitter into the synapse.

Unlike the resting potential, which is ordinarily maintained at a steady voltage, the action potential fluctuates over time, with a rapid depolarization followed by a less rapid return to the resting potential (Figure 2.24). When the threshold is reached, a large number of sodium channels in the cell membrane open up, and sodium ions flood into the neuron, overwhelming the sodium-potassium pump. This is measured as a rapid depolarization to 0 mV and beyond to +30 mV or more, as sodium ions stream into the neuron unchecked. At the peak of the action potential, sodium stops its movement into the cell, and potassium rushes out of the cell, which causes the voltage to fall from above +30 mV to below −70 mV. Because both potassium and sodium leave the neuron when the internal potential becomes positive, the internal charge drops to nearly −100 mV. This state, when the internal charge of the cell is more negative than the resting potential, is called **hyperpolarization.** The sodium-potassium pumps restores the resting potential by pumping out the remaining sodium ions and pumping in escaped potassium ions. Therefore, the action potential begins at threshold, becomes depolarized, then repolarized, then hyperpolarized, and finally polarized to the negative resting potential. And, all of this takes place in a matter of 1 or 2 milliseconds.

How do we know that sodium ions and potassium ions are responsible for producing action potentials? Hodgkin and Huxley's research on the giant axon of the squid demonstrated that the action potential consists of two components: inflowing sodium followed by outflowing potassium. Figure 2.24 shows the time course of the movement of sodium and potassium during an action potential. When the diffusion of sodium or potassium in or out of the neuron is interrupted, the action potential is disrupted, as *For Further Thought* illustrates.

hyperpolarization: a state in which a neuron becomes more negatively charged than normal

neurotoxins: chemicals that target and destroy specific neurons or impair their function

What Puffer Fish, Bees, Scorpions, and Snakes Can Tell Us About Ion Channels

Some animals, like puffer fish, bees, scorpions, and snakes, produce venoms that immobilize prey or repel predators. These venoms are called **neurotoxins** because they have their poisonous effect on neurons in the central and peripheral nervous systems. Research has demonstrated that these neurotoxins interfere with the flow of ions in and out of neurons by blocking sodium or potassium channels.

For example, the puffer fish is a poisonous, spiny fish that is capable of swallowing a great deal of air or water, which makes it swell up in size to scare away predators. For further protection, the puffer fish secretes a neurotoxin, known as *tetrodotoxin* or *TTX*. Tetrodotoxin blocks sodium channels, thereby preventing action potentials. In large doses, this neurotoxin leaves the victim feeling weak or unable to move, and it can be fatal. In very small doses, as when a person eats a properly prepared puffer fish, tetrodotoxin will produce a tingling sensation in the mouth. However, fatalities can occur when people eat a puffer fish that contains too much tetrodotoxin.

Scorpions, snakes, and bees produce a number of different venoms that act as neurotoxins. Bees, for example, release several toxins from their stingers, including apamin and mast cell degranulating peptide. Depending on their species, poisonous snakes secrete any of a number of neurotoxins, such as dendrotoxin, toxin I, bungarotoxin, taipoxin, and crotoxin. For instance, the green mamba snake releases dendrotoxin when it bites, whereas the black mamba releases toxin I. Likewise, specific neurotoxins (charybdotoxin, Imperatoxin, P01) are associated with different species of scorpions. The neurotoxins produced by scorpions, snakes, and bees are quite similar in function: They block potassium channels and prevent potassium from leaving neurons. When potassium channels are blocked, potassium cannot leave the cell during an action potential, and hyperpolarization does not occur at the end of the action potential. Thus, these neurotoxins cause overexcitation of neurons, allowing them to fire rapidly, over and over. Seizures and immobilization can result from high doses of these toxins.

Special Properties of an Action Potential The action potential has a number of special properties that we need to discuss because we will be coming back to the action potential again and again over the course of this textbook. First of all, action potentials follow a rule known as the **all-or-none law.** According to the all-or-none law, after threshold has been reached and an action potential has begun, it always goes all the way to completion, that is, to its particular positive peak. If a neuron has a threshold of -55 mV and a peak of +30 mV, its action potential will always be measured as peaking at +30 mV. This is true no matter how intense the stimulus is that triggers the action potential. A weak stimulus, as long as it is above threshold, will produce the same size action potential as a very strong stimulus.

If a neuron responds with the same-size action potential to all stimuli, no matter how weak or strong, then how does that neuron communicate information about the intensity of the stimulus? This is an important question because neurons, especially sensory neurons, must be able to convey information about intensity, as you will learn in Chapter 7. To understand the answer to this question, you must know something about refractory periods—another special property of neurons.

A *refractory period* is the period of time following an action potential during which the neuron cannot fire again. For a few milliseconds following the firing of an action potential, the neuron can absolutely not fire again; this is called the **absolute refractory period.** During the absolute refractory period, no stimulus of any intensity can produce another action potential. The **relative refractory period** follows the absolute refractory period. During the relative refractory period, another action potential can be produced, but only by larger-than-normal stimuli. Over time, the neuron becomes less refractory and will fire once again to normal stimuli. This means that most neurons can generate only 200 action potentials or fewer per second (Fischbach, 1992).

How can refractory periods help explain the encoding of intensity by neurons? With a very intense stimulus, one that is larger than normal, an action potential is produced. During the absolute refractory period, there can be no new action potential. But, if the intense stimulus continues, it will evoke another action potential during the relative refractory period, a few milliseconds after the initial action potential. These action potentials will continue, about 2 or 3 milliseconds apart, as long as the intense stimulation continues. A weaker stimulus, however, is not strong enough to cause an action potential during the relative refractory period. This means that a lag of 4 or 5 or even more milliseconds will occur between action potentials. That is, intensity of stimulation is encoded by the neuron as frequency of the action potential. The stronger the stimulus, the more frequently the neuron fires. The weaker the stimulus, the slower the rate of action potentials. Remember that some stimuli are so weak that they evoke no action potentials whatsoever.

Axonal Propagation **Axonal propagation** is another property of the axon potential that you will encounter in later chapters of this textbook. The term *axonal propagation* refers to the movement of the action potential down the axon. In an unmyelinated axon, the action potential begins at the axon hillock (Figure 2.25). Depolarization initially takes place in a very narrow region of the axon in the area of the axon hillock, opening sodium channels in the membrane at this site. As sodium ions rush into the axon, they depolarize the membrane a bit farther down

Figure 2.24 The action potential

When an action potential is initiated, sodium ions flood into the neuron, causing a surge of depolarization. At the peak of the action potential, sodium movement into the neuron is slowed, and potassium continues to exit the neuron. The sodium-potassium pump restores the resting potential by pumping sodium out of the cell and potassium back into the neuron.

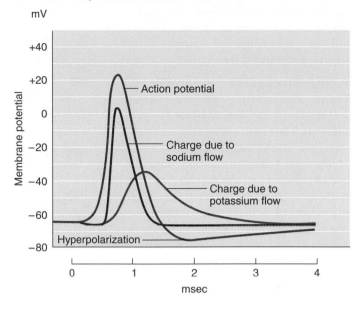

all-or-none law: a rule that the action potential always goes all the way to completion if threshold stimulation has been reached and an action potential is initiated

absolute refractory period: a period of time following an action potential during which no stimulus can initiate another action potential

relative refractory period: a period of time following an action potential during which an action potential can be initiated only by a stronger-than-normal stimulus

axonal propagation: the movement of the action potential down an axon

from the cell body. This depolarization leads to the entry of more sodium ions, which causes depolarization of the membrane farther down the axon. Bit by bit, the action potential moves down the axon as depolarization spreads from one site to the next, until the action potential reaches the terminal buttons, triggering the release of neurotransmitters. We will examine this phenomenon in greater detail in Chapter 3.

Axonal Propagation in Myelinated Axons Propagation of the action potential in myelinated axons is quite different. First of all, the cell membrane under the myelin cannot be depolarized, which means that the action potential cannot move down the myelinated axon in a step-by-step fashion as it does in the unmyelinated neuron. The only places along the cell membrane that can be depolarized are at the nodes of Ranvier. Therefore, the action potential in a myelinated axon can occur only at the nodes of Ranvier, where sodium ions can enter the axon. The action potential jumps from node of Ranvier to node of Ranvier as it moves down the axon (Figure 2.26). This jumping of the action potential is called **saltatory conduction.**

You can imagine that an action potential that jumps from node of Ranvier to node of Ranvier moves a lot faster down an axon than does an action potential that spreads down the axon bit by bit. In fact, axonal propagation down the axon can be as much as 200 times faster in a myelinated axon than in an unmyelinated axon. Another factor that affects the speed with which an axon potential moves down an

Figure 2.25 Movement of the action potential down an unmyelinated axon

Depolarization moves in a stepwise fashion down the axon. When one section of the axon becomes depolarized, Na⁺ channels in the adjacent area open, allowing Na⁺ to flow into the axon at that point, which depolarizes that section of the axon.

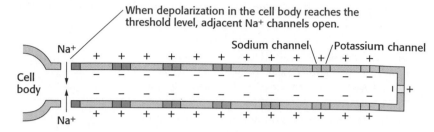

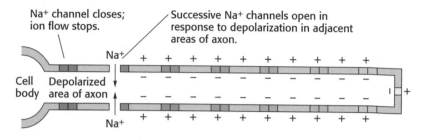

saltatory conduction: the jumping of an action potential along a myelinated axon

Figure 2.26 Movement of the action potential down a myelinated axon

In a myelinated axon, Na⁺ can only enter the axon through ion channels located at the nodes of Ranvier (the gaps in the myelin sheath). Depolarization at one node of Ranvier causes Na⁺ channels to open in the adjacent node of Ranvier, allowing Na⁺ to flow into the axon at that point, which depolarizes that section of the axon. The action potential appears to leap from one node of Ranvier to the next as it moves down the myelinated axon.

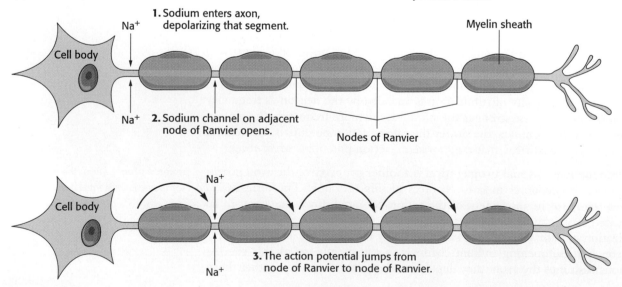

axon is the diameter of the axon. Diameters of axons can vary from 1 micron to 1 millimeter. The smaller the diameter of the axon, the slower the axon potential travels down its length. As a general rule, action potentials travel most rapidly down thick, myelinated axons, and they travel most slowly down thin, unmyelinated axons.

Summation

Before an action potential can begin, the membrane potential must reach threshold, as you've already learned. How does this occur? The threshold is nothing more than a depolarization of the neuron 10–20 mV above the resting potential. Neurons are capable of depolarizing other neurons, either through chemical or electrical synapses. In the electrical synapse, remember that positive charges flow into a more negatively charged neuron, causing depolarization. Neurotransmitters are released into the synapse at chemical synapses, and these neurotransmitters cause ion channels to open on the postsynaptic neuron.

The important point to remember here is that one neuron by itself is not typically capable of producing an action potential in another neuron. That is, one neuron cannot alter another neuron's membrane potential by 10 to 20 mV all by itself. It takes many neurons firing over a brief period of time to raise a neuron's membrane potential from −70 mV to −55 mV. A special mechanism called summation is needed.

Figure 2.27 illustrates a simplified representation of input that one neuron receives from other neurons. By "simplified" I mean that, in Figure 2.27, the postsynaptic neuron is receiving input from only six other neurons, whereas a real neuron receives input from up to 10,000 other neurons. Neurons A, B, C, D, E, and F in Figure 2.27 cannot individually depolarize the postsynaptic neuron from −70 mV to −55 mV. In fact, most neurons can change a postsynaptic neuron's membrane potential by about 0.5 mV.

In order for the postsynaptic neuron to reach threshold, a number of different presynaptic neurons must fire at the same time. This requires that the postsynaptic neuron process input from many different neurons and add them together in order to reach threshold and initiate an action potential. **Spatial summation** refers to the addition of the input from many different presynaptic neurons. If neurons A through F were to stimulate the postsynaptic neuron in Figure 2.27 at the same time, the postsynaptic neuron would use spatial *summation* to cumulate the input from these presynaptic neurons.

However, even six neurons cannot, as a group, produce an action potential in a postsynaptic neuron. Assume that the each of the neurons (A–F) can depolarize the postsynaptic neuron by 0.5 mV. Adding these depolarizations gives a total of 3.0 mV:

$$(0.5 \text{ mV} + 0.5 \text{ mV} + 0.5 \text{ mV} + 0.5 \text{ mV} + 0.5 \text{ mV} + 0.5 \text{ mV}) = 3.0 \text{ mV}.$$

A depolarization of 3.0 mV takes the postsynaptic neuron only from −70 mV to −67 mV, which is not close to the threshold required to initiate an action potential. If these neurons were to fire several times over a brief period of time, the postsynaptic neuron could add all of these depolarizations in a process called **temporal summation**. In

spatial summation: addition of input from many different presynaptic neurons

temporal summation: addition of input from one presynaptic neuron over a brief period of time

Figure 2.27 Summation
Presynaptic neurons A–F make a synaptic connection with a postsynaptic neuron. A postsynaptic neuron typically receives input from thousands of presynaptic neurons.

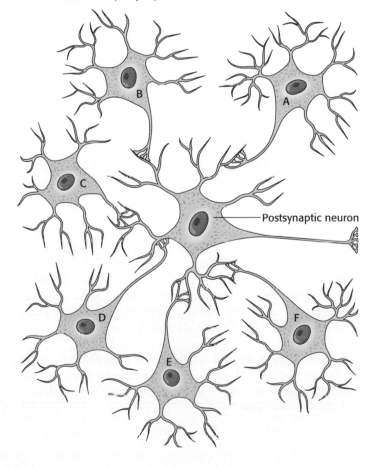

Postsynaptic neuron

temporal summation, the input from one presynaptic neuron over time is added by the postsynaptic neuron.

The postsynaptic neuron uses both spatial summation and temporal summation to process all the stimulation coming in from presynaptic neurons. It adds the stimuli bombarding it from many different sources, and it sums these stimuli over time. Remember that intensity of the stimuli is encoded by the presynaptic neuron as frequency. That is, a very strong stimulus will cause a neuron to fire very rapidly. A presynaptic neuron that is firing very rapidly will produce many action potentials in a very brief period of time, which means that, due to temporal summation, the postsynaptic neuron will receive a lot of stimulation from that one presynaptic neuron. One presynaptic neuron firing very rapidly can produce the same amount of stimulation as several presynaptic neurons firing slowly.

Let's complicate the picture just a bit. Not all presynaptic neurons cause depolarization in the postsynaptic neuron. Some presynaptic neurons actually produce hyperpolarization. As you will learn in Chapter 3, some neurotransmitters released by presynaptic neurons cause sodium channels to open, and some cause potassium channels to open. Recall that, when sodium channels open, sodium rushes in to the cell, producing depolarization. When potassium channels open, potassium leaves the cell, making the inside of the neuron more negative and producing hyperpolarization. Therefore, the postsynaptic neuron is bombarded by a host of depolarizations and hyperpolarizations, which it must summate.

Excitation and Inhibition

Some presynaptic neurons release neurotransmitters that depolarize the postsynaptic neurons. They are called *excitatory neurons* because they cause the postsynaptic neuron to become more positive. On the other hand, *inhibitory neurons* release neurotransmitters that hyperpolarize the postsynaptic neuron, making it more negative. A postsynaptic neuron receives stimulation from both excitatory and inhibitory neurons. The excitatory neuron causes an **excitatory postsynaptic potential** of approximately +0.5 mV in the postsynaptic neuron, whereas the inhibitory neuron causes an **inhibitory postsynaptic potential** of about −0.5 mV in the postsynaptic neuron.

Imagine in Figure 2.27 that neurons A, B, C, and D are excitatory neurons and that neurons E and F are inhibitory neurons. If all six presynaptic neurons fire once at the same time, they would have a net effect of raising the membrane potential of the postsynaptic neuron by +1.0 mV. That is, the potential of the resting postsynaptic neuron would increase from −70 mV to −69 mV. Do you understand how this would happen? Neurons A, B, C, and D would increase the postsynaptic potential by 4 times (+0.5 mV), or +2.0 mV, whereas neurons E and F would decrease the potential by 2 times (−0.5 mV), or −1.0 mV, for a net effect of (+2.0 mV) + (−1.0 mV), or +1.0 mV. If these six neurons fired many times in very rapid succession, they could raise the postsynaptic potential to threshold, initiating an action potential in the postsynaptic neuron.

Remember that this example that we've just used is a very simplistic representation of what actually occurs in the brain. Hundreds or thousands of neurons are activated in producing most behaviors. Another point to remember here is that inhibition is a very important process in the brain. Inhibition serves to control or check the activities of excitatory neurons. Think what would happen if you acted on every impulse that you experience. Inhibitory neurons prevent postsynaptic neurons from responding to all impulses from excitatory neurons. They provide needed checks and balances to the nervous system.

In Chapter 3 we will continue our discussion of the roles of excitatory and inhibitory neurons. We will examine neurotransmitters released by excitatory and inhibitory neurons and consider various drugs and chemicals that affect neurotransmitter function.

excitatory postsynaptic potential: a small increase (~ +.5 mV) in the charge across a postsynaptic membrane

inhibitory postsynaptic potential: a small decrease (~ −.5 mV) in the charge across a postsynaptic membrane

A neuron at rest has a (a)_____ difference of approximately −70 mV across the cell membrane, with the inside of the neuron being more negative than the outside. The unequal distribution of ions across the cell membrane, the high concentrations of (b)_____ inside the neuron, and the high concentrations of sodium outside, produces the negative resting potential. When a neuron becomes depolarized, its membrane potential becomes more (c)_____. If the depolarization reaches 10–20 mV above the resting potential, an (d)_____ potential is initiated and moves down the axon, triggering the release of neurotransmitter in the terminal buttons of the axon. (e)_____ summation involves the addition of input from many different presynaptic neurons, whereas (f)_____ summation involves the addition of input from one presynaptic neuron over time. A postsynaptic neuron receives stimulation from excitatory neurons, which produce an (g)_____ postsynaptic potential (_PSP), and from inhibitory neurons, which produce an (h)_____ postsynaptic potential (_PSP).

Chapter Summary

The Organization of the Nervous System

▶ The nervous system is one of the body's many systems, including the digestive system, the respiratory system, the cardiovascular system, and the reproductive system.

▶ The nervous system has two divisions, the central nervous system, which is composed of the brain and the spinal cord, and the peripheral nervous system, which is composed of all the other nervous tissue outside the brain and spinal cord.

▶ The peripheral nervous system is divided into the somatic system, which controls skeletal muscles, and the autonomic nervous system, which controls smooth and cardiac muscles.

▶ The autonomic nervous system is divided into the sympathetic nervous system, which is activated when a person becomes excited or aroused, and the parasympathetic nervous system, which is activated when a person relaxes.

Neurons and Glial Cells

▶ Neurons and glia are the main cells that comprise the nervous system.

▶ Like other cells in the body, neurons possess a soma, cytoplasm, a cell membrane, and numerous organelles including a nucleus (which contains the genetic information of the cell stored in chromosomes), ribosomes (which are involved in protein production), mitochondria (which produce ATP), dendrites, and one axon.

▶ The function of neurons is to communicate with other neurons, muscles, and glands, and they possess special processes, called dendrites and axons, for receiving and sending information.

▶ Neurons can be classified as monopolar (containing only one axon), bipolar (containing one axon and one dendrite), or multipolar neurons (containing many dendrites and one axon), or they can be classified as motor neurons, sensory neurons, or interneurons.

▶ Glial cells function to support the activity of neurons, including providing nourishment to neurons (astrocytes), removing waste products (microglia and astocytes), forming scar tissue in the nervous system (astrocytes), guiding the development of the nervous system (radioglia), providing insulation for neurons (oligodendrocytes and Schwann cells), contributing to the blood-brain barrier (astrocytes), communicating with neurons through gap junctions (astrocytes), and functioning as the brain's immune system (microglia).

▶ Multiple sclerosis is a disorder caused by degeneration of the myelin covering of axons.

The Function of Neurons

▶ Neurons provide a communication network linking the central nervous system and the peripheral nervous system. They communicate with each other across chemical synapses, which involve neurotransmitters released by presynaptic terminals, and across electrical synapses, which involve ions passed through gap junctions.

▶ Electrical synapses allow for rapid communication between neurons, whereas chemical synapses involve the release of neurotransmitters from a presynaptic neuron, which carry a message to postsynaptic neurons. Information flow across a chemical synapse is unidirectional (flows in one direction from the presynaptic neuron to the postsynaptic neuron), whereas information flow across the synapse is bidirectional (flows in both directions depending on the charge of the neurons).

▶ In an electrical synapse, information flows from the more positive neuron through the gap junction to the more negative neuron.

▶ A neuron at rest has a voltage difference of approximately –70 mV across the cell membrane, with the inside of the neuron being more negative than the outside.

▶ The unequal distribution of ions across the cell membrane, with high concentrations of potassium inside the neuron and high concentrations of sodium outside, produces the negative resting potential.

▶ When a neuron becomes excited, sodium enters the neuron, producing depolarization. When a neuron becomes depolarized, its membrane potential becomes more positive. If the depolarization reaches 10–20 mV

above the resting potential, an action potential is initiated.

▶ Axonal propagation of the action potential triggers the release of neurotransmitters into the synaptic cleft.

▶ Before an action potential can begin, spatial summation and temporal summation of excitatory and inhibitory postsynaptic potentials occur, thereby increasing the membrane potential from –70 mV to some threshold level. Spatial summation involves the addition of input from many different presynaptic neurons, whereas temporal summation involves the addition of input from one presynaptic neuron over time.

▶ A postsynaptic neuron receives stimulation from both excitatory neurons, which produce an excitatory postsynaptic potential (EPSP), and inhibitory neurons, which produce an inhibitory postsynaptic potential (IPSP).

Key Terms

absolute refractory period   (p. 47)
action potential   (p. 45)
adenosine triphosphate
   (ATP)   (p. 29)
all-or-none law   (p. 47)
astrocytes   (p. 33)
autonomic nervous system   (p. 24)
axon   (p. 29)
axon hillock   (p. 29)
axonal propagation   (p. 47)
Bell-Magendie law   (p. 32)
bipolar neuron   (p. 31)
cell membrane   (p. 27)
central nervous system   (p. 24)
chemical synapse   (p. 40)
chromosome   (p. 28)
cytoplasm   (p. 27)
dendrite   (p. 29)
dendritic spines   (p. 29)
depolarization   (p. 44)
DNA   (p. 28)
dorsal   (p. 31)
electrical synapse   (p. 41)
excitatory postsynaptic
   potential (p. 50)
ganglia   (p. 32)

gap junctions   (p. 38)
genome   (p. 28)
glia   (p. 27)
gliosis   (p. 35)
hyperpolarization   (p. 46)
inhibitory postsynaptic
   potential   (p. 50)
interneuron   (p. 31)
ion   (p. 38)
ion channel   (p. 43)
microglia   (p. 34)
mitochondrion   (p. 29)
monopolar neuron   (p. 31)
motor neuron   (p. 31)
multipolar neuron   (p. 31)
myelin   (p. 35)
negative resting potential   (p. 43)
nervous system   (p. 24)
neuron   (p. 27)
nodes of Ranvier   (p. 35)
neurotoxins   (p. 46)
nuclei   (p. 32)
nucleus   (p. 28)
oligodendrocytes   (p. 35)
organelle   (p. 27)

parasympathetic nervous
   system   (p. 25)
peripheral nervous system   (p. 24)
postsynaptic neuron   (p. 40)
potassium   (p. 43)
presynaptic neuron   (p. 40)
radial glia   (p. 34)
relative refractory period   (p. 47)
ribosomes   (p. 28)
RNA   (p. 28)
saltatory conduction   (p. 48)
Schwann cells   (p. 35)
sensory neuron   (p. 32)
sodium   (p. 44)
soma   (p. 27)
somatic nervous system   (p. 24)
spatial summation   (p. 49)
sympathetic nervous
   system   (p. 25)
synapse   (p. 40)
synaptic cleft   (p. 40)
temporal summation   (p. 49)
terminal buttons   (p. 29)
ventral   (p. 31)
vesicle   (p. 40)

Questions for Thought

1. Describe the physical symptoms you would expect in a person with an overactive sympathetic nervous system.

2. What would you predict would occur if a person injures the ventral aspect of his or her spinal cord?

3. When are electrical synapses necessary? When are chemical synapses most useful?

Questions for Review

1. What are the major differences between the somatic and autonomic nervous systems?

2. Identify the mitochondrion and the nucleus of a cell. How are they alike? How are they different?

3. Discuss the functions of glial cells and neurons.

4. Describe how sodium ions and potassium ions contribute to the maintenance of a neuron's resting potential. How do they contribute to the initiation of an action potential?

Suggested Readings

Abramsky, O., & Ovadia, H. (1997). *Frontiers in multiple sclerosis: Clinical research and therapy*. St. Louis: Mosby.

Aicardi, J. (1998). *Diseases of the nervous system in childhood*. London: MacKeith Press.

Bennett, R. L. (1999). *The practical guide to the genetic family history*. New York: John Wiley.

Bignami, A. (1991). *Glial cells in the central nervous system*. Amsterdam; New York: Elsevier.

Crick, F. (1994). *The astonishing hypothesis: The scientific search for the soul*. New York: Scribner.

Special series of articles on dendrites in *Science, 2000,* Vol. 290, pp. 735–758.

Web Resources

For a chapter tutorial quiz, direct links to the Internet sites listed below and other features, visit the book-specific website at **www.wadsworth.com/product/ 0155074865**. You may also connect directly to the following annotated websites:

http://psych.hanover.edu/Krantz/neural/ actionpotential.html
You can view simulations of basic physical principles associated with action potentials on this site, then take a quiz on what you have learned.

http://medic.med.uth.tmc.edu/edprog/histolog/ nerve/hist-04.htm
This site provides high magnification images of different tissues in the nervous system.

http://www.sci.sdsu.edu/histology/ne01.htm
This site contains a neuron under high magnification. You can turn the labels off and on to test yourself about the anatomy of the neuron.

http://faculty.washington.edu/chudler/bbb.html
Explore the blood-brain barrier here.

http://faculty.washington.edu/chudler/toxin1.html
This site lists neurotoxins, their animal sources, and mechanisms of action.

For additional readings and information, check out InfoTrac College Edition at **http://www.infotrac-college.com/wadsworth**. Choose a search term yourself or enter the following search terms: chromosome, fragile X syndrome, nervous system, neurons, neurotoxic agents, Ramon y Cajal.

CD-ROM: Exploring Biological Psychology

The Neuron Structure
    Animation: The Parts of a Neuron
    Virtual Reality: The Structure of the Neuron
    Interactive Puzzle: The Neuron
Conduction of Information within Neurons
    Animation: The Action Potential

Animation: Na^+ Ions
Animation: The Resting Potential
Animation: Postsynaptic Potentials
Interactive Recaps
Chapter 2 Quiz
Connect to the Interactive Biological Psychology Glossary

3

Chemical Synapses, Neurotransmitters, and Drugs

Matt celebrated his 21st birthday with a keg party at his apartment. The first few beers when down smoothly, and he felt no ill effects from the alcohol at first. However, when he began dancing with his girlfriend, he found that he lost his balance easily and that he could not coordinate his movements to the music. As the party continued, Matt drank several more beers. He soon began staggering around the apartment, hugging the walls as he moved from one room to the next. When people talked to him, he had a hard time following the conversation. His speech became slurred and effortful. After a few more beers, Matt nearly fell over when his girlfriend kissed him. She giggled and led him to his bedroom, where he staggered to his bed, lay down, and promptly fell asleep.

In Chapter 2, you learned about *intraneuronal communication*. In this chapter, we will examine *interneuronal communication*, or communication between neurons [*intra* = inside; *inter* = between, Greek]. Remember that there are two types of junctions betweeen neurons, electrical synapses and chemical synapses. This means that some neurons communicate electrically, through the exchange if ions, and that other neurons communicate via chemicals released (called neurotransmitters) by the presynaptic neuron.

This chapter will focus on the function of *chemical synapses*. You will be introduced to a variety of chemicals that influence the activity of neurons. Some of these chemicals are neurotransmitters manufactured by the neurons themselves, and some are substances, such as alcohol, that are ingested and then transported across the blood-brain barrier.

Alcohol is a good example of an ingested substance that affects the functioning of neurons. The opening vignette describes how overconsumption of alcohol affected Matt's nerve system. Actually, there are many differ- ent types of alcohol (Figure 3.1), all having a different chemical structure. However, only one of these alcohols, *ethanol,* is safe for human consumption. Ethanol is the alcohol found in beer, wine, and distilled spirits, like whiskey and vodka. Another type of alcohol, propanol, is probably known to you as "rubbing alcohol." The other types of alcohol, if consumed even in small amounts, produce vio- lent illness or death. Ethanol can make you sick or kill you, but only if ingested in large amounts.

Let's look at how ethanol affects most neurons. Recall from Chapter 2 that, in order to excite a neuron, the membrane must be depolarized. Depolarization takes place when the inside of the neu- ron becomes more positive following the flow of positively charged Na^+ ions (usually Na^+ ions) into the neuron. Ethanol blocks the flow of Na^+ into the neuron, thereby preventing the cell from getting excited and producing an action potential. That's why alcohol is clas- sified as a depressant: It depresses, or decreases, the activity of neu- rons. In the opening vignette, ethanol interfered with Matt's ability to walk, talk and maintain his balance by inhibiting the neurons that control these functions.

In fact, all chemicals that affect neurons cause a change in the activity of neurons. Some chemicals, like ethanol, decrease the activ- ity of neurons, and other chemicals increase the activity of neurons. The chemicals produced by neurons, called **neurotransmitters,** typi- cally affect a neuron's activity by opening particular ion channels. As you learned in Chapter 2, opening Na^+ channels increases a neuron's activity because Na^+ rushes into the neuron when the Na^+ channel is open, depolarizing the neuron. Opening Ca^{++} channels can also pro- duce depolarization. When the inside of a neuron becomes more negative than its resting potential of -70 mV, the neuron's activity is depressed because the neuron requires more stimulation in order to produce an action potential. A neuron's activity is inhibited when K^+ or Cl^- channels are opened. Let's examine how this happens.

The concentration of ions on either side of the cell membrane determines the direction in which the ions flow. In Chapter 2, you learned that Na^+ has a much higher concentration outside the neuron compared to the inside. The same is true with Cl^- and Ca^{++}. For example, the concentration of Ca^{++} is 1,000 times greater outside the neuron than inside. This means that Na^+, Ca^{++}, and Cl^- will move into the neuron when their respective ion channels are opened (Figure 3.2). On the other hand, K^+ has a higher concentration inside the neuron and, therefore, will flow out of the neuron when the K^+ channel is opened, with a net effect of making the inside of the neuron more negative.

When ion channels open, ions flow in or out of the neuron, causing the inside of the neuron to become more positive or negative. Na^+ and Ca^{++} bring positive charges into the cell and, thus, make the inside of the neuron more pos- itive. That is, Na^+ and Ca^{++} depolarize the neuron's membrane. In contrast,

Figure 3.1 Many types of alcohol.
A few examples of different types of alcohol are shown. Notice that each has a different chemical structure. Of these, only ethanol is safe for human consumption.

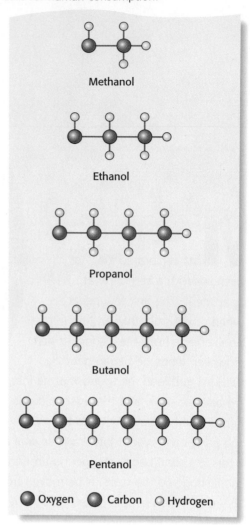

Methanol

Ethanol

Propanol

Butanol

Pentanol

Oxygen   Carbon   Hydrogen

neurotransmitter: chemical released by neurons to signal neurons and other cells

Figure 3.2 Movement of ions across ion channels.
(a) When the ion channel is closed, a high concentration of Na$^+$ is found on the outside of the neuron and a low concentration is found on the inside. (b) When the ion channel opens, Na$^+$ ions move from a region of high concentration to a region of low concentration.

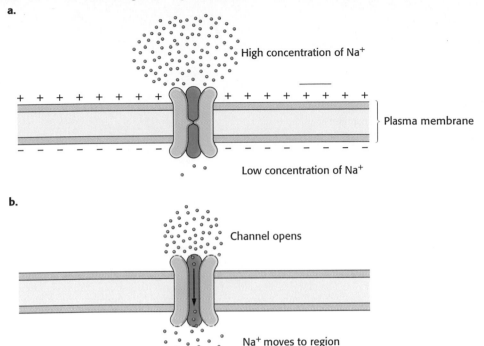

a.

High concentration of Na$^+$

Plasma membrane

Low concentration of Na$^+$

b.

Channel opens

Na$^+$ moves to region
of lower concentration

opening of K$^+$ or Cl$^-$ channels hyperpolarizes the neuron. When Cl$^-$ ion channels open, Cl$^-$ enters the neuron, causing the inside to become more negative. Opening K$^+$ channels also makes the inside of the neuron negative because K$^+$ ions flow out of the cell, taking their positive charge with them. ●

Opening Ion Channels

Ion channels obviously play an important role in determining the activity of neurons. What causes ion channels to open? There are actually four different types of ion channels, and each type is opened by a different mechanism (Cooper, Bloom, & Roth, 1996).

The first type of ion channel is a **ligand-gated channel.** Ligand-gated channels are ion channels that have a special protein, called a **receptor,** attached (Figure 3.3). Receptors are embedded in the cell membrane and have special places along its molecular structure that bind to other chemicals. Chemicals that bind to neuronal receptors are called **ligands,** and, therefore, these channels are referred to as ligand-gated channels. When a neurotransmitter or other chemical, such as a drug, binds to the ligand-gated receptor, the chemical reaction causes the shape of the ion channel to change, opening the channel. (Recall from Chapter 2 that ion channels are special proteins that are capable of changing shape.)

The other three types of ion channels are *voltage-gated channels, ion-gated channels,* and *nongated channels.* As its name implies, a voltage-gated channel is sensitive to changes in the membrane potential. When the cell membrane becomes depolarized, voltage-gated channels open, allowing ions to enter or leave the neuron. Ion-gated channels are sensitive to particular ion concentrations within the neuron.

ligand-gated channel: ion channels that have a special protein attached that binds with a neurotransmitter or other chemical

receptor: a specialized sensory cell that responds to a specific stimulus

ligand: a chemical that binds to receptors on neurons

Figure 3.3 A receptor and its associated ion channel.
(a) When the receptor site on the ligand-gated channel is empty, the channel remains closed.
(b) When a neurotransmitter binds to the receptor site, the channel opens.

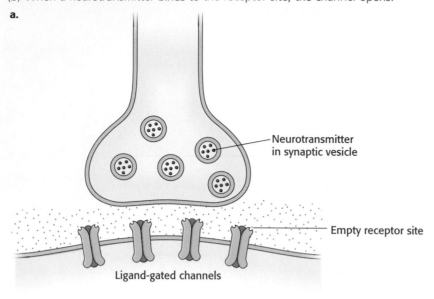

a.

Neurotransmitter in synaptic vesicle

Empty receptor site

Ligand-gated channels

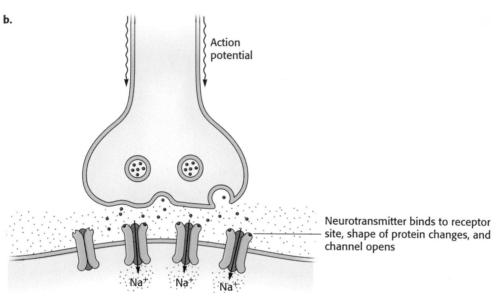

b.

Action potential

Neurotransmitter binds to receptor site, shape of protein changes, and channel opens

Na⁺ Na⁺ Na⁺

The opening of these ion channels is governed by the intracellular concentration of particular ions. Nongated channels are always open, allowing ions to leak in or out of the neuron. For example, as you learned in Chapter 2, some K^+ channels on the neuronal membrane are continuously open, permitting K^+ ions to leak into the extracellular fluid, where they are pumped back into the neuron by the Na^+-K^+ pump.

All four types of ion channels play important roles in the function of a neuron, especially voltage-gated and ligand-gated channels. To show you how these ion channels participate in the life of a neuron, let's review how action potentials are initiated and propagated in neurons that communicate via chemical synapses.

Propagation of the Action Potential

Recall from Chapter 2 that action potentials are initiated when the membrane potential reaches some threshold level, generally 15 to 20 mV above the resting potential. *Propagation of the action potential* refers to the movement of the action potential down the axon. The action potential usually begins in the axon hillock, due to lowered threshold levels in the hillock, and travels down the axon to the terminal buttons.

In the unmyelinated axon, the action potential moves down the axon in a step-wise process (see Figure 2.25). When the action potential begins, a tiny segment of the neuronal membrane next to the axon hillock becomes depolarized, which causes Na^+ channels in that region to open. The inflow of Na^+ through the opened channels causes depolarization of the membrane nearest the open Na^+ channels, thus opening more Na^+ channels in that segment of the cell membrane. The action potential advances down the axon one tiny segment at a time, with each consecutive segment becoming depolarized and causing contiguous Na^+ channels to open. This process is very much like the chain reaction that occurs when the first of many neatly arranged dominoes (placed on their ends) is tipped over. The first domino knocks over the second which knocks over the next, and so forth, until the entire length of dominoes has fallen down. The same process occurs in myelinated axons except that, in myelinated axons, membrane depolarization can occur only at the nodes of Ranvier. (Refer to Chapter 2 for a review of saltatory conduction down a myelinated axon.) Thus, voltage-gated Na^+ channels are responsible for the propagation of the action potential down the axon.

Storage and Release of Neurotransmitters

Neurotransmitters are manufactured inside the neuron and immediately stored in little sacs called *vesicles*. These neurotransmitter-containing vesicles are then transported to the terminal buttons of the axon, where they remain until their contents are released into the synapse (Figure 3.4). For the release of neurotransmitter to occur, voltage-gated Ca^{++} channels are required. Voltage-gated Ca^{++} channels open when the membrane potential is depolarized.

When the action potential reaches the terminal buttons of the axon, the membrane at the terminal site becomes depolarized, causing Ca^{++} channels to open and Ca^{++} ions to rush into the terminal buttons. The presence of Ca^{++} ions in the terminal site induces fusion of the vesicle with the presynaptic membrane. The exact mechanism by which the vesicle fuses with the membrane is unknown, but it appears that, after the vesicle fuses with the presynaptic membrane, the neurotransmitter is rapidly expelled into the synapse. Thus, voltage-gated Ca^{++} channels are necessary for neurotransmitter release, whereas voltage-gated Na^+ channels are required for propagation of the action potential down the axon.

Figure 3.4 Storage and release of neurotransmitters.
Neurotransmitter molecules are stored in synaptic vesicles in the terminal buttons of axons (1). When an action potential reaches the terminal button, the vesicles fuse with the cell membrane of the presynaptic axon (2) and discharge the neurotransmitter into the synapse (3).

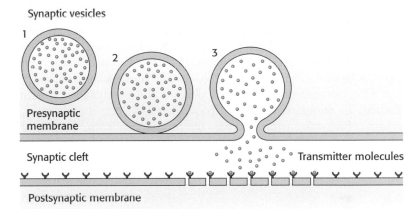

Initiation of the Action Potential

In a chemical synapse, neurotransmitters released by the presynaptic neuron diffuse across the synapse and bind with receptors on the postsynaptic membrane. **Classical neurotransmitters** are neurotransmitters that bind to a receptor that is attached to a ligand-gated ion channel. When a neurotransmitter binds to a receptor coupled to a ligand-gated channel, the chemical reaction causes the ion channel to change shape. The ion channel opens up and allows ions to follow their concentration gradient into or out of the neuron.

Some neurotransmitters bind with ligand-gated Na^+ channels. Following an action potential in the presynaptic neuron, these neurotransmitters are released, diffuse across the synapse, and bind with the ligand-gated Na^+ channels. The Na^+ channels open for 10 to 100 milliseconds, permitting Na^+ to rush into the cell, which

classical neurotransmitter: a neurotransmitter that binds to a receptor that is attached to a ligand-gated ion channel produces an excitatory postsynaptic potential (EPSP), as described in Chapter 2. If enough neurotransmitter is released, multiple EPSPs are produced, and the membrane potential is elevated to threshold, triggering an action potential. Therefore, opening numerous ligand-gated Na$^+$ channels in the postsynaptic neuron initiates an action potential. There is evidence that opening ligand-gated Ca^{++} channels will also trigger an action potential in some neurons.

Inhibition of the Action Potential

Inhibition of the neuron occurs when K$^+$ or Cl$^-$ channels are opened or when Na$^+$ or Ca^{++} channels are blocked. Two mechanisms produce inhibition in neurons: **presynaptic inhibition** and **postsynaptic inhibition.** You learned about postsynaptic inhibition in Chapter 2 when we discussed inhibitory postsynaptic potentials (IPSPs). Postsynaptic inhibition takes place in the postsynaptic dendrite following the release of an inhibitory neurotransmitter from a presynaptic axon (Figure 3.5). In contrast, presynaptic inhibition occurs at axoaxonic synapses, where terminal buttons from one axon release inhibitory neurotransmitters that bind with receptors on the membrane of a second axon. Let's review postsynaptic inhibition first.

Neurotransmitters that bind with ligand-gated Cl$^-$ or K$^+$ channels will produce IPSPs. Do you understand how? Recall that when Cl$^-$ or K$^+$ channels are opened, Cl$^-$ flows into the neuron or K$^+$ flows out, causing hyperpolarization of the neuron's membrane. IPSPs are produced when inhibitory neurotransmitters bind to receptors that open Cl$^-$ or K$^+$ channels. In contrast, EPSPs are produced when excitatory neurotransmitters bind to receptors attached to Na$^+$ or Ca^{++} channels. In order for a neuron to become excited and for an action potential to be initiated, enough EPSPs have to be produced to raise the membrane potential to threshold. When IPSPs outnumber EPSPs, the membrane potential becomes hyperpolarized, making it less likely that the postsynaptic neuron will fire.

The purpose of IPSPs is to prevent the postsynaptic neuron from getting excited. In comparison, the purpose of presynaptic inhibition is to prevent the release of neurotransmitters from the presynaptic axon. That is, presynaptic inhibition prevents an already excited axon from releasing neurotransmitters into the synapse. An IPSP is analogous to the gate of a fence to keep a horse inside. Presynaptic inhibition is like lassoing an escaped horse.

presynaptic inhibition: inhibition at axoaxonic synapses that occurs when the presynaptic axon releases inhibitory neurotransmitters that block the release of neurotransmitters from the postsynaptic axon

postsynaptic inhibition: inhibition that takes place in the postsynaptic dendrite following the release of an inhibitory neurotransmitter from a presynaptic axon

Figure 3.5 Presynaptic and postsynaptic inhibition.
(a) Neurotransmitter is released by the presynaptic neuron, and an IPSP is produced in the postsynaptic dendrite. (b) Neurotransmitter is released by a presynaptic axon, which opens K$^+$ channels in the postsynaptic axon and hyperpolarizes its membrane.

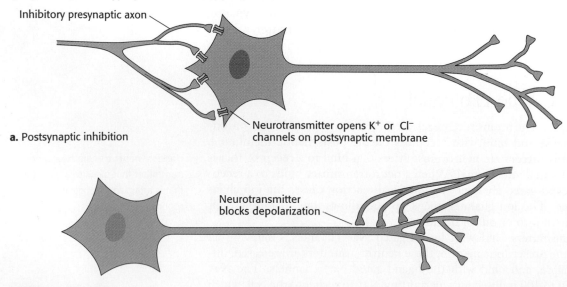

Inhibitory presynaptic axon

Neurotransmitter opens K$^+$ or Cl$^-$ channels on postsynaptic membrane

a. Postsynaptic inhibition

Neurotransmitter blocks depolarization

b. Presynaptic inhibition

Figure 3.5 illustrates how presynaptic inhibition works. One axon terminates on the endplate of another axon. An action potential in the first axon initiates the release of neurotransmitters that bind to K^+-channel receptors on the postsynaptic membrane of the second axon. That is, the neurotransmitters that produce presynaptic inhibition typically open K^+ channels, which hyperpolarizes the membrane of the postsynaptic axon, making it impossible for the voltage-gated Ca^{++} channels to open. If the voltage-gated Ca^{++} channels cannot open, neurotransmitter cannot be released from the postsynaptic axon.

One example of presynaptic inhibition involves a special type of receptor called an **autoreceptor.** Autoreceptors are found on the terminal endings of some axons. As their name implies, autoreceptors bind with neurotransmitters released from their own axon, producing presynaptic inhibition. Consider what this means for a moment. Every time an axon releases neurotransmitter into the synapse, some of this neurotransmitter binds with autoreceptors located on the axon. These autoreceptors in turn inhibit firing of the axon. This means that autoreceptors control the release of neurotransmitter from their own axon. When the autoreceptors are stimulated by the neurotransmitter released from their own axon, they inhibit the axon from releasing more neurotransmitter.

I know that this discussion has been quite technical, and I hope you are not too overwhelmed or confused. However, you will need to understand this material thoroughly in order to understand the effects of specific neurotransmitters and drugs that affect behavior. Indeed, this material forms the foundation for the rest of the topics we will cover in this book. Table 3.1 summarizes the roles that various ion channels play in neuronal function. Let me review the concept of ligand-gated channels one more time, using the action of a specific neurotransmitter, **acetylcholine,** as an example.

autoreceptor: a receptor found on the terminal buttons of some neurons that binds with neurotransmitters released from their own axon

acetylcholine: the first neurotransmitter to be discovered, binds with nicotinic and muscarinic receptors

Table 3.1

Ion Channels and Their Functions

Type of Ion Channel	Action	Examples of Function in Neurons
ligand-gated	neurotransmitters bind with receptors on these channels and open channel	initiation of action potential; inhibition of action potential
voltage-gated	depolarization of cell membrane opens this channel	propagation of the action potential down the axon; neurotransmitter release
ion-gated	increased intracellular concentration of a particular ion opens this channel	cellular secretion
non gated	always open	K^+ channels on cell membrane permit K^+ to leak out of neuron

Recap 3.1: Opening Ion Channels

There are four types of ion channels: ligand-gated channels, voltage-gated channels, (a)_____-gated channels, and non-gated channels. Voltage-gated Na^+ channels are responsible for the propagation of the action potential down the (b)_____. Voltage-gated Ca^{++} channels are required for the (c)_____ of neurotransmitters. Classical neurotransmitters bind to a receptor that is attached to a (d)_____-_____ ion channel, producing EPSPs and IPSPs. Neurotransmitters that produce (e)_____ _____ open K^+ channels, which hyperpolarize the membrane of the presynaptic axon. (f)_____ bind with neurotransmitters released from their own axon, producing presynaptic inhibition.

Types of Receptors

Ligand-Gated Ion Channel Receptors

Acetylcholine was the first neurotransmitter to be discovered and identified. In 1921, a German physiologist named Otto Loewi was trying to figure out how the *vagus nerve* slows the heartbeat. He connected two hearts with a tube containing a salt solution and then electrically stimulated the vagus nerve going to one of the hearts (Heart #1). Stimulation of the vagus nerve caused Heart #1 to slow its heartbeat, as was expected. However, to Loewi's surprise, a minute or so later, the other heart (Heart #2) slowed its heartbeat, even though its vagus nerve had not been stimulated. Loewi reasoned that a chemical released by the vagus nerve, rather than electrical stimulation, caused the heart to slow its beat. According to Loewi's hypothesis, the chemical released by the vagus nerve diffused in the salt solution from Heart #1 to Heart #2, thereby affecting both hearts. He isolated the chemical in the salt solution and determined through chemical analysis that it was a small molecule called *acetylcholine*.

Since its discovery, acetylcholine has been shown to play an important role in many human behaviors, including learning and memory. In fact, a severely disabling disorder, *Alzheimer's disease*, which is characterized by dementia and profound memory loss, is associated with diminished levels of acetylcholine in the brain (Coyle, Price, & Delong, 1983). Like other neurotransmitters, acetylcholine is synthesized by neurons and released into the synapse when an action potential arrives at the terminal button containing acetylcholine-laden vesicles. When acetylcholine diffuses across the synaptic gap to reach the postsynaptic neuron, individual acetylcholine molecules bind with acetylcholine receptors that are embedded in the membrane of the postsynaptic dendrites. These acetylcholine receptors are **ligand-gated ion channel receptors.**

Acetylcholine-gated ion channel receptors have a distinct shape. Each receptor is made up of five subunits: two alpha subunits, one beta subunit, one delta subunit, and one gamma subunit. The five subunits form a ring around a central pore (or ion channel), which traverses the entire thickness of the cell membrane. Acetylcholine binds with a specific region on the alpha subunits (Changeux, 1993). That is, the receptor site for acetylcholine is on the alpha subunit. Binding of acetylcholine to both alpha subunits of the receptor causes a chemical reaction, which causes the proteins that make up the subunits to change their shape. As the subunits change shape, the central pore opens, allowing Na^+ to rush into the neuron.

Thus, this acetylcholine receptor is connected to a ligand-gated Na^+ channel. The Na^+ channel opens when acetylcholine binds chemically with the alpha subunits of the receptor. When the channel opens, Na^+ ions enter the postsynaptic neuron, depolarizing it and producing an EPSP. An interesting fact about this acetylcholine receptor is that several other substances also bind with it. One of these substances is *nicotine*, the active ingredient found in cigarettes and other tobacco products. Nicotine binds with the receptor, causing the Na^+ channel to open. For this reason, the acetylcholine-gated Na^+ channel is also referred to as the **nicotinic receptor.**

G Protein-Linked Receptors

However, nicotine does not bind with all acetylcholine receptors, which led investigators to discover another type of acetylcholine receptor, the **muscarinic receptor.** This second type of acetylcholine receptor gets its name from a poisonous mushroom called *Amanita muscaria*. When this particular mushroom is ingested, its active ingredient, known as *muscarine*, binds to the muscarinic receptor and produces some acetylcholine-like effects, such as constriction of the pupils (Barondes, 1993).

ligand-gated ion channel receptor: a protein on the cell membrane that is attached to a ligand-gated channel and binds with a specific neurotransmitter

nicotinic receptor: a ligand-gated ion channel receptor that binds with both nicotine and acetylcholine

muscarinic receptor: a G protein-linked receptor that binds with both muscarine and acetylcholine

The muscarinic receptor is not connected to a ligand-gated ion channel, and binding to this receptor does not open any ion channels. Think about that for a moment. What do you think happens when acetylcholine binds with the muscarinic receptor? How can acetylcholine stimulate the postsynaptic neuron if it doesn't open any ion channels? The muscarinic receptor is a totally different type of receptor from the nicotinic receptor. It is classified as a **G protein-linked receptor,** whereas the nicotinic receptor is a ligand-gated ion channel receptor (Wilcox & Gonzales, 1995). This means that the muscarinic receptor is associated with a special protein called a *G protein.* (The *G* stands for *guanine,* a nucleotide found in the cell, as you learned in Chapter 2.) Let's look at how a G protein-linked receptor works.

A G protein-linked receptor, such as the muscarinic receptor, is a protein that is embedded in the neuronal membrane. It is a long protein that snakes its way across the cell membrane, permitting information to be conducted from the outside of the neuron to the inside. When acetylcholine binds with a muscarinic receptor, it causes the protein to change shape, which activates G protein inside the neuron (Figure 3.6). The G protein stays activated for many seconds, a relatively long time. While the G protein is activated, it in turn activates any number of enzymes within the neuron. Most commonly, activated G protein targets *adenylate cyclase,* an enzyme responsible for the manufacture of *cyclic AMP* within the neuron. The G protein activates adenylate cyclase, which in turn changes ATP into cyclic AMP, producing a large number of cyclic AMP molecules. Cyclic AMP diffuses throughout the interior of the neuron, influencing other enzymes inside the neuron. One important enzyme activated by cyclic AMP is *protein kinase A,* which changes the excitability of ion channels. Thus, acetylcholine does influence ion channels via muscarinic receptors, but the pathway is quite rambling and involves a **second messenger,** cyclic AMP.

I've slipped in a new term here: *second messenger.* With G protein-linked receptors, changes in ion channels are not produced directly by the neurotransmitter. Rather, the neurotransmitter binds with the receptor on the outside of the neuron and activates G protein, which in turn activates an enzyme that activates a second messenger. It is the second messenger that delivers the neurotransmitter's message to the inside of the neuron. The second messenger is like the person who delivers a subpoena to you when a judge wants you to appear in court. The judge (that is, the neurotransmitter) prepares a subpoena that is given to the person who delivers subpoenas (the messenger), and this messenger carries the subpoena to you, therefore stimulating action by you.

In the case of muscarinic receptors, the second messenger is cyclic AMP. Cyclic AMP activates protein kinase A, which alters certain ion channels on the postsynaptic membrane. This alteration of ion channels by protein kinase A can last for several minutes. In addition, cyclic AMP can enter the nucleus of a neuron and affect particular genes. For example, in Chapter 14, we will examine the long-term changes in gene expression that are caused by certain neurotransmitters associated with stress. In Chapter 9, we will also look at the role of cyclic AMP on the expression of particular proteins necessary for the creation of long-term memories.

Comparing Nicotinic and Muscarinic Acetylcholine Receptors

A comparison of nicotinic and muscarinic acetylcholine receptors yields two major differences. First, nicotinic receptors are linked to an ion channel, and binding of acetylcholine to this receptor causes a Na^+ channel to open. In contrast, as you've just learned, binding of acetylcholine to the muscarinic receptor activates G protein, which in turn activates a second messenger that alters the excitability of particular ion channels. The second difference between nicotinic and muscarinic receptors is related to their long-term effects within the postsynaptic neuron. When acetylcholine binds to a nicotinic receptor, the chemical reaction opens the ion channel for only 10 to 100 milliseconds. Then, the ion channel goes back to its original, closed conformation, and the Na^+-K^+ pump quickly goes to work, ferrying the Na^+ ions out of the neuron. Thus, stimulation of a nicotinic receptor has a short term effect on the postsynaptic neuron. Activation of the muscarinic receptor, on the

G protein-linked receptor: a protein embedded in a cell membrane that binds with a specific neurotransmitter, which activates G protein inside the neuron

second messenger: a chemical activated when a neurotransmitter binds with a G protein-linked receptor, which alters a neuron's function

Figure 3.6 Activation of a G protein-linked receptor.

(a) The G protein-linked receptor is embedded in the neuronal membrane. (b) When a neurotransmitter binds with the G protein-linked receptor, the receptor changes shape and activates G protein inside the neuron. (c) When G protein is activated, it activates adenylate cyclase, which changes ATP into cyclic AMP. (d) Cyclic AMP moves throughout the interior of the neuron, activating protein kinase (which opens ion channels) and other target proteins.

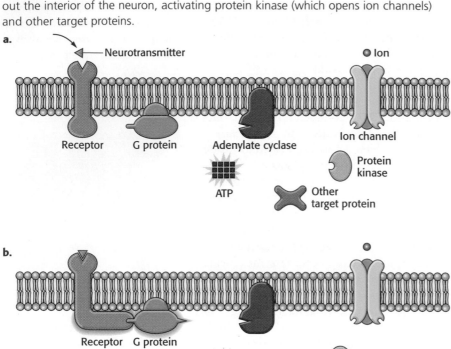

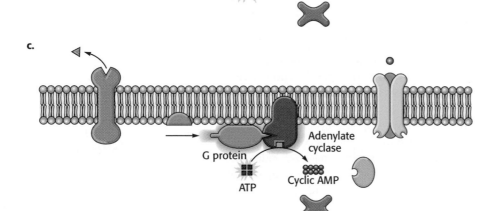

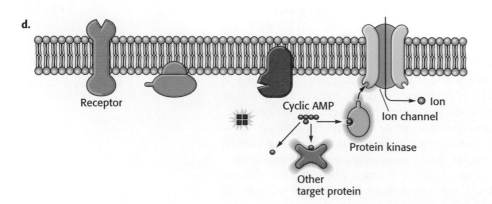

other hand, has much longer-lasting effects because G protein and cyclic AMP are active for many seconds after acetylcholine binds with the muscarinic receptor.

Some investigators use the terms *ionotropic* and *metabotropic* to differentiate between nicotinic and muscarinic receptors. Indeed, these terms can be used to distinguish between all ligand-gated ion channel and G protein-linked receptors. **Ionotropic receptors** are those receptors that directly open an ion channel, like the nicotinic acetylcholine receptor. These receptors have a very short-lived effect on the neuron, on the order of 10–100 milliseconds. The effect of **metabotropic receptors,** as G protein-linked receptors are called, is longer lasting because G protein and cyclic AMP stay active in the neuron for several seconds after the neurotransmitter binds with the receptor.

ionotropic receptor: a receptor that directly opens an ion channel
metabotropic receptor: receptor that activates second messengers

Other Types of Receptors

So far, you've been introduced to two types of receptors: ligand-gated ion channel receptors, like the acetylcholine nicotinic receptor, and protein G-linked receptors, like the acetylcholine muscarinic receptor. Investigators have identified at least five different types of receptors (Wilcox & Gonzales, 1995). The other types of receptors include tyrosine kinase receptors, growth factor receptors, and hormone receptors. At present, not much is known about these last three types of receptors. Tyrosine kinase receptors bind with proteins that direct the growth of axons and dendrites and, thus, may play a role in brain development and repair (Berninger & Poo, 1999). Hormone receptors in neurons probably permit chemicals that are produced by glands outside the brain to alter the activity of neurons (Lustig, 1994; Steckler & Holsboer, 1999). Growth factor receptors probably play a role in cell growth and maintenance (Conti et al., 2001). You can be sure that other types of neuronal receptors will be discovered as neuroscientists continue to study how neurons function.

Before we leave this discussion of receptors, I want to impress you with one more point. Thus far, I've led you to believe that acetylcholine binds with two receptors: the nicotinic receptor and the muscarinic receptor. In truth, there are really four different acetylcholine nicotinic receptors and five different acetylcholine muscarinic receptors, for a total of nine acetylcholine receptors (Kebabian & Neumeyer, 1994). Table 3.2 lists the best-known neurotransmitters and the number of receptors associated with each. Some investigators estimate that there may be as many as 1,000 different receptors on neurons in the central and peripheral nervous systems (Cooper et al., 1996).

Table 3.2

Selected Neurotransmitters and Their Receptors

Neurotransmitter	Receptor Subtypes
acetylcholine	nicotinic (4 types) muscarinic (5 types)
glutamate	ionotropic (5 types) metabotropic (8 types)
GABA	$GABA_A$ (17 types) $GABA_B$ (3 types)
serotonin	$5HT_1$, $5HT_2$, $5HT_3$, $5HT_4$, $5HT_5$, $5HT_6$, $5HT_7$
dopamine	D1, D2, D3, D4, D5
epinephrine	$alpha_1$, $alpha_2$, $beta_1$, $beta_2$
endorphin	mu_1, mu_2, $kappa_1$, $kappa_2$, $delta_1$, $delta_2$
anandamide	CB1, CB2

Think about what it means to have 1,000 different receptors. It means that each neurotransmitter is capable of stimulating or inhibiting a neuron in a wide variety of ways. The control of behavior is indeed a very complicated process, involving chemicals that play different roles depending on their location in the nervous system, as you will learn in Chapter 4.

Don't forget that many *exogenous* chemicals—those chemicals that come from a source outside the body (as opposed to *endogenous* chemicals, which have an internal source)—also bind with postsynaptic receptors. Alcohol not only has a general effect of blocking Na+ channels in all neurons, but it also binds with particular receptors known as GABA receptors. (*GABA* is the abbreviation for a neurotransmitter called gamma-aminobutyric acid.) In this chapter, we will consider the effects of various drugs on behavior as they bind with specific receptors on neurons.

Psychopharmacology is the study of chemical substances that affect the activity of neurons. Therefore, much of the information that we have about drug action in the brain comes from the research of psychopharmacologists. Some drugs are classified as **agonists,** and others are classified as **antagonists.** Agonists are chemical substances that bind with a receptor and activate the receptor, much like a neurotransmitter does. In contrast, antagonists also bind with a receptor, but they do not activate the receptor. Instead, antagonists block the action of the neurotransmitter by preventing the neurotransmitter from binding with its receptor (Figure 3.7). We will examine the roles of well-known neurotransmitter agonists and antagonists in our discussion of neurotransmitters.

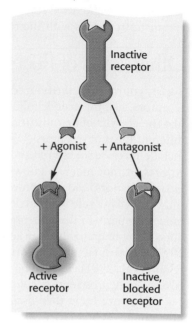

Figure 3.7 Action of agonists and antagonists.
Agonists bind with the receptor and activate it, like a neurotransmitter. Antagonists bind with the receptor and block the action of the neurotransmitter by preventing the neurotransmitter from binding with its receptor.

agonist: a chemical that binds with and activates a receptor

antagonist: chemical that binds with a receptor, blocking the action of the neurotransmitter

Recap 3.2: Types of Receptors

The neurotransmitter, (a)_____, binds with both ligand-gated ion channel receptors, and G protein-linked receptors. The acetylcholine-gated Na$^+$ channel receptor is called the (b)_____ receptor. The G protein-linked acetylcholine receptor is called the (c)_____ receptor. G protein-linked receptors make use of a second messenger, such as (d)_____ _____, which indirectly influences the excitability of ion channels. At least three other types of receptors have been identified, including tyrosine kinase receptors, (e)_____ factor receptors, and (f)_____ receptors.

Neurotransmitters

In this section, we will examine a wide variety of chemicals that are synthesized and used by neurons to transmit information across chemical synapses. Dozens of these transmitter substances have been identified. However, I will focus only on the neurotransmitters that play an important role in the regulation of human behavior. These neurotransmitters are listed in Table 3.3.

Originally, I referred to acetylcholine as a *classical neurotransmitter.* A classical neurotransmitter, as you'll recall, is a neurotransmitter that binds with ligand-gated ion channels. We use the term *classical* because this was the first type of neurotransmitter function that scientists identified. However, we now know that neurotransmitters can bind with other types of receptors and have longer-lasting effects on neurons. A neurotransmitter that binds with G protein-linked receptors is often referred to as a **neuromodulator,** although the distinction between neurotransmitters and neuromodulators is often blurred (Cooper et al., 1996). Therefore, to simplify things a bit, I will use the term *neurotransmitter* to refer to any substance that is released by a presynaptic neuron into a chemical synapse. This makes sense given that most neurotransmitters bind with both ion channel receptors and G protein-linked receptors.

neuromodulator: a neurotransmitter that binds with a G protein-linked receptor

Table 3.3

Neurotransmitter Families

Family Name	Associated Neurotransmitters
Amino acid	glutamate, aspartate, glycine, gamma-aminobutyric acid
Peptide	substance P, cholecystokinin, endorphins
Monoamine	serotonin, norepinephrine, dopamine, histamine
Unknown	acetylcholine
Unknown	nitric oxide
Unknown	anandamide

neurohormone: a chemical released into the bloodstream that travels to target neurons

epinephrine: a neurohormone, also known as adrenaline, that is released by the adrenal gland and activates the sympathetic nervous system

glutamate: a neurotransmitter that is the most abundant excitatory neurotransmitter in the brain.

gamma-aminobutyric acid (GABA): a neurotransmitter that is the most abundant inhibitory neurotransmitter in the brain

peptide: a short chain of amino acids

endorphin: endogenous opiate neurotransmitters that inhibit pain messages

cholecystokinin: a peptide released from the duodenum that inhibits eating

Another type of chemical, called a **neurohormone,** is synthesized by certain brain structures or by organs outside of the brain, is released into the bloodstream, and travels to target neurons. Neurohormones bind with G protein-linked receptors, hormone receptors, and growth factor receptors. Like neuromodulators, neurohormones generally have longer-lasting effects on the action of neurons. For example, **epinephrine,** which is also known as *adrenaline*, is a neurohormone that is released by the adrenal gland, a structure located above the kidney. When released into the bloodstream, epinephrine travels to neurons in the sympathetic nervous system, activating those neurons and producing the physiological effects that we associate with sympathetic arousal: increased heart rate, rapid breathing, pupil dilation, constriction of blood vessels in the gut, and increased flow of blood to skeletal muscles (Figure 3.8).

Classifying Neurotransmitters

Neuroscientists have attempted to classify neurotransmitters and group them into "families." But, neurotransmitters are difficult to classify due to their wide variety. However, some are easy to group together. For example, some neurotransmitters are simple *amino acids*, like **glutamate** or **gamma-aminobutyric acid (GABA).** Amino acids are relatively simple compounds that contain a NH_2 (amino) group and COOH (acid) group (Figure 3.9a). **Peptides,** such as **endorphin** and **cholecystokinin,** form another class of neurotransmitters. Peptides are nothing more than a short chain of amino acids joined end to end (Figure 3.9b).

Figure 3.8 Release and action of epinephrine.

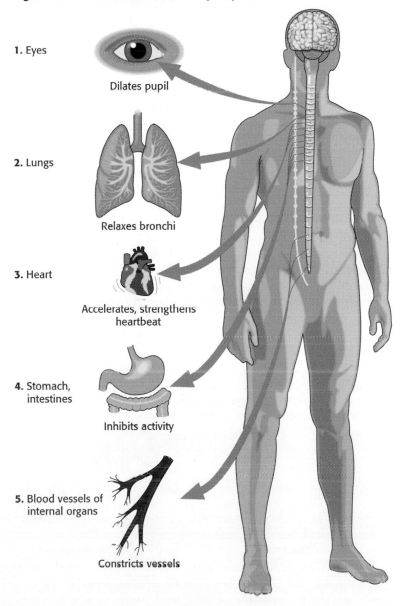

1. Eyes — Dilates pupil

2. Lungs — Relaxes bronchi

3. Heart — Accelerates, strengthens heartbeat

4. Stomach, intestines — Inhibits activity

5. Blood vessels of internal organs — Constricts vessels

Figure 3.9 Structure of amino acids and peptides.
(a) Amino acids are simple molecules composed of a NH_3^+ group and a COOH- group.
(b) Peptides consist of a string of amino acids that are bound together chemically.

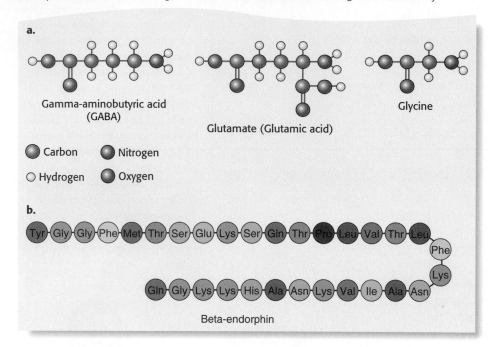

a.

Gamma-aminobutyric acid
(GABA)

Glutamate (Glutamic acid)

Glycine

- Carbon
- Nitrogen
- Hydrogen
- Oxygen

b.

Tyr–Gly–Gly–Phe–Met–Thr–Ser–Glu–Lys–Ser–Gln–Thr–Pro–Leu–Val–Thr–Leu–Phe–Lys

Gln–Gly–Lys–Lys–His–Ala–Asn–Lys–Val–Ile–Ala–Asn

Beta-endorphin

Another well-known family of neurotransmitters are the **monoamines,** which are derivatives of amino acids that contain one amine (NH_2) group. Monoamines that have been demonstrated to act as neurotransmitters include **serotonin, norepinephrine,** and **dopamine** (Figure 3.10). Serotonin is derived from the amino acid *tryptophan,* which is found in foods that you eat every day. In fact, there is evidence that you can alter brain serotonin levels by changing your diet (see *For Further Thought*). Norepinephrine and dopamine come from another amino acid, *tyrosine,* which is commonly found in a variety of foods. Together with epinephrine, norepinephrine and dopamine form a special class of monoamines known as *catecholamines* because they each contain a catechol ring and one amine (NH_2) group.

Other transmitter substances synthesized by neurons, such as acetylcholine, **anandamide,** and **nitric oxide,** do not fit neatly into a particular family of neurotransmitters. These substances are not derived from amino acids. Nitric oxide, for example, contains no carbon and is an inorganic compound. Perhaps, in the future, neuroscientists will discover related chemicals that function as neurotransmitters. For the present, acetylcholine, anandamide, and nitric oxide are the sole occupants of their respective family trees (Table 3.3).

monoamine: a chemical compound that contains one amino group

serotonin: a monoamine neurotransmitter that plays a role in sleep, vigilance, mood, appetite, and repetitive movements

norepinephrine: a monoamine neurotransmitter that plays a role in mood, drive reduction, sleep, arousal, cognition, and emotions

dopamine: a monoamine neurotransmitter that is a precursor of norepinephine and epinephrine

anandamide: a recently discovered neurotransmitter that binds with cannabinoid receptors

nitric oxide: an atypical neurotransmitter that readily diffuses across the cell membrane of a neuron

Figure 3.10 Structure of monoamines.
Monoamines are derivatives of amino acids that contain one amine (NH_2) group.

Dopamine

Norepinephrine

Serotonin (5-hydroxytryptamine)

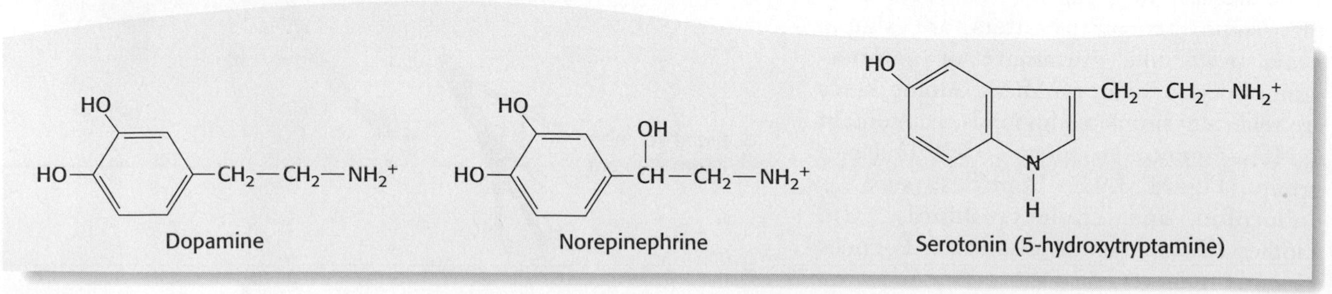

Serotonin and Diet

What you eat can affect serotonin levels in your brain. Recall that serotonin is derived from the amino acid *tryptophan*. When tryptophan crosses the blood-brain barrier, it is converted to 5-hydroxytryptophan, which in turn becomes 5-hydroxytryptamine (5-HT, or serotonin). However, tryptophan has to compete with other large amino acids to get into the brain. Because tryptophan is present in very small quantities in most foods, especially compared to other large amino acids, it is usually outnumbered by molecules of other amino acids vying to cross the blood-brain barrier and cannot easily get into the brain.

Foods high in protein contain relatively large quantities of other amino acids, compared to tryptophan. Thus, consuming foods rich in protein tends to prevent tryptophan from crossing the blood-brain barrier. In contrast, foods that are poor in protein have tiny amounts of all amino acids. This means that, when low-protein foods are con-

sumed, tryptophan has less competition when crossing the blood-brain barrier and enters the brain more readily. Research has demonstrated that meals that contain less than 5% protein cause an increase in serotonin production in the brain (Fernstrom, 1987).

In addition, meals rich in carbohydrates promote the passage of tryptophan across the blood-brain barrier. Carbohydrates stimulate the release of insulin in the body, and the more carbohydrates consumed, the more insulin is released. Tryptophan requires insulin to cross the blood-brain barrier, which means that larger quantities of insulin in the blood will transport larger amounts of tryptophan into the brain. Hence, meals rich in carbohydrates and poor in protein will facilitate the entry of tryptophan into the brain, resulting in increased synthesis of serotonin, which in turn may elevate mood (Silverstone, 1993).

Recap 3.3: Neurotransmitters

A neurotransmitter that binds with G protein-linked receptors is called a (a)_____. A neurohormone is released into the (b)_____ and travels to target neurons. (c)_____ is a neurohormone that is released by the adrenal gland and activates neurons of the sympathetic nervous system. Some neurotransmitters, such as glutamate and gamma-aminobutyric acid (GABA) are simple (d)_____ _____. Other neurotransmitters, such as endorphin and cholecystokinin, are (e)_____. The neurotransmitters serotonin, norepinephrine, and dopamine are classified as (f)_____. Other neurotransmitters, such as acetylcholine, anandamide, and (g)_____ _____, do not fit neatly into a family of neurotransmitters.

The Roles of Neurotransmitters in Human Behavior

Let's examine the roles that major neurotransmitters play in regulating human behavior. You are already familiar with acetylcholine, so we'll begin our discussion with this neurotransmitter. Next, we'll take a look at the major amino acid, peptide, and monoamine transmitter substances, and we'll conclude with a discussion of two recently discovered neurotransmitters: nitric oxide and anandamide.

Acetylcholine

Acetylcholine receptors are found throughout the central and peripheral nervous systems, and acetylcholine is believed to play an important role in a wide range of behaviors. For example, acetylcholine is the neurotransmitter that initiates contraction in all smooth and skeletal muscles, as you will learn in Chapter 6. Thus, acetylcholine is necessary for the functioning of the somatic and autonomic nervous systems. Chemicals, such as *curare* and cobra snake venom, that block the action of acetylcholine can interfere with muscle contraction, causing paralysis. Curare, for example, is derived from a South American plant and is still used by native hunters there as a poison on the tip of their arrows. When a curare-tipped arrow strikes a prey animal, the curare binds with acetylcholine receptors in the animal, preventing acetylcholine from reaching its muscle receptors. Consequently, the animal becomes paralyzed and drops to the ground, which makes it easy to capture. Curare has several useful medical applications because of its ability to paralyze muscles.

Two life-threatening illnesses, caused by bacteria, are associated with the interference of acetylcholine transmission in skeletal muscles. *Tetanus*, also known as "lockjaw," usually results from a wound (typically a deep puncture wound) that is not cleaned properly, allowing the bacterium *Clostridium tetani* to multiply in the area surrounding the wound. The *Clostridium* bacterium produces a powerful *exotoxin*, a poison that is released into the bloodstream, which interferes with acetylcholine function by blocking the release of neurotransmitters that inhibit acetylcholine. That is, the tetanus toxin stops the inhibition of muscle contraction. A person afflicted with tetanus experiences prolonged, unmitigated muscle contractions that can lead to death, if not treated. Another illness, known as *botulism*, results from ingestion of a bacterium called *Clostridium botulinum*, which is found in canned and preserved foods that have not been properly prepared. This bacterium, after it is ingested, is not destroyed by enzymes in the digestive tract and gets into the bloodstream, where it multiplies and produces an exotoxin that inhibits acetylcholine release at the junction between the presynaptic neuron and the muscle fiber (Pellizzari, Rossetto, Schiavo, & Montecucco, 1999). Botulism causes weakness and eventual paralysis of all skeletal muscles, including the muscles needed for breathing. Death due to suffocation results in several hours to days, if the illness goes untreated.

In addition to the important role that acetylcholine plays in muscle contraction, acetylcholine plays a number of other important roles in the central and peripheral nervous systems. Recall that there are two types of acetylcholine receptors: nicotinic and muscarinic receptors. When acetylcholine binds with muscarinic receptors in the peripheral nervous system, a number of parasympathetic responses are observed, including decrease in heart rate, increase in rhythmic contractions in the stomach and small and large intestines, constriction of the pupil of the eye, and increase in secretions of various glands, including salivary glands and other glands associated with the digestive system. Muscarinic receptors also play an important role in the central nervous system, particularly in learning, memory, attention, arousal, electrical brain wave activity, and the control of posture (Blokland, 1996; Ehlert, Roeske, & Yamamura, 1995; Felder et al., 2001; Mesulam, 1995; Reiner & Fibiger, 1995; Schwarz et al., 1999).

Although most research focuses on the important role that muscarinic receptors play in learning and memory, there is some evidence that nicotinic receptors are involved in a variety of cognitive processes, such as decision making (Decker, Brioni, Bannon, & Arneric, 1995; Levin & Simon, 1998). Nicotinic receptors have also been implicated in the control of blood flow to the cerebral cortex and in the reduction of anxiety. However, most nicotinic receptors are located in the peripheral nervous system, rather than in the brain (Edmonds, Gibb, & Colquhoun, 1995; McGehee & Role, 1995). In the peripheral nervous system, nicotinic receptors are located predominantly at neuromuscular junctions (that is, at the synapses between motor neurons and skeletal muscles). Acetylcholine is released from the terminal buttons of motor neurons and binds with receptors on muscle fibers, opening Na^+ channels and causing contraction of the muscle.

Drugs Associated with Acetylcholine Receptors

Keeping in mind that there are two major classes of acetylcholine receptors, you shouldn't be surprised to learn that different chemical substances bind to nicotinic

Figure 3.11 Comparison of acetylcholine, nicotine, and muscarine molecules.
Nicotine and muscarine resemble acetylcholine structurally. Note that the N atom is bonded with CH_3 in each molecule.

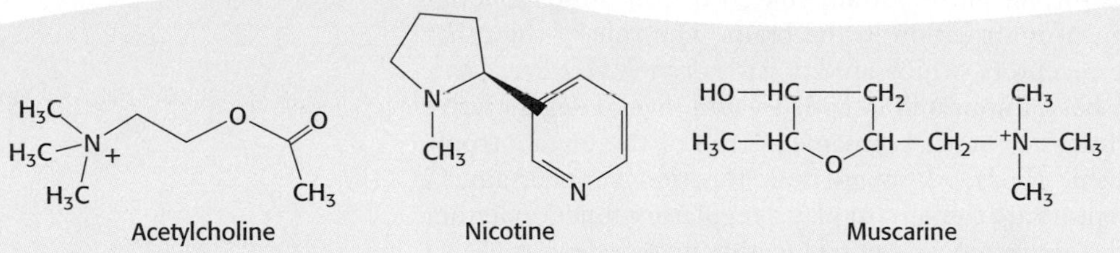

Acetylcholine   Nicotine   Muscarine

and muscarinic acetylcholine receptors. **Curare**, as you learned earlier, binds with nicotinic receptors, preventing acetylcholine from activating the receptor. It is a nicotinic antagonist. **Nicotine,** on the other hand, is a nicotinic agonist. Whether derived from tobacco or from nicotine gum or patches, nicotine enters the bloodstream, crosses the blood-brain barrier, and activates nicotinic receptors. This is because nicotine has a molecular shape that is very similar to the acetylcholine molecule (Figure 3.11; Domino, 1998). Nicotine has been demonstrated to improve cognitive processing, increase cerebral blood flow, and decrease anxiety—functions associated with activation of nicotinic receptors (Decker, Brioni, Bannon, & Arneric, 1995). We will examine how nicotine addiction develops in Chapter 13.

You have already learned about one agonist of the muscarinic acetylcholine receptor, **muscarine** (Figure 3.11). Muscarine binds with the muscarinic receptor, producing a number of parasympathetic responses, including constriction of the pupil of the eye (Barondes, 1993). A muscarinic antagonist that has a number of medical applications is *atropine*. Like muscarine, nicotine, and curare, atropine is a natural substance that is derived from a plant. It can fit into the muscarinic receptor and prevent acetylcholine from binding with the receptor. In ancient times, atropine was used as a poison. Today it has many useful medical applications. For example, it is used to produce dilation of the pupil, so that the physician may examine the interior of the eyeball. Recall that muscarine has the opposite effect: pupillary constriction. Atropine is sometimes used as an adjunct to surgery, to reduce salivary and mucous secretions while the person or animal is under general anesthesia.

curare: a nicotinic antagonist that produces paralysis
nicotine: a nicotinic agonist, binds with acetylcholine ligand-gated ion channels

muscarine: a muscarinic agonist, binds with G protein-linked acetylcholine receptor

Amino Acid Neurotransmitters

Amino acid neurotransmitters are the most common transmitter substances found in the human nervous system. Unfortunately, because amino acids are found inside all cells in the body, scientists overlooked their role as neurotransmitters for many years. Ionotropic receptors for the amino acids, *glutamate, aspartate, glycine,* and *gamma-aminobutyric acid,* have been identified in the cell membranes of neurons, and these amino acids are now regarded as true neurotransmitters. Glutamate and aspartate bind with receptors that open Na^+ channels and, hence, are excitatory neurotransmitters. Glycine and gamma-aminobutyric acid (GABA) open Cl^- channels and are inhibitory neurotransmitters. I focus on glutamate and GABA in this discussion because the roles of glutamate and GABA in regulating human behavior are well documented, whereas the functions of glycine and aspartate are not well understood.

Glutamate

Table 3.2 (p. 65) showed that there are at least 13 different receptors for glutamate: 5 ionotropic glutamate receptors and 8 metabotropic glutamate receptors. Most neurons in the brain use glutamate to produce rapid excitation in postsynaptic neurons. That is, most presynaptic neurons in the brain excite postsynaptic neurons via ionotropic glutamate receptors in the postsynaptic membrane. These ionotropic receptors fall into two classes: one group of receptors that binds with a synthetic chemical called N-methyl-D-aspartate (NMDA) and another group of receptors that does not bind with NMDA. The receptors that bind with NMDA, called the *NMDA receptors*, are believed to play an important role in the encoding of long-term memory and the storing of information in the brain. The role of the other class of ionotropic glutamate receptors, which are known as *non-NMDA receptors*, is not clear, although they've been implicated in epilepsy and several degenerative brain diseases such as Alzheimer's disease. The same is true of the metabotropic glutamate receptors (Nakanishi, 1992). Although their function is uncertain, G protein-linked glutamate receptors are thought to play a regulatory function, either augmenting or suppressing the activation of ionotropic glutamate receptors.

Chemicals Associated with Glutamate Receptors Although a large number of synthetic drugs have been created that bind with glutamate receptors, I will focus on two better-known chemical substances that we encounter every day. The first substance is *caffeine*, which is found in most coffee, tea, and carbonated beverages. Caffeine's main effect is to increase the activity of glutamate receptors that activate heart muscle, which elevates cardiac output and increases the flow of oxygen to the brain. Caffeine does not bind with glutamate receptors directly, but instead it blocks the action of adenosine, a neurotransmitter that inhibits glutamate release. That is, caffeine binds with adenosine receptors, preventing adenosine from binding with its own receptors. When adenosine cannot bind with its own receptors, it cannot inhibit the release of glutamate. Thus, caffeine blocks the action of adenosine and indirectly increases glutamate release. Some people are especially sensitive to caffeine and report that caffeine makes them feel extremely anxious, shaky, and unable to concentrate. This extreme effect is due to caffeine increasing the release of glutamate in the brain.

The second substance that I will mention in conjunction with glutamate receptors is *monosodium glutamate*, also known as *MSG*, which is used in some types of cuisine to enhance the flavor of food. (Chinese restaurants, for example, typically use MSG in their dishes, although some do not use MSG and promote themselves as being MSG-free.) MSG does not cross the blood-brain barrier, so it has no effect on the brain. However, because the blood-brain barrier is not fully developed in the very young, MSG can cross the blood-brain barrier in young children. MSG does bind with glutamate receptors in the peripheral nervous system and can produce tingling, burning, loss of sensation, ringing in the ears, and other peripheral symptoms in people who are sensitive to MSG or who have ingested too much of the substance (Settipane, 1987).

GABA

GABA is considered to be the most important inhibitory neurotransmitter in the brain (Paul, 1995). There are several types of GABA receptors, each of which produces inhibition in a different way. $GABA_A$ receptors are ionotropic receptors that are linked to Cl^- channels, which produce IPSPs when the Cl^- channels are opened. In contrast, $GABA_B$ receptors are metabotropic, G protein-linked receptors. Their inhibitory effect is longer lasting. In addition, as you might well imagine, a wide variety of different $GABA_A$ and $GABA_B$ receptors have been discovered in the human nervous system. Therefore, like the other neurotransmitters we have considered to this point, GABA plays a number of different roles in the brain, many of them still undiscovered.

The $GABA_A$ receptor has received a great deal of study. It is a large complex that contains receptor sites for other substances in addition to GABA. Figure 3.12 illustrates a typical $GABA_A$ receptor complex. The receptor itself is a protein composed of five subunits that form an ion channel. It is embedded in the cell membrane, with receptor sites for GABA located on the surface

Figure 3.12 The $GABA_A$ receptor complex.
The $GABA_A$ receptor is a complicated structure that contains binding sites for GABA, alcohol, barbiturates, and benzodiazepine.

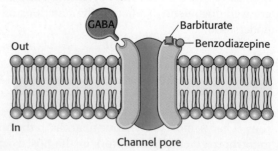

of the neuron. Some subunits also have receptor sites for other substances, including the antianxiety agents known as **benzodiazepines,** barbiturates, alcohol, general anesthetics, and certain steroids (Mihic, Sanna, Whiting, & Harris, 1995).

Although investigators are beginning to understand the structure of $GABA_A$ receptors, they are still far away from linking specific receptor types to specific behaviors. Certainly, the wide variety of $GABA_A$ receptors that exist point to an enormous range of behaviors and functions that are regulated by GABA (Barnard, 1995; Luddens, Korpi, & Seeburg, 1995). Some investigators believe that very minor alterations in the $GABA_A$ receptor structure can profoundly affect receptor function and may be implicated in a number of behavior disorders, including anxiety disorders, alcohol abuse, epilepsy, sleep disorders, and certain degenerative disorders such as Huntington's disease (Ali et al., 1999; Malizia & Richardson, 1995; Mihic et al., 1995).

The $GABA_B$ receptor type is not well understood. Its structure has not yet been determined, nor has its role in the brain been established (Ramirez et al., 1997). We do know that it is a G protein-linked receptor and that it is not as abundant in the brain as are $GABA_A$ receptors. At present, research indicates that activation of $GABA_B$ receptors attenuates the release of a wide variety of neurotransmitters and hormones (Cooper et al., 1996; Paul, 1995).

Drugs Associated with $GABA_A$ Receptors Many chemical substances are associated with the $GABA_A$ receptor complex. For example, a variety of compounds have been synthesized that bind directly with the GABA receptor site, acting as GABA agonists or antagonists. These compounds are useful for research purposes when comparing the various receptor types, but they are not important for you, the student of behavior, to study. Instead, I would like to focus on several well-known drugs that bind with different receptor sites on the $GABA_A$ receptor complex. Because they do not bind directly with the GABA site, they do not act as GABA agonists or antagonists. But, these drugs do act as modulators, changing the rate at which the Cl$^-$ channel opens and closes. The drugs we will examine in this context are *benzodiazepines, barbiturates, alcohol,* and *general anesthetics.*

Benzodiazepines are a class of drugs that were first developed in the 1950s (Ballenger, 1995). These drugs are chiefly prescribed as antianxiety agents and have sedative and muscle relaxant effects as well. Benzodiazepines can also be used to control epileptic convulsions. In 1977, several investigators working in different laboratories discovered that benzodiazepines bind to receptor sites on $GABA_A$ receptor complexes. It is important to point out here that benzodiazepine does not bind to all $GABA_A$ receptors, only those $GABA_A$ receptor complexes that have specific binding sites for benzodiazepine. Benzodiazepines increase Cl$^-$ channel opening indirectly by increasing GABA binding to its receptor. That is, benzodiazepines have no effect on the GABA receptor, except in the presence of GABA. Hence, benzodiazepines enhance the effect of GABA.

Like benzodiazepines, barbiturates are antiepileptic agents, but they are also used to induce sleep or unconsciousness in patients. Drugs that induce sleep are called *hypnotics;* drugs that induce unconsciousness are called *general anesthetics.* Barbiturates can be used as an antiepileptic, a hypnotic, or a brief-acting general anesthetic. They bind to different sites on the $GABA_A$ receptor complex than do benzodiazepines (Figure 3.12). Their effect on the receptor is quite a bit different, too. At lower doses, barbiturates increase GABA binding to its receptor, much like benzodiazepines. At higher doses that produce anesthesia or unconsciousness, barbiturates open Cl$^-$ channels by themselves, without GABA being present (Paul, 1995).

Ethanol also binds to specific sites on the $GABA_A$ receptor complex. Similar to benzodiazepine in action, ethanol augments GABA binding to its receptor, producing increased opening of Cl$^-$ channels and increased inhibition. This inhibitory action most likely produces the anxiety-reducing and sedative effects of alcohol. General anesthetics, used during surgery to induce unconsciousness in the surgical patient, also bind with the $GABA_A$ receptor complex, increasing the inhibitory function of GABA (Mihic et al., 1995). Thus, it appears that one of GABA's functions in the brain is to calm a person down and to induce sleep and unconsciousness as GABA activity increases.

Peptide Neurotransmitters

Neuroscientists have identified nearly 50 different peptides that are made by neurons and used as transmitter substances. These peptide neurotransmitters, or *neuropeptides*, as they're often called, differ from other neurotransmitters because they are synthesized in ribosomes in the soma of the neuron, whereas other neurotransmitters are manufactured in the axon near the site of release. The neuropeptides are then packaged in vesicles and transported to the terminal buttons to await release into the synapse. In addition, peptide neurotransmitters are almost always released by the presynaptic neuron in conjunction with another neurotransmitter (Hokfelt, Castel, Morino, Zhang, & Dagerlind, 1995). This observation (that neuropeptides do not act alone as a signaling transmitter) has raised many questions about the role of peptides as neurotransmitters. Some investigators believe that neuropeptides are just primitive transmitters that have been superceded through evolution by more sophisticated neurotransmitters. However, most neuroscientists believe that neuropeptides enrich the message by modulating the effect of the other neurotransmitter. At present, the functions of very few peptide neurotransmitters are truly understood. I will focus on only three neuropeptides in this chapter, although you will learn about more in later chapters.

Substance P

Substance P gets its funny name from the fact that it was first identified as an active substance in a powder made from brain extract. It is found in many parts of the brain and spinal cord, especially those parts of the nervous system associated with the sensation of pain. Currently, substance P is believed to be the primary neurotransmitter that signals pain.

substance P: a neurotransmitter used by pain receptors to signal the presence of tissue damage and pain

It also is released in conjunction with acetylcholine and serotonin in particular parts of the brain, although its roles in this regard are uncertain. Several investigators have demonstrated that substance P is released in response to stress and that it may play a role in depression, as you will learn in Chapter 15 (Burnet & Harrison, 2000; Kramer et al., 1998; Wahlestedt, 1998).

Cholecystokinin (CCK)

CCK is a neurohormone synthesized by cells in the small intestine and in the nervous system. It is released into the blood and travels to the central nervous system, where it binds with CCK receptors on neurons. CCK's main function involves transmitting signals about satiety following a meal. However, CCK also appears to play a role in blocking pain and reducing anxiety (Hawranko & Smith, 1999; Zwanzger et al., 2001; Wiesenfeld-Hallin et al., 1997).

Endorphins and Other Endogenous Opiate Peptides

The term *endorphin* is actually a contraction of *endogenous morphine*, so called because this class of neuropeptides is synthesized by neurons and functions like morphine in countering pain and reducing stress. At least six different peptides have been identified as endogenous opiate peptides, including a group of peptides known as *enkephalins* and another group known as *dynorphins*. Endogenous opiate peptides bind with **opioid receptors** on the membranes of neurons. These opioid binding sites are G protein-linked receptors located in particular areas of the brain. In addition to reducing pain, endogenous opiate peptides have also been implicated in the regulation of blood pressure, stress responses, food intake, sexual behavior, temperature regulation, and memory (Bremner, Southwick & Charney, 1999; Cooper et al., 1996; Mercer & Holder, 1997; Wagner & Chavkin, 1995; Wei & Loh, 1997).

opioid receptors: receptors on the cell membranes of neurons that bind with endogenous opiates and opiate drugs

Drugs Associated with Opioid Receptors Typically, neurotransmitters are first identified by neuroscientists, and then their respective receptors are located and characterized. In the case of endorphins, these two steps were reversed. The opioid receptor was isolated and identified first, and *then* researchers discovered the

Figure 3.13 Structures of various opiate drugs and endorphins.
(a) The three-dimensional structures of enkephalin and morphine have similarities, which are indicated by arrows. (b) The two synthetic opiate drugs shown have similar chemical structures.

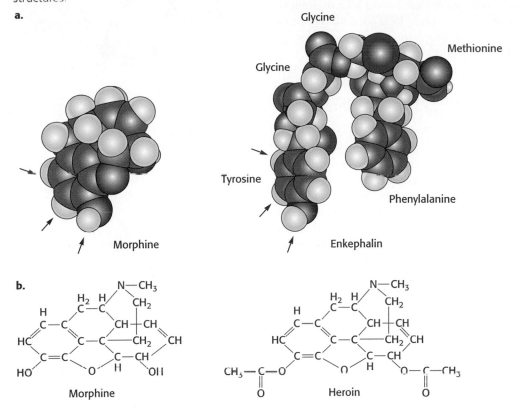

endogenous transmitter that binds to the receptor (Snyder, 1980.) Why was this discovery process reversed for opioid receptors?

Opium, a derivative of the poppy plant, has been known for centuries to produce sedation and euphoria in the user. Other drugs that are derived naturally or synthetically from opium, called **opiates** or *narcotics*, were developed in the 19th and 20th centuries. These new opiates, including *morphine, heroin, codeine,* and *demerol*, were effective in alleviating pain (Figure 3.13). Researchers reasoned that opium and its derivatives must interact with neurons to produce their effects, and some began searching for receptor sites on neurons that bind with opiates. In 1973, Candice Pert and Solomon Snyder at Johns Hopkins University discovered the receptor binding site for opiate drugs. After the opioid receptor was identified, investigators embarked on a search for endogenous ligands, that is, chemicals in the nervous system that bind to the opioid receptor. In 1974 and 1975, researchers in Europe and the United States found a brain extract that competes with opiates and binds to the opioid receptor (Hughes, 1975; Pasternak, Goodman, & Snyder, 1975; Terenius & Wahlstrom, 1974). Hence, it was the discovery of the opioid receptors in the brain that prompted the search for endorphins.

opiates: drugs that are derived naturally or synthetically from opium, such as morphine, heroin, codeine, and demerol

Monoamine Neurotransmitters

Earlier in this section on neurotransmitters, you learned that serotonin, norepinephrine, and dopamine belong to the same family, called monoamine neurotransmitters. Collectively, these neurotransmitters play an important role in regulating mood, sleep, appetite, and memory (Barker & Blakely, 1996). Individually, these three neurotransmitters each have a particular distribution in the brain and have been implicated in special functions. Other amines, such as *histamine*, have been identified in the central nervous system, but their roles are unclear at present. Therefore, I will focus on serotonin, norepinephrine, and dopamine in this section.

Serotonin

Serotonin was discovered over a hundred years ago in the serum of blood, hence its prefix: *sero-*. The suffix *-tonin* comes from the observation that this blood-borne substance increases muscle *tone* in smooth muscle in the gut (Azmitia & Whitaker-Azmitia, 1995). Recall that serotonin is derived from the amino acid tryptophan and therefore has the chemical name 5-hydroxytryptamine (abbreviated as 5-HT).

Seven classes of serotonin receptors have been identified, each with its own distribution in the brain and its own function. For example, one type of receptor (5-HT$_1$ receptors) is implicated in anxiety, aggression, and depression, whereas another type (5-HT$_2$ receptors) seems to be involved in appetite and motor control, and a third type (5-HT$_3$ receptors) appears to play a role in nausea, vomiting, anxiety, and schizophrenia (Azmitia & Whitaker-Azmitia, 1995; Glennon & Dukat, 1995; Scalzitti & Hensler, 1997). Of these different receptor types, only the 5-HT$_3$ receptor is an ionotropic ion channel receptor (Jackson & Yakel, 1995; Shih, Chen, & Gallaher, 1995). The rest are believed to be G protein-linked receptors. The fact that serotonin has so many different types of receptors tells us that serotonin plays many roles in the brain. In fact, no other neurotransmitter has been implicated in so many important human functions (Jacobs & Fornal, 1995).

Serotonin's most important function appears to be the regulation of sleep. But, it has also been demonstrated to be involved in vigilance, mood regulation, appetite (especially appetite for carbohydrates), and stereotyped or repetitive movements, such as response to pain. For example, high levels of serotonin are associated with a decrease in total caloric intake and a decrease in carbohydrate intake (Blundell, 1984). As you will learn in later chapters, serotonin has also been implicated in a host of disorders, including mood disorders, anxiety disorders, obsessive-compulsive disorder, schizophrenia, eating disorders, migraine headaches, and sleep disorders (Aghajanian, 1995; Heninger, 1995; Porsolt, 1993; Tollefson, 1996).

Drugs Associated with Serotonin Receptors   Given that there are at least 15 different serotonin receptor subtypes, there are dozens of drugs that I could discuss in this section. However, I will limit my discussion to two illicit drugs, l̲ysergic acid d̲iethylamide (LSD), and m̲ethylene-d̲i̲oxym̲eth̲amphetamine (MDMA), that appear to interact with serotonin receptors but that are not generally prescribed for medical purposes. The molecular structure of LSD is strikingly similar to that of serotonin (Figure 3.14), and, hence, LSD is able to fit into serotonin receptor sites. LSD's effect is hallucinogenic, producing hallucinations and altering cognition and sensory experiences. The active ingredient in psychedelic mushrooms, called *psilocybin*, also resembles serotonin in chemical structure (Figure 3.14). Like LSD, psilocybin fits into the serotonin receptor and causes hallucinations.

MDMA, known as *ecstasy* for the short-term surge of euphoria and feeling of well-being that it produces, also binds with some serotonin receptors. However, exposure to MDMA appears to be toxic to neurons. Damage to the axons of serotonin neurons has been observed in the brains of people who have taken MDMA more than 200 times (McCann, Szabo, Scheffel, Dannals, & Ricaurte, 1998). Using a radiolabel that binds to 5-HT markers on the axons of neurons that release serotonin, McCann and colleagues (1998) were able to show in brain scans that axon terminals in serotonin neurons were destroyed in human subjects who used large doses of MDMA over the course of 4 to 5 years, compared to control subjects who had never used MDMA. This damage was dose-related because the damage observed was greater in subjects who used MDMA more times (400 versus 100 doses).

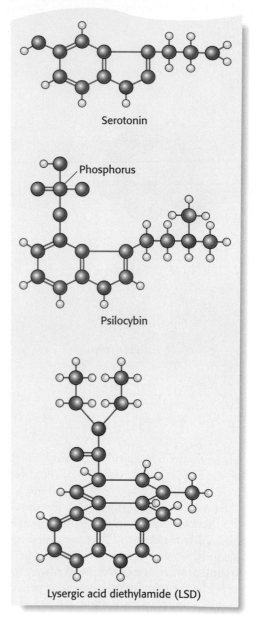

Figure 3.14 Molecular structure of LSD, psilocybin, and serotonin.

Serotonin

Phosphorus

Psilocybin

Lysergic acid diethylamide (LSD)

Norepinephrine

Norepinephrine and its catecholamine cousin, epinephrine, bind to the same adrenergic receptors. Altogether, there are four subtypes of adrenergic receptors (alpha$_1$-, alpha$_2$-, beta$_1$-, and beta$_2$-), each having its own agonists and antagonists and each having its own distribution in the brain. The adrenergic receptors are all G protein-linked receptors, but the similarity among them ends there. For example, the two alpha-adrenergic receptors each utilize a different second messenger (Morilak, 1997). The beta-adrenergic receptors can be differentiated from each other by comparing their tendencies to bind with norepinephrine versus epinephrine: Beta$_1$ binds more readily with norepinephrine than epinephrine, and beta$_2$ binds more readily with epinephrine (Cooper et al., 1996).

It is quite interesting that a neurotransmitter and a neurohormone would bind to the same receptors, but it tells us that both norepinephrine and epinephrine are involved in sympathetic activation. Both produce an increase in heart rate, respiration rate, sweating, and pupil dilation. In addition, norepinephrine plays a role in mood, drive reduction, sleep, arousal, cognition, and emotions (Foote & Aston-Jones, 1995; Morilak, 1997). Epinephrine, on the other hand, is present in very low levels in the brain. Norepinephrine also has been implicated in a number of behavioral disorders, including depression, posttraumatic stress disorder, anxiety disorder, and withdrawal symptoms associated with drug addiction (Leonard, 2001; Placidi et al., 2001; Robbins & Everitt, 1995; Valentino & Aston-Jones, 1995). You will learn a great deal more about norepinephrine in Chapters 9–14 as we discuss sleep, eating, sexual behavior, emotions, addiction, and response to stress.

Drugs Associated with Adrenergic Receptors Recall that the four adrenergic receptor subtypes each have their own agonists and antagonists. That means that we could discuss any of a large number of possible drugs here. I have chosen to focus on two drugs, *clonidine* and *yohimbine*, because these are the best known and because they have important implications for human behavior. Clonidine is an agonist of the alpha$_2$-adrenergic receptor, and yohimbine is an antagonist of the alpha$_2$-adrenergic receptor. Because these two drugs have opposite effects on the same receptor, you would expect them to have opposing behavioral effects—and they do! Clonidine has a sedative or calming effect when administered, whereas yohimbine agitates the subject and can provoke anxiety. However, the effects of these drugs are not straightforward. For example, clonidine has been demonstrated to interfere with learning and memory in healthy people and to improve cognitive ability in brain-damaged alcoholics (Robbins & Everitt, 1995). You will learn more about clonidine in Chapter 10 when we discuss learning and memory, and we will examine the effects of yohimbine on people who have posttraumatic stress disorder in Chapter 14.

Dopamine

Dopamine is considered by some investigators to be the most important catecholamine in the brain (Jaber, Robinson, Missale, & Caron, 1996). It is actually a metabolic precursor of norepinephrine and epinephrine, which means that norepinephrine and epinephrine are derived from dopamine, and any dysfunction in the synthesis of dopamine is likely to affect norepinephrine and epinephrine function as well (Figure 3.15). Dopamine has its own receptors, a total of five different subtypes, and is distributed along four major pathways in the brain, as you will learn in Chapter 4 (Baldessarini & Tarazi, 1996). Each dopamine pathway in the brain is associated with a different function of dopamine: motor control, thinking, affect, and hormone secretion. In addition, dopamine has been implicated in the control of emotions and feelings of pleasure and euphoria. An impressive number of disorders are associated with dopamine, including movement disorders such as Parkinson's disease, psychotic disorders such as schizophrenia, and drug addiction (Ng, George, & O'Dowd, 1997).

Dopamine appears to be involved in a wide range of behaviors, due in part to its many different receptors. Originally, only two dopamine receptors were identified: D1 and D2. The other receptors, D3, D4, and D5, were discovered more recently. All dopamine receptors are G protein-linked receptors, which means that dopamine acts as a neuromodulator in the brain. Investigators have grouped the five receptor subtypes in two families: D1-like receptors and D2-like receptors. D1 and D5 receptors make up the D1-like family, whereas the others (D2, D3, and D4) are members of the D2-like family (Seeman, 1995). When dopamine binds with D1-like receptors, cyclic AMP activity is increased. The opposite effect occurs with D2-like receptors: Activation of the D2-like receptor inhibits cyclic AMP (Cooper et al., 1996; Jaber, Robinson, Missale, & Caron, 1996; Ng, George, & O'Dowd, 1997). As a result, different kinds of behaviors are associated with D1-like and D2-like receptors. For example, D2-like receptors appear to play a role in schizophrenia, as antipsychotic agents bind with receptors in the D2-like family.

Drugs Associated with Dopamine Receptors The best known of the drugs associated with dopamine receptors are the D2-receptor antagonists, which include *chlorpromazine, clozapine,* and *haloperidol.* If you ever work in the mental health field, you will quickly become familiar with these drugs because they are prescribed to treat schizophrenia and other psychotic conditions. (See Chapter 15 for a full description of schizophrenia and other psychoses.) Because dopamine antagonists are so effective in eliminating many symptoms of schizophrenia, many investigators believe that dysfunction of the dopamine system is the underlying cause of schizophrenia.

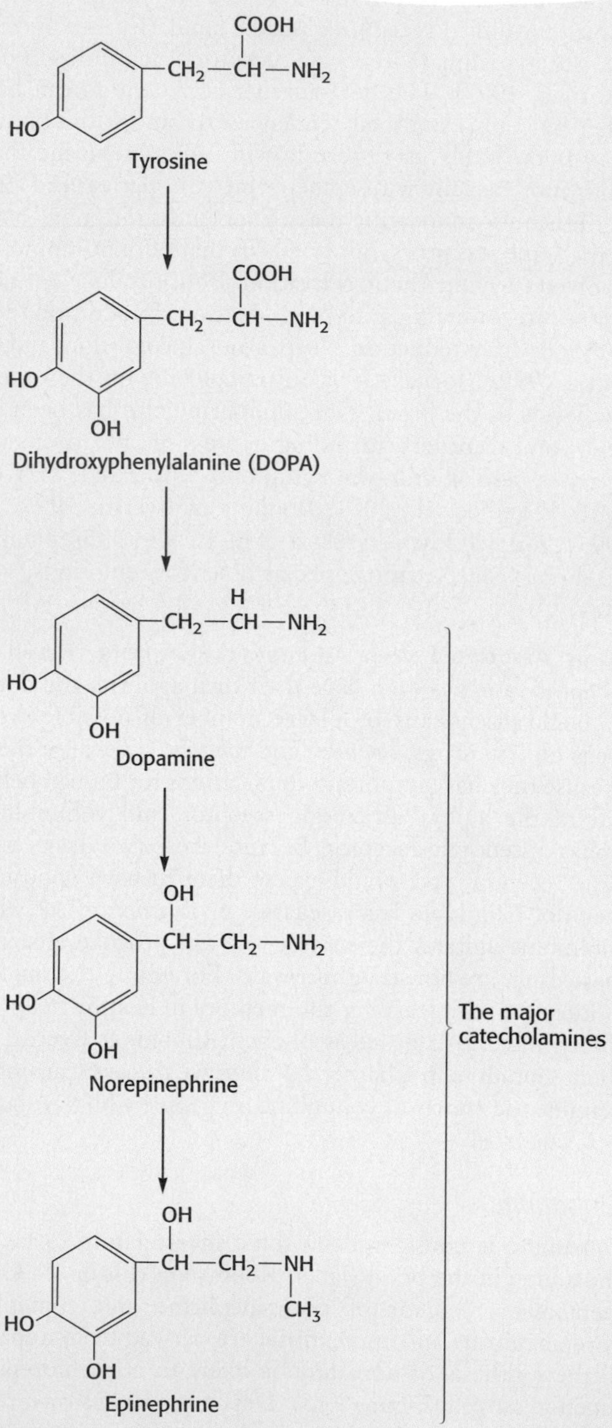

Anandamide

Anandamide is an endogenous ligand that binds with **cannabinoid receptors** in the nervous system. Do you remember the term *endogenous ligand?* I used this term earlier when discussing endorphins. An endogenous ligand is a compound that: (1) is synthesized in the nervous system and (2) binds with receptors embedded in the cell membrane of neurons. Like the endorphins, anandamide is found in discrete areas of the brain, where it binds with its own special receptors, called cannabinoid receptors. And, like the endorphins, the cannabinoid receptor was isolated and identified *before* anandamide was discovered. These discoveries have been relatively recent. Cannabinoid receptors were first identified in 1988, and the endogenous ligand, anandamide, was discovered in the same laboratory at Hebrew University in Israel in 1992 (Devane, Dysarz, Johnson, Melvin, & Howlett, 1988; Devane, Hanus, Breuer, Pertwee, Stevenson, et al., 1992). The word *anandamide* is derived from the Sanskrit word for "bliss," *ananda,* and the suffix *-amide* refers to its chemical structure.

Figure 3.15 Metabolic pathway from tyrosine to epinephrine.

Tyrosine is converted into DOPA, which is further converted to dopamine, then norepinephrine and finally epinephrine.

Tyrosine

Dihydroxyphenylalanine (DOPA)

Dopamine

Norepinephrine

Epinephrine

The major catecholamines

cannabinoid receptor: a newly discovered receptor that binds with anandamide and tetrahydrocannabinol

Since the discovery of the original cannabinoid receptor, a second cannabinoid receptor has been identified. It now appears that there are two cannabinoid receptors: CB1 and CB2. The CB1 receptor is found primarily in the central nervous system, and the CB2 receptor is found primarily in the peripheral nervous system. At present, it is believed that CB1 and CB2 are G protein-linked receptors that use cyclic AMP as a second messenger (Matsuda, 1997). The location of cannabinoid receptors in the brain indicates that these receptors probably play a role in emotion, cognition, and motor control (Barinaga, 2001; Lallemand et al., 2001; Martin, 1995; Meschler et al., 2001; Sullivan, 2000). However, the exact role that anandamide and these receptors play is not known.

Drugs Associated with Cannabinoid Receptors

The word *cannabinoid* comes from *cannabis sativa*, a leafy hemp plant that is best known as *marijuana*. For centuries, cannabis has been used for both medicinal and recreational purposes. The active ingredient in cannabis, tetrahydrocannabinol (THC), is an agonist that binds to cannabinoid receptors in the brain, producing a number of effects, including changes in mood, thinking, and sensory perception (Figure 3.16). Moderate cannabis intoxication can impair memory and motor coordination. Other adverse side effects include feelings of depersonalization, panic attacks, and disturbances in thinking that closely resemble a psychosis (Emrich, Leweke, & Schneider, 1997; Martin, 1995).

Figure 3.16 Comparison of THC and anandamide molecules.

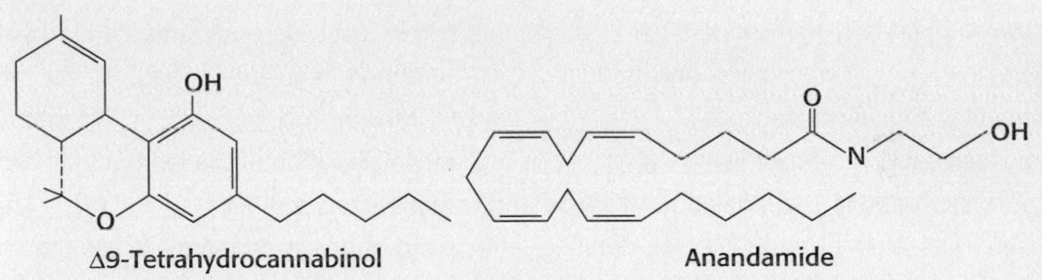

Δ9-Tetrahydrocannabinol   Anandamide

Nitric Oxide

Nitric oxide was first identified as a neurotransmitter in 1987 when investigators discovered that acetylcholine produces dilation of blood vessels only when nitric oxide is present (Ignarro, Buga, Wood, Byrnes, & Chaudhuri, 1987; Palmer, Ferrige, & Moncada, 1987). Since that time, neuroscientists have been trying to understand how this gaseous compound functions in the nervous system. You see, nitric oxide presents a bit of a problem to researchers. It is produced by neurons, but it is not stored in vesicles and is not released into the synapse like other neurotransmitters (Cooper et al., 1996). In fact, nitric oxide easily diffuses across the cell membrane, which means it can readily leave one neuron and enter another (Garthwaite & Boulton, 1995; Lane & Gross, 1999). However, the action of nitric oxide is short lived because it is an unstable compound that can exist for only a few seconds before converting into a more stable, but inactive form (Gross & Wolin, 1995).

Inside the postsynaptic neuron, nitric oxide appears to stimulate a second messenger called cyclic GMP. However, the mechanism by which nitric oxide works is not at all clear. Psychologists conducting research in this area have found that nitric oxide, perhaps through activation of cyclic GMP, plays a role in learning and memory and sexual, aggressive, and ingestive behaviors (Nelson, Kriegsfeld, Dawson, & Dawson, 1997). For example, inhibition of nitric oxide interferes with memory formation. In addition, decreased nitric oxide levels in the brain result in decreased sexual activity, increased aggression, and decreased eating. Nitric oxide appears to work with other neurotransmitters in the brain, as well as in the peripheral nervous system. In order for nitric oxide to affect eating behavior, for example, the presence of serotonin neurons is required. Its role in learning and memory appears to involve glutamate and the glutamate-NMDA receptor (Gross & Wolin, 1995). Nitric oxide also plays an important role in pituitary hormone release, particularly in the release of hormones that affect sexual behavior and stress responses (Nelson et al., 1997). The importance of nitric oxide has been recognized by the Nobel

Prize Committee, which awarded the 1998 Nobel Prize in Medicine to investigators Robert F. Furchgott, Louis J. Ignarro, and Ferid Murad for their pioneering research on nitric oxide.

✏️ Recap 3.4: The Role of Neurotransmitters in Human Behavior

(a)_____ initiates contraction of muscles, stimulates parasympathetic responses, and plays a role in learning, memory, and arousal. Curare, nicotine and (b)_____ are drugs associated with acetylcholine receptors. Glutamate typically produces rapid excitation in postsynaptic neurons and is believed to play an important role in the formation of (c)_____-_____ memory. (d)_____ is the most important inhibitory neurotransmitter in the brain. Benzodiazepines, barbiturates, (e)_____, and general anesthetics bind with receptor sites on the GABA receptor. Substance P is the neurotransmitter that signals (f)_____. Cholecystokinin is a neurohormone that signals (g)_____ following a meal. Endorphins and other (h)_____ opiates function to reduce pain and to regulate blood pressure, stress responses, and food intake. Opiates or naracotics, such as morphine, heroin, codeine, and demerol, bind with (i)_____ receptors and reduce pain. Serotonin regulates mood, sleep, and appetite. Two illicit drugs, (j)_____ and MDMA (or "(k)_____") interact with serotonin receptors. (l)_____ is involved in activation of the sympathetic nervous system and in the regulation of mood and responses to stress. (m)_____ has been implicated in motor control, thinking, affect, and hormone secretion. Drugs that are used to treat (n)_____ bind with dopamine receptors. Anandamide binds with cannabinoid receptors and is believed to play a role in emotion, (o)_____, and motor control. The drug (p)_____ also binds with cannabinoid receptors. (q)_____ _____ is an unusual neurotransmitter that is involved in learning and sexual, aggressive, and eating behaviors.

The End of the Story: Removing Neurotransmitters from the Synapse

What happens after neurotransmitters have been released into the synapse and bind with postsynaptic receptors? Do they merely stay attached to the receptor forever? Think about what this would mean, if the neurotransmitter were to remain bound to the receptor for a long time. In the case of ion channel receptors, a neurotransmitter bound indefinitely to that type of receptor would keep the ion channel open, producing prolonged depolarization or hyperpolarization—which would have devastating effects on brain function. On the other hand, a neurotransmitter that is bound for an overly long time to a G protein-linked channel would activate a second messenger excessively, again impairing brain function. So, proper brain function requires that neurotransmitters bind rapidly with their respective receptor sites and then just as rapidly detach from the receptor and disappear from the synapse. How is this accomplished?

There are two main mechanisms by which neurotransmitters are removed from the synapse following an action potential: (1) degradation by enzymes and (2) reuptake into the presynaptic neuron.

Degradation by Enzymes

The removal of acetylcholine from the synapse is a good example of degradation by enzymes. After its release from the presynaptic terminal, acetylcholine binds briefly with its postsynaptic receptor and then detaches. As it detaches from its receptor and slips back into the synapse, acetylcholine is immediately attacked and deactivated by an enzyme, **acetylcholinesterase** (Figure 3.17). Acetylcholinesterase deactivates acetylcholine by breaking the neurotransmitter into two components: acetyl and choline. Choline is taken back up by the presynaptic neuron, where it is rejoined with acetyl to make acetylcholine. Thus, acetylcholine is able to stimulate the postsynaptic receptor for only a brief period of time.

acetylcholinesterase: an extracellular enzyme that deactivates acetylcholine

Figure 3.17 Deactivation of acetylcholine by acetylcholinesterase

(a) Acetylcholine, formed from acetyl-CoA and choline molecules, is released into the synaptic cleft. (b) Acetylcholinesterase (red triangle) attacks acetylcholine and breaks it into two components, acetyl (purple triangle) and choline (green circle). Choline is taken back up by the presynaptic neuron.

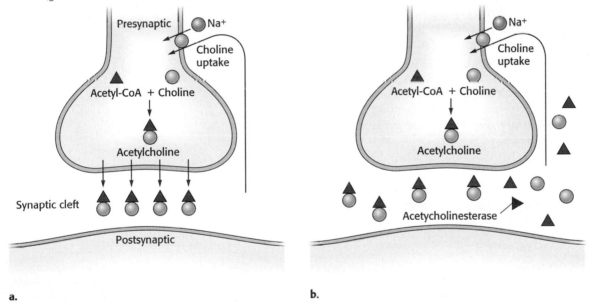

In later chapters, we will examine how neuropharmacologists have taken advantage of the action of acetylcholinesterase to fashion drugs that prolong or reduce the effect of acetylcholine. Think about it for a moment. A drug that mimics acetylcholinesterase will quickly eliminate acetylcholine from the synapse, thereby reducing acetylcholine's effect. A drug that inhibits acetylcholinesterase (an *acetylcholinesterase inhibitor*) will hinder the enzyme's action and allow acetylcholine to accumulate in the synapse, prolonging the neurotransmitter's effect. For example, in Chapter 10, we will look at the effect of acetylcholinesterase inhibitors and enhancers on memory. Because acetylcholine plays an important role in memory, a drug that enhances the activity of acetylcholinesterase (and reduces acetylcholine at the synapse), such as *scopalamine*, will interfere with memory. In contrast, an acetylcholinesterase inhibitor, like *physostigmine*, increases acetylcholine in the synapse and enhances memory (Asthana et al., 1999).

Reuptake by the Presynaptic Neuron

Unlike acetylcholine, the monoamines are not deactivated by a synaptic enzyme but, instead, rely on a reuptake mechanism to remove them from the synapse. Hence, they are removed from the synapse much more slowly than acetylcholine. After their release into the synapse following an action potential, monoamines bind briefly with their postsynaptic receptors before detaching and drifting freely in the synapse. A cellular presynaptic transport mechanism, located in the membrane of the axon, pumps the monoamine back inside the presynaptic neuron.

After it is inside the neuron, the monoamine is attacked by a number of enzymes that break it down so it can be removed from the brain and excreted from the body. Two enzymes that have received much study in this regard are **monoamine oxidase (MAO)** and **catechol-O-methyltransferase (COMT)**. MAO breaks down all monoamines, including dopamine, norepinephrine, and serotonin. In contrast, COMT breaks down only the catecholamines dopamine and norepinephrine.

The reuptake and enzymatic mechanisms that remove and deactivate monoamines have provided neuroscientists with important clues about how monoamine levels in the brain can be controlled. Altogether, there are three ways to increase the availability of monoamines in the synapse: (1) increase the release of monoamines into the synapse, (2) block the reuptake transport system that pumps monoamines back into the presynaptic neuron, and (3) inhibit the enzymes, MAO or COMT, that break down monoamines. The arousing effects of two highly abused drugs, *amphetamine* and *cocaine*, are the result of elevated catecholamine levels in the brain. Amphetamine appears to increase catecholamine levels in the synapse by stimulating the release of catecholamines and by blocking the reuptake by the presynaptic neuron. Cocaine increases dopamine levels in the synapse by blocking the dopamine reuptake transport mechanism. In addition, cocaine also blocks the reuptake of the other monoamines, norepinephrine and serotonin.

For nearly half a century, physicians have been prescribing *MAO inhibitors* to treat patients who are depressed (Healy, 1998). MAO inhibitors block the deactivation of the monoamines by MAO and increase the availability of serotonin, norepinephrine, and dopamine in the brain. Is it possible that low levels of monoamines cause depression? Certainly some investigators think so, and the clinical evidence supports such a suggestion. Another class of drugs that is used to treat

monoamine oxidase (MAO): an intracellular enzyme that deactivates monoamines

catechol-O-methyltransferase (COMT): an intracellular enzyme that deactivates catecholamines

---

Choosing the Best Drug to Treat Depression

Mika was an international student enrolled in an American university when she went to the university's counseling center, complaining of depression. The psychologist who talked to Mika ascertained that she needed medication and referred her to a physician at the university health center for a prescription for an antidepressant. The physician prescribed a SSRI for Mika.

A week later, Mika met with her psychologist. She was still depressed, but she now had an additional symptom: She could not stay awake. While the psychologist was talking to her, Mika nodded off and fell asleep repeatedly. The psychologist consulted with the physician who prescribed the SSRI and advised her of Mika's sleepy state. Mika was then taken off the SSRI and prescribed a norepinephrine reuptake inhibitor, which eliminated her sleepiness.

However, Mika's depression did not lift until she'd been taking the new antidepressant for over 5 weeks. This is typical for antidepressant medications: They require 4 to 6 weeks before their antidepressant effects become apparent. The reason for this time lag is yet unknown but is probably due to changes that take place within neurons in response to the medication. Many people who are treated pharmacologically for depression get no relief from their symptoms, even after 6 weeks of self-administration of the prescribed drug. Often a different antidepressant medication is prescribed that does improve the patient's mood, but it takes several weeks more before the new medication takes effect.

Table 3.4

Effects of Various Antidepressants

Drug	Effect	Neurotransmitter Activity	
		Norepinephrine	Serotonin
Celexa	Blocks serotonin reuptake	No Change	↑
Paxil	Blocks serotonin reuptake	No Change	↑
Prozac	Blocks serotonin reuptake	No Change	↑
Zoloft	Blocks serotonin reuptake	No Change	↑
Elavil	Blocks norepinephrine reuptake	↑	No change
Norpramin (desimipramine)	Blocks norepinephrine reuptake	↑	No change
Imipramine	Blocks serotonin and norepinephrine reuptake	↑	↑
Effexor	Blocks serotonin and norepinephrine reuptake	↑	↑
Wellbutrin	Weakly blocks serotonin and norepinephrine reuptake	Unknown	Unknown
Parnate	Inhibits monoamine oxidase	↑	↑

depression is called *tricyclic antidepressants*. These tricyclic antidepressants are believed to block the reuptake transport systems for norepinephrine, dopamine, and serotonin, elevating monoamine levels in the brain. In addition, a class of drugs known as *selective serotonin reuptake inhibitors* (SSRIs) is also prescribed to treat depression in some patients. As their name implies, SSRIs function by inhibiting the serotonin reuptake transport mechanism, thereby increasing serotonin levels in the brain. In contrast, another antidepressant drug, *desipramine*, blocks the reuptake of norepinephrine but has no effect on the reuptake of serotonin. Table 3.4 summarizes the effects of drugs used to treat depression. Norepinephrine, serotonin, and dopamine seem to play a role in depression, but their exact roles are not clear, as you will learn in Chapter 15 when we return to a consideration of depression. In fact, selecting a drug to treat depression is not always easy (see *Case Study*).

You've finally come to the end of this chapter on chemical synapses. By now, you should have a good idea of how neurons signal to each other with chemicals, and you should understand how the chemicals affect the functioning of neurons. Remember, however, that many neurons communicate with their neighbors using gap junctions or electrical synapses. Chemical synapses are necessary for sending information to cells in other parts of the nervous system. In the next chapter, you will learn the names and functions of the various regions of the central and peripheral nervous systems. And you will learn that the neurons in each region have receptors for some types of neurotransmitters but not for others. The entire picture is quite complicated, and even leading experts in the field don't understand all the intricacies. In the chapters to come, I will try to keep the material as uncomplicated as I can, giving you only information that is relevant for our study of behavior.

Recap 3.5: Removing Neurotransmitters from the Synapse

Neurotransmitters are removed from the (a)_____ by means of two mechanisms, degradation by enzymes and reuptake into the presynaptic neuron. Acetylcholinesterase is an enzyme that deactivates (b)_____. The enzyme monoamine oxidase (MAO) breaks down (c)_____, norepinephrine, and dopamine. Catechol-O-methyltransferase (COMT) deactivates only dopamine and (d)_____. Two highly abused drugs, amphetamine and (e)_____, produce arousing effects by blocking the reuptake of catacholamines. MAO inhibitors and tricyclic antidepressants increase the availability of monoamines and are used to treat (f)_____. (g)_____s block the reuptake of serotonin and are also prescribed to treat depression.

Chapter Summary

Opening Ion Channels

▶ Many neurons communicate chemically, via neurotransmitters that diffuse across a chemical synapse.

▶ Ion channels play an important role in regulating the activity of neurons.

▶ There are four types of ion channels, ligand-gated channels, voltage-gated channels, ion-gated channels, and non-gated channels. Ligand-gated channels are ion channels that have a special protein, called a receptor, attached. A voltage-gated channel is sensitive to changes in the membrane potential. Ion-gated channels are sensitive to particular ion concentrations within the neuron. Non-gated channels are always open, allowing ions to leak in or out of the neuron.

▶ Voltage-gated Na^+ channels are responsible for the propagation of the action potential down the axon. Voltage-gated Ca^{++} channels are required for the release of neurotransmitters.

▶ Classical neurotransmitters bind to a receptor that is attached to a ligand-gated ion channel, producing EPSPs and IPSPs.

▶ Neurotransmitters that produce presynaptic inhibition open K^+ channels, which hyperpolarize the membrane of the presynaptic axon. Autoreceptors bind with neurotransmitters released from their own axon, producing presynaptic inhibition.

Types of Receptors

▶ Neurotransmitters bind with five different types of receptors, including ionotropic receptors, which directly open ion channels, or metabotropic receptors, such as the G protein-linked receptor that uses cyclic AMP as a second messenger.

▶ Other types of receptors include tyrosine kinase receptors, growth factor receptors, and hormone receptors, but not much is known about these last three types of receptors.

▶ The neurotransmitter acetylcholine binds with both ligand-gated ion channel receptors, and G protein-linked receptors. The acetylcholine-gated Na^+ channel receptor is called the nicotinic receptor. The G protein-linked acetylcholine receptor is called the muscarinic receptor.

Neurotransmitters

▶ A neurotransmitter that binds with G protein-linked receptors is called a neuromodulator. A neurohormone is released into the bloodstream and travels to target neurons. Epinephrine is a neurohormone that is released by the adrenal gland and activates neurons of the sympathetic nervous system.

▶ Some neurotransmitters can be classified as amino acids, peptides, or monoamines, although other neurotransmitters, such as acetylcholine, anandamide, and nitroc oxide, are difficult to group together.

▶ Acetylcholine, the first neurotransmitter to be discovered, binds with nicotinic (ionotropic) receptors and muscarinic (metabotropic) receptors. Acetylcholine initiates contraction of muscles, stimulates parasympathetic responses, and plays a role in learning, memory, and arousal. Curare and nicotine are drugs that bind with nicotinic receptors. Muscarine and atropine are drugs that bind with muscarinic receptors.

▶ All neurotransmitters bind with several different types of receptors, which indicates that each neurotransmitter can excite or inhibit other neurons in a wide variety of ways.

Amino acid neurotransmitters include glutamate, aspartate, glycine, and GABA. Glutamate typically produces rapid excitation in postsynaptic neurons and is believed to play an important role in the formation of long-term memory. Caffeine and monosodium glutamate are two chemicals associated with glutamate action. GABA is the most important inhibitory neurotransmitter in the brain. Benzodiazepines, barbiturates, alcohol, and general anesthetics bind to receptor sites in the $GABA_A$ receptor.

Nearly 50 different peptide neurotransmitters have been identified, including substance P, cholescystokinin, and endorphins. Substance P is the neurotransmitter that signals pain. Cholecystokinin is a neurohormone that signals satiety following a meal. Endorphins and other endogenous opiates function to reduce pain and to regulate blood pressure, stress responses, and food intake. Narcotic drugs, such as morphine, heroin, codeine, and demerol, bind with endorphin receptors and are effective in alleviating pain.

Serotonin, dopamine, norepinephrine, and the neurohormone epinephrine are the best-known monoamines. Serotonin regulates mood, sleep, and appetite. Two illicit drugs, lysergic acid diethylamide (LSD) and methylenedioxymethamphetamine (MDMA, or "ecstacy"), interact with serotonin receptors. Norepinephrine is involved in activation the sympathetic nervous system and in the regulation of mood and responses to stress. Two drugs, clonidine (a sedative) and yohimbine (anxiety-producer), bind with adrenergic receptors. Dopamine has been implicated in motor control, thinking, affect, and hormone secretion. The best known of the drugs associated with dopamine receptors are the D2-receptor antagonists, which are used to treat schizophrenia and other psychotic conditions.

Anandamide is an endogenous ligand that binds with cannabinoid receptors in the nervous system and is believed to play a role in emotion, cognition, and motor control. Marijuana is a drug that also binds with cannabinoid receptors.

Nitric oxide is an atypical neurotransmitter that plays a role in learning and memory, and sexual, aggressive, and eating behaviors.

The End of the Story: Removing Neurotransmitters from the Synapse

There are two main mechanisms by which neurotransmitters are removed from the synapse following an action potential: (1) degradation by enzymes and (2) reuptake into the presynaptic neuron.

Acetylcholinesterase deactivates acetylcholine by breaking the neurotransmitter into two components, acetyl and choline. A drug that inhibits acetylcholinesterase (an *acetylcholinesterase inhibitor*) will hinder the enzyme's action and allow acetylcholine to accumulate in the synapse, prolonging the neurotransmitter's effect.

The monoamines are not deactivated by a synaptic enzyme but, instead, rely on a reuptake mechanism to remove them from the synapse. Once inside the neuron, the monoamine is attacked by a number of enzymes that break it down so it can be removed from the brain and excreted from the body. The enzyme, monoamine oxidase (MAO), breaks down serotonin, norepinephrine, and dopamine. Catechol-O-methyltransferase (COMT) deactivates only dopamine and norepinephrine. Amphetamine and cocaine increase catecholamine levels in the synapse by stimulating the release of catecholamines and by blocking the reuptake by the presynaptic neuron.

MAO inhibitors, tricyclic antidepressants, and selective serotonin reuptake inhibitors (SSRIs) have been prescribed to treat patients who are depressed.

Key Terms

acetylcholine (p. 61)
acetylcholinesterase (p. 81)
agonist (p. 66)
anandamide (p. 68)
antagonist (p. 66)
autoreceptor (p. 61)
benzodiazepine (p. 73)
cannabinoid receptor (p. 78)
catechol-O-methyltransferase (COMT) (p. 82)
cholecystokinin (p. 67)
classical neurotransmitter (p. 59)
curare (p. 71)
dopamine (p. 68)
endorphin (p. 67)
epinephrine (p. 67)

G protein-linked receptor (p. 63)
gamma-aminobutyric acid (GABA) (p. 67)
glutamate (p. 67)
ionotropic receptors (p. 65)
ligand (p. 57)
ligand-gated channel (p. 57)
ligand-gated ion channel receptor (p. 62)
metabotropic receptor (p. 65)
monoamine (p. 68)
monoamine oxidase (MAO) (p. 82)
muscarine (p. 71)
muscarinic receptor (p. 62)
neurohormone (p. 67)
neuromodulator (p. 66)

neurotransmitter (p. 56)
nicotine (p. 71)
nicotinic receptor (p. 62)
nitric oxide (p. 68)
norepinephrine (p. 68)
opiates (p. 75)
opioid receptors (p. 74)
peptide (p. 67)
postsynaptic inhibition (p. 60)
presynaptic inhibition (p. 60)
receptor (p. 57)
second messenger (p. 63)
serotonin (p. 68)
substance P (p. 74)

Questions for Thought

1. How might an investigator demonstrate that a certain neurotransmitter regulates a particular behavior? For example, how might a psychologist show that cholecystokinin plays a role in eating behavior?

2. When a person becomes addicted to nicotine, what changes take place in the nervous system of the addicted person? What might happen when that person tries to quit smoking?

Questions for Review

1. Identify the functions of ligand-gated, voltage-gated, ion-gated, and non-gated ion channels.

2. What are some differences between ionotropic and metabotropic receptors?

3. How does nitric oxide differ from other neurotransmitters?

4. Name drugs that increase the activity of receptors associated with acetylcholine, serotonin, dopamine, norepinephrine, anandamide, and endorphins.

Suggested Readings

Barondes, S. H. (1993). *Molecules and mental illness.* New York: Scientific American Library.

Briley, M. (2000). *Understanding antidepressants.* London: Martin Dunitz Ltd.

Cox, P. A., & Ballick, M. J. (1994, June). The ethnobotanical approach to drug discovery. *Scientific American, 271,* 82–87.

Dressler, D., & Potter, H. (1993). *Discovering enzymes.* New York: Scientific American Library.

Web Resources

For a chapter tutorial quiz, direct links to the Internet sites listed below, and other features, visit the book-specific website at **www.wadsworth.com/product/ 0155074865**. You may also connect directly to the following annotated websites:

http://faculty.washington.edu/chudler/chnt1.html
This detailed site gives information about types of neurotransmitters, the synthesis of neurotransmitters, and the inactivation of neurotransmitters

http://ifcsun1.ifisiol.unam.mx/Brain/trnsmt.htm
At this site you can read more about neurotransmitters and link to related topics like presynaptic neurons, ion channels, second messenger signaling, depolarization, and action potentials.

For additional readings and information, check out InfoTrac College Edition at **http://www.infotrac-college.com/wadsworth**. Choose a search term yourself or enter the following search terms: benzodiazepines, neurotransmitters.

CD-ROM: Exploring Biological Psychology

Communicating between Neurons
    Animation: Cholinergic
    Animation: Release of ACh
    Animation: AChE Inactivates ACh
    Animation: AChE Inhibitors
Psychoactive Drugs
    Animation: Opiate Narcotics

    Animation: CNS Depressants
    Animation: CNS Stimulants
    Animation: Hallucinogenics
Interactive Recaps
Chapter 3 Quiz
Connect to the Interactive Biological Psychology
    Glossary

4

The Organization of the Nervous System

On a Saturday night shortly before midnight, 15-year-old Tyler was carried by his worried parents into the emergency room of a large medical center. Tyler was conscious but unable to speak. In addition, he appeared to be paralyzed on the right side of his body. The doctors who examined him were puzzled: Here was a teenager who appeared to have suffered a stroke, a disorder typically associated with older adults. Tyler's symptoms, inability to speak and right-sided paralysis, suggested damage to the left side of his brain. Although Tyler couldn't speak, he could nod "yes" or shake his head "no" when questioned by the emergency room doctors. At first, Tyler refused to answer the doctors' questions, but he began to cooperate when he was told that the doctors couldn't help him unless he told them what he'd been doing earlier that evening.

The doctors surmised that Tyler had been trying to get high on some type of inhalant. Their questions focused on determining the chemical he had used. It turned out that Tyler and his friends had been sniffing butane, the propellant used in disposable lighters. Butane is known to cause spasms in the muscular walls of blood vessels. In Tyler's case, the butane he inhaled caused sudden, extreme constriction of the arteries in his brain, causing a major artery in his left hemisphere to develop an infarct or blockage. Neurons in that side of his brain were deprived of oxygen as a result of the infarct and were damaged, producing a loss of function associated with the left hemisphere in the brain.

The World Congress of Neuroscience has hailed the 21st century as the "Century of the Brain." The Century of the Brain! How much do you know about the brain? Do you understand the mechanisms by which it controls behavior? If you do, you should be able to explain how brain damage caused by sniffing butane affects behavior.

To help prepare you for the 21st century, this chapter will introduce you to the brain and its organization. As you read this chapter, you will learn about the important structures in the brain and how each participates in the control of bodily functions and behavior. Later in this book, we will look at vital human behaviors such as speech, reasoning, and emotions. We will examine how the brain is involved in mental illness. And we will explore the role of the brain in behaviors that we have in common with other animals, such as eating, sleeping, drinking, and sexual behavior. We will also probe the brain's regulation of movement and sensory processes like vision, taste, smell, touch, and hearing.

Remember from Chapter 2 that the nervous system has two divisions: the *central nervous system* and the *peripheral nervous system.* The central nervous system is composed of the brain and the spinal cord. All of the neurons located outside the brain and spinal cord comprise the peripheral nervous system. In this chapter, we will focus on the organization of the nervous system and, in particular, on the structure of the principal organ of the nervous system, which is the brain. Let's consider the organization of the central nervous system first. ●

An Overview of the Central Nervous System

The primary function of the central nervous system is to process information that it receives from the peripheral nervous system and then organize a response to that information. For example, imagine that a spider climbs onto your ankle and begins to walk up your leg. The tickling sensation travels through your peripheral nervous system to your central nervous system. This information travels up your spinal cord to your brain, which then processes this information and send messages back to your peripheral nervous system, directing your eyes to look at your leg for the source of the tickling and your hand to brush the offending creature off your leg.

The brain can also initiate behavior on its own, without prompting from the peripheral nervous system. You might, for example, suddenly think of your sister in a faraway city and decide to telephone her. Your central nervous system in this case directs the movements that would take you to the telephone, pick up the receiver, and dial your sister's phone number.

Protecting the Central Nervous System

The central nervous system is so important to your survival that it is encased in bone for protection. The brain is surrounded by the skull, and the spinal cord is protected by the column of vertebral bones that you know as the backbone. Underneath these bones, three layers of tissues, called the **meninges,** cover the brain and spinal cord, providing further protection (Figure 4.1).

The outermost layer of the meninges is known as the **dura mater.** The dura mater is a tough, fibrous protective coating that helps maintain the integrity of the brain and spinal cord. Beneath the dura mater is the **arachnoid layer,** which gets it name from its spider weblike appearance. The arachnoid layer's web is composed of blood vessels and other vasculature containing a special fluid, found only in the central nervous system, called **cerebrospinal fluid.** Cerebrospinal fluid is manufactured in a structure (called the *choroid plexus*) located near the top of the brain, and

meninges: protective covering for the central nervous system

dura mater: tough outer layer of the meninges

arachnoid: middle weblike layer of the meninges

cerebrospinal fluid: a watery fluid found in the ventricles of the brain and in the spinal cord it flows down through the brain and spinal cord through a system of canals, known as **ventricles.** The word *cerebrospinal* comes from *cerebrum*, which is the Latin word for "brain," and *spinal*, which refers to the spinal cord. When the cerebrospinal fluid reaches the base of the spinal cord, it travels back up the spinal cord through the arachnoid layer of the meninges to the brain.

Scientists are still debating the purpose of the cerebrospinal fluid (Spector & Johanson, 1989). Certainly, it acts as a watery cushion to protect the central nervous system from smacking against the skull or backbone following a sudden jarring. But, is this its only function? Chemicals produced by the brain are transported in the cerebrospinal fluid to the spinal cord, although the role of these chemicals in the cerebrospinal fluid is unknown. Chemicals found in the cerebrospinal fluid can tell us a lot about the brain. For example, they can indicate the presence of an infection in the brain or a chemical imbalance.

Cerebrospinal fluid, then, is a window into the brain—it can tell us what is happening in the brain. A number of investigators have linked certain chemicals found in the cerebrospinal fluid, such as cholecystokinin (CCK) and 5-hydroxyindoleacetic acid (5-HIAA), to a greater risk of depression and suicidal behavior (Asberg, 1997; Loefberg, Agren, Harro, & Oreland, 1998; Singareddy & Balon, 2001). The compound 5-HIAA is a primary metabolite (or by-product) of serotonin. When serotonin levels are reduced, levels of 5-HIAA are also reduced. A *spinal tap* is a medical procedure that is used to extract cerebrospinal fluid from the arachnoid layer of the meninges. This procedure can inform physicians about the state of the brain without their actually going into the brain.

The innermost layer of the meninges is called the **pia mater.** This delicate tissue is in direct contact with the surface of the brain and spinal cord.

Sometimes bacteria or other microorganisms can invade the meninges, producing a disorder known as *meningitis*. Meningitis is a life-threatening illness that can produce long-term disabilities in those fortunate enough to survive. In meningitis, the meninges swell in response to the infection by the microorganism, putting pressure on the spinal cord or brain, which can kill neurons or produce permanent brain damage. The onset of the illness is very rapid. A healthy individual will develop a fever and flulike symptoms, which rapidly progress to rigidity of the neck and severe headache. If the infection is left untreated, the individual will lapse into a coma and eventually die. Even with antibiotic treatment, 10% of people who contract meningitis will die (Moore & Broome, 1994). In the United States, meningitis is quite rare, occurring in less than 3 out of every 100,000 people each year.

The Spinal Cord

You have already been introduced to the spinal cord in Chapter 2. Recall that, in cross-section, the spinal cord resembles a gray butterfly surrounded by a white

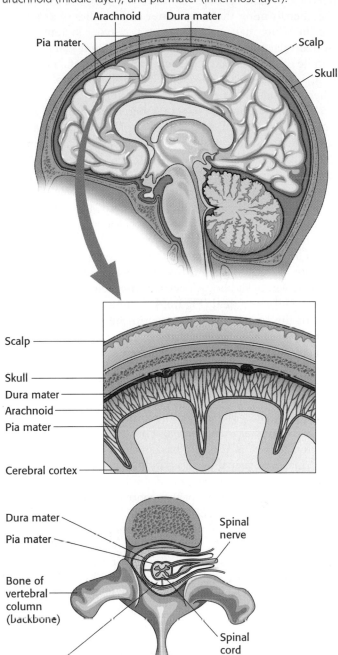

Figure 4.1 The meninges, the protective covering of the central nervous system
The meninges consist of three layers, the dura mater (outer layer), arachnoid (middle layer), and pia mater (innermost layer).

ventricle: a cavity in the brain that contains cerebrospinal fluid
pia mater: innermost layer of the meninges

background (Figure 4.2). The gray "butterfly" is actually composed of neuronal soma, and the white matter is composed of bundles of axons. We see this pattern repeated throughout the nervous system: groups of neuronal cell bodies clustered together forming the gray matter and bundles of axons forming the white matter. In the central nervous system, a cluster of neuronal soma is called a **nucleus** (plural is *nuclei*), and a bundle of axons is called a **tract.** In the peripheral nervous system, a cluster of soma is called a **ganglion** (plural is *ganglia*), whereas a bundle of axons is called a **nerve.**

It is also important to remember, as you learned in Chapter 2, that the spinal cord is organized in such a way that sensory functions are located in the *dorsal* aspect of the spinal cord and motor functions are regulated in the *ventral* portion (Figure 4.2). Sensory information coming from the peripheral nervous system travels up the tracts located in the white matter on the dorsal side of the spinal cord. Information about movement is transmitted down tracts found in the white matter on the ventral side of the spinal cord.

The spinal cord extends from the base of the skull to the tailbone. It is divided into five sections based on its location within the body: **cervical, thoracic, lumbar, sacral,** and **coccygeal** (Figure 4.3). The *cervical* portion of the spinal cord is located in the neck. As its name implies, the thoracic portion of the spinal cord is that section that runs through the chest area or thorax. The *lumbar* section is located within the vertebrae that make up the small of the back. The *sacral* portion of the spinal cord is found within the backbones that are attached to the *pelvic girdle*, the circle of bones that comprise your hips and pelvis. The *coccygeal* portion, which is located at the very base of the spinal cord, is very small and virtually useless in humans.

Each of the five segments of the spinal cord receives information from and controls the muscles and organs in a particular part of the body. The cervical portion of the spinal cord innervates the shoulders, arms, and hands. The thoracic portion of the spinal cord regulates the functioning of muscles and organs in the chest and upper abdomen. The lower abdominal muscles and organs, as well as muscles in the legs and feet, are controlled by the lumbar portion of the spinal cord. Finally, the sacral portion of the spinal cord directs the workings of the organs within the pelvis, including the reproductive organs, the bladder, and rectum. In an animal with a tail, the coccygeal region of the spinal cord controls tail movements and receives sensory information from the tail. In humans, the coccygeal spinal cord controls only a small group of muscles above the anus.

Spina bifida is a disorder in which the bony spinal column fails to close properly during development, leaving a part of the spinal cord exposed. The amount of exposed spinal cord varies, depending on the extent of the opening in the backbone. Approximately 1 out of every 1,000 children born has spina bifida, although the disorder can be detected early in pregnancy. Because the spinal cord protrudes out of

Figure 4.2 The spinal cord viewed in cross-section
In cross-section, the spinal cord looks like a gray butterfly surrounded by a white background. The gray "butterfly" is composed of neuronal soma, and the white matter consists of bundles of myelinated axons.

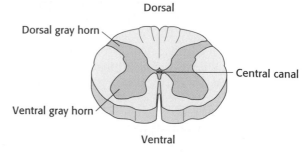

nucleus: cluster of neuronal soma (cell bodies) in the central nervous system
tract: bundle of axons in the central nervous system

Figure 4.3 The five segments of the spinal cord

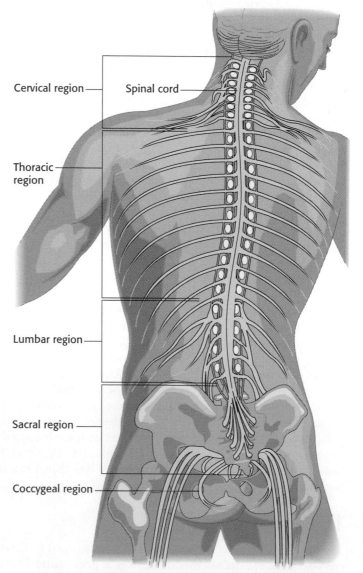

the backbone in spina bifida, it is vulnerable to infection and damage, which can leave the afflicted child severely physically and sometimes mentally handicapped. Surgical treatment, including closure of the bony defect, can sometimes help children born with this disorder.

Recap 4.1: An Overview of the Central Nervous System

Three layers of tissues, called the (a)_____, cover the brain and spinal cord. The outermost layer of the meninges is the (b)_____ mater, the middle layer is the (c)_____ layer, and the innermost layer is the (d)_____ mater. Vessels in the arachnoid layer contain a fluid found only in the central nervous system called (e)_____ fluid. (f)_____ is an infection of the meninges in which the meninges swell, putting harmful pressure on the brain or spinal cord. The spinal cord is divided into five segments: cervical, (g)_____, lumbar, (h)_____, and coccygeal. (i)_____ _____ is a disorder in which the spinal cord is left exposed, due to failure of the backbone to close during development.

The Brain

I remember the first time I saw an MRI scan of my own brain. I was fascinated *and* disappointed to find that my brain looked just like any other healthy human brain I'd ever seen. You can see it for yourself in Figure 4.4. I'm sure my brain looks just like your brain. Most of us have identical structures situated in the same locations within the skull.

Furthermore, our human brains bear a close resemblance to the brains of other mammals (Figure 4.5). In fact, if you are really observant, you will notice many similarities between your brain and the brains of other vertebrates, like fish, amphibians, reptiles, and birds. For all vertebrates, the brain can be divided into three parts: the **forebrain,** the **midbrain,** and the **hindbrain.** These terms make a lot of sense if you consider the brain of a typical animal, one that is oriented horizontally with respect to the ground. The hindbrain is situated in the back of the brain, toward the animal's hindquarters. The forebrain is situated in the front of the brain, and the midbrain is situated in the middle. In humans and other animals that have a vertical orientation, the hindbrain is located at the bottom, the midbrain is located on top of the hindbrain, and the forebrain, which is enormous in humans, sits on top, covering not only the tiny midbrain but also the larger hindbrain. Figure 4.6 shows the positions of the forebrain, midbrain, and hindbrain in the human brain.

Psychologists and other brain investigators use standard anatomical terms when referring to direction or location in the brain, instead of terms like *top/bottom* or *under/over* (Figure 4.7 on page 96). The terms *dorsal* and *ventral* are somewhat confusing because they are used differently when referring to structures in the spinal cord as opposed to structures in the brain. As you've already learned, when discussing the spinal cord, *dorsal* means *toward the back,* and *ventral* means *toward the belly.* In the brain, *dorsal* means *toward the top,* and

ganglion: cluster of neuronal soma in the peripheral nervous system

nerve: bundle of axons in the peripheral nervous system

cervical: region of the spinal cord located in the neck

thoracic: region of the spinal cord located in the chest

lumbar: region of the spinal cord located in the lower back

sacral: region of the spinal cord located in the pelvic girdle

coccygeal: region of the spinal cord located at the base of the spine

forebrain: the largest part of the brain, contains the cerebrum, basal ganglia, limbic system, thalamus, and hypothalamus

midbrain: the mesencephalon, consists of the tectum, the tegmentum, and a ventral region that contains the reticular formation

hindbrain: the part of the brain immediately superior to the spinal cord, consists of the medulla, pons, and cerebellum; also known as the rhombencephalon

Figure 4.4 MRI of the author's brain

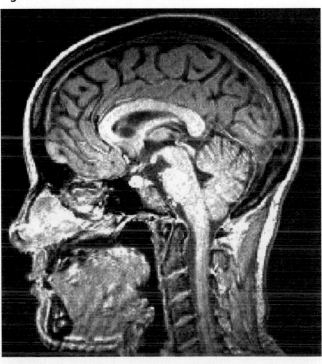

Figure 4.5 Comparison of the human brain with the brains of other vertebrates

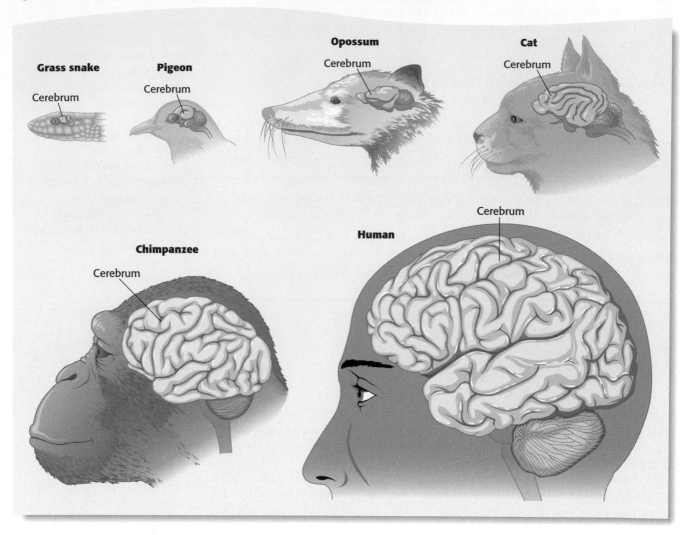

ventral means toward the bottom. Because of this confusion, the terms superior and inferior are often used when referring to direction in the brain, in place of dorsal and ventral, respectively.

If you read specialized journals and books in the neuroscience field, you will quickly learn that scientists sometimes use different terminology when referring to the parts of the brain. The forebrain is often called the **prosencephalon,** the midbrain is called the **mesencephalon,** and the hindbrain is called the **rhombencephalon.** The root, -encephalon, comes from the Greek word for "brain." The prefixes pro-, mes-, and rhomb- are Greek in origin, too. Let's consider the rhombencephalon first.

prosencephalon: forebrain
mesencephalon: midbrain
rhombencephalon: hindbrain

The Rhombencephalon

As its Greek name implies, the hindbrain is shaped like a rhombus. Three structures comprise the rhombencephalon: the medulla, the pons, and the cerebellum (Figure 4.8 on page 97).

The **medulla** is located directly above, or superior to, the spinal cord. This means that all information coming from and going to the spinal cord must pass through the medulla. Indeed, the medulla contains a great deal of white matter, or tracts, that relays information between the spinal cord and higher brain areas. Gray matter is also found in the medulla, however. Clusters of neurons, known as nuclei, are scattered throughout the medulla. Each nucleus has a specific function, as you will learn in later chapters. Some nuclei regulate life-support functions, such as breathing, coughing, or vomiting. Damage to these nuclei can result in death.

medulla: hindbrain structure that controls life-support functions

Figure 4.6 The forebrain, midbrain, and hindbrain

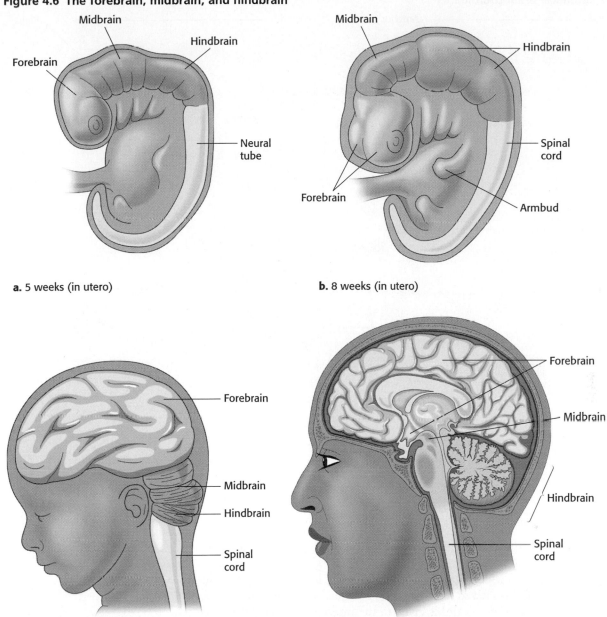

a. 5 weeks (in utero)

b. 8 weeks (in utero)

c. 7 months (in utero)

d. Adult

Other nuclei receive sensory information directly from the peripheral nervous system, and others send commands to particular muscles in the head, neck, chest, and upper abdomen. The nuclei in the medulla communicate with each other and with neurons in other parts of the brain to produce all sorts of behaviors.

Superior to the medulla is the **pons**. The pons is a bridge-like structure that is composed almost entirely of white matter, or tracts conveying information between the higher brain regions and the medulla and spinal cord. I'm sure that, sometime during your elementary school career, you learned that the right side of your brain controls the left side of your body and vice versa. Information leaving the right side of your forebrain travels down tracts through your midbrain to your hindbrain, where the tracts cross over to the left side of your pons and continue down the left side of your medulla and spinal cord. The same is true for neural impulses that are sent from the left forebrain: Tracts carrying these impulses cross over to the right side in the pons. Many neural messages coming from the medulla and spinal cord also cross over in the pons before traveling to higher brain areas, as you will learn in later chapters.

pons: hindbrain structure that relays information from the spinal cord and medulla to the higher brain structures

Figure 4.7 Anatomical brain coordinates

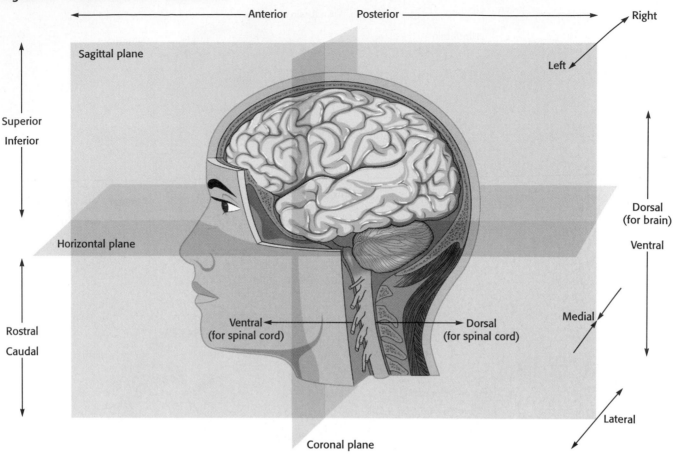

The **cerebellum** lies dorsal to both the medulla and the pons. We will discuss its structure in greater detail in Chapter 6. For now, you should know that it is divided into two hemispheres: right and left. Each hemisphere contains a cerebellar cortex (gray matter) and underlying white matter. This architecture (gray matter situated over tracts of white matter) gives the cerebellum a characteristic treelike appearance when it is viewed in cross-section (Figure 4.9). The name *arbor vitae* [*arbor* = tree; *vitae* = of life, Latin] is given to the internal architecture of the cerebellum.

The neurons in the cerebellum are responsible for coordinating muscular activities, especially those involved in rapid and repetitive movements. Alcohol is known to especially impair the functioning of the cerebellum, causing intoxicated persons to lose their muscle coordination. Sobriety tests performed by police officers are designed to detect impairment of the cerebellum (see *For Further Thought* on page 99).

The Mesencephalon

The midbrain is the smallest of the three major divisions of the brain. In the human brain, it is roughly the size of a large acorn. The mesencephalon can be divided into three parts: the dorsal portion, the ventral portion, and the *tegmentum*, which lies between the dorsal and ventral areas. The dorsal area is also known as the *tectum*, and it contains four structures that look like little hills, the **superior colliculi** and the **inferior colliculi.** You have two superior colliculi and two inferior colliculi in your midbrain: one on the left side of your brain and one on the right side. Located above the inferior colliculi, the *superior colliculi* are important in processing visual information, as you will learn in Chapter 7. The *inferior colliculi* are involved in relaying auditory information to the cerebellum and forebrain. The tegmentum

cerebellum: hindbrain structure that controls motor coordination and coordinates movement in response to sensory stimuli

superior colliculus: a midbrain structure that receives visual information and processes the location of objects in the environment
inferior colliculus: a midbrain structure that receives and processes auditory information

Figure 4.8 Major structures in the brain

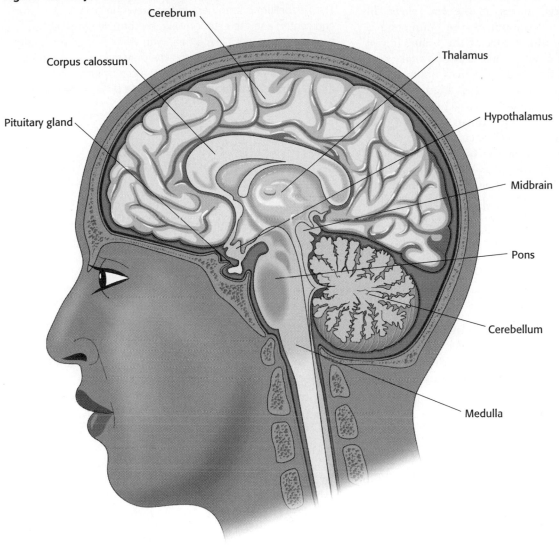

contains a number of important structures, such as the *red nucleus*, the *periaqueductal gray*, and the *substantia nigra*, that we will cover later in this book, structures that play a vital role in attention, pain control, emotions, and sensory processing. For the most part, the ventral area of the mesencephalon consists of tracts relaying neural information between the hindbrain and the forebrain.

The **reticular formation**, which runs from the hindbrain to the forebrain, takes up a large portion of the midbrain. As you will discover in Chapter 10, the reticular formation plays an important role in keeping you awake and alert. When your alarm goes off, it is your reticular formation that rouses you to consciousness. The reticular formation also arouses you when someone calls your name, when some creepy-crawlie slithers up your arm, or when someone yells *"Help!"* Damage to the reticular formation can produce a state of unconsciousness called a *coma*, in which a person is unable to respond to external stimuli. We will discuss the comatose state in Chapter 10.

reticular formation: group of neurons located in the brain stem that alerts the forebrain to important stimuli

The Prosencephalon

The largest part of the human brain is the forebrain, or *prosencephalon* (see Figure 4.6). This area of the brain produces the most interesting human behaviors, such as thinking, creating, eating, speaking, and emotions. It can be divided into two parts: the **diencephalon** and the **telencephalon.**

diencephalon: forebrain area that contains the thalamus and hypothalamus

telencephalon: forebrain area that contains the basal ganglia, limbic system structures, and the cerebrum

The *diencephalon*, together with the mesencephalon and rhombencephalon, makes up the *brain stem*. In terms of evolutionary development, the brain stem is considered to be the oldest part of the brain. If you examine the brain of a reptile, like that of a snake or a turtle, you would find that the reptilian brain is very similar to the human brain stem (see Figure 4.5). In fact, the well-known Canadian psychologist Paul MacLean (1990) described the human brain as being composed of three layers, a *reptilian* core surrounded by an *old mammalian* brain, which in turn is topped with what MacLean called the *new mammalian* brain. According to MacLean's conceptualization of the brain, the diencephalon is part of the reptilian brain, and the telencephalon contains both the old mammalian and new mammalian brains.

The Diencephalon

The diencephalon is located directly superior to the mesencephalon. Information from the mesencephalon must pass through the diencephalon in order to reach the higher parts of the forebrain. As its prefix *di-* implies, two structures comprise the diencephalon. These two structures are the **thalamus** and the **hypothalamus** (see Figure 4.8). Hence, the *hypothalamus* lies below, or inferior to, the thalamus.

The shape of the *thalamus* resembles an egg that has been flattened on one side. It is composed of a large number of nuclei, or clusters of neurons, that relay information to and from structures in the telencephalon, especially the largest structure, which is called the **cerebrum.** The cerebrum is considered the seat of consciousness by most behavioral neuroscientists. That is, you do not become consciously aware of a stimulus unless neural information about the stimulus makes its way to the cerebrum. It is the function of the nuclei in the thalamus to process incoming information and pass it on to the cerebrum. Thus, the thalamus acts like a switchboard operator, relaying information between the cerebrum and other parts of the brain. More recently, there is evidence that the thalamus also receives information from the cerebrum, which modifies the way the thalamus processes incoming information (Sillito, Jones, Gerstein, & West, 1994).

The hypothalamus is located on the ventral surface of the brain superior to the midbrain (see Figure 4.8). Below or ventral to the hypothalamus lies the **pituitary gland,** which is attached to the hypothalamus by a stalk called the *infundibulum* [*infundibulum* = funnel, Latin]. The hypothalamus directly controls the activity of the pituitary gland by releasing **hormones** that are sent to the pituitary gland via the infundibulum. Hormones are specialized chemicals that are released by one structure in the body, typically called a *gland*, and affect another structure in the body. The hypothalamus directs the activity of the pituitary gland with hormones, and the pituitary gland uses hormones to control the activity of other glands in the body, as you will learn in Chapters 11–13.

Figure 4.9 The structure of the cerebellum

The cerebellum is seen here in two views, in cross-section (top and center) and the exterior view (bottom). In cross-section, the cerebellum looks like a tree, with white matter appearing as the branches of the tree and the gray matter appearing as the leaves. The outside surface of the cerebellum is convoluted. These convolutions are called *folia* [*folia* = leaves, Latin].

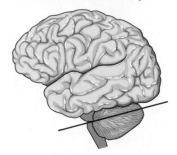

Cross-section of cerebellum

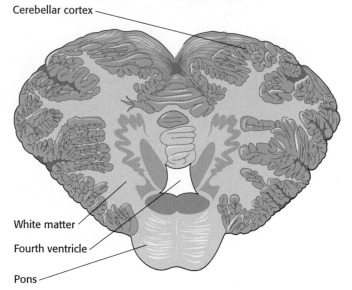

Cerebellar cortex

White matter

Fourth ventricle

Pons

External view of cerebellum

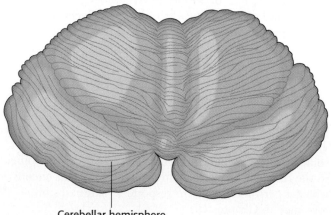

Cerebellar hemisphere

thalamus: structure in the diencephalon that relays information from the brain stem to the cerebrum

Sobriety Tests: Evaluating Cerebellar Impairment

Alex left a bar in Atlanta with four friends. He had drunk six beers but felt that he could drive safely. Within minutes, he was stopped at a roadblock by police who were looking for drunk drivers.

Alcohol affects the functioning of neurons throughout the brain, including the cerebellum. Because the cerebellum controls coordinated movements, alcohol interferes with coordination. A sobriety test allows police officers to check for signs of cerebellar dysfunction that are caused by alcohol intoxication.

A police officer approached Alex's car and asked for his driver's license. Nervously, Alex fumbled in his wallet for his license. The officer scanned it briefly, then asked Alex to say the alphabet as quickly as he could. Alex did well until he got to "L, M, N, O, P." Because he was intoxicated, his tongue stumbled over those letters.

The police officer asked Alex to get out of the car and walk along a straight line that was painted on the pavement. Alex had a difficult time walking the line. He stag-gered, weaving from side to side, and nearly fell over at one point. Finally, the officer told Alex to close his eyes, extend his right arm, then touch his nose with his right index finger. Alex closed his eyes and tried to touch his nose, but he slammed his hand into his face very hard.

Alex failed all three phases of the sobriety test. He demonstrated fine motor impairment when he slipped up saying the letters of the alphabet. Impairment of gross movement was evident when Alex could not walk along a straight line. In addition, Alex failed the finger-to-nose test, a test that assesses the ability of the cerebellum to locate the position of a particular limb in space and to direct the movement of that limb based on its location.

After Alex failed the sobriety test, he was subjected to a Breathalyzer test, which measures alcohol content of the expired breath. This test indicated that the level of alcohol in Alex's body was above the legal limit. Alex was given a ticket for DUI, his car was towed away, and he and his intoxicated friends had to take a taxi home.

In addition, the hypothalamus is involved in the regulation of many motivated behaviors, such as eating, drinking, sleeping, temperature control, sexual behavior, and emotions. Like the thalamus, the hypothalamus contains many tiny clusters of neurons called *nuclei*. Each nucleus in the hypothalamus plays a role in the regulation of a specific motivated behavior. We will examine the functions of the hypothalamus in Chapters 10–13.

hypothalamus: a structure in the diencephalon that controls the pituitary gland and regulates motivated behaviors

cerebrum: largest structure in the brain, believed to be the seat of consciousness

pituitary gland: structure connected to the hypothalamus by a stalk that regulates the activity of other major glands in the body; master gland located below the ventral surface of the brain, which receives commands from the hypothalamus

hormone: a chemical released by a gland

Recap 4.2: The Brain Stem

The medulla, (a)_____, and (b)_____ are three structures in the rhombencephalon. Neurons in the (c)_____ regulate life-support functions, receive sensory information, or send motor commands to muscles in the head, neck, and trunk. The pons permits passage of information between the (d)_____ _____ and higher regions of the brain. The cerebellum coordinates muscular activity and is especially vulnerable to (e)_____, which impairs its functioning. The mesencephalon is divided into three regions: the dorsal area, the ventral area, and the (f)_____. The dorsal area is also known as the tectum and consists of the (g)_____ colliculus, which processes visual information, and the (h)_____ colliculus, which processes auditory information. The (i)_____ formation runs from the hindbrain to the forebrain through the midbrain and plays an important role in keeping the individual awake and alert. The largest part of the human brain is the forebrain or (j)_____. It is divided into two parts, the diencephalon and the (k)_____. The (l)_____ is comprised of two structures, the thalamus and the hypothalamus. The (m)_____ contains a cluster of nuclei that relay information to and from the cerebrum. The hypothalamus is involved in the regulation of the (n)_____ gland and motivated behaviors, such as sleeping, eating and drinking.

The Telencephalon

The *telencephalon* contains many structures, some that we will examine briefly in this chapter and others that will be introduced to you in later chapters. As you've just learned, the largest structure in the telencephalon—indeed, the largest structure in the brain—is the *cerebrum*.

Other structures in the telencephalon include the **hippocampus,** the **amygdala,** the **septum,** and the **basal ganglia,** which are buried deep within the white matter of the cerebrum. We will examine each of these brain structures below.

The Limbic System

The hippocampus, amygdala, and septum, together with a handful of regions in the midbrain, diencephalon, and cerebrum, comprise the **limbic system.** It was Paul MacLean who coined the term *limbic system. Limbic* comes from the Latin word *limbus,* meaning "boundary." To MacLean's mind, the limbic system formed a boundary between the brainstem and the higher centers of the brain. The limbic system functions in the production and experience of emotion, as you will learn in Chapter 13.

The *hippocampus* gets its name from its seahorse-like shape [*hippo* = horse; *kampus* = sea monster, Greek]. In addition to the role it plays in emotions, the hippocampus is responsible for some types of learning and for the creation of permanent, or *long-term*, memories. Damage to the hippocampus can interfere with and produce memory loss (Chapter 9).

The *amygdala* is located at the tail end of the hippocampus's seahorse shape. It is oval in appearance and has two distinct regions: one that produces fear and escape behaviors when stimulated and another that elicits rage and aggressive attack behavior when activated, as you will learn in Chapter 13. This is the brain area most directly concerned with *fight versus flight* behavior. *Rabies*, which is caused by a virus that attacks the telencephalon, especially in the region of the amygdala, produces a lack of natural fear, as well as vicious attack behavior, in infected or *rabid* animals.

The *septum* is a complex forebrain structure that contains a number of different nuclei with diverse functions. Until 1954, the function of the septum was unknown. Studies by James Olds and Peter Milner in the early 1950s demonstrated that stimulation of a particular area of the septum produces feelings of intense pleasure in the animal being stimulated (Olds & Milner, 1954). We will examine this structure of the brain more closely in Chapter 13 when we discuss emotions and addictions. Other regions of the septum appear to be involved in the regulation of aggressive behavior.

The Basal Ganglia

The term *basal ganglia* is a misnomer. Think about it: As you've already learned, *ganglia* refers to clusters of neurons found in the peripheral nervous system. But, the basal ganglia consist of several clusters of neurons found in the base of the forebrain. The basal ganglia are composed of two distinct structures: an egg-shaped nucleus that contains the putamen and globus pallidus, and a tail-shaped structure called the caudate [*cauda* = tail, Latin]. Together, these structures are responsible for the production of movement. For example, you notice that your hands are dirty and decide to wash your hands. The basal ganglia initiate this washing behavior. Hand-washing compulsions, in which people feel compelled to wash their hands hundreds of times a day, are a common manifestation of obsessive-compulsive disorder (Chapter 13). According to research psychologist Judith Rapoport (1991), faulty circuits between the basal ganglia and other brain structures may cause obsessive-compulsive disorders. The basal ganglia have also been implicated in a number of movement disorders, such as Parkinson's disease and Huntington's chorea, as you will learn in Chapter 6.

hippocampus: limbic system structure that plays a role in emotions and memory

amygdala: an almond-shaped structure located in the medial temporal lobe that is implicated in the experience of negative emotions

septum: limbic system structure associated with pleasurable feelings

basal ganglia: a group of subcortical nuclei that sends and receives information about movement to and from the cerebrum

limbic system: the two brain circuits that regulate emotions

The Cerebrum

The *cerebrum* (*cerebrum* = brain, Latin) gets its name from the fact that it is by far the largest structure in the brain—so large, in fact, that when the skull is removed from the top of a person's head, the only structure that can be seen is the cerebrum (Figure 4.10). The rest of the forebrain, the midbrain, and the hindbrain are tucked underneath the cerebrum in the skull. This means that damage to the skull, as in a skull fracture, will have its greatest impact on the cerebrum. In Chapter 16, we will look at different effects of damage to the cerebrum.

The cerebrum is organized like the cerebellum, with a cortical layer called the **cerebral cortex,** which consists of five to seven layers of neurons, and white matter beneath the cortex. The white matter is composed of axons leaving and entering the cerebral cortex. Some axons carry information from nuclei in the thalamus to particular regions of the cortex. Other axons carry information from the cerebral

cerebral cortex: outermost layers of the cerebrum that contain neurons

Figure 4.10 The cerebrum in two views: in the skull and removed from the skull

a.

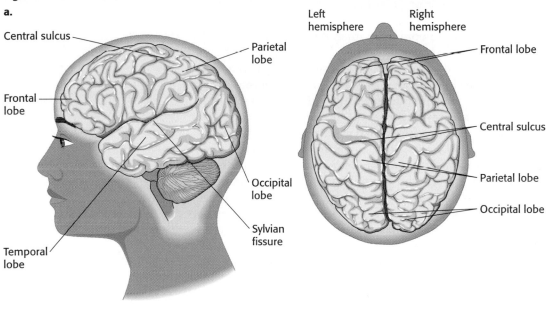

Anatomical areas (left lateral view)

Anatomical areas (top view)

b.

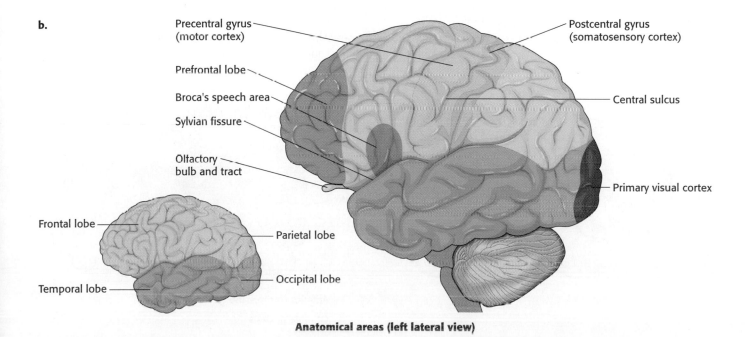

Anatomical areas (left lateral view)

cortex to specific nuclei in the thalamus. Most axons in the white matter of the cerebrum, however, carry information from one area of the cortex to another.

Like all of the brain structures that we have discussed thus far, the cerebrum has two halves, called **cerebral hemispheres.** That is, you have a left cerebral hemisphere and a right cerebral hemisphere. Four *lobes* make up each cerebral hemisphere: the **frontal lobe,** the **parietal lobe,** the **temporal lobe,** and the **occipital lobe** (Figure 4.10). Although each lobe has specialized functions, the four lobes in each hemisphere communicate with each other and with the lobes in the other hemisphere. Communication between the hemispheres is made possible by several tracts of axons that connect neurons. These tracts that link the two cerebral hemispheres are known as the **corpus callosum** and the **anterior commissure** (Figure 4.11). The corpus callosum is a large, thick tract that connects neurons in the left and right frontal, parietal, and occipital lobes. In contrast, the anterior commissure is much smaller and links neurons in the left and right temporal lobes. The anterior commissure also connects contralateral neurons in the hippocampus and amygdala, which are buried deep within the temporal lobe. Another tract, the **posterior commissure,** is composed of axons that link neurons in the right and left diencephalon and mesencephalon.

The surface of the cerebrum is not smooth but, rather, is covered with bumps and grooves. The grooves are called *sulci* (singular: **sulcus**) or fissures, whereas the raised areas or bumps are called *gyri* (singular: **gyrus**). The sulci and gyri serve as landmarks that help us determine the boundaries of the lobes of the cerebrum. The **central sulcus** runs from the top of the cerebrum inferiorly to the **Sylvian fissure,** which is also known as the *lateral sulcus.* In Figure 4.10, you can see that the central sulcus forms the boundary between the frontal and parietal lobes.

The most posterior region of the frontal lobe is the **precentral gyrus,** the ridge that is located just anterior to, or in front of, the central sulcus. The precentral gyrus, as we will discuss in Chapter 6, plays an important role in coordinating fine movements and is also known as the *motor cortex.* Directly posterior to the central sulcus is the **postcentral gyrus,** which is the most anterior region of the parietal lobe. The prefixes *pre-* and *post-* should help you remember where these gyri are located: The *pre*central gyrus is found *before* the central sulcus, in the frontal lobe, and the *post*central gyrus is found *behind* the central sulcus, in the parietal lobe. The other distinction between the precentral and postcentral gyri that you should remember is that the precentral gyrus processes motor functions, and the

cerebral hemispheres: the two (left and right) halves of the cerebrum

frontal lobe: most anterior lobe of the cerebrum, which contains the motor cortex and other centers of executive function

parietal lobe: region of the cerebrum, located immediately posterior to the frontal lobe, that processes somatic information relayed from the body

temporal lobe: most inferior lobe of the cerebrum, which processes auditory, smell, and taste information and contains the hippocampus and amygdala

occipital lobe: most posterior lobe of the cerebrum that processes visual information

corpus callosum: large tract that connects neurons in the left and right cerebral hemispheres

anterior commissure: tract that connects neurons in the left and right hippocampus and amygdala

posterior commissure: tract that connects neurons in the right and left diencephalon and mesencephalon

sulcus: grooves or fissures in the surface of the cerebrum

gyrus: raised area in the surface of the cerebrum

central sulcus: a groove that separates the frontal lobe from the parietal lobe

Figure 4.11 The cerebrum in cross-section

The cerebrum is seen in two views in cross-section: mid-sagittal cross-section (left) and coronal cross-section (right). In the coronal view, the major nuclei of the basal ganglia (putamen, globus pallidus, and caudate nucleus) are visible.

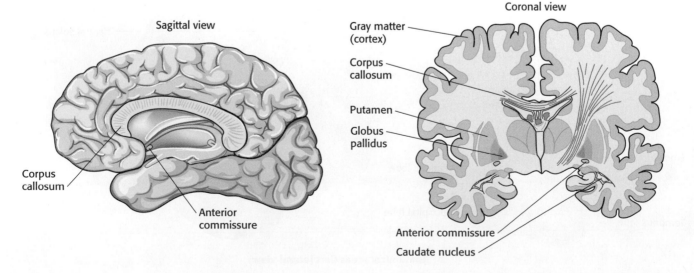

postcentral gyrus processes sensory information. The *Sylvian fissure*, or lateral sulcus, separates the temporal lobe from the other lobes of the cerebrum (see Figure 4.10). The parietal-occipital sulcus forms the boundary between the occipital lobe and the parietal lobe. Beneath the convolutions of the cerebral cortex, myelinated axons connect the four lobes of the cerebrum, allowing each lobe to contribute specialized information as they work together as a unit. Let's examine the specialized functions of each of the lobes of the cerebrum.

The Frontal Lobes   Brain investigators divide the frontal lobe into three separate regions, each with its own special functions: the **motor cortex,** the **premotor cortex,** and the **prefrontal cortex.** You have already been introduced to the motor cortex, or precentral gyrus, which directs fine motor coordination. The premotor cortex is located immediately anterior to the motor cortex. Some investigators use the term *primary motor cortex* when referring to the precentral gyrus and the term *supplementary motor cortex* when referring to the premotor cortex, to differentiate between their functions. The neurons in the precentral gyrus communicate directly with the motor neurons that control muscle contractions, whereas the neurons in the premotor cortex process information about intended movements and send that information on to the motor cortex.

The prefrontal cortex contains a number of regions that have been demonstrated to control a number of executive functions, including short-term memory, working memory, decision making, and prioritizing behaviors. When you are trying to decide whether you should do your laundry, watch television, or call your mother, it is your prefrontal cortex that weighs the alternatives and empowers you to make a decision. Throughout this book, we will make many references to the frontal lobe because it plays an important role in who you are and what you do.

The Parietal Lobes   Located directly posterior to the frontal lobes, the parietal lobes consist of the postcentral gyrus, or primary somatosensory cortex, and the secondary somatosensory cortex. The prefix *somato-* is derived from the Latin word *soma*, which means "body." *Somatosensation* refers to sensations that arise from the body. The principal function of the parietal lobes, then, is to process sensory information coming in from the body, whether it be a stomach ache or the sensation of someone stroking your arm or cold toes on a wintry day. You will learn more about the parietal lobe in Chapters 7 and 8.

The Occipital Lobes   The occipital lobes are situated at the posterior end of the cerebrum, posterior to the parietal lobes. The principal function of the occipital lobes is to process visual information coming from the eyes. As you will learn in Chapter 8, neurons in the occipital lobe receive information about the images detected by the eyes, analyze that information by breaking each image into tiny components, and then reconstitute the image after consulting with neurons in the frontal, parietal, and temporal lobes.

The Temporal Lobes   Separated from the rest of the cerebrum by the Sylvian fissure, the temporal lobes play a role in a number of important functions. The senses of taste, smell, and audition are processed in the temporal lobes. Language comprehension, too, is regulated in the temporal lobe, as is recognition of visual objects and faces. In addition, several structures, including the amygdala and the hippocampus, are located deep beneath the cortex of the temporal lobe. Therefore, damage to the temporal lobe can affect hearing, taste, smell, comprehension of language and facial expressions, mood, and memory.

Left or Right?   Psychologists, like Roger Sperry at the California Institute of Technology, have demonstrated that the left and right cerebral hemispheres have specialized functions, too. The new brain-scanning technologies have confirmed that the cerebrum divides its work asymmetrically across the two hemispheres. For most people, the left hemisphere plays an important role in speech and language comprehension. Arithmetic and scientific reasoning also appear to be controlled by the left hemisphere. In contrast, neurons in the right hemisphere process information

Sylvian fissure: the lateral sulcus that separates the temporal lobe from the rest of the cerebrum

precentral gyrus: the gyrus immediately anterior to the central sulcus, also known as the motor cortex

postcentral gyrus: the gyrus immediately posterior to the central sulcus, also known as the somatosensory cortex

motor cortex: located in the precentral gyrus, directs fine motor coordination

premotor cortex: an area of the frontal lobe involved in planning, organizing, and integrating movements of the head, trunk, and limbs

prefrontal cortex: most anterior region of the frontal lobe, composed of three divisions: dorsolateral, medial, orbitofrontal

about emotional expression, face recognition, music, and other time-space relationships. We will examine Dr. Sperry's Nobel Prize-winning research and the specialized roles of the left and right hemispheres in Chapter 10. However, it is important to remember that the differences between the left and right hemispheres are not clear cut. More recent research has suggested that some people lack specialized hemispheric skills (Gazzaniga, 1989). We will also discuss this research in more detail in Chapter 8.

✎ Recap 4.3: The Telencephalon

The telencephalon contains many structures, including the cerebrum, the hippocampus, the amygdala, the septum, and the basal ganglia. The (a)_____ is a seahorse-shaped structure that plays a role in the creation of long-term memories. The (b)_____ is involved in emotional behaviors such as fear, escape, rage, and aggression. Composed of a cluster of neurons located in the base of the telencephalon, the (c)_____ _____ play a role in the production of movement. The largest structure in the brain is the (d)_____. It has an outer layer of gray matter called the cerebral (e)_____ and is composed of four lobes: the frontal, parietal, occipital, and temporal lobes. The three tracts that link the two cerebral hemispheres are called the corpus callosum, the (f)_____ commissure, and the (g)_____ commissure. The (h)_____ lobes can be divided into three regions; the motor cortex, the premotor cortex, and the prefrontal cortex. Processing of somatosensation is the principal function of the (i)_____ lobes, whereas processing of vision is the principal function of the (j)_____ lobes. The (k)_____ lobes are involved in a number of functions including hearing, taste, smell, and emotions.

lateral ventricle: ventricle located in the telencephalon

third ventricle: ventricle located in the diencephalon

The Ventricles

When Greek scientists in Hippocrates's and Aristotle's time dissected the brains of human cadavers, they were quite impressed with the size of the empty chambers in those brains (Figure 4.12). Actually, these chambers are not empty in living people and in other living animals but rather are filled with *cerebrospinal fluid,* which you learned about earlier in this chapter. A canal system is formed by these chambers, which allows the cerebrospinal fluid to flow from the telencephalon, through the mesencephalon and rhombencephalon to the spinal cord. Let's take a closer look at this system of canals, called ventricles.

The telencephalon contains the largest of the ventricles, the **lateral ventricles.** You have two lateral ventricles: one in the left cerebral hemisphere and the other in the right cerebral hemisphere. At the top of the lateral ventricle is a tuft of vessels called the *choroid plexus,* which produces cerebrospinal fluid. A special type of glial cells, known as *ependymal cells,* covers the walls of the ventricles and assists in the production of cerebrospinal fluid (Hammond, 1996). Cerebrospinal fluid flows from the lateral ventricles to the **third ventricle,** which is located in the diencephalon. In the mesencephalon, the ventricles narrow to a constricted

Figure 4.12 The ventricles
The ventricles permit the circulation of cerebrospinal fluid through the brain: lateral ventricle (telencephalon), third ventricle (diencephalon), aqueduct of Sylvius (mesencephalon), and fourth ventricle (rhombencephalon).

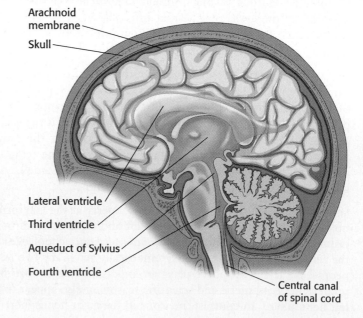

Arachnoid membrane
Skull
Lateral ventricle
Third ventricle
Aqueduct of Sylvius
Fourth ventricle
Central canal of spinal cord

opening, called the **aqueduct of Sylvius** (Figure 4.12). The aqueduct of Sylvius opens into the **fourth ventricle** in the hindbrain, which in turn narrows to become the **central canal** of the spinal cord.

Thus, cerebrospinal fluid flows from the lateral ventricle (in the telencephalon) to the third ventricle (in the diencephalon) to the aqueduct of Sylvius (in the mesencephalon) to the fourth ventricle (in the rhombencephalon) to the central canal of the spinal cord. It flows down the spinal cord in the central canal until it reaches the bottom of the spinal cord. From there, the cerebrospinal fluid flows up along the outside of the spinal cord in the arachnoid layer of the meninges and ultimately is absorbed into the bloodstream or passes through tiny vessels in the cerebrum back into the lateral ventricle.

Blockage of these vessels or of any part of the ventricle system causes cerebrospinal fluid to build up in the brain, producing a disorder known as *hydrocephalus* (Figure 4.13). You can imagine that, as fluid builds up in the brain due to a blockage of the ventricle system, pressure on neurons in the brain increases, and neurons are damaged or destroyed. Therefore, hydrocephalus is a serious condition that can produce death or permanent damage to the nervous system. We will discuss hydrocephalus in greater detail in Chapter 16.

Recap 4.4: The Ventricles

The brain contains a system of canals, called (a)_____, which contain cerebrospinal fluid. The (b)_____ ventricle is located in the telencephalon, and the (c)_____ ventricle is located in the diencephalon. The aqueduct of Sylvius is located in the mesencephalon, and the (d)_____ ventricle is located in the rhombencephalon. Cerebrospinal fluid flows through the ventricles in the brain and down through the (e)_____ canal of the spinal cord.

Figure 4.13 Photo of child with hydrocephalus
In hydrocephalus, a portion of the ventricles is blocked, causing accumulation of cerebrospinal fluid in the brain. Because the bones of the skull are not fixed in very young children, the head of the infant with hydrocephalus will swell as pressure from accumulating cerebrospinal fluid builds. In the newborn infant shown below, light placed behind the head shines through the skull because cerebrospinal fluid has compressed and replaced brain tissue.

aqueduct of Sylvius: ventricle located in the midbrain
fourth ventricle: ventricle located in the hindbrain
central canal: channel that runs down the center of the spinal cord and contains cerebrospinal fluid

The Distribution of Neurotransmitters in the Brain

In Chapter 3, you learned about a wide variety of neurotransmitters that are released from neurons to influence the activity of other neurons. Anatomical studies of the brain using sophisticated labeling and staining techniques, which you will learn about in the next chapter, have demonstrated that most neurotransmitters do their work in particular regions of the brain. In this section, we will examine the distribution of neurotransmitters in the brain. That is, we will trace the pathways from the neuronal soma to the release of neurotransmitters in specific parts of the brain for each of the major neurotransmitters discussed in Chapter 3.

Norepinephrine

Neurons that release norepinephrine are generally found in the reticular formation. Earlier in this chapter, you learned that the reticular formation alerts the rest of the brain that something important has happened. Therefore, norepinephrine plays an important role in alerting diverse parts of the brain at the same time. The majority of cells that produce norepinephrine are found in an area of the reticular formation called the **locus coeruleus,** which is located on the ventral border of the fourth ventricle. You will learn more about the function of the locus coeruleus when we discuss sleep in Chapter 10 and the stress response in Chapter 14. The axons that leave the locus coeruleus carry messages to all parts of the brain, including the thalamus, hypothalamus, the limbic system, and the cerebral cortex (Figure 4.14).

locus coeruleus: hindbrain structure that produces norepinephrine and regulates arousal

Dopamine

There are three major dopamine pathways in the brain. These are known as the *mesolimbic*, the *mesocortical*, and the *nigrostriatal* systems (Figure 4.15). Each pathway is comprised of neurons whose cell bodies are in the midbrain and whose axons project to one or more areas in the forebrain. In the mesolimbic system, neurons in the ventral tegmental area of the mesencephalon release dopamine in subcortical areas of the limbic system, including the hippocampus, amygdala, septum, and the hypothalamus. The mesocortical pathway also begins in the ventral tegmental area in the midbrain, but it projects primarily to the prefrontal cortex. The nigrostriatal pathway projects from the substantia nigra to the caudate nucleus and putamen of the basal ganglia. Put this together with what you know about brain function: Dopamine influences emotion and motivation in the mesolimbic system, thinking and other cognitive processes in the mesocortical system, and movement in the nigrostriatal system. A fourth, minor dopamine pathway, called the *tuberoinfundibular* system, extends from the hypothalamus to the pituitary gland and regulates hormone release by the pituitary.

Serotonin

Neurons that produce serotonin are found in several cell groups called the **raphe nuclei,** which are located in the midbrain and the pons. The axons of these neurons project to many areas in the brain, including the thalamus, hypothalamus, basal ganglia, hippocampus, septum, and cerebral cortex (Figure 4.16). Thus, serotonin affects many functions in the brain, such as those involved in movement, emotions, cognition, sleep, eating, and other motivated behaviors.

raphe nuclei: hindbrain structures that produce serotonin

GABA

The distribution of GABA in the brain differs significantly from that of the monoamines. Instead of being distributed along discrete pathways that extend from one region of the brain to another, this important inhibitory neurotransmitter appears to have mainly local effects. That is, most neurons that release GABA in the brain and spinal cord are interneurons (Paul, 1995). You learned in Chapter 2 that interneurons are neurons whose axons do not extend beyond their local cell cluster. Therefore, the neurons that release GABA affect only the activity in a restricted area of the brain. However, GABA-releasing neurons are found in abundance everywhere in the brain and spinal cord. In the rat brain, these neurons are most abundant in the diencephalon and mesencephalon and less abundant in the rhombencephalon and telencephalon (Cooper et al., 1996).

Glutamate

Recall from Chapter 3 that there are many different types of glutamate receptors. The distribution of glutamate in the brain is determined by the location of these different glutamate receptors. For example, NMDA receptors are found in high concentration in the hippocampus, where they play a role in memory, as you will learn in Chapter 11. In general, all glutamate receptors are found in highest abundance in the forebrain, although they are also found in high concentration in the cerebellum (Cotman et al., 1995).

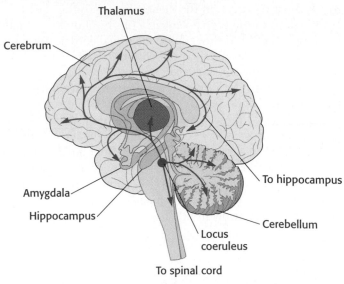

Figure 4.14 Norepinephrine pathways in the brain
Norepinephrine is produced by neurons in the locus coeruleus in the hindbrain and is released in the forebrain, midbrain, cerebellum, and spinal cord.

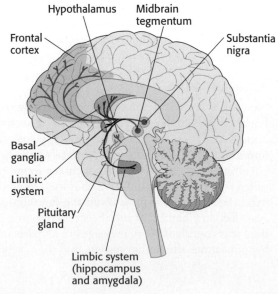

Figure 4.15 Dopamine pathways in the brain
There are three major dopamine pathways in the brain: (a) from the midbrain to the frontal lobes (blue), (b) from the midbrain to the limbic system (purple), and (c) from the substantia nigra to the basal ganglia (red). A minor dopamine pathway extends from the hypothalamus to the pituitary gland (green).

Acetylcholine

There are two types of acetylcholine receptors: *nicotinic* and *muscarinic* receptors, as you learned in Chapter 3. Nicotinic receptors are found in highest concentration in the thalamus, cerebral cortex, and midbrain, although most nicotinic receptors are found the peripheral nervous system (Domino, 1998). This distribution of nicotinic receptors in the brain reflects the involvement of these receptors in cognitive and emotional processes. Muscarinic receptors are also most abundant in the forebrain, where they play an important role in learning, memory, and attention (Ehlert et al., 1995).

Anandamide

Anandamide binds with cannabinoid receptors in the brain. The cannabinoid receptors, as you will recall from Chapter 3, are the binding sites for marijuana in the brain. Cannabinoid receptors have been found in highest concentration in the basal ganglia, cerebellum, hippocampus, cerebral cortex, and amygdala (Kreitzer & Regehr, 2001; Maneuf et al., 1996; Martin, 1995; Ohno-Shosaku, Maejima, & Kano, 2001; Wilson & Nicoll, 2001). This distribution reflects marijuana's effect on movement, memory and cognition, and the experience of reward.

This discussion of the distribution of neurotransmitters in the brain was meant to serve as an introduction to the topic. You will learn more about the distribution and action of neurotransmitters in later chapters as we examine different types of behavior. Neurons that release a particular neurotransmitter are often referred to as _____*ergic* neurons. (The name of the neurotransmitter is supplied in the blank.) For example, neurons that release serotonin are called *serotonergic* neurons, and those that release GABA are *GABAergic* neurons. Table 4.1 lists the names given to neurons associated with specific neurotransmitters.

Figure 4.16 Serotonin pathways in the brain

Serotonin is produced by neurons in the raphe nuclei located in the pons and is released throughout the cerebrum, limbic system, hypothalamus, midbrain, and cerebellum.

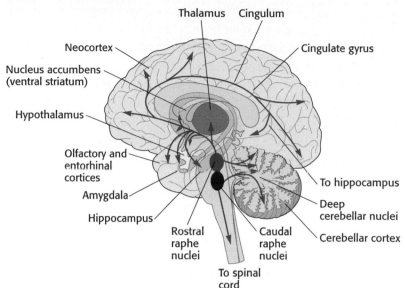

Table 4.1	
Names of Neurons Associated with Specific Neurotransmitters	
Neurotransmitters	**Associated Neurons**
acetylcholine	cholinergic
serotonin	serotonergic
dopamine	dopaminergic
norepinephrine	noradrenergic
epinephrine	adrenergic
glutamate	glutaminergic
GABA	GABAergic
anandamide	cannabinergic

Neurons in the locus coeruleus, located in the reticular formation, produce (a)_____. The mesolimbic, mesocortical, and the nigrostriatal systems are the major (b)_____ pathways in the brain, which carry it from the midbrain to the forebrain. Neurons in the raphe nuclei in the hindbrain produce (c)_____. Most neurons that release GABA in the brain and spinal cord are (d)_____. (e)_____ receptors are found in high concentration in the forebrain and cerebellum. (f)_____ acetylcholine receptors are most abundant in the thalamus, cerebral cortex, midbrain, and peripheral nervous system, and muscarinic receptors are most abundant in the (g)_____. (h)_____ receptors are found in the basal ganglia, cerebellum, cerebral cortex, and nucleus accumbens, brain areas associated with movement, memory, and reward.

The Peripheral Nervous System

Recall from Chapter 2 that the peripheral nervous system has two divisions: the **somatic nervous system** and the **autonomic nervous system.** The somatic nervous system innervates *striated muscles*, which are under your voluntary control. In contrast, the autonomic nervous system innervates *smooth muscles* (and *cardiac*, or heart, muscles) and is not under your conscious control. It acts automatically, in response to signals from the central nervous system.

The autonomic nervous system is composed of two divisions: the **sympathetic nervous system** and the **parasympathetic nervous system.** The sympathetic nervous system becomes activated when a person is excited, aroused, or in another highly emotional state. On the other hand, the parasympathetic nervous system plays an energy-conserving role and is associated with a relaxed, vegetative state.

Both the sympathetic and parasympathetic nervous systems innervate all organs and body structures containing smooth muscles. However, the two divisions of the autonomic nervous system have opposite effects on the structures that they stimulate. For example, recall from Chapter 2 that the sympathetic nervous system speeds up the heart, and the parasympathetic system slows it down. Sympathetic activation causes the pupils in the eyes to dilate, and parasympathetic activation causes the pupils to constrict. Likewise, when the sympathetic nervous system is activated, salivary glands produce a thick saliva in small quantities, whereas parasympathetic stimulation of the salivary glands causes copious secretion of a thin, watery saliva.

I've used the word *innervate* several times in the preceding paragraphs. Notice that the root of *innervate* is *nerve.* The peripheral nervous system transmits information over relatively long distances in the body by way of nerves. To *innervate,* then, means to send information by way of nerves. Usually this information serves to control or regulate the body structure that is innervated.

The peripheral nervous system transmits information to the entire body by way of 12 pairs of **cranial nerves** and 31 pairs of **spinal nerves,** or 43 pairs of nerves altogether. I use the term *pairs of nerves* because, due to the bilateral nature of the central nervous system, nerves exit from the right and left halves of the brain and spinal cord. That means that you have a left optic nerve that connects your left eye to your brain and a right optic nerve that connects your right eye. The same is true for all the nerves that we will discuss in this section. Each nerve is paired with a nerve on the opposite side of the body. Let's consider the cranial nerves first.

somatic nervous system: a division of the peripheral nervous system that controls skeletal muscles

autonomic nervous system: a division of the peripheral nervous system, controls smooth muscles

sympathetic nervous system: a division of the autonomic nervous system, producing fight-or-flight responses

parasympathetic nervous system: a division of the autonomic nervous system, concerned with energy conservation

cranial nerves: twelve pairs of nerves that enter and exit the brain through holes in the skull

spinal nerves: nerves that enter and exit the spinal cord between bones of the spinal column

Cranial Nerves

The cranial nerves permit direct communication between the brain and the peripheral nervous system. Cranial nerves allow for: (1) sensory input from the head, neck, and upper abdomen to the brain; (2) motor output from the brain to the skeletal muscles in the head and neck; and (3) parasympathetic output to smooth muscles in the head, neck, and upper abdomen. These nerves gain access to the brain via holes, or *foramena* [plural of *foramen*, or hole], in the skull. Cranial nerves I and II go to the forebrain. Cranial nerves III and IV arise from the midbrain, and cranial nerves V–XII enter and exit the hindbrain. Table 4.2 summarizes the functions of the twelve cranial nerves. Note that Roman numerals are used to denote each cranial nerve.

Cranial nerve I, the **olfactory nerve,** carries information about odors from the smell receptors in the roof of the nose. Like cranial nerve I, cranial nerve II, or the **optic nerve,** transmits sensory information to the brain. The optic nerve arises from the retina in the eye and carries information about light to the brain. These nerves will be examined more closely in Chapter 7.

Cranial nerves III, IV, and VI have both *sensory* and *motor* functions. These three cranial nerves innervate the muscles that control eye movement. Cranial nerve V, the **trigeminal nerve,** gets its name from the Latin words *tri-* (three) and *gemina-* (roots) because it splits into three separate branches as it leaves the brain. One branch of the trigeminal nerve innervates the forehead and side of your head, a second branch innervates your top jaw, and the third branch innervates your lower jaw. Altogether, the trigeminal nerve controls the muscles of mastication, that is, the muscles that produce chewing movements. The trigeminal nerve also

olfactory nerve: cranial nerve I, which carries information about odors from the nose to the brain

optic nerve: cranial nerve II, which carries information about vision from the eye to the brain

trigeminal nerve: cranial nerve V, which carries sensory information from the mouth and face and controls facial muscles of mastication

Table 4.2

Functions of the Cranial Nerves

Cranial Nerve	Function
Olfactory (I)	Sensory: smell
Optic (II)	Sensory: vision
Oculomotor (III)	Sensory: eye muscles Motor: eye muscles
Trochlear (IV)	Sensory: eye muscle (superior oblique) Motor: eye muscle
Trigeminal (V)	Sensory: skin of face, jaws, teeth Motor: muscles of mastication
Abducens (VI)	Sensory: eye muscle (lateral rectus) Motor: eye muscle
Facial (VII)	Sensory: taste, facial muscles Motor: muscles of facial expression
Auditory (VIII)	Sensory: hearing, vestibular senses
Glossopharyngeal (IX)	Sensory: tongue, throat Motor: muscles of tongue and throat
Vagus (X)	Sensory: taste, organs of chest and upper abdomen Motor: smooth muscles in neck, chest, upper abdomen
Accessory (XI)	Motor: skeletal muscles of neck
Hypoglossal (XII)	Sensory: muscles in lower jaw, tongue Motor: muscles in lower jaw, tongue

relays *sensory* information from the tongue, lips, and jaws to the brain. For example, information about a toothache is transmitted to the brain via cranial nerve V.

Cranial nerve VII, the **facial nerve,** is sometimes confused with the trigeminal nerve. Whereas the trigeminal nerve controls the facial muscles of mastication, the facial nerve innervates the muscles of facial expression. Place your hands on your face and make chewing movements. The muscles that you can feel contracting are the muscles innervated by cranial nerve V. Now smile, then frown. These muscles are controlled by cranial nerve VII. The facial nerve also carries *sensory* information (taste from the tongue) to the brain. Bell's palsy is caused by a viral infection in cranial nerve VII and usually lasts from a few days to several weeks, although some people retain the symptoms of Bell's palsy permanently. A person afflicted with Bell's palsy loses control of the muscles on the side of the face that has the affected nerve, which causes the face to have a lopsided appearance for the duration of the infection.

The next cranial nerve, cranial nerve VIII or the **auditory nerve,** has *sensory* functions only. Some of the axons that make up cranial nerve VIII conduct auditory information from the inner ear to the brain. Other axons carry information about equilibrium and the head's position with respect to gravity to the brain. We will discuss this nerve in greater detail in Chapter 7.

Cranial nerve X, also known as the **vagus nerve,** is my personal favorite. As its Latin name implies [*vagare* = to wander], the vagus nerve leaves the brain and winds its way down the neck and body trunk to innervate structures in the neck, chest, and upper abdomen. Your heart and stomach, for example, receive information from the brain via the vagus nerve. The vagus nerve also carries sensory information from these organs to the brain, and it relays taste sensations from the taste receptors located deep in your throat and in your larynx. You will learn more about this important nerve in Chapter 11 when we discuss the regulation of eating behavior.

Let me summarize the most important functions of the 12 pairs of cranial nerves. Cranial nerves I, II, and VIII have *sensory* functions only. Cranial nerves III, IV, and VI control eye movement, and cranial nerves V and VII control face muscles. Muscles of the throat and tongue are controlled by cranial nerves IX and XII, and muscles in the neck are controlled by cranial nerve XI. Cranial nerve X, the wanderer, innervates organs and muscles in the neck, chest, and abdomen. The next time a person rolls his or her eyes, winks, smiles, or nods at you, try to figure out which cranial nerves are being used.

Spinal Nerves

In addition to the cranial nerves, the peripheral nervous system contains 31 pairs of spinal nerves. The spinal nerves are bundles of axons that exit and enter the spinal cord. Recall from our earlier discussion of the spinal cord that axons entering the dorsal aspect of the spinal cord are carrying sensory information and that axons leaving the ventral aspect of the spinal cord are carrying motor information to muscles. Each spinal nerve, then, is composed of a sensory branch and a motor branch (Figure 4.17). All spinal nerves are paired, with one nerve associated with the left side of the spinal cord and one nerve associated with the right side.

You have already learned that the spinal cord is divided into five regions: cervical, thoracic, lumbar, sacral, and coccygeal. The spinal nerves are named after the region of the spinal cord from which they arise. Because the spinal cord is encased within the vertebral column, the spinal nerves can enter and exit the spinal cord only where there are breaks in the column of bones that make up your backbone (Figure 4.18). Therefore, the number of nerves that arise from each region of the spinal cord is determined by the number of vertebral bones that cover and protect that region. In Figure 4.3, you can see that 8 pairs of nerves arise from the cervical region of the spinal cord, 12 pairs of nerves arise from the thoracic region, 5 pairs of nerves from the lumbar region and 5 from the sacral region, and 1 pair of nerves from the coccygeal region, for a grand total of 31 pairs of nerves.

facial nerve: cranial nerve VII, which controls the muscles of facial expression

auditory nerve: cranial nerve VIII, which carries information from the inner ear to the brain

vagus nerve: cranial nerve X, which carries sensory information from the upper abdomen, chest, and neck to the brain and carries motor information from the brain to smooth muscles in those areas of the body

Figure 4.17 The sensory and motor branches of spinal nerves
Sensory nerves enter the dorsal aspect of the spinal cord. Motor nerves exit from the ventral aspect of the spinal cord.

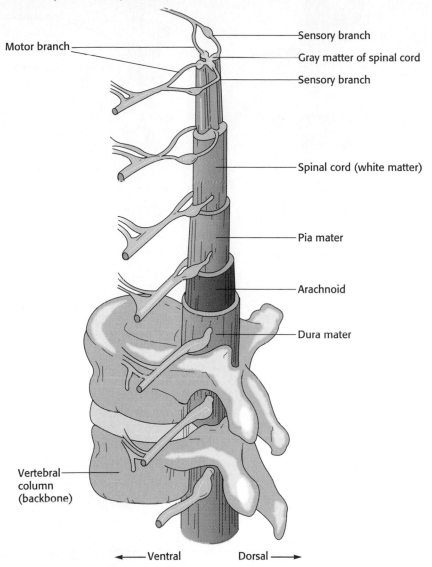

Motor branch

Sensory branch

Gray matter of spinal cord

Sensory branch

Spinal cord (white matter)

Pia mater

Arachnoid

Dura mater

Vertebral column (backbone)

◄— Ventral   Dorsal —►

Each spinal nerve is named after the region of the spinal cord from which it arises. A nerve from the cervical region is named C1 through C8, depending on where it arises, with C1 being the most superior nerve and C8 the most inferior of the cervical nerves. Thoracic nerves are named T1 through T12, with T1 being most superior and T12 most inferior. Likewise, lumbar nerves are named L1, L2, L3, L4, and L5, and sacral nerves are named S1, S2, S3, S4, and S5. Each spinal nerve innervates a specific area of the body. The body area innervated by one spinal nerve is called a *dermatome*. Figure 4.19 illustrates the dermatomes associated with each spinal nerve.

When a person suffers an injury to the spinal cord, we identify the injury by its location on the spinal cord. If a woman breaks her neck between the third and fourth cervical vertebrae, we say that she has a C4 injury. In general, the higher the lesion on the spinal cord, the more impairment of movement and sensation we expect to see. A person with a C4 injury, or an injury to the spinal cord above C4, is likely to develop *quadriplegia*, a disability in which the motor and sensory functions of all four limbs are impaired. If you look closely at Figure 4.19, you will see that the hands and forearms receive innervation from C6, C7, and C8. This means that some arm function may be spared with a C5 injury, and the person with a C4 injury will have weak or limited motor control of the forearms. The actor Christopher Reeve was thrown from a horse while attempting a jump and damaged his spinal cord at C3. Because of the high level of his spinal cord injury, Reeve has retained only weak control of his shoulder muscles. He can no longer move his limbs or trunk. He is now a quadriplegic, confined to a motorized wheelchair, and requires a mechanical ventilator to breathe (Figure 4.20).

The Organization of the Peripheral Nervous System

In this final section, I want you to gain an understanding of how the peripheral nervous system is distributed across the cranial and spinal nerves. So far, you've learned that the peripheral nervous system is comprised of 12 cranial nerves and 31 spinal nerves. You've also learned that the peripheral nervous system has two divisions: the somatic and autonomic nervous systems, and you've learned that the autonomic nervous system is further divided into the sympathetic and parasympathetic nervous systems.

Except for cranial nerves I, II, and VIII, all cranial and spinal nerves innervate skeletal muscles and, thus, are part of the somatic nervous system. (Recall that cranial nerves I, II, and VIII carry sensory information only and have no motor component.) Not all cranial and spinal nerves innervate smooth muscles, however. Therefore, the autonomic nervous system is not distributed across all nerves. Of the cranial nerves, only cranial nerves III, V, VII, IX, and X innervate smooth muscles and glands (Figure 4.21). Similarly, only the spinal nerves arising from the thoracic, lumbar, and sacral regions of the spinal cord relay information from the autonomic nervous system.

The two divisions of the autonomic nervous system, the sympathetic and the parasympathetic nervous systems, are also distributed unevenly across the spinal and cranial nerves. The sympathetic nervous system arises from the *thoracic* and *lumbar* regions of the spinal cord. Thus, only the

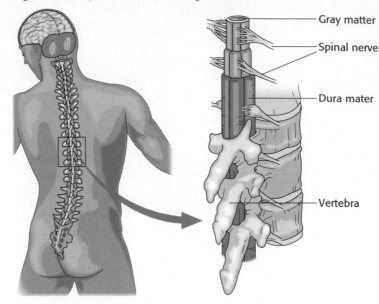

Figure 4.18 Spinal nerves exiting between vertebrae

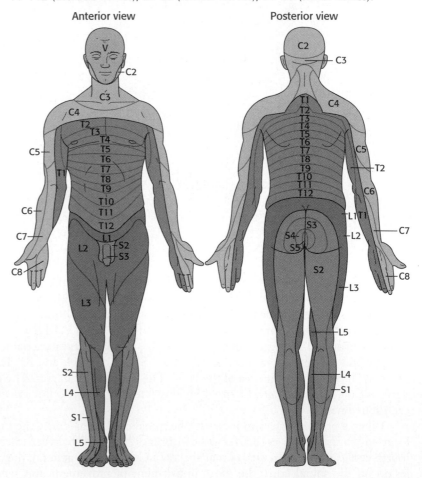

Figure 4.19 Dermatomes
Spinal nerves innervate specific areas of the body: C1–C8 (cervical nerves), T1–T12 (thoracic nerves), L1–L5 (lumbar nerves), S1–S5 (sacral nerves).

thoracic and lumbar nerves carry sympathetic information. These nerves send a short branch to a chain of ganglia, called the *sympathetic ganglia*, which is located just lateral to the thoracic and lumbar regions of the spinal cord (Figure 4.21). From the sympathetic ganglia, messages from the sympathetic nervous system are sent via nerves to various organs and glands throughout the body, preparing the body to deal with arousing or stressful stimuli. Nerves arising from the sympathetic ganglia innervate smooth muscles and glands in the head, neck, trunk, and limbs. The *Case Study* describes the case of a young boy with cancer of the sympathetic nervous system.

The sympathetic nervous system is sometimes referred to as the *thoracolumbar system* because it arises from the thoracic and lumbar regions of the spinal cord. Similarly, the parasympathetic nervous system is called the *craniosacral system* because only certain cranial nerves and nerves from the sacral region of the spinal cord relay parasympathetic information to smooth muscles and organs. Cranial nerves III, V, VII, IX and X conduct information from the parasympathetic nervous system to smooth muscles and glands in the head and neck. In addition, cranial nerve X carries parasympathetic stimulation to smooth muscles and organs in the

Figure 4.20 Christopher Reeve, an actor who damaged his spinal cord at C3

Figure 4.21 Distribution of the autonomic nervous system

The sympathetic nervous system arises from the thoracic and lumbar regions of the spinal cord. The parasympathetic nervous system arises from the sacral region of the spinal cord and from the brain (via cranial nerves).

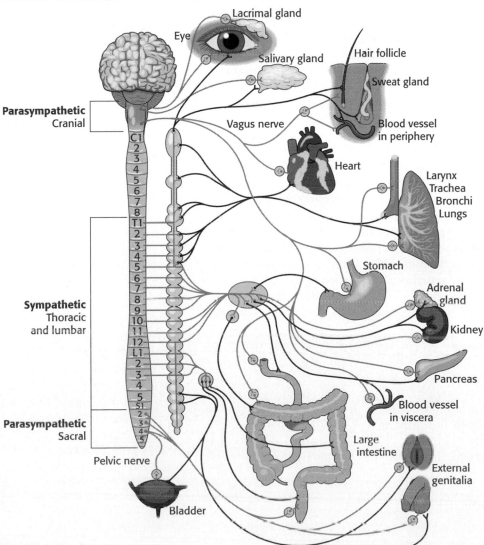

Neuroblastoma

Robyn was a happy, friendly baby who had big blue eyes and a ready smile. Soon after he first learned to walk, Robyn began to complain of pain in his back. He would take a few steps, grab his sides, and groan. When he started to talk, his first words included "Ow!" and "Hurt!"

Robyn's mother took Robyn to his pediatrician, the first of many physicians who examined Robyn. The pediatrician was doubtful that Robyn was really experiencing pain and suggested that he was just calling for more attention. However, Robyn continued to complain about pain in his back, especially when he walked. His mother had him examined by two other pediatricians who could not find anything wrong. When Robyn was 3 years old, his mother took him to a family practitioner who referred him to a physician who specialized in the treatment of arthritis. The arthritis specialist examined Robyn carefully before he said to Robyn's mother, "Your son does not have arthritis. He has *neuroblastoma.*"

Neuroblastoma is a form of cancer that strikes the neurons of the sympathetic nervous system. Tumors were found in the sympathetic ganglia in the thoracic and lumbar areas of Robyn's back, a common origin of neuroblastoma. That explained why Robyn experienced pain in the middle of his back. Over time, tumors spread along the entire distribution of Robyn's sympathetic nervous system, to his lungs, liver, and other organs. Tumors developed even in Robyn's eyes, blinding him. A cheerful little boy until the end, Robyn died shortly before his 5th birthday.

chest and upper abdomen, such as the heart and the stomach. Sacral nerves relay parasympathetic stimulation to the smooth muscles and organs of the lower abdomen and pelvic area. Figure 4.21 illustrates the distribution of the parasympathetic nerves.

Go back and read the introductory material on the autonomic nervous system on pages 24–27. In general, the sympathetic and parasympathetic nervous systems innervate the same muscles and organs but tend to have opposite effects on those structures. Different neurotransmitters are associated with the two divisions of the peripheral nervous system, which probably accounts for their different effects. Norepinephrine is the neurotransmitter that is released by neurons in the sympathetic ganglia, whereas acetylcholine is released by nerves carrying parasympathetic information. Sympathetic stimulation arises from the chain of sympathetic ganglia located next to the thoracic and lumbar regions of the spinal cord and affects all organs at the same time. (The sympathetic nervous system gets its name from the fact that the sympathetic ganglia cause all organs to work in concert, or *in sympathy*, with each other.) In contrast, parasympathetic information is relayed along cranial and sacral nerves to individual ganglia located near the affected organ. Therefore, parasympathetic stimulation is more fine tuned and organ specific than is sympathetic stimulation.

We will come back to a discussion of the autonomic nervous system many times during the course of this book, when we are examining eating behavior (Chapter 11), sexual behavior (Chapter 12), emotion (Chapter 13), and the reaction to stress (Chapter 14). Autonomic arousal, especially activation of the sympathetic nervous system, can also affect perception, attention, learning, and a number of cognitive processes, as you will learn in Chapters 8, 9, and 10. Therefore, it is important that you understand thoroughly the differences between the two divisions of the autonomic nervous system, the sympathetic and parasympathetic nervous systems.

The peripheral nervous system consists of (a)_____ spinal nerves and (b)_____ cranial nerves. The (c)_____ nerve (cranial nerve I) transmits olfactory information to the brain, whereas the (d)_____ nerve (cranial nerve II) transmits visual information. The (e)_____ nerve (cranial nerve V) innervates the muscle of mastication, and the (f)_____ nerve (cranial nerve VII) innervates the muscles of facial expression. The (g)_____ nerve (cranial nerve VIII) transmits auditory and vestibular information to the brain. Unlike the other cranial nerves, the (h)_____ nerve (cranial nerve X) courses through the head, neck, chest, and upper abdomen, innervating the structures in those regions. Spinal nerves are named after the five regions of the spinal cord: (i)_____, (j)_____, (k)_____, (l)_____, and (m)_____. The body region innervated by one spinal nerve is called a (n)_____. The sympathetic nervous system arises from the (o)_____ and (p)_____ regions of the spinal cord, whereas the parasympathetic nervous system arises from the (q)_____ and (r)_____ regions of the spinal cord.

Chapter Summary

An Overview of the Central Nervous System

▶ The central nervous system is comprised of the brain and spinal cord.

▶ The central nervous system is protected by bone and the meninges, which has three layers. The outermost layer of the meninges is the dura mater, the middle layer is the arachnoid layer, and the innermost layer is the pia mater. Vessels in the arachnoid layer contain a fluid found only in the central nervous system called cerebrospinal fluid.

▶ The spinal cord is divided into five sections: cervical, thoracic, lumbar, sacral, and coccygeal, each of which controls the muscles and organs in a specific area of the body.

The Brain

▶ The brain has three subdivisions: the hindbrain (or rhombencephalon), the midbrain (mesencephalon), and the forebrain (prosencephalon).

▶ The medulla, pons, and cerebellum are the major structures in the rhombencephalon. Neurons in the medulla regulate life-support functions, receive sensory information, or send motor commands to muscles in the head, neck, and trunk. The pons permits passage of information between the spinal cord and higher regions of the brain. The cerebellum coordinates muscular activity and is especially vulnerable to alcohol, which impairs its functioning.

▶ In the mesenchephalon are located the superior and inferior colliculi, the tegmentum, and the reticular formation. The superior colliculus processes visual information, and the inferior colliculus processes auditory information. The reticular formation runs from the hindbrain to the forebrain, through the midbrain and plays an important role in keeping the individual awake and alert.

▶ The largest part of the human brain is the forebrain or prosencephalon. It is divided into two parts, the diencephalon and the telencephalon.

▶ The diencephalon is composed of the thalamus and hypothalamus. The thalamus contains a cluster of nuclei that relay information to and from the cerebrum. The hypothalamus is involved in the regulation of the pituitary gland and motivated behaviors, such as sleeping, eating, and drinking.

▶ Together, the mesencephalon, rhombencephalon, and diencephalon make up the brain stem, which regulates our most primitive behaviors, such as breathing, sleep, sexual behavior, drinking, and eating.

▶ The telencephalon contains structures of the limbic system, the basal ganglia, and the cerebrum. The hippocampus is a seahorse-shaped structure that plays a role in the creation of long-term memories. The amygdala is involved in emotional behaviors such as fear, escape, rage, and aggression. The basal ganglia are composed of a cluster of neurons located in the base of the telencephalon and play a role in the production of movement.

▶ The cerebrum is the largest structure in the brain and is organized like the cerebellum with two hemispheres, a cortical layer (the cerebral cortex, which contains the cell bodies of hundreds of millions of neurons), and underlying white matter. Mental activities requiring consciousness are processed in the four lobes of the cerebrum. The frontal lobes consist of three regions, the motor cortex, the premotor cortex, and the prefrontal cortex. Processing of somatosensation is the principal function of the parietal lobes, and processing of vision is the principal function of the occipital lobes. The temporal lobes are involved in a number of functions including hearing, taste, smell, and emotions.

▶ The ventricles form a canal system in the brain. Although its function is uncertain, cerebrospinal fluid, produced in the lateral ventricle, circulates through the brain and spinal cord.

▶ Each of the neurotransmitters has a specific distribution in the brain. Norepinephrine and serotonin are produced in the hindbrain and are carried to diverse areas in the forebrain. There are three major dopamine pathways in the brain, the mesolimbic, mesocortical, and the nigrostriatal systems, which carry dopamine from the midbrain to the forebrain.

The Peripheral Nervous System

▶ The peripheral nervous system is composed of 12 cranial and 31 spinal nerves.

▶ Spinal nerves are named after the five regions of the spinal cord: cervical, thoracic, lumbar, sacral, and coccygeal. The body region innervated by one spinal nerve is called a dermatome.

▶ The somatic nervous system innervates skeletal muscles by way of all cranial and spinal nerves except for cranial nerves I, II, and VIII, which carry sensory information only. The olfactory nerve (cranial nerve I) transmits olfactory information to the brain, whereas the optic nerve (cranial nerve II) transmits visual information. The auditory nerve (cranial nerve VIII) transmits auditory and vestibular information to the brain.

▶ The sympathetic nervous system arises from thoracic and lumbar spinal nerves, whereas the parasympathetic nervous system communicates via nerves arising from the sacral segments of the spinal cord and via cranial nerves III, V, IX, and X.

Key Terms

amygdala (p. 100)
anterior commissure (p. 102)
aqueduct of Sylvius (p. 105)
arachnoid layer (p. 90)
auditory nerve (p. 110)
autonomic nervous system (p. 108)
basal ganglia (p. 100)
central canal (p. 105)
central sulcus (p. 102)
cerebellum (p. 96)
cerebral cortex (p. 101)
cerebral hemispheres (p. 102)
cerebrospinal fluid (p. 90)
cerebrum (p. 99)
cervical (p. 93)
coccygeal (p. 93)
corpus callosum (p. 102)
cranial nerves (p. 108)
diencephalon (p. 97)
dura mater (p. 90)
facial nerve (p. 110)
forebrain (p. 93)
fourth ventricle (p. 105)
frontal lobe (p. 102)
ganglion (p. 93)
gyrus (p. 102)

hindbrain (p. 93)
hippocampus (p. 100)
hormones (p. 99)
hypothalamus (p. 99)
inferior colliculi (p. 96)
lateral ventricles (p. 104)
limbic system (p. 100)
locus coeruleus (p. 105)
lumbar (p. 93)
medulla (p. 94)
meninges (p. 90)
mesencephalon (p. 94)
midbrain (p. 93)
motor cortex (p. 103)
nerve (p. 93)
nucleus (p. 92)
occipital lobe (p. 102)
olfactory nerve (p. 109)
optic nerve (p. 109)
parasympathetic nervous system (p. 108)
parietal lobe (p. 102)
pia mater (p. 91)
pituitary gland (p. 99)
pons (p. 95)
postcentral gyrus (p. 103)

posterior commissure (p. 102)
precentral gyrus (p. 103)
prefrontal cortex (p. 103)
premotor cortex (p. 103)
prosencephalon (p. 94)
raphe nuclei (p. 106)
reticular formation (p. 97)
rhombencephalon (p. 94)
sacral (p. 93)
septum (p. 100)
somatic nervous system (p. 108)
spinal nerves (p. 108)
sulcus (p. 102)
superior colliculi (p. 96)
Sylvian fissure (p. 103)
sympathetic nervous system (p. 108)
telencephalon (p. 97)
temporal lobe (p. 102)
thalamus (p. 98)
third ventricle (p. 104)
thoracic (p. 93)
tract (p. 92)
trigeminal nerve (p. 109)
vagus nerve (p. 110)
ventricles (p. 91)

Questions for Thought

1. Which parts of the brain are highly developed in alligators? In birds?
2. How do you think the limbic system influences the functioning of the cerebrum?
3. How does the function of the cerebellum differ from that of the basal ganglia?

Questions for Review

1. Name the three layers of the meninges. What does each do?

2. What are the four lobes of the cerebrum? How do their functions differ?

3. How does the parasympathetic nervous system differ from the sympathetic nervous system?

4. What are the functions of each structure in the hindbrain?

Suggested Readings

Calvin, W. H., & Ojemann, G. A. (1998). *Conversations with Neil's brain: The neural nature of thought and language*. Reading, MA: Perseus Books.

Sacks, O. (1986). *The man who mistook his wife for a hat*. New York: Penguin Press.

Thompson, R. F. (1984). *The amazing brain*. Boston: Houghton Mifflin.

Web Resources

For a chapter tutorial quiz, direct links to the Internet sites listed below, and other features, visit the book-specific website at **www.wadsworth.com/product/0155074865**. You may also connect directly to the following annotated websites:

http://www.braininfo.rprc.washington.edu
This is a whole brain catalog! You can view a whole brain and then zoom in on structures (with accompanying imaging scans) or search by term.

http://www.loni.ucla.edu/
This site provides graphic images and animation of the basic brain anatomy, the developing brain, the diseased brain, and more.

http://webct.downstate.edu:8900/courseware/neuro/
This site allows you to view different cross-sections of the brain and illustrates the location of the major structures within each cross-section.

http://predator.pnb.uconn.edu/beta/virtualtemp/nervous/Brainregions.htm
Explore the different regions of the brain and their functions.

For additional readings and information, check out InfoTrac College Edition at **http://www.infotrac-college.com/wadsworth**. Choose a search term yourself or enter the following search terms: Brain, Nerve, Spinal Cord.

CD-ROM: Exploring Biological Psychology

Viewing the Brain: Planes of Section
    Virtual Reality: Head Planes
    Virtual Reality: Body Planes
    Interactive Puzzle: The Planes
Viewing the Brain: Structure and Function
    Sagittal Section: Right Hemisphere 1
    Sagittal Section: Right Hemisphere 2
    Sagittal Section: Right Hemisphere 3
    Virtual Reality: The Brain
    Interactive Puzzle: The Brain

Viewing the Brain: Cerebral Cortex
    Left Hemisphere Function 1
    Left Hemisphere Function 2
    Sagittal Plane
    Virtual Reality: The Brain
    Interactive Puzzle: The Cortex
Interactive Recaps
Chapter 4 Quiz
Connect to the Interactive Biological Psychology Glossary

5

Neuroscientific Research Methods

In the campus newspaper, Evan saw an ad soliciting male volunteers for a study of the effects of alcohol on the brain. According to the ad, participants in the study were paid $200. Because he needed money for spring break, Evan called to volunteer for the study. The woman who answered the phone asked him a lot of questions about his drinking habits, his experiences with drugs, and his medical history. When he finished answering all the questions, the woman told him that he qualified for the study and made an appointment for Evan to go to a nearby medical center for the study.

On the appointed day, Evan went to the medical center where he was met by a nurse who asked him to read a ten-page consent form that explained the purpose of the study, the procedure, and the risks involved. After he signed the consent form, the nurse drew blood from his arm and took him to the office of a neuropsychologist who gave him a number of memory, motor coordination, and pen-and-paper tests. The neuropsychologist also asked him questions about any head injuries he might have had. Next, the nurse brought him to the office of a physician who gave Evan a brief physical exam and again asked him about any previous head injuries. When the physician was finished with his examination, Evan was taken to a room where he put on a dressing gown and was asked to lie on a table on his back. A needle was inserted into a vein in his left arm, and his head was immobilized by velcro straps. As he lay on the table, it rolled toward a huge brain scanning machine, until his head was in the center of the scanner. While the PET machine scanned his brain, the nurse asked Evan to put a series of letters and numbers in alphabetical/numerical order. She read one series after another to him for almost 20 minutes, forcing him to hold the numbers and letters in his memory while he put them into the correct order. Evan was then led to another clinic in the hospital to undergo an MRI scan of his brain, a procedure that took nearly 40 minutes. He was really exhausted when he finished participating in the study, but he was happy to have an extra $200 in his pocket.

Evan participated in a study that I am currently conducting on the effects of alcohol abuse on glucose metabolism in the brains of college-aged people. *Glucose metabolism* refers to the uptake of glucose from the blood and to its breakdown by neurons to produce ATP and other by-products. It is, therefore, an indication of activity in neurons. Studies of older, chronic alcoholics have demonstrated that glucose metabolism is significantly reduced in particular regions of their brains, compared to the brains of age-matched nondrinkers. In my study, I am interested in determining whether alcohol can produce alterations in brain activity in youthful drinkers who have been abusing alcohol for less than 5 years.

To conduct this study, I am using a brain-imaging method known as *positron emission tomography (PET),* which I will describe later in this chapter. However, I cannot conduct this study alone, nor can I conduct the study in my own laboratory at the university where I teach. The equipment needed to do PET scans is very expensive and is available at only a limited number of research centers. To conduct this study, I need to send my participants to a neuroscience institute in a nearby city to have their PET scans performed. In addition, I do not administer the PET scans personally. That is, I work with a team of neuroscientists, including a physicist, a radiochemist, a physician, a clinical neuropsychologist, and a computer scientist, to obtain my data.

Today, neuroscience research is conducted in this manner at many institutions. Scientists from many disciplines work together as a team to conduct research. Physiological psychologists bring a special expertise to the research team, including expert knowledge of the effects of physiological processes on behavior and training in research design and data analysis. In this chapter, we will look at many different research methods used to study the biological bases of behavior. As you read the following sections, please keep in mind that many of these methods require teamwork, especially those that make use of sophisticated equipment and chemical analyses. ●

Brain Lesions and Brain Stimulation

Brain Lesions

Early investigators used two techniques to study the brain: lesioning and stimulation. **Lesioning** involves damaging or disrupting the function of a particular area of the brain. If a region of the brain is destroyed, then it cannot perform its usual function. The investigator would typically produce a lesion in an area of interest in the brain of an *anesthetized* animal. When the experimental subject recovered from the surgery, its behavior was observed for any signs of deficits. Lesioning, then, demonstrates what happens when a brain structure is *not* functioning normally.

lesioning: destroying or disrupting the function of a specific brain structure

The function of that brain structure is inferred from the resulting behavioral problem. If the subject is rendered deaf by the lesioning procedure, for example, it is assumed that the lesioned area was involved in hearing.

Most of the earliest lesioning studies involved **ablation,** or removal of a part of the brain, particularly the cortex, which was most accessible. In the first studies, the brain region to be removed was merely ladled out with a sharp spoon. However, this rather crude procedure created a bruised area in the brain that became scarred and prone to produce epileptic seizures.

Karl Lashley, the American psychologist whom you learned about in Chapter 1, used a technique called hot wire **thermocautery.** After preparing his subject for the procedure, which involved anesthetizing it and opening its skull, Lashley placed the tip of a red-hot wire in the brain to burn away the area to be lesioned (Figure 5.1). This technique produced a neat lesion, with little bleeding, but it did not eliminate scarring, which caused uncontrollable seizures.

Penfield perfected a suctioning technique to lesion the brain. He used a pipette, which looks like a medicine dropper, to draw out the brain tissue. This technique was superior to Lashley's because it produced minimal, if any, scarring. All brain cells that did not have a good blood supply were easily removed, which meant that no *necrotic* tissue was left in the brain after surgery. Penfield's suctioning technique is still used today by neurosurgeons and neuroscience investigators to remove brain matter.

ablation: removal of a part of the brain
thermocautery: to cut away tissue using heat

Figure 5.1 Hot wire thermocautery: a lesioned (cauterized) brain

Subcortical Lesions

Ablation techniques work fine when a cortical area of the brain is under investigation. However, an entirely different technique is needed when lesioning a structure beneath the cortex. Think about the problems that would be encountered in lesioning a **subcortical** structure. First of all, the subcortical structure is not visible when the skull is opened, and it has to be located underneath the overlying cortex. In addition, care must be taken to lesion the subcortical structure without damaging the overlying brain. How is it possible to locate and lesion subcortical structures?

Think about how you might get to a city that you have never visited before. For starters, you might ask a friend how to get there, or you could pick up a road atlas and locate the city. And that's exactly how brain investigators find unfamiliar brain structures: They consult with a colleague or read a published paper that describes another scientist's research on that structure, or they use a stereotaxic brain atlas. A brain atlas contains dozens of maps of the brain, each map representing a slice through a particular region of the brain. There are atlases for human brains, dog brains, cat brains, rat brains, monkey brains, even for several species of bird brains. A structure is located by a set of three coordinates: inferior/superior, medial/lateral, and anterior/posterior (Figure 5.2). The **inferior/superior** coordinate tells the investigators how far below the surface the structure is. The **medial/lateral** coordinate tells how far over from midline the structure is, and the **anterior/posterior** coordinate tells how far from the front or back of the head the structure is.

A piece of apparatus, called the **stereotaxic instrument,** was developed in 1908 by Horsley and Clark to enable investigators to locate brain structures with precision because subcortical structures can be quite small and easy to miss if measurements are not precise. The stereotaxic instrument consists of a platform on which the subject's head is held securely in place

subcortical: located below the cortex
inferior: lower, below
superior: upper, above
medial: toward the midline
lateral: toward the side
anterior: toward the front
posterior: toward the back, behind
stereotaxic instrument: an apparatus that allows investigators to locate subcortical brain structures with great precision

Figure 5.2 A page from a stereotaxic brain atlas showing a rat brain

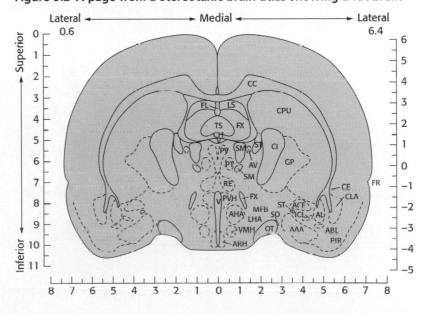

and a measuring device that allows measurements based on the three coordinates discussed above. Figure 5.3 illustrates a stereotaxic instrument used for human patients.

Equipped with a brain atlas and stereotaxic instrument, a neuroscientist is able to locate subcortical structures and lesion them. To produce a subcortical lesion, an insulated conducting wire, called an **electrode,** is inserted into the brain. Some of the earliest electrodes were merely sewing needles insulated with melted glass (Valenstein, 1973). In small animals, lesions are made with direct current (DC) electricity. Radio-frequency (RF) waves are used to produce a lesion in a larger animal, including humans. Because the brain has the consistency of a thick pudding, passing a wire down through it does not cause noticeable damage to brain structures in the wire's path. Only those structures surrounding the uninsulated tip of the electrode are destroyed during lesioning.

electrode: electrical conducting medium

Today, neurosurgeons use sophisticated imaging techniques when performing stereotaxic surgery, instead of relying solely on stereotaxic brain atlases. Brain surgery is based on the precise knowledge of the spatial position of the target structure and of its relationships with other brain structures. Imaging techniques provide accurate localization of structures buried deep within the brain. Modern imaging systems allow minimal invasion of the brain and provide instant and continual navigational information during surgery. The *For Further Thought* box describes one modern neuronavigation technique. We will discuss additional imaging techniques later in this chapter.

Other lesioning techniques have been developed by brain investigators. Chemical lesions are produced by inserting a **cannula,** or miniature tube, stereotaxically into the brain area under investigation and injecting minute amounts of a chemical that kills neurons in the desired structure. Some neuroscientists make lesions by freezing tiny areas of the brain. They insert a **cryoprobe,** which looks like an electrode, into the targeted brain area with a stereotaxic instrument. The temperature at the tip of the cryoprobe is lowered to below 0°C, freezing the surrounding tissue (Campeau & Davis, 1990; Valenstein, 1986).

cannula: miniature tube used to carry chemicals into the brain

cryoprobe: probe that is inserted into the brain to cool specific regions

Figure 5.3 Human stereotaxic instrument

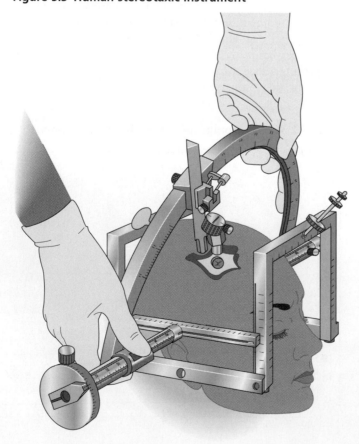

Neuronavigation

For many neurosurgeons today, brain surgery involves using technologically advanced systems that enable surgeons to localize and work in specific regions of the brain. In the past, stereotaxic instruments were the only apparatus available to locate targets in the brain. Today's neurosurgeon has an array of neuronavigational devices that permit faster, more accurate, and less invasive surgeries. In the photo on the left, you can see a typical modern surgery room, with computers and computer monitors providing a visual image of the patient's brain as the surgeon moves a hand-held localization device about the surgical site.

The localization device is an interactive tool that links movement of the surgeon's hand with the view of the brain presented on the computer screen. This localization device can help the surgeon visualize the position of major blood vessels and other brain structures that the surgeon will want to avoid during surgery. It also permits the surgeon to assess how much tumor remains hidden during surgery to remove a brain tumor. The main benefit of neuronavigational systems is that their use reduces the size of the craniotomy (skull flap) and the amount of brain tissue that is disturbed during surgery.

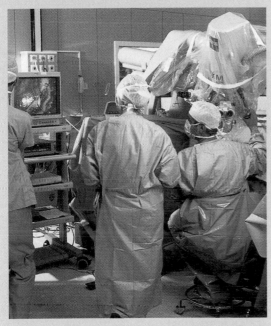

Surgeon views computer monitor to ascertain position of the localization probe in the brain.

Close up of the surgery to remove the tumor.

More recently, investigators have used **neurotoxins** to make functional lesions. Neurotoxins are chemicals that target specific neurons and interfere with the synthesis of a particular neurotransmitter, effectively depleting that neurotransmitter. To produce such a lesion, a specific neurotoxin is administered to a particular area of the brain by means of a cannula. For example, *6-hydroxydopamine* (6-OHDA) is a neurotoxin that destroys dopamine-containing neurons. When applied to the *substantia nigra* (a structure that contains dopamine-producing neurons), 6-OHDA kills dopamine-producing neurons, thus preventing the synthesis and release of dopamine. As a result, neurons in the basal ganglia do not receive stimulation from dopamine and do not function properly, producing a movement disorder that resembles Parkinson's disease (Blum et al., 2001; Tillerson et al., 2001; Tseng et al., 2001). Thus, 6-OHDA can be used to produce Parkinson's disease in laboratory animals, which allows investigators to study the development and treatment of Parkinson's disease in the laboratory.

The most modern subcortical lesioning techniques employ converging beams of ionizing radiation in procedures involving the gamma knife, the cyclotron, or linear accelerators. The area to be lesioned is located stereotaxically, and the lesioning rays focused on that precise area of the brain. This noninvasive technique is preferred for producing lesions in human brains because the overlying and

neurotoxins: chemicals that target and destroy specific neurons

surrounding brain tissues are unaffected by the penetrating radiation. Only at the point where the rays come together does tissue destruction occur.

Remember that neurons do not typically grow back after they have been destroyed. Therefore, exposing brain tissue to DC electricity, RF waves, ionizing radiation, toxic chemicals, or freezing cryoprobes produces permanent damage to the brain. *Temporary lesions* can be produced in one of two ways: (1) injecting a potassium chloride (KCl) solution into a stereotaxically implanted cannula aimed at the brain region under study, or (2) cooling the brain area below 25°C (but not below freezing) using a cryoprobe. In either case, after the KCl has been absorbed into the bloodstream, or after the brain has been permitted to warm to body temperature (about 37°C), brain functioning returns to normal.

Figure 5.4 The gamma knife hemisphere
In the gamma knife procedure, the patient's head is placed into a fixed helmet, which delivers 201 converging beams of gamma radiation. Each individual beam is very weak and cannot damage brain tissue. Tissue destruction occurs where the beams converge and meet.

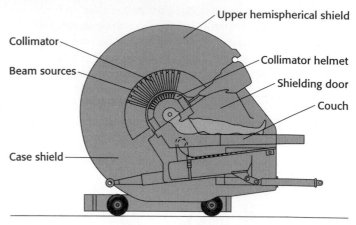

Upper hemispherical shield
Collimator
Beam sources
Collimator helmet
Shielding door
Couch
Case shield

Brain Stimulation

Brain lesioning is an indirect method for determining the function of a specific area of the brain. An investigator can only infer the function of a particular brain region when observing a subject with a lesion in that region. For example, a subject might appear to be blind following a brain lesion, and the investigator might conclude that a brain region involved in visual processing was destroyed. It could be, however, that the visual processing center works perfectly fine but that attentional processes have been altered. That is, the subject might be unable to respond to visual stimuli because it can no longer pay attention to stimuli.

Stimulation of the brain is a more direct method of assessing the functions of specific brain regions. The stimulation method involves causing a part of the brain to become active. This can be accomplished either by excitatory chemicals injected into the brain via cannulas or by electrodes conducting alternating current (AC) electricity. The earliest investigators, like Fritsch and Hitzig, who stimulated the brains of dogs (discussed in Chapter 1), studied the effects of stimulation in anesthetized subjects. While a dog was unconscious, they opened its skull and touched electrodes to the surface of the motor cortex, passing a stimulating electrical current into the brain and noting contractions of the dog's muscles.

Obviously, the amount of information to be gained from the stimulation of brains of immobile, unconscious subjects is quite limited. In 1896, another German investigator, Ewald, developed a technique in which electrodes were permanently attached to the skull using ivory screws. The electrodes were implanted during a surgical procedure in which the subject was anesthetized, and electricity was passed through the electrodes after the subject had fully recovered from the surgery. This new development permitted Ewald to stimulate the brains of fully awake dogs that were restrained only by a leash (Valenstein, 1973).

Subcortical brain stimulation became possible following the invention of the stereotaxic instrument. Electrodes were implanted stereotaxically in anesthetized subjects and anchored to their skulls; electrical stimulation was performed after the subjects regained consciousness (Figure 5.5). Stimulation of deep brain structures produced behaviors that were strikingly different from those produced by stimulation of the cortex. In the United States, much of the pioneering brain stimulation research was conducted in fully awake

stimulation: a method of studying the brain that involves causing a part of the brain to become active

Figure 5.5 Rat with implanted electrode

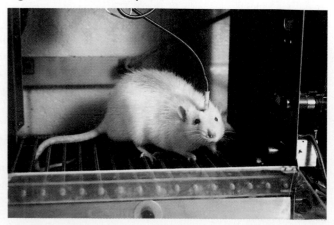

human subjects in the 1940s and 1950s. Electrical stimulation of subcortical structures was studied in patients with epilepsy, chronic schizophrenia, or movement disorders, such as tics or spasticity (Ramey & O'Doherty, 1960).

A new stimulation technique, called **transcranial magnetic stimulation,** is noninvasive and does not require surgery. With this procedure, magnetic impulses are delivered to the brain via coils that do not touch the head. Transcranial magnetic stimulation permits the investigator to directly stimulate neurons in the cerebral cortex (Civardi et al., 2001; DiLazzaro et al., 2001; George, Wasserman, & Post, 1996; Rosler, 2001). Thus far, it has been used to map functions, such as movement, attention, speech, and vision, on the cortex.

transcranial magnetic stimulation: a noninvasive treatment for depression that involves directly stimulating neurons in the cerebral cortex

---

Recap 5.1: Brain Lesions and Brain Stimulation

(a)_____ involves disrupting the function of a particular area of the brain. (b)_____ involves removing a part of the brain. A (c)_____ technique is used today by neurosurgeons and neuroscience investigators to remove brain matter. To produce a subcortical lesion, the subcortical structure must be located using a (d)_____ brain atlas and (e)_____ instrument. Subcortical lesions can be made using an (f)_____ or cannula, which are inserted into the brain. Lesions can be made with chemicals that target specific neurons, called (g)_____. Permanent damage to brain structures can be produced by exposing the brain to direct current (DC) electricity, radio frequency (RF) waves, ionizing radiation, neurotoxins, or freezing cryoprobes. (h)_____ involves causing a part of the brain to become active and can be accomplished by excitatory chemicals or by alternating current (AC) electricity. (i)_____ _____ stimulation is a noninvasive technique that directly stimulates neurons in the cerebral cortex.

Recording Brain Activity

Brain lesioning and stimulation experiments have provided much information about the localization of function in the brain. A newer technique, **recording** of the brain, has enabled investigators to pinpoint active brain regions in a normally functioning human brain. The earliest brain recordings were conducted by Richard Caton, who was David Ferrier's classmate in medical school in Scotland (Spillane, 1981). Using a galvanometer, which measures small electrical currents, he measured the electrical activity in the brains of rabbits and monkeys while these subjects were exposed to flashing lights, sounds, smells, and tactile stimulation. He noted that the brain's response varied depending on whether the subject was awake or asleep and that the electrical activity ceased at death.

recording: a method of studying the brain that enables investigators to pinpoint active brain regions

Electroencephalography

The Austrian psychiatrist Hans Berger is usually credited with the development of **electroencephalography** (EEG). In 1924, using his young son as his subject, he pasted two pieces of silver foil on his son's scalp, attached wires to the foil, and connected the wires to a galvanometer. Berger recorded the galvanometer's response on a roll of paper and observed that his son's brain emitted a rhythmic electrical signal, which he termed the "alpha rhythm." The alpha rhythm disappeared whenever his son concentrated on arithmetic problems, demonstrating that these rhythms reflected underlying brain processes.

electroencephalography: a recording technique that measures the electrical activity of the brain

At first, scientists and the general public alike believed that electroencephalography would enable scientists to "read minds." However, even with great technological advances in the second half of the 20th century, these electrical brain records, or electroencephalograms (EEGs), have not unlocked the secrets of the billions of cells located beneath the skull. First, the electrical signal coming from the brain is very weak, measured in hundred-thousandths of volts. Second, most EEG investigators use scalp electrodes (Figure 5.6), which are disks of precious metal, usually gold or platinum, that are positioned on the subject's scalp. These scalp electrodes pick up signals from millions of brain cells, which makes interpretation of function difficult.

Computer technology has been coupled with electroencephalography to make EEGs more useful to investigators. The computer permits high-speed processing of the recorded electrical activity, which enables investigators to measure brain responses in milliseconds, or thousandths of seconds. In the **evoked potential** or **event-related potential** (ERP) procedure, EEG responses are recorded by a computer while a subject is presented with the same stimulus over many trials or performs the same task repeatedly. For example, the subject might be shown patterns of flashing lights and asked to identify the pattern. The computer analysis of the EEGs indicates the timing and location of the brain's response to the flashing pattern and also the timing and location of brain activity when the subject identifies the pattern.

Figure 5.7 illustrates a computer-generated image of patterns of EEG activity in right-handed men responding to numeric stimuli (Gevins et al., 1987). These human subjects were instructed to press a button with precise pressure (0.1 to 0.9 kg) in response to visual stimuli, the numbers 1 to 9. For each trial, the subject was presented with a 300-millisecond cue that indicated whether the right or left hand was to be used. One second later the numeric stimulus (1 to 9) was presented, and the subject pressed the button with the force indicated by the stimulus. The electrical activity of brain cells was recorded by 26 electrodes placed on the scalp and analyzed by a computer for patterns of response.

You can see in Figure 5.7 that the brain activity is quite different during the period between the cue and the numeric stimulus, when the subject is preparing to respond, depending on whether the subject used his right or left hand and depending on whether the subject made a correct or incorrect response. For the right or dominant hand, many areas of the left cortex appear to be working together when the subject makes an accurate response, but very little coordinated brain activity occurs when the right hand makes an inaccurate response. With the left or nondominant hand, the pattern is different. When correct responses are made by the left hand, coordinated brain activity is recorded in specific regions of the right and left cortex; incorrect responses by the left hand are accompanied by complex, *bilateral* brain patterns.

Some brain scientists have used **microelectrodes** (very tiny electrodes that can be inserted into individual neurons) to record from one neuron at a time. Single-cell recording with microelectrodes has provided investigators with precise information about the function of particular neurons in specific areas of the brain. For example, some cells deep in the brain fire rapidly when cocaine is administered, and others in the same region suppress their activity when cocaine is administered (Pederson, Wolske, Peoples, & West, 1997).

Typically, however, single-cell recording by microelectrodes inserted directly into a neuron is an **in vitro** procedure, which means that the recordings are conducted in cultured cells in a dish on the laboratory bench. (Techniques that are performed on tissues or nonliving specimens are called *in vitro* techniques, whereas those that are performed on living animals are referred to as *in vivo* techniques.) In an **in vivo** study, single-cell recording is normally done in anesthetized or unconscious subjects—*not* in awake, freely moving animals. In conscious, unrestrained subjects, *extracellular* microelectrodes are used to record single-cell electrical activity. That

Figure 5.6 Scalp electrodes
Electrodes are taped on the scalp of a human subject.

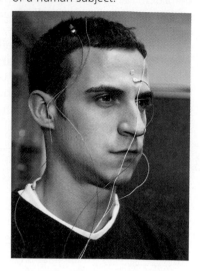

evoked potential: a type of event-related potential, or a change in recorded brain activity as measured by EEG, produced in response to a specific stimulus

event-related potential: measured change in brain activity following the presentation of a stimulus

Figure 5.7 Computer-generated EEG image
These images show that when a right-handed man makes a correct response with his dominant (right) hand, the left cerebral cortex is active in preparing his response. When the left hand is used, activity in both hemispheres is recorded.

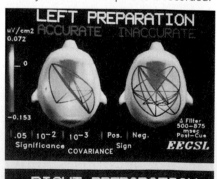

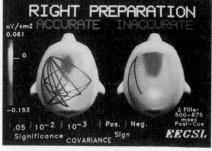

is, an *intracellular* placement of a microelectrode is a very fragile preparation that cannot be preserved in a freely moving animal. Therefore, in an awake animal engaging in a behavior, single-cell recordings are done extracellularly (Ludvig et al., 2000).

Another type of single-cell recording is the **voltage clamp technique.** This procedure is always conducted in vitro and is used to study the activity of voltage-gated ion channels. The voltage clamp technique permits investigators to hold the membrane at a particular voltage or membrane potential. By setting the membrane potential at various voltages, investigators can measure ion currents at these different voltages.

Imaging Techniques

Other, more modern technologies have been developed to enable scientists to measure brain activity. These include **magnetoenccphalography** (MEG), **computed tomography** (CT), **single photon emission computed tomography** (SPECT), **positron emission tomography** (PET), and **functional magnetic resonance imaging** (fMRI). Table 5.1 summarizes the strengths and weaknesses of each neuroimaging technique.

Magnetoencephalography

This relatively new technique, developed by David Cohen in 1968, enables investigators to measure the magnetic fields generated by active brain cells. Just as an electric current flowing through a wire produces a magnetic field, so do the incredibly small electrical currents generated by neurons also produce tiny magnetic fields. These magnetic fields are measured using dozens of antenna coils that are mounted in a "captor," which is lowered over the subject's head (Figure 5.8). A superconducting quantum interference device (SQUID), which can detect minuscule magnetic fields, is used to measure the magnetic fields generated by neurons. At first, there were great hopes for the applicability of the MEG technique, in research

microelectrode: tiny electrode used to measure the electrical activity of individual neurons

in vitro: in cultured cells on a lab bench

in vivo: in a living body

voltage clamp technique: an in vitro technique used to study the activity of voltage-gated ion channels

magnetoencephalography: a recording technique that measures magnetic fields generated by the brain

computed tomography (CT): a recording technique that provides a three-dimensional image of the brain as a result of passing a series of X rays through the head at various angles

single photon emission computed tomography (SPECT): a recording technique that is an extension of the CT technique and is used to localize the highest concentrations of photon-emitting isotopes in the brain, which are associated with brain activity

positron emission tomography (PET): a recording technique that is used to localize the source of positrons emitted from radioactive isotopes in the brain, which is associated with brain activity

functional magnetic resonance imaging (fMRI): a recording technique that is based on MRI technology and permits localization of accumulation of oxygenated hemoglobin in the brain, which is associated with brain activity

Table 5.1

Comparison of Brain-Imaging Techniques

Technique	Benefits	Drawbacks
EEG	Noninvasive; relatively low cost of equipment; accurately records brain activity within milliseconds	Difficult to localize exact source of electrical activity; some distortion as electrical currents pass through skull
MEG	Noninvasive; no distortion as magnetic fields pass through bone; accurately records brain activity within milliseconds	Expensive equipment; does not allow precise localization of brain activity; cannot pick up deep signals in brain
SPECT	Better than EEG or MEG in localizing brain activity; cheaper than PET imaging	Requires administration of a radioisotope; time lag >20 seconds; can't be used in studies of cognition
PET	Better localization of brain activity than SPECT; can be used to localize specific neurotransmitter receptors in the brain	Extremely expensive radioisotopes required; some health risk associated with radioisotopes; time lag >1 minute
fMRI	Noninvasive; precise localization of brain activity; less expensive than PET; time lag <1 second, better than PET	Time lag does not permit study of cognitive processes; instruments not yet standardized; subject must be still

and in the clinic. Investigators hailed MEG as much better at localization of brain activity than is EEG (Hari & Lounasmaa, 1989). Research by Cohen, "the father of MEG," however, demonstrated that MEG is no better at localization than is EEG (Cohen et al., 1990).

Like the EEG technique, MEG accurately records brain activity within milliseconds. It is superior to EEG because magnetic fields can pass easily through bone and skin without distortion, and electrical currents cannot. However, like the EEG, the MEG does not allow precise localization of brain activity. And, MEG is very expensive, requiring much more costly instrumentation than does EEG. Whereas EEG is capable of measuring electrical signals from the cortex and from brain stem regions, MEG cannot pick up signals from deep within the brain. Therefore, EEG is preferred by most investigators today (Crease, 1991; Wheless et al., 1999).

Figure 5.8 MEG captor lowered over subject's head

Computed Tomography

Also known as computerized axial tomography or computer-assisted tomography (CAT), the computed tomography (CT) scan provides a three-dimensional image of the brain. Tomography involves passing X rays through the head at various angles and obtaining a large number of two-dimensional X-ray images or slices, which are then converted into a three-dimensional image by the computer. First introduced in 1973 by South African physicist Allan Cormack and British engineer Sir Godfrey Hounsfield, this method is used to establish links between behavior and specific brain regions (Raichle, 1994b). If a person is having visual difficulties, for example, and a lesion near the back of the head is detected on the CT scan, we infer that this region of the brain is involved with visual processes. Figure 5.9 is a CT scan of a patient who has dementia.

CT, like all X-ray images, works best for hard tissue, such as bone. The brain is soft tissue and, hence, does not image well with this method. A dye that is radiopaque (that is, a dye that does not allow X rays to pass through it) is injected into the vein of an individual before a CT scan. The dye is pumped through the blood vessels throughout the entire body and coats the walls of these blood vessels. A CT scan of the brain, then, shows the distribution of blood vessels in the brain. A tumor or other abnormality appears as a disruption in the normal pattern of blood vessels.

Figure 5.9 CT scan of a patient with dementia
The ventricles are enlarged and the cerebral cortex has deteriorated, producing deep sulci.

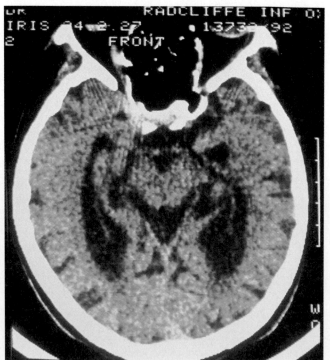

Single Photon Emission Computed Tomography

SPECT is an extension of the CT technique. In the SPECT technique, the subject is injected with an isotope that emits single photons, such as ^{123}I, an isotope of iodine. The radioisotope is then transported in the bloodstream to the subject's brain. Because *blood flow is increased in active parts of the brain*, active regions will contain the highest concentration of photon-emitting isotopes. The location of these emitted photons is detected with a scanner, enabling investigators to measure blood flow in the brain (Figure 5.10). SPECT is useful for localizing brain activity and does a better job at localization than EEG or MEG (Ricker & Zafonte, 2000). But, it has a time lag of over 20 seconds, much slower than EEG or MEG, and is therefore not terribly useful for processing cognitive activities, which take fractions of seconds to occur.

Positron Emission Tomography

Many investigators use PET scans in their studies of brain function because the images produced by PET are much more detailed and, hence, provide more information than do SPECT scans. In the PET technique, the subject either inhales a positron-emitting radioactive isotope or is injected with a radioactive isotope bound to glucose or water. The radioisotopes most commonly used in PET are ^{15}O, ^{11}C, and ^{18}F, which are isotopes of oxygen, carbon, and fluoride, respectively (Grasby, Malizia, & Bench, 1996). Remember that blood flow in the brain is increased in those regions that are most active. This means that active regions contain the most radioactive isotopes and release the most radiation. A detection device is placed around the subject's head while the subject is performing a task, such as looking at a word or pointing to a stimulus. As the subject participates in the task, certain brain areas become active, and blood flow increases in those areas. Positrons that are emitted from the radioactive isotopes collide with electrons and are annihilated, producing two photons (or gamma rays) that go off in opposite directions and are measured by the detection device. The gamma-ray detection device sends the information to a computer, which produces detailed images of the areas of activity in the brain.

When studying the use of PET to determine brain function, the **paired-image subtraction method** is employed (Raichle, 1994a). Typically, a subject is asked to perform a control task, such as gazing at a fixation point, and a PET image is generated as the subject gazes at the point. Then the subject is directed to view a more complicated visual stimulus, like a word, and another PET scan is done. The images obtained during the control task are subtracted from those generated during the second task to produce an image in which the shared areas of brain activity between the two tasks are cancelled out. Only the brain regions uniquely activated by the second task are displayed in the resulting image (Figure 5.11).

Studies that utilize PET technology are producing a wealth of information about how the brain divides its work. One example is a recent experiment by Haxby and his colleagues (1996) at the National Institute of Mental Health, in which they studied changes in cerebral blood flow associated with encoding and recognizing a face. In this experiment, 10 healthy young men and women were asked to perform four tasks: face encoding, face recognition, face perception control, and sensorimotor control tasks. On the face-encoding task, the subjects were instructed to commit 32 faces to memory and told that they would be tested for recognition of these faces later. On the face-recognition task, subjects were asked to identify faces that they had memorized. The other two tasks were control tasks, and the PET images obtained during the performance of these tasks were subtracted from the images obtained during face encoding and recognition. The results were striking (Figure 5.12). During face

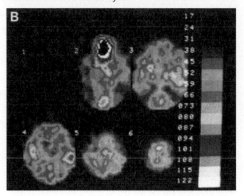

Figure 5.10 SPECT image
This image of an elderly man with Alzheimer's shows large areas of the cortex as blue or black, indicating areas of reduced brain activity.

paired-image subtraction method: an analytical method used in functional brain imaging in which an image obtained while a subject is engaged in a control task is subtracted from an image obtained while the same subject performs a behavior of interest, producing an image that indicates the brain areas uniquely activated by the behavior of interest

Figure 5.11 Paired-image subtraction method
In this method a difference image is obtained by subtracting the PET scan of a control state from that of a task state (top row). Images from different subjects are averaged to obtain a mean difference image.

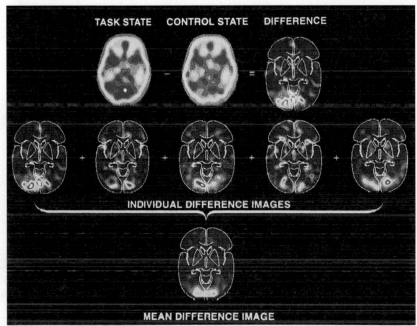

TASK STATE   CONTROL STATE   DIFFERENCE

INDIVIDUAL DIFFERENCE IMAGES

MEAN DIFFERENCE IMAGE

encoding, when the subjects were memorizing the faces, the *left* prefrontal cortex was activated. In contrast, the *right* prefrontal cortex was activated during the face-recognition task.

More recently, the PET technique has been modified to allow study of neurotransmitter systems in the brain (Laruelle & Huang, 2001). Investigators have developed chemicals tagged with a radioactive element that are capable of binding with specific types of receptors. These chemicals, called **radioligands,** allow investigators to study the location and density of different types of neurotransmitter receptors. Other radioactive-labeled compounds bind directly with substances in the brain and provide an indication of the presence of various substances in the brain. For example, Figure 5.13 illustrates PET scans from the brains of a cigarette smoker and a nonsmoker who have been administered a chemical, labeled with a radioactive element, that binds to a brain enzyme called MAO-B. MAO-B is an enzyme that breaks down dopamine, a neurotransmitter that is associated with pleasure and reward. As you can see in Figure 5.13, MAO-B activity is very much reduced in the brain of a smoker compared to that of a nonsmoker, which means that dopamine activity is most likely increased in the brains of smokers.

We will examine many more applications of PET imaging in behavioral research in later chapters of this book. The information to be gained from PET studies is important, but unfortunately it is an extremely costly technique. For example, the radioactive isotopes used in PET are very expensive to produce. Very few radioactive isotopes release positrons; most release photons, which makes SPECT a cheaper technique to use. Also, using these isotopes puts the subject and experimenter at considerable health risk, and their use is limited by federal guidelines, which does not make repeated trials on the same subject feasible. PET scans are better at localizing brain functions than are SPECT scans because two photons are produced with each positron emitted, making localization more precise. However, like SPECT, PET cannot accurately record the time course of many cognitive activities. It takes minutes to make a PET image, and most cognitive functions occur in less than a second.

Functional Magnetic Resonance Imaging

Developed in 1990 by Seiji Ogawa and his colleagues at Bell Laboratories, fMRI is a measurement technique that is based on conventional magnetic resonance imaging (MRI) technology (Belliveau et al., 1991; Savoy, 2001). Whereas MRI is used to produce detailed, static images of the brain, fMRI permits measurement of blood flow through a brain region, which is an indicator of activity in that region. The fMRI technique is designed to detect the differences between oxygenated and deoxygenated blood, based on the fact that hemoglobin carrying oxygen has different magnetic properties than deoxygenated hemoglobin. The strange thing about neurons is that they increase their glucose consumption when active, but not their oxygen consumption. This means that, when blood flow through an active brain region increases, oxygenated hemoglobin builds up

Figure 5.12 PET activation image
Haxby and his colleagues (1996) demonstrated in this PET study that the left prefrontal cortex is activated when human participants *memorize* faces. The right prefrontal cortex is activated when they *recognize* human faces.

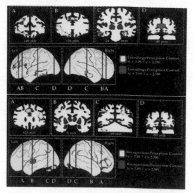

radioligands: chemicals tagged with a radioactive element that bind with specific receptors

Figure 5.13 PET scan showing reduced MAO-B in the brains of cigarette smokers
Yellow and red in this PET scan indicate high levels of MAO-B activity. In a healthy nonsmoker, MAO-B activity is quite high. MAO-B activity is reduced in the brain of a cigarette smoker.

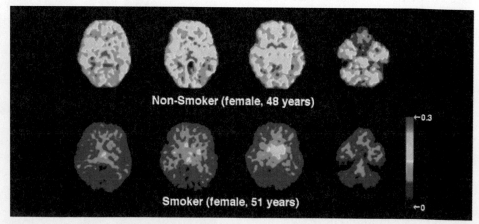

in the blood vessels. Functional MRI detects this increase in blood oxygen and thus is able to pinpoint active brain regions. As with the PET technique, a control image is produced while the subject engages in a passive control activity and is compared to successive images obtained while the subject participates in a task.

Figure 5.14 is an fMRI image showing the location of a region that processes language in the brain of a 9-year-old boy (Benson et al., 1996). As you can see, the images produced by fMRI are as detailed as PET scans, and fMRI has many advantages over PET. For example, the fMRI technique is noninvasive and does not require administration of radioactive chemicals, which means that subjects can be tested repeatedly, without risk of exposing the subjects to radiation. Functional MRI is also a less expensive technique to use than PET. Moreover, fMRI has a time lag of about a second (Stehling, Turner, & Mansfield, 1991), which is far superior to that of PET. EEG and MEG are capable of recording brain activity within milliseconds of its occurrence and, hence, provide a more accurate measure of the time course of brain activity than does fMRI. However, fMRI is much better for localization studies than are EEG or MEG.

The main disadvantage of the fMRI technique is that the instruments and measuring techniques have yet to be standardized (Raichle, 1994a). It appears that fMRI studies require instruments with higher magnetic field strength than standard MRI scanners used in hospitals, but there is little agreement among investigators as to the field strength requirements (Savoy, 2001). For fMRI experiments, the subject's entire body must be placed into the scanner, which is shaped like a narrow tube. As a result, some subjects become claustrophobic and uncomfortable during fMRI studies. Any movement by the subject destroys the image being produced, so the subject must lie very still, which increases the subject's discomfort and renders impossible the study of behaviors involving movement of the head, such as speaking. The type of study conducted in the fMRI scanner is also limited by the high magnetic field in the scanner. For example, the instruments used to present stimuli to subjects in PET studies cannot be used in the magnetic environment of the fMRI scanner.

Microdialysis

Neuroscientists employing bottom-up research strategies have their own recording techniques. One of the most widely used of these techniques is **microdialysis,** introduced in 1966 (Bito, Davson, Levin, Murray, & Snider, 1966), which involves the sampling of brain chemicals in live, active subjects. Microdialysis, then, is an in vivo technique in which a tube-shaped probe is inserted, with the aid of a stereotaxic instrument, into the region of the brain under investigation. At the tip of the probe is a

microdialysis: an in vivo technique that permits sampling of brain chemicals

Figure 5.14 fMRI images of language production in 9-year-old boy

When a 9-year-old boy thought of words beginning with a particular letter (Letter Fluency Task) or read words silently, the left hemisphere was activated more than the right. (Yellow indicates areas of highest activation.)

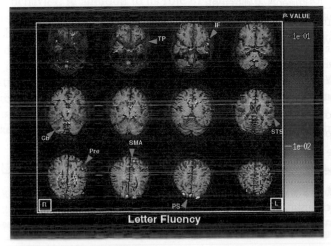

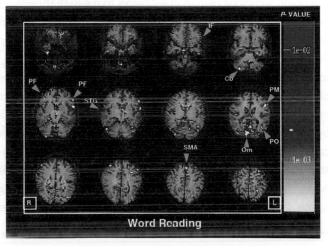

response to "foreign" substances and the antibodies' tendency to attack these substances when they are encountered. In immunocytochemistry, antibodies can be raised against any cellular component that the investigator chooses to study, including an enzyme, a neurotransmitter, or a particular molecule on the cell membrane. Histological techniques involve the microscopic examination of tissues and cells, typically using special stains designed to highlight cells of interest. The chemical techniques used in immunocytochemistry typically are sophisticated procedures that are sensitive to the biological properties of the cells under study and allow measurement or identification of a particular substance. Immunocytochemistry is a powerful technique that is used to map the brain chemically. That is, it is used to identify the pathways associated with various chemicals, such as neurotransmitters or specific receptors.

One immunocytochemical procedure involves the use of **c-*fos***, a protein produced in the soma of neurons following excitation of the neuron (Sagar, Sharp, & Curran, 1988). In this procedure, the brains of animals that have received a particular type of stimulation are compared to those that have received no stimulation. Those animals that receive the experimental stimulation will have c-*fos* in the neurons that are excited by the stimulation. For example, Neophytou and his colleagues (2000) compared the distribution of c-*fos* expression in the brains of two strains of rats that show different responses to high-frequency sounds. When exposed to a continuous, high-frequency (20,000 Hz) sound, Lister rats (white rats with black hoods) show escape behavior by running away. However, Wistar (albino) rats do not run but freeze immediately when the high-frequency sound is turned on. Immunocytochemical analysis of c-*fos* expression in the brains of these rats following exposure to the high-frequency sound revealed that c-*fos* was present in different brain areas in the two strains. In the Lister rats, c-*fos* was found in the *dorsal* region of the periaqueductal gray, which means that the dorsal periaqueductal gray was activated in this strain when they were exposed to high-frequency sounds. In contrast, c-*fos* was present in the *ventral* periaqueductal gray region of Wistar rats following exposure to high-frequency sounds. Thus, this c-*fos* study demonstrates that different areas of the brain are associated with escape-versus-freezing behaviors.

c-fos: a protein produced in a neuron following excitation of the neuron

Chromatography

Chromatography is a type of chemical analysis that permits investigators to isolate, identify, and measure a specific substance. A mixture of compounds (for example, extracellular fluid extracted from the brain) is separated into its components by passing the liquid, called the *mobile phase*, through a *stationary phase*, which is typically a column of porous solid material. Because substances with different chemical compositions travel at different speeds through the column, the different substances spread out along the column and are thus separated from each other. The substance under study is then collected from the column for further analysis.

chromatography: a type of chemical analysis that permits the isolation, identification, and measurement of a specific chemical substance

The most widely used form of chromatography in neuroscience research is **high performance liquid chromatography** (usually called **HPLC**). Compared to classic chromatography, HPLC is more sensitive and has more resolution, which means it permits better separation of substances that are chemically similar. When HPLC is used, the mobile phase is pushed through the stationary phase under high pressure, causing rapid separation of the chemical compounds in the mobile phase. Electrochemical recordings are usually conducted after the separation is complete. These recordings allow investigators to measure the relative amounts of each compound in the mobile phase. This technique is typically used in conjunction with microdialysis studies to determine the identity of the substance that has been extracted from the brain.

high performance liquid chromatography (HPLC): a type of chromatography that is widely used in neuroscience research because of its great sensitivity

Neuroscientists who study behavior have many techniques and tools at their disposal to study the brain. Lesioning, stimulation, and recording techniques all have their distinct strengths and weaknesses. And, each contributes uniquely to our understanding of brain functioning. Lesioning tells us what happens when a particular region of the brain stops functioning. Stimulation demonstrates the behaviors that are produced when a particular region becomes activated. Together, lesioning and stimulation studies indicate which brain structures are critical for a particular function. By contrast, recording techniques disclose brain areas that participate in that function (Clarke, 1994).

Recap 5.3: Other Chemical Methods of Studying the Brain

(a)_____ is a labeling method in which a radioactively tagged chemical is injected into a specific brain region in order to trace pathways in the brain from the soma of neurons to the endplates of their axons. Horseradish peroxidase is an enzyme that permits both anterograde and (b)_____ tracing. Immunocytochemistry uses immunological, (c)_____, and chemical methods to trace brain activity from neuron to neuron. One procedure involves the use of c-fos, a chemical that is produced in neurons following (d)_____. (e)_____ is a type of chemical analysis that allows the isolation and identification of a substance.

Genetic Studies of Behavior

In Chapter 2, you learned about genes and chromosomes and their relationship to some behaviors. As investigators learn more and more about the human genome, we are becoming more aware of the important role that **genetics,** or the inheritance of genes, plays in the development of certain behavior disorders. You've already learned that Huntington's disease, for example, is inherited through a dominant gene. In later chapters, you'll encounter other disorders, such as schizophrenia and manic-depressive disorder, that also appear to have a genetic basis. Certainly, there is plenty of evidence that environment can also play a vital role in the development of a disorder, as you will learn in Chapter 16. Genetic analyses attempt to assess the extent of the effect that heredity plays in the genesis of a disorder.

genetics: the study of the inheritance of genes

In addition, genetic studies may try to determine how the disorder under study is inherited. Sometimes an individual possesses the gene that produces a certain characteristic but shows no observable sign of that characteristic. We use the terms **genotype** and **phenotype** to explain this situation. Genotype refers to the genes that an individual possesses and that are encoded in the individual's DNA. Phenotype refers to the expression of a gene as evidenced by the presence of an observable characteristic that is associated with that gene. For example, I can possess the gene for left-handedness without actually being left-handed. If I were left-handed (that is, if I used my left hand predominantly in motor activities involving my hands), I would possess the phenotype as well as the genotype for left-handedness. There are a number of models that attempt to explain the pathway from the genotype to the phenotype.

genotype: the genes that a person possesses
phenotype: the expression of a gene, in which an observable characteristic associated with the gene is present

Genetic Analysis

A number of methods are used to determine whether a disorder is hereditary. The first step usually involves **family studies,** which examine the rates of occurrence of a disorder within affected families. The number of first-degree relatives, which include parents, siblings, and offspring, with the disorder is considered especially

family studies: a type of genetic analysis that examines the rate of occurrence of a disorder within affected families

important. Family studies cannot tell us for certain that a disorder is inheritable because families also share environments as well as genetic backgrounds.

Twin studies permit us to compare rates of occurrence of a disorder in identical versus fraternal (nonidentical) twins. Identical, or *monozygotic*, twins develop from the same fertilized egg and therefore share the same genes (Figure 5.16). In contrast, fraternal twins are *dizygotic*, which means they develop from two different fertilized eggs, and they share about 50% of their genes, like other, nontwin siblings. In twin studies, investigators measure the *concordance rate*, which is the number of pairs of twins sharing the disorder divided by the total number of twin pair studies (Figure 5.16). Concordance rates in identical and fraternal twins are compared in twin studies because it is assumed that, whereas both identical and fraternal twins share the same environment, only identical twins share the same genes. If identical twins have a much greater concordance rate for a particular disorder than fraternal twins do, investigators conclude that there is strong evidence that genetics contributed to the development of the disorder. For example, Prescott, Aggen, and Kendler (1999) studied 1,546 pairs of identical and 2,551 pairs of nonidentical twins for rates of alcoholism and found a significantly higher concordance rate for identical twins compared to nonidentical twins. As a result, these investigators concluded that alcoholism has a major genetic component.

In **adoption studies,** investigators study children with a particular disorder who were raised by adoptive parents. Rates of occurrence of the disorder in the adoptive parents are compared with the occurrence rates of the same disorder in the biological parents, to measure the effect of nature (the genetic contribution of the biological parents) versus nurture (the contribution of the adoptive parents). If genetics plays an important role in the development of a disorder, the disorder should occur more in biological parents than in adoptive parents. For example, a number of studies have demonstrated that adopted children are much more likely to be alcoholic if their biological parents are alcoholic than if their adoptive parents are alcoholic, leading investigators again to conclude that genetic factors contribute to alcoholism (Sigvardsson, Bohman, & Cloninger, 1996).

Special statistical analyses have been developed to determine the location of genes related to the disorder. **Segregation analysis** allows the investigator to examine whether the pattern of inheritance of a disorder over several generations of a family agrees with a hypothetical pattern that would be expected if a particular mode of inheritance were true. For example, if a disorder was inherited through a dominant gene, we would expect that approximately 50% of the offspring would inherit the disorder. This is true in the case of Huntington's disease.

Another type of statistical genetic analysis is **linkage analysis.** This type of analysis makes use of a known **biological marker,** which is an abnormality associated with the disorder. In linkage analysis, investigators try to ascertain whether the gene associated with the biological marker is linked to or is part of the gene responsible for the disorder. The main purpose of this type of analysis is to determine the location of the gene or genes that produce the disorder.

Genetic Models

A number of models have been developed to explain the mode of inheritance of a disorder. These models can be classified as single gene or *monogenic* models, *polygenic* models, and *multifactorial* models.

The monogenic model was first proposed by Gregor Mendel in 1866, long before the discovery of genes and chromosomes. Mendel was a monk who tended

twin studies: a type of genetic analysis that compares the rates of occurrence of a disorder in identical versus fraternal twins

adoption studies: a type of genetic analysis that compares the rates of occurrence of a disorder in adoptive parents with the rates of occurrence of the disorder in biological parents

segregation analysis: a type of genetic analysis that examines whether the pattern of inheritance of a disorder in a family agrees with an expected pattern of inheritance

linkage analysis: a type of genetic analysis that studies whether a gene associated with a biological marker is linked to the gene responsible for the disorder

Figure 5.16 Twin studies
Twin studies compare concordance rates of a disorder in identical (bottom) versus fraternal (top) twins.

gardens in the monastery where he lived, and he studied plants as a hobby. When he crossed a tall pea plant with a short one, he was at first surprised that he got a tall plant, rather than a plant of medium height. After many years of study and a mountain of statistical calculations, Mendel concluded that the "tall" trait was dominant and that it masked the "short" trait. According to Mendel, a single gene produces a particular trait. For this reason, his model is called a single gene model. Most authorities agree that a single gene model cannot explain the inheritability of most disorders.

A polygenic model, on the other hand, proposes that a disorder is caused by several genes found in several different regions of different chromosomes. The model that has found the most acceptance is the multifactorial model. According to this model, a combination of genetic and environmental factors produces a disorder. This model assumes, like the polygenic model, that more than one gene is involved, but it also emphasizes the role of the environment, including prenatal influences, brain development, and psychosocial factors.

Behavioral Genetics

Investigators in the field of **behavioral genetics** study the genetic basis of behavior and attempt to apply this knowledge to the treatment of various behavioral and neurodegenerative disorders. They have developed a wealth of techniques that enables them to examine the role of specific genes in certain behaviors. Long-lasting changes in neuronal function, which are associated with learning and development, are controlled by the expression of particular genes. Recall from Chapter 3 that activation of a second messenger can cause certain genes to be expressed. Each gene controls a specific event within the neuron, which can affect behavior. The *Case Study* describes the case of a patient whose brain tumor was treated with experimental gene therapy.

One widely used technique, called the **knockout model,** involves eliminating a single gene to determine its role in a particular behavior. To study a behavior, an intact, behaving animal is required. Therefore, in the knockout model, a whole animal (minus one gene) is tested to see if the absent gene affects the behavior under investigation. To obtain a knockout animal, a specific gene is cloned and altered to disable important regulatory regions of the gene. (Recall that genes consist of strings of nucleic acids. Interruption of the order of these nucleic acids will render the gene inoperable.) The altered gene is combined with the DNA of stem cells, which give rise to altered cells that lack the knockout gene. Crossbreeding of animals with the knockout gene will produce offspring (called *knockout mutants*) that lack the targeted gene.

Knockout technology has helped investigators determine the genetic basis of normal behaviors (such as learning, memory, feeding, and response to pain) and specific disorders, such as anxiety, depression, schizophrenia, Alzheimer's disease, and drug addiction (Crawley, 1999; Martinez & Derrick, 1996). For example, a particular opioid receptor, called the *mu-opioid receptor,* has been implicated in alcohol (or ethanol) self-administration and addiction. Amanda Roberts and her colleagues at the Scripps Research Institute compared the ethanol drinking behavior of normal mice with that of knockout mice that lacked the gene for the mu-opioid receptor (Roberts, McDonald, Heyser, Kieffer, Matthes, Koob, & Gold, 2000). Knockout mice that lack the gene for the mu-opioid receptor do not possess any mu-opioid receptors. These knockout mice showed an aversion to alcohol, refusing to barpress for it or drink it, whereas normal mice drank it readily. This finding indicates that endogenous opiates enhance the rewarding effects of ethanol.

biological markers: abnormalities shared by members of a particular sub-population that are presumed to be evidence of an underlying biological problem

behavioral genetics: a discipline that studies the genetic basis of behavior and attempts to apply this knowledge to the treatment of behavioral disorders

knockout model: a technique in which a single gene is eliminated to determine its role in a particular behavior

Gene Therapy for Treating Brain Tumors

Brad was 43 years old when he first noticed something was wrong with his left leg. At first, his leg felt weak and unable to support his body when he walked upstairs. Within a week, Brad walked with a pronounced limp. He soon began to have trouble walking across a room. At this point, Brad decided to see his physician.

Brad's physician was troubled by Brad's symptoms, and he ordered MRI scans of Brad's brain. The scans indicated a suspicious mass near the top of Brad's brain, in the area of the right motor cortex. Brad was then referred to a neuro-surgeon, who removed a walnut-sized tumor from his brain. A biopsy of the tumor revealed that it was an aggressive, fast-growing glioma. Brad was then given radia-tion treatment to kill any remaining cancerous cells that the surgeon might have left behind.

Brad's prognosis was quite poor. He was informed that the type of tumor found in his brain typically recurs within a year. The neurosurgeon told Brad about a number of experimental treatment programs around the nation,

including a gene therapy program at that hospital. After conferring with his wife and other family members, Brad elected to take part in the gene therapy treatment at his local medical center.

When the neurosurgeon removed Brad's glioma, the tumor was preserved for the experimental gene therapy treatment. Gliomas secrete a substance, called transform-ing growth factor-ß (TGF-ß), which suppresses the action of the immune system and enhances growth of the tumor. The first step of the treatment was to alter the tumor cells genetically by blocking the gene that codes for TGF-ß. Thus, the altered glioma cells suppress TGF-ß secretion. These genetically altered cells were cultured and then injected into Brad. Research with animals conducted by Habib Fakhrai and his colleagues (1996) has demonstrated that immunization with tumor cells altered to suppress the action of TGF-ß will eradicate any remaining glioma cells. Thus far, Brad has survived for over 2 years with no signs of recurring tumor.

Recap 5.4: Genetic Studies of Behavior

(a)_____ refers to the genes that are encoded in an individual's DNA, whereas (b)_____ refers to the expression of the gene that results in an observable charac-teristic. In genetic analysis, (c)_____ studies examine the rate of occurrence of a disorder within affected families, and (d)_____ studies examine the rate of occur-rence of a disorder in monozygotic versus dizygotic twins. Adoption studies compare the rate of the disorder in adoptive parents with the occurrence rates of the same disorder in (e)_____ parents. The (f)_____ model, proposed by Gregor Mendel, is also called a single gene model. According to a (g)_____ model, a disorder is caused by several genes found on different chromosomes. According to the (h)_____ model, a combination of genetic and environmental factors produce a disorder. The knockout model involves eliminating a single (i)_____ in a living ani-mal to determine its role in a particular behavior.

Experimental Design

In this chapter, you have learned about a wide variety of techniques used to study the brain and behavior. We've examined surgical techniques, like brain lesioning and stimulation, and we've discussed the neurobehavioral applications of the most modern imaging, chemical, and behavioral genetic techniques. To derive useful information from the application of these techniques, psychologists and other investigators employ rigorous experimental standards when they design experi-ments and collect data. In this section, we will review standard protocols used when studying the relationship between the brain and behavior.

An experiment is only as good as its design. In order to get useful, valid results, an experiment must be well designed. However, not all investigators conduct experiments as they attempt to draw connections between the brain and behavior. Some researchers make use of **case studies,** in which one or more patients are thoroughly examined for behavioral disorders and associated brain abnormalities. Case studies yield valuable information, but experiments allow investigators to control and manipulate variables, which permits them to draw conclusions about the cause and effect of the variables.

Investigators follow a number of general rules when designing experiments. For example, when studying the effect of a particular treatment, the behavior of the subjects who receive the treatment should always be compared to the behavior of **control subjects,** who do not receive the treatment. Furthermore, the control subjects should be matched as closely as possible to the *experimental subjects*, that is, the subjects who receive the treatment, in terms of age, gender, intelligence, medical history, socioeconomic status, and education level. The choice of control subjects is tricky when studying a population with a particular type of disorder. When studying a hospitalized population with schizophrenia, for example, the proper control group is most likely another hospitalized population, rather than a group of healthy control subjects.

Double Blind Studies

In studies with a repeated measures design, in which the participant receives the treatment on some trials but not on others, it is best if both the participant and the experimenter are unaware of whether the treatment is being administered. For example, if a drug for pain relief is being tested, participants in the experiment might imagine that they feel pain relief if they believe that they are receiving a pain medication. The experimenter would have certain expectations, too, if he or she knew that a pain relief medication was administered to the subject. Therefore, a **double blind study** is usually conducted in which both the participant and the investigator are blind to the treatment. Neither the participant nor the investigator knows what the participant is getting in a double blind study.

In a double blind study, a second experimenter, or a research assistant, packages and labels the drugs to be administered with a secret code, and only this person knows whether the participant is actually receiving the *test drug* (the medication being tested) or a **placebo** (an inactive compound that is packaged to look just like the test drug). The principal (or blind) experimenter collects data from the participants during all trials, and at the end of the study, the secret code is given to this experimenter, which allows the experimenter to determine if the test drug produced different results from the placebo.

When testing the efficacy of a drug or other treatment, the best design involves a **crossover** procedure, in which all groups of subjects sometimes receive the treatment under study at one time and receive the control condition (or placebo) at another time. A *double blind, crossover study* is considered to be the gold standard in experimental design because this type of experiment combines the benefits of a double blind study with those of a crossover design. In a double blind, crossover study, all participants receive the experimental treatment and the control treatment at different times during the study, but neither the experimenter nor the participants know which treatment is being administered at any time.

However, when a surgical manipulation is used, a crossover design is usually impossible to use because the investigator cannot reverse the surgery. Surgeries that involve the removal of an organ or other tissue in the body typically end with the suffix *-ectomy*, as in *gonadectomy*, or removal of the gonads. In contrast, surgeries that involve cutting through body tissues are given the suffix *-otomy*, such as *vagotomy*, a procedure in which the vagus nerve is severed. The appropriate control group in studies that involve these types of irreversible surgeries are **sham-operated controls.** A sham operated control is a control subject that receives the same surgical preparation, anesthesia, and incision that the experimental subjects

case studies: a method of investigation in which one or more patients are thoroughly examined for behavioral disorders and associated brain abnormalities

control subjects: participants in a study who do not receive the treatment under investigation

double blind study: an experiment in which neither the participant nor the experimenter knows if the participant is getting the experimental treatment

placebo: an inactive compound that looks just like the test drug

crossover: a type of experimental procedure in which all subjects receive the treatment under study at some time during the experiment and receive the control condition (or placebo) at another time during the experiment

sham-operated control: a participant that undergoes surgery, like the experimental subject, but does not receive the experimental manipulation

Figure 5.17 Double dissociation study in rat subjects

Lesions of the fornix interfere with learning a spatial task, whereas striatal lesions interfere with learning a nonspatial task.

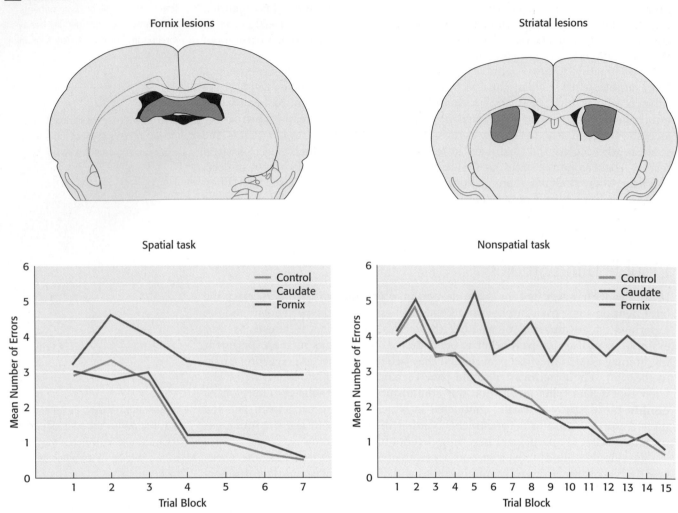

receive. The only difference is that the sham-operated control does not receive the experimental manipulation. For example, in a study of the effects of testosterone on memory in male rats, the experimental group would receive a gonadectomy, and the sham-operated control group would undergo the same surgery but would not have their testes removed.

Double Dissociation Studies

Brain-lesioning studies often make use of a special paradigm called **double dissociation.** In a double dissociation study, two groups of subjects receive lesions in different parts of the brain. After they recover from the surgery, the two groups of subjects are tested on two different behavioral tests. If the two lesioned brain areas mediate different behaviors, then the subjects in the two groups should show different deficits when tested on the different tasks.

For example, using a double dissociation design, Packard and McGaugh (1992) lesioned the brains of two groups of rats. One group received a lesion in an area of the brain called the *fornix*, and the other group received a lesion in the *striatal*. Rats were then tested on two tasks: a spatial task and a nonspatial task. Lesions of the fornix disrupted learning of a spatial task and didn't interfere with learning of the nonspatial task. In contrast, striatal lesions interfered with nonspatial learning but not spatial learning (Figure 5.17).

double dissociation: a type of experiment in which two groups of subjects receive lesions in different regions of the brain and are tested on two different behavioral tasks following recovery

In the following chapters, we will look at a number of behavioral phenomena including movement, sensation, sleep, thinking, memory, consummatory and sexual behavior, and emotions. When discussing each type of behavior, I will present the results of well-designed studies that have been published in peer-reviewed journals. Papers and reports that appear in peer-reviewed journals have been read and approved for publication by other investigators in the field. Reviewers for these journals carefully consider the appropriateness of the experimental design as well as the conclusions drawn before approving the paper for publication.

Recap 5.5: Experimental Design

In (a)_____ studies, one or more patients are thoroughly examined for behavioral disorders and associated brain abnormalities. In experiments in behavioral neuroscience, the behavior of subjects who receive the experimental treatment is compared to the behavior of (b)_____ subjects who do not receive the treatment. In a (c)_____ _____ study, both the subject and the experimenter are unaware of whether the treatment is being administered. In a (d)_____ study, all groups of subjects receive the treatment under study at one time and receive the control condition at another time. When a surgical manipulation is used in an experiment, (e)_____-_____ controls (control subjects that receive the same surgical preparation, anesthesia, and incision that experimental subjects receive) are required. In a (f)_____ _____ study, two groups of subjects receive lesions in two different brain regions and then are tested on two different behavioral tests.

Chapter Summary

Brain Lesions and Brain Stimulation

▶ The earliest techniques used to study the brain and behavior were brain lesioning and stimulation.

▶ Lesioning involves disrupting the function of a particular area of the brain. Ablations are typically performed to remove tissue from the cerebral cortex, whereas subcortical lesions are produced by direct current (DC) electricity, radio frequency current, ionizing radiation, cooling the brain, and neurotoxins and other chemicals.

▶ Brain stimulation involves causing a part of the brain to become active and can be accomplished using alternating current (AC) electricity, chemicals administered through a cannula, or transcranial magnetic stimulation.

Recording Brain Activity

▶ Brain activity can be recorded using electroencephalography (EEG), magnetoencephalography (MEG), single photon emission computed tomography (SPECT), positron emission tomography (PET), and functional magnetic resonance imaging (fMRI).

▶ Electroencephalography (EEG) permits recording the electrical activity of the brain. In the evoked potential

procedure, the timing and location of brain activity in response to a stimulus are identified.

▶ Magnetoencephalography (MEG) permits measuring the magnetic fields generated by active brain cells.

▶ Computed tomography (CT) provides three-dimensional images of the brain. Single photon emission computed tomography (SPECT) permits identification of active brain regions by detecting the emission of single photons from an injected radioisotope.

▶ Positron emission tomography (PET) provides detailed information about active brain areas, due to the release of positrons by the injected radioisotope used in PET imaging.

▶ Functional magnetic resonance imaging (fMRI) permits measurement of blood flow through a brain region, which is an indicator of brain activity in that region.

▶ Microdialysis involves sampling brain chemicals in live, active subjects.

Other Chemical Methods of Studying the Brain

▶ Autoradiography is a labeling method in which a radioactively tagged chemical is injected into a specific brain region in order to trace pathways in the brain from the soma of neurons to the endplates of their axons.

▶ Horseradish peroxidase is an enzyme that permits tracing of pathways in the brain.

▶ Immunocytochemistry uses immunological, histological, and chemical methods to trace brain activity from neuron to neuron.

▶ Chromatography is a type of chemical analysis that allows the isolation and identification of a substance.

Genetic Studies of Behavior

▶ Genetic studies, involving genetic analysis and genetic models, assess the effects of heredity in the development of a particular disorder and determine how a disorder is inherited.

▶ Genotype refers to the genes that are encoded in an individual's DNA, whereas phenotype refers to the expression of the gene that results in an observable characteristic.

▶ The monogenic model, proposed by Gregor Mendel, is also called a single gene model. According to the polygenic model, a disorder is caused by several genes found on different chromosomes. According to the multifactorial model, a combination of genetic and environmental factors produce a disorder.

▶ Behavioral genetics investigates the genetic basis of behavior, using a wealth of techniques, including knockout technology. The knockout model involves eliminating a single gene in a living animal to determine its role in a particular behavior.

Experimental Design

▶ In case studies, one or more patients are thoroughly examined for behavioral disorders and associated brain abnormalities.

▶ Rigorous experimental methods guarantee useful research data that permit investigators to draw conclusions about the cause and effect of specific biological and behavioral factors.

▶ In experiments in behavioral neuroscience, the behavior of subjects who receive the experimental treatment is compared to the behavior of control subjects who do not receive the treatment.

▶ In a double blind study, both the subject and the experimenter are unaware of whether the treatment is being administered.

▶ In a crossover study, all groups of subjects receive the treatment under study at one time and receive the control condition at another time.

▶ The use of control subjects and double blind, crossover procedures are required when testing the efficacy of a particular treatment or drug.

▶ Sham-operated controls are control subjects that receive the same surgical preparation, anesthesia, and incision that experimental subjects receive. In a double dissociation study, two groups of subjects receive lesions in different brain regions and then are tested on two different behavioral tests.

Key Terms

ablation (p. 121)
adoption studies (p. 136)
anterior (p. 121)
autoradiography (p. 133)
behavioral genetics (p. 137)
biological markers (p. 136)
c-*fos* (p. 134)
cannula (p. 122)
case studies (p. 139)
chromatography (p. 134)
computed tomography (CT) (p. 127)
control subjects (p. 139)
crossover (p. 139)
cryoprobe (p. 122)
double blind study (p. 139)
double dissociation (p. 140)
electrode (p. 121)
electroencephalography (EEG) (p. 125)
event-related potential (ERP) (p. 126)
evoked potential (p. 126)

family studies (p. 135)
functional magnetic resonance imaging (fMRI) (p. 127)
genetics (p. 135)
genotype (p. 135)
high performance liquid chromatography (HPLC) (p. 134)
horseradish peroxidase labeling (p. 133)
immunocytochemistry (p. 133)
in vitro (p. 126)
in vivo (p. 126)
inferior (p. 121)
knockout model (p. 137)
lateral (p. 121)
lesioning (p. 120)
linkage analysis (p. 136)
magnetoencephalography (MEG) (p. 127)
medial (p. 121)
microdialysis (p. 131)
microelectrode (p. 126)
neurotoxins (p. 123)

paired-image subtraction method (p. 129)
phenotype (p. 135)
placebo (p. 139)
positron emission tomography (PET) (p. 127)
posterior (p. 121)
radioligands (p. 130)
recording (p. 125)
segregation analysis (p. 136)
sham-operated controls (p. 139)
single photon emission computed tomography (SPECT) (p. 127)
stereotaxic brain atlas (p. 121)
stereotaxic instrument (p. 121)
stimulation (p. 124)
subcortical (p. 121)
superior (p. 121)
thermocautery (p. 121)
transcranial magnetic stimulation (p. 125)
twin studies (p. 136)
voltage clamp technique (p. 127)

Questions for Thought

1. What techniques might investigators use to study brain changes in Alzheimer's disease?
2. How might twin studies and family studies be used to investigate the influence of genes on alcoholic behavior?
3. Is the use of knockout technology ethical?

Questions for Review

1. How are subcortical brain lesions produced?
2. What are the benefits and drawbacks of EEG, MEG, SPECT, PET, and fMRI?
3. Distinguish among monogenic, polygenic, and multifactorial genetic models.

Suggested Readings

Belliveau, J. W., Kennedy, D. N., McKinstry, R. C., Buchbinder, B. R., Weisskoff, R. M., Cohen, M. S., Vevea, J. M., Brady, T. J., & Rosen, B. R. (1991). Functional mapping of the human visual cortex by magnetic resonance imaging. *Science, 254*, 716–719.

Bergman, H., Chertkow, H., Wolfson, C., Stern, J., Rush, C., Whitehead, V., & Dixon, R. (1997). HM-PAO (CERETEC) SPECT brain scanning in the diagnosis of Alzheimer's disease. *Journal of the American Geriatric Society, 45*, 15–20.

Penfield, W. (1975). *The mystery of the mind*. Princeton, NJ: Princeton University Press.

Raichle, M. E. (1994). Visualizing the mind. *Scientific American, 270*, 58–64.

Valenstein, E. S. (1986). *Great and desperate cures*. New York: Basic Books.

Web Resources

For a chapter tutorial quiz, direct links to the Internet sites listed below and other features, visit the book-specific website at **www.wadsworth.com/product/ 0155074865**. You may also connect directly to the following annotated websites:

http://www.ruf.rice.edu/~lane/rvls.html
This is a clear, simple how-to site for statistics.

http://www.humanbrainmapping.org/
This database of brain images is shared by scientists from around the world

http://faculty.washington.edu/chudler/image.html
Compare the look of different imaging techniques used for CT, PET and MRI and see advantages and disadvantages of each.

For additional readings and information, check out InfoTrac College Edition at **http://www.infotrac-college.com/wadsworth**. Choose a search term yourself or enter the following search terms: brain mapping, ct imaging, electroencephalography, genetics, pet imaging, placebo.

CD-ROM: Exploring Biological Psychology

Animation: Josephine Wilson's Brian Scans
Interactive Recaps

Chapter 5 Quiz
Connect to the Interactive Biological Psychology Glossary

6

Control of Movement

Larissa was a beautiful baby with huge brown eyes and dimpled cheeks. Nearly 2 years of age, she was a bright, happy chatterbox, using full sentences to express herself. However, Larissa's motor development was abnormally slow. She couldn't sit up unassisted until she was nearly 11 months old, and she still wasn't walking when her parents brought her in for her two-year examination. (Most babies can sit up by themselves by the age of 7 months and walk by 15 months.) The pediatrician looked concerned as she examined Larissa. She applied a firm touch to the sole of Larissa's right foot and frowned as Larissa's toes fanned out in response, her big toe bending upward. Then she tested Larissa's left foot. Again, the toes on her left foot fanned in response to the pediatrician's touch.

The pediatrician explained to Larissa's parents that the fanning of her toes was called a positive Babinski reflex and was perfectly normal in young babies. However, a positive **Babinski reflex** is normally absent in children as old as Larissa. To determine the cause of the delay in Larissa's motor development, the pediatrician ordered a number of tests for Larissa, including scans of her brain and spinal cord. MRI scans of Larissa's spinal cord revealed a tiny, fluid-filled cyst in the cervical region of her spinal cord, a condition known as *syringomyelia*. The pediatrician explained that Larissa was probably born with the fluid-filled cyst in her spinal cord and that the cyst was interfering with the transmission of messages from her brain to the motor neurons in her spinal cord. Although surgery was risky, the pediatrician advised Larissa's parents to consult a pediatric neurosurgeon because the cyst could grow over time, causing Larissa to become severely disabled. Just after her second birthday, Larissa underwent surgery to

Babinski reflex: positive when a touch to the ball of the foot causes the toes to fan; negative when a touch to the ball of the foot causes the toes to curl

145

destroy the cyst in her spinal cord. She began walking soon after the surgery, and her motor development continued normally after that.

The Babinski reflex is one example of a reflex that is seen in very young infants but disappears as the baby gets older. If you firmly touch the bottom of the foot of an infant who is less than 6 months old, the baby's toes will extend and spread apart (Figure 6.1). This fanning of the toes in response to a touch on the bottom of the foot is called a positive Babinski reflex. By the time the infant is approximately 6 months of age, the cerebral cortex develops inhibitory control of motor neurons in the spinal cord. This means that the cerebral cortex begins to send inhibitory messages down the spinal cord, which inhibits the Babinski reflex. Therefore, if you stroke the sole of the foot of an older child (one who is older than 6 months of age), the child's toes will flex and curl inward in response to the touch. This is referred to as a negative Babinsk reflex.

Clinicians make use of reflexes when testing for damage to the nervous system (Fiorentino, 1973). Adults with intact, or undamaged, nervous systems exhibit a negative Babinski reflex when touched on the sole of their foot. This is a normal response for people with healthy nervous systems. However, those with spinal cord or brain damage do not always curl their toes when tested with a firm touch to the bottoms of their feet. The *Case Study* describes the case of a young man, named Kevin, who damaged his spinal cord in a car accident when he was 16. Touching the bottom of Kevin's foot produces a positive Babinski reflex. That is, Kevin's toes fan out, just like a young baby's, when the sole of his foot is stroked. Damage to Kevin's spinal cord has destroyed the axons that carried inhibitory messages to the motor neurons that control Kevin's feet. Thus, the Babinski reflex is not inhibited when the bottom of Kevin's foot is touched, and Kevin exhibits a positive Babinski reflex.

Movement is the result of muscle contractions, and muscles are controlled by the nervous system. Damage to the nervous system, then, disrupts normal muscle function. In this chapter, we will examine normal muscle function and

Figure 6.1 The Babinski reflex
Fanning of the toes in response to a touch on the bottom of the foot is called a positive Babinski reflex. When the foot of an older child is touched, the toes flex and curl (negative Babinski reflex).

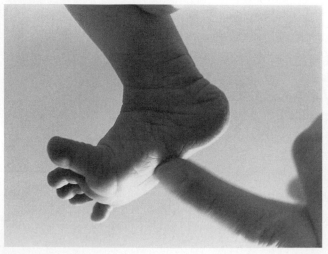 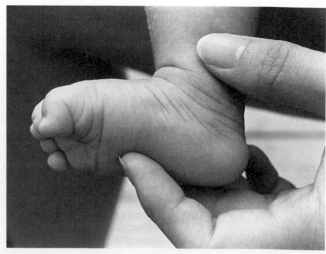

Partial Spinal Cord Injury

Kevin was 16 when his parents bought a fast, red sports car. He had just obtained his driver's license and was ordinarily a safe, careful driver. One evening, his parents let him borrow the car to go to a friend's house on an isolated rural road. On the way home, Kevin decided to see how fast the sports car could really go. He raced up the center of the empty road as fast as he could. When the road twisted sharply to the left, Kevin lost control of the car. His car went off the right shoulder and struck a tree. In the impact, Kevin was flung against the steering wheel, breaking his sternum, or breastbone, and several ribs. In addition, Kevin's spinal cord was injured at the T4 level. The damage to his spinal cord was limited to the ventral aspect.

This meant that Kevin's motor function was impaired, but his sensory function was left intact. Kevin's injury is referred to as an *incomplete spinal cord injury*. Some axons at the T4 level, the point of injury, survived in spite of the damage, especially those in the dorsal region of Kevin's spinal cord.

Today, the effects of the spinal cord damage are obvious. Kevin can stand on his legs, but he cannot walk without support. His gait is spastic, characterized by overextension of the joints in his legs. Motor function of the autonomic nervous system is also affected. For example, Kevin does not sweat any place on his body below the level of T4.

---

disorders that cause abnormal muscle function. We will also consider the roles of the brain and spinal cord in controlling movement, and we will compare reflexes with voluntary movement. Let's start by looking at the structure and function of muscles. ●

muscle fiber: a long, thin muscle cell

endplate: chemically sensitive region on the muscle fiber that responds to acetylcholine

neuromuscular junction: synapse between the axon of the motor neuron and a muscle fiber

Muscle Structure and Function

Like all body tissues, muscles are composed of cells. Each cell is called a **muscle fiber** (Figure 6.2). Muscle fibers are similar to all cells in that they have a nucleus, mitochondria, and other typical cellular components. Muscle fibers are different from other cells because they contain contractile fibrils made of filaments. There are two kinds of filaments in muscle fibers: thin filaments that contain a protein called *actin* and thick filaments that contain *myosin*. The filaments are arranged in such a way that actin filaments and myosin filaments are lined up side by side with their ends overlapping (Figure 6.3). Actin filaments are attached to structures known as Z-lines, which makes them easy to identify. Contraction of the muscle fiber occurs when a chemical process causes the actin filaments to slide along the myosin filaments, pulling the Z-lines closer together and shortening the muscle fiber. There is still a great deal of debate over exactly how the actin and myosin filaments interact. But, most investigators believe that tiny appendages, called *crossbridges*, on the myosin filament bind with actin, creating a force that moves the actin filament.

What causes muscle contractions? To begin to answer this question, recall that muscle fibers resemble neurons in one important aspect. Like neurons, each muscle fiber has a chemically sensitive region known as an **endplate.** The endplate of a muscle fiber contains receptor sites for the neurotransmitter *acetylcholine.* Axons from motor neurons terminate on the endplates of muscle

Figure 6.2 Muscles and muscle fibers
Muscles are composed of cells, and each cell is called a muscle fiber.

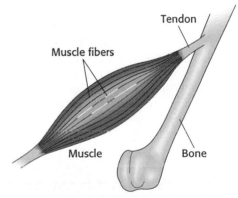

Figure 6.3 The role of muscle filaments in muscle contraction
During a muscle contraction, actin filaments slide along the myosin filaments, pulling the Z-line close together and shortening the muscle fiber.

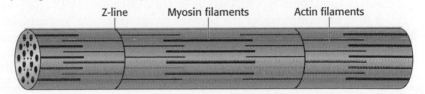

fibers, and acetylcholine is released from the terminal buttons of the motor neurons whenever the motor neurons get excited and fire. This means that motor neurons initiate muscle contraction by releasing acetylcholine into the junction between the axon terminus (or ending) and the muscle fiber, called the **neuromuscular junction** (Figure 6.4). When acetylcholine binds with its receptor sites on the muscle fiber, it causes Na^+ channels to open, depolarizing the fiber, which allows Ca^{++} to enter the neuron. Ca^{++} initiates the chemical process that causes myosin and actin filaments to slide past each other, shortening the fiber.

In order for a muscle contraction to occur, ATP is necessary. ATP is the fuel that propels the actin filaments along the myosin crossbridges, causing the muscle fiber to shorten. If a muscle is depleted of ATP, it will stop contracting and become stiff. This stiffened state of the muscle is referred to as *rigor*. At death, when all cellular processes cease and ATP is no longer synthesized, muscles in the body stiffen as ATP stores are exhausted, producing a state known as *rigor mortis* (*mortis* = death, Latin).

Contraction of a muscle occurs when its fibers shorten. Please keep in mind that each muscle contains hundreds or thousands of muscle fibers. Each muscle fiber receives innervation from one axon, which means that each motor neuron stimulates contraction in only one muscle. However, an axon from a motor neuron often branches near its terminus, and individual branches terminate on endplates of different fibers. That is, one motor neuron can innervate many different fibers in one muscle. The total number of fibers innervated by one motor neuron is referred to as a *motor unit*. Damage to a particular motor neuron will interfere with the functioning of the entire motor unit that receives innervation from that motor neuron. Muscles that require fine motor control, such as the muscles that control eye movement, have very small motor units, with each motor neuron innervating only a few muscle fibers. In contrast, muscles that are used mainly for maintaining posture have large motor units, in which a single motor neuron communicates with thousands of muscle fibers (Keynes & Aidley, 1991).

The term **muscle tone** refers to the vigor of a muscular contraction. When muscle tone in a particular muscle is increased, more fibers in that muscle contract at the same time. When muscle tone is decreased, fewer muscle fibers contract together. A muscle with a great deal of tone feels firm to the touch, whereas a muscle with low tone feels soft or flabby. Investigators demonstrated a long time ago that muscle tone increases in a systematic fashion within a muscle (Denny-Brown & Pennybacker, 1938; Henneman, 1957). When a muscle first starts to contract, small motor units are stimulated first. As the muscle tone increases, larger motor units are recruited into action, causing large numbers of muscle fibers to contract.

Different Muscle Types

You learned in Chapter 2 that there are three types of muscles: *skeletal*, *smooth*, and *cardiac* muscles. **Skeletal muscle** is the muscle tissue that is connected to the bones and cartilage of the skeleton. Contraction of the skeletal muscles causes the bones of the skeleton to move. They are the muscles that are under our voluntary control and, thus, are innervated by the *somatic nervous system*. When I tap my finger on the desktop or smile at a friend, I am using skeletal muscles to perform these voluntary activities.

Skeletal muscle can be classified by its color (Bagshaw, 1993). Red muscle contains a high concentration of the protein myoglobin. Like hemoglobin, which is found in the blood, myoglobin binds with oxygen. This means that red muscle relies on oxygen and the process of oxidation to produce ATP, which allows the muscle to engage in sustained activity without fatiguing. In contrast, white muscle does not rely on oxidation to produce ATP and quickly goes into oxygen debt during muscle

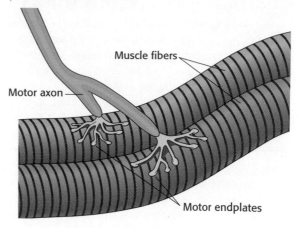

Figure 6.4 The neuromuscular junction
The axons of motor neurons synapse with motor endplates on muscle fibers.

Muscle fibers

Motor axon

Motor endplates

muscle tone: the vigor of a muscular contraction

skeletal muscle: muscle that is attached to bones and cartilage of skeleton

contraction. For this reason, white muscle is used for rapid muscle contractions that take place in short bursts. White muscle contracts rapidly and fatigues quickly, whereas red muscle contracts more slowly over a long period of time.

Birds and other vertebrates possess muscles that have red or white fibers exclusively. That is, they have muscles that are all red or all white. For example, when carving a turkey the other day just before dinner, I stopped to give my sons an anatomy lesson, pointing out to them that the breast meat was white and the legs and thighs were dark. Turkeys spend most of their time running around on their legs. Hence, their leg and thigh muscles are composed of red muscles, which allow the turkeys to strut about for long periods of time without tiring. In contrast, turkeys are capable of brief flights during which they beat their wings furiously. Because breast muscles of turkeys are composed of white fibers, they fatigue quickly, which means that turkeys cannot fly for long periods of time. In mammals, on the other hand, red and white muscle fibers are found in the same muscle. When you sprint across a parking lot to your car during a downpour, you are making use of your white muscle fibers. When you hike a 5-mile trail in a state park, you are using your red muscle fibers.

Smooth muscles are found in the walls of blood vessels and in the walls of many organs, including the stomach, the small and large intestines, the bladder, and the uterus. They are also found in the skin and in the ducts of glands. As you learned in Chapter 4, smooth muscles control the constriction and dilation of blood vessels and of the pupil of the eye. Smooth muscles are responsible for *peristalsis*, the rhythmic contractions of the digestive organs, and they also control the opening and closing of sphincters and ducts throughout the body. In general, smooth muscles contract more slowly, although more efficiently, than striated muscles. However, smooth muscle contraction is not well understood (Warshaw, McBride, & Work, 1987). Therefore, we will limit our focus to the action of skeletal muscles in the remainder of this chapter.

flexion: a movement that bends a limb

extension: a movement that straightens a limb

antagonists: muscles that produce opposite movements around a joint

Skeletal Muscle Function

Skeletal muscles are attached to the bones of the skeleton by tough strands of connective tissue known as *tendons*. The bones themselves are joined together at *joints*, which typically are enclosed in a capsule (Figure 6.5). Inside the joint capsule is a greasy *synovial fluid* that allows bones to slide past each other easily as the bones are moved by contracting muscles. Many joints are structured in such a way that movement around the joint is permitted in two opposing directions only. For example, movement around the elbow joint is limited to **flexion** and **extension** of the arm (Figure 6.5). Flexion of a limb refers to a movement that bends the limb, whereas extension is a straightening of the limb.

Two muscles on either side of the elbow joint, called the *biceps* and the *triceps* muscles, produce flexion and extension of the arm. Contraction of the biceps muscle causes the arm to bend at the elbow joint. In contrast, contraction of the triceps muscle produces extension of the arm. Muscles that produce opposite movements around a joint are called **antagonists.** Thus, the biceps and triceps muscles are antagonist muscles. Likewise, the muscles that open your mouth and the muscles that close it are antagonists.

Please keep in mind that muscles do their work by contracting. My arm bends because my biceps muscle contracts, and my arm straightens because my triceps muscle contracts. Muscle relaxation is a passive process. It occurs when a muscle stops contracting. Motor neurons initiate muscle contraction by releasing acetylcholine at the neuromuscular junction. When a motor neuron stops firing, the associated muscle fibers stop contracting, and muscle relaxation takes place.

Movement occurs when one or more muscles contract. For example, as you've just learned, contraction of the biceps muscle bends the arm.

Figure 6.5 Attachment of muscles to bones around the elbow joint
Extensor and flexor muscles are positioned on opposite sides of a joint. Flexor muscles bend the limb, and extensor muscles straighten the limb.

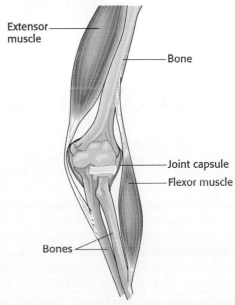

Extensor muscle

Bone

Joint capsule

Flexor muscle

Bones

This type of muscle contraction is called **isotonic contraction.** As its name implies [*iso-* = same, *-tonic* = tone, Greek], muscle tone remains unchanged during this type of contraction. Isotonic contraction occurs when a muscle shortens in length, pulling the attached bones in the direction of the contraction.

Isometric contraction is another type of contraction. During isometric contraction, the muscle does not shorten but rather remains the same length. How does this happen? The bones remain in a fixed position during isometric contraction, so the muscle cannot shorten.

Try it out for yourself. First, contract your right biceps muscle isotonically, which will cause your arm to flex. When you do this, keep your left hand on your biceps as you bend your right arm and feel that the muscle tone does not change. Next, contract your right biceps muscle isometrically. To do this, you need to assume the stance of a bodybuilder with your right arm in a semiflexed position. After your arm is in a fixed position, continue to contract your right biceps muscle, keeping your left hand over the right biceps to monitor muscle tone. When a bodybuilder performs an isometric contraction of the biceps muscle, you can see the biceps bulge and pop out of the arm. Isometric contractions take place in your arms and back when you are carrying a load that you do not want to drop or tip, whereas isotonic contractions produce movement.

> **isotonic contraction:** shortening of a muscle that causes movement of a body part
>
> **isometric contraction:** contraction of a muscle that is fixed in length, causing an increase in muscle tone

Recap 6.1: Muscle Structure and Function

Each muscle cell is called a muscle (a)_____, which has a chemically sensitive endplate that is sensitive to the neurotransmitter (b)_____. This fiber contains two kinds of filaments, actin and (c)_____, which are responsible for contraction of the fiber. The synapse between the axon of a motor neuron and the endplate of a muscle fiber is called a (d)_____ junction. The total number of muscle fibers innervated by one motor neuron is called a (e)_____ _____. (f)_____ muscle is muscle tissue that is connected to the bones of the skeleton. It can be classified by its two colors, (g)_____ (which contains myoglobin, permitting the muscle to engage in sustained behavior) and (h)_____ (which is used for short bursts of rapid muscle contractions). (i)_____ muscles are found in the walls of blood vessels and many internal organs, in the skin, and in the ducts of glands. (j)_____ of a limb is movement that bends a limb, and (k)_____ is a straightening of the limb. During (l)_____ contraction, a muscle shortens in length. During (m)_____ contraction, muscle tone increases.

Spinal Control of Movement

Many movements of the arms, trunk, and legs are regulated by spinal cord mechanisms. Think about this for a moment. Consider what happens when you touch something very hot with your bare hand. You immediately jerk your hand away from the offending object, don't you? This reaction happens instantaneously. It happens so fast, in fact, that you don't have time to think about it. Your reaction occurs so quickly because the painful sensation is processed in the spinal cord. That is, the information about the painful stimulus goes directly to your spinal cord, where it is sent to the motor neurons that stimulate the contraction of muscles that pull your hand away from the painful object (Figure 6.6). It would take far too long for you to react if the information had to travel up the spinal cord to be processed in the brain, and then motor directions were sent from the brain to the muscle.

These rapid, automatic responses to particular stimuli that are mediated by the spinal cord are called **reflexes.** Reflexes can be simple movements, or they can be postural adjustments that involve many muscles. However, reflexes always occur the same way in response to a particular stimulus. The reflex that I described in the preceding paragraph is called the **withdrawal reflex,** or the *flexion reflex.* This reflex involves an immediate withdrawal movement that is made in response to a painful or noxious stimulus. I am so certain of the speed of this reflex that I once sat and watched my son, Jacob, at 2 years of age, stick his finger into a flame of a candle. I didn't bother to rush to his aid because I knew that his withdrawal reflex would remove his hand from the flame before I could reach him. (And it did!)

Reflexes also occur in the head and neck, but these are not typically mediated by the spinal cord. Motor nuclei in the brain stem control these reflexes. In this section, we will focus solely on spinal reflexes. We will consider reflexes that occur in the head and neck in Chapters 7 and 9.

Review the structure of the spinal cord in Figure 6.6. Sensory information enters the spinal cord through the dorsal horn, and the motor neurons are situated in the gray matter in the ventral aspect of the spinal cord. When a withdrawal reflex occurs, an axon carrying sensory information from a receptor relays this information directly to motor neurons, which respond to the information by initiating muscle contractions that cause flexion.

The withdrawal reflex is a **unisynaptic reflex,** involving only one synapse between the receptor and the motor neuron. Most other reflexes are **polysynaptic,** involving more than one synapse. Information from receptors is carried by axons into the spinal cord. In the central gray matter of the spinal cord, these axons terminate on interneurons. The axons of the interneurons, in turn, terminate on the dendrites of motor neurons, releasing neurotransmitters that excite or inhibit the motor neurons. Sometimes a chain of two or more interneurons may be involved in a reflex. Because more synapses are involved in a polysynaptic reflex than in a unisynaptic reflex, there is a greater time lapse between the introduction of the stimulus and the initiation of movement in polysynaptic reflexes. In contrast, unisynaptic reflexes occur nearly instantaneously, in under 50 milliseconds.

The motor neurons that control the skeletal muscles in the arms, trunk, and legs are all located in the spinal cord. A close inspection of the motor neurons under the microscope reveals that there are small motor neurons and large motor neurons. The large motor neurons are called **alpha motor neurons,** and the small ones are called **gamma motor neurons.** Action potentials travel rapidly down the axons of alpha motor neurons, which have large diameters, and they travel more slowly down the thinner axons of gamma motor neurons.

You can imagine that, if two types of motor neurons carry action potentials to muscles at different speeds, they probably terminate on different types of muscle fibers. And, indeed, there are two types of fibers in skeletal muscles: **extrafusal fibers** and **intrafusal fibers.** The larger alpha motor neurons transmit information to the extrafusal fibers, whereas the gamma motor neurons transmit information to the intrafusal fibers. Let's look at the differences between these two types of fibers and the roles they play in muscle contraction.

Figure 6.6 The withdrawal reflex

Axons from receptors in the skin terminate directly on the dendrites of motor neurons. A painful stimulus stimulates an axon potential in the axon of the receptor, which causes excitatory neurotransmitter molecules to be released into the synapse. The motor neurons become excited and initiate muscle contractions that pull the limb away from the noxious stimulus.

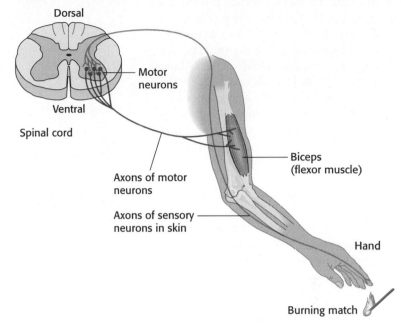

reflex: a rapid, automatic set of muscle contractions made in response to a particular stimulus

withdrawal reflex: flexion of a limb in response to a painful or noxious stimulus

unisynaptic reflex: a reflex that involves only one sensory and one motor neuron and one synapse

polysynaptic reflex: a reflex involving a sensory neuron, a motor neuron, and one or more interneurons

alpha motor neurons: large motor neurons that innervate extrafusal muscle fibers

gamma motor neurons: small motor neurons that innervate intrafusal muscle fibers

extrafusal fibers: long muscle fibers that run the entire length of the muscle

intrafusal fibers: muscle fibers located inside muscle spindles

Extrafusal and Intrafusal Fibers

Extrafusal fibers are long muscle fibers that run the entire length of the muscle (Figure 6.7). On the other hand, intrafusal fibers are shorter and do not extend from one end of the muscle to the other end. Instead, intrafusal fibers are found in **muscle spindles,** which are interspersed among the extrafusal muscle fibers. That is, intrafusal fibers are located inside the spindle, and extrafusal fibers are located outside the spindle. A muscle spindle is composed of several intrafusal fibers that are joined to a centralized structure called a *nuclear bag* (Figure 6.7). Inside the nuclear bag is a special receptor, known as an **annulospiral receptor,** that is sensitive to being stretched. Axons from annulospiral receptors carry information to the spinal cord, where they terminate on motor neurons that stimulate extrafusal fibers in the muscle in which they are located, causing that muscle to contract. That is, when annulospiral receptors are stretched, they activate motor neurons, which initiate muscle contraction.

How does an annulospiral receptor get stretched? In the laboratory, investigators can isolate a muscle spindle and mechanically stretch the receptor by pulling or tugging on the spindle. Therefore, stretching a muscle or part of a muscle will excite annulospiral receptors. Relaxation of the muscle can stretch annulospiral receptors, too, especially when the muscle becomes very relaxed and loses much of its tone. In fact, the annulospiral receptor is the most important mechanism we have for maintaining muscle tone.

The Stretch Reflex

Have you ever watched someone falling asleep in class? As that person starts to drop off to sleep, his or her head begins to fall forward. But, the head goes down only so far when it jerks back up again. This sequence might occur many times, over and over again: Head starts to sink, then it springs back up quickly, waking the napper momentarily. Consider what happens. The head begins to fall forward because muscles in the back of the neck and shoulders lose their muscle tone as the person falls asleep. The head continues to drop until these muscles are stretched so much that annulospiral receptors fire. When the annulospiral receptors get excited, they activate motor neurons, which stimulate muscle fiber contraction to restore muscle tone. This unisynaptic reflex is called the **stretch reflex.** This reflex can be elicited whenever a muscle is stretched. A gentle tap below the kneecap, for example, stretches the extensor muscle in the leg, causing the muscle to contract and the leg to extend (Figure 6.8).

Reciprocal Innervation

Consider a problem inherent in the design of the stretch reflex: Contraction of one muscle produces stretching of its antagonist muscle. Take the biceps muscle, for example. Contraction of the biceps muscle bends the arm at the elbow, which stretches the triceps muscle. When the triceps muscle is stretched, the annulospi-

Figure 6.7 Extrafusal and intrafusal muscle fibers
Stretching the muscle spindle causes the annulospiral receptor in the nuclear bag to be stretched. When stretched, the annulospiral receptor gets excited, and an action potential travels down its axon to the spinal cord, where the axon terminates on several motor neurons. The motor neurons then become excited and stimulate contraction of fibers in the muscle. Thus, stretching the annulospiral receptor in a muscle results in contraction of that muscle.

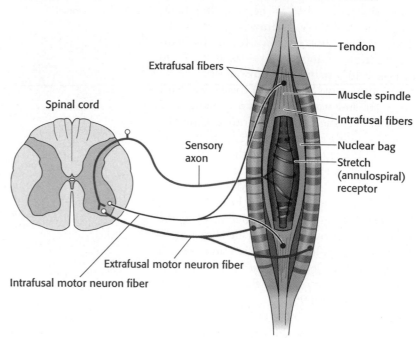

Tendon

Extrafusal fibers

Muscle spindle

Intrafusal fibers

Spinal cord

Sensory axon

Nuclear bag

Stretch (annulospiral) receptor

Extrafusal motor neuron fiber

Intrafusal motor neuron fiber

muscle spindles: composed of several intrafusal fibers that are joined to a nuclear bag containing an annulospiral receptor

annulospiral receptor: a receptor that fires when stretched

stretch reflex: contraction of a muscle in response to stretching of the annulospiral receptors in that muscle

ral receptors in that muscle fire, exciting motor neurons that should cause contraction of the triceps muscle. This means that every time you bend your arm, your arm should automatically straighten. And, every time you straighten your arm, which stretches the biceps muscle, your arm should bend reflexively. But, this doesn't happen. Why not?

Reciprocal innervation explains why we are able to bend our arms and hold them in a bent position for as long as we want, without initiating a stretch reflex in the antagonist muscles. With reciprocal innervation, axons arising from motor neurons branch before leaving the spinal cord. Some of these branches terminate on inhibitory neurons in the central gray region of the spinal cord (Figure 6.9). As their name implies, the function of these inhibitory cells is to inhibit other neurons, namely, the motor neurons of antagonist muscles. Hence, reciprocal innervation involves the inhibition of antagonist muscles by motor neurons of contracting muscles.

The Tendon Reflex

Recall that tendons connect muscles to bone and cartilage. Stretch receptors, called **Golgi tendon organs,** are located in tendons. The purpose of a Golgi tendon organ is to provide feedback to the nervous system about muscle contraction. When a muscle contracts powerfully, the tendon that attaches the muscle to the skeleton is stretched, which stretches the Golgi tendon organ. Like all stretch receptors, Golgi tendon organs fire when stretched. Their axons carry information about tendon stretching to the spinal cord, where they terminate on inhibitory neurons. When excited, these interneurons inhibit the motor neurons that are producing the powerful muscle contraction that is causing the tendon to be stretched (Figure 6.10). The overall effect of stretching the Golgi tendon organ is to inhibit muscle contraction in a muscle that is contracting too vigorously.

Thus, we have two feedback systems that relay information about muscle function to the spinal cord. Annulospiral receptors fire when the muscle relaxes and muscle fibers stretch, and the Golgi tendon organ fires when its respective muscle contracts too vigorously, stretching the tendon. The annulospiral receptor and the Golgi tendon organ stimulate opposite effects in the spinal cord. In response to neurotransmitters released by annulospiral receptors, motor neurons increase their firing and produce muscle contraction. The Golgi tendon organ, in contrast, inhibits the firing of motor neurons, causing a decrease in muscle contraction. Together, these two feedback systems maintain the correct muscle tone necessary for optimum muscle function.

These two feedback systems also send information to the brain about the contraction and relaxation of muscles in the body. This information allows the brain to plan future movements based on the present state of the muscles. In addition, information from the muscles, particularly information from contracting muscles, can affect neurotransmitter function. Jacobs (1994) has demonstrated that repetitive muscle contractions increase serotonin activity in the brain (see *For Further Thought*).

Figure 6.8 The patellar stretch reflex
A tap on the tendon beneath the kneecap stretches the extensor muscle of the leg, causing that muscle to contract and the leg to extend.

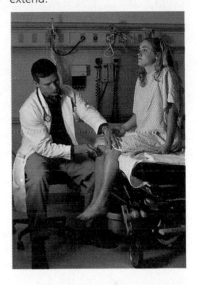

Figure 6.9 Reciprocal innervation
Axons of motor neurons branch before leaving the spinal cord. These branches terminate on inhibitory cells, which inhibit the motor neurons of antagonist muscles. When a flexor motor neuron fires, it excites muscle fibers in the flexor muscle, and it excites inhibitory cells. When the inhibitory cell is excited, it inhibits the antagonist (extensor) motor neurons.

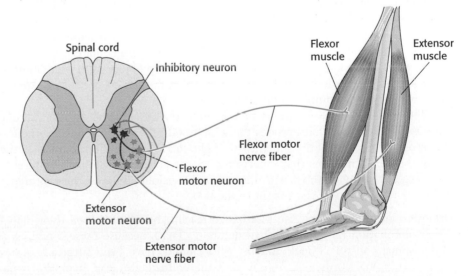

Other Spinal Reflexes

The importance of reflexes has been recognized for centuries. Seventeenth- and eighteenth-century investigators studied and cataloged most of the reflexes that are known today (Swazey, 1969). For example, in the mid-1700s, Robert Whytt, at the University of Edinburgh, studied spinal reflexes in decapitated frogs and tortoises. You see, frogs without heads are frogs without brains, which means that any elicited behavior in these specially prepared subjects is mediated by the spinal cord. Whytt studied a number of reflexes that could be produced in headless frogs, including the withdrawal reflex and the *scratch reflex*. As its name implies, the scratch reflex is a scratching movement made by one of the frog's limbs when the frog's skin is tickled. Stimulation of sensory receptors on the frog's skin is translated into action potentials that travel down axons to the spinal cord, where they excite motor neurons that initiate contractions in muscles that produce scratching movements by the frog's limb. This scratching behavior occurs even when the brain is absent.

Probably the most important and most comprehensive study of reflexes was conducted by the British physician and scientist Sir Charles Scott Sherrington. From 1884 to 1935, Sherrington studied many reflexes, including the withdrawal reflex, the scratch reflex, and the knee jerk reflex, in monkeys, dogs, and cats. He is credited with discovering reciprocal innervation and for introducing the term *synapse*. Two important principles about movement have emerged from Sherrington's research. The first principle, the *principle of the common path*, refers to the role of the motor neuron as the final step in the pathway to the muscle. Any commands to a muscle, whether from the brain or the spinal cord, must pass through the motor neuron to get to the muscle. The second principle that emerged from Sherrington's research involves the *integrative action of neurons*. According to Sherrington, all neurons in the body work together to permit smooth, precise movement.

Figure 6.10 Golgi tendon organ reflex
Vigorous contraction of a muscle stretches the tendons of that muscle, exciting the stretch receptors (called Golgi tendon organs) in the tendons. When excited, the Golgi tendon organs stimulate inhibitory cells in the spinal cord, which inhibit firing of motor neurons and, thus, inhibit contraction of the muscle.

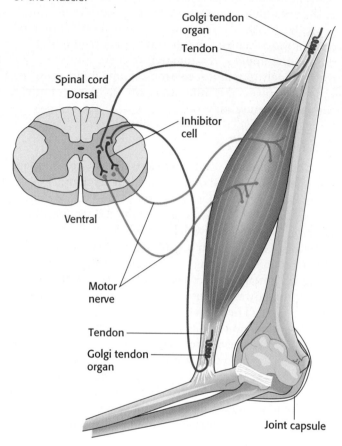

The Crossed Extensor Reflex   One spinal reflex that Sherrington studied intensively is the **crossed extensor reflex**. This reflex is an example of Sherrington's concept of the integrative action of neurons because it typically occurs in conjunction with another reflex, the withdrawal reflex. Consider what happens when you step on a sharp object when walking in your bare feet. Immediately, the involved leg flexes to withdraw the injured foot from the sharp object. But, what about the other leg? If one leg is flexed, it is important that the other leg remain extended. Otherwise, you will tumble to the floor.

The crossed extensor reflex is stimulated by the onset of the withdrawal reflex. The sensory receptor that initiates the withdrawal reflex also excites interneurons that cross the midline of the spinal cord (Figure 6.11). These interneurons, in turn, excite the motor neurons that innervate extensor muscles in the contralateral leg. As a result, when one limb is withdrawn from a noxious stimulus, the contralateral limb extends to support the weight of the body.

crossed extensor reflex: extension of a limb in response to a noxious stimulus applied to the contralateral limb

Urination and Defecation   No one has to teach babies how to soil their diapers. Their elimination functions happen naturally. That's because these functions are under spinal control. Spinal animals, whose brains have been surgically severed from their spinal cords, continue to defecate and urinate, even assuming typical

Movement and the Raphe Nucleus

In chapter 4, you learned that neurons in the raphe system, which is located in the hindbrain, release serotonin when stimulated. Barry Jacobs (1994; Jacobs & Fornal, 1997, 1999) has demonstrated that the activity of these serotonin neurons is closely related to motor activity. For example, some serotonin neurons in the raphe system begin to fire right before a movement is initiated. In addition, many serotonin neurons increase their firing rate as the rate of muscle contractions increases. If a person walks rapidly, neurons in the raphe nucleus fire faster than if the same person walks at a more leisurely pace. This is especially true for repetitive movements like chewing or running.

Most of Jacobs's experiments have focused on the activity of neurons in the raphe nuclei of cats because this area of the cat's brain has been studied extensively in the past by others, and its properties are well known. Jacobs observed that, when a cat runs on a treadmill, serotonin neurons in the raphe system fire at the same rate as the animal's gait. These neurons appear to mediate gross motor functions (that is, extrapyramidal system functions) rather than fine motor (or pyramidal system) control. Thus, neurons in the raphe system appear to enable gross movements of the torso and limbs but not movements of the eyes or fingers.

When a cat hears a sudden noise, such as the slamming of a door, the cat stops what it is doing and turns toward the source of the sound to determine its significance. This "what is it?" reaction is called an *orienting response*, which we will discuss in detail in Chapter 9. During an orienting response, when the cat stops all movement to concentrate on a particular stimulus, serotonin neurons in the raphe do not fire. These same neurons become active again when the individual begins to move once more. Hence, serotonin neurons in the raphe increase their firing rate when large muscle groups are contracting and decrease their firing rate when movement ceases or when the individual makes a "what is it?" response to an environmental distraction.

---

eliminatory positions. In spinal animals and in young infants, urination and defecation are caused by stretch reflexes. Let's consider the urination and defecation reflexes separately.

The organ that collects urine, called the *bladder*, is lined with smooth muscle. Like all muscles, the muscle in the bladder wall contains stretch receptors. As the bladder fills with urine, the wall of the bladder becomes stretched, causing the stretch receptors to fire. The axons of these stretch receptors terminate on motor neurons in the spinal cord that control bladder muscles. Stretching of stretch receptors in the bladder produces contraction of bladder muscle, which forces urine out of the body through a passageway called the *urethra*. Thus, the bladder empties as a result of a stretch reflex.

Defecation involves a stretch reflex, too. The large intestine, including the region (called the *rectum*) closest to the anus, is also lined with smooth muscles and stretch receptors. As the rectum fills with feces, the walls of the rectum stretch, causing stretch receptors to fire. The stretch receptors stimulate motor neurons in the spinal cord that initiate contraction of rectal muscles, expelling feces from the body.

Toilet training takes urination and defecation out of reflexive control and places it under conscious control. A child being toilet trained learns to use skeletal muscles to open and close the sphincter muscles of the bladder and anus. This training cannot be done with a very young child because the frontal lobes are not developed enough to take control of bladder and bowel function.

People with spinal cord injuries typically have incomplete communication between the brain and neurons in

Figure 6.11 The crossed extensor reflex
A painful stimulus to one limb causes flexion of that limb (withdrawal reflex) and extension of the contralateral limb (crossed extensor reflex).

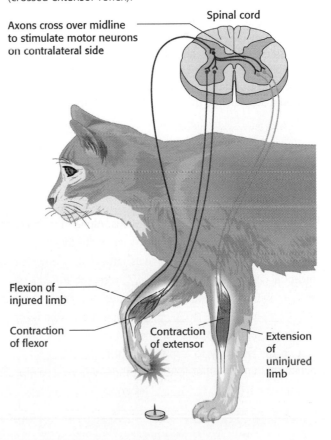

Spinal cord

Axons cross over midline to stimulate motor neurons on contralateral side

Flexion of injured limb

Contraction of flexor

Contraction of extensor

Extension of uninjured limb

the spinal cord. Often, following the injury, they lose conscious control of their bladder and bowels. However, the stretch reflexes that produce urination and defecation remain intact. Some people with spinal cord injuries can learn to control bladder function by taking advantage of the intact stretch reflex in the bladder. For example, the bladder wall can be stretched by tugging on the skin of the abdomen. Thus, people with spinal cord injuries can initiate urination by stretching the abdominal wall.

Sexual Reflexes   Many of the components of sexual activity, including erection of the penis and ejaculation, are under spinal control (Agmo, 1999). Adequate stimulation will produce penile erection in men with spinal cord injuries and in male animals whose brains have been surgically separated from their spinal cords. Continued stimulation will induce ejaculation of semen in these male subjects. Sensory receptors associated with the penis excite motor neurons in the sacral area of the spinal cord that cause dilation of blood vessels, producing erection of the penis. Genital receptors also excite motor neurons that cause the rhythmic contraction of muscles associated with ejaculation in the male and orgasmic response in the female.

Some sexual response can be brought under conscious control. For example, thinking erotic thoughts can produce sexual excitement leading to penile erection in the man or engorgement of the clitoris and vaginal lubrication in the woman. However, these responses can also be stimulated reflexively and are difficult, if not impossible, to stop after they have begun. For that reason, premature ejaculation cannot be halted when it occurs because the motor neurons that initiate the ejaculatory muscle contractions have been excited reflexively. A man who is trying to prevent premature ejaculation must do so by sending inhibitory signals from his brain down to the motor neurons in his spinal cord. Another way to control premature ejaculation is the use of anesthetic creams that are applied to the genital area to reduce sensation in that area and, thus, decrease stimulation of sensory neurons that excite the ejaculatory motor neurons.

We have examined a number of reflexes that involve sensory neurons in the peripheral nervous system and motor neurons in the spinal cord. These reflexes serve to protect the body, to produce postural adjustments, or to support important biological functions such as respiration, elimination, and reproduction. All of these reflexes take place without prompting from higher brain structures and do not require conscious control. However, in line with Sherrington's concept of the final common path, you should keep in mind that motor neurons receive innervation both from the peripheral nervous system and from the brain. That is, skeletal muscles that are under reflexive control can also be brought under conscious control. In the final sections of this chapter, we will look at how the brain controls movement.

Recap 6.2: Spinal Control of Movement

Rapid, automatic responses to particular stimuli are called (a)_____. The withdrawal, or (b)_____, reflex involves an immediate withdrawal movement that occurs in response to a painful stimulus. Alpha motor neurons innervate (c)_____ fibers, and gamma motor neurons innervate (d)_____ fibers. (e)_____ fibers are found in muscle spindles, attached to a nuclear bag, which contains a stretch receptor called the (f)_____ receptor. (g)_____ _____ involves the inhibition of antagonist muscles by motor neurons of contracting muscles. (h)_____ _____ organs are stretch receptors found in tendons. According to the principle of the common path, the (i)_____ _____ is the final step in the pathway to a muscle. In the (j)_____ _____ reflex, one leg extends when the other flexes to withdraw from a painful stimulus. Urination and defecation involve a (k)_____ reflex.

Control of Movement by the Brain

The brain controls movement by means of two motor systems: the **pyramidal motor system** and the **extrapyramidal motor system**. These two systems arise from different regions of the brain, and each has many distinguishing features, which we will examine. However, these systems do not act independently because there is a good deal of communication between the pyramidal and extrapyramidal systems. In addition, both systems terminate on motor neurons, the final common path to the skeletal muscles.

The Pyramidal Motor System

The pyramidal motor system arises from the **primary motor cortex** in the frontal lobe (Figure 6.12). It sends information to the motor neurons by way of axons that leave the primary motor cortex and extend without synapsing to the appropriate motor neurons. From the primary motor cortex to the motor neurons in the spinal cord, the axons of the pyramidal system are bundled together in a tract known as the **dorsolateral corticospinal tract.**

Recall that the left hemisphere of the brain controls the right side of the body and that the right hemisphere controls the left side of the body. This means that the dorsolateral corticospinal tracts arising from the left and right hemispheres have to cross over to the other side of the brain. The axons from the left primary motor cortex cross over to the right side of the brain, and those from the right primary motor cortex cross over to the left side, in pyramid-shaped structures on the ventral surface of the medulla. The pyramidal system gets its name from these medullary pyramids where the crossover, or *decussation*, of the dorsolateral corticospinal tract occurs.

The primary motor cortex, which is also called the *precentral gyrus*, is organized topographically, as you learned in Chapter 1. Each muscle in the body is controlled by neurons located in specific places in the primary motor cortex. Figure 6.12 illustrates the location of neurons in the primary motor cortex of a chimpanzee that control particular body parts, the result of research conducted by Sherrington and his colleague, Grunbaum, in 1901 and 1902. Recall from Chapter 1 that Fritsch and Hitzig mapped the primary motor cortex of the dog in 1863 and that Penfield mapped the human primary motor cortex in the 1940s. Research conducted in many species (for example, Sherrington and Grunbaum studied the primary motor cortex of the chimpanzee, orangutan, and gorilla) confirms that the primary motor cortex is organized in such a way that the location of the neurons is essentially the same for all mammalian species, with neurons at the superior aspect of the primary motor cortex controlling the feet of the hind limbs and neurons at the inferior aspect of the primary motor cortex controlling the face and mouth.

Other regions of the frontal lobe assist the primary motor cortex in the production of movement. Recall from Chapter 4 that the frontal lobe is composed of several areas, including the prefrontal cortex, the premotor cortex, and the primary motor cortex. The *prefrontal cortex* appears to organize the response to sensory stimuli, especially when some stimuli need to be ignored. The *premotor cortex* and the *supplementary motor cortex* are both located in the frontal lobe, immediately anterior to the primary motor cortex. Axons from the premotor cortex, which lies on the lateral aspect of

pyramidal motor system: the motor system that arises from the primary motor cortex in the frontal lobe and directs fine motor control of skeletal muscles

extrapyramidal motor system: the motor system that coordinates gross postural adjustments and arises from the cerebral cortex, basal ganglia, cerebellum, and reticular formation

primary motor cortex: the precentral gyrus, which sends impulses involving fine motor control to motor neurons

dorsolateral corticospinal tract: group of axons that carries messages from the primary motor cortex to motor neurons in the spinal cord

Figure 6.12 The motor cortex in the frontal lobe

Neurons in the motor cortex stimulate motor neurons that control specific muscles in the body.

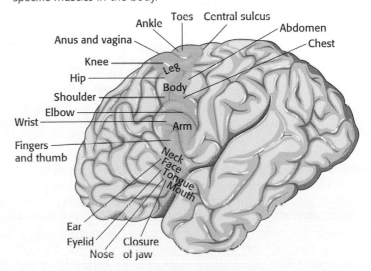

the frontal lobe, join axons from the primary motor cortex to form the dorsolateral corticospinal tract of the pyramidal system, although the specific function of the premotor cortex is not clear. The supplementary motor cortex, located on the medial aspect of the frontal lobe, plays a role in organizing complex, rapid movements. We will examine the functions of these regions in more detail in Chapters 8 and 9.

The function of the pyramidal motor system is fine motor control of skeletal muscles. Using scissors requires fine motor control of the muscles of the hands and fingers, for example. Neurons in the primary motor cortex organize the movements necessary to open and close scissors and send commands to the appropriate motor neurons in the spinal cord. Under direction of the primary motor cortex, these motor neurons stimulate muscles in the hand, producing movements that open and close the scissors smoothly and accurately. Whenever you learn a new motor task that requires fine motor control, the primary motor cortex directs the motor neurons, thereby regulating the muscle contractions needed to produce the new movement.

The Extrapyramidal Motor System

The function of the extrapyramidal motor system is to coordinate gross movements and postural adjustments. This system generally develops before the pyramidal system because gross motor control is learned before fine motor control. For example, children learn to patty-cake before they learn to hold a crayon. In addition, not all gross movements develop at the same time. A baby learns to hold her head upright before she masters the ability to sit, and she learns to sit before she stands.

The extrapyramidal system arises from many parts of the brain, including the cerebral cortex, the thalamus, the cerebellum, the basal ganglia, and the reticular formation. As its name implies, the extrapyramidal system is distributed outside the pyramidal system and does not pass through the pyramids in the medulla [*extra-* = outside, Latin]. And, unlike the pyramidal system, the extrapyramidal system synapses profusely, permitting much intercommunication among the structures in the forebrain, midbrain, and hindbrain that comprise the extrapyramidal motor system.

The primary motor cortex contributes to the functioning of the extrapyramidal motor system, as well as the pyramidal motor system. Axons from the primary motor cortex and the supplementary motor cortex form the **ventromedial corticospinal tract** and synapse with other neurons in the extrapyramidal motor system. Unlike the dorsolateral corticospinal tract, the ventromedial corticospinal tract does *not* cross to the opposite side of the brain but, instead, continues down to the ipsilateral spinal cord. The *basal ganglia* and the *cerebellum* perhaps play the most important roles in the extrapyramidal motor system. Let's examine the roles of these structures separately.

ventromedial corticospinal tract: pathway from the primary motor cortex and supplementary motor cortex that synapses with neurons in the extrapyramidal motor system

The Cerebellum

As you learned in Chapter 4, the function of the cerebellum is to coordinate movement in response to sensory stimuli. The cerebellum receives sensory information from muscles and tendons, from the reticular formation, from the inner ear, and from the eyes, nose, and ears. The muscles and tendons inform the cerebellum about the state of all the muscles in the body. Therefore, the cerebellum knows which muscles are contracted and which are relaxed before it sends out commands to motor neurons.

The reticular formation responds whenever the nervous system is exposed to a new or important stimulus. It relays information about the important stimulus to the cerebellum, and the cerebellum organizes the response. For example, when my reticular formation detects that my name has been spoken, it alerts my cerebellum. In response, my cerebellum stops my ongoing behavior and turns my head in the direction where my name was spoken. From the inner ear, the cerebellum gets information about balance. The cerebellum coordinates muscle contractions to restore balance whenever we start to fall. The receptors in the eyes, ears, and nose all send information to the cerebellum about the presence of objects in the environment. After communicating with the cerebrum and the basal ganglia, the cerebellum coordinates movements toward or away from those objects.

No one is certain exactly how the cerebellum coordinates movement. Undoubtedly, accurate movements require that both the force and timing of muscle contractions are carefully controlled. And, research with patients with cerebellar injuries indicates that the cerebellum is intimately involved in regulating the force and timing of muscle contractions (Wickelgran, 1998b).

The organization of the cerebellum gives us some clues about how it might coordinate movement (Figure 6.13). The cerebellum's outer layer, called the **cerebellar cortex,** appears to govern coordination of movement (Bastian et al., 1998). The cerebellar cortex contains five types of neurons (Purkinje, Golgi, stellate, basket, and granule cells), but only the axons of Purkinje cells carry information out of the cerebellum. Each Purkinje cell in the cerebellar cortex is believed to control one specific muscle in the body. Linking the Purkinje cells are millions of parallel axons that run through the cerebellar cortex. The parallel axons are thought to activate certain muscles simultaneously, producing coordinated movement.

The cerebellum is especially adept at coordinating rapid, well-learned movements. For example, when you are first learning to play a musical scale on the piano, your primary motor cortex directs the movement of your fingers on the piano keyboard. But, after the scale has become well learned, control shifts to the cerebellum. In fact, the cerebellum appears to take over control of all well-learned movements, allowing the individual to perform the movements subconsciously, without involvement of the cerebrum. Often, when I drive to work in the morning, I get into my car, put the car in gear, and suddenly find myself pulling into the parking lot at the university. I don't remember anything about the drive: I don't remember stopping for red lights or passing any landmarks. That's because I used my cerebellum to drive while I used my cerebrum to think about upcoming events of the day.

cerebellar cortex: the cerebellum's outermost layer, which contains Purkinje, Golgi, stellate, basket, and granule cells

Figure 6.13 Organization of the cerebellum

The cerebellar cortex contains a number of different neurons, including Purkinje, stellate, basket, granular, and Golgi cells. The Purkinje cells carry information out of the cerebellum.

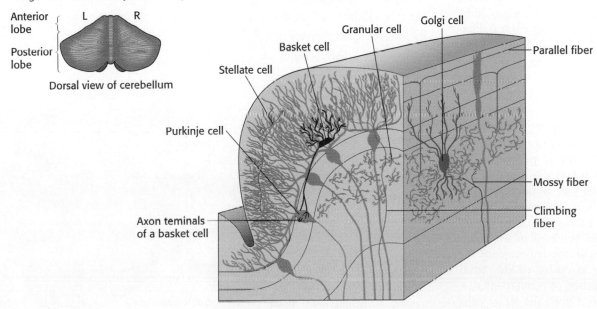

Anterior lobe
Posterior lobe
Dorsal view of cerebellum
Stellate cell
Basket cell
Granular cell
Golgi cell
Parallel fiber
Purkinje cell
Axon teminals of a basket cell
Mossy fiber
Climbing fiber

The Basal Ganglia

The basal ganglia play an important role in relaying information to and from the cerebral cortex, although the specific functions of the basal ganglia with respect to movement are unclear (Schmidt & Kretschmer, 1997). Recall from Chapter 4 that the basal ganglia are actually a group of nuclei, or clusters of neuronal cell bodies, located beneath the cerebral cortex. That is, the basal ganglia are composed of a diverse group of subcortical nuclei, including the **striatum,** the **globus pallidus,** the **substantia nigra,** and the **subthalamic nucleus.** The striatum itself contains several nuclei: the **caudate nucleus, putamen,** and the **nucleus accumbens.** The function of the striatum is to receive information from the cerebral cortex and send it on to the globus pallidus. The caudate nucleus is associated with the processing of cognitive information, whereas the putamen appears to be responsible for relaying motor signals. The globus pallidus processes that information and sends new information back to the thalamus and on to the cerebral cortex, including the primary motor cortex, thereby influencing behavior. The striatum also receives information from the thalamus and from the amygdala, which functions in the expression of emotion (Davis, 1992; Steriade, McCormick, & Sejnowski, 1993). This information, too, gets relayed from the basal ganglia to areas of the cerebral cortex involved in planning and execution of movement.

In summary, information comes into the basal ganglia from the cerebral cortex, is processed there, and then is sent back to the cerebral cortex. Information coming into the striatum from diverse regions of the cerebral cortex remains segregated in the striatum and does not mix. At least five independent pathways have been identified in the basal ganglia (Weiner & Lang, 1995). For example, one circuit receives information from the somatosensory cortex and sends it to the premotor cortex just anterior to the primary motor cortex. Another circuit gets input from association areas in the cerebral cortex and relays that input to the prefrontal cortex. The purpose of these circuits is unclear, although we do know that GABA is the most abundant neurotransmitter in the axons that extend from neurons in the output areas of the basal ganglia to the cerebrum. Thus, we can infer that the most important function of the basal ganglia is to inhibit particular regions of the cerebral cortex (Folstein, 1989).

The initiation, acceleration, deceleration, and termination of movement appear to be controlled by a pathway that stretches from the cerebral cortex to the spinal cord. This pathway receives inputs from the cerebral cortex, limbic system, basal ganglia nuclei (putamen, globus pallidus, substantia nigra, subthalamic nucleus), the reticular formation, and the cerebellum (Figure 6.14). Messages from the nuclei of the basal ganglia to this pathway are inhibitory. Overactivity of basal ganglia nuclei will interfere with movement, as you will learn in the next section.

Recall from Chapter 4 that the nigrostriatal dopamine pathway projects from the substantia nigra to the caudate nucleus and putamen of the basal ganglia. This means that stimulation of the substantia nigra causes dopamine to be released in the striatum. Thus, dopamine is necessary for the proper functioning of the basal ganglia. A number of movement disorders associated with the basal ganglia, which we will discuss in the next

striatum: part of the basal ganglia that is composed of the caudate nucleus, putamen, and the nucleus accumbens

globus pallidus: a group of neurons that is part of the basal ganglia and receives information from the striatum

substantia nigra: a cluster of cells in the basal ganglia that produces dopamine

subthalamic nucleus: a nucleus that is part of the basal ganglia

caudate nucleus: a structure in the striatum of the basal ganglia that processes cognitive information

putamen: a nucleus in the striatum of the basal ganglia that relays motor information

nucleus accumbens: a forebrain nucleus where dopamine is released, producing pleasurable feelings

Figure 6.14 Organization of the basal ganglia

The basal ganglia consist of a group of nuclei, including the striatum (which contains the caudate nucleus, the putamen, and nucleus accumbens), the globus pallidus, the substantia nigra, and the subthalamic nucleus.

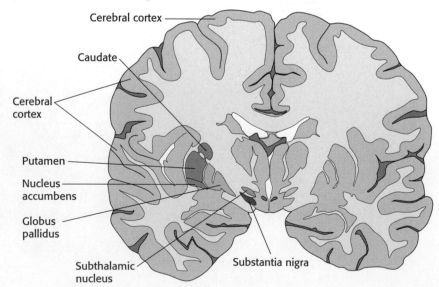

section, result from the presence of too much or too little dopamine in the striatum.

Recap 6.3: Control of Movement by the Brain

The brain has two motor systems, the (a)_____ motor system and the (b)_____ motor system. The pyramidal motor system arises from the (c)_____ _____ cortex and travels to motor neurons in the spinal cord by way of the dorsolateral corticospinal tract. Fine motor control is regulated by the (d)_____ system, whereas gross movements and postural adjustments are coordinated by the (e)_____ system. The extrapyramidal system arises from the (f)_____ cortex, the cerebellum, the basal ganglia, and the reticular formation. The function of the (g)_____ is to coordinate well-learned movements and movements made in response to sensory stimuli. The (h)_____ _____ are involved in relaying information to and from the cerebral cortex. The basal ganglia are composed of a number of (i)_____, including the globus pallidus, substantia nigra, subthalamic nucleus, and the (j)_____, which includes the caudate nucleus, putamen and nucleus accumbens.

Movement Disorders

Damage to muscles, motor neurons, the spinal cord, the pyramidal system, or the extrapyramidal system can cause a movement disorder. Let's take a look at the types of disorders associated with damage to each of these structures or systems.

Damage to Muscles

Skeletal muscles must be intact and healthy in order to function properly. For example, when a muscle is separated from the skeleton, as happens with a torn tendon, contraction of the muscle does not produce the expected movement. Another disorder, **muscular dystrophy,** causes wasting of the muscle fibers, which weakens muscular contraction. There are several forms of muscular dystrophy, each of which is most prevalent in certain age groups. However, all forms of this disorder appear to have a genetic basis, and all result in progressive muscle weakness and physical disability. Although a cure for muscular dystrophy has not yet been found, much research is currently underway to find such a cure. Recently, Italian investigators have reported that cells from bone marrow can grow into new muscle fibers to replace damaged muscle fibers in mice (Ferrari, Cusella-De Angelis, Coletta, Paolucci, Stornaiuolo, Cossu, & Mavilio, 1998). Further research is needed to determine whether bone marrow transplants can help people with muscular dystrophy.

muscular dystrophy: a disorder characterized by wasting of the muscle fibers, which causes muscular weakness

Myasthenia gravis is a movement disorder associated with the progressive degeneration of acetylcholine receptors located at neuromuscular junctions. It is an autoimmune disease in which antibodies attack and destroy acetylcholine receptors on skeletal muscles, leaving the afflicted individual with muscle weakness and rapidly fatiguing muscle contractions. This disorder occurs most often in women between the ages of 20 and 30, although men are more likely than women to develop the disorder after the age of 40. Although no cure for myasthenia gravis presently exists, the disorder can be treated with drugs that inhibit acetylcholinesterase, the enzyme that breaks down acetylcholine in the synapse. By

myasthenia gravis: a disorder characterized by progressive loss of acetylcholine receptors in the neuromuscular junction

blocking the action of acetylcholinesterase, these drugs (called *anticholinesterases*) increase the amount of acetylcholine that is available at the synapse to stimulate the remaining neuromuscular receptor sites. A blood-filtering process, known as *plasmapheresis*, is also used to remove the muscle-attacking antibodies from the blood (Spring & Spies, 2001).

Damage to Motor Neurons

Motor neurons, as you learned earlier in this chapter, are the final common path leading to muscles. Damage to motor neurons would most certainly affect movement adversely. One disorder, known as **amyotrophic lateral sclerosis** or **ALS,** is caused by the degeneration of motor neurons in the spinal cord and brain. (This disorder, which typically first appears in middle or late adulthood, is also referred to as Lou Gehrig's disease, named after the famous baseball player who was stricken with it.) As more and more motor neurons die, the symptoms of ALS progress from muscle weakness to muscle wasting and extreme impairment of movement. Abnormal, excessive glutamate activity is thought to produce the motor neuron degeneration seen in ALS (Plaitakis & Shashidharan, 1995). Currently, no treatment or cure is available for individuals with ALS (Charles & Swash, 2001).

amyotrophic lateral sclerosis (ALS): a progressive disorder caused by degeneration of motor neurons in the spinal cord and brain

Damage to the Spinal Cord

Spinal cord injuries can produce a range of disorders, depending on the location of the injury. Damage to the cervical spinal cord is a common injury that occurs in diving, skiing, and automobile accidents. Recall from Chapter 4 that actor Christopher Reeve suffered a C3 injury when he was hurt in a horseback-riding accident. Damage to the cervical spinal cord typically results in **quadriplegia.** As its name implies, quadriplegia involves paralysis, or loss of motor function, of all four limbs.

quadriplegia: disability involving impairment of motor and sensory functions in all four limbs

Often, damage to the cervical spinal cord does not result in total loss of movement in the arms and hands. Recall from Chapter 4 that innervation for most muscles is typically spread over several segments of the spinal cord. For example, the motor neurons that control muscles in the arms and hands are located in spinal cord segments C3, C4, C5, C6, C7, C8, T1, T2, and T3. The total aggregate of motor neurons that control one muscle is known as a **motor pool.** The motor pool for the biceps muscle consists of motor neurons scattered over segments C5, T2, and T3. Damage to the spinal cord at C6, for example, would impair biceps muscle fibers that receive innervation from motor neurons in T2 and T3. However, those muscle fibers in the biceps that receive innervation from motor neurons in C5 would be spared, and weak control of the biceps muscle would be observed with a C6 injury.

motor pool: the total aggregate of all motor neurons that controls one muscle

Damage to the thoracic or lumbar area of the spinal cord usually produces **paraplegia.** In paraplegia, the hind limbs lose their motor function. The forelimbs, or arms, escape impairment in paraplegia because the cervical spinal cord is not injured and remains intact. However, damage to the thoracic or lumbar area interrupts communication between the brain and the motor neurons that control muscles in the legs and feet. Thus, voluntary movement of the hind limbs is impaired.

paraplegia: a disorder involving loss of motor function to the lower limbs

Most spinal cord injuries do not involve complete transections or breaks of the spinal cord. In most cases, only partial damage occurs. People with partial damage to the spinal cord are often *ambulatory*, or able to walk, with or without assistance (Little, Ditunno, Stiens, & Harris, 1999). Keep in mind that sensory axons enter the spinal cord on the dorsal side. Thus, damage to the spinal cord can produce sensory, as well as motor, impairment.

Whenever damage to the spinal cord occurs, **spinal shock,** a condition in which no reflexes can be elicited, is observed immediately following the injury. Spinal shock can last for hours, days, or weeks following the injury and involves a total loss of spinal reflex activity. As you learned earlier in this chapter, spinal reflexes remain intact following surgical severance of the spinal cord. However, immediately following damage to the spinal cord, no reflexes can be elicited. It

spinal shock: condition seen immediately following damage to the spinal cord in which no spinal reflexes can be elicited

appears that the spinal cord goes into a state of shock following disconnection from the brain. In rats, dogs, and cats, spinal reflexes return within a few hours or days of the spinal injury, although the animal remains paralyzed and cannot engage in voluntary movement.

Unfortunately, for monkeys, apes, and humans, recovery from spinal shock does not typically occur (Creed, Denny-Brown, Eccles, Liddell, & Sherrington, 1932). Following injury to the spinal cord, primates do not recover spinal reflexes as fully as lower animals do. Even the withdrawal reflex cannot ordinarily be elicited. In humans, the urination and defecation reflexes shut down immediately following spinal cord injury, and the injured patients require urinary catheterization (a tube placed into the bladder to remove urine) and special assistance in bowel function to maintain elimination of wastes. It appears that motor neurons in the spinal cords of primates rely profoundly on innervation from the brain. When this innervation is interrupted because of damage to the spinal cord, the motor neurons cannot function normally, and reflexive action is disrupted.

Damage to the Pyramidal System

Damage to any part of the pyramidal system will affect movement, especially fine motor control. The primary motor cortex, which is located at the top of the brain directly under the skull, is particularly vulnerable to damage from trauma, such as a blow to the head. Discrete damage to the primary motor cortex will affect only a small set of muscles. For example, a small tumor on the most superior aspect of the primary motor cortex will impair walking or foot movement, whereas a tumor on the inferior aspect of the primary motor cortex will affect jaw movement. Recent research has demonstrated that the primary motor cortex is more flexible than originally believed. When one area of the primary motor cortex is damaged, other areas of the primary motor cortex can take over the function of the damaged area.

Damage to any part of the corticospinal tract results in **transient flaccid paralysis.** Let's take the term *transient flaccid paralysis* apart. You know what *paralysis* is: an inability to move voluntarily. The word *transient* refers to the fact that this paralysis is temporary, and the word *flaccid* means that there is a loss of muscle tone. Damage to the pyramidal system results in a temporary state of paralysis in which the patient has no muscle tone. The limbs feel like limp noodles when tested. If, following an automobile accident, a person comes into the emergency room on a stretcher and is paralyzed with a loss of muscle tone, you can be sure that that individual has suffered damage to the pyramidal motor system.

transient flaccid paralysis: complete loss of muscle tone, with paralysis, seen immediately after damage to the pyramidal motor system

Transient flaccid paralysis usually lasts for only a few days or weeks following pyramidal damage. It is gradually replaced by a more permanent state of **hyperreflexia,** in which the injured individual has extremely reactive reflexes. For example, when a knee jerk reflex is tested immediately following pyramidal damage, no reflex is elicited. However, when tested for a knee jerk reflex several weeks following pyramidal injury, the patient will typically give an extremely strong extension response.

hyperreflexia: a state in which reflexes are extremely reactive and exaggerated

The primary motor cortex receives information from other areas of the cerebrum, including the prefrontal cortex, the parietal lobe, and the temporal lobe. Sometimes damage to these areas of the brain will have an adverse effect on the functioning of the primary motor cortex and on fine motor control. In one disorder, called **apraxia,** the individual cannot organize movements into a productive sequence (Roy & Square, 1994). For example, when given an envelope and a sheet of paper, the person with apraxia cannot figure out how to fold the paper and put it into the envelope, even after being shown how to do it. The person with apraxia cannot complete a series of movements that must be carried out sequentially. The primary motor cortex is typically intact and undamaged in apraxia, but other areas of the cortex are impaired, particularly those areas of the parietal and prefrontal cortex in the left hemisphere that relay information to the primary motor cortex about the sequence of movements to be performed.

apraxia: a disorder caused by cerebral damage in which a person cannot organize movements into a productive sequence and can no longer perform previously familiar movements with the hands

Damage to the Extrapyramidal System

Recall that many diverse brain structures comprise the extrapyramidal system. Damage to any of these structures produces impairment of the motor system. In contrast to the pyramidal system, damage to the extrapyramidal motor system does *not* produce transient flaccid paralysis. Instead, immediately following extrapyramidal damage, hyperreflexia is observed in the injured person. Often a *loss of reciprocal innervation* accompanies the hyperreflexia. This means that, when a reflex is tested, a vigorous movement is elicited, which immediately stimulates contraction of the antagonist muscles. Usually reciprocal innervation inhibits the antagonist muscles from contracting when a particular muscle contracts, but damage to the extrapyramidal system interferes with this inhibition, which tends to exaggerate the stretch reflex in the antagonist muscles.

I know this is a bit complicated, so let me give you an example. Consider the knee jerk reflex. Let's take a person with extrapyramidal damage and test the knee jerk reflex. Tapping the tendon beneath the knee cap stretches the extensor (or quadriceps) muscle in the leg, as you've already learned. When this tendon is tapped, stretch receptors in the extensor muscle initiate contraction of that muscle, and the leg extends (see Figure 6.8). However, when the extensor muscle contracts, it stretches the flexor muscle of the leg. Normally, contraction of the flexor muscle is inhibited by reciprocal innervation. But, in a person with extrapyramidal damage, this inhibition is diminished, and the stretch reflex in the flexor muscle occurs, flexing the leg and stretching the extensor muscle. Stretching the extensor muscle sets off the stretch reflex in the extensor muscle once again, causing contraction of the extensor muscle and stretching of the flexor muscle.

This process of contraction → stretching of antagonist → contraction of antagonist → stretching of antagonist's antagonist → contraction of antagonist's antagonist and so on produces a series of jerks, known as **clonus,** in the limb. As the opposing muscles continue to trigger each other's stretch reflexes, *rigidity* of the limb sets in. Together, clonus and rigidity produce **spasticity.** In other words, damage to the extrapyramidal system causes hyperreflexia, which leads to spasticity. Spasticity interferes with normal smooth movement of the limbs. As the injured person attempts to move a limb, stretch reflexes in antagonist muscles are called into action, and the limb moves in a jerky fashion until rigidity sets in, halting movement altogether.

clonus: a series of jerks produced in a limb that is stretched following extrapyramidal damage

spasticity: a disorder that is produced by clonus and rigidity, which interferes with smooth movement of a limb

Damage to the Basal Ganglia

Damage to particular extrapyramidal structures produces specific movement disorders. For example, damage to the basal ganglia causes a number of problems, including **tics** and **choreas.** Tics are brief, involuntary contractions of skeletal muscles produced by the basal ganglia (Leckman, Pauls, & Cohen, 1995). Usually these tics are confined to the head and neck and typically consist of a twitch in one or more facial or shoulder muscles. Choreas involve more elaborate involuntary movements of the head, arms, and legs. *Hemiballismus* is a form of chorea that includes uncontrolled flailing of the arms and legs.

These uncontrolled movements, especially choreas and hemiballismus, are observed in some individuals with **cerebral palsy.** Cerebral palsy is a movement disorder that is caused by damage to the motor areas of the cerebrum, including the motor cortex and basal ganglia (Hadders-Algra, 2001). Although the cause of most cases of cerebral palsy is unknown, it can develop in infants before birth or shortly after birth (Collins et al., 2001; Schendel, 2001). Many different forms of cerebral palsy exist, depending on the extent and location of cerebral damage. Damage to the basal ganglia in cerebral palsy can result in spasticity, disturbed con-

tic: a brief, involuntary contraction of specific skeletal muscles produced by damage to the basal ganglia

chorea: involuntary contractions that produce movements of the head, arms, and legs

cerebral palsy: a motor disorder caused by damage to the developing brain

trol of balance, and uncontrolled movements, including *athetoid* (or writhing) movements. You will learn more about cerebral palsy in Chapter 16.

Huntington's Disease

Perhaps the best-known chorea is the disorder known as Huntington's chorea or **Huntington's disease,** which we discussed in Chapter 2. Functioning of the basal ganglia becomes disrupted in Huntington's disease, producing tics and uncontrollable muscle contractions early in the disease and culminating in dementia and psychosis in the end stages of the illness. Research has demonstrated that Huntington's disease is linked to a dominant gene on chromosome 4, which increases glutamate activity in the striatum. This increase in glutamate ultimately interferes with basal ganglia function by destroying GABA-releasing neurons in the striatum and the globus pallidus (Fischer, 1997; Nicholson & Faull, 1996; Trottier & Mandel, 2001). Figure 6.15 illustrates the brain **atrophy,** or destruction of tissue, that is seen in Huntington's disease.

No known cure exists for Huntington's disease at present. In the early stages of the illness, antipsychotic medication, which reduces the activity of dopamine in the brain, is used to treat the involuntary muscle contractions. However, no treatment helps much in the end stages of the illness. If it is true that glutamate over-activity is responsible for the degeneration of neurons in the basal ganglia, drugs that treat epilepsy by decreasing glutamate activity or increasing GABA activity might prove useful for treating and even preventing Huntington's disease (Fischer, 1997).

Parkinson's Disease

Another well-known illness associated with damage to the basal ganglia is **Parkinson's disease.** Parkinson's disease appears to be caused by destruction of dopamine-producing cells in the substantia nigra, resulting in a depletion of dopamine in the basal ganglia. (In 2000, Arvid Carlsson received the Nobel Prize in physiology for his research on dopamine and its role in Parkinson's disease in the 1950s.) As dopamine levels decline, movement becomes impaired in Parkinson's disease. The first motor symptoms include tremor, especially of the hands, and unsteadiness and loss of balance, which leads to falls. Rigidity and inability to complete a movement occur later in the course of the illness. Parkinson's disease is a progressive illness that ultimately leaves persons unable to care for themselves. Because dopamine levels in the brain are diminished in Parkinson's disease, psychological depression is often a component of the disorder that must be treated.

Parkinson's disease is most frequently seen in the elderly, although individuals in their 30s or 40s (or, in rare cases, even younger) may be diagnosed with this disorder. In addition, men are more likely to develop this disorder than are women. Actor Michael J. Fox was first diagnosed with Parkinson's disease at age 30, whereas Pope John Paul II and former U.S. Attorney General Janet Reno developed Parkinson's later in life (Figure 6.16).

The exact cause of Parkinson's disease is unknown. That is, no one can explain how or why dopamine-producing cells in the substantia nigra are destroyed. However, studies of young people in California who inadvertently injected themselves with a bad batch of synthetic heroin that contained a lethal by-product, called methyl-phenyl-tetrahydropyridene or MPTP, gave investigators a clue as

Figure 6.15 A normal brain and a brain with Huntington's disease

The ventricles are enlarged, and the basal ganglia and cerebral cortex are much reduced in the brain of an individual with Huntington's disease (right), compared to the normal brain (left).

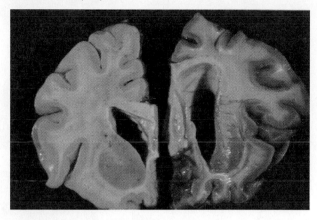

Huntington's disease: a genetic disorder, linked to chromosome 4, which increases glutamate activity in the striatum, producing tics and uncontrollable muscle contractions

atrophy: deterioration of tissue

Parkinson's disease: a movement disorder caused by destruction of dopamine-producing cells in the substantia nigra, with symptoms of tremor, loss of balance, and rigidity of limbs

Figure 6.16 Diagnosed with Parkinson's disease: Michael J. Fox, Pope John Paul II, former U.S. Attorney General Janet Reno

to how Parkinson's disease develops. These young drug users developed dramatic cases of Parkinson's disease after using the MPTP-contaminated drug repeatedly for several days. Several of the afflicted people became so immobile that they could move only their eyes. Following the discovery of the effects of MPTP in humans, investigators at the National Institute of Mental Health tried to produce the same results in monkeys. They found that injections of MPTP into monkeys produced full-blown Parkinson's disease in those animals (Burns et al., 1983). Postmortem examination of the monkeys' brains revealed destruction of the nigrastriatal dopamine system following injection of MPTP. Recently, Timothy Greenamyre and his colleagues demonstrated that a widely used pesticide, rotenone, produces Parkinson's-like symptoms in rats (Betarbet, et al., 2000). Rotenone is structurally similar to MPTP (and its metabolite MPP+) and is found in hundreds of products, including flea and tick powders and plant pesticides.

Classical antipsychotic drugs, which decrease dopamine activity in the brain, produce symptoms that resemble Parkinson's disease. These symptoms are labeled *extrapyramidal side effects* and include tremors, muscular rigidity, and a shuffling gait. Another extrapyramidal side effect sometimes observed is *akathisia*, which involves feelings of restlessness and a need to keep moving, resulting in restless movement, such as pacing. The extrapyramidal side effects are believed to be the result of decreased dopamine activity and increased acetylcholine activity in the nervous system. Drugs that decrease acetylcholine activity, called *anticholinergic medications*, and drugs that increase dopamine activity, called *dopaminergic medications*, reduce extrapyramidal side effects (Stanilla & Simpson, 2001).

Treatment for Parkinson's Disease Investigators are still trying to find a cure or lasting treatment for Parkinson's disease. Because dopamine is depleted in the basal ganglia in Parkinson's disease, you would think that it would be an easy matter just to give the person a pill containing dopamine. Unfortunately, dopamine cannot cross the blood-brain barrier, so a dopamine pill won't work. But, a precursor of dopamine, a substance that is readily converted to dopamine in the brain, can cross the blood-brain barrier. This precursor is called **L-dopa**, or *levodopa*. L-dopa, when taken orally, enters the bloodstream, crosses the blood-brain barrier, and is converted into dopamine in the brain. This drug is especially helpful in the early stages of the illness. However, L-dopa has a number of unwelcome side effects, including uncontrolled, extraneous muscle contractions, increased blood pressure, occasional psychotic symptoms, and headaches (Duty, Henry, Crossman, & Brotchie, 1996). It cannot be used every day, on a long-term basis. Hence, researchers are looking for alternative treatments for Parkinson's disease.

L-dopa: a drug, used to treat Parkinson's disease, which crosses the blood-brain barrier and is converted to dopamine in the brain

A number of alternative treatments for Parkinson's disease appear promising. These treatments are especially useful when patients are receiving the maximal daily dose of L-dopa with no improvement in symptoms or when patients develop dyskinesias (movement problems, such as choreas) in response to L-dopa. Alternative drugs therapies, such as *glutamate antagonists*, are currently under investigation to determine their efficacy in treating Parkinson's disease. The interaction between glutamate and dopamine systems in the basal ganglia is quite complicated. Destruction of neurons in the substantia nigra results in hyperactivity of the subthalamic nucleus and its projections, producing tremors, rigidity, and other Parkinsonian symptoms. Neurons in the subthalamic nucleus are excited by glutamate, *and* they release glutamate when excited, which suggests that Parkinson's disease is a glutamate hyperactivity disorder. Thus, reducing glutamate activity should inhibit activity of the subthalamic nucleus and decrease clinical manifestations of Parkinson's disease. Experiments with rats treated with antipsychotic drugs (which block dopamine activity, producing rigidity and immobility in rats) and with monkeys injected with MPTP demonstrate that glutamate antagonists can reduce Parkinsonian symptoms (Marin et al., 2000; Ossowska et al., 1998; Papa & Chase, 1996; Starr, 1995).

Surgical treatments for Parkinson's disease fall into three categories: *destructive*, *nondestructive*, and *restorative* (Follett, 2000). Destructive surgical treatments for Parkinson's disease involve ablating or making surgical cuts through the ventral thalamus **(thalamotomy)** or the globus pallidus of the basal ganglia **(pallidotomy)**. Surgical cuts in these regions are believed to interfere with the transmission of excitatory messages that produce the clinical manifestations of Parkinson's disease. Both thalamotomy and pallidotomy reduce the rigidity and tremors observed in Parkinson's patients, improving their posture, gait, and locomotion. Pallidotomy is also associated with an improvement in mood and cognitive function in patients with Parkinson's (Narabayashi, 1996).

thalamotomy: a surgical procedure used to treat Parkinson's disease, involving surgical cuts through the ventral thalamus

pallidotomy: a surgical procedure used to treat Parkinson's disease, involving surgical cuts through the globus pallidus of the basal ganglia

Nondestructive surgical treatments for Parkinson's disease involve stimulation of structures located deep within the brain, such as the subthalamic nucleus. Subthalamic stimulation produces significant improvement in Parkinson's patients and appears to be more promising than pallidotomy as a treatment for Parkinson's disease (Levesque, Taylor, Rogers, Le, & Swope, 1999). That is, stimulation of the subthalamic nucleus reduces Parkinsonian symptoms without resulting in destruction of a region of the brain.

Restorative surgical treatments for Parkinson's disease include *fetal tissue trans-plantation* and *gene therapy*. Fetal tissue transplantation involves implanting grafts of dopamine-rich midbrain tissue from very young (6- to 9-week-old) human fetuses into the putamen-caudate nucleus regions of patients with Parkinson's disease. Clinical studies of people who have received these grafts indicate that many patients enjoy a progressive reduction of their symptoms and improvement in mobility for months after the grafts (Lindvall et al., 1990; Thompson, 1992). PET scans of these patients a year after the implantation showed increased dopamine production, which indicates that the implanted grafts had survived and remained functional. However, not all Parkinson's patients show improvement following implantation of fetal grafts, and the use of brain tissues from aborted fetuses in this procedure raises ethical concerns for some people.

Gene therapy for Parkinson's disease is still in the experimental stages (Olson, 2000). In order to do gene therapy, a gene that will treat the cause or symptoms of Parkinson's disease must be introduced into the brain. One way to introduce a gene into the brain is to insert the gene into *astroglial cells* (a special type of glial cell, as you learned in Chapter 2, which are also referred to as *astrocytes*) and implant these altered glial cells back into the brain, where they act as tiny drug factories, pumping out the necessary chemicals to treat Parkinson's disease. A gene can also be introduced by way of a virus, like herpes simplex virus cells, which readily attack neurons. The virus crosses the blood-brain barrier and infects neurons by injecting its genes into the DNA of the host cell, thus causing the neuron to manufacture the target gene. A number of candidate genes are under investigation in the search for a treatment for Parkinson's disease. These genes direct the production of a specific protein, such as *glial cell line-derived neurotrophic factor* (GDNF), *human tyrosine hydroxylase* (TH), or *aromatic l-amino acid decaroxylase* (AADC), which have been shown to increase or restore the secretion of dopamine by neurons (Bankiewicz et al., 2000; Connor et al., 1999; Kordower et al., 2000; Leone et al., 2000; Shen et al., 2000; Yurek & Fletcher-Turner, 2001). So far, these techniques have been studied only in rats or nonhuman primates. Investigators hope to test one or more of these techniques in clinical trials in people in the near future.

Damage to the Cerebellum

Damage to the cerebellum interferes with the ability of this brain structure to coordinate movement. Depending on the extent of the damage, movement impairments can vary. For example, tumors in the cerebellum produce a variety of problems related to the location of the tumor. Tumors in the posterior cerebellum disrupt communication with the vestibular system and interfere with balance, whereas tumors that affect midline cerebellar structures disturb bilateral coordination of the limbs and trunk (Bastian, Mink, Kaufman, & Thach, 1998).

People with cerebellar damage show a number of problems, including **ataxia,** which is an inability to walk or move in a coordinated fashion, and **disequilibrium,** a loss of balance. Staggering or a foot-dragging gait is evidence of cerebellar damage. Other individuals may be unable to perform rapid, well-learned movements following damage to the cerebellum. Instead, their movements become hesitant and slow.

As you know, the cerebellum is extremely dependent upon the senses as it coordinates movement. For example, as I walk across a room, the cerebellum receives information from my eyes about the presence and location of objects in the room, allowing me to cross the room without tripping over shoes and other items on the floor. In Chapter 7, we will examine the various sensory systems, and we will look at a number of sensory disorders that can disrupt cerebellar function.

ataxia: an inability to walk in a coordinated fashion

disequilibrium: a loss of balance

(a)_____ disorders associated with damage to (b)_____ include muscular dystrophy and myasthenia gravis. Amyotrophic lateral sclerosis is caused by degeneration of (c)_____ neurons. Damage to the cervical spinal cord typically results in (d)_____, whereas damage to the thoracic or lumbar spinal cord causes (e)_____. Damage to the corticospinal tract results in (f)_____ _____ paralysis. Immediately following (g)_____ damage, hyperreflexia is observed. Damage to the (h)_____ _____ causes a number of disorders including tics, choreas, Huntington's disease, and Parkinson's disease. (i)_____ disease is caused by destruction of dopamine-producing cells in the substantia nigra. Treatments for Parkinson's disease include drug therapy, involving (j)_____ and glutamate antagonists, and surgical treatments. Damage to the (k)_____ produces a number of problems including ataxia and disequilibrium.

Chapter Summary

Muscle Structure and Function

▶ Each muscle cell is called a muscle fiber, which contain contractile tissue. This fiber contains two kinds of filaments, actin and myosin, which are responsible for contraction of the fiber.

▶ Each muscle fiber has a chemically sensitive endplate that contains receptors for acetylcholine. Acetylcholine stimulates contraction of the muscle fibers in skeletal, smooth, and cardiac muscle.

▶ The synapse between the axon of a motor neuron and the endplate of a muscle fiber is called a neuromuscular junction. The total number of muscle fibers innervated by one motor neuron is called a motor unit.

▶ Skeletal muscles are attached to the bones of the skeleton and produce flexion and extension movements of the limbs. Skeletal muscle can be classified by its color, red (which contains myoglobin, permitting the muscle to engage in sustained behavior) and white (which is used for short bursts of rapid muscle contractions).

▶ Smooth muscles are found in the walls of blood vessels and many internal organs, in the skin, and in the ducts of glands.

Spinal Control of Movement

▶ The spinal cord mediates rapid, automatic responses to stimuli, called reflexes.

▶ A large number of unisynaptic and polysynaptic reflexes are organized in the spinal cord, including the stretch reflex, tendon reflex, withdrawal reflex, crossed extensor reflex, elimination reflexes, and sexual reflexes. The withdrawal, or flexion, reflex involves an immediate withdrawal movement that occurs in response to a painful stimulus. In the crossed extensor reflex, one leg extends when the other flexes to withdraw from a painful stimulus. Urination and defecation involve a stretch reflex.

▶ Alpha motor neurons innervate extrafusal fibers, and gamma motor neurons innervate intrafusal fibers. Intrafusal fibers are found in muscle spindles, attached to a nuclear bag, which contains a stretch receptor called the annulospiral receptor.

▶ Reciprocal innervation involves the inhibition of antagonist muscles by motor neurons of contracting muscles.

▶ According to the principle of the common path, the motor neuron is the final step in the pathway to a muscle.

Control of Movement by the Brain

▶ The brain controls movement by means of the pyramidal motor system and the extrapyramidal motor system.

▶ Arising from the primary motor cortex, or precentral gyrus, the pyramidal system traverses the spinal cord through the dorsolateral corticospinal tract. Axons leaving the precentral gyrus pass without synapsing to target motor neurons in the ventral horn of the spinal cord.

▶ The extrapyramidal system arises from the cerebral cortex, the basal ganglia, the cerebellum, and the reticular formation. The function of the cerebellum is to coordinate well-learned movements and movements made in response to sensory stimuli. The basal ganglia are involved in relaying information to and from the cerebral cortex.

▶ The pyramidal system develops later than the extrapyramidal system and regulates fine motor control, whereas the extrapyramidal system controls gross postural adjustments and other movements produced by large muscles.

Movement Disorders

▶ Damage to muscles, motor neurons, the spinal cord, the pyramidal system, or the extrapyramidal system can result in a movement disorder.

▶ Muscular dystrophy and myasthenia gravis are associated with progressive damage to muscle fibers.

▶ Amyotrophic lateral sclerosis (ALS) is caused by damage to motor neurons.

▶ Damage to the cervical spinal cord typically results in quadriplegia, whereas damage to the thoracic or lumbar spinal cord causes paraplegia.

▶ Damage to the pyramidal system results in transient flaccid paralysis, which eventually is replaced by hyperreflexia, damage to the extrapyramidal system immediately produces hyperreflexia.

▶ Damage to the basal ganglia can produce tics, choreas, as seen in Huntington's disease, and Parkinson's disease. Parkinson's disease is caused by destruction of dopamine-producing cells in the substantia nigra. Treatments for Parkinson's disease include drug therapy, involving L-dopa and glutamate antagonists, and surgical treatments.

▶ Damage to the cerebellum can result in ataxia, disequilibrium, and disruption of rapid, well-learned movements.

Key Terms

alpha motor neuron (p. 151)
amyotrophic lateral sclerosis
   (ALS) (p. 162)
annulospiral receptor (p. 152)
antagonists (p. 149)
apraxia (p. 163)
ataxia (p. 168)
atrophy (p. 165)
Babinski reflex (p. 145)
caudate nucleus (p. 160)
cerebellar cortex (p. 159)
cerebral palsy (p. 164)
chorea (p. 164)
clonus (p. 164)
crossed extensor reflex (p. 154)
disequilibrium (p. 168)
dorsolateral corticospinal
   tract (p. 157)
endplate (p. 147)
extension (p. 149)
extrafusal fibers (p. 151)
extrapyramidal motor
   system (p. 157)

flexion (p. 149)
gamma motor neuron (p. 151)
globus pallidus (p. 160)
Golgi tendon organ (p. 153)
Huntington's disease (p. 165)
hyperreflexia (p. 163)
intrafusal fibers (p. 151)
isometric contraction (p. 150)
isotonic contraction (p. 150)
L-dopa (p. 167)
motor pool (p. 162)
muscle fiber (p. 147)
muscle spindles (p. 152)
muscle tone (p. 148)
muscular dystrophy (p. 161)
myasthenia gravis (p. 161)
neuromuscular junction (p. 148)
nucleus accumbens (p. 160)
pallidotomy (p. 167)
paraplegia (p. 162)
Parkinson's disease (p. 165)
polysynaptic reflex (p. 151)
primary motor cortex (p. 157)

putamen (p. 160)
pyramidal motor system (p. 157)
quadriplegia (p. 162)
reciprocal innervation (p. 153)
reflex (p. 151)
skeletal muscle (p. 148)
spasticity (p. 164)
spinal shock (p. 162)
stretch reflex (p. 152)
striatum (p. 160)
substantia nigra (p. 160)
subthalamic nucleus (p. 160)
thalamotomy (p. 167)
tic (p. 164)
transient flaccid paralysis (p. 163)
unisynaptic reflex (p. 151)
ventromedial corticospinal
   tract (p. 158)
withdrawal reflex (p. 151)

Questions for Thought

1. Why do some reflexes develop later than others during development?

2. Give an example of how you use isometric muscle contraction everyday. Give an example of isotonic contraction.

3. If you had a brain tumor at the superior aspect of your primary motor cortex, movement to which parts of your body might be affected?

Questions for Review

1. Explain how the annulospiral receptors and Golgi tendon organs regulate muscle tone.

2. Name three differences between the pyramidal and extrapyramidal motor systems.

3. What are the effects of spinal shock?

4. Describe several treatments available for Parkinson's disease.

Suggested Readings

Harper, P. S. (1996). *Huntington's disease*. London: W. B. Saunders.

Jacobs, B. L. (1994). Serotonin, motor activity, and depression related disorders. *American Scientist, 82,* 456–463.

Ohyc, C., Kimura, M., & McKenzie, J. S. (1994). *Basal ganglia V*. New York: Plenum Press.

Sacks, O. W. (1983). *Awakenings*. New York: Dutton.

Stern, G. M. (1999). *Parkinson's disease*. Philadelphia: Lippincott Williams & Wilkins.

Web Resources

For a chapter tutorial quiz, direct links to the Internet sites listed below and other features, visit the book-specific website at **www.wadsworth.com/product/ 0155074865**. You may also connect directly to the following annotated websites:

http://www.furman.edu/~einstein/general/ development/reflexes.htm
This site will introduce you to eight different types of infant reflexes.

http://neurologychannel.org
Search this online library for more information about a variety of movement disorders including ALS (Lou Gehrig's disease), Huntington's disease, Parkinson's disease and myasthenia gravis.

http://www.parkinsonsinfo.com/about_parkinsons/
On this detailed site you can learn more about Parkinson's disease, how people live with it and the latest disease research.

For additional readings and information, check out InfoTrac College Edition at **http://www.infotrac-college.com/wadsworth**. Choose a search term yourself or enter the following search terms: amyotrophic, apraxia, lateral sclerosis, muscular dystrophy, myasthenia gravis, Parkinson's Disease.

CD-ROM: Exploring Biological Psychology

Animation: The Withdrawal Reflex
Animation: The Crossed Extensor Reflex
Video: The Brain Pacemaker

Interactive Recaps
Chapter 6 Quiz
Connect to the Interactive Biological Psychology Glossary

Sensory Processes

At the age of nineteen months, Helen Keller became deaf and blind following an illness that damaged her nervous system. With the help of a skilled, devoted teacher named Anne Sullivan, Helen learned to communicate with other people by using the manual alphabet of the deaf, a system of hand signals used to spell out words. She also learned to read Braille, using her fingertips to feel the raised bumps of the Braille symbols. At the age of 10, she learned how to speak after only one month of lessons. Helen was such an intelligent, diligent student that she was accepted into Radcliffe College and graduated from Radcliffe with honors in 1904 (Figure 7.1). Although she was unable to process visual and auditory information, Helen learned at a very young age to identify objects in her environment by their smell, taste, or feel. This tells us that different sensations reach the brain by different pathways. In Helen Keller's case, the pathways for vision and audition were not functional, and information about light and sound could not be transmitted to her brain. All of her other pathways were intact, however, which enabled her to experience all the other sensations that we feel every day.

What are these sensations? They include taste, smell, touch, pain, warm and cold, dizziness, a full stomach, a sore muscle, and movement of our limbs. We have specialized sensory cells, called **receptors,** that respond to specific stimuli and send information about those stimuli to the central nervous system. In this chapter, we will examine a variety of receptors associated with the various sensory systems and discuss how these cells encode information about stimuli. We will also explore the pathways between receptors and areas of the brain that process sensory information.

receptor: a specialized sensory cell that responds to a specific stimulus

Sensory Stimuli and Receptors

Internal and External Stimuli

Receptors are activated by **stimuli.** These stimuli can come from outside the body *(external stimuli)* or from within the body *(internal stimuli).* Examples of external stimuli that stimulate our receptors are light, sound, tastes, odors, pressure, and changes in temperature. Internal stimuli occur within the body and include stretching of muscles or tendons, blood pressure, and chemicals carried in the blood, such as glucose or hormones.

Stimuli generally take one of two forms: *chemical* or *mechanical.* Chemical stimuli are molecules that bind with receptor sites on receptors. For example, molecules that are dissolved in water (such as salt or NaCl) excite receptors on the tongue. Chemicals located inside the body, like blood glucose, stimulate receptors located deep within the body. Receptors that are stimulated by chemical stimuli are called **chemoreceptors.**

Mechanical stimuli exert physical force, such as pushing, pulling, or vibrating. Like chemical stimuli, mechanical stimuli can be external or internal. A tap on the skin is an example of an external mechanical stimulus, whereas stretching of a muscle is an internal mechanical stimulus. **Mechanoreceptors** are receptors that respond to mechanical stimuli.

Light cannot be classified as a chemical or mechanical stimulus. It is released in discrete packets of energy, called **photons.** Photons are emitted by the sun and other sources of light and travel at a speed of 186,000 miles per second (the speed of light) until they are absorbed. Most objects in our environment absorb photons, although many surfaces, such as glass or polished metal, reflect light. Visual receptors in the eyes contain special chemical molecules, known as *photopigments,* that absorb photons.

Characteristics of Waves

Many external stimuli are transmitted through the environment as waves. For example, vibrations and sound travel in waves. Electromagnetic radiation, which comes from the sun and other sources of radiant energy, also travels in waves. Figure 7.2 illustrates the many forms of electromagnetic radiation, including visible light.

Waves have a number of characteristics that you should know about in order to understand the material in this chapter. **Wavelength** refers to the distance between corresponding parts of two consecutive waves (Figure 7.3). Like other forms of electromagnetic radiation, light is characterized by its wavelength. As you can see in Figure 7.2, each color of the rainbow (red-orange-yellow-green-blue-indigo-violet) is associated with a particular wavelength. Red, which has a wavelength of approximately 700 nanometers (or 10^{-9} meters), is considered *long-wavelength light.* In contrast, blue, with a wavelength of about 500 nanometers, is called *short-wavelength light.* Visible light makes up a very small proportion of the electromagnetic spectrum, which ranges from a wavelength of 10^{-14} meters for cosmic rays to a wavelength of 10^6 meters for radio waves (Figure 7.2).

We can also characterize waves by their **frequency,** which is the number of waves that occurs in a certain period of time. One complete wave is called a *cycle* (Figure 7.3). Thus, the frequency of a wave is expressed as *cycles per second* (cycles/second). The International System of Units uses the term

Figure 7.1 Helen Keller at her graduation from Radcliffe College in 1904

stimuli: objects or events that excite a sensory neuron or receptor

chemoreceptors: receptors that respond to chemical stimuli

mechanoreceptors: receptors that respond to mechanical stimulation, such as pulling, stretching, or vibrating

photon: discrete packet of light energy

wavelength: the distance between two corresponding parts of a wave

frequency: the number of waves that occurs in a specified period of time, usually a second

Figure 7.2 Various forms of electromagnetic radiation

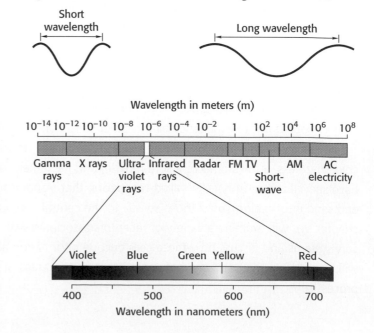

Hertz (named for a German scientist, Heinrich Hertz, who studied waves in the late 19th century) as the unit for frequency. Sound waves are usually described by their frequency. For example, women's voices typically have a frequency between 200 and 1,000 Hz, and men's voices typically have a frequency between 60 and 500 Hz. (*Hz* is the abbreviation for *Hertz*.) This demonstrates that higher frequency sounds are perceived as having a higher pitch than lower frequency sounds. Frequency is a physical characteristic of waves, and *pitch* is the corresponding perceptual experience of frequency.

Light can also be described in terms of frequency. Blue light, for example, has a frequency of approximately 660 trillion Hz, or 660×10^{12} Hz. More commonly, however, we think of blue light in terms of wavelength. The opposite is true for sound. We could easily use wavelength to characterize sound, but we don't. According to convention, light is described in wavelength units (meters) and sound in Hz units.

Another characteristic of waves is **amplitude** (Figure 7.3). The amplitude is the height of the wave from the lowest to the highest points. The amplitude of a sound wave corresponds to the psychological phenomenon known as **loudness.** A large amplitude is associated with a loud sound, and a small amplitude is associated with a softer, less loud sound. We use the unit **decibel** (named after Alexander Graham Bell, who studied the transmission of sound and invented the telephone) to measure loudness. The decibel scale ranges from 0 (least perceptibility) to about 160 (extremely loud, causing extreme pain).

Receptors

Receptors are specialized cells that inform the central nervous system about changes in the internal or external environment. Some receptors are neurons, which means that they have true axons that produce an action potential in response to a stimulus that is above threshold and release neurotransmitters. Other receptors are cells that alter the functioning of a neuron by depolarizing or hyperpolarizing it. Let's consider examples of each of these types of receptors.

Olfactory receptors are neurons that respond to chemicals associated with particular odors. Because they are *bipolar neurons*, each olfactory receptor has an axon and a dendrite (Figure 7.4). At the end of each dendrite is a dendritic knob from which many fine hairlike projections, called *cilia*, extend. These cilia have receptor sites that bind with specific chemicals. When an airborne chemical binds with a receptor site, an excitatory potential called a **receptor potential** (or *generator potential*) is generated. A receptor potential is a graded potential like the excitatory postsynaptic potential (EPSP). This means that, if the stimulus is strong, the receptor potential will be greater than it would be if the stimulus is weak. If threshold is reached, an action potential is initiated, which causes neurotransmitters to be released at the axon terminal. Thus, olfactory receptors use neurotransmitters to signal to the brain that an odor is present.

Hertz: a unit of frequency (1 Hertz = 1 cycle/second)

amplitude: the height of a wave from its lowest to highest points

loudness: a psychological phenomenon that corresponds to amplitude of sound waves

decibel: unit used to measure loudness

olfactory receptors: neurons that respond to chemicals associated with odors

receptor potential: an excitatory or generator potential that occurs when a receptor is stimulated

Figure 7.3 Characteristics of a wave

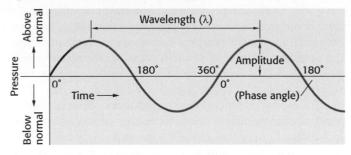

Diagram of sound wave

Figure 7.4 Olfactory receptors
The olfactory receptor is a bipolar neuron with a dendritic knob located at the end of the dendrite. Cilia on the dendritic knob contain receptor sites for odorants.

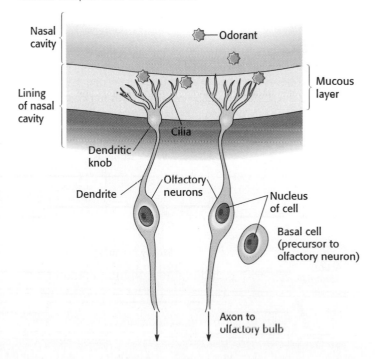

In contrast, **taste receptors** do not have dendrites or axons. Taste receptors have tiny finger-like processes, called *microvilli*, that project into the mouth, where they come into contact with chemicals that act as taste stimuli. The taste stimuli cause changes in the receptor membrane, either opening sodium channels or closing potassium channels, which depolarizes the receptor cell. Information about this depolarization is sent to the brain by way of neurons that communicate with the receptor cells.

All receptors function as **transducers.** That is, they transduce or convert one form of energy, such as chemical energy or mechanical energy, to an electrochemical form of energy, specifically a membrane potential (such as a generator potential, postsynaptic potential, or action potential). As you know, neurons communicate by means of action potentials, which initiate the release of neurotransmitters into synapses. The function of receptors, therefore, is to provide information about specific stimuli to neurons in the central nervous system by translating qualitative information about the stimuli into patterns of action potentials. Receptors are sensitive to the quality of stimuli, and they send quantitative information to the brain about the quality of stimuli.

How do receptors translate information into patterns of action potentials? You should recall from Chapter 2 that, according to the All-or-None Law, action potentials do not vary in amplitude. This means that, after an action potential is activated, it always goes to completion, reaching the same positively charged peak each time. Receptors use action potentials to transmit information about stimuli to the brain. When the stimulus is intense, the action potential does not increase in size. Rather, the frequency of the action potentials increases with an increase in stimulus intensity. That is, with a more intense stimulus, more action potentials per second are sent to the brain; and, with a less intense stimulus, fewer action potentials per second are transmitted to the brain (Figure 7.5). Thus, intensity of the stimulus is encoded as frequency of action potentials.

When a receptor is continuously stimulated by the same stimulus, the receptor will decrease its firing in response to that stimulus (Figure 7.5). This decrease in responsivity by the receptor to constant or repeated stimulation is called **adaptation.** All types of receptors show adaptation, even pain receptors. For example, imagine that you walk into your apartment after your roommate has spent the entire afternoon baking brownies. At first, the smell of chocolate is very intense and pleasant. But, after a few seconds, you can no longer smell the brownies because of adaptation of your olfactory receptors. We will examine other examples of adaptation when we discuss other sensory systems.

taste receptors: specialized cells that respond to chemicals dissolved in water

transducer: something that can convert one form of energy to another

adaptation: a decrease in the firing of a receptor to repeated stimulation

Figure 7.5 Coding information about stimuli

The strength of a stimulus is encoded by the frequency of the action potential. A strong stimulus produces more action potentials per second than a weaker stimulus does. Notice that the size of the action potential does not change. During adaptation, a neuron decreases its rate of firing in response to repeated or prolonged stimulation.

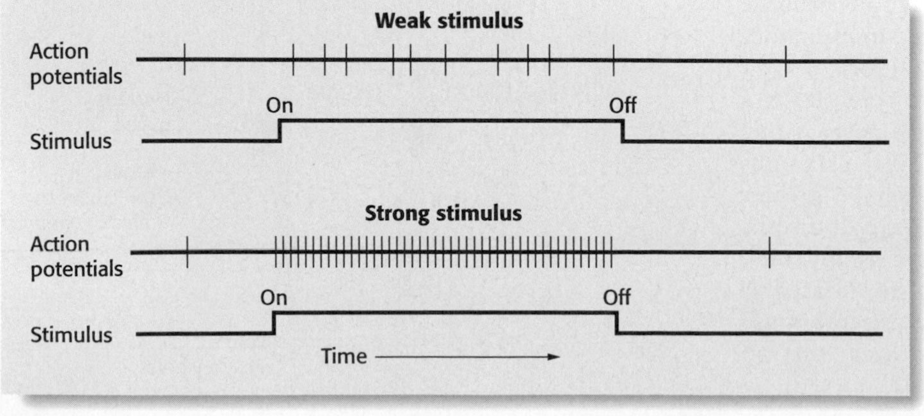

Specialized sensory neurons, called (a)_____, respond to specific stimuli. (b)_____ respond to chemical stimuli, and (c)_____ respond to mechanical stimuli. Vibrations and sound travel in (d)_____. (e)_____ is the distance between corresponding parts of two consecutive waves. (f)_____ refers to the number of waves that occur in a given period of time. The (g)_____ of a wave is the height of a wave from its lowest to highest points. The receptor potential, also called a (h)_____ potential, is a graded potential that is produced when a receptor is excited by a stimulus. Receptors are (i)_____, which means that they convert one form of energy to an electrochemical form of energy. (j)_____ is the decrease in responsiveness of a receptor to repeated stimulus. The network of neurons that form a pathway from the receptor to the cerebrum is called a (k)_____ system.

We have various receptors that respond to specific types of stimuli: taste receptors for taste stimuli, visual receptors for photons, mechanoreceptors in the skin for touch, and so forth. The receptors communicate with neurons that, in turn, communicate with other neurons that process information about the stimuli and relay it to the cerebral cortex, where conscious processing of the stimuli takes place. This network of neurons that form a pathway from the receptor to the cerebrum is known as a **sensory system.** In this chapter, we will examine a number of sensory systems, including the systems that process information about visual images, sounds, skin and muscle sensations, odors, taste, and head position.

sensory system: a network of neurons that form a pathway from the receptor to the cerebrum

visual field: that part of the environment from which visual receptors receive information

The Visual System

Compared to the other sensory systems, the visual system has received the most scientific investigation. Hence, our knowledge about the visual system is quite sophisticated. However, we are still a long way from understanding how visual images are processed and identified in the brain. In this section, we will examine how a visual image is encoded by visual receptors and then transmitted to the brain.

The Nature of Visual Stimuli

Visual receptors are stimulated by *photons*, which (as you've already learned) are discrete packets of light energy. Photons are emitted from various sources of light, such as the sun or a light bulb, and then bounce off objects in the environment, forming a visual image of each object that is relayed to the receptors in the eye (Figure 7.6). Only photons bouncing off objects in that part of the environment called the **visual field** can stimulate the visual receptors. It is important to keep in mind, however, that the

Figure 7.6 Stimulation of the visual receptors
The object in the visual field is the distal stimulus, and the image on the retina is the proximal stimulus. Note that the retinal image is actually upside down.

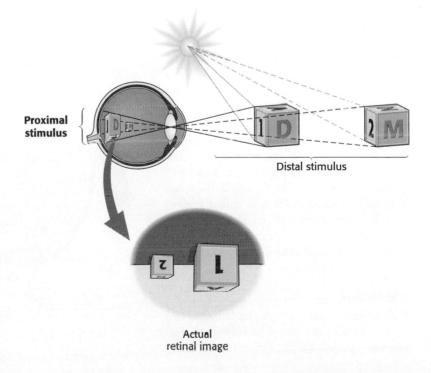

visual field changes every time the eyes shift their gaze. The object in the visual field is referred to as the **distal stimulus,** whereas the visual image that stimulates the visual receptors is referred to as the **proximal stimulus.** The proximal stimulus differs from the distal stimulus in a number of ways. For example, the distal stimulus is typically a three-dimensional object, and the proximal stimulus is a two-dimensional representation of that object. In addition, the proximal stimulus is oriented upside down, compared to the distal stimulus (Figure 7.6).

distal stimulus: object in the visual field

proximal stimulus: the visual image that stimulates the visual receptors

Anatomy and Function of the Visual System

The visual receptors are located in the **retina,** a flat, multilayered tissue situated in the back of the eye (Figure 7.7). The human eyeball is attached to the skull and held in the eye socket by means of six tiny muscles, which permit movement of the eye. The tough, white outer layer of the eye is called the *sclera.* Toward the front of the eye, the sclera disappears and is replaced by a transparent covering, called the **cornea.** Those of you who wear contact lenses to correct your vision are quite familiar with the cornea because that is the tissue on which the contact lenses are placed. The cornea is composed of several layers of cells that get their nourishment from the watery *aqueous humor* located behind it (Figure 7.7). Because the cornea contains no blood vessels, the cells that comprise the cornea get their oxygen from the air and from the aqueous humor. For that reason, depriving the cornea of contact with the air can damage or kill cells in the cornea.

retina: a flat, multilayered tissue at the back of the eyes that contains the visual receptors

cornea: transparent covering on the front of the eye that aids in focusing light as it enters the eye

To reach the visual receptors in the retina, photons must pass through the cornea and aqueous humor. Next the photons must enter the eyeball through the **pupil,** which is the hole in the center of the **iris,** the circular, colored structure of the eye. The iris contains smooth muscle, which regulates the diameter of the pupil. Recall from Chapter 2 that smooth muscles are controlled by the autonomic nervous system. The sympathetic nervous system, which becomes activated when an individual is aroused or in an emotional state, causes dilation of the pupil. In contrast, the parasympathetic nervous system produces constriction of the pupil. A constricted pupil allows less light into the eye but produces a sharper image on the retina.

pupil: the hole in the center of the iris through which light passes to stimulate receptors in the retina
iris: the circular, colored structure in the front of the eye that regulates the diameter of the pupil
lens: a yellowish, transparent structure located inside the eyeball that focuses light on the retina
accommodation: the process by which the lens changes shape in order to focus light

After the photons pass through the pupil and enter the eye, they encounter the **lens,** a transparent structure that focuses the visual image produced by the photons on the retina. The shape of the lens is controlled by specialized smooth muscles called *ciliary muscles,* which alter the shape of the lens to compensate for the distance of the distal stimulus to the eye. When the distal stimulus is far away from the eye, the lens becomes flattened in shape in order to produce a sharp image of the object on the retina. On the other hand, the lens becomes rounder and fatter when the distal stimulus is located close to the eye. This process in which the lens changes shape to focus the image on the retina is called **accommodation.** As we age, the lens loses its elasticity, and accommodation becomes impaired. This condition is called *presbyopia.* You may have noticed that your parents began to wear glasses while reading or switched to bifocal lenses in their forties, a sure sign of presbyopia.

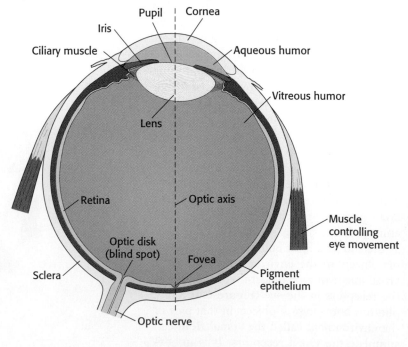

Figure 7.7 Anatomy of the visual system

Human eye

The Retina

The photons pass through the lens and the *vitreous humor,* the jelly-like substance that fills the interior of the eyeball behind the lens, to reach the retina. There are five layers of cells in the retina: (1) *visual receptors*, (2) *horizontal cells*, (3) *bipolar cells*, (4) *amacrine cells*, and (5) *ganglion cells*. These five layers are arranged with the **visual receptors** located at the back of the retina and the **ganglion cells** located nearest the vitreous humor. In other words, in order for the photons to reach the visual receptors, they have to pass through the ganglion cells, the amacrine cells, the bipolar cells, and the horizontal cells. This may seem like a very strange arrangement to you (and it is!), to have the receptors in the back of the retina rather than in front, but the receptors need plenty of nourishment (especially oxygen, glucose, and special enzymes), which they get from the blood vessels in the lining, called the *pigment epithelium*, in the back of the eye.

The pigment epithelium is a dark layer of tissue located behind the retina, at the back of the eye, and it serves two purposes. The first purpose is to provide nourishment to the cells in the retina, via blood vessels that course through the pigment epithelium. The second purpose is to absorb stray photons that are not absorbed by photopigments in the visual receptors. If the stray photons were allowed to bounce around inside the eyeball, they would distort the visual images on the retina. Many other mammals, such as dogs, cats, and cattle, do not have a pigment epithelium but instead have a reflective lining called a *reflecting tapetum* behind the retina. Have you ever seen a cat's eyes glow in the light of a flashlight? This reflecting tapetum reflects the stray photons back through the retina, where they stimulate visual receptors. Thus, the purpose of the reflecting tapetum is to maximize the light-activating visual receptors, which is important in animals that are active at night.

The cells of the retina also receive nourishment from blood vessels that lie in front of the retina. The root of the word *retina* comes from *ret-*, which means *net* or *network*, referring to the fact that a network of blood vessels covers the front of the retina. Figure 7.8 is a photograph of the inside of the eyeball as seen through an instrument, called an *ophthalmoscope*, that is used to view the interior of the eye. You can see the multitude of blood vessels that crisscross in front of the retina. Why don't you see these blood vessels in your own eyes? Certainly, as photons pass through these blood vessels to stimulate visual receptors on the retina, they produce shadows of these blood vessels on the retina. However, due to adaptation, the visual receptors do not respond to the constant stimulation produced by the blood vessels situated in front of the retina. Hence, we are normally unaware of their presence.

Visual Receptors

There are two types of visual receptors: **rods** and **cones.** These structures derive their names from their appearance. That is, as you can see in Figure 7.9a, rods are rod shaped, and cones have a tapered appearance. There are a number of other differences between rods and cones. In the human eye, there is only one type of rod and three types of cones. However, the rods outnumber the cones: approximately 120 million rods to 5 million cones. Cones are concentrated in the center of the retina in the *area centralis* (central area), particularly in the region of a tiny dimple in the retina known as the **fovea.** In contrast, the rods are dispersed throughout the retina, with a very low concentration in the area centralis.

The fovea is located along the *optic axis*, an imaginary straight line that runs from the center of the distal stimulus through the pupil and lens to the retina (see Figure 7.7). Photons that follow this imaginary line into the eye stimulate cone receptors in the fovea. These cone receptors permit us to see fine detail, whereas rods are insensitive to detail. Rods, on the other hand, provide us with peripheral vision, and cones do not, because there are few cones located in the periphery of the retina. In addition, rods respond better to movement than do cones.

Most importantly, rods and cones differ in their sensitivity to light. Rods are extremely sensitive to light and work best in dim light. In contrast, cones are less sensitive to light and work best in bright light. For this reason, we refer to rod vision as *scotopic vision* and refer to cone vision as *photopic vision* [*skotos* = darkness; *photos* = light, Greek]. As we will discuss in greater detail later, humans possess three types of cone receptors, each one of which is sensitive to different wave lengths of light. This means that cones give us information about colors in our

visual receptors: rods and cones, which are excited by photons

ganglion cells: cells on the retina whose axons form the optic nerve

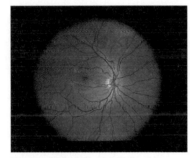

Figure 7.8 View of the interior of the eye through an ophthalmoscope

rod: a visual receptor that responds best in dim light

cone: a visual receptor that responds best in bright light

fovea: a tiny dimple in the center of the retina where cones are concentrated

Figure 7.9 Anatomy of visual receptors

(a) The outer segment of visual receptors, which are rod-shaped in rods and cone-shaped in cones, contains the photopigments that absorb photons entering the eye. (b) The photopigment 11-cis-retinal converts to all-trans-retinal, changing shape, when it absorbs a photon.

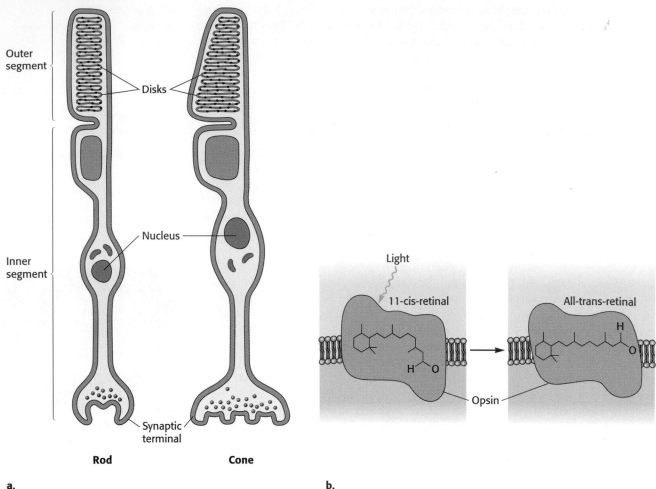

visual world. Rods are not sensitive to wavelength of light and, thus, cannot provide information about color.

All visual receptors are composed of two distinct regions: an *inner segment* and an *outer segment*. In the inner segment are found the nucleus and other important organelles of the receptor cell. The outer segment contains the **photopigments** that absorb the photons entering the eye. Billions of photopigment molecules are embedded in membranous disks located in the outer segment (Figure 7.9a). The photopigment in rods is called **rhodopsin,** and it has been studied in great detail by investigators in many laboratories. Because there are different types of cones, the name of the photopigment in cones varies.

When photons enter the eye and strike the visual receptors, each photon is absorbed by one photopigment molecule. The photopigment molecule is composed of a derivative of vitamin A called *11-cis-retinal*, which is bound to a protein called an *opsin*. Normally, 11-cis-retinal has the shape shown in Figure 7.9b. When the photopigment absorbs a photon, 11-cis-retinal changes shape, or *isomerizes*, to *all-trans-retinal*. During isomerization from 11-cis-retinal to all-trans-retinal, the photopigment also changes color and becomes *bleached*. After a photopigment is bleached, it becomes inactive and cannot absorb any more photons until the photopigment reverts to its original shape, 11-cis-retinal. The photopigment becomes unbleached in the dark, after the light has been removed, in a process called **dark adaptation.**

photopigments: chemicals that absorb photons entering the eye

rhodopsin: the photopigment found in rods

dark adaptation: a process in which the photopigments become unbleached in the dark, which allows the receptor to become sensitive to light again

In a very bright light, many photons stimulate visual receptors at the same time, bleaching the photopigments. You learned earlier that rods are more sensitive to light than cones are. This means that the photopigments in rods bleach faster and more completely when exposed to light. A bright light will bleach the rods entirely, whereas the same light will bleach only a small proportion of cone photopigments. Thus, the cones function well in bright light, but rods cannot because of overbleaching. Of course, extremely bright light will bleach out even entire cones. For example, a person who is exposed to the sun reflecting off snow on a very sunny day will experience a sense of blindness in which everything in the entire visual field disappears and is replaced by a uniform grayness. This phenomenon is referred to as *snow blindness* and is caused by overbleaching of cone photopigments.

The bleaching of a photopigment starts a biochemical change in the receptor that results in a change in the membrane potential of the receptor. Recall that this change in potential is called a *receptor potential* and that it is a graded potential. The receptor potential hyperpolarizes the visual receptor, which decreases its release of the neurotransmitter *glutamate*. That is, when a photon is absorbed by a photopigment molecule in a visual receptor, the receptor *decreases* its release of glutamate. This means that, in the absence of light, rods and cones continually release glutamate at their terminal endplates. Light stimulation, on the other hand, causes the receptors to become hyperpolarized, which results in less glutamate being released.

Transmission of Visual Information Through the Retina   The visual receptors use glutamate to signal to horizontal and bipolar cells (Figure 7.10). Horizontal cells receive information from nearby rods or cones and send signals back to those receptors, modifying their release of glutamate. When light strikes a visual receptor, causing a decrease in glutamate in the synapse between the receptor and the horizontal cell, the horizontal cell responds to this decrease in glutamate by sending messages to the receptor, which cause the receptor to increase its release of glutamate. That is, the function of the horizontal cell is to antagonize or oppose the action of the receptor. Investigators are not certain of the mechanism or the purpose of horizontal cells, although they appear to enhance light contrast, which improves our ability to see.

For example, horizontal cells appear to play a role in *lateral inhibition*, a process in which a neuron inhibits neighboring neurons. When light strikes a visual receptor, the receptor decreases its release of glutamate, which activates its postsynaptic horizontal cell. In response, the horizontal cell sends inhibitory signals to its postsynaptic cells (receptor cells), inhibiting them. This means that all receptors near an excited receptor are inhibited by the horizontal cell. Thus, lateral inhibition enhances contrast between edges by selectively decreasing the output of receptors adjacent to excited receptors.

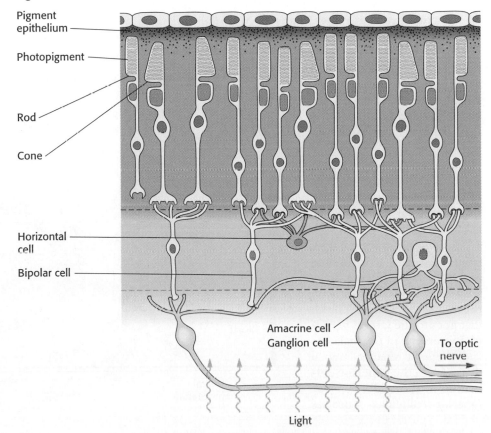

Figure 7.10 Transmission of information across the retina

Pigment epithelium

Photopigment

Rod

Cone

Horizontal cell

Bipolar cell

Amacrine cell

Ganglion cell

To optic nerve

Light

The dendrites of bipolar cells also synapse with the terminal buttons of visual receptors. In the absence of light, receptors send a steady stream of glutamate molecules into the synapse between themselves and bipolar cells, which decreases the activity of the bipolar cells. However, in the presence of light, when glutamate release decreases, bipolar cells become active. Activation of bipolar cells affects the activity of amacrine and ganglion cells in the retina.

As with horizontal cells, which provide feedback to the rods and cones, the role of amacrine cells is to provide feedback to bipolar and ganglion cells. The ganglion cells receive information from amacrine and bipolar cells and transmit this information in the form of action potentials to neurons in the brain (Figure 7.10). The information that the ganglion cells receive from amacrine and bipolar cells is in the form of neurotransmitters: glutamate from bipolar cells and glutamate or GABA from amacrine cells. Thus, whether or not a ganglion cell generates action potentials depends on the balance of glutamate and GABA it receives from presynaptic neurons. The pattern of action potentials that ganglion cells send to the brain is the net result of activity of visual receptors, horizontal cells, bipolar cells, and amacrine cells.

Transmission of Visual Information from the Retina to the Brain The axons of ganglion cells come together to form *cranial nerve II*, or the **optic nerve,** which exits the retina at a spot called the **optic disk.** Another name for the optic disk is the *blind spot* because no receptors are present at the place where the ganglion axons leave the retina. Thus, photons striking the blind spot do not register an image. You are not normally aware of this blind spot because the other eye and the cerebral cortex fill in the missing information. (It is important to keep in mind that the cerebral cortex constructs the visual image from bits of information that it receives from cells in the retina, as we will examine in greater detail in Chapter 8.)

The optic nerve carries information from the ganglion cells of the retina to the brain. Just anterior to the pituitary gland and inferior to the hypothalamus, the optic nerves from the left and right eyes converge to form the **optic chiasm** (Figure 7.11). In humans (but not in most animals), action potentials coming from ganglion cells in the half of the retina nearest to the nose, called the **nasal hemiretina,** cross over to the other side of the brain. Action potentials coming from the **lateral hemiretina,** the half of the retina nearest to the side of the head, do not cross over but rather continue on to the ipsilateral, or same, side of the brain. Study Figure 7.11 closely. Information from the right visual field goes to the nasal hemiretina of the right eye and the lateral hemiretina of the left eye. Because information from the nasal hemiretina crosses and that from the lateral hemiretina does not, images of objects in the right visual field are projected to the left side of the brain. The opposite is true for visual stimuli in the left visual field.

The **optic tract** emerges from the optic chiasm and enters the brain (Figure 7.11). This tract actually splits into two branches: a larger branch that goes to the **lateral geniculate nucleus** of the thalamus and a much smaller branch that goes to the **superior colliculus** in the midbrain. The superior colliculus processes

optic nerve: cranial nerve II, which carries information about vision from the eye to the brain

optic disk: the blind spot on the retina where the axons that form the optic nerve exit the retina

optic chiasm: the structure formed by the merging of the left and right optic nerves

nasal hemiretina: the half of the retina nearest to the nose

lateral hemiretina: the half of the retina nearest to the side of the head

optic tract: the axons that emerge from the optic chiasm and enter the brain

lateral geniculate nucleus (LGN): a nucleus in the thalamus that receives information directly from the ganglion cells in the retina and relays it on the visual cortex

superior colliculus: a midbrain structure that receives visual information and processes the location of objects in the environment

Figure 7.11 Anatomy of the visual pathway to the brain

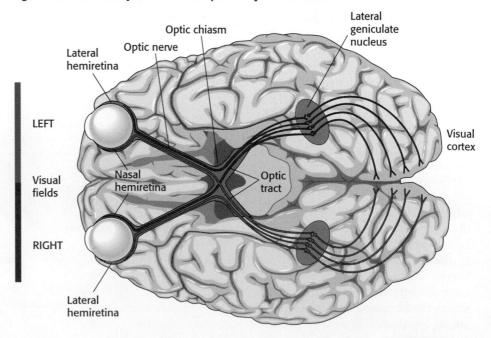

information about the location of the visual stimulus in the visual field and assists the eyes in moving and tracking visual stimuli. In contrast, information that goes to the lateral geniculate nucleus is sent on to the **occipital lobe** of the cerebrum for conscious processing. We will examine visual processing in the lateral geniculate nucleus and in the cerebrum in greater detail in Chapter 8.

occipital lobe: most posterior lobe of the cerebrum that processes visual information

Evolution of the Eye

The complicated anatomy of the human eye can be best understood by examining the eyes of more primitive animals. Simple animals, such as worms, do not have eyes at all. Instead, they have photoreceptors distributed over the entire external surface of their bodies. Worms can discriminate between the presence and absence of light, but they are unable to recognize objects in their environment. In order to recognize objects, the receptors must be grouped together in such a way that each receives light from a specific region of the environment. The eye of the nautilus is an example of a primitive "pinhole" eye in which the photoreceptors are grouped together and line the inside of a hollow sphere (Figure 7.12). Light enters the eye through a tiny hole, or pinhole, and strikes a particular region of receptors, depending on the location of its source. This anatomical arrangement permits the nautilus to localize the source of the light, but the nautilus eye lacks any focusing mechanisms that would allow the animal to see clearly.

The octopus eye represents an elaboration and improvement of the pinhole eye. Instead of having a layer of flattened skin cells over the exterior of the pinhole eye, the octopus eye is covered with a transparent cornea that helps refract (or bend) light, concentrating it to a single point of focus. In addition, a lens, which further bends and focuses light, is inserted in the octopus eye between the cornea and the receptors on the retina (Figure 7.12). In some vertebrates, the lens moves forward and backward, much like the lens of a camera, to bring the image into sharp focus. The primate eye has a special adaptation that allows accommodation, or changing the shape of the lens, to bring the image into focus on the receptors at the back of the eye.

The process of evolution has produced numerous varieties of eyes, permitting various species of animals to occupy different environmental niches. For example, nocturnal animals (animals active only at night, such as owls) have only rods, which are highly sensitive in dim light, on their retinas. Day-active, or diurnal, animals (such as chipmunks and pigeons) have retinas that contain only cones. Humans and other animals that are active during the day and night have both rods and cones on their retinas. The dolphin's eye contains 7,000 times more rods than the human

Figure 7.12 Evolution of the eye

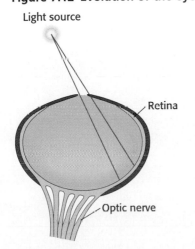

"Pinhole" eye of nautilus

"Lens" eye of the octopus

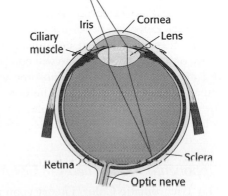

Cross section through the mammalian eye

eye, which enables the dolphin to see underwater at great depths. Fish see nearby objects very well, due to their flat cornea and spherical lens that does not change shape. In contrast, birds see distant objects extremely well because their eyeballs are elongated, which causes large images of distant objects to be focused on the retina. The human eye is designed in such a way that we are able see minute detail in focus at close range in bright light. This adaptation enables us to work and move safely through our environments in daylight or under artificial lighting.

Color Vision

Trichromatic Color Theory

The ability to see color comes from the fact that we have three types of cones, each sensitive to different wavelengths of light. Working independently, Thomas Young (1773–1829) and Hermann von Helmholtz (1821–1894) were the first to propose that as few as three different receptors are needed in order for people to see all the 200 shades of color that we perceive. They based their theory, now called the **Young-Helmholtz** or **Trichromatic Color Theory,** on the results of experiments that demonstrated that people can match any color stimulus using three primary colors: red, green, and blue. However, not until the late 1970s, with the development of the *microspectrophotometer,* a device that measures the wavelengths absorbed by cones, did investigators know for certain that people actually have three types of cones. Indeed, it turned out that Young and von Helmholtz were quite correct! Humans have three types of cones: *S cones* that absorb short-wavelength or blue light, *M cones* that absorb medium-wavelength or green light, and *L cones* that absorb long-wavelength or red light. Only primates have three types of cones. Other mammals have only two types of cones, S cones and *LM cones,* which are an intermediate type of cone between L and M cones, responding to yellow light (Rodieck, 1998).

The ability to see color requires three different types of cones. If an individual has fewer than three functional types of cones, then color vision will be impaired. **Trichromats** are individuals who have all three functional cone types (S, M, and L) and have normal color vision. **Dichromats** have only two functional cone types. As you've already learned, nonprimate mammals are dichromats. People who have a nonfunctional M or L cone type are also dichromats. To human dichromats, the rainbow appears blue at the inside of the arc, turns to a colorless gray in the middle, and changes to yellow at the outside of the arc. **Monochromats** have only one functional cone type and, thus, have impaired color vision because at least two cone types are needed in order to make wavelength comparisons and perceive color. To them, a rainbow looks like an arc of bright light (Rodieck, 1998).

People with impaired color vision are often referred to as *color blind.* Color blindness is typically an inherited disorder because the cones we possess are controlled by gene expression. The genes for cones are found on the X chromosome, which normally contain genes for S, M, and L cones (Neitz & Neitz, 2000). However, people who are color blind inherit X chromosomes that carry defective or missing genes for one or more cones. In order for a woman to be color blind, she must inherit two X chromosomes (one from her mother and one from her father) that carry defective genes for cones. Therefore, women are unlikely to be color blind, unless they inherit defective genes from both parents, because the normal genes on one X chromosome will compensate for the abnormal genes on the other. If a man inherits an X chromosome with defective genes for cones, he will have impaired color vision because he does not have another X chromosome to offset the X chromosome with the defective gene. You probably know someone who is color blind. Nearly 10% of all men possess an X chromosome that carries genes for defective or missing cones.

Opponent-Process Theory of Color Vision

The Trichromatic Color Theory cannot explain all perceptual experiences involving color. For example, the theory proposed by Young and von Helmholtz cannot

Young-Helmholtz or Trichromatic Color Theory: a theory of color vision that proposes that only three different receptors are needed to see all shades of all colors

trichromat: an individual with three functional cone types who has normal color vision

dichromat: an individual with two functional cone types who has impaired color vision

monochromat: an individual who possesses only one functional cone type and sees only black and white and grays

explain why staring at the green, black, and yellow flag in Figure 7.13 produces a red, white, and blue afterimage, called a *negative afterimage*. In 1878, Ewald Hering proposed another theory of color vision, called the **Opponent-Process Theory,** which could account for phenomena that the Trichromatic Color Theory could not explain.

According to the Opponent-Process Theory, three opponent processes, which Hering conceptualized as three pairs of opposing colors (red-green, blue-yellow, black-white) code for color in the nervous system. Individual neurons in the visual system function as a single opponent process. That is, one neuron, called a *red-green opponent process cell*, increases its firing in response to the presence of red (or long-wavelength light) and decreases its firing in response to green (or medium-wavelength light). Another neuron, called a *blue-yellow opponent process cell*, shows a differential response to blue versus yellow. The third type of neuron, the *black-white opponent process cell*, responds to changes in brightness, increasing its firing in response to white and decreasing in response to black.

When Hering proposed his theory, there was no physiological evidence to support the presence of an opponent-process mechanism in the visual system. However, experiments since Hering's time have demonstrated that opponent-process coding is present in ganglion cells (Boynton, 1979). Thus, the Trichromatic Color Theory explains the mechanism by which cones code for color, and the Opponent-Process Theory explains how color coding is accomplished by ganglion cells and other neurons in the visual pathway that leads to the cerebral cortex. We will examine color perception in more detail in Chapter 8.

Opponent-Process Theory: a theory of color vision, which proposes that three pairs of opposing colors (red-green, yellow-blue, black-white) code for color in the nervous system

Disorders of the Visual System

Visual disorders are the result of damage to or disease of the eye or the brain. In this section, we will focus on eye problems that impair vision. In Chapter 8, we will examine brain disorders that cause visual problems.

Cornea

The cornea must be smooth and transparent in order for light to enter the eye without distortions. An injury to the cornea that causes scarring will interfere with the transmission of light through the cornea, causing blurring. When the surface of the cornea is irregular, light rays are scattered as they pass through the cornea. This problem is known as an *astigmatism*. A person with an astigmatism can see perfectly well in some orientations but will experience blurring in others.

Figure 7.13 Negative afterimage

For thirty seconds, focus your eyes on the star in the bottom right corner. Then move your eyes to the blank rectangle to the right. What do you see? (You should see a negative afterimage as described in the text.)

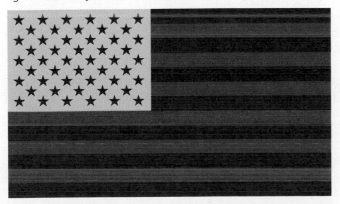
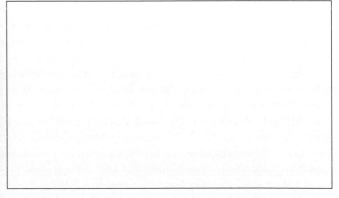

Aqueous Humor

The eyeball maintains its shape due to the pressure of fluid within the eye. To keep the pressure inside the eye (called the *intraocular pressure*) from getting too high, the aqueous humor drains off through tiny ducts in the eye. When a blockage prevents drainage of the aqueous humor, the intraocular pressure increases, producing a condition known as **glaucoma.** In glaucoma, the intraocular pressure becomes so high that pressure on the optic nerve causes damage to the nerve, which interferes with transmission of information from the retina to the brain (Nicolela, Drance, Broadway, Chauhan, McCormick, & LeBlanc, 2001). Glaucoma is the leading cause of blindness in the United States today.

glaucoma: a condition in which the intraocular pressure increases, producing damage to the optic nerve

Lens

For proper transmission and focusing of light on the retina, the lens must be elastic and transparent. As we age, the lens loses its elasticity and its transparency. We discussed **presbyopia** earlier in this chapter. At age 16, the lens begins to lose its elasticity, and by age 50, accommodation is seriously compromised, meaning that the lens can no longer attain a spherical shape needed to bring near objects into focus. People with presbyopia have trouble seeing close objects clearly and require corrective lenses.

presbyopia: a condition found in older people in which the lens loses its ability to accommodate

Years of exposure to bright sunlight and ultraviolet radiation cause the lens to darken and lose its transparency. When this happens, images become blurred and indistinct. In some people, the lens becomes opaque, and vision is totally obstructed. This condition is known as a **cataract.** Treatment for a cataract involves surgical removal of the damaged lens. Of course, after the lens is removed, the patient's ability to focus light on the retina is eliminated. To correct this problem, a plastic artificial lens is sewn in place of the old lens (Hwang & Olson, 2001). This artificial lens is flat, allowing for focusing of light coming from a distance. For near vision, the cataract patient must wear corrective lenses. One way to decrease the risk of developing cataracts is to wear sunglasses with a good ultraviolet (UV) block that shields the eyes from the sun's harmful radiation.

cataract: a visual disorder in which the lens becomes opaque and vision is obstructed

Sometimes the shape of a person's eyes makes it impossible for the lens to bring light into focus on the retina. For example, when the eyeball is too long along the optic axis, the lens brings the light to focus in front of the retina. This problem is called **myopia,** or nearsightedness. A person with myopia is unable to see clearly objects in the distance, although vision for near objects is unimpaired. In contrast, in **hyperopia,** when the eyeball is too short, the lens cannot bring light coming from near objects into focus on the retina. Another name for hyperopia is farsightedness. A person who is farsighted cannot see near objects clearly but can bring far objects into focus. Corrective lenses are used to treat myopia and hyperopia.

myopia: nearsightedness, in which an individual cannot see far objects clearly

hyperopia: farsightedness, in which a person cannot bring near objects into focus

Retina

Damage to neurons on the retina will impair vision. Most commonly, retinal disease involves the rods and cones. **Macular degeneration** is a leading cause of blindness in the elderly. The **macula lutea** is a yellowish spot that contains the fovea in the area centralis of the retina. In this disorder, the cones in the macula lutea die, leaving the patient unable to read or see detail. Eventually, all of the receptors on the retina are affected, producing blindness (Sun & Nathans, 2001).

Retinitis pigmentosa is a genetic disorder involving chromosome 8 that affects rhodopsin in rods (Blanton et al., 1991; Sullivan et al., 1999). This disorder often strikes in childhood, although some forms of the disease affect only adults. The first symptoms are night blindness and *tunnel vision*, in which peripheral vision is lost and the visual field is limited to central or cone vision. These symptoms indicate that rods are impaired or nonfunctional. In most forms of the disorder, loss of vision spreads to the cones, and total blindness ensues.

Diabetes, which you learned about in Chapter 2, can also produce blindness. People with diabetes have very fragile capillary blood vessels that rupture easily and heal slowly. This is a problem in the eye because there are so many blood vessels

macular degeneration: a disorder in which cones in the macula lutea die, causing blindness

macula lutea: yellowish spot in the center of the retina that contains the fovea

retinitis pigmentosa: a genetic disorder that first destroys rods but eventually spreads to the cones, causing total blindness

lining the retina. Some diabetic individuals experience rupturing of these blood vessels, which spills blood into the vitreous humor, obscuring vision, and deprives the neurons on the retina of oxygen and other nutrients. Laser surgery is used to stop the bleeding inside the eye.

Recap 7.2: The Visual System

Visual receptors are stimulated by discrete packets of light energy called (a)_____. The visual receptors, called (b)_____ and (c)_____, are located in the retina of the eye. The retina contains five layers of cells: receptors, horizontal cells, bipolar cells, (d)_____ cells, and (e)_____ cells. The visual receptors contain (f)_____ that absorb photons entering the eye. Axons of the ganglion cells form the (g)_____ nerve, which carries information from the retina to the brain. Information from the (h)_____ hemiretina crosses to the other side of the brain over the optic chiasm. Information from visual receptors is transmitted from the retina to the (i)_____ _____ nucleus of the thalamus to the occipital lobe in the cerebrum. According to the (j)_____ _____ Theory, the ability to see color comes from three types of cones, S cones, M cones, and L cones. According to the (k)_____-_____ Theory, three opponent processes (red-green, blue-yellow, black-white) code for color in the nervous system. An (l)_____ results from an irregularly shaped cornea. The leading cause of blindness is (m)_____, which is caused by increased intraocular pressure. Disorders associated with the lens of the eye include (n)_____ and (o)_____. Macular degeneration causes blindness beginning with the death of cones in the macula lutea, whereas (p)_____ _____ causes blindness beginning with the death of rods in the periphery of the retina.

The Auditory System

Helen Keller could not hear, but she could feel vibrations. Although she was deaf, Helen could tell when people were entering or leaving the house, she could identify people by their footfall, and she could distinguish musical instruments being played in an orchestra. Vibrations stimulated receptors in her skin, her bones, and other structures in her body, and she was able to use this information the same way we use auditory information. That is, auditory information comes to us in the form of vibrations or oscillations of air molecules. Those of us who are not deaf have functional auditory receptors, called **hair cells,** that relay information about vibrations to the brain.

hair cells: specialized receptors in the auditory system, located in the cochlea

The Nature of Auditory Stimuli

At the beginning of this chapter, you learned about the characteristics of waves. We think of sounds as traveling in waves. Vibrating objects create a pattern of air flow in which a band of compressed air molecules alternates with a partial vacuum in which few air molecules are found. Thus, sound waves are composed of peaks, which represent the band of compressed air molecules, followed by troughs, where there are few air molecules. When we talk about sound waves, we usually refer to their frequency and their amplitude. The human auditory system is sensitive to sound waves that have a frequency between 20 and 20,000 Hz. Any vibrations that have a frequency less than 20 Hz or greater than 20,000 Hz cannot be detected by our auditory systems. Other animals have different ranges of auditory sensitivity. Have you ever blown a dog whistle? You can't hear a thing when you blow it, except for your breath coming out of your mouth. But, dogs can hear it. That's because the whistle puts out air vibrations with a frequency of about 50,000 Hz, which is way above our upper sensitivity limit. Dogs can hear frequencies over 50,000 Hz, and rats have an even higher range, over 100,000 Hz.

We perceive the amplitude of sound waves as loudness, which as you've learned is measured in decibels (abbreviated *dB*). Our ability to detect a sound at a particular dB level depends on the frequency of the sound. That is, the human auditory system is constructed in such a way that we hear sounds with frequencies between 1,000 and 5,000 Hz best. Typically, humans with normal hearing can detect these sounds at around 0–10 dB. However, for low-frequency sounds (less than 200 Hz), the sound must be at least 20–60 dB before we can hear it (Betke, 1991; Sivian & White, 1933).

Anatomy and Function of the Auditory System

The peripheral portion of the auditory system can be divided into three parts: the **outer ear,** the **middle ear,** and the **inner ear.**

The Outer Ear

The outer ear consists of the *pinna* and the *external auditory meatus*. The pinna is the outer, fleshy part of the ear, which acts as a sound collector. Some animals have the ability to move their pinna in different directions to catch sound waves better. Humans, however, typically have immobile pinna, although some people can wiggle their pinna slightly. The external auditory meatus is the ear canal or opening into the temporal bone, where the middle and inner ears are located (Figure 7.14). This canal is about 1¼ inches long and is shaped in such a way that it amplifies sound waves with a frequency of 2,000 to 5,000 Hz.

outer ear: the outermost part of the ear, consisting of the pinna and auditory canal

middle ear: the part of the ear that contains the eardrum, three ossicles, and the eustachian tube

inner ear: the innermost part of the ear, consisting of the cochlea

The Middle Ear

Vibrating air is collected by the pinna and is guided into the external auditory meatus toward the middle ear, which begins at the *tympanic membrane,* or **eardrum.** The eardrum is a thin, flexible membrane that is stretched across the ear canal

eardrum: the tympanic membrane, which is stretched across the end of the ear canal

Figure 7.14 Anatomy of the ear
(a) The parts of the outer, middle, and inner ear. (b) The three canals of the cochlea.

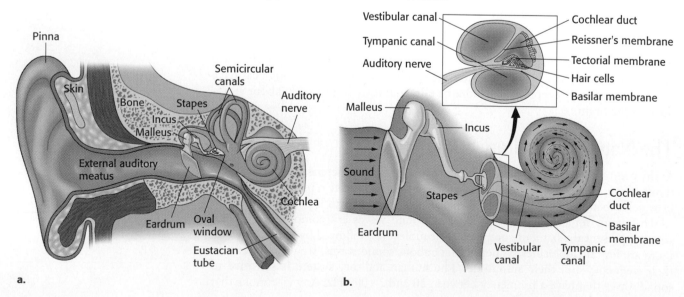

(Figure 7.14). Attached to the eardrum is a chain of three tiny bones, or *ossicles*. The first ossicle, which is directly connected to the eardrum, is called the **hammer** or *malleus* [*malleus* = hammer, Latin]. Vibration of the eardrum causes the hammer to vibrate, which in turn produces vibration of the second ossicle, called the **anvil** or *incus* [*incus* = anvil, Latin], and then the third ossicle, the **stirrup** or *stapes* [*stapes* = stirrup, Latin].

The middle ear, therefore, is comprised of the eardrum, the ossicles, and one other structure, called the **eustachian tube.** The eustachian tube is a canal that runs from the chamber of the middle ear to the throat. Although it plays no role in the transmission of vibrations from the air to the auditory receptors, the eustachian tube assists in hearing by allowing air to enter or escape from the middle ear in order to equalize the pressure on both sides of the eardrum. Have you ever ridden in a car going through the mountains and felt your ears "pop"? Or, perhaps you've felt your ears "pop" while seated in a jet that is landing. This popping sensation is the sound of air rushing in or out of your middle ear.

The Inner Ear

Vibrating air in the ear canal causes the eardrum to vibrate, which produces vibration of the ossicles. Thus, vibrating air is translated into vibrating membrane and then vibrating bone. In the inner ear, vibrations of the stirrup are translated into vibrating membrane again, as the stirrup vibrates against the **oval window,** a thin membrane that covers the opening to the inner ear. The inner ear itself is located in the **cochlea,** a spiral-shaped canal located in the temporal bone.

The cochlea contains three chambers: the **scala vestibuli** (or *vestibular canal*), the **scala media** *(cochlear duct)*, and the **scala tympani** *(tympanic canal)*. The oval window opens into the scala vestibuli, and vibration of the oval window causes the fluid in the scala vestibuli to vibrate. The scala vestibuli and scala tympani are connected at the apex of the cochlea, through a tiny opening called the *helicotrema* (Figure 7.14b). When the fluid in the scala vestibuli vibrates, these vibrations stimulate movement of the fluid in the scala tympani.

The scala media is located between, or in the middle of, the scala vestibuli and the scala tympani. Between the scala tympani and the scala media is a thin, flexible membrane called the **basilar membrane.** The receptors, or hair cells, are found on top of the basilar membrane. These receptors get their name from the tufts of hairs that protrude from the top of these cells. The hairs of the receptor cells are embedded in a stiff membrane, called the **tectorial membrane,** that lies on top of the hair cells (Figure 7.14b).

Vibration of the oval window causes the fluid in the scala vestibuli and scala tympani to vibrate, which makes the basilar membrane vibrate. When the basilar membrane moves, the hair cells on top of it move, causing their hairs to be pulled and bent. Remember that auditory receptors are mechanoreceptors, which means that they are excited by mechanical forces like tugging or pulling. The hair cells are located between a very elastic, moveable membrane (the basilar membrane) and a stiff, inflexible membrane (the tectorial membrane). Therefore, movement of the basilar membrane puts mechanical force on the hairs of the hair cells, and this mechanical force is translated into an action potential in the hair cell.

Two types of hair cells sit on top of the basilar membrane: *inner hair cells* and *outer hair cells* (Figure 7.15). The inner hair cells fire in response to the vibration of the basilar membrane, and they transmit information about vibrations to the brain. The function of the outer hair cells, on the other hand, is not clear. They not only send information to the brain, but they also receive information from auditory centers in the brain. In addition, the outer hair cells contain proteins that contract like muscles, which allows them to produce movements in the underlying basilar membrane. Investigators believe that outer hair cells play an important role in the perception of pitch (Cho, 2000; Dallos & Evans, 1995; Geisler, 1993; Reuter & Zenner, 1990; Teas, 1989).

hammer: the first ossicle in the middle ear, which receives vibrations from the eardrum and relays them to the anvil

anvil: the second ossicle in the middle ear, which receives vibrations from the hammer and relays them to the stirrup

stirrup: the third ossicle in the middle ear, which receives vibrations from the anvil and transmits them to the oval window

eustachian tube: a canal that runs from the middle ear to the throat

oval window: the opening to the inner ear covered by a thin membrane that vibrates in response to vibrations by the stapes bone

cochlea: a spiral-shaped canal that contains the inner ear

scala vestibuli: the vestibular canal in the cochlea that receives vibrations from the oval window

scala media: the middle chamber of the cochlea that contains the hair cells

scala tympani: the tympanic canal in the cochlea that receives vibrations from the scala vestibuli

basilar membrane: the thin, flexible membrane in the cochlea that supports the hair cells

tectorial membrane: a stiff membrane located on top of the hair cells

Figure 7.15 Hair cells

The inner and outer hair cells have "hairs" or stereocilia that are embedded in the tectorial membrane.

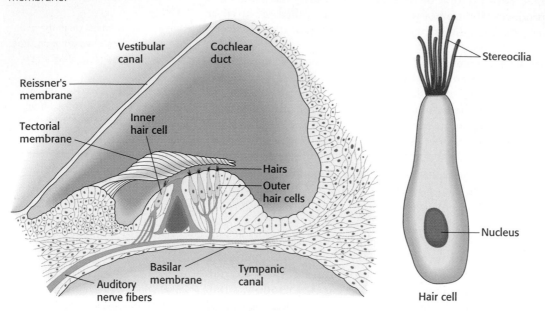

Auditory Pathway to the Brain

Axons from sensory neurons in the cochlea relay information from the hair cells to the brain. These axons come together to form the *auditory branch of cranial nerve VIII*, the **auditory nerve.** The auditory nerve enters the medulla in the hindbrain and synapses with neurons in the **cochlear nucleus** (Figure 7.16). From the cochlear nucleus, axons go to the **superior olive,** a structure located in the hindbrain, which processes information about pitch. Two pathways emerge from the superior olive: One goes to the reticular formation and on to the cerebellum, and the other goes to the **inferior colliculus** in the midbrain. From the inferior colliculus, axons go to a nucleus in the thalamus called the **medial geniculate nucleus,** which processes auditory information and sends it on to the auditory cortex in the temporal lobe. We will examine the processing of auditory information in the auditory cortex in Chapter 8.

auditory nerve: cranial nerve VIII, which carries information from the inner ear to the brain

cochlear nucleus: a group of neurons in the medulla that receives auditory information from the auditory nerve

superior olive: hindbrain structure that processes auditory information before sending it on to the midbrain

inferior colliculus: a midbrain structure that receives and processes auditory information

Locating Sound

Localization of sound takes place in the brain below the level of the cerebrum, in the brain stem. However, higher level processing of sound location takes place in the prefrontal cortex, as you will learn in Chapter 8. Picture yourself sitting at your desk when suddenly a picture falls off the wall and slams onto the floor. You immediately turn your head in the direction of the noise to see what happened. Turning toward a sound happens unconsciously, and we are quite accurate at locating the direction and source of a sound. Let's look at how we do this.

Humans, like all mammals, have an ear on each side of their head. These two ears are located in different places in space, and hence the sounds reaching each ear will be a little different. For example, a sound coming from

Figure 7.16 Auditory pathway to the cerebrum

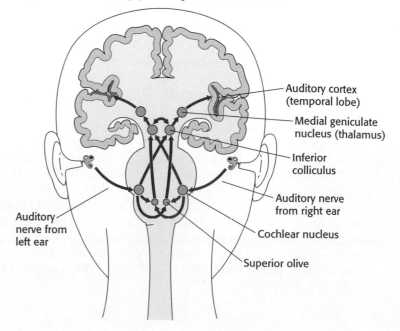

the left will sound louder to the left ear than it does to the right ear. Your head acts as a sound barrier, blocking the sound from reaching the ear on the other side of your head. Neurons in the brain calculate the **loudness difference** and determine the location of the sound. This method for localizing sound works best for high-frequency sounds above 5,000 Hz. Rodents and mammals with tiny heads use the loudness difference almost exclusively to calculate the direction of sound.

The brain also uses **phase differences** to localize sound. Recall that sound waves are patterns of peaks and troughs, representing air compression and decompression. Waves are said to be *in phase* when their peaks and troughs occur simultaneously. Waves are *out of phase* when their peaks and troughs do not correspond. Because the ears are separated in space, sound waves arrive at the ears out of phase. Phase differences are used by neurons in the brain to determine the direction of the sound. Phase differences provide good information for sounds with a frequency less than 1,000 Hz.

In summary, loudness differences work best for locating sounds with frequencies greater than 5,000 Hz, and phase differences work best for locating sounds with frequencies less than 1,000 Hz. But, what about sounds between 1,000 and 5,000 Hz? We have a difficult time localizing these sounds. Have you ever been driving in your car and heard a siren near you? You probably had a hard time figuring out which direction the siren was coming from because most sirens have a frequency between 1,500 and 3,500 Hz.

Pitch Perception

The hair cells of the cochlea have to process both the amplitude and the frequency of the sound wave and send this information to the brain. Von Helmholtz proposed the **Place Theory of pitch perception** more than 100 years ago. According to von Helmholtz, different hair cells along the basilar membrane are particularly sensitive to certain frequencies. Georg von Bekesy, in the 1950s, did a series of studies of the cochlea that earned him a Nobel Prize. Von Bekesy's research demonstrated that von Helmholtz's notion of place theory was indeed correct: Different regions of the cochlea are most sensitive to particular frequencies. For example, low-frequency sounds maximally stimulate hair cells in the apex of the cochlea, whereas high-frequency sounds maximally stimulate hair cells in the base of the cochlea.

The Place Theory does not adequately explain how frequencies below 500 Hz are perceived. Another theory, called **Frequency Theory,** has been proposed to explain the perception of low frequencies. According to Frequency Theory, vibrations of incoming sounds are translated into vibrations of the basilar membrane, which are further translated into frequencies of action potentials. Simply put, this means that a sound of 60 Hz is transmitted to the brain by a neuron firing 60 times per second. However, most neurons cannot fire over 200 times per second. To transmit information about sounds with frequencies between 100 and 500 Hz, a number of neurons must fire together, producing a volley of action potentials that duplicates the frequency of the sound. This suggestion that neurons work together to produce a volley of action potentials that correspond to the frequency of the sound is known as the **volley principle** (Wever, 1970). According to the volley principle, a sound of 350 Hz would stimulate the firing of a group of neurons that *together* relays a total of 350 action potentials per second to the brain.

Disorders of the Auditory System

A diminished ability to hear, called *hearing loss*, occurs when transmission of auditory information along the auditory system is impaired. *Conductive hearing loss* is a hearing disorder in which vibrations are not effectively transmitted from the eardrum to the hair cells of the cochlea. **Deafness** is the extreme form of hearing loss in which the individual cannot perceive auditory stimuli. In general, there are five kinds of deafness: (1) outer ear deafness, (2) middle ear deafness, (3) inner ear deafness, (4) nerve deafness, and (5) central deafness.

medial geniculate nucleus: a thalamic nucleus that receives auditory information from the midbrain and sends it to the auditory cortex in the temporal lobe

loudness difference: difference in the intensity of the sound reaching each ear

phase difference: difference in the pattern of peaks and troughs striking the two ears

Place Theory of pitch perception: a theory that proposes that different regions of the basilar membrane are particularly sensitive to certain frequencies

Frequency Theory: a theory that proposes that vibrations of incoming sounds are translated into frequencies of action potentials

volley principle: a theory that proposes hair cells in the cochlea work together to produce a series of action potentials that duplicate the frequency of the sound

deafness: a condition in which an individual cannot perceive auditory stimuli

Outer Ear Deafness

Blockage of the external auditory meatus will cause hearing loss or deafness. For example, a waxy substance, which acts as a natural bug repellent, is produced in the walls of the external auditory meatus. Excess buildup of this waxy substance can clog the ear canal and interfere with the passage of sound waves down the canal. A tumor or other obstruction, like a foreign object placed in the ear, can also impede hearing. Some individuals, such as those born to mothers with syphilis or German measles, are born with no external auditory meatus. Obviously, the absence of an ear canal makes it impossible for auditory stimuli to excite the nervous system, and these individuals are deaf.

Middle Ear Deafness

Damage to any of the structures in the middle ear will interfere with transmission of auditory information and produce middle ear deafness. For example, a ruptured or torn eardrum cannot vibrate effectively. Fortunately, eardrums often heal following rupture. If healing is not possible, the damaged eardrum can be replaced with an artificial eardrum constructed from the patient's own body tissue. As we age, our joints become stiff due to arthritis and rheumatism, and movement is slowed. This is true of the joints between our ossicles, too. That is, in old age, vibration of the hammer produces slower, diminished vibrations of the other ossicles, impairing conduction of auditory information. This conduction problem is usually corrected with a hearing aid. The *For Further Thought* box discusses how a hearing aid works.

The eustachian tube, too, can be the source of middle ear deafness. Infections that begin in the throat can travel up the eustachian tube to the middle ear, which impedes vibration of the eardrum and ossicles. A child who suffers from chronic middle ear and throat infections can develop scarring and blockage of the eustachian tube. A blocked eustachian tube interferes with air pressure balance in the middle ear, making it difficult for the eardrum to vibrate effectively. To treat a scarred, blocked eustachian tube, a tiny tube is inserted into the eardrum. The tube allows air to enter or leave the middle ear to equalize air pressure on both sides of the eardrum and improves hearing ability by allowing the eardrum and ossicles to vibrate freely.

Inner Ear Deafness

Damage to the hair cells in the cochlea produces inner ear deafness. This type of deafness is seen in people who are exposed to loud sounds over a long period of time, such as rock musicians, dentists, and farmers and other workers who operate loud machinery. Extremely loud sounds are transmitted in the form of large-amplitude sound waves. These sound waves are translated into large-amplitude movements of the basilar membrane, which causes violent rocking of the hair cells that tears and damages the hairs of the hair cells. A damaged hair cell cannot be repaired or replaced. Another form of inner ear deafness is *progressive hearing loss*, which involves degeneration of hair cells. Progressive hearing loss is an inherited disorder that begins as early as young adulthood (Steele, 1998).

Experts used to believe that inner ear deafness is noncorrectable. However, the development of **cochlear implants,** tiny electrodes placed in the cochlea that send auditory signals to the auditory nerve, has helped a number of people with inner ear deafness to hear again (Rauschecker & Shannon, 2002). A tiny microphone is tucked behind the ear of the hearing-impaired person and picks up sound, which is sent to a processor. The processor, which is about the size of a wallet and is worn under clothing, digitalizes the sound. The digitalized signals are transmitted through the skin to the cochlear implant, which stimulates the auditory nerve.

cochlear implant: a device that is surgically placed in the brain where it can stimulate the auditory nerve

Nerve Deafness

Damage to the auditory nerve can occur as a result of trauma or infection. In some people, an inherited degenerative disease causes the auditory nerve to waste away, causing progressive deafness. No treatment is currently available for this type of deafness.

Conductive Deafness and Hearing Aids

Nearly 1 out of every 10 people has a hearing loss that can be corrected by a hearing aid. A hearing aid is a deceptively simple device that collects sound waves, amplifies them, and transmits the amplified waves directly into the ear canal close to the eardrum. Thus, a hearing aid has three components, which correspond to each of its functions: a microphone that picks up sound waves, an amplifier that boosts the sound, and a receiver that delivers the amplified sound into the ear, plus tiny replaceable batteries.

There are many varieties of hearing aids. Behind-the-ear (BTE) hearing devices fit behind the pinna and have a plastic tube that is inserted into the ear canal to deliver the amplified sound directly to the middle ear. Some people who wear eyeglasses have special frames that contain a hearing aid in the earpiece that goes behind the ear. As with standard BTE aids, these hearing aids have a plastic tube that is placed in the ear canal. The in-the-ear (ITE)

device is a popular type of hearing aid, developed in the 1970s, that is placed directly in the ear canal. However, this type of aid is quite difficult to use with a telephone because the wearer gets a feedback noise whenever anything is held too close to the microphone of the hearing aid.

A newer kind of hearing aid is the completely-in-the-canal (CIC) device. The CIC hearing aids are custom-made to fit completely in the ear canal. The microcanal aid is even smaller and fits deeper in the ear canal. A nylon string is attached to the microcanal hearing aid to enable the wearer to remove it from the canal. These two styles are the most popular aids available today because they are nearly invisible to the casual observer. Because they are located deep in the ear canal, these hearing aids do not produce any feedback noise when the wearer is using a telephone.

Central Deafness

Damage to any of the brain structures in the auditory pathway to the auditory cortex will produce central deafness. Trauma or disease, such as a brain tumor, can cause central deafness. In Chapter 8, we will examine the effect of damage to the auditory cortex and other cortical areas involved with sound perception.

Recap 7.3: The Auditory System

Auditory receptors are called (a)_____ cells. The frequency of sound waves are measured in (b)_____ (Hz) units, whereas loudness is measured in (c)_____ (dB). The outer ear consists of the (d)_____ and external (e)_____ _____. The middle ear consists of the (f)_____, three (g)_____, and (h)_____ tube. The inner ear is found in the (i)_____, which contains three chambers, the scala (j)_____, scala (k)_____, and scala (l)_____. The hair cells are located on the (m)_____ membrane in the scala media. The (n)_____ nerve (cranial nerve VIII) transmits information from the cochlea to the cochlear nucleus. From the cochlear nucleus, auditory information is transmitted to the (o)_____ olive, and on to the (p)_____ colliculus and then to the (q)_____ geniculate nucleus in the thalamus before terminating in the auditory cortex in the temporal lobe. To locate a sound, the brain uses (r)_____ difference and (s)_____ difference. According to the (t)_____ Theory of pitch perception, low-frequency sounds stimulate hair cells best in the apex of the cochlea, and high-frequency sounds stimulate hair cells best in the base of the cochlea. The (u)_____ Theory of pitch perception has been proposed to explain the perception of frequencies below 500 Hz. (v)_____ _____ are used to correct a conductive hearing loss. (w)_____ _____ are used to correct inner ear deafness.

The Somatosensory System

The root of the word *somatosensory* is *soma*, which, as you've already learned, means "body" in Greek. Thus, the **somatosensory system** relays information about the body to the brain. **Somatosensory receptors** include receptors in the skin as well as receptors in muscles, joints, and tendons. Therefore, the somatosensory system is comprised of skin senses *and* the senses of **kinesthesia, proprioception,** and **interoception.** The word *kine* means "to move" in Greek. Hence, *kinesthesia* refers to the ability to sense movement. *Proprioception* is the ability to know where a body part is in space. Recall from Chapter 2 that many body organs are lined with smooth muscles, which contain somatosensory receptors that inform the brain when stretching takes place in the muscle. Thanks to our somatosensory system, we can tell when our stomachs are full and when our bladders are in need of emptying. This sensation from internal organs is called *interoception.*

somatosensory system: the sensory system that relays information about the body to the brain

somatosensory receptors: receptors in the skin, muscles, joints, and tendons

kinesthesia: the ability to sense movement

proprioception: the ability to know where a body part is in space

interoception: the sense that arises from one's internal organs

The Nature of Somatosensory Stimuli

Most somatosensory receptors are mechanoreceptors, which means that they respond to physical forces like pulling or stretching. In Chapter 6, you learned about the function of stretch receptors in muscles and tendons. Stretching of a muscle excites the stretch receptors, called *annulospiral receptors,* in that muscle. On the other hand, stretching of the tendon stimulates the *Golgi tendon organs,* which are the stretch receptors in tendons.

Recall that Helen Keller could sense vibrations through her skin. The receptors in the skin provide information about pressure, temperature, pain, and vibration. Pressure and vibration directly stimulate mechanoreceptors. Temperature can also stimulate mechanoreceptors because cold causes shrinkage of tissue, and warmth produces expansion. However, temperature changes can also affect chemoreceptors because some chemicals such as enzymes are active at certain temperatures but not at others.

Pain, too, can be relayed to the brain by way of chemoreceptors and mechanoreceptors. Certainly, too much pressure on the skin, as when the skin is pinched, can produce pain. But, certain stimuli, such as a bee sting, produce pain indirectly through chemoreceptors. That is, a bee sting causes the release of chemicals like *bradykinin* and *prostaglandin.* These chemicals stimulate chemoreceptors that send pain signals to the brain.

Figure 7.17 Anatomy of the skin

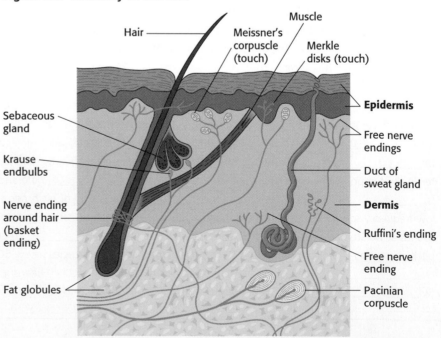

Hair — Meissner's corpuscle (touch) — Muscle — Merkle disks (touch) — Epidermis — Free nerve endings — Duct of sweat gland — Dermis — Ruffini's ending — Free nerve ending — Pacinian corpuscle

Sebaceous gland — Krause endbulbs — Nerve ending around hair (basket ending) — Fat globules

Anatomy and Function of the Somatosensory System

Numerous receptors are found in the skin. Figure 7.17 illustrates the many varieties of receptors located in the skin. *Pacinian corpuscles* are skin receptors that consist of a central sensory fiber surrounded by concentric layers of tissue. These receptors appear to respond to pressure.

Other receptors include *Ruffini's endings, Krause endbulbs, Meissner's corpuscles, Merkel's disks, basket cells,* and *free nerve endings.*

The functions of many of these are not clear. There is evidence that free nerve endings respond to painful stimuli, although any receptor can produce the sensation of pain if it is overstimulated. In addition, Ruffini's endings appear to respond to warm stimuli, and Krause endbulbs are excited by cold stimuli. However, many areas on the body lack Ruffini's or Krause receptors, yet these areas still respond to warm or cold stimuli. Thus, Ruffini's endings and Krause endbulbs may transmit information about temperature to the brain, but they are not necessary for the sensation of temperature. Sound confusing? I assure you that it is confusing, even for experts in the area of somatosensation.

The stretch receptors located in muscles, tendons, and joints send information to the brain about stretching. That is, when a muscle or tendon or joint is stretched, action potentials are transmitted to the brain. The brain, in turn, uses this information to create a *body image* of which muscles are contracted, which muscles are relaxed, and which limbs are bent or straight. You can tell where your limbs are in space, even when your eyes are closed. This is the essence of body language: knowing the position of all of your body parts without visually checking. Kinesthesia and proprioception work together to produce one's body image.

Two separate pathways, the **lemniscal pathway** and the **extralemniscal pathway,** carry information about somatosensation to the brain. The lemniscal pathway relays information about pressure and stretching to the brain by way of **A-fibers,** which are myelinated axons that have a large diameter. In contrast, the extralemniscal pathway relays information about pain and temperature by way of thin, unmyelinated axons called **C-fibers.** Recall from Chapter 2 that action potentials travel very rapidly down thick, myelinated axons, and they move most slowly down thin, unmyelinated axons. Therefore, information about pressure and stretch travels quickly to the brain, and information about pain and temperature is relayed more slowly.

Have you ever stepped into a bathtub filled with hot water? At first, you are not aware of the water's temperature. But, after a second or two, the sensation of warmth builds in your foot and eventually feels so hot that you withdraw your foot from the water. Sensations of pain and temperature are quite primitive and developed before touch sensations. Thus, they travel to the brain by way of evolutionarily older pathways, those without myelin.

A- and C-fibers carry action potentials to the central nervous system. Recall that information coming from body areas below the neck enters the dorsal root of the spinal cord, and information from the head and neck is transmitted to the brain by way of cranial nerves. Information from A-fibers travels up the spinal cord in the dorsal columns (Figure 7.18). In contrast, information about pain and temperature is not transmitted through the *dorsal columns* but rather is sent to the brain by way of several tracts, including *Lissauer's tract,* the *neospinothalamic tract*, and the *paleospinothalamic tract.*

Somatosensory information that is relayed up the dorsal columns enters the brain and crosses over to the contralateral side of the brain in the hindbrain. This information is next transmitted to a region in the midbrain called the *medial lemniscus.* Under the microscope, the medial lemniscus looks like a stack of plates [*lemniscus* = plate, Latin]. Therefore, the lemniscal pathway, which carries information about pressure and stretching, gets its

lemniscal pathway: the somatosensory pathway that relays information about pressure and stretching to the brain

extralemniscal pathway: the somatosensory pathway that relays information about pain and temperature to the brain

A-fiber: a myelinated axon that has a large diameter

C-fibers: thin, unmyelinated axons

Figure 7.18 Somatosensory pathways to the cerebrum

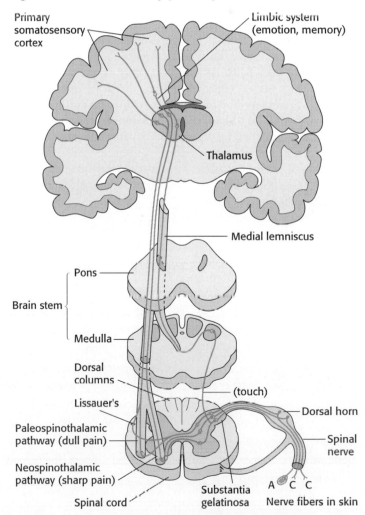

name from the fact that it synapses with neurons in the medial lemniscus of the midbrain. The extralemniscal pathway does not send information to the lemniscal region of the midbrain. Hence, the extralemniscal pathway is *outside* of the lemniscal system.

From the medial lemniscus, the lemniscal pathway carries information to the *ventral basal nuclei* of the thalamus. Finally, information about pressure and stretching is relayed from the thalamus to the **primary somatosensory cortex** in the *postcentral gyrus* in the parietal lobe (Figure 7.18). We will examine the primary somatosensory cortex in more detail in Chapter 8.

Extralemniscal information about pain and temperature is relayed to the contralateral side of the brain as it enters the hindbrain. In the midbrain, information about pain and temperature is transmitted to the reticular formation for processing and is sent on to the *posterior nuclei* in the thalamus. From the posterior nuclei in the thalamus, the extralemniscal pathway carries information about pain and temperature to the **secondary somatosensory cortex,** which is located in the parietal lobe, posterior to the postcentral gyrus. In Chapter 8, we will discuss conscious processing of pain and temperature stimuli.

Disorders of the Somatosensory System

Because of the diverse nature of the somatosensory system, the disorders of this sensory system take many forms. For example, viral infections can interfere with signals coming from the stretch receptors of the proprioceptive system, which will leave the patient without a body image. When carrying an object, one patient had to watch her hands constantly (Sacks, 1985). Otherwise, she would not be aware of the object in her hands, and she would drop whatever she was holding. Another patient would stumble and fall in dark rooms because he could not walk if he couldn't see his feet (Cole, 1995).

One rare, but extremely interesting, disorder occurs in people born without pain receptors. These individuals retain all of their other somatosensations, but they cannot feel pain. As children, they require constant supervision and care because they get no clues from their environment as to what is dangerous. For example, extremely hot food can burn their mouths, and they must be taught to blow on their food to cool it down. In some hereditary forms of pain insensitivity that are accompanied by mental retardation, self-mutilation and repeated injury to the same site due to pain insensitivity are seen (Berkovitch et al., 1998).

We will examine other somatosensory disorders, such as pain in phantom limbs, in Chapter 8 because these disorders result from faulty connections within the central nervous system.

primary somatosensory cortex: the postcentral gyrus in the parietal lobe, which processes sensory information from the skin and muscles

secondary somatosensory cortex: the area of the parietal lobe posterior to the postcentral gyrus, which receives information from the primary somatosensory cortex for "what" and "where" processing

Recap 7.4: The Somatosensory System

Somatosensory receptors are found in the skin, (a)_____, (b)_____, and tendons. (c)_____ is the ability to sense movement of the body, whereas (d)_____ is the sensation that arises from internal organs. The (e)_____ can sense pressure, temperature, pain, and vibration. (f)_____ corpuscles respond to pressure, (g)_____ nerve endings respond to pain, (h)_____ endings respond to warm sensations, (i)_____ endbulbs respond to cold, and (j)_____ receptors respond to stretch in muscles, tendons, and joints. The (k)_____ system relays information about pressure and stretch by way of large-diameter, myelinated A-fibers. The (l)_____ system relays information about temperature and pain by way of thin, unmyelinated C-fibers. The primary somatosensory cortex is located in the postcentral gyrus in the (m)_____ lobe.

The Olfactory System

Our sense of smell, or **olfaction,** provides us with a tremendous amount of information about our environment. Most other animals rely on their sense of smell for survival: for finding mates, locating food, and avoiding predators. In contrast, humans tend to rely on their eyes and ears, more than on their noses, for information about the world around them. But, imagine how you would learn to know the world if you could not see or hear. Helen Keller used her sense of smell to identify objects around her. For example, she could distinguish a wide variety of flowers by their smell, as she described in the book she wrote about her life:

> I used to feel along the square stiff boxwood hedges, and, guided by the sense of smell, would find the first violets and lilies . . . Here, also, were trailing clematis, drooping jasmine, and some rare sweet flowers called butterfly lillies . . . But the roses—they were loveliest of all. (Keller, 1954, pp. 24–25)

You might assume, as many people do, that deaf or blind people have a much better sense of smell than people with normal hearing or vision. Research comparing the olfactory ability of blind human subjects with sighted subjects has demonstrated that blind subjects are not significantly better than sighted subjects in odor detection or odor discrimination (Smith, Doty, Burlingame, & McKeown, 1993). In fact, sighted subjects who were employed as water quality evaluators did far better than blind and untrained sighted subjects on tests of taste and smell ability. Helen Keller, and others with visual or auditory impairments, must *learn* to use their sense of smell to obtain information about the world around them.

Although we humans don't depend on our noses to find food or mates, our sense of smell is quite acute. Most people can recognize about 10,000 odors and can detect a drop of perfume that evaporates in a room the size of a large classroom. Human subjects have demonstrated that they can correctly sort T-shirts into two piles—those that have been worn by men and those that have been worn by women—based on their smell alone (Lord & Kasprzak, 1989; Schleidt, Hold, & Attili, 1981). Even very young human infants, just a few weeks old, can identify the scent of their own mothers, preferring T-shirts worn by their mothers to T-shirts worn by other lactating women (Russell, 1976). There is also evidence that men and women can differentiate among human vaginal odors associated with ovulation and premenstrual vaginal odors (Doty, 1997; Doty, Ford, Preti, & Huggins, 1975).

The Nature of Odors

Odors are produced by chemicals that are dissolved in the air. That is, in order for a chemical to have a smell, it must be volatile, which means it must be gaseous at room temperature. The shape of the chemical molecule determines its smell. The chemical structures of molecules associated with two well-known odors are illustrated in Figure 7.19.

Not all chemicals dissolved in the air have an odor. For example, water vapor has no smell. In general, substances that contain carbon *(organic substances)* have an odor, although not all organic matter has an odor. Molecules that have an odor are called *odorants*.

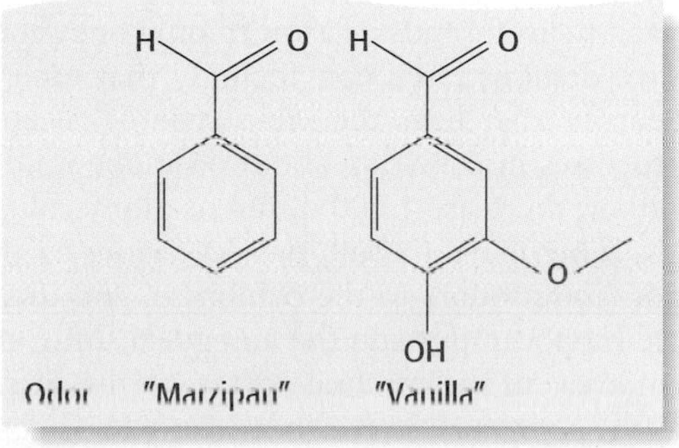

Anatomy and Function of the Olfactory System

Olfactory receptors are located at the top of the nasal cavity. The cell bodies of these neurons are embedded in the *olfactory epithelium,* which lines the skull. A mucous layer, called the *olfactory mucosa,* covers the cilia. To reach the receptor sites on the cilia, chemical

Figure 7.19 Chemical structures of two common odors

The molecular structures of marzipan and vanilla, which have similar odors.

molecules that communicate information about odors must diffuse through the olfactory mucosa.

The human nose contains approximately 10 million olfactory receptors on each side. Dogs have 10 times more receptors than humans do. They also have more cilia and thus more receptor sites per olfactory receptor, which contributes to their superior sense of smell. For example, bloodhounds need only a few molecules of an odorant to detect an odor. When tracking a scent, bloodhounds are able to follow a scent to a riverbank, swim across the river, and pick up the scent on the other bank.

Also located in the olfactory epithelium is another type of cell called a *neuronal stem cell*. Neuronal stem cells give rise to new neurons. You learned in Chapter 2 that neurons are not usually replaced when they die. However, olfactory sensory neurons die and are sloughed off with the outer layers of the olfactory epithelium about once a month. New olfactory receptors are generated by the stem cells to replace the dead cells.

On the surface of each cilia of the olfactory sensory neuron are special proteins that act as binding sites for odorants. The receptor sites on olfactory sensory neurons are G protein-coupled receptors, which you learned about in Chapter 3. Each protein receptor site binds with one and only one chemical. John Amoore (1971) has proposed the **Stereochemical Theory of Odor** to explain how specific odorants excite olfactory sensory neurons. According to the Stereochemical Theory, each odorant is a chemical substance that has a particular shape, and each shape fits into the receptor site like a key fits into a lock. That is, when a molecule has the correct shape, it fits precisely into the binding site, which produces a depolarization that generates an action potential in the olfactory neuron. This theory is considered too simplistic today, but its general concept of a molecule fitting into a specific receptor site is correct.

If we can recognize 10,000 different odors, how do neurons code for each of these smells? Research by Richard Axel and his colleagues (Axel, 1995) has demonstrated that each olfactory sensory neuron contains only one type of receptor site on its cilia. Altogether, according to Axel's research, we have 1,000 different receptor proteins, which means we have 1,000 different types of olfactory sensory neurons. In order to detect 10,000 different odors, odorants must bind with more than one type of receptor protein. For example, the odorant vanillin, which produces a vanilla odor, has a number of functional units that are capable of binding with various receptor sites on different neurons. Groups of sensory neurons forward axon potentials to the brain, with different groups of neurons being activated for different smells (Yoshihara, Nagao, & Mori, 2001).

Approximately 10 million axons, from each side of the nose, leave the olfactory epithelium and pass through the skull to form the **olfactory nerve,** or *cranial nerve I* (Figure 7.20). The skull bone in this region is called the *cribiform plate*. It is very porous, due to the millions of holes that allow the olfactory axons to exit the nasal cavity, and thus is quite weak. For example, any object that can pass through the nostril, such as a pencil, can very easily shatter the cribiform plate and enter the brain.

The olfactory nerve goes directly to the **olfactory bulb,** which is situated between the cribiform plate and the frontal lobe (Figure 7.20). Axons coming from the olfactory sensory neurons, which make up the olfactory nerve, separate and individually project to special structures, called **glomeruli,** in the olfactory bulb. Each neuron sends its axon to only one glomerulus. Axel (1995) and his colleagues have demonstrated convincingly that each glomerulus receives information from neurons that bear the same type of receptor protein. That is, each glomerulus processes information about only one kind of odor (Yoshihara et al., 2001). Altogether, there are 1,000 different glomeruli in the olfactory bulb.

The olfactory bulb projects axons to the thalamus, which sends the information about odors to the cerebrum, and to structures in the limbic system, such as the hippocampus and the amygdala. Information about smell is sent to two different areas in the cerebral cortex: to the **olfactory cortex** in the temporal lobe and to the *prefrontal cortex*, where the odor is consciously detected and identified. Some

Stereochemical Theory of Odor: a theory that proposes that each odorant is a chemical substance that has a particular shape that fits into a specific receptor site

olfactory nerve: cranial nerve I, which carries information about odors from the nose to the brain

olfactory bulb: brain structure that receives olfactory information directly from the receptors and processes this information before relaying it on to the cerebral cortex

glomeruli: special structures in the olfactory bulb that each process information about one kind of odor

olfactory cortex: the area in the temporal lobe that processes information from the olfactory bulb

Figure 7.20 Anatomy of the olfactory system

Odor molecules bind with receptors on the cilia of olfactory receptors located on the roof of the nasal cavity. The axons of the receptors form cranial nerve I as they pass through the skull to the olfactory bulb.

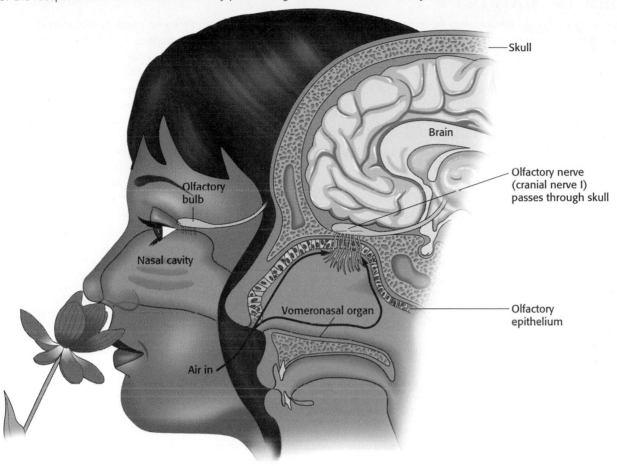

information from the olfactory bulb goes directly to the cerebral cortex without going to the thalamus first. We will discuss the role of the frontal and temporal lobes in more detail in Chapter 8.

An Accessory Olfactory System

Like other animals, humans appear to have two olfactory systems (Bartoshuk & Beauchamp, 1994; Takami et al., 1993). The primary olfactory system, which you've just learned about, allows us to detect and recognize odors. The second system, called the *accessory olfactory system*, transmits information about **pheromones,** the chemical signals that regulate sexual and social behaviors. In many species, including rodents and farm livestock, pheromones released by the female of the species signal that she is available for mating, which initiates sexual behavior in the male (Wysocki & Meredith, 1987). Lesions in the accessory olfactory system suppress male sexual behavior in these species. In humans, the role of pheromones and the accessory olfactory system is much less important in controlling or initiating behavior.

Sensory neurons for the accessory olfactory system are located in the **vomeronasal organ** in the floor of the nasal cavity (Figure 7.20). When the neurons in the vomeronasal organ are stimulated by pheromones, action potentials race down their axons to signal to neurons in the hypothalamus and other areas of the brainstem. Information from the accessory olfactory system is *not* processed by the olfactory bulb and, therefore, does not reach the cerebrum, where conscious processing of odors occurs. Thus, processing of olfactory information in the accessory

pheromones: chemical signals that regulate sexual and social behaviors in some species

vomeronasal organ: a structure located in the floor of the nasal cavity that contains receptors for the accessory olfactory system

A Case of Anosmia

Chris was a senior in high school when he had what he considers to be the worst case of flu he's ever had in his life. He had the usual sore throat, headache, fatigue, and nasal congestion that one would expect with a bad viral infection, and he also found that his food lost its flavor, which he blamed on his stuffy nose. However, when his flu symptoms went away, his sense of taste was still disturbed. What's more, Chris had developed anosmia—an inability to detect odors.

After several weeks, when his sense of smell did not recover, Chris's parents took him to his family doctor, who assured him that his olfactory sense would return. He waited over a month and, in the meantime, lost a good deal of weight because he no longer liked to eat. Eating had become a chore because he could not smell the food on his plate and the food itself seemed to have no flavor.

He went next to a series of specialists when his olfactory sense did not return after 6 weeks. The specialists ordered CAT scans, examined his nasal cavity using tiny cameras, and took biopsies from his oral and nasal pharynx [pharynx = throat, Greek]. The results of all these tests were inconclusive. One specialist noted a good deal of scar tissue in the nasal cavity and suggested that, when the scar tissue shrank, Chris's sense of smell would return.

About 5 months after the onset of anosmia, Chris's olfactory sense began to recover. At first, he was bothered by phantom odors that would occur randomly during the day. For example, he was sitting in class one day when he suddenly smelled the swimming pool where he had worked as a lifeguard the summer before. As Chris approached complete recovery, other strange odors began to haunt him more frequently. Chris's sense of smell returned to normal 7 months after he first developed anosmia.

olfactory system is largely unconscious. That is, we are generally unaware when our vomeronasal organ is stimulated. For example, women who live together tend to menstruate at the same time (McClintock, 1971; Preti et al., 1986). Investigators believe this menstrual synchrony occurs because the women exchange chemical signals by way of the accessory olfactory system. In addition, women who live with men tend to have shorter, more regular menstrual cycles. Chemicals in men's sweat have been shown to affect women's menstrual cycles (Cutler et al., 1986).

Disorders of the Olfactory System

The olfactory disorder that has received the most study is **anosmia,** which is an inability to smell. Some people have *total anosmia* and cannot detect any odors whatsoever. For example, individuals with a genetic disorder known as *Kallman's syndrome* present with a number of abnormalities, including lack of development of the olfactory system and the reproductive organs. In addition, viral infections that invade the olfactory system can produce temporary or permanent anosmia. See the *Case Study*. In fact, any condition that blocks the nasal cavity or damages the olfactory system can produce anosmia, including sinus disease, nasal tumors or polyps, head injury, and upper respiratory infections, like the common cold, that induce the production of large quantities of mucous that block the nasal passages.

anosmia: an inability to smell odors

Some people have a *specific anosmia*, which means that they cannot smell a particular odor. For example, nearly 30% of all people tested cannot smell androstenone, a chemical molecule found in human sweat, whereas most of us are very sensitive to that odor (Labows & Wysocki, 1984). Recall that each odor is associated with a specific set of receptor proteins. The inability to smell a specific odor is believed to be related to a missing or altered gene because receptor proteins are coded by specific genes. An aberrant gene might result in the failure to produce a particular receptor protein needed to detect a particular odor. John Amoore (1977) has suggested that counting and cataloging specific anosmias will permit scientists to identify primary odors associated with specific receptor sites.

Olfactory deficits have been observed in a number of brain-related disorders, including schizophrenia, Parkinson's disease, Alzheimer's disease, Huntington's disease, and head trauma (Bylsma et al., 1997; Doty et al., 1997; Doty et al., 1991; Mesholam et al., 1998; Moberg & Doty, 1997; Moberg et al., 1999; Moberg et al., 1997). For example, compared to nonschizophrenic control subjects, schizophrenic patients had impairments in odor detection, identification, discrimination, and memory (Moberg et al., 1999). These olfactory deficits appear to be associated with abnormalities of the right hemisphere because a number of brain-imaging studies have indicated reduced glucose metabolism on the right side of the brain in schizophrenic patients with severe olfactory deficits (Bertollo, Cowen, & Levy, 1996; Clark, Kopala, & Hurwitz, 1991). Very low-weight anorexics also have an impaired ability to detect and identify odors, even after lengthy hospitalization and significant weight gain (Federoff, Stoner, Andersen, Doty, & Rolls, 1995). The severe, prolonged self-starvation that is a hallmark of anorexia is suspected to produce permanent damage to the olfactory system.

Recap 7.5: The Olfactory System

Substances that have an odor are called (a)_____. Olfactory receptors, located at the top of the nasal cavity, send information about odors to the olfactory bulb by way of the (b)_____ nerve (cranial nerve I). The olfactory bulb contains special structures, called (c)_____, that process information about only one type of odor. Information about smell is sent to two different areas in the cerebral cortex, the olfactory cortex in the (d)_____ lobe and the (e)_____ cortex. An accessory olfactory system transmits information about (f)_____ to the brain. Sensory receptors for the accessory olfactory system are located in the (g)_____ organ in the floor of the nasal cavity (h)_____ is the inability to smell. Olfactory (i)_____ have been observed in Kallman's syndrome, schizophrenia, Parkinson's disease, Alzheimer's disease, Huntington's disease, and head trauma.

The Taste System

Your sense of taste provides you with information about the foods you are ingesting. Sweet-tasting substances are generally a ready source of calories, whereas poisons and spoiled foods typically have a bitter taste. Human breast milk, for example, is an excellent source of nutrition and is sweet tasting. For that reason, we usually react positively to sweet-tasting substances and negatively to bitter-tasting substances. Studies of very young infants have demonstrated that reactions to different tastes appear to be innate (Figure 7.21). Babies offered sweet-tasting food will appear to smile and move toward the food source. When a bitter-tasting substance is placed on a baby's tongue, the baby screws up its face in disgust and pulls away from the experimenter.

The Nature of Taste Stimuli

Taste stimuli are chemicals that are dissolved in water. Saliva, which is mostly water, dissolves solid food particles, permitting them to interact with taste receptors.

Figure 7.21 Reactions of babies exposed to sweet, sour, and bitter tastes

These three babies were exposed to various tastes between birth and their first feeding. (1) no taste stimulus (at rest). (2) Reaction to distilled water (control). (3) Response to a sweet stimulus. (4) Response to a sour stimulus. (5) Response to a bitter stimulus.

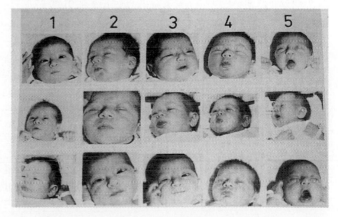

If dry salt or sugar is sprinkled on the surface of a dry tongue, the salt or sugar crystals will have no taste because the crystals are incapable of stimulating taste receptors in their dry, undissolved state. But, if salt or sugar is sprinkled on a wet tongue, the crystals will dissolve in the saliva on the tongue and stimulate taste receptors, producing a salty or sweet taste.

In the previous section, you learned that people possess about 1,000 different receptors that respond to at least 10,000 different odors. The taste system, on the other hand, responds to four **primary tastes**: *sweet, sour, salty,* and *bitter.* Certainly you can detect and identify more than four different tastes. Recently, investigators have identified a fifth primary taste, the taste of glutamate, called *umami*, which has its own specific receptors on the tongue and a special processing area in the cerebral cortex (Rolls, 2000). Psychologists and other neuroscientists are working together to discover how taste receptors respond to taste stimuli to produce the many different tastes that we experience daily.

Salty sensations are produced by substances that contain sodium (Na^+). As Figure 7.22 illustrates, Na^+ ions directly enter the receptor cells through sodium channels in the membrane of the microvilli, depolarizing the receptor cells (Kinnamon, 1988). Other positively charged ions, or *cations*, such as lithium (Li^+) or potassium (K^+), can also produce a salty taste, but the mechanism by which these chemicals stimulate taste receptors is unknown (Bartoshuk & Beauchamp, 1994).

Sour tastes are produced by substances that are acidic. Acidic substances contain positively charged hydrogen ions (H^+), which block K^+ channels or affect ion channel activity in other ways (Figure 7.22). A wide range of substances produces a sweet or bitter taste, and the receptor mechanisms for these primary tastes are still being debated. Sweet and bitter substances may bind with specific ligand-gated receptors, or they may require a second messenger to produce depolarization (Walters, DuBois, & Kellogg, 1993; Levitan & Kaczmarek, 1997). Most substances that taste sweet or bitter are organic substances, such as sugars or amino acids, that contain carbon. However, some metals (for example, lead), which contain no carbon, have a sweet taste. Lead poisoning occurs in children who are attracted to the sweet taste of peeling lead paint or other lead-based products and eat significant quantities of these substances.

Stimulation of a taste receptor by one food can produce *adaptation* in that receptor, which will alter the taste of other foods that are introduced to the mouth after adaptation has taken place. For example, if you eat a piece of chocolate fudge cake with chocolate icing and then drink a sip of cola, the cola will taste bitter and not sweet. This is because the chocolate cake will stimulate sweet receptors intensely, producing adaptation of those receptors. Therefore, when the cola is introduced to the sweet receptors, they do not respond. Only the bitter and salty receptors respond because cola has a weak bitter and salty taste, as well as a powerful sweet taste.

Another phenomenon, called **potentiation**, also occurs in taste receptors. With potentiation, one taste stimulus causes a receptor to respond more intensely to another stimulus. Have you ever drunk orange juice after brushing your teeth? Ugh, what an awful taste! This is a great example of potentiation. The detergent in the toothpaste alters the bitter receptors on your tongue, increasing their ability to respond. So, when you drink orange juice immediately after brushing your teeth, the bitter receptors in your mouth increase their activity, producing a sensation of bitterness when stimulated by orange juice.

Flavor is a sensory quality that combines olfaction and taste. When you have a bad cold that clogs up your nasal passages, making it impossible for odorants to come in

primary tastes: pure sweet, sour, salty, or bitter tastes

potentiation: a phenomenon in which one taste stimulus causes a receptor to respond more intensely to another stimulus

Figure 7.22 Stimulation of taste receptors by taste stimuli

Different hypotheses have been proposed to explain how the primary tastes stimulate taste receptors. Sour stimuli block the movement of potassium out of the cell, causing depolarization. Sodium derived from salty stimuli pass into the cell, depolarizing it. Sweet and bitter stimuli are believed to bind with specific receptor sites and use second messengers to close potassium or open sodium channels.

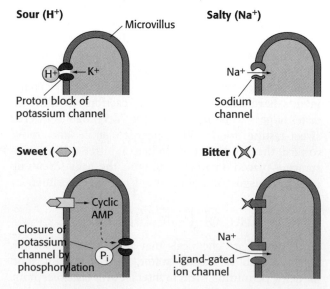

contact with olfactory receptors, the flavors of the food you eat are distorted. That is, stimulation of the taste receptors alone does not elicit the complete sensation of flavor.

Anatomy and Function of the Taste System

Like the olfactory system, the taste (or *gustatory*) system contains chemoreceptors. The chemoreceptors of the taste system, called taste receptors, are embedded in the linings of the mouth and throat. However, most taste receptors are found on the tongue in structures known as **taste buds.** Taste buds are located on the surface of the little bumps, called *papillae* (singular = *papilla*), that cover the tongue. The taste receptors have little hairlike projections, or *microvilli*, that protrude through pores in the surface of the tongue (Figure 7.23). When taste stimuli come in contact with these microvilli, they initiate a receptor potential, which excites neurons that send information about taste stimuli to the brain.

Three cranial nerves carry information about taste to the brain. Cranial nerve VII, the *facial nerve,* transmits information from taste receptors in the anterior two-thirds of the tongue. Taste receptors in the posterior one-third of the tongue and throat send their information to the brain by way of cranial nerve IX, the *glossopharyngeal nerve.* The *vagus nerve,* also known as cranial nerve X, carries information from taste receptors in the lower part of the throat, including the larynx. These three cranial nerves converge in the **nucleus of the solitary tract,** where taste information is initially processed before being relayed through the **ventral posterior medial nucleus** of the thalamus to the **primary taste cortex,** which is located in the frontal lobe just anterior to the temporal lobe. Information about the intense burning produced by spicy or "hot" foods is transmitted to the brain by way of cranial nerve V, the *trigeminal nerve.* We will examine the effects of *capsaicin,* the ingredient in hot peppers that causes burning and pain, in Chapter 8 when we discuss the sensation of pain.

Figure 7.23 A papilla with taste receptors
Taste receptors are found in taste buds on the tongue.
(a) These taste buds are located on the surface of tongue papillae. (b) Taste stimuli bind with receptor sites on the microvilli of the taste receptor.

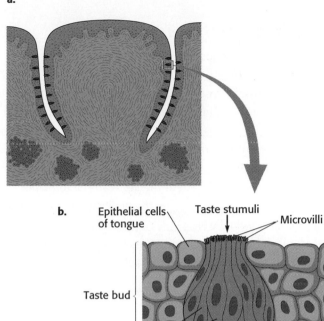

Disorders of the Taste System

Ageusia is the inability to taste. Rarely do people have *total ageusia,* which is a complete absence of the ability to taste. However, a few genetic disorders do produce total ageusia, and head trauma and viral infections can produce temporary total ageusia. Most forms of ageusia are *specific ageusias* in which an individual cannot sense a particular taste or family of tastes. One well-researched example is the substance *phenylthiocarbamide,* or *PTC,* which produces a bitter taste in people who have inherited the ability to taste this chemical. About 25% of all Americans cannot taste PTC, although they can taste other bitter substances (Bartoshuk, Duffy, & Miller, 1994; Guo & Reed, 2001).

Perhaps the most disturbing taste disorder for any individual is **dysgeusia,** in which the individual has a disagreeable taste in the mouth that is due to a nose, mouth, or throat infection, medication, or chemotherapy (Bartoshuk & Beauchamp, 1994). Sometimes the dysgeusia is due to "phantoms" caused by damage to the taste system. In the case of taste phantoms, there are no physical stimuli

taste buds: tiny structures that contain taste receptors

nucleus of the solitary tract: a nucleus in the medulla that receives information from the gut and other receptors by way of cranial nerves VII, IX, and X

ventral posterior medial nucleus: a group of neurons in the thalamus that processes taste information

primary taste cortex: an area of the frontal lobe just anterior to the temporal lobe that receives information about taste stimuli from the thalamus

ageusia: an inability to taste

dysgeusia: a disagreeable taste in the mouth due to infection, medication, tumors, or chemotherapy

in the mouth or saliva that elicit the dysgeusia. Rather, irritation of the peripheral or central nervous system produces the sensation of a bad taste in the mouth. For example, El-Deiry and McCabe (1990) reported the case of a 54-year-old man with a tumor in his temporal lobe that caused a phantom foul, bitter taste in his mouth.

Recap 7.6: The Taste System

The taste system responds to five primary tastes: (a)_____, (b)_____, (c)_____, (d)_____, and (e)_____. With (f)_____, one taste stimulus causes a taste receptor to respond more intensely to another stimulus. The taste receptors are found in the linings of the mouth and throat, especially in structures called (g)_____ _____ that are located on papillae on the tongue. Three cranial nerves carry information about taste to the brain: the (h)_____ nerve (cranial nerve VII), the (i)_____ nerve (cranial nerve IX), and the (j)_____ nerve (cranial nerve X). These nerves carry information to the nucleus of the (k)_____ _____ in the hindbrain. Taste information is transmitted to the primary taste cortex in the (l)_____ lobe. (m)_____ is the inability to taste, whereas (n)_____ is a disagreeable taste in the mouth produced by an infection, medication, brain tumor, or chemotherapy.

The Vestibular System

When he was much younger, my youngest son loved to spin around in circles. Arms outstretched, he would go around and around. Then he would stop abruptly and wait for that dizzy feeling, that sensation that the world was still spinning even though he was not. This spinning sensation arises from the **vestibular system.** Usually you are not aware when your vestibular system is working. But, when something is wrong, like when your eyes and vestibular system send contradictory messages to the brain, you become consciously aware of the vestibular system. In this section, we will examine this sensory system that you largely take for granted.

vestibular system: the sensory system that responds to changes in head movement and to gravity

The vestibular system shares many similarities with the auditory system. Like the auditory system, the vestibular system is located in the temporal bone in the same cavity as the inner ear. A series of canals comprising the vestibular system is located deep within the temporal bone and is referred to as the *bony labyrinth*. For this reason, the vestibular system is sometimes called the *labyrinth system*. The vestibular receptors are mechanoreceptors called *hair cells*, identical in appearance to those in the auditory system. In addition, information from the vestibular hair cells is forwarded to the brain by way of the *vestibular branch of the auditory nerve*, cranial nerve VIII.

The Nature of Vestibular Stimuli

The main function of the vestibular system is to detect changes in head movement in order to assist the eyes in vision. Your eyes are like two cameras mounted on a moving tripod. Have you ever seen a video that was filmed while the video camera was bouncing around? For example, perhaps you've seen the film *Blair Witch Project*. That's what the image that is sent to your brain looks like. But, the vestibular system informs your brain of head movements, and the visual system compensates for these movements, the net result being a visual image that appears clear and stable. Therefore, any changes in head movement, such as speeding up or slowing down or turning the head, act as stimuli that excite vestibular receptors. Static head positions (that is, head positions that do not change) are also registered by certain receptors in the vestibular system. These receptors are particularly sensitive to the position of the head with respect to gravity.

Anatomy and Function of the Vestibular System

The hair cells are located in three organs that make up the vestibular system: the **utricle,** the **saccule,** and the **semicircular canals.** You have one utricle, one saccule, and three semicircular canals on either side of your head (Figure 7.24). In the utricle and saccule, the hair cells are found in a sensitive encapsulated area called the *macula* (plural = *maculae*). The macula contains endolymph (the same fluid found in the scala media of the cochlea) and tiny pieces of calcium carbonate, in addition to the hair cells. In the utricle, the macula is oriented horizontally, along the base of the organ. When a person is sitting or standing, with the head in an upright position, gravity pushes down on the calcium carbonate particles, forcing them down on top of the hair cells, which bends the hairs of the hair cells. This means that the hair cells in the utricle get stimulated when the head is upright.

In the saccule, the macula is oriented vertically along the medial wall. When the head is in an upright position, gravity pushes the calcium carbonate particles down, so that they are piled up at the bottom of the saccule, and few hair cells are affected. However, when the head is in a horizontal position, the hair cells of the saccule are maximally stimulated. For example, when you are lying in bed or lying on the sofa watching television, the hair cells in your saccule fire wildly.

The primary function of the hair cells in the utricle and saccule is to gather information about the static position of the head with respect to gravity. They are our gravity detectors. In contrast, the hair cells in the semicircular canals relay information about head movement.

There are three semicircular canals, oriented at 90° to each other, on each side of the head (Figure 7.24). At the ends of each of the canals are swellings, called *ampullae* (singular = *ampulla*), where the hair cells are located. There are no macula in the semicircular canals. Rather, the hair cells are found in *cristae* (singular = *crista*). One crista is found in each ampulla. Each crista contains a cluster of hair cells covered by a gelatinous *cupola* or covering. Movement of the head causes fluid in the semicircular canals to move. As the fluid in the semicircular canals moves, it causes movement of the gelatinous cupola, which tugs and pulls at the hairs of the hair cells, producing action potentials.

Brain Pathways Carrying Vestibular Information

Action potentials produced by cells in the utricle, saccule, and semicircular canals are relayed to the brain by way of the vestibular portion of cranial nerve VIII, the auditory nerve. As you have already learned, the auditory nerve enters the brain at the level of the medulla. The vestibular branch of the auditory nerve goes to the vestibular nucleus. From the vestibular nucleus, axons carrying information from the vestibular system travel in bundles to various regions of the central nervous system.

Many axons leaving the vestibular nucleus synapse with neurons associated with cranial nerves III, IV, and VI, the nerves that control eye movement. Recall that the vestibular system's main function is to assist with vision. Movement of the head causes compensatory movement of the eyes. Look at yourself in the mirror, keeping your eyes on your eyes in the mirror. Move your head to the left, and you'll observe that your eyes will move to the right. When you fix your gaze on an object, your vestibular system works with the nerves that control your eye muscles, in

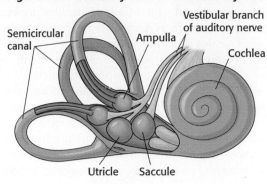

Figure 7.24 Anatomy of the vestibular system

utricle: a vestibular structure that signals information about the position of the head with respect to gravity

saccule: a vestibular structure that signals information about the position of the head with respect to gravity

semicircular canals: vestibular structures that respond to changes in head movement

order that you keep your eyes on the object as you move your head. These automatic eye movements that are made in response to head movements are called **oculovestibular reflexes.**

Nystagmus is another example of an oculovestibular reflex. Continuous stimulation of the vestibular system (for example, the stimulation produced by spinning in circles) induces nystagmus, or oscillation of the eyes, in which an individual's eyes move laterally a short distance before jumping back to their original position and then start to move laterally again. The eyes move in response to messages being sent to the brain by the semicircular canals. These messages inform the brain that the head is moving, and the neurons controlling eye movement produce compensatory movements of the eyes.

Some axons from the vestibular nucleus travel to the cerebellum and reticular formation, and others travel to the spinal cord, via the *vestibulospinal tract* (Figure 7.25). These axons carry information that is used to coordinate reflexes that help us maintain an upright posture with respect to gravity and maintain balance (Wilson, Boyle, Fukushima, Rose, Shinoda, Sugiuchi, & Uchino, 1995). For example, the *righting reflex* permits us to recover our upright posture when we stumble or fall over.

In addition, a number of axons coming from the vestibular nucleus synapse with neurons associated with the *nucleus of the solitary tract* and with cranial nerve X, the vagus nerve. You learned earlier in this chapter that the nucleus of the solitary tract processes information about taste. In Chapter 14, you will learn that this nucleus receives a great deal of information from the peripheral nervous system, including information carried by the vagus nerve to the brain. Recall that the vagus nerve innervates structures in our upper abdomen, chest, and neck, including the stomach. Overstimulation of the vestibular system produces *motion sickness*, with which an individual feels nauseous and may even vomit. For example, a roller coaster ride may trigger vomiting because stimulation of the vestibular system triggers the vagus nerve, which stimulates the stomach to eject its contents. For some people, even mild stimulation of the vestibular system, such as a car ride or jet flight, produces motion sickness.

Finally, some axons leaving the vestibular nucleus send their information to the cerebral cortex. This information first goes to the thalamus and then on to the vestibular sensory cortex in the temporal lobe.

Disorders of the Vestibular System

The vestibular system is not necessary for our survival, as studies of people born without this sensory system have demonstrated. Often, people whose pregnant mothers had syphilis or German measles are born without vestibular systems. These people are able to stand upright with respect to gravity and can even dive blindfolded into a swimming pool, thanks to the receptors in their muscles and joints. Therefore, disorders of the vestibular system produce annoying, but not life-threatening, symptoms. For example, those individuals with disease of the peripheral vestibular system, such as viral infections that invade the vestibular organs, have difficulty determining visual vertical. They typically are 5°–30° off from vertical when asked to indicate vertical on various testing instruments. However, the symptoms of

Figure 7.25 Vestibular pathways
From the vestibular nuclei, axons carry vestibular information to the motor neurons that control eye movement, to the cerebellum and reticular formation, to the spinal cord, and to the vagus nerve.

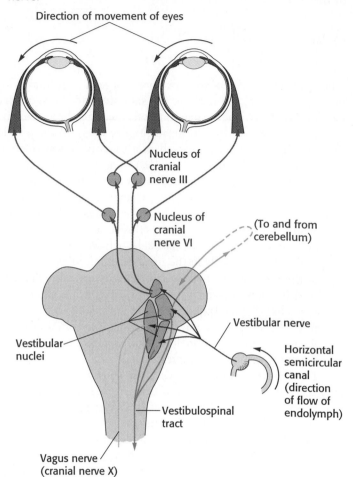

Direction of movement of eyes

Nucleus of cranial nerve III

Nucleus of cranial nerve VI

(To and from cerebellum)

Vestibular nerve

Vestibular nuclei

Horizontal semicircular canal (direction of flow of endolymph)

Vestibulospinal tract

Vagus nerve (cranial nerve X)

oculovestibular reflexes: automatic eye movements made to compensate for movements of the head
nystagmus: oscillation of the eyes following stimulation of the vestibular system

some vestibular disorders can be thoroughly debilitating, as in *Meniere's disease*, which produces symptoms of dizziness and unsteadiness (Anderson & Harris, 2001; DiGirolamo et al., 2001). Some individuals with Meniere's disease are helped by surgical removal of the vestibular system (Neely, 2001).

The vestibular system relies on movement of fluid in the semicircular canals and in the utricle and saccule to produce stimulation of the hair cells. Due to the physical property of inertia (resistance to movement), the fluid in these vestibular organs moves slowly. And, when a change in direction occurs, the endolymph changes direction after a considerable time lag. For this reason, the information reaching the brain from the vestibular system is largely inaccurate. Many of the disorders involving the vestibular system are due to the inaccuracies of this sensory system.

For example, dizziness, or **vertigo**, occurs when there is a conflict in the information coming from the vestibular system and that coming from the visual system (Bles et al., 1998; Probst & Schmidt, 1998). For example, when an individual spins around in circles, the fluid in that person's semicircular canals moves in the opposite direction. However, when that individual stops suddenly, the fluid continues in the original direction and then abruptly changes direction, much like a person riding in a car that makes a sudden stop. Think about what happens when you slam on the brakes of your car. At first, your body lurches forward because you are heading in a forward direction, and then your body is flung backward. Your vestibular system reacts in the same way. When you stop spinning, the fluid in the semicircular canals pushes your hair cells in the opposite direction to which they were originally pulled, and the message is sent to the brain that the body is now moving in the opposite direction. The eyes, however, tell the brain that the body has stopped moving, and *postrotational vertigo* results [*post-* = after, Latin].

Adaptation of the vestibular system can lead to problems, too. Have you ever been on a cruise that lasted for several days? I haven't, but once I took a train from Chicago to San Francisco, a trip that lasted three days, with the same effect. At first, while on a cruise (or on a train), you are very aware of the movement of the vessel and might even feel seasick, due to prolonged stimulation of the vestibular system. But, after a day or so, you are no longer aware of the movement because of adaptation of the vestibular system. However, when you get off the boat or train, the earth under your feet feels as if it is moving and rolling. This hallucination occurs because your vestibular system, which had adapted to the movement of the boat (or train), suddenly begins firing again, and the brain misinterprets this sudden activation of the vestibular system as movement.

People who spin for a living, like ballerinas and figure skaters, have vestibular systems that are permanently adapted. We can demonstrate this by having the ballerina or skater spin in circles and then observe his or her eyes. A normal person who spins in circles will show nystagmus, or oscillation of the eyeballs, as you learned earlier in this section. However, a professional dancer or skater will not show any evidence of nystagmus, which is a sign that the vestibular system is not responding to the spinning movement.

As people age, their vestibular systems deteriorate, producing problems, such as dizziness and faulty vestibular reflexes, in many elderly individuals (Matheson, Darlington, & Smith, 1999). For most people, a great deal of compensation takes place within the central nervous system, so that they do not show signs of vestibular deterioration. However, for those aged individuals with extremely impaired vestibular systems, the resulting dizziness has profound effects, producing anxiety and loss of confidence.

In the next chapter, we will examine how sensory information is processed by the cerebral cortex. Unfortunately, very little is known about cortical processing of vestibular information, except where it interacts with visual or somatosensory information. Therefore, in Chapter 8, we will not look at how the cerebral cortex decodes vestibular information. We will, however, discuss how information from the other sensory systems (visual, auditory, somatosensory, olfactory, and taste) is interpreted in the brain and translated into perceptual experiences.

vertigo: dizziness

The vestibular receptors are mechanoreceptors called (a) _____, which are sensitive to head movements and head position with respect to gravity. The vestibular hair cells are located in the utricle, (b)_____, and (c)_____ canals. Information from the vestibular receptors is transmitted to the brain by way of the vestibular branch of the (d)_____ nerve (cranial nerve VIII). (e)_____ is the oscillation of the eyes following continuous stimulation of the vestibular system. (f)_____ _____ occurs when stimulation of the vestibular system triggers the vagus nerve. (g)_____ disease is a vestibular disorder that produces dizziness and unsteadiness. Dizziness, also called (h)_____, occurs when the brain receives conflicting information from the vestibular and visual systems.

Chapter Summary

Sensory Stimuli and Receptors

▶ Specialized sensory neurons, called receptors, respond to specific stimuli. Chemoreceptors respond to chemical stimuli, and mechanoreceptors respond to mechanical stimuli. Receptors act as transducers to convert chemical or mechanical energy into action potentials.

▶ Many external stimuli are transmitted through the environment as waves, which possess special characteristics, including wavelength, frequency, and amplitude. Wavelength is the distance between corresponding parts of two consecutive waves. Frequency refers to the number of waves that occur in a given period of time. The amplitude of a wave is the height of a wave from its lowest to highest points.

▶ Receptors show a number of special characteristics, including generator potentials and adaptation. The receptor potential, also called a generator potential, is a graded potential that is produced when a receptor is excited by a stimulus.

▶ Adaptation is the decrease in responsiveness of a receptor to a repeated stimulus.

▶ The network of neurons that form a pathway from the receptor to the cerebrum is called a sensory system.

The Visual System

▶ Visual receptors, called rods and cones, are stimulated by photons, which pass through the cornea, pupil, lens, and vitreous humor to reach the retina.

▶ The retina contains five layers of cells: receptors, horizontal cells, bipolar cells, amacrine cells, and ganglion cells. Information about the photons is transmitted from the receptors to horizontal, bipolar, amacrine, and ganglion cells in the retina to the optic nerve and then on to the lateral geniculate nucleus of the thalamus and the primary visual cortex in the occipital lobe.

▶ According to the Trichromatic Color Theory, the ability to see color comes from the fact that we have three different types of cone (S cones, M cones, and L cones), each sensitive to different wavelengths of light. According to the Opponent-Process Theory, three opponent processes (red-green, blue-yellow, black-white) code for color in the nervous system.

▶ Damage to various structures in the visual system will impair vision, producing blindness, astigmatism, glaucoma, presbyopia, cataract, retinitis pigmentosa, and macular degeneration. An astigmatism results from an irregularly shaped cornea. The leading cause of blindness is glaucoma, which is caused by increased intraocular pressure. Disorders associated with the lens of the eye include presbyopia and cataracts. Macular degeneration causes blindness beginning with the death of cones in the macula lutea, whereas retinitis pigmentosa causes blindness beginning with the death of rods in the periphery of the retina.

The Auditory System

▶ Auditory receptors are called hair cells. These hair cells are located on the basilar membrane of the cochlea and respond to vibrations that have a frequency between 20 and 20,000 Hz.

▶ The frequency of sound waves are measured in Hertz (Hz) units, whereas loudness is measured in decibels (dB).

▶ The outer ear consists of the pinna and external auditory meatus. The middle ear consists of the eardrum, three ossicles, and eustachian tube. The inner ear is found in the cochlea, which contains three chambers, the scala vestibuli, scala tympani, and scala media.

▶ The vibrations pass through the outer and middle ear to reach the cochlea in the inner ear.

- The auditory nerve (cranial nerve VIII) transmits information from the cochlea to the cochlear nucleus. From the cochlear nucleus, auditory information is transmitted to the superior olive, and on to the inferior colliculus and then to the medial geniculate nucleus in the thalamus before terminating in the auditory cortex in the temporal lobe.

- To locate a sound, the brain uses loudness difference and phase difference.

- According to the Place Theory of pitch perception, low frequency sounds stimulate hair cells best in the apex of the cochlea, and high frequency sounds stimulate hair cells best in the base of the cochlea. The Frequency Theory of pitch perception has been proposed to explain the perception of frequencies below 500 Hz.

- Damage to specific structures in the auditory system produce different types of deafness or hearing loss, including outer ear deafness, middle ear deafness, inner ear deafness, nerve deafness, and central deafness. Hearing aids are used to correct a conductive hearing loss associated with middle ear deafness. Cochlear implants are used to correct inner ear deafness.

The Somatosensory System

- Somatosensory receptors are located in the skin, muscles, joints, and tendons and typically respond to mechanical stimuli.

- Somatosensation includes skin sensations, kinesthesia, proprioception, and interoception. Kinesthesia is the ability to sense movement of the body, whereas interoception is the sensation that arises from internal organs. The skin can sense pressure, temperature, pain, and vibration.

- Pacinian corpuscles respond to pressure, free nerve endings respond to pain, Ruffini's endings respond to warm sensations, Krause endbulbs respond to cold, and stretch receptors respond to stretch in muscles, tendons, and joints.

- The lemniscal system relays information about pressure and stretch by way of large diameter, myelinated Λ-fibers. The extralemniscal system relays information about temperature and pain by way of thin, unmyelinated C-fibers.

- The primary somatosensory cortex is located in the postcentral gyrus in the parietal lobe.

The Olfactory System

- Substances that have an odor are called odorants.

- Olfactory receptors are located at the top of the nasal cavity and are chemoreceptors stimulated by chemicals carried in the air.

- The olfactory nerve (cranial nerve I) relays information about odorants from the receptors to the olfactory lobe, which contains special structures, called glomeruli, that process information about only one type of odor.

- Information about smell is sent to two different areas in the cerebral cortex, the olfactory cortex in the temporal lobe and the prefrontal cortex.

- An accessory olfactory system transmits information about pheromones to the brain. Sensory receptors for the accessory olfactory system are located in the vomeronasal organ in the floor of the nasal cavity.

- Anosmia is the inability to smell and can be caused by infections, genetic abnormalities, head trauma, brain disorders, and tumors.

The Taste System

- Taste receptors are chemoreceptors, which respond to five primary tastes: sweet, sour, salty, bitter, and umami.

- Taste receptors respond to chemicals dissolved in water.

- The taste receptors are found in the linings of the mouth and throat, especially in structures called taste buds that are located on papillae on the tongue.

- Information about taste is sent from the taste receptors, via cranial nerves VII, IX, and X, to the nucleus of the solitary tract and on to the thalamus and the primary taste cortex in the frontal lobe.

- Ageusia is the inability to taste, whereas dysgeusia is a disagreeable taste in the mouth produced by an infection, medication, brain tumor, or chemotherapy.

The Vestibular System

- The vestibular system, like the somatosensory system, has mechanoreceptors, which are located in the utricles, saccules, and semicircular canals. These receptors, called hair cells, are sensitive to head movements and head position with respect to gravity.

- Information from the vestibular receptors is transmitted to the brain by way of the vestibular branch of the auditory nerve (cranial nerve VIII).

- A number of different pathways carry information from the hair cells in the vestibular system to various structures in the central nervous system, including the cerebellum, motor neurons that control eye movements, the spinal cord, and the vagus nerve. Nystagmus is the oscillation of the eyes following continuous stimulation of the vestibular system.

- Disorders associated with the vestibular system include motion sickness, Meniere's disease, and vertigo. Motion sickness occurs when stimulation of the vestibular system triggers the vagus nerve. Meniere's disease is a vestibular disorder that produces dizziness and unsteadiness. Dizziness, also called vertigo, occurs when the brain receives conflicting information from the vestibular and visual systems.

Key Terms

A-fibers (p. 195)
accommodation (p. 178)
adaptation (p. 176)
ageusia (p. 203)
amplitude (p. 175)
anosmia (p. 200)
anvil (p. 189)
auditory nerve (p. 190)
basilar membrane (p. 189)
cataract (p. 186)
C-fibers (p. 195)
chemoreceptors (p. 174)
cochlea (p. 189)
cochlear implants (p. 192)
cochlear nucleus (p. 190)
cones (p. 179)
cornea (p. 178)
dark adaptation (p. 180)
deafness (p. 191)
decibel (p. 175)
dichromat (p. 184)
distal stimulus (p. 178)
dysgeusia (p. 203)
eardrum (p. 188)
eustachian tube (p. 189)
extralemniscal pathway (p. 195)
fovea (p. 179)
frequency (p. 174)
Frequency Theory (p. 191)
ganglion cells (p. 179)
glaucoma (p. 186)
glomeruli (p. 198)
hair cells (p. 187)
hammer (p. 189)
Hertz (p. 175)
hyperopia (p. 186)
inferior colliculus (p. 190)
inner ear (p. 188)
interoception (p. 194)
iris (p. 178)
kinesthesia (p. 194)
lateral geniculate nucleus (p. 182)
lateral hemiretina (p. 182)

lemniscal pathway (p. 195)
lens (p. 178)
loudness (p. 175)
loudness difference (p. 191)
macula lutea (p. 186)
macular degeneration (p. 186)
mechanoreceptors (p. 174)
medial geniculate nucleus (p. 190)
middle ear (p. 188)
monochromat (p. 184)
myopia (p. 186)
nasal hemiretina (p. 182)
nucleus of the solitary
    tract (p. 203)
nystagmus (p. 206)
occipital lobe (p. 183)
oculovestibular reflexes (p. 206)
olfaction (p. 197)
olfactory bulb (p. 198)
olfactory cortex (p. 198)
olfactory nerve (p. 198)
olfactory receptors (p. 175)
Opponent-Process Theory (p. 185)
optic chiasm (p. 182)
optic disk (p. 182)
optic nerve (p. 182)
optic tract (p. 182)
outer ear (p. 188)
oval window (p. 189)
phase difference (p. 191)
pheromones (p. 199)
photons (p. 174)
photopigments (p. 180)
Place Theory of pitch
    perception (p. 191)
potentiation (p. 202)
presbyopia (p. 186)
primary somatosensory
    cortex (p. 196)
primary taste cortex (p. 203)
primary tastes (p. 202)
proprioception (p. 194)
proximal stimulus (p. 178)

pupil (p. 178)
receptor potential (p. 175)
receptors (p. 173)
retina (p. 178)
retinitis pigmentosa (p. 186)
rhodopsin (p. 180)
rods (p. 179)
saccule (p. 205)
scala media (p. 189)
scala tympani (p. 189)
scala vestibuli (p. 189)
secondary somatosensory
    cortex (p. 196)
semicircular canals (p. 205)
sensory system (p. 177)
somatosensory receptors (p. 194)
somatosensory system (p. 194)
Stereochemical Theory of
    Odor (p. 198)
stimuli (p. 174)
stirrup (p. 189)
superior colliculus (p. 182)
superior olive (p. 190)
taste buds (p. 203)
taste receptors (p. 176)
tectorial membrane (p. 189)
transducer (p. 176)
trichromat (p. 184)
Trichromatic Color
    Theory (p. 184)
utricle (p. 205)
ventral posterior medial
    nucleus (p. 203)
vertigo (p. 207)
vestibular system (p. 204)
visual field (p. 177)
visual receptors (p. 179)
volley principle (p. 191)
vomeronasal organ (p. 199)
wavelength (p. 174)
Young-Helmholtz color
    theory (p. 184)

Questions for Thought

1. Give an example of sensory adaptation that you've experienced.
2. Why do cats see better at night than humans do?
3. Explain why the flavor of food changes when you have a cold.
4. Is the vestibular system really necessary?

Questions for Review

1. Which sensory systems contain chemoreceptors, and which contain mechanoreceptors?

2. How do rods differ from cones?

3. Trace the pathway of a vibration as it travels from the air to the hair cell in the cochlea. Where does information about sound go after it leaves the cochlea?

4. Identify nuclei in the thalamus that relay information from the sensory receptors to the cerebral cortex.

5. Explain the difference between kinesthesia, proprioception, and interoception.

Suggested Readings

Axel, R. (1995). The molecular logic of smell. *Scientific American, 273,* 154–159.

Beauchamp, G. K., & Bartoshuk, L. (1997). *Tasting and smelling.* San Diego: Academic Press.

Palmer, S. E. (1999). *Vision science: Photons to phenomenology.* Cambridge, MA: MIT Press.

Rodieck, R. W. (2000). *The first steps in seeing.* Sunderland, MA: Sinauer.

Web Resources

For a chapter tutorial quiz, direct links to the Internet sites listed below and other features, visit the book-specific website at **www.wadsworth.com/product/ 0155074865**. You may also connect directly to the following annotated websites:

http://members.aol.com/nocolorvsn/color3.htm
Learn more about why people are colorblind and what it is like to be colorblind.

http://www.nidcd.nih.gov/
This site, from the National Institute on Deafness and Other Communication Disorders, provides extensive information on audition and deafness.

http://www.cf.ac.uk/biosi/staff/jacob/teaching/ sensory/olfact1.html
Does fear have a smell? How is your sense of smell tied to your memory? Does aromatherapy work? Answer these questions and more when you visit this website.

For additional readings and information, check out InfoTrac College Edition at **http://www.infotrac-college.com/wadsworth**. Choose a search term yourself or enter the following search terms: cochlear implants, pheromones, presbyopia, and myopia.

CD-ROM: Exploring Biological Psychology

Anatomy of the Eye
    Animation: The Retina
    Animation: Inverted Vision
    Virtual Reality: The Eye
Interactive Puzzle: The Hearing Process

Interactive Somesthetic Experiment
Interactive Recaps
Chapter 7 Quiz
Connect to the Interactive Biological Psychology Glossary

Perceptual Processes

Amadou Diallo, an emigrant from West Africa, returned home to his apartment building in New York City after a hard day at work, unaware that he was being followed by four undercover police officers who mistook him for a gun-toting rapist. He stopped in the lobby of his building to see if he had any mail. Standing in front of his mailbox, Amadou reached into his pants pocket and pulled out a small dark object. "Gun!" one of the officers shouted, and the police officers immediately opened fire on Amadou, killing him. To the surprise and dismay of the police officers when they examined Amadou's body after the shooting, they found a wallet, not a gun, in his hand.

Receptors, as you learned in Chapter 7, are excited by specific stimuli. The function of receptors is to encode information about stimuli and relay that sensory information to the brain.

When this information reaches the appropriate neurons in the brain, those neurons begin to process the information, registering "what" and "where" the stimulus is. **Perception** involves the interpretation of information that comes from the receptors. Most of the time, the brain accurately interprets the information sent by the receptors. However, sometimes, as in the example just given, an inaccurate interpretation is made, sometimes with disastrous results, as in the shooting of Amadou Diallo.

perception: a process that involves the interpretation of information that comes from the receptors

In Chapter 4, you learned that the cerebrum is composed of four lobes: the *frontal, parietal, temporal,* and *occipital* lobes. In this chapter, we will examine the specific perceptual functions associated with each lobe. Before we turn to a discussion of perceptual processes, let's look at the organization of the cerebrum.

The Cerebrum's Role in Perception

The four lobes of the cerebrum get their names from the overlying bones of the skull (Figure 8.1). For example, the frontal lobes are located under the frontal bones, the occipital lobes under the occipital bones, and so forth. However, this method of classifying cerebral structures is quite gross and does not tell us a lot about specific regions within the cerebrum. Early research employing *retrograde tracing* (a lesioning technique in which axons are destroyed and then their soma are located) indicated that specific nuclei in the thalamus project to particular areas of the cerebral cortex. For example, destruction of axons in the auditory cortex results in the death of neurons in the medial geniculate nucleus of the thalamus. Thus, each lobe of the cerebrum contains many areas that each have a specific function.

Many investigators in the first half of the 20th century attempted to identify specific areas of the cerebrum by examining the cerebral cortex under the microscope. The process of classifying individual areas of the cerebrum based on their microscopic appearance is called *cytoarchitectonic typing*. Perhaps the best-known example of cerebral mapping based on cytoarchitectonic typing is **Brodmann's classification system** (Figure 8.2). According to Brodmann (1909), the cerebral cortex can be divided into approximately 50 areas, based on their microscopic appearance. Brodmann's system was a very popular and convenient way to classify functional areas of the cerebrum. Even today, many of us in this field still refer to the primary visual cortex in the occipital lobe as Brodmann's *area 17*. However, finer distinctions of cortical areas have been made as a result of research using autoradiographic techniques and behavioral studies.

Brodmann's classification system: a system of cerebral mapping that divides the cortex into approximately 50 areas, based on their microscopic appearance

Microscopic examination of the cerebrum has revealed that it is comprised of two parts: (1) cortex composed of five or six layers of neurons and (2) underlying white matter that contains axons that carry action potentials to and from the neurons in the cerebral cortex. The outermost layer of the cerebral cortex, called the *plexiform layer*, contains no neuronal cell bodies but instead consists of tips of dendrites and axons. The inner layers are composed of predominately two types of neurons: **stellate cells** and **pyramidal cells.**

Stellate, or star-shaped, cells get their name from the fact that they have many short dendrites that extend from the soma. In general, axons coming from neurons in the thalamus and other parts of the brain will synapse with the dendrites of stellate cells. Axons of the stellate cells synapse with the dendrites of pyramidal and other cells in the cerebral cortex. Thus, the pyramidal cells receive their innervation from stellate cells and transmit this information via axons going down into the white matter beneath the cortex, carrying the information to other areas of the brain. This means that the cortex is organized in narrow columns of neurons

stellate cells: star-shaped neurons in the cerebral cortex

pyramidal cells: neurons shaped like pyramids that are located in the cerebral cortex

Figure 8.1 Lobes of the cerebrum and overlying skull bones

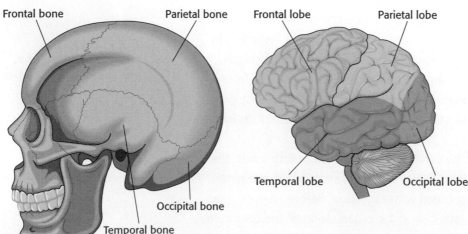

Frontal bone Parietal bone Frontal lobe Parietal lobe

Occipital bone

Temporal bone

Temporal lobe Occipital lobe

arranged in five or six layers, with information coming into the stellate cells in that column and leaving via the axons of pyramidal cells in the same column.

Depending on the function of a specific area of the cerebral cortex, five or six layers of neurons can be identified (Brodmann, 1909; Mignard & Malpeli, 1991). Many areas have distinctive microscopic appearances that make them easy to identify. For example, the primary visual cortex in the occipital lobe is often referred to as the *striate cortex* due to the presence of many myelinated axons from the thalamus that extend into layer 4 of the cortex in that region of the occipital lobe, giving it a striated appearance.

Today our maps of the cerebrum are based on microscopic examination *and* behavioral testing. The cerebrum of the macaque monkey has been studied extensively by many investigators in experiments that involved recording, stimulation, and lesioning of the macaque brain. As a result of these experiments, at least 32 different regions of the primate cerebrum have been identified as being associated with visual processing, each region having a specific function (Van Essen, Anderson, & Felleman, 1992). Of these 32 areas, 7 are also involved in processing information from other sensory systems.

Let's begin our study of perceptual functions by examining the processing of visual information in the cerebrum. Visual perception has received a great deal of research, and we understand it much better than other types of perceptual processing. However, please be aware that we are far from having a thorough knowledge of visual processes.

Figure 8.2 Brodmann's classification system
Brodmann divided the cerebral cortex into 52 regions based on their microscopic appearance.

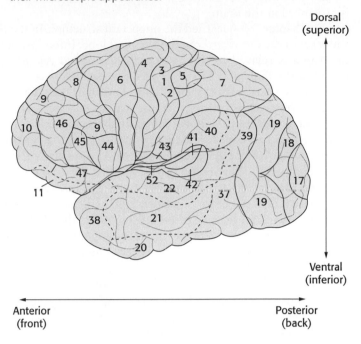

Dorsal (superior)

Ventral (inferior)

Anterior (front)

Posterior (back)

Recap 8.1: The Cerebrum's Role in Perception

The four lobes of the cerebrum are named for the overlying (a)_____ of the skull. The process of identifying areas of the cerebrum based on their microscopic differences is called (b)_____ typing. The best known example of cerebral mapping based on microscopic appearance is (c)_____ classification system, which divides the cerebral cortex into more than 50 distinct areas. The cerebrum has two parts, a (d)_____ composed of neuronal cell bodies and underlying (e)_____ _____ that contains myelinated axons. Two types of neurons are found in the cerebral cortex, (f)_____ cells (which receive information from the thalamus and other parts of the cerebrum) and (g)_____ cells (which transmit information from the cortex to other parts of the brain).

Visual Processing

I have a number of objects on the desk in front of me: a coffee cup, stapler, tape dispenser, keyboard, mouse, mouse pad, monitor, and a box of tissues. Each of these objects appears to me as distinctly different. Each has a particular shape and color, and each is located in a different place on my desktop. On the monitor, my screensaver moves across the screen, over and over, its position constantly changing.

Visual perception allows me to identify and locate all of the items on my desk. It permits me to perceive the screensaver moving across the monitor screen. Thus, visual perception involves a number of functions: (1) processing color, (2) processing shape or form, (3) locating objects in three-dimensional space, and (4) processing motion. In this section, we will examine how each of these perceptual functions is processed in the brain.

In Chapter 7 you learned the important structures in the pathway from the *rods* and *cones* to the *visual cortex* in the occipital lobe. Information from the receptors in the retina is relayed to the neurons in the *lateral geniculate nucleus* (abbreviated LGN) of the thalamus. From the LGN, axons carry visual information directly to the primary visual cortex, which is also known as the striate cortex or **area V1.**

Let's retrace this pathway because it is actually two pathways carrying information about color, form, motion, and spatial relationships. The two pathways begin with the rods and cones. The first pathway, called the **ventral stream,** ends in the inferior temporal lobe and is concerned with processing information about color and form (Figure 8.3). The second pathway, called the **dorsal stream,** terminates in the posterior parietal lobe and is involved in detecting motion and the location of objects in the visual field (Goodale & Milner, 1992; Ungerleider & Mishkin, 1982). Due to their functions, the ventral stream is often called the **"What" system,** and the dorsal stream is called the **"Where" system** (Palmer, 1999). Table 8.1 summarizes the differences between the "What" and the "Where" systems.

Recall from Chapter 7 that cones are sensitive to wavelength, which corresponds to the psychological attribute that we call color, and they also permit us to see detail. Rods, on the other hand, respond best to motion. Information from the rods and cones ultimately is transmitted to ganglion cells, whose axons converge to form the optic nerve. Ganglion cells come in two sizes: large and small. Investigators have applied a numbers of names to these different-sized ganglion cells. The large ganglion cells, which make up about 10% of all ganglion cells, receive their information primarily from rods and are known as *magnocellular,* or *parasol, ganglion cells,* due to their shape. The smaller *parvocellular,* or *midget,* ganglion cells account for more than 80% of the ganglion cells on the retina and receive their input from cones [*magno-* = large; *parvo-* = small, Latin]. From the ganglion cells, information from the rods and cones is transmitted to separate layers in the LGN.

Altogether, the LGN is comprised of six layers of neurons: four layers of **parvocellular** neurons on the top and two layers of **magnocellular** neurons on the bottom (Livingstone & Hubel, 1988). Information from cones is relayed from the parvocellular ganglion cells to the parvocellular layers of the LGN, and information from rods is carried from the magnocellular ganglion cells to the magnocellular layers of the LGN. Thus, the parvocellular layers process information about color, form, and detail, whereas the magnocellular layers receive information about form, spatial relations, and motion. The parvocellular system is particularly well developed in primates.

area V1: the primary visual cortex located in the occipital lobe, also known as the striate cortex or Brodmann's area 17

ventral stream: a visual pathway that is concerned with processing information about color and form; the "What" system

dorsal stream: a visual pathway that is involved in detecting motion and the location of objects in the visual field; the "Where" system

"What" system: the visual pathway concerned with processing color and form

"Where" system: the visual pathway concerned with detecting motion and the location of objects in the visual field

parvocellular layers: four top layers of the lateral geniculate nucleus that process information about color, form, and detail

magnocellular layers: two bottom layers of the lateral geniculate nucleus that process information about form, spatial relations, and motion

Table 8.1

Comparison of the Parvocellular ("What") and Magnocellular ("Where") Pathways

	Parvocellular ("What")	Magnocellular ("Where")
Type of Information Processed	color, form, detail	form, motion, spatial relations
Source of Information	cones	rods
Type of Associated Ganglion Cell	midget, or parvocellular	parasol, or magnocellular
Location in Thalamus	top four layers	bottom two layers
Target in V1	blob regions	interblob region

Figure 8.3 Anatomy of the visual system
(a) Medial (sagittal) view of the brain. (b) Lateral (exterior) view of the brain.

a.

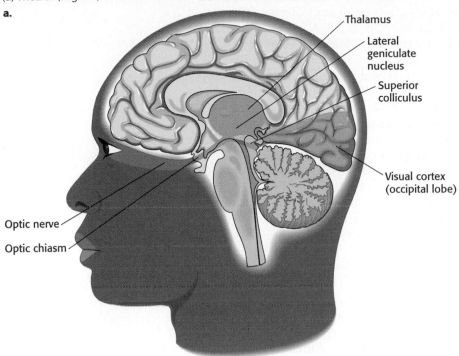

Thalamus

Lateral geniculate nucleus

Superior colliculus

Visual cortex (occipital lobe)

Optic nerve

Optic chiasm

b.

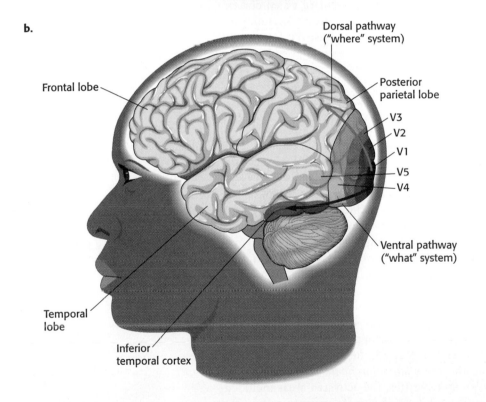

Dorsal pathway ("where" system)

Frontal lobe

Posterior parietal lobe

V3

V2

V1

V5

V4

Ventral pathway ("what" system)

Temporal lobe

Inferior temporal cortex

One interesting aspect of the LGN is that each eye sends information to different layers of the LGN. That is, the left eye relays action potentials to two parvocellular layers and one magnocellular layer, whereas the right eye sends its information to the two other parvocellular layers and the other magnocellular layer. This means that each layer in the LGN receives information from only one eye. In other words, the LGN processes *monocular* information.

Axons from the magnocellular and parvocellular layers of the LGN project to different regions of the striate cortex, or area V1, in the occipital lobe. When examined under the microscope with a special stain that reveals an enzyme called *cytochrome oxidase*, area V1 appears to contain areas that look like *blobs* surrounded by nonbloblike regions, called *interblobs* [*inter-* = between, Latin] (Horton & Hubel, 1981). Axons coming from the parvocellular layers of the LGN synapse with neurons in the blob regions, and axons from the magnocellular layers innervate neurons in the interblob regions. Thus, the separation of the rod information and cone information continues into the primary visual cortex, where the ventral and dorsal streams begin.

Information from neurons in V1 is then passed on to area V2 of the occipital lobe. V2 functions like a post office, delivering messages to the correct addresses in the cerebral cortex. In general, information in V2 is sent to one of the major visual processing centers, called V3, V4, or V5. Microscopic analysis of V2 reveals that it is composed of areas that resemble *thick stripes* or *thin stripes* and areas in between the stripes, called the *interstripe* regions (Livingstone & Hubel, 1982). Neurons in the thick stripe regions of V2 receive their input from the interblob regions of V1 and transmit this information to V5. In contrast, the thin stripes receive their innervation from the blobs of V1 and transmit this information to V4. Input to V3 is a bit more complicated. The neurons in the interstripe regions of V2 get information from both the blob and interblob regions of V1. From the interstripe region of V2, axons project to area V3.

In summary, the blobs of V1 send their information to the thin stripes and interstripes of V2, and the interblobs of V1 send their information to the thick stripes and interstripes of V2. Information from the interstripes of V2 goes to V3, information from the thin stripes of V2 goes to V4, and information from the thick stripes of V2 ends up in V5 (Zeki, 1992). As it enters the primary visual cortex, visual information is immediately routed along one of three pathways, ending in V3, V4, or V5. To understand how the primate brain processes visual information, let's examine each perceptual function individually.

The Ventral Stream or "What" System

Processing of Color

The pathway for color processing begins with cones and ends in the inferior temporal and frontal lobes (Zeki & Marini, 1998). Information about color is relayed to the blobs in V1 by way of parvocellular neurons in the LGN. From the blobs in V1, color information is sent to the thin stripes in V2 and, from there, to V4. Neurons in V4 appear to analyze the wavelength of objects and make wavelength comparisons among objects in the visual field. This information is then relayed to the inferior temporal and frontal lobes for further processing.

Using functional MRI, Zeki and Marini (1998) examined brain activity in nine men who were shown colored or black-and-white visual stimuli. When the subjects were exposed to colored objects, a pathway extending from V1 to V4 was activated. In addition, the inferior temporal and frontal lobes were activated by the colored stimuli. However, different areas of the frontal lobe were activated, depending on whether the objects were colored appropriately or inappropriately. For example, when the men were shown red strawberries, V1, V2, V4, the inferior temporal cortex, the hippocampus, and an area on the *ventrolateral prefrontal cortex* were activated. When the men were shown blue strawberries, the activated areas included V1, V2, V4, the inferior temporal cortex, and the *dorsolateral prefrontal cortex*. The hippocampus was most likely activated with red strawberries because the appropriately colored strawberries stimulated a memory process. (Recall from Chapter 4 that the hippocampus is involved in long-term memory formation.) The abnormally colored objects activated the dorsolateral frontal cortex, whereas the normally colored objects activated the ventrolateral frontal cortex, which demonstrates that the frontal lobe plays a role in analyzing the color of objects in our visual space.

Processing of Form

Information about orientation, lines, and edges is sent to the brain via the parvo-cellular and magnocellular pathways. In V1 are neurons that are sensitive to the orientation and features of objects. Experiments conducted by David Hubel and Torsten Wiesel (1962), for which they were awarded the Nobel Prize in 1981, revealed that different neurons in V1 respond to different types of stimuli. For example, certain neurons, which Hubel and Wiesel named *simple cells*, respond best to a line or edge in a particular orientation, whereas other cells (called *complex cells*) are most sensitive to lines or edges with a particular orientation or to moving edges. Simple cells are thought to be part of the parvo- system, with its emphasis on form, and complex cells can be considered part of the magno- system, with its emphasis on movement. A third type of neuron in V1 identified by Hubel and Wiesel is the *hypercomplex cell*, which is even more selective in its response to visual stimuli, pre-ferring stimuli with a particular length or width in a particular orientation. These cells signal the presence of particular lines and edges in the visual field to cells in the interstripe regions of V2.

The neurons in the interstripe region of V2 project their axons to area V3, which processes information about form. Some information about form (especially form associated with color) is also processed in V4. But, V3 appears to be the area that is primarily responsible for form perception. Like V1 and V2, V3 is located in the occipital lobe (Corballis, 1994). Information from V3 is relayed to the inferior temporal cortex, where the forms are further analyzed and identified. Identification of objects occurs in the inferior temporal lobe (Milner, 1995; Van Essen et al., 1992; Zeki, 1992). Studies measuring functional MRI responses to visual stimuli have demonstrated that one region of the inferior temporal lobe located on the border between the temporal and occipital lobes, called the *fusiform face area*, is activated strongly when a human subject views pictures of faces, but responds weakly when the person views pictures of other classes of objects (Druzgal & D'Esposito, 2001; Haxby, Ungerleider, Clark, Schouten, Hoffman, & Martin, 1999; Kanwisher, McDermott, & Chen, 1997; McCarthy, Puce Gore, & Allison, 1997; Tzourio-Mazoyer et al., 2002). In contrast, a medial region of the inferior temporal cortex, called the *parahippocampal place area*, is activated strongly by pho-tographs of indoor and outdoor scenes, but is not activated at all by faces (Epstein & Kanwisher, 1998; Hudson & Grace, 2000). However, investigators disagree over how the inferior temporal lobe permits us to distinguish faces from other objects (Helmuth, 2001). Damage to the inferior temporal lobe interferes with an individ-ual's ability to recognize objects, as you will learn later in this chapter.

Recordings of electrical activity in the brains of monkeys have also confirmed that the inferior temporal cortex is actively involved in the recognition and identi-fication of visual stimuli (Thorpe & Fabre-Thorpe, 2001). Sheinberg and Logothetis (2001) trained monkeys to search large color photographs for a small, hidden figure, similar to "Where's Waldo?" puzzles. When a monkey's eyes landed on the target, neurons in the inferior temporal cortex began to fire wildly. How-ever, these same neurons did not fire when the monkey was examining the rest of the photo. A recent study by David Freedman and his colleagues at MIT, in which they recorded electrical activity in the brains of monkeys, has demonstrated that the prefrontal cortex is also involved in recognizing and categorizing visual stimuli (Freedman, Miller, Poggio, & Riesenhuber, 2001).

The Dorsal Stream or "Where" System

Processing of Motion

The ability to detect motion permits us to follow objects with our eyes and to avoid moving objects. Rods can rapidly detect visual events, which makes them especially sensitive to motion. Information about motion is relayed to the interblob regions of V1 by way of the magnocellular pathway. From the interblobs in V1, this infor-mation is sent to the thick stripes of V2 and on to V5, which is located in the temporal lobe, adjacent to area V4. (V5 is sometimes referred to as *area MT*, for *middle temporal cortex*, where it is located.) Axons from area V5 project to the posterior parietal lobe, where information about motion is analyzed.

Processing of Depth and Spatial Relations

The ability to move through the environment or to reach for an item requires a visual system that allows us to accurately perceive the location of objects in three-dimensional space (Lappin & Craft, 2000). Rods and cones both register information about spatial relations. This information reaches V1 by way of the parvocellular and magnocellular pathways and is then relayed to V3, V5, and other areas of the visual cortex. From V3 and V5, the information about depth and spatial relations is transmitted to the posterior parietal cortex, where the location of objects in space is determined.

Recall from Chapter 7 that the optic nerve divides into two branches as it enters the brain: a major tract that goes to the LGN and a minor tract that innervates the *superior colliculus* in the midbrain. The superior colliculus, as you know, also processes the location of objects in the environment. Anatomical studies have indicated that the superior colliculus projects directly to V5, bypassing V1 (Corballis, 1995). Thus, information received by the superior colliculus is shared with neurons in the posterior parietal lobe that process location in three-dimensional space.

In summary, the "What" and the "Where" systems shoulder the two basic tasks of vision: *object recognition* and *object location*. These two systems can (and often do) function independently. The "What" system permits us to recognize objects in the environment regardless of their location. In contrast, the "Where" system allows us to move around in an environment in which nothing is identifiable and enables us to pick up unfamiliar objects. Research examining visual deficits in monkeys following lesions of the inferior temporal lobe or the posterior parietal lobe has demonstrated that object recognition is impaired by lesions of the inferior temporal lobe, and judgments of object location are impaired by lesions of the posterior parietal cortex (Goodale & Milner, 1992). Studies of people who have damage in these cortical areas confirm the findings of this monkey research, as you will learn in the section on disorders of visual processing.

Binding

Before we turn to a consideration of human visual perceptual disorders, I want to stress that the pathways you have just learned about do *not* act independently and are *not* isolated from the other pathways. That is, the inferior temporal lobe receives information about spatial relations. And, the posterior parietal cortex gets some information from V3 and V4 about form and color. One unsolved mystery concerning visual perception is called the *binding* problem: how our brains combine information from the "What" system and the "Where" system to produce a unified perception (Crick, 1984; Damasio, 1989; Friedman-Hill, Robertson, & Treisman, 1995).

Chenchal Rao, Gregor Rainer, and Earl Miller (1997) at the Massachusetts Institute of Technology attempted to solve the binding mystery by recording the electrical activity of 195 neurons in the prefrontal cortex of two monkeys. These monkeys were trained to make eye movements in a task that combined activation of the "What" and "Where" systems. While a monkey stared at a fixation point, an object was flashed on the screen. The object was followed by a brief delay period (delay 1), after which two test objects were flashed on the screen, one of which matched the original object flashed in the first screen. The monkey's task was to remember the location of the matching test object during a short delay period (delay 2) and then move its eyes in the direction of the correct location when a choice screen was shown.

The study conducted by Rao and his colleagues (1997) was designed to determine whether neurons in 195 locations in the prefrontal cortex responded to information from the "What" system, or from the "Where" system, or from both.

Neuronal activity recorded during delay 1 was presumed to reflect activity from the "What" system because the monkey's task during this delay was to identify an object. In contrast, neuronal activity during delay 2 was associated with activity in the "Where" system because the monkey was retaining location information during this delay period. Of the neurons that fired during the delay periods, 7% were active only during delay 1 (that is, were responsive only to information from the "What" system), and 41% were active only during delay 2 (indicating input from the "Where" system only). Over 50% of the neurons were extremely active during both delays, which meant that they contributed to the processing of both "What" information and "Where" information.

Rao and his colleagues (1997) concluded from their study of the electrical activity of neurons in monkey brains that the prefrontal cortex integrates "What" information and "Where" information. However, this study does not provide definitive answers about how and where binding actually takes place. Please keep in mind, too, that at least 32 areas in the primate brain process information about vision, and we have examined only a few of the best-studied areas.

Another line of research has demonstrated an association between *40-Hz oscillations* of neural activity and visual binding in humans, monkeys, and cats (Elliott & Muller, 2000; Singer & Gray, 1995; Tallon-Baudry, Bertrand, Delpuech, & Pernier, 1996). Some neurons in the cerebral cortex fire together at the same time, producing synchronous firing patterns, called oscillations. Bursts of synchronous neural activity in the visual cortex, the right temporal cortex, and the left frontal cortex that occur at a rate of 40 times per second (40 Hz) are associated with visual binding. The 40-Hz oscillations are observed in the brains of 8-month-old human infants but are absent in the brains of 6-month-old infants (Csibra, Davis, Spratling, & Johnson, 2000). Infants that are 7 months or older are able to bind together various visual features to perceive visual illusions, whereas younger infants cannot. For example, infants older than 7 months can perceive the illusory Kanizsa square shown in Figure 8.4, and younger infants cannot. Visual binding is required to perceive this illusion. Thus, the presence of 40-Hz oscillations in cortical neural activity appears to be necessary for visual binding.

Figure 8.4 Kanizsa square
The small black square in the center of this figure is a visual illusion. Binding is necessary to perceive such an illusion.

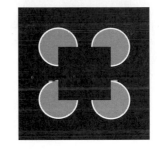

Disorders of Visual Processing

Visual perceptual disorders are associated with damage to a particular area of the visual cortex. You learned in the preceding section that each area of the visual cortex is responsible for a specific function, processing information about color, form, space, or motion, or integrating this information with other information. In this section, we will examine disorders caused by damage to the major areas of the visual cortex.

Damage to V1

Figure 8.5 illustrates how the visual field is mapped onto V1, with the left visual field represented on the right visual cortex and the right visual field represented on the left visual cortex. Damage to a tiny area of V1 produces a **scotoma,** which is a blind spot in the part of the visual field that corresponds with the damaged area (Corballis, 1994). A person with a scotoma cannot see objects that are located in that part of the visual field associated with the damaged region of V1. Damage to one hemisphere in the region of V1, either in the left half or the right, causes **hemianopia,** in which the patient cannot see the visual field *contralateral* to the damaged side of the cerebrum. That is, a person with complete damage to V1 on the *right* side of the brain would be unable to see objects in the *left* visual field.

Blindness typically results from complete destruction of V1 on both sides of the cerebrum, leaving the individual unable to see and recognize objects. However, some individuals who have total, bilateral damage to V1 show a phenomenon called **blindsight,** in which the individual cannot see or describe an object but will reach accurately toward the object (Milner, 1995; Weiskrantz, Cowey, & Hodinatt-Hill, 2002). In addition, individuals with blindsight can move through the environment

scotoma: a blind spot in a part of the visual field

hemianopia: a disorder in which a brain-damaged individual cannot see the visual field contralateral to the damaged side of the cerebrum

blindness: a disorder in which a person is unable to see and recognize objects visually

blindsight: a phenomenon in which a person cannot see an object but will reach accurately toward the object

Figure 8.5 Mapping the visual field onto the primary visual cortex

The left primary visual cortex (V1) processes information from the right visual field, and the right primary visual cortex processes information from the left visual field.

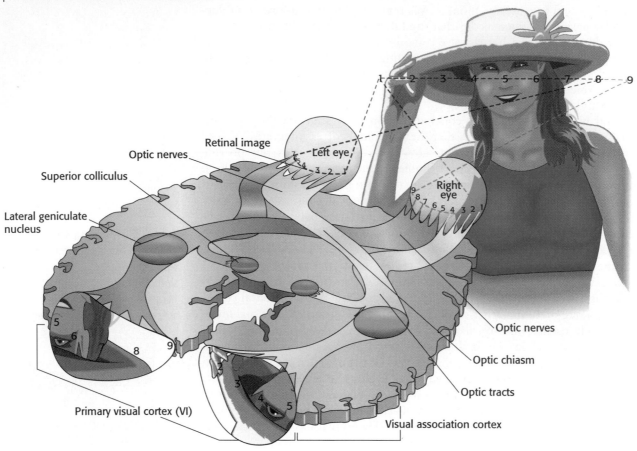

easily, avoiding obstacles, and their eyes can accurately follow a moving target. The explanation for this amazing phenomenon, in which the individual is blind but appears to be able to know the location of objects in space, is that the posterior parietal lobe continues to receive visual information even after the total destruction of V1. Experiments with monkeys have demonstrated that V3 and V5 continue to function after lesioning V1, whereas V4 cannot function without input from V1 (Milner, 1995). Information from the superior colliculus is transmitted directly to V5, as you learned earlier, and this information is then relayed to the posterior parietal cortex, where information about location and movement is integrated, even in the absence of input from V1.

Damage to V2 and V3

Due to their location in the occipital lobe in close proximity to V1, it is nearly impossible to damage V2 or V3 without also sustaining damage to V1. This means that damage to V2 or V3 will ordinarily result in total blindness in the affected person.

Damage to V4

Damage to V4 results in a visual disorder called **achromatopsia,** in which the affected individual cannot see color. The person is able to perceive form and can recognize objects, but the forms and objects are seen in shades of gray, without color. Achromatopsia is different from color blindness caused by abnormalities in cone receptors, which was discussed in Chapter 7. Patients with achromatopsia have no concept for color and cannot even remember seeing colors before the damage to V4 occurred (Zeki, 1992).

achromatopsia: a visual disorder associated with damage to V4 in which the affected individual cannot see color

Damage to V5

Recall that information about motion is processed in V5. Therefore, damage to V5 causes the affected person to be unable to perceive movement or moving objects, a disorder known as **akinetopsia.** An individual with akinetopsia can see an object when it is stationary, but not when it is moving. For some patients with akinetopsia, visual images of moving objects cannot be integrated. For example, when one patient with akinetopsia poured tea into a cup, the stream of tea looked like a frozen column to her (Corballis, 1994). If you've ever been in a darkened room lit by a strobe light, you might be able to imagine what it is like to have damage to area V5. Under strobe lighting, movement appears to disappear, and the visual experience of movement is replaced by a series of discrete images in which the object is located in a different place in successive images.

Damage to the Inferior Temporal Lobe

Damage to the inferior temporal lobe produces a number of disorders, collectively called **visual agnosia,** which involve the inability to recognize familiar objects in the visual field. Patients with *visual object agnosia* cannot identify or name objects but can describe the color, motion, and details of those objects. In severe cases, called *apperceptive agnosia*, affected individuals cannot identify or report knowledge of even the simplest shapes and forms (Milner, 1995).

Another form of visual agnosia is **prosopagnosia,** in which the patients with damage to the right inferior temporal lobe, or bilateral damage to the inferior temporal lobes, cannot recognize faces of people who are familiar to them. People with prosopagnosia sometimes cannot recognize other natural objects, such as animals or vegetables. In contrast, damage to the left inferior temporal lobe results in a disorder called **pure alexia.** Individuals with pure alexia can often identify individual letters but cannot put the letters together to read them as whole words (Corballis, 1994; DeRenzi, 2000; Jones & Tranel, 2001; Mendez, 2001).

Damage to the Posterior Parietal Lobe

As you learned earlier in this chapter, the posterior parietal cortex integrates information from V3 and V5 to analyze the location and motion of objects in the visual field. Damage to this area of the cortex results in a disturbance in the ability to locate and reach for objects in the environment. For example, in *Balint's syndrome*, bilateral damage to the occipital and posterior parietal lobes produces a disturbance in visually guided reaching, an inability to systematically scan the environment or fixate the eyes on an object, and an inability to be aware of more than one object at a time (Damasio, 1995).

Another disorder associated with unilateral damage to the posterior parietal cortex is **visual extinction** (Corballis, 1994). Individuals with visual extinction can perceive an object anywhere in their visual fields. However, when two objects are presented, one in the left and one in the right visual field, affected individuals will ignore the object that is located in the visual field contralateral to the damaged site. Visual extinction is probably due to a disruption of normal attention, which is caused by damage to the posterior parietal lobe. We will examine attention in great detail in Chapter 9.

Michael McCloskey and his colleagues (1995) at Johns Hopkins University reported the case of a female college student with a deficit in visually localizing objects, which is associated with damage to the posterior parietal cortex. Figure 8.6 shows the student's copy of a test stimulus. You can see that her drawing is full of mislocations and misorientations,

akinetopsia: a visual disorder associated with damage to V5 in which the affected individual cannot perceive movement or moving objects

visual agnosia: a visual disorder caused by damage to the inferior temporal lobe in which the affected individual cannot recognize familiar objects in the visual field

prosopagnosia: a form of visual agnosia in which affected individuals cannot recognize faces of people familiar to them

pure alexia: a form of visual agnosia associated with damage to the left inferior temporal lobe in which affected individuals can identify individual letters but cannot put letters together to read them as a whole word

visual extinction: a visual disorder associated with unilateral damage to the posterior parietal cortex in which the affected individual will ignore an object located in the visual field contralateral to the damaged site

Figure 8.6 Deficits in visually localizing objects
This student's drawing is full of mislocations and misorientations. Damage to the posterior parietal lobe is associated with a deficit in visually localizing objects.

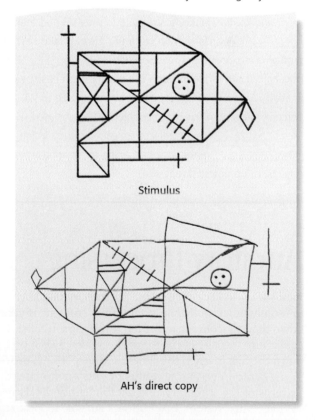

Stimulus

AH's direct copy

mistakes that indicate that her disorder involves localizing parts of an object relative to each other. This student also made many errors (63 errors in 96 trials) when asked to point to a 3-cm cube placed in front of her on a table when the cube was located to her left or right. Typically she would reach to the left when the cube was on her right and vice versa. As you can imagine, a disorder of this type would interfere with an individual's comprehension of written text. For example, this student made a number of errors when reading, including: (1) reading "snail" as "nails," (2) reading "John gave Mary" as "Mary gave John," (3) reading "pen" as "den," and (4) reading the number 93 as "thirty-nine."

Other areas of perceptual processing, such as taste processing or auditory processing, have not been studied as thoroughly or as intensely as has visual processing. In the remainder of this chapter, we will examine research in a number of other fields of perceptual processing, including the perception of pain, touch, taste, and smell. Let's turn to a discussion of auditory perception next and consider how speech and music are processed in the cerebral cortex.

Recap 8.2: Visual Processing

Information from rods and cones is relayed to neurons in the (a)_____ _____ nucleus (LGN) of the thalamus. From the LGN, (b)_____ information is relayed to the primary visual cortex, also called area V1. Two pathways in the brain process visual information: a (c)_____ stream (the "What" system) that processes information about color and form and a (d)_____ stream (the "Where" system) that processes information about motion and the location of objects in the visual field. The (e)_____ neurons in the LGN receive information from cones on the retina and transmit that information to blob regions of V1. The (f)_____ neurons in the LGN receive information from the rods and relay this information to the interblob regions of V1. The processing of (g)_____ involves area V4, which sends information on to the inferior temporal cortex and the prefrontal cortex. Information about form is relayed to area V3 and then to the inferior (h)_____ _____. Information about movement and spatial relations is relayed to area V5 and then to the posterior (i)_____ _____. Information from the "What" and "Where" systems are combined in the prefrontal cortex in a process called (j)_____. People with (k)_____ cannot see but can move through the environment easily, avoiding obstacles. (l)_____ (inability to see color) is associated with damage to V4, and (m)_____ (inability to perceive movement or moving objects) is associated with damage to V5. Damage to the (n)_____ temporal cortex can produce visual agnosia, whereas damage to the (o)_____ parietal lobe results in an inability to accurately locate and reach for objects in the environment.

Auditory Processing

I am sitting in my office in the psychology building at Wittenberg University on an unusually quiet afternoon. One of my students is taking a makeup exam in a room down the hall from me to the left. From time to time, I can hear the rustling of papers as she turns a page in the exam. I can also hear footsteps and muffled voices farther down the hall to my right. These auditory stimuli provide a good deal of information to my central nervous system about my environment. The frequency and temporal patterns of the stimuli enable me to identify the nature of the sound, much like the "What" visual system. In addition, I am able to localize the sound, based on the loudness and echo qualities of the auditory stimuli, comparable to the "Where" visual system. Thus, it appears that my brain, like yours, contains auditory "What" and "Where" systems.

Anatomical studies of the brains of rhesus monkeys have demonstrated that the auditory areas of the primate cerebral cortex are indeed connected to two pathways or streams (Romanski, Tian, Fritz, Mishkin, Goldman-Rakic, & Rauschecker, 1999). One pathway, the **auditory "What" stream,** begins in the rostral part of the **primary auditory cortex** in the temporal lobe and ends in the **ventrolateral prefrontal cortex,** which also processes visual "what" information (Figure 8.7). In contrast, the **auditory "Where" stream** originates in the caudal portions of the primary auditory cortex and terminates in the **dorsolateral prefrontal cortex,** which is a

Figure 8.7 The "What" and "Where" streams of the auditory system
The auditory "What" stream begins in the rostral end of the primary auditory cortex in the temporal lobe and ends in the ventrolateral prefrontal cortex. The auditory "Where" stream begins in the caudal end of the primary auditory cortex and ends in the dorsolateral prefrontal cortex.

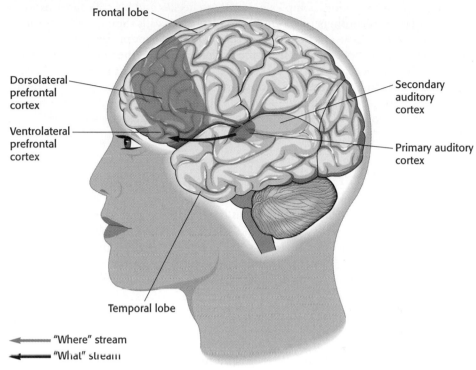

spatial processing area. However, it is important to remember that, as in the visual system, a great deal of interaction and sharing of information takes place between the auditory "What" and "Where" streams (Kaas & Hackett, 1999).

Identifying a sound and determining the location of its source are the functions of the auditory "What" and "Where" streams, respectively. Analysis of the frequencies of the sound as well as of the temporal patterns of the sound permits us to identify a sound. Much research has been conducted on frequency perception, but research on timing and sound pattern analysis is in its early stages. In Chapter 7, you learned about the major theories of pitch perception and sound localization. In this chapter, we will examine what modern brain-imaging and recording studies have taught us about auditory processing.

Processing of Complex Sounds Versus Pure Tones

Most of the sounds we hear are quite complex, consisting of many different frequencies arriving at the ear at the same time. Pure tones, which consist of a single frequency, are typically produced in the laboratory and rarely occur in our everyday experience. Obviously, pure tones require less analysis than complex sounds, just as spots of light are easier to analyze than a complex visual image. Research with anesthetized rhesus monkeys exposed to pure tones or complex auditory stimuli has demonstrated that wider areas of the cortex are activated when complex sounds are heard (Rauschecker, Tian, & Hauser, 1995).

Josef Rauschecker and his colleagues, Biao Tian and Marc Hauser (1995), placed electrodes in the cerebral cortex on both sides of the lateral (Sylvian) fissure in seven adult monkeys and presented the monkeys with pure tones or sounds composed of wide ranges of frequencies. The primary auditory cortex produced evoked potentials to both pure tones and complex acoustic stimuli. However, cortical areas lateral and superior to the primary auditory cortex, called the **secondary auditory cortex,** are activated by complex sounds but not by pure tones. In fact, these

auditory "What" stream: an auditory pathway that begins in the rostral part of the primary auditory cortex and ends in the ventrolateral prefrontal cortex
primary auditory cortex: an area of the temporal cortex that receives information directly from the medial geniculate nucleus of the thalamus
ventrolateral prefrontal cortex: an area of the prefrontal cortex that processes visual and auditory "What" information
auditory "Where" stream: an auditory pathway that originates in the caudal part of the primary auditory cortex and ends in the dorsolateral prefrontal cortex
dorsolateral prefrontal cortex: a region of the prefrontal cortex that processes auditory "Where" information

secondary auditory cortex: cortical areas lateral and superior to the primary auditory cortex in the temporal lobe that process complex sounds

secondary auditory areas preferred complex sounds to pure tones, as evidenced by their increased firing rate to complex auditory stimuli (Rauschecker, Tian, & Hauser, 1995). This means that the secondary auditory areas integrate and process auditory information over a large range of frequencies, which is necessary for the processing of sounds used in communication.

In addition to random complex noise, Rauschecker and his colleagues exposed the monkeys to recordings of seven different monkey calls. Single-cell recordings revealed that many neurons in the secondary auditory cortex prefer one or two calls over others, firing more vigorously to the preferred than to the nonpreferred monkey calls (Rauschecker et al., 1995; Tian, Reser, Durham, Kustov, & Rauschecker, 2001). This finding is extremely interesting because the cortical area where the electrodes were placed, called the *superior temporal gyrus*, is the area in the human brain that is involved in the perception of speech sounds, as you will learn in the next section.

Processing of Speech

Speech is one of the several ways in which humans communicate. We also use body language, including facial expressions and hand gestures, and written language to communicate. **Language** is a formalized system of symbolic representations that we use to communicate ideas, questions, and commands. Most languages have both a spoken form and a written form, although some languages of native peoples do not have a written form. **American Sign Language** (ASL) is a standard system of hand gestures used by deaf people to communicate and has neither a spoken nor a written form.

The basic units of spoken language are called **phonemes.** For example, the American dialect of the English language contains about 40 different phonemes. We combine phonemes to produce **morphemes,** which are meaningful units of sounds. To form the morpheme "cape," the phonemes *k*, long *a*, and *p* are combined. To create complex strings of morphemes (such as sentences), we follow rules of **grammar** that stipulate how morphemes are to be combined. Phonemes, morphemes, and grammatical rules vary for each spoken language. You should keep in mind, too, that speech involves two processes: *production* and *comprehension*. As you will learn in this section, different areas of the brain are associated with the production and comprehension of speech.

Because speech is a uniquely human capacity, research with animal subjects is not possible when studying the neural basis of speech, although experiments with monkeys (like the one described in the preceding section by Josef Rauschecker and his colleagues) are useful in helping us understand the behavior of neurons in the auditory areas of the cortex. Our knowledge about speech processing in the brain is the result of research conducted in the 19th and 20th centuries. The earliest research involved studies of individuals with communication disorders who had suffered damage to specific areas of the brain (Goodglass, 1993). Today, functional imaging studies are confirming the findings of earlier research of brain-damaged individuals. Let's review these findings.

The Effects of Brain Damage on Speech Processing

Damage to Broca's Area   Recall from Chapter 1 that **Broca's area** was one of the first areas of the cerebral cortex to be associated with a specific function, namely the production of speech (Figure 8.8). Remember Tan, the man who could utter only one syllable ("tan") after a stroke damaged the inferior portion of the frontal lobe? Since Broca's original research on Tan, many studies of brain-injured individuals have confirmed Broca's finding that speech production is associated with a specific area in the inferior frontal lobe. Today this area is called Broca's area, in honor of its discoverer (Buckner et al., 1996; Whitaker & Kahn, 1994). Damage to Broca's area produces disorders of language production known collectively as forms of **expressive aphasia.**

language: a formalized system of symbolic representations that we use to communicate ideas, questions, and commands

American Sign Language: a standard system of hand gestures used by deaf individuals to communicate

phonemes: the basic units of spoken language

morphemes: meaningful units of sounds

grammar: rules that specify how morphemes are to be combined

Broca's area: an area of the inferior frontal cortex associated with the production of speech

expressive aphasia: disorders of language production

Figure 8.8 Classic speech centers

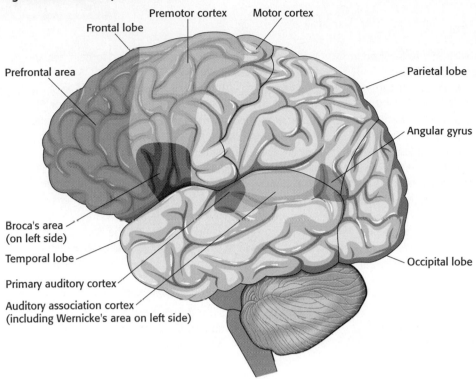

Depending on the extent and location of damage to Broca's area, any of a number of symptoms are observed. In extreme cases, people with expressive aphasia are unable to speak at all or can speak only one word or a phrase. I remember working with an elderly woman who could utter only a curse, "son of a bitch," following a stroke that damaged Broca's area. I'd ask her, "How are you feeling today?" And she would answer, "Son of a bitch, son of a bitch, son of a bitch." Another young man could say only "no." When asked how he was feeling, he answered, "No-o-o-o."

Some stroke patients lose their ability to speak or write one part of speech. For example, Caramazza and Hillis (1991) studied two patients: one who could not say verbs and one who could not write verbs, although they had no problem with nouns, adjectives, adverbs, and prepositions. Both patients could use the word *crack* as a noun but could not produce it when it was used as a verb in a sentence. Research with these and similar patients suggests that the brain sorts words by grammatical class. In addition, written words and spoken words appear to be stored in different locations in the cortex (Caramazza & Hillis, 1991; Petersen, Fox, Posner, Mintun, & Raichle, 1988).

Many other people with damage to Broca's area exhibit symptoms of **Broca's aphasia,** which is also referred to as *verbal aphasia*. Symptoms of Broca's aphasia include: (1) nonfluent speech that is effortful, with long pauses inserted between short phrases, (2) grammatical errors in which words are jumbled and function words like prepositions are missing, and (3) errors involving repetition, omission, or addition of sounds. As an example, one patient described his presurgical preparation in the following way: "when they had me to get ready that is they shaved off all my hair was and a few odd parts of pencil they quive me in the fanny" (Penfield & Roberts, 1959). People with Broca's aphasia often exhibit **anomia** (also called *nominal aphasia*), in which they cannot name familiar objects. However, they typically have no problem comprehending spoken language or reading written material, and they also are aware of their impairment. The *Case Study* describes the case of a college-aged woman with verbal aphasia.

Broca's aphasia: a disorder of language production associated with damage to Broca's area, also called verbal aphasia

anomia: a language disorder in which the affected individual cannot name familiar objects

Verbal Aphasia

LaDonna was a college freshman when she was involved in a car accident, in which she was flung from the car through the windshield. She lay in a coma for 3 months before slowly regaining consciousness. As a result of the accident, LaDonna sustained damage to her left frontal cortex, including the motor cortex and Broca's area. This brain damage caused temporary paralysis of her right arm and leg, which eventually developed into permanent weakness of those limbs. More devastating was the damage to Broca's area because it left LaDonna unable to express herself clearly.

As is typical with Broca's aphasia, LaDonna's speech was slow and halting. She found she had to search for words, and, when she tried to say them, often a different word or sound would pop out. She was constantly surprised and dismayed at the words that came out of her mouth.

A good example of this difficulty was an event that occurred a short while after LaDonna had awakened from her coma. One day LaDonna needed to use the toilet and

decided that, rather than ring for a nurse to help her, she would hop on her good leg to the bathroom. She got herself to the edge of the bed. But, when she tried to stand up on her good leg, she immediately fell to the floor. She had no idea how weak she was or how heavy the useless left side of her body was. As she lay on the floor, LaDonna tried to reach the bell to call for the nurse but couldn't quite get her hand on it. She was forced to remain on the floor, helpless, until someone discovered her. To add to her humiliation, she had urinated on herself during her fall.

A nurse came into the room about 10 minutes later and was horrified to find LaDonna on the floor. She asked LaDonna what happened. LaDonna looked up sheepishly and replied, "I'm taking a walk in the rain." That's not what she had meant to say at all. She had meant to tell the nurse about her need to use the toilet and about how she fell, but her words did not match her intention. This is the kind of communication problem that LaDonna had to learn to deal with following her accident.

Damage to Wernicke's Area **Wernicke's area** is located close to the primary auditory cortex in the superior temporal gyrus and the *planum temporale*. Damage to Wernicke's area produces a disturbance in language comprehension called **receptive aphasia,** which is characterized by an inability to understand what is being said or to follow simple commands. An individual with receptive aphasia typically speaks fluently, using long phrases with little hesitation. Some people who have damage to Wernicke's area exhibit a phenomenon called *word deafness*, in which they cannot understand spoken words, although they can perceive nonverbal sounds in the environment and can read, write, and talk normally (Corballis, 1994; Nakakoshi et al., 2001).

Associated with receptive aphasia are characteristic speech problems, including anomia, *paraphasia*, and *jargon aphasia*. Paraphasia involves the substitution of one phoneme for another phoneme or one word for another word. For example, a patient with paraphasia might say, "I wand to hatch mobile," when he meant to say "I want to have more." With jargon aphasia, the patient speaks fluently, using expansive, grammatically correct phrases. However, the content of the phrases is nonsensical in jargon aphasia. One patient, when asked to explain the function of a key, replied, "indication of measurement of piece of apparatus or intimating the cost of apparatus in various forms" (Brain, 1961). Unlike patients with Broca's aphasia, those with receptive aphasia are often unaware of their impairment. Table 8.2 compares the symptoms of expressive and receptive aphasias.

Damage to the Arcuate Fasciculus Broca's and Wernicke's areas communicate through a bundle of axons known as the **arcuate fasciculus.** You can imagine that damage to the arcuate fasciculus would result in a lack of communication between the cortical area responsible for speech production and the area responsible for language comprehension. This disruption in communication produces a disorder called **conduction aphasia,** in which affected individuals have relatively good language production and comprehension but cannot repeat what is said to them. Individuals with conduction aphasia can sometimes accurately repeat meaningful words

Wernicke's area: an area in the superior temporal gyrus associated with language comprehension

receptive aphasia: a disturbance in language comprehension

arcuate fasciculus: the bundle of axons that connects Broca's and Wernicke's areas

conduction aphasia: a communication disorder in which affected individuals have good language production and comprehension but cannot repeat what is said to them

Table 8.2

Comparison of Expressive and Receptive Aphasia

	Expressive aphasia	Receptive aphasia
Cortical Area Implicated	Broca's area	Wernicke's area
Associated Syndromes	Broca's (verbal) aphasia, anomia	paraphasia, anomia, jargon aphasia
Speech Characteristics	nonfluent, effortful speech; long pauses, short phrases; grammatical errors; function words missing; repetition, omission, or addition of sounds; aware of impairment	disturbed language comprehension; fluent speech long phrases, substitution of phonemes or words; content is nonsensical; often unaware of impairment

but not meaningless "nonsense" syllables, indicating that these patients have an impaired ability to parrot word sounds.

Damage to the Cerebellum   Damage to the *cerebellum* also produces impairment in speech production (Gordon, 1996). Recall from Chapters 2 and 6 that the cerebellum is involved in coordinating muscle contractions to produce smooth, accurate movements. The cerebellum receives information from the cerebrum and participates in the planning and execution of speech sounds. The most common impairment observed following cerebellar damage is **dysarthria,** a disorder in which affected persons cannot control the rate, volume, or rhythm of their speech. In addition, articulation of phonemes is usually disturbed in patients with dysarthria. Removal of tumors from the cerebellum sometimes results in *cerebellar mutism*, in which the affected individual cannot speak following surgery. Young children who develop mutism after cerebellar surgery typically recover within several months, and they exhibit severe dysarthria when they begin speaking again (Gordon, 1996).

dysarthria: a disorder in which affected individuals cannot control the rate, volume, or rhythm of their speech

Results of Brain-Imaging Studies

A number of brain-imaging studies have revealed that the area of the human temporal lobe containing Wernicke's area is activated when speech sounds are heard. In Wernicke's area, speech sounds produce stronger activation than do tones, indicating that this area responds best to spoken language (Binder et al., 1994; Calvert et al., 1997; Demonet et al., 1992; Petersen et al., 1988; Zatorre et al., 1992). Helen Neville and her colleagues (1998) conducted a study using functional MRI to determine areas of brain activation in normally hearing and congenitally deaf (deaf since birth) people processing sentences in English and American Sign Language. They compared brain activation records of three groups of subjects: (1) normally hearing people who did not know ASL and who were native English speakers, (2) congenitally deaf people whose native language was ASL and who learned English later in life, and (3) normally hearing, bilingual people who were born to deaf parents and had both ASL and English as native languages. All subjects were presented with English sentences and nonsense consonant strings that they had to read and a video of a native deaf signer who produced sentences in ASL and nonsign gestures. For all subjects, functional MRI scans were conducted for both hemispheres.

Neville and her colleagues (1998) found that Broca's area and Wernicke's area became activated in deaf and hearing subjects when they were exposed to their native language, English versus American Sign Language (Figure 8.9). Normally hearing subjects, including those with deaf parents for whom ASL was a native language, displayed significant activation of Broca's area and Wernicke's area in the left hemisphere when they read English sentences, with very weak activation of the right hemisphere. Deaf subjects did not show left hemisphere activation when they

Figure 8.9 fMRI scans of hearing and deaf individuals

(Left) Broca's and Wernicke's areas in the left hemisphere are activated when normal hearing participants read English sentences. Deaf participants showed activation of the right hemisphere when they read English sentences. (Right) When processing ASL, deaf participants showed significant activation of Broca's and Wernicke's areas in the left hemisphere.

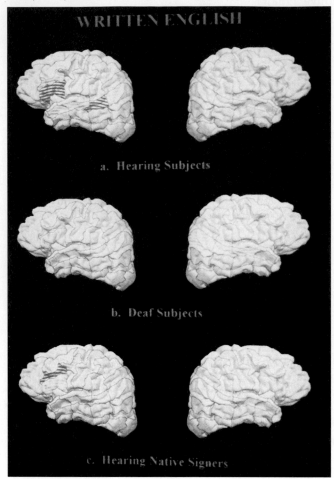

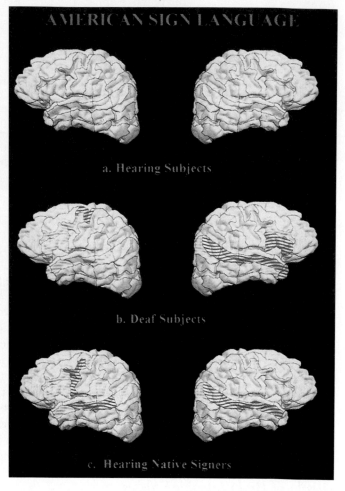

read English sentences, but they showed activation of corresponding areas of the right hemisphere instead. When processing ASL (their native language), deaf subjects showed significant activation of Broca's and Wernicke's areas in the left hemisphere, as well as corresponding areas in the right hemisphere. Normally hearing individuals who had ASL as a native language showed the same activation pattern as deaf participants. Thus, all subjects who processed sentences in their native language displayed activation of Broca's and Wernicke's areas in the left hemisphere, regardless of whether the language was auditory (English) or visual (ASL).

In addition, Neville's lab discovered that another area of the cortex, called the **angular gyrus,** was also activated when English or American Sign Language was processed (Neville et al., 1998). The angular gyrus is located at the junction of the temporal, parietal, and occipital lobes (Figure 8.8) and is believed to integrate visual, auditory, and somatosensory information. Damage to this cortical area has been implicated in reading disorders as well as a writing disorder known as *agraphia*. People with agraphia often have trouble forming letters when using a pen or pencil, have spelling errors, and cannot space words and letters uniformly across a page when writing. However, people with agraphia typically have no difficulty speaking or understanding spoken language (Grossman et al., 2001; Levine, Mani, & Calvano, 1988; Whitaker & Kahn, 1994).

angular gyrus: an area of the cortex located at the junction of the temporal, parietal, and occipital lobes that integrates visual, auditory, and somatosensory information

Other imaging studies have demonstrated that the highly specific speech functions attributed to Broca's area and Wernicke's area are actually shared by a number of regions in the cerebral cortex, including the *dorsolateral prefrontal cortex* and the *superior temporal gyrus*. These brain areas appear to process language independently of the sensory modality or structure of the language. That is, these brain areas probably mediate the more cognitive aspects of language. We will examine cognitive processing in the cerebral cortex in Chapter 9.

Lateralization of Language Functions

Pierre Paul Broca was the first investigator to report that language functions were localized to the left cerebral hemisphere (Broca, 1861). Since then, a large number of investigations, including case studies of stroke patients and other brain-injured individuals as well as brain-imaging studies, have confirmed Broca's finding that the left hemisphere is specialized for language (Muller et al., 1999; Whitaker & Kahn, 1994). For example, 95% of all patients with aphasia have damage in the left hemisphere (Provins, 1997). American Sign Language also appears to be processed predominately in the left hemisphere in native signers (Corina, Vaid, & Bellugi, 1992; Neville et al., 1998). Left hemispheric damage in deaf individuals produces *sign language aphasia*, in which signing is disturbed (Poizner, Klima, & Bellugi, 1987).

In further support of Broca's finding, Geschwind and Levitsky (1968) examined 100 brains of people who had recently died and discovered that the planum temporale, which contains Wernicke's area, was significantly larger on the left side of the brain, compared to the right, in 65% of the brains. Geschwind's research team went on to describe other asymmetries in the size of auditory and other language centers, with those on the left being significantly larger (Galaburda, LeMay, Kemper, & Geschwind, 1978). However, Broca's and Wernicke's areas are not confined to the left hemisphere in all individuals. A small percentage of people have these language centers on both sides of the brain, and an even smaller percentage have language centers only on the right side of the brain.

No one knows why left hemispheric lateralization of language occurs in most, but not all, people (Provins, 1997). Studies of individuals with damage in language centers of the cortex have revealed that brain damage can affect the organization of language in the brain. For example, research comparing PET scans of people who incurred brain damage before 5 years of age to healthy people and to people who incurred brain damage after 20 years of age indicates a significant difference in the distribution of language areas among these three groups (Muller et al., 1999). When listening to sentences, the healthy controls showed activation in the left hemisphere predominately. In contrast, the right hemisphere was dominant during language tasks in adults who incurred brain damage in the left hemisphere when they were very young. Bilateral activation was observed in those individuals who incurred brain damage as adults. These results indicate that other areas of the brain can take over language functions when a normal language center is damaged, especially if the damage occurs at an early age. We will discuss this finding in greater detail when we examine recovery from brain damage in Chapter 16.

When the normal left lateralization for language is disrupted, speech abnormalities are produced. For example, **stuttering** is a disturbance of speech production characterized by disfluency, abnormal timing (such as long pauses or drawn-out syllables), and uncontrolled repetition of phonemes. The biological basis for this disorder is unknown, although brain-imaging studies are helping us understand the brain mechanisms involved. Peter Fox and his colleagues (1996) compared PET scans of 10 men who stuttered since early childhood with 10 male normal controls. PET imaging was conducted while both groups of subjects read a paragraph by themselves or as part of a chorus. When chorus reading, stutterers do not stutter and read normally, with no disfluency. (That is, chorus reading induces fluency in the speech of a stutterer.) PET scans of the stutterers indicated overactivation of the right cerebral hemisphere and the cerebellum when they were

stuttering: a disturbance of speech production characterized by disfluency, abnormal timing, and uncontrolled repetition of phonemes

Figure 8.10 PET scans of stutterers
During stuttering, overactivation of the right cerebral hemisphere is observed, and left lateralization of language is absent.

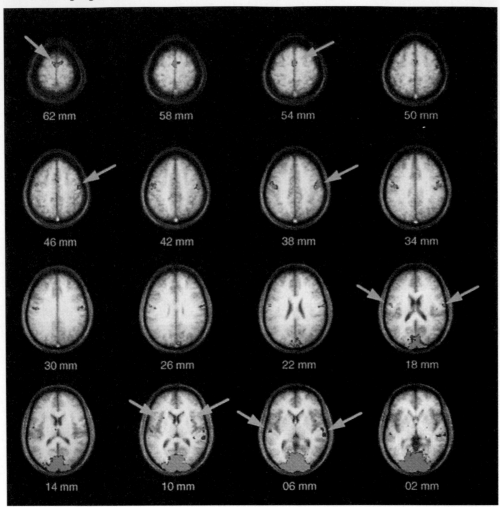

stuttering. In addition, left lateralization of speech was absent during stuttering (Figure 8.10). However, when the chronic stutterers read fluently during the chorus reading condition, the speech and motor areas in the left hemisphere became dominant, indicating that disruption of the normal lateralization of speech is associated with speech disfluency.

Processing of Music

Music is a complex auditory phenomenon that has various components, including *melody, rhythm,* and sometimes verbal *lyrics.* Melody consists of a sequence or pattern of various frequencies, whereas rhythm is the temporal component that dictates the length of time that the individual frequencies are heard as well as the length of the pauses. Musical compositions can be distinguished on the basis of their melody, rhythm, and lyrics (the words that are sung). For example, "Mary Had a Little Lamb" and "Merrily We Roll Along" have identical melodies but can be distinguished by their rhythm and lyrics. Different musical instruments can be distinguished by the pattern of frequencies that each produces, with each instrument emitting a characteristic pattern of frequencies. From the cochlea to the cerebral cortex, neurons in the auditory system are organized in such a way that they respond only to specific frequencies (Merzenich, Kaas, & Roth, 1976; Rauschecker et al., 1995).

As with the perception of language, the perception of music involves many different parts of the brain and appears to be lateralized (Riecker et al., 2000; Zatorre, 1998). However, the localization of music functions in the brain appears to be different for musicians and nonmusicians. For nonmusicians, music is divided between the left and right hemispheres, with melody being processed on the right and rhythm on the left (Bever & Chiarello, 1974; Boucher & Bryden, 1997; Corballis, 1994; Liegeois-Chauvel et al., 1998; Maess, Koelsch, Gunter, & Friederic: 2001; Matteis et al., 1997). Musicians tend to use the left hemisphere almost exclusively when playing or listening to music.

In musicians, large areas of the cerebral cortex are involved in processing music (Hirata, Kuriki, & Pantev, 1999; Pantev, Oostenveld, Engelien, Ross, Roberts, & Hoke, 1998). In general, the earlier the age at which musical training began, the larger the music-processing areas in the brain (Pantev et al., 1998). For example, MRI studies have revealed that the corpus callosum is 10–15% thicker in musicians who began studying music before the age of 7, compared to nonmusicians and people who study music later in life. A thicker corpus callosum would allow abundant communication between the two hemispheres to coordinate movements that produce intricate musical compositions (Schlaug, 2001; Schlaug et al., 1994).

Damage to brain areas that are associated with music perception produces impairments in music perception, known as **amusia.** Damage to frontal areas of the cortex results in *expressive amusia*, the inability to produce music, and damage to more posterior areas in the temporal lobe results in *receptive amusia* (Corballis, 1994). The impairments associated with receptive amusia vary depending on the hemisphere involved. Damage to the right hemisphere, especially in the area of the superior temporal gyrus, produces an overall impairment of music perception that interferes with the recognition of melodies. Damage to the left temporal cortex results in an inability to process rhythm (Liegeois-Chauvel et al., 1998; Schuppert, Munte, Wieringa, & Altenmuller, 2000).

amusia: an impairment in music perception

Recap 8.3: Auditory Processing

The auditory "What" streams begins in the rostral part of the primary auditory cortex in the (a)_____ lobe and ends in the (b)_____ prefrontal cortex. The auditory "Where" stream begins in the caudal part of the primary auditory cortex and ends in the (c)_____ prefrontal cortex. The secondary auditory cortex is activated by complex sounds but not by (d)_____. Spoken language is comprised of (e)_____ _____ (the basic units of language) that are combined to form meaningful units of sounds called (f)_____. Damage to Broca's area produces (g)_____ aphasia. (h)_____ is the inability to name familiar objects. Damage to (i)_____ area produces receptive aphasia. (j)_____ involves the substitution of one phoneme for another. Damage to the arcuate fasciculus produces a disorder called (k)_____ aphasia. The most common disorder following damage to the cerebellum is (l)_____. When deaf individuals are exposed to their native language (American Sign Language or English), both (m)_____ area and (n)_____ area become activated in the left hemisphere. PET scans of stutterers show overactivation of the (o)_____ hemisphere and cerebellum when they are stuttering. For nonmusicians, melody is processed in the (p)_____ hemisphere and rhythm is processed in the (q)_____, whereas musicians tend to use the (r)_____ hemisphere exclusively when playing or listening to music. Impairments in music perception are referred to as (s)_____.

Somatosensory Processing

Imagine that a fly lands on your left arm while you are reading. You don't see it or hear it, but you know the fly is there because you can feel it on your skin. Without looking at it, you can tell that it is very light, almost weightless. You can also feel its movement up your arm, from your wrist to just below your elbow. Immediately, you perceive that there is an insect on your arm ("What"), and you swat at it with your right hand ("Where").

The sensations that arise from the body are transmitted to the brain by way of the somatosensory system. This information, especially from the skin and muscles, is important because it tells us about the location of our limbs in space and about objects in the environment that are touching us. Recall from Chapter 7 that somatosensory information travels to the brain by way of two pathways: *A-fibers*, which are large-diameter, myelinated axons, and *C-fibers*, which are small-diameter, unmyelinated axons. This information, after passing through several synapses in the midbrain and thalamus, is projected to the **primary somatosensory cortex** in the *postcentral gyrus* of the parietal lobe (Figure 8.11a).

You were introduced to the primary somatosensory cortex in Chapter 1. Recall that it is topographically organized, with each neuron in the primary somatosensory cortex receiving information from a specific area of the body. For example, information from the big toe on my right foot goes to neurons in the superior aspect of my left postcentral gyrus, and information from the left side of my face goes to neurons in the inferior aspect of my right postcentral gyrus (Figure 8.11b). Studies of brain-injured individuals and single-cell recordings in the brains of macaques have revealed that the somatosensory information may be processed along "What" and "Where" streams, much like the visual and auditory systems (Reed, Caselli, & Farah, 1996). Information received by the primary somatosensory cortex is sent on to other cortical regions, collectively known as the **secondary somatosensory cortex,** for "What" and "Where" processing.

primary somatosensory cortex: the postcentral gyrus in the parietal lobe, which processes sensory information from the skin and muscles

secondary somatosensory cortex: the area of the parietal lobe posterior to the postcentral gyrus, which receives information from the primary somatosensory cortex for "What" and "Where" processing

Figure 8.11 Primary and secondary somatosensory areas
The primary and secondary somatosensory areas are located in the parietal lobe. Like the motor cortex, the primary somatosensory cortex is topographically organized.

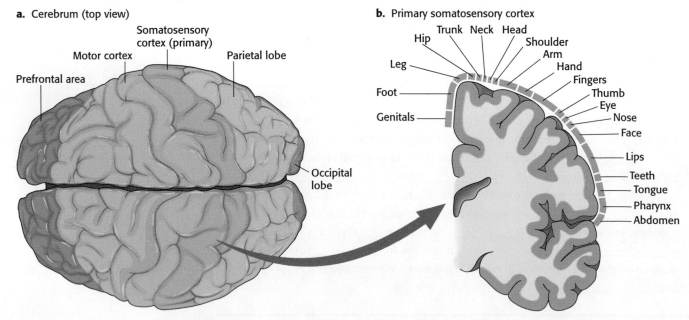

a. Cerebrum (top view)

Prefrontal area
Motor cortex
Somatosensory cortex (primary)
Parietal lobe
Occipital lobe

b. Primary somatosensory cortex

Hip
Trunk Neck Head
Shoulder
Arm
Hand
Leg
Fingers
Foot
Thumb
Eye
Genitals
Nose
Face
Lips
Teeth
Tongue
Pharynx
Abdomen

The "What" and "Where" Systems

Damage to the *inferior parietal cortex* produces a disorder called **tactile agnosia,** in which the affected individuals cannot recognize objects through touch (Caselli, 1991; Reed & Caselli, 1994; Valenza et al., 2001). The affected individuals perform well on tests of spatial ability and can recognize the objects visually. In addition, there is no impairment of their ability to detect tactile stimuli. However, when asked to identify an object through the sense of touch, people with damage to the inferior parietal cortex can accurately judge the length and size of the object, but they cannot recognize it. Therefore, the "What" system appears to be associated with the inferior parietal cortex.

The *posterior parietal cortex* processes "Where" information from the somatosensory system. Recall that this area of the cortex also receives "Where" information from the visual system. However, the regions that process somatosensory input exclusively appear to be separate from the visual spatial processing areas (Duhamel, Colby, & Goldberg, 1998). In the primate brain, information from visual and somatosensory spatial processing areas are combined in an area in the parietal cortex immediately posterior to the primary somatosensory cortex (Graziano, Cooke, & Taylor, 2000). This area processes visual and somatosensory input simultaneously to produce a sense of "body image" that guides movement and postural adjustments. Movement of tactile stimuli across the skin, as well as the location of the stimuli and their spatial relationship to other tactile stimuli, is processed in the posterior parietal lobe.

tactile agnosia: a somatosensory disorder in which the affected individual cannot recognize objects through touch, associated with damage to the inferior parietal cortex

Plasticity of the Somatosensory Cortex

A number of investigators have demonstrated that the topographical map of the primary somatosensory cortex is quite plastic and can be reorganized. For example, specific tactile experiences can change the organization of the somatosensory cortex. Evoked potential recordings of brain activity of blind individuals revealed that the fingertip used for reading Braille sends input to a larger area of the somatosensory cortex than do the fingers not used for reading (Pascual-Leone & Torres, 1993). In addition, the fingers on the left hands of violinists activate larger areas on the primary somatosensory cortex than do the fingers of nonmusicians, as MEG recordings have shown (Elbert, Pantev, Weinbruch, Rockstroh, & Taub, 1995).

The topographical organization of the primary somatosensory cortex is also altered following amputation of a limb (Florence, Taub, & Kaas, 1998; Merzenich, 1998). That is, the neurons in the postcentral gyrus that formerly received input from the missing limb come to respond to receptors located in the trunk and face, as well as the stump of the amputated limb (Figure 8.12). The end result is that a touch on the face of an individual with an amputated limb will induce a sensation that feels as if it is coming from the missing limb (Ramachandran et al., 1992). This large-scale reorganization of the primary somatosensory cortex is not

Figure 8.12 Reorganization of the primary somatosensory cortex following amputation of an arm

Following amputation of an arm, areas of the primary somatosensory cortex that formerly responded to sensations in the arm will come to respond to sensations in the leg, trunk, and face.

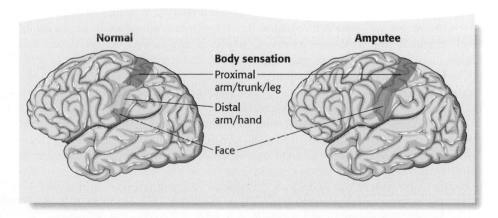

well understood but may be caused by degeneration of particular areas in the thalamus due to loss of innervation from receptors in the amputated limb. We will discuss this phenomenon in more detail in Chapter 16.

However, the ability of the primary somatosensory cortex to reorganize may contribute to the experience of chronic pain, especially a type of chronic pain known as *phantom limb pain*, in which an individual who has had a limb amputated continues to feel pain in the missing limb long after it has been amputated. Phantom limb pain is seen in many individuals who have suffered amputation of a limb. Flor and his colleagues (1998) have discovered that the severity of phantom limb pain experienced is directly related to the extent of the reorganization of the somatosensory cortex, with more pain being associated with greater reorganization within the cortex. To understand this finding, let's examine the cortical processes responsible for the perception of pain.

Perception of Pain

Have you ever noticed that an ache or pain hurts worse when you are hungry or tired? The sensation of pain results from a complex interplay of signals from pain receptors and inhibitory messages that descend from the brain. That is, the experience of pain is influenced by many factors, including a person's level of motivation, attitude toward and expectations about pain, and attention paid to the painful stimulus. The amount of tissue damage, by itself, does not predict the amount of pain felt. The intensity of pain perceived depends on the pattern of action potentials generated by pain receptors *and* the amount of inhibition that is generated by specific areas of the brainstem and cerebral cortex.

Melzack and Wall (1965) were the first investigators to explain the curious observation that people respond in different ways under different circumstances to identically painful stimuli. Their explanation is called the **Gate-Control Theory of Pain** (Figure 8.13). According to this theory, C-fibers carry information about pain to neurons in the **substantia gelatinosa,** which is located in the dorsal horn of the spinal cord and extends into the medulla. From the substantia gelatinosa, information about pain is relayed to the brain stem and on to the cerebral cortex, where pain is consciously experienced. However, pain messages can be prevented from reaching the cortex by "closing the gate," a metaphor that Melzack and Wall used to describe the inhibitory influence of brain structures and A-fibers on the substantia gelatinosa (Melzack & Wall, 1994). Two areas of the brain stem, the **periaqueductal gray** and the **periventricular gray,** send axons down to the substantia gelatinosa, which release neurotransmitters that inhibit transmission of pain information to the brain. A-fibers that carry tactile information can also "close the gate" to stop pain information from reaching the brain.

Neurochemical Explanation of the Gate-Control Theory

Pain receptors use a neurotransmitter known as **substance P** to signal the presence of tissue damage and pain to the central nervous system. Substance P is released by small-diameter, unmyelinated axons (C-fibers) in the substantia gelatinosa and excites neurons whose axons carry information about pain to the brain (Figure 8.13). However, centers in the cerebrum and brainstem project axons down to the substantia gelatinosa. These axons release neurotransmitters that alter the pain information that actually reaches the cerebrum.

Two classes of neurotransmitters inhibit pain messages being sent to the brain (Watkins & Mayer, 1982). The first class of neurotransmitters is the endogenous opiate transmitters, called **endorphins,** which you learned about in Chapter 3. Input from higher brain centers causes neurons in the periaqueductal gray and periventricular gray areas to release endorphins at their terminal buttons in the substantia gelatinosa (Figure 8.13b). These terminal buttons form axo-axonal synapses with the axons of the neurons that release substance P. Therefore, the

Gate-Control Theory of Pain: a theory proposed by Melzack and Wall to explain how reactions to pain can be modified by inhibitory processes in the brain stem and A-fibers

substantia gelatinosa: an area in the dorsal horn of the spinal cord and medulla where the transmission of pain messages to the cerebrum can be inhibited

periaqueductal gray: area in the midbrain that contains neurons that release neurotransmitters that inhibit the transmission of pain messages in the substantia gelatinosa

periventricular gray: a region of the hypothalamus located next to the third ventricle, which is associated with the expression of negative emotions

substance P: a neurotransmitter used by pain receptors to signal the presence of tissue damage and pain

endorphins: endogenous opiate neurotransmitters that inhibit pain messages

substantia gelatinosa is open, information about pain (traveling in C-fibers) is sent to the cere-
es consciousness. (b) In the substantia gelatinosa, C-fibers release substance P, which activates a
to the cerebrum. Endorphin-producing neurons in the periaqueductal gray (in the midbrain) have
axons that terminate on the axons of C-fibers in the substantia gelatinosa and inhibit the release of substance P.

a.   b.

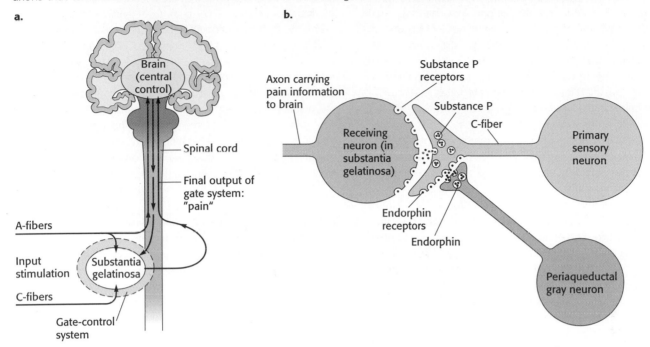

release of endorphins in the substantia gelatinosa causes presynaptic inhibition, preventing substance P from being released to signal pain. Endorphins are also released by the pituitary gland in response to painful or stressful situations, further inhibiting pain, as you will learn in Chapter 14.

The second class of neurotransmitters that inhibit pain messages is **nonopiate transmitters.** These neurotransmitters are also released by neurons whose cell bodies are located in the brainstem, although the exact location of these neurons is not certain. Axons from these neurons descend into the spinal cord, forming synapses with neurons that release substance P. These nonopiate neurotransmitters also inhibit the release of substance P, producing **analgesia,** or an absence of pain.

nonopiate transmitters: a second class of neurotransmitters that inhibit pain messages

analgesia: an absence of pain

What causes a football player to be able to play to the end of a game after breaking a rib? We've all heard stories of people with horrible injuries who are somehow able to ignore pain and finish the task at hand. The explanation is found in Melzack and Wall's Gate-Control Theory. Higher brain centers send input via the periaqueductal and periventricular gray and other brainstem areas that blocks pain messages coming from the receptors. If a person switches his or her attention to winning the game or rescuing a loved one, pain messages can be suppressed by the descending pain inhibition systems.

Treatment for Pain

Many treatments for pain can be explained by the Gate-Control Theory. The *For Further Thought* box describes the action of various drugs, including some new experimental substances, used to treat pain. Other (nonpharmacological) methods for treating pain include *counterirritation, acupuncture, transcutaneous electrical nerve stimulation,* and *hypnosis.*

Pharmacological Treatments for Pain

Drugs have been used to treat pain for thousands of years, but our understanding of the biological mechanisms underlying such pharmacological treatments has just begun. As investigators discover how particular painkillers work, we are learning that pain control is indeed a very complicated process in the nervous system. Drugs that treat pain are typically classified into one of two categories: *opiate* or *nonopiate* drugs. Regardless of their classification, all painkilling drugs vary in their effectiveness in treating different kinds of pain. Aspirin, for example, is not effective in blocking postoperative pain, whereas opiates are not very effective in inhibiting pain associated with movement (MacPherson, 2000).

Opiate drugs, as you learned in Chapter 3, are chemically similar to *opium,* which is derived from the poppy plant. The best-known opiates that are used to treat pain are *morphine, demerol, darvon, codeine,* and *percodan,* although a number of opiates that have been around for a long time (such as *hydromorphone, oxycodone,* and *dihydrocodeine*) are coming back into favor again to treat severe pain. These drugs are all known to produce analgesia via stimulation of the mu-opioid receptor. A wide variety of techniques are used to administer opiate medication, including oral, rectal, intravenous, transdermal (through the skin), inhalation, and epidural (into the meninges of the spinal cord) administration. Adverse side effects of opiate painkillers include respiratory depression (producing death in drug overdoses), nausea, and other types of gastrointestinal upset.

Nonopiate analgesics treat pain in many different ways. Over-the-counter analgesics, such as *aspirin, acetaminophen,* and *ibuprofen,* block the production of prostaglandins, chemicals that are released when body tissue is damaged and causes pain, fever, and inflammation (Garavito, 1999). *Anticonvulsants* (drugs that stop seizures) inhibit pain by blocking Na^+ channels. Certain *antidepressants* also have analgesic effects, but they work by blocking reuptake of norepinephrine and serotonin. *Tramadol* is an interesting drug because it blocks pain by binding with the mu-opioid receptor *and* by inhibiting reuptake of norepinephrine and serotonin. Other classes of nonopiate painkillers include drugs that bind with alpha2 adrenergic receptors (for example, *clonidine*) and drugs that antagonize the glutamate NMDA receptors (for example, *ketamine*).

A number of drugs are currently being tested in clinical trials in humans for their safety and effectiveness in treating pain. *Epibatidine* is an alkaloid derived from the skin of a poisonous frog and has been demonstrated to produce analgesia in rats. Studies have shown that epibatidine stimulates nicotinic acetylcholine receptors. Another new analgesic drug currently under investigation, called *nitroaspirin,* is a combination of aspirin and NO (the neurotransmitter nitric oxide). Clinical trials are also underway to test in double-blind, controlled studies the effectiveness of *cannabinoids* in treating pain.

Thus, pain control is achieved through a variety of neurotransmitter systems. Increasing opioid, serotonin, norepinephrine, epinephrine, acetylcholine, NO, and cannabinoid activity, as well as decreasing glutamate activity, is associated with pain relief. In addition, blocking Na^+ channels also appears to cause analgesia. Alcohol (that is, ethanol) most likely achieves its painkilling effect in this manner, by blocking Na^+ channels.

Counterirritation involves using a brief irritating stimulus to counteract ongoing pain. It is a technique that has been used for centuries to alleviate pain. Acupuncture is a pain control method developed by Chinese doctors over 4,000 years ago. In some ways, acupuncture works like counterirritation. Thin needles are inserted into the skin at special points, often far from the site of pain, and vibrated slightly. For example, to alleviate tooth pain, Mayer (1975) stimulated acupuncture points in the subjects' hands. Another form of counterirritation is transcutaneous electrical nerve stimulation (abbreviated *TENS*). This technique involves sending a tiny current to the skin to stimulate receptors in the area of the injury to induce analgesia (Carroll, et al., 2001). Often, people who are receiving TENS will wear a little box clipped to a belt, with wires extending from the box to the site of stimulation. These three forms of treatment—counterirritation, acupuncture, and TENS—appear to activate both the endorphin and the nonopiate pain-inhibitory systems (Watkins & Mayer, 1982).

Hypnosis has also proven effective in treating pain. Studies using naloxone, an opiate antagonist, have demonstrated that naloxone does not block analgesia produced by hypnosis (Barber & Mayer, 1977). If endorphins mediated the analgesia produced by hypnosis, then naloxone should reverse the effect of hypnosis. However, naloxone does not affect the analgesia induced by hypnosis. In contrast, naloxone does block analgesia produced by counterirritation, acupuncture, and TENS, which demonstrates that endorphins are involved in inhibiting pain with these techniques. Thus, hypnosis activates only nonopiate pain-inhibitory systems, whereas counterirritation, acupuncture, and TENS activate opiate and nonopiate systems.

Cortical Processing of Pain

Pain perception actually has three dimensions: *sensory-discriminative*, *motivational-affective*, and *cognitive-evaluative* (Craig & Rollman, 1999). The sensory-discriminative dimension involves detecting pain and identifying its source. The motivational-affective dimension involves the emotional and motivational aspects of the pain, whereas the cognitive-evaluative dimension involves determining the meaning of the pain (for example, determining how serious the pain is and how it should be dealt with). Different cortical systems process the three dimensions of pain separately.

Information about all body sensations, including pain, first go to the primary somatosensory cortex upon reaching the cerebrum. Next, information about pain is relayed to the secondary somatosensory cortex. The sensory-discriminative components of pain perception appear to be processed in these regions of the cortex. From these areas in the parietal lobe, pain information is sent to the frontal lobe for processing of the motivational-affective and cognitive-evaluative components of pain (Rainville, Duncan, Price, Carrier, & Bushnell, 1997).

Evaluation of the motivational-affective dimension of pain, such as its unpleasantness and whether it can be endured, appears to involve the **anterior cingulate cortex** in the frontal lobe. Patients with prefrontal lobotomies that destroyed the cingulate cortex can still feel pain, but they do not find it unpleasant or distressing (Rainville et al., 1997). With PET imaging, Bud Craig and his colleagues (1996) found that the anterior cingulate cortex becomes active when subjects touch painfully hot or cold stimuli but remains inactive when the same subjects touch warm or cool stimuli. Pierre Rainville and his colleagues (1997) used hypnotic suggestion to increase or decrease the unpleasantness of a stimulus (hot water), without actually changing the intensity of the pain stimulus. PET scans revealed that the anterior cingulate cortex became very active when the hypnotic suggestion increased the unpleasantness of the painful stimulus and that it became significantly less active when hypnotic suggestion directed a decrease in the unpleasantness. In contrast, the activation levels of the primary somatosensory cortex and secondary somatosensory cortex did not change when the perceived unpleasantness of the hot water was altered by hypnotic suggestion. A number of other investigators have concurred that the suffering associated with pain is experienced in the anterior cingulate cortex (Jones, Friston, & Frackowiak, 1992; Talbot et al., 1991).

The cognitive-evaluative dimension of pain is also processed in the *prefrontal cortex*. Research in Alexander Ploghaus's (1999) laboratory has demonstrated, using functional MRI scans, that discrete areas of the human prefrontal cortex and the *insula*, an area of the frontal lobe just superior to the Sylvian fissure, become activated when pain is anticipated. The posterior parietal lobe may also play a role in the evaluation of certain aspects of pain, particularly its intensity and spatial features (Talbot et al., 1991).

It is important to remember that the cerebral cortex communicates with subcortical structures, such as the hippocampus, the hypothalamus, and the periaqueductal and periventricular gray areas, about the presence and quality of pain (Hsieh et al., 1996). The hippocampus processes this information, laying down memories of the painful stimulus, which will influence subsequent emotional reactions to the stimulus. The hypothalamus contributes to the inhibition of pain by stimulating the pituitary gland to release endorphins. As you learned earlier in this section,

anterior cingulate cortex: an area of the prefrontal cortex that appears to be part of the central executive system that coordinates working memory, especially attentional processes

stimulation of the periaqueductal and periventricular gray areas causes neurons in these areas to release endorphins and other nonopiate neurotransmitters that inhibit pain.

A recent PET study by Jon-Kar Zubieta and his colleagues (2000) at the University of Michigan has demonstrated that sustained jaw pain produced in healthy human subjects triggers the release of endogenous opioids and activation of mu-opioid receptors in a number of cortical and subcortical brain regions, including the anterior cingulate cortex, lateral prefrontal cortex, insual, thalamus, hypothalamus, and amygdala. As mu-opioid receptor activity increased, the subjects reduced their subjective ratings of the pain experience. Thus, pain that is experimentally induced in the laboratory activates the release of endorphins in cortical and subcortical areas associated with sensory, affective, and cognitive dimensions of pain.

Thus, the experience of pain results from the activation of pain receptors in the peripheral nervous system and the responses of cortical and subcortical structures in the brain to that activation. In people who have experienced devastating tissue injury, the central nervous system can continue to issue pain responses in the absence of stimulation from the peripheral nervous system, as is the case with phantom limb pain. Additionally, reorganization of the somatosensory cortex can cause a mix-up in the processing of signals reaching the brain. For example, **allodynia** is an abnormal pain response to a normally nonpainful stimulus that is observed in individuals who have suffered tissue and nerve damage. A light touch on the skin can produce horrible pain in patients with allodynia. The brains of these patients come to interpret many nonpain messages as painful, which activates the emotional and cognitive centers to respond to the nonpainful stimulus as if it were a source of excruciating pain.

As we conclude this discussion of pain perception, please keep in mind that we are a long way from understanding precisely how pain is processed in the central nervous system. Investigators who study pain have not reached a consensus concerning the role of the cerebral cortex in the perception of pain. We know even less about the mechanisms of smell perception and taste perception in the brain—topics that we will examine next in this chapter.

allodynia: an abnormal pain response to a normally nonpainful stimulus that is observed in individuals who have suffered tissue and nerve damage

Recap 8.4: The Somatosensory System

Information for somatosensory processing is relayed to the primary somatosensory cortex in the (a)_____ lobe. From there, information is sent to the (b)_____ somatosensory cortex for "What" and "Where" processing. The somatosensory "What" system involves the (c)_____ parietal cortex. Damage to this area results in (d)_____ _____, a disorder in which a person cannot identify objects by their touch. The somatosensory "Where" system involves the (e)_____ parietal lobe, an area also involved in processing visual "Where" information. The ability of the primary somatosensory cortex to reorganize following injury to the body may contribute to the experience of (f)_____ _____ pain, in which a person continues to feel pain in a missing limb. Melzack and Wall proposed the (g)_____ Theory of Pain, to explain wide variety of responses to identical pain stimuli. Axons from the (h)_____ gray and the (i)_____ gray areas release pain-inhibiting neurotransmitters in the substantia gelatinosa. These neurotransmitters are of two types: (j)_____ (endogenous opiate transmitters) and (k)_____ transmitters. They reduce pain sensations by inhibiting the release of substance (l)_____. Treatments for pain include drugs, (m)_____, (n)_____, (o)_____ (p)_____ (q)_____ stimulation, and hypnosis.

Olfactory and Taste Processing

Olfactory Processing

Natural odors consist of many different molecules mixed together. The task of the olfactory system is to sort out these various chemicals and identify the odor present at any given time. When you consider all the thousands of volatile chemicals that can possibly stimulate the olfactory receptors, the job of the olfactory system seems impossibly hard.

On the other hand, the olfactory system is remarkably simple, compared to the visual, auditory, or somatosensory systems. The olfactory processing center in the cerebral cortex is only two synapses away from the receptors. In addition, the olfactory system does not appear to separate into functional streams, like the "What" and "Where" streams of the other perceptual systems that we've studied (Laurent, 1999).

Recent research at Stanford University has identified the location of the **primary olfactory cortex** and the **secondary olfactory cortex** in humans. Using functional MRI, Sobel and his colleagues (1998) discovered that when a human subject sniffs, an area of the ventral temporal lobe known as the **piriform cortex,** as well as an area of the frontal cortex immediately anterior to the piriform cortex, is activated (Figure 8.14). That is, the primary olfactory cortex in people is located in both the temporal and frontal lobes. When a human subject becomes aware of an odor, the secondary olfactory cortex is activated. The secondary olfactory cortex is found in the lateral and anterior *orbitofrontal prefrontal cortex*, an area of the frontal lobe directly behind the eyeball socket in the skull (Sobel, Prabhakaran, Desmond, Glover, Goode, Sullivan, & Gabrieli, 1998).

primary olfactory cortex: the region of the cerebral cortex, located in both the frontal and temporal lobes, that receives olfactory information from the olfactory lobe

secondary olfactory cortex: an area involved in the identification of odors that is located in the orbitofrontal prefrontal cortex

piriform cortex: an area of the ventral temporal lobe where part of the primary olfactory cortex is located

Gender Differences in Olfactory Ability

In tests of odor detection and odor identification, women consistently outperform men. This superiority in olfactory ability in women has been demonstrated in black American, white American, Korean American, and native Japanese subjects (Doty, Applebaum, Zusho, & Settle, 1985). These findings have been corroborated by brain-recording and brain-imaging studies. For example, women have larger evoked potentials to olfactory stimuli than do men (Evans, Cui, & Starr, 1995). David Yousem and his colleagues (1999) presented a variety of pleasant and unpleasant odors to eight men and eight women while their brains were being scanned, using functional MRI. The images of the women's brains showed up to eight times more activation in the frontal lobes than those of the men when they received olfactory stimulation (Figure 8.15). In both men and women, the right frontal lobes showed more activation associated with olfaction than did the left. However, for both the left and right frontal lobes, the level of activation in response to odors is greater in women than in men.

Taste Processing

Investigators are just beginning to understand the mechanisms by which taste is

Figure 8.14 The primary and secondary olfactory centers
The primary olfactory cortex is located in the piriform cortex in the temporal lobe and an area in the frontal lobe immediately anterior to the piriform cortex. The secondary olfactory is found in the orbitofrontal prefrontal cortex.

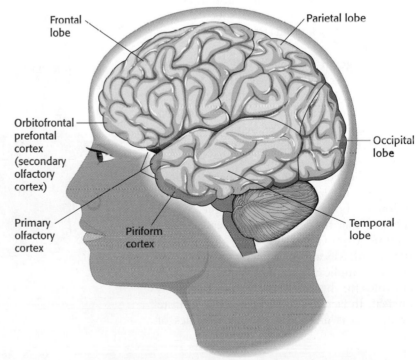

processed in the cerebral cortex. As you learned in Chapter 7, information from taste receptors reaches the brain by way of three cranial nerves, which synapse with neurons in the nucleus of the solitary tract. From the hindbrain, information about taste is transmitted to the ventromedioposterior (VPM) nucleus of the thalamus and then on to the **primary taste cortex,** in the **insula.** Bornstein (1940) studied a dozen men with bullet wounds in an area just superior to the Sylvian fissure, which includes the insula (Figure 8.16). Bornstein's subjects all exhibited taste impairments, implicating the peri-Sylvian area of the cortex in taste perception [*peri-* = around, Latin]. Since Bornstein's original research, a number of lesioning experiments in monkeys and recording studies in human and monkey subjects have verified that the primary taste cortex in primates is located in the insula (Pritchard, Macaluso, & Eslinger, 1999).

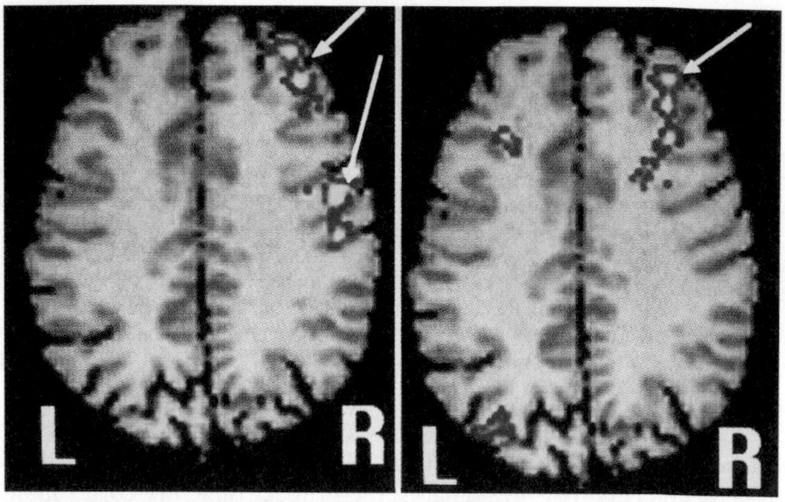

Single-cell recording of neurons in the primary taste cortex of macaque monkeys has revealed a number of interesting findings. Fewer than 10% of the neurons in the primary taste cortex actually respond to taste stimuli. About 25% of the neurons fire in response to mouth or jaw movements, and fewer than 5% respond to tactile stimulation of the mouth and tongue. This means that the function of nearly 65% of the neurons in the primary taste cortex is unknown (Scott & Plata-Salaman, 1999). Of the neurons that do respond to taste stimuli, most responded to only one of four primary tastes: sweet, sour, salty, or bitter (Scott, Giza, & Yan, 1999; Scott & Plata-Salaman, 1999). However, tastes are not topographically organized on the primary taste cortex. That is, neurons that respond to a specific taste are not located in a specific region of the insula. Rather, the neurons that respond to a specific taste appear to be scattered across the primary taste cortex.

Damage to the insula will impair taste perception, as Bornstein first noted in 1940. Patients with lesions in the primary taste cortex demonstrate both a loss of taste sensitivity and an inability to recognize previously familiar tastes. Damage to the right insula causes impairment of sensitivity and recognition on the left side of the tongue. However, damage to the left insula impairs taste recognition on both sides of the tongue, which suggests that the left insula processes information from both sides of the tongue (Pritchard, Macaluso, & Eslinger, 1999).

The implication of this finding of different roles for the left versus the right insula is unclear. In fact, the role of the insula in taste perception is unknown, although studies of

Figure 8.15 fMRI scans of the olfactory activation in men and women

In both men and women, the right frontal lobe shows more activation in response to an olfactory stimulus than does the right. In addition, the level of activation in response to odors is greater in women than in men.

primary taste cortex: an area of the frontal lobe just anterior to the temporal lobe that receives information about taste stimuli from the thalamus

insula: area of the frontal lobe superior to the Sylvian fissure where the primary taste cortex is located

Figure 8.16 The primary taste cortex
The primary taste cortex is located in the insula, located in the frontal lobe, just superior to the Sylvian fissure.

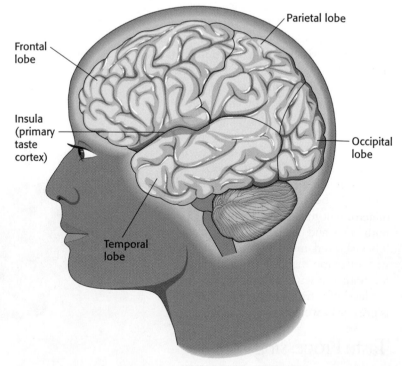

brain-damaged individuals indicate that it plays a role in the conscious processing and identification of specific tastes. However, identification of tastes also appears to occur in the brain stem, as studies of lesioned rats and human infants born without a cerebrum (called **anencephalic** infants) have shown. Anencephalic babies show the same reaction as do babies with intact brains when exposed to different tastes (Steiner, 1977). When a sweet taste is placed on their tongues, anencephalic and normal infants make a pleased expression and move toward the food source. Like normal babies, anencephalic babies screw up their faces in disgust when offered a bitter-tasting substance (Figure 8.17).

Compared to our knowledge of visual perceptual processes, our understanding of taste perception is quite limited. But, even our models of visual processing are imprecise and speculative at this time. In Chapter 9, we will examine cognitive processes, such memory and attention, in the brain. This topic is a logical extension of our discussion of perceptual processes because cognitive processes make use of perceptions to make comparisons, form memories, and manipulate ideas.

Figure 8.17 Facial responses of anencephalic babies to taste stimuli
Anencephalic babies and normal controls were exposed to various tastes between birth and their first feeding. (A) no taste stimulus (at rest). (B) Reaction to distilled water (control). (C) Response to a sweet stimulus. (D) Response to a sour stimulus. (E) Response to a bitter stimulus.

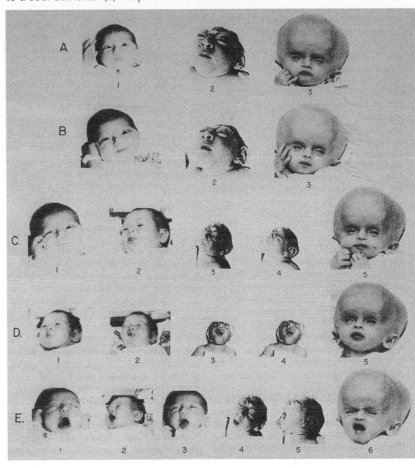

Recap 8.5: Olfactory and Taste Processing

The primary olfactory cortex is located in the (a)_____ cortex in the temporal lobe and an adjacent area of the (b)_____ cortex. The secondary olfactory cortex is in the (c)_____-_____ prefrontal cortex, located directly behind the eyeball sockets. Women consistently perform better than men in tests of (d)_____ detection and identification. The primary taste cortex is located in the (e)_____ in the frontal lobe.

anencephalic: a condition in which the individual has no cerebrum

Chapter Summary

The Cerebrum's Role in Perception

▶ Perception is the process by which the brain interprets the information it receives from receptors.

▶ The four lobes of the cerebrum are named for the overlying bones of the skull.

▶ Most perceptual processing takes places in the cerebral cortex, which is composed of five or six layers of neurons.

▶ The process of identifying areas of the cerebrum based on their microscopic differences is called cytoarchitectonic typing. The best known example of cerebral mapping based on microscopic appearance is Brodmann's classification system, which divides the cerebral cortex into more than 50 distinct areas.

▶ The cerebrum has two parts, a cortex composed of neuronal cell bodies and underlying white matter that contains myelinated axons. Two types of neurons are found in the cerebral cortex, stellate cells (which receive information from the thalamus and other parts of the cerebrum) and pyramidal cells (which transmit information from the cortex to other parts of the brain).

▶ The functions of specific areas of the cortex have been identified by experiments that involved recording, imaging, lesioning, or stimulation of the brain.

Visual Processing

▶ Information from rods and cones is relayed to neurons in the lateral geniculate nucleus (LGN) of the thalamus.

▶ From the LGN, visual information is relayed to the primary visual cortex, also called area V1, in the occipital lobe and then on to V2, V3, V4, and V5.

▶ The parvocellular neurons in the LGN receive information from cones on the retina and transmit that information to blob regions of V1. The magnocellular neurons in the LGN receive information from the rods and relay this information to the interblob regions of V1.

▶ Visual processing takes place along two pathways, the ventral ("What") stream that processes information about color and form and a dorsal stream (the "Where" system) that processes information about motion and the location of objects in the visual field.

▶ The processing of color involves area V4, which sends information on to the inferior temporal cortex and the prefrontal cortex. Information about form is relayed to area V3 and then to the inferior temporal cortex. Information about movement and spatial relations is relayed to area V5 and then to the posterior parietal lobe.

▶ It is uncertain how the brain combines information from the "What" and "Where" systems in a theoretical process called binding.

▶ Visual perceptual disorders are associated with damage to particular areas of the cerebral cortex, including scotoma, hemianopia, blindsight, achromatopsia, akinetopsia, and visual agnosia. Damage to a tiny region in area V1 will produce a scotoma, whereas complete damage to V1 in one hemisphere can cause hemianopia. People with blindsight cannot see but can move through the environment easily, avoiding obstacles. Achromatopsia (inability to see color) is associated with damage to V4, and akinetopsia (inability to see color) is associated with damage to V5. Damage to the inferior temporal cortex can produce visual agnosia, whereas damage to the posterior parietal lobe results in an inability to accurately locate and reach for objects in the environment.

Auditory Processing

▶ Auditory perceptual processing also takes place along "What" and "Where" streams that end in the prefrontal cortex. The auditory "What" stream begins in the rostral part of the primary auditory cortex in the temporal lobe and ends in the ventrolateral prefrontal cortex. The auditory "Where" stream begins in the caudal part of the primary auditory cortex and ends in the dorsolateral prefrontal cortex.

▶ A variety of different sounds, including pure tones, complex sounds, speech, and music, are processed in the primary auditory cortex and adjacent areas. The secondary auditory cortex is activated by complex sounds but not by pure tones.

▶ Spoken language is comprised of phonemes (the basic units of language) that are combined to form meaningful units of sounds called morphemes.

▶ Damage to Broca's area causes a number of expressive aphasias, including Broca's (or verbal) aphasia. Anomia is the inability to name familiar objects.

▶ Damage to Wernicke's area produces receptive aphasia. Paraphasia involves the substitution of one phoneme for another.

▶ Damage to the arcuate fasciculus produces a disorder called conduction aphasia.

▶ The most common disorder following damage to the cerebellum is dysarthria.

▶ When deaf individuals are exposed to their native language (American Sign Language or English), both Broca's area and Wernicke's area become activated in the left hemisphere.

▶ PET scans of stutterers show overactivation of the right hemisphere and cerebellum when they are stuttering.

▶ For nonmusicians, melody is processed in the right hemisphere and rhythm is processed in the left, whereas musicians tend to use the left hemisphere exclusively when playing or listening to music. Impairments in music perception are referred to as amusia.

Somatosensory Processing

▶ Information for somatosensory processing is relayed to the primary somatosensory cortex in the parietal lobe.

▶ Somatosensory information may also be processed along "What" and "Where" streams in the secondary somatosensory cortex. The somatosensory "What" system involves the inferior parietal cortex. Damage to this area results in tactile agnosia, a disorder in which a person cannot identify objects by their touch. The somatosensory "Where" system involves the posterior parietal lobe, an area also involved in processing visual "Where" information.

▶ The gate-control theory of pain has been proposed to explain how we respond to and control the response to painful stimuli. Axons from the periaqueductal gray and the periventricular gray areas release pain-inhibiting neurotransmitters in the substantia gelatinosa. These neurotransmitters are of two types: endorphins (endogenous opiate transmitters) and nonopiate transmitters. They reduce pain sensations by inhibiting the release of substance P.

▶ Treatments for pain appear to activate the endorphin or the nonopiate pain-inhibitory systems or both. Treatments for pain include drugs, counterirritation, acupuncture, transcutaneous electrical nerve stimulation, and hypnosis.

▶ The sensory-discriminative component of pain perception is processed in the secondary somatosensory cortex, the motivational-affective component is processed in the anterior cingulate cortex of the frontal lobe, and the cognitive-evaluative component is processed in the prefrontal cortex and the insula.

Olfactory and Taste Processing

▶ Perceptual processing of olfactory and taste stimuli is not well understood.

▶ Unlike the other perceptual systems discussed in this chapter, the olfactory and taste systems do not appear to separate into functional "What" and "Where" streams.

▶ The primary olfactory cortex is located in the piriform cortex in the temporal lobe and an adjacent area of the frontal cortex. The secondary olfactory cortex is in the orbito-frontal prefrontal cortex, located directly behind the eyeball sockets.

▶ Women consistently perform better than men in tests of odor detection and identification.

▶ The primary taste cortex is located in the insula in the frontal lobe.

Key Terms

achromatopsia (p. 222)
akinetopsia (p. 223)
allodynia (p. 240)
American Sign Language (p. 226)
amusia (p. 233)
analgesia (p. 237)
anencephalic (p. 243)
angular gyrus (p. 230)
anomia (p. 227)
anterior cingulate cortex (p. 239)
arcuate fasciculus (p. 228)
area V1 (p. 216)
auditory "What" stream (p. 225)
auditory "Where" stream (p. 225)
blindness (p. 221)
blindsight (p. 221)
Broca's aphasia (p. 227)
Broca's area (p. 226)
Brodmann's classification system (p. 214)
conduction aphasia (p. 228)
dorsal stream (p. 216)
dorsolateral prefrontal cortex (p. 225)

dysarthria (p. 229)
endorphins (p. 237)
expressive aphasia (p. 226)
Gate-Control Theory of Pain (p. 236)
grammar (p. 226)
hemianopia (p. 221)
insula (p. 242)
language (p. 226)
magnocellular (p. 216)
morphemes (p. 226)
nonopiate transmitters (p. 237)
parvocellular (p. 216)
perception (p. 213)
periaqueductal gray (p. 236)
periventricular gray (p. 236)
phonemes (p. 226)
piriform cortex (p. 241)
primary auditory cortex (p. 225)
primary olfactory cortex (p. 241)
primary somatosensory cortex (p. 234)
primary taste cortex (p. 242)
prosopagnosia (p. 223)

pure alexia (p. 223)
pyramidal cells (p. 214)
receptive aphasia (p. 228)
scotoma (p. 221)
secondary auditory cortex (p. 225)
secondary olfactory cortex (p. 241)
secondary somatosensory cortex (p. 234)
stellate cells (p. 214)
stuttering (p. 231)
substance P (p. 236)
substantia gelatinosa (p. 236)
tactile agnosia (p. 235)
ventral stream (p. 216)
ventrolateral prefrontal cortex (p. 225)
visual agnosia (p. 223)
visual extinction (p. 223)
visual "What" system (p. 216)
visual "Where" system (p. 216)
Wernicke's area (p. 228)

Questions for Thought

1. Imagine what it would be like if you suffered damage to your "What" visual system. How would damage to the "What" visual system differ from damage to the "What" auditory stream?

2. Do brain-imaging studies indicate any similarity between spoken language and American Sign Language?

3. Why do some forms of pain control work better than other forms?

4. Can you explain why women generally have a better sense of smell than men?

Questions for Review

1. What is the difference between blindness and blindsight?

2. Describe the pathway from the outer ear to the primary auditory cortex.

3. What kinds of information are processed in the primary somatosensory cortex? What about the secondary somatosensory cortex?

4. Which brain areas have been implicated in the perception of smell and taste?

Suggested Readings

Crick, F. (1994). *The astonishing hypothesis: The scientific search for the soul.* New York: Scribner.

Lappin, J. S., & Craft, W. D. (2000). Foundations of spatial vision: From retinal images to perceived shapes. *Psychological Review, 107,* 6–38.

Logothetis, N. K. (1999). Vision: A window on consciousness. *Scientific American, 28,* 69–75.

Neville, H. J., Bavelier, D., Corina, D., Rauschecker, J., Karni, A., Lalwani, A., Braun, A., Clark, V., Jezzard, P., & Turner, R. (1998). Cerebral organization for language in deaf and hearing subjects: Biological constraints and effects of experience. *Proceedings of the National Academy of Sciences, 95,* 922–929.

Stern, P., & Marx, J. (1999). Making sense of scents (special section on olfaction). *Science, 286,* 703–728.

Web Resources

For a chapter tutorial quiz, direct links to the Internet sites listed below and other features, visit the book-specific website at **www.wadsworth.com/product/ 0155074865**. You may also connect directly to the following annotated websites:

http://dragon.uml.edu/psych/illusion.html
Check out over 20 different optical illusions that demonstrate characteristics of our sensory and perceptual systems.

http://www.aphasia.org/NAAfactsheet.html
For more information about aphasias visit this detailed fact sheet.

http://thalamus.wustl.edu/course/bassens.html
This highly detailed site follows the basic somatosensory pathways using actual photographs of the cerebral cortex, the midbrain and pons through to the lumbar section of the spinal cord.

For additional readings and information, check out InfoTrac College Edition at **http://www.infotrac-college.com/wadsworth**. Choose a search term yourself or enter the following search terms: analgesia, articulation disorders, blindness, Broca's area, and stuttering.

CD-ROM: Exploring Biological Psychology

Animation: Visual Pathways
Video: Hearing Loss
Interactive Recaps

Chapter 8 Quiz
Connect to the Interactive Biological Psychology Glossary

9

Cognitive Processes

Ken wanted to become a member of Mensa, an organization that strictly limits its membership to people who have an extremely high IQ (intelligence quotient, a measure of intelligence), in the top 2% of the population. To join Mensa, Ken had two options: he could take a standardized intelligence test that was administered by a licensed psychologist, or he could go to a regional Mensa office and take the Mensa test. Being a typical college student, Ken could not afford to go to a psychologist for an intelligence test. Instead, he made an appointment to take a Mensa test in a nearby city. When he sat down to take the Mensa test, he was surprised by the questions. He was expecting questions that tested his knowledge base, like the questions asked on popular TV game shows. However, the questions on the Mensa test were little puzzles, requiring him to solve word games or to complete a complicated series of numbers. Some questions asked him to analyze patterns in pictures, like the example in Figure 9.1.

Try to solve the puzzle in Figure 9.1. Now think about the process that you used to solve the puzzle. You probably examined each individual domino carefully, and then tried to figure out a pattern in the dots. To do this, you had to hold certain dot patterns in your memory while you manipulated others. You probably tried arithmetic functions, like addition, subtraction, and multiplication, to arrive at the correct solution. Highly intelligent people can perform these problem-solving tasks easily.

To solve this puzzle, you made use of cognitive processes, such as thinking, memory, and attention. We will explore the nature of cognitive processes in this chapter, focusing on current research in cognitive neuroscience. Cognitive

Figure 9.1 Domino puzzle
To solve this puzzle, you must hold numbers in your memory while you make comparisons between them.

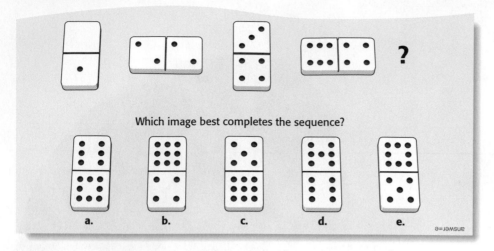

Which image best completes the sequence?

a.   b.   c.   d.   e.

answer=e

psychologists study how we acquire, process, store, retrieve, and use information. Cognitive neuroscientists relate these processes to brain structure and function.

Much of the research that I presented in Chapter 8 was conducted by cognitive neuroscientists. In fact, many psychologists consider perception to be just one of many cognitive functions. I chose to separate visual and other types of sensory perception from the material in Chapter 9 because I wanted to emphasize the role of the primary sensory cortex in *receiving* information from receptors and then *relaying* that information to other centers in the cortex for further processing. In this chapter, our discussion begins with processing centers beyond the primary sensory cortex. We will take an in-depth look at three cognitive processes: memory, attention, and learning. As you will soon learn, many of the processing centers concerned with cognition are located in the frontal lobe. Therefore, let's start our discussion of cognitive processes by examining the organization of the frontal cortex.

The Frontal Lobe's Role in Cognition

The frontal lobe is the largest brain structure, comprising about one-third of the entire brain. It is usually divided into three functional zones: the **prefrontal cortex,** the **premotor cortex,** and the **motor cortex** (or *precentral gyrus*). Of these three zones, the prefrontal cortex is the largest (Figure 9.2). Lesioning and recording studies of monkey brains, as well as functional brain-imaging research with human subjects, have indicated that the prefrontal cortex plays an important role in cognitive functions. The premotor cortex and motor cortex, on the other hand, are involved in planning, organizing, and integrating fine movements of the head, trunk, and limbs.

The prefrontal cortex can be roughly divided into three regions: *dorsolateral, medial,* and *orbitofrontal.* The dorsolateral region comprises the most superior and lateral aspects of the prefrontal cortex. The medial region contains the midline structures of the prefrontal cortex, such as the anterior cingulate cortex, which you

prefrontal cortex: most anterior region of the frontal lobe, composed of three divisions: dorsolateral, medial, orbitofrontal

premotor cortex: an area of the frontal lobe anterior to the motor cortex that processes information about intended movements and sends that information to the motor cortex

motor cortex: located in the precentral gyrus, directs fine motor coordination

Figure 9.2 The organization of the frontal lobe

The frontal lobe has three functional zones: the prefrontal cortex, the premotor cortex, and the motor cortex.

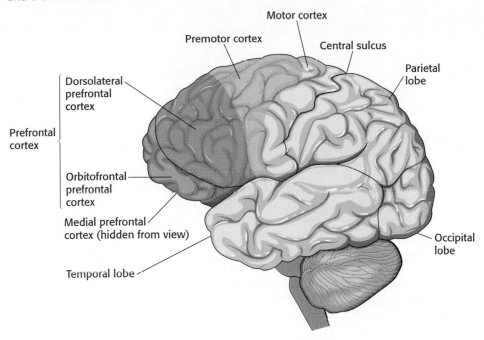

learned about in Chapter 8. The orbitofrontal region is the most anterior region of the prefrontal cortex, including areas located around the eye sockets.

Recall from Chapter 8 that Brodmann (1908) divided the cerebral cortex into 50 or so areas based on their microscopic anatomical differences. Figure 8.2 shows the organization of the cortex according to Brodmann's scheme. You can see in this figure that the premotor cortex and the motor cortex each comprise one entire area. (Brodmann's area 4 is the motor cortex, and area 6 is the premotor cortex.) In contrast, the prefrontal cortex is composed of over 10 Brodmann areas, each having a different microscopic appearance and presumably different function. Ongoing research is attempting to discover the role of each of the areas in the prefrontal cortex.

Think of all the discoveries that have come about since the invention of the telescope and the microscope. For cognitive neuroscientists, modern imaging techniques, such as PET and functional MRI, are producing the same sorts of astounding discoveries that telescopes have provided for astronomers and microscopes for biologists. Before the development of these imaging techniques, cognitive neuroscientists were limited to studying the effects of lesions on cognitive activity in monkeys and to single-cell recording in monkey brains. Because monkeys do not use language and arithmetic functions to the extent that people do, experiments using monkeys were restricted to studying memory, attention, and decision making. Research with human subjects, using EEG recordings, was conducted, but EEG recordings are not accurate in localizing a function to a precise area of the cortex, as you learned in Chapter 5. The development of noninvasive brain-imaging techniques, like PET and functional MRI, has permitted cognitive neuroscientists to identify cortical structures involved in complex cognitive processes in human subjects (Posner, 1993). Brain-imaging studies have allowed investigators to confirm the findings of earlier experiments with monkeys and case studies of humans with brain damage. Our understanding of the brain processes underlying memory has especially benefited from the availability of brain-imaging technology.

The largest structure in the brain is the (a)_____ _____. It is divided into three functional zones: the (b)_____ cortex, the (c)_____ cortex, and the motor cortex. The prefrontal cortex plays an important role in cognitive functions and can be further divided into three regions: (d)_____, medial, and (e)_____.

Biological Basis of Memory

The concepts of **long-term memory** and **short-term memory** have been with us since the time of the famous American psychologist William James (1890). Short-term memory has been conceptualized as a limited memory system capable of holding around seven pieces of information at any one time (Miller, 1956). Information in short-term memory remains there for about 30 seconds before decaying, unless it is held there for longer periods through rehearsal. Donald Hebb (1949) postulated that short-term memory is produced by *reverberating neural circuits* in the frontal lobes. A process called **consolidation** was proposed by Hebb to describe the shift of information from short-term memory to long-term memory. In long-term memory, huge amounts of information are held indefinitely, for long periods of time. According to Hebb (1949), long-term memory is the result of *structural changes* within neural memory circuits.

There is ample evidence that two such systems of memory, long-term and short-term, exist. Patients with impairment of long-term memory often have intact short-term memory processes (Baddeley & Warrington, 1973; Milner, 1971). For example, a patient who is unable to remember past events will have no difficulty recalling short spans of numbers (digit spans) immediately after they are presented.

The concept of consolidation, however, was called into question by Warrington and Shallice (1969) following their intensive study of a patient (K. F.) who suffered brain damage in a motorcycle accident. K. F. had virtually no ability to recall digit spans after they were presented, indicating a short-term memory deficit, but could learn lists of paired words. Somehow, K. F. was able to put items into long-term memory (such as the lists of paired words) even though his short-term memory was impaired. Shallice and Warrington (1970) reasoned that information does not have to go through short-term memory to get to long-term memory.

Today, because our concept of short-term memory has evolved, we are able to explain the case of K. F. without discarding the concept of consolidation (Squire, Knowlton, & Musen, 1993). Research with monkeys and people has demonstrated that short-term memory is not just one temporary storage facility but rather is composed of many different temporary processes functioning at different sites in the cortex (Baddeley & Hitch, 2000; Courtney, 1996; Goldman-Rakic, 1987; Smith, Jonides, & Koeppe, 1996). That is, short-term memory appears to consist of several storage depots, one for *memories of objects*, one for *spatial memories*, and another for *verbal memories*, which are linked by a central executive system that coordinates all of the stored information (Smith & Jonides, 1998). In fact, the concept of short-term memory has now been discarded in a favor of a new concept, **working memory.**

Working Memory

Baddeley and Hitch introduced the concept of working memory in 1974. They conceptualized working memory as a series of different operations carried out at different sites in the cortex, coordinated by a central executive system. Working memory permits you to add numbers in your head, to read, and to solve problems

long-term memory: a memory system in which large amounts of information are stored indefinitely

short-term memory: a memory system in which limited amounts of information are stored briefly

consolidation: a process in which memories are transferred from short-term memory to long-term memory

working memory: a series of operations carried out at different sites in the cerebral cortex

Intelligence and Working Memory

The capacity of a person's working memory has been linked to two measures of intelligence: language comprehension and pattern reasoning. Meredyth Daneman and Patricia Carpenter (1980) measured the capacity of verbal working memory by having college students read or listen to a group of unrelated sentences and remember the last word in each sentence. Students who recalled the most words (and therefore had the largest working-memory capacities) also scored highest on the verbal SAT. Thus, the size of working-memory capacity is highly correlated with language-comprehension ability. This finding was confirmed in another study conducted by Daneman and her colleague Philip Merikle (1996), who combined the data from 77 previously published studies involving over 6,000 participants and reanalyzed them.

Pattern reasoning is another dimension of intelligence that is measured on standard IQ tests. One such test is *Raven's Progressive Matrices*, in which the person being tested must figure out the pattern in a series of stimuli. An example is shown in Figure 9.3. In this example, only one answer correctly completes the matrix. (Can you figure out which is the correct answer?) This is a relatively easy matrix. The more difficult ones require that you juggle many rules in your mind at once. Carpenter and her colleagues Marcel Just and Peter Shell (1990) found that students who score highest on these types of intelligence tests can hold the most concepts in their working memory.

Figure 9.3
In the Raven's matrices test, the individual must select the diagram that best completes the matrix.

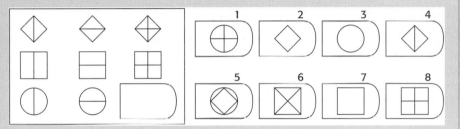

like the one at the beginning of the chapter. Different bits of information are stored temporarily in various sites and processed there. The ability to think and reason involves working memory. In fact, a person's intelligence may be linked to the capacity of his or her working memory (see *For Further Thought*).

The evidence for different working memory sites is quite convincing. Research with monkeys by Patricia Goldman-Rakic and her colleagues (Wilson, O'Scalaidhe, & Goldman-Rakic, 1993) at Yale University demonstrated that one area of the prefrontal cortex is associated with working memory for objects and that another prefrontal area is involved in working memory for spatial locations. Goldman-Rakic and her colleagues recorded neural activity in the *ventral* region of the prefrontal cortex of two monkeys trained to perform delayed-response tasks. The monkeys were exposed to two types of delayed-response trials. On *spatial* delayed-response trials, visual stimuli were flashed on the left or right side of a screen, while the monkey's gaze was fixed on a fixation point in the center of the screen. After a 2.5-second delay, the fixation point faded away, and the monkey moved its eyes in the direction of the remembered location of the stimulus. On *pattern* delayed-response trials, monkeys were presented with one of two stimulus patterns. After a delay of 2.5 seconds, a monkey was required to move its eyes to the left for one stimulus pattern or to the right for the other pattern. In other words, the monkeys responded to the *location* of the stimulus in the spatial delayed-response trials and to the *stimulus pattern* in the pattern delayed-response trials.

Goldman-Rakic and her colleagues found that neurons in the *ventral prefrontal cortex* responded vigorously during the pattern delayed-response trials (Wilson, O'Scalaidhe, & Goldman-Rakic, 1993). Only 3% of neurons studied in the ventral prefrontal cortex responded to the location of the stimulus. Some neurons in the pattern delayed-response trials were highly responsive to one stimulus pattern, and other neurons responded strongly to the other pattern. These investigators compared their results with earlier findings by Goldman-Rakic (1987), in which she demonstrated that neurons in the *dorsolateral prefrontal* area are specialized to respond to the location of stimuli.

PET studies of humans have revealed that the human brain has specific sites in the prefrontal cortex for object, location, and verbal working memories (Courtney, Ungerleider, Keil, & Haxby, 1996; D'Esposito et al., 1998). Furthermore, John Jonides and his colleagues at the University of Michigan (Smith, Jonides, & Koeppe, 1996) found that activation in the *right* prefrontal cortex occurred when human subjects recalled the spatial location of dots and that activation of the *left* prefrontal cortex occurred when the subjects recalled the *identity* of letters. In their study, human participants were required to retain for 3 seconds either four letters (using *verbal memory*) or the position of three dots (*spatial memory*). Using PET imaging, the investigators demonstrated a striking *double dissociation* (Chapter 5): The *verbal* task activated regions in the *left hemisphere*, and the *spatial* task activated only regions in the *right hemisphere*.

Let's examine the circuits responsible for object, location, and verbal working memories, as well as the central executive system that coordinates the activities of the different working memories.

Working Memory for Object Identification

The working memory for object identification allows an individual to hold an object or series of objects in mind. This operation permits us to make comparisons and matches with objects in working memory and to put a series of objects in order. For example, face recognition is accomplished by this working memory. Functional MRI and PET scans of monkeys and people engaged in tasks that utilize the working memory for object identification indicate that the *inferior temporal cortex* and the *prefrontal cortex* are involved. In Chapter 8, you learned about the inferior temporal cortex and its role in visual object recognition. Working memory for object identification somehow connects the workings of the inferior temporal lobe with storage centers in the prefrontal cortex (Brewer et al., 1998; Miller, Erickson, & Desimone, 1996; Jiang et al., 2000; Miller, Li, & Desimone, 1991).

Working Memory for Spatial Location

Recalling the locations of objects and storing information about these locations briefly are the tasks of the working memory for spatial location. This working memory is especially important if you are engaged in an activity that requires that you know the location of several items at once, as when you are playing chess. Functional brain-imaging studies and single-cell recordings from monkey brains have revealed that areas in the right hemisphere, including the *posterior parietal cortex*, the *right hippocampus*, the *premotor cortex*, and the *dorsolateral prefrontal cortex*, are activated when this working memory is used (Courtney et al., 1998; Jonides et al., 1993; Maguire et al., 1998; Steinmetz & Constantinidis, 1997; Di Pellegrino & Wise, 1993; Zironi et al., 2001).

Working Memory for Verbal Information

Mental operations involving words are executed by the working memory for verbal information. Figure 9.4 illustrates the cortical areas that are activated when a person thinks of uses for nouns that are presented visually on a screen while the person lies in the scanner (Posner, 1993). As you can see, *Broca's area* and *Wernicke's area* (the classic speech centers in the left hemisphere that you learned about in Chapter 8) are activated when a person is using the working memory for verbal information. In addition, the *anterior cingulate cortex*, which is located in the medial aspect of the prefrontal cortex, is activated when this working memory is used. Other studies employing different verbal tasks have shown that the left *premotor cortex* is also activated when the working memory for verbal information is functioning, indicating that human subjects are rehearsing the verbal material sub-

Figure 9.4 PET scan of activated brain areas with working memory for verbal information
This PET scan shows the cortical areas that are activated when a person thinks of uses for nouns. "Naive" refers to scans made when the person is first given a list. "Practiced" refers to scans made after the person is familiar with the list. "Novel" refers to scans made when the person is given a new (second) list of words. Broca's and Wernicke's areas, as well as the anterior cingulate cortex, are activated when a person is using working memory for verbal information.

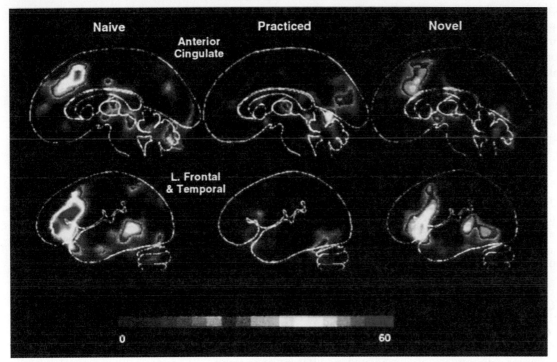

vocally (Smith & Jonides, 1999). Table 9.1 summarizes the differences among object, location, and verbal working memories.

The Central Executive System

Studies of brain-injured individuals have shown that working memory has two components: (1) the individual short-term storage systems described in the previous sections and (2) an executive system that coordinates and directs the operations of the working memory. That is, some patients have intact temporary storage mechanisms but impaired executive processes, whereas others have impaired short-term

Table 9.1

Comparison of Object, Location, and Verbal Working Memory

| | Type of Working Memory | | |
	Object Identification	Spatial Location	Verbal Information
Functions performed	briefly store one or more objects, make comparisons and matches, put series of objects in order	recall location of objects, briefly store information about location of an object	mental operations involving words (for example, thinking of uses of a word or spelling a word)
Brain areas involved	inferior temporal cortex, prefrontal cortex	posterior parietal cortex, right hippocampus, premotor cortex, dorsolateral prefrontal cortex	Broca's area, Wernicke's area, anterior cingulate cortex, left premotor cortex

storage but intact executive functions (D'Esposito & Postle, 1999). For example, individuals with damage to the prefrontal cortex that results in **frontal lobe syndrome** have severe impairment of the executive operations of working memory (Hernandez et al., 2002). They have difficulty organizing and planning tasks, and they have attention deficits, being easily distracted or unable to switch their attention from one task to another. On the other hand, the short-term storage systems of patients with frontal lobe syndrome are typically unimpaired.

The executive operations of working memory include attending to relevant stimuli and ignoring irrelevant ones, managing and planning tasks, and monitoring data in short-term storage (Smith & Jonides, 1999). Although research in this area is still in its earliest phase, we know that these executive operations are associated with particular areas of the prefrontal cortex.

For example, the **anterior cingulate cortex** is activated whenever any type of working memory is used (Corbetta et al., 1991; Posner, 1993). The functioning of the anterior cingulate cortex does not seem to be restricted to any modality (visual, spatial, or verbal) and appears to play a role in attention, which we will examine later in this chapter. Smith and Jonides (1999) have suggested that the anterior cingulate cortex may also be involved in resolving conflicts when an individual is required to choose between competing stimuli or responses. Other areas of the left prefrontal cortex, however, are also activated when there is cognitive conflict. Another executive operation, task management, appears to involve the anterior cingulate cortex, as well as Brodmann's area 46, which is part of the dorsolateral prefrontal cortex (D'Esposito et al., 1997; Quintana & Fuster, 1999; Smith & Jonides, 1999).

Long-Term Memory

Like the concept of short-term memory, the concept of long-term memory has evolved since the time of William James. Today, we think of long-term memory as comprised of several different components, each mediated by different brain structures. The two main components of long-term memory are **declarative memory** (also called *explicit memory*) and **nondeclarative memory** (also called *implicit memory* or *procedural memory*). Declarative memory involves the conscious retention of facts and events, as when you remember the name of your kindergarten teacher or recall that two plus two equals four. In contrast, nondeclarative memory refers to nonconscious memory for learned behaviors. For example, when you learn to ride a bicycle, you cannot say exactly what you have learned because this information is stored in nondeclarative memory. Declarative memory is formed quickly, can be accessed by any of the processing channels of working memory, and is subject to error or forgetting. On the other hand, nondeclarative memory develops slowly over time, can be accessed only by the brain system in which the learning originally occurred, and is reliable (not typically subject to error).

Studies of brain-injured individuals have provided convincing support that two distinct long-term memory systems exist. People with impaired declarative memory, who cannot recall events from the past or who consistently fail standard memory tests in the laboratory, will often have intact nondeclarative memory. For example, an individual might not remember taking piano lessons but can play the piano beautifully. Further examination of these brain-injured patients has indicated that different brain systems are involved in declarative and nondeclarative memory. Let's explore these two types of long-term memory more closely.

Declarative Memory

The ability to consciously recall facts and events appears to require an intact **hippocampus.** Recall from Chapter 4 that the hippocampus is located deep within the medial temporal lobe (Figure 9.5). Individuals with damage to the hippocampus show symptoms of **amnesia,** or loss of declarative memory. At present, most investigators believe that information in temporary storage in working memory is transferred to long-term, declarative memory by way of a *consolidation process* that takes place in the *hippocampus*. Damage to the hippocampus appears to disrupt that

frontal lobe syndrome: a disorder caused by damage to the prefrontal cortex, characterized by impairment in attention and in organizing and planning tasks

anterior cingulate cortex: an area of the prefrontal cortex that appears to be part of the central executive system that coordinates working memory, especially attentional processes

declarative memory: explicit memory, or the conscious retention of facts and events
nondeclarative memory: implicit memory, or nonconscious memory for learned behaviors

hippocampus: limbic system structure that plays a role in emotions and memory
amnesia: loss of declarative memory

process, interfering with the formation and retrieval of declarative memory.

The extent of hippocampal damage will influence the type of amnesia produced. **Retrograde amnesia,** for example, is a loss of declarative memory from some point in time backward. That is, a person with retrograde amnesia will not remember certain events that occurred before he or she suffered brain injury. Some people have loss of memory for a few hours before the brain injury, others have loss of memory for 1 to 2 years, and still others have loss of memory for several decades or all of their adult lives (Squire et al., 1993; Zola-Morgan et al., 1986). Damage to a limited area of the hippocampus or minimal damage is associated with shorter periods of memory loss.

Another memory disorder, called **anterograde amnesia** or *global amnesia*, results from bilateral damage to the hippocampus. One well-studied case is a patient known as H. M., who developed anterograde amnesia following surgical removal of the hippocampus on the left and right sides of his brain. (This surgery was performed on H. M. to relieve recurrent, incapacitating bouts of epileptic seizures.) Following the surgery, H. M. showed the classic symptom of anterograde amnesia: an inability to form new declarative memories. Although he could recall memories from his youth, H. M. could not remember anything that happened since his surgery (James & MacKay, 2001; Milner, 1966; Sagar et al., 1985; Spiers, Maguire, & Burgess, 2001). He continually lost his way around the hospital following the surgery, and, when his parents moved to a new location, he could not remember how to get to their new house. Anterograde amnesia has also been produced as a result of bilateral hippocampal destruction by *viral encephalitis*, which you learned about in Chapter 2.

However, the hippocampus and medial temporal lobe are not the sites of long-term storage. Experiments with monkeys and rodents have demonstrated that, if hippocampal damage occurs at a time long after learning has taken place, the damage has no effect on memory for the learned event (Squire et al., 1993; Zola-Morgan & Squire, 1990). This means that the hippocampus must be working at the time of learning, but it is not necessary for the retrieval of stored memories. In the first stage of consolidation, as functional MRI studies have shown, the hippocampus binds together information from all the various sites active in the cerebral cortex at the time of learning (Fernandez et al., 1999; Naya, Yoshida, & Miyashita, 2001; Rugg, 1998). At first, immediately after learning has occurred, the hippocampus stores the entire memory and can readily retrieve it. But, over a period of weeks and months, the cerebral cortex takes over the storage and retrieval of the memory (McClelland, McNaughton, & O'Reilly, 1995). This consolidation process can take a relatively long time, which explains why damage to the hippocampus can result in the retrieval problems observed in retrograde amnesia. After long-term memory is stored in the cerebral cortex, memory retrieval is performed by the prefrontal cortex (Hasegawa, Fukushima, Ihara, & Miyashita, 1998). Figure 9.6 illustrates the phases of memory consolidation, from short-term memory to long-term memory. Memory encoding takes place primarily in the hippocampus, and declarative memory retrieval takes place in the prefrontal cortex (Markowitsch, 1995).

Declarative memory has two forms: **episodic memory** and **semantic memory.** Episodic memory is the memory for the events in one's own life, whereas semantic memory is general knowledge, such as knowing the multiplication tables or state capitals (Tulving, 1989). With both episodic memory and semantic memory, we are aware when we are

Figure 9.5 The hippocampus
The hippocampus is located deep within the medial temporal lobe.

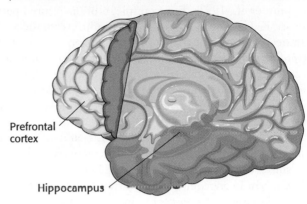

Prefrontal cortex

Hippocampus

retrograde amnesia: loss of declarative memory from some point in time backward

anterograde amnesia: global amnesia, an inability to form new declarative memories

episodic memory: memory for events in one's own life
semantic memory: memory for general knowledge

Figure 9.6 Phases of memory consolidation

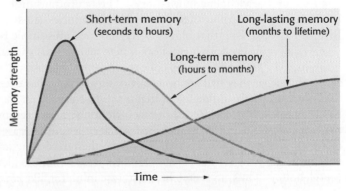

Memory strength

Short-term memory (seconds to hours)

Long-term memory (hours to months)

Long-lasting memory (months to lifetime)

Time

trying to retrieve information from storage. Individuals with retrograde amnesia show greater impairment of episodic memory than semantic memory, although the reason for this difference is unclear (Squire et al., 1993). For example, a brain-injured patient, referred to as "K. C." in the literature, has both retrograde and anterograde amnesia and cannot remember any personal events in his entire life (*episodic memory*), either before or after the motorcycle accident that caused his head injury (Figure 9.7). However, his knowledge of history, geography, music, and politics is intact (*semantic memory*). Thus, K. C. has unimpaired semantic memory and essentially nonfunctional episodic memory.

Brain-imaging studies using PET and SPECT have demonstrated that the retrieval of semantic memory and episodic memory is subserved by different cerebral hemispheres. That is, the *left hemisphere* is engaged in the retrieval of *semantic memory*, and the *right hemisphere* is engaged in the retrieval of *episodic memory* (Markowitsch, 1995; Markowitsch et al., 1997).

Figure 9.7 The patient, K.C.
K.C. has no episodic memory, but his semantic memory is intact. In this photograph, he is shown playing chess, although he can't remember learning to play chess or playing chess before.

The Effects of Emotion on the Consolidation of Long-Term Memory

You've probably noticed that you remember well experiences that occurred when you were emotionally aroused. For example, you might easily recall a particular time when your roommate made you angry or when you experienced a very embarrassing moment. There is a very good biological explanation for why memories for emotional experiences are quite strong. As you will learn in Chapters 13 and 14, when you are feeling emotionally aroused or stressed, the hormones *epinephrine* and *cortisol* are released. These hormones enhance consolidation processes by activating the amygdala (Gold & McCarty, 1995; McGaugh, 2000). Lesioning studies involving rat subjects indicate that the amygdala plays a vital role in memory by enhancing consolidation in the hippocampus.

Research with human subjects has revealed that drugs that block the effects of epinephrine interfere with memory formation, whereas drugs that increase adrenergic activity improve memory (Cahill et al., 1994; Soetens et al., 1995; van Stegeren et al., 1998). PET studies have confirmed the role of the amygdala in memory consolidation (Cahill et al., 1996; Hamann et al., 1999). For example, *increased activation of the amygdala* in PET scans during learning is related to *enhanced long-term memory*.

A number of investigators have speculated that epinephrine and cortisol enhance memory by increasing glucose availability in the brain (Gold & McCarty, 1995; McGaugh, 2000). Both epinephrine and cortisol have gluconeogenic properties [*gluco-* = glucose; *-neo-* = new; *-genic* = creation, Latin]. That is, both hormones promote glucose production, and glucose is believed to facilitate memory formation. You might have read or heard that a natural herb called *ginkgo biloba* has been shown to enhance memory. At present, the results of studies of this herb are mixed. However, if the claims about ginkgo biloba prove to be true, ginkgo biloba most likely enhances memory by increasing blood flow to (and, thus, glucose availability in) the brain (Gajewski & Hensch, 1999).

The Role of Acetylcholine in Memory The neurotransmitter *acetylcholine* appears to be necessary in forming new declarative memories (Rosenzweig, 1996; Sarter & Bruno, 1997). A drug that blocks acetylcholine's muscarinic receptors, such as *scopolamine*, will interfere with formation of new memories (Gruber, Stone, & Reed, 1967; Hasselmo, 1999). For example, college students administered scopolamine could not remember what they had for breakfast or any of the other events that occurred while they were under the influence of that drug. In contrast, an *acetylcholinesterase inhibitor* has the opposite effect. Recall that acetylcholinesterase removes acetylcholine from the synapse, reducing its availability. An acetylcholinesterase inhibitor reverses the effect of acetylcholinesterase. If acetylcholinesterase functions to decrease acetylcholine at the synapse, then acetylcholinesterase inhibitors increase the availability of acetylcholine. Thus, an acetylcholinesterase inhibitor, like *physostigmine*, will improve memory formation (Furey, Pietrini, & Haxby, 2000). A decrease in acetylcholine has been associated with memory disorders, such as Alzheimer's disease (Everitt & Robbins, 1997).

Nondeclarative Memory

Nondeclarative memory refers to an unrelated collection of learned behaviors that are acquired slowly but that, once stored, can be retrieved reliably. They are grouped together under the name *nondeclarative memory* because each is accessed without conscious awareness. Examples of nondeclarative memory include skills, habits, conditioned responses, and priming.

Skills are procedures that are learned to accomplish a particular task. A skill, like riding a bike or driving a car, is acquired without conscious awareness of what has been learned. The same is true for the acquisition of *habits*, which are tendencies to behave in a certain way given a specific set of stimuli. For example, I have developed a bad habit of driving with the emergency brake of my car engaged. I don't know how this habit developed, but I find myself, several times a day, driving around town in my car with the emergency brake on. Because this habit is nonconscious, I typically don't notice that my emergency brake is on until I smell it burning.

For skills and habits (and, indeed, for all forms of nondeclarative memory), the brain structures involved do not include the hippocampus. This means that an intact hippocampus is not required for the acquisition of skills and habits. H. M., the man with bilateral lesions of the hippocampus, was able to acquire the skill of tracing a star while watching his hand in a mirror, but he could not form any new explicit memories. The acquisition of skills and habits involves the *cerebellum* and the pathway, called the **corticostriatal system,** that projects from the cerebral cortex to the *basal ganglia* (Gabrieli, 1998; Squire et al., 1993; Thach, 1998). Recall that Parkinson's disease is caused by disturbed function of the basal ganglia and the corticostriatal system. Individuals with Parkinson's disease often show impairment in acquiring cognitive skills but have unimpaired declarative memory (Saint-Cyr et al., 1988).

Reza Shadmehr and Henry Holcomb (1997) used PET scans to measure activity changes in human volunteers who learned a motor skill. When the participants were first learning the skill, the prefrontal cortex was most active (Figure 9.8). However, within 6 hours of acquiring the skill, the brain shifts control of this skill from the prefrontal cortex to the premotor cortex, the posterior parietal lobe, and the cerebellum. Thus, an established skill is stored in a stable form in more posterior parts of the brain. The premotor cortex appears to be involved in the retrieval of the learned skill, the parietal lobe integrates somatic and visual information, and the cerebellum executes the motor skill.

Classical conditioning, also known as *Pavlovian conditioning* in honor of its discoverer Ivan Pavlov, produces another form of nondeclarative memory, the *conditioned response.* Pavlovian conditioning makes use of an unconditioned or unlearned stimulus (US) that reflexively elicits an unconditioned response (UR). In his original paradigm, Pavlov presented powdered meat (the US) to a dog, eliciting drooling in the dog (the UR). Drooling is a reflexive response that dogs make to meat. This reflex is not learned but rather happens automatically. Pavlov then used a bell as a *conditioned stimulus* (CS). Keep in mind that dogs do not ordinarily drool to the sound of a bell. However, when the bell (CS) is paired repeatedly with the meat (US), over time the bell will come to elicit drooling (Figure 9.9).

Drooling in response to a bell is a conditioned, or learned, response (CR). After the dog has associated the presence of meat with the bell, the dog will reliably drool when it hears the bell. Research with rabbits that have acquired a conditioned eyeblink response indicates that classically conditioned responses are stored in the *cerebellum* (Krupa, Thompson, & Thompson, 1993; Thompson, 1986). Conditioned responses develop in people, too. One good example is *conditioned fear,* in which people come to associate previously benign stimuli with frightening ones. A person with an anxiety disorder known as *agoraphobia* [*agora-* = marketplace; *-phobia* = fear, Greek] might come to fear standing in line at the

corticostriatal system: pathway that projects from the cerebral cortex to the basal ganglia, which is involved in the formation of nondeclarative memories

classical conditioning: a form of implicit learning in which a conditioned stimulus is associated with an unconditioned stimulus and comes to produce a conditioned response, also known as Pavlovian conditioning

Figure 9.8 PET scans that show skill learning
(a) In learning a skill, the motor cortex and somatosensory cortex in the left hemisphere are active. (b) During early learning of a skill, the right prefrontal cortex is active. (Red and yellow indicate regions with the greatest activation.)

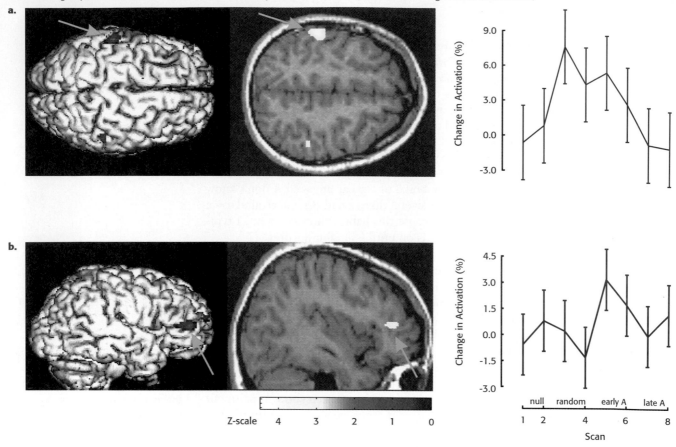

checkout counter in the grocery store. This fear develops without conscious awareness, and it is retrieved nonconsciously, so that the feeling of fear comes upon the person "from out of the blue." We will discuss conditioned fears in more detail in Chapters 13 and 14.

Priming has probably received more research than other forms of nondeclarative memory (Squire et al., 1993). It is an increase or improvement in the ability to recognize particular stimuli after previous experience with them (Figure 9.10). For example, in a word-stem completion task, an individual may be presented with a list of words (such as *garden, window, tennis*) and, at a later time, be asked to complete word stems like *gar-, tar-, sin-*. Typically, people can produce completions faster for fragments that they've seen before. (In this example, an individual would come up with *garden* faster than he or she would *single* because of previous exposure to the word *garden*.)

Priming occurs nonconsciously, outside of our awareness. Subjects in priming experiments are not permitted to rehearse the original list of stimuli, in order to keep the stimuli in working memory or transfer them to long-term storage. Thus, priming is a phenomenon that is distinct from declarative memory.

Figure 9.9 Pavlovian conditioning
In Pavlov's experiment, the sight of meat (US) caused salivation (UR) in a dog. When the sound of a bell (CR) is paired with meat (US), the bell (CS) will come to elicit salivation (CR).

Pavlov's experiment

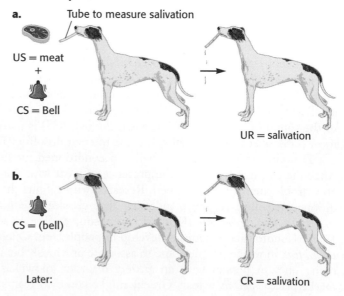

Figure 9.10 The priming effect
(a) The participant is first presented with a list of words. (b) The participant can then produce completions faster for fragments that they've seen before.

a. Time 1

b. Time 2

Patients with impaired declarative memory (either retrograde or anterograde amnesia) show normal priming effects (Cave & Squire, 1992; Cermak et al., 1985; Musen & Squire, 1992; Schacter & Buckner, 1998; Smith & Oscar-Berman, 1990). In addition, priming can last a long time, over a year in some cases following exposure to a list of compound words (Sloman et al., 1988). Keep in mind that priming can also occur with nonverbal stimuli, such as pictures of objects or nonsense drawings. PET research has indicated that priming is associated with areas in the *posterior parietal and occipital lobes* known to process *visual* information and the *left inferior frontal lobe (Broca's area)* to process *conceptual* information (Schacter & Buckner, 1998; Schacter et al. 1996; Squire et al., 1993).

Disorders of Memory

Amnesia

The most common form of memory disorder is amnesia, which affects declarative memory. Earlier in this section, you learned about retrograde and anterograde amnesia, the two most common forms of amnesia. Both of these disorders are caused by cerebral trauma or disease, like viral encephalitis. Often, people with amnesia will show retention for events that they deny remembering. It may be that, in amnesia, stored memories cannot be consciously accessed (Rugg, 1995).

Another type of amnesia is called **psychogenic amnesia,** which is typically caused by stress or psychological trauma. Individuals with psychogenic amnesia cannot retrieve information that is stored in long-term memory. The *Case Study* presents the cases of two patients with psychogenic amnesia. Both of these individuals could recall nothing about their past lives. That is, their *episodic memories* were impaired. PET scans of these patients indicated abnormal activity in the *right cerebral hemisphere*, which is believed to play an important role in the retrieval of episodic memory (Markowitsch et al., 1997; Yasuno et al., 2000).

Apraxia

Another disorder, **apraxia,** involves an inability to perform previously familiar movements with the hands, like brushing one's teeth or waving goodbye. Apraxia typically results from damage to left hemispheric areas, including the parietal lobe and prefrontal cortex. The *left hemisphere* appears to organize the movements of both hands because damage to the parietal cortex on the left side of the brain produces apraxia in both hands (Roy & Square, 1994). This disorder is not due to a

priming: an improvement in the ability to recognize particular stimuli following previous exposure to them

psychogenic amnesia: a memory disorder associated with stress or psychological trauma in which episodic memories cannot be retrieved

apraxia: a disorder caused by cerebral damage in which a person cannot organize movements into a productive sequence and can no longer perform previously familiar movements with the hands

Psychogenic Amnesia

Hans Markowitsch and his colleagues (1997) in Germany and Fumihiko Yasuno and his colleagues (2000) in Japan have studied memory retrieval processes in two patients with psychogenic amnesia. The German patient was a 30-year-old man, B. T., who could not remember any of his past. Just before losing his declarative memory, B. T. went to a bank and withdrew a large sum of money from his account. He was found penniless along a roadside in the Czech Republic, unable to remember his identity or anything about his past. B. T. was treated in a psychiatric clinic and diagnosed with psychogenic amnesia. Although his intelligence and short-term and nondeclarative memories were unimpaired, B. T. could not recall any autobiographical memories. After 6 months of treatment, he was able to answer some questions about his personal history correctly (for example, his date of birth), but he was uncertain whether his answers truly reflected his past (Markowitsch et al., 1997).

The Japanese patient examined by Yasuno and colleagues was a 33-year-old woman who, before the onset of psychogenic amnesia, had been overwhelmed with a number of financial and legal problems. In an unsuccessful suicide attempt, she took an overdose of sleeping pills.

When she regained consciousness in the hospital, she had lost all of her declarative memory, including her name. Neuropsychological testing showed that she had no other impairments except for an inability to recall autobiographical memories, including information about her family or her job history. A year later, she was able to answer correctly questions about her personal past, claiming that she had relearned all the facts of her past history. That is, she did not recover her episodic memory, but rather she relearned facts about her past (Yasuno et al., 2000).

In both of these cases, the patient had been troubled by severe financial and legal difficulties prior to the onset of psychogenic amnesia. This extreme stress somehow interfered with underlying brain mechanisms and resulted in an inability to retrieve personal, emotion-laden memories. (We will examine the effect of stress on memory in greater detail in Chapter 14.) PET scans of these patients revealed a functional abnormality in brain areas believed to be involved in the retrieval of episodic memory, including the hippocampus, the right temporal lobe, the anterior cingulate cortex, and the prefrontal cortex (Markowitsch et al., 1997; Yasuno et al., 2000).

---

motor dysfunction, however, or to an impairment in language comprehension or object recognition. Instead, apraxia seems to involve a failure of nondeclarative memory systems used to program specific hand movements or, more likely, to a failure of the executive system that integrates and coordinates these memory systems (Koski et al., 2002). Often, individuals with apraxia can imitate a hand gesture immediately following its demonstration (for example, combing one's hair or folding a sheet of paper), but they cannot perform the appropriate movements in response to a verbal command.

Alzheimer's Disease

Alzheimer's disease is a neurodegenerative disorder that is characterized by severe memory loss, deficits in reasoning, inappropriate emotional responses, and a general decline in intellectual and physical functioning that progresses to death. Of these symptoms, memory loss is often the first to be diagnosed and is the most prominent symptom in Alzheimer's disease (Butters, Delis, & Lucas, 1995). The types of memory loss found in Alzheimer's patients include anterograde amnesia for both episodic memory and semantic memory, as well as retrograde amnesia. Nearly 2% of the population in the United States has Alzheimer's, with most cases occurring in the elderly population. We will discuss the neuronal pathology and cause of Alzheimer's disease in Chapter 16. However, at this point, you should know that the brains of individuals with Alzheimer's disease have severely reduced levels of acetylcholine. Recall in our discussion of declarative memory that I stressed the importance of acetylcholine in memory processes. Drug therapies for Alzheimer's patients typically include a drug that increases acetylcholine levels or replaces acetylcholine in the brain, but these therapies have proven to produce variable results, especially in people with advanced Alzheimer's disease (Everitt & Robbins, 1997; Marin, Davis, & Speranza, 1997).

Alzheimer's disease: the most common form of senile dementia, whose symptoms include memory and related cognitive deficits, with a progressive decline in all intellectual and physical functions that leads to death

(a)_____-_____ memory is a limited memory system that can hold about seven pieces of information for approximately 30 seconds. Huge amounts of information are stored in (b)_____-_____memory for long periods of time. The transfer of information from short-term to long-term memory occurs in a process called (c)_____. The concept of (d)_____ memory has replaced that of short-term memory. (e)_____ memory consists of several storage depots: for object identification, for spatial location, for verbal information, and a central executive system. This central executive system is associated with particular areas of the prefrontal cortex, including the (f)_____ _____ cortex. The two main components of long-term memory are (g)_____ memory (which involves the conscious retention of facts and events) and (h)_____ (which involves nonconscious memory for learned behaviors). The (i)_____ plays an important role in the consolidation of long-term, declarative memories. Damage to the (j)_____ produces amnesia. Declarative memory has two forms: (k)_____ memory (the memory for the events in one's like) and (l)_____ memory (general knowledge). The (m)_____ plays an important role in memory by enhancing consolidation in the hippocampus. The hormones (n)_____ and (o)_____ enhance memory by increasing glucose availability in the brain. The neurotransmitter (p)_____ is important in forming new declarative memories. (q)_____ memory involves a collection of learned behaviors that are acquired slowly and are reliably retrieved, including skills, habits, conditioned responses, and priming. Disorders of memory include (r)_____ (with its three forms: anterograde, retrograde, and psychogenic), (s)_____ (an inability to use the hands to perform familiar movements), and (t)_____ disease (a neurodegenerative disorder of the elderly that severely affects memory).

Biological Basis of Attention

"Please pay attention!"

How often we've heard this phrase. But, what is attention? The concept of attention is quite complex and, for that reason, is difficult to study. **Attention** can refer to being alert, or to orienting to specific stimuli, or to one of the executive functions of working memory, which you learned about in the preceding section. In addition, attention can be affected by one's motivational level or emotional state. For example, students who want to do well in a class pay more attention to their professors in lectures than do their less-motivated classmates. Likewise, overly excited or distraught individuals have a difficult time focusing on what is going on around them.

Attention is also selective, capable of ignoring some stimuli while tuning in to others. You could be at a crowded party chatting with a friend, oblivious to all other conversations in the room, until you hear your name spoken in another conversation several feet away, which shifts your attention to that conversation. This demonstrates that attention is a high-level process that occurs *after* a good deal of sensory and perceptual processing, such as processing the meaning of words, has taken place. That is, visual, auditory, and other types of stimuli are processed and decoded in the absence of attention, without us having to pay attention to the stimuli.

Historically, research on attention has relied on lesioning studies and EEG recordings of subjects who are attending to particular stimuli. More recently, functional imaging techniques have enhanced our understanding of the biological processes underlying attention. Let's examine that research more closely.

attention: a state of being alert or orienting to a specific stimulus or processing information in working memory

Electrophysiological Studies of Attention

Recordings of the electrical activity of neurons have provided us with important information concerning attention. One electroencephalographic (EEG) technique, called **event-related potential (ERP)** or *evoked potential*, allows investigators to measure the response of the brain to individual stimuli. In most human ERP studies, scalp electrodes are used to pick up electrical changes in the brain underlying the skull. These electrodes are pasted or taped to the scalp over various sites of interest in the brain (see Figure 5.6). In animal subjects and in people undergoing brain surgery, electrodes are implanted directly in the brain at the sites under investigation, and evoked potentials are measured from cells adjacent to the implanted electrodes. Typically, to detect an ERP, the stimulus is presented repeatedly, and the resulting electrical changes are summed and averaged by a computer.

<aside>event-related potential: measured change in brain activity following the presentation of a stimulus</aside>

When a person is presented with a stimulus, a number of areas in the brain are activated, culminating with a response in the cerebral cortex. Take an auditory stimulus, for example. First, the hair cells in the cochlea are activated, and information is sent to the cochlear nucleus and then on to other brain stem structures, including the superior olive, inferior colliculus, and the medial geniculate nucleus of the thalamus. From the thalamus, information about the auditory stimulus is relayed to the primary auditory cortex in the temporal lobe and then to Wernicke's area, before being sent to memory and attention centers in the cerebral cortex. As the information passes from one structure to the next, electrical activity in that brain structure indicates that neurons are excited and are sending the information elsewhere.

Therefore, for auditory stimuli, we can see a shift in electrical activity from brain stem centers to auditory processing centers to higher cerebral centers. Evoked potentials are manifestations of the electrical activity elicited in a particular area of the brain by a specific stimulus. Given the orderly transmission of information in the various sensory systems, different components of the evoked potential occur at precise time intervals following the occurrence of a stimulus or event. For example, 20 msec after the presentation of a stimulus, an *early component of the evoked potential* is recorded over the appropriate primary sensory cortex. For auditory stimuli, the early component would be best detected over the temporal lobe. For visual stimuli, it is recorded over the occipital lobe. This early component represents the response of the sensory system to the stimulus.

In contrast, a *late component of the evoked potential* is recorded about 100 msec or more after the presentation of a stimulus. This late component is typically recorded over the vertex of the skull, rather than over a primary sensory cortex, and reflects cognitive processing of the meaning of the stimulus. The late component appears to represent the brain's attentional response to the stimulus because there is a *direct relationship* between attention and the size of the late component of the evoked potential. That is, a larger late component ERP is recorded when more attention is paid to a stimulus (Carretie et al., 2001; Turak et al., 2002).

The Orienting Response and Habituation

Individuals make a behavioral response when they pay attention to a novel, or newly introduced, stimulus. They stop whatever they are doing, and they turn toward the stimulus, focusing their receptors (eyes, ears, nose) on the new stimulus. When someone calls your name, for instance, you turn to look in the direction of the voice. This focusing of receptors on a novel or important stimulus is called an **orienting response.** The orienting response is an easily observed behavioral response to a stimulus. You can readily see when your pet or an animal in the wild is making an orienting response. Just call your pet's name, and watch its response to you.

<aside>orienting response: the focusing of receptors on a novel or important stimulus</aside>

However, if the novel stimulus is presented over and over, the individual will begin to show **habituation** to the stimulus. Habituation is a response of the central nervous system to stimuli that do not contribute useful information. For example, if you were to call your pet's name repeatedly, your pet would readily ascertain

<aside>habituation: a decrease in response of the nervous system to a repeated stimulus, such as a chronic stressor</aside>

that no consequences follow its response to its name, and it would show habituation, which is observed as an *absence of an orienting response*. Habituation is a decrease in response by the brain to repeated stimulation. It is different from *adaptation*, which you learned about in Chapter 7. Adaptation involves a decrease in the response of *receptors* to repeated stimulation. In habituation, the receptors are firing normally, as the large early component of the evoked potential reveals. However, the late component is much reduced in habituation, which indicates that attentional centers have reduced their response to the stimulus (Figure 9.11).

Dishabituation occurs when a habituated individual is suddenly presented with a new or different stimulus. For example, when you first turn on the clothes dryer, you are aware of the swishing sound of your clothes going around and around in the dryer. After a minute or so, you become habituated to the noise and no longer pay attention to the sound of the dryer. But, if the dryer suddenly starts making a thumping noise, you show dishabituation: You look up and turn toward the dryer attentively. The reappearance of an orienting response signifies that dishabituation has taken place in a previously habituated individual. When ERPs are recorded, dishabituation is characterized by a large late component of the evoked potential.

The orienting response is generated by a midbrain structure called the **ascending reticular activation system,** or the *reticular formation* (Figure 9.12). The reticular formation is a diffuse system of axons that extends from the hindbrain to the thalamus. As its name implies, the ascending reticular activating system sends messages *up* to the forebrain to *activate* attentional processes in the cerebrum. Whenever the reticular formation receives information about important or novel stimuli, it produces an orienting response to the stimulus, *and* it sends an activating message to the cerebrum. The reticular formation even functions during sleep, arousing you to wakefulness when your alarm goes off, for example. Lesions to the midbrain portion of the reticular formation, particularly to an area called the **tegmentum,** will eliminate orienting responses (Horn, 1963; Sprague, Chambers, & Stellar, 1961).

For the most part, electrophysiological studies of attention have focused on the response of the individual to a single stimulus or to a simple pattern of stimuli. In the next section, we will examine how attention to more complex stimuli is studied.

Functional Brain-Imaging Studies of Attention

Cognitive research has identified a number of attentional processes. In an attempt to relate these processes to brain function, cognitive neuroscientists have employed lesioning and single-cell recording techniques in monkeys, as well as functional imaging of primate brains. In this section, we will review this research and draw some conclusions regarding the role of the cerebral cortex in attention.

Selective Attention

During our waking moments, we are bombarded by a host of stimuli. The function of attention is to select among these stimuli, processing information about

Figure 9.11 Habituation in ERP recording
Large waves represent relaxation. When a tone is sounded, the cat's brain shows activation (smaller, faster brain waves). After 36 or 37 repetitions of the tone, the cat's brain shows very little response to the tone.

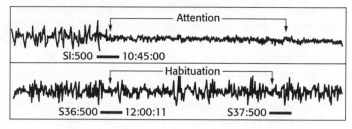

dishabituation: an orienting response in a habituated individual to a new or different stimulus

ascending reticular activation system: reticular formation, a diffuse system of axons extending from the hindbrain to the thalamus that activates attentional systems in the cerebrum

tegmentum: an area of the reticular formation that is associated with the production of orienting responses

Figure 9.12 The reticular formation
The reticular formation extends from the hindbrain to the thalamus.

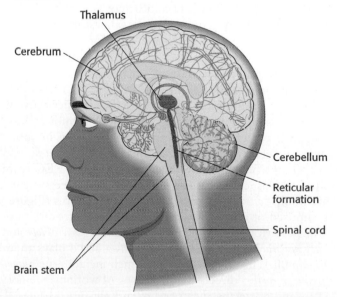

relevant stimuli and ignoring irrelevant ones. This process by which brain systems select stimuli for processing is called **selective attention.** One current explanation for selective attention suggests that neural representations of different stimuli active in the brain at any one time suppress each other, and selective attention acts to *increase suppression of irrelevant stimuli* and to *decrease suppression of relevant stimuli* (Desimone & Duncan, 1995; Duncan, 1984). Recent research by Kastner and his colleagues (1998) using functional MRI has demonstrated that attention does indeed decrease suppression of attended stimuli in human subjects.

Attentional processes are associated with each of the working memory modalities (object identification, spatial, verbal) that you learned about in the preceding section. For example, **visual spatial attention** is a type of selective attention used when an individual is required to look or search for objects in a particular location. The posterior parietal lobe appears to play a role in this type of attention because damage to this area produces *neglect* of stimuli in the visual space contralateral to the damage. Persons with damage to the right posterior parietal cortex, for example, will ignore objects located on their left side (Hillis, Mordkoff, & Caramazza, 1999; Posner, Petersen, Fox, & Raichle, 1988). Brain-imaging studies have demonstrated that areas V3, V4, or V5 also become active when a person pays attention to particular aspects of a visual stimulus, such as its shape, color, or location, respectively (Kastner et al., 1998; Posner, 1993).

Attention for Action

Another type of attentional process is associated with the executive system that directs the various components of working memory. This attentional process is referred to as **attention for action.** Attention for action is not related to any one sensory system but, rather, receives information from all working memory modalities and coordinates this information in order to complete the task at hand. Because we are not able to do many tasks at once (for example, we can't listen to two conversations at the same time), attention for action selects which stimuli will control our actions at any given moment. In the laboratory, attention for action can be tested by giving subjects two tasks to do at once. Using functional MRI, Mark D'Esposito and his colleagues (1997) discovered that **area 46** in the prefrontal cortex became active when subjects had to do two tasks (a mental rotation and a verbal task) simultaneously. However, when subjects had to complete only one of these tasks, area 46 was not activated, which demonstrates that area 46 plays a role in switching of attention between two or more tasks.

Attention for action has also been associated with activation of another area of the prefrontal cortex—the *anterior cingulate cortex*, which we discussed in Chapter 8 and earlier in this chapter. Recall that, earlier in this chapter, you learned that the anterior cingulate cortex becomes active when there is cognitive conflict. Cognitive conflict can be produced in the laboratory with the Stroop test, in which subjects are shown names of colors ("red," for example) printed in a different color of ink (Figure 9.13). When they are asked to name the color of the ink, cognitive conflict is created: Subjects have to suppress their response to the printed word and pay attention only to the color of the ink. PET images of the brains of these subjects reveal that the anterior cingulate cortex becomes active when people are forced to attend to some stimuli but ignore others (Smith & Jonides, 1999). The anterior cingulate cortex also plays an important role in monitoring performance and detecting errors during task completion (Carter et al., 1998).

On the basis of brain-imaging studies and EEG recordings in monkey brains, Michael Posner (1994) has suggested that three systems are involved in selective attention: *posterior, anterior,* and *vigilance* systems (Figure 9.14). These systems are comprised of many brain areas that you've already learned about in this chapter. The posterior system includes the *posterior parietal lobe* and two thalamic nuclei, the *pulvinar nucleus* and the *reticular nucleus,* and it plays an important role in orienting to stimuli. The anterior system, which includes the *anterior cingulate gyrus* and the *premotor cortex,* directs the processes of working memory, including attending to ideas and retrieving memories from long-term storage. Finally, the vigilance sys-

Figure 9.13 Examples of Stroop stimuli

a. Read through this list of color names as quickly as possible.

RED	YELLOW	BLUE	GREEN
RED	GREEN	YELLOW	BLUE
YELLOW	GREEN	BLUE	RED
BLUE	RED	GREEN	YELLOW
RED	GREEN	BLUE	YELLOW

b. Name each of these color patches as quickly as possible.

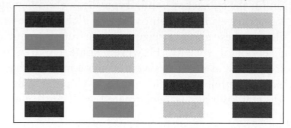

c. Name the color of ink in which each word is printed as quickly as possible.

RED	BLUE	GREEN	YELLOW
YELLOW	BLUE	RED	GREEN
BLUE	YELLOW	GREEN	RED
GREEN	BLUE	YELLOW	RED
BLUE	YELLOW	RED	GREEN

tem is responsible for keeping the individual awake and alert. In addition, the vigilance system allows for *sustained attention*, in which an individual maintains attention to a stimulus for long periods of time (Coull, 1998). Brain areas that comprise the vigilance system include structures that you will learn more about in Chapter 10, including the locus coeruleus, reticular formation, and the right frontal and parietal lobes.

In summary, cognitive functions are not limited to one area of brain. Rather, many cortical and subcortical areas work together to perform a cognitive task, such as attention (Farrah, 1994). Two areas of the prefrontal cortex seem to play a particularly important role in executive cognitive functions such as attention and task management, namely the anterior cingulate cortex, which is located in the medial aspect of the prefrontal cortex, and Brodmann's area 46, which is located in the dorsolateral prefrontal cortex. Functional brain-imaging studies have shown conclusively that both of these areas are involved in working memory and attention.

Attentional Disorders

Disorders of attention range from barely perceptible impairments of attention to debilitating states in which the person cannot live independently because of the severity of the attentional deficits. The milder forms of attention disorders include *petit mal epilepsy* and *attention deficit disorder* (or a related syndrome, *attention deficit/ hyperactivity disorder*), although the extreme forms of these disorders can be quite disabling. *Akinetic mutism* and *autism* are more debilitating disorders. Let's take a look at each.

Petit Mal Epilepsy

Petit mal epilepsy is a condition that is seen primarily in children, although most outgrow this problem before adolescence. As its name implies, petit mal epilepsy is an epileptic, or seizure, disorder. Unlike **grand mal** (or *generalized*) **seizures,** which are characterized by convulsions with bouts of clonus (Chapter 6) followed by a period of unconsciousness, petit mal seizures do

petit mal epilepsy: a seizure disorder in which the affected individual has absence seizures and cannot focus attention on the subject at hand

grand mal seizure: a seizure disorder characterized by convulsions with bouts of clonus followed by unconsciousness

Figure 9.14 Three selective attention systems
Three systems are involved in selective attention: posterior (controls orienting response), anterior (directs working memory), and vigilance (sustains attention to a stimulus for long periods of time).

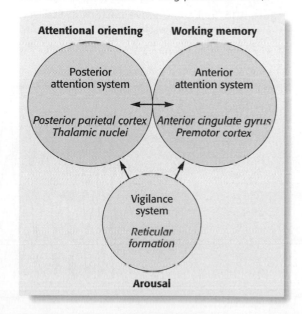

not cause prolonged unconsciousness. Rather, people with petit mal epilepsy will have momentary episodes, called **absence seizures,** in which they cannot focus their attention on the subject at hand. Typically, a child having a petit mal episode will exhibit fluttering eyelids accompanied by a blank stare or eyes rolled upward. For most children, these absence seizures occur very infrequently and do not cause problems in school or socially. However, some children have these petit mal episodes so frequently, as often as several times a minute, that the seizures come to interfere with their intellectual and social development. Because this is a seizure disorder, petit mal epilepsy is best treated with antiepileptic or anticonvulsant medication.

absence seizures: a type of seizure disorder characterized by an inability to focus on the subject at hand

An EEG record from a 22-year-old woman having a petit mal seizure is shown in Figure 9.15. A hallmark of this disorder is a rhythmic spike-and-wave pattern. As you will learn in the next chapter, EEG records from awake individuals normally show irregular brain waves. The presence of regular brain wave patterns during wakefulness indicates pathology, or disease. One test that confirms the presence of petit mal epilepsy is the *continuous performance test.* In this test, an individual is asked to watch a screen while letters are displayed, one at a time. The individual is instructed to press a button when a particular letter is seen, like an "X." Typically, a person with petit mal epilepsy will perform well on this test, pressing the button without error whenever the "X" is presented on the screen. However, when an absence seizure begins, the person will not be aware of any "X" on the screen and will not press the button. In addition, a spike-and-wave pattern is observed in the EEG record, indicating the presence of a seizure.

Attention Deficit Disorder

A relatively common disorder, affecting 3–7% of all children, is *attention deficit disorder* or, as it is formally named by the American Psychiatric Association, **attention deficit/hyperactivity disorder** (or **ADHD**). This disorder is not restricted to children, however. Nearly 50% of children with ADHD will continue to show symptoms in adulthood (Gold, 1998). Individuals with ADHD exhibit a variety of symptoms that reflect impairment of working memory and the prefrontal cortex, including: (1) a deficit in planning, organizing, and executing tasks; (2) an inability to persist in a task in the face of temptation, frustration, or interruption; and (3) impulsivity. The deficit in working memory limits the ability of people with ADHD to hold information in short-term storage while they retrieve other information. All of these symptoms involve the prefrontal cortex and its connections with the basal ganglia (Barkley, 1997).

attention deficit/hyperactivity disorder: an attentional disorder that impairs the ability of affected individuals to hold information in working memory while they retrieve other information

Figure 9.15 Spike-and-wave pattern in EEG record during petit mal epilepsy
Low voltage, desynchronized brain waves are normally seen in the awake, conscious individual. During a petit mal episode, the brain waves become slower, larger, and regular.

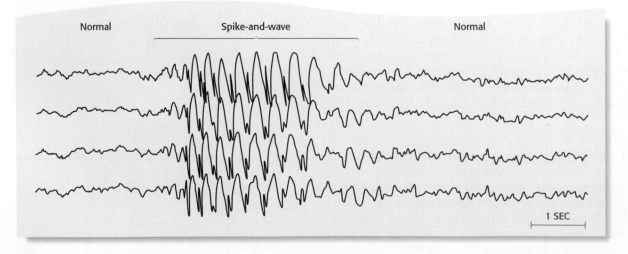

The neurotransmitters *norepinephrine* and *dopamine* appear to play a role in ADHD. Drugs used to treat this disorder, like *dextroamphetamine* or Ritalin, increase norepinephrine and dopamine levels in the brain. Norepinephrine is associated with maintaining alertness. Low levels of norepinephrine activity in the brains of individuals with ADHD contribute to their inability to stay focused on a stimulus or set of stimuli. Dopamine release in the brain has been shown, in recent studies, to draw attention to new or important stimuli (Horvitz et al., 1997; Schultz, Dayan, & Montague, 1997). Individuals with ADHD are overly distracted by stimuli that other people's brains filter out. That is, their attention gets drawn to far too many stimuli, making it difficult for them to concentrate on the stimuli at hand.

Multiple attentional systems are affected by ADHD. The anterior attention system, including the anterior cingulate cortex, which is associated with working memory and attending to ideas, is influenced by both norepinephrine and dopamine. In contrast, the activity of the posterior attentional system, which controls orienting responses to new stimuli, is affected by norepinephrine only. Thus, a dysfunction in the norepinephrine and dopamine systems impairs both the selection of stimuli to be attended and orienting responses to new stimuli. The vigilance system may also be impaired because brainstem structures, such as the *locus coeruleus*, appear to be dysfunctional in ADHD (Pliszka, McCracken, & Maas, 1996).

Akinetic Mutism

Akinetic mutism is a disorder in which an individual is unable to make orienting responses. Persons afflicted with this disorder typically spend the day sitting in the same position, staring blankly, although they may occasionally shift the direction of their gaze in an aimless fashion. Akinetic mutism leaves affected individuals with no social or sexual interests. For this reason, patients with akinetic mutism require around-the-clock care. Research with laboratory animals and case studies of human patients indicate that lesions of the midbrain reticular formation produce symptoms of akinetic mutism (Alexander, 2001). Lesions of the anterior cingulate cortex also result in akinetic mutism (Damasio & Van Hoesen, 1983).

akinetic mutism: a disorder in which the affected individual is unable to make orienting responses due to damage to the reticular formation

Autism

The disorder **autism** is characterized by a severe impairment of cognitive and social skills that is obvious in affected children by the age of 3 years (Ciaranello, 1996; Frith, 1993). Although symptoms can range from mild to severe, autistic children typically have impaired language and social interactions, cannot interpret the emotional responses of others, engage in bizarre and repetitive behaviors, and do not show normal attentional processes, often becoming focused on one stimulus or activity to the exclusion of others (Figure 9.16). Associated with autism are a number of brain malformations that suggest that autism develops very early in embryonic life, perhaps within 3 weeks of conception: a shortened brainstem, absence of the superior olive, defective motor neurons controlling facial muscles (causing a lack of facial expression in autistic people), and reduced numbers of neurons in the cerebellum. The forebrains of individuals with autism appear to be normal, however (Rodier, 2000).

autism: an attentional disorder characterized by a severe impairment of cognitive and social skills

The symptoms of autism can be readily explained by brainstem dysfunction. The extraordinary sensitivity to auditory and visual stimuli is probably related to brainstem problems. Recall that the cerebellum plays an important role in language and other cognitive processes, including organizing movements (Daum et al., 1993; Gordon, 1996). The most obvious symptom of autism—the inability to disengage attention from one stimulus to a different one—is related to a failure in

Figure 9.16 A child with autism

the orienting response, which is also controlled by brainstem structures. Other authors have implicated impairments in the hippocampus, amygdala, and parietal and temporal lobes as the source of autism (Waterhouse, Fein, & Modahl, 1996).

Older theories about the origins of autism have focused on altered neuro-transmitter function. For example, Herman and Panksepp (1978) and others have proposed that autism is related to increased activity of the endogenous opioid system. Much of the support for this theory is based on research with humans and other animals that shows that opioids like heroin cause behaviors that resemble autistic symptoms, such as reduced social interaction and repetitive stereotyped movements. However, this theory has received little empirical support. Opiate antagonists which decrease opioid activity in the brain, have little positive effect on autistic individuals (Gillberg, 1995).

Startle Disorder

Hyperekplexia, also known as *familial startle disorder,* involves an overreactive orienting response. A loud noise or sudden stimulus, such as a unexpected touch, produces an exaggerated startle response in affected individuals. This disorder is seen in infants and persists into adulthood. Investigators have identified a mutant gene that produces this disorder (Rajendra et al., 1994; Shiang et al., 1993). This mutant gene makes glycine receptors in the spinal cord 400 times less sensitive to glycine than are normal receptors. This means that glycine, an inhibitory neurotransmitter, has a difficult time binding with its receptor in the spinal cord, which *decreases* spinal inhibition. Thus, in people with hyperekplexia, a sudden stimulus initiates an orienting response that continues out of control due to lack of inhibition from the spinal cord.

We have examined only five of a variety of disorders involving attention. Because individuals with schizophrenia have impairments in the dorsolateral prefrontal cortex, some investigators regard schizophrenia as an attentional disorder. We will explore schizophrenia and related disorders in Chapter 15.

hyperekplexia: a familial startle disease, a disorder characterized by an overreactive orienting response

Recap 9.3: Biological Basis of Attention

Electrophysiological studies of attention use a technique called the (a)_____-_____ _____ (ERP), or evoked potential. The early component of the evoked potential is recorded over the (b)_____ sensory cortex. There is a direct relationship between attention and the size of the (c)_____ component of the evoked potential. The focusing of attention on a new or important stimulus is called an (d)_____ response. (e)_____ occurs when a stimulus is presented repeatedly and is seen as an absence of the orienting response. The orienting response is activated by the (f)_____ formation in the midbrain. (g)_____ attention is the process by which brain systems select stimuli for processing. (h)_____ _____ _____ is an attentional process that receives information from all working memories and coordinates the information to complete the task at hand. Area 46 and the anterior cingulate cortex have been implicated in the control of attention for (i)_____. Three systems are involved in selective memory: posterior, (j)_____, and (k)_____ systems. Attentional disorders include (l)_____ _____ epilepsy, (m)_____ _____ _____ disorder (an impairment characterized by a deficit in executing tasks, inability to persist in the face of frustration, and impulsivity), (n)_____ _____ (a disorder in which the individual is unable to make orienting responses), (o)_____ (a severe impairment of cognitive and social skills), and (p)_____ (familial startle disorder).

Biological Basis of Learning

We use the word *learn* all the time. Right now you are enrolled in a college course to *learn* about the biological foundations of behavior. But, what does it mean to *learn something?*

The classical definition of *learning* has three components: Learning is a *relatively permanent change in behavior* that *results from experience*. The first italic phrase, *relatively permanent*, refers to the fact that learning produces a long-term, rather than transient, change. If you know a classmate's name today but don't know it tomorrow, then you have not learned that classmate's name. The second italic phrase indicates that learning is characterized by a *change in behavior*. We know that learning has occurred when we see a change in behavior. For example, when I learn a person's name, I am able to greet that person by name in the future, rather than smiling and merely saying, "Hi." The third italic phrase, *results from experience*, emphasizes that learning is more than a permanent change in behavior. It is a change that is produced because something in the environment has changed, and that change has stimulated neurons to change the way they respond to a stimulus.

Different types of learning produce different types of memory, as you've learned earlier in this chapter. In general, there are two basic types of learning, *explicit* and *implicit*, each associated with a particular form of memory. **Explicit learning** refers to a change that has taken place with conscious awareness, as when you learn someone's name. As its name implies, explicit learning causes a change in explicit or declarative memory. **Implicit learning** involves the acquisition of behaviors for which we have no conscious awareness. It is nonconscious learning and results in the formation of implicit or nondeclarative memories. Recent research has revealed that these two types of learning come about as a result of different brain mechanisms. Let's examine those mechanisms now.

explicit learning: a change in behavior that has taken place with conscious awareness

implicit learning: the acquisition of behaviors for which we have no conscious awareness

Explicit Learning

For explicit learning to occur, two stimuli must occur simultaneously or as close in time as possible (Kandel & Hawkins, 1992). For example, when you learn a person's name, you are presented with his or her face and name at the same time. I might show you a picture of my sister, Gina, and tell you, "This is my sister, Gina." Or, I might bring Gina to you in person and introduce you to her. "Meet my sister, Gina." In either case, two stimuli, the *visual* image of my sister and the *auditory* information, "Gina," occur simultaneously, which permits explicit learning (that is, the conscious learning of associations) to take place. This learned association is then processed by neurons in the hippocampus and eventually stored in declarative memory.

Long-Term Potentiation

Cells in the hippocampus show tremendous plasticity in their functioning that allows them to incorporate learned associations. This plasticity was discovered in 1973 by Timothy Bliss and Terge Lomo in Oslo, Norway, when they repeatedly stimulated particular presynaptic neurons in the hippocampus and found that this stimulation increased the synaptic strength between the pre- and postsynaptic neurons. Following repeated stimulation of certain presynaptic cells in the hippocampus, the postsynaptic neuron fires readily when the presynaptic neuron is excited. For example, after you've learned the association between a person's face and name, the sight of that person's face readily causes his or her name to come to mind. This synaptic strengthening is called **long-term potentiation (LTP).** Many investigators believe that long-term potentiation may constitute the physiological basis of explicit learning (Rioult-Pedotti, Friedman, & Donoghue, 2000).

The synapses in the hippocampus that exhibit LTP are called *CA1 synapses*, and they utilize *glutamate* as the neurotransmitter. Two types of glutamate receptors are required for the development of LTP: **NMDA receptors** and non-NMDA

long-term potentiation: an increase in the readiness of a postsynaptic neuron to fire following repeated stimulation by the presynaptic neuron

NMDA receptors: a type of glutamate receptor, associated with long-term potentiation, that is typically blocked with magnesium

receptors, called **AMPA receptors.** The NMDA receptors are usually nonfunctional because magnesium blocks the ion channel associated with the NMDA receptor (Figure 9.17). In order for LTP to be induced, the magnesium block on the NMDA receptor has to be removed.

The first step in LTP induction is the *removal of the magnesium block* from the NMDA receptors on the postsynaptic neuron. This is accomplished by the release of glutamate from the presynaptic neuron (Figure 9.17). That is, the presynaptic neuron must strongly stimulate the postsynaptic neuron by releasing huge quantities of glutamate. Glutamate crosses the synapse and binds with the AMPA receptor, producing a large depolarization of the postsynaptic neuron. This depolarization causes the magnesium blockage in the NMDA receptor to be removed.

The second step in LTP induction is the *activation of protein kinases* in the postsynaptic cell. As the presynaptic cell continues to release glutamate, glutamate is now able to bind with the NMDA receptor, which opens up the calcium ion channel associated with the NMDA receptor. Calcium ions flow into the postsynaptic cell and activate a number of different protein kinases that alter the functioning of the postsynaptic neuron for several days or weeks. For example, protein kinases probably induce changes in the dendritic spines of the postsynaptic neuron, which increase the availability of AMPA receptors to bind with glutamate (Malenka & Nicoll, 1999).

Figure 9.17 Long-term potentiation

To initiate long-term potentiation, glutamate binds with AMPA receptors, depolarizing the neuron and removing the magnesium block from the NMDA receptor. Glutamate then binds with the NMDA receptor, which opens calcium channels, allowing calcium to enter the cell and stimulate the release of nitric oxide. Nitric oxide diffuses back to the presynaptic neuron, where it stimulates the continued, enhanced release of glutamate.

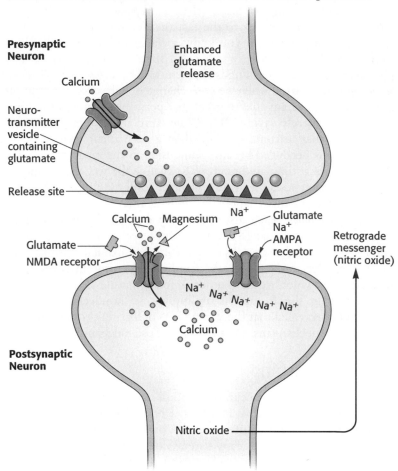

However, to keep LTP operative, a third step is necessary: *continued, enhanced release of glutamate* by the presynaptic neuron. To accomplish this step, a messenger is needed to carry a message *from* the postsynaptic neuron *to* the presynaptic cell. This messenger is believed to be the neurotransmitter *nitric oxide* (Bohme et al., 1991; Chapman et al., 1992; O'Dell Hawkins, Kandel, & Arancio, 1991; Schuman & Madison, 1991). Recall from Chapter 3 that nitric oxide is an unusual transmitter substance because it readily diffuses across cell membranes. The protein kinases activated by calcium in the postsynaptic cell increase the production of nitric oxide in the postsynaptic neuron (Figure 9.17). Nitric oxide diffuses out of the postsynaptic cell, crosses the synapse, and enters the presynaptic cell, where it stimulates the release of glutamate. Due to the action of nitric oxide, glutamate continues to be released from the presynaptic cell and binds with NMDA receptors on the postsynaptic neuron, activating more protein kinases. Thus, LTP is maintained by a long-term increase in the release of glutamate by the presynaptic neuron.

Many investigators believe that LTP serves to keep associations alive in the hippocampus (Martinez & Derrick, 1996; Schmizu, Tang, Rampon, & Tsien, 2000). These associations are the fragments of learned material that are initially stored in the hippocampus before being shifted to long-term memory. As long as LTP is maintained between two neurons, that association continues to be stored in the hippocampus. However, learned explicit associations are eventually moved to

AMPA receptors: a type of glutamate receptor, associated with long-term potentiation, that binds readily with glutamate, producing depolarization of the neuron

long-term storage in the cerebral cortex. The mechanism for long-term storage is not yet known, although it may require activation of genes, growth of new dendritic or axonal projections, or the manufacture of new proteins (Kandel & Hawkins, 1992).

Implicit Learning

Implicit learning involves strengthening the association between sensory and motor neurons involved in the learning task. A number of investigators have attempted to explain how this association is strengthened, but the simplest and best-known explanation was proposed by psychologist Donald O. Hebb at McGill University. According to Hebb's (1949) model, the presynaptic neuron *and* the postsynaptic neuron must fire at the same time in order for an association to be learned. When the presynaptic neuron and postsynaptic neuron fire together repeatedly, some change takes place between the neurons that strengthens the connection between them (Figure 9.18). Thus, over time the firing of the presynaptic neuron automatically causes the postsynaptic neuron to fire. This strengthened connection between two neurons, called the **Hebb synapse,** has been advanced by many scholars as the basis for implicit learning, although other, more complicated models have also been proposed.

As you learned earlier in this chapter, examples of implicit learning include learning a skill, developing a habit, habituation, classical conditioning, and priming. Of these, the cellular mechanisms underlying classical conditioning are best understood. Therefore, we will focus on classical conditioning in this section.

Classical Conditioning

By now, you know the basic paradigm in classical conditioning: A conditioned stimulus (CS) is presented and is immediately followed by the presentation of an unconditioned stimulus (US), which elicits an unconditioned response (UR). Following many presentations of the CS-US pairing, the CS presented alone will elicit a conditioned response (CR). In classical conditioning, an association is learned between the CS and the US, and the behavior that originally followed the US comes to be elicited by the CS (Figure 9.19). Because the relationship between the US and the UR is a reflex, we know that activation of neurons by the US directly excites motor neurons that produce the UR. Somehow, the neurons activated by the CS also come to excite these same motor neurons.

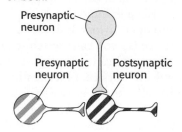

Figure 9.18 Hebb synapse
According to Hebb, the connection between the presynaptic (orange striped) and postsynaptic neurons is strengthened due to repeated simultaneous firing of both.

Presynaptic neuron

Presynaptic neuron   Postsynaptic neuron

Hebb synapse: an increase in the synaptic strength between two neurons produced by repeated simultaneous firing of the two neurons

Figure 9.19 Classical conditioning of the *Aplysia*
Activation of the sensory neuron by the US leads to excitation of a modulatory neuron. The axon of the modulatory neuron terminates on the axon of the CS neuron and influences the release of neurotransmitters by the CS neuron. However, the modulatory neuron can only influence the CS neuron when the CS neuron is active. When the CS and US are paired, the modulatory neuron is activated by the US neuron *at the same time* that the CS neuron is activated, causing greater than normal amounts of neurotransmitter to be released by the CS neuron.

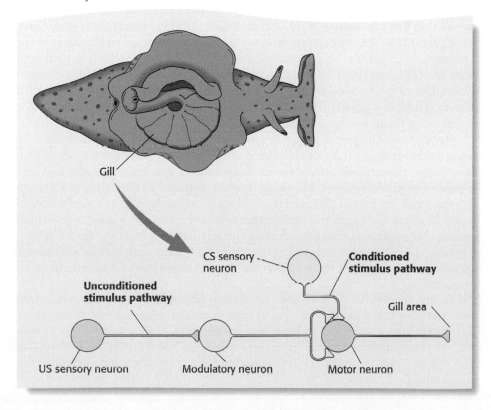

Classical conditioning occurs in people and other mammals, and it takes place even in very simple animals, like the sea slug *Aplysia*, which has relatively few neurons and no brain. Eric Kandel and his colleagues at Columbia University have studied this sea slug for decades in an attempt to determine the cellular basis of learning. Thanks to their careful research, we have a very good understanding about how classical conditioning occurs in the *Aplysia*. Kandel received the Nobel Prize in medicine in 2001 for his research on learning in the *Aplysia*.

Keep in mind that a simple animal like the sea slug has a rather limited repertoire of behaviors. It doesn't move around much, its mouth is located on its ventral surface (so you can't watch it eat), and it has no limbs to speak of. About the only activity you can see in this animal is the rhythmic movement of the gill, located on its dorsal surface, as it breathes. Kandel and his colleagues were able to make use of a reflex that was easy to observe: gill withdrawal elicited by a spray of water (Figure 9.19). That is, spraying water (the US) at the *Aplysia* causes it to stop breathing and momentarily retract its gill (UR).

Poking the *Aplysia*, on the other hand, appears to have no effect on the animal. The gill continues to move up and down, without hesitation, following a poke. Therefore, investigators in Kandel's lab devised a classical conditioning paradigm in which a poke (CS) was paired with a spray of water (US). After many pairings, the poke (CS) began to elicit gill withdrawal (CR) when it was presented alone, demonstrating classical conditioning (Figure 9.19).

Kandel and his colleagues went on to study this effect at the cellular level by examining the activity of individual neurons involved in eliciting this conditioned response. The cell of interest is the neuron that is activated by the CS (the CS neuron). How does this neuron come to excite the motor neuron that causes gill withdrawal (the CR)? To answer this question, Kandel and others studied the pathway from the sensory neuron stimulated by the US (the US neuron) to the motor neuron that produces the UR (Figure 9.19).

Activation of the sensory neuron by the US leads to excitation of a *modulatory neuron* (Hawkins, Abrams, Carew, & Kandel, 1983). The axon of the modulatory neuron terminates on the axon of the CS neuron (Figure 9.19). This means that the modulatory neuron can influence the release of neurotransmitters by the CS neuron. However, the modulatory neuron can influence the CS neuron only when the CS neuron is active. When the CS and US are paired, the modulatory neuron is activated by the US neuron *at the same time* that the CS neuron is activated. Serotonin released by the modulatory neuron binds with receptors on the axon of the CS neuron, activating a second messenger in the CS neuron, which in turn activates protein kinase. Protein kinase causes greater than normal amounts of neurotransmitter to be released by the CS neuron. Thus, future excitation of the CS neuron results in a greater than normal release of neurotransmitter that is capable of activating the motor neuron that produces gill withdrawal.

Recall from Chapter 3 that, after they are activated, protein kinases remain active in the neuron for a relatively long time. Protein kinases are known to produce many changes within a neuron; for example, altering its production and release of neurotransmitter. However, protein kinases can also alter RNA transcription and have been demonstrated to cause alterations in the expression of genes. You have learned in this section that protein kinases play a major role in both explicit and implicit learning by altering the way neurons function. In the future, as we learn more about how learning occurs and how long-term memory is formed, we will also gain a better understanding about the role of protein kinases in cellular processes.

In this chapter, we have focused on three cognitive processes: memory, attention, and learning. Certainly, we could have examined other aspects of cognition, such as reasoning, decision making, and imagination. Unfortunately, our knowledge of the biological underpinnings of these functions is still quite limited. We also did not look at another very important aspect of cognition, namely, consciousness. In Chapter 10, we will consider brain mechanisms underlying consciousness and sleep.

Recap 9.4: Biological Basis of Learning

(a)_____ is a relatively permanent change in behavior that results from experience. (b)_____ learning involves a change that has taken place with conscious awareness. (c)_____ learning involves the acquisition of behavior for which we have no conscious awareness. Repeated stimulation of certain presynaptic neurons in the hippocampus causes (d)_____ strengthening between presynaptic and postsynaptic neurons. This synaptic strengthening is called (e)_____-_____ _____ (LTP). Synapses that exhibit LTP are called CA1 synapses and utilize the neurotransmitter (f)_____. Classical conditioning is one example of (g)_____ learning. Eric Kandel's research with the *Aplysia* has demonstrated that activation of a sensory neuron by the unconditioned stimulus produces excitation in a modulatory neuron that releases (h)_____, which leads to an increase in neurotransmitter release by the neuron that elicits the conditioned response.

Chapter Summary

The Frontal Lobe's Role in Cognition

▶ Many cognitive processing centers are located in the frontal lobes, the largest structure in the human brain.

▶ The frontal lobe is divided into three functional zones: the prefrontal cortex, the premotor cortex, and the motor cortex.

▶ The prefrontal cortex plays an important role in cognitive functions and can be further divided into three regions: dorsolateral, medial, and orbitofrontal.

Biological Basis of Memory

▶ Short-term memory is a limited memory system that can hold about seven pieces of information for approximately 30 seconds. Huge amounts of information are stored in long-term memory for long periods of time. The transfer of information from short-term to long-term memory occurs in a process called consolidation.

▶ The concept of working memory has replaced that of short-term memory. Working memory consists of several storage depots: for object identification, for spatial location, for verbal information, and a central executive system.

▶ Long-term memory has two main components, declarative memory (which involves the conscious retention of facts and events) and nondeclarative memory (which involves nonconscious memory for learned behaviors).

▶ Temporary storage in working memory is transferred to long-term memory by way of a consolidation process that takes place in the hippocampus. Damage to the hippocampus produces amnesia.

▶ Declarative memory involves the conscious retention of facts and events. It has two forms: episodic memory (the memory for the events in one's life) and semantic memory (general knowledge).

▶ The amygdala plays an important role in memory by enhancing consolidation in the hippocampus. The hormones epinephrine and cortisol enhance memory by increasing glucose availability in the brain. The neurotransmitter acetylcholine is important in forming new declarative memories.

▶ Nondeclarative memory refers to an unrelated collection of learned behaviors, such as skills, habits, conditioned responses, and priming, that can be accessed without conscious awareness.

▶ Memory disorders include retrograde, anterograde, and psychogenic amnesia, apraxia (an inability to use the hands to perform familiar movements), and Alzheimer's disease (a neurodegenerative disorder of the elderly that severely affects memory).

Biological Basis of Attention

▶ Attention can refer to being alert, or orienting to specific stimuli, or one of the executive functions of working memory.

▶ Electrophysiological studies of attention use a technique called the event-related potential (ERP), or evoked potential. The early component of the evoked potential is recorded over the primary sensory cortex.

▶ When people pay attention to a newly introduced stimulus, they make a behavioral response, called an orienting response, which is generated by the reticular formation.

▶ Habituation occurs when a stimulus is presented repeatedly and is seen as an absence of the orienting response.

- Selective attention is the process by which brain systems select stimuli for processing. Three systems are involved in selective memory: posterior, anterior, and vigilance systems.

- Attention for action is an attentional process that receives information from all working memories and coordinates the information to complete the task at hand.

- Attentional disorders include petit mal epilepsy, attention deficit disorder (an impairment characterized by a deficit in executing tasks, inability to persist in the face of frustration, and impulsivity), akinetic mutism (a disorder in which the individual is unable to make orienting responses), autism (a severe impairment of cognitive and social skills), and hyperekplexia (familial startle disorder).

Biological Basis of Learning

- Explicit learning refers to a change that takes place with conscious awareness, whereas implicit learning involves the acquisition of behavior without conscious awareness.

- Long-term potentiation may be the physiological basis of explicit learning. Repeated stimulation of certain presynaptic neurons in the hippocampus causes synaptic strengthening between presynaptic and postsynaptic neurons.

- Classical conditioning is one form of implicit learning. Eric Kandel's research with the *Aplysia* has demonstrated that activation of a sensory neuron by the unconditioned stimulus produces excitation in a modulatory neuron that releases serotonin, which leads to an increase in neurotransmitter release by the neuron that elicits the conditioned response.

Key Terms

absence seizures   (p. 268)
akinetic mutism   (p. 269)
Alzheimer's disease   (p. 262)
amnesia   (p. 256)
AMPA receptors   (p. 272)
anterior cingulate cortex   (p. 256)
anterograde amnesia   (p. 257)
apraxia   (p. 261)
area 46   (p. 266)
ascending reticular activating system   (p. 265)
attention   (p. 263)
attention deficit/hyperactivity disorder (ADHD)   (p. 268)
attention for action   (p. 266)
autism   (p. 269)
classical conditioning   (p. 259)
consolidation   (p. 252)

corticostriatal system   (p. 259)
declarative memory   (p. 256)
dishabituation   (p. 265)
episodic memory   (p. 257)
event-related potential (ERP)   (p. 264)
explicit learning   (p. 271)
frontal lobe syndrome   (p. 256)
grand mal seizure   (p. 267)
habituation   (p. 264)
Hebb synapse   (p. 273)
Hippocampus   (p. 256)
Hyperekplexia   (p. 270)
implicit learning   (p. 271)
long-term memory   (p. 252)
long-term potentiation (LTP)   (p. 271)
motor cortex   (p. 250)

NMDA receptors   (p. 271)
nondeclarative memory   (p. 256)
orienting response   (p. 264)
petit mal epilepsy   (p. 267)
prefrontal cortex   (p. 250)
premotor cortex   (p. 250)
priming   (p. 260)
psychogenic amnesia   (p. 261)
retrograde amnesia   (p. 257)
selective attention   (p. 266)
semantic memory   (p. 257)
short-term memory   (p. 252)
tegmentum   (p. 265)
visual spatial attention   (p. 266)
working memory   (p. 252)

Questions for Thought

1. How might stress affect storage in long-term memory?
2. Explain the difference between adaptation and habituation.
3. What is the role of protein kinase in long-term potentiation and in classical conditioning in the *Aplysia?*

Questions for Review

1. Why is autism considered by some investigators to be a disorder of the brain stem?

2. What roles do the hippocampus and the corticostriatal system play in the formation of long-term memory?

3. Which brain structures are associated with each of the three systems of selective attention: the posterior, anterior, and vigilance systems?

Suggested Readings

Cognitive neuroscience (special section). (1997). *Science, 275*, 1579–1610.

Ernst, M., & Zametkin, A. (1995). The interface of genetics, neuroimaging, and neurochemistry in attention-deficit hyperactivity disorder. In F. E. Bloom & D. J. Kupfer (Eds.), *Psychopharmacology: The fourth generation of progress.* New York: Raven Press.

Hermelin, B. (2001). *Bright splinters of the mind. A personal story of research with autistic savants.* Philadelphia: Jessica Kingsley.

Malenka, R. C., & Nicoli, R. A. (1999). Long-term potentiation—A decade of progress? *Science, 285*, 1870–1874.

Rodier, P. M. (2000). The early origins of autism. *Scientific American, 282*, 56–63.

Roy, E. A., & Square, P. A. (1994). Neuropsychology of movement sequencing disorders and apraxia. *Neuropsychology.* New York: Academic Press.

Rugg, M. D. (1995). Memory and consciousness: A selective review of issues and data. *Neuropsychologia, 33*, 1131–1141.

Web Resources

For a chapter tutorial quiz, direct links to the Internet sites listed below and other features, visit the book-specific website at **www.wadsworth.com/product/ 0155074865**. You may also connect directly to the following annotated websites:

http://faculty.washington.edu/chudler/hippo.html
Are memories formed in the corners or center of the brain? Find out when you search this site.

http://www.autism-society.org/whatisautism/ autism.html#types
If you have further questions about autism check out this site.

http://www.nimh.nih.gov/publicat/adhd.cfm
This site by the National Institute of Mental Health discusses Attention Deficit Hyperactivity Disorder in detail. Case studies are included to help you better understand the disorder.

For additional readings and information, check out InfoTrac College Edition at **http://www.infotrac-college.com/wadsworth**. Choose a search term yourself or enter the following search terms: amnesia, attention deficit-hyperactivity disorder, epilepsy, and seizures (medicine).

CD-ROM: Exploring Biological Psychology

Video: Classic Conditioning
Video: Alzheimer's Patient
Video: Amnesiac Patient
Video: Attention Deficit Disorder

Interactive Recaps
Chapter 9 Quiz
Connect to the Interactive Biological Psychology Glossary

10

Consciousness and Sleep

Priscilla is a 20-year-old college student with a history of sleepwalking. In fact, Priscilla has been sleepwalking since she was 3 or 4 years old. A junior in college, she shares an apartment with two other women, each having her own bedroom. Nearly every night, Priscilla wakens one or both of her roommates with her sleepwalking "antics." Often, Priscilla sleepwalks into their rooms while they are sleeping and wakens them to tell them some bit of nonsense, such as "I'm locked out of the house, and I can't get back in." Other nights, her roommates are awakened because of the noise she makes in the apartment while sleepwalking. For example, one night she pulled down the draperies in the living room as she tried to climb them in her sleep. Before her junior year in college, Priscilla had a different roommate every semester because her constant sleepwalking scared them away. One roommate left before the end of the semester after Priscilla wakened her one night, standing naked before her bed, and announced in French, "I am a man."

Sleepwalking is a state in which a person appears to be conscious but is actually asleep. But, what does it mean *to be conscious?* In this chapter we will examine the states of consciousness and sleep. We will also examine those in-between states, such as sleepwalking, dreaming, and coma, in our attempt to understand what consciousness is and how it occurs. ●

Consciousness

Consciousness, like many of the cognitive concepts that we covered in Chapter 9, is difficult to define. It refers to an awareness of one's self and one's surroundings. But, consciousness seems to be more than that. Some investigators believe that consciousness requires a state of wakefulness, although others consider dreaming to be a state of consciousness. Obviously, there is no consensus about the nature of consciousness (Damasio, 1999). Early psychologists studied consciousness by examining **metacognition,** or the subjects' awareness of their own mental processes (Nelson, 1996). In a typical experiment, subjects were exposed to specific stimuli and then asked to make reports about their introspections, or thought processes, concerning these stimuli. These early studies were loaded with methodological problems and really didn't tell us much about important aspects of consciousness, including alertness and attention.

More recently, Jean Delacour (1995) has suggested that consciousness is characterized by six main features: (1) behavior that is coherent and controlled; (2) detection of novel stimuli and orienting responses to those stimuli; (3) behavior that is goal directed and flexible; (4) production and comprehension of language; (5) evidence of declarative memory; and (6) presence of metacognition. Working memory and attention are important components of consciousness because working memory is involved in goal-directed task completion, and attention is involved in responding to selected stimuli and retrieving ideas from declarative memory. According to Delacour's six criteria for consciousness, the behaviors exhibited while a person is sleepwalking are not considered conscious behavior because these behaviors are neither coherent nor goal directed. Metacognition is absent during sleepwalking, too. That is, a person is not aware of his or her own thought processes while sleepwalking.

According to Delacour (1995), varying degrees of consciousness are present in nonhuman animals. For example, many animals have behavior that is integrated, goal directed, and flexible. The squirrels that try to eat from the squirrel-proof birdfeeder in my backyard exhibit a variety of clever behaviors in their attempts to steal birdseed. My dog will sit at the window for hours watching the squirrels, alert and attentive. Great apes show higher levels of consciousness. They can recognize themselves in a mirror, use tools, and engage in pretend play and deceptive behavior (Cheney & Seyfarth, 1990; Gallup & Suarez, 1991; Griffin, 1992). Linguistic experts argue whether the ability to use language creatively is limited to humans. Chimpanzees and gorillas that have been trained to use sign language appear to communicate their thoughts and desires (Figure 10.1). In the wild state, these apes use distinctive vocalizations to communicate information about emotional states and the presence of particular threats in their environment.

Figure 10.1 Ape using ASL

A close examination of Delacour's criteria reveals that consciousness appears to involve structures in the frontal lobe, particularly the prefrontal cortex. Keep in mind that many activities that you perform while awake are performed unconsciously. For example, as you learned in Chapter 9, retrieving information from implicit or procedural memory is an unconscious process. On many days, I back my car out of my driveway as I prepare to drive to work, and, the next thing I know, I'm pulling into the parking lot outside my office building, with no conscious recollection whatsoever of driving to work, stopping at traffic signals, and so forth. Somehow, although awake, I got to my office unconsciously, with no awareness of the actions that I performed to reach my destination.

Thus, consciousness appears to be more than merely being awake. Behaviors that are performed automatically or activities that make use of nondeclarative memory do not require conscious processing. In contrast, unexpected events and novel, complex tasks are processed consciously. You might have noticed that, when you consciously attend to a well-learned automatic behavior, such as climbing the stairs, your performance of that behavior is slowed down and less accurate. The next time you walk up a flight a stairs, try to pay attention to every movement of your legs. You will find that your movements become awkward when you switch the performance of automatic behaviors from unconscious to conscious processing.

Disorders of Consciousness

To obtain a better understanding of consciousness, let's consider a number of cognitive disorders that we examined in Chapter 9, such as amnesia, frontal lobe syndrome, autism, and akinetic mutism, which are characterized by impairment of consciousness. In this section, we will also examine two disorders, *coma* and *locked-in syndrome*, whose primary symptoms include disturbance of consciousness. *Dissociative states* will also be discussed because these states represent a disruption of consciousness.

Amnesia

Individuals with retrograde or anterograde amnesia exhibit impairment of declarative memory. Recall from Chapter 9 that *retrograde amnesia* involves an inability to retrieve past memories, and *anterograde amnesia* involves an ability to form new declarative memories. According to Delacour's criteria for consciousness, accessing declarative memory is necessary for conscious processing to occur. This means that any impairment of declarative memory interferes with conscious processing.

Frontal Lobe Syndrome

Injury to the frontal lobe produces impairments of attention, metacognition, goal-directed behavior, and other aspects of working memory required for conscious behavior. One of the most striking features of *frontal lobe syndrome* is **goal neglect,** in which the affected individual disregards instructions and ignores requirements of a task, although the individual is able to explain the instructions or rules for task completion (Duncan, 1995). Except for goal neglect, impairment of conscious processes is minimal in patients with frontal lobe syndrome. The *Case Study* describes a famous case of frontal lobe syndrome.

goal neglect: a disorder in which the affected person disregards instructions and ignores requirements of a task, although the person can explain the instructions or rules

Autism

Recall from Chapter 9 that *autism* is an attentional disorder in which affected individuals cannot easily shift their attention from a stimulus that preoccupies them to another stimulus. Thus, an autistic individual might not make an orienting response to a stimulus that most of us would find important, like a human voice. Other evidence of impaired consciousness in autistic people includes behaviors that are not coherent, flexible, and goal oriented and an absence or near absence of language. **Asperger's syndrome** is a form of autism in which the affected individuals are high functioning, displaying excellent language skills and evidence of metacognition (Channon et al., 2001; Koning & Magill-Evans, 2001). People with Asperger's syndrome can describe their inner feelings and report their thoughts, thus possessing a consciousness that is less impaired than that normally found in autism.

Asperger's syndrome: a form of autism in which the affected individual is high functioning, with excellent language skills and evidence of metacognition

Akinetic Mutism

The most extreme form of impaired attention is *akinetic mutism.* Individuals with akinetic mutism are unable to make orienting responses to new or important stimuli, a requirement of consciousness. They remain motionless hour after hour, not responding to anything in their immediate environment. Although these individuals are awake, they are not conscious of stimuli or events that are occurring around them.

Loss of Psychic Self-Activation

Individuals with bilateral lesions of the basal ganglia often present with an interesting symptom referred to as **loss of psychic self-activation,** which resembles akinetic mutism in some respects (Desfontaines, Pillon, Deweer, Dubois, &

loss of psychic self-activation: a disorder characterized by mental and motor inactivity except when the individual is stimulated by environmental demand

The Story of Phineas Gage

Phineas Gage was a highly intelligent, hard-working man who was well liked by his coworkers before he suffered a tragic accident in 1848. At the time of his accident, he was 25 years old and a foreman for a construction crew that was laying railroad tracks in Vermont. To lay tracks in the mountainous, rocky terrain of Vermont, the crew had to use blasting powder to break up big rocks that were in the path of the tracks. Normally the men would drill a hole in a rock, pour blasting powder into the hole, put a fuse on top, and then cover the powder and fuse with sand. A long metal rod was then used to tamp or pack the sand down before the fuse was lit.

One day, however, Phineas was distracted for a moment and began tamping down the blasting powder before the sand was added. The impact of the tamping rod on the blasting powder ignited a huge explosion, causing the rod to shoot up and rip through Phineas's head. The rod, which was about 42 inches long and over 1 inch in diameter, entered just below his left cheekbone, destroying his left eye, and exited through the top of his head. Miraculously, Phineas survived this terrible accident. He stood up immediately after the impact knocked him off his feet, began talking normally, and was able to walk away with his men.

Within a few months, Phineas had recovered well enough to return to work. He had lost his left eye, but his speech, memory, and intelligence were unaffected by the accident. However, his personality had changed dramatically. Formerly a polite, socially responsible man, he became extremely rude, and he began to curse routinely, lie to his coworkers, and show up for work irregularly. He seemed to have lost all sense of social awareness and was eventually fired from his job. After losing his job, he wandered around the United States and South America until his death in 1861 in San Francisco, where he was buried without an autopsy.

Five years after Phineas's death, the country doctor who had treated him asked Phineas's family to have the body exhumed so that he could examine Phineas's skull. Phineas's doctor later sent the skull and the tamping rod to Harvard University, where they are currently exhibited at the Warren Anatomical Medical Museum. In 1993, Hannah Damasio at the University of Iowa reconstructed a three-dimensional image of the damaged skull and brain, using computerized brain-imaging techniques. The computer images are shown in Figure 10.2. From these images, Damasio has determined that the tamping rod passed through the medial portion of the frontal lobes in both hemispheres. This region of the prefrontal cortex is believed to play an important role in decision making and conscious awareness.

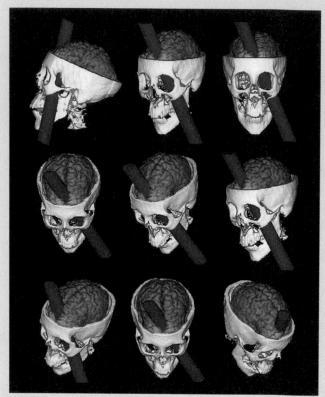

Figure 10.2 Computer-generated images of Phineas Gage's damaged skull and brain

Laplane, 1996). This disorder is characterized by both mental and motor inactivity except when the individual is stimulated by an environmental demand. That is, the individual with loss of psychic self-activation remains inactive for hours on end unless something in the external environment provides stimulation. People with this disorder are unable to initiate thoughts or actions on their own, although they will respond normally when called upon to act. In their inactive state, they don't experience boredom, but they feel indifferent or mentally empty. However, they *are* conscious and can respond to external stimuli, even in their inactive state, unlike patients with akinetic mutism.

Coma

Coma is defined as a state of unconsciousness in which the eyes are closed. This is a very broad, nonspecific definition because many different levels of awareness are observed in coma. The Glasgow Coma Scale (Teasdale & Jennett, 1974) is used to assess the level of functioning in an individual in a coma state. Table 10.1 describes the various stages of the Glasgow Coma Scale. To obtain a Glasgow Scale score, the clinician must assess eye opening, motor response, and verbal response of the comatose patient. In general, a low score on the scale is associated with a poor prognosis for recovery (Masson et al., 2001). Approximately 45% of people who have a Glasgow Coma Scale score of less than 5 will die before waking from the coma, whereas only 3% of people with a score greater than 12 will die. Some people who do survive enter a *permanent vegetative state* in which their eyes are open but their behaviors are reflexive and primitive. For example, individuals in a permanent vegetative state will often cry when they are distressed or in pain. (Crying is a primitive response.) Speech is never observed in a person in a permanent vegetative state.

Coma results from brain damage caused by trauma, anoxia (oxygen deprivation), or disease. For example, coma is often associated with head injuries received in car accidents. Typically, in a car accident, when the car slams to a halt, people inside are first pitched forward, as their bodies continue in the forward motion of the car, and then are tossed backward due to the force of inertia (Figure 10.3). This means that injuries occur in the front of the brain (or frontal lobes) as a person's body is propelled forward in space after the impact, and injuries also occur in the back of the brain (parietal and occipital lobes) when the body is jerked backward in space. In general, damage that is limited to one hemisphere does not produce a coma state. That is, both hemispheres must be injured to induce coma. Other areas implicated in coma include the midbrain and pontine reticular formation.

coma: a state of unconsciousness in which the eyes remain closed

Locked-In Syndrome

This rare disorder occurs in individuals whose motor systems become permanently detached from conscious control. People with **locked-in syndrome** appear to be unconscious and in a coma because their eyes are closed and they do not move or

locked-in syndrome: a disorder in which the person's motor system is detached from conscious control, although the person is fully conscious and aware

Table 10.1

The Glasgow Coma Scale

Score	Clinical Signs
	Eye Opening
E4	Opens eyes spontaneously
3	Opens eyes on command
2	Opens eyes when pinched
1	Does not open eyes to pain
	Motor Response
M6	Follows simple commands
5	Withdraws body part when pinched
4	Pulls away examiner's hand when pain applied
3	Flexes body inappropriately to pain
2	Body becomes rigid in response to pain
1	Has no response to a pinch
	Verbal Response
V5	Carries on normal conversation, oriented for time and place
4	Talks to examiner but makes no sense
3	Seems confused or disoriented
2	Makes sounds that examiner doesn't understand
1	Makes no noise

Coma Score (E + M + V) = 3 to 15

Source: Teasdale & Jennett (1974)

Figure 10.3 Brain damage seen following a vehicular accident

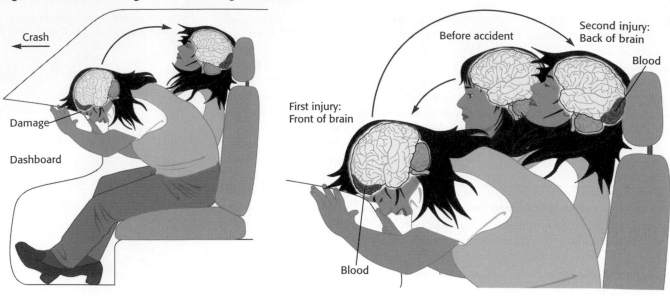

respond to stimuli. However, these individuals are fully conscious and aware of their surroundings. Sometimes an individual with locked-in syndrome is able to move an eyelid and can communicate by means of blinking (such as, one blink means "yes," and two blinks mean "no"). Using eye blinks, a journalist named Jean-Dominique Bauby was able to dictate a whole book, *The Diving Bell and the Butterfly*, an amazing account of his life following a stroke that left him impaired with locked-in syndrome. Locked-in syndrome is usually associated with damage to the hindbrain, particularly in the area of the pons.

Dissociative States

In this chapter, you've learned that one of the most prominent characteristics of consciousness is the integration of all sensory and memory components of the conscious experience, which results in a unified consciousness. In **dissociative states,** this integration becomes disrupted, and affected individuals can experience altered sensory perceptions, amnesia, attentional disorders, and distortion of time perception and identity (Krystal, Bennett, Bremner, Southwick, & Charney, 1995). For example, a person with dissociative symptoms may experience **flashbacks,** in which the emergence of vivid memories causes a past event to be experienced as happening all over again. Persons having a flashback may experience altered auditory and visual perceptions that cause them to feel as if they are reliving the past event. A disturbance in identity function can result in **multiple personality disorder,** in which an individual can exhibit a number of different personae, some of whom are unaware of the existence of other personae, or *fugue states*, in which affected persons do not know their own identity and have no memory of their past.

Norepinephrine has been linked to flashbacks and other dissociative states (Krystal et al., 1995). For example, a drug that increases norepinephrine activity, called **yohimbine,** has been demonstrated to initiate flashbacks and panic attacks in individuals who have experienced a previous traumatic event. (We will examine the effects of yohimbine in greater detail in Chapter 15.) Three classes of drugs produce dissociative states in healthy people: (1) anesthetics that act as glutamate antagonists, like phencyclidine (PCP) and ketamine; (2) marijuana and related cannabinoids; and (3) hallucinogens that increase serotonin activity, such as LSD. These drugs all have the effect of altering sensory perceptions, distorting attention and memory, and causing a state of **depersonalization,** in which affected individuals feel as if they are outside of their own body.

dissociative state: a disorder in which the affected individual experiences altered sensory perceptions, memory loss, and distortion of time perception and identity

flashback: the emergence of vivid memories that causes a past event to be experienced as happening all over again

multiple personality disorder: a disturbance in identity function in which the affected person can have a number of different personae, some of whom are unaware of the other personae

yohimbine: a drug that blocks the alpha-2 adrenergic receptor and produces an increase in the release of norepinephrine

depersonalization: a state in which affected individuals feel as if they are outside their own body

Research on Consciousness

Research with brain-injured patients, as well as functional brain-imaging and electroencephalographic studies, has contributed to our understanding of the biological bases of consciousness. For example, as you learned in the preceding section, studies of individuals with cognitive disorders due to brain injury or faulty brain development have indicated that specific brain dysfunctions can result in characteristic impairments of consciousness. Other research has examined consciousness in patients who have undergone brain surgery to correct a neurological problem or to remove a brain tumor.

In 1981, Roger Sperry, a professor at the California Institute of Technology, received a Nobel Prize for his research on cerebral function in individuals who had undergone a *callosotomy*, or surgical division of the **corpus callosum** [*callos-* = callosum, as in *corpus callosum; -otomy* = to cut, Latin]. Recall from Chapter 4 that the corpus callosum is a thick band of axons that connects the two halves of the cerebrum (Figure 10.4). Severing the corpus callosum produces a permanent loss of communication between the two cerebral hemispheres and is performed only on patients with severely disabling seizure disorders who do not respond well to traditional drug treatment. These individuals are often referred to as **split-brain patients** after the surgery.

Immediately following callosotomy, split-brain patients appear disoriented and unable to coordinate their hand movements to work together. One man, for example, started to button his shirt with one hand, and the other hand immediately began unbuttoning the shirt! Because the left hand is controlled by the right side of the brain and the right hand by the left side, severing the corpus callosum leaves the postsurgical patient in a state where one hand does not know what the other hand is doing. However, within a month or so, the two cerebral hemispheres learn to work together, typically through the visual and auditory senses, which relay information to both halves of the cerebrum, and the postsurgical patient's behavior looks smooth and normal.

corpus callosum: large tract that connects neurons in the left and right cerebral hemispheres

split-brain patients: individuals who have undergone a callosotomy

Figure 10.4 The corpus callosum

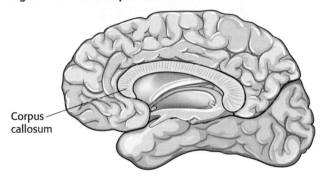

Corpus callosum

The participants in Roger Sperry's experiments were split-brain individuals who had had surgery several years prior to the experiments, and they looked essentially normal in their everyday behavior. However, the experiments conducted in Sperry's laboratory were able to demonstrate that something very unusual was taking place in the participants: They appeared to have a *left-brain consciousness* and a *right-brain consciousness*. When an object was placed in the left hand of one of Sperry's subjects (out of the subject's view; see Figure 10.5), the information was relayed to the right cerebral hemisphere only. (If the subject were able to see the object, information about that object would be sent to both sides of the cerebrum.) When asked to name the object in the left hand, these individuals could not identify the object because only the left hemisphere can produce language. However, when asked to pick out the object among a group of several objects behind a screen, the left hand could easily choose the correct object, and the right hand could not. The opposite was true for objects placed in the right hand: Split-brain subjects could name the object placed in their right hand and could select the correct object behind a screen, whereas the left hand could not.

This experiment demonstrates that information about touch is sent to the contralateral hemisphere and that only that hemisphere is aware of that information in split-brain individuals. This phenomenon is not true for just the sense of touch. For example, visual information in the left or right visual field is not shared between hemispheres in people with a severed corpus callosum. When a photograph with a split image is presented to split-brain subjects, the image on the left is transmitted

Figure 10.5 Sperry's split-brain studies

(a) Patient's left hemisphere did not see the word, so the patient could not name it. The right hemisphere, which did see the word, controls the left hand that writes "cat." (b) The feeling of spoon in the left hand goes to the right hemisphere. Patient cannot name item and merely guesses. The left hemisphere produces language, but the left hemisphere has no knowledge of the spoon.

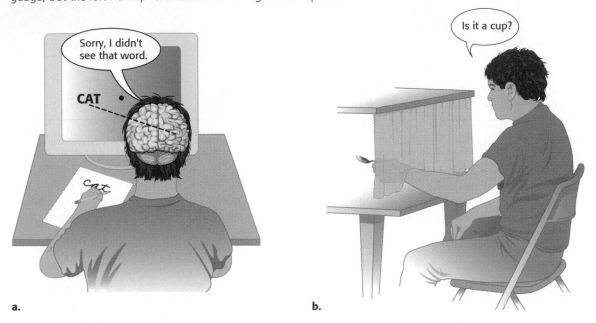

a. b.

to the right side of the brain, and the image on the right is transmitted to the left side of the brain. When asked to describe the photograph, split-brain subjects describe the image on the right side of the photograph because only the left hemisphere has control of speech.

Sperry and his colleagues were surprised to discover that each hemisphere has a consciousness or awareness of its own (Gazzaniga, Bogen, & Sperry, 1962, 1992; Sperry, Gazzaniga, & Bogen, 1969). In split-brain patients, neither mind-right nor mind-left is aware of the other hemisphere's consciousness. That is, little, if any, cognitive or perceptual information is shared between the two cerebral hemispheres. However, a split-brain patient experiences a unitary consciousness, just like you and I, and is aware of only one mind and one set of sensory experiences and memories (Gazzaniga, 1989).

More recent research with split-brain patients has demonstrated that this sense of unified conscious awareness is due to a special role of the left hemisphere in consciousness (Gazzaniga, 1989; Gazzaniga & Ledoux, 1978). Because the left hemisphere contains the language centers necessary for the production of speech, carefully designed studies can give us a clear understanding of the function of the left hemisphere in consciousness. For example, in a test of concept association, when the right hemisphere of a split-brain patient was shown an image of a wintry, snow-covered scene, and the left hemisphere was shown an image of a chicken claw, the patient pointed to an image of a chicken with the right hand and pointed to an image of a shovel with the left hand. When asked why the chicken and the shovel were selected, the split-brain patient responded that chickens have claw feet and that the shovel was needed to clean out the chicken house. The left hemisphere did not have knowledge of the snow-covered scene, but it readily concocted an explanation for why the left hand selected a picture of a shovel (Gazzaniga, 1989). This experiment shows quite clearly that the left hemisphere is involved in interpreting incoming data based on the knowledge that it has.

(a)_____ refers to an awareness of one's self and one's surroundings, whereas (b)_____ is an awareness of one's own mental processes. (c)_____ is an impairment of declarative memory and, thus, interferes with conscious processing. Goal neglect is an impairment associated with (d)_____ _____ syndrome. In (e)_____ syndrome, individuals exhibit a consciousness that is less impaired than that observed in most autistic individuals. Individuals with (f)_____ _____ are unable to make orienting responses to novel stimuli. A loss of (g)_____ _____ is characterized by an inability to initiate thoughts or actions in the absence of external stimulation. (h)_____ is a state of unconsciousness in which the eyes are closed. In contrast, a permanent (i)_____ state is a state of unconsciousness in which the eyes are open but behaviors are reflexive and primitive. People with (j)_____ syndrome appear to be unconscious because their eyes are closed, but they are fully conscious, only unable to move or respond to stimuli. Roger Sperry received a Nobel Prize for his research on consciousness in patients who have undergone a surgical division of the (k)_____ _____. His research demonstrated that each cerebral hemisphere has a consciousness of its own, although the (l)_____ hemisphere plays a special role in consciousness because it contains the language centers.

Sleep

Studies of split-brain patients have provided us with a great deal of insight into the role of the cerebral hemispheres in the conscious processing of information. Research using EEG recordings of human brains during sleeping and waking states has helped us better understand the neural mechanisms underlying sleep and consciousness. Let's examine the findings of EEG research next.

Electrophysiology of Consciousness and Sleep

Electrical activity in the brain can be measured in two ways, as you learned in Chapter 5: through *scalp electrodes* pasted onto the skin overlying the skull and through *intracranial electrodes* inserted into the brain [*intra-* = inside; *-cranial* = referring to the cranium or skull, Latin]. The intracranial electrodes are typically microelectrodes that record the electrical activity of one or more neurons located near the tip of the electrode. In contrast, the changes in electrical activity recorded by scalp electrodes reflect the activity of hundreds or thousands of neurons lying directly beneath the electrode on the scalp. Both types of recordings have revealed important information about brain activity underlying sleep and consciousness.

Intracranial Recording

Recent research has demonstrated that the unified character of consciousness may be explained by **synchronous oscillations,** which occur when neurons fire at the same time at the same rate of 40 times per second in different parts of the brain (Delacour, 1995). Much of the research on synchronous firing in neurons has involved the process of *binding*, which we examined in Chapter 8. Recall that different aspects of a visual image (for example, its color, shape, movement, location) are analyzed separately in different regions of the visual cortex. Binding involves combining these different pieces of information about the image and producing a single, unified representation of the visual object. A number of animal studies have indicated that binding occurs as a result of synchronous oscillations of groups of

synchronous oscillations: firing patterns of 40 action potentials per second that occur in several neurons at the same time

neurons in the visual cortex (Crick, 1994; Eckhorn et al., 1988; Gray & Singer, 1989; Gray et al., 1989; Singer, 1993). Thus, consciousness may be the product of unification of information analyzed separately by different areas of the brain.

Recording with Scalp Electrodes

Research involving EEG measures recorded via scalp electrodes has revealed that brain activities associated with sleep and waking are quite different. In general, **synchronized brain waves** are the hallmark of deep sleep. Synchronized brain waves are large, slow, regular waves (Figure 10.6). In contrast, **desynchronized brain waves,** which are rapid, irregular brain waves, are observed during conscious states. States of high excitation or emotional states are associated with very fast and highly irregular EEG recordings. The fast, irregular brain waves associated with arousal are called **beta waves.** Beta waves occur at a frequency of approximately 13–50 waves per second and are associated with activation of the sympathetic nervous system. In addition, cognitive and emotional tasks that require intake of information, such as counting verbs in a written passage, checking for arithmetic errors, or looking at provocative slides, are associated with increased beta activity (Ray & Cole, 1985).

On the other hand, **alpha waves** are observed during periods of relaxed wakefulness, when the parasympathetic nervous system is active. Alpha waves occur at a rate of 8–12 waves per second. Tasks that require attention to internal processing, such as performing mental arithmetic, creating sentences that begin with a particular letter, and mentally rotating geometric figures, are associated with increased alpha wave activity (Ray & Cole, 1985).

When alpha waves disappear and give way to slower brain waves, sleep occurs. Thus, sleep and wakefulness appear to be states along a continuum of brain activity levels, with wakefulness being associated with beta and alpha brain waves and sleep being associated with slower brain waves. During periods of drowsiness, as when you are sitting in a boring lecture and begin to drift off, EEG records indicate that brain activity fluctuates between alpha and slower, more regular waves, called **theta waves.** Theta waves occur at a rate of 3–7 waves per second and are usually associated with light sleep.

Stages of Sleep

EEG studies have shown us that sleep occurs in four stages, each with its own characteristic brain wave activity. The stages of sleep are referred to as Stage I, II, III, or IV, with Stage I being the lightest stage of sleep and Stage IV being the deepest. Desynchronized theta waves are found primarily in **Stage I sleep** (Figure 10.7). Like Stage I sleep, **Stage II sleep** is characterized by desynchronized brain waves. However, synchronized brain waves are also present in Stage II sleep, as are other hallmarks, including **sleep spindles** and **K-complexes.** Sleep spindles are bursts of brain waves with a frequency of 7–14 waves per second that last for several seconds and recur every 3 to 10 seconds (Steriade, McCormick, & Sejnowski, 1993). They are present in all stages of sleep but are most prevalent in Stage II sleep and are associated with a loss of perceptual awareness. On the other hand, K-complexes are seen only in Stage II sleep. K-complexes appear as large changes in measured voltage in EEG records, with a sharp positive peak followed by a sharp negative peak.

In **Stage III sleep,** synchronized brain waves called **delta waves** are observed, indicating a deeper stage of sleep. Delta waves are very slow, regular brain waves that occur at a rate of approximately two waves per second. **Stage IV sleep** is associated with a preponderance of delta waves in the EEG record (Figure 10.7). That is, in Stage IV sleep, over 50% of the EEG record indicates delta wave activity, whereas delta waves occur less than 50% of the time in Stage III sleep. During Stage IV sleep, heart rate and breathing are slow, and the individual is in the deepest stage of sleep. These stages of sleep, during which the EEG record exhibits large, slow brain waves, are often referred to collectively as **slow-wave sleep** or *quiet sleep.* Table 10.2 summarizes the characteristics of each stage of sleep.

Figure 10.6 Four types of brain waves

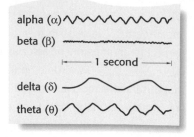

synchronized brain waves: large, slow, regular waves associated with deep sleep

desynchronized brain waves: rapid, irregular brain waves that are observed during conscious states

beta waves: fast, irregular brain waves associated with states of excitation that occur at a frequency of 13–50 Hz

alpha waves: desynchronized brain waves observed during periods of relaxed wakefulness that occur at a frequency of 8–12 Hz

theta waves: slow, irregular brain waves associated with Stage I sleep that occur at a rate of 3–7 Hz

Stage I sleep: the lightest stage of sleep characterized by desynchronized theta waves

Stage II sleep: the stage of sleep characterized by desynchronized brain waves, sleep spindles, and K-complexes

sleep spindles: bursts of brain waves with a frequency of 7–14 Hz that are most prevalent in Stage II sleep

K-complexes: large changes in voltage in EEG records observed only in Stage II sleep

Stage III sleep: the stage of sleep characterized by less than 50% synchronized delta waves

delta waves: large synchronized brain waves with a frequency of 0.5–2.5 Hz that are observed in deeper stages of sleep

Stage IV sleep: the deepest stage of sleep characterized by more than 50% synchronized delta waves

slow-wave sleep: stages of sleep that exhibit large, slow brain waves

Figure 10.7 Stages of sleep

Brain waves (EEG) become large, slow, and regular in Stage IV sleep, whereas they are fast, low voltage, and irregular in REM sleep. Eye movements (EOG) increases dramatically in REM sleep, but muscle tension (EMG) disappears in REM sleep.

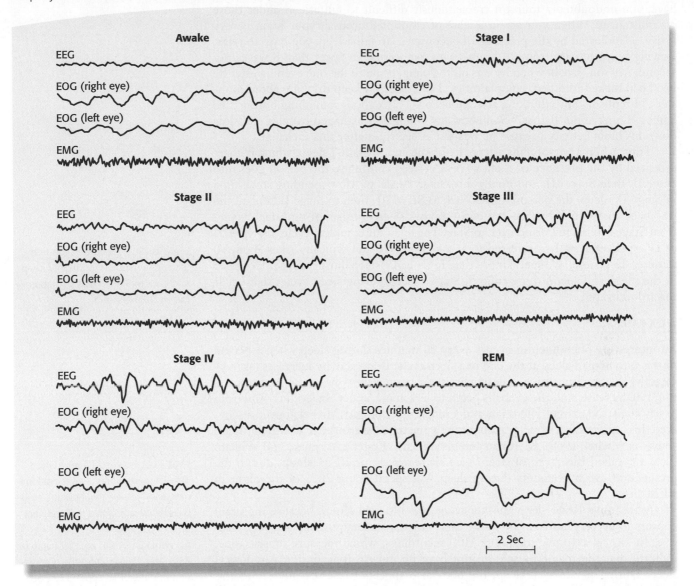

Table 10.2

Stages of Sleep

Stage	EEG Activity	Muscle Tone	Eye Movements
I	primarily theta wave activity	moderate	slow, rolling
II	mostly synchronized, with sleep spindles, K-complexes	moderate	none
III	synchronized, with some delta wave activity (<50%)	low-moderate	none
IV	>50% delta wave activity	low-moderate	none
REM	desynchronized, increased brain activity	none	rapid, jerking eye movements

A person who falls asleep first enters Stage I. However, to fall asleep, a person must be in a relaxed state, with alpha waves present in the EEG record. Have you ever tried to sleep when you were really excited or upset about something? If you have, you undoubtedly found it tremendously difficult to fall asleep under those circumstances. When you are in a state of emotional arousal, your brain is very active, as indicated by the presence of beta waves. To fall asleep, you have to relax, slowing brain activity from 20 brain waves per second to fewer than 8 waves per second. My son, Jacob, when he was quite young, came to me one evening after he had been tucked into bed, complaining, "I can't sleep. I keep thinking about monsters." I replied, "Stop thinking abut monsters. Think about something boring, like llamas. Think about llamas." Somehow my young son managed to relax and slow down his brain activity because he was fast asleep soon after this exchange.

Thus, when a person falls asleep, he or she enters Stage I sleep, which is characterized by the presence of theta waves. As sleep continues, the person goes into Stage II, then Stage III, and finally into Stage IV sleep. After spending some time in Stage IV sleep, the person moves back to Stage III, then to Stage II, and all the way back to Stage I. In fact, the entire night's sleep consists of repeated cycling from Stage I to Stage IV and back to Stage I again. This complete cycle, I → II → III → IV → III → II → I, is referred to as a **sleep cycle** and typically takes about 90 minutes. In general, we spend more time in Stage IV sleep during sleep cycles early in the night and spend more time in Stage I sleep during sleep cycles that occur toward morning.

sleep cycle: a complete cycle from Stage I sleep down to Stage IV sleep and back to Stage I that lasts approximately 90 minutes

REM Sleep

An interesting phenomenon occurs every 90 minutes during sleep when a person moves into Stage I sleep at the end of a sleep cycle: Brain activity increases (as indicated by the predominance of desynchronized brain waves), heart rate and respiration rate increase, and the eyeballs begin to jerk about under the eyelids. American psychologist Nathaniel Kleitman and French psychologist Michel Jouvet discovered this unique stage of sleep at about the same time (Aserinsky & Kleitman, 1953; Jouvet & Michel, 1968). Kleitman and his students, Eugene Aserinsky and William Dement, called this stage of sleep *rapid eye movement* or **REM sleep,** due to the presence of eye movements during sleep. We spend about 20% of the night in REM sleep.

Jouvet gave REM sleep another name, **paradoxical sleep,** because the brain appears to be very active at the same time that the skeletal muscles are very inactive. In fact, electromyographic (EMG) recordings, which measure muscle tone, indicate that the major muscle groups have no muscle tone during paradoxical sleep. During paradoxical sleep, the body also appears to be sexually excited, as indicated by penile erection in men and vaginal lubrication in women. Men will notice that they often awaken with a penile erection in the morning. Recall from the preceding paragraph that we spend more time in Stage I sleep toward morning. This means that we are most likely to be in paradoxical or REM sleep just before we awaken and thus will be coming out of a stage of sexual arousal.

REM sleep: a sleep stage in which desynchronized brain waves predominate and the sleeping individual's eyeballs move rapidly in a jerky fashion under closed eyelids
paradoxical sleep: another name for REM sleep derived from the observation that the brain appears very active while skeletal muscles are very inactive

Another paradoxical feature of REM sleep is the lack of awareness of sensory stimulation despite increased activity of the thalamus and cerebral cortex (Pare & Llinas, 1995). That is, somatosensory, auditory, or olfactory stimuli can be applied to a person in REM sleep, and that person will not be consciously aware of the stimuli. However, electrical activity of the entire forebrain is virtually identical for waking and REM states, which means that a cognitive response to sensory stimuli should be induced. Pare and Llinas (1995) have suggested that REM sleep operates very much like automatic, implicit or nonconscious processing, relying on previously stored data rather than responding to incoming sensory stimulation.

Also associated with REM sleep are two unique EEG phenomena: *theta waves* recorded in the hippocampus and simultaneous electrical activity in the pons, lateral geniculate nucleus, and occipital lobe, called *PGO spikes*. All mammals show hippocampal theta waves and PGO spikes when they are in REM sleep. On the other hand, birds do not have these EEG markers of REM when they are in active sleep. In addition, of all the bird species, only geese and ducks exhibit loss of muscle tone during REM sleep.

Aquatic mammals, such as whales and dolphins, show a remarkable adaptation to their watery existence: Only one cerebral hemisphere sleeps at a time, while the other hemisphere remains awake, allowing the animal to swim to the surface periodically to breathe. EEG records show desynchronization associated with wakefulness in one hemisphere and slow synchronized brain waves in the sleeping hemisphere. Many sleep with one eye open, in order that the awake hemisphere can monitor the environment visually while the other hemisphere sleeps. Even more unusual, some species (for example, the bottlenose dolphin) have no REM sleep whatsoever, which allows the animal to swim continuously (Mukhametov, 1985, 1988).

REM sleep typically does not occur when we first fall asleep. As we move from a relaxed state into Stage I sleep at the beginning of the night's sleep, theta waves are present, but movement of the eyes under the closed eyelids and dreaming are not present. REM sleep does not usually occur until the end of the first sleep cycle. In general, the appearance of REM immediately after falling asleep is a sign of pathology, as in a sleep disorder called *narcolepsy*, which will be discussed later in this chapter. The presence of REM at the onset of sleep has also been associated with drug or alcohol addiction, depression, or sleep deprivation.

Alcohol and other drugs that depress the central nervous system, such as barbiturates and marijuana, affect the amount of time spent in the various stages of sleep during a sleep cycle. That is, if you drink alcohol or smoke marijuana or take a barbiturate before going to bed, you will descend quickly from Stage I to Stage IV sleep, and you will spend more time than normal in Stage IV sleep. In fact, you will spend so much time in Stage IV sleep that you will not get enough REM sleep. People who take barbiturates on a regular basis find that they have very vivid dreams and horrifying nightmares when they stop using the pills. We see this **REM rebound** effect in people who are deprived of REM sleep. Normally, we spend about 20% of our sleeping time in REM sleep. However, following REM deprivation, people can spend over 30% of their sleep in REM.

REM rebound: an increase in REM sleep observed in individuals who have been deprived of REM sleep

Recap 10.2: Sleep

Intracranial recording has demonstrated that the unified character of consciousness may be explained by (a)_____ _____ that occur at a rate of 40 times per second. EEG research has revealed that (b)_____ brain waves are associated with deep sleep and (c)_____ brain waves are associated with active, conscious states. (d)_____ waves are observed when an individual is aroused, and (e) waves are associated with relaxed wakefulness. Theta waves are found primarily in Stage (f)_____ sleep, whereas sleep spindles and K-complexes are present in Stage (g)_____ sleep. Delta waves occur more than 50% of the time in Stage (h)_____ sleep and less than 50% of the time in Stage (i)_____ sleep. A (j)_____ _____ from Stage I to Stage IV and back to Stage I again takes about 90 minutes. In (k)_____ sleep, brain activity increases, heart rate increases, and skeletal muscles are inactivated, except for eye muscles, which cause the eyeballs to jerk about under closed eyelids. Two unique phenomena are also associated with (l)_____ sleep: hippocampal theta waves and PGO spikes. (m)_____ _____ is seen in people who are deprived of REM sleep.

Brain Mechanisms of Sleep and Consciousness

Brain lesioning and stimulation studies using animal subjects have demonstrated that a number of brain stem structures play crucial roles in sleep and consciousness. These structures include the *reticular formation, locus coeruleus, raphe*, and various hypothalamic and thalamic nuclei (Figure 10.8). In addition, examination of human patients who have damage to these areas reveals that these structures are also important in regulating sleep and consciousness in people. Table 10.3 summarizes the roles that these structures play. Let's take a look at each of these structures individually.

The Reticular Formation

You learned about the **reticular formation** in Chapter 9 when we examined attention and the orienting response.

Recall that lesioning the reticular formation at the level of the midbrain results in an inability to make orienting responses to novel or important stimuli. Earlier research by Bremer (1935) revealed that the reticular formation also plays an important arousal function. Bremer compared two groups of cats. One group, the *encephale isolé* [*isolated brain*, French] group, received a surgical lesion below the medulla, which severed the brain from the spinal cord. The other group of cats, the *cerveau isolé* [*isolated mind*, French] group, received a surgical cut through the midbrain above the superior colliculus (Figure 10.9). The encephale isole group showed normal sleeping and waking patterns. In contrast, the cerveau isole group remained in a sleeping state following surgery and could not be wakened.

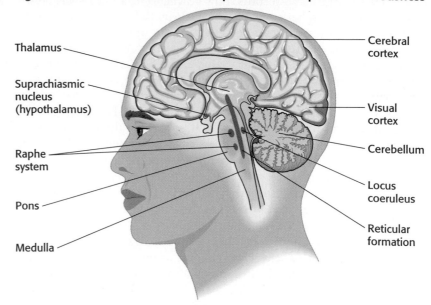

Figure 10.8 Brain stem structures implicated in sleep and consciousness

Thalamus

Suprachiasmic nucleus (hypothalamus)

Raphe system

Pons

Medulla

Cerebral cortex

Visual cortex

Cerebellum

Locus coeruleus

Reticular formation

reticular formation: a group of neurons located in the brain stem that alerts the forebrain to important stimuli

---

Table 10.3

Brain Structures Involved in Sleep and Consciousness

Brain Structure	Function
Reticular formation	produces cerebral arousal and vigilance, initiates orienting response
Raphe system	lesions of raphe produce sleeplessness in rats; stimulation induces sleep
Locus coeruleus	produces and regulates arousal, initiates a state of alert attentiveness
Suprachiasmic nucleus of the hypothalamus	regulates biological clock
Reticular thalamic nucleus	in non-REM sleep, blocks transmission of sensory information to cerebrum and limbic system
Intralaminar nucleus of the thalamus	transmits information from the hindbrain to the cerebrum

Bremer (1936) originally interpreted his findings as supporting the **passive theory of sleep.** According to the passive theory of sleep, the brain is a passive organ and requires stimulation in order to be active. This means that we are awake as long as the brain receives stimulation. Bremer reasoned that the encephale isole group showed normal sleep and waking because the brain was receiving stimulation from all of the cranial nerves, although no information from the spinal nerves could reach the brain. On the other hand, the cerveau isole group could receive stimulation only from cranial nerves I and II, which was not enough to keep the cats awake, according to Bremer's reasoning. However, shortly after Bremer's study, investigators in a lab in Italy (Moruzzi & Magoun, 1949) discovered the reticular formation, and the explanation for the permanent sleep of the cerveau isole group became clear: The reticular formation produces cerebral arousal, and Bremer had severed the reticular formation in the cerveau isole group.

The Raphe

In Chapter 4, the **raphe system** was identified as the principal source of the neurotransmitter *serotonin* in the brain. Because serotonin plays an important role in regulating sleep, the raphe undoubtedly is crucial in the control of sleep. Lesions of the raphe produce sleeplessness in rats, whereas stimulation of the raphe induces sleep (Jouvet, 1999). A case study of a patient with a tumor in the raphe system revealed that the patient was unable to sleep and remained awake for about 2 weeks until his death (Arpa et al., 1994).

Neurons in the raphe exhibit a firing pattern that is unlike that of other neurons in the brain (Jacobs, 1994). These neurons fire spontaneously at a slow, steady rate. Even when the neurons are surgically removed from the brain and cultured in a dish on the lab bench, these serotonin cells continue to fire their characteristic rhythm pattern. The rate of firing of raphe cells changes in response to alterations in the level of consciousness. For example, when an individual is relaxed but awake, the serotonin neurons fire at a rate of about three spikes per second (Figure 10.10). The number of spikes per second generated by the serotonin neurons increases when an individual is awake and aroused. As the individual falls into slow-wave (non-REM) sleep, the number of spikes per second decreases. However, during REM sleep when the cortex shows increased activation associated with dreaming, the neurons in the raphe system *stop firing* altogether. Just before the individual awakens, the neurons in the raphe resume their three-per-second pattern.

The Locus Coeruleus

Recall from Chapters 3 and 4 that norepinephrine is produced by neurons in the **locus coeruleus.** Norepinephrine is involved in producing and regulating arousal, which is necessary for consciousness. For example, the release of norepinephrine from the locus coeruleus is responsible for the shift from sleep or decreased

Figure 10.9 Bremer's encephale isole and cerveau isole preparations

(a) In the encephale isole preparation, a lesion was made between the medulla and the spinal cord. (b) In the cerveau isole preparation, a lesion was made between the diencephalon and the mesencephalon.

a. Encephale isole

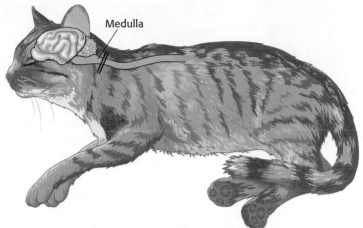

Medulla

b. Cerveau isole

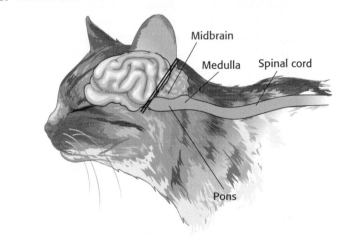

Midbrain

Medulla

Spinal cord

Pons

passive theory of sleep: an explanation of sleep that proposes that the brain is a passive organ and requires stimulation to remain active

raphe system: a hindbrain area that produces serotonin and regulates sleep behavior

locus coeruleus: hindbrain structure that produces norepinephrine and regulates arousal

Figure 10.10 Spike activity in the raphe associated with various states of consciousness
Activity of neurons in the raphe varies, depending on the state of consciousness, with very high rates of activity associated with active waking and no activity associated with REM sleep.

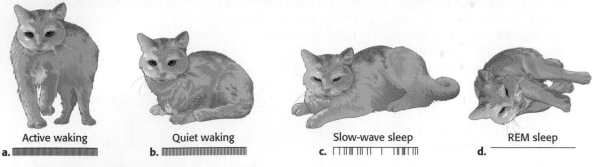

a. Active waking   b. Quiet waking   c. Slow-wave sleep   d. REM sleep

Serotonin neuronal activity

5 seconds

consciousness to alert wakefulness (Bremner, Krystal, Southwick, & Charney, 1996). For that reason, neurons in the locus coeruleus are active when we are awake and comparatively inactive when we are asleep (Abercrombie & Zigmond, 1995). In addition, the locus coeruleus becomes active when a novel or important stimulus is presented, initiating a state of alert attentiveness. The locus coeruleus also appears to play a role in selecting between a well-learned behavior or a more flexible behavior, which requires conscious execution, in an unfamiliar situation (Usher, Cohen, Servan-Schreiber, Rajkowski, & Aston-Jones, 1999).

The Suprachiasmic Nucleus of the Hypothalamus

The **suprachiasmic nucleus** of the hypothalamus is located in the anterior hypothalamus just above, or superior to, the optic chiasm. This nucleus has been demonstrated to play a crucial role in regulating sleep-wake cycles, or what is known as the **biological clock.** Research on many species indicates that each species is active at certain hours of the day and is inactive at others. Reptiles, birds, and mammals appear to undergo a period of quiescence that we call *sleep.* Studies of human participants have shown that most people have a rhythm, called a **circadian rhythm,** that is a little over 24 hours long for both young and elderly individuals (Czeisler et al., 1999). For most people, this means that we feel sleepy sometime during the evening and typically fall asleep within an hour or two thereafter. If we manage to stay awake past our usual sleeping time, we feel extremely tired in the middle of the night. However, toward morning, we get a second wind and feel wide awake once again.

The suprachiasmic nucleus is believed to contain the pacemaker that controls the circadian rhythm. Not only does this rhythm regulate our levels of sleepiness and awakeness, but it also controls hormonal levels and body temperature and metabolism (Schibler, Ripperger, & Brown, 2001; Wirz-Justice, 1995). For example, our body temperature reaches a peak at 8 p.m. and then drops throughout the night, reaching a low at about 5 a.m., when it starts rising again. The pituitary hormone *adrenocorticotropin* (ACTH, which regulates our response to stress, as you will learn in Chapter 14) increases slowly during the night and shows a marked increase about 1 hour before spontaneous awakening (Born, Hansen, Marshall, Molle, & Fehm, 1999). Our brain activity and sensory abilities follow a circadian rhythm, too. At 8 p.m., most of our senses (taste, smell, hearing) are at a peak, and our hearing remains sharp all night. Most of our senses, including our sense of pain, are lowest in the morning.

This rhythm continues despite changes in lighting, diet, hormonal state, drugs, and illness (Richter, 1955). People and other animals living in constant light or constant darkness continue to go to sleep and wake up right on schedule according

suprachiasmic nucleus: a nucleus of the hypothalamus that controls the biological clock
biological clock: a mechanism controlled by the suprachiasmic nucleus that regulates sleep-wake cycles
circadian rhythm: a sleep-wake cycle that is approximately 24 hours long in most people

to their biological clock. However, events in the environment can reset the biological clock. For example, if you live in New York and fly three time zones west to California, you feel very tired at 9 p.m. California time because your body is still on New York time (which is midnight). But, in a few days, your biological clock is reset, and you adjust to California time and no longer feel like sleeping at 9 p.m. Any number of things can reset your biological clock, including natural or artificial light, your alarm clock, or other environmental demands. Anything that resets the biological clock is called a **zeitgeber.**

When the biological clock is disturbed, as when an individual remains awake longer than usual, changes take place in the brain to restore the sleep-wake cycle. Using a microdialysis technique, Tarja Porkka-Heiskanen and her colleagues (1997) at Harvard Medical School studied the effects of prolonged wakefulness in cats. Electrodes and cannulae for microdialysis probes were implanted into the brains of cats in order that EEG records and neurotransmitter samples could be obtained from freely moving subjects. When cats were kept awake for 6 hours beyond their normal sleeping time, adenosine levels in the hypothalamus increased. Adenosine is known to inhibit the activity of neurons that release acetylcholine. Therefore, the results of Porkka-Heiskanen's experiment suggest that prolonged wakefulness results in an increase in extracellular adenosine levels, which causes an inhibition of cholinergic neurons, inducing sleep. During recovery sleep, the level of adenosine declines to normal levels.

The Effect of Light

Information about light is relayed from the *retina* to the suprachiasmic nucleus of the hypothalamus by way of the **retinohypothalamic tract** (Figure 10.11). The suprachiasmic nucleus processes this information and sends it to the **pineal gland.** The pineal gland is an unpaired structure that is located just anterior to the midbrain and posterior to the diencephalon. The main function of the pineal gland appears to be the release of a hormone called **melatonin.** Information from the suprachiasmic nucleus directly affects the release of melatonin from the pineal gland because melatonin release follows a circadian rhythm with low levels of melatonin being released during the light cycle and high levels being released during the dark. Melatonin, in turn, signals information about the environmental light/dark cycle to the rest of the brain (Arendt, 1988; Cardinali, 1981; Golombek, Pevet, & Cardinali, 1996). In addition, melatonin receptors in the suprachiasmic nucleus permit melatonin to influence and even alter the circadian rhythm (Reppert et al., 1988; Reppert 1997). The *For Further Thought* describes how melatonin can reset the biological clock.

However, the retinohypothalamic tract is not the only pathway by which information about light reaches the brain. Scott Campbell and Patricia Murphy (1998) at Cornell University demonstrated that shifts in the circadian rhythm occurred following light pulses administered to the back of the knees of human participants who were unaware that light was being administered. Although Campbell and Murphy do not know exactly how information about this type of light stimulation was transmitted to the brain, they suggested that the stimulation of light receptors in the blood, such as hemoglobin in red blood cells, causes nitric oxide to signal the presence of light to the suprachiasmic nucleus, altering the biological clock.

Many investigators now believe that genes control the biological clock. Earlier research with fruit

zeitgeber: anything, such as light or an alarm clock, that resets the biological clock

retinohypothalamic tract: a band of axons that connects the retina with the suprachiasmic nucleus, relaying information about the presence of light in the environment

pineal gland: an unpaired brain structure that releases melatonin

melatonin: a hormone that signals information about the environmental light/dark cycle to the rest of the brain

Figure 10.11 Pathways to and from the suprachiasmic nucleus
Information from the retina reaches the supraciasmic nucleus via the retinohypothalamic tract. Light striking the retina causes the suprachiasmic nucleus to signal the pineal gland to reduce its secretion of melatonin.

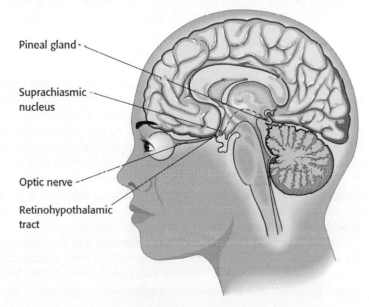

Pineal gland

Suprachiasmic nucleus

Optic nerve

Retinohypothalamic tract

Resetting the Biological Clock with Melatonin

Melatonin is a hormone that is used by the brain to signal the presence or absence of environmental light. This signal conveys information about the circadian cycle as well as the light changes associated with seasonal variations. Because melatonin is so closely tied to the sleep-wake cycle, it has been used to treat a number of disorders associated with disturbance of the circadian rhythm. For example, it has been used effectively to reduce sleepiness and lapses in alertness associated with jet lag and shift work (Golombek, Pevet, & Cardinali, 1996).

When taken as a drug, melatonin can reset the biological clock. However, the time of day has an important impact on the effect of melatonin in the body. That is, when melatonin is taken at dusk, it shifts the circadian rhythm forward, which is useful if you are traveling to a different time zone in the east. In contrast, when melatonin is taken at dawn, it shifts the biological clock backward in time, preparing a person to adjust to a new time zone in the west.

A dose of 2.0 to 5.0 mg of melatonin will normally induce sleep. A much smaller dose of 0.5 mg simulates the changes produced naturally by diminishing light associated with sunset. When 0.5 mg is taken in the afternoon, it simulates an earlier sunset in the body and prepares the body for an earlier bedtime. Therefore, a person traveling from California to New York might take 0.5 mg in the afternoon for 2 or 3 days before flying east, which should prepare that person to eat and sleep at appropriate hours on the East Coast. When 0.5 mg of melatonin is taken in the early morning, it will simulate a delay of dawn, which will allow a person who travels from the East Coast to the West Coast to remain asleep longer in the morning and thus make a better adjustment to a more western time zone.

flies and bread mold has demonstrated that circadian rhythms in these organisms are controlled by genes. More recent research with hamsters and mice has shown that their biological clocks, too, appear to be controlled by genes (Morris et al., 1998; Antoch et al., 1997). For example, Joseph Takahashi and his colleagues at Northwestern University have located the gene, which Takahashi has labeled the **Clock gene,** responsible for producing the circadian rhythm in mice (Antoch et al., 1997). Mice with defective Clock genes have a circadian rhythm that is 4 hours longer than normal. Of much interest to researchers is the discovery that one segment of the gene contains the same sequence of amino acids found in the genes that control the biological clocks in fruit flies and bread mold. Similarly, Clock genes, called *per* genes, have also been discovered in humans (Fu & Ptacek, 2001). Although no one currently understands how these genes ultimately control the biological clock, it may be that all organisms share the same basic clock mechanism.

Clock gene: a gene in mice that produces their circadian rhythm

Thalamic Nuclei

The neural pathways between the thalamus and the cerebral cortex, called the **thalamocortical system,** appear to play an important role in determining our conscious experience (Pare & Llinas, 1995; Tononi & Edelman, 1998). Recall that the reticular formation relays its information to the thalamus for action by the cerebrum. The posterior areas of the thalamocortical system are associated with perceptual processing and categorization, and the anterior areas are associated with memory and planning. These areas work together to produce a unified consciousness, in which all components of the conscious experience (visual, auditory, taste, olfactory, somatosensory, data from memory, and other components) are integrated, and incongruent elements are combined or ignored (Damasio, 1999).

As you learned in Chapter 4, the thalamus acts as a filter or gate that controls the transmission of sensory information to the cerebral cortex, amygdala, and hippocampus. EEG studies have indicated that, in non-REM sleep, certain thalamic nuclei, including the **reticular thalamic nucleus,** produce slow synchronous oscil-

thalamocortical system: a neural pathway between the thalamus and the cerebral cortex, which plays a role in determining our conscious experience

reticular thalamic nucleus: a nucleus in the thalamus that blocks access of sensory information to the cerebrum and limbic system

lations that appear to block the access of sensory information to the cerebrum and limbic system (Krystal et al., 1995; Steriade, McCormick, & Sejnowski, 1993). During REM sleep and wakefulness, another EEG pattern is observed in the thalamus that is believed to promote transmission of sensory stimulation to the cortex. Thus, during dreaming, the thalamocortical system sends internally generated sensory information from the limbic system to the cerebral cortex to create the experience we know as dreams.

The **intralaminar nuclei** of the thalamus have been shown to control the transmission of information from the hindbrain to the cerebrum. These nuclei receive information directly from the ascending reticular activating system and sends that information to different parts of the cortex, including the *anterior cingulate cortex,* which (as you learned in Chapter 9) is involved in shifting attention and cognitive processing. Together with the thalamic reticular nucleus, the intralaminar nuclei play an important role in alerting the cortex and determining which stimuli receive conscious attention. PET studies of human participants revealed activation of the midbrain reticular formation and the intralaminar nuclei when the participants shifted from a relaxed state to a vigilant, aroused state (Figure 10.12), indicating that the reticular formation and intralaminar nuclei play a central role in arousal and vigilance (Kinomura, Larsson, Gulyas, & Roland, 1996).

REM Sleep and the Brain

Investigators are uncertain as to the exact brain structures that control REM sleep. Certain areas of the pons appear to be associated with certain aspects of REM sleep. For example, stimulation of acetylcholine receptors in the posterior-dorsal region of the pons produces rapid eye movement but no other components of REM sleep, whereas stimulation of acetylcholine receptors in the posterior-ventral pons produces desynchronized brain waves characteristic of REM sleep and PGO spikes (Baghdoyan, Rodrigo-Angulo, McCarley, & Hobson, 1984; Katayama, DeWitt, Becker, & Hayes, 1984). In addition, acetylcholine injected into the dorsal-lateral pons causes loss of muscle tone. Thus, acetylcholine appears to play an important role in maintaining REM sleep, although glutamate has been demonstrated to be involved in the loss of muscle tone in REM sleep (Lai & Siegel, 1988). In contrast, serotonin neurons in the raphe system and norepinephrine neurons in the locus coeruleus are typically inactive during REM sleep.

Neuroanatomists (people who study brain anatomy) have discovered many anatomical interconnections between the brain structures involved in cortical arousal. Interconnections exist between all of the structures described in the

Figure 10.12 PET activation of the reticular formation and intralaminar nuclei in a vigilance task

These PET images were generated by the paired-image subtraction method, in which PET scans obtained while participants were resting with their eyes open were subtracted from scans obtained while participants were engaged in a reaction-time task. Significant activations were found in the reticular formation (midbrain tegmentum, C, D) and the intralaminar nucleus of the thalamus, A, B, E.

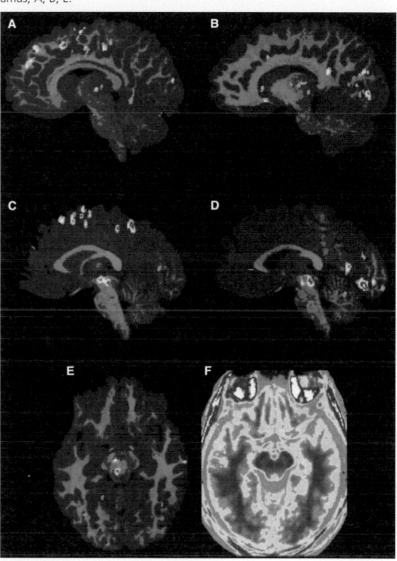

intralaminar nucleus: a nucleus of the thalamus that controls the transmission of information from the hindbrain to the cerebrum

preceding sections, including the reticular formation, the raphe system, the locus coeruleus, and various hypothalamic and thalamic nuclei. Information appears to run in both directions, to and from these interconnected sites, which means that a good deal of data is shared among these brain structures. The unified nature of consciousness can be explained by the simultaneous activation of all of these structures (Delacour, 1995).

Recap 10.3: Brain Mechanisms of Sleep and Consciousness

In Bremer's sleep experiment, cats in the *cerveau isole* group remained in a permanent sleeping state following surgery because Bremer had severed the (a)_____ _____, which alerts the cerebrum when important stimuli occur. The (b)_____ system is the principal source of serotonin in the brain and, thus, plays a role in regulating sleep. Neurons in the locus coeruleus produce (c)_____, which is involved in producing arousal and consciousness. The (d)_____ nucleus (SCN) of the hypothalamus plays a crucial role in regulating the biological clock. The SCN relays information about light to the pineal gland, which releases (e)_____. The (f)_____ system is the pathway between the thalamus and cerebral cortex that plays a role in determining our conscious experience. (g)_____ appears to play a role in maintaining REM sleep.

The Function of Sleep

No one knows why we sleep, although people since the dawn of humankind have tried to explain the function of sleep. Primitive people believed that, when we sleep, our spirits leave our bodies to cavort with other spirits (living and dead). According to this primitive view, dreams are a glimpse of our interactions with these other spirits.

More modern explanations of sleep include the *passive theory* of sleep, which you learned about earlier in this chapter, the *active theory* of sleep, the *restorative theory* of sleep, and the *evolutionary theory* of sleep. The discovery of the reticular formation caused the passive theory of sleep to fall out of favor. Ivan Pavlov, who won a Nobel Prize for his work on salivary function in 1904, proposed the **active theory of sleep.** According to the active theory of sleep, the brain is normally active. (Recall that the passive theory of sleep maintained that the brain is passive.) Sleep occurs in the active brain when a wave of depression sweeps over the cerebrum. Pavlov never explained the mechanism for this wave of depression, and, in fact, no wave of depression has ever been measured (except when the surface of a brain is carelessly allowed to dry out during surgery). The active theory of sleep has been discarded because no underlying brain mechanism for sweeping cortical depression has ever been uncovered.

According to the **restorative theory of sleep,** sleep is a time when waste products in the nervous system are removed and neurotransmitters and other chemicals are restored. On an intuitive level, this theory makes a lot of sense. When we are awake, neurons are very active and produce a lot of waste products and discharge huge quantities of neurotransmitters. However, after a very busy day, you do not require more sleep than you do after a day during which you've done very little. There is evidence that our sleep pattern changes after a physically vigorous day, such as after running a marathon, but there is no evidence that we actually do more restoration of tissue and neurochemicals after a hard day's work.

active theory of sleep: an explanation of sleep that proposes that the brain is normally active and that sleep arises from a wave of depression that spreads across the cerebrum

restorative theory of sleep: an explanation of sleep that proposes that sleep is a state during which waste products are removed from the brain and neurotransmitters are restored

The **evolutionary theory of sleep** maintains that all animals occupy an environmental niche and sleep to conserve energy during times when it is dangerous to be awake. For example, humans do not see well in the dark and could not easily escape predators if they were being chased at night. For that reason, according to the evolutionary theory, people sleep at night because it's safer for them to be asleep then. Other animals, known as **nocturnal animals,** are active at night and sleep during the day. These animals have evolved with sensory abilities (acute olfactory and auditory senses, scotopic vision) that permit them to find food and mates safely at night.

evolutionary theory of sleep: an explanation of sleep that proposed that all animals sleep to conserve energy during times when it is dangerous or not necessary for them to be awake
nocturnal animals: animals that are active at night and sleep during the day

The support for the evolutionary theory of sleep is largely circumstantial. Large grazing animals, like elephants, horses, and cows, spend only a few hours sleeping and many hours each day (up to 20 hours per day) eating because their caloric needs are so great. Prey animals, such as rabbits and mice, that have safe hiding places have long periods of sleep. Prey animals that live in an open, vulnerable environment, like herding antelope, display light sleep for short periods of time. In contrast, predators, like wolves and lions, sleep deeply for long periods of time. A common domestic cat, for example, will sleep about 18 hours a day.

According to the evolutionary theory of sleep, humans sleep because consciousness has high energy costs. When we are awake or in REM sleep, heart rate, respiration rate, and brain activity are increased. Thus, consciousness and REM sleep are accompanied by high metabolic rates. Even when we are awake, most brain activities are unconscious. Delacour (1995) has suggested that conscious brain activity requires more energy than unconscious brain activity and that therefore, we engage in conscious behavior sparingly. For this reason, well-learned behaviors are transferred over to the unconscious, or implicit, memory systems for execution (Kavanau, 1997). Conscious processing is reserved for new or unexpected events and for retrieving stored data from declarative memory, although there is evidence that some novel stimuli can be processed in the absence of conscious awareness (Berns, Cohen, & Mintun, 1997).

The Function of REM Sleep

If the function of sleep is unknown, the function of REM sleep is even more unclear. For some unknown reason, newborns spend about 50% of their sleeping time in REM sleep. What could they be dreaming about? Many investigators believe that memory consolidation occurs during REM sleep. Other investigators have suggested that REM sleep in newborns is important for strengthening neural networks.

Although the function of REM sleep is still unknown, we do know that deprivation of REM sleep can impair thinking and disturb behavior. For example, REM deprivation is associated with increased eating and weight gain, an inability to concentrate, and increased anxiety and irritability. When a REM-deprived person is permitted to get a full night of undisturbed sleep, REM rebound is observed. As you learned earlier in this chapter, *REM rebound* refers to an increase in REM sleep, which is accompanied by an increase in dreaming.

The Nature of Dreaming

Psychologists and other theorists have proposed a variety of explanations for the function of dreams. Undoubtedly, in other psychology courses, you have learned about Sigmund Freud's theory of dreams. According to Freud (1900), dreams symbolically express our unconscious desires and fears. For example, dreaming about money, Freud believed, might indicate a person's anxiety concerning anal functions.

A more modern view of dreams is the **activation-synthesis hypothesis** of dreaming, proposed by Robert McCarley and J. Allan Hoffman (1981). According to the activation-synthesis hypothesis, our cerebral cortex processes and interprets incoming sensory information, even during sleep. Thus, dreams arise when the brain attempts to make sense out of disjointed sensory input (for example, visual

activation-synthesis hypothesis: an explanation of how dreams arise, based on the processing and interpretation of sensory information by the cerebral cortex

images produced by random activation of the visual system) during sleep. One morning just before awakening, I dreamed that I was at a party dancing to music, then abruptly awoke to find that my clock radio was playing. I had obviously incorporated the music blaring from my radio into my dream.

Dement and Kleitman (1957) attempted to determine when dreaming occurs during the course of a night. Participants in their study slept in Dement and Kleitman's laboratory, with EEG electrodes pasted to their scalps to permit recording of brain activity while they slept. The investigators monitored the participants' EEG records while they slept and awakened participants during REM and non-REM sleep. When the participants were awakened during REM sleep, they reported dreaming about 80% of the time. In contrast, they reported dreaming about 20% of the time when awakened during non-REM sleep. Hence, dreaming occurs during both REM and non-REM sleep (Foulkes, 1993).

Subsequent research has demonstrated that the quality of REM dreams differs from the quality of dreams generated during non-REM sleep. REM dreams are experienced as vivid and well organized, albeit sometimes illogical or fantastical (for example, dreaming that you are flying with your arms outstretched). The content of non-REM dreams is less organized and appears to be related to ongoing life events or concerns. This difference in dream content and quality may be related to differences in brain physiology during REM sleep and non-REM sleep. REM sleep is characterized by an *increase in excitatory input* to the cerebral cortex from the ascending reticular activating system and a *reduction in inhibitory input* to the cortex, with only dopamine pathways being active (Gottesmann, 1999). Thus, dreams during REM sleep are often illogical or irrational, due to the absence of inhibitory influences that normally regulate activity in the cerebral cortex. During non-REM sleep, brain stem input to the cerebral cortex via dopamine, norepinephrine, serotonin, and histamine pathways is largely inhibitory, producing less intense and more rational mental activity (Gottesmann, 1999).

Recap 10.4: The Function of Sleep

According to the (a)_____ theory of sleep, the natural state of the brain is to be asleep. In contrast, according to the (b)_____ theory of sleep, the brain is normally active. The (c)_____ theory of sleep maintains that sleep is a time when waste products are removed and vital chemicals restored. The (d)_____ theory of sleep maintains that sleep conserves energy at times when it is dangerous to be awake. The function of (e)_____ sleep is unknown. According to the (f)_____-_____ hypothesis of dreams, dreams arise when the brain tries to make sense out of incoming sensory information during sleep. When subjects were awakened from (g)_____ sleep, they reported dreaming 80% of the time, compared to subjects awakened during (h)_____-_____ sleep, who report dreaming 20% of the time.

Sleep Disorders

Sleep disorders tell us a great deal about the processes underlying the continuum between sleep and consciousness. Let's review a number of these disorders as we seek to understand sleeping and waking states.

Insomnia

Insomnia is a disorder in which the affected individual has difficulty falling asleep or staying asleep. All of us have had this trouble at one time or another. In fact, for people between the ages of 18 and 25, insomnia is a common problem. A person may have trouble sleeping because he or she is excited or worried about something. Recall that earlier in the chapter I stressed that a person must be in a relaxed state before sleep can occur. Sometimes a college student can get into a vicious cycle where he or she lies in bed worrying, "Here I go again. I can't fall asleep. If I don't sleep tonight, I'll be too tired to study for my exam tomorrow night. Then I'll fail the exam and end up flunking out of school . . ." These kinds of thoughts are accompanied by beta wave activity, which is not conducive to falling asleep. Whereas younger people have trouble falling asleep, older people who experience insomnia have trouble staying asleep (Reynolds, Buysse, & Kupfer, 1995).

Sometimes prescription sleep medication is prescribed for individuals who have insomnia, although most people with insomnia do not seek medical treatment for this disorder but rather use over-the-counter medications or alcohol to fall asleep (Nowell, Buysse, Morin, Reynolds, & Kupfer, 1998). Many over-the-counter medications contain antihistamines, which block histamine receptors. (Recall from Chapter 3 that histamines cause arousal of the nervous system.) Benzodiazepines have been found to be the most effective for treating insomnia. As you learned in Chapter 3, benzodiazepines bind with GABA receptors, producing relaxation. Barbiturates can also induce sleep, but tolerance to the drugs occurs in a few days, requiring higher and higher doses to be administered to achieve sleep. Withdrawal from barbiturates can produce insomnia, increased REM sleep, and vivid nightmares (Nishino, Mignot, & Dement, 2001). Also, melatonin has been demonstrated to be somewhat useful in treating insomnia.

Relaxation exercises and meditation can help a person learn to relax and fall asleep. Other behavioral treatments include *cognitive behavioral therapy*, *sleep restriction therapy*, and *stimulus control therapy*. In cognitive behavioral therapy, the patient learns to identify and modify thought patterns that maintain insomnia. Sleep restriction therapy involves initially restricting the amount of time that a person has to sleep and gradually increasing the time for sleep as the person's ability to fall asleep improves. In stimulus control therapy, people with insomnia are allowed to use the bedroom only for sleep. That is, they cannot read, work, or watch television in their bedroom and must leave their bedroom if they are unable to sleep for 20 minutes, returning only when they feel sleepy. All of these behavioral techniques have proven to be helpful (Nowell et al., 1998).

insomnia: a disorder in which the affected individual has difficulty falling asleep or staying asleep

Narcolepsy

This disorder is characterized by episodes of *cataplexy* in which the affected individual suddenly loses all muscle tone and falls asleep. These sleeping attacks resemble epileptic seizures, hence the term **narcolepsy.** Typically, a person with narcolepsy will experience an *aura*, or sensory illusion, such as a particular odor or a visual image, immediately before the sleep attack, and different environmental stimuli (especially emotional stimuli) have been observed to trigger an episode of cataplexy. For example, laughter is the most common trigger for cataplexy in people. EEG recordings of people during cataplexy reveal that they go immediately into REM sleep when they collapse into sleep. The loss of muscle tone during cataplexy also indicates that the affected individual is in REM sleep. However, the most prominent symptom for most people with narcolepsy is the excessive daytime sleepiness and periods of intense drowsiness that occur every 3 to 4 hours, requiring a short nap. The individual with narcolepsy is typically not aware of these periods of drowsiness and often will deny falling asleep. EEG studies of individuals with narcolepsy have revealed that narcolepsy is associated with decreased delta wave activity during non-REM sleep (Guilleminault et al., 1998).

narcolepsy: a disorder characterized by seizure-like attacks in which the affected individual loses all muscle tone and falls asleep

Narcolepsy has also been detected in dogs, and much research has been conducted on narcoleptic dogs in order to gain a better understanding of this puzzling disorder (Takahashi, 1999). For over a decade, William Dement has maintained a colony of narcoleptic Dobermans and Labradors at Stanford University (Figure 10.13). Because the genetic pedigree of the Stanford dogs is well known, Mignot and his colleagues have been able to identify the gene that causes canine narcolepsy (Lin et al., 1999). This gene codes for a receptor of a particular neuropeptide called **orexin,** which regulates eating behavior. By inactivating the orexin gene in mice, Yanagisawa and his colleagues (Chemelli et al., 1999) have been able to produce narcoleptic attacks in mice. Investigators are uncertain as to the role that orexin plays in sleep, but recent evidence suggests that narcolepsy may be caused by the loss of cells in the hypothalamus that produce orexin (Siegel, 2000).

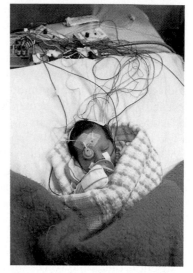

Figure 10.13 A narcoleptic dog

Sleep Apnea

The word *apnea* literally means "without breath" [*a-* = without; *-pnea* = breath, Latin, Greek]. Thus, **sleep apnea** is a disorder in which breathing is temporarily suspended during sleep. This disturbance can occur at any age from birth to old age and is most prevalent in obese adults. Obviously, when an individual stops breathing, asphyxiation sets in, and death can result. Most cases of **sudden infant death syndrome (SIDS),** in which a healthy infant is placed in its crib and is discovered dead sometime later, have been attributed to sleep apnea. That is, in these infants, the breathing reflex is not fully developed or reliable, and, when they stop breathing, the brain does not induce inhalation as it should. Sleep apnea is especially common in premature babies, who have to be monitored constantly for any signs of breathing cessation (Figure 10.14). In addition, some medications can cause sleep apnea. People taking certain muscle relaxants, for example, may wake up gasping for air, which can be a frightening experience.

Somnambulism

Sleepwalking is the common word for **somnambulism.** As you learned at the beginning of this chapter, people can engage in very complicated behaviors (such as speaking in French or climbing stairs) while sleepwalking. However, sleepwalking generally occurs in non-REM sleep, when the brain is relatively inactive. This means that people are unconscious of their behavior when somnambulating. Remember that during REM sleep the major muscle groups do not have any tone and are incapable of producing movement. On the other hand, muscle tone is present during non-REM sleep, and behavior can be initiated by unconscious or implicit brain systems, out of the person's conscious control.

Figure 10.14 Infant with an apnea monitor

REM Sleep Behavior Disorder

Some individuals with Parkinson's disease and other neurodegenerative disorders show excessive motor activity during REM sleep. **REM sleep behavior disorder** is characterized by normal skeletal muscle tone during REM sleep and motor activity associated with the content of the ongoing dream. That is, people with REM sleep behavior disorder do *not* lose their muscle tone during REM sleep and are capable of moving and acting out their dreams. Often the dreams have emotional content that is frightening or threatening to the dreamer (requiring the dreamer to defend himself or herself from an attack), which causes the dreamer to assault his or her bed partner (Ferini-Strambi & Zucconi, 2000; Olson, Boeve, & Silber, 2000). Benzodiazepines have been demonstrated to reduce motor activity during REM sleep in people who are troubled with this disorder.

Nocturnal Enuresis

Nocturnal enuresis is also known as *bed-wetting*. Many young children have accidents and urinate in their sleep. But, persistent bed-wetting after the age of 9 is

orexin: a class of peptides that stimulates food intake and also appears to play a role in producing narcolepsy

sleep apnea: a disorder in which breathing is temporarily suspended during sleep

sudden infant death syndrome (SIDS): a disorder associated with sleep apnea in which a seemingly healthy infant is placed in a crib to sleep and is found dead sometime later

somnambulism: sleepwalking associated with non-REM sleep

REM sleep behavior disorder: a disorder characterized by normal skeletal muscle tone during REM sleep and motor activity associated with dream content

nocturnal enuresis: bed-wetting, which occurs in non-REM sleep

regarded as a medical problem. Nocturnal enuresis occurs in non-REM sleep, when conscious processing is absent in the brain. Thus, bed-wetting happens unconsciously, and the person is not aware that he or she is urinating when it happens, which makes this disorder very difficult to treat (Butler, 2001; Jensen & Kristensen, 2001; Lawless & McElderry, 2001).

Psychologists employ classical conditioning to treat bed-wetting. An alarm is used as the US, which awakens the affected individual. (Waking is the UR to the alarm.) This alarm is wired to a sensor that detects wetness, and the sensor is attached to the individual's pajama bottoms (Figure 10.15). Therefore, when the individual begins to urinate during sleep, the sensor detects the urine, causing the alarm to ring. Urination is the CS that is paired with the alarm (the US). This treatment is based on the theory that, when urination (the CS) occurs, the individual will awaken (the CR).

Night Terror

A **nightmare**, as you know, is a "bad" dream or a dream loaded with negative emotional content. Some nightmares can be so disturbing that the autonomic arousal that they induce wakens us from our sleep. Nightmares occur typically during REM sleep. In contrast, **night terror** takes place during non-REM sleep. A person experiencing night terror awakens from deep sleep frightened and showing signs of autonomic arousal, including increased heart rate and blood pressure. Often the individual experiencing night terror will begin to scream and then wake up, confused and frightened. Whereas a person awaking from a nightmare can usually describe the content of the bad dream in detail, an individual awaking with night terror has no idea why he or she feels scared. Night terror is common in young children and usually disappears as they get older, although some people continue to experience night terror in adulthood.

Sleep Disorders Associated with Alterations of the Circadian Rhythm

A number of disorders are associated with alterations of the circadian rhythm, including *advanced-sleep-phase syndrome, delayed-sleep-phase syndrome,* and *jet lag.* Individuals with **advanced-sleep-phase syndrome** generally feel tired due to disturbed phasing of their circadian rhythm, several hours earlier than their normal sleep time. A person with advanced-sleep-phase syndrome, for example, may shows signs of sleepiness at 5 or 6 p.m., instead of at 10 or 11 p.m. In contrast, those with **delayed-sleep-phase syndrome** do not feel tired until many hours after their normal sleep time and awake much later than normal. **Jet lag** is caused by taking long flights that cross several time zones, which causes an abrupt shift in the sleep-wake cycle. Although it lasts only a day or so, people with jet lag feel tired and cannot think clearly during normal waking hours and have trouble falling asleep at bedtime.

One disorder, called *familial advanced sleep-phase syndrome,* is believed to be associated with a mutation in a gene on chromosome 2 (Toh et al., 2001). This gene, known as h*Per2*, disrupts the normal functioning of the human biological clock when a single base-pair mutation of the gene occurs. People with familial advanced

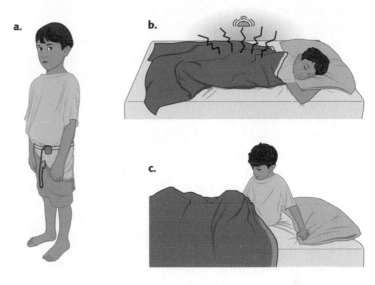

Figure 10.15 A treatment for nocturnal enuresis
(a) Before the child goes to bed, a moisture sensor is clipped to the child's pajamas. (b) When the child begins to urinate during sleep, the sensor detects the wetness and activates an alarm. (c) The child is awakened. Thus, urination (CS) is paired with the alarm (US). Over time, the initiation of urination (CS) will cause the child to awaken (CR).

nightmare: a dream loaded with negative emotional content
night terror: a phenomenon that occurs during non-REM sleep in which affected individuals awaken from deep sleep frightened and showing signs of autonomic arousal

advanced-sleep-phase syndrome: a disorder in which affected individuals feel tired several hours earlier than their normal sleep time
delayed-sleep-phase syndrome: a disorder in which affected individuals do not feel tired until many hours after their normal sleep time and awaken much later than normal
jet lag: a disturbance of the sleep-wake cycle caused by taking a long flight that crosses several time zones

sleep-phase syndrome tend to rise very early in the morning, at about 4:00 a.m. In fact, the biological clocks of these individuals tend to run fast, approximately 4 hours ahead of normal. Many members of the same family, who share this altered gene, fall asleep very early in the evening and awaken well before dawn.

Shift work can also produce sleep disorders, especially when the worker is forced to work different shifts during different weeks; for example, working 3 p.m. to 11 p.m. one week and 11 p.m. to 7 a.m. the next. Changing shifts on a weekly or monthly basis is quite disruptive for the endogenous biological clock, causing the individual to feel sleepy and inattentive while awake and to have problems falling asleep at bedtime. Sleepiness can disrupt performance and cause the sleepy person to make more mistakes than usual (Akerstedt, 1985). In addition, confused and very ill patients often have a **reversed sleep-wake cycle,** remaining asleep during the day and awake at night (Wirz-Justice, 1995). Bright light has been used with some success as treatment for all of these disorders (Campbell et al., 1993; Eastman et al., 1994; Lack et al., 1996; Oren & Terman, 1998). Light has an activating effect, probably caused by light-induced release of norepinephrine, and it improves performance.

> **reversed sleep-wake cycle:** a disorder in which the affected individual remains asleep during the day and is awake at night

The research of cognitive psychologists and behavioral neuroscientists is improving our understanding of the states we call *sleep* and *consciousness*. Some scholars firmly believe that we will never fully understand consciousness because of the problems presented by the mind studying the mind (Horgan, 1994). They question whether the human mind can really examine itself objectively. Nonetheless, studies that involve recording the electrical activity of the brain or functional brain imaging have greatly enhanced our knowledge of sleep and consciousness and will continue to do so in the future. Most cognitive neuroscientists today agree that consciousness results from the integration of many discrete cortical functions that are distributed across the cerebrum.

But, remember that brain stem structures also play an important role in sleep and consciousness. For example, the biological clock, which determines when we sleep and when we're awake, is regulated by the suprachiasmic nucleus of the hypothalamus. As you will learn in Chapter 11, the hypothalamus directs behaviors associated with a number of drives, in addition to the drive to sleep.

Recap 10.5: Sleep Disorders

(a)_____ is a disorder in which a person has difficulty falling or staying asleep. Antihistamines, benzodiazepines, and barbiturates can (b)_____ sleep. (c)_____ is characterized by excessive daytime sleepiness and episodes of cataplexy in which a person loses all muscle tone and falls asleep. (d)_____ _____ is a disorder in which breathing is temporarily suspended during sleeping. People with (e)_____ typically sleepwalk during non-REM sleep. (f)_____ _____ _____ disorder is characterized by normal skeletal muscle tone and activity during REM sleep. The formal term for bed-wetting is (g)_____ _____. Nightmares generally occur during (h)_____ sleep, and night terror takes place during (i)_____ sleep. A person with (j)_____-sleep-phase syndrome will become sleepy early in the evening and awaken in the early morning hours. In contrast, a person with (k)_____-sleep-phase syndrome does not feel sleepy until several hours after normal sleep time and awakens hours later than normal.

Chapter Summary

Consciousness

▶ Consciousness refers to an awareness of one's self and one's surroundings, but investigators disagree as to its exact nature. Metacognition is an awareness of one's own mental processes.

▶ Consciousness appears to involve structures in the frontal lobe, especially the prefrontal cortex.

▶ The study of disorders of consciousness has provided some insight into the nature of consciousness.

▶ Amnesia is an impairment of declarative memory and, thus, interferes with conscious processing.

▶ Goal neglect is an impairment associated with frontal lobe syndrome.

▶ In Asperger's syndrome, individuals exhibit a consciousness that is less impaired than that observed in most autistic individuals.

▶ Individuals with akinetic mutism are unable to make orienting responses to novel stimuli.

▶ A loss of psychic self-activation is characterized by an inability to initiate thoughts or actions in the absence of external stimulation.

▶ Coma is a state of unconsciousness in which the eyes are closed. In contrast, a permanent vegetative state is a state of unconsciousness in which the eyes are open but behaviors are reflexive and primitive.

▶ Experiments with split-brain patients conducted by Roger Sperry and others have demonstrated the important role that the cerebral hemispheres play in the conscious processing of information. Roger Sperry received a Nobel Prize for his research on consciousness in patients who have undergone a surgical division of the corpus callosum. His research demonstrated that each cerebral hemisphere has a consciousness of its own, although the left hemisphere plays a special role in consciousness because it contains the language centers.

Sleep

▶ Intracranial recordings of the electrical activity of neurons have suggested that the unified character of consciousness may be explained by synchronous oscillations of neurons firing at the same rate of 40 times per second in different parts of the brain.

▶ EEG studies using scalp electrodes have shown that synchronized brain waves are associated with deep sleep and desynchronized brain waves are associated with active, conscious states.

▶ Beta waves are observed when an individual is aroused, and alpha waves are associated with relaxed wakefulness. Theta waves are found primarily in Stage I sleep, whereas sleep spindles and K-complexes are present in Stage II sleep. Delta waves occur more than 50% of the time in Stage IV sleep and less than 50% of the time in Stage III sleep.

▶ In REM sleep, brain activity increases, heart rate increases, skeletal muscles are inactivated (except for eye muscles, which cause the eyeballs to jerk about under closed eyelids), and sexual arousal occurs. Two unique phenomena are also associated with REM sleep: hippocampal theta waves and PGO spikes. REM rebound is seen in people who are deprived of REM sleep.

Brain Mechanisms of Sleep and Consciousness

▶ A number of brain structures play crucial roles in sleep and consciousness, including the reticular formation, the raphe system, the locus coeruleus, the suprachiasmic nucleus of the hypothalamus, and specific thalamic nuclei.

▶ In Bremer's sleep experiment, cats in the *cerveau isole* group remained in a permanent sleeping state following surgery because Bremer had severed the reticular formation, which alerts the cerebrum when important stimuli occur.

▶ The raphe system is the principal source of serotonin in the brain and, thus, plays a role in regulating sleep.

▶ Neurons in the locus coeruleus produce norepinephrine, which is involved in producing arousal and consciousness.

▶ The suprachiasmic nucleus (SCN) of the hypothalamus plays a crucial role in regulating the biological clock. The SNC relays information about light to the pineal gland, which releases melatonin.

▶ The thalamocortical system is the pathway between the thalamus and cerebral cortex that plays a role in determining our conscious experience.

▶ Acetylcholine appears to play a role in maintaining REM sleep.

The Function of Sleep

▶ Many theories have been advanced to explain why we sleep, although the evidence for each theory is largely circumstantial. According to the passive theory of sleep, the natural state of the brain is to be asleep. In contrast, according to the active theory of sleep, the brain is normally active. The restorative theory of sleep maintains that sleep is a time when waste products are removed and vital chemicals restored. The evolutionary theory of sleep maintains that sleep conserves energy at times when it is dangerous to be awake.

▶ The function of REM sleep is unknown.

▶ According to the activation-synthesis hypothesis of dreams, dreams arise when the brain tries to make sense out of incoming sensory information during sleep.

▶ When subjects were awakened from REM sleep, they reported dreaming 80% of the time, compared to subjects awakened during non-REM sleep, who report dreaming 20% of the time.

▶ Deprivation of REM sleep can impair thinking and disturb behavior, as well as produce REM rebound.

Sleep Disorders

▶ Insomnia is a disorder in which a person has difficulty falling or staying asleep. Antihistamines, benzodiazepines, and barbiturates can induce sleep.

▶ Narcolepsy is characterized by excessive daytime sleepiness and episodes of cataplexy in which a person loses all muscle tone and falls asleep.

▶ Sleep apnea is a disorder in which breathing is temporarily suspended during sleeping.

▶ People with somnambulism typically sleepwalk during non-REM sleep.

▶ REM sleep behavior disorder is characterized by normal skeletal muscle tone and activity during REM sleep.

▶ Nightmares generally occur during REM sleep, and night terror takes place during non-REM sleep.

Key Terms

activation-synthesis hypothesis   (p. 299)
active theory of sleep   (p. 298)
advanced-sleep-phase syndrome   (p. 303)
alpha waves   (p. 288)
Asperger's syndrome   (p. 281)
beta waves   (p. 288)
biological clock   (p. 294)
circadian rhythm   (p. 294)
Clock gene   (p. 296)
coma   (p. 283)
consciousness   (p. 280)
corpus callosum   (p. 285)
delayed-sleep-phase syndrome   (p. 303)
delta waves   (p. 288)
depersonalization   (p. 284)
desynchronized brain waves   (p. 288)
dissociative state   (p. 284)
evolutionary theory of sleep   (p. 299)
flashback   (p. 284)
goal neglect   (p. 281)
insomnia   (p. 301)

intralaminar nucleus   (p. 297)
jet lag   (p. 303)
K-complex   (p. 288)
locked-in syndrome   (p. 283)
locus coeruleus   (p. 293)
loss of psychic self-activation   (p. 281)
melatonin   (p. 295)
metacognition   (p. 280)
multiple personality disorder   (p. 284)
narcolepsy   (p. 301)
nightmare   (p. 303)
night terror   (p. 303)
nocturnal animals   (p. 299)
nocturnal enuresis   (p. 302)
orexin   (p. 302)
paradoxical sleep   (p. 290)
passive theory of sleep   (p. 293)
pineal gland   (p. 295)
raphe system   (p. 293)
REM rebound   (p. 291)
REM sleep   (p. 290)
REM sleep behavior disorder   (p. 302)

restorative theory of sleep   (p. 298)
reticular formation   (p. 292)
reticular thalamic nucleus   (p. 296)
retinohypothalamic tract   (p. 295)
reversed sleep-wake cycle   (p. 304)
sleep apnea   (p. 302)
sleep cycle   (p. 290)
sleep spindle   (p. 288)
slow-wave sleep   (p. 288)
somnambulism   (p. 302)
split-brain patient   (p. 285)
Stage I sleep   (p. 288)
Stage II sleep   (p. 288)
Stage III sleep   (p. 288)
Stage IV sleep   (p. 288)
sudden infant death syndrome   (p. 302)
suprachiasmic nucleus   (p. 294)
synchronized brain waves   (p. 288)
synchronous oscillations   (p. 287)
thalamocortical system   (p. 296)
theta waves   (p. 288)
yohimbine   (p. 284)
zeitgeber   (p. 295)

Questions for Thought

1. Do dogs experience consciousness? Do autistic children experience consciousness?

2. In a split-brain patient, which hemisphere is most likely to produce a sense of conscious awareness? Why?

3. Can sleepwalking occur during REM sleep? Why or why not?

4. How does shift work affect sleeping and consciousness?

Questions for Review

1. List Delacour's criteria for consciousness and give a real-life example of each.

2. What is the difference between being in a coma and having locked-in syndrome?

3. What roles do structures in the hindbrain, hypothalamus, and thalamus play in the production of sleep and consciousness?

4. Explain the difference between advanced-sleep-phase syndrome and delayed-sleep-phase syndrome.

Suggested Readings

Damasio, A. R. (1999). *The feeling of what happens: Body and emotion in the making of consciousness.* New York: Harcourt Brace.

Delacour, J. (1995). An introduction to the biology of consciousness. *Neuropsychologia, 33,* 1061–1074.

Dement, W. C. (1978). *Some must watch while some must sleep.* New York: Norton.

Gottesmann, C. (1999). Neurophysiological support of consciousness during waking and sleeping. *Progress in Neurobiology, 59,* 469–508.

Tulving, E. (1989). Remembering and knowing the past. *American Scientist, 77,* 361–367.

Web Resources

For a chapter tutorial quiz, direct links to the Internet sites listed below and other features, visit the book-specific website at **www.wadsworth.com/product/ 0155074865**. You may also connect directly to the following annotated websites:

http://www.sleephomepages.org/sleepsyllabus/a.html
This site provides information about sleep, dreams, and sleep disorders

http://faculty.washington.edu/chudler/narco.html
Learn about treatment and symptoms of narcolepsy on this site.

http://faculty.washington.edu/chudler/yawning.html
Yawning: Why do we yawn and why are yawns contagious?

http://www.nimh.nih.gov/publicat/bioclock.cfm
Discover how the biological clock works.

For additional readings and information, check out InfoTrac College Edition at **http://www.infotrac-college.com/wadsworth**. Choose a search term yourself or enter the following search terms: Asperger syndrome, multiple personality disorder, and sleep apnea.

CD-ROM: Exploring Biological Psychology

Video: Sleep Cycle
Stages of Sleep on an EEG
    Simulation: EEG
    Animation: Awake
    Animation: Stage 1
    Animation: Stage 2

    Animation: Stage 3
    Animation: Stage 4
    Animation: REM
Interactive Recaps
Chapter 10 Quiz
Connect to the Interactive Biological Psychology Glossary

11

The Regulation of Motivated Behaviors

A resident of Fresno, California, Dan decided to visit a friend in Arizona. Rather than take the expressway, he decided to drive along Route 190, which runs through Death Valley. It is a lonely stretch of road, and cars pass by very infrequently. About 20 miles east of Darwin (near the center of Death Valley), smoke began to pour out from under the hood of his car, and the indicator on the car's temperature gauge warned that the engine's temperature was dangerously high. Dan pulled off the road quickly and opened the hood. Steaming liquid poured out of a crack in the radiator hose. Standing outside his car, Dan quickly noticed the intense heat of the afternoon sun. He retreated back inside his car, to get out of the sun. Next Dan devised a fan by folding up a newspaper and fanned himself to cool down. But, the sweat just poured off him, and he felt hot and miserable. Less than an hour later, he became aware of the fact that he was extremely thirsty. His lips were dry, his throat was parched, and all he could think about was a cool drink of water. Once help arrived and Dan was ensconced in air-conditioned luxury with a tall glass of ice water, he suddenly felt hungry and realized that he hadn't eaten for hours.

Hunger, thirst, and hyperthermia [*hyper-* = more than normal; *-thermia* = heat or temperature, Latin] are drive states. A **drive** is a condition that motivates an individual to perform a particular behavior or set of behaviors in order to eliminate that condition. That is, when you are hungry, you fix a sandwich, or open a bag of chips, or drive to a fast-food restaurant, to satisfy that drive state. The same is true for being thirsty or overheated (or underheated). You engage in appropriate behaviors to satisfy the state of imbalance produced by the drive

drive: a condition that motivates an individual to perform a particular behavior or set of behaviors

In this chapter, we will look at the regulation of motivated behaviors such as eating, drinking, and temperature regulation. These behaviors appear to be controlled by particular regions of the **hypothalamus,** a brain structure that plays an important role in *homeostatic regulation.* **Homeostasis** is derived from two Greek words, *homeo- (homos)* meaning "same" and *-statis* meaning "to stand." Thus, homeostasis involves maintaining certain biological variables, such as body temperature, body weight, and body fluid volume, at a constant level. Obviously, homeostatic regulation by the hypothalamus is not perfect. For example, some people overeat and gain weight, thereby overriding their homeostatic mechanism that regulates eating.

Let's examine how temperature, food intake, and body fluids are regulated. I have placed a greater emphasis on food intake regulation in this chapter because physiological psychologists have conducted a vast amount of research on eating behavior. ●

hypothalamus: a structure in the diencephalon that controls the pituitary gland and regulates motivated behaviors

homeostasis: an internal mechanism that maintains certain biological variables at a constant level

Regulation of Body Temperature

We have a number of classification systems that categorize animals according to their ability to regulate their body temperatures. Aristotle proposed one of the earliest classification systems, categorizing animals as either *warm blooded* or *cold blooded.* According to Aristotle's classification system, warm-blooded animals are warm to touch, and cold-blooded animals are cool to touch. However, Aristotle's system runs into trouble when we try to categorize a reptile, like a lizard, that has been lying in the sun. This lizard feels warm to touch after it has been lying in the sun for some time, although it feels cool after it has been lying in the shade. Certainly, an animal cannot be both warm blooded and cold blooded. Scientists have developed more precise classification systems since Aristotle's time.

One modern classification system categorizes animals as **endotherms** or **ectotherms,** based on their body's source of heat. Endotherms are animals that have an internal source of heat, whereas *ectotherms* are animals that get their body heat from sources outside their own bodies. Endotherms produce heat through *oxidation* of substances such as fats, proteins, and carbohydrates. Oxidation is a process of combustion in which substances are combined with oxygen. Although ectotherms also make use of oxidative processes in their bodies, the heat produced is not controlled or harnessed by an ectotherm's central nervous system. In general, endotherms maintain a constant core body temperature and, thus, are **homeothermic.** (*Core body temperature* refers to the temperature of the body core, which includes the internal organs and the brain.) Ectotherms, on the other hand, tolerate a wide range of core body temperatures and are sometimes called *poikilotherms* [*poikilo-* = various, *-therm* = temperature, Greek]. Birds and mammals are endotherms, and all other animals are ectotherms.

endotherms: animals that have an internal source of heat

ectotherms: animals that have an external source of heat

homeothermic: animals that maintain a constant core body temperature

Balancing Heat Production and Heat Loss

It is nearly impossible to think about *heat production* without also thinking about *heat loss* because these two processes are closely linked in homeothermic animals (also called *homeotherms*). In order for a homeotherm to maintain the same body temperature, heat production must be equal to heat loss. However, it is easier to discuss the mechanisms of heat production independent from heat loss, so I will present the mechanisms of heat production first, followed by a discussion of heat loss.

Heat Production

Endotherms produce heat by means of two mechanisms: **shivering thermogenesis** and **nonshivering thermogenesis.** Shivering thermogenesis is the production of heat by the rhythmic muscular contractions that we call *shivering.* When the hypothalamus detects that the core body temperature has decreased, it stimulates neurons in the cerebellum that initiate shivering. The cerebellum coordinates shivering by relaying rhythmic impulses down the spinal cord to motor neurons, which stimulate rhythmic muscle contraction. When muscles contract, they produce a great deal of heat. If you jog for a block or so, you will notice immediately that you start to sweat and feel overheated after a few minutes of exercise. Shivering produces a lot of heat because many muscles are contracting at once, generating much heat. The colder you become, the more vigorously you shiver. I remember that once I was so cold that I could barely talk because my teeth were chattering so violently.

Nonshivering thermogenesis refers to all the other ways in which we produce heat (besides shivering). The primary mechanism of nonshivering thermogenesis is **basal metabolism.** Basal metabolism is the minimum amount of energy expended while a person is at rest. When you are resting, your heart is beating, you are breathing, and a reduced number of neurons in your brain are active, but that's about all that's happening in your body. However, the muscles in your chest (that is, your heart muscle and the muscles between your ribs) produce heat, even when you are resting. In fact, when you are resting, over 75% of your body's heat is produced in your chest and head. In contrast, when you are shivering, over 75% of your body's heat is produced by your skeletal muscles. Thus, basal metabolism is an important source of heat production.

Basal metabolism is controlled by **calorigenic hormones,** released by the **thyroid gland,** that cause an increase in body temperature. The thyroid gland is a butterfly-shaped organ located in the neck (Figure 11.1). Its functioning is controlled by the **pituitary gland,** like many of the body's glands.

Recall from Chapter 4 that the hypothalamus regulates the activity of the pituitary gland. When neurons in the **anterior hypothalamus** detect a drop in the core body temperature, a command is sent from the hypothalamus to the anterior pituitary gland to increase body temperature. In response to the command from the hypothalamus, the anterior pituitary releases *thyrotropin-releasing hormone* into the bloodstream. Thyrotropin-releasing hormone arrives at the thyroid gland via the bloodstream and stimulates the thyroid gland to release a number of calorigenic hormones, including *thyroxin.* These calorigenic hormones increase the core body temperature by increasing basal metabolism (Andersson, Ekman, Gale, & Sundsten, 1963). Think for a moment about how this mechanism works: Basal metabolism is the amount of heat produced at rest. If basal metabolism is increased, then heart rate and respiration rate speed up, producing more muscle contractions per minute and, thus, more heat.

Another mechanism of nonshivering thermogenesis is **brown fat metabolism.** Human babies are born with very immature nervous systems and are incapable of shivering until they are about 6 months of age. However, newborn humans are born with deposits of brown fat located in strategic areas of their bodies, at the back of the head and in the chest (McCance & Widdowson, 1977). When the hypothalamus of a newborn detects a decrease in core body temperature, the hypothalamus directs the burning of brown fat, which produces a good deal of heat, thereby raising the baby's core body temperature (Blumberg, Deaver, & Kirby, 1999; Friedman, 1967). (Most fat in the body is white and produces less heat than brown fat when burned.)

shivering thermogenesis: the production of heat by shivering

nonshivering thermogenesis: the production of heat by processes other than shivering

basal metabolism: the minimum amount of energy expended while a person is at rest

calorigenic hormones: hormones released by the thyroid gland that produce an increase in body temperature

thyroid gland: a butterfly-shaped gland located in the neck that controls the body's metabolic rate

pituitary gland: a structure connected to the hypothalamus by a stalk, that regulates the activity of other major glands in the body; master gland located below the ventral surface of the brain, which receives commands from the hypothalamus

anterior hypothalamus: area of the hypothalamus that participates in temperature and water intake regulation

brown fat metabolism: a mechanism of nonshivering thermogenesis that involves burning brown fat to produce heat

Figure 11.1 The location of the thyroid gland and other endocrine glands

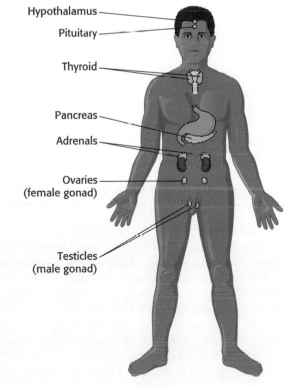

Hypothalamus
Pituitary
Thyroid
Pancreas
Adrenals
Ovaries (female gonad)
Testicles (male gonad)

Heat Loss

Heat loss occurs constantly as we lose heat to the environment in several ways. When a person dies, metabolic processes (including oxidation) cease, and the body stops producing heat. Within a short period of time, the temperature of the corpse drops to room temperature, due to heat loss, and the corpse feels cool to the touch. Therefore, in the absence of heat production, heat loss causes body temperature to decrease. In the living endotherm, heat production offsets any drop in body temperature due to heat loss.

Evaporation is the most effective mechanism that we have for losing heat. It is the process by which liquid is turned into a gas or vapor. To turn a liquid into vapor requires a lot of heat, approximately one calorie per gram of liquid for each degree of heat. The heat needed to produce evaporation comes from the body, which results in heat loss for the body (Figure 11.2). To enhance heat loss through evaporation, humans produce sweat, which is released onto the surface of the skin and subsequently evaporates, producing heat loss.

Most mammals cannot sweat, but they utilize the mechanism of evaporation in other ways. For example, dogs and cats (and most other mammals) lose heat through panting. They produce a bolus of saliva on their tongue and breathe fast and rhythmically through their mouths, causing the saliva to evaporate, which causes heat loss. Pigs and hippos wallow in mud and then emerge to cool off by letting the wet mud evaporate from their bodies. In a similar manner, rats, guinea pigs, and kangaroos lick themselves, spreading their saliva all over the surfaces of their bodies. As the saliva evaporates, it removes heat from their bodies, cooling them (Hainsworth & Epstein, 1966).

We also lose heat through **conduction** of body heat to the surrounding air or to solid objects in the environment. For example, when you stand on a cold sidewalk, you lose heat through the soles of your shoes, due to conduction. You might notice that, during the December holiday season, volunteers for the Salvation Army stand out in the cold for long periods of time. Their secret? They stand on a piece of corrugated cardboard, which acts as an insulator between their feet and the frozen sidewalk. The corrugated cardboard traps air between the sheets of cardboard and the cold sidewalk. Air is a poor conductor of heat, which means that heat does not readily flow from the feet through the cardboard to the sidewalk. When you sit in a chair, you lose heat to the chair through radiation. Feel the seat of the chair when you get up. You will notice that the seat is warm. That warmth came from your bottom, which was in contact with the chair.

Vascular Control of Heat Loss Blood vessels play an important role in the regulation of body temperature, particularly the **superficial blood vessels** that are found in the skin. When the blood vessels in the skin *dilate*, blood flow to the surface of the body increases, and heat loss to the environment is *increased*. In contrast, *constriction of blood vessels* in the skin reduces blood flow to the body's surface and, thus, *decreases heat loss* through the skin. Therefore, when we become cold or when we are exposed to a cold environment, our superficial blood vessels constrict, reducing heat loss. When we are overheated or exposed to a hot environment, our superficial blood vessels dilate, which increases heat loss to the environment.

Insulation Responses Recall that air is a poor conductor of heat. The *insulation response* takes advantage of this principle in order to *reduce heat loss* to the environment. Birds and mammals have smooth muscles in their skin that encircle the roots of feathers (birds) or hairs (mammals). When these smooth muscles contract, the feathers or hairs are pulled up to an erect position (Figure 11.3). This insulation response is called **piloerection.** When piloerection occurs, air is trapped between the erect hairs or feathers. This layer of air insulates the body because air is a poor conductor of heat. Hence, the animal's body heat is not readily lost to the environment when piloerection occurs.

Piloerection is quite effective in preventing heat loss in hairy animals. For example, the arctic fox has such extremely thick fur insulation that shivering is

Figure 11.2 Mechanisms of heat loss
To enhance heat loss through evaporation, humans produce sweat, which is released onto the surface of the skin and evaporates (top). By contrast, hippos wallow in mud and then emerge to cool off by letting the wet mud evaporate from their bodies (bottom).

evaporation: a heat loss mechanism that involves turning a liquid into a gas
conduction: a heat loss mechanism that involves losing heat to the surrounding air or objects in the environment

superficial blood vessels: blood vessels located in the skin

piloerection: an insulation response in which the hairs covering the body are pulled into an erect position, which allows air to become trapped between the hairs

Figure 11.3 The insulation response
(a) Wolf in temperate environment. (b) Wolf when cold.

Piloerection

a.

b.

unnecessary until the temperature falls to −40°C (Scholander, Hock, Walters, Johnson, & Irving, 1950). However, in relatively hairless animals like humans, piloerection is not very effective. When we get cold, the insulation reflex is triggered in our skin, causing smooth muscles that surround hair follicles to contract. You can see the contraction of these smooth muscles as your skin gets a bumpy appearance when they contract, resulting in what is sometimes referred to as "goose bumps." Because piloerection is not effective in humans, we make behavioral responses to compensate for our lack of insulation, such as putting on more clothes.

The central nervous system of a homeotherm struggles to maintain a stable core body temperature. This is a difficult task because heat loss continues constantly, and the body must produce enough heat, but not too much, to counterbalance the heat lost through evaporation and conduction. Figure 11.4 summarizes the body's response when it is exposed to a hot environment and a cold environment.

Brain Mechanisms Involved in Temperature Regulation

You've already learned about the brain mechanisms that control shivering and the release of thyroid hormones, which increase basal metabolic rate. Both of these heat production processes are regulated by a region in the anterior hypothalamus called the **preoptic area** (Figure 11.5). In fact, heat production and heat loss are both controlled by the preoptic area of the hypothalamus, as research with nonhuman animal subjects has demonstrated (Ishiwata et al., 2001; Jha, Islam, & Mallick, 2001). For example, when the preoptic area of a rat is lesioned, the rat is unable to maintain a normal core body temperature and will not shiver or show nonshivering thermogenesis when it is exposed to a cool environment (Satinoff, Valentino, & Teitelbaum, 1976). Electrical stimulation of the preoptic area in rats produces both shivering and nonshivering thermogenesis (Thornhill & Halvorson, 1994). Stimulation of the *medial preoptic area* induces an increase in core body temperature caused by nonshivering thermogenesis, whereas stimulation of the *lateral preoptic area* induces shivering. Thus, shivering thermogenesis and nonshivering thermogenesis are controlled by different neurons in the preoptic area.

Neurons in the preoptic area appear to be *thermosensitive*, or sensitive to temperature. Laudenslager (1976) applied heat and cold to neurons in the preoptic area of rhesus monkeys. When Laudenslager cooled the neurons in the preoptic area of monkeys, the monkeys pressed a lever continuously to turn on a sunlamp. The

preoptic area: a region of the anterior hypothalamus that regulates heat loss and production

Figure 11.4 Balancing heat production and heat loss

(a) Exposure to a hot environment. When we are exposed to a hot environment or when we become overheated, our bodies make a number of adjustments to prevent hyperthermia. The first response of the body is to dilate superficial blood vessels. The second response of the body is sweating, which increases heat loss through evaporation. If you remain for an extended period of time in a hot environment, your hypothalamus directs your pituitary gland to decrease basal metabolism by reducing the output of your thyroid gland.

(b) Exposure to a cold environment. When exposed to a cold environment, our bodies' first response is to increase the insulation response, or produce "goose bumps" by piloerection. The second response of the body is to decrease blood flow to the skin by constricting superficial blood vessels. The next response is shivering, which typically produces a great deal of body heat. If you are a very young infant and are unable to shiver, you would burn brown fat. Finally, if you are exposed to a cold environment for a long time, your hypothalamus directs your pituitary gland to increase basal metabolism by increasing the release of thyroid hormones.

a.

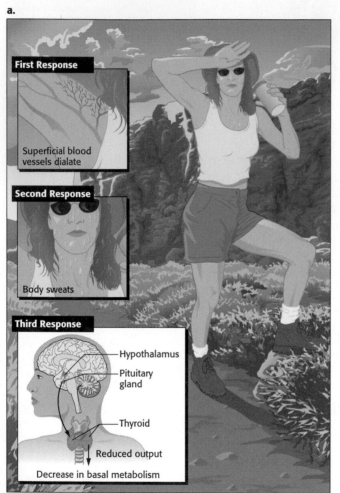

b.

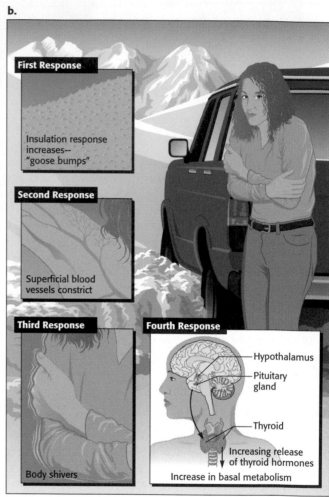

monkeys pressed a lever to receive cool air when the preoptic neurons were heated. Forster and Ferguson (1952) demonstrated that warming thermosensitive neurons in the hypothalamus of cats produced panting in those animals. Similarly, cooling the preoptic area produces shivering, and warming the same area suppresses shivering in rats (Kanosue et al., 1994; Zhang et al., 1995).

Behavioral Regulation of Heat Production and Heat Loss

Ectotherms cannot shiver and, thus, cannot produce heat by shivering thermogenesis. However, this does *not* mean that ectotherms cannot regulate body temperature. When ectotherms become cold, they seek shelter in a warm place or they huddle together. I remember, when I was a graduate student at Columbia University and living in New York City, finding a most disgusting pile of cockroaches gathered around the pilot light of my gas oven one December afternoon. Likewise, ectotherms can also decrease their body temperatures by behavioral means when they become overheated. For example, ants will carry water in their mouths when they get too hot, allowing evaporation of the transported water to cool them off.

Endotherms, too, use behavioral means to increase or decrease body temperature. For example, people will stamp their feet and flap their arms when they are cold. The muscular contractions that are produced when feet are stamped and arms are flapped generate a good deal of heat, although not as much as shivering does. We also put on coats, scarves, and hats when we are cold to prevent heat loss. To enhance heat loss when we are too hot, we might sit in front of a fan (which increases heat loss through convection), take off excess clothing (increasing heat loss through conduction), jump into a pool of water (to increase heat loss through evaporation), or move into a cooler environment.

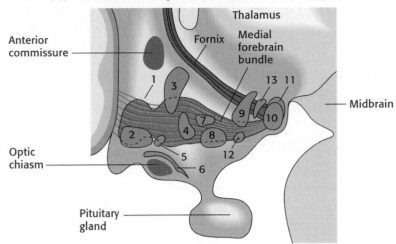

Figure 11.5 Anatomy of the hypothalamus
The hypothalamus consists of a collection of nuclei. In this sagittal section, you can see the locations of the medial preoptic nucleus (1), lateral preoptic nucleus (2), paraventricular nucleus (3), anterior hypothalamic nucleus (4), supraoptic nucleus (5), suprachiasmic nucleus (6), lateral hypothalamic nucleus (7), and the mammillary nuclei (8–12).

Disorders of Temperature Regulation

Fever

We've all experienced a fever. It typically accompanies a cold or a flu, ailments that are caused by infectious microorganisms. A **fever** is an increase in core body temperature above its normal level. In fact, although we regard a fever as a sign of dysregulation of our body temperature, the spike in temperature that is the hallmark of a fever is actually orchestrated by the hypothalamus in response to stimulation by the immune system. The function of the immune system, as you will learn in Chapter 14, is to identify foreign agents that threaten the well-being of the body. When a microorganism infects a region of your body, your immune system mobilizes to deal with the intruder and informs the hypothalamus that the body is under attack. In response, the preoptic area of the hypothalamus directs an increase in core body temperature (Saper, 1998). Bacteria and viruses are quite fragile and can survive within only a narrow range of temperatures. When the body temperature rises above 99°F, viruses and bacteria begin to die. Thus, the hypothalamus produces a state of fever to fight an infection by microorganisms. We feel quite miserable when we have a fever and core body temperature is above 99°F. But, we can usually survive a slight fever. When core body temperature goes above 105°F, however, enzymes in our brains and bodies cannot work effectively, and our body systems begin to shut down.

fever: an increase in core body temperature above its normal level

Menopausal Dysregulation

The menstrual cycle in women is controlled by hormones produced by the pituitary gland and the ovaries, as you will learn in Chapter 12. Core body temperature in women fluctuates over the course of the menstrual cycle, with the highest temperatures recorded at ovulation and the lowest recorded just before menstruation. Thus, sex hormones appear to influence the regulation of body temperature in women. Some women experience a significant drop in core body temperature, which causes insomnia, 1 or 2 days before menstruation (Manber & Armitage, 1999).

When a woman ages and the production of sex hormones ceases, it results in a state called **menopause,** during which regulation of core body temperature can be disrupted. Many menopausal women experience a sudden increase in core body temperature from time to time, referred to as a **hot flash.** In response to an erratic release of pituitary hormones, the preoptic area of the hypothalamus directs an increase in heat production, which produces a sudden rise in body temperature (Woodward & Freedman, 1994). Recall what happens when the body becomes overheated: Vasodilation and flushing of the skin occur, followed by perfuse sweating. A woman experiencing a hot flash feels overly warm, clammy with sweat, and very uncomfortable. For some women, hot flashes occur so frequently that they are a source of great embarrassment. Hormonal supplements, which increase the levels of estrogen and progesterone in a woman's body, can alleviate the symptoms of temperature dysregulation caused by menopause.

menopause: a period in a woman's life following the cessation of the production of sex hormones

hot flash: a sudden increase in core body temperature that happens spontaneously in menopausal women

Energy Balance

We've just examined how homeotherms balance heat production and heat loss to maintain a constant body temperature. Heat production is also closely associated with food intake. For healthy endotherms that maintain the same body weight over a period of time, the following equation is true:

$$\text{Energy}_{IN} = \text{Energy}_{OUT}$$

In this equation, *energy* is measured in units called **calories.** *Energy*$_{IN}$ refers to the calories we take in as food. *Energy*$_{OUT}$ refers to the many ways in which we expend energy, such as movement and exercise, growth, maintenance of body tissues, basal metabolism, and heat production. The food that we eat is burned to produce energy that allows us to move, grow, maintain our tissues, and produce heat. Thus, food intake is closely associated with the regulation of body temperature. Healthy, well-nourished endotherms (humans included) will maintain the same body weight if the amount of energy they take in as food is equal to the amount of energy that they need for muscle contractions, growth and maintenance, and heat production.

calorie: a unit of heat energy

When food intake exceeds the energy expended (that is, when Energy$_{IN}$ > Energy$_{OUT}$), weight gain occurs. In the next section of this chapter, we will examine a variety of reasons why people gain weight. For example, people gain weight when they increase their food intake without increasing their energy output (Energy$_{IN}$ increases, and Energy$_{OUT}$ remains the same). They also gain weight when they switch from an active to a sedentary lifestyle without making a compensatory decrease in their food intake (Energy$_{IN}$ remains the same, and Energy$_{OUT}$ decreases). Moving from a cold to a warm climate can also produce a decrease in Energy$_{OUT}$ because the person who has moved to the warmer climate no longer needs to produce as much body heat. *For Further Thought* discusses individual differences in weight gain caused by variations in fidgeting, maintaining good posture, and other activities.

In contrast, when the energy expended exceeds food intake (Energy$_{IN}$ < Energy$_{OUT}$), weight loss occurs. For example, when a person goes on a diet, Energy$_{IN}$ decreases. In the case of a dieter, Energy$_{OUT}$ can exceed Energy$_{IN}$ if the dieter decreases food intake without simultaneously decreasing exercise level. You can imagine that, if a person diets and increases exercise output (that is, if Energy$_{IN}$ decreases and Energy$_{OUT}$ increases), even more weight loss will occur. However, dieting can induce a reduction in basal metabolism (decreasing Energy$_{OUT}$), especially in people who have been dieting for a long time (Gingras, Harber, Field, & McCargar, 2000). The hypothalamus responds to a decrease in Energy$_{IN}$ by reducing Energy$_{OUT}$. Therefore, people who try to lose weight by dieting will typically find it difficult to lose weight due to their reduced basal metabolic rate. Exercise,

Activity and Resistance to Weight Gain

When people consume more calories than they burn, they tend to put on weight. But, some individuals resist weight gain when they overeat, whereas others get fat. We all know people who can eat huge amounts of food and remain quite thin. What is their secret?

At the Mayo Clinic, James Levine and his colleagues, Norman Eberhardt and Michael Jensen (1999), have studied how different people expend excess calories when they overeat. For 8 weeks, the adult participants in their experiment consumed 1,000 extra kcal every day, eating between 2,200 and 3,800 kcal per day. As a result of daily overconsumption of calories, the participants gained an average of 10.3 pounds over 8 weeks. However, not all people in the study gained the same amount of weight. Some gained as little as 3 pounds, and some gained nearly 16 pounds.

The investigators were able to measure both fat gain and energy expenditure in each of the overfed participants. They found that, on a daily basis, participants stored a mean of 432 kcal of the excess energy consumed as fat and burned a mean of 531 kcal as increased energy expenditure. However, the range among the participants was actually quite large. One person stored only 58 kcal as fat each day, whereas another stored 687 kcal as fat each day.

Levine and his colleagues then determined how the participants expended their excess energy intake. They restricted the participants to a low level of sports and fitness types of activities (including walking), which they measured. The remaining energy expenditure of the participants was due to nonexercise activity, such as fidgeting, spontaneous muscle contractions, and maintaining posture. The investigators' analysis of the data indicated that nonexercise activity determines who gained weight. The change in nonexercise activity for the participants ranged from −98 kcal (which represents a *decrease* in activity) to +692 kcal per day. Those people who spent more time fidgeting, sitting, and standing gained less weight than fellow participants who lounged around and did not exhibit much spontaneous muscular activity. You can view all the data collected by Levine and his colleagues in this study at *www.sciencemag.org/feature/data/982662.shl*

on the other hand, increases basal metabolic rate and can enhance weight loss in people who are dieting (Thompson, Manore, & Thomas, 1996).

The interaction between body temperature and food intake is undeniable. However, food intake is influenced by many variables besides temperature regulation. Let's take a look at the current research on food intake and body weight regulation.

Recap 11.1: Regulation of Body Temperature

(a)_____ are animals that generate their own body heat, whereas ectotherms cannot generate their own body heat. Endotherms maintain a constant core body temperature and are (b)_____ (c)_____ thermogenesis and (d)_____ thermogenesis are two mechanisms used by endotherms to produce heat. The primary mechanism of nonshivering thermogenesis is basal (e)_____. Under the influence of the (f)_____, the anterior pituitary gland releases thyrotropin-releasing factor, which stimulates the thyroid gland to release (g)_____ hormones. (h)_____ fat metabolism is used by newborn humans to produce heat. The most effective mechanism for losing heat is (i)_____. To reduce loss of body heat, blood vessels in the skin (j)_____ in response to cold environments. (k)_____ occurs when smooth muscles contract in response to cold, pulling hairs or feathers up on end to trap air and reduce loss of body heat. Heat production and heat loss are regulated by the (l)_____ _____ of the hypothalamus. (m) _____ is an increase in core body temperature above its normal level and normally occurs in response to an infection. Energy is measured in units called (n)_____.

Regulation of Food Intake

Food intake and food selection are affected by many variables, both biological and psychological. Psychological variables are typically related to individual differences, such as preferences for certain flavors or food textures. We will examine psychological variables briefly in this chapter, but our main focus will be on biological factors that determine food intake. We will look at brain mechanisms, as well as mechanisms in the peripheral nervous system, that control the onset and offset of eating. In addition, we will review the research on the effects of neurotransmitters and hormones on eating. Let's start by exploring the role that homeostasis plays in food intake regulation.

Homeostasis and Allostasis

Homeostasis was first described by Walter Cannon (1929), a professor of physiology at Harvard University, as the set of mechanisms that maintains steady states in the body, including constant levels of glucose and water, among other things. According to Cannon, homeostatic mechanisms cause an individual to drink when water levels in the body fall or to eat when glucose levels decline. However, homeostasis cannot explain fully why individuals begin to eat or drink. That is, we do not always eat because our blood glucose levels have dropped. Sometimes we eat when we have no need for food. A concept called **allostasis** has been introduced to explain the nonhomeostatic cues that initiate eating and drinking. Allostasis takes into account an individual's expectations and readiness to alter behavior to meet changing demands in the environment (Schulkin, McEwen, & Gold, 1994). For example, most of us have been forced to nibble a piece of birthday cake after a very filling meal when we were not hungry at all.

> **allostasis:** a concept that explains nonhomeostatic cues that initiate eating and drinking

Thus, homeostasis is a nonflexible mechanism that requires systems to have **set points,** or optimum levels of various physiological factors, such as body temperature or blood glucose levels, which the nervous system struggles to maintain. When a measure deviates from a set point, as when blood glucose levels drop below some optimal level, homeostatic mechanisms in the brain initiate behavior to bring the level back to the set point level. Allostasis, on the other hand, is a flexible system that allows for learning and adaptation to changing circumstances. Together, homeostasis and allostasis control eating, which means that the regulation of eating is very complicated (Winn, 1995).

> **set point:** an optimal level set by the hypothalamus for each of several physiological factors, including body temperature and body weight

Humans are **omnivores,** which means they eat a variety of foods, including meats, vegetables, and grains, to obtain the energy that they need. Omnivores face a unique predicament that vegetarian (strictly plant-eating) and carnivorous (strictly meat-eating) animals do not: They must carefully select foods in their diet to obtain the complete balance of nutrients that they need. Thus, besides eating to obtain energy, omnivores also eat to obtain needed nutrients. Let's review what these essential nutrients are.

> **omnivores:** animals that eat a variety of foods

Macronutrients

Basically, there are two classes of nutrients: **macronutrients** and micronutrients. Macronutrients are nutrients that we need in large supply. They include *carbohydrates, proteins,* and *fats.* Carbohydrates can take a simple form, like *sugars,* or a complex form, like *starches.* All carbohydrates are readily converted to glucose in the body and are burned for energy or converted to glycogen or fat. Excess energy is stored as *glycogen* in the liver or as *fat* in adipose or fat cells. Glycogen is composed of the simple sugar, glucose, and is a ready source of energy when muscles need it quickly.

> **macronutrients:** nutrients that we need to eat in large quantities

Proteins are derived from many sources, including meat, dairy, and vegetable products. In the process of digestion, proteins are broken down into amino acids. (You learned about the structure of amino acids in Chapter 3.) Amino acids are necessary for the manufacture of other substances in the body, including certain neurotransmitters, enzymes, and hormones. Amino acids can be oxidized to produce energy, and excess amino acids can be converted into fat.

Fats are digested and broken down into fatty acids. Fatty acids play a number of important roles in the body, and they can be burned to produce energy. Like excess carbohydrates and proteins, excess fatty acids are stored as fat. However, it is important to keep in mind that increased intakes of carbohydrates and proteins lead to increased oxidation (that is, burning) of sugars and amino acids, which means that increased intake of carbohydrates and proteins does not necessarily lead to increased fat storage. In contrast, increased fat intake does not stimulate increased fat oxidation but goes directly into fat stores, which means that high-fat diets can induce obesity (Swinburn & Ravussin, 1993).

Micronutrients

Micronutrients are nutrients that are needed in minuscule supply. *Vitamins* and *minerals* are the major classes of micronutrients. These vitamins and minerals are essential for cellular processes to occur. For example, calcium is needed by neurons and muscles in order for neurotransmitters to be released and muscle contraction to take place. Typically, the recommended minimum daily requirements for micronutrients are measured in milligrams or smaller units. In contrast, the recommended minimum daily requirements for macronutrients are measured in grams. Table 11.1 gives the recommended minimum daily requirement for macronutrients and selected micronutrients.

As we begin to consider the mechanisms that control food intake, you should keep in mind that eating has two distinct phases: It begins, and it ends. That is,

micronutrients: nutrients that we need to eat in minuscule quantities

---

Table 11.1

Recommended Minimum Daily Requirements for Macronutrients and Micronutrients

Minimum Daily Requirement

Macronutrients	
Carbohydrates	315 g
Protein	25 g
Fat	65 g

Micronutrients	
Vitamin A	5000 IU
B vitamins:	
Thiamin	1.5 mg
Riboflavin	1.7 mg
Niacin	20 mg
B_6	2 mg
Folic acid	400 mcg
B_{12}	6 mcg
Vitamin C	60 mg
Vitamin D	400 IU
Vitamin K	30 IU
Potassium	4 g
Calcium	1 g
Iron	18 mg
Chloride	3.6 g
Zinc	15 mg
Copper	2 mg

Units of Measurement:

g = gram
IU = International Unit
mg = milligram (10^{-3} g)
mcg = microgram (10^{-6} g)

food intake consists of two processes: (1) onset of eating and (2) offset of eating. Let's examine each of these processes separately.

Onset of Eating

The onset of eating is controlled by both homeostatic and allostatic mechanisms. Typically, we do not wait until our energy supplies are depleted before we start eating. Most of us, most of the time, eat in *anticipation* of our needs. For the most part, we rely on allostatic, rather than homeostatic, mechanisms to begin eating. This allostatic mechanism, which involves implicit learning, is evident in the way eating habits are established. We all have regular, appointed hours at which we consume food. Those of us who eat breakfast every day feel quite hungry by midmorning if we haven't eaten, whereas those who regularly skip breakfast do not feel like eating until lunchtime. Some people acquire a habit of eating ice cream in the evening before bedtime. If you have this habit and happen to skip your ice cream treat in the evening, you feel hungry at bedtime. This means that some allostatic mechanism "learns" when your regular or habitual eating times occur, and it prompts you to eat when the appointed eating hour approaches.

Central Onset Mechanisms

Allostatic Mechanisms   You might be wondering about the location of this allostatic mechanism that prompts you to eat. Some investigators believe that the **lateral hypothalamus,** working in conjunction with the *prefrontal cortex,* is responsible for the allostatic mechanism regulating eating behavior (Winn, 1995). Recall from Chapter 9 that the frontal cortex organizes attention and behavioral output. Many anatomical interconnections exist between the lateral hypothalamus and prefrontal cortex, which means that there is a great deal of communication between these two brain sites. Output from the lateral hypothalamus to the prefrontal cortex initiates processes in the frontal lobe that organize the execution of eating behavior.

lateral hypothalamus: an area of the hypothalamus responsible for the initiation of allostatic eating

Early research demonstrated that bilateral lesions of the lateral hypothalamus produced a failure to eat, or **aphagia,** and weight loss in rats (Anand & Brobeck, 1951). That is, following destruction of the lateral hypothalamus in both hemispheres, rats refused to eat or drink and eventually died from starvation unless measures were taken to provide nutrients to them. Investigators prematurely concluded that the lateral hypothalamus is responsible for the initiation of eating, referring to the lateral hypothalamus as the *feeding center* (Grossman, 1967; Stellar, 1954). However, subsequent studies showed that dopamine-transmitting axons pass through the lateral hypothalamus on their way from the substantia nigra to the basal ganglia and raised the question of whether lesioning the dopamine axons caused aphagia (Figure 11.6). Indeed, lesioning this *dopamine pathway* with a **neurotoxin** that destroys dopamine-containing neurons, called *6-hydroxydopamine* (6-OHDA), did produce aphagia and weight loss in rats, despite the fact that no neurons in the lateral hypothalamus were injured (Marshall, Richardson, & Teitelbaum, 1974; Ungerstedt, 1973). Thus, the notion that the lateral hypothalamus acts as a feeding center that initiates eating was called into question.

aphagia: a failure or refusal to eat

neurotoxins: chemicals that target and destroy specific neurons or impair their function

The development of a new family of chemicals called **excitotoxins,** which destroy cell bodies of neurons by overexciting them, allowed investigators to lesion the neurons in the lateral hypothalamus without injuring the dopamine axons that pass through it (Clark, Clark, Bartle, & Winn, 1991; Winn, Tarbuck, & Dunnett, 1984). It is important to keep in mind that the electrical lesions of the lateral hypothalamus that were performed in the 1950s and 1960s destroyed both the neurons in the lateral hypothalamus *and* the dopamine pathway that passed through it. Lesioning the lateral hypothalamus with excitotoxins, such as *ibotenic acid* or *NMDA,* damages only the neurons in the lateral hypothalamus and not the dopamine pathway (Figure 11.6). Remarkably, destroying the neurons in the lateral hypothalamus with excitotoxins also produces aphagia and weight loss. Thus, after a decade or more of skepticism, the lateral hypothalamus was shown to play an important role in the control of eating.

excitotoxins: a chemical that destroys cell bodies of neurons by overexciting them

Single-cell recordings of neurons in the lateral hypothalamus of macaque monkeys have provided additional support for a role for the lateral hypothalamus in food intake regulation. Neurons in the lateral hypothalamus fire in response to the sight of food, but not to the sight of nonfood items, and to the taste of food in hungry monkeys (Burton, Rolls, & Mora, 1976). Thus, the response of the lateral hypothalamus depends on the motivational state of the monkey and occurs only when the monkey is motivated to eat. Interestingly, when a monkey was fed a particular food until the animal was quite full, the neurons in the lateral hypothalamus stopped firing in response to the sight of that food. However, if the full animal was shown another food, which it had not yet eaten, the neurons in the lateral hypothalamus began firing again, even though the monkey was already full (Rolls, Murzi, Yaxley, Thorpe, & Simpson, 1986; Rolls & Rolls, 1982). Thus, these studies demonstrate that neurons in the lateral hypothalamus become activated when they receive information about the presence of an interesting, edible food item. The firing of cells in the lateral hypothalamus in response to food always precedes eating behavior.

Figure 11.6 The effects of lesioning the lateral hypothalamus and the nigrostriatal bundle

(a) The nigrostriatal (dopaminergic) bundle of axons courses through the lateral hypothalamus. (b) When neurons in the lateral hypothalamus of a rat are lesioned with an excitotoxin (such as ibotenic acid), the rat stops eating. (c) When the nigrostriatal bundle of a rat is lesioned with a neurotoxin (such as 6-OHDA), the rat also stops eating.

a.

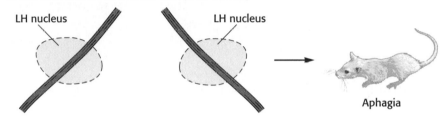

b. Lesion cells in LH with excitotoxin (ibotenic acid)

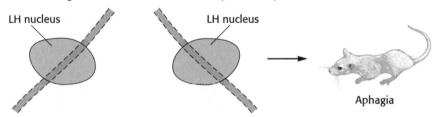

c. Lesion in nigrostriatal bundle with 6-OHDA (neurotoxin)

There is also evidence that neurons in the lateral hypothalamus change their firing response as a result of learning (Rolls, 1994; Wilson & Rolls, 1990). This means that the lateral hypothalamus provides flexibility in the response of the individual to food. The *orbitofrontal cortex* appears to change eating behavior in response to learning and relays this information to the lateral hypothalamus. For example, taste and smell information are integrated in the orbitofrontal cortex and affect the reward value of food, which alters the way the individual responds to the food. The orbitofrontal cortex relays information to the lateral hypothalamus, increasing the motivation to eat. In turn, the lateral hypothalamus and the cerebral cortex stimulate the *basal ganglia*, which initiate eating (Rolls, 1994). Table 11.2 summarizes the roles of brain structures involved in homeostasis and allostasis.

Homeostatic Mechanisms According to Nigel Lawes (1988), homeostatic regulation takes place in the *paraventricular system*, which includes the **paraventricular nucleus** of the hypothalamus and a number of other brain structures that have anatomical connections with the paraventricular nucleus (Figure 11.7). The paraventricular system receives information from the body and organizes behavior to respond to changes in internal body states. For example, the paraventricular system receives information about blood glucose levels and water balance and directs the brain's response to changes in these variables. When blood glucose levels fall, the paraventricular system initiates eating to restore optimal blood glucose levels. In

paraventricular nucleus: a cluster of neurons in the hypothalamus that organizes behavior, including eating, to respond to changes in internal body states

Table 11.2

Role of Brain Structures in Homeostasis and Allostasis of Food Intake

Brain Structure	Function
Lateral hypothalamus	Initiates eating when the individual is motivated to eat (allostatic)
Prefrontal cortex	Organizes attention to food and execution of eating behavior (allostatic)
Orbitofrontal cortex	Changes eating behavior in response to learning (allostatic)
Basal ganglia	Initiates eating under influence of lateral hypothalamus and prefrontal cortex (allostatic)
Paraventricular nucleus (hypothalamus)	Organizes eating behavior in response to changes in internal body states (homeostatic)
Ventromedial nucleus (hypothalamus)	Relays information from the nucleus of the solitary tract to the paraventricular nucleus (homeostatic)

contrast, the neurons in the lateral hypothalamus do not respond directly to changes in blood glucose or water balance (Winn, 1995).

A number of theories have been proposed to explain the homeostatic mechanism underlying the regulation of eating behavior. These theories include the *glucostatic theory*, the *thermostatic theory*, and the *lipostatic theory*. You will notice that each of these theories makes use of the suffix *-static*, which refers to a steady state. Thus, these theories postulate that a steady state is maintained in the body by a homeostatic mechanism.

The **glucostatic theory**, first proposed by Mayer (1953), maintains that *glucose levels* are regulated in the body. According to this theory, whenever blood glucose levels fall below some optimal level, glucose receptors in the brain fire and stimulate eating. When blood glucose levels rise, eating is terminated. This theory has quite a bit of empirical support but has proven to be an inadequate explanation for the control of eating (Smith, 1996). When regulating food intake behavior, the brain is influenced by many factors in addition to blood glucose levels, as you will learn in this chapter. Body fat supplies, hormone levels, and learning are just a few of the many influences that determine when and what an individual eats.

The **thermostatic theory** postulates that *core body temperature* drives eating behavior [*thermo-* = temperature or heat, Greek]. When body temperature falls below some optimal level, eating is triggered. In contrast, a rise in body temperature will cause eating to cease. According to this theory, heat is produced during the course of a meal as a result of smooth contractions in the gut following ingestion of food. This rise in body temperature that accompanies ingestion of food triggers a mechanism that terminates eating of a meal. That is, as body temperature begins to rise during a meal, temperature receptors fire in response to

glucostatic theory: a theory that postulates that glucose levels control food intake

thermostatic theory: a theory that postulates that core body temperature drives eating behavior, causing us to eat when core body temperature is lower than normal and to stop eating when core body temperature is elevated

Figure 11.7 The paraventricular system in the rat brain
The paraventricular nucleus of the hypothalamus receives information about the peripheral nervous system from the nucleus of the solitary tract and information about fat stores and blood sugar from other areas of the hypothalamus. Together, the paraventricular nucleus (homeostatic control) and the lateral hypothalamus (allostatic control) direct food intake.

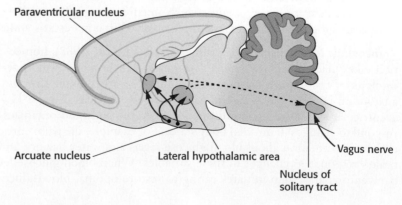

Paraventricular nucleus

Arcuate nucleus

Lateral hypothalamic area

Vagus nerve

Nucleus of solitary tract

the increase in body temperature and excite neurons in parts of the brain that stop eating. Temperature receptors that respond to very small changes in internal body temperature are located in the body cavity along the dorsal wall, where they can detect the heat produced by digestive processes (Riedel, 1976). However, core body temperature alone cannot explain why eating begins and stops.

The prefix *lipo-* refers to *fat* or fatty tissue. Thus, the **lipostatic theory** of food intake regulation is based on the notion that a central homeostatic mechanism monitors and maintains an optimal level of body fat. The "optimal" level of body fat appears to depend on a number of factors, including genetics. That is, some individuals have inherited a predisposition for more fat storage than others. According to the lipostatic theory, the brain stimulates eating when fat stores fall below an optimal level and terminates eating when fat storage is excessive. This theory has some support. **Leptin** is a hormone that is secreted by fat cells and suppresses food intake (Fulton, Woodside, & Shizgal, 2000). Investigators have determined that the more fat an individual has stored, the more leptin that is released. Therefore, leptin regulates fat storage by suppressing food intake when fat stores get too large. Although the action of leptin may explain how fat storage is regulated in the body, it is doubtful whether the lipostatic theory can explain why an individual starts and stops eating a particular meal.

In summary, the glucostatic theory focuses on blood glucose levels as the controlling factor for eating behavior, whereas the thermostatic theory focuses on core body temperature and the lipostatic theory focuses on fat storage. However, none of these theories can, by themselves, explain why an individual starts and stops eating.

Effects of Drugs and Neurotransmitters Two classes of drugs, *barbiturates* and *benzodiazepines*, have been shown to stimulate food intake. Recall from Chapter 3 that barbiturates and benzodiazepines are both classes of sedatives that act as depressants of brain activity. Benzodiazepines increase *GABA* activity in the brain and have been demonstrated to produce **hyperphagia,** or overeating [*hyper-* = more than normal; *-phagia* = to eat, Latin], in a wide variety of species, including baboons, cattle, cats, dogs, hamsters, horses, humans, mice, monkeys, pigeons, pigs, rabbits, rats, sheep, and wolves (Cooper & Higgs, 1994). They appear to increase food intake by enhancing the palatability (that is, the tastiness) of the ingested food. Recall from earlier in this chapter that the lateral hypothalamus, in conjunction with the frontal cortex, mediates changes in responsiveness to food stimuli. Thus, benzodiazepines act by stimulating the reward system that acts through the lateral hypothalamus, making foods appear to be more tasty and, therefore, increasing their intake.

Morphine, too, produces hyperphagia (Doyle, Berridge, & Gosnell, 1993). In contrast, the opiate antagonist *naloxone* reduces food intake. This demonstrates that the *endorphin* system plays a role in food intake regulation. Although the data are not yet conclusive, endorphins appear to increase the palatability of food, just like benzodiazepines do (Cooper & Higgs, 1994). By increasing the tastiness of food, the endogenous opioid neurotransmitters stimulate eating through the allostatic system, encouraging individuals to eat even when they are no longer hungry.

Effects of Neuropeptides Two brain peptides, **galanin** and **neuropeptide Y,** have been demonstrated to stimulate eating behavior and to control energy balance via the paraventricular nucleus of the hypothalamus (Leibowitz, 1995; Leibowitz, Akabayaski, Alexander, & Wang, 1998; Wang, Akabayashi, Yu, Dourmashkin, Alexander, Silva, Lighter, & Leibowitz, 1998). However, these neuropeptides have different effects on eating behavior. Galanin appears to control fat intake, fat metabolism, and fat storage (Leibowitz, 1998). In rats, galanin produces increased fat consumption, and it stimulates fat consumption most vigorously at puberty. Neuropeptide Y triggers intake of carbohydrates and promotes the storage of excess carbohydrates as body fat (Leibowitz, 1995). Thus, both galanin and neuropeptide Y encourage fat storage and weight gain.

Another newly discovered class of peptides, called **orexins,** also stimulates food intake (Sakurai et al., 1998). Whereas galanin and neuropeptide Y are released

lipostatic theory: a theory that postulates that we eat to maintain an optimum level of body fat

leptin: a hormone secreted by fat cells that suppresses food intake

hyperphagia: overeating

galanin: a brain peptide that stimulates fat consumption

neuropeptide Y: a brain peptide that stimulates the intake of carbohydrates

orexins: a class of peptides that stimulates food intake and also appears to play a role in producing narcolepsy

in several locations in the brain, orexins are found only in the lateral hypothalamus, which means that their functions are quite limited. You learned about orexins in Chapter 10 when we discussed narcolepsy. Recall that dogs and mice that cannot make orexins become narcoleptic. Although the function of orexins is still unknown, Masashi Yanagisawa and his colleagues (Sakurai et al., 1998) found that rats ate three to six times more food than did controls after orexins were injected directly into the lateral hypothalamus. When the rats were food deprived, levels of orexins in the lateral hypothalamus increased tremendously, indicating that orexins do indeed play a role in the regulation of food intake.

In summary, a number of drugs and neuropeptides stimulate eating, including barbiturates, benzodiazepines, morphine, galanin, neuropeptide Y, and orexin. Table 11.3 summarizes the action of these chemicals in the brain.

Peripheral Onset Mechanisms

The peripheral nervous system appears to play an important role in stimulating eating behavior. Signals from the gut are transmitted to the brain by way of the **vagus nerve,** also known as *cranial nerve X* (Figure 11.8). This information is relayed to the **nucleus of the solitary tract** in the hindbrain and from there is sent to the *paraventricular nucleus and the lateral nucleus* of the hypothalamus. Information from the mouth, such as information about the taste of food, which can stimulate eating, is also sent to the nucleus of the solitary tract for processing (Zeigler, 1994).

A review of the research concerning peripheral factors that trigger eating indicates that no single factor initiates eating by itself. Instead, several signals impact the central nervous system simultaneously to trigger eating (Mei, 1994). Among these many signals are neural messages relayed to the brain via the vagus nerve and hormonal messages sent from the gut to the brain. For example, stomach contractions produce feelings of hunger that trigger eating, as research by Walter Cannon (1912) has shown. Cannon had his graduate student swallow a balloon that was inflated in the stomach through a tube that passed down the throat and the esophagus (Figure 11.9). When the balloon was inflated, Cannon was able to measure the force of smooth muscle contractions as the stomach squeezed the balloon with each stomach contraction. The student was asked to indicate when he felt hungry, and Cannon discovered that stomach contractions were most vigorous when the student reported feeling very hungry. Thus, Cannon concluded that stomach contractions signal hunger. This finding shouldn't come as a surprise to you. Certainly, your grumbling stomach must have prompted you to eat on more than one occasion.

vagus nerve: cranial nerve X, which carries sensory information from the upper abdomen, chest, and neck to the brain and carries motor information from the brain to smooth muscles in those areas of the body

nucleus of the solitary tract: a nucleus in the medulla that receives information from the gut and other receptors by way of cranial nerves VII, IX, and X

Table 11.3

Actions of Drugs, Neuropeptides, and Hormones on the Onset of Eating

Chemical Agent	Function	Allostasis or Homeostasis?
Drugs		
Barbiturates	Stimulate eating (increases palatability)	Allostasis
Benzodiazepines	Stimulate eating (increases palatability)	Allostasis
Morphine	Stimulates eating (increases palatability)	Allostasis
Neuropeptides		
Galanin	Stimulates eating (increases fat consumption)	Homeostasis
Neuropeptide Y	Stimulates eating (increases carbohydrate consumption)	Homeostasis
Orexin	Stimulates eating (function unknown)	Allostasis?
Hormones		
Adrenal steroids	Stimulate eating	Homeostasis
Ovarian hormones	Inhibit eating (decrease palatability)	Allostasis

Figure 11.8 The vagus nerve and its pathway

The vagus nerve transmits information from the duodenum, stomach, liver, and pancreas to the nucleus of the solitary tract in the hindbrain.

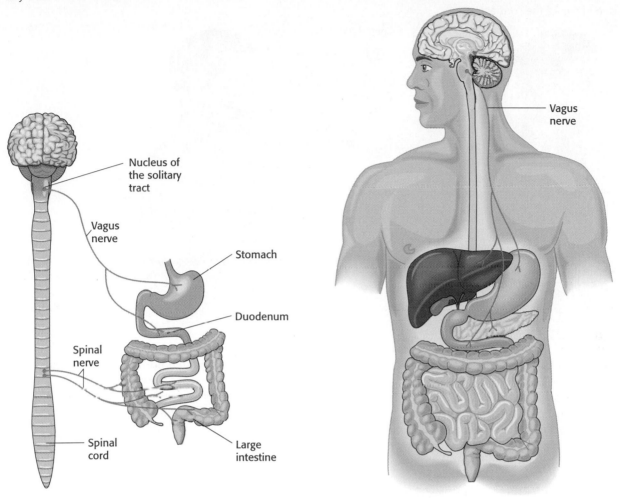

However, other factors besides the stomach must signal a need to eat. Research on people who have had their stomachs surgically removed for medical reasons indicates that these individuals begin to eat normally, without external prompting, just like people who have intact stomachs. Therefore, stomach contractions are not necessary to produce eating, but they do stimulate eating in people who have stomachs. Individuals without stomachs rely on other peripheral and central signals to trigger eating, such as hormonal cues.

Effects of Hormones Hormones produced by the adrenal gland, called **adrenal steroids,** also stimulate food intake. (You will learn more about adrenal steroids in Chapter 14.) They cause overeating and obesity in rodents that are genetically predisposed to be obese (McEwen, 1995c). In addition, removal of the adrenal glands, which eliminates the production of adrenal steroids, reduces hyperphagia and weight gain in rats that have lesions in the ventromedial hypothalamus (McEwen, Spencer, & Sakai, 1993).

Estrogen and **progesterone** are two hormones produced by the ovaries in women. (You will learn more about these hormones in Chapter 12.) These two hormones have an effect on women's food intake and food selection throughout the menstrual cycle. Energy intake is highest just before menstruation when estrogen and progesterone levels are lowest. Energy intake is lowest at ovulation, in the

adrenal steroids: hormones produced by the cortex of the adrenal gland

estrogen: a gonadal hormone produced by the ovaries

progesterone: a gonadal hormone produced by the ovaries that prepares the female body for pregnancy

Figure 11.9 Walter Cannon's experiment
(a) The student swallowed an uninflated balloon attached to a tube. The balloon is then inflated, and pressure from the stomach wall is recorded. (b) When the stomach contracts, it puts pressure on the balloon, causing a pen to move and record the contraction.

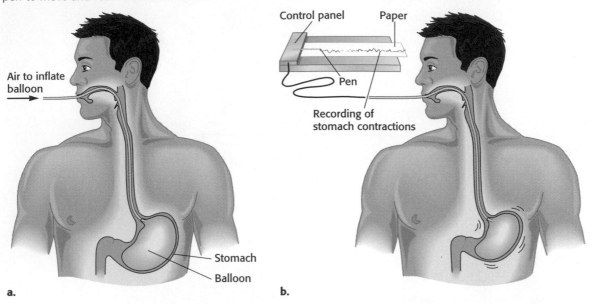

middle of the menstrual cycle (Figure 11.10), when estrogen levels are highest. Thus, high levels of ovarian hormones appear to suppress eating during the menstrual cycle, whereas low levels of ovarian hormones are associated with increased food intake. In addition, carbohydrate intake and fat intake are at a minimum about 2 days after ovulation. Foods are perceived as tasting "sweeter" just before menstruation, which increases consumption of sweets during the premenstrual phase (Buffenstein, Poppitt, McDevitt, & Prentice, 1995; Danker-Hopfe, Roczen, & Lowenstein-Wagner, 1995).

Adrenal hormones and ovarian hormones appear to have opposite effects on eating onset. Adrenal steroids stimulate food intake, whereas estrogen and progesterone suppress intake. Table 11.3 summarizes the actions of these hormones.

Offset of Eating

Did you ever think about why you put down your fork, push yourself away from the table, and stop eating? Brobeck (1955) introduced the concept of **satiety** to explain why you stop eating. Satiety has the same root as *satisfaction*, which is *satis*, a Latin word meaning "enough." That is, you stop eating when you've had enough. But, how does your brain know when you've had enough?

Satiation is an unconscious physiological process that stops eating (Blundell, 1979; Smith, 1998). In this section, we will look at the various factors that produce satiation and regulate the end of a meal. These factors include brain mechanisms as well as sensory signals from the gut and hormonal signals. Let's examine brain mechanisms first.

Figure 11.10 Effects of ovarian hormones on eating
Food intake is reduced at ovulation (when estrogen levels are highest) and is greatest in the premenstrual phase (when levels of ovarian hormones are declining).

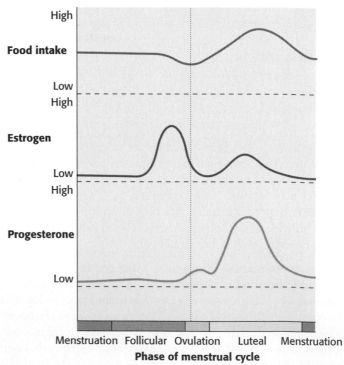

satiety: an unconscious physiological process that stops eating

Central Offset Mechanisms

In the previous section, you learned that the *paraventricular nucleus* of the hypothalamus appears to regulate homeostatic eating. Therefore, in addition to the onset of eating, the paraventricular nucleus plays an important role in the *offset* of homeostatic eating. Closely related to the paraventricular nucleus in this regard is the **ventromedial nucleus of the hypothalamus (VMH).** The ventromedial nucleus, as its name implies, is located in the ventral and medial region of the hypothalamus (see Figure 11.5). Early research by Hetherington and Ranson (1940) demonstrated that bilateral lesions of the VMH produced *hyperphagia* and *obesity* (Figure 11.11). In contrast, electrical stimulation of the VMH caused a hungry animal to stop eating. As a result of lesioning and stimulation studies, the VMH was regarded as the "satiety center" of the brain that regulates the offset of eating (Stellar, 1954).

However, as with the lateral hypothalamus, many axons pass through the VMH. Lesioning the VMH produces damage to the neurons in the ventromedial nucleus *and* to the axons that pass through the nucleus. Likewise, electrical stimulation of the VMH excites both the cell bodies located in the VMH *and* the axons that pass through that region. Most of the axons that pass through the VMH form a pathway between the *nucleus of the solitary tract* and the *paraventricular nucleus* of the hypothalamus. Thus, damage to this pathway disrupts regulation of eating behavior, producing overeating. Table 11.2 on page 322 summarizes the roles of the brain structures involved in food intake regulation.

Effects of Drugs   Early research on the effects of drugs on eating was conducted in the clinic rather than the laboratory (Cooper & Higgs, 1994). One of the first published observations was on the appetite-reducing effect of *amphetamine* (Nathanson, 1937). For many years (before its negative side effects were recognized), amphetamine was widely used therapeutically as a weight-loss drug. *Fenfluramine* was another drug that was observed to reduce food intake in rodents and people (Munro, Seaton, & Duncan, 1966; Silverstone, Cooper, & Begg, 1970; Woodward, 1970). These two drugs, which both produce decreased eating and weight loss, have different effects on the brain. Amphetamine acts through *catecholamine* pathways that utilize *norepinephrine* and *dopamine* as their neurotransmitters and is believed to inhibit those parts of the brain that initiate eating. In contrast, fenfluramine increases activity in *serotonin* pathways and stimulates the satiety center in the ventromedial and paraventricular hypothalamus (Blundell, 1981; Blundell, Latham, & Lesham, 1976). Drugs that enhance activity at serotonin receptors, particularly the 5-HT$_{1B}$ and the 5-HT$_{2C}$ receptors, produce satiety and decrease the amount of food eaten at a meal (Simansky, 1998).

Thus, amphetamine reduces food intake by inhibiting the onset of eating, and fenfluramine reduces food intake by stimulating satiety centers in the brain. The actions of these drugs are summarized in Table 11.4.

Peripheral Offset Mechanisms

As food passes through the upper part of the digestive tract (that is, through the mouth, down the throat and esophagus, through the stomach and small intestine), it stimulates receptors located in the lining of these structures (Figure 11.12). These receptors send sensory messages about the presence of food by way of the *trigeminal, facial, glossopharyngeal,* and *vagus nerves* (cranial nerves V, VII, IX, X) to the central nervous system, which signal satiation and, therefore, cause eating to stop. It is interesting that these peripheral signals occur and satiation begins before nutrients are absorbed into the blood. Satiety is apparently elicited by food in the digestive tract before absorption has occurred and energy stores have been replaced (Smith, 1998).

Oral Cues   Food placed into the mouth stimulates receptors that line the oral cavity and the throat and starts the development of satiety (Figure 11.13). Research with dogs and rats has demonstrated that stimulation of oral and pharyngeal [*pharynx* = throat, Greek] receptors only can produce satiety (Kraly et al., 1978;

Figure 11.11 Effects of lesioning the ventromedial nucleus of the hypothalamus
When a lesion in made in the ventromedial nucleus of the hypothalamus of a rat, the rat becomes hyperphagic, which produces obesity.

ventromedial nucleus of the hypothalamus (VMH): a nucleus of the hypothalamus that transmits information about the state of the body to the paraventricular nucleus, inhibiting eating

Table 11.4

Actions of Drugs and Hormones on the Offset of Eating

Chemical Agent	Function	Allostasis or Homeostasis?
Drugs		
Amphetamines	Appetite-reducing (inhibit initiation of eating)	Allostasis
Fenfluramine	Appetite-reducing (stimulates satiation)	Homeostasis
Hormones		
apo A-IV	Appetite-reducing (stimulates satiation)	Homeostasis
Bombesin	Appetite-reducing (stimulates satiation)	Homeostasis
Cholecystokinin	Appetite-reducing (stimulates satiation)	Homeostasis
Glucagon	Appetite-reducing (stimulates satiation)	Homeostasis
Insulin	Appetite-reducing (stimulates satiation)	Homeostasis
Leptin	Appetite-reducing (reduces palatability)	Allostasis

Smith, 1995). A surgical procedure developed by Ivan Pavlov, called the **esophageal fistula,** produces an opening in the esophagus that leads directly to the outside of the neck (Figure 11.13). Food that is chewed and swallowed by the animal subject ordinarily travels down the esophagus to reach the stomach. However, in an animal with an esophageal fistula, food that is swallowed ends up on the floor under the animal's neck, producing what is known as **sham feeding.** Therefore, only receptors in the mouth and throat are stimulated by food in an animal with an esophageal fistula because the food never reaches the stomach or intestines.

Kraly and his colleagues (1978) showed quite convincingly that satiety occurs in rats with esophageal fistulas. Rats with esophageal fistulas will swallow twice as much food as normal during a meal, but they do eventually stop eating, which indicates that satiety has occurred. Sham-feeding rats begin their next meal sooner than normal, waiting 25 minutes before eating again instead of waiting 56 minutes as they normally do because their eating onset mechanisms are activated sooner by the lack of nourishment that occurs with sham feeding.

Stomach Cues Food in the stomach can also produce satiety (Smith, 1998). Think about how you feel after you've consumed an enormous meal, like Thanksgiving dinner. Your stomach is distended from all the mashed potatoes and stuffing you've consumed, and you feel that you can't eat another bite. This

Figure 11.12 Major organs of the digestive tract

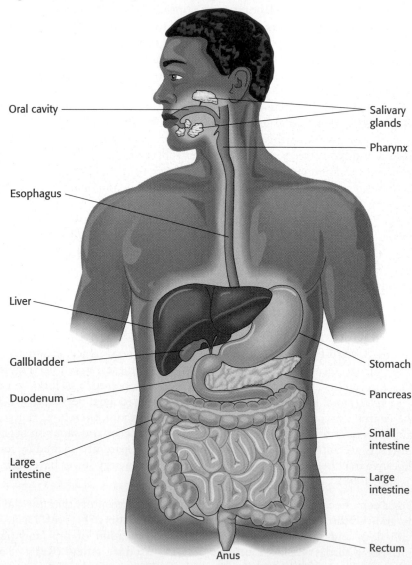

Oral cavity

Salivary glands

Pharynx

Esophagus

Liver

Gallbladder

Duodenum

Large intestine

Anus

Stomach

Pancreas

Small intestine

Large intestine

Rectum

Figure 11.13 The esophageal fistula and sham eating

To create an esophageal fistula, the esophagus is closed off and an opening (called a fistula) is made in the animal's neck. All food that is swallowed passes out of the animal's body through the fistula. This is called sham eating because food cannot reach the animal's stomach but instead is spilled on the floor.

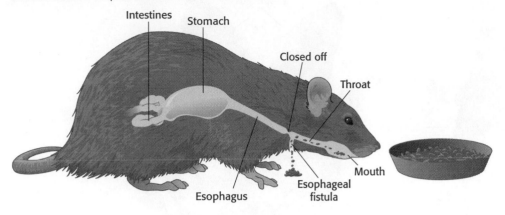

same effect can be produced in the laboratory. An inflatable cuff, devised by Young and Deutsch (1981), is placed around the constriction between the stomach and the small intestine, called the **pyloric sphincter.** When the cuff is inflated, food cannot pass from the stomach to the small intestine. Satiety is readily produced in an animal when the pyloric cuff is inflated just prior to a meal. Rats with an inflated pyloric cuff stop eating immediately after consuming a normal-sized meal, indicating that satiety can occur before food has been absorbed into the blood from the small intestine.

Intestinal Cues   The small intestine, which is located between the stomach and the large intestine, also plays an important role in the development of satiety (Greenberg, 1998). The **duodenum** (the section of the small intestine nearest the stomach) provides a good deal of information to the central nervous system that induces feelings of satiety in the individual (Figure 11.12). Research with dogs, rats, pigs, and human participants has shown that food injected directly into the duodenum of a hungry individual inhibits food intake (Ehman et al., 1971; Houpt, 1982; Welch et al., 1985; Yin & Tsai, 1973.) Thus, food in the duodenum stimulates receptors that signal the brain, producing satiety.

Studies using **parabiotic rats** have also demonstrated that the duodenum is instrumental in producing satiation. Rats joined parabiotically typically share the same blood supply because their skin and the muscles on their sides are sutured together (Figure 11.14). In parabiotic rats that have their intestines crossed, with the stomach of one rat connected to the duodenum of the other and vice versa, the food in the stomach of one rat is passed on to the duodenum of the other. Study Figure 11.14 carefully to make sure you understand this surgical preparation. In experiments in which parabiotic rats with crossed intestines are deprived of food for several hours and then allowed to eat, only one animal is permitted to at first. When one rat eats, the food leaves its stomach and goes directly into the duodenum of the second rat, producing satiety in the second rat. The second rat never starts to eat because its duodenum is full, whereas the first rat continues to eat because both its stomach and its duodenum are empty (Lepkovsky et al., 1975).

Effects of Hormones and Neurotransmitters   The mechanisms by which receptors in the stomach and intestines produce satiation are largely unknown. Certainly, neural messages transmitted by way of the vagus nerve to the nucleus of the solitary tract and the paraventricular nucleus of the hypothalamus play a role in the inhibition of eating. There is also evidence that chemical substances that act as hormones are released into the blood when food stimulates receptors in the stomach and

esophageal fistula: an opening in the esophagus that leads directly to the outside of the neck

sham feeding: eating that occurs with an esophageal fistula, in which food that is swallowed spills out of the esophagus onto the floor before reaching the stomach

pyloric sphincter: a muscular constriction between the stomach and the duodenum

duodenum: the first segment of the small intestine connected directly to the stomach

parabiotic rats: rats joined surgically that share the same blood supply

Figure 11.14 Parabiotic rats

(a) Parabiotic rats with shared blood supply only. Each rat has its own digestive system. (b) Parabiotic rats with crossed intestines. The duodenum of rat A (left) is surgically attached to the stomach of rat B (right), and the duodenum of rat B is surgically attached to the stomach of rat A.

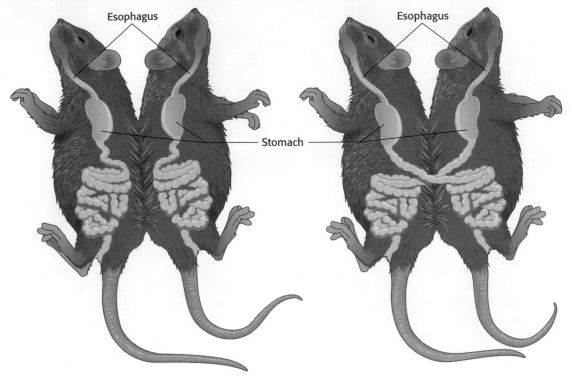

a. Parabiotic rats with shared blood supply   **b.** Parabiotic rats with crossed intestines

duodenum. A number of hormones released in the gut induce the termination of eating behavior. These hormones are peptides, which means that they can also act as neurotransmitters and bind with receptors on neurons. We will examine the role of *cholecystokinin, bombesin, glucagon, insulin,* and *leptin* in this section.

    Cholecystokinin (CCK) is a peptide that is released from the duodenum in response to ingested food. Gibbs, Young, and Smith (1973) demonstrated that intraperitoneal injections of CCK (that is, administration of CCK into the abdomen via a needle) produced inhibition of eating in rats. Since then, research with rats and other animals (including people) has demonstrated that CCK has a satiating effect and can regulate meal size (Smith & Gibbs, 1992, 1998). This suggests that food in the duodenum triggers the release of CCK, which in turn inhibits eating. CCK appears to inhibit food intake by means of two mechanisms: as a *hormone* or as a *neurotransmitter.* Acting as a neurotransmitter, CCK produces stimulation of the vagus nerve by binding with CCK receptors on vagal neurons in the duodenum. CCK also works like a hormone, traveling in the blood to the brain, where it binds with CCK receptors in the paraventricular nucleus of the hypothalamus and inhibits eating (Halmi, 1995; Smith, 1998).

    Bombesin is a peptide that has been isolated in amphibians and has been demonstrated to inhibit food intake in rodents, cats, birds, baboons, and people when administered into the abdomen. However, bombesin is not produced by birds or mammals. Two peptides released into the stomachs and intestines of mammals, called *gastrin-releasing peptide* and *neuromedin,* are chemically related to bombesin. Receptors for gastrin-releasing peptide and neuromedin also bind with bombesin, which implicates these peptides in the inhibition of food intake. Indeed, administration of gastrin-releasing peptide and neuromedin has been shown to decrease food intake and produce satiety (Kirkham et al., 1995; Smith, 1998). Gastrin-releasing peptide and neuromedin are large molecules, too large to cross the blood-

cholecystokinin: a peptide released from the duodenum that inhibits eating

bombesin: an amphibian peptide that inhibits food intake

Tab

Met

Heig

4'10"

4'11"

5'0"

5'1"

5'2"

5'3"

5'4"

5'5"

5'6"

5'7"

5'8"

5'9"

5'10'

5'11'

6'0"

Met

Heig

5'2"

5'3"

5'4"

5'5"

5'6"

5'7"

5'8"

5'9"

5'10'

5'11'

6'0"

6'1"

6'2"

6'3"

6'4"

Weigh
weighi
Source

brain barrier, which means that they act locally in the gut as neurotransmitters to terminate eating. Signals produced by these peptides are transmitted by the vagus nerve to the nucleus of the solitary tract, where these mediate food intake.

Two hormones produced by the pancreas, **glucagon** and **insulin,** are also implicated in the offset of eating. The primary role of glucagon is to break down glycogen, which is stored in the liver, into glucose to raise blood glucose levels. In contrast, insulin lowers blood glucose levels by transporting glucose out of the bloodstream and into cells. However, they both appear to play a role in the offset of eating.

Glucagon inhibits food intake and produces satiety when it is injected into rats and people (Geary, 1998). In addition, glucagon is released in the body during a meal, immediately after onset of the meal, which means that it could act as a signal that induces satiety and termination of the meal. Glucagon appears to stimulate the vagus nerve, which transmits information to the nucleus of the solitary tract, producing satiation. Glucagon receptors have also been found in the brain, particularly in the nucleus of the solitary tract and in the medial and paraventricular areas of the hypothalamus (Geary, 1998). Secretion of glucagon also appears to stimulate the release of insulin.

Insulin appears to produce satiation, too. Insulin is released during a meal as soon as food enters the mouth (Strubbe & Steffens, 1975). As the meal continues, more and more insulin is released, increasing insulin's ability to produce satiety. VanderWeele (1998) maintains that insulin is one of many factors that works to terminate a meal. These factors send redundant signals to the brain by way of the vagus nerve, reducing appetite and decreasing the palatability or tastiness of the consumed food.

Another hormone that suppresses food intake is *leptin*, which you learned about earlier in this chapter. Leptin is secreted by fat cells and circulates in the blood to reach the *lateral* and the *ventromedial hypothalamus*, where it has its principal effects. The role of leptin is to regulate fat storage by suppressing food intake when fat stores get too large. The effect of leptin on the lateral hypothalamus appears to be opposite the effect of benzodiazepines and endorphins. Whereas benzodiazepines and endorphins increase the palatability and reward value of food (which induces food intake), leptin reduces the reward value of food in the lateral hypothalamus (Fulton, Woodside, & Shizgal, 2000). Receptors for leptin are also found in the ventromedial hypothalamus, where leptin directly triggers termination of eating behavior.

More recently, another hormone called *apolipoprotein A-IV* (apo A-IV) has been found to suppress food intake (Tso, Liu, & Kalogeris, 1999; Tso, Liu, Kalogeris, & Thomson, 2001). Apo A-IV is synthesized in the small intestine and is released whenever a meal containing fat is consumed. The release of apo Apo A-IV rapidly follows the absorption of fat from the intestine into the bloodstream. Apo A-IV travels in the bloodstream to the hypothalamus, where it suppresses food intake (Liu et al., 2001). Unfortunately, when an individual eats a high-fat diet regularly the release of apo A-IV declines. This means that chronic ingestion of high-fat diets results in reduced apo A-IV release and less suppression of food intake, which may explain why people who eat high-fat diets tend to become obese (Tso et al., 2001).

Cholecystokinin, bombesin, gastrin-releasing peptide, neuromedin, glucagon, insulin, leptin, and apo A-IV are hormones that have been demonstrated to suppress food intake. The specific actions of these hormones are summarized in Table 11.4.

Role of the Liver   The **liver** appears to play a central role in digestion and metabolism. Recall that glycogen is stored in the liver and is broken down when the body is in need of glucose. Several hormones, including glucagon and insulin, affect the activity of the liver. For example, glucagon initiates the breakdown of glycogen, and insulin is involved in carbohydrate storage and glycogen production in the liver. Some investigators believe that the liver regulates short-term food intake, based on these hormonal mechanisms (Friedman & Tardoff, 1986; Russek, 1981;

glucagon: a hormone produced by the pancreas that inhibits eating

insulin: a pancreatic hormone that produces satiation

liver: an organ in the digestive system that produces and stores glycogen and may play a role in the regulation of short-term food intake

On the other hand, **hypogonadism** in men, accompanied by reduced levels of testosterone, has also been associated with obesity (Marin & Arver, 1998). For reasons as yet unknown, accumulation of fat in the abdomen occurs with low levels of testosterone in men, whereas normal levels of testosterone counteract this accumulation of fat.

The type of food consumed may affect hormone release, appetite, and weight gain. Recall that the neuropeptide *galanin* stimulates the intake of *fatty foods*, whereas *neuropeptide Y* stimulates *carbohydrate* consumption. Unfortunately, eating fatty foods increases the production of galanin, which in turn stimulates the consumption of even more fat. This same vicious cycle is evident for neuropeptide Y. Intake of carbohydrates increases the release of neuropeptide Y, which produces cravings for more carbohydrates. There is evidence from research with female rats that increased levels of galanin and neuropeptide Y contribute to overeating and increased weight gain (Leibowitz et al., 1998).

In summary, insulin, thyroid hormones, testosterone, galanin, and neuropeptide Y are all associated with weight gain. Increased levels of insulin and decreased levels of thyroid hormone have been implicated in weight gain. In addition, both excessively high and low levels of testosterone are linked to obesity syndromes. Galanin and neuropeptide Y contribute to weight gain by increasing intake of fats and carbohydrates, respectively.

Genetic Factors

The link between genetics and obesity is still unclear. Certainly, researchers have observed that obese people are more likely to have obese children than are people of normal weight. However, obese people are also more likely to have obese adopted children *and* obese pets, which calls into question a genetic explanation of obesity. That word of caution aside, investigators have discovered two animal strains that are genetically obese: the ob/ob mouse and the Zucker fatty yellow rat. Both strains of animals produce offspring that, due to a defective gene, are grossly obese (Figure 11.16). The Zucker fatty yellow rat gets its name from the fact that this rat produces so much fat that the excess fat literally oozes through the animal's skin and coats its hair.

In the ob/ob mouse, the defective gene, called the *obesity* or **ob gene,** has been identified and cloned. Research with the ob gene has indicated that body fat in adult rats and mice is regulated by leptin acting on the hypothalamus to inhibit eating (Kiess et al., 1998). As you learned in the previous section, the release of leptin increases as fat stores increase. In genetically obese rodents, the defective ob gene produces a *leptin deficiency*, which causes a failure to inhibit eating as fat stores increase. That is, as the rodents get fatter and fatter, correspondingly large amounts of leptin are *not* secreted because of the leptin deficiency, and eating is not inhibited. A defective ob gene has recently been shown to produce severe obesity in human children (Kiess et al., 1998). These children have a leptin deficiency due to a mutation in the ob gene.

Behavioral Factors

Personality and eating habits can certainly play a role in the way we eat, the foods we select, and our attitudes toward food, although these variables have received relatively little study. For example, individuals who eat rapidly consume a great deal of food before satiety signals terminate a meal. Members of a subclass of the population, called *restrained eaters*, control their eating behavior very rigorously in a manner that predisposes them to obesity when their controls break down (Polivy & Herman, 1976; Wardle, 1990). Stanley Schachter and his colleagues at Columbia University compared the eating behaviors of obese humans and hyperphagic rats with lesions in the ventromedial nucleus of the hypothalamus. They found that, compared to normal controls, obese rats and humans were finicky eaters who avoid bad-tasting food, did not like to work to obtain their food, and were highly

Figure 11.16 The ob/ob mouse
The ob/ob mouse (left) is genetically obese. A normal mouse is shown at right.

hypogonadism: a disorder in which a man has reduced levels of testosterone

ob gene: a defective gene found in genetically obese mice

emotional. Most importantly, Schachter and Rodin (1974) discovered that obese rats and humans did not respond as much to internal signals as they did to external cues to eat, whereas normal controls were more aware of their internal signals. An obese person who had just eaten a large meal had more difficulty passing up delicious-smelling pastries than did a normal control with a similarly full stomach.

In addition, the environment can affect food intake. Normal rats typically eat the same amount of lab chow every day and rarely get obese. However, when they are offered a variety of foods (marshmallows, peanut butter, crackers, sausage, cheese, and so forth) and allowed to eat cafeteria style, rats overeat and gain weight (Kanarek & Hirsch, 1977). This effect has also been demonstrated in people. *Cafeteria-style eating* might explain why freshman college students often gain weight when they enter college. Like rats offered a cafeteria-style diet, students who dine in the college cafeteria select a wide variety of foods to consume and overeat.

Other environmental stimuli have been shown to produce overeating or hyperphagia in rats. For example, a mild tail pinch elicits overeating in rats (Antelman & Szechtman, 1975), and white noise has also been shown to produce hyperphagia (Kupfermann, 1964; Wilson & Cantor, 1986). **Schedule-induced hyperphagia** has been produced in rats that press a lever for pleasurable brain stimulation on an intermittent reinforcement schedule. That is, when pleasurable brain stimulation is available once every 90 seconds, rats will spend the first 60 seconds or so of that waiting period eating, if food is made available. During the last 20–30 seconds, the rats go to the lever and begin pressing it in anticipation of receiving a pleasurable brain stimulation. Rats that are placed in an experimental chamber for several hours a day and permitted to press for rewarding brain stimulation with food available will overeat and gain weight (Wilson & Cantor, 1987). Although these phenomena have not been demonstrated in people to date, it is extremely probable that environmental stimuli like noise or schedules can affect eating behavior in people, too.

schedule-induced hyperphagia: overeating that occurs when an individual is on a schedule waiting for a nonfood reward

Producing Obesity in the Laboratory

Animal models of obesity have been used by scientific investigators to gain an understanding of the chemical and cellular basis of obesity. A number of techniques allow psychologists and other scientists to study obesity in laboratory animals. At this point, you should understand how each of these techniques produces obesity. Obesity can be induced by a number of surgical techniques, including *lesioning the ventromedial nucleus of the hypothalamus* and *electrical stimulation of the lateral hypothalamus*. Injecting a normal, healthy rat with *insulin* will also produce obesity in that animal. Behavioral methods used to produce hyperphagia and obesity include the tail-pinch procedure and cafeteria-style eating. Investigators who are interested in the genetic basis of obesity study animals that have inherited a genetic flaw that makes them obese, such as the ob/ob mouse and the Zucker rat.

Bulimia Nervosa

Bulimia nervosa occurs in less than 4% of the population, although its occurrence is limited mostly to adolescent girls and women (Garfinkel et al., 1995). Investigators believe that bulimia nervosa and the related disorder, anorexia nervosa, develop in people who are unhappy with the shapes of their bodies and who take extreme measures to control their body weights. Bulimia nervosa is characterized by binge eating followed by self-induced vomiting or laxative use. A person with bulimia may eat normally much of the time, although she often diets for extended periods of time. However, cycles of uncontrollable binging and purging interrupt the bulimic individual's day, producing a sense of distress and shame. A bulimic college student told me once, "I can be sitting in a friend's house or my boyfriend's apartment, and this feeling will come over me, and I will tell a lie, anything, so I can go back to my house and binge." During binge-eating episodes, people eat enormous quantities of foods, typically foods high in carbohydrates and fats, like cake, ice cream, or pizza, but they also will eat bizarre food items, such as a bag of

bulimia nervosa: an eating disorder characterized by binge eating followed by self-induced vomiting or laxative use

flour or a frozen TV dinner. Sometimes so much food can be consumed that the stomach will rupture (Casper, 1998).

Depending on the purging method used, a number of physical problems can emerge as a result of bulimia, including erosion of enamel from the teeth and digestive system disorders involving the stomach, small intestine, or large intestine. Vomiting and laxative use can also deplete potassium levels in the blood, causing **hypokalemia**, which can interfere with heart and kidney function. Studies of bulimic individuals indicate that they have reduced serotonin activity compared to anorexic patients and normal controls (Kaye et al., 1998, 2000). In a recent PET study, Walter Kaye and his colleagues (2001) at the University of Pittsburgh found that reduced levels of serotonin bound with $5HT_{2A}$ receptors in the medial orbital frontal cortex of recovered bulimics compared to healthy, age-matched volunteers. (The medial orbital frontal cortex is associated with impulse control, anxiety, and depression.) Drugs that increase serotonin activity, such as selective serotonin reuptake inhibitors (SSRIs, as you learned in Chapter 3), are useful in reducing bingeing episodes, although relapse occurs when use of these drugs is continued over a long period of time or when use of these drugs is discontinued (Halmi, 1995; Mauri et al., 1996; Walsh & Devlin, 1995). Cognitive-behavioral therapy is the treatment of choice for bulimia nervosa (Wilson & Fairburn, 1999).

Anorexia Nervosa

Anorexia nervosa is rarer than bulimia nervosa and is found in one of two forms: **restricting anorexia** and **anorexia nervosa-bulimic subtype.** Restricting anorexia is characterized by severe reduction in food intake, which produces an emaciated appearance due to a loss of body fat, especially fat stored under the skin or *subcutaneous fat* [*sub-* = under; *-cutaneous* = skin] (Figure 11.17). People with restricting anorexia lose from 15 to 60% of their body weight due to reduced caloric intake, and they also eat selectively, avoiding certain "forbidden" foods, which leads to malnutrition and vitamin deficiencies. In contrast, individuals with the bulimic subtype of anorexia nervosa engage in abnormal eating behavior patterns that resemble bulimic behavior, including gorging followed by vomiting or other forms of purging, in addition to periodic bouts of severe food restriction.

Research on treatments for anorexia nervosa lags far behind research on treatments for bulimia nervosa (Wilson & Fairburn, 1999). Nutritional and cognitive-behavioral counseling can help the anorexic patient gain weight, and SSRIs have been demonstrated to be helpful in controlling depression and compulsive behaviors associated with anorexia (Kaye, 1997; Kaye et al., 1998; Wilson & Fairburn, 1999). Treatment can be given in either an inpatient or outpatient setting. The *Case Study* describes the case of a woman who required hospitalization, or inpatient treatment, for her severe restricting anorexia.

A number of physiological and neurochemical abnormalities accompany anorexia nervosa. For the restricting subtype of the disorder, these abnormalities resemble the effects of starvation and include slowed metabolic rate, lowered body temperature, abnormal EEG record, and disorders of the digestive system, the cardiovascular system, and the kidneys. The changes in body temperature and metabolic rate reflect dysfunction of the hypothalamus (Casper, 1998). Other problems associated with anorexia that indicate hypothalamic involvement are sleep disorders, including insomnia and early morning wakening, changes in pituitary gland function, reduced gonadal function, including absence of menstruation in women, and depression. Reduction in body fat, as signaled by reduced levels of leptin and other hormones, affects hypothalamic function, which in turn affects activity of the pituitary gland (Baranowska et al., 1997; Casper, 1997; Kiess et al., 1998). For example, a loss of body fat can interfere with reproductive function, via the hypothalamic-pituitary-gonadal pathway, which is adaptive in times of starvation because it prevents a starving woman from getting pregnant.

Brain-imaging studies have revealed that adolescent girls with anorexia nervosa may develop permanent brain cell loss due to their illness. Katzman and his col-

hypokalemia: the depletion of potassium levels in the blood

anorexia nervosa: an eating disorder in which the individual restricts food intake and loses significant body weight

restricting anorexia: a form of anorexia nervosa that is characterized by severe reduction of food intake, which leads to an emaciated appearance

anorexia nervosa-bulimic subtype: a form of anorexia nervosa in which the affected individual engages in bingeing and purging, in addition to bouts of food restriction

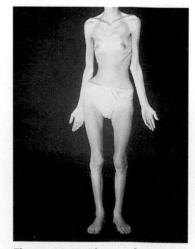

Figure 11.17 Photo of anorexic patient

Anorexia

Laura was quite popular in elementary school, but her social life flagged when she made the transition to junior high school. The "cool" kids no longer called her and invited her on their outings, and Laura was stuck hanging out with the less popular girls, who tended to be a bit overweight. When Laura's mother made an offhand comment one day about one of Laura's best friends ("That poor girl would be so much prettier if she lost some weight!"), Laura looked in a mirror and said to herself, "I'm ugly. I need to lose weight." She immediately began restricting her food intake. Laura made up a secret list of foods that she could not eat because they contained too much fat. Before eating anything, she studied the package label carefully to see how much fat the food contained.

While she was in high school, Laura had to work hard to deceive her mother, who always seemed to be watching her. She was able to skip breakfast by getting up late and claiming there was no time to eat. When her mother forced her to take something to eat on the way to school, Laura promptly dumped it into the nearest trash can she passed. She didn't eat lunch at school, either. Dinner was a problem because her family always sat down to eat together, and she was forced to pretend to eat, although most food ended up in her napkin, which Laura tossed into the trash. Laura became involved in athletics: field hockey in the fall, basketball in the winter, and track in the spring, because practice took place during dinnertime.

When she arrived at college, Laura weighed about 98 pounds, which was much too thin for her 5'6" frame. However, college provided Laura with a good deal of freedom. No one was concerned with whether she ate or not, although at first her roommate would invite her to come to the dining hall with her and sometimes brought back food for her, which Laura never touched. Laura was extremely proud of her ability to resist food and of her self-control. However, she was afraid that, if she started to eat, she would lose control and not be able to stop eating.

Laura's parents were startled at her gauntness when she came home the summer after her first year. Laura had lost nearly 10 pounds in college, and her hair was thin and had lost its natural sheen. When she refused to take off her favorite sweatshirt on a very warm day in July, claiming she was cold (which she was), her mother took her to talk with a local psychologist. Laura insisted to the psychologist and her mother that her appetite was good and that she ate regularly. She saw the psychologist every week over the summer and ate more than she wanted to, to please her mother and the psychologist.

Laura was relieved to go back to college at the end of the summer so that she could eat the way she wanted, which amounted to a handful of vitamins, one cup of chicken broth, and a tablespoon or so of applesauce each day. At Thanksgiving, she weighed about 85 pounds, and her parents promptly called the health center at her college and asked for help. The physician who examined Laura was alarmed. She looked absolutely skeletal and was weak and apathetic. He told Laura that she had to come to the health center every day and, if her weight dropped below 85 pounds, she would have to leave the college to get treatment. The physician also insisted that Laura see the school counselor twice a week.

Every day Laura reported for her weigh-in at the health center. Often she would consume two cups of broth right before the weigh-in and then promptly vomit it up after she left the health center. In January, Laura came down with the flu and was "too sick" to come to the health center for the daily weigh-in. When she did come in, 4 days later, her weight had slipped to 82 pounds. Her parents were called, and they came and took Laura home, where she immediately was enrolled in an inpatient eating disorder clinic at a local university hospital. Laura was promptly placed on intravenous (IV) nutrition therapy to restore needed nutrients and electrolytes to her body. Psychotherapy, nutritional therapy, and occupational therapy were soon added to her treatment. Laura was released after 8 weeks of inpatient treatment, but she remained in treatment as an outpatient for 3 more years while she attended a local college near her parents' home.

leagues (1996) in Toronto compared MRI scans of the brains of 13 low-weight adolescent girls with anorexia nervosa with the brains of 8 healthy, age-matched controls. The brains of the anorexic subjects had significantly enlarged ventricles and associated reductions in gray matter and white matter. That is, the brains of adolescents with restricting anorexia had significantly less brain matter than did the brains of healthy controls. A year later, 6 of the 13 girls had recovered and gained weight. MRI scans were conducted for all 13 original patients and 18 healthy controls (Katzman, Zipursky, Lambe, & Mikulis, 1997). Although white matter volume in the recovered anorexic patients had increased significantly, gray matter was still severely reduced in the brains of recovered anorexics. Another MRI study comparing the brain scans of 12 women who had recovered from anorexia 1 to 23 years prior to the study with MRI scans of 18 healthy controls and 13 low-weight anorexic patients demonstrated that the former anorexics had a significantly smaller volume of gray matter in their brains than did the healthy controls (Lambe, Katzner, Mikulis, Kennedy, & Zipursky, 1997). Both the former anorexics and the low-weight anorexics had reduced amounts of gray matter in their brains, which suggests that anorexia causes permanent changes in the brain that are not affected by treatment and recovery.

Pica

When an individual is deprived of certain nutrients, due to adverse dietary, cultural, or economic circumstances, a condition called **specific hunger** occurs. **Specific hunger** refers to a deprivation state in which an individual lacks a particular nutrient or group of nutrients in the diet. In the laboratory, a state of specific hunger is produced by depriving the laboratory subject of a particular nutrient, such as an amino acid or a vitamin. Animals deprived of a specific nutrient will increase their intake of foods that contain the needed nutrient (Kratz & Levitsky, 1979; Leung, Rogers, & Harper, 1968; Pant, Rogers, & Harper, 1972). When these foods are unavailable, laboratory animals will engage in **pica,** or eating of nonnutritive substances such as wood chips or their own feces. Malnourished human children and pregnant women, who have special dietary needs due to the rapid growth they are experiencing, have been observed engaging in pica (Hamilton et al., 2001; Prasad, 2001; Sule & Madugu, 2001). For example, children who are deprived of protein will eat dirt and clay, which provide little nutritional value (Donovick & Burright, 1992).

specific hunger: a deprivation state in which the affected individual lacks a specific nutrient in the diet

pica: the eating of nonnutritive substances

Recap 11.3: Eating Disorders

(a)_____ and (b)_____ are the two most prominent eating disorders in Western society. People who chronically overeat show (c)_____, due to secretion of large amounts of insulin. Chronic hyperinsulinemia can produce (d)_____ _____ diabetes, in which a person fails to respond to the insulin he or she produces. When a person overproduces insulin, (e)_____ results because the large amounts of insulin cause more glucose than normal to be transported out of the blood. As a result of hypoglycemia, the (f)_____ detects an abnormally low level of blood glucose and initiates eating, which can produce overeating and weight gain. People who do not produce insulin have Type 1 diabetes, which causes glucose to accumulate in the blood, called (g)_____. In older people, (h)_____ gland function is reduced, which can produce weight gain in those who do not reduce their food intake. In genetically obese mice, the defective ob gene produces a deficiency of (i)_____, a hormone that inhibits food intake. (j)_____ _____ is characterized by binge-eating followed by self-purging. The two forms of anorexia nervosa are (k)_____ _____ (severe reduction in food intake) and (l)_____ _____-_____ _____ (food restriction plus periodic binging and purging). When an individual is deprived of one or more essential nutrients, the eating of nonnutritive substances, called (m)_____, may occur.

Regulation of Water Intake

Water intake is intimately linked to temperature regulation and food intake. For example, sweating depletes the body's water supplies, causing thirst. Eating highly salty food can also affect water levels within the cells of the body and produce thirst. Ingestion of cold water causes heat loss because it takes one calorie to raise one gram of water one degree C. Thus, you burn a large number of calories for every 8 ounces of ice cold water that you drink.

Controlling water levels in the body is important because two-thirds of the body is composed of water. All of the water in the body can be divided into two components: the **intracellular compartment** and the **extracellular compartment**. Most of the body's water, about 70%, is found in the intracellular compartment. As its name implies, the intracellular compartment refers to all the water located inside the cells of the body. The remaining 30–35% of body's water supply is found outside of cells, such as in the blood, in glands, in the lymph system, and in the cavities of body organs like the stomach or bladder. This means that you lose water from your extracellular compartment whenever you sweat, vomit, bleed, or urinate.

The central nervous system, particularly neurons in the *anterior hypothalamus*, controls water balance in the intracellular and extracellular compartments. Two different homeostatic mechanisms regulate water levels in these compartments. For the intracellular compartment, the homeostatic mechanism involves preserving a *constant concentration of solutes* (particles in solution, such as salts, acids, and other chemical molecules) within the cell. You might recall from high school or college chemistry classes that concentrations are measured in terms of the number of solutes per unit of water. Thus, by increasing water within a cell, the concentration of solutes is decreased. Decreasing water, or taking water out of a cell, increases the concentration of solutes within a cell. This is an important concept, so examine Figure 11.18 to make sure you understand how water affects intracellular concentration. For the extracellular compartment, the homeostatic mechanism involves maintaining a *constant volume of fluid* in the extracellular compartment. Thus, water intake is regulated by two homeostatic mechanisms: one that preserves a constant concentration in the intracellular compartment and one that maintains a constant volume in the extracellular compartment.

Figure 11.18 Water and intracellular concentration
Water flows across a semipermeable membrane from an area of low osmotic pressure (dilute solution) to an area of higher osmotic pressure (more concentrated solution).

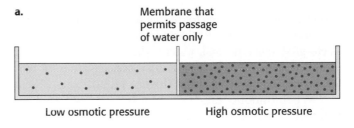

Regulating the Concentration of the Intracellular Compartment

The anterior hypothalamus maintains the internal concentration of cell at a concentration of 0.15 M. (A 1.0 M solution has a concentration equal to the molecular weight of the solute added to enough water to make one liter of solution.) Whenever the concentration of the intracellular compartment becomes greater than 0.15 M, *osmotic thirst* occurs in the affected individual. Let's take a look at how intracellular concentrations rise.

Recall from Chapter 2 that cell membranes are semipermeable, which means that they allow some molecules to pass readily across a membrane while other substances are trapped inside or outside of the cell. Water, for example, passes readily across the cell membrane, whereas sodium and chloride cannot. Cells get their water from the blood that flows in nearby blood vessels (Figure 11.19). The concentration within a cell depends on the concentration of the blood that flows by. That is, when intracellular fluid in the cells is more concentrated than the blood, water is drawn from the blood into the cells. When the blood is more concentrated, it draws water from the cells.

Think about what happens when you eat a large bag of salty chips. The salty chips are digested, and the salt passes from your small intestine into your

Figure 11.19 Osmotic thirst

a. Normal state

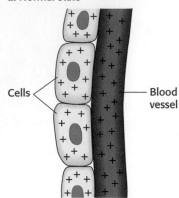

Cells ⟨ Blood vessel

b. Osmotic thirst

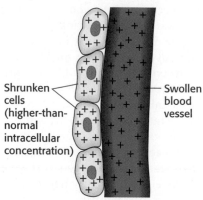

Shrunken cells (higher-than-normal intracellular concentration)

Swollen blood vessel

In normal state, the concentrations of ions in the blood and inside of cells (intracellular compartment) are equal.

After a salty meal, the concentration of ions in the blood is greater than that inside cells.

Water is drawn out of cells into the blood, producing osmotic thirst.

bloodstream. If you eat a lot of this salty food, the concentration of salt in your blood increases to a higher level than normal. Because the concentration of salt in the blood is elevated above normal, water is drawn from the cells into the blood. When water is pulled from the cells, the internal concentration of the cells increases above 0.15 M, producing **osmotic thirst** (Figure 11.19).

When osmotic thirst occurs, it sets off a series of events that results in drinking behavior. Special receptors, called **osmoreceptors,** in the *lamina terminalis* in the anterior hypothalamus monitor the intracellular concentration (Ramsay & Thrasher, 1990; Verney, 1947). When the concentration increases above 0.15 M, these osmoreceptors fire and excite neurons in the *paraventricular nucleus* and *supraoptic nucleus* of the hypothalamus, which in turn stimulate the *pituitary gland.* The pituitary gland reacts to stimulation from the hypothalamus by releasing a hormone called **antidiuretic hormone,** or *ADH* (Bargmann & Scharrer, 1951). Antidiuretic hormone, which is also known as *vasopressin,* travels in the blood to the *kidneys,* where it signals to the kidneys to stop producing urine (Nielsen, Frokiaer, Marples, Kwon, Agre, & Knepper, 2002). The purpose of antidiuretic hormone, then, is to regulate water loss, through suppressing urination, from the body. The lamina terminalis relays information about increased osmotic pressure to the *lateral preoptic area* of the hypothalamus, which induces drinking behavior, although the mechanism that causes drinking is unknown. Thus, osmotic thirst produces two end results: It stops water loss through the kidneys, and it initiates drinking.

In the laboratory, osmotic thirst is produced by injecting *hypertonic saline* into the experimental subject [*hyper-* = more than normal; *-tonic* = concentration]. That is, a salt solution with a concentration greater than 0.15 M is injected into the subject. This solution acts just like a big bag of salty chips in your bloodstream: It draws water from the intracellular compartment and produces osmotic thirst, which causes the subject to begin drinking. In contrast, when control subjects are injected with *hypertonic urea,* no drinking occurs because urea (a waste product produced by all cells) diffuses readily across the cell membrane. This means that, even though the concentration of the urea solution is greater than 0.15 M, osmotic thirst does not occur because the urea does not stay in the extracellular compartment when it is injected into an experimental subject. Instead, the urea diffuses into the intracellular compartment, pulling in water with it as it enters the cells of the body. Therefore, the concentration of the intracellular compartment does not change, and no drinking is observed. Osmotic thirst is produced when the concentration of solutes in the cells of the body is increased above the normal physiological level.

osmotic thirst: thirst that occurs when the concentration of the intracellular compartment becomes greater than normal

osmoreceptors: special receptors in the anterior hypothalamus that monitor intracellular concentration

antidiuretic hormone: a hormone produced by the pituitary gland that inhibits the production of urine, also known as vasopressin

Regulating the Volume of the Extracellular Compartment

A second type of thirst, called **hypovolemic thirst,** is produced when fluid in the extracellular compartment becomes *reduced in volume* (Stricker, 1966; Stocker, Stricker, & Sved, 2001). Loss of fluid from the extracellular compartment through profuse sweating, vomiting, diarrhea, or hemorrhage can produce hypovolemic thirst. For example, a bad case of the flu or a heavy menstrual flow can result in hypovolemic thirst. A nursing woman feels thirsty more often and drinks more due to depletion of her fluid stores caused by lactation.

In the laboratory, hypovolemic thirst is typically produced by drastically reducing blood pressure in the laboratory subject. Tying off, or *ligating*, a major blood vessel such as the inferior vena cava (the large vein that carries blood from the lower part of the body back to the heart) will cause a large reduction in blood pressure, resulting in hypovolemic thirst and drinking in the affected animal. Obviously, blood pressure must be high enough to permit blood to flow against the force of gravity to reach the brain. When blood pressure is drastically reduced, blood cannot get to the brain, causing unconsciousness, seizures, and even death. Therefore, the body needs a mechanism like hypovolemic thirst to maintain blood pressure in order that the brain receives the nourishment that it needs.

To maintain the volume of fluid in the extracellular compartment, receptors called **baroreceptors,** which are located in large veins, monitor blood pressure. When blood pressure drops, the baroreceptors fire, initiating drinking behavior. A reduction in blood pressure also stimulates the kidney to release a hormone called **renin** (Ramsay & Thrasher, 1990). Renin is secreted into the blood, where it binds with another hormone called **angiotensin I** to produce a third hormone called **angiotensin II.** Angiotensin II is the active form of angiotensin. In the bloodstream, it causes blood vessels to constrict, which increases blood pressure. Angiotensin II also binds with receptors in a part of the hypothalamus called the **subfornical organ,** which in turn stimulates the *preoptic area*, stimulating drinking behavior (Fitzsimons, 1998). Thus, hypovolemic thirst causes angiotensin II to become activated, which in turn increases blood pressure and initiates drinking, restoring blood pressure to normal levels. For example, after running a marathon, a runner's extracellular fluid volume will be reduced due to excessive sweating. Baroreceptors in the runner's body will fire, causing the kidneys to release renin, which binds with angiotensin I to produce angiotensin II. Angiotensin II will cause the runner to feel thirsty and drink.

Nonhomeostatic Drinking

As with eating, not all drinking occurs when an individual has a need for water. That is, people do not ordinarily wait until their blood pressure drops or their intracellular concentration rises before they start to drink. Most of our drinking behavior is nonhomeostatic or **secondary drinking. Primary drinking** occurs when an individual experiences osmotic or hypovolemic thirst. In contrast, secondary drinking occurs in the absence of thirst.

What stimulates secondary drinking? For many people, eating acts as a cue for drinking behavior. In fact, most drinking is **prandial drinking,** or drinking that occurs when an individual is eating. Personally, I find it impossible to eat unless I have some liquid to sip on during the meal. However, this is just a habit because some people are able to eat very comfortably without drinking during the meal. Other types of secondary drinking include drinking when the mouth feels dry or drinking a cool beverage on a hot day or a hot beverage on a cool day. Drinking something because it tastes good is yet another example of secondary drinking.

In the laboratory, secondary drinking can be produced when an individual is working for a reward on a schedule. In the previous section on obesity, you learned

hypovolemic thirst: thirst that is produced when fluid in the extracellular compartment becomes reduced in volume

baroreceptors: receptors located in large veins that monitor blood pressure

renin: a hormone produced by the kidneys that becomes activated by hypovolemic thirst

angiotensin I: an inactive hormone that floats in the blood, precursor to angiotensin II

angiotensin II: a hormone activated when renin binds with angiotensin I, which causes constriction of blood vessels and stimulates drinking behavior

subfornical organ: a region of the hypothalamus that stimulates drinking

secondary drinking: nonhomeostatic drinking that occurs in the absence of thirst

primary drinking: drinking that occurs in response to osmotic or hypovolemic thirst

prandial drinking: drinking that occurs when eating food during a meal

about schedule-induced eating. Schedule-induced drinking (usually referred to as **schedule-induced polydipsia**) was first demonstrated in rats and has since been reported in many other species, including humans (Falk, 1961, 1971, 1977). Animals, including people, will often drink huge quantities of liquids when they are working for food or other rewards (such as money or pleasurable brain stimulation) that become available every minute or so.

Likewise, some people will drink large quantities of alcohol in order to get drunk. This, too, is an example of secondary drinking. We will examine alcohol drinking in greater detail in Chapter 13. As we conclude this chapter, it is important to keep in mind that not all eating and drinking are controlled by homeostatic mechanisms. Eating and drinking disorders arise when homeostatic mechanisms break down, but they also arise as a result of environmental or behavioral causes. Investigators are just beginning to understand how these disorders occur, especially those disorders that develop as a result of psychological, rather than purely biological, triggers. For example, we are still a long way from knowing how anorexia and bulimia nervosa develop. How can a fear of gaining weight translate into a life-threatening illness that affects eating behavior, the nervous system, and, ultimately, all body systems?

schedule-induced polydipsia: over-drinking that occurs when the individual is on a schedule waiting for a nonfluid reward

---

Recap 11.4: Regulation of Water Intake

About 70% of the body's water is found in the (a)_____ compartment, which is located inside the cells of the body. The (b)_____ compartment refers to water found in the blood, in glands, in the lymph system, and in the cavities of body organs. (c)_____ thirst arises when the internal concentration within a cell becomes higher than normal, which occurs when salty food is ingested. In response to firing of osmoreceptors, the pituitary gland releases (d)_____ hormone (ADH), which causes the kidneys to stop production of urine and initiates drinking. (e)_____ thirst is produced when fluid in the extracellular compartment becomes reduced in volume, due to hemorrhage, sweating, vomiting, or diarrhea. (f)_____ monitor blood pressure and fire when blood pressure drops, initiating drinking behavior. In addition, the kidneys release the hormone (g)_____ in response to low blood pressure. Renin is secreted into the blood where it binds with (h)_____ I (the inactive form) to produce (i)_____ II (the active form, which causes constriction of blood vessels, increasing blood pressure). (j)_____ drinking occurs when a person experiences osmotic or hypovolemic thirst, whereas (k)_____ drinking occurs in the absence of thirst. (l)_____-_____ _____ is produced in individuals who are working or waiting for food or other rewards.

Chapter Summary

Regulation of Body Temperature

▶ The hypothalamus plays an important role in homeostatic regulation of body temperature and food and water intake.

▶ Endotherms are homeothermic animals that can produce their own heat and maintain a constant core body temperature. Ectotherms cannot generate their own body heat.

▶ Shivering thermogenesis and nonshivering thermogenesis are two mechanisms used by endotherms to produce heat. The primary mechanism of nonshivering thermogenesis is basal metabolism.

- Under the influence of the hypothalamus, the anterior pituitary gland releases thyrotropin-releasing factor, which stimulates the thyroid gland to release calorigenic hormones. Brown fat metabolism is used by newborn humans to produce heat.

- Heat loss occurs through evaporation and conduction. The most effective mechanism for losing heat is evaporation.

- To reduce loss of body heat, blood vessels in the skin constrict in response to cold environments. Piloerection occurs when smooth muscle contract in response to cold, pulling hairs or feathers up on end to trap air and reduce loss of body heat.

- Heat production and heat loss are regulated by the preoptic area of the hypothalamus.

- Fever and menopausal dysregulation are the most common examples of disorders of temperature regulation.

- Energy balance is affected by both heat production and food intake. Energy is measured in units called calories.

Regulation of Food Intake

- Homeostasis maintains steady states in the body, whereas allostasis involves nonhomeostatic cues that initiate eating and drinking.

- As omnivores, we have to select carefully to obtain needed macronutrients (protein, fat, carbohydrates, which we need in large supply) and micronutrients (vitamins and minerals, which we need in tiny amounts).

- Both the onset and offset of eating are controlled by peripheral and central mechanisms.

- The lateral hypothalamus, together with the prefrontal cortex, regulates allostatic food intake mechanisms. Bilateral lesions of the lateral hypothalamus produce aphagia.

- Homeostatic regulation of food intake involves the paraventricular nucleus of the hypothalamus.

- Barbiturates, benzodiazepines, and endorphins stimulate food intake by enhancing the palatability of the ingested food. The brain peptides, galanin, neuropeptide Y, and orexin, also stimulate food intake. In addition, adrenal steroids, which are hormones produced by the adrenal gland, stimulate food intake.

- Signals from the gut stimulate eating by way of the vagus nerve, which relays information to the nucleus of the solitary tract.

- The ventromedial nucleus of the hypothalamus, together with the paraventricular nucleus, are involved in the homeostatic offset of eating.

- Amphetamine and fenfluramine reduce food intake.

- The stomach and the small intestine, particularly the duodenum (the section of the small intestine nearest the stomach) play an important role in satiety.

- Several hormones, including cholecystokinin (released by the duodenum), bombesin (found in amphibians), glucagon and insulin (both released by the pancreas), and leptin (secreted by fat cells) are involved in the offset of eating.

- The liver plays a central role in metabolism by controlling glycogenolysis and glycogenesis.

Eating Disorders

- Eating disorders include obesity, bulimia nervosa, anorexia nervosa, and pica.

- People who chronically overeat show hyperinsulinemia, due to secretion of large amounts of insulin. Chronic hyperinsulinemia can produce Type 2 diabetes, in which a person fails to respond to the insulin he or she produces.

- When a person overproduces insulin, hypoglycemia results because the large amounts of insulin cause more glucose than normal to be transported out of the blood. As a result of hypoglycemia, the hypothalamus detects an abnormally low level of blood glucose and initiates eating, which can produce overeating and weight gain.

- People who do not produce insulin have Type 1 diabetes, which causes glucose to accumulate in the blood, called hyperglycemia.

- In older people, thyroid gland function is reduced, which can produce weight gain in those who do not reduce their food intake.

- In genetically obese mice, the defective ob gene produces a deficiency of leptin, a hormone that inhibits food intake.

- Bulimia nervosa is characterized by binge-eating followed by self-induced purging.

- The two forms of anorexia nervosa are restricting anorexia (severe reduction in food intake) and anorexia nervosa-bulimic subtype (food restriction plus periodic binging and purging).

- When an individual is deprived of one or more essential nutrients, the eating of non-nutritive substances, called pica, may occur.

Regulation of Water Intake

- About 70% of the body's water is found in the intracellular compartment, which is located inside the cells of the body. The extracellular compartment refers to water found in the blood, in glands, in the lymph system, and in the cavities of body organs.

- Osmotic thirst arises when the internal concentration within a cell becomes higher than normal, which occurs when salty food is ingested. In response to firing of osmoreceptors, the pituitary gland releases antidiuretic hormone (ADH), which causes the kidneys to stop production of urine and initiates drinking.

- Hypovolemic thirst is produced when fluid in the extracellular compartment becomes reduced in volume, due to hemorrhage, sweating, vomiting, or diarrhea. Baroreceptors monitor blood pressure and fire when blood pressure drops, initiating drinking behavior. In addition, the kidneys release the hormone, renin, in response to low blood pressure. Renin is secreted into the blood where it binds with angiotensin I (the inactive form) to produce angiotensin II (the active form, which causes constriction of blood vessels, increasing blood pressure).

▶ Most of our drinking is nonhomeostatic in nature. Primary drinking occurs when a person experiences osmotic or hypovolemic thirst, whereas secondary drinking occurs in the absence of thirst.

Key Terms

adrenal steroids (p. 325)
allostasis (p. 318)
angiotensin I (p. 343)
angiotensin II (p. 343)
anorexia nervosa (p. 338)
anorexia nervosa-bulimic subtype (p. 338)
anterior hypothalamus (p. 311)
antidiuretic hormone (ADH) (p. 342)
aphagia (p. 320)
baroreceptor (p. 343)
basal metabolism (p. 311)
bombesin (p. 330)
brown fat metabolism (p. 311)
bulimia nervosa (p. 337)
calorie (p. 316)
calorigenic hormones (p. 311)
cholecystokinin (p. 330)
conduction (p. 312)
drive (p. 309)
duodenum (p. 329)
ectotherm (p. 310)
endotherm (p. 310)
esophageal fistula (p. 329)
estrogen (p. 325)
evaporation (p. 312)
excitotoxin (p. 320)
extracellular compartment (p. 341)
fever (p. 315)
galanin (p. 323)
glucagon (p. 331)
glucostatic theory (p. 322)

glycogenesis (p. 332)
glycogenolysis (p. 332)
homeostasis (p. 310)
homeothermic (p. 310)
hot flash (p. 316)
hyperglycemia (p. 335)
hyperinsulinemia (p. 334)
hyperphagia (p. 323)
hypoglycemia (p. 334)
hypogonadism (p. 336)
hypokalemia (p. 338)
hypothalamus (p. 310)
hypovolemic thirst (p. 343)
insulin (p. 331)
intracellular compartment (p. 341)
Klein-Levin syndrome (p. 335)
lateral hypothalamus (p. 320)
leptin (p. 323)
lipostatic theory (p. 323)
liver (p. 331)
macronutrients (p. 318)
menopause (p. 316)
micronutrients (p. 319)
neuropeptide Y (p. 323)
neurotoxin (p. 320)
nonshivering thermogenesis (p. 311)
nucleus of the solitary tract (p. 324)
ob gene (p. 336)
obesity (p. 332)
omnivore (p. 318)
orexins (p. 323)
osmoreceptor (p. 342)
osmotic thirst (p. 342)

parabiotic rats (p. 329)
paraventricular nucleus (p. 321)
pica (p. 340)
piloerection (p. 312)
pituitary gland (p. 311)
prandial drinking (p. 343)
preoptic area (p. 313)
primary drinking (p. 343)
progesterone (p. 325)
pyloric sphincter (p. 329)
renin (p. 343)
restricting anorexia (p. 338)
satiety (p. 326)
schedule-induced hyperphagia (p. 337)
schedule-induced polydipsia (p. 344)
secondary drinking (p. 343)
set point (p. 318)
sham feeding (p. 329)
shivering thermogenesis (p. 311)
specific hunger (p. 340)
subfornical organ (p. 343)
superficial blood vessels (p. 312)
testosterone (p. 335)
thermostatic theory (p. 322)
thyroid gland (p. 311)
Type 1 diabetes (p. 334)
Type 2 diabetes (p. 334)
vagus nerve (p. 324)
ventromedial nucleus of the hypothalamus (VMH) (p. 329)

Questions for Thought

1. How do whales manage to stay warm in cold ocean waters?
2. Why are so many people in this country overweight?
3. Give several examples of secondary drinking.
4. Explain how the controls of eating, drinking, and body temperature are interrelated.

Questions for Review

1. How does the pituitary gland control body temperature regulation? What role does the pituitary gland play in water intake regulation?

2. Contrast shivering thermogenesis with nonshivering thermogenesis.

3. Which drugs increase food intake? Which decrease food intake? What is the mechanism by which these drugs affect eating?

4. List the hormones involved in eating, drinking, and temperature regulation. Where is each hormone produced? What role does each play?

Suggested Readings

Halmi, K. A. (1995). Basic biological overview of eating disorders. In F. E. Bloom & D. J. Kupfer (Eds.), *Psychopharmacology: The fourth generation*. New York: Raven Press.

Legg, C. R., & Booth, D. (1994). *Appetite: Neural and behavioural basis*. Oxford: Oxford University Press.

Smith, G. P. (1998). *Satiation: From gut to brain*. New York: Oxford University Press.

Wilson, G. T., & Fairburn, C. G. (1998). Treatments for eating disorders. In P. E. Nathan & J. M. Gorman (Eds.), *A guide to treatments that work*. New York: Oxford University Press.

Web Resources

For a chapter tutorial quiz, direct links to the Internet sites listed below and other features, visit the book specific website at **www.wadsworth.com/product/ 0155074865**. You may also connect directly to the following annotated websites:

http://arbl.cvmbs.colostate.edu/hbooks/pathphys/ digestion/pregastric/foodintake.html
This site discusses control of food intake and body weight

http://arbl.cvmbs.colostate.edu/hbooks/pathphys/ digestion/pregastric/fatgenes.html
Learn about the genetics of obesity on this site.

http://www.nimh.nih.gov/publicat/eatingdisorder. cfm#ed1
Find coverage of eating disorders and the search for a solution on this site from The National Institute of Mental Health.

http://www.cdc.gov/nccdphp/dnpa/obesity/ index.htm
Get the facts about obesity on this site from the National Center for Chronic Disease Prevention and Health Promotion.

For additional readings and information, check out InfoTrac College Edition at **http://www.infotrac-college.com/wadsworth**. Choose a search term yourself or enter the following search terms: obesity, hypoglycemia, hyperglycemia, diabetes, bulimia, and anorexia.

CD-ROM: Exploring Biological Psychology

Video: Anorexia Patient—Susan
Video: Stress and Fat
Interactive Recaps

Chapter 11 Quiz
Connect to the Interactive Biological Psychology Glossary

12

Regulation of Sexual Behavior

Molly is a girl who was born a boy. That is, she possesses the sex chromosomes of a male (one X and one Y chromosome), and she was born with testes and a scrotum. However, she was born without a penis, a rare defect known as *cloacal exstrophy.* Her surprised and dismayed parents elected for Molly to have reconstructive surgery that involved removing the testes and giving Molly the appearance of having female external genitalia. And, Molly was raised a girl. She was dressed in girls' clothing, given girls' toys to play with, and was socialized to be a girl. However, she was always a bit different, compared to other girls. She preferred the rough-and-tumble games of boys. In fact, she preferred playing with boys. By the time Molly reached puberty, she felt more like a boy than a girl, despite her family's attempts to raise her as a girl.

Molly's story is similar to the stories of many children whose parents elected to raise them in a gender role that is not consistent with their biological sex. In a recent study, 14 out of 25 children who were reassigned sex at birth feel that they are the wrong sex (Reiner et al., 1999). That is, in most cases, biological boys who have been raised as girls feel like boys. This suggests that sex hormones affect the development of the brain before birth, making an indelible impression on the fetus that cannot be taken away by a surgeon's knife. In this chapter, we will look at how sex hormones affect behavior. We will examine their influence on physical development, perceptual ability, and sexual behavior. ●

Sexual Differentiation

Sexual differentiation, the process by which we become biological males or females, begins at conception. A female embryo develops when a *sperm* cell bearing an X chromosome and an egg or *ovum*, which always carries an X chromosome, are united. On the other hand, a male embryo develops when a sperm bearing a **Y chromosome** fertilizes an ovum. Recall from Chapter 2 that the Y chromosome is much smaller than the X chromosome and contains relatively little genetic material. In fact, the Y chromosome appears to have one function: to direct the development of the testes.

The embryo has the ability to differentiate into a male or a female. We all start out with the same equipment that is capable of taking a male or female form. The developing embryo has two **primordial gonads,** each of which contains a cortex (outer layer) and medulla (inner layer). In an embryo with a Y chromosome, the Y chromosome directs the cortex of both primordial gonads to develop into male gonads, or **testes** (Sinclair et al., 1990). (*Testis* is the singular of *testes*.) The medulla of the primordial gonads disappears in male embryos as the testes develop and grow (Figure 12.1).

In the *absence* of the Y chromosome, the female reproductive system develops. The medulla of the primordial gonad develops into the female gonad or **ovary,** and

sexual differentiation: the process by which we become biological males or females

Y chromosome: the tiny sex chromosome that directs the development of the testes

primordial gonads: the undifferentiated gonads found in the developing embryo

testis: male gonad (plural: testes)

ovary: female gonad

Figure 12.1 Sexual differentiation

Sexual appearance of baby at second to third month of pregnancy — Genital tubercule, Genital groove, Anus, Urethrolabial fold, Labioscrotal swelling — **Male and female identical**

Sexual appearance of baby at third to fourth month of pregnancy — **Female:** Genital tubercule, Vulval groove, Anus, Inner labial fold, Outer labial swelling; **Male:** Genital tubercule, Urethral groove, Anus, Urethral fold, Scrotal swelling

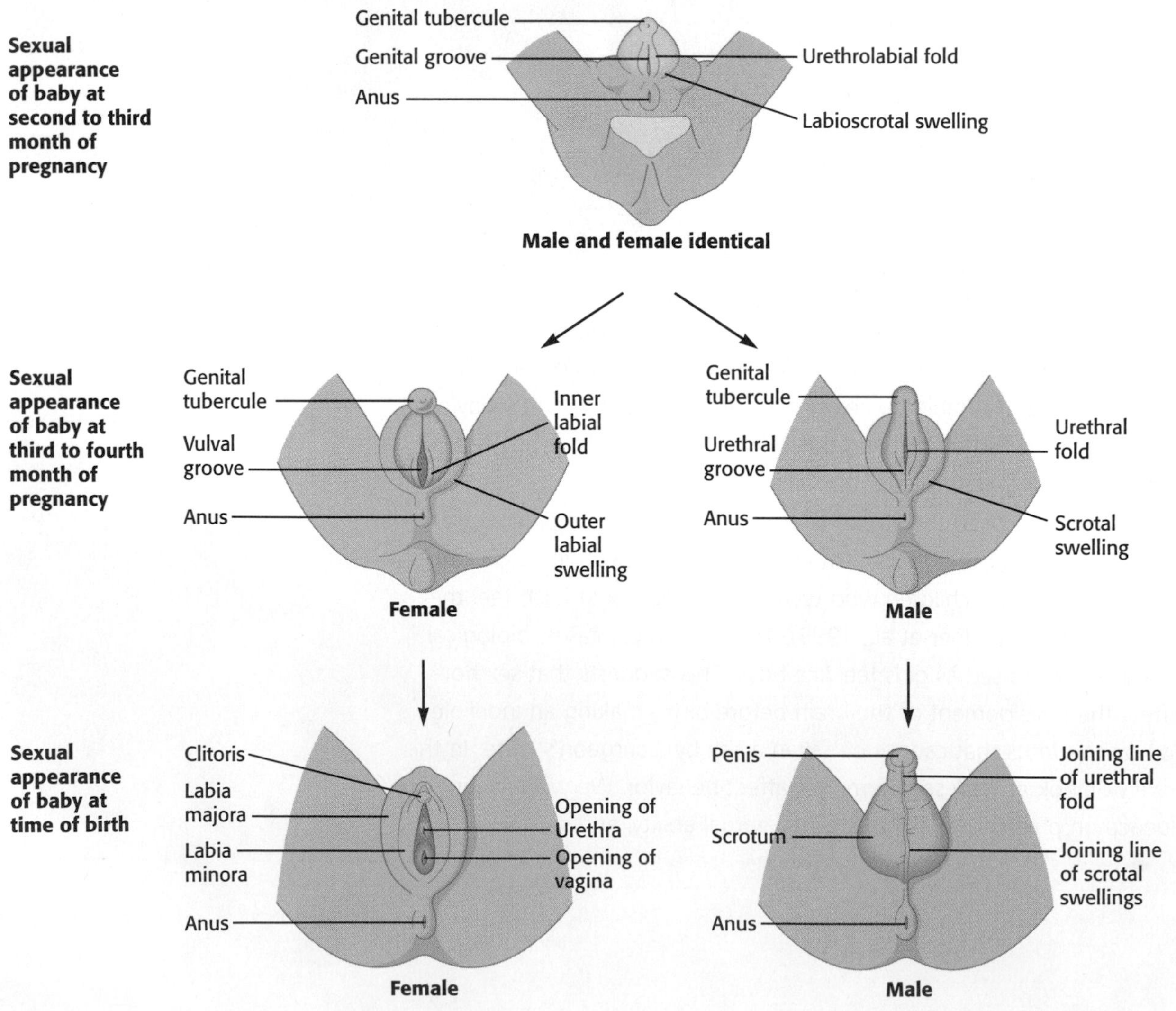

Sexual appearance of baby at time of birth — **Female:** Clitoris, Labia majora, Labia minora, Anus, Opening of Urethra, Opening of vagina; **Male:** Penis, Scrotum, Anus, Joining line of urethral fold, Joining line of scrotal swellings

the cortex of the primordial gonad disappears, when the Y chromosome is missing. The ovary can be characterized as the default gonad because it emerges if the Y chromosome is absent.

Organizational Effects of Hormones

The gonads produce hormones, called **gonadal hormones,** which direct the development of the structures that determine sexual function: the *internal genitalia* and *external genitalia*. These hormones have two effects on body tissues and behavior. During embryonic development, gonadal hormones have *organizational effects*, which are permanent and cannot be reversed. That is, gonadal hormones influence the development of the reproductive system and the nervous system. Gonadal hormones also have *activational effects* in adulthood, causing changes in behavior and body function when the circulating hormone levels are high. Activational effects of gonadal hormones are temporary and disappear when the levels of circulating hormone decline (MacLusky & Naftolin, 1981).

As soon as the testes develop, they begin to produce a hormone called **testosterone.** Testosterone is released into the bloodstream, where it travels to other parts of the body, including the brain. The developing brain is especially vulnerable to the effects of testosterone, which alters the formation of the hypothalamus, the cerebrum, and other areas, as you will learn later in this chapter. Testosterone also affects the development of the internal genitalia and external genitalia.

gonadal hormone: hormone produced by the male or female gonads

testosterone: a hormone produced by the male gonads or testes

Internal Genitalia

The internal genitalia include the *vas deferens, epididymis,* and associated glands, such as the *prostate gland,* in the male body and the *vagina, uterus,* and *fallopian tubes* in the female. However, in the earliest embryonic stages, male and female alike have the ability to develop male or female internal genitalia. This is because embryos possess two sets of internal organs, called the **Wolffian** and the **Müllerian ducts.** The Wolffian ducts are the precursors of the male internal genitalia. Under the influence of testosterone, the Wolffian ducts flourish and develop into the internal plumbing of the normal male reproductive system. The testes also secrete another hormone known as **Müllerian inhibiting substance.** This hormone does exactly what its name implies: It inhibits the development of the Müllerian ducts. Thus, the testicular hormones, testosterone and Müllerian inhibiting substance, orchestrate the development of the male internal reproductive system by stimulating the growth of the Wolffian system and preventing the growth of the Müllerian ducts. Female internal genitalia, which arise from the Müllerian system, are the default structures that develop when testes and testicular hormones are absent.

Because the ovaries develop in the female body, no Müllerian inhibiting substance is produced. In addition, the ovaries produce ovarian gonadal hormones, including *estrogen* and *progesterone,* which are believed to inhibit the action of testosterone in the female body (Novy & Resko, 1981). This means that the Wolffian ducts do not develop because they require testosterone for their development, and, thus, the Wolffian ducts wither away. The Müllerian ducts, however, flourish and grow because there is no Müllerian inhibiting substance to prevent their development. Therefore, the vagina, uterus, and fallopian tubes grow and mature in the female body due to the absence of testosterone and Müllerian inhibiting substance.

Wolffian ducts: the precursors of the male internal genitalia

Müllerian ducts: the precursors of the female internal genitalia

Müllerian inhibiting substance: a hormone produced by the testes that inhibits the development of the Müllerian ducts

External Genitalia

The final form of the external genitalia is also determined by the presence of testosterone. In its earliest stages, the embryo possesses a unisex external appearance. Both male and female embryos have protruding tufts of flesh called the *genital tubercle, urethrogenital folds,* and *labioscrotal swellings* (Figure 12.1). In the male's body, testosterone is converted to **dihydrotestosterone,** which in turn changes the external appearance of the embryonic genitalia. The presence of dihydrotestosterone

dihydrotestosterone: the androgen that converts the embryonic external genitalia into the penis and scrotum

causes the genital tubercle to transform into the glans (or head) of the penis, the urethrogenital folds to close up to form the body of the penis, and the labioscrotal swelling to become the scrotum that holds the testes. The testes actually descend into the scrotum later in development.

In contrast, the external genitalia become female when dihydrotestosterone is not present. The genital tubercle transforms into the clitoris, the urethrogenital folds become the labia minora, and the labioscrotal swellings develop into the labia majora, in the absence of testosterone (Figure 12.1). The female reproductive system can be characterized as the default system: The body takes a female form if the Y chromosome or testicular hormones are missing, as you will learn in the next section.

Variations in Sexual Differentiation

For most individuals, sexual differentiation goes smoothly, and the body's sexual appearance at birth is normal and appropriate for their chromosomal designation. However, some people develop abnormally due to genetic variations or exposure to hormone-like chemicals in the mother's uterus (Hiort, 2000; Hiort & Holterhus, 2000). In this section, we will consider a number of syndromes that alter sexual differentiation.

Genetic Variations

Human beings typically have 46 chromosomes, 22 pairs of autosomal chromosomes and 1 pair of sex chromosomes, as you learned in Chapter 2. Human males normally have the chromosomal designation 46, XY, whereas human females normally have the chromosomal designation 46, XX. It is important to keep in mind that not all people have 46 chromosomes. For example, some individuals have fewer than 46 chromosomes, as in the case of people with **Turner's syndrome** who are missing a sex chromosome and have a chromosomal designation of 45, XO. Because these individuals lack a Y chromosome, they do not develop testes and, therefore, do not produce testosterone or Müllerian inhibiting substance. This means that individuals with Turner's syndrome have the "default body," with female internal and external genitalia. However, because they are missing a sex chromosome, individuals with Turner's syndrome have a sterile female gonad or ovary and cannot become pregnant. These individuals are raised as girls and develop with a female gender identity. They are typically short in stature and often have a short neck or a neck with a webbed appearance.

In contrast, individuals with Klinefelter's syndrome have the chromosomal designation 47, XXY. That is, they have an extra sex chromosome. People with Klinefelter's syndrome have functional testes, because they possess a Y chromosome, and therefore have typical male internal and external genitalia, although sometimes they have a penis that is smaller than normal. Keep in mind that the presence or absence of a Y chromosome determines whether or not testes will develop and whether or not testosterone will be produced. Whether a person has a chromosomal designation of XY, XXXY, or XXXXXY, the presence of a Y chromosome dictates that testes will develop and, as a consequence, that male internal and external genitalia will form. Individuals with a 45, YO chromosomal designation (an unpaired Y chromosome) have not been identified. Having an unpaired Y chromosome most likely results in miscarriage or embryonic death (Weekes, 1994).

Some individuals, referred to as **true hermaphrodites,** are born with both ovarian and testicular tissue. Typically, true hermaphrodites have a chromosomal designation of 46, XX. However, a fragment of the Y chromosome that directs the growth of testes is translocated to the X chromosome or an autosome (Kojima et al., 1998; Margarit et al., 2000). This means that, although hermaphroditic individuals do not actually have a Y chromosome, they inherit a fragment of the Y chromosome from one parent, which causes one or more testes to be produced. Testosterone is produced by the testis and released into the bloodstream, where it promotes the growth of male internal and external genitalia. Müllerian inhibiting

Turner's syndrome: a syndrome in which affected individuals have chromosomal designation of 45, XO, which results in the development of female internal and external genitalia and sterile ovaries

true hermaphrodite: an individual born with both ovarian and testicular tissue

substance may or may not be produced, and thus the individual may or may not develop female internal genitalia. At puberty, estrogen produced by the ovary will stimulate the growth of breasts and curvature of the hips. If female internal genitalia are present, menstruation will begin. Because true hermaphrodites are usually born with a penis or a structure resembling a phallus, they are typically raised as boys, even if a vagina is also present. In this case, surgical removal of the ovaries and other female organs is performed to enable the adoption of a male gender identity. On the other hand, when no phallus is present, a female gender assignment is usually given. Typically, the parents make gender assignments shortly after the individual's birth. A number of investigators have questioned the appropriateness of gender assignment by the parents before the individual is able to choose the gender that is most comfortable for them (Fausto-Sterling, 1999; Nussbaum, 2000; Kuhnle & Krahl, 2002).

Some genetic variations leading to faulty sexual differentiation are not due to the absence of a sex chromosome or to the presence of an extra sex chromosome. Instead, they are due to a mutation on an autosomal chromosome. For example, due to a recessive gene on an autosome, some biological males with a chromosomal designation of 46, XY are born with female external genitalia (Figure 12.2). These males have a genetic mutation that causes a deficiency of the enzyme *5-alpha-reductase*, which prevents the conversion of testosterone to dihydrotestosterone (Cai et al., 1996). Recall that testosterone is capable of stimulating growth of the Wolffian system, but it cannot stimulate development of the penis and scrotum. Thus, these boys are born with *male* internal genitalia and *female* external genitalia. At puberty, however, the surge in hormonal release from the testes produces enough testosterone to stimulate the growth of the penis. To the amazement of the affected individual and family, the girl transforms into a boy as the penis grows, the testes descend into the scrotum, and secondary sex characteristics associated with the male body develop. This condition is nicknamed *guevedoces*, or "eggs (testes) at twelve" [*gueve-* = eggs; *-doces* = twelve, Spanish]. Although these individuals are raised as girls, they readily adopt a male gender identity, dressing and acting like men, after they develop male external genitalia (Imperato-McGinley et al., 1974). In the culture in which individuals with guevedoces live, men have higher status than women. This may explain why these individuals readily adopt a male sex role. In addition, testosterone was present during brain development in these individuals, which may contribute to the adoption of a male sex role. Some

Figure 12.2 Guevedoces syndrome
Due to a deficiency of 5-alpha-reductase, dihydrotestosterone is not produced. The lack of dihydrotestosterone results in the development of feminized external genitalia. At puberty, a surge of testosterone stimulates the growth of the penis and scrotum.

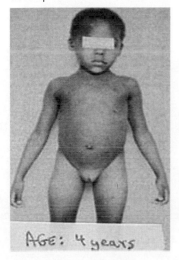 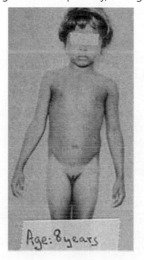 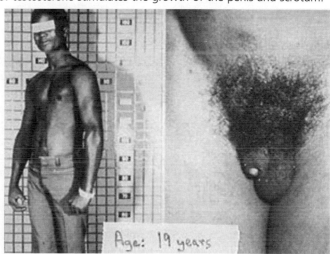

individuals with this disorder do not adjust well to their life as a man, however (Aartsen et al., 1994).

Another genetic mutation leads to a disorder known as **androgen insensitivity syndrome.** The word *androgen* refers to all male hormones, including testosterone. Individuals with this disorder have the chromosomal designation 46, XY. However, they are insensitive to the testosterone produced by their own testes. That is, because they have a Y chromosome, testes develop. The testes secrete testosterone and Müllerian inhibiting substance. The Müllerian inhibiting substance prevents the growth of the Müllerian system, and the individual's insensitivity or inability to respond to testosterone prevents the development of the Wolffian system. Thus, the individual with androgen insensitivity syndrome has neither male nor female internal genitalia. The external genitalia, however, take the default female form because the individual's body cannot respond to testosterone and acts as if no testosterone is present. When the child is born, it appears to be a girl and is raised female. For many individuals with androgen insensitivity syndrome, no problem is noticed until puberty. At the time of puberty, these individuals may develop breasts due to the increased release of estrogen from the adrenal gland, but menstruation does not occur. A gynecological exam quickly reveals the problem: Undescended testes are found in the abdominal cavity, but no uterus or ovaries are found. Because such individuals are insensitive to testosterone and other androgens, hormone therapy cannot transform a woman with androgen insensitive syndrome into a man, even though she has a Y chromosome. Indeed, because the individual has been raised female and because testosterone has not affected the development of her nerous system, she is typically comfortable in that gender role and is happy to remain a woman. Estrogen hormone treatments stimulate the growth of breasts and other female secondary sex characteristics, although the affected woman will never be able to get pregnant because she lacks ovaries and a uterus. The *Case Study* describes the case of a young woman with androgen insensitivity syndrome.

Hormonal Variations

Other anomalies in sexual differentiation are produced by exposure to hormones or hormone-like chemicals. For example, in one disorder, called **adrenogenital syndrome,** female and male embryos are exposed to high levels of androgens in the uterus. This exposure to androgens is caused by the drugs administered to the mothers to prevent a miscarriage or by a disorder of the adrenal glands, called **congenital adrenal hyperplasia,** which causes androgens to build up in the fetus's body. Typically, these conditions cause blood androgen levels to be elevated later in the pregnancy, after the internal genitalia have developed but before the development of the external genitalia. This means that the internal genitalia develop normally. Because the affected female embryo has a chromosomal designation of 46, XX, she has ovaries and develops a vagina, uterus, and fallopian tubes. However, the high blood androgen levels have a disastrous impact on the formation of her external genitalia. The high levels of androgen masculinize the external genitalia of the female embryo, in extreme cases transforming the genital tubercle and urethrogenital folds into a penis and the labioscrotal swelling into a scrotum. The affected individual is born with the external appearance of a male baby, although the scrotum is empty, and is often raised as a boy. Keep in mind, however, that this individual has ovaries and female internal genitalia. Imagine what happens at puberty: Estrogen released from the ovaries causes the breasts to develop, and menstruation begins, with menstrual fluid oozing out of the urethral opening of the penis. This can be extremely upsetting and confusing for an individual who has been raised as a boy. Often, these individuals elect to remain males because they have a masculine gender identity and because high levels of androgens have masculinized their brains. Surgical removal of the ovaries, uterus, and breast tissue and androgen therapy permits these individuals to remain male. Other individuals elect to revert to their biological sex and undergo reconstructive surgery to create female external genitalia (Schnitzer & Donahoe, 2001; White, 2001).

androgen insensitivity syndrome: a disorder in which the affected individual is insensitive to all androgens, including testosterone

adrenogenital syndrome: a disorder in which embryos are exposed to high levels of androgens in the uterus, which masculinizes the female embryo

congenital adrenal hyperplasia: a disorder of the adrenal glands that elevates androgen levels in the blood

Androgen Insensitivity Syndrome

Carolyn was a college freshman with an embarrassing problem: She had no vagina. When she was 14, her mother took her to her gynecologist because she was worried that her daughter had not begun menstruating and showed few signs of sexual maturation. Because of Carolyn's youth, the female gynecologist performed a pelvic exam by inserting a finger into Carolyn's rectum. The gynecologist could not locate a uterus in Carolyn's pelvis, but she did find two firm, egg-shaped structures that she knew were not ovaries.

An ultrasound test and blood tests were ordered for Carolyn. The ultrasound confirmed the absence of a uterus and the presence of two testes in Carolyn's pelvic cavity. The blood tests showed high levels of testosterone and very low levels of estrogen in her blood. What's more, a chromosome test indicated that Carolyn had both X and Y chromosomes in each cell of her body. Very gently, the gynecologist told Carolyn and her mother that Carolyn had a rare disorder called androgen insensitivity syndrome. The doctor explained that Carolyn would never be able to have a baby because she had no uterus or ovaries.

Carolyn didn't understand much of what the doctor told her. At 14 years of age, Carolyn was not thinking about having babies. But, she began to worry that nobody would marry her because she couldn't have babies. The physician also told Carolyn that she had no vagina, but that she could have a vagina surgically constructed when she was older. Carolyn asked if doctors couldn't also construct a uterus for her so that she could have babies. The doctor laughed softly, shook her head, and, using diagrams in a book, explained to Carolyn why only a vagina could be replaced. Carolyn blushed when the doctor showed her the pictures of women's bodies, and she didn't like talking about embarrassingly intimate parts of her body.

The gynecologist asked for a family history, because androgen insensitivity syndrome is so rare. Carolyn's father had married the daughter of his first cousin, which meant that Carolyn and her mother shared one set of great-grandparents. Although the physician couldn't say for certain whether that was why Carolyn had her unusual disorder, she assured Carolyn and her mother that most people with Carolyn's disorder did not have close intermarriages in their families.

Carolyn was placed on estrogen therapy, which caused her pubic hair and breasts to grow. Tall and lanky, she developed into a very attractive and feminine young woman. In high school, she had a series of boyfriends and felt sexually attracted to them. However, she avoided sexual contact with them because she feared that they would discover that she was "different."

In the summer after her first year of college, Carolyn underwent surgery for vaginal reconstruction in a large hospital on the West Coast. The surgeon first made an incision in the shallow vaginal opening between Carolyn's urethra and anus. Then, mucous membrane transplants from her labia were used to enlarge the vaginal opening. Strips of flesh were also removed from the insides of her thighs to line the vagina, in order to give the vagina more depth. By the time Carolyn returned to campus in the fall to begin her sophomore year, she was completely healed. She was no longer afraid of rejection by prospective male partners because she believed that she was now a complete woman.

As a result of genetic variations or hormonal irregularities, some individuals are born with ambiguous genitalia, such as an enlarged clitoris or a penis with unclosed urethrogenital folds. Other individuals, as you have learned in this chapter, are born with internal or external genitalia that do not match their chromosomal sex. In both cases, these individuals are referred to as **intersexed,** or pseudohermaphrodites. Typically, intersexed individuals have gonads that are congruent with their chromosomal designation (that is, individuals who are 46, XY have testes, and those who are 46, XX have ovaries). Androgen insensitivity syndrome and androgenital syndrome are the two most common causes associated with pseudohermaphrodism (Al-Agha, Thomsett, & Batch, 2001; Farkas & Chertin, 2001).

In most cases in which the female embryo is exposed to large quantities of androgens, some masculinization occurs, but the girl is not born with a penis. Sometimes the girl has an enlarged clitoris, but typically the effects of early exposure to androgens are limited to changes in behavior. For example, girls who have been exposed to androgens in the uterus are often "tomboys" who prefer boys' games and excel at them (Berenbaum & Hines, 1992; Ehrhardt, Epstein, & Money, 1968; Ehrhardt & Meyer-Bahlburg, 1981). Research with rats demonstrates that a female embryo that develops between two male embryos is exposed to more testosterone

intersexed: a condition in which a person has an atypical reproductive anatomy

Figure 12.3 Rat embryos in utero

A female embryo that develops between two male embryos is exposed to more testosterone than is a female embryo that develops between two female embryos.

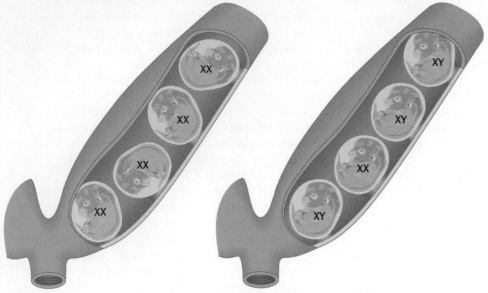

a. All female   **b.** One female fetus surrounded by male fetuses

than a female embryo that develops between two female embryos (Hernandez-Tristan et al., 1999; Figure 12.3). Female rat pups that are exposed to higher levels of testosterone in the uterus display masculine behaviors soon after birth, including male sexual behaviors (de Jonge et al., 1988; VandePoll et al., 1986, 1988). Thus, it appears that testosterone and other androgens masculinize the developing brain, which ultimately affects behavior. Testosterone is believed to increase GABA and glutamate activity in the developing brain, which produces permanent changes in the male brain (McCarthy, Davis, & Mong, 1997). In the next section, we will examine the effects of testosterone on the brain.

Sex Differences in the Brain

Research using brain-imaging techniques has provided a good deal of information about sex differences in brain structure and brain activity. Bottom-up research with animal subjects has also added to our understanding of the influence of sex hormones on brain development. For example, recall from Chapter 1 that a series of studies with baby monkeys demonstrated that testosterone slows the development of area TE of the cortex and speeds up the maturation of the orbitofrontal cortex (Bachevalier et al., 1990; Clark & Goldman-Rakic, 1989). In this section, we will examine the effects of sex hormones on the structure and function of the brain.

It is important to keep in mind that men produce estrogen in their adrenal glands and testes and that women produce androgens, including testosterone, in both their adrenal glands and ovaries. Thus, estrogen is *not* found exclusively in female, and testosterone is *not* found exclusively in males. The difference between hormone levels in men and women is a matter of degree. Typically, women have between 100 and 400 picograms (10^{-12} grams) of estrogen per milliliter of blood, whereas men have less than 50 picograms per milliliter. Men have between 300 and 900 nanograms (10^{-9} grams) of testosterone per deciliter of blood, and women have much less than 100 nanograms per deciliter. The roles of androgens in women and estrogens in men are largely unknown, although androgens are believed to contribute to sex drive in women, as they do in men.

It is also important to remember that sex differences can result from different experiences that boys and girls (and men and women) have, given their gender roles. For example, boys are typically given toys that require or enhance visuospatial skills, whereas girls are typically given toys that require or enhance fine motor skills. Thus, a particular brain structure may be more active in boys than in girls, or vice versa, due to the effect of playtime activities, rather than due to biological influences. Keep in mind, then, that a strong environmental component may contribute to the observed male–female differences.

Sex Differences in Brain Structure

The gonadal hormones, testosterone and estrogen, have organizational effects on the development of the brain, producing permanent sex differences in brain structure and function. These sex differences include differences in the size of organelles within neurons, differences in dendritic branching and axonal terminals, and differences in the size of certain nuclei or cell groups in the brain (MacLusky & Naftolin, 1981; Segovia et al., 1999). Many areas of the developing brain are directly affected by the action of estrogen and testosterone.

Overall, men's brains are approximately 15% larger than women's, whereas men's bodies are only about 8% larger than women's (Gibbons, 1991). At birth, the brains of boys and girls are the same size, and they remain the same size until the age of 2 years. Then, boys' brains grow faster until full adult brain size is reached at 6 years of age. Androgens have been implicated in this increased growth of the male brain. In addition to overall size differences, a number of individual brain structures show sex-based size differences.

One striking difference between the brains of men and women is the size of the *corpus callosum*. Recall from Chapter 4 that the corpus callosum is a wide band of axons that permits communication between the two cerebral hemispheres. A number of studies have revealed that the corpus callosum is thicker in women than in men (Allen et al., 1991; de Lacoste et al., 1990; de Lacoste & Holloway, 1982). Although the reason for this difference is unknown, the thicker corpus callosum in women allows for more intercommunication between the two halves of the cerebrum (Kimura, 1992). Thus, men tend to have larger asymmetries in function than do women. That is, women tend to use both sides of their brains for speech and spatial functions, whereas men use only one hemisphere for each (Hiscock et al., 1999; Lambe, 1999; Shaywitz et al., 1995). The increased interconnectivity between the two cerebral hemispheres in women might explain why women show fewer and less severe neurological deficits following damage to one hemisphere (Majewska, 1996; McGlone, 1978). In addition, progesterone appears to reduce swelling of the brain following head trauma in females compared to males (Roof et al., 1993).

Research with rats and humans has demonstrated that androgens contribute to the increased asymmetry seen in the brains of males (Geschwind & Galaburda, 1985). The cerebral cortex in the right hemisphere is thicker in the male brains of rats and human fetuses than in female brains (Diamond, 1991; de Lacoste et al., 1991). Jane Stewart and Bryan Kolb (1988) have shown that androgens act on the developing brain by *suppressing* the growth of the *left* cerebral cortex. Investigators are still debating whether these structural differences can explain the differences in verbal and spatial abilities observed in men and women. For example, learning and language disabilities are more common in males than in females, which might result from the suppressive effect of androgens on the left hemisphere (Geschwind & Galaburda, 1985; Hier, 1979; Lambe, 1999).

Other sex differences involve enlargements in certain areas of the hypothalamus that regulate sexual behavior, presumably due to the influence of testosterone. The *third interstitial nucleus* of the anterior hypothalamus, for example, is larger in men than in women (Allen et al., 1989). An analogous nucleus in rats, called the *sexually dimorphic nucleus* in the preoptic area of the hypothalamus, is also larger in male than in female rats (Gorski et al., 1978, 1980). These differences are so large that they are visible without a microscope (Breedlove, 1994). Interestingly, the third interstitial nucleus is smaller in homosexual men than in heterosexual men, although the biological basis for this difference in unknown (LeVay, 1991). *For Further Thought* discusses the evidence for a biological explanation of homosexuality.

Biological Explanations of Homosexuality

Less than 5% of the human population is exclusively homosexual (that is, attracted only to members of their own sex). Most women prefer men as sexual partners, and most men prefer women. Because most people are heterosexual, we have come to think that heterosexual behavior is biologically based, especially because it produces offspring. But if heterosexual behavior is controlled by biology, is it not possible that biology can also influence homosexual behavior? A number of investigators have produced evidence that suggests that biology can determine a person's sexual orientation.

The evidence for a biological basis for homosexual orientation comes from anatomical, genetic, and psychological research. The earliest evidence came from anatomists. Reporting that the suprachiasmic nucleus is enlarged in homosexual men, Swaab and Hofman (1990) were the first to describe a difference between the brains of gay and straight men. More importantly, LeVay (1991) found a significant difference in the size of a specific brain structure (the third interstitial nucleus of the anterior hypothalamus) that is directly implicated in the control of male sexual behavior. According to LeVay's findings, this interstitial nucleus is two to three times larger in heterosexual men than in women or homosexual men. That is, LeVay has demonstrated that a gay man has the interstitial nucleus of a woman, which may affect his sexual behavior.

Although LeVay is a highly regarded scientist who conducted this study following stringent research protocols, a number of criticisms have been levied against his research. For example, LeVay's findings assume that all people are exclusively homosexual or exclusively heterosexual and, hence, do not reflect the gradations of sexual activity that fall in between those two extremes. In addition, all of LeVay's homosexual subjects died of AIDS, which suggests

that AIDS can affect the size of the third interstitial nucleus. However, six of the heterosexual men in LeVay's study also died of AIDS, but their interstitial nuclei were all twice as large as those of gay men. Admittedly, there was wide variation in the size of the nuclei studied by LeVay, with much overlap between homosexual and heterosexual men. In many cases, the difference between the size of the interstitial nucleus in gay and straight men was negligible (Fausto-Sterling, 1992).

Another line of research that suggests a biological basis for homosexuality involves genetic studies. Studies of twins have demonstrated that identical twins are twice as likely to both be gay than are fraternal twins and five times more likely to both be gay than adopted brothers are (Bailey & Pillard, 1991). Dean Hamer and his colleagues at the National Institutes of Health (NIH) located a region on the X chromosome, at position q28, that is shared by gay brothers but is not shared by heterosexual brothers (Hamer, Hu, Magnuson, Hu, & Pattatucci, 1993). A study by Stacey Cherny and her colleagues (Hu et al., 1995) supported Hamer's findings by demonstrating that homosexual brothers, but not their heterosexual brothers, were likely to share the q28 marker on the X chromosome. However, Cherny's group did not find shared Xq28 markers for lesbian sisters. Hamer's research has come under attack by some investigators (Fausto-Sterling & Balaban, 1993; Rice, Anderson, Risch, & Ebers, 1999), but several new studies have confirmed the linkage between male homosexuality and the q28 marker on the X chromosome, which suggests that male homosexuality may be inherited from one's mother.

In addition, genetic studies of "fruitless" fruit flies by Angela Pattatucci and Dean Hamer at NIH have also supported the notion that homosexuality has a genetic basis

(continued)

Later in this chapter, you will learn that the *hypothalamus* regulates gonadal hormone release and, thus, organizes sexual behavior. One obvious difference between men and women is that women's bodies undergo periodic fluctuations in the levels of ovarian hormones, which lead to the production of mature eggs for fertilization. The hypothalamus of the male is defeminized early in brain development by testosterone, eliminating ovulatory cycles in the male body. In contrast, estrogen feminizes the brain. The brain of the male rodent embryo is protected from its mother's estrogen by a substance in its blood plasma known as *alpha-fetoprotein*, which binds with estrogen, inactivating it (MacLusky & Naftolin, 1981). It is not certain if this same mechanism serves to protect the male human embryos from feminization by its mother's estrogen.

Sex Differences in Brain Activity

PET scan studies have demonstrated differences in brain activity between men and women (Majewska, 1996). For example, women have 15% greater cerebral cortical

(continued)

(anonymous, 1992). The fruitless mutant is a male fruit fly that has functional sperm and sex organs but does not mate with females. Instead, this fruitless male is attracted to other males and, when in the presence of another male, will scurry around to the back end of the other and lick its genitals—behavior that is very unusual for normal fruit flies. Figure 12.4 shows a chain of fruitless males licking the tail-parts of another male. Certainly human sexual behavior is more complicated than that of a fruit fly, but there is convincing evidence that some gene causes "fruitless" male fruit flies to engage in this atypical behavior and, at the same time, to avoid mounting and inseminating females.

Psychological studies have also demonstrated biological differences between homosexual and heterosexual people. Dennis McFadden and Edward Pasanen (1999) at the University of Texas in Austin measured tiny echoes (called otoacoustic emissions) produced by the inner ears of 237 college-aged people. Typically, the inner ears of women produce much stronger echoes than those of men. However, McFadden and Pasanen found that lesbian and bisexual women produced significantly weaker echoes than strictly heterosexual women, whereas there was no difference between homosexual and straight men. Cheryl McCormick and Sandra Witelson at McMaster University in Canada have also studied biological differences between homosexual and heterosexual individuals. For example, they have found that gay men and lesbians are more likely to show a left-hand preference for many tasks than are heterosexual men and women (McCormick, Witelson, & Kingstone, 1990; McCormick & Witelson, 1991). More recently, they have demonstrated that right-handed heterosexual men and women show greater left hemispheric specialization for language than left-handed heterosexuals, whereas handedness does not affect cerebral dominance for language in gay men or lesbians (McCormick & Witelson, 1994).

It is important to remember for all of these studies that correlation does not prove causation. That is, the fact that a particular gene is found only in gay men or that a particular brain structure is bigger or smaller in homosexual individuals does not mean that that gene or that brain structure causes homosexual behavior. The scientific debate about the biological basis of homosexuality is not over and is likely to continue for a long time.

Figure 12.4 Homosexual fruit flies
"Fruitless" male fruit flies do not mate with and show no interest in female fruit flies. However, when presented with a male fruit fly, they lick its genitals, an unusual behavior for fruit flies.

blood flow than men do and significantly greater global (or overall) glucose metabolism (Gur & Gur, 1990). PET studies have also revealed that women have higher activity levels in the cingulate gyrus, whereas men have higher activity levels in the temporal lobe, limbic system, and cerebellum (Gur et al., 1995). In some cases, these differences mirror gender differences in ability or behavior. For example, men and boys learn routes faster and with fewer errors than women and girls, although women and girls can recall more landmarks along the route (Galea & Kimura, 1992; Gibbs & Wilson, 1999). A recent functional MRI study in Germany at the University of Ulm indicated that different parts of the brain are activated when men and women learn a route (Gron et al., 2000). The right side of the cerebrum concerned with spatial relationships and landmarks is activated when women learn a route. In contrast, the left prefrontal cortex and left hippocampus are activated when men learn a route. This sex difference may explain the differences in the ways men and women learn to navigate space.

The process by which we become biological males or females is called (a)_____ _____ . Normally, a biological female has two (b)_____ chromosomes, whereas a biological male has one (c)_____ and one (d)_____ chromosome. The Y chromosome directs the development of the (e)_____, which produces two hormones, testosterone and Müllerian inhibiting substance. (f)_____ affects the development of the internal and external genitalia, stimulating the growth of the Wolffian ducts and the penis and scrotum. (g)_____ _____ _____ prevents the growth of the Müllerian ducts, which normally develop into female internal genitalia. Individuals with (h)_____ syndrome have a chromosomal designation of 45, XO and are typically raised as girls. Individuals with (i)_____ syndrome have a chromosomal designation of 47, XXY, possess testes and are typically raised as boys. (j)_____ _____ syndrome occurs in individuals with a chromosomal designation of 46, XY, who are born with testes but are insensitive to testosterone. In (k)_____ syndrome, embryos are exposed to high levels of androgens, which masculinize the external genitalia of female embryos. The (l)_____ callosum is larger in women than in men. In contrast, the (m)_____ nucleus of the hypothalamus is larger in men than in women. Male sex hormones, called (n)_____, appear to suppress the growth of the left cerebral cortex, causing the right cortex to be thicker than the left cortex in male rats and humans.

Regulation of Female Sexual Behavior

Eggs, or *ova*, are produced by the ovaries in female animals, whereas sperm are produced by the testes in male animals [*ova* = eggs, Latin; *ovum* = singular form of *ova*]. The term *sexual behavior* refers to the behavior in which animals engage to bring eggs and sperm together. For aquatic animals, sexual behavior involves the female laying eggs and the male of the same species spraying the eggs with sperm. Sexual behavior in land-dwelling animals requires that the male deposit sperm into the genital tract of the female. Typically, female insects mate once during their lifetime, during which time they receive all the sperm they need from the males of the species. In some species, the female insect "thanks" the male by killing him so that he won't share his sperm with other females. Most land-dwelling animals mate during a *breeding season*, when food and climate are optimal. Humans, like several other species, including dogs, cats, and rats, engage in sexual behavior year around, regardless of the season.

Sexual behavior is one component of **reproductive behavior.** Reproductive behavior involves producing children and nurturing them until they are able to live on their own. Thus, reproductive behavior consists of sexual behavior (bringing egg and sperm together) and *parenting behavior* (nurturing offspring). For most species, both sexual and parenting behaviors are driven by hormones. As we begin this discussion, you will need to keep in mind two concepts: *gonadal hormones* and *gonadotrophic hormones*. Gonadal hormones are hormones that are produced by the *gonads*. For example, estrogen is a gonadal hormone that is produced in the ovaries, and testosterone is a gonadal hormone that is produced in the testes. In contrast, **gonadotrophic hormones** are hormones that are secreted by the pituitary gland and affect (or change) the gonads. Let's examine how hormones regulate the sexual

reproductive behavior: behavior that produces offspring and nurtures them until they are able to live on their own

gonadotrophic hormones: hormones secreted by the pituitary gland that alter the function of the gonads

behavior of most mammalian species. We'll start by looking at how hormones control female sexual behavior.

In most species, the female determines when *mating*, or sexual behavior, will occur. Her *receptivity*, or willingness to accept a male for sexual purposes, is determined by her hormonal status. The female animal experiences a series of hormonal fluctuations that is associated with the production and availability of ova for fertilization by sperm. These hormonal fluctuations are periodic and involve an interplay between gonadotrophic and gonadal hormones. The term **ovarian cycle** refers to the rhythmic fluctuations in the release of ovarian hormones, which produce a number of changes in the female's body and in her behavior.

At the beginning of the ovarian cycle, before an egg is ready for fertilization, the hypothalamus directs the anterior pituitary gland to begin the cycle. The hypothalamus communicates with the anterior pituitary gland by means of a hormone called **gonadotropin-releasing hormone,** which is released by the hypothalamus. Under the influence of the gonadotropin-releasing hormone, the anterior pituitary releases a gonadotrophic hormone called **follicle-stimulating hormone (FSH).** FSH travels in the bloodstream to the ovary, where it stimulates the maturation of one or more eggs. Each immature egg is stored in its own sac or *follicle*, and FSH causes one or more eggs to grow and mature (Figure 12.5). In addition, FSH also stimulates the ovary to produce the gonadal hormone, **estrogen.** Thus, FSH has two roles: It stimulates the maturation of one or more eggs, and it stimulates the production of estrogen.

Estrogen is released into the bloodstream, where it travels to the brain and binds with estrogen receptors in the hypothalamus. Over time, under the influence of FSH, the ovary continues to pump out estrogen, and estrogen levels in the blood increase. A mechanism in the hypothalamus serves as a *negative feedback loop*. When estrogen levels rise to a certain level, neurons in the hypothalamus send a message to the anterior pituitary gland to stop the production of FSH and to begin the production of another gonadotrophic hormone called **luteinizing hormone (LH).** LH is transported in the bloodstream to the ovary, where it has a number of effects.

ovarian cycle: the rhythmic fluctuations in the release of ovarian hormones

gonadotropin-releasing hormone: a hormone released by the hypothalamus that signals the anterior pituitary to release follicle-stimulating hormone

follicle-stimulating hormone (FSH): a gonadotrophic hormone that stimulates the maturation of immature egg and sperm

estrogen: a gonadal hormone produced by the ovaries

luteinizing hormone (LH): a gonadotrophic hormone that initiates ovulation and stimulates the development of the corpus luteum

Figure 12.5 Ovarian cycle during which conception has occurred
If fertilization of the ovum occurs, the fertilized ovum implants in the wall of the uterus, and the corpus luteum continues to secrete high levels of progesterone and estrogen.

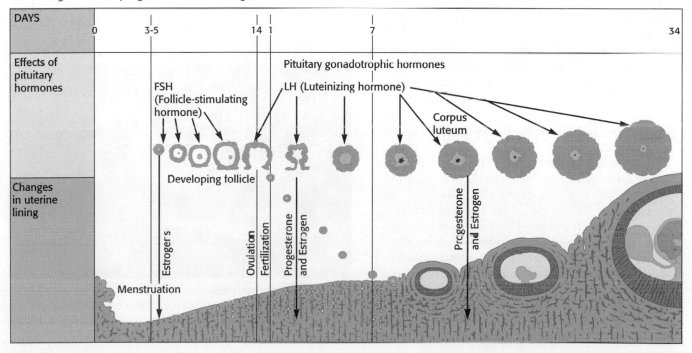

First, LH causes the mature egg to burst out of its follicle in a process called **ovulation.** The egg (ovum) is drawn into the fallopian tubes, which are located at the ends of the horns of the uterus, and it drifts down into the uterus. After the egg has been released from the ovaries, it is ready for fertilization by sperm, should sperm be present in the female's genital tract. Typically, sperm meet the egg in the fallopian tubes. The fertilized egg then implants in the lining of the uterus, although sometimes it implants in the fallopian tubes or outside of the uterus, producing a *tubal* or *ectopic pregnancy*, which is lethal for the embryo (Figure 12.6).

After the egg has erupted from the follicle, LH stimulates the ruptured follicle to become a **corpus luteum** (see Figure 12.5). Under stimulation by LH, the corpus luteum produces two gonadal hormones: estrogen and **progesterone.** The purpose of progesterone is to prepare the body for pregnancy. For example, progesterone causes the uterine wall to thicken in preparation for pregnancy.

As long as the pituitary gland continues to secrete LH, the corpus luteum stays intact and produces estrogen and progesterone. If the egg is fertilized by a sperm cell, pregnancy ensues. After the fertilized egg implants in the lining of the uterus, a specialized network of blood vessels, called a *placenta*, develops between the fertilized egg and uterine wall (Figure 12.7). Hormones released by the placenta trigger the continued release of LH, which stimulates the corpus luteum to produce progesterone and estrogen. As the pregnancy continues, the levels of estrogen and progesterone in the blood increase. The graph in Figure 12.8 illustrates the fluctuations in the levels of gonadal hormones through the ovarian cycle and throughout pregnancy. Note that ovulation takes place in the middle of the cycle.

At ovulation, the female has one or more eggs available for fertilization. These eggs (ova) can survive for up to 72 hours, but they wither away if they are not fertilized during this period. If no sperm is available to fertilize the eggs, pregnancy does not occur, and no placenta is formed. This means that, during ovarian cycles that do not result in pregnancy, the eggs degenerate, and no placental hormones are produced. In the absence of placental hormones, the pituitary gland stops producing LH, which causes the corpus luteum in the ovary to wither away, too. As the corpus luteum degenerates, it stops producing progesterone and estrogen, causing the levels of both of these gonadal hormones to plummet. This drop in gonadal hormones signals the end of the ovarian cycle.

In humans, the drop in estrogen and progesterone levels causes the uterus to shed its inner lining, which was thickened by the rise in progesterone. When the uterus sheds its lining, it produces a bloody discharge that is released through the vagina, in a process called **menstruation.** During the period of time just before menstruation, which is called the *premenstrual period*, estrogen and progesterone levels are at their lowest (Figure 12.8). As you learned in Chapter 11, this premenstrual period is associated with an increase in appetite, especially for fats and carbohydrates. Retention of

Figure 12.6 The human female reproductive system
(a) The ovaries are suspended by ligaments from the uterus. (b) An ectopic or tubal pregnancy occurs when the fertilized ovum implants in the wall of a fallopian tube.

a.
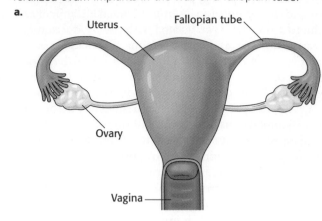

b.
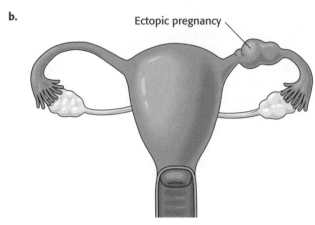

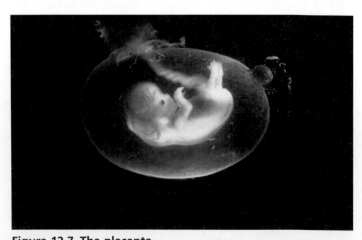

Figure 12.7 The placenta
The placenta (red structure at top of photo) is a specialized network of blood vessels that provide oxygen and nutrients to the developing fetus.

electrolytes in the abdomen also occurs during the premenstrual period, causing bloating due to increased water retention. Lowered levels of serotonin, which produces insomnia and changes in mood, are also associated with this premenstrual period in women.

You might be wondering how the cycle starts up again. Recall the negative feedback loop that controls the release of FSH. As you've already learned, when estrogen levels rise due to the effects of FSH on the ovary, the hypothalamus directs the pituitary to stop producing FSH. However, after a pregnancy or during the premenstrual cycle, estrogen levels fall precipitously, prompting the hypothalamus to initiate FSH release by the anterior pituitary. Thus, the ovarian cycle begins again when estrogen levels fall to some threshold level.

Figure 12.8 Estrogen and progesterone levels throughout the ovarian cycle
When estrogen levels reach a peak, luteinizing hormone is released, stimulating ovulation. Following ovulation, a corpus luteum is formed and progesterone is released.

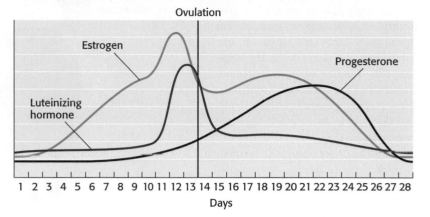

The graphs in Figure 12.8 depict a 28-day ovarian cycle for women. In fact, the ovarian cycle varies among women, although most women have ovarian cycles that range from 12 to 55 days. *Oral contraceptives*, or birth control pills, prevent ovulation by tricking the hypothalamus. These pills contain a synthetic estrogen. When a woman swallows one oral contraceptive pill, the synthetic estrogen is sufficient to stimulate the negative feedback loop that turns off the production of FSH. That is, as long as a woman takes a pill each day, estrogen levels in her blood remain high, which suppresses the release of FSH and prevents a new cycle from starting. However, if a woman forgets to take a pill, her estrogen levels fall, which could trigger the release of FSH and cause an egg to begin maturing in its follicle. When a woman completes taking all the pills in the 21-day cycle, the estrogen levels in her blood plummet, and the premenstrual period begins, culminating in menstruation within a day or two. Following menstruation, the woman who is trying to avoid pregnancy begins taking the contraceptive pills again, one a day, to prevent the release of FSH from the pituitary gland.

ovulation: a process in which the mature ovum bursts out of the ovarian follicle and is available for fertilization

corpus luteum: a yellowish structure in the ovary, which was formerly a ruptured follicle, that produces progesterone

progesterone: a gonadal hormone produced by the ovaries that prepares the female body for pregnancy

menstruation: a process in the human female body in which the uterus sheds its lining, producing a bloody discharge, when estrogen and progesterone levels fall

Sexual Receptivity in the Female

Ovulation is usually associated with sexual receptivity in the females of most species, including primates (Adams, Gold, & Burt, 1978; Etgen et al., 1999; Slob et al., 1995). Typically, in the period just before and during ovulation, nonhuman female animals change their behavior in ways that signal to males of their species that they are ready to mate. Many female animals release pheromones from glands in their genital tracts, which also communicate to the male that the female is sexually receptive. The term **estrus** refers to this period when a female is sexually receptive or "in heat." (For that reason, the term *estrous cycle* is sometimes used to describe the ovarian cycle in nonmenstruating animals. Humans and other primates that menstruate are said to undergo *menstrual cycles*.)

For example, a female rat is normally a shy and retiring animal that prefers to keep to herself. However, when she is in estrus, she can become quite fearless and aggressive, presenting herself to males for mating. If a male tries to copulate with her when she is not in estrus, the female rat will roll over on her back and will kick, squeal, and bite at the male. However, when she is in estrus and has mature eggs available for fertilization, she will permit the male to mount her sexually and will assume a position, called **lordosis,** in which her hindquarters are lifted slightly to make intromission of the penis easier for the male (Meyerson, Frohlich, & Morgan, 2002; Pfaff, 1968; Figure 12.9).

estrus: a time period during which a nonhuman female is sexually receptive

lordosis: a position assumed by the receptive female animal, in which her hindquarters are raised to permit intromission of the penis into the vagina

In some species, due to hormonal changes associated with ovulation, the female undergoes a change in her physical appearance, which signals to the males of the species that she is in estrus. For example, the female stickleback fish develops a large red spot on her side when she is ready to lay eggs, and the females of some primate species have a "sex skin" (labia of the external genitalia) that swells and darkens in color when they are in estrus.

On the other hand, the females of most primate species are sexually receptive and will copulate with males throughout the ovarian cycle. In some species, sexual receptivity and copulation are used to communicate affection or high emotion. Bonobo monkeys, for example, copulate with friends, newcomers, and family members to communicate a welcome or greeting. Field studies have described incidents in which a female ape will present sexually to a male of the same species to avoid a beating or to gain a favor, such as a banana. All of this probably makes you wonder about human sexual behavior because female humans are sexually receptive throughout their ovarian cycles and even when they are pregnant. This state of perpetual sexual receptivity in women might be an evolutionary adaptation to keep the males of the species (that is, men) around for protection and to help provide food for their offspring.

Although women engage in sexual activity throughout their ovarian cycle, masturbation and female-initiated sexual behavior occur with a significantly higher frequency at the time of ovulation. Adams, Gold, and Burt (1978) asked female participants to complete detailed daily questionnaires describing their sexual activity and found that female-initiated sexual behavior increased at ovulation for women who did not use oral contraception. Women who used oral contraception did not show an increase in sexual behavior at the time of ovulation because oral contraceptives suppress hormonal activity associated with ovulation. Also, sexual behavior initiated by their male partners also did not correlate with ovulation in the female participants. Similarly, Kloos Slob and his colleagues (1996) at Erasmus University in the Netherlands observed that women became more sexually aroused while watching an erotic video during the period just before ovulation, compared to the period following ovulation. (Progesterone levels in the blood were measured to determine the correct phase of their ovarian cycle.) Thus, women show greater sexual arousal and increased sexual activity around the time of ovulation.

The cause of the observed increase in sexual arousal and activity in women at ovulation is unclear. Certainly, estrogen levels are high during this period, but progesterone levels are much lower. Testosterone levels in the blood peak during ovulation, and this rise in testosterone may explain the increased sexual activity observed at ovulation (Morris, Udry, Khan-Dawood, & Dawood, 1987). When testosterone is administered to healthy, sexually functional women, testosterone causes an increase in sexual arousal in these women, who report increased "genital sensations" and "sexual lust" (Tuiten, Van Honk, Koppeschaar, Bernaards, Thijssen, & Verbaten, 2000). Testosterone is used to treat impaired sexual arousal in women and produces an increase in sexual fantasies, masturbation, and other sexual activity in women with reduced sexual desire (Davis, 2000; Shifren et al., 2000). Alan and Elizabeth Riley (2000) compared the testosterone levels in a group of women with a lifelong history of reduced sexual drive to the testosterone levels in a group of healthy, sexually functional women. Women with reduced sexual drive

Figure 12.9 A female rat showing lordosis
When a female rat is in estrus, she will display lordosis, arching her back and pulling her tail aside.

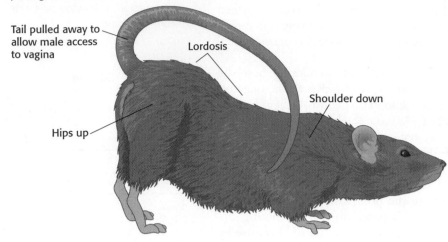

Tail pulled away to allow male access to vagina

Lordosis

Shoulder down

Hips up

were found to have significantly lower levels of testosterone than women with normal sexual drives.

Sex drive and sexual receptivity are observed in women who have had their ovaries surgically removed and in women who have gone through **menopause,** an aging process in which the ovaries stop functioning and cease their production of hormones. Thus, sex drive and sexual receptivity are not dependent on female gonadal hormones. In women, sex drive appears to be associated with the release of androgens by the adrenal glands and ovaries because drugs that increase androgen levels have been shown to increase sex drive in women (Rissman, 1995; Tuiten et al., 2000). On the other hand, the female gonadal hormones estrogen and progesterone do appear to play a role in the regulation of mood in women (Janowsky, Halbreich, & Rausch, 1996), as you will learn in Chapter 14.

menopause: a period in a woman's life following the cessation of the production of sex hormones

Sexual Disorders in Women

Sexual disorders in women fall into three general categories: disorders related to the ovarian cycle, fertility disorders, and disorders involving sexual response.

Amenorrhea

Amenorrhea, or the absence of menstrual cycles, has two forms: *primary amenorrhea* and *secondary amenorrhea*. In primary amenorrhea, the ovarian cycles never begin, although the young woman often shows signs of puberty onset. In secondary amenorrhea, menstruation ceases prematurely, as when a woman develops the eating disorder *anorexia nervosa*. Both types of amenorrhea can be caused by a dysfunction of the ovaries or pituitary gland, which would interfere with the production of gonadal or gonadotrophic hormones. Developmental or genetic disorders, such as Turner's syndrome or androgen insensitivity disorder, result in primary amenorrhea due to sterile or absent ovaries.

amenorrhea: the absence of menstrual cycles

Infertility

Infertility is a condition in which the woman cannot conceive and get pregnant. Obviously, a woman without ovaries cannot get pregnant, nor can a woman who has had a *hysterectomy*, or surgery in which the uterus is removed [*hyster-* = uterus, *-ectomy* = to remove, Latin]. However, infertility can also be caused by hormonal dysfunction, as when a woman does not produce FSH or progesterone. This condition can often be corrected with hormone replacement therapy. Some women have blocked fallopian tubes as a result of scarring or excessive growth of the *endometrium*, which lines the uterus. Although women with blocked fallopian tubes have regular ovarian cycles, the eggs cannot get into the uterus, and sperm cannot reach the eggs for fertilization. *In vitro fertilization* is the treatment of choice for blocked fallopian tubes. As the term *in vitro* implies, eggs and sperm are mixed together on the lab bench, and fertilization takes place in a test tube. The fertilized eggs are then placed in the woman's uterus for implantation. Typically, more than one fertilized egg are transferred to the uterus because the failure rate is quite high with this procedure, and most fertilized eggs do not survive.

infertility: a condition in which a woman cannot conceive and become pregnant

Dysmenorrhea

Dysmenorrhea, or painful menstruation, occurs in about 25% of all women under the age of 25. Younger women usually experience *spasmodic dysmenorrhea*, which begins at the onset of menstruation and is characterized by severe cramping and abdominal pain. *Congestive dysmenorrhea* occurs primarily in older women. It occurs premenstrually and is experienced as abdominal pain and tenderness. Dysmenorrhea was once thought to be psychological in origin, but research has demonstrated that the pain experienced is associated with the production of *prostaglandin* in the uterus (Deligeoroglou, 2000). Recall from Chapter 3 that prostaglandin is one of several chemicals that stimulates pain receptors, producing a sensation of pain. Dysmenorrhea is usually treated with analgesics, or pain

dysmenorrhea: a condition in which a woman experiences painful menstruation

relievers, and hormones. Contraceptive pills are a ready source of estrogen and are often prescribed to reduce prostaglandin production.

Loss of Sex Drive

Some women suffer from a loss of sex drive, or loss of *libido*. A loss of libido may be associated with a decline in estrogen levels following hysterectomy or menopause, painful intercourse, depression, anxiety, or chronic stress (Graziottin, 2000). Typically, women with diminished libido are not interested in engaging in sexual behavior, have reduced genital sensitivity, and are not aroused by stimuli that most women would find sexually exciting. Other women have difficulty achieving an orgasm. For most disorders involving loss of sex drive, effective treatment includes estrogen replacement therapy, androgen therapy (including testosterone treatment), and psychotherapy (Berman et al., 2000; Sarrel, 2000; Shifren et al., 2000).

Recap 12.2: Regulation of Female Sexual Behavior

(a)_____ hormones are hormones produced by the ovaries or testes. (b)_____hormones are hormones produced by the pituitary gland that stimulate changes in the gonads. (c)_____-_____ hormone (FSH) is released by the pituitary gland and causes maturation of immature eggs in the ovary. (d)_____ hormone (LH) is released by the pituitary when estrogen levels reach an optimum level. LH causes (e)_____ (the process by which mature ova burst out of the ovarian follicle) and stimulates the development of the corpus luteum in the ovary, which produces (f)_____. Ovulation is associated with (g)_____ _____ in most female animals. (h)_____ refers to the absence of menstrual cycles, which can be caused by hormonal, genetic, or developmental disorders. (i)_____ is a condition in which a woman cannot conceive and get pregnant. Painful menstruation, called (j)_____ , occurs in about one-fourth of all women under the age of 25.

Regulation of Male Sexual Behavior

In general, male animals can be divided in two groups: *seasonal breeders* and *nonseasonal breeders*. **Seasonal breeders** are those animals that mate only during a particular time of the year, typically when food supplies are abundant. In contrast, **nonseasonal breeders** are animals that mate throughout the year, regardless of the season or the availability of food. Most animals are seasonal breeders, although many species, such as humans, rats, dogs, and cats, are nonseasonal breeders. Let's examine the sexual behavior of seasonal breeders first.

seasonal breeders: animals that mate only during a particular time of the year

nonseasonal breeders: animals that mate throughout the year, regardless of season

Seasonal Breeders

Seasonal breeders are sexually active only during a particular time of the year. During most of the year, the male seasonal breeder is sexually immature, with immature gonads and a shrunken penis. Somehow, his hypothalamus gets the message that breeding season is approaching, and it begins the process that prepares the male's body for sexual activity. The passing of seasons may be signaled to the brain as lengthening or shortening of daylight via the retinohypothalamic tract, which you learned about in Chapter 10, or as a change of temperature that may be detected by the anterior hypothalamus, as you learned in Chapter 11.

At the start of the breeding season, the hypothalamus releases gonadotropin-releasing hormone to signal to the anterior pituitary gland to begin the process of sexual maturation. In response to the hypothalamus, the anterior pituitary releases two gonadotrophic hormones: follicle-stimulating hormone (FSH) and **interstitial cell–stimulating hormone (ICSH).** These two gonadotrophic hormones travel in the bloodstream to the male gonads, the testes, where they have their effect (Figure 12.10). FSH stimulates the production of sperm cells in the testes. As its name implies, ICSH stimulates interstitial cells in the testes, which produce testosterone. Thus, ICSH initiates the production of testosterone. At the beginning of the breeding season, then, sperm production and testosterone production begin. (As an aside, ICSH is chemically identical to luteinizing hormone, or LH, the gonadotrophic hormone found in female animals. Therefore, the anterior pituitary glands in male and female animals produce the same two gonadotrophic hormones: FSH and LH, or ICSH.)

Testosterone is a gonadal hormone released by the testes into the bloodstream. It has effects throughout the male animal's body. For example, testosterone causes the male's penis and testes to grow, and it stimulates certain neurons in the hypothalamus, increasing the male animal's sex drive. It also produces *secondary sex characteristics*, which vary according to the male's species. The male white-tailed deer is a seasonal breeder whose secondary sex characteristics include a prominent white chest and antlers. At the beginning of the breeding season, the penis and scrotum of the male white-tailed deer grow, and he develops a magnificent chest of white fur and a set of antlers. These secondary sex characteristics signal to the female of the species that the male is sexually mature and ready to mate.

At the end of the breeding season, the hypothalamus signals to the pituitary gland to stop production of FSH and ICSH. When production of these gonadotrophic hormones ceases, the testes revert back to their immature state. Sperm production stops, as does the production of testosterone. The absence of testosterone results in shrinkage of the penis and testes. In addition, as testosterone levels in the blood decrease, male secondary sex characteristics recede. For example, the male white-tailed deer loses his magnificent chest and antlers at the end of the breeding season, his penis and scrotum shrink, and he loses his sex drive. In fact, a male deer during the nonbreeding season is nearly indistinguishable from his female counterpart in appearance. People walking through the woods will sometimes find a set of antlers that has been shed by a male deer at the end of the breeding season.

interstitial cell–stimulating hormone: a gonadotrophic hormone that stimulates the release of testosterone

Figure 12.10 Hormonal changes in the seasonal breeder
(a) Nonbreeding season. (b) Breeding season.

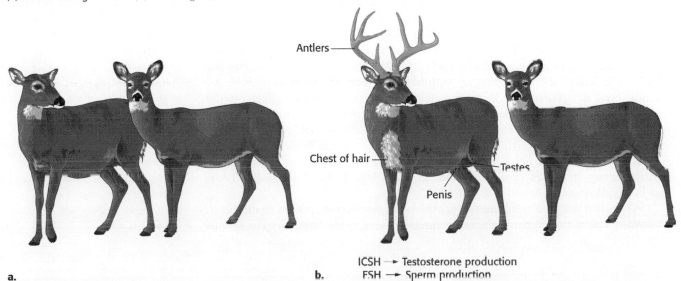

Antlers

Chest of hair

Penis

Testes

ICSH ⟶ Testosterone production
FSH ⟶ Sperm production

a.

b.

Nonseasonal Breeders

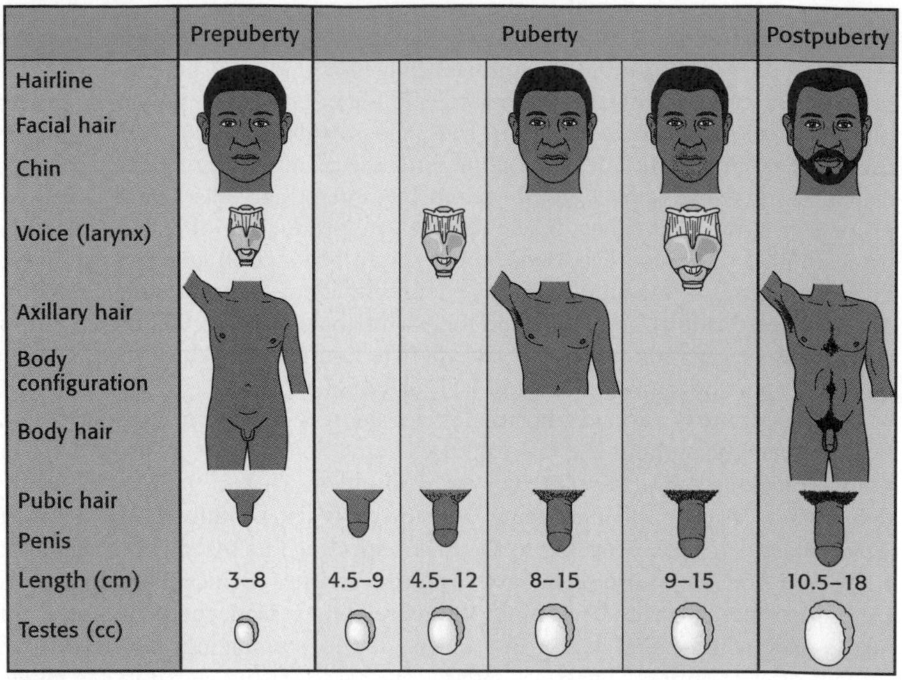

Nonseasonal breeders are sexually active throughout the year, regardless of season. They undergo a physical change called **puberty**, which involves sexual maturation. As puberty begins, the hypothalamus of the male nonseasonal breeder releases gonadotropin-releasing hormone to direct the anterior pituitary gland to release FSH and ICSH. As in the case of the seasonal breeder, FSH and ICSH cause sexual maturation. FSH stimulates the production of sperm cells in the testes, and ICSH stimulates the production of testosterone. Testosterone induces the growth of the penis and testes, as well as the development of secondary sex characteristics. Most importantly, testosterone binds with neurons in the hypothalamus, producing sex drive. However, unlike the seasonal breeder, the pituitary gland of the nonseasonal breeder continues to secrete FSH and ICSH continuously for the rest of the male's life. Thus, the male nonseasonal breeder is always ready to copulate after puberty takes place.

In the male human, secondary sex characteristics that arise during puberty include the growth of facial hair and hair on the legs, chest, armpits, and groin area. Testosterone also stimulates growth of the larynx, or voice box, which causes the voice to deepen, and it stimulates skeletal muscle development, as well as skeletal or bone growth (Figure 12.11). Because FSH and ICSH continue to be secreted until a man is well into his 80s, testosterone and sperm are produced in his testes until very late in life. This means that a man in his 70s or 80s still has a sex drive and is capable of impregnating a fertile woman.

Figure 12.11 Changes in the male human at puberty

	Prepuberty	Puberty				Postpuberty
Hairline						
Facial hair						
Chin						
Voice (larynx)						
Axillary hair						
Body configuration						
Body hair						
Pubic hair						
Penis						
Length (cm)	3–8	4.5–9	4.5–12	8–15	9–15	10.5–18
Testes (cc)						

puberty: a physical change that involves sexual maturation and occurs in nonseasonal breeders

Regulation of Sexual Behavior in Males

Our understanding of how the male brain regulates sexual behavior is quite sophisticated. The **medial preoptic area** of the hypothalamus appears to be responsible for the expression of sexual behavior in males, because lesions of this area impair or eliminate sexual behavior in a wide variety of species (van Furth, Wolterink, & van Ree, 1995). The medial preoptic area receives input from many different areas of the brain, including the cerebral cortex, amygdala, nucleus accumbens, and the ventral tegmental area. In general, **opioids** (whether endogenous opioids or administered drugs like opium or morphine) have an inhibitory effect on the medial preoptic area and interfere with sexual performance (Argiolas, 1999). In contrast, **dopamine** has an excitatory effect on the medial preoptic area and facilitates sexual behavior in males. Release of dopamine from the nucleus accumbens results in increased sex drive and stimulates the medial preoptic area, producing sexual activity in males (Hull, Lorrain, et al., 1999; Melis & Argiolas, 1995; van Furth, Wolterink, & van Ree, 1995).

Whereas dopamine facilitates sexual behavior, **serotonin** appears to inhibit it. Following ejaculation in the male, serotonin is released in the lateral hypothalamus

medial preoptic area: an area of the hypothalamus that appears to regulate the expression of male sexual behavior

opioids: chemicals (neurotransmitters or synthetic drugs) that bind with opioid receptors

dopamine: a monoamine neurotransmitter that is a precursor of norepinephrine and epinephrine

serotonin: a monoamine neurotransmitter that plays a role in sleep, vigilance, mood, appetite, and repetitive movements and the medial preoptic area. This release of serotonin reduces sex drive by inhibiting the release of dopamine in the nucleus accumbens (Hull et al., 1999). Thus, dopamine promotes sexual arousal, and serotonin stimulates sexual satiation. For this reason, selective serotonin reuptake inhibitors (SSRIs), which increase serotonin activity, interfere with sexual arousal and orgasm. Both men and women who take an SSRI antidepressant experience diminished genital sensitivity and a reduced ability to achieve orgasm.

Sexual Disorders in Men

Sexual disorders observed in men include fertility problems and sexual arousal dysfunction. *Fertility problems* include a low sperm count or sperm with low motility (that is, sperm that do not move as fast or as far as normal). Obviously, either of these problems can result in a failure to impregnate a woman. The causes for these disorders are unknown, but they have been associated with a number of factors, including heredity, chronic marijuana use, and wearing tight underwear that holds the testes close to the body. The scrotum that holds the testes hangs from a man's body because sperm cells require storage in a temperature that is lower than core body temperature. Sperm cells are less viable when they are exposed to temperatures close to core body temperature. Thus, tight underwear that holds the testes close to the body lowers sperm count by killing or inactivating sperm cells due to the increase in temperature.

Sexual arousal in men causes erection of the penis, which allows for intromission of the penis into a woman's vagina and permits sperm to be deposited into her vaginal canal. Erection of the penis is caused by the *relaxation of smooth muscles* at the base of the penis. When relaxed, these muscles press against the veins that drain blood from the penis, resulting in a pooling of blood in the spongy tissues of the penis (Figure 12.12). To initiate an erection, conscious or unconscious signals from the cerebral cortex or limbic system are relayed to the hypothalamus. In turn, the hypothalamus stimulates the parasympathetic nervous system, causing *acetylcholine* to be released in the base of the penis. Acetylcholine induces the release of *nitric oxide*, which causes relaxation of the smooth muscles and, consequently, erection of the penis. Norepinephrine, released by the sympathetic nervous system, antagonizes this process, by inducing *contraction of the smooth muscles* at the base of the penis. Thus, cold temperatures, anxiety, or fear, which stimulate the activity of the sympathetic nervous system, cause norepinephrine to be released in a man's body, resulting in temporary shrinkage of the penis.

About 10% of the male population experiences erectile dysfunction, due to nerve damage, hormonal disorders, alcoholism, cigarette smoking, or cardiovascular problems, such as high blood pressure and hardening of the arteries, that cause decreased blood flow to the penis (Melman & Christ, 2001). Approximately 20% of men with erectile dysfunction have significantly lower levels of testosterone levels in the blood than normal (Nehra, 2000). A number of treatments have been tried to treat erectile dysfunction disorder, including semirigid and inflatable penile implants, vacuum pumps, hormone treatments, and injections of muscle relaxants into the penis. Currently, the drug *sildenafil* (better known by its brand name, Viagra) is considered the most effective treatment for erectile dysfunction disorders.

Viagra triggers an erection by blocking an enzyme that breaks down *cyclic guanine monophosphate* (cGMP), a molecule activated by nitric oxide to relax smooth muscles (Melman, 1999). That is, Viagra's chief effect is to increase the availability of cGMP in smooth muscles in the penis, causing relaxation of those muscles and, thus, penile erection. However, Viagra is effective only in the presence of nitric oxide, which is released in response to sexual stimulation. If a man is not sexually aroused, Viagra does not stimulate penile erection.

Figure 12.12 Control of penile erection

In order for penile erection to occur, smooth muscles at the base of the penis press against veins that drain the penis, causing blood to pool in the spongy tissue of the penis.

a. Male pelvis: side view

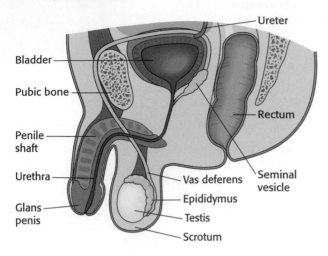

- Ureter
- Bladder
- Pubic bone
- Rectum
- Penile shaft
- Urethra
- Vas deferens
- Seminal vesicle
- Epididymus
- Glans penis
- Testis
- Scrotum

b. Penile erection: Blood pools in spongy tissue of the penis, as smooth muscles at the base of the penis press against the veins that drain the penis.

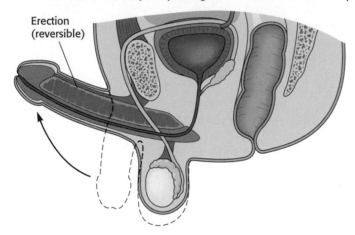

Erection (reversible)

c. Sequence leading to erection of the penis

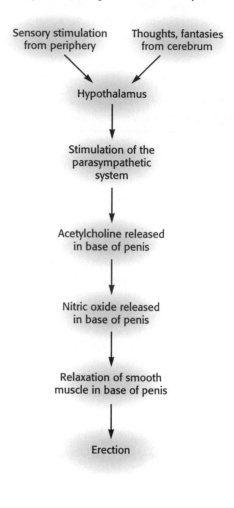

Sensory stimulation from periphery → Thoughts, fantasies from cerebrum

Hypothalamus

↓

Stimulation of the parasympathetic system

↓

Acetylcholine released in base of penis

↓

Nitric oxide released in base of penis

↓

Relaxation of smooth muscle in base of penis

↓

Erection

Recap 12.3: Regulation of Male Sexual Behavior

Male animals are either (a)_____ breeders, which mate only during a particular time of the year, or (b)_____ breeders, which mate throughout the year. The (c)_____ gland of a seasonal breeder releases FSH and interstitial cell–stimulating hormone (ICSH) at the beginning of the mating season. FSH stimulates the production of (d)_____ cells, and ICSH stimulates interstitial cells, which produce (e)_____. Nonseasonal breeders undergo a physical change, called (f)_____, which brings about sexual maturation. At puberty, (g)_____ and (h)_____ are released by the pituitary gland, stimulating the production of sperm and testosterone. Release of FSH and ICSH is terminated at the end of the mating season in seasonal breeders, but release of these hormones continues throughout the life of the nonseasonal breeder. The (i)_____ _____ area of the hypothalamus regulates sexual behavior in male animals. (j)_____ stimulates sexual behavior in males, whereas (k)_____ inhibits it.

Deviant Sexual Behavior

Deviant sexual behavior, or **paraphilia**, is a problem for some men and women. *Voyeurism, exhibitionism,* and *pedophilia* are three of the most common paraphilias. **Voyeurism** is a problem behavior in which the affected individual (called a *voyeur* or a "peeping Tom") gets sexual gratification from surreptitiously watching others disrobe or engage in sexual activity. An individual who displays **exhibitionism** gets sexual gratification from exposing his or her genitals to others, especially strangers. **Pedophilia** is a disorder in which a person is sexually aroused by children and desires to have sexual contact with them. Although these deviant (and illegal) sexual behaviors can occur in both men and women, their incidence is significantly higher in men.

Treatment for these paraphilias includes surgical castration, psychotherapy, and antiandrogen drugs (Rosler & Witztum, 1998, 2000). Antiandrogens produce chemical castration and work in one of two ways: by blocking the activity of androgens or by inhibiting the secretion of testosterone. Androgen antagonists are drugs that block the action of testosterone at the receptor. Unfortunately, androgen antagonists have unwelcome side effects, which limits their usefulness. Drugs that mimic the activity of gonadotropin-releasing hormone selectively inhibit the secretion of testosterone. These analogues of gonadotropin-releasing hormone are the drug of choice in treating paraphilias because they have few negative side effects and are long-lasting in their effect, requiring an injection once every 1 to 3 months (Rosler & Witztum, 2000). Recall that androgens, including testosterone, induce sex drive in both men and women. Antiandrogens reverse the action of the androgens, which in turn decreases sex drive and the urge to engage in these deviant sexual behaviors. Surgical castration has the same effect as antiandrogens, reducing testosterone activity in the body (Rosler & Witztum, 1998, 2000). However, the effect of antiandrogens is readily reversible, whereas surgical castration is not. Therefore, surgical castration is rarely used to treat paraphilia and is reserved for extreme cases.

Whereas antiandrogens are quite effective in the treatment of voyeurism, exhibitionism, and pedophilia, they are not effective in treating rapists. This tells us that rape is not so much a sexual behavior as it is an act of aggression. If rape were a disorder caused solely by increased sex drive, an antiandrogen should produce a diminished drive to commit rape in rapists. However, these drugs do not reduce rape behavior. In Chapter 13, we will examine emotional behavior, including aggression and aggressive disorders.

paraphilia: deviant sexual behavior

voyeurism: a paraphilia in which the affected individual gets sexual gratification from surreptitiously watching others disrobe or engage in sexual behavior

exhibitionism: a paraphilia in which the affected individual gets sexual gratification from exposing his or her genitals to others, especially strangers

pedophilia: a paraphilia in which the affected individual is sexually aroused by children and desires sexual contact with them

---

Recap 12.4: Deviant Sexual Behavior

Deviant sexual behavior is referred to as (a)_____. Three of the most common forms of deviant sexual behaviors are (b)_____ (in which sexual gratification is obtained by watching others disrobe or engage in sex), (c)_____ (in which sexual gratification is obtained by exposing one's private parts to others), and (d)_____ (in which sexual gratification is obtained by sexual contact with children). (e)_____ drugs are used to treat deviant sexual behaviors, and they work in one of two ways: blocking the action of testosterone at the receptor or inhibiting the secretion of testosterone.

Comparing the Regulation of Male and Female Sexual Behaviors

In this chapter, we have examined the regulation of sexual behavior. Although our understanding of how the male brain regulates sexual behavior is quite sophisticated, our understanding of the regulation of human female sexual behavior is quite sketchy. Estrogen appears to produce sexual motivation in the female rat, but its role in human female sexual behavior is not clear. As you learned in this chapter, sexual interest is greatest, and female-initiated sexual activity is most frequent, during ovulation when estrogen levels are high. But, testosterone levels are also highest at ovulation, and it may be that testosterone increases sexual drive and activity in women, as it does in men.

Dopamine has an excitatory effect on the medial preoptic area of the hypothalamus and facilitates male sexual behavior, increasing the frequency of sexual activity and coordinating genital reflexes, such as erection of the penis and ejaculation (Figure 12.13). Testosterone stimulates the release of dopamine in the medial preoptic area in males and females. Injections of estrogen followed by progesterone in female rats produced a significant increase in dopamine release in the medial preoptic area of those females, which is associated with sexual receptivity and copulation (Hull, Lorrain, et al., 1999). Estrogen also stimulates dopamine release in women in the basal ganglia, which coordinates sequential movements necessary in sexual activity (Hull, Lorrain, et al., 1999; Frohlich, Ogawa, Morgan, Burton, & Pfaff, 1999). Therefore, dopamine may facilitate sexual behavior in women as well as men. In contrast, serotonin appears to promote sexual satiation in both men and women because SSRIs interfere with sexual arousal and orgasm in both sexes.

Figure 12.13 Dopamine and male sexual behavior

Using a microdialysis technique, Phillips and his colleagues (1993) measured increased release of dopamine in the nucleus accumbens of a male rat just before the rat copulated with a female.

Oxytocin

Serotonin is believed to suppress sexual arousal by blocking the action of **oxytocin,** a neuropeptide produced in the hypothalamus. The best-known biological functions of oxytocin are to stimulate contractions of the uterine wall and ejection of milk from the nipple. However, oxytocin has also been found to promote sexual activity in both male and female animals (Argiolas, 1999). In humans, oxytocin levels increase as a person advances from the stage of initial sexual arousal through orgasm (Carmichael, Warburton, Dixen, & Davidson, 1994). Higher levels of oxytocin are associated with the experience of orgasm in men and women.

In addition, injections of oxytocin have been demonstrated to reverse the inhibitory effects of SSRIs on ejaculation in male rats (Cantor, Binik, & Pfaus, 1999). That is, male rats that receive daily doses of an SSRI show an inability to ejaculate, although they copulate avidly with a receptive female. When oxytocin is administered to male rats receiving chronic SSRI injections, the males are able to ejaculate normally. Thus, SSRIs are believed to inhibit the action of oxytocin, thereby interfering with ejaculation and orgasm. Oxytocin also increases sexual behavior in female rats (Bale, Davis, Auger, Dorsa, & McCarty, 2001).

Another important function of oxytocin is the regulation of social behaviors, particularly species-specific sociosexual behavior and social attachment or bonding (Carter, 1998). Oxytocin controls sexual behavior in monogamous male rodents, for example. It also functions in the regulation of maternal behavior and infant separation distress (Insel, 1992). In humans, oxytocin is believed to play an important role in affiliation with others and in the development of feelings of love (Carter, 1998). Green, Fein, Modahl, Feinstein, Waterhouse, and Morris (2001) recently discovered that oxytocin levels are significantly reduced in autistic children. This finding suggests that oxytocin abnormalities in autistic individuals may be responsible for the social impairments, such as reduced social attachment, associated with autism.

In Chapter 13, we will examine the role of dopamine and serotonin in the regulation of emotions. The hypothalamus and basal ganglia, which stimulate and coordinate sexual behavior, also play an important role in emotional behavior, as do

oxytocin: a hormone produced by the paraventricular nucleus that regulates lactation and childbirth and is released in response to specific stressors; it also appears to regulate sexual and social behaviors in male and female animals

other structures, including the limbic system and the prefrontal cortex. We did not explore the role of the prefrontal cortex in sexual behavior, mainly because the research in that area is nearly nonexistent. Obviously, the prefrontal cortex must play some role in sexual behavior, particularly in the selection of the target of sexual desire. The roles of the prefrontal cortex and the limbic system in the regulation of emotional behavior are much better understood, as you will learn in Chapter 13.

Recap 12.5: Comparing the Regulation of Male and Female Sexual Behavior

(a)_____ appears to produce sexual motivation in the female rat, but its role in human female sexual behavior is not clear. (b)_____ may increase sexual drive in women, as it does in men. Testosterone stimulates the release of (c)_____ in the medial preoptic area in males and females. (d)_____ also stimulates dopamine release in women in the basal ganglia, which coordinates sequential movements necessary in sexual activity. (e)_____ appears to promote sexual satiation in both men and women, as SSRIs interfere with sexual arousal and orgasm in both sexes. Serotonin suppresses sexual arousal by blocking the action of (f)_____, a neuropeptide produced in the hypothalamus. High levels of oxytocin are associated with the experience of (g)_____ in men and women. In humans, (h)_____ is believed to play an important role in affiliation with others and in the development of feelings of love.

Chapter Summary

Sexual Differentiation

▶ The process by which we become biological males or females is called sexual differentiation.

▶ Sexual differentiation, which begins at conception, is largely determined by the chromosomes carried by the egg and the sperm to the fertilized egg. Normally, a biological female has two X chromosomes, whereas a biological male has one X and one Y chromosome.

▶ The Y chromosome directs the development of the testes, which produces two hormones, testosterone and Müllerian inhibiting substance. Testosterone affects the development of the internal and external genitalia, stimulating the growth of the Wolffian ducts and the penis and scrotum. Müllerian inhibiting substance prevents the growth of the Müllerian ducts, which normally develop into female internal genitalia.

▶ The presence or absence of male gonadal hormones affect the development of internal and external genitalia. In the absence of a Y chromosome, the ovaries develop, and female internal and external genitalia develop.

▶ Individuals with Turner's syndrome have a chromosomal designation of 45, XO and are typically raised as girls. Individuals with Klinefelter's syndrome have a chromosomal designation of 47, XXY, possess testes and are raised as boys. Androgen insensitivity syndrome occurs in individuals with a chromosomal designation of 46, XY, who are born with testes but are insensitive to testosterone. In adrenogenital syndrome, embryos are exposed to high levels of androgens, which masculinize the external genitalia of female embryos.

▶ The brain is also influenced by sexual differentiation, which alters brain structures and activity. The corpus callosum is larger in women than in men. In contrast, the interstitial nucleus of the hypothalamus is larger in men than in women. Male sex hormones, called androgens, appear to suppress the growth of the left cerebral cortex, causing the right cortex to be thicker than the left cortex in male rats and humans.

Hormonal Regulation of Female Sexual Behavior

▶ Gonadal hormones are hormones produced by the ovaries or testes. Gonadotrophic hormones are hormones produced by the pituitary gland that stimulate changes in the gonads.

▶ Sexual behaviors in nonhuman animals are regulated by hormonal activity, and some human sexual behavior has been linked to gonadal hormones as well.

▶ In female animals, ovulation is produced by an interplay of pituitary (FSH, LH) and gonadal (estrogen, progesterone) hormones. Follicle-stimulating hormone (FSH) causes maturation of immature eggs in the ovary and luteinizing hormone (LH) is released by the pituitary when estrogen levels reach an optimum level causing ovulation.

▶ Amenorrhea refers to the absence of menstrual cycles, which can be caused by hormonal, genetic, or developmental disorders. Infertility is a condition in which a woman cannot conceive and get pregnant. Painful menstruation, called dysmenorrhea, occurs in about one-fourth of all women under the age of 25.

Hormonal Regulation of Male Sexual Behavior

▶ The pituitary gland of a seasonal breeder releases FSH and interstitial cell–stimulating hormone (ISCH) at the beginning of the mating season. FSH stimulates the production of sperm cells, and ICSH stimulates interstitial cells, which produce testosterone.

▶ Nonseasonal breeders undergo a physical change, called puberty, which brings about sexual maturation. At puberty, FSH and ICSH are released by the pituitary gland, stimulating the production of sperm and testosterone.

▶ Release of FSH and ICSH is terminated at the end of the mating season in seasonal breeders, but release of these hormones continues throughout the life of the nonseasonal breeder.

▶ Sexual disorders in men include fertility problems and erectile dysfunction.

▶ The medial preoptic area of the hypothalamus regulates sexual behavior in male animals. Dopamine stimulates sexual behaviors in males, whereas serotonin inhibits it.

Deviant Sexual Behaviors

▶ Three of the most common forms of deviant sexual behaviors are voyeurism (in which sexual gratification is obtained by watching others disrobe or engage in sex), exhibitionism (in which sexual gratification is obtained by exposing one's private parts to others), and pedophilia (in which sexual gratification is obtained by sexual contact with children).

▶ Treatment for paraphilia include psychotherapy and antiandrogen drugs. Antiandrogen drugs work in one of two ways: blocking the action of testosterone at the receptor or inhibiting the secretion of testosterone.

Comparing the Regulation of Male and Female Sexual Behavior

▶ Estrogen appears to produce sexual motivation in the female rat, but its role in human female sexual behavior is not clear.

▶ Testosterone may increase sexual drive in women, as it does in men. Testosterone stimulates the release of dopamine in the medical preoptic area in males and females.

▶ Estrogen also stimulates dopamine release in women in the basal ganglia, which coordinates sequential movements necessary in sexual activity.

▶ Serotonin appears to promote sexual satiation in both men and women, as SSRIs interfere with sexual arousal and orgasm in both sexes. Serotonin suppresses sexual arousal by blocking the action of oxytocin, a neuropeptide produced in the hypothalamus.

▶ High levels of oxytocin are associated with the experience of orgasm in men and women. In humans, oxytocin is believed to play an important role in affiliation with others and in the development of feelings of love.

Key Terms

Questions for Thought

1. What does it mean to be male? What does it mean to be female?
2. Can autosomes play a role in sexual differentiation?
3. What is the relationship between the hypothalamus and the pituitary gland?

Questions for Review

1. What causes the Wolffian system to develop? What causes the Müllerian system to develop?
2. What role do pituitary hormones play in the female ovarian cycle?
3. What role do pituitary hormones play in male sexual behavior?
4. How do dopamine and serotonin affect sexual behavior?

Suggested Readings

Ellis, L., & Ebertz, L. (1998). *Males, females, and behavior: Toward biological understanding.* Westport, CT: Praeger.

Frohlich, J., Ogawa, S., Morgan, M., Burton, L., & Pfaff, D. (1999). Hormones, genes, and the structure of sexual arousal. *Behavioral Brain Research,* 105, 5–27.

Jensvold, M. F., Halbreich, U., & Hamilton, J. A. (1996). *Psychopharmacology and women.* Washington, DC: American Psychiatric Press.

LeVay, S. (1993). *The sexual brain.* Cambridge, MA: MIT Press.

Web Resources

For a chapter tutorial quiz, direct links to the Internet sites listed below and other features, visit the book-specific website at **www.wadsworth.com/product/0155074865**. You may also connect directly to the following annotated websites:

http:www.dhushara.com/book/socio/kimura/kimura/htm
Learn more about sex differences in the brain on this site.

http://www.apa.org/pubinfo/orient.html
The American Psychological Association answers some basic questions about sexual orientation and homosexuality on this site.

http://www.isna.org/
Visit this site to learn more about intersex individuals and how the Intersex Society of North America is helping to end the shame, secrecy, and unwanted genital surgeries for people born with atypical reproductive anatomies.

For additional readings and information, check out InfoTrac College Edition at **http://www.infotrac-college.com/wadsworth**. Choose a search term yourself or enter the following search terms: cloacal exstrophy and Turner's syndrome.

CD-ROM: Exploring Biological Psychology

Animation: Menstruation Cycle
Video: Erectile Dysfunction
Video: Sex Dysfunction in Women

Interactive Recaps
Chapter 12 Quiz
Connect to the Interactive Biological Psychology Glossary

13

Biological Bases of Emotion and Addiction

Emotion

Theories of Emotion

Emotional Pathways in the Central Nervous System

The Locus Coeruleus

The Limbic System

The Cerebral Cortex

The Medial Forebrain Bundle and Periventricular Circuits

Negative Emotions

The Role of the Amygdala

Rage and Agression

Fear

Disorders Associated with Negative Emotions

Case Study: Obsessive-Compulsive Disorder

Positive Emotions

Disorders Associated with Positive Emotions

Addiction

Definition of Addiction

For Further Thought: Withdrawal from Alcohol

Role of Neurotransmitters in Addiction

The Development of an Addiction

Treatment for Addiction

Chapter Summary

While picnicking with a companion, Walter is suddenly overcome by a strange feeling. He imagines seeing two large white male dogs fighting, but is puzzled because he knows only one such dog is really present. Intrigued, he chases them, but the dogs run away and vanish "into nothing" as they jump over a river. In their place, Walter sees a fisherman in waders holding out a fly rod. Suddenly, Walter charges the man—a total stranger toward whom he harbored no ill feelings—and pushes him underwater, saying, "I'll teach you how to fish like a bear." The man, in his forties, finds a rock and tries to hit Walter in the face. Meanwhile, Walter's picnic companion arrives, grabs his head, and shouts, "No! No! Don't do it!" But Walter, seemingly emotionless, bites her finger and holds the man under until he drowns. He then tries to drown his companion, too, but he suddenly comes to his senses and lets her go (LoPiccolo, 1996, p. 52).

Walter was a handsome man in his early 20s at the time of this homicide. People who knew Walter called him mild mannered and a social loner. His police report indicated that he had no criminal record and no history of violence. A forensic psychiatrist was called in to examine Walter because the homicide he committed was so bizarre. Most homicides, approximately 90% of them, are committed by a murderer who has a motive and a plan. Most murderers feel strong emotions, such as rage, greed, or jealousy, when they commit their murders. But Walter had no motive, no plan, and no feelings of emotion as he drowned the stranger who happened to be fishing nearby. What caused Walter to commit murder?

To understand the answer to this question, you will need to learn how emotions are produced and controlled by the brain. In this chapter, we will examine the biological basis of emotions. We will also take a look at addictions because these behaviors use many of the same brain structures and mechanisms as emotional behavior does. Let's begin by defining *emotion*. ●

Emotion

We talk about emotions all the time. *I'm so happy to see you! Dad was thrilled when he found his watch. Polly was very angry at the interruption. Jamil was sad when the trip was over. Tika loved the gift you bought her. Kevin got scared when the trees began to fall over.* Each of these statements describes a feeling or emotional reaction to a stimulus. For example, seeing someone you care for causes happiness, finding a lost watch produces pleasure, an interruption causes anger, and so forth. An emotion doesn't occur on its own. A stimulus is needed to initiate the reaction we call an emotion.

An emotion is a complicated response to a particular stimulus. The formal definition of an emotion has three components: An **emotion** is a *cognitive experience* that is accompanied by an *affective reaction* and a characteristic *physiological response*. That is, an emotion involves thought processes (cognitive experience), alterations in mood (affective reaction), and a bodily reaction (physiological response). When you are experiencing an emotion, you are consciously aware that the emotion is occurring as you are thinking about the stimulus and your response to that stimulus. Your mood changes when you experience an emotion, becoming more positive or negative. This affective component of emotion is referred to as *feeling* (Panksepp, 1989). In addition, the **sympathetic nervous system** is activated when you experience an emotion. Recall from Chapter 2 that the sympathetic nervous system produces a number of changes in your body when it is activated: Your pupils dilate, your heart beats faster, your breathing rate speeds up, you begin to sweat, your saliva becomes thicker, your blood leaves your gut and flows to your muscles, and so forth. These physiological responses accompany all emotional states.

Expression of emotions appears to be universal across all cultures. Regardless of the culture in which an individual is raised, similar facial expressions are used to communicate emotion. Figure 13.1 illustrates a series of faces expressing various emotions. See if you can determine the emotion being expressed in each photograph. When you experience an emotion, the **somatic nervous system** reflexively initiates contraction of certain muscles in your face by way of cranial nerve VII, the facial nerve, which innervates the muscles of facial expression. For example, when you are happy, muscles in your face contract to pull the corners of your mouth up and back. These muscle contractions are produced reflexively in response to certain stimuli.

When we think about emotions, they seem to fall into one of two categories: 1) *positive emotions* and 2) *negative emotions*. Positive emotions are those that make us feel better, and they tend to draw us toward the eliciting stimulus. In contrast, negative emotions are accompanied by feelings of anxiety, depression, or hostility, and they tend to make us avoid the eliciting stimulus. Emotions organize our behavior in such a way as to motivate us to approach pleasant stimuli (as in the case of positive emotions) or avoid unpleasant or noxious stimuli (as in the case of negative emotions). Thus, emotions are important for our survival.

In general, emotions such as happiness, love, and euphoria are considered positive emotions. Anger, hatred, disgust, and fear are considered negative emotions. These negative emotions have also been called *emotions of self-preservation* because they function to produce defensive responses by an individual to an arousing stimulus. For example, when I picked up what I thought was a dead snake from my driveway one day, the snake's tail began to move. In response, I reflexively dropped the snake and ran down the driveway away from the snake. Thus, I displayed self-

emotion: a cognitive experience accompanied by an affective reaction and characteristic physiological response

sympathetic nervous system: a division of the autonomic nervous system, producing fight-or-flight responses

somatic nervous system: a division of the peripheral nervous system that controls skeletal muscles

Figure 13.1 Facial expression of emotion
Characteristic facial expressions are used to communicate emotion.

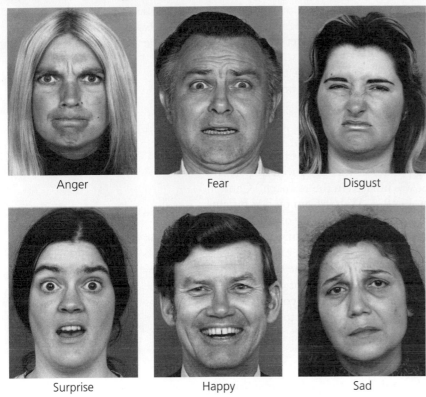

Anger Fear Disgust

Surprise Happy Sad

preservation as I dashed away from the snake that was still very much alive. Walter Cannon, in 1927, referred to these negative emotional reactions as **fight-or-flight responses.** Emotions of self-preservation produce either *fight behavior*, in which an individual strikes out at a threatening stimulus in an attempt to eliminate it, or *flight behavior*, in which the individual runs from the emotion-inducing stimulus (as I did from the snake).

Both positive and negative emotions are associated with activation of the sympathetic nervous system. Whether you are in love or so angry that you could scream, your body has the same reaction: dilation of the pupils, increased heart rate and sweating, cessation of peristalsis in the gut. Investigators who study emotions do not agree as to whether each emotion produces a specific pattern of physiological responses (Ekman, 1992; Ortony & Turner, 1990). It may be that the autonomic arousal (that is, arousal of the sympathetic nervous system) experienced during an emotional reaction is nonspecific, or identical for all emotions, which means that the brain must distinguish among emotions based on cognitive or other nonphysiological cues. Later in this chapter, we will discuss how activation of the sympathetic nervous system occurs. Before we get to that discussion, I want you to consider how emotions are generated and experienced. A number of investigators have proposed theories to explain how emotions arise. Let's examine the best known of these theories.

fight-or-flight responses: Walter Cannon's term for negative emotional reactions

Theories of Emotion

James-Lange Theory
William James and Carl Lange published separate papers at about the same time— James in the United States and Lange in Europe—that detailed the same explanation

of emotion (James, 1890; Lange & James, 1922). Today we call that explanation the **James-Lange theory of emotion,** in honor of the two psychologists who proposed it. According to the James-Lange theory, a stimulus produces a physiological response, and the physiological response produces an emotion (Figure 13.2). The classic example goes like this: You are walking in the woods and meet a bear. Seeing the bear makes your heart pound, and you run away. Running away with a pounding heart causes you to feel afraid. That is, according to the James-Lange theory of emotion, you feel afraid *after* you experience the physiological responses produced by the sympathetic and somatic nervous systems.

James-Lange theory of emotion: an explanation of emotion that maintains that the physiological response to a stimulus produces an emotion

Cannon-Bard Theory

You may recall Walter Cannon's name from Chapter 12, when we examined stomach contractions and the initiation of eating. (Cannon was the psychologist who had his grad student swallow the balloon that was inflated in the stomach.) Cannon is also well known for his theory on emotion. In 1927, Walter Cannon and his student, Phil Bard, wrote a paper that refuted the James-Lange theory of emotion and proposed an alternative theory, known as the **Cannon-Bard theory of emotion** (Cannon, 1927). According to the Cannon-Bard theory, a stimulus causes an emotion, and that emotion produces physiological changes. That is, the Cannon-Bard theory maintains that a stimulus is directly followed by an emotional reaction, which then elicits a bodily response (Figure 13.2). For example, if you meet a bear in the woods, you feel fear (an emotion) and run away. According to the Cannon-Bard theory, you run away because you feel afraid.

Cannon-Bard theory of emotion: an explanation of emotion that maintains that a stimulus elicits an emotion, which produces physiological changes

Schachter-Singer Theory

At Columbia University, Stanley Schachter and his student, Jerome Singer, designed an ingenious experiment to test whether the James-Lange or the Cannon-Bard theory is correct (Schachter & Singer, 1962). In their experiment, they had three groups of male participants, who were told that the study involved testing the effects of vitamin A on vision. The first group was administered an injection of epinephrine but was uninformed about its effect *(Epi-Uninformed group).* The participants in this group were told that they had been injected with vitamin A but that it would have no side effects. Recall from Chapter 3 that epinephrine is a powerful stimulant of the sympathetic nervous system. The second group also received epinephrine but was told that the "vitamin A" injection would cause them to feel shaky and excited *(Epi-Informed group).* The third group received an injection of saline (salt water) and was told that the vitamin A shot would have no side effects *(Placebo group).* Thus, the Epi-Uniformed group experienced physiological arousal but had no explanation for that arousal, the Epi-Informed group experienced physiological arousal and knew that the injection produced that arousal, and the Placebo group experienced no physiological arousal.

Following the injection, each participant was placed individually in a room where a confederate was completing a survey. (A confederate is a person who is paid to act like a participant in the study.) The participant was asked to complete the same survey while he waited for the "vitamin A" to be absorbed into his bloodstream. As the participant completed the survey, the confederate began to act either euphoric or angry. In the euphoria condition, the confederate began laughing at the questions on the survey and folded the pages into paper airplanes, which he sailed across the room. In the anger condition, the confederate became angry over the questions in the survey and wadded each page into a ball, which he angrily threw across the room. Schachter and Singer were interested in observing how the participants reacted when the confederate began to display emotion.

As Schachter and Singer predicted, the participants in the Epi-Uninformed group displayed emotional behavior when exposed to a confederate who was displaying emotional behavior. For example, those in the euphoria condition were observed to laugh and make airplanes with the confederate, whereas those in the

Figure 13.2 Major theories of emotion

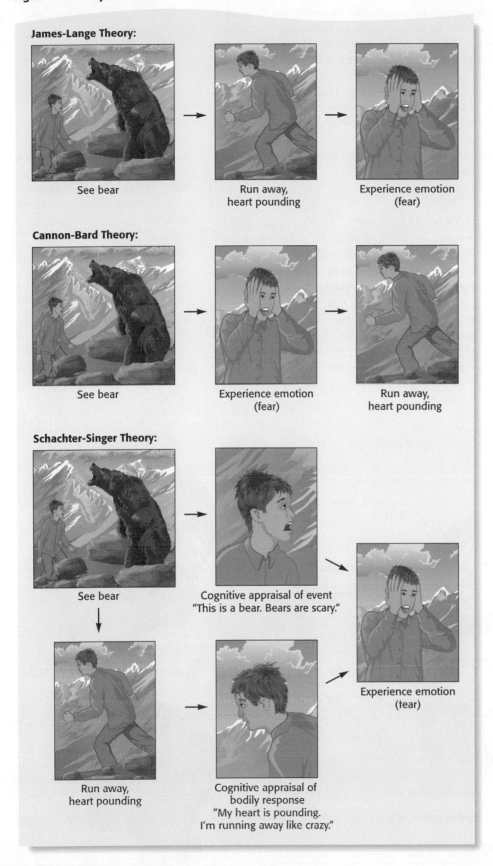

James-Lange Theory:

See bear → Run away, heart pounding → Experience emotion (fear)

Cannon-Bard Theory:

See bear → Experience emotion (fear) → Run away, heart pounding

Schachter-Singer Theory:

See bear → Cognitive appraisal of event "This is a bear. Bears are scary."

Run away, heart pounding → Cognitive appraisal of bodily response "My heart is pounding. I'm running away like crazy." → Experience emotion (fear)

anger condition tore up their surveys in anger. These participants in the Epi-Uninformed group experienced physiological arousal due to the injection of epinephrine, but they attributed this arousal to an emotional state, euphoria or anger, depending on the behavior of the confederate. On the other hand, subjects in the Epi-Informed and Placebo groups did not display emotional behavior. Those participants in the Epi-Informed group experienced physiological arousal, but they attributed that arousal to the drug that was injected because they were informed of the true effects of the drug. Those in the Placebo group did not display emotional behavior because they did not experience physiological arousal. Thus, according to the **Schachter-Singer theory of emotion,** in order to experience an emotion, an individual needs to experience physiological arousal *and* has to attribute the physiological arousal to an appropriate stimulus (Figure 13.2).

Vascular Theory of Emotion

A more recent theory of emotion was described by Zajonc, Murphy, and Inglehart in 1989. As its name implies (*vascular* refers to blood vessels), the **vascular theory of emotion** is based on changes in blood flow through particular blood vessels in the face. These blood vessels drain into the **cavernous sinus,** a large venous pool of blood that collects at the base of the skull before being carried back to the heart (Figure 13.3). The cavernous sinus is central to the vascular theory of emotion because blood draining from the superficial layers of the face is cooler than core body temperature and, thus, cools the brain. A number of studies conducted by Zajonc and others have demonstrated that increasing the temperature of the brain (just a few tenths of a degree) produces negative emotions like anger and sadness,

Schachter-Singer theory of emotion: an explanation of emotion that maintains that to experience an emotion, an individual needs to experience physiological arousal *and* has to attribute the arousal to an appropriate stimulus

vascular theory of emotion: an explanation of emotion that maintains that warming the brain produces negative emotions and cooling the brain produces positive emotions

cavernous sinus: a large pool of venous blood that pools at the base of the skull

Figure 13.3 Vascular theory of emotion
(a) Parts of the vascular system involved in emotional expression. (b) Face smiling. (c) Face frowning.

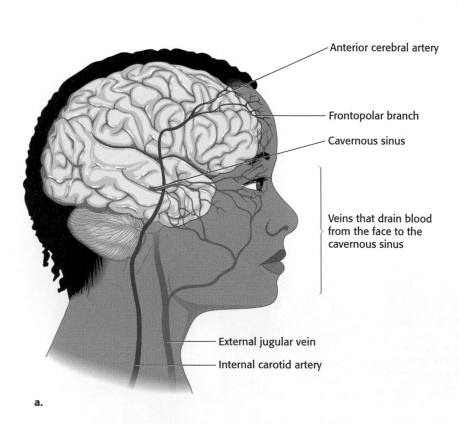

Anterior cerebral artery

Frontopolar branch

Cavernous sinus

Veins that drain blood from the face to the cavernous sinus

External jugular vein

Internal carotid artery

a.

b. Cool blood from the superficial layer of face (skin, muscle) drains into cavernous sinus, cooling the brain.

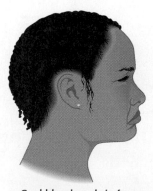

c. Cool blood pools in face and does not drain into cavernous sinus, warming the brain

whereas cooling the brain produces feelings of happiness (Zajonc et al., 1989). These minute changes in brain temperature are believed to alter the activity of enzymes and neurotransmitters in the brain, which could affect the experience of emotion.

According to the vascular theory of emotion, muscular contractions that produce *smiling* cause blood to drain rapidly from the face into the cavernous sinus, which *lowers the temperature* of the brain, producing a positive emotion (Figure 13.3). For example, when human participants hold a pencil in their teeth, blood drains out of the face into the cavernous sinus, and, after several minutes, a feeling of happiness or well-being is induced. Put a pencil between your canine teeth and look at yourself in the mirror. You will appear to be smiling. Thus, smiling causes blood to drain from your face into the cavernous sinus, cooling your brain and producing a positive emotion. In contrast, when participants hold a pencil with their lips only, producing a frown, their mood declines, and they report feeling sad or unhappy (Figure 13.3). Muscle contractions that produce a *frown* cause blood to pool in the face, rather than drain into the brain, which *increases the temperature* of the brain.

The vascular theory of emotion may explain why facial expression of emotions appears to be universal across all cultures. Because smiling causes blood to drain from the face and frowning causes blood to pool in the face, these facial expressions are directly implicated in the control of brain temperature. However, it is unclear whether smiling occurs before or after the experience of a happy emotion in a natural setting, as when someone gives you an unexpected gift. In the laboratory, Zajonc proposed that smiling precedes the experience of the emotion because smiling lowers the temperature of the brain and, consequently, stimulates those areas of the brain that cause us to feel a positive emotion (Zajonc et al., 1989).

The James-Lange theory would also predict that smiling (the physiological response) precedes the experience of happiness. The Cannon-Bard theory requires that happiness (the emotion) be felt first, followed by smiling. In contrast, the Schachter-Singer theory predicts that smiling would occur before the experience of happiness but that happiness would be experienced only if the smiling person could attribute the smile to some appropriate stimulus. That is, if the individual could not explain why he or she were smiling, or if the individual were to reason, "I'm not really smiling, I'm holding a pencil in my teeth," the Schachter-Singer theory of emotion would lead us to predict that happiness would not be experienced. Thus, each theory of emotion that we have examined in this section would lead us to a different interpretation of smiling behavior.

Recap 13.1: Emotion

An (a)_____ is a cognitive experience that is accompanied by a characteristic affective reaction and physiological response. The (b)_____ nervous system becomes activated when an emotion is experienced. (c)_____ emotions make us feel better and draw us to the eliciting stimulus, whereas (d)_____ emotions are accompanied by feelings of anxiety, sadness, or hostility. According to the (e)_____-_____ theory of emotion, a stimulus produces a physiological response, which in turn produces an emotion. According to the (f)_____-_____ theory of emotion, a stimulus produces an emotion, which in turn produces a physiological response. According to the (g)_____-_____ theory of emotion, an individual must experience physiological arousal and have an appropriate cognitive attribution in order to experience an emotion. According to Zajonc's (h)_____ theory of emotion, smiling causes blood to drain rapidly from the face, (i)_____ the blood in the cavernous sinus, which produces a positive emotion. In contrast, frowning causes blood to pool in the face, which (j)_____ the temperature of the brain and produces a negative emotion.

Emotional Pathways in the Central Nervous System

The theories presented in the previous section all emphasize physiological factors that produce emotions. These physiological factors are associated with activation of certain regions of the central and peripheral nervous systems. Thus far, you have learned that activation of two divisions of the peripheral nervous system, the sympathetic and somatic nervous systems, produces the physical reactions that we associate with emotions. In this section, we will examine the brain regions that initiate and control the experience of emotion.

The Locus Coeruleus

At this point, you should be familiar with the location and function of the **locus coeruleus** because we've discussed this structure in a number of prior chapters, including the chapter on sleep and consciousness. Recall from Chapter 4 that the locus coeruleus is a hindbrain structure that contains neurons that produce *norepinephrine*, the neurotransmitter responsible for heightened arousal and vigilance. The locus coeruleus receives inputs from many areas of the brain concerned with homeostasis and internal body states, including the hypothalamus (Figure 13.4). Excitation of the locus coeruleus activates the sympathetic nervous system, stimulating the release of norepinephrine throughout the brain *and* the release of the neurohormone **epinephrine** from the adrenal glands (Bremner et al., 1996; Shan & Krukoff, 2001). In turn, the release of epinephrine produces the physical changes that we associate with stimulation of the sympathetic nervous system, such as increased heart and respiration rates, pupil dilation, increased sweating, and changes in blood flow.

locus coeruleus: hindbrain structure that produces norepinephrine and regulates arousal

epinephrine: a neurohormone, also known as adrenaline, that is released by the adrenal gland and activates the sympathetic nervous system

Figure 13.4 The locus coeruleus
The locus coeruleus receives information about the internal state of the body from all parts of the brain including the hypothalamus. Excitation of the locus coeruleus activates the sympathetic nervous system, stimulating the release of norepinephrine throughout the brain and the release of epinephrine from the adrenal gland.

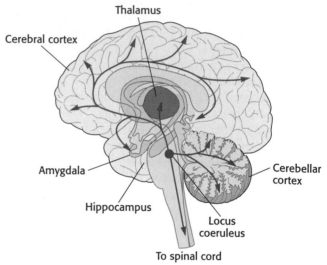

The Limbic System

Early investigators who studied emotion attempted to identify the brain structures responsible for the experience of emotion. Cannon (1927) proposed that the thalamus initiates emotions, although Bard, his former student, disagreed and suggested that the hypothalamus produces emotions, based on his research involving hypothalamic lesions in rats (Bard, 1934). As a result of a large body of lesioning research in animals, Papez (1937) concluded that a pathway between subcortical structures in the forebrain is responsible for generating emotions. According to Papez, these structures include the *hypothalamus, anterior thalamus, cingulate gyrus,* and *hippocampus.* The pathway between this group of brain structures is sometimes referred to as the *Papez circuit*. Another, more lateral circuit that mediates emotional behavior was described by Yakovlev (1948). Yakovlev's circuit includes the *orbitofrontal cortex,* the *anterior temporal cortex, amygdala,* and *dorsomedial thalamus.* However, in 1949, Paul MacLean used the term **limbic system** to refer to the two circuits (that is, the Papez and Yakovlev circuits) that are involved in emotion, a term that most scholars continue to use today.

The structures that comprise the limbic system are located beneath the cerebral cortex, in the white matter of the cerebrum. They include the **hippocampus,** the **septum** and its adjacent neighbor, the **nucleus accumbens,** and the **amygdala.** Many investigators also consider the **olfactory bulb** to be a part of the limbic sys-

limbic system: the two brain circuits that regulate emotions

hippocampus: structure in the limbic system associated with emotions and consolidation of long-term memories

septum: structure in the limbic system associated with positive emotions

nucleus accumbens: a forebrain nucleus where dopamine is released, producing pleasurable feelings

amygdala: an almond-shaped structure located in the medial temporal lobe that is implicated in the experience of negative emotions

olfactory bulb: brain structure that receives olfactory information directly from the receptors and processes this information before relaying it on to the cerebral cortex

Figure 13.5 The limbic system

(a) The major structures of the limbic system. (b) The limbic system situated in the human brain.

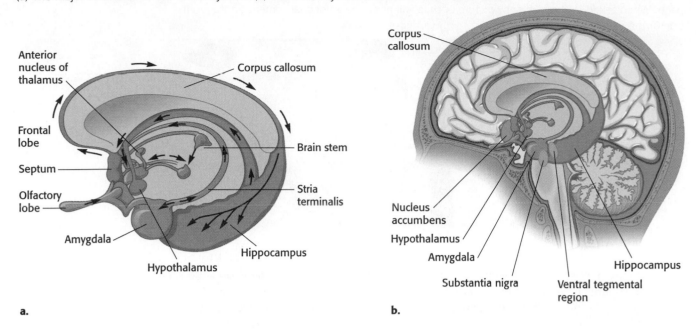

a.

b.

tem, based on research studying rats, although it's not clear that the sense of smell plays an important role in human experience of emotion. In addition, parts of the prefrontal cortex, the cingulate gyrus, the hypothalamus, the thalamus, and the midbrain are also considered to be part of the limbic system (Figure 13.5). PET studies of human participants who were exposed to different stimuli, such as films, pictures, and emotional memories, that produced feelings of happiness, sadness, or disgust revealed that the thalamus, hypothalamus, midbrain, and prefrontal cortex are all activated when an individual is experiencing positive or negative emotions (Lane et al., 1996, 1997). In contrast, Richard Lane and his colleagues (1997) observed that the amygdala was activated with negative emotions but not with positive emotions. Thus, particular emotions appear to activate different parts of the limbic system.

The Cerebral Cortex

Whereas early theorists in the first half of the 20th century focused on the role of subcortical structures in the expression of emotions, investigators over the past 3 decades have come to recognize the important role that the cerebral cortex plays in the experience of emotions. Modern techniques such as electroencephalography and brain imaging have demonstrated that both anterior and posterior cortical regions interact with subcortical areas to enable us to experience emotions. A number of investigators have distinguished the *expression* of emotion from the *understanding* and *feeling* of emotion because each function is processed in different areas of the cerebrum. The understanding and expression of emotion appear to be processed in the *right hemisphere* (Heller, Nitschke, & Miller, 1998). In contrast, both hemispheres are involved in the feeling of emotion.

For example, a variety of research methodologies have demonstrated that the *left* frontal lobe is active when a person is feeling a positive emotion, whereas the frontal regions of the *right* hemisphere are more active when a person is experiencing a negative emotion (Davidson, 1992). Patients with lesions in the left hemisphere often show signs of anxiety or sadness following a stroke or surgery (Gianotti, 1972; Goldstein, 1948). In contrast, euphoria often results in patients with right hemisphere lesions (Babinski, 1914; Denny-Brown, Meyers, & Horenstein, 1952; Gianotti, 1972; Heller et al., 1998). During Wada tests, which are used

Figure 13.6 Examples of sad and happy pictures drawn by children

When asked to draw a sad picture, a child will place the emotional content on the left side of the page. When asked to draw a happy picture, a child will place the emotional content on the right side of the page.

to determine hemispheric dominance for speech, selective anesthesia of the cerebral hemispheres is produced by injection of short-acting barbiturate into the left or right carotid artery. When the barbiturate is injected into the left carotid artery, anesthetizing the left hemisphere, patients exhibit sadness or anxiety. Injection into the right carotid artery, which produces short-term anesthesia of the right cerebral hemisphere, induces euphoria in the affected patient (Rossi & Rosadini, 1967).

Wendy Heller (1994) reasoned that hemispheric differences in processing emotions would be reflected in the way people represent emotion in drawings. That is, she hypothesized that sad images would be drawn on the left side of a piece of paper because sad emotions activate the right hemisphere more, which should direct the eyes to the left. She also hypothesized that happy images would be displaced to the right side of a page due to the higher level of activation of the left hemisphere by positive emotions. She asked 200 children between the ages of 5 and 12 to draw a picture of something that made them happy and another picture showing something that made them sad. As Heller predicted, sad images were drawn left of center, and happy images were drawn right of center (Heller, 1994). Figure 13.6 illustrates examples of sad and happy pictures drawn by the children in Heller's studies.

The Medial Forebrain Bundle and Periventricular Circuits

Two different circuits in the brain are implicated in the regulation of positive and negative emotions. Positive emotions are associated with stimulation of the **medial forebrain bundle,** a bundle of axons that courses through the center of the forebrain. In contrast, negative emotions, or emotions of self-preservation, are associated with activation of the amygdala and the **periventricular** and **periaqueductal gray regions** of the diencephalon and midbrain. The periventricular region of the diencephalon is located in the hypothalamus and is involved in mediating the stress response to noxious stimuli, as you will learn in Chapter 14. The periaqueductal gray region is found in the midbrain, and it contains neurons that produce *endorphins* and *GABA*—neurotransmitters implicated in the experience of negative emotions, such as fear and anxiety. These pathways are not the same circuits as those described by Papez and Yakovlev. In fact, a large number of circuits control the experience of emotion in the brain. On the basis of his and others' research on emotion, Jaak Panksepp at Bowling Green State University has proposed that a separate circuit exists for each emotion (Panksepp, 1989, 1992).

Because different areas of the brain are activated by different emotions, we will consider the brain mechanisms involved in regulating negative and positive emo-

medial forebrain bundle: a bundle of neurons that courses through the center of the forebrain, which is associated with positive emotions

periventricular gray region: a region of the hypothalamus located next to the third ventricle, which is associated with the expression of negative emotions

periaqueductal gray region: a region in the midbrain that contains neurons that produce endorphins and GABA

tions separately. In the next section, we will examine the brain mechanisms involved in the production and regulation of the emotions of self-preservation, that is, the fight-or-flight emotions.

Recap 13.2: Emotional Pathways in the Central Nervous System

Neurons in the (a)_____ _____ release norepinephrine and activate the sympathetic nervous system in response to an emotional stimulus. Structures in the (c)_____ circuit include the hypothalamus, anterior thalamus, and cingulate gyrus. Structures in (d)_____ circuit include the orbitofrontal cortex, the anterior temporal cortex, amygdala, and dorsomedial thalamus. The term (e)_____ _____ is used to refer to both circuits. The left frontal lobe is activated during (f)_____ emotions, and the right frontal lobe is activated during (g)_____ emotions. Positive emotions are also associated with a bundle of axons that run through the center of the forebrain called the (h)_____ _____ bundle. Activation of the periventricular and periaqueductal (i)_____ regions are associated with negative emotions.

Negative Emotions

The emotions of self-preservation motivate an individual to deal with an unpleasant or aversive stimulus by eliminating it or avoiding it. Thus, *rage* and *fear* are two prime examples of negative emotions. We will focus our discussion on these two emotions in this section. The amygdala plays an important role in regulating the expression of rage and fear. For example, rage is often expressed as *aggression*, an emotional response that involves attacking a noxious stimulus. Before moving to a discussion of rage, aggression, and fear, let's examine the role of the amygdala in the generation of negative emotions.

The Role of the Amygdala

When we consider negative emotions, the role of the *amygdala* cannot be ignored. The amygdala is an almond-shaped structure located in the medial temporal lobe, adjacent to the hippocampus (Figure 13.7). It is comprised of a number of nuclei, including the lateral nucleus, the basolateral nucleus, the accessory basal nucleus, and the central nucleus. Research with rats has demonstrated that the *lateral nucleus of the amygdala* receives sensory information from many parts of the brain, including the thalamus and the cerebrum. In turn, the lateral nucleus processes this information and sends it to the other nuclei in the amygdala. These nuclei relay this information to other parts of the brain, such as the basal ganglia, for action. For example, when sensory information about a noxious stimulus is transmitted to the lateral nucleus, the lateral nucleus relays that information to the *central nucleus*, which activates neurons in the brain stem, causing autonomic arousal (Le Doux, 1994). The central nucleus also relays

Figure 13.7 The amygdala
The amygdala is an almond-shaped structure located in the medial temporal lobe.

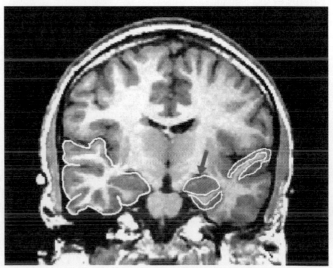

information to the *periaqueductal gray area* of the midbrain to produce *defensive reactions* in response to the noxious stimulus (LeDoux, 1995).

Although we know a great deal about the anatomy and physiology of the amygdala in animals, very little is known about how the amygdala functions in emotional behavior in humans (Aggleton, 1992). We assume that the human amygdala functions similarly to the way the amygdala functions in rats. In the example that I used earlier in this chapter, we might assume that, when I picked up the "dead" snake and then saw that the snake was moving, this visual information was transmitted to the lateral nucleus of my amygdala, which stimulated the central nucleus (Figure 13.7). In response, the central nucleus of my amygdala alerted my locus coeruleus, activating my sympathetic nervous system. Obviously, because I dropped the snake and ran away from it, other motor systems were also activated, probably by way of the amygdala's effect on the *basal ganglia*, which organize and initiate behavior. However, my *prefrontal cortex*, rather than my amygdala, could have organized my response to the snake. Investigators are just beginning to learn about the roles of the cerebrum and the amygdala in the human experience of emotion.

Bilateral damage to the part of the temporal lobe that contains the amygdala produces a bizarre disorder known as **Kluver-Bucy syndrome.** This syndrome was originally described by Kluver and Bucy in their classical studies of bilateral lesions of the anterior temporal lobe (Kluver & Bucy, 1937). Monkeys with bilateral damage to their temporal lobes, which included damage to the amygdala on both sides of the brain, exhibited a loss of fear of their human handlers, a lack of emotional responsiveness, increased and inappropriate sexual behavior, and indiscriminate eating and mouthing of items that are inedible or were previously rejected. This loss of emotionality led a number of investigators to propose that the amygdala plays an important role in emotion (LeDoux, 1992). However, monkeys and people with Kluver-Bucy syndrome have an impaired ability to make discriminations and to associate stimuli with rewards, which tells us that the amygdala is also important in processes that involve learning about consequences. The alterations in emotionality and in eating and sexual behavior seen in Kluver-Bucy syndrome may reflect an impairment in the ability to link stimuli with reward and punishment (Rolls, 1992).

The role of the amygdala in humans for the expression of emotions may actually be limited, compared to its central role in other animals (Halgren, 1992). However, we cannot deny that the amygdala plays some role in human emotions because the rare cases of Kluver-Bucy syndrome indicate that damage to the amygdala disrupts emotional responsiveness. In addition, stimulation of the amygdala in human patients produces fits of uncontrolled rage or feelings of fear (Charney, Deutch, Southwick, & Krystal, 1995; Mark & Ervin, 1975), and PET studies have demonstrated that the amygdala is activated when a person is experiencing fear (Phelps et al., 2001).

Studies of patients with another extremely rare condition, called *Urbach-Wiethe disease*, have demonstrated that the amygdala also plays an important role in emotional memories. Urbach-Wiethe disease involves bilateral brain damage that is limited to the amygdala. Compared to healthy controls, patients with this disorder have markedly impaired declarative memories for emotionally arousing events (Markowitsch, Calabrese, Wuerker, Durwen, et al., 1994). For example, individuals with Urbach-Wiethe disease had difficulty remembering an emotionally arousing story that was presented to them, whereas they had no problem remembering a neutral story (Adolphs, Cahill, Schul, & Babinsky, 1997). In a study that compared one 30-year-old woman with Urbach-Wiethe disease to 12 brain-damaged patients and 7 healthy controls, the woman with bilateral amygdaloid damage was unable to recognize fear in facial expressions and also had difficulty judging other emotional facial expressions (Adolphs, Tranel, Damasio, & Damasio, 1994). Another patient with Urback-Wiethe disease could not recognize vocal expressions of fears, although he was able to recognize vocal expressions of joy, anger and sadness (Ghika-Schmid et al., 1997). Thus, the amygdala appears to be involved in the recognition of emotions in human facial and vocal expressions.

Kluver-Bucy syndrome: a disorder caused by bilateral damage to the anterior temporal lobe that is characterized by a loss of fear, a lack of emotional responsiveness, inappropriate sexual behavior, and indiscriminate mouthing of inedible items

In summary, the amygdala appears to stimulate the behavioral response to emotionally arousing stimuli by activating the periaqueductal gray and the basal ganglia. The amygdala also plays an important role in learning about consequences and in forming declarative memories involving emotional events. However, cognitive processes directed by the prefrontal cortex are vital in the expression of human emotions. For example, whether an individual reacts with fear or aggression to a noxious stimulus, such as a snake or stinging insect, is largely a product of the individual's memory, reasoning, and decision-making processes, which are controlled by the prefrontal cortex (Halgren, 1992; LeDoux, 1992).

Rage and Aggression

Human aggression is usually associated with rage, which causes individuals to lash out physically or verbally at others. Most of us, at one time or another, have experienced this emotion. However, some people have uncontrollable bouts of aggressive behavior, in which they strike out at loved ones for little or no reason. Study of these individuals has aided our understanding of the mechanisms underlying rage and aggression.

Head trauma is associated with increased levels of aggression (Kavoussi, Armstad, & Coccaro, 1997). Approximately 70% of patients with brain lesions due to head injury show aggression and increased irritability. Men who batter their spouses are significantly more likely to have suffered head trauma in the past compared to other men. Abnormal CT scans and EEG recordings in the *temporal lobes* are most commonly associated with episodic aggression, in which an individual has bouts of aggressive behavior. Lesions in the *prefrontal cortex* are also associated with increased physical and verbal aggression.

Individuals with **temporal lobe seizures** will sometimes exhibit aggression with little or no provocation (Gloor, 1992; Mark & Ervin, 1975). As with other forms of epileptic seizures, patients with temporal lobe epilepsy will often experience an aura, or altered perceptual episode, immediately before the seizure. They may also show a sudden change in mood or thought, or they may experience physiological symptoms, such as stomach upset, nausea, or pain. An individual with temporal lobe epilepsy will often exhibit vacant staring and lip smacking or chewing movements at the onset of the seizure. As the seizure progresses, the individual will become aggressive, striking out at the nearest individual or object. Vernon Mark and Frank Ervin (1975) reported the case of one patient, a quiet, reserved 34-year-old engineer, who experienced episodic bouts of aggression due to temporal lobe seizures:

> The assault against his wife characteristically began after a complaint of severe abdominal or facial pain. During the ensuing conversation, he would seize upon some innocuous remark and interpret it as an insult. At first, he would try to ignore what she had said, but could not help brooding; and the more he thought about it, the surer he felt that his wife no longer loved him and was "carrying on with a neighbor." Eventually he would reproach his wife for these faults, and she would hotly deny them. Her denials were enough to set him off into a frenzy of violence. He would sometimes pick his wife up and throw her against the wall; he did this to her even when she was pregnant. He did the same thing to his children. These periods of rage usually lasted for 5 to 6 minutes, after which he would be overcome with remorse and grief and sob as uncontrollably as he had raged. He would then go to sleep for a half-hour or so and wake up feeling refreshed and eager to work. (Mark & Ervin, 1975, pp. 93–94)

This patient was treated with antiepileptic medications, which are used to treat seizures, but these did not stop the seizures and bouts of aggression. Typically, antiepileptic medications are the first line of treatment in patients with temporal lobe epilepsy, and they are often successful in halting the attacks. Stereotaxic surgery was performed on the patient whose case was just described, and small bilateral lesions were made in the amygdala. Following surgery, this patient never had an episode of aggression again. Because antiepileptic medications are usually successful in controlling temporal lobe seizures, surgery is rarely performed. However, surgery may be indicated when medication does not work in preventing seizures.

temporal lobe seizures: epileptic seizures caused by damage to the temporal lobes, which produce aggressive behaviors with little or no provocation

It may be that Walter, whose case was described at the beginning of this chapter, also suffered an epileptic seizure in his limbic system at the time that he drowned the unsuspecting fisherman (LoPiccolo, 1996). He first experienced visual hallucinations of two dogs fighting, and hallucinations and confused thinking often precede a temporal lobe seizure. After he began his aggressive attack, no amount of reasoning or pleading could make him stop. In humans, the frontal lobes generally function to hold emotions and emotional behavior in check. In Walter and others experiencing seizures in the limbic system, the electrical storm produced by the seizures appears to disrupt the usual communications between the frontal lobes and the limbic system, allowing the limbic system to produce unchecked aggressive behavior. However, we are still far from understanding how the frontal lobes control the limbic system and how the limbic system generates aggression.

Research with cats has shown that the medial hypothalamus and the periaqueductal gray in the midbrain mediates rage behavior when a cat is attacked (that is, defensive rage behavior). The lateral hypothalamus mediates predatory attack behavior in cats, as when a cat attacks a mouse (Gregg & Siegel, 2001). The amygdala, hippocampus, and areas of the frontal lobe, including the cingulate gyrus and the prefrontal cortex, communicate with these areas of the hypothalamus and may regulate the intensity of the rage and attack behavior.

Although the brain mechanisms that mediate aggression in people are not well understood, we do know quite a bit about the effects of neurotransmitters and certain hormones on aggression. *Serotonin, norepinephrine, dopamine,* and certain *hormones* play an important role in controlling aggression. Let's examine the relation of each of these neurochemicals with aggressive behavior.

Serotonin

Research with cats, rats, and mice, as well as humans, has demonstrated that serotonin plays a central role in the inhibition of aggression (Kavoussi et al., 1997). Low levels of serotonin are associated with aggressive behavior in every species studied. People who have histories of uncontrolled aggressive behavior have low levels of the serotonin metabolite *5-hydroxyindolacetic acid* (5-HIAA) in their cerebral spinal fluid (Asberg et al., 1976; Brown et al., 1989; Linnoila et al., 1989). Suicide (aggression toward oneself) is also associated with low levels of serotonin or 5-HIAA (Mann, Arango, & Underwood, 1990; Roy, Dejong, & Linnoila, 1989). Genetic mutations that produce a faulty enzyme or a missing 5-HT receptor, resulting in a disturbance in serotonin function, have been related to increased aggression in mice and humans (Kavoussi et al., 1997). In addition, drugs that increase serotonin activity in the brain have been demonstrated to reduce aggressive behavior.

Norepinephrine

High levels of norepinephrine activity in rats, mice, monkeys, and humans are associated with increased aggression. For example, human subjects who were chronic "Ecstasy" users had significantly more aggressive responses and higher norepinephrine blood levels than control subjects in an experiment designed to elicit aggression (Gerra et al., 2001). In addition, increased levels of norepinephrine receptor binding have been measured in people who died as a result of violent suicide, compared with those who died in accidents (Arango et al., 1992). Increased norepinephrine activity in the brain is also related to an increase in externally directed aggression (Siever & Davis, 1991). Further evidence for the role of norepinephrine in aggression comes from studies that demonstrate that drugs that block norepinephrine receptors reduce aggressive behavior (Kavoussi et al., 1997).

Dopamine

Increased dopamine activity causes animals to respond aggressively to environmental stimuli. This increase in dopamine activity may be the result of supersensitive dopamine receptors, which have a greater-than-normal response to dopamine

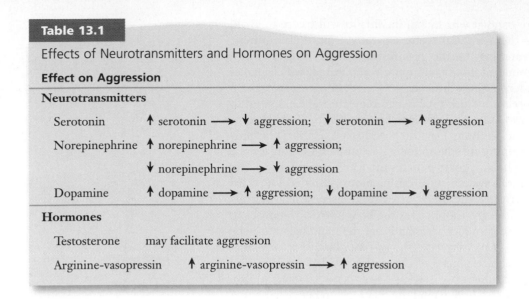

Table 13.1

Effects of Neurotransmitters and Hormones on Aggression

Effect on Aggression	
Neurotransmitters	
Serotonin	↑ serotonin ⟶ ↓ aggression; ↓ serotonin ⟶ ↑ aggression
Norepinephrine	↑ norepinephrine ⟶ ↑ aggression;
	↓ norepinephrine ⟶ ↓ aggression
Dopamine	↑ dopamine ⟶ ↑ aggression; ↓ dopamine ⟶ ↓ aggression
Hormones	
Testosterone	may facilitate aggression
Arginine-vasopressin	↑ arginine-vasopressin ⟶ ↑ aggression

(Winchel & Stanley, 1991). Tranquilizers that reduce dopamine activity in the brain are used to control aggression in agitated patients (Fava, 1997).

Testosterone

Testosterone appears to be associated with aggressive behavior, although the nature of that association is unclear (Kavoussi et al., 1997). For example, fighting among male animals increases following puberty, when testosterone levels are higher. Studies comparing men who commit violent crimes to those who commit nonviolent crimes revealed that violent offenders have significantly higher testosterone levels. However, whereas drugs that block androgen activity are useful in treating paraphilias, as you learned in Chapter 12, these antiandrogens are not effective in reducing aggressive behavior. Thus, testosterone may facilitate aggressive behavior, but it does not appear to control aggression.

Arginine-vasopressin has also been implicated in the expression of aggressive behavior. This hormone is produced in the hypothalamus and has its aggressive effects in the anterior hypothalamus. Whereas serotonin inhibits aggressive behavior, arginine-vasopressin promotes aggression (Delville et al., 1998). Increased aggression in people is associated with high levels of arginine-vasopressin and low levels of the serotonin metabolite 5-HIAA in human cerebrospinal fluid (Coccaro et al., 1998).

Table 13.1 summarizes the effects of neurotransmitters and hormones on aggressive behavior.

arginine-vasopressin: a hormone produced by the paraventricular nucleus that regulates salt and water balance and increases ACTH release when working with CRH

Fear

Ned Kalin and Steven Shelton at the University of Wisconsin have been studying the development of fear in infant rhesus monkeys in order to understand the brain mechanisms that underlie this complex emotion. These investigators have found that young monkeys make three different fear responses when they are separated from their mothers (Figure 13.8). When frightened, the infants cry to their mothers, making cooing sounds, or they sit very still (freeze) to avoid detection by a predator, or they make a threatening face, baring their teeth and growling (Kalin & Shelton, 1989). The fear response that the baby monkeys make depends on the environmental stimuli. That is, if they are separated from their mothers and left alone, they coo. If they are separated from their mothers and can see a

Figure 13.8 Fear responses by monkeys
When a baby monkey is separated from its mother and is stared at, it will bare its teeth and growl.

human who does not make eye contact with them, the infants will freeze to avoid detection. If a human stares at them when they are separated from their mothers, the young monkeys make threatening, hostile gestures toward the human. Thus, fear responses, even of very young monkeys, are quite complicated, which makes identifying their biological underpinnings difficult.

Three structures in the forebrain work together to regulate the expression of fear: the *prefrontal cortex*, the *amygdala*, and the *hypothalamus* (Bakshi, Shelton, & Kalin, 2000; Kalin, 1993; Kalin, Shelton, Davidson, & Kelley, 2001). The prefrontal cortex interprets the meaning of environmental stimuli and organizes the fear response to those stimuli. The amygdala initiates the fear response, including stimulating the sympathetic nervous system and arousing motor systems. The third structure, the hypothalamus, activates the body's stress responses, which permits the body to defend itself. You will learn more about the body's stress responses in Chapter 14. In the meantime, you should understand that the hypothalamus activates the *pituitary gland*, which in turn stimulates the *adrenal gland* to release hormones, called *steroids*, that alter the responses of the cardiovascular, nervous, and immune systems to the fearful stimulus.

Investigators are just beginning to understand the relationship between neurotransmitters and fear. Kalin and his colleagues have determined that two neurotransmitter pathways, those involving **endogenous opiates** and those involving receptors for **benzodiazepines,** are associated with fear responses. Recall from Chapter 3 that benzodiazepines are minor tranquilizers that bind with particular sites on GABA receptors. Benzodiazepines are antianxiety agents that produce a feeling of calm. A decrease in activity in the endogenous opiate pathway causes increased cooing behavior but has no effect on freezing or threatening behavior when an individual is afraid (Kalin, 1993). As you might expect, an increase in activity in endogenous opiate receptors (for example, produced by an injection of morphine) decreases cooing behavior but again has no effect on defensive responses. In contrast, increased activity at benzodiazepine receptors has no effect on cooing, but it does decrease freezing and threatening behaviors in response to a fearful stimulus. Thus, endorphins appear to mediate crying behavior when an individual is afraid, and GABA mediates freezing and threatening behaviors.

endogenous opiates: neurotransmitters that bind with opiate receptors
benzodiazepines: minor tranquilizers that stimulate GABA activity and produce a feeling of calm

The responses that animals make to threatening or frightening stimuli vary according to their species. For example, as you've just learned, a baby rhesus monkey will cry, freeze, or make threatening gestures when confronted with a fear-inducing stimulus, depending on the nature of the stimulus. Robert Bolles (1970) called these defensive responses *species-specific defense reactions*. Michael Fanselow and his colleagues at UCLA and at the University of Tüebingen in Germany have spent many years examining how the brain in a rat controls species-specific defense reactions, particularly how it selects specific responses to different stimuli. Their research suggests that the amygdala in rats activates a freezing reaction in response to stimuli that elicit low or moderate fear, whereas the midbrain organizes vigorous defensive responses, such as defensive attack, in response to stimuli that elicit high levels of fear (Fanselow, DeCola, De Oca, & Landeira-Fernandez, 1995; Fendt & Fanselow, 1999). The *amygdala* and the *periaqueductal gray area* appear to work together to select different modes of defensive behavior in rats, depending on the nature of the threatening stimulus.

Disorders Associated with Negative Emotions

Negative emotions are accompanied by defensive fight-or-flight reactions. Let's consider what would happen if one of these reactions went awry, as in the case when an individual experiences too much fight (that is, excessive aggression) or too much flight (excessive anxiety).

Aggressive Disorders

Pathologic anger and aggression are associated with a number of brain disorders, which are listed in Table 13.2. Typically, treatment of these disorders is the physi-

Table 13.2

Brain Disorders Associated with Pathologic Aggression

▶ Dementia	▶ Autism
▶ Huntington's disease	▶ Seizure disorder
▶ Brain injury	▶ Drug or alcohol intoxication
▶ Korsakoff's syndrome	▶ Drug or alcohol withdrawal
▶ Brain tumors	▶ Premenstrual dysphoric disorder
▶ Mental retardation	▶ Attention deficit disorder

Source: Fava (1997)

cian's primary goal. Sometimes the treatment, as for bipolar disorder or seizure disorder, will prevent the occurrence of attacks of aggression. However, when the medication given to treat the primary disorder does not stop aggressive behavior, additional medications are administered. Recall that low levels of serotonin and high levels of norepinephrine are implicated in aggressive behavior. Therefore, drugs that *increase serotonin* activity, such as *serotonin specific reuptake inhibitors*, and those that *decrease norepinephrine* activity, such as medications that *block norepinephrine receptors* (for example, adrenergic *beta-blockers*) are prescribed to control aggression and violent behavior (Fava, 1997).

The diagnosis of **intermittent explosive disorder** is given when the pathologic aggression is not associated with another brain disorder. According to the *Diagnostic and Statistical Manual* of the American Psychiatric Association (*DSM-IV*), intermittent explosive disorder is characterized by episodes of uncontrolled, aggressive outbursts that result in assaults causing personal injury or destruction of property (American Psychiatric Association, 1994). The cause of this disorder is unknown. Treatment of intermittent explosive disorder usually involves counseling or psychotherapy, in addition to administration of drugs, such as serotonin reuptake inhibitors, beta-blockers, or tranquilizers that decrease dopamine activity.

Self-mutilation, or an act of deliberate harm to one's own body, occurs in a number of populations, including mentally retarded people, psychotic patients, individuals in prisons, and people with personality disorders, such as borderline personality disorder (which we will discuss in Chapter 15). Typically, this self-injurious behavior is done without the aid of another person, and the injury results in tissue damage (Winchel & Stanley, 1991). Like other acts of aggression, self-mutilation is associated with low levels of serotonin and high levels of dopamine activity. This disorder is difficult to treat successfully, especially when it occurs in people with personality disorders.

intermittent explosive disorder: a disorder characterized by episodes of uncontrolled, aggressive outbursts that result in assaults causing personal injury or property damage

Anxiety Disorders

Uncontrolled bouts of fear and overactivation of the fear system have been implicated in the development of **anxiety disorders.** Anxiety is sometimes difficult to distinguish from fear. Freud, for example, did not make a distinction between fear and anxiety in his writings. Most authors base their distinctions on the stimuli that arouse fear versus anxiety and the responses to these stimuli. For example, *fear* might be described as a realistic, defensive response to a threatening stimulus that is present, whereas *anxiety* might be described as an overly fearful response made to a stimulus that most would not consider threatening or to a threatening stimulus that is not present and perhaps unlikely to occur. Anxiety also has a cognitive component that is missing in a fear response. This cognitive component involves an awareness of the changes occurring in the body, such as pounding heart, dizziness, and visual blurring (Craig, Brown, & Baum, 1995).

anxiety disorders: disorders characterized by uncontrolled bouts of fear or overactivation of the fear system

We have all experienced anxiety at one time or another, because anxiety serves to alert us to future or impending danger and allows us to prepare for this danger. (Fear, on the other hand, alerts us to danger that is present and must be dealt with immediately.) However, anxiety becomes pathologic when it disrupts normal behavior. That is, when an individual makes repeated inappropriate responses to some unknown or unreal threat, an anxiety disorder is present. A number of anxiety disorders have been identified, including *generalized anxiety disorder, panic disorder, phobias, obsessive-compulsive disorder,* and *post-traumatic stress disorder.* We will examine post-traumatic stress disorder in detail in Chapter 14. In the meantime, let's look at the remaining types of anxiety disorders and discuss the biological basis of each.

Generalized anxiety disorder is a syndrome characterized by excessive apprehension about unknown future events. The affected individual will report feeling a sense of impending doom, as if something terrible is going to happen. These feelings are accompanied by persistent, bothersome physical symptoms, such as trembling or twitching, shortness of breath, pounding or palpitating heart, profuse sweating, nausea, or difficulty concentrating. These symptoms are all associated with activation of the sympathetic nervous system.

generalized anxiety disorder: a syndrome characterized by excessive apprehension about unknown future events

Panic disorder is characterized by bouts of intense fear or terror that are unpredictable and appear to occur "out of the blue." That is, the onset of panic attacks does not appear to correlate with environmental stimuli. The attacks can be so severe and incapacitating that affected individuals may be unable to leave their homes and may feel as if they are going to die or going crazy. A person with panic disorder experiences symptoms of autonomic arousal during a panic attack, including trembling, dizziness, chest pains, breathing difficulties, increased heart rate, or faintness. Some investigators have suggested that panic attacks take place because of an instability in the brain's fight–flight mechanism, which produces bouts of unprovoked autonomic arousal and an intense desire to escape or flee (Deakin, 1998).

panic disorder: a disorder characterized by bouts of intense fear or terror that are unpredictable and appear to occur "out of the blue"

Many individuals with panic disorder become anxious when exercising, which indicates an abnormality in lactate metabolism that affects acid–base balance. In fact, an injection of sodium lactate produces panic attacks in 50–70% of individuals with panic disorder and in less than 10% of people without the disorder (Liebowitz et al., 1984; Pohl et al., 1988). The mechanism that produces panic attacks is unclear, although lactate may cause hyperventilation, which in turn induces a panic attack (Stein & Uhde, 1997). It may be that people with panic disorder are especially sensitive to carbon dioxide levels in their blood and that changes in carbon dioxide levels produce hyperventilation, which elicits a panic attack.

Panic disorder can also be accompanied by **phobias,** particularly *agoraphobia.* Phobias are intense fears generated by stimuli that most people do not consider to be overly threatening. Three classes of phobias have been distinguished: *agoraphobia, social phobias,* and *specific phobias. Agoraphobia* refers to a disorder in which affected individuals feel tremendous anxiety when they are in places or situations where they can't easily escape or be helped, such as riding in a jet or standing in the line at the grocery store. Some people with panic disorder come to fear these situations, especially if they experience a panic attack while in the situations, and will avoid them. In fact, some people with agoraphobia are so anxious that they cannot leave their homes, even if accompanied by a loved one whom they trust.

phobias: intense fears generated by specific stimuli

Social phobias are characterized by an overwhelming fear of being in situations in which one might be evaluated or scrutinized by others. In contrast, *specific phobias* are unreasonable, excessive fears of a particular object or situation, such as needles. As with other anxiety disorders, phobias are accompanied by symptoms of autonomic arousal, including dizziness, nausea and other gastrointestinal symptoms, chest pain and heart palpitations, and loss of bladder or bowel control.

Obsessive-compulsive disorders are characterized by repetitive thoughts, or obsessions, that intrude into a person's consciousness and ritualized behaviors that are performed repeatedly (compulsions). These obsessions and compulsions disrupt the affected individual's normal activities. For example, a person with obsessive-compulsive disorder may have to wash his hands dozens of times a day,

obsessive-compulsive disorder: an anxiety disorder characterized by repetitive thoughts and ritualized behaviors that are performed repeatedly

Obsessive-Compulsive Disorder

Ted was a college sophomore on academic probation when he first visited the university counselor. He had just failed another test in his American history class, and he knew he needed help. Before he left for his appointment with the counselor, Ted vacuumed his apartment. He started to go out the door when he noticed a piece of fuzz on the carpet. Without hesitation, he got the vacuum back out and went over the entire carpet in his three-room apartment again, this time moving all the furniture, including the couch and heavy dresser. Then Ted found a crumb on the carpet in the hallway. He knew he had to go, but he felt he must vacuum the apartment one more time to make sure it was really clean. Finally, he went out the door, 10 minutes late for his appointment.

The counselor seemed very friendly and warm, which put Ted at ease. His problem was quite embarrassing, but he found it was easy to tell the counselor about how crazy he felt. Ted told her that he was afraid he was going to flunk out of school. The counselor asked him about his study habits. That was the problem, Ted admitted. He tried to study, but he couldn't study unless the apartment was "in order." Ted explained that he couldn't study unless the carpet was immaculately clean. He couldn't bear to have even a speck of dust on the floor, so he vacuumed the rug over and over.

After he was certain that the carpet was clean, he set up his desk to study. Ted owned about 50 pens, which he arranged by color and size on top of his desk. The pens had to be lined up straight, in a row. If one pen looked crooked, he had to start all over again, lining up the pens carefully, all parallel, all in a row. This process often took over an hour. If a pen happened to fall on the floor, Ted got out the vacuum cleaner to vacuum the area where the pen dropped. When the pens were lined up to his satisfaction, he next arranged the books on his desk, again by size and color. Ted felt that the books had to be perfectly straight and lined up parallel with his pens. By the time he got around to studying, it was usually after 10 P.M., which left him little time to study.

The counselor listened carefully and seemed to understand his dilemma. She talked to him about obsessive-compulsive behaviors, and Ted had to admit that it sounded like his problem in a nutshell. He agreed to see the counselor on a weekly basis to learn to control his compulsions. In addition, the counselor arranged for Ted to begin taking a selective serotonin reuptake inhibitor (SSRI). The SSRI made him feel less anxious when he sat down to study. If the urge to vacuum came over him, Ted found that he could ignore it and focus on his studying. In his sessions with the counselor, Ted learned to identify his compulsions when they occurred, and he began to relabel those troubling thoughts and urges and, thus, gained control over them.

or else he feels extremely anxious. Another person with obsessive-compulsive disorder may have a difficult time leaving for work in the morning because she has to keep checking to make sure the appliances are unplugged. Still another may feel compelled to keep thinking the same words over and over in order to feel secure. Although the individual is aware that the behavior is senseless and disruptive, that individual cannot stop performing it without experiencing a great deal of anxiety and apprehension (see the *Case Study*).

Treatment of Anxiety Disorders

Because activation of the sympathetic nervous system is implicated in all forms of anxiety disorders, drugs that decrease activity of the sympathetic nervous system would be expected to alleviate the symptoms of these disorders (Charney, Bremner, & Redmond, 1995). Some forms of social anxiety are treated successfully with *beta-blockers*, which decrease activity at epinephrine and norepinephrine receptors. However, one of the most effective treatments for anxiety disorders is *imipramine*, a drug that blocks the reuptake of catecholamines and, therefore, increases norepinephrine activity. Likewise, buspirone (trade name Buspar), which acts as both an agonist and antagonist of dopamine as well as an agonist of serotonin, is effective in treating anxiety (Ballenger, 2001; Goldberg & Finnerty, 1979; Paul & Skolnick, 1982; Taylor et al., 1982). It is unclear why these drugs and some other antidepressants, like monoamine oxidase (MAO) inhibitors, can alleviate anxiety disorders.

Benzodiazepines are widely used for the control of anxiety. As you learned earlier in this chapter, benzodiazepines alleviate freezing and other defensive behaviors in baby monkeys. By binding with sites on GABA receptors, benzodiazepines augment the inhibiting activity of GABA throughout the brain. Investigators are uncertain about where the antianxiety actions of GABA occur in the brain, but benzodiazepines are unquestionably successful in reducing anxiety in people (Malizia, Coupland, & Nutt, 1995). It is interesting that alcohol, which also binds with GABA receptors, has an *anxiolytic*, or anxiety-reducing, effect on people, too. This demonstrates that GABA must be an important mediator of anxiety.

However, the symptoms of obsessive-compulsive disorder are *not* alleviated by benzodiazepines. Although individuals with this disorder experience a great deal of anxiety, this anxiety is not reduced by benzodiazepines. Instead, people with obsessive-compulsive disorder get the most relief with a special class of antidepressants that increases serotonin activity in the brain, known as *selective serotonin reuptake inhibitors (SSRIs)*. Figure 13.9 illustrates the change in brain activity in a patient with severe obsessive-compulsive disorder following administration of an SSRI. In contrast, antidepressants that block the reuptake of norepinephrine, such as *desipramine*, do not reduce obsessive-compulsive symptoms. Thus, obsessive-compulsive behaviors appear to be related to decreased serotonin activity in the brain (Baumgarten & Grozdanovic, 1998).

Figure 13.9 Brain activity in a person with obsessive-compulsive disorder

This figure shows PET scans of the brain of a patient with severe obsessive-compulsive disorder. Plane 8 is taken at the level of the basal ganglia, and plane 12 is taken at the level of the nucleus accumbens and the orbital prefrontal cortex. These scans were made before and after six weeks of treatment with an SSRI. The paired-image subtraction method produces the image in the third column, which shows that the basal ganglia, the nucleus accumbens, and the orbital prefrontal cortex are active in obsessive-compulsive disorder. The figures on the far right show (in red) where the differences are most striking.

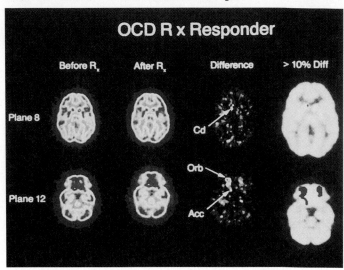

Recap 13.3: Negative Emotions

The (a)_____, located in the medial temporal lobe, appears to play an important role in the activation of negative emotions. Bilateral damage to the medial temporal lobe produces (b)_____-_____ syndrome, a disorder in which affected individuals exhibit a loss of emotionality and an impaired ability to associate stimuli with consequences. Individuals with (c)_____-_____ disease, which is caused by bilateral damage limited to the amygdala, have difficulty remembering emotionally arousing events. Head trauma is associated with increased levels of (d)_____. Individuals with (e)_____ lobe seizures may exhibit aggression with very little or no provocation. (f)_____ levels of serotonin and (g)_____ levels of norepinephrine or dopamine are associated with aggressive behavior. The prefrontal cortex, the amygdala, and the hypothalamus work together to control the expression of (h)_____. The neurotransmitters, (i)_____ and GABA, appear to mediate behaviors associated with fear. Disorders associated with negative emotions include (j)_____ disorders and (k)_____ disorders. Treatment of these disorders involve blocking (l)_____ activity or increasing (m)_____ activity.

Positive Emotions

Euphoria, happiness, being in love, joy—these positive emotions are all associated with stimulation of the **mesolimbic dopamine pathway.** This pathway extends from the *ventral tegmentum* in the midbrain to the *nucleus accumbens* in the forebrain (Figure 13.10). It has projections to the *limbic system* and the *prefrontal cortex*, which allow it to communicate with a large group of structures that regulate emotional behavior. In the diencephalon, this pathway of dopamine fibers is known as the *medial forebrain bundle.*

Research involving the medial forebrain bundle led to the accidental discovery of this pleasure system. In 1954, James Olds and Peter Milner at McGill University were conducting a study of the brain's alerting system in rats. Electrodes were mistakenly inserted in the medial forebrain bundle, and then electrical stimulation was passed down the electrodes into the brains of the rats. Careful observation of the rats that received electrical stimulation of the medial forebrain bundle revealed that the rats found the brain stimulation to be rewarding. When a lever was placed in the cage and the rats trained to press the lever for stimulation of the medial forebrain bundle, the rats pressed the lever almost continuously, up to 5,000 times per hour (Figure 13.11). This indicated that the rats found this brain stimulation to be very pleasurable because a rat will normally make 300 to 500 barpresses per hour for food reinforcement.

Histological examination of the brains of Olds and Milner's rat revealed that the electrodes that produced pleasure were located in the medial forebrain bundle in the hypothalamus (Olds & Milner, 1954). Since that time, investigators have found that pleasurable brain stimulation can be produced in a number of brain regions, from the midbrain to the forebrain, that contain dopamine fibers (Wise & Rompre, 1989). Electrical stimulation of these brain regions in humans has produced two types of sensations: either an intense feeling of sexual arousal ("as if I'm about to have an orgasm") or a feeling of lightheadedness that erased negative thoughts (Hall, Bloom, & Olds, 1977; Olds & Olds, 1969). Thus, pleasure in the human brain is linked to this dopamine pathway.

In addition to dopamine, other neurotransmitters are involved in the generation of pleasurable feelings, including *serotonin, endorphin,* and *GABA.* The **cascade theory of reward** has been proposed to explain how these neurotransmitters work together to produce feelings pleasure or well-being (Blum et al., 1996; Blum et al., 1997). According to this theory, pleasurable feelings arise when dopamine is released and binds with neurons in the nucleus accumbens and hippocampus. However, the cascade begins in the hypothalamus, where serotonin is released by excitatory neurons (Figure 13.12). The release of serotonin causes endorphins to be released in the ventral tegmental area of the midbrain, which inhibits the release of GABA. Normally, GABA inhibits the release of dopamine. But, when endorphins inhibit the release of GABA, no GABA is present in the ventral tegmental area to inhibit the release of dopamine. Therefore, dopamine neurons in the ventral tegmental area are permitted to fire, and they release dopamine at their axonal endplates in the nucleus accumbens and hippocampus, producing a feeling of well-being or pleasure. Many different stimuli can cause the release of dopamine in the nucleus accumbens and hippocampus, including food and water reward, gratifying social experiences, and drugs, such as alcohol, cocaine, nicotine, and opiates.

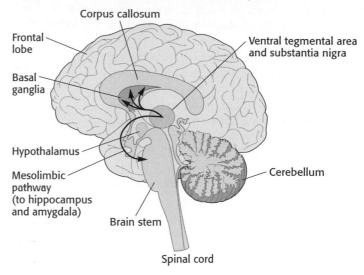

Figure 13.10 The mesolimbic dopamine pathway
The mesolimbic dopamine pathway extends from the ventral tegmental area of the midbrain to the limbic system.

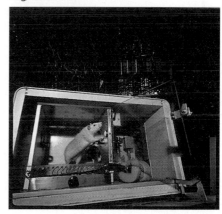

Figure 13.11 Rat exhibiting barpressing behavior

mesolimbic dopamine pathway: a dopamine pathway associated positive emotions that extends from the ventral tegmentum in the midbrain to the limbic system

cascade theory of reward: an explanation of how serotonin, endorphin, and GABA participate in the release of dopamine in the nucleus accumbens and hippocampus to produce feelings of pleasure or well-being

Please remember that the cascade theory of reward is just that: a theory. Although there is considerable experimental evidence that supports this theory, pleasurable feelings may not arise from the mechanism just described. The idea that dopamine is responsible for the experience of pleasure and reward is accepted by most investigators, but some investigators believe that dopamine does not produce feelings of pleasure. Instead, these investigators believe that dopamine functions to draw attention to important stimuli (Gray, Young, & Joseph, 1997; Sarter & Bruno, 1997; Wickelgren, 1997). That is, the release of dopamine in the nucleus accumbens may influence processing in the prefrontal cortex that motivates an individual to pay more attention to certain stimuli and to be more aware of sensory stimulation from these stimuli.

Although the exact brain mechanisms underlying positive emotions are not known, there is no denying that we have the ability to experience a range of pleasurable feelings. Whether we are sharing a laugh with friends, glowing from praise for a job well done, or smiling into the eyes of a loved one, certain brain regions are activated, and certain neurochemicals are released. Most current evidence from lesioning, stimulation, and recording experiments indicates that dopamine plays an important role in most, if not all, rewarding experiences (Koob & Le Moal, 1997; Wise & Rompre, 1989). In addition, PET studies using radioactive ligands that bind with specific receptors have demonstrated that activation of dopamine receptors is important for the experience of pleasure (Volkow, Fowler, & Wang, 1999; Volkow et al., 1999).

Functional imaging studies of human brains have also increased our understanding of positive emotion by revealing which brain structures are active during rewarding episodes. For example, in one PET study (Thut et al., 1997), cerebral blood flow was measured in human participants performing a task during two conditions: one in which they were rewarded by a simple "okay" and the other in which they were rewarded with money. Money reward, which presumably provided more pleasure, was associated with significantly higher levels of activation in the dorsolateral prefrontal cortex and the orbitofrontal cortex. With respect to subcortical structures, a functional MRI study revealed that certain subcortical structures—namely, the nucleus accumbens and amygdala—are activated by pleasurable rewards in human participants (Breiter & Rosen, 1999). A more recent functional MRI study indicated that winning a competitive tournament was associated with activation of the left amygdala and losing was associated with activation of the right amygdala (Zalla et al., 2000). Recall that earlier in this chapter you learned that the *left* hemisphere is active during positive emotions and that the *right* hemisphere is more active during negative emotions. The findings of Zalla and his colleagues reflect the hemispheric asymmetry associated with the processing of positive and negative emotions.

Figure 13.12 The cascade theory of reward

The reward cascade begins with the release of serotonin by neurons in the hypothalamus. The release of serotonin stimulates the release of endorphins in the ventral tegmental region, which inhibits the release of GABA, allowing dopamine to be released in the nucleus accumbens and hippocampus.

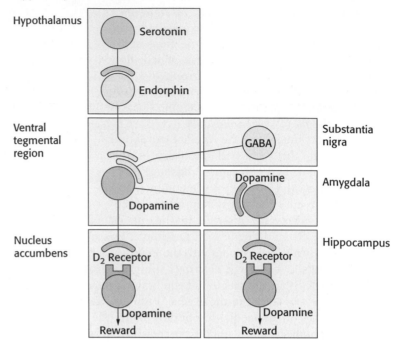

Disorders Associated with Positive Emotions

Disorders associated with positive emotions may present as too much positive emotion, as in the case of *mania*, or too little, as in the case of *depression*. In some cases, an individual may not be able to recognize or experience pleasure, as sometimes happens in *schizophrenia*. One or more monoamines (serotonin, norepinephrine, or dopamine) have been implicated in these disorders. We will discuss these disorders and their biological bases in detail in Chapter 15.

In some individuals, the reward system can fail to function properly, as in the **reward deficiency syndrome.** This disorder is characterized by decreased activity of neurons in the nucleus accumbens and hippocampus, which produces *dysphoria* (the opposite of euphoria), negative emotions, and cravings for substances that can increase dopamine activity. Recall that a variety of substances can induce the release of dopamine in the nucleus accumbens and hippocampus, including food, sex, and drugs. People with reward deficiency syndrome may overeat, take drugs, or engage in risky behaviors, like gambling or unsafe sex, in order to increase dopamine activity in their brains and thus enhance their feeling of well-being. For example, recent research has linked cigarette smoking and nicotine addiction with reward deficiency syndrome (Lerman, 1999).

Kenneth Blum and his colleagues (Blum et al., 1996; Blum et al., 1997; Blum et al., 2000) have determined that a variant of a specific gene, called the *A1 allele*, in some individuals is associated with reward deficiency syndrome. In these individuals, the A1 allele codes for an inactive dopamine D_2 receptor, which is less likely to bind with dopamine and severely reduces excitation of neurons in the nucleus accumbens and hippocampus. Thus, a decrease in the activity of dopamine D_2 receptors can produce the symptoms of reward deficiency syndrome.

A person who abuses a drug over a long period of time can also experience a decrease in the availability of dopamine D_2 receptors (Volkow et al., 1993). For example, chronic exposure to cocaine is associated with a decrease in dopamine D_2 receptors in the brain. This decrease in dopamine D_2 receptors is believed to produce craving for the drug. Thus, people with reward deficiency syndrome will experience dysphoria and cravings due to decreased dopamine activity in the limbic system. Baum suggests that these cravings can lead to a variety of problem behaviors, including *compulsive overeating*, *substance abuse*, or *addiction*.

reward deficiency disorder: a disorder characterized by decreased activity of neurons in the nucleus accumbens and hippocampus, which produces dysphoria and cravings for substances that increase dopamine activity

---

Recap 13.4: Positive Emotions

Positive emotions are associated with the mesolimbic dopamine pathway, known as the (a)_____ _____ bundle in the diencephalon. Stimulation of the medial forebrain bundle is (b)_____, and rats will barpress continuously for it. According to the cascade theory of reward, feelings of pleasure arise when (c)_____ binds with receptors in the hippocampus and nucleus accumbens. According to this theory, release of serotonin by neurons in the hypothalamus causes (d)_____ to be released in the midbrain, which inhibits the release of GABA, producing an increased release of dopamine in the forebrain (e)_____ _____ syndrome is characterized by feelings of dysphoria and craving, which are associated with decreased activity of neurons in the hippocampus and nucleus accumbens.

Addiction

People talk about addictions nearly every day. Someone may say, "He's a real alcoholic," or "She's trying to kick her nicotine addiction." Others speak of being a "chocoholic" or a "workaholic." Still others complain of their addiction to shopping or to exercise. What does it mean to be an addict? Can a person truly be addicted to chocolate or exercise? In this section, we will examine the nature of addiction. In addition, we will look at how an addiction develops and how it is treated.

Definition of Addiction

An **addiction** is a disorder in which the affected person loses control over his or her intake of a particular substance and demonstrates *psychological dependence* and *physical dependence* on the substance. An addicted individual craves the abused substance when it is not available for consumption. This craving is called **psychological dependence.** The abused substance also causes **physical dependence,** a state characterized by severe physical **withdrawal** symptoms, such as tremors, seizures, hallucinations, or nausea, when the individual abstains from taking the substance. Different abused substances are associated with specific withdrawal symptoms (Figure 13.13). *For Further Thought* describes the withdrawal symptoms of chronic alcoholics who stop drinking for more than a few hours.

Many investigators and clinicians disagree over the exact definition of *addiction.* Most require both psychological dependence and physical dependence in their definition. However, this very stringent definition creates problems when some drugs are considered. For example, there is convincing evidence that marijuana produces psychological dependence. But withdrawal symptoms are not observed when a person stops using marijuana because tetrahydrocannabinol is absorbed by fat cells in the body and remains in the body for several weeks after a person abstains. Thus, physical dependence is not seen in chronic marijuana users who stop smoking. For this reason, some authorities claim that marijuana is not addicting.

By the same token, because physical withdrawal symptoms are not apparent when a compulsive shopper refrains from shopping or a compulsive gambler refrains from gambling, most investigators and clinicians assert that an individual cannot really be addicted to shopping or gambling. The term *dependence* is used instead to characterize these compulsive behaviors, as in *shopping dependence* or *gambling dependence.* The same is true for compulsive exercising, which is referred to as *exercise dependence* (Cockerill & Riddington, 1996). People who engage in obligatory exercise spend most of their waking hours either exercising or planning their next run or next weight-training session, that is, thinking about their next opportunity to exercise even when they are not actually exercising, often at a great cost to their family life or career. However, even though some people will organize their

addiction: a disorder in which the affected person lose control over intake of a particular substance and demonstrates psychological dependence and physical dependence

psychological dependence: craving or discomfort experienced when a substance is not available for consumption

physical dependence: a state characterized by severe physical withdrawal symptoms when an individual abstains from taking an abused substance

withdrawal: severe physical symptoms, such as tremors, seizures, hallucinations or nausea, associated with abstinence from an abused substance

Figure 13.13 Withdrawal

(a) Drug intake is sporadic at first and is accompanied by positive mood changes. When drug dependence develops, drug intake becomes more regular, and negative mood changes are experienced when the drug is not available for consumption. Withdrawal from the drug is accompanied by physical dependence (which is short-term) and psychological dependence (which is long-term). (b) Although withdrawal from morphine and ethanol are accompanied by distinctly different withdrawal symptoms, dysphoria is associated with both.

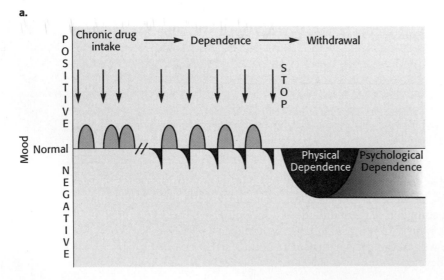

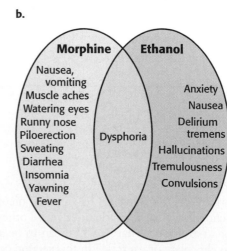

Withdrawal from Alcohol

When a person abuses alcohol for a long period of time, changes take place in that person's brain that lead to physical dependence. People who are physically dependent on alcohol will develop withdrawal symptoms when they stop drinking for even a few hours, and these symptoms can be fatal. Every year, thousands of people die due to alcohol withdrawal (USDHHS, 1987). Three phases of alcohol withdrawal have been identified, based on their time of onset after a person has stopped drinking.

Phase I occurs within a few hours after drinking has stopped. In Phase I, a person develops uncontrollable shakes, profuse sweating, and feelings of agitation and weakness. That person may also complain of headache, nausea, vomiting, and abdominal cramps. If the abstaining individual goes more than a few hours without alcohol, auditory and visual hallucinations may be experienced. A person in Phase I also feels an overwhelming urge to resume drinking, and many alcoholics begin drinking again when Phase I withdrawal symptoms occur, avoiding the more severe and life-threatening withdrawal symptoms associated with Phase II and III.

Phase II occurs within 24 hours of abstaining from alcohol. Grand mal seizures, in which a person loses consciousness, are seen in this phase. Some people in this phase of alcohol withdrawal will have only one seizure, whereas some suffer severe seizures that continue without interruption until treated by a medical professional. Other alcoholics who abstain from alcohol do not have any seizures at all in Phase II.

Phase III occurs after 30 or more hours of abstention from alcohol. In this stage, the individual is extremely agitated and confused, is disoriented for time and place, and suffers from frightening hallucinations. Very often, the alcoholic in Phase III of withdrawal will feel as if bugs are crawling on his or her skin and clothing, or the individual will experience visual hallucinations of bugs or small animals crawling about. Physically, the person may have an extremely high fever and tachycardia (abnormally rapid heart rate). This phase may last for three or four days, if untreated, and is often referred to as delirium tremens (DTs). This is the stage during which an alcoholic in withdrawal is most likely to die, due to very high fever, heart failure, or self-injury resulting from delusions and hallucinations. Initial treatment for alcohol withdrawal normally includes antiseizure medications, including antianxiety agents such as benzodiazepines, and drugs to treat fever, dehydration, and other physical symptoms, as well as supportive psychotherapy.

lives around these compulsive activities (shopping, gambling, exercising), with devastating effects on family and work, there is little consensus as to whether these behaviors constitute addictions.

Role of Neurotransmitters in Addiction

Drugs that are frequently abused, such as *alcohol*, *cocaine*, or *opiates* (for example, *morphine* or *heroin*), induce release of dopamine in the limbic system when ingested (Koob & Bloom, 1988; Sell et al., 1999; Ortiz et al., 1996; Volkow, Fowler, & Wang, 1999). *Nicotine* and *tetrahydrocannabinol* (the active ingredient in marijuana) also induce release of dopamine in the nucleus accumbens (Chen et al., 1991; Tanda et al., 1997). Thus, addictive substances produce the same effects as pleasurable emotions in the brain. Ingvar and associates (1998) conducted PET scans on 13 male, nonalcoholic participants to localize the brain areas that are activated by consumption of moderate doses of alcohol. The alcohol ingested produced inebriation and a feeling of enhanced well-being in the subjects, and it increased brain activity in the medial temporal lobe (where the hippocampus and amygdala are located) and in the septum and nucleus accumbens (Ingvar et al., 1998). That is, a moderate amount of alcohol selectively activates the brain structures associated with reward and positive emotions.

Like positive emotions, alcohol has been demonstrated to activate the reward cascade that you learned about in the preceding section (Koob & Bloom, 1988). Alcohol stimulates the release of *serotonin*, which activates the release of *endorphins* and, ultimately, results in the release of *dopamine* in the nucleus accumbens. Consequently, drugs that increase the activity of serotonin, endorphins, or dopamine in the brain will decrease craving for alcohol in alcoholic individuals and will prevent relapse in recovered alcoholics (Johnson & Ait-Daoud, 1999; Verheul, van den Brink & Geerlings, 1999).

Addictive drugs also have biological effects similar to positive emotions in that they are associated with stimulation of D_2 dopamine receptors. For example, research with rats has demonstrated that D_2 receptor activity is related to alcohol intake in rats, increasing alcohol intake in alcoholic rats when D_2 activity is low and reducing alcohol intake when D_2 activity is high (Dyr et al., 1993; McBride et al., 1993). The aberrant A1 allele, which we discussed in conjunction with reward deficiency syndrome, is found in most people who have a severe form of alcoholism (Blum et al., 1997). This means that the D_2 receptor activity is drastically reduced in most human alcoholics. Similarly, Nora Volkow and her colleagues (1999) have conducted PET studies using the radiochemical [11C]raclopride (containing the radioactive isotope carbon-11), which binds with D_2 dopamine receptors. Their research has revealed that low levels of D_2 receptors are associated with liking for and abuse of cocaine and other psychostimulant drugs (Volkow, Fowler, & Wang, 1999; Volkow et al., 1999). Thus, a number of investigators have suggested that *reduced dopamine D_2 receptor activity* leads to compulsive drug abuse and addiction (Blum et al., 1996; Blum et al., 1997; Volkow, Fowler, & Wang, 1999; Volkow et al., 1999). The reduction in D_2 receptor activity results in decreased activation of the nucleus accumbens and hippocampus, producing dysphoria, craving for the abused substance, and compulsive self-administration of the drug.

To summarize, substances that are associated with addiction induce the release of dopamine in the limbic system and activate the pleasure–reward system associated with positive emotions. Hence, self-administration of the substance makes the individual feel good. Addiction appears to be related to low levels of D_2 dopamine receptor activity. Some individuals are born with the abnormal A1 allele, which produces D_2 receptors that are defective and less active than normal D_2 receptors. These individuals with abnormal D_2 receptors appear to be prone to develop addictions. However, chronic drug use can alter brain function, changing brain metabolism, receptor function, gene expression, and responsiveness to drug-related cues in the environment (Leshner, 1997). Specific drugs have unique effects on the brain. However, all addictive substances share common effects on the brain that reflect an underlying mechanism associated with all addictions.

The Development of an Addiction

When a person begins to use a drug, that drug use is sporadic and voluntary. But after an addiction develops, the addicted individual is compelled to seek out the drug and consume it. This compulsive drug use is the hallmark of addiction. Addicts lose control over their drug intake. They have a difficult time thinking of anything but acquiring the drug, and they will forsake all kinds of social obligations (including family life and work) in order to obtain and use the drug. We still do not know for sure how an addiction develops, but research in this area has given us some clues.

Most people who use drugs do not become addicts. Genetics, stress, life circumstances, and drug availability all determine who develops an addiction and who does not. George Koob and Michel Le Moal (1997) have proposed a model of **hedonic homeostatic dysregulation,** involving alterations in the reward pathway, to explain how an addiction develops. This model explains not only how drug addiction occurs but also how other compulsive behaviors like binge eating and compulsive gambling develop. According to this model, addiction is a downward spiraling process that proceeds from an initial failure in self-regulation to a large-scale breakdown in self-regulation (Figure 13.14). The mesolimbic dopamine system is central to this model because addicting drugs produce their rewarding effects through the release of dopamine by neurons in this system.

The hedonic homeostatic dysregulation model is based on the three stages of the addiction cycle: *preoccupation-anticipation*, *binge-intoxication*, and *withdrawal–*

hedonic homeostatic dysregulation: a model that explains how an addiction develops, based on alterations in the reward pathway

negative affect. That is, an addict (or a person developing an addiction) is always in one of these stages. The addict is either: (1) preoccupied with procuring the drug and anticipating its ingestion (preoccupation-anticipation), or (2) ingesting the drug in an uncontrolled manner and reeling from the effects of the drug (binge-intoxication), or (3) abstaining from the drug and feeling miserable (withdrawal–negative affect). As the individual spirals downward into addiction, these stages are repeated, each time altering the function of the brain a bit more (Koob & Le Moal, 1997).

Studies of the neurochemistry of addiction have suggested that certain neurotransmitters and stress hormones are implicated in the development of addiction. As the individual enters the preoccupation-anticipation stage, dopamine levels increase, as do the levels of endorphins and stress hormones. In the binge-intoxication stage, dopamine and endorphin levels remain high, producing a rewarding effect. This rewarding effect acts like a **positive reinforcer.** (Recall from your introductory psychology course that a positive reinforcer is any stimulus that increases the likelihood of the behavior that precedes it.) Thus, taking the drug is rewarded or positively reinforced by the pleasurable feelings that arise from the release of dopamine in the limbic system.

The last stage, withdrawal–negative affect, is characterized by reduced levels of dopamine and endorphin and increased levels of stress hormones. These chemical changes have the effect of producing withdrawal symptoms and negative emotions, which are experienced as intolerable. Thus, the physical and emotional symptoms of this stage act as a **negative reinforcer.** A negative reinforcer is a stimulus whose *removal* increases the likelihood of a behavior. This means that the individual caught in this addictive cycle takes the drug to remove the symptoms of withdrawal–negative affect produced by decreased levels of dopamine and endorphin.

In the addictive cycle, positive reinforcement works with negative reinforcement to maintain drug intake. After a person is trapped in this cycle, it is tremendously difficult for her or him to stop the cycle and abstain from the drug. In addition, the problem of **tolerance,** in which a person requires more of the drug in order to get the desired effect, compounds the difficulty faced by the addict. Tolerance occurs because dopamine and serotonin levels are systematically reduced in the nucleus accumbens with the passing of each withdrawal–negative affect stage (Weiss et al., 1992, 1996). Thus, in order to experience the rewarding effects of the drug, the addicted individual must ingest more and more of the drug to make up for the lost dopamine and serotonin. Ahmed and Koob (1998) have suggested that a *hedonic set point* may be reset higher and higher as a result of exposure to the drug, which causes the addicted individual to ingest progressively more of the drug over time to maintain a higher level of intoxication.

Research has also demonstrated that *glutamate* activity is altered during the development of an addiction. Repeated exposure to the drug causes neurons to make adaptations to the drug, including changes in cAMP levels within the neurons, which can lead to altered gene expression and neurotransmitter release (Nestler & Aghajanian, 1997). For example, chronic exposure to a drug reduces the ability of some genes to produce necessary proteins in the cell. Another effect of altered gene function is to increase the availability of glutamate receptors in the ventral tegmental area, which increases glutamate activity. Increased glutamate activity causes an increase in dopamine release, enhancing the effect of the drug (Wickelgren, 1998). This mechanism explains drug **sensitization** observed in some addicts. Sensitization is characterized by a progressive increase in the effect of a drug with repeated administration. For example, people who are addicted to

Figure 13.14 The Hedonic Homeostatic Dysregulation model

Neurotransmitter activity associated with the three stages of the model.

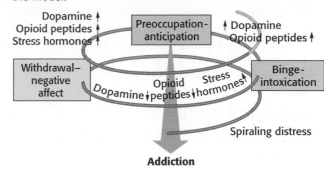

positive reinforcement: a stimulus that increases the likelihood of the behavior that precedes it

negative reinforcement: a stimulus whose removal increases the likelihood of the behavior that precedes its removal

tolerance: a progressive decrease in the effect of a drug with repeated administration

sensitization: a progressive increase in the effect of a drug with repeated administration

cocaine or amphetamine will experience increased anxiety and drug craving with repeated exposure to the drug. Thus, sensitization is believed to contribute to compulsive drug-seeking.

Stress can also contribute to the addiction because stress increases circulating levels of stress hormones. This increase in stress hormones will contribute to drug-seeking behavior in the preoccupation-anticipation stage or will increase the intolerable symptoms associated with the withdrawal–negative affect stage, which will also encourage drug-taking behavior (Figure 13.14). You will learn more about the effects of stress on behavior in Chapter 14.

Treatment for Addiction

Initially, treatment for addiction is focused on treating the withdrawal symptoms associated with drug abstinence. In many cases, these withdrawal symptoms can be life-threatening, as you learned in *For Further Thought*. However, long after the symptoms of physical dependence have disappeared, psychological dependence continues to be a problem (Figure 13.13). A number of pharmacological treatments have been developed to ease cravings and other aspects of psychological dependence.

Pharmacological treatment of addiction involves restoring neurotransmitter levels that have been altered by the addiction. Drugs that increase dopamine function, particularly those that increase D_2 receptor function, can be used to help the addicted person remain abstinent (Koob & Le Moal, 1997). In addition, drugs that increase endorphin or serotonin activity are helpful in preventing relapse and maintaining abstinence. Antianxiety agents, which increase GABA activity, are also used to help reduce the symptoms, associated with the withdrawal–negative affect phase, that the abstaining addict experiences. Drugs that antagonize the effect of glutamate, such as *acamprosate*, have been shown to be effective in reducing craving and compulsive drug-seeking in addicts (Wickelgren, 1998).

Addiction is a disorder that is long-term and prone to relapse. Typically, a recovering addict will have periods of abstinence interrupted by relapses characterized by compulsive drug-seeking and use. Some investigators question whether a cure for addiction is possible, given the chronic nature of the disorder (Leshner, 1997). Treating a chronic disorder like an addiction is difficult due to the many structural, functional, cellular, and biochemical changes in the brain that have occurred as a result of the addiction. In addition, social and other environmental stimuli act as cues that prompt the addictive behavior (Siegel, 1979; Siegel, Baptista, Kim, McDonald, & Weiss-Kelly, 2000). For example, a person who is trying to quit smoking will find it extremely difficult to refuse a cigarette at a party, especially if he or she has been drinking. Treatment for addiction involves changing the way an individual thinks about and responds to environmental cues, in addition to compensating for altered brain function caused by the addiction.

In this chapter, we have examined the biological basis of emotion and addiction. Negative emotions are associated with activation of the periventricular and peraqueductal gray areas of the hypothalamus and midbrain, whereas positive emotions are associated with the stimulation of the hippocampus. Addiction appears to involve these same brain structures. During the preoccupation-anticipation and binge-intoxication stages of the addiction cycle, the nucleus accumbens and periventricular and periaqueductal gray areas are activated. During the withdrawal–negative affect stage, the periventricular area in the hypothalamus stimulates the release of stress hormones. We will examine how stress hormones affect the brain and behavior in Chapter 14.

Recap 13.5: Addiction

Drugs that are frequently abused stimulate the release of (a)_____ in the limbic system. Addictive drugs are also associated with stimulation of (b)_____ dopamine receptor. (c)_____ dependence is characterized by intense craving for a substance when it is not available for consumption. (d)_____ dependence is characterized by severe withdrawal symptoms. The (e)_____ _____ _____ model has been proposed to explain how an addiction develops. According to this theory, an addict is always in one of three stages: (f)_____-_____, (g)_____-_____, or (h)_____-_____ _____. In the (i)_____-_____ stage as the addict prepares to procure the substance, dopamine, endorphin, and stress hormones increase. In the (j)_____-_____ stage when the addict is consuming the substance, dopamine and endorphin levels are high, producing a rewarding effect. In the (k)_____-_____ affect stage when the addict feeling miserable because the effects of the drug have disappeared, dopamine and endorphin levels are low. (l)_____ activity is also increased during development of an addiction, which causes increased dopamine release and enhances the effect of the abused drug. Pharmacological treatment of addiction includes drugs that increase (m)_____, (n)_____, or (o)_____ activity.

Chapter Summary

Emotion

▶ An emotion is a complicated response to a stimulus, involving an alteration of mood, cognition, and physiology, including activation of the sympathetic nervous system.

▶ According to the James-Lange theory of emotion, a stimulus produces a physiological response, which in turn produces an emotion.

▶ According to the Cannon-Bard theory of emotion, a stimulus produces an emotion, which in turn produces a physiological response.

▶ According to the Schachter-Singer theory of emotion, an individual must experience physiological arousal and have an appropriate cognitive attribution in order to experience an emotion.

▶ According to Zajonc's vascular theory of emotion, smiling causes blood to drain rapidly from the face, cooling the blood in the cavernous sinus, which produces a positive emotion. In contrast, frowning causes blood to pool in the face, which increases the temperature of the brain and produces a negative emotion.

Emotional Pathways in the Central Nervous System

▶ Particular regions of the brain have also been implicated in the regulation of emotions, including the locus coeruleus, the limbic system, the cerebral cortex, the medial forebrain bundle, and periventricular circuits.

▶ Neurons in the locus coeruleus release norepinephrine and activate the sympathetic nervous system in response to an emotional stimulus.

▶ Structures in the Papez circuit include the hypothalamus, anterior thalamus, and cingulate gyrus. Structures in Yakolev's circuit include the orbitofrontal cortex, the anterior temporal cortex, amygdala, and dorsomedial thalamus. The term *limbic system* is used to refer to both circuits.

▶ The left frontal lobe is activated during positive emotions, and the right frontal lobe is activated during negative emotions.

▶ Positive emotions are also associated with a bundle of axons that run through the center of the forebrain called the medial forebrain bundle. Activation of the periventricular and periaqueductal gray regions are associated with negative emotions.

Negative Emotions

▶ The amygdala relays information about sensory stimuli to different parts of the brain, including the frontal lobe and periaqueductal gray area, which produces defensive reactions. Bilateral damage to the medial temporal lobe produces Kluver-Bucy syndrome, a disorder in which affected individuals exhibit a loss of emotionality and an impaired ability to associate stimuli with consequences. Individuals with Urbach-Wiethe disease, which is caused

14

Stress and the Nervous System

Marcy was married nearly 20 years when her husband disappeared, leaving her alone to care for their five children ages 4 to 17 years. He was finally located 3 years later, living in a distant state with another woman. In the interim, Marcy was forced to seek public assistance before finding a job that allowed her to support her family.

Immediately after her husband left, Marcy was extremely upset. Whenever she worried about paying the bills or losing her house, her heart would begin to pound, and she got "the shakes." She had trouble sleeping and was edgy and irritable with her children. Marcy also had trouble concentrating on anything for very long. To treat these symptoms, Marcy's physician prescribed a minor tranquilizer for her to take.

Over the next few years, her oldest children left home to go to college or get married. As each child left, Marcy became more and more despondent. When her youngest child was diagnosed with juvenile-onset diabetes, a serious chronic illness that required that the child receive several injections of insulin daily, Marcy became so depressed that her doctor prescribed an antidepressant for her. Despite the medication, Marcy's depression worsened. Six years to the day after her husband left her, Marcy tried to commit suicide. Her suicide note read, "There is nothing to live for," which was far from the truth because her youngest children were very dependent on her.

What caused Marcy's depression? Many psychologists believe that stress causes depression. Certainly Marcy had a lot of stress to deal with: being abandoned by her husband, raising five children on her own, seeing her children leaving the nest one by one, treating her youngest child's illness. But Marcy also had a serious medical problem of her own, an underactive thyroid gland, and she was menopausal. (Recall from Chapter 12 that some women experience postmenopausal depression.)

In this chapter, you will learn that stress affects the brain and the body in a number of ways. Stress produces hormonal changes that alter neurotransmitter levels in the nervous system. Some of these changes can produce depression. Other hormones, in addition to stress hormones, can affect neurotransmitter activity, too. In Marcy's case, stress and other hormonal problems contributed to her depression. We'll examine how stress interacts with other factors to produce depression and other disorders later in this chapter. But first let's look at the nature of stress. ●

Defining Stress

Stress is a state of imbalance produced by **stressors.** Stressors are people, objects, places, or events that disrupt *homeostasis* in the nervous system (Cullinan, Herman, Helmreich, & Watson, 1995; Michelson, Licinio, & Gold, 1995; Walker & Diforio, 1997). As you learned in Chapter 11, the hypothalamus works very hard to maintain homeostasis in the nervous system *and* elsewhere in the body. Whenever homeostasis is challenged, the hypothalamus organizes the body's response to the challenge. For example, when the body temperature rises drastically, the hypothalamus initiates changes that ultimately result in a lower body temperature. The hypothalamus also responds to the disruption of homeostasis produced by stressors.

Stressors can alter homeostasis in a variety of ways. For example, imagine the nonhomeostatic state induced when you lock yourself, while dressed in jeans and a T-shirt, out of the house on a cold day. Or imagine the disruption that occurs when you discover you've lost your checkbook. In the first example, the stressor is primarily a physical one. In the second, it is psychological. Both physical and psychological stressors disrupt homeostasis in the body, and the stress response to both types of stressors is the same, as you will learn later in this chapter.

Stress is a negative experience that is accompanied by characteristic emotional, behavioral, biochemical, and physiological reactions (Baum, 1990). These stress reactions enable the individual to adapt to the stressor or to escape from it. In this chapter, we will discuss how the body and brain respond to stressors. As you think about stress, it may occur to you that stressors are different for different people. That is, one person might find a particular circumstance very stressful, whereas another person might not be bothered by it at all. For example, my family recently went to a large theme park that has an aerial tramway suspended about 50 feet above the ground. My youngest son begged me to go on the tramway with him, and I reluctantly agreed to do it. During the entire tram ride, I was scared to death and had white knuckles and a pounding heart to prove it. In contrast, my son was thrilled with the experience. He just loved being up so high and viewing the entire park from above.

The fact that we are not all stressed by the same things means that our brains have a mechanism that evaluates stimuli and determines whether the stimuli are good or bad for us and whether we can cope with a particular stimulus or control it. Those stimuli that are judged to be stressors initiate stress responses in the nervous system (LeDoux, 1995). Unfortunately, the bulk of neuroscience research that has focused on stress has been conducted on nonhuman animals. There are two reasons for this. First, to study stress, the investigator must expose the subject to a stressor, and it is quite difficult to get people to volunteer for studies in which they will be stressed. Second, studying the effects of stress on the brain requires that blood chemistry and brain dissection data be collected, which is often not possible with human participants. Therefore, we understand quite well the brain mecha-

stress: a negative experience accompanied by characteristic emotional, behavioral, biochemical, and physiological responses
stressor: a person, object, place, or event that disrupts homeostasis in the nervous system

nisms involved in stress responses in rats and monkeys, and we infer that the same brain mechanisms
are at work in stressed humans.

For example, behavioral neuroscientists have
studied the effects of physical and psychological
stressors in rats by exposing rats to very hot or very
cold temperatures (a physical stressor) or to physical restraint (a psychological stressor). Either type
of stressor leads to the same stress response in rats.
Thus, we assume that humans make the same
response ultimately to physical and psychological
stressors.

Sometimes, however, identical treatments with
rats and humans do not produce the same kind of
stress. Take, for example, separating a newborn rat
and an infant human from their mothers (Figure
14.1). Separation from its mother is a physical stres-
sor for a newborn rat because the separation produces *hypothermia*, or decreased
body temperature (refer to Chapter 10), in the hairless little rat pup. In contrast,
separating 9-month-old human babies from their mothers causes a good deal of
anxiety and emotional upset in these infants, producing psychological stress. Yet
both newborn rats and human babies show the same physiological response (for
example, an increase in certain hormones in the blood) to the stress of separation
from their mothers (Larson, Gunnar, & Hertsgaard, 1991). This is more evidence
that psychological and physical stressors produce the same effect in the body.

Please keep in mind that stressors can be very pleasant as well as unpleasant.
Any stimulus that challenges the body's homeostasis will produce stress. A wedding,
therefore, can be as stressful as a funeral because both disrupt normal functioning
of the body. To help you understand this better, let's examine how information
about stressors reaches the nervous system and how the nervous system, in turn,
responds to this information.

Stress Pathways in the Central Nervous System

Stress can be produced by environmental (external) or psychical (internal) events
[*psyche* = mind, Greek]. Thus, a number of pathways carrying information about
stressors have been identified in the central nervous system, some that carry information from the periphery to the brain and others that originate in the brain.
Because the hypothalamus organizes the body's response to homeostatic disruptions, it is the ultimate recipient of information about stress. Many axons that relay
information about stressors terminate in a particular region of the hypothalamus
known as the **paraventricular nucleus.**

Environmental stimuli excite *sensory neurons* in the peripheral nervous system.
Information about these stimuli is sent to the brain via sensory tracts in the spinal
cord and cranial nerves. The *vagus nerve* is especially important in conducting
information about the gut and chest organs to the brain. These pathways are well
known to neuroscientists and have been studied extensively. Less certain, however,
are the stress pathways and relay stations located within the brain. Although we
understand the role of the paraventricular nucleus in stress responses, we do not
know with certainty how information gets to this region of the hypothalamus or
the roles that other parts of the brain play in responding to stress.

Investigators have a number of research tools at their disposal when they
attempt to identify brain structures associated with stress. Those who conduct
research in this area make use of *lesioning* and *stimulation* techniques, *electrophysiological recording, microdialysis,* and *c-fos* analyses. These are all techniques that you
learned about in Chapter 5. After a potential stress pathway has been identified,
investigators will lesion a section of the pathway to determine if damage to the

Figure 14.1 A human infant separated from its mother

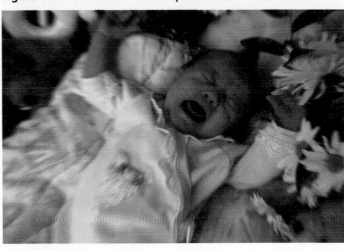

paraventricular nucleus: a nucleus
of neurons in the hypothalamus that
organizes behavior, including eating,
to respond to changes in internal
body states

pathway disrupts the stress response. We expect that damage to a pathway will interfere with the function of the axons that comprise that pathway.

Either electrical or chemical stimulation is used to test particular brain structures that are suspected to play a role in stress. With chemical stimulation, neurotransmitters or other chemical substances thought to excite or inhibit the stress response are administered via a cannula to a specific region of the brain. Following the administration of the test substance, the subject's behavior is observed closely to examine whether the substance enhances or reduces the stress response.

Microdialysis is used to determine which hormones or neurotransmitters are released in particular structures believed to play a role in stress. Tiny probes are inserted into the brain region under study before the subject is exposed to a stressor. During and after the stress, minute amounts of chemicals are extracted from the brain and analyzed. In this way, investigators have identified the neurotransmitters that stimulate the release of hormones in the paraventricular nucleus in response to stress. (We will examine the roles of various neurotransmitters later in this chapter.)

As you learned in Chapter 5, c-*fos* is a useful substance to study because its presence indicates recent activation of a neuron. That is, when a neuron becomes excited due to challenge by a stressor, several genes, including c-*fos*, are activated. Immunohistochemical techniques are employed to test for the presence of c-*fos* in particular neurons thought to mediate stress responses. Research using c-*fos* markers has demonstrated that neurons in many regions of the brain, including the paraventricular nucleus, are excited when the body is exposed to either physical or psychological stressors (Akil & Morano, 1996; Zigmond, Finlay, & Sved, 1995).

Neurons from many regions of the brain send their axons to the paraventricular nucleus of the hypothalamus (Figure 14.2). A number of structures in the hindbrain, midbrain, and forebrain serve as relay stations, gathering information about stressors from numerous inputs and then sending that information on to the paraventricular nucleus (Cullinan et al., 1995). Let's examine the major stress relay stations in the brain. Please keep in mind that our knowledge about these regions and how they are related to specific stressors is quite vague at present (Akil & Morano, 1996).

Figure 14.2 Diverse inputs to the paraventricular nucleus
The paraventricular nucleus (PVN) of the hypothalamus receives input from the limbic system and cerebral cortex via the bed nucleus of the stria terminalis (BST), from other parts of the hypothalamus, and from brain stem structures, such as the nucleus of the solitary tract, the tegmentum and reticular formation, the periaqueductal gray, the locus coeruleus, and the raphe system.

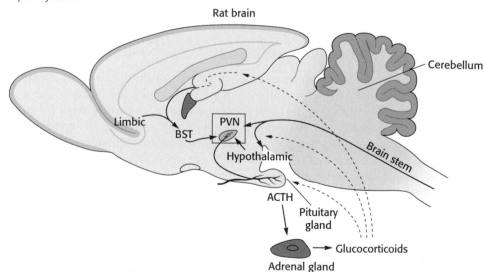

Processing Internal Stressors: The Nucleus of the Solitary Tract

Information about stressors coming from the gut or other internal receptors is relayed via the vagus and other cranial nerves to the *nucleus of the solitary tract* in the medulla (Figure 14.3). For example, information about choking is sent to the nucleus of the solitary tract by way of the *glossopharyngeal nerve*. We discussed this hindbrain structure in Chapter 7 when discussing the sensation of taste. Thus, all sorts of sensory information are sent to the nucleus of the solitary tract for processing. Somehow, this nucleus sorts out the stress-inducing stimuli from the other signals and sends information about these stressors to the paraventricular nucleus. Axons from the nucleus of the solitary tract excite neurons in the paraventricular nucleus by releasing *norepinephrine* and other *catecholamines* (Cullinan et al., 1995; Zigmond et al., 1995).

Processing Somatosensory Stressors: Tegmentum and Reticular Formation

Somatosensory information from the skin and stretch receptors in muscles is sent to relay stations in the pons and midbrain. These relay areas include the *tegmentum* and particular regions of the *reticular formation*. As you learned in Chapter 8, the tegmentum is involved in attentional processes, and the reticular formation is responsible for arousing the nervous system in response to novel or important stimuli. The tegmentum appears to relay visual and auditory information, in addition to news about somatosensory stimuli, to the paraventricular nucleus.

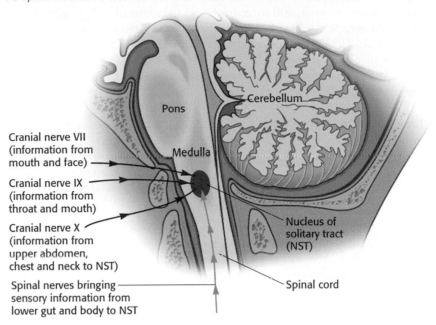

Figure 14.3 Inputs to the nucleus of the solitary tract
The nucleus of the solitary tract receives input from the mouth and face via cranial nerve VII, from the mouth and throat via cranial nerve IX, from the upper abdomen, neck, and chest via cranial nerve X, and from lower parts of the body via spinal nerves.

Cranial nerve VII (information from mouth and face)

Cranial nerve IX (information from throat and mouth)

Cranial nerve X (information from upper abdomen, chest and neck to NST)

Spinal nerves bringing sensory information from lower gut and body to NST

Pons

Cerebellum

Medulla

Nucleus of solitary tract (NST)

Spinal cord

The tegmentum and reticular formation have direct projections to the paraventricular nucleus. Like the axons coming from the nucleus of the solitary tract, axons from the tegmentum and reticular formation also release *catecholamines*, stimulating the paraventricular nucleus. *Acetylcholine*, which also has excitatory effects on the paraventricular nucleus, is released by some axons coming from these structures. Because no direct pathways have been identified between the somatosensory cortex and the paraventricular nucleus, investigators have concluded that these structures in the pons and mesencephalon relay most of the information regarding somatosensory stressors to the hypothalamus (Cullinan et al., 1995).

Processing Painful Stressors: The Periaqueductal Gray and Central Gray Areas

Recall from Chapter 8 that the *periaqueductal gray area* of the midbrain and *central gray area* of the pons play an important role in the response to pain. Certainly, any type of pain would function as a stressor and set in motion a response by the nervous system to deal with the pain. Pathways have been identified between these areas and the paraventricular nucleus of the hypothalamus. Axons in the pathways between the periaqueductal gray and central gray areas and the paraventricular nucleus release acetylcholine and substance P, both of which have excitatory effects on the paraventricular nucleus.

Processing Homeostatic Challenges: The Locus Coeruleus

You first learned about the locus coeruleus in Chapter 4 when we discussed the distribution of neurotransmitters in the brain. Recall from that discussion that the cells of the *locus coeruleus* produce almost all of the norepinephrine found in the brain. This structure is located in the pons along the ventral aspect of the fourth ventricle in an area that is considered to be part of the reticular formation (Zigmond et al., 1995). Many of the pathways going to and from the locus coeruleus are feedback loops that allow this structure to play a role in homeostatic regulation.

The locus coeruleus is also sensitive to physical sensations and changes in heart rate and blood pressure. Experiments using microdialysis, electrophysiological recordings in awake animals, and c-*fos* analyses all have demonstrated an increase in locus coeruleus activity (and an increase in the release of norepinephrine from the cells of the locus coeruleus) following exposure to stressors like foot shock, forced swimming, exposure to cold, and forced exercise (Abercrombie & Jacobs, 1987; Aston-Jones, Chiang, & Alexinsky, 1991; Glavin et al., 1983; Maynert & Levi, 1964; Tanaka et al., 1983; Van Bockstaele et al., 2001; Zigmond et al., 1995). As further evidence that the locus coeruleus is involved in initiating stress responses in the brain, a direct pathway from the locus coeruleus to the paraventricular nucleus has been identified (Bremner et al., 1996).

Processing Emotional Stressors: The Raphe System

Recall from Chapter 4 that the raphe system in the brain stem is the sole source of *serotonin* in the brain (Figure 14.4). Researchers have discovered a pathway carrying axons from the raphe system to the paraventricular nucleus of the hypothalamus (Akil & Morano, 1996). Therefore, stressors impacting the raphe system are believed to stimulate stress responses in the paraventricular nucleus. Lesioning studies have indicated that the serotonergic pathway from the raphe to the paraventricular nucleus relays information about only certain types of stressors, especially those *emotional stressors* that activate the cerebral cortex and limbic system (Cullinan et al., 1995).

Processing Homeostatic Challenges: The Hypothalamus

Recall that the *hypothalamus* is composed of many clusters of neurons, called *nuclei*.

Figure 14.4 Serotonin pathways in the brain
Serotonin is produced by neurons in the raphe nuclei in the hindbrain and is released in all parts of the central nervous system, including the cerebral cortex, hippocampus, amygdala, basal ganglia, thalamus, hypothalamus, cerebellum, and the spinal cord.

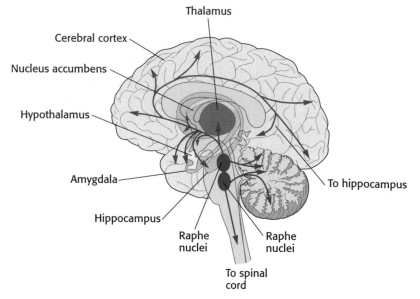

The paraventricular nucleus is just one of those many nuclei. Investigators have determined that nearly all hypothalamic nuclei send axons to the paraventricular nucleus (Swanson, 1987). This means that diverse nuclei in the hypothalamus, most of which monitor homeostatic processes such as blood glucose or osmotic pressure, relay information about changes in homeostasis to the paraventricular nucleus. In addition, axons from numerous neurons in the limbic system carry information from the limbic system to other hypothalamic nuclei, which in turn relay that information to the paraventricular nucleus. These nuclei have been demonstrated to have both excitatory and inhibitory effects on the paraventricular nucleus. Hence, their effect on the paraventricular nucleus is complicated and not well understood.

Processing Cognitive and Emotional Stressors: The Limbic System

Structures in the *limbic system*, including the *hippocampus*, the *septum*, and the *amygdala*, have been shown experimentally to play a role in stress responses (Cullinan et al., 1995). Cognitive and emotional stressors stimulate these limbic system structures, which in turn excite the paraventricular nucleus. However, only a few areas of the amygdala have direct projections to the paraventricular nucleus. Most information from the limbic system arrives at the paraventricular nucleus indirectly. One forebrain structure, the **bed nucleus of the stria terminalis,** appears to receive inputs from numerous areas of the limbic system (Wang, Cen, & Lu, 2001).

bed nucleus of the stria terminalis: a forebrain structure that relays information from the limbic system to the paraventricular nucleus

Thus, the bed nucleus is believed to be a major relay station between the limbic system and the paraventricular nucleus.

Processing Cognitive and Emotional Stressors: The Cerebral Cortex

Emotional and cognitive stressors can certainly be generated or moderated by the cerebrum, particularly the prefrontal cortex. The cerebral cortex undoubtedly plays an important role in monitoring and interpreting stimuli, determining which are stressors and which are benign. But there are no direct projections from the cerebral cortex to the paraventricular nucleus. The bed nucleus of the stria terminalis is thought to be a relay station between the cerebrum and the hypothalamus. The evidence for this is uncertain, however, and investigators are still trying to determine how information about stressors from the cerebral cortex reaches the paraventricular nucleus.

Recap 14.1: Defining Stress

(a)_____ are people, objects, places or events that disrupt homeostasis in the nervous system. (b)_____ is a state of imbalance produced by a stressor. When homeostasis is disrupted, the (c)_____ nucleus of the hypothalamus organizes the body's response. This nucleus receives information about the presence of stressors from a number of brain structures including the nucleus of the (d)_____ _____, which relays information from the gut and other internal receptors. Somatosensory information is sent to midbrain structures, including the (e)_____ and (f)_____ formation, before being sent to the paraventricular nucleus. Information about pain is sent to the (g)_____ _____ area and then on to the paraventricular nucleus. The limbic system and the cerebral cortex send information about stressors to (h)_____ nucleus of the stria terminalis, which relays this information to the hypothalamus.

The Response to Acute Stress

I have just summarized all that neuroscientists know about pathways and relay points in the brain concerned with the stress response. As you've just learned, most of the details are still vague, and a lot of questions remain unanswered. Now let's examine the stress response. A tremendous amount of research has been conducted in this area, and we understand this process quite well.

First, let's take an example of an acute stressor and consider what happens when you are exposed to this stressor. An **acute stressor** is one that occurs infrequently and for a limited period of time. For example, think about what your reaction would be if you stumble and break your wrist. First of all, information from muscles and pain receptors would alert your central nervous system that something is wrong. Broken blood vessels at the location of the injury would start to hemorrhage, causing swelling and more pain. This information, too, is relayed to the central nervous system. When the information about the injury reaches the central nervous system, your attention is drawn to the site of the break. You begin to worry about the swelling and whether you will be able to take the three exams scheduled for next week. If nerves have been injured and you cannot move your fingers, you might also begin to fret about possible long-term disuse of your hand or even paralysis or amputation.

A physical stressor, such as a broken wrist, begins in the peripheral nervous system. Information about this stressor is rapidly sent to the central nervous system.

acute stressor: a stressor that occurs infrequently and for a limited period of time

After the central nervous system is activated, the cerebral cortex and limbic system react to the stressor, supplying a cognitive/emotional response. That is, a physical stressor is typically amplified by an accompanying cognitive/emotional reaction. In contrast, a psychological stressor is initiated by the cerebral cortex or limbic system. This type of stressor produces a physiological reaction as part of the stress response.

Overall, the purpose of the stress response is twofold: (1) to prepare the individual to respond to the stressor and the disequilibrium produced by the stressor, and (2) to inhibit behaviors that would not be adaptive in dealing with the stressor (Michelson, Licinio, & Gold, 1995). Examples of adaptive behaviors that enable the individual to respond effectively to the stressor include increased blood flow, increased breathing rate, increased energy availability, and increased alertness and vigilance. In contrast, functions like sleep, eating, growth, and reproduction are suppressed during the stress response. For example, disruptions in fertility, such as a cessation of menstruation, have been observed in women who are exposed to stress (Stout, 1995). Stress also affects the functioning of the immune system.

Stress and the Immune System

As you learned earlier, the immune system is the body's line of defense against microorganisms and aberrant cells, like those found in tumors. Your skin, the mucus in your respiratory tract, and blood cells (called **macrophages**) that chew up and destroy invading microorganisms act together in a nonspecific way to protect you from a variety of pathogens. Other white blood cells, particularly **T-cells** and **B-cells,** target specific microorganisms, although it may take several days to activate T-cells and B-cells.

Numerous studies involving rat and human subjects have shown that acute stressors suppress the functioning of the immune system by inhibiting macrophages, T-cells, and B-cells. In rats, acute stressors-such as exposure to electric shock, vestibular stimulation, a fight with a powerful foe, separation from one's mother, a cold water bath, a loud noise, physical restraint, and a stick with a hypodermic needle—suppress the function of macrophages, T-cells, and B-cells (reviewed by Maier, Watkins, & Fleshner, 1994). In humans, acute stressors, like final exams and sleep deprivation, suppress immune function, causing an increase in illness and visits to the college infirmary (Dorian, Garfinkel, Brown, Shore, Gladman, & Keystone, 1982; Kiecolt-Glaser et al., 1987; Marshall et al., 1998; Palmblad, Petrini, Wasserman, & Akerstedt, 1979). Sheldon Cohen and his colleagues at Carnegie Mellon University (1991) assessed stress levels in 394 healthy people and then exposed them to a cold virus. Those participants who reported psychological stress had increased rates of respiratory illness following exposure to the virus.

However, stressors do not uniformly affect the immune system in the same manner in all people. Psychological factors and coping skills can alter the effect of acute stressors. For example, loneliness and high anxiety can increase the immunosuppressive effects of acute stressors (Maier et al., 1994; Miller et al., 1997). That is, a lonely, anxious person who is exposed to a stressor is more likely to develop an illness than is a calm individual with plenty of social support who is exposed to the same stressor.

The field of **psychoneuroimmunology** has developed over the past 4 decades in response to laboratory findings that psychological or physical stressors can affect the functioning of the immune system. More recently, research has revealed that certain behavioral strategies can improve immune function by reducing the immunosuppressive effects of stressors (Nathan et al., 1997). Today, investigators in the field of psychoneuroimmunology study the interactions among the nervous system, the endocrine system, the immune system, and behavior. The cells of the immune system, the endocrine system, and the nervous system bear receptors that respond to the same neurotransmitters, neurohormones, and neuropeptides. Thus, a neurotransmitter or hormone that is released in response to a stressor by one system will affect all three systems simultaneously.

macrophage: a blood cell that is part of the immune system and destroys invading microorganisms in a nonspecific way

T-cell: a white blood cell that is part of the immune system and functions by targeting specific intruders inside cells

B-cell: a white blood cell that is part of the immune system and functions by targeting specific microorganisms using antibodies

psychoneuroimmunology: a field of study that examines the interactions among the nervous system, endocrine system, immune system, and behavior

You might wonder why the body's response to stress includes suppression of the immune system. Stress-induced immunosuppression hardly seems adaptive, compared to the adaptations we considered earlier in this section. Steven Maier and his colleagues at the University of Colorado have suggested that suppression of the immune system allows the body to mobilize its energy resources to deal with the stressor (Maier et al., 1994; Maier & Watkins, 1998). A functioning immune system produces reactions like inflammation and fever, both of which require relatively large amounts of the body's energy. In a stress response, energy is shunted from the immune system to skeletal muscles and the brain.

At present, research indicates that the response to a stressor has two components: one involving the *locus coeruleus* and the other involving the *paraventricular nucleus of the hypothalamus*. Let's examine each of these components separately.

The Stress Response Initiated by the Locus Coeruleus

You learned about the first component of the stress response in Chapter 13 when we examined the arousal of the *sympathetic nervous system*. Excitation of the locus coeruleus activates the sympathetic nervous system, which stimulates the release of norepinephrine from neurons everywhere in the brain (Bremner et al., 1996). One of the main effects of activation of the locus coeruleus is an increase in arousal and vigilance, which permits the individual to respond effectively to the stressor (DeSauza & Grigoriadis, 1995; Nestler, Alreia, & Aghaianian, 1999). Recall from Chapter 13 that activation of the sympathetic nervous system also causes the neurohormone *epinephrine* to be released from the medulla of the adrenal gland. In turn, epinephrine has a number of effects in the peripheral and central nervous systems, such as increased heart rate and increased respiration rate, all of which help the individual deal with stress. In addition, activation of the locus coeruleus and the sympathetic nervous system turns on the second stress–response system in the brain, involving the paraventricular nucleus.

The Stress Response Initiated by the Paraventricular Nucleus

The second component of the stress response begins with the stimulation of the paraventricular nucleus. When the paraventricular nucleus is excited, it releases a number of chemical substances, including **corticotropic-releasing hormone,** or **CRH.** During the stress response, CRH is released into the blood flowing through the *infundibulum* to the **pituitary gland** (Figure 14.5). CRH is transported to the *anterior lobe* of the pituitary gland, where it stimulates the release of the pituitary hormone **adrenocorticotropic hormone,** or **ACTH.** As its name implies, ACTH produces a change in the cortex of the adrenal gland, stimulating the synthesis and release of yet another hormone, **glucocorticoid.**

Glucocorticoids are *steroid* substances that are derived from the cortex of the adrenal gland, and they are found in a number of forms. In rats, the predominant glucocorticoid is called **corticosterone.** It is called **cortisol** in humans. The main function of glucocorticoids is to increase the production and availability of blood glucose in order to provide energy to deal with the stress. Glucocorticoids also inhibit the immune system, decrease inflammatory reactions, and activate a host of proteins and enzymes that enable the individual to respond to the stressor (Akil & Morano, 1996; Michelson et al., 1995). In addition, glucocorticoids affect gene transcription in the nuclei of cells, thus having long-term as well as immediate effects on the body. In fact, the effects of glucocorticoids can linger long after the stressor has been removed, setting the stage for a number of physical and psychological disorders, as you will learn later in this chapter and in Chapter 15.

In summary, when the paraventricular nucleus of the hypothalamus is activated by information about a stressor, it releases CRH, which is transported to the anterior pituitary. In response to CRH, the anterior lobe of the pituitary gland releases

corticotropic-releasing hormone (CRH): a hormone released by the paraventricular nucleus that stimulates the release of ACTH from the anterior pituitary gland

pituitary gland: structure, connected to the hypothalamus by a stalk, that regulates the activity of other major glands in the body; master gland located below the ventral surface of the brain, which receives commands from the hypothalamus

adrenocorticotropic hormone (ACTH): a hormone released by the paraventricular nucleus that stimulates the adrenal cortex to produce glucocorticoids

glucocorticoid: a steroid hormone derived from the cortex of the adrenal gland

corticosterone: a glucocorticoid produced by rats

cortisol: a glucocorticoid produced by humans

Figure 14.5 The hypothalamic-pituitary-adrenal response to stress

(a) In response to a stressor, the paraventricular nucleus of the hypothalamus releases CRH, which stimulates the release of ACTH from the pituitary gland. In response to ACTH, the adrenal gland releases cortisol. (b) A negative feedback loop controls the release of cortisol by the adrenal gland.

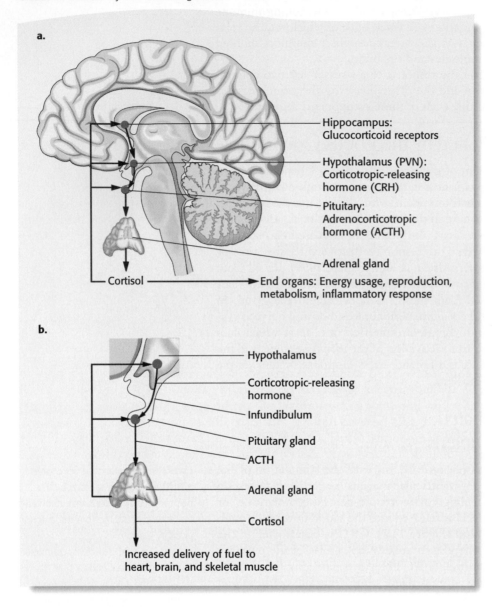

a.

Hippocampus: Glucocorticoid receptors

Hypothalamus (PVN): Corticotropic-releasing hormone (CRH)

Pituitary: Adrenocorticotropic hormone (ACTH)

Adrenal gland

Cortisol — End organs: Energy usage, reproduction, metabolism, inflammatory response

b.

Hypothalamus

Corticotropic-releasing hormone

Infundibulum

Pituitary gland

ACTH

Adrenal gland

Cortisol

Increased delivery of fuel to heart, brain, and skeletal muscle

---

ACTH into the blood. ACTH is transported to the cortex of the adrenal gland, where it stimulates the release of glucocorticoids (Figure 14.6). Glucocorticoids, in turn, travel in the blood to various sites of action in the body, especially in the brain, preparing the individual to deal with the stressor. This response to stress, which is mediated by the *h*ypothalamus, *p*ituitary, and *a*drenal gland, is often referred to as the **HPA axis** response.

HPA axis: the connection between the hypothalamus, pituitary gland, and adrenal gland

Other Actions of CRH

In addition to activating ACTH, CRH stimulates widespread areas throughout the brain. Its main effects on the brain involve heightened arousal and attention, which increase readiness to respond to a stressor (Britton et al., 1982; DeSouza & Grigoriadis, 1995; Sutton et al., 1982). Also, CRH has been demonstrated to inhibit eating, sexual behavior, and growth—functions that are not adaptive when dealing with stress (Michelson et al., 1995; Rivier & Vale, 1984). The paraventricular nucleus secretes CRH in minute amounts throughout the day, even when no stressors are present. The role of CRH in the absence of stress is unclear. We do know that the level of CRH fluctuates during the day and that the variation in CRH levels affects our ability to respond to stressors.

The Relationship Between the Paraventricular Nucleus and the Locus Coeruleus

As you've just learned, there are two components of the stress response: one initiated by the paraventricular nucleus and one initiated by the locus coeruleus. You might be wondering how these two brain structures work together to enable us to respond to stress effectively, and, in fact, many investigators have wondered about this, too. Research indicates that the relationship between the locus coeruleus and the paraventricular nucleus is reciprocal. That is, excitation of one structure produces excitation of the other. This relationship is characterized as a *positive feedback loop* (Figure 14.6).

Figure 14.6 Positive feedback loop between the locus coeruleus and the paraventricular nucleus
Excitation of the paraventricular nucleus (PVN) of the hypothalamus initiates excitation of the locus coeruleus. Likewise, excitation of the locus coeruleus initiates excitation of the paraventricular nucleus.

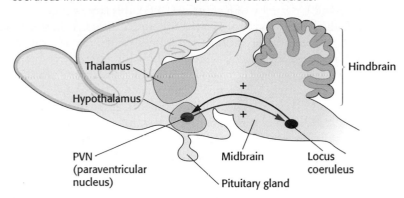

Chemical stimulation studies of rats have demonstrated that CRH (which is secreted by the paraventricular nucleus) increases activity of the locus coeruleus and that norepinephrine (which is released by the locus coeruleus) activates the paraventricular nucleus (Calogero et al., 1988; Valentino, Foote, & Aston-Jones, 1983). Moreover, both the locus coeruleus and the paraventricular nucleus are activated by serotonin and acetylcholine, and both are inhibited by GABA and endorphins. Hence, these two structures appear to work together because they are both turned on and off by the same neurochemicals (Michelson et al., 1995).

Other Hormones Associated with the Stress Response

Epinephrine, CRH, ACTH, and cortisol are not the only hormones released in response to stress. When stimulated, the paraventricular nucleus secretes over a dozen hormones and neuropeptides. Under the microscope, this nucleus appears to be composed of large cells in the *magnocellular* region and small cells in the *parvicellular* region [*magno-* = large; *parvi-* = small, Latin]. Each of these regions in the paraventricular nucleus releases different chemical substances. For example, CRH is synthesized and secreted by parvicellular neurons only.

Neurons in the magnocellular layer produce *arginine-vasopressin* and *oxytocin*, both of which are associated with the stress response and are transported to the posterior lobe of the pituitary gland (Akil & Morano, 1996; Cullinan et al., 1995; Michelson et al., 1995). Oxytocin plays an important role in lactation and childbirth but has also been demonstrated to be released when an individual is exposed to particular stressors. The other hormone, arginine-vasopressin, regulates salt and water balance.

Arginine-vasopressin is also produced in the parvicellular region of the paraventricular nucleus, although the bulk of this hormone is synthesized in the magnocellular neurons. Like CRH, arginine-vasopressin can stimulate the release of ACTH in the anterior pituitary. By itself, arginine-vasopressin has a weak effect on ACTH release. However, working with CRH, arginine-vasopressin can dramatically increase ACTH release, activating a strong stress response. As you will learn later in this chapter, arginine-vasopressin is believed to be responsible for maintaining a prolonged stress response, which can have tragic effects on physical and mental health.

The parvicellular region of the paraventricular nucleus also secretes a large number of other substances, including many hormones that you've learned about in earlier chapters: *thyrotropin-releasing hormone*, *growth hormone–releasing hormone*, *somatostatin*, *dopamine*, *enkephalin*, *cholecystokinin (CCK)*, and *angiotensin*. Many of these hormones, such as thyrotropin-releasing hormone and somatostatin, stimulate the release of hormones from the anterior pituitary gland. The others control functions related to the stress response, such as relief of pain (enkephalin) or inhibition of eating (CCK).

Why would neurons that secrete CRH also secrete these additional substances? According to William Cullinan and his colleagues at the University of Michigan and University of Kentucky (1995), this large variety of hormones enable the individual to respond to a wide range of stressors. Whereas CRH produces a standard response to a stressor regardless of its nature, the other hormones secreted by the paraventricular nucleus allow for a specific response to a particular stressor, be it hemorrhage or hypoglycemia or hypothermia (Stout et al., 1995).

The wide variety of chemical substances released from the paraventricular nucleus with CRH also allow the individual to respond completely and appropriately to a stressful situation. That is, a stressful event is often comprised of many stressors being presented at once. For example, if you are involved in a car accident, you might experience pain (a physiological stressor) and fear (a psychological stressor) and any number of other stressors. To deal with this constellation of stressors, you need many systems to be activated at once. One example of this phenomenon is **stress-induced analgesia** (Coutinho et al., 2002; Stout et al., 1995). Recall from Chapter 7 that *analgesia* refers to an absence of pain. In response to a stressor, enkephalin and other opioid neurotransmitters are released with CRH. These opioid neurotransmitters produce analgesia even in an animal that is exposed to a psychological stressor such as restraint. Stress-induced analgesia also occurs in people and may be seen following a traumatic accident in which the individual sustains extensive injury to some body part but experiences no pain.

stress-induced analgesia: an absence of pain produced when a stressor stimulates the release of opioid neurotransmitters

Controlling the Release of Glucocorticoids

You've just learned that glucocorticoids affect a wide range of body functions. To keep the body functioning optimally, the release of glucocorticoids must be closely controlled because too much or too little of this steroid substance can cause widespread damage. In addition, glucocorticoids must be released promptly in response to a stressor, and their release must be terminated immediately when the stressor is removed. Recall that excitation of the paraventricular nucleus initiates glucocorticoid activity. The rapid release of CRH stimulates secretion of ACTH, which causes glucocorticoid levels in the blood to increase quickly in response to a stressor. Under normal conditions, when the stressor is removed, release of ACTH stops immediately, terminating glucocorticoid synthesis in the adrenal gland.

How does the nervous system prevent excessive elevation of glucocorticoid levels in response to stress? In Chapter 12, you learned that a *negative feedback loop* regulates estrogen levels in a woman's body. This is precisely the same mechanism that controls glucocorticoid levels in the blood (Figure 14.5). Let's explore how this negative feedback loop works. When glucocorticoid is released by the cortex of the adrenal gland into the circulating bloodstream, it is transported to glucocorticoid receptor sites throughout the body. Glucocorticoid binds with receptors on particular neurons in the brain and pituitary gland, exciting those neurons. These same neurons, when activated by glucocorticoids, inhibit neurons in the paraventricular nucleus that produce CRH and neurons in the anterior pituitary that release ACTH. Thus, increased levels of glucocorticoids in the blood produce inhibition of CRH and ACTH release, which ultimately leads to a reduction in glucocorticoid synthesis.

Dexamethasone is a form of synthetic glucocorticoid. When dexamethasone is administered to an individual, it acts like glucocorticoid, inhibiting the cells that release CRH and ACTH. Therefore, administration of dexamethasone is expected to suppress the release of glucocorticoid because it activates the negative feedback loop that controls the secretion of glucocorticoid (Figure 14.5). The **dexamethasone suppression test** is used to assess the ability of the HPA axis to regulate glucocorticoid release. Cortisol release in healthy people is suppressed following the administration of dexamethasone. However, individuals with impaired regulation of the HPA axis will fail to respond appropriately to a dexamethasone challenge by decreasing cortisol release. For example, depressed people have impaired function of the HPA axis and typically show an increase in cortisol following a dexamethasone challenge. Thus, the dexamethasone suppression test is used to diagnose depression.

Glucocorticoid receptors have been found throughout the brain and pituitary gland, and they are especially prevalent in the hypothalamus and hippocampus. In fact, two different types of glucocorticoid receptors are located in the hippocampus, which suggests that the hippocampus plays an important role in regulating glucocorticoid levels (Akil & Morano, 1996; Cullinan et al., 1995; Michelson et al., 1995). Because the hippocampus also functions in learning and memory, the glucocorticoid receptors in the hippocampus may provide information to this structure about the stress response as it encodes memories about the stressor. By encoding information about stressors into memory, the hippocampus influences the future perception of the stressors and our reaction to them.

Coping Successfully with Acute Stress

Successful coping reduces the release of norepinephrine and glucocorticoid to their basal levels. That is, when an individual has successfully coped with a stressor, and the effect of the stressor has been removed, the activation of the HPA axis and the locus coeruleus should be terminated promptly. In the previous section, you learned about the negative feedback loop that regulates the release of glucocorticoid. This is an important first step in terminating the stress response. In addition, norepinephrine and serotonin play an important role in coping with stress.

As you've learned, norepinephrine is released following activation of the locus coeruleus. Actually, there are two pathways from the locus coeruleus to the paraventricular nucleus. One pathway terminates on *alpha adrenergic receptors* in the paraventricular nucleus, and the other pathway innervates *beta adrenergic receptors*. When norepinephrine binds with the alpha adrenergic receptors in the paraventricular nucleus, CRH is released, and the HPA axis is activated. On the other hand, the beta adrenergic receptors in the paraventricular nucleus inhibit the release of CRH when they are excited by norepinephrine. Therefore, when the stressor is dealt with successfully, beta adrenergic receptors are stimulated, and activity of the HPA axis is suppressed (McEwen, 1995).

Serotonin also inhibits the activity of the HPA axis. Recall from Chapter 4 that serotonin is released from neurons located in the raphe system in the hindbrain. Axons from the raphe cells terminate on $5HT_{1A}$ receptors in the paraventricular nucleus. When serotonin binds with these receptors, CRH release is suppressed, and activation of the HPA axis is terminated, which stops the stress response. Thus, removal of a stressor activates cells in the locus coeruleus and raphe system, which in turn inhibit the release of CRH via beta adrenergic and $5HT_{1A}$ receptors. It is important that the HPA axis and the stress response be shut down when the stressor is removed because prolonged activation of the stress response can produce a number of negative consequences, as you will learn in the next section.

dexamethasone: a form of synthetic glucocorticoid that inhibits the release of CRH and ACTH

dexamethasone suppression test: a test that assesses the ability of the HPA axis to regulate glucocorticoid release, which can be used to diagnose depression

An (a)_____ stressor is one that occurs infrequently and for a limited period of time. The stress response has two purposes: (1) to prepare the person to respond to the stressor (with (b)_____ blood flow, breathing rate, and alertness), and (2) to inhibit behaviors that interfere with dealing with the stressor (by (c)_____ sleep, eating, growth, and reproduction). Acute stressors also suppress the functioning of the (d)_____ system, by inhibiting macrophages, T-cells, and B-cells. In response to an acute stressor, the locus coeruleus releases (e)_____ and activates the sympathetic nervous system, stimulating the release of (f)_____. The paraventricular nucleus of the hypothalamus responds to a stressor by releasing (g)_____ _____ _____ (CRH), which stimulates the pituitary gland to release (h)_____ _____ (ACTH). ACTH travels to the cortex of the adrenal gland, where it stimulates the release of glucocorticoid, called (i)_____ in humans. The main function of cortisol is to (j)_____ the availability of blood glucose to provide energy to deal with stress. The (k)_____ axis involves the hypothalamus, the pituitary gland, and the adrenal gland. The relationship between the paraventricular nucleus and the locus coeruleus is characterized as a (l)_____ feedback loop because CRH released by the paraventricular nucleus increases activity of the locus coeruleus and norepinephrine from the locus coeruleus activates the paraventricular nucleus. The release of cortisol is controlled by a (m)_____ feedback loop. In the dexamethasone suppression test, administration of dexamethasone (n)_____ the release of cortisol in healthy individuals but (o)_____ cortisol levels in depressed people. When an individual has successfully coped with a stressor, activation of the HPA axis and the locus coeruleus is (p)_____.

The Response to Chronic Stress

We have just examined the nervous system's response to acute stressors. In response to an acute stressor, both the HPA axis and the locus coeruleus are activated, and glucocorticoids and catecholamines (especially epinephrine and norepinephrine) are released. When the acute stressor is removed, the release of glucocorticoids and catecholamines is promptly terminated. Hence, the effect of an acute stressor is short-term and reversible.

In contrast to an acute stressor, a **chronic stressor** occurs repeatedly or for prolonged periods of time. If an individual is unable to terminate or avoid the stressor, the nervous system makes neurochemical and behavioral adaptations to the stressor (Deakin, 1998). In addition, chronic stressors, such as experiencing a divorce or caring for a relative with Alzheimer's disease, suppress functioning of the immune system (Maier et al., 1994). Chronic stressors, therefore, can have long-lasting, sometimes irreversible effects on the nervous system. For example, chronic overexercising can have negative long-term effects on the nervous system (see *For Further Thought*).

The concept of *chronic stress* is quite complicated. On the one hand, it can refer to a person's response to a chronic stressor that is present for a prolonged period of time. On the other hand, chronic stress can persist long after a stressor has been removed. Andrew Baum's studies of people exposed to the accident at the nuclear power plant at Three Mile Island in 1980 revealed that chronic stress continued to be experienced by people living close to the accident site for up to 6 years following the accident (Baum, 1990; Baum, Cohen, & Hall, 1993; Davidson, Fleming, &

chronic stressor: a stressor that occurs repeatedly or for prolonged periods of time

Effects of Excessive Exercise

Regular exercise has a number of well-documented health benefits, including improved respiration and cardiovascular health, enhanced muscular and skeletal function, and reduced risk of obesity and other chronic disorders. However, extreme physical exercise performed on a regular basis may introduce some adverse health effects (McEwen, 1995). These adverse effects result from the increased activity of the sympathetic nervous system and the HPA axis associated with a stress response.

Chronic excessive exercise produces a stress response in the body that is accompanied by elevated levels of glucocorticoids and, eventually, a significant increase in the size of the medulla and cortex of the adrenal glands (McEwen, 1995; Buuck, Tharp, & Brumbaugh, 1976; Tharp, 1975). Recall that glucocorticoids increase the availability of glucose in the body, which is helpful for athletes because physical exercise requires a great deal of glucose. However, glucocorticoids also suppress the functioning of the immune system. Investigations of immune response in men who regularly engage in extreme physical activity have revealed reduced immune function in these men. For exam-

ple, a study of male swimmers on a university intercollegiate swim team showed that the level of salivary immunoglobulins (a measure of immune response) was significantly lower at the end of the competitive swim season following several months of chronic exercise, which increased the vulnerability of these swimmers to upper respiratory infections (Tharp & Barnes, 1990).

Highly trained athletes who engage in extreme physical exertion over several years will eventually show a blunted HPA-axis response to stress. Wittert, Livesey, Espiner, and Donald (1996) examined cortisol levels in ultra-marathon runners who had been training for many years and found that blood cortisol levels were reduced in these athletes. The HPA axis adapts to the high levels of CRH released by the paraventricular nucleus during chronic physical exertion. This means that, over time, much lower levels of ACTH and cortisol are released in response to stress in these athletes. Adaptation of the pituitary gland and adrenal cortex to stress can severely limit a person's ability to respond adequately to stress (Tharp, 1975).

Baum, 1987; Davidson & Baum, 1986; Schaeffer & Baum, 1984; Collins, Baum, & Singer, 1983). That is, chronic stress persisted in the absence of a physical stressor in people living near Three Mile Island. Let's take a close look at the response of the nervous system to chronic stress.

Effect of Chronic Stress on the Locus Coeruleus–Norepinephrine System

Most studies of the effect of chronic stress on the locus coeruleus have employed animal subjects, particularly rats. For example, chronic stress can be induced in rats by restraining them for 1 hour a day for 3 or more weeks. Chronic exposure to a stressor produces a long-term change in the excitation of the locus coeruleus (Bremner et al., 1996). Studies with rat subjects have indicated that a variety of responses are possible when an animal is exposed to chronic stress, including **habituation** and **sensitization**.

Habituation involves a decrease in the release of norepinephrine in the stressed rat when it is repeatedly exposed to a given stressor (Figure 14.7). Recall that, in response to an acute stressor, the locus coeruleus increases its firing rate, which increases the release of norepinephrine. If that stressor is presented repeatedly, the locus coeruleus responds to the stressor by *decreasing* its firing rate, thus causing a decrease in the release of norepinephrine (Zigmond et al., 1995). This effect is similar to the *tolerance* to drugs seen in addicted individuals, which you learned about in Chapter 13.

Sensitization is an enhanced response observed when a chronically stressed individual is presented with a new or different stressor (Figure 14.7). For example, Nisenbaum, Zigmond, Sved, and Abercrombie (1991) kept rats in a cold environment for several weeks and then exposed them to tail shock. In this procedure, cold was the chronic stressor, and tail shock was the new stressor. The investigators used

habituation: a decrease in the response of the nervous system to a repeated stimulus, such as a chronic stressor

sensitization: an enhanced response observed when a chronically stressed individual is presented with a new or different stressor

Figure 14.7 Habituation versus sensitization

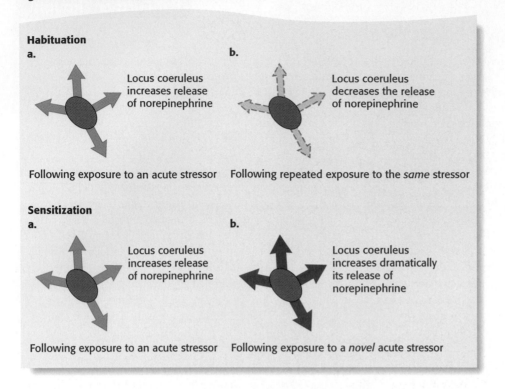

Habituation

a.

Locus coeruleus increases release of norepinephrine

Following exposure to an acute stressor

b.

Locus coeruleus decreases the release of norepinephrine

Following repeated exposure to the *same* stressor

Sensitization

a.

Locus coeruleus increases release of norepinephrine

Following exposure to an acute stressor

b.

Locus coeruleus increases dramatically its release of norepinephrine

Following exposure to a *novel* acute stressor

microdialysis to measure the amount of norepinephrine released by neurons in the locus coeruleus. Compared to control subjects that received only tail shock, chronically stressed rats had significantly more norepinephrine released in their brains when they were exposed to tail shock. Chronically stressed people are believed to show a sensitization response when they are confronted with a novel stressor: They typically overreact to the novel stressor.

Effect of Chronic Stress on the HPA Axis

Far less is known about the role of the HPA axis in chronic stress compared to its role in acute stress (Michelson et al., 1995). And, we are just beginning to understand the effects of chronic stress on this axis. Studies of rats and primates exposed to a variety of chronic stressors indicate that glucocorticoid levels remain high in chronically stressed animals. That is, the HPA axis continues to remain active and pump out glucocorticoids in response to chronic stress, unlike the locus coeruleus system, which habituates to the presence of chronic stressors.

One problem with studying the effect of chronic stress on the HPA axis in humans is obtaining a good measure of HPA activation. With rats and other animal subjects, we can measure the release of CRH, ACTH, glucocorticoid, or neurotransmitters directly in the brain using microdialysis. In humans, we measure cortisol levels in hopes that these reflect HPA activity. However, measuring cortisol levels in the blood is problematic because the stress of being poked with a needle while blood is drawn causes cortisol to be released and, hence, is an inaccurate measure of chronic stress (Yehuda, 1997). A better measure of HPA activity in chronic stress is urinary cortisol levels, in which the amount of cortisol in the urine is measured.

Chronic stress can produce permanent changes in the HPA axis (Sapolsky, 1997; Walker & Diforio, 1997). For example, the negative feedback loop that controls the release of glucocorticoids can become impaired (Figure 14.8). When this feedback loop breaks down, glucocorticoids circulating in the bloodstream do not turn off the neurons in the paraventricular nucleus that release CRH or the cells in the anterior pituitary that release ACTH. Thus, glucocorticoid continues to be synthesized and released, even as glucocorticoid levels rise higher and higher. The final result is persistently elevated levels of glucocorticoid under chronic or repeated stress (McEwen, 1995).

Another factor that contributes to the breakdown of the negative feedback loop that controls glucocorticoid release is the hormone *arginine-vasopressin*, which is produced with CRH in the paraventricular nucleus and which also stimulates the release of ACTH. Research with rats and humans indicates that arginine-vasopressin may maintain high glucocorticoid levels in the brain and throughout the body in response to repeated or prolonged stress. Recall that arginine-vasopressin is *not* part of the negative feedback loop that regulates glucocorticoid release. Glucocorticoids inhibit the release of CRH and ACTH but not the release of arginine-vasopressin. Although the physiological mechanism is not understood, chronic stress appears to produce high levels of glucocorticoids that are maintained by arginine-vasopressin acting on cells that secrete ACTH, which in turn stimulate the release of glucocorticoids (Michelson et al., 1995). Because glucocorticoids inhibit the release of CRH, CRH levels are reduced in an individual exposed to chronic stress. Therefore, chronic stress is associated with reduced levels of CRH and increased levels of arginine-vasopressin, ACTH, and glucocorticoids. Table 14.1 summarizes the effects of chronic stress.

Effect of Chronic Stress on the Brain

High levels of glucocorticoids caused by chronic stress can have a devastating effect on the brain, especially the *hippocampus* (Hoschl & Hajek, 2001). Rats exposed to chronic stress and, therefore, high glucocorticoid levels for several weeks experience *atrophy*, or wasting away, of dendrites of *pyramidal neurons* in the hippocampus (Sapolsky, 1996). This damage to the dendrites is reversible, however, and can be repaired if the chronic stressor is removed. Permanent, irreversible loss of hippocampal neurons is observed in rats that have been exposed to chronic stress for several months. That is, chronic stress causes cell death in the rat hippocampus.

Brain-imaging studies suggest that increased levels of glucocorticoids also cause damage to hippocampal neurons in humans (Figure 14.9). People with Cushing's syndrome overproduce cortisol due to a tumor in the hypothalamus, pituitary, or adrenal gland. MRI studies of their brains indicate hippocampal damage, with atrophy of the hippocampus on both sides of the brain (Starkman et al., 1999). Hippocampal atrophy was also observed in MRI scans of the brains of depressed patients with chronically high cortisol levels (Sheline et al., 1996). In addition, MRI scans of the brains of patients with post-traumatic stress disorder showed significant reductions in the size of the hippocampus, compared to those of controls (Gurvits et al., 1993; Bremner et al., 1993).

The observed damage to the hippocampus is believed to be due to the elevated levels of glutamate in the hippocampus (Horger & Roth, 1995; Sapolsky, 1996; Walker & Diforio, 1997). As you will learn in Chapter 16, too much glutamate can have a **cytotoxic** effect on neurons, destroying them. Glucocorticoids increase glutamate levels by interfering with the regulation of glutamate release. Because the

Figure 14.8 Impairment of the negative feedback loop in chronic stress

Chronic stress can impair the negative feedback system that controls the release of glucocorticoids. As a result of this impairment, glucocorticoids in the bloodstream fail to inhibit the release of CRH and ACTH, which causes glucocorticoid levels to rise higher and higher. (SCN = suprachiasmic nucleus, PVN = paraventricular nucleus, AVP = arginine-vasopressin)

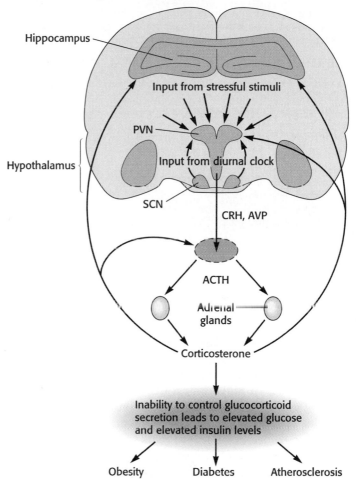

cytotoxic: having a destructive effect on cells

Table 14.1

Summary of the Effects of Chronic Stress

Effect on Locus Coeruleus–Norepinephrine System

Habituation: Decrease in release of norepinephrine to repeated stressor
Sensitization: Increase in release of norepinephrine to new or different stressor

Effect on HPA Axis

Continued release of glucocorticoids to chronic stressor
Impairment of negative feedback loop that controls glucocorticoid release
Persistently elevated levels of glucocorticoids

Effect on Brain

Atrophy of dendrites of pyramidal neurons in the hippocampus
Death of hippocampal neurons
Disruption of action of dopamine in the prefrontal cortex that enables coping responses

Effect on Behavior

Habituation
Sensitization
Fear conditioning
Learned helplessness
Seizures
Memory impairment

negative feedback loop that controls glucocorticoid synthesis becomes impaired with chronic stress, glucocorticoid production and release continue uncontrolled, which means that high levels of cortisol are present in the body of a chronically stressed person. As cortisol levels increase, so do glutamate levels increase in the hippocampus. The elevated levels of glutamate, in turn, damage the dendrites of pyramidal neurons and then eventually destroy these neurons in the hippocampus.

The death of hippocampal neurons caused by excessive levels of glucocorticoids must certainly lead to impairment of learning and memory (Akil & Morano, 1996; Walker & Diforio, 1997). But, think for a moment about what the death of hippocampal cells means in terms of glucocorticoid regulation. Earlier in this chapter you learned that the hippocampus plays an important role in the negative feedback loop that inhibits the release of glucocorticoids. Recall that the hippocampus contains numerous glucocorticoid receptors and is believed to send inhibitory signals to the paraventricular nucleus of the hypothalamus, which terminates the release of CRH. Damage to the hippocampus means that inhibition of the CRH neurons is reduced, which in turn leads to increased release of glucocorticoids (Figure 14.9). The increase in circulating glucocorticoids further damages the hippocampus, leading to even less inhibition of CRH-secreting neurons and further release of glucocorticoids. This vicious cycle is self-perpetuating and demonstrates the devastating effects of chronic stress (Akil & Morano, 1996).

The neurotransmitter *serotonin* has also been implicated in the damage to dendrites of pyramidal neurons in the hippocampus. The evidence is indirect, however. For example, antidepressant medication that increases serotonin availability in the brain stops destruction of the dendrites of hippocampal cells (McEwen, 1995). Other

Figure 14.9 Effect of hippocampal damage on negative feedback loop

Normally, the hippocampus inhibits the release of CRH by the hypothalamus. Activation of the HPA axis increases levels of circulating cortisol, producing damage in the hippocampus. Hippocampal damage reduces inhibition of the CRH-producing neurons in the paraventricular nucleus of the hypothalamus.

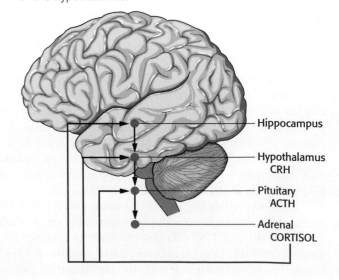

Hippocampus

Hypothalamus
CRH

Pituitary
ACTH

Adrenal
CORTISOL

evidence demonstrates that persistently elevated levels of glucocorticoid produced by chronic stress are associated with altered serotonin function in the hippocampus. Together, hippocampal damage and changes in serotonin function can negatively affect cognitive processes, especially those needed to cope with the stressor.

How does glucocorticoid alter serotonin activity in the hippocampus? The answer to this question is quite complicated. Recall from Chapter 4 that serotonin is produced by neurons located in the raphe system in the hindbrain. Axons from these raphe neurons project to many different regions in the brain, including the hippocampus. Two pathways from the raphe system terminate in the hippocampus: (1) a pathway that has an **anxiogenic,** or anxiety-producing, function; and (2) a pathway from the medial raphe that has an **anxiolytic,** or anxiety-reducing, function (Figure 14.10). The anxiogenic pathway originates in the dorsal raphe and terminates on $5HT_2$ receptors in the hippocampus and amygdala. In contrast, the anxiolytic pathway originates in neurons in the medial raphe and innervates $5HT_{1A}$ receptors in the hippocampus. The anxiolytic pathway plays an important role in coping with stress because it reduces emotional responding to stimuli associated with past aversive experiences (McEwen, 1995). However, when glucocorticoid levels remain elevated in response to chronic stress, glucocorticoid blocks the response of $5HT_{1A}$ receptors, thereby suppressing the activity of the anxiolytic pathway, and it also enhances $5HT_2$ receptor function, increasing anxiety in the chronically stressed individual (Duman, 1995).

Another area of the brain that is affected by chronic stress is the *prefrontal cortex*, especially the regions near the midline, called the *mesoprefrontal cortex*, and regions near the eye socket, called the *orbitoprefrontal cortex* [*meso-* = toward the middle; *orbito-* = referring to the eye socket, Latin] (Figure 14.11). The prefrontal cortex contains receptors for the neurotransmitters norepinephrine, serotonin, dopamine, and acetylcholine, all of which are involved in the stress response. For example, dopamine release is very sensitive to stress because even mild stressors can produce a dramatic increase in the release of dopamine in the prefrontal cortex (Horger & Roth, 1996). The role of dopamine in the prefrontal cortex is believed to be to enable coping responses because dopamine inhibits the same neurons that receive excitatory input from glutamate, which is released by fear-invoking neurons located in the amygdala (Deutch & Young, 1995). In other words, dopamine helps an individual cope with stress by counteracting emotional responses generated by the amygdala. Chronic exposure to stress appears to disrupt dopamine release, which interferes with an individual's ability to make appropriate coping responses (Horger & Roth, 1996).

Effect of Chronic Stress on Behavior

Chronic stress and traumatic stress can both produce persistent symptoms that interfere with normal behavior. These symptoms include *habituation, sensitization, fear conditioning, failure of extinction, learned helplessness, seizures,* and *memory impairment.* You've probably learned about these symptoms in other psychology courses, but I want to review them here in the context of stress-related problems.

Habituation

We touched upon the concept of habituation in an earlier section of this chapter and in Chapter 9. In the context of chronic stress, habituation occurs to a stressor that is presented repeatedly or for a long period of time. The original response to the stressor is a bona fide stress response mediated by the locus coeruleus and the

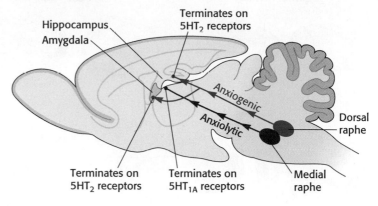

Figure 14.10 Serotonin pathways from the raphe system to the hippocampus

anxiogenic: anxiety-producing
anxiolytic: anxiety-reducing

Figure 14.11 Regions of prefrontal cortex affected by chronic stress

Squirrel monkey

Cat

Rhesus monkey

Dog

Chimp

Human

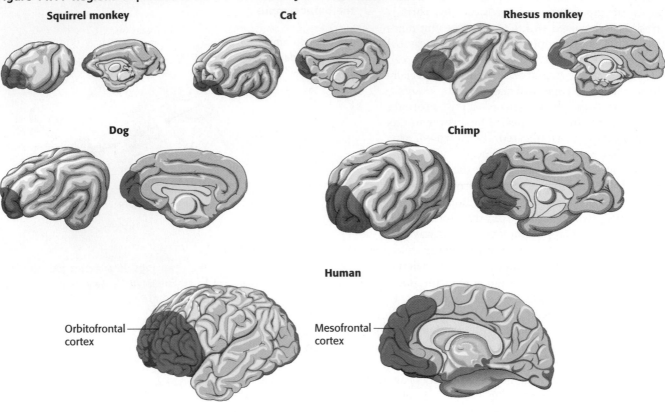

Orbitofrontal cortex

Mesofrontal cortex

HPA axis. This stress response causes the individual to be vigilant, attentive to the stressor, and highly aroused. However, when a stressor is chronic, the individual can habituate to it. That is, the individual will fail to respond to the stressor with a stress response (Gold & McCarty, 1995). This can be a problem, especially when the person needs to respond to the stressor. For example, parents with a young child on an apnea monitor that sounds an alarm when the child stops breathing [*a-* = without; *-pnea* = air, Latin] need to respond to that alarm immediately. At first, parents respond to the alarm promptly and with a great deal of distress. But, after repeated alarms, some parents fail to wake up immediately when the alarm sounds because of habituation.

Sensitization

Sensitization is another concept that we've already examined in this chapter. As opposed to habituation, sensitization is an *increase* in responsiveness to a stressor (Charney, Deutch, Southwick, & Krystal, 1995). Some investigators have examined the phenomenon of sensitization to a novel stressor, which causes an individual to make inappropriate responses to a stimulus, as we discussed earlier. However, sensitization can also occur to a stressor that has been presented repeatedly or chronically. An example of this might be a person who needs to have blood drawn repeatedly for medical testing purposes, such as a person with AIDS who needs to have T-cell levels monitored. Every time a needle is inserted in this person's arm to draw blood, the sensitized person makes a greater-than-normal stress response to the needle.

Fear Conditioning

You learned about fear conditioning in Chapter 13. In **fear conditioning,** an individual learns to fear a neutral stimulus that has been paired with a fear-inducing

fear conditioning: a process in which an individual learns to fear a neutral stimulus that has been paired with a fear-inducing stimulus

stimulus (Figure 14.12). In a classic experiment, John Watson conditioned a fear response in a young infant referred to as Little Albert. Using a classical conditioning paradigm, Watson repeatedly presented Little Albert with a white rat paired with a loud, fear-evoking noise. As a consequence, Little Albert developed a fear of white fuzzy objects. Fear conditioning can occur in people who are exposed to a traumatic, fear-inducing stressor (Charney et al., 1995). These people begin to fear stimuli that were associated with the traumatic stressor. For example, a child who has been sexually abused in a boat may show a fear or avoidance response to boats or water. Norepinephrine has been implicated as playing a key role in fear conditioning because its increased release in the hippocampus and the amygdala may elicit a conditioned response (Bremner et al., 1996).

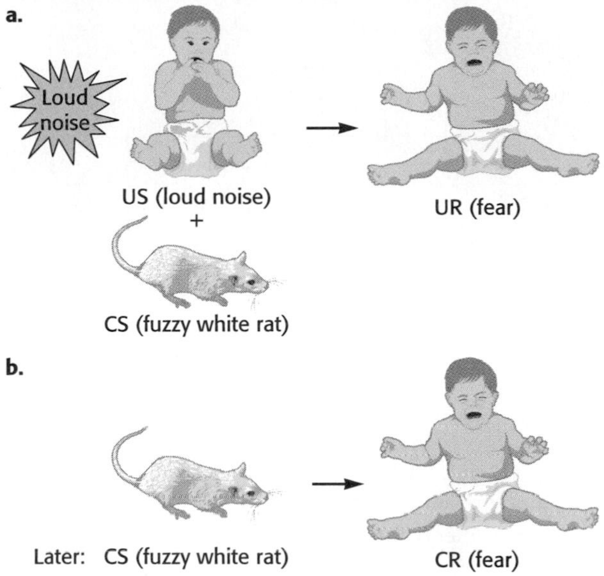

Failure of Extinction

Extinction refers to the absence of response to a stimulus. In a classical conditioning paradigm, extinction is a loss of conditioned response (CR) to the conditioned stimulus (CS) after the conditioned stimulus has been presented repeatedly without the unconditioned stimulus (US). Following chronic or traumatic stress, extinction can fail to occur. **Failure of extinction** is observed when an individual continues to make a conditioned response to a stimulus in the absence of the unconditioned stimulus. That is, a person who has suffered excessive stress may continue to respond to stimuli associated with the stressor long after the stimuli and the stressor have been paired (Charney et al., 1995). For example, a veteran who has been exposed to chronic stress on the battle front may continue to respond to loud noises with an intense stress response, even though the loud noise is not associated with battle. Bremner and his colleagues (1996) at Yale University have proposed that chronic or traumatic stress results in increased release of norepinephrine in the hippocampus and amygdala, which elicits a conditioned response in the absence of the US.

Learned Helplessness

Seligman and Maier (1967) first demonstrated **learned helplessness** in dogs that were exposed to inescapable shocks. When escape from the shocks was later made possible, the dogs with learned helplessness failed to escape the shocks. Rather, they just lay on the floor, shaking in fear, waiting for the shocks (Figure 14.13). This phenomenon is believed to be mediated by the neurotransmitter norepinephrine, which is released in response to uncontrollable stressors (Bremner et al., 1996; McEwen, 1995). Learned helplessness is associated with depletion of brain norepinephrine because the production of norepinephrine cannot keep up with the demand for it when an individual is exposed to chronic, inescapable stress (Petty et al., 1993). Symptoms of learned helplessness, such as decreased motor activity and decreased avoidance, have been observed in humans who have been exposed to long-term uncontrollable stress, such as law students or abused children (Cerezo & Frias, 1994; Satterfield, Monahan, & Seligman, 1997). In addition, learned helplessness has been used by some investigators as an animal model of depression because the symptoms associated with learned helplessness so closely resemble those of depression.

Seizures

Numerous investigators have examined the relationship between stress and **seizures**. In fact, Chi-Wan Lai and Michael Trimble (1997) have reviewed nearly

Figure 14.12 Fear conditioning paradigm

In John Watson's experiment, a loud noise (US) induces fear and crying (UR) in a baby. When a white, fuzzy rat (previously an unfeared object, the CS) is paired with the loud noise (US), the rat (CS) will come to elicit fear and crying (CR).

Fear conditioning: (Watson's experiment)

a.

Loud noise

US (loud noise) + CS (fuzzy white rat)

UR (fear)

b.

Later: CS (fuzzy white rat)

CR (fear)

failure of extinction: continuing to respond to a stimulus long after the stimulus (conditioned stimulus) and the stressor (unconditioned stimulus) have been paired

learned helplessness: decreased motor activity and decreased avoidance in response to exposure to an inescapable stressor

seizures: epileptic episodes in which abnormal electrical activity is detected in the brain, producing inattentiveness (petit mal seizures) or unconsciousness (grand mal seizures)

Figure 14.13 Dog in learned helplessness paradigm

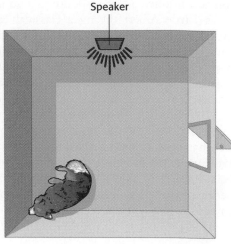

a. Tone signals that shock (electric) is about to occur

b. When shock is applied, dog runs about room, frantically trying to escape (inescapable shock)

c. Later, after repeated pairings of tone and inescapable shock, dog merely huddles and shivers in a corner when tone plays, even when the door is open and escape is possible

100 published studies that looked at the ability of stress to induce epileptic seizures. Abnormal electroencephalographic (EEG) waves, accompanied by observable seizures, were recorded in human adults and children during stressful interviews or other traumatic events (Berkhout, Walker, & Adey, 1969; Groethuysen et al., 1957; Stevens, 1959; Stores & Lwin, 1981). Most studies of the effect of stress on seizure activity have been conducted with human participants who are epileptic. That is, stress appears to produce seizures in individuals who have a history of seizures. Only one study of first-time seizures induced by stress has been published (Ferrie et al., 1994). Ferrie and his colleagues examined 9 clinical patients who had seizures for the first time while playing video games and reviewed published case histories of 18 additional individuals who experienced their first seizures while playing video games. The stress of sleep deprivation, overexcitement, and intense cognitive processing was believed to be responsible for the development of seizures in these young patients. The neurotransmitters serotonin and GABA, as well as the HPA axis hormones CRH, ACTH, and glucocorticoids, all appear to play a role in the development of stress-related seizures (Lai & Trimble, 1997).

Memory Impairment

Memory impairment is a critical symptom in a number of stress-related disorders. Recall from Chapter 10 that moderate stress and the release of norepinephrine improve memory, especially encoding and retrieval. However, chronic stress or exposure to a highly traumatic stressor will interfere with memory storage and working memory. Although the mechanism is not understood, the increased release of catecholamines in response to chronic or traumatic stressors is believed to disrupt memory processes (Bremner et al., 1996; Gold & McCarty, 1995). Some patients with stress-related disorders often show a loss of memory for events surrounding a stressful experience, and others have extremely sharp memories for a few details related to the traumatic event. These problems with long-term memory may be related to hippocampal damage resulting from chronic stress (Gold & McCarty, 1995; McEwen, 1995a; Sapolsky, 1996). In addition, short-term memory can become impaired due to stress-related activation of the prefrontal cortex or damage to the hippocampus (Bremner et al., 1996; Deutch & Young, 1995; Horger & Roth, 1996).

memory impairment: a symptom associated with a number of disorders, including stress-related disorders, in which memory storage or retrieval is disrupted

A (a)_____ stressor occurs repeatedly or for prolonged periods of time. (b)_____ and sensitization are observed when an individual is exposed to chronic stress. Habituation involves a (c)_____ in the release of norepinephrine from the locus coeruleus in response to a chronic stressor. Sensitization involves an (d)_____ in the release of norepinephrine in response to a chronic stressor. Chronic stress can produce permanent changes in the HPA axis, impairing the (e)_____ feedback loop that controls the release of glucocorticoids (cortisol in humans). Chronic stress also affects brain structures, such as the (f)_____, where it destroys the dendrites of pyramidal neurons. Elevated levels of (g)_____, caused by increased levels of cortisol, damage hippocampal neurons, impairing learning and memory. The prefrontal cortex is also affected by chronic stress, especially the (h)_____ cortex and the (i)_____ cortex. Chronic stress also disrupts (j)_____ release, which interferes with ability of the stressed individual to cope. Abnormal behaviors are associated with chronic or traumatic stress, including (k)_____ (failure of response to the stressor), (l)_____ (increase in responsiveness to a stressor), (m)_____ _____ (fearing a neutral stimulus that are associated with a traumatic stressor), (n)_____ of (o)_____ (continuation of a response to a stimulus that is no longer associated with a traumatic stressor), (p)_____ _____ (decreased motor activity and failure to respond when exposed to a chronic, inescapable stressor), (q)_____ (abnormal brain activity produced by traumatic or chronic stressors), and (r)_____ _____ (disruption in encoding and retrieval of information associated with the chronic or traumatic stressor).

Disorders Associated with Stress

When people are exposed to chronic stress or when the stress response is not terminated immediately following the removal of a stressor, dysregulation of the stress response can occur. Particularly vulnerable are those behaviors that are typically suppressed by the stress response, such as eating, sleeping, and sexual behavior. In many disorders associated with stress, eating, sleeping, or sexual behavior can be disrupted (Akil & Morano, 1996). Dysfunction of the locus coeruleus system or the HPA axis can lead to problematic behaviors such as sensitization, learned helplessness, or memory impairment. In this section, we will examine a number of disorders, including *post-traumatic stress disorder*, *major depressive disorder*, and *fatigue disorders*. Although animal models exist for each of these disorders, I will focus my discussion on research involving human patients. We will look at the theoretical causes as well the treatments for each of these disorders.

Before we examine each of the stress-related disorders individually, I must emphasize that not everybody who experiences chronic stress develops a stress-related disorder. In fact, most of us experience a traumatic, stressful experience sometime in our lives, but only a small percentage of us acquire post-traumatic stress disorder or depression. What makes some people more vulnerable than others to stress-related disorders? At this point, investigators are uncertain about the answer to this question. Some people may have a genetic predisposition to develop a stress-related disorder. That is, those individuals with a stress-related disorder may have inherited a genetic mutation, or an alteration in a normal gene, that causes neurons to react to stressors or stress hormones in nonadaptive ways—for example, to release too much or too little of an important enzyme, which would alter the functioning of the neurons (Duman, 1995).

Post-Traumatic Stress Disorder

Post-traumatic stress disorder has only recently been recognized as a formal disorder. The third edition of the *Diagnostic and Statistical Manual (DSM-III)* published by the American Psychiatric Association first listed post-traumatic stress disorder as a bona fide disorder in 1980. Table 14.2 gives the *DSM-IV* criteria for post-traumatic stress disorder. (*DSM-IV* is the most recent edition of the *Diagnostic and Statistical Manual.*) All individuals with post-traumatic stress disorder have experienced one or more traumatic events (an extreme stressor like a car accident, or rape, or exposure to acts of violence) prior to the development of the disorder. To give you a better understanding of this disorder, a Vietnam veteran with post-traumatic stress disorder is presented in the *Case Study*. The most striking or definitive symptoms are vivid recurrent memories for certain aspects of the traumatic event and **flashbacks** in which the individual feels as if he or she is actually re-experiencing the traumatic event. Research on this disorder began with the study of "shell-shocked" soldiers after World War I, but intensive study of post-traumatic stress disorder did not begin until after 1980 (Southwick, Yehuda, & Morgan, 1995).

In post-traumatic stress disorder, the locus coeruleus remains hyperactive, causing a sensitization response to all stressors, especially those that resemble the original traumatizing event (Bremner et al., 1996; Zigmond et al., 1995). For example, the sound of a car backfiring might make you jump a bit, but it causes an enhanced stress response in a veteran with post-traumatic stress disorder because it reminds the veteran of gunfire during a battle. Norepinephrine is released in elevated amounts throughout the nervous system in response to this harmless sound, activating the sympathetic nervous system.

Studies of the effects of **yohimbine,** a norepinephrine-receptor antagonist, on patients with post-traumatic stress disorder provide further evidence that excessive release of norepinephrine may play an important role in the development of post-traumatic stress disorder. Yohimbine blocks a specific norepinephrine receptor, called the *alpha-2 adrenergic receptor.* Alpha-2 adrenergic receptors function as autoreceptors on presynaptic terminals in neurons that release norepinephrine. In Chapter 3, you learned that presynaptic inhibition can be produced by autorecep-

post-traumatic stress disorder: a disorder, caused by exposure to one or more traumatic events, that is characterized by recurrent distressing memories of the event and feeling as if the traumatic event were recurring

flashback: the emergence of vivid memories that causes a past event to be experienced as happening all over again

yohimbine: a drug that blocks the alpha-2 adrenergic receptor and produces an increase in the release of norepinephrine

---

Table 14.2

Summary of *DSM-IV* Criteria for Post-Traumatic Stress Disorder

Has experienced traumatic event(s) that threatens the self or others
Reexperiencing criteria (one required)
Experiencing recurrent distressing memories, dreams, or flashbacks
Experiencing intense psychological or physiological reactions to stimuli that resemble or symbolize the traumatic event (one required)

Avoidance criteria (three required)
Avoidance of thoughts, feelings, or activities associated with the traumatic event
Memory loss for important aspect of the trauma
Markedly reduced interest in important activities
Feelings of detachment from others
Restricted affect or numbing
Sense of foreshortened future

Arousal criteria (two required)
Insomnia
Irritability or angry outbursts
Impaired concentration
Constantly on guard, hypervigilant
Abnormal or exaggerated startle reaction

Symptoms must be present for at least 1 month
Distress or impairment must be clinically significant

Post-Traumatic Stress Syndrome

Doug graduated from high school in 1966 and was almost immediately drafted into the Army. As soon as he finished boot camp, he was sent to Vietnam. He was installed with his platoon in a primitive camp on the edge of the jungle. The men in his camp were all extremely jumpy because mines were hidden everywhere in the jungle and fields near the camp and nearly everyday one or more exploded with a loud thud that was hair raising. They learned pretty quickly to trust no one who was Vietnamese, and they lived a tense, lonely existence far from the comforts and distractions of a city.

One night, Doug awoke to the sound of gunfire. He instinctively ran from his barrack and hid in the jungle near the camp. From his hiding place, Doug could hear the screams of his fellow soldiers as they were shot. He was so frightened that he urinated in his pants as he crouched beneath some brush, listening to the rat-tat-tat of the automatic gunfire. It was dark, so he couldn't see the attackers. But he could hear them call to each other, although he couldn't understand their language. Doug remained very still as a few of the attackers ran through the edge of the jungle, looking for escapees. Finally, the attackers departed.

For a long time, Doug hid in the brush, without moving. He listened for sounds of life in the camp but heard none. Afraid that some attackers remained in the camp, he stayed in his hiding place until the sun was quite high in the sky the next morning. The sight that greeted his eyes was harrowing. Everyone in his platoon had been murdered—everyone but him. He radioed for help and was soon transported away from that place of death.

Doug was never the same after that awful night when his buddies were massacred. He returned to the United States but was unable to hold a job or stay in a relationship for long. His sleep was troubled by recurring dreams of being wakened by the sound of gunfire, and he awoke, shaking and frightened, most nights. Doug had difficulty concentrating or listening when others were talking, and he had a hard time controlling his temper, especially when he drank.

When he arrived back in the States, people his age were protesting the presence of American troops in Vietnam. He was invited to speak at rallies but found that he couldn't remember anything about Vietnam. He couldn't recall even the names of his buddies who were killed. Living on disability, Doug spent most of his time in his apartment alone. He kept the television turned off because he couldn't bear to hear any reports about the war in Vietnam or the protests against the war.

What bothered Doug most were the flashbacks. These occurred mostly when he was drinking. Unfortunately, Doug had little to do but drink. He would be sitting in his living room, drinking whiskey, when, all of a sudden, he could hear gunshots and the sound of people running everywhere. His vision darkened, and he would run blindly out of the apartment, into the street, screaming. Doug could see and hear his attackers. He could feel them chasing him. Each flashback felt as vivid and real as that awful night in Vietnam. In fact, the flashbacks are as troublesome and real today, over 35 years later, as they were when Doug first returned from Vietnam.

tors that bind with the neurotransmitter that is released by the presynaptic neuron. The release of norepinephrine from a presynaptic neuron is controlled by alpha-2 adrenergic receptors on that neuron. That is, norepinephrine binds with alpha-2 adrenergic receptors on the presynaptic endings of norepinephrine-releasing neurons, which inhibit subsequent release of norepinephrine (Figure 14.14). Yohimbine blocks this autoreceptor, thereby preventing presynaptic inhibition and allowing additional norepinephrine to be released. Ultimately, yohimbine administration results in an increase in the release of norepinephrine.

When yohimbine is administered to patients with post-traumatic stress disorders, it produces panic attacks (discussed in Chapter 13), feelings of dissociation (discussed in Chapter 9), and flashbacks (Krystal et al., 1995; Southwick et al., 1995). In contrast, yohimbine does not produce these effects in healthy controls or in individuals with schizophrenia, major depression, obsessive-compulsive disorder, or generalized anxiety disorder (Charney et al., 1990). Because yohimbine administration results in increased norepinephrine release, the symptoms of post-traumatic stress disorder must be produced by excessive norepinephrine activity. Bremner and his colleagues (1997) administered yohimbine in a randomized, double-blind design to 10 Vietnam veterans with post-traumatic stress disorder and 10 healthy controls and then compared PET images of the brains of the two

Figure 14.14 Alpha-2 adrenergic autoreceptors

When norepinephrine is released in the synapse, it binds with alpha-2 adrenergic receptors, which inhibit the release of additional norepinephrine.

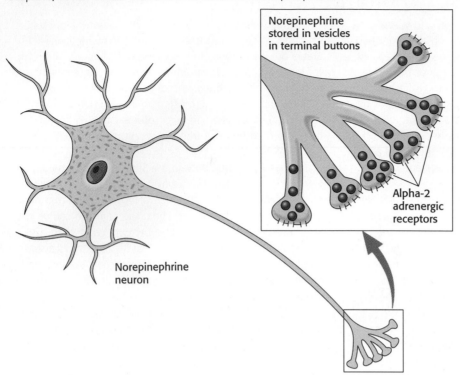

groups. Whereas all veterans with post-traumatic stress disorder experienced increased anxiety following injections of yohimbine, none of the controls did. In addition, significant differences were observed in glucose metabolism in the critical areas of brain between these two groups, indicating that yohimbine causes enhanced norepinephrine release in the brains of individuals with post-traumatic stress disorder.

Individuals with post-traumatic stress disorder experience symptoms like flashbacks, dissociation, and panic only intermittently. On the other hand, they are constantly hyperaroused [*hyper-* = more than normal, Latin] and overly vigilant. The chronically high levels of norepinephrine observed in people with post-traumatic stress disorder most likely produce the increased arousal and vigilance associated with this disorder. The episodic symptoms, such as flashbacks and panic, are possibly triggered by trauma-related stressors that, due to sensitization, cause a massive disruption of norepinephrine regulation (Southwick et al., 1995).

Investigators disagree, however, about the function of the HPA axis in post-traumatic stress disorder (Michelson et al., 1995). There is some evidence that urinary cortisol levels are lower than normal in most patients with post-traumatic stress disorder (Stout et al., 1995). This decrease in circulating cortisol is most likely due to enhanced responsiveness of the negative feedback loop that regulates cortisol levels (Yehuda, 1997). In patients with post-traumatic stress disorder, the pituitary gland is especially responsive to cortisol, which inhibits the release of ACTH, thereby preventing the release of additional cortisol. The chronically low levels of cortisol seen in post-traumatic stress disorder cause the person with this disorder to be more sensitive to stimuli in the environment and particularly sensitive to stressors. Stimuli that vaguely resemble sensations associated with the traumatic event are capable of triggering a rapid, intense stress response.

Treatment of Post-Traumatic Stress Disorder

The current treatment for post-traumatic stress disorder is *antidepressant medication*, which was originally designed to treat depression (Davidson et al., 2001; Cantz &

Buchalter, 2001; Marshall, Beebe, Oldham & Zaninelli, 2001). Refer back to Table 3.4 for a description of various antidepressant drugs. Long-term administration of antidepressant medication causes a sustained decrease in the firing of neurons in the locus coeruleus, which results in a decreased demand for norepinephrine (Duman, 1995). Because excitation of the locus coeruleus is increased in individuals with post-traumatic stress disorder, antidepressant drugs help relieve symptoms of the disorder by decreasing the activity of the locus coeruleus. Antidepressant medications also increase monoamine availability at the synapse, which improves signaling between neurons and within neurons (Duman, 1995).

Medications that are used to treat post-traumatic stress disorder do not eliminate the memories of the traumatic event that cause the patient so much trouble. Psychotherapy is needed to help the patient deal with the traumatic memories. After antidepressant medication has subdued the overarousal caused by increased activation of the locus coeruleus, a clinical psychologist can begin work to alter the way the patient thinks and feels about the traumatic event. This therapy may focus on reducing the loss of memory for the traumatic event and discharging unacknowledged emotions about the event (Krystal, Bennett, Bremner, Southwick, & Charney, 1995).

Major Depressive Disorder

Major depressive disorder (often referred to informally as *depression*) is a mood disorder characterized by lethargy, sad affect, diminished interest in all activities, cognitive disturbances, and eating and sleeping abnormalities. Animal models of depression typically use chronic stress to induce symptoms of depression in the nonhuman animals under study (Leonard, 1997). These animal models have demonstrated that chronic stressors produce symptoms of depression in animals as well as alter their neurotransmitter, hormone, and immune functions. Unfortunately, whereas observable behaviors such as motor activity, facial expression, eating, and sleep can be studied in animal models of depression, disturbances of mood and feelings cannot (Viguera & Rothschild, 1996). We will examine depressive disorders in greater detail in Chapter 15. In this chapter, we will focus on disturbances of the HPA axis that may contribute to depression.

major depressive disorder: a mood disorder characterized by lethargy, sad affect, diminished interest in all activities, cognitive disturbances, and eating and sleeping abnormalities

HPA Axis Dysfunction

For some reason not yet understood, about half of all patients with major depressive disorder have cortisol levels that are significantly higher than normal. It may be that major depressive disorder causes disruption of the HPA axis, or it may be that dysregulation of the HPA axis produces or maintains depression (Akil & Morano, 1996). Certainly the symptoms of increased vigilance and decreased vegetative functions like sleeping suggest that the depressed person has a hyperactive HPA axis (DeSouza & Grigoriadis, 1995; Michelson et al., 1995; Stout et al., 1995).

Unlike healthy controls, many people with major depressive disorder fail to suppress cortisol release following administration of dexamethasone in the dexamethasone suppression test. Recall that cortisol release should decrease following administration of dexamethasone because dexamethasone acts like cortisol, the human equivalent of glucocorticoid, in the negative feedback loop that controls glucocorticoid release. However, depressed people with a hyperactive HPA axis do not suppress cortisol release because of a chronic excess of CRH (DeSouza & Grigoriadis, 1995; Michelson et al., 1995). The increased release of CRH leads to elevations of circulating cortisol in individuals with major depression. These elevations of cortisol are not diminished by administration of dexamethasone.

There is a great deal of indirect evidence that excess secretion of CRH in the brains of depressed individuals might maintain their depressive symptoms. For example, investigators have found reduced numbers of CRH receptors in the frontal cortex of suicide victims (DeSouza & Grigoriadis, 1995). You see, the brain's response to excess levels of a transmitter substance is to decrease the numbers of receptor sites for that substance. This is called **down-regulation.** That is,

down-regulation: a reduction in the number of receptor sites available for an overabundant neurochemical in the brain

down-regulation decreases the number of receptor sites available for an overabundant neurochemical in the brain. Thus, the number of CRH receptor sites in the brains of depressed patients is reduced because there is an excess release of CRH.

Depression is often seen in patients with *anorexia nervosa*, which we discussed in Chapter 11. These patients have been demonstrated to have hypersecretion of CRH and, as a consequence, increased levels of cortisol. Interestingly, administration of CRH to rats inhibits food consumption in the rats. It may be that excess release of CRH in people with anorexia nervosa is contributing to their restricted intake of food (DeSouza & Grigoriadis, 1995).

Depression also occurs in another stressed population: those individuals with cancer. David Spiegel at Stanford University (1996) has estimated that about 50% of all cancer patients are depressed. Research conducted by Spiegel and his colleagues (Blake-Mortimer et al., 1999) has demonstrated that treatment for depression can increase the cancer patient's survival time and often reduces the patient's cancer-related pain, particularly for those patients with breast cancer, lymphoma, and malignant melanoma.

Fatigue Disorders

Fatigue disorders are characterized by lethargy, a loss of drive, and an increase in vegetative behaviors like sleeping and eating. These disorders include **chronic fatigue syndrome, atypical depression, seasonal affective disorder,** and **fibromyalgia** (Michelson et al., 1995). The major symptoms and treatments for these disorders are given in Table 14.3. In contrast to major depressive disorder—which, as you've just learned, is associated with increased levels of CRH—these fatigue disorders are associated with chronically low levels of CRH (Bradley et al., 2000; Cleare et al., 2001). If an individual is unable to release large amounts of CRH in response to a stressor, that individual has an impaired stress response system. Reduced CRH secretion leads to a decreased ability to respond to stress. This means that the systems that typically become activated during stress, including the

fatigue disorders: a cluster of disorders characterized by lethargy, loss of drive, and an increase in vegetative disorders such as sleeping and eating

chronic fatigue syndrome: a disorder characterized by symptoms of weakness, lethargy, tiredness, impaired concentration or memory, sore throat, and/or muscle and joint pain that last for more than 6 months

atypical depression: a mood disorder characterized by fatigue, lethargy, sleeping more than normal, and overeating

seasonal affective disorder: a mood dysfunction or depressive disorder that occurs most commonly in the winter

fibromyalgia: a disorder characterized by fatigue, headaches, and numbness accompanied by widespread bone and muscle pain

Table 14.3

Major Symptoms and Treatment for Representative Fatigue Disorders

Fatigue Disorder	Major Symptoms	Treatment
Chronic fatigue syndrome	Lethargy, weakness, tiredness; unrefreshing sleep; impaired memory, concentration; sore throat, tender lymph nodes in neck or armpit; muscle or joint pain; headaches; feelings of malaise following exertion. Symptoms present for >6 months.	Graded exercise program; cognitive behavioral therapy; *not effective:* antiviral medication, SSRIs, immunoglobulin treatment
Seasonal affective disorder	In winter months: lethargy, sleeping more than normal, hyperphagia, carbohydrate craving	Light therapy (2,500 lux for 2 hours daily); SSRIs
Atypical depression	Lethargy, sleeping more than normal, hyperphagia, sensitive to rejection by others	SSRIs; MAO inhibitor
Fibromyalgia	Fatigue, headaches, numbness; widespread pain in muscles and/or joints, in absence of signs of inflammation	SSRIs; graded exercise program; *not effective:* opioids, corticosteroids

HPA axis and the locus coeruleus, do not respond fully in the face of stress in a person who has a fatigue disorder. As a result, the central nervous system responses usually observed in a stress response, such as increased vigilance and attention and heightened arousal, are weak or absent in fatigue disorders. Although very little research has been conducted in this area, people with chronic fatigue syndrome and seasonal affective disorder generally have reduced levels of cortisol. This observation supports the hypothesis that low levels of CRH are responsible for maintaining some of the symptoms of fatigue disorders because low levels of CRH would produce low levels of circulating cortisol.

Stress has been implicated in the development of other psychological disorders, including *schizophrenia* and *bipolar disorder* (Diforio & Walker, 1997). However, we have not included them in the discussion here because the relationship between these disorders and stress is less straightforward. We will consider these disorders with other psychotic disorders in Chapter 15 because additional brain mechanisms and neurotransmitter systems appear to be involved.

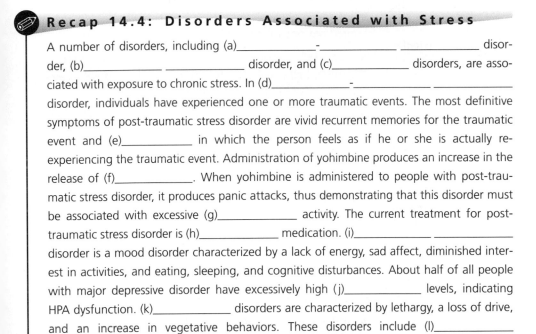

Recap 14.4: Disorders Associated with Stress

A number of disorders, including (a)_____-_____ _____ disorder, (b)_____ _____ disorder, and (c)_____ disorders, are associated with exposure to chronic stress. In (d)_____-_____ _____ disorder, individuals have experienced one or more traumatic events. The most definitive symptoms of post-traumatic stress disorder are vivid recurrent memories for the traumatic event and (e)_____ in which the person feels as if he or she is actually re-experiencing the traumatic event. Administration of yohimbine produces an increase in the release of (f)_____. When yohimbine is administered to people with post-traumatic stress disorder, it produces panic attacks, thus demonstrating that this disorder must be associated with excessive (g)_____ activity. The current treatment for post-traumatic stress disorder is (h)_____ medication. (i)_____ _____ disorder is a mood disorder characterized by a lack of energy, sad affect, diminished interest in activities, and eating, sleeping, and cognitive disturbances. About half of all people with major depressive disorder have excessively high (j)_____ levels, indicating HPA dysfunction. (k)_____ disorders are characterized by lethargy, a loss of drive, and an increase in vegetative behaviors. These disorders include (l)_____ _____ syndrome, (m)_____ _____ disorder, and (n)_____.

Chapter Summary

Defining Stress

▶ Stressors are people, objects, places or events that disrupt homeostasis in the nervous system. Stress is a state of imbalance produced by a stressor.

▶ Information about stressors reaches the paraventricular nucleus of the hypothalamus by way of the nucleus of the solitary tract (which relays information from the gut and other internal receptors), the tegmentum and reticular formation (which receive somatosensory information), the periaqueductal and central gray areas (which process information about pain), the locus coeruleus, the raphe system, and the bed nucleus of the stria terminalis (which receives input from the limbic system and the cerebral cortex).

▶ When homeostasis is disrupted, the paraventricular nucleus of the hypothalamus organizes the body's response.

The Response to Acute Stress

▶ The response to acute stressors is reversible. An acute stressor is one that occurs infrequently and for a limited period of time.

▶ The stress response has two purposes: 1) to prepare the person to respond to the stressor (with increased blood flow, breathing rate, and alertness), and 2) to inhibit behaviors that interfere with dealing with the stressor (suppress sleep, eating, growth, and reproduction).

▶ Acute stressors also suppress the functioning of the immune system, by inhibiting macrophages, T-cells, and B-cells.

▶ The locus coeruleus responds to acute stress by activating the sympathetic nervous system, which stimulates the release of norepinephrine and epinephrine.

▶ The paraventricular nucleus responds to acute stress by releasing a number of chemicals including corticotropic-releasing hormone (CRH), which stimulates the release of ACTH from the pituitary gland.

▶ In response to ACTH, the cortex of the adrenal gland secretes glucocorticoid (called cortisol in humans). The main function of cortisol is to increase the availability of blood glucose to provide energy to deal with stress.

▶ The HPA axis involves the hypothalamus, the pituitary gland, and the adrenal gland.

▶ The relationship between the paraventricular nucleus and the locus coeruleus is characterized as a positive feedback loop because CRH released by the paraventricular nucleus increases activity of the locus

coeruleus and norepinephrine from the locus coeruleus activates the paraventricular nucleus.

▶ The release of cortisol is controlled by a negative feedback loop. In the dexamethasone suppression test, administration of dexamethasone suppresses the release of cortisol in healthy individuals but increases cortisol levels in depressed people.

▶ When an individual has successfully coped with a stressor, activation of the HPA axis and the locus coeruleus is terminated.

The Response to Chronic Stress

▶ A chronic stressor occurs repeatedly or for prolonged periods of time.

▶ Chronic stress affects the locus coeruleus–norepinephrine system, the HPA axis, the hippocampus and prefrontal cortex, and behavior.

▶ Habituation and sensitization are observed when an individual is exposed to chronic stress. Habituation involves a decrease in the release of norepinephrine from the locus coeruleus in response to a chronic stressor. Sensitization involves an increase in the release of norepinephrine in response to a chronic stressor.

▶ Chronic stress can produce permanent changes in the HPA axis, impairing the negative feedback loop that controls the release of glucocorticoids (cortisol in humans). In response to a chronic stressor, levels of glucocorticoids are persistently elevated, which has devastating effects on the brain and immune system.

▶ Chronic stress also affects brain structures, such as the hippocampus, where it destroys the dendrites of pyramidal neurons. Elevated levels of glutamate, caused by increased levels of cortisol, damage hippocampal neurons, impairing learning and memory.

▶ The prefrontal cortex is also affected by chronic stress, especially the mesoprefrontal cortex and the orbitoprefrontal cortex.

▶ Chronic stress also disrupts dopamine release, which interferes with ability of the stressed individual to cope.

▶ Abnormal behaviors are associated with chronic or traumatic stress, including habituation (failure of response to the stressor), sensitization (increase in responsiveness to a stressor), fear conditioning (fearing a neutral stimulus that are associated with a traumatic stressor), failure of extinction (continuation of a response to a stimulus that is no longer associated with a traumatic stressor), learned helplessness (decreased motor activity and failure to respond when exposed to a chronic, inescapable stressor), seizures (abnormal brain activity produced by traumatic or chronic stressors), and memory impairment (disruption in encoding and retrieval of information associated with the chronic or traumatic stressor).

Disorders Associated with Stress

▶ Dysregulation of the stress response can produce a number of disorders, including post-traumatic stress disorder, major depressive disorder, and fatigue disorders.

▶ In post-traumatic stress disorder, individuals have experienced one or more traumatic events. The most definitive symptoms of post-traumatic stress disorder are vivid recurrent memories for the traumatic event and flashbacks in which the person feels as if he or she is actually re-experiencing the traumatic event.

▶ Administration of yohimbine produces an increase in the release of norepinephrine. When yohimbine is administered to people with post-traumatic stress disorder, it produces panic attacks, thus demonstrating that this disorder must be associated with excessive norepinephrine activity.

▶ The current treatment for post-traumatic stress disorder is antidepressant medication.

▶ Major depressive disorder is a mood disorder characterized by a lack of energy, sad affect, diminished interest in activities, and eating, sleeping, and cognitive disturbances.

▶ About half of all people with major depressive disorder have excessively high cortisol levels, indicating HPA dysfunction.

▶ Fatigue disorders are characterized by lethargy, a loss of drive, and an increase in vegetative behaviors. These disorders include chronic fatigue syndrome, seasonal affective disorder, and fibromyalgia.

Key Terms

acute stressor   (p. 415)

adrenocorticotropic hormone
   (ACTH)   (p. 417)

anxiogenic   (p. 427)

anxiolytic   (p. 427)

atypical depression   (p. 436)

B-cell   (p. 416)

bed nucleus of the stria
   terminalis   (p. 414)

chronic fatigue syndrome   (p. 436)

chronic stressor   (p. 422)

corticosterone   (p. 417)

corticotropic-releasing hormone
   (CRH)   (p. 417)

cortisol   (p. 417)

cytotoxic   (p. 425)

dexamethasone   (p. 421)

dexamethasone suppression
   test   (p. 421)

down-regulation   (p. 435)

failure of extinction   (p. 429)

fatigue disorders   (p. 436)

fear conditioning   (p. 428)

fibromyalgia   (p. 436)

flashbacks   (p. 432)

glucocorticoid   (p. 417)

habituation   (p. 423)

HPA axis   (p. 418)

learned helplessness   (p. 428)

macrophage   (p. 416)

major depressive disorder   (p. 435)

memory impairment   (p. 430)

paraventricular nucleus   (p. 411)

pituitary gland   (p. 417)

post-traumatic stress
   disorder   (p. 432)

psychoneuroimmunology   (p. 416)

seasonal affective disorder   (p. 436)

seizure   (p. 428)

sensitization   (p. 423)

stress   (p. 410)

stress-induced analgesia   (p. 420)

stressor   (p. 410)

T-cell   (p. 416)

yohimbine   (p. 432)

Questions for Thought

1. Can you remember a time when you became ill after experiencing stress?

2 Which system is more important in dealing with stress: the locus coeruleus–norepinephrine system or the HPA axis?

3 How can stress contribute to depression?

Questions for Review

1. Describe the various pathways by which information about stressors reaches the paraventricular nucleus of the hypothalamus.

2. What techniques have investigators used to study the brain's response to stress?

3. How do the effects of acute stress differ from the effects of chronic stress?

4. Describe the stress response initiated by the paraventricular nucleus.

5. Which brain systems are disturbed in post-traumatic stress disorder?

Suggested Readings

Baum, A. (1990). Stress, intrusive imagery, and chronic distress. *Health Psychology, 9,* 653–675.

Friedman, M. J., Charney, D. S., & Deutch, A. Y. (1995). *Neurobiological and clinical consequences of stress: From normal adaptation to PTSD.* Philadelphia: Lippincott-Raven.

Maier, S. F., & Watkins, L. R. (1998). Cytokines for psychologists: Implications of bidirectional immune-to-brain communication for understanding behavior, mood, and cognition. *Psychological Review, 105,* 83–107.

Yehuda, R., & McFarlane, A. C. (1997). *Psychobiology of posttraumatic stress disorder.* New York: New York Academy of Sciences.

Web Resources

For a chapter tutorial quiz, direct links to the Internet sites listed below and other features, visit the book-specific website at **www.wadsworth.com/product/ 0155074865**. You may also connect directly to the following annotated websites:

http://165.112.78.61/stressanddrugabuse.html
For information on the role of stress in drug addiction check out this site.

http://www.ncptsd.org/
This site from the National Center for Post-Traumatic Stress Disorder provides a variety of different resources to help you understand the aftereffects of trauma.

http://stress.about.com/library/weekly/ aa012901a.htm
This site provides additional information on cortisol, the hormone that is released in the body during stressed or agitated states.

For additional readings and information, check out InfoTrac College Edition at **http://www.infotrac-college.com/wadsworth**. Choose a search term yourself or enter the following search terms: post traumatic stress and seasonal affective disorder.

CD-ROM: Exploring Biological Psychology

Simulation: Stress and Health
Video: Stress and the Brain
Interactive Recaps

Chapter 14 Quiz
Connect to the Interactive Biological Psychology Glossary

Disordered Behavior

As a young boy, Joseph was described as "the kindest boy you'd ever meet." Mild mannered and shy, he worked in his father's neighborhood grocery store from 6 A.M. to closing every day of the week, taking time out only to go to school, from the age of 7 until he graduated from high school. His father was a domineering man who had immigrated to the United States in his late teens, established a chain of grocery stores with his older brother, then returned to his native land to find a wife. He married a woman much younger than himself and brought her back to America with him. They had nine children in rapid succession, and Joseph was the oldest.

Joseph's father controlled all aspects of his family's lives, dictating when they should work, when they could go out, and with whom they could associate. His mother never left the house, except to go to church or to the hospital to have another baby. She spoke no English and had no friends. Joseph and his siblings were not encouraged to make friends, either. Indeed, they were too busy working in the family business or doing schoolwork to have time for normal leisure or social activities.

After high school, Joseph enlisted in the Army and went off to boot camp. He then was sent overseas to join American troops fighting in a foreign war. After less than 6 months in battle, Joseph was given a medical discharge from the Army. His diagnosis was paranoid schizophrenia.

When he returned home, Joseph was angry and hostile toward his family. On his first morning home he flung a cup of hot coffee in his father's face. He had loud conversations with the voices in his head. He believed that people armed with guns were looking in the windows at him, trying to get him. He paced constantly, gesticulating and talking nonsense.

What caused Joseph to become schizophrenic? Was it his rigid, domineering father? His mother, who was emotionally inaccessible? His restricted social life as a teenager? Was it the pressures of Army life, or the horrors of war? Or was it a genetic problem—a maternal aunt also had been diagnosed as schizophrenic? And why didn't any of his brothers or sisters develop schizophrenia? These are the kinds of questions we will try to answer in this chapter.

Until very recently students of behavior were taught that psychological disorders are either of biological or psychological origin. The American Psychiatric Association's *Diagnostic and Statistical Manual of Mental Disorders*, which is used by clinical psychologists and psychiatrists to diagnose patients with behavior disorders, originally classified disorders as organic or psychogenic. Organic disorders were defined as those syndromes that are due to damage to the nervous system, biochemical abnormalities, or some other biological cause. In the latest (fourth) edition of the *Diagnostic and Statistical Manual of Mental Disorders (DSM-IV,* American Psychiatric Association, 1994), however, the term *organic* has been abandoned, and the term *disorder due to a general medical condition* has been substituted for all disorders for which a biological cause has been established. The authors wanted to eliminate any impression that some disorders are of biological origin and others are not. There is widespread agreement today among neuroscientists and practitioners that all behaviors are regulated by the brain and, therefore, that all disordered behaviors have a biological basis.

Nearly a century ago, Emil Kraepelin, who is regarded by many scholars as the father of modern psychiatry, pulled together a group of outstanding brain scientists at the Psychiatric Clinic of Munich University to study brain abnormalities associated with mental illness (Andreasen, 1988). This group included distinguished investigators whose names you should recognize: Alzheimer, Brodmann, and Nissl. Unfortunately, these scientists had only 19th-century technology at their disposal. Using limited chemical analyses, the compound microscope, and stains developed by Dr. Nissl, they could not find any specific brain abnormalities associated with most mental illnesses. This led them to conclude that many mental illnesses, most notably schizophrenia and mood disorders, have no specific underlying neural mechanism. Today's investigators have a number of modern technologies available, as you learned in Chapter 5, to identify in great detail the anatomical and neurochemical bases of disordered behavior.

In this chapter we will examine a variety of disorders commonly seen in the clinical setting, including psychoses, mood disorders, and personality disorders. We will focus on the anatomical, biochemical, and hereditary underpinnings of these disorders, looking at basic research that takes a "bottom-up" approach and at those imaging studies that take a "top-down" approach. Let's turn to the study of psychotic disorders first.

Psychoses

Many people confuse the term *psychotic* with the term *schizophrenic*, or they use the terms interchangeably, believing that they mean the same thing. Actually, schizophrenia is one of many different psychotic syndromes. **Psychoses** are severe mental disorders in which thinking is so disturbed that the afflicted person is not well oriented for person, time, and place. A good way to test this is to ask three simple questions: "What is your name?" "What is today's date?" "Who is the president of the United States?" A normal person would have no trouble answering these questions. A psychotic person, however, would have difficulty coming up with the correct answers.

Let me give you an example of the disordered thought processes that are characteristic of a psychosis. Here is the transcript of an interview with a young man (T) who was diagnosed as psychotic.

psychosis: a severe mental disorder in which thinking is disturbed and the affected individual is not well oriented for person, time, and place

DR: Can you tell me your name?
T: Tommy.
DR: Okay, Tommy—?
T: Tommy, you know, like the rock opera, *Tommy*. The Who?
DR: Tommy, okay. And what is your last name?
T: It's just Tommy.
DR: Uh-huh. What is your father's last name?
T: Oh. I was created when the needle hit the record, a flash of electricity, er, energy.

Most people are aware that they have parents, and they can tell you their last name without hesitation. A psychotic person has difficulty with even the simplest questions, often choosing a ridiculous answer over an obviously correct one. Thinking is so disturbed that a person with a psychosis cannot distinguish between rational and irrational ideas. This lack of judgment interferes with work and social behaviors, making it difficult for those with psychotic disorders to survive on their own. Often irrational thinking in a psychotic disorder is accompanied by delusions, hallucinations, and inappropriate emotional responses.

In Chapter 13, we examined the biological bases of anxiety disorders. Anxious people, unlike psychotic individuals, are well oriented for time and place. The overwhelming symptom of people with anxiety disorders is anxiety, which may make them unhappy or cause them to behave in embarrassing ways. But anxious individuals do not generally experience hallucinations, delusions, or irrational thoughts.

For most psychotic disorders, the biological cause is well documented. These disorders are referred to as "psychotic disorders due to a general medical condition" (American Psychiatric Association, 1994). Another term often used in conjunction with these disorders is **dementia,** which involves cognitive impairment (a decline in memory, thinking, and emotional functions) and poor judgment (Gottfries, 1988). Dementia and psychosis are both defined as "madness" (Gershon & Rieder, 1992). As with most psychoses, the diagnosis of dementia is usually coupled with a documented organic basis, such as arteriosclerosis (hardening of the arteries), malnutrition, brain tumor, or other degenerative brain disorder. We will examine dementias in Chapter 16, but I mention them here because they are often accompanied by psychotic symptoms. As we begin our discussion of psychotic disorders, let's first turn to disorders that have been linked to an organic brain problem.

dementia: a disorder that involves an impairment of memory, thinking, and emotional function

Reversible and Irreversible Psychoses

Not all psychoses are permanent conditions. Some people have one brief psychotic episode and then return to a normal state of mind. Other individuals have recurrent bouts of psychosis but remain functional much of the time. Most dementias, however, are irreversible because they are caused by some underlying neural problem that cannot be corrected. A person diagnosed with dementia is likely to remain mentally incapacitated for life. Less than 20% of all dementia cases are reversible. Psychosis or dementia may be treatable (that is, reversible) when the cause is an infectious disease, malnutrition, or drug related (Robinson, 1997).

Infections, especially those caused by bacteria that produce powerful toxins, such as diphtheria and some forms of bacterial pneumonia, can produce **toxic psychoses,** with symptoms of restlessness, loss of orientation for time and place, hallucinations, inattention, and perceptual distortions. These psychotic symptoms disappear when the infection is successfully treated. Likewise, the psychotic symptoms that accompany **viral encephalitis,** an inflammation of the brain caused by viruses so tiny that they can pass through the filters imposed by the blood–brain barrier, are not permanent. Sometimes meningitis, an inflammation of the meninges usually caused by a bacterial infection, will result in temporary disorientation for time and place, impaired memory and confusion, and hallucinations. Advanced liver or kidney disease can also produce brain dysfunction that causes psychotic symptoms.

toxic psychosis: a psychotic disorder caused by bacteria that produce powerful toxins

viral encephalitis: an infection of the brain caused by a virus that passes through the blood–brain barrier

Some brain tumors, particularly those located in the frontal, temporal, or parietal lobes or in the limbic regions, will produce psychotic symptoms (Craven, 2001; Lisanby, Kohler, Swanson & Gur, 1998; Lu & Yeh, 2001). In fact, patients with brain tumors are sometimes misdiagnosed as psychotic when they first come in for medical treatment, especially when their presenting symptoms are inappropriate emotional response, apathy, confusion, hallucinations, and loss of orientation for time and place. These symptoms generally subside when the tumor is removed.

Reversible psychotic symptoms can also be produced by abuse of stimulants, such as amphetamine, cocaine, and PCP or "angel dust," which were all discussed in Chapter 3. For example, large doses of amphetamine taken repeatedly will induce paranoid delusions similar to those observed in people with schizophrenia. This is true of amphetamine addicts and normal subjects. Studies of normal volunteers who were administered large doses of amphetamine daily under controlled conditions revealed that 100% of the subjects developed paranoid delusions within 1 week of the start of the study (Barondes, 1993). Repeated use of cocaine will also induce suspiciousness and paranoid delusions, as well as auditory hallucinations. Abuse of PCP produces hallucinations, paranoia, disordered thought, and sometimes catatonic movement disorders that are typically seen in schizophrenia. Remember that both amphetamine and cocaine augment catecholamine activity in the brain. (You might want to refer back to Chapter 3 for their specific actions.) PCP binds with the NMDA receptor, discussed in Chapter 10, and blocks the action of glutamate. For abusers of these drugs, the psychotic symptoms disappear after drug use has stopped.

Traumatic injuries to the brain, such as cerebral concussions, contusions, and lacerations, are often followed temporarily by impaired memory, confusion, and loss of orientation for time and place. A person regaining consciousness after being knocked unconscious in an accident will frequently look around quite blankly and ask, "Where am I? What happened?" However, with severe brain injury, these psychotic symptoms may be permanent. One example of an irreversible psychotic state caused by trauma to the brain is **dementia pugilistica,** a disorder found in people who have suffered repeated blows to the head, such as boxers (Jordan, 2000).

dementia pugilistica: an irreversible psychotic state caused by brain trauma that results from repeated blows to the head

Recap 15.1: Psychoses

(a)_____ are severe mental disorders in which thinking is disturbed and the affected individual is not well oriented for person, time, and place. (b)_____ is a disorder that involves cognitive impairment and poor judgment. (c)_____ psychoses are reversible psychoses produced by bacterial infections, which induce systems of restlessness, loss of orientation for time and placer, hallucinations, inattention, and perceptual distortions. Reversible psychoses are also produced by (d)_____ _____ (a brain inflammation caused by a virus) and (e)_____ (an inflammation of the meninges caused by an infection). Abuse of stimulants, such as amphetamine, cocaine, and PCP, can also produce (f)_____ psychoses. An irreversible psychotic state called (g)_____ _____ is observed in some boxers who have suffered repeated blows to the head.

Schizophrenia

Schizophrenia was first described at the beginning of the 20th century by two European psychiatrists, Emil Kraepelin in Germany and Eugen Bleuler in Switzerland. Impressed by the progressive intellectual deterioration of the schizophrenic patients that he examined, Kraepelin called the disorder *dementia praecox*. He maintained that dementia praecox is due to deterioration of the brain.

Bleuler, on the other hand, named the disorder **schizophrenia** because he believed that the most striking symptom of the disorder is the disorganization of associations, which leads to disconnected thoughts, words, and emotions. He did not agree with Kraepelin that patients with schizophrenia get progressively worse. Bleuler observed that his schizophrenic patients sometimes functioned normally and sometimes functioned abnormally. As a result, Bleuler concluded that schizophrenia is caused by a transient physiological dysfunction in the brain and is *not* due to degeneration of the brain.

Today the cause of schizophrenia is still not known. In fact, some scholars wonder whether it is really one illness or a collection of related illnesses (Heinrichs, 1993). According to the *DSM-IV* (1994), the criteria for a diagnosis of schizophrenia include a decline in functioning and any two of the following symptoms: delusions, hallucinations, disorganized speech or behavior, blunted mood, or apathy. However, a person is diagnosed as schizophrenic only after all other possible organic causes of psychosis are ruled out. Schizophrenia is the label people are given when their psychotic symptoms cannot be explained by drug intoxication or some other medical condition, such as a nutritional deficiency, cerebrovascular disease, Huntington's disease, or hepatic encephalopathy.

Given the *DSM-IV* criteria for schizophrenia, one person diagnosed as schizophrenia may have delusions, but no hallucinations. Another may have delusions *and* hallucinations. Still another person diagnosed as schizophrenic may have no delusions or hallucinations but may have disorganized speech and social isolation instead. Do these people all have the same illness? The *DSM-IV* actually distinguishes among five types of schizophrenia, but research does not support these distinctions (Heinrichs, 1993).

Crow (1980) has attempted to sidestep the problem of subtypes of schizophrenia by classifying the symptoms associated with schizophrenia into two categories: **positive symptoms** and **negative symptoms.** Positive symptoms are those behaviors observed in schizophrenics that most people typically do not have. That is, positive symptoms occur in addition to normal behaviors. Examples of positive symptoms include disturbed thinking, hallucinations, delusions, and movement disorders. In schizophrenia, thinking can be so disorganized that it resembles the cognitive deterioration of dementia. Thoughts are loosely connected, and the afflicted person will jump from one subject to the next in the same breath, for example, remarking "riding on the coattails of the law, paw, dog, number 1 dawg, that's Jesus's way."

Negative symptoms represent diminished functioning. Blunted mood, poverty of speech, inability to experience pleasure, apathy, poor insight and judgment, and inattention are examples of negative symptoms. Whereas sane people exhibit a wide range of emotions, readily engage in conversation, can experience fun and pleasure, generally have good judgment, and show interest in their surroundings, schizophrenic people often lack these behaviors.

Crow (1980) tried to distinguish between positive schizophrenia and negative schizophrenia on the basis of whether a patient showed positive or negative symptoms. However, most patients do not show exclusively positive or negative symptoms. That is, most schizophrenic individuals will experience both types of symptoms, often at the same time. Positive and negative symptoms appear to arise from different parts of the brain, as you will learn in the next section. Any biological explanations of schizophrenia will need to address the occurrence of positive and negative symptoms in most schizophrenic patients.

Biological Explanations of Schizophrenia

Biological explanations of schizophrenia are based on four universal observations about schizophrenia: (1) the presence of positive and negative symptoms, which implicates disturbances in widely different parts of the brain; (2) the effective

schizophrenia: a psychotic disorder of unknown origin that is characterized by the disorganization of associations, producing disconnected thoughts, words, and emotions

positive symptoms of schizophrenia: those behaviors, such as hallucinations and delusions, observed in individuals with schizophrenia that most people typically do not exhibit

negative symptoms of schizophrenia: those behaviors observed in schizophrenic individuals who demonstrate diminished functioning

treatment of schizophrenic symptoms by drugs that reduce dopamine activity in the brain; (3) the role played by stress in the onset and worsening of schizophrenic symptoms; and (4) peak age of onset for schizophrenia, which is late adolescence or early adulthood. In addition, a number of neurotransmitter circuits appear to function abnormally in schizophrenia (Figure 15.1). Most hypotheses that I will discuss can explain only one or two of these observations. Others, such as the neural diathesis–stress model, can address at least three. What is needed, as you shall find out, is a comprehensive model that ties together all the facets of this complicated illness.

The Dopamine Hypothesis

For several decades, the leading biological explanation of schizophrenia, known as the **dopamine hypothesis,** has focused upon overactivity of particular dopamine pathways (Seeman et al., 1997). There are two lines of evidence that suggest that dopamine might play a role in schizophrenia. First of all, drugs that stimulate dopamine receptors, such as cocaine and amphetamine, can produce psychotic symptoms in normal human subjects. In addition, when dopamine agonists are administered to schizophrenic patients, their symptoms worsen. Second, drugs that counter the action of dopamine reduce or eliminate positive schizophrenic symptoms. All drugs used today to treat schizophrenia are dopamine antagonists, to some extent, and are known as **neuroleptics** (Davis, Kahn, Ko, & Davidson, 1991).

It is not known what produces the overactivation of dopamine pathways in schizophrenia. We do know that dopamine levels in schizophrenic individuals are *not* significantly higher than those in normal controls. For example, schizophrenic patients do not have higher-than-normal levels of *homovanillic acid*, which is an end product of dopamine metabolism. In fact, there is evidence that schizophrenics have *decreased* levels of homovanillic acid (Andreasen, 1988). Therefore, it is unlikely that excess dopamine actually produces schizophrenic symptoms (Davis et al., 1991). Instead, two alternative proposals have been advanced to explain how overactivity in dopamine pathways occurs in schizophrenia: (1) an increase in the density of dopamine receptors, which means more neural activity in response to a normal amount of released dopamine or (2) an imbalance in dopamine activity in the brain, in which some areas of the brain are more active than normal and others are less active. Most investigators agree that one particular subfamily of dopamine receptors, the D_2 subfamily, is primarily involved in the etiology of schizophrenia, as we discussed in Chapter 3.

Increased Density of D_2 Receptors Postmortem examination of normal and schizophrenic brains suggests that schizophrenia may be due to an increase in the density of D_2 receptors in the limbic system (Seeman, Guan, & Van Tol, 1993). Although not all studies indicate that there is in fact an increase in D_2 receptor density in schizophrenia, a complete review of the literature by Davis and his associates (1991) prompted them to conclude that D_2 receptor density in subcortical limbic areas is greater in schizophrenic than in normal subjects, regardless of medication history. In contrast, D_2 receptor organization in the temporal cortex is abnormally underdeveloped, which may contribute to the appearance of positive symptoms, such as hallucinations, in schizophrenia (Joyce, Goldsmith, & Gurevich, 1997).

Figure 15.1 Main neuronal circuits and neurotransmitters dysregulated in schizophrenia

GABA, dopamine (DA) from the ventral tegmental area (VTA), and serotonin from the raphe nuclei (R) regulate the activity of neurons in the cerebral cortex. The cerebral cortex communicates with the basal ganglia and limbic system using glutamate (GLU) primarily. Any of these neurotransmitter systems can be disrupted in schizophrenia.

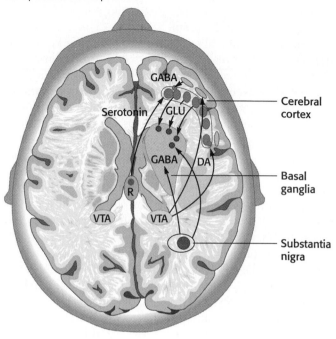

dopamine hypothesis of schizophrenia: the leading biological explanation of schizophrenia that focuses on the role of dopamine in the development and maintenance of schizophrenia

neuroleptics: dopamine antagonists used to treat schizophrenia

The D$_3$ receptor is a member of the D$_2$ subfamily of dopamine receptors, as you learned in Chapter 3. Eugenia Gurevich and her colleagues have compared the density of D$_3$ receptors in the brains of deceased schizophrenics with those of deceased control subjects (Gurevich, Bordelon, Shapiro, Arnold, Gur, & Joyce, 1997; Gurevich & Joyce, 1999; Joyce et al., 1997; Joyce & Gurevich, 1999). They found elevated concentrations of the D$_3$ receptor in the limbic system of schizophrenic patients who did not receive antipsychotic medication for at least a month before their deaths, compared to control subjects and to schizophrenic patients who received antipsychotic medication. That is, schizophrenic patients receiving antipsychotic medication had the same number of D$_3$ receptors in their limbic systems as did nonschizophrenic subjects, whereas unmedicated schizophrenic patients had twice the number of D$_3$ receptors as the other groups (Gurevich et al., 1997). Their findings suggest that antipsychotic medications reduce the number of D$_3$ receptors in the mesolimbic dopamine system and restore balance among the dopamine pathways (Figure 15.2).

Regional Imbalances in Dopamine Activity Recall from Chapter 4 that there are three major dopamine pathways in the brain. These are known as the mesolimbic, the mesocortical, and the nigrostriatal systems (Figure 15.2). Each pathway is comprised of neurons that have their cell bodies in the midbrain and whose axons project to one or more areas in the forebrain. In the mesolimbic system, neurons in the ventral tegmental area of the mesencephalon release dopamine in subcortical areas of the limbic system, including the hippocampus, amygdala, nucleus accumbens,

Figure 15.2 Dopamine (DA) pathways in the brain
D$_2$ receptors are concentrated in the nigrostriatal pathway (motor pathway), and D$_3$ receptors are concentrated in the mesolimbic dopamine pathway. Antipsychotic medications act on D$_2$ subfamily of receptors to eliminate positive symptoms of schizophrenia. Some antipsychotics also act on the prefrontal cortex to restore serotonin activity balance.

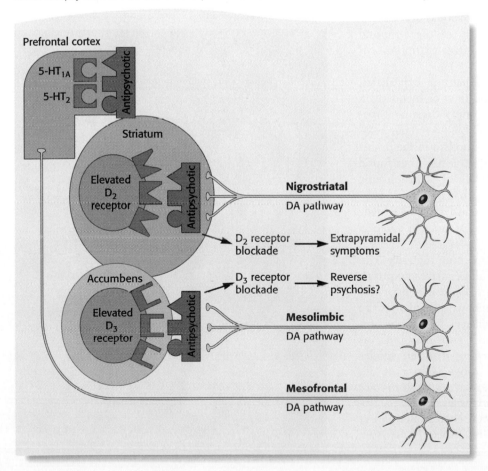

and the hypothalamus. The mesocortical pathway also begins in the ventral tegmental area in the midbrain, but it projects primarily to the prefrontal and other regions of the cerebral cortex. The nigrostriatal pathway projects from the substantia nigra to the caudate nucleus and putamen of the basal ganglia. Put this together with what you know about brain function: Dopamine influences emotion and motivation in the mesolimbic system, thinking and other cognitive processes in the mesocortical system, and movement in the nigrostriatal system.

Neuroleptic medications have different actions on the three dopamine systems, which suggests that not all pathways are equally active in schizophrenia. There is indeed a great deal of evidence that regional imbalances in dopamine activity occur in the brains of individuals with schizophrenia (Davis et al., 1991; Volkow et al., 1986; Weinberger, 1987), prompting Davis and his associates to propose a *modified dopamine hypothesis of schizophrenia*. According to this modified hypothesis, in schizophrenia, dopamine activity in the cerebral cortex is decreased, whereas dopamine activity in subcortical areas of the brain is increased. That is, in schizophrenia, the mesocortical system becomes underactive and the mesolimbic system becomes overactive (Figure 15.3). A number of investigators agree that underactivity of the prefrontal cortex is responsible for the negative symptoms of schizophrenia and that overactivity of the mesolimbic system and underactivity of the temporal cortex are responsible for the positive symptoms of schizophrenia.

In support of the modified dopamine hypothesis, imaging studies that measure blood flow or metabolism indicate an imbalance in the functioning dopamine systems in schizophrenia. Using PET, Volkow and her associates (1986) measured glucose metabolism in the brains of 18 schizophrenic and 12 normal subjects. They found that metabolism in the frontal lobes of schizophrenic subjects was *decreased* compared to that of normal subjects and was *increased* in the subcortical areas of schizophrenic patients compared to that of normal subjects (Figure 15.4).

Regional imbalances in dopamine activity can explain the presence of positive and negative symptoms in schizophrenia. Overactivation of the subcortical areas of the temporal lobe, which would involve the hippocampus and amygdala, produces hallucinations, perceptual distortions, delusions and paranoia, as demonstrated in studies of recording from electrodes placed deep into the temporal lobes (Gloor et al., 1982; Halgren et al., 1978). Negative symptoms are associated with damage to the prefrontal cortex, particularly in the dorsolateral prefrontal cortex (Berman et al., 1986; Weinberger et al., 1986; Stuss & Benson, 1984).

Figure 15.3 Regional imbalances in dopamine (DA) activity
Compared to the normal state, the mesocortical dopamine system is weakened and the mesolimbic dopamine system is overactive in schizophrenia.

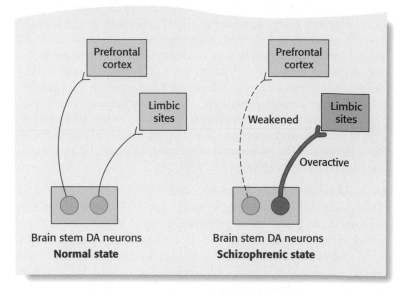

Figure 15.4 PET images of dopamine imbalances in the brains of schizophrenic patients
Binding of D_3 receptors in the basal ganglia is significantly greater in a schizophrenic patient not taking antipsychotic medication (c), compared to a healthy control (a) and a schizophrenic patient taking antipsychotic medication (b). In this scan, red indicates highest levels of activity and blue indicates lowest.

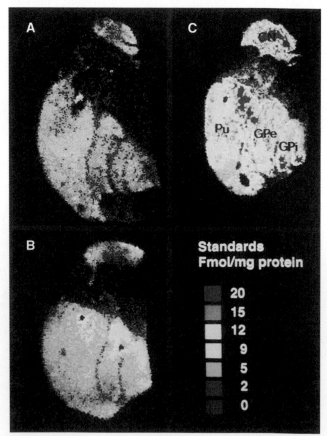

Other support for the dopamine hypothesis comes from research on movement abnormalities in schizophrenia. In Chapter 5, you learned about the role that excess dopamine activity plays in movement disorders associated with the basal ganglia, such as Huntington's disease. Walker, Savoie, and Davis (1994) studied home movies of infants who later became schizophrenic and their healthy siblings. Infants who developed schizophrenia later in life showed evidence of movement disorders or dyskinesias, whereas their healthy siblings did not. These investigators proposed that overactivation of D_2 receptors could disrupt the functioning of the pathway between the basal ganglia and cortex, which could produce both motor disturbances and psychotic symptoms.

The role of dopamine in reinforcement, which was discussed in Chapter 13, cannot be ignored in our consideration of the biological bases of schizophrenia. Recall that the release of dopamine in the nucleus accumbens is associated with reward, which causes behaviors to be repeated. This might explain why schizophrenic individuals become obsessed with a delusion (for example, that the CIA is monitoring their thoughts) or have recurring hallucinations. One young schizophrenic woman remarked to me, "I keep seeing evil faces on the walls, and they scare me." If something is frightening, a normal response would be to try to shut it out. But, in schizophrenia, overactivation of the mesolimbic dopamine synapses might lead to stimulation of the reward system, which in turn would produce repeated episodes of the frightening hallucinations.

However convincing the evidence is in favor of the dopamine hypothesis, there is also considerable evidence that schizophrenia is not caused by one single neurotransmitter dysfunction (Emrich, Leweke, & Schneider, 1997; Weinberger, 1987). For example, a new class of powerful drugs used to treat schizophrenia, called *atypical neuroleptics*, appears to increase serotonin levels as well as block dopamine in the brain. In fact, dysfunctions in any of several neurotransmitter systems could produce schizophrenic symptoms. Remember that psychotic symptoms are quite complex and involve cognitive, perceptual, social, and emotional processes. This means that schizophrenia may be caused by impaired interaction between different neurotransmitter systems. Investigators are currently examining the possible roles of glutamate, GABA, serotonin, acetylcholine, and other peptides in schizophrenia. Let's turn now to a review of some of the most recent biological explanations of schizophrenia.

The NMDA Receptor Hypofunction Hypothesis

Olney and Farber (1995) have developed a model, called the **NMDA receptor hypofunction hypothesis,** linking glutamate with schizophrenia. Remember from Chapter 12 that the NMDA receptor is a type of glutamate receptor. Interestingly, substances that block the NMDA receptor, such as PCP or "angel dust," can produce psychotic symptoms or worsen them in psychotic individuals. According to Olney and Farber (1995), hypofunction of the NMDA receptor is associated with schizophrenia. A decrease in the functioning of NMDA receptors can also cause damage to the hippocampus, amygdala, and cortical areas that are abnormal in schizophrenia.

The NMDA receptor hypofunction hypothesis is *not* incompatible with the dopamine hypothesis. One of dopamine's many functions is to inhibit the release of glutamate. Therefore, the overactivity of the mesolimbic dopamine pathway in schizophrenics can result in decreased stimulation of NMDA receptors, which can induce psychotic symptoms. Hypofunction of NMDA receptors could very well produce the pattern of dopamine activity imbalance described earlier, impairing the function of the prefrontal cortex, which could lead to subcortical overactivation (Greene, 2001; Weinberger, 1987; Walker & Diforio, 1997).

The Cannabinoid Hypothesis of Schizophrenia

Use of *Cannabis sativa*, better known as marijuana, has been associated with a number of cognitive, motor, and mood alterations. The most common adverse effects

NMDA receptor hypofunction hypothesis: one explanation of schizophrenia that focuses on the role of underactive NMDA (glutamate) receptors in the development of schizophrenia

include paranoid psychosis and acute panic. In addition, chronic consumption of cannabis may produce changes that resemble the negative symptoms of schizophrenia. Although these adverse effects of cannabis use look very much like the clinical symptoms of schizophrenia, this does not prove that cannabis can cause schizophrenia. However, some investigators have been studying the effects of marijuana intoxication to gain a better understanding of the disturbances that are hallmarks of schizophrenia (Skosnik, Spatz-Glenn, & Park, 2001).

For example, Emrich, Leweke, and Schneider (1997) have examined similar perceptual distortions that are experienced by schizophrenic individuals and by healthy, cannabis-intoxicated participants. This research has led them to propose a **cannabinoid hypothesis of schizophrenia.** According to this hypothesis, dysfunction of the endogenous cannabinoid system plays a direct role in the cognitive impairments observed in schizophrenia, particularly those distortions due to reduced internal censorship (Lewekc et al., 1999). Because cannabinoid receptors were first identified very recently (Devane et al., 1988), little is known about their function. These receptors appear to be clustered in the hippocampus, basal ganglia, and the cerebellum (Herkenham et al., 1990, 1991), which can explain the effects of marijuana on the motor system and memory. However, much more research is needed before the cannabinoid hypothesis can be given serious attention.

cannabinoid hypothesis of schizophrenia: one explanation of schizophrenia that focuses on the role of endogenous cannabinoids in cognitive impairments observed in schizophrenia

The Diathesis–Stress Model of Schizophrenia

If you take a course in abnormal psychology, you will undoubtedly learn about the **diathesis–stress model of schizophrenia.** This theoretical model has been used for decades to explain the development of schizophrenia. According to this model (Rosenthal, 1970), people who are predisposed to develop schizophrenia have a biological "weakness" or diathesis that makes them vulnerable to the effects of stress. Furthermore, schizophrenic individuals have an intensified response to stress, and stress worsens their symptoms. Until recently, very few investigators studied the biological aspects of this model. Most research to date has focused upon the nature of the stressors associated with schizophrenia.

diathesis–stress model: a theoretical model that proposes that people who are predisposed to develop schizophrenia have a biological weakness that makes them vulnerable to the effects of stress

In Chapter 14, you learned that cortisol levels in the blood and urine become elevated during stress, due to activation of the hypothalamic-pituitary-adrenal (HPA) axis. Although a number of cortisol abnormalities have been reported in schizophrenic individuals, these abnormalities are not sufficient to explain the onset of schizophrenic symptoms. However, schizophrenia is also associated with a pronounced dopamine response to activation of the HPA axis. It is important to remember that stress induces changes in a number of neurotransmitter systems in all people. But, in schizophrenic people, stress causes the release of cortisol from the adrenal gland, which in turn produces a massive increase in dopamine activity in the mesolimbic system (Walker & Diforio, 1997).

Figure 15.5 illustrates Walker and Diforio's diathesis–stress model. This model suggests that both biological insults and psychosocial stress can produce activation of the HPA axis and release of cortisol, which then activates the subcortical dopamine pathways that run from the midbrain to the limbic system. Overactivation of this subcortical dopamine pathway is believed to result in schizophrenic symptoms. This model can also explain why late adolescence or early adulthood is the peak period for the onset of schizophrenic symptoms. Human cortisol release rises rapidly during adolescence, producing overactivation in the mesolimbic dopamine system in individuals who are vulnerable to developing schizophrenia.

Structural Abnormalities Associated with Schizophrenia

Modern imaging techniques allow us not only to study the binding of chemicals to brain receptors but also to visualize structural changes in the brains of schizophrenics. The finding reported most often in imaging studies concerns the size of the ventricles in schizophrenic patients. Over three dozen published papers have reported enlarged *third* and *lateral ventricles* in the brains of schizophrenics, as a result of CT or MRI studies. Remember that the ventricles themselves do not have

Figure 15.5 Walker and Diforio's neural diathesis–stress model

The release of cortisol triggered by stress can stimulate overactivity in the mesolimbic dopamine system and produce or worsen symptoms of schizophrenia.

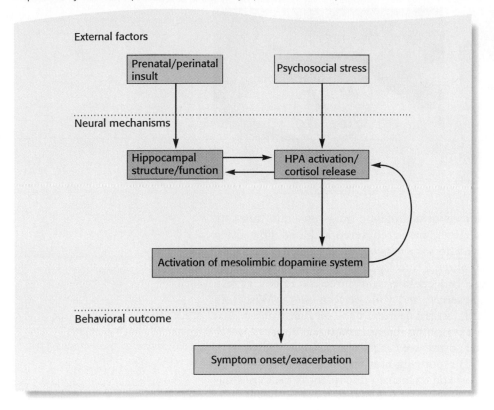

a particular function, except to hold cerebrospinal fluid. An increase in the size of the ventricles generally means that the volume of periventricular structures is reduced [*peri-* = around; *-ventricular* = ventricle, Latin].

MRI studies have revealed that the *prefrontal cortex, hippocampus* and *amygdala* are smaller in schizophrenics than in normal subjects (Breier, Buchanan, Elkashef, Munson, Kirkpatrick, & Gellad, 1992; Szeszko et al., 2002). A number of other investigators have reported a reduction in the size of the hippocampus in schizophrenic subjects (Bogerts et al., 1990; Suddath et al., 1990; DeLisi et al., 1988). Other studies have demonstrated reduced mass in the precentral cortex (Andreasen et al., 1986; Shelton, Karson, Doran, Pickar, Bigelow, & Weinberger, 1988). In addition, postmortem examination of the brains of schizophrenics has revealed a number of irregularities in the neurons in the hippocampus and other periventricular limbic areas, as well as in the prefrontal cortex (Bogerts & Falkai, 1995; Weinberger, 1987; Bogerts et al., 1985). These abnormalities, illustrated in Figure 15.6, include decreased volume of cells, decreased number of cells, gliosis, and disarray of pyramidal cell orientation in the hippocampus (Jeste & Lohr, 1989; Kovelman & Scheibel, 1984).

One of the best methods to determine structural abnormalities associated with schizophrenia is to compare the brain of a schizophrenic individual with the brain of his or her nonschizophrenic, monozygotic twin. Using MRI, Suddath and his colleagues (1990) studied 15 pairs of identical twins who were discordant for schizophrenia. (**Discordant** means that one twin is affected by the disorder whereas the other is not; **concordant** means that both twins are affected.) The hippocampus was found to be smaller in the schizophrenic twin in 14 of the 15 pairs of twins. As well, the lateral and third ventricles were determined to be larger in 13 of 15 of the schizophrenic twins. These differences between discordant twins, however, may be due to drug treatment because the schizophrenic twin in each pair had received neuroleptic drugs to control symptoms and the unaffected twin had not.

discordant: twins who do not share a particular trait

concordant: sharing a particular trait

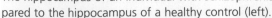

Figure 15.6 Cellular irregularities in the hippocampus of schizophrenic individual
The hippocampus of an individual with schizophrenia (right) is much reduced in size compared to the hippocampus of a healthy control (left).

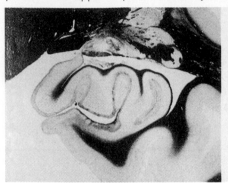
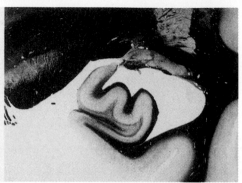

In a study that examined the effects of neuroleptic drugs on brain function, Karen Berman and her associates (1992) measured cerebral blood flow using SPECT in 8 pairs of identical twins who were concordant for schizophrenia, 10 pairs who were discordant for schizophrenia, and 3 pairs who were all well. Cerebral blood flow was measured in each subject in each of three conditions: at rest, during a control (number matching) exercise, and while performing the Wisconsin Card Sorting (WCS) Test. The WCS Test is a neuropsychological instrument that assesses problem-solving and abstract reasoning ability. It requires the use of working memory and, thus, the prefrontal cortex (see *For Further Thought*).

Berman and her associates (1992) reported a number of interesting findings. Cerebral blood flows for schizophrenic and unaffected discordant twins were similar at rest and during the control task. During the WCS Test, however, blood flows in the prefrontal cortex were significantly lower in schizophrenic twins compared to their unaffected twin (Figure 15.7). Comparisons of prefrontal blood flows in concordant schizophrenic twins revealed that those twins who received higher levels of neuroleptic drugs actually had higher prefrontal blood flows than their less medicated twin. This finding suggests that hypoactivity of the prefrontal cortex, which appears to be characteristic of schizophrenia, is not associated with drug intake.

Another structure that appears to be disturbed in schizophrenic patients is the *thalamus*. Nancy Andreasen and her colleagues (1994) at the University of Iowa compared MRI scans of the brains of 47 healthy and 39 schizophrenic male subjects. Like other investigators, they found that schizophrenic patients had enlarged ventricles compared to the healthy volunteers. In addition, this research team discovered that the thalamus, particularly on the right side, was significantly smaller in schizophrenics and that the white matter surrounding the thalamus (that is, the axons leaving and entering the thalamus) was also smaller. Both the medial dorsal regions of thalamus, which sends axons to the prefrontal cortex, and the lateral thalamus, which projects to the parietal and temporal association areas, were abnormal. You learned in Chapter 4 that the main function of the thalamus is to control input to the cerebrum and other forebrain structures. It may be that abnormalities in the structure of the thalamus could interfere with the ability of the thalamus to filter out unimportant sensory input, overwhelming the schizophrenic individual with stimuli.

Prenatal Influences on Brain Structure

Structural abnormalities in the brain, particularly those in the hippocampus, have been linked to prenatal dis-

Figure 15.7 SPECT images of schizophrenics and their nonschizophrenic twins
During the Wisconsin Card Sorting Test, the activity of the prefrontal cortex (left on each scan) is much reduced in individuals with schizophrenia compared to their nonschizophrenic twins. Blue indicates low activity; yellow and red indicate high activity levels.

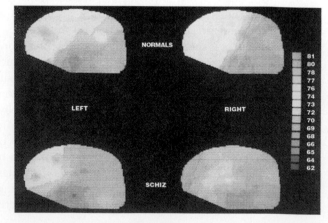

The Wisconsin Card Sorting Test

The Wisconsin Card Sorting Test is a neuropsychological instrument that identifies dysfunction of the frontal lobes. It detects impairment of executive functions, such as abstract thinking and concept formation, which are necessary for effective problem solving at work and in social interactions. PET studies have indicated that the frontal lobes (in particular, the *dorsolateral prefrontal cortex*), as well as the inferior parietal lobes, the visual association cortex, and inferior temporal cortex, are activated when normal human participants complete this test (Berman, Ostrem, Randolph, Gold, Goldberg, Coppola, Carson, Herscovitch, & Weinberger, 1995). Schizophrenic individuals show marked impairment on this test, which suggests that one or more of these brain regions are not functioning normally in schizophrenia.

In the Wisconsin Card Sorting Test, 128 cards are typically used. Each card bears one to four symbols, in one of four colors (red, yellow, green, blue). Only one type of symbol (triangle, star, cross, or circle) is printed on a card, as shown in the examples. Thus, a card might contain two blue stars, or three green circles, or a red triangle. The test taker is instructed to sort the cards into piles, based on stimulus cards that indicate a given category (color of symbols, number of symbols, or shape of symbols on the card). After the test taker has sorted approximately 10 cards, the stimulus cards (and, therefore, the category) are changed without explanation, and the test taker must sort the cards according to the new category. The test taker must be able to correctly identify the new category indicated by the stimulus cards and then shift his or her sorting strategy to match the new category. People with frontal lobe impairments have a good deal of difficulty switching categories and show *perseveration,* which is a failure to switch cognitive set.

A number of computerized versions of this test now exist. In one version, the test taker is first presented with a target card and four reference cards and is asked to match the target card to one of the reference cards, based on one of the three possible categories. The test taker is not told which dimension (color, number, shape) is to be matched but must figure out the relevant dimension by trial and error. After several matching trials, the relevant dimension is changed, without the test taker's knowledge. The test taker is forced to change his or her cognitive set to identify the new relevant dimension.

This modified procedure requires that the test taker pay close attention to the task at hand, keep patterns of stimuli in short-term memory, and, most importantly, be able to identify a change and shift from one concept (for example, color) to another (for example, number). Schizophrenic individuals have difficulty identifying the new concept and adjusting their behavior to select the correct match. They typically continue to make the same mistakes repeatedly, showing perseveration (Figure 15.8).

Wisconsin Card Sorting Test

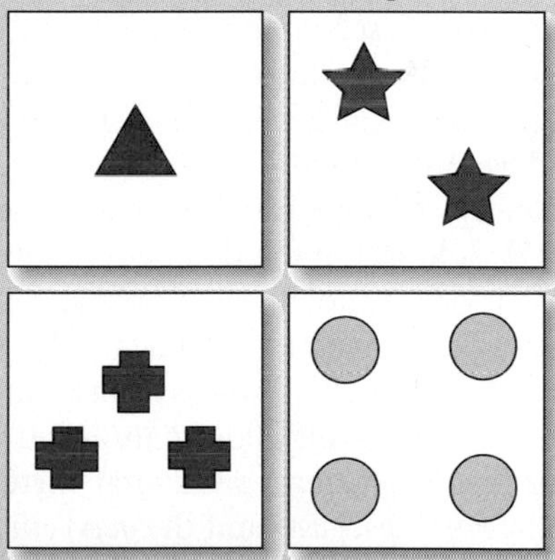

Figure 15.8 Wisconsin Card Sorting Test stimuli

turbances in laboratory animals and people. These disturbances include viral infection, nutritional deficiency, hypoxia, or acute stress in the pregnant mother. Interestingly, these same prenatal stressors have been demonstrated to be significantly correlated with the development of schizophrenia (Mednick et al., 1987; Walker & Diforio, 1997).

For example, exposure of the fetus to any of a number of viruses, including the virus that produces polio, during the second trimester of pregnancy may be related to the development of schizophrenia (Davis & Phelps, 1995; Squires, 1997). Studies of people born to mothers who starved in the Netherlands during the winter of 1944–45 following a Nazi blockade suggest that malnutrition of a mother during the first trimester of pregnancy may produce schizophrenia in her offspring (Hulshoff et al., 2000; Susser & Lin, 1992; Susser, Neugebauer, Hoek, Brown, Lin, Labovitz, & Gorman, 1996). In addition, schizophrenia is associated with neurological damage caused by an incompatibility between the blood of a mother and her developing fetus (Hollister, Laing, & Mednick, 1996).

In summary, all of these reported brain abnormalities are nonspecific and subtle. The imaging and postmortem studies do not indicate a specific, consistent brain pathology that can be associated with schizophrenia. Only a small reduction in tissue volume or slight neuronal irregularity has been found in the brains of schizophrenic patients, and the differences obtained are statistical, not qualitatively obvious to the untrained eye. These subtle differences were overlooked by researchers during the first half of the 20th century, before the development of sophisticated pathological and imaging techniques, which led early investigators to conclude that no brain pathology is associated with schizophrenia.

The Dorsolateral Prefrontal Cortex

Today it is clear that schizophrenia is a disease of the brain, in which certain areas of the brain become damaged early in life, perhaps prenatally in some cases. However, onset of the illness does not occur until brain maturation is complete, usually in late adolescence (Olney & Farber, 1995; Walker & Diforio, 1997; Weinberger, 1987). One of the last brain areas to mature is the *dorsolateral prefrontal cortex*, which reaches functional maturity in early adulthood. Because this area of the brain matures in late adolescence, prenatal damage to this area of the brain would not be evident during childhood. The social and cognitive deficits (the negative symptoms of schizophrenia) associated with damage to the dorsolateral prefrontal cortex would not be apparent until after this area has fully developed (Figure 15.9).

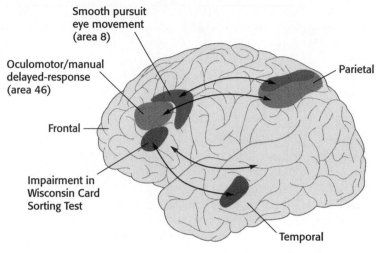

Figure 15.9 Areas of the dorsolateral prefrontal cortex that have been linked to deficits observed in schizophrenia

Smooth pursuit eye movement (area 8)

Oculomotor/manual delayed-response (area 46)

Frontal

Impairment in Wisconsin Card Sorting Test

Parietal

Temporal

This is clearly demonstrated in experiments with monkeys (Goldman & Alexander, 1977). A lesion in the dorsolateral prefrontal cortex has no effect on the behavior of infant or preadolescent monkeys. However, these same lesions significantly impair the performance of adult monkeys on delayed-response tasks. Brain damage may not be clinically obvious at the time of the lesion, but symptoms may develop later in life following brain maturation.

Damage to the dorsolateral prefrontal cortex could explain both the *underactivation of the mesocortical pathway* and the *overactivation of the mesolimbic system*, which are believed to underlie the symptoms of schizophrenia (Davis et al., 1991; Weinberger, 1987). Pycock, Kerwin, and Carter (1980) demonstrated that chronic overactivity of the subcortical dopamine system is produced when dopamine receptors in the prefrontal cortex of rats are destroyed. This finding suggests that the mesocortical dopamine pathway controls or inhibits mesolimbic dopamine activity. Damage to the prefrontal cortex, then, will result in increased activity in the mesolimbic dopamine system, producing the positive symptoms of schizophrenia.

Hallucinations

Hallucinations are among the most commonly reported positive symptoms of schizophrenia. These hallucinations are abnormal perceptual experiences that occur in the absence of external stimuli. This means that hallucinations most likely arise from abnormal brain activity. Using PET imaging, a team of investigators from London and New York has examined the brain areas activated during auditory and visual hallucinations (Silbersweig et al., 1995). As you might expect, activation of the auditory-linguistic association cortex in the temporal lobe did occur in all subjects experiencing auditory hallucinations. Likewise, visual hallucinations were associated with activation of the visual association cortex (Figure 15.10). This activation in the association areas of the cortex rather than in the primary sensory cortex makes sense given the internally generated nature of the hallucinations. Also

hallucination: an abnormal perceptual experience that occurs in the absence of external stimuli

Figure 15.10 PET image of a hallucinating schizophrenic brain
Brain areas with significantly increased activity during visual and auditory hallucinations are highlighted.

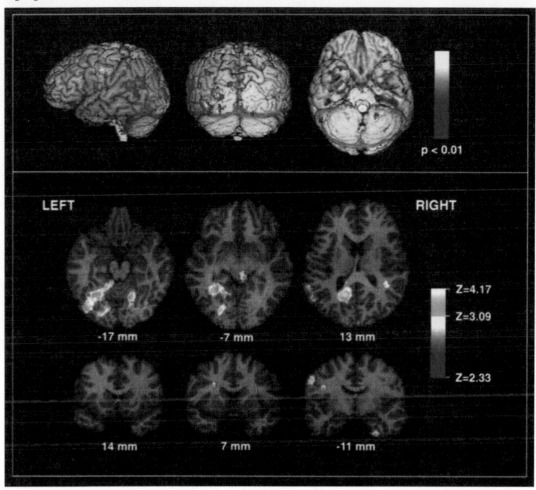

activated during both visual and auditory hallucinations were subcortical structures located deep within the brain, including the thalamus and hippocampus. Major dopamine and glutamine pathways connect these structures with each other and with other structures in the limbic system. The relative absence of activation in the prefrontal cortex in the brains of hallucinating schizophrenic patients is consistent with our earlier discussion of reduced activity in the mesocortical pathway.

Functional Abnormalities Associated with Schizophrenia

A number of dysfunctions associated with schizophrenia have been identified, including abnormalities in eye movements, event-related brain potentials, and attention and information processing (Emrich et al., 1997). These abnormalities that are commonly found in schizophrenic individuals are called **biological markers** because they are presumed to be evidence of an underlying physiological problem in the brain. All biological explanations of schizophrenia need to take these biological markers into account and attempt to explain why they are prevalent in schizophrenic but not in other individuals.

Straube and Oades (1992) have conducted an exhaustive review of the schizophrenia literature. Their review has revealed that the conclusions of many older studies and anecdotal reports have not been confirmed by the findings of more recent, well-controlled experiments. In addition, Straube and Oades have discovered that

biological markers: abnormalities shared by members of a particular subpopulation that are presumed to be evidence of an underlying biological problem

some dysfunctions are observed only in some subtypes of schizophrenia but not in others. Other reported dysfunctions are not specific to schizophrenia but are also common in depression or other disorders. Let's examine closely what Straube and Oades have found concerning these biological markers.

Eye Movements

Motor coordination appears to be a prominent problem in schizophrenia. This may be due to a dysfunction involving the nigrostriatal dopamine pathway, or it may be a consequence of taking neuroleptic medication, which interferes with dopamine activity in the brain. Much research has focused on eye movements in schizophrenic individuals (Obayashi et al., 2001). When tested with fixed targets, the reflexive eye movements of schizophrenic subjects were quite similar to those of control subjects. However, schizophrenics had more difficulty than controls did with voluntary tasks, such as switching their gaze from a fixation point to a peripheral stimulus.

Schizophrenic individuals have even more difficulty following a moving object with their eyes (Mahlberg et al., 2001). These movements of the eyes following a moving object are called **smooth pursuit eye movements.** In studies of this type of eye movement, schizophrenic subjects have been found to have irregular smooth eye pursuit movements. These deviations from normal include: (1) frequent interruptions of the tracking movement, (2) pursuit movements lagging behind the stimulus, and (3) overshooting of the target (Straube & Oades, 1992). In addition, these deviations are observed in both medicated and nonmedicated patients, so these deviations appear to be not related to the effects of neuroleptic medication (Hutton et al., 2001). Poor smooth pursuit eye movements do occur in normal subjects when they are distracted. Therefore, it is likely that this disturbance is due to an attentional disorder in schizophrenia.

The **gating hypothesis of schizophrenia** has been employed for many years to explain the sensorimotor deficits observed in schizophrenic patients (Olney & Farber, 1995). According to this hypothesis, an inhibitory filter or gating mechanism is present in sensorimotor systems in the brain. This gating mechanism is believed to be located in the thalamus, and its function is to regulate the amount of information that is sent to the cerebral cortex for processing. In schizophrenia, this gating mechanism doesn't function properly (Figure 15.11). As a result, the cortex becomes flooded with uncensored and irrelevant information, which impairs thinking, attention, and sensorimotor functions, such as smooth pursuit eye movements. In support of this hypotheses, Andreasen and her colleagues (1994) have found structural changes in the medial thalamus in schizophrenic patients, as I discussed earlier. These changes could disrupt the filtering mechanism and leave schizophrenic individuals feeling overwhelmed by the resulting flood of thoughts, sensations, and emotions.

Event-Related Brain Potentials

In Chapter 9, you learned about the various components of the evoked potential. Each of these components occurs at a certain time interval following a presented stimulus, reflecting

smooth pursuit eye movements: the movements that the eyes make when following a moving target

gating hypothesis of schizophrenia: one explanation of schizophrenia that proposes that the filtering process that controls the relay of information to the cortex is faulty in schizophrenic people

Figure 15.11 Disturbed filtering process in schizophrenia may involve the thalamus
Normally, activation of one circuit in the thalamus suppresses competing circuits between the thalamus and the cerebral cortex (neocortex). In schizophrenia, this filtering process is disturbed, due to the absence of suppression of competing circuits by the basal ganglia and the thalamus. Several circuits between the thalamus and cerebral cortex can be activated simultaneously in schizophrenic patients, impairing attention and reason.

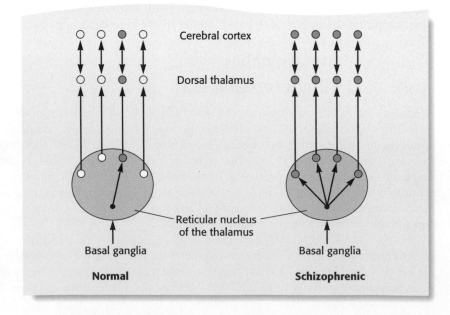

the level of brain processing. The earliest occurring components represent the lowest levels of processing; for example, brain stem processing occurs 10 msec or less after the stimulus. Later components reflect more complex processing; for example, decision making occurs 300 msec or more after the stimulus.

As you might expect, the earliest components of the event-related potentials recorded in schizophrenic subjects do not differ from those of normal controls. Brain stem processing and projection to primary sensory areas in the cerebral cortex appear to be unaffected in most schizophrenics. Evoked potentials in the 100–200 msec range, which are an indication of the amount of attention paid to the stimulus, are reduced in schizophrenic subjects (Straube & Oades, 1992). This is additional evidence that attention deficits are prominent features of schizophrenia. Schizophrenic subjects also show reduced late evoked potentials, demonstrating that they have difficulty assessing the meaningfulness and relevance of stimuli. These reductions are most pronounced when the stimuli are auditory. These data, taken all together, indicate disturbances in attention and information processing in the brain.

Attention and Information Processing

In addition to the electrophysiological evidence described in the preceding paragraph, the results of neuropsychological testing suggest that attention and information processing are disturbed in schizophrenia. For example, as was discussed earlier, schizophrenic subjects perform poorly on the Wisconsin Card Sorting Test, which requires that they change strategies while problem solving. These subjects repeat incorrect responses and seem unable to stop making the same errors over and over again. This type of impairment indicates a dysfunction of the frontal lobes, particularly the dorsolateral prefrontal cortex.

Another test on which schizophrenic patients perform poorly is the Continuous Performance Test, Identical Pairs Version. I described the Continuous Performance Test in Chapter 9. The Identical Pairs Version differs from the original version in that the patient is required to signal when two identical stimuli are presented in a row. Remember that the Continuous Performance Test measures sustained attention. Individuals with schizophrenia do significantly worse on this test than do control subjects, indicating impaired attention (Roitman et al., 1997). Schizophrenics also perform worse than controls on the Trail-Making Test, Part B, which measures executive cognitive function and ability to change cognitive set (Trestman et al., 1995). Thus, cognitive deficits, characterized by impaired attention, flexibility, and problem solving, are biological markers of schizophrenia.

A pharmacological animal model that mimics this type of cognitive impairment has recently been developed at Yale University by Robert Roth and his colleagues (Jentsch et al., 1997). Vervet monkeys were administered phencyclidine (PCP) twice a day for 2 weeks and then were given a behavioral test that required taking a slice of banana out of a transparent cube that was open on one side only. Control and PCP-treated monkeys both acted instinctively at first and tried to grab for the banana through the transparent wall. The control subjects learned very quickly to reach around to the open side to grab the banana. But, the treated monkeys acted just like monkeys whose dorsolateral prefrontal cortex have been lesioned: They kept trying to grab the banana through the wall of the cube. This type of error perseveration is exactly what is seen in schizophrenia. The PCP-treated monkeys couldn't seem to stop themselves from making the same error repeatedly. What's more, the Yale researchers examined dopamine usage in the prefrontal cortex following PCP treatment. They discovered that PCP treatment reduced dopamine usage in two areas only: in the dorsolateral prefrontal cortex and in the prelimbic cortex, which is believed to control behavioral inhibition.

Other types of impairments in information processing associated with schizophrenia include disturbances of conceptual and abstract thinking, inaccurate selection of stored information, and slowed reaction times. These, however, are not specific to schizophrenia. People who are depressed, those who are manic, or those with brain damage show similar impairments. In addition, some subtypes of schizophrenia are associated with specific impairments. For example, paranoid schizophrenics have a hard time distinguishing between important stimuli and background noise. Because many of these cognitive disturbances are either not specific to schizophrenia or observed with only some subtypes, investigators do not try to fold these types of impairments into their models of schizophrenia.

Genetic Bases of Schizophrenia

Schizophrenia appears to run in some families, fueling speculation that there might be a genetic basis for schizophrenia. Certainly, the data suggest the existence of a genetic basis, but the inheritance pattern of schizophrenia does not follow simple Mendelian genetics, which emphasizes the presence of dominant and recessive genes (Emrich et al., 1997). Let's take a look at the inheritance data for schizophrenia and some of the proposed genetic explanations.

All published reports agree that a schizophrenic individual is more likely to have a blood relative who is also schizophrenic than a nonschizophrenic individual is. The likelihood of developing schizophrenia is highest if one has a monozygotic twin who is also schizophrenic. Likewise, the likelihood is quite high in those who have two schizophrenic parents. On the other hand, 90% of the people who develop schizophrenia have no close relatives with schizophrenia (McGue & Gottesman, 1989; Straube & Oades, 1992). What does this tell us about the inheritance of schizophrenia?

According to classical Mendelian rules, if schizophrenia were carried by a dominant gene, the concordance rate in monozygotic twins would be expected to be 100%, and the rate in dizygotic twins would approach 50%. In reality, the concordance rate for monozygotic twins is 44% and that for dizygotic twins is only 12% (McGue & Gottesman, 1989). Obviously, we must discard Mendelian genetics as an explanation for the incidence of schizophrenia. But, there must be *some* influence of genetic inheritance because schizophrenia is more likely to occur in monozygotic twins, who share identical genes, than in dizygotic twins, who share approximately 50% of their genes. In addition, adopted children who have schizophrenic biological parents but are raised by healthy adoptive parents are more likely to become schizophrenic than are adopted children with healthy biological parents. Again, the influence of heredity is obvious.

The Mendelian model postulates that a single gene located in one region of a specific chromosome produces a particular trait. Most authorities agree that a single major locus model cannot explain the inheritability of schizophrenia. Polygenic models can help explain the various subtypes and symptoms of schizophrenia. For example, positive symptoms might be produced by one gene and negative symptoms by another. However, these models have no clear support, either (McGue & Gottesman, 1989).

The model that has found the most acceptance is the *multifactorial model*. According to this model, a combination of genetic and environmental factors produces schizophrenia. This model assumes, like the polygenic model, that more than one gene is involved, but it also emphasizes the role of the environment, including prenatal influences, brain development, and psychosocial factors. That is, according to this model, schizophrenia develops in those who have the appropriate genetic background *and* certain environmental exposures that make them susceptible to the illness. Molecular geneticists who study the inheritance of schizophrenia have been searching for a gene locus on chromosomes 5, 6, 9, 19, 20, and 22. The locus on chromosome 5 is particularly interesting because it is near the locus that controls metabolism of corticosteroids, which are important in stress reactions (Straube & Oades, 1992).

Support for the multifactorial model of schizophrenia comes from studies of monozygotic twins. Some pairs of monozygotic twins are **monochorionic,** which means that they shared the same placenta, whereas other pairs are **dichorionic,** which means that each twin had his or her own placenta. Identical twins who shared the same placenta have a concordance rate of 60% for schizophrenia. In contrast, identical twins who are dichorionic have a concordance rate of only 10.7% (David,

monochorionic: sharing the same placenta

dichorionic: having two separate placentas

Phelps, & Bracha, 1995). Thus, monochorionic monozygotic twins are much more likely to both be schizophrenic than are dichorionic monozygotic twins. This finding suggests that environmental factors also play a role in the development of schizophrenia. Monochorionic/monozygotic twins share the same blood circulation and are more likely to share infections than are dichorionic monozygotic twins. For this reason, a number of investigators have proposed that a prenatal viral infection, together with a genetic predisposition, can contribute to the development of schizophrenia later in life (Davis et al., 1995; David & Phelps, 1995; Squires, 1997).

In summary, there appear to be a large number of biochemical, structural, and functional abnormalities associated with schizophrenia. Dopamine overactivity, glutamate hypofunction, and disturbed cannabinoid systems have all been implicated in this illness. Structural changes involving the prefrontal cortex, the thalamus, the hippocampus, and other limbic structures have been associated with schizophrenic symptoms. However, at the present time, it is unclear whether any of these abnormalities actually cause schizophrenia or whether they are the result of having schizophrenia. Some of these abnormalities might even be produced by the medication that is administered to control schizophrenic symptoms, for example, problems with motor coordination. It may be, as Heinrichs (1993) has pointed out, that we will never find a unitary cause for schizophrenia because schizophrenia as we know it today may not be one single illness. Instead, schizophrenia may actually be *many* illnesses, which means that there will be different causes for each subtype of this devastating disorder.

Recap 15.2: Schizophrenia

The symptoms associated with schizophrenia can be classified into two categories, (a)_____ symptoms (behaviors observed in addition to normal behaviors, such as hallucinations, disturbed thinking, or delusions) or (b)_____ symptoms (diminished functioning, such as blunted mood, apathy, poor judgment). The dopamine hypothesis of schizophrenia is based on the observation that drugs used to treat schizophrenia are dopamine antagonists called (c)_____. One particular type of dopamine receptor, called the (d)_____ receptor, is associated with schizophrenia. According to the (e)_____ _____ hypothesis of schizophrenia, dopamine activity is diminished in the prefrontal cortex and is increased in the subcortical brain regions. According to the (f)_____ _____ _____ hypothesis, a decrease in the activity of NMDA receptors is associated with schizophrenia. The (g)_____-_____ model of schizophrenia proposes that stress causes the release of cortisol from the adrenal cortex, which produces a massive increase in dopamine in the mesolimbic system of schizophrenic individuals. Imaging studies have revealed a number of structural abnormalities associated with schizophrenia, including enlarged (h)_____ and reductions in the size of the (i)_____, (j)_____ cortex, and thalamus. The social and cognitive deficits of schizophrenia have been associated with damage to the (k)_____ prefrontal cortex, which is one of the last brain areas to mature. Functional abnormalities observed in schizophrenic individuals are called (l)_____ _____, because they are presumed to be evidence of an underlying biological problem. These functional abnormalities include irregular (m)_____ _____ eye movements and disturbances in (n)_____ and (o)_____ processing. Schizophrenic individuals perform (p)_____ on the Wisconsin Card Sorting Test, the Continuous Performance Test (Identical Pairs Version), and the Trail-Making Test. The genetic model that has found the most acceptance in explaining the inheritance of schizophrenia is the (q)_____ model, which proposes that a combination of genetic and environmental factors produce schizophrenia.

Mood Disorders

Mood disorders are characterized by states of extreme mood in which the affected individual experiences severe depression or wild elation (mania). There are two categories of mood disorders, depressive disorders (in which the individual has one or more episodes of depression) and bipolar disorders (in which the individual experiences mood swings from severe depression to mania to depression, often with a return to normal mood in between). In Chapter 14, you learned about a number of depressive disorders that are associated with stress. In this chapter, we will examine the biological bases of major depressive disorder and bipolar disorders.

Major Depressive Disorder

Major depressive disorder is a mood disorder characterized by lethargy, sad affect, diminished interest in all activities, cognitive disturbances, and eating and sleeping abnormalities. Table 15.1 gives the *DSM-IV* criteria for major depressive disorder. A number of subtypes of the disorder exist, which makes generalizations about depression impossible. For example, some individuals with depression are psychotic and have major thought disturbances, such as delusions and hallucinations, but most individuals with this disorder do not have psychotic symptoms. Others experience depression only during specific seasons of the year, but most people with major depressive disorder experience symptoms that are not seasonal. Therefore, as we examine the results of studies of people with major depressive disorder, please keep in mind that some of the inconsistent findings are most likely due to the many forms of depressive illness that comprise the syndrome known as major depressive disorder. That is, people with different symptom presentations might have dysfunctions in distinctly different regions of the brain.

major depressive disorder: a mood disorder characterized by lethargy, sad affect, diminished interest in all activities, cognitive disturbances, and eating and sleeping abnormalities

---

Table 15.1

Summary of *DSM-IV* Criteria for Major Depressive Disorder

Symptoms listed must cause distress or impair social or occupational functioning and must not be due to the effects of a drug or a medical condition.

At least one of the following must be present for at least 2 weeks
    Depressed mood most of the time
    Marked loss of interest or pleasure in all activities

Four or more of the following symptoms must also be present at the same time for at least 2 weeks:
    Significant weight loss when not dieting
    Insomnia nearly every day
    Hypersomnia [*hyper-* = more than normal; *-somn* = sleep] nearly every day
    Restlessness that is noticeable to others
    Movements markedly slowed down
    Fatigue or loss of energy nearly every day
    Feelings of worthlessness or excessive guilt nearly every day
    Unable to think, concentrate, or make decisions nearly every day
    Recurrent thoughts of death, suicidal ideation with or without a specific plan, suicide attempt

---

Biological Explanations of Major Depressive Disorder

Biological explanations of depression have been around since ancient times (Thase & Howland, 1995). Hippocrates, for example, taught that depression, or *melancholia* as it was called back then (literally, black bile), is due to an excess of black bile in the body [*melan-* = black; *-chole* = bile, Greek]. Our explanations have become more sophisticated since Hippocrates' time, thanks to the development of chemical and imaging techniques that allow investigators to determine the activity levels of neurotransmitters, hormones, and enzymes in the brain. In this section we will examine neurotransmitter and hormonal explanations for the development of major depressive disorder. Keep in mind that these "explanations" are merely hypotheses that require further testing.

Neurotransmitter-Based Explanations of Major Depressive Disorder

Monoamine Hypothesis of Depression Antidepressant medication selectively increases the availability of *monoamines* (that is, norepinephrine, dopamine, and serotonin) in the brain. For that reason, the **monoamine hypothesis of depression** is currently the most widely recognized and accepted theoretical explanation for the development of depression (Leonard, 1997b). According to the monoamine hypothesis, depression occurs when the availability or activity of one or more monoamines is reduced. Antidepressant treatment produces an immediate increase in the availability of serotonin and/or norepinephrine in the brain. Chronic administration of antidepressant medication also causes changes in the density of receptor binding sites for serotonin and norepinephrine, as well as an increase in dopamine activity in the nucleus accumbens (Gessa, 1996).

Norepinephrine Hypotheses The *catecholamine hypothesis of depression* was the earliest attempt to explain the cause of major depressive disorder. According to this hypothesis, major depressive disorder is caused by deficits of norepinephrine in critical areas of the brain (Schildkraut, 1965). The evidence in support of this hypothesis was abundant. In the early 1960s, a number of investigators observed that drugs that severely deplete norepinephrine in the brain (for example, reserpine) cause depression. Soon after that, drugs that increase norepinephrine levels in the brain, such as **tricyclics** and **MAO inhibitors,** were found to act as effective antidepressants. When end products of norepinephrine metabolism were measured in the urine, blood, or cerebrospinal fluid, early studies demonstrated that levels of these metabolites were reduced, indicating that norepinephrine was depleted in the brains of depressed individuals. However, more recent studies of norepinephrine levels in the urine, blood, and cerebrospinal fluid have shown that norepinephrine levels are actually increased in people with major depressive disorder, which is not consistent with the original norepinephrine hypothesis of depression (Viguera & Rothschild, 1996).

Abnormalities of norepinephrine function unquestionably exist in people with major depressive disorder, and thus norepinephrine probably plays an important role in the development of depression (Ressler & Nemeroff, 1999). But what can this role be? Siever and Davis (1985) have proposed a *dysregulation hypothesis*, which suggests that depression results from a failure in the regulation of the norepinephrine system, rather than from a deficit or excess of norepinephrine. According to their hypothesis, the firing of neurons in the locus coeruleus in depressed individuals is erratic and greatly increased, which interferes with the responsiveness of the locus coeruleus system.

One paradoxical finding with antidepressant medication is that norepinephrine levels increase immediately upon administration of the medication, but relief of depressive symptoms does not occur immediately. It often takes 2 weeks or more for the medication to actually have an effect on the patient's mood and behavior. The reason for this delay in therapeutic effect may be that antidepressants cause structural changes in the neuron, in addition to increasing norepinephrine availability. Antidepressants have been observed to cause dendritic sprouting and increase the density of beta-adrenergic receptors in the brain (Racagni et al., 1991; Wong, Bruck, & Farbman, 1991). Therefore, the therapeutic effect of antidepressants may be related to their ability to repair structural changes caused by chronic stress.

Serotonin Hypothesis The *serotonin hypothesis* was proposed in 1968, based on several lines of evidence that serotonin deficiency plays an important role in the development of major depressive disorder (Coppen, 1968). First of all, all antidepressants, including tricyclic antidepressants and MAO inhibitors, have been demonstrated to

monoamine hypothesis of depression: the most widely accepted explanation of depression that proposes that depression occurs when the availability or activity of one or more monoamines is reduced

tricyclic antidepressant: a medication that increases norepinephrine availability at the synapse

MAO inhibitor: an antidepressant medication that inhibits the enzyme that breaks down monoamines, thereby increasing their availability at the synapse

increase serotonin activity at the synapse. The development of specific serotonin reuptake inhibitors (SSRIs), which selectively increase serotonin availability at the synapse, in the 1980s was seen as additional support for this hypothesis. Another line of support for this hypothesis was the finding of decreased levels of the serotonin metabolic end product, **5-hydroxyindolacetic acid (5-HIAA),** in the cerebrospinal fluid of suicide victims (Stanley & Mann, 1983).

Like the norepinephrine hypothesis, a major problem with the serotonin hypothesis is that antidepressants increase serotonin availability in the synapse immediately following their administration, but depressive symptoms continue for 2 weeks or more after chronic administration of the antidepressant medication has begun. Thus, a deficiency of serotonin does not appear to cause depressive symptoms because increasing serotonin availability does not relieve depressive symptoms. On the other hand, there is evidence that antidepressants reduce the number of 5HT2 receptors (Gonzalez-Heydrich & Peroutka, 1990). Recall from our discussion of chronic stress that 5HT2 receptors in the hippocampus and amygdala receive input from an anxiogenic pathway that interferes with coping ability. Therefore, antidepressants might relieve depressive symptoms by eliminating a number of 5HT2 receptors, which ultimately results in decreased anxiety and distress in the depressed individual.

Dopamine Hypothesis Because tricyclic antidepressants block norepinephrine reuptake more effectively than dopamine reuptake, dopamine was not considered to be a factor in the development of depression until recently. Gessa (1996) has proposed a *dopamine hypothesis of depression.* According to this hypothesis, reduced firing in the mesolimbic dopamine system may be responsible for symptoms of depression. This hypothesis is based on evidence that withdrawal from the chronic use of cocaine or amphetamine produces symptoms resembling those of depression, including depressed mood, lethargy, and fatigue. In addition, studies of animal models of depression, such as learned helplessness, have demonstrated depletion of dopamine in the animal subjects that show signs of helplessness or despair.

Cholinergic Hypothesis According to the *cholinergic hypothesis of depression,* acetylcholine functions with norepinephrine to regulate mood, and imbalances in the availability of acetylcholine and norepinephrine produce depression (Janowsky, El-Yousef, Davis, & Sekerke, 1972). Increased levels of acetylcholine have been associated with major depressive disorder, and drugs that increase acetylcholine activity in the brain have been shown to induce symptoms of depression. In addition, treatments for depression, including antidepressant medication and electroconvulsive treatment, reduce brain levels of acetylcholine (Kapur & Mann, 1993).

GABA Hypothesis As you learned in Chapter 3, GABA is the most abundant inhibitory neurotransmitter in the brain. One of its many functions is to inhibit firing of cells in the locus coeruleus. A number of investigators have demonstrated that GABA levels in the blood and cerebrospinal fluid are lower than normal in individuals with major depressive disorder (Viguera & Rothschild, 1996). Moreover, some GABA agonists have significant antidepressant effects (Petty, Triveldi, Fulton, & Rush, 1995). Petty (1995) has proposed a GABA hypothesis for mood disorders based on this evidence of a relationship between GABA and depressive disorders. According to Petty's (1995) hypothesis, people with low levels of GABA may have inherited a vulnerability to develop a depressive disorder.

Substance P Dysfunction Substance P is a neuropeptide that you learned about in Chapter 8 when we discussed pain perception. However, substance P appears to have receptors throughout the central nervous system, which suggests that it plays a role in a variety of neural functions in addition to the perception of pain. For example, substance P has been implicated in the development of depression (Baby, Nguyen, Tran, & Raffa, 1999). Recently, a drug that antagonizes the action of substance P has been demonstrated to effectively treat depression (Argyropoulos & Nutt, 2000; Baby et al., 1999; Hokfelt, Pernow, & Wahren, 2001; Kramer et al.,

5-hydroxyindolacetic acid (5-HIAA): a serotonin metabolite used to estimate the levels of serotonin activity in the central nervous system

1998; Nutt, 1998). This is the first time that a drug not directly related to monoamine function has been shown to be effective in the treatment of depression. Substance P's role in depression is unknown, but suppression of its action can bring about an improvement in depressive symptoms.

Many explanations have been proposed to account for the underlying cause of depression. Of these, the monoamine hypothesis is the most widely accepted. Table 15.2 summarizes the main evidence for each biological explanation for depression.

Table 15.2

Biological Explanations for Depression

Neurotransmitter-Based Explanations

Monoamine hypothesis	Decreased monoamine (serotonin, norepinephrine, dopamine) activity produces depression.
Norepinephrine hypothesis	Norepinephrine deficits cause depression.
Serotonin hypothesis	Serotonin deficiencies or an overabundance of $5HT_2$ receptors contributes to depression.
Dopamine hypothesis	Reduced firing in the mesolimbic dopamine system may lead to depression.
Cholinergic hypothesis	Imbalances in the availability of acetylcholine and norepinephrine produce depression.
GABA hypothesis	Reduced GABA levels may lead to depression.
Substance P dysfunction	Increased substance P activity may contribute to depression.

Hormonal Explanations

HPA axis dysfunction	Increased cortisol levels are related to depression.
Hypothalamic-pituitary-thyroid axis dysfunction	Deficiencies in thyroid activity are associated with depression.
Hypothalamic-pituitary-gonadal axis dysfunction	Low levels of estrogen can trigger depression.
Melatonin dysfunction	Disruption of the melatonin system, causing a phase advancement, can produce depression.

Hormonal Explanations of Major Depressive Disorder

Hypothalamus-Pituitary-Adrenal Axis Dysfunction   You learned in Chapter 14 that about half of all patients with major depression have cortisol levels that are significantly higher than normal, indicating dysregulation of the hypothalamus-pituitary-adrenal axis (Akil & Morano, 1996; Boyer, 2000). This dysfunction may contribute to the abnormal neurotransmitter levels, particularly norepinephrine levels, observed in most depressed patients. Refer back to Chapter 14 to review the research on hypothalamus-pituitary-adrenal axis dysfunction associated with depression.

Hypothalamus-Pituitary-Thyroid Axis Dysfunction   In Chapter 11, you learned about the control of metabolism by the thyroid gland. Thyrotropin-releasing hormone is secreted by neurons in the hypothalamus and stimulates the anterior pituitary gland to release thyroid-stimulating hormone into the bloodstream. As its name implies, thyroid-stimulating hormone stimulates the thyroid gland to release thyroid hormones, which have a number of effects in the body, including increasing metabolic rate. Deficiencies in thyroid activity, referred to as a **hypothyroid** condition, have been observed in some individuals with major depressive disorder.

The **thyrotropin releasing hormone stimulation** test has been used extensively by investigators studying the effect of thyroid activity on depression (Nathan

hypothyroid: a condition caused by a deficiency in thyroid activity

thyrotropin-releasing hormone stimulation test: a test used to study the response of the thyroid gland when thyrotropin-releasing hormone is administered

et al., 1996). Normally, administration of thyrotropin-releasing hormone would induce an increase in the release of thyroid-stimulating hormone by the pituitary gland. However, thyrotropin-releasing hormone produces very little increase in thyroid-stimulating hormone release in 25–30% of patients with major depressive disorder. This demonstrates that, in some depressed individuals, the response of the thyroid system is impaired.

Hypothalamic-Pituitary-Gonadal Axis Dysfunction   Low levels of estrogen associated with menopause, childbirth, and the premenstrual (or late luteal) stage of the menstrual cycle have been shown to be correlated with mood disorders (Parry & Newton, 2001). In addition, estrogen has been used successfully to treat some forms of severe persistent depression (Klaiber et al., 1979). The role that estrogen plays in the development of depression is unknown at present. However, we do know that estrogen and other reproductive hormones can affect the function of all the neurotransmitters associated with depression, including norepinephrine, serotonin, dopamine, and acetylcholine. These gonadal hormones can also alter the activity of other hormone systems, such as cortisol, thyroid, and melatonin, which regulates the biological clock. Thus, estrogen may exert its influence on moods through its effect on other hormonal or neurotransmitter systems.

Melatonin Dysfunction   Sleep abnormalities are observed in many individuals with major depressive disorder (Wirz-Justice, 1995; Seifritz, 2001). Most suffer from an inability to fall asleep and an inability to stay asleep. Others complain that they feel sleepy all the time. Electroencephalographic (EEG) studies of depressed patients have demonstrated that brain wave abnormalities are present in many cases of major depressive disorder, including reduced levels of slow-wave sleep and altered distribution of REM sleep throughout the night. One common feature seen in the EEG records of depressed individuals is increased REM activity, which is typically suppressed by antidepressant medication (Thase & Howland, 1995).

Anderson and Wirz-Justice (1991) have proposed that a disruption in the melatonin system, which controls circadian rhythms, as you learned in Chapter 9, is responsible for the sleep disturbances observed in depressed individuals. This disruption causes a **phase advancement** of the circadian rhythm. The term *phase advancement* refers to the fact that hormonal and other physiological processes, which fluctuate throughout the day according to regular, predictable patterns in healthy individuals, appear to be shifted several hours forward in people who are depressed. For that reason, many depressed individuals wake up earlier and go into REM sleep sooner during the night. In addition, the circadian rhythm for norepinephrine and cortisol release shows evidence of phase advancement in many people with major depressive disorder.

Phase advancement explains why traveling west over several time zones often induces depression in the traveler who has a history of mood disorder. Individuals who travel west from New York to California find themselves in a time zone that is several hours behind their own internal clocks. The disruption of the circadian rhythm caused by westward travel leads to sleep and other neurophysiological disruptions that are associated with depression. Likewise, depriving a depressed person of sleep typically causes a short-term relief of depression because the sleep deprivation temporarily resets the phase-advanced circadian rhythm of the depressed individual (Wu & Bunney, 1990). The rapid return of depression following sleep recovery suggests that melatonin plays an important role in the regulation of mood.

Nearly all of the research concerned with the biology of depression that has been conducted to date, especially the human studies, is correlational in nature. Thus, we cannot impute causation from it. That is, we cannot infer that low levels of norepinephrine or high levels of cortisol cause depression. Rather, it may be that depression causes low levels of norepinephrine and high levels of cortisol. Because it is unethical to deliberately try to cause depression in human subjects, we may never know exactly what causes major depressive disorder. However, the research that can be ethically conducted should help us to find effective methods of treatment for all subtypes of the disorder.

phase advancement: the shift of hormonal and other physiological functions several hours forward in time

Treatment of Major Depressive Disorder

A variety of medications and procedures are used to treat major depressive disorder. In the preceding sections, I described the actions of *antidepressant drugs* on various neurotransmitter and hormonal systems. New classes of antidepressants are under development, including GABA agonists, CRH antagonists, and acetylcholine antagonists (Berman, Krystal, & Charney, 1996). Some of these drugs, particularly GABA agonists, have been demonstrated to be as clinically effective as traditional antidepressants (Petty et al., 1995). Some of the newest drugs (for example, a drug that blocks the receptors for substance P) appear to successfully treat major depressive disorder, but they don't fit neatly into any of the explanations of depression that we've explored in this chapter (Kramer et al., 1998). In the future, our understanding of the mechanisms underlying depression will improve as we study the action of new medications on the nervous system.

One procedure that has been demonstrated to be quite successful in treating profoundly depressed patients is **electroconvulsive therapy (ECT),** in which an electric current is passed across the patient's brain, producing a seizure (Sackeim, Devanand, & Nobler, 1995; Szuba, O'Reardon, & Evans, 2000). This procedure has been in use since the late 1930s, although its use has declined quite a bit since the development of modern antidepressant medications. However, it is still used regularly with patients with major depressive disorder, especially with those who are severely depressed and not responding to medication.

Investigators are uncertain how electroconvulsive therapy relieves depressive symptoms in the depressed patient. One observation is that CRH levels in the cerebrospinal fluid are diminished following electroconvulsive therapy, which suggests that excess secretion of CRH in the brain maintains symptoms of depression (De Souza et al., 1995). Electroconvulsive therapy also alters monoamine, acetylcholine, and GABA activity in the brain, as you learned earlier in this chapter. One of the negative side effects of electroconvulsive therapy is memory loss and disorientation in the patient.

Transcranial magnetic stimulation is a relatively new method of treating depression. This is a noninvasive method that involves directly stimulating neurons in the cerebral cortex (George, Wasserman, & Post, 1996; Szuba et al., 2000). Originally, transcranial magnetic stimulation was used as a research tool to map functions, like memory, movement, speech, and vision, on the cortex, much like the electrical stimulation studies that were conducted on patients undergoing brain surgery over 50 years ago. However, early investigators observed a temporary elevation in mood in people tested with this procedure, and some began testing the procedure informally on depressed patients, with inconclusive results (Kirkcaldie, Pridmore, & Pascual-Leone, 1997).

More recently, investigators have applied knowledge derived from PET studies of depressed people to improve the ability of transcranial magnetic stimulation to treat depression. That is, brain-imaging studies of depressed patients have demonstrated decreased cerebral activity in the anterior regions of the brain, especially on the left side of the brain. When high-frequency repetitive transcranial magnetic stimulation is applied to the left prefrontal cortex of a depressed individual, it increases activity in that area of the brain and produces short-term relief of depression. This effect has been demonstrated in well-designed studies that use a placebo control and a double-blind procedure (George et al., 1996; Figiel et al., 1998; Kirkaldie et al., 1997). Depressed patients who fail to suppress cortisol release in response to the dexamethasone suppression test will show a suppression following treatment with transcranial magnetic stimulation, an effect also seen with antidepressant medication (Pridmore, 1999; Reid & Pridmore, 1999). In addition, unlike electroconvulsive therapy, transcranial magnetic stimulation does not require anesthesia, does not produce seizures in patients, and appears to have no negative side effects (Post et al., 1999).

electroconvulsive therapy: a procedure, used to treat profoundly depressed patients, in which a high-voltage electrical current is passed through the patient's brain, producing a seizure

transcranial magnetic stimulation: a noninvasive treatment for depression that involves directly stimulating neurons in the cerebral cortex

Bipolar Disorder

Bipolar disorder, or *manic-depressive disorder* as it is sometimes called, can present with psychotic symptoms and, thus, is discussed in this chapter with other psychotic disorders. Persons with bipolar disorder can show symptoms of depression at times and symptoms of mania, or high excitability, at other times. When in a manic state, persons with bipolar disorder will experience generally elevated mood and self-esteem, feeling that their abilities and/or beliefs are superior to those of others. They also have high levels of energy, don't seem to require much sleep, and can have irrational thinking that is accompanied by poor judgment, delusions, and hallucinations. PET images of the brain of an individual with bipolar disorder indicate that the metabolic activity of the brain is increased on days of the manic phase and is decreased on days of the depressed phase (Figure 15.12).

A number of alterations in neurotransmitter and hormone functions have been associated with bipolar disorder. For example, in Chapter 14 you learned that major depressive disorder is associated with higher-than-normal levels of cortisol. The same is true of bipolar disorder, which indicates that regulation of the HPA axis may be disrupted in this disorder. Abnormalities of the thyroid system have also been reported in patients with bipolar disorder (Nathan et al., 1996).

Abnormalities in serotonin, norepinephrine, and dopamine have been implicated in the cause of bipolar disorder. Serotonin activity is reduced in bipolar disorder, whereas norepinephrine activity is increased (Prange et al., 1974; Alda, 2001). This pattern differs from that observed in patients with major depressive disorder, who have depressed levels of serotonin and norepinephrine activity. Increased dopamine levels have been observed in patients with psychotic mania and psychotic depression (Thase & Howland, 1995). In addition, bipolar disorder appears to be an inheritable condition and has been associated with genes on chromosomes 4, 18, and 21, as well as the X chromosome (Asherson et al., 1998; Berrettini, 1998; Curtis, 1999; Kennedy et al., 1999; Van Broeckhoven et al., 1999).

bipolar disorder: a mood disorder in which the affected individual will show symptoms of depression at some times and symptoms of mania at others

Figure 15.12 PET scan of brain of bipolar individual
Yellow indicates areas of high levels of brain activity. When the patient was depressed (May 17 and May 27), brain activity was low. During a manic phase (May 18), brain activity was very high.

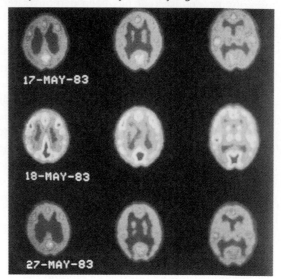

Treatment of Bipolar Disorder

Treatment of bipolar disorder has centered on relieving the manic or depressive symptoms and providing prophylactic or preventive therapy (Mitchell & Malhi, 2002). Lithium is used to treat manic symptoms. It also works as a prophylactic treatment, stabilizing mood and preventing the individual with bipolar disorder from cycling into a manic or depressive phase. Administered as a salt, lithium takes the form of a positively charged ion (Li^+), like sodium (Na^+) and potassium (K^+), in body tissues. The therapeutic action of lithium is still under debate, but it appears to affect a number of systems that might be involved in bipolar and other affective disorders (Lenox & Manji, 2001; Muller-Oerlinghausen et al. 2001). For example, lithium increases serotonin activity, which appears to be decreased in both bipolar and major depressive disorders. Lithium's antimanic activity seems to come from its ability to reduce dopamine transmission. Its effect on the norepinephrine system is unclear, although it has been demonstrated to produce an increase in norepinephrine in urine and blood. Lithium also alters the circadian rhythm, slowing down the biological clock.

A number of other medications are sometimes prescribed, in conjunction with lithium or alone, for patients with bipolar disorder. For example, antidepressants may be prescribed for bipolar individuals experiencing severe depressive symptoms. Antipsychotic agents may also be given to those individuals with symptoms of psychotic depression or mania, such as delusions or hallucinations. Atypical antipsychotic medications appear to be more effective and safer to use with lithium than are traditional antipsychotics (Ghaemi & Goodwin, 1999). Anticonvulsant drugs, which are primarily used to treat seizure disorders, have also been found to be effective in the treatment of some individuals with bipolar disorder (Schaffer, Schaffer, & Caretto, 1999).

Recap 15.3: Mood Disorders

(a)_____ _____ disorder is a mood disorder characterized by lethargy, sad affect, diminished interest in activities, cognitive disturbances, and eating and sleeping abnormalities. The most widely accepted explanation for the development of depression is the (b)_____ hypothesis, which is based on the observation that drugs that increase the availability of serotonin, norepinephrine, and dopamine relieve symptoms of depression. (c)_____ increase the availability of monoamines in the synapse, but depressive symptoms continue for two or more weeks after drug administration has begun. Increased levels of the neurotransmitter, (d)_____, have been associated with major depressive disorder. Hormonal abnormalities associated with major depressive disorder include higher than normal levels of cortisol 9 (as indicated by the (e)_____ suppression test), deficiencies in (f)_____ activity (as indicated by the thyrotropin-releasing hormone stimulation test), low levels of (g)_____ (associated with menopause, childbirth, and the premenstrual phase of the menstrual cycle), and (h)_____ dysfunction associated with sleep abnormalities and phase advancement of the circadian rhythm. Treatment for major depressive disorder include (i)_____ drugs, (j)_____ therapy, and (k)_____ _____ stimulation. (l)_____ _____ is characterized by the presence of depressed symptoms for a period of time and symptoms of mania (high excitability, elevated mood and self-esteem) at other times. Abnormalities of (m)_____, (n)_____, and (o)_____ are associated with bipolar disorder. Treatment for bipolar disorder includes (p)_____, (q)_____ medication, (r)_____ mediation, and (s)_____ medication.

Personality Disorders

A **personality disorder** is characterized by a *consistent, abnormal pattern of behavior* that is used *over a long period of time* by the affected individual. Whereas healthy people may at times show symptoms of one personality disorder or another, the behavioral disturbances observed in individuals with a true personality disorder are much more severe than those seen in healthy people. On the other hand, the severe symptoms associated with psychosis or depression, such as hallucinations, delusions, and anxiety, are not generally associated with personality disorders.

The *DSM-IV* identifies 10 personality disorders. The symptoms for each of these are summarized in Table 15.3. Some people will present with the symptoms of only one personality disorder, whereas others will present with the symptoms of two or more disorders. In addition, some personality disorders are characterized by less severe symptoms that may best be described as an exaggeration of normal human behavior. Examples of these less severe symptoms include dependence and passivity, which all of us exhibit to some extent at times. Other personality disorders, such as paranoid or schizotypal, have symptoms that resemble those of schizophrenia, although they are not nearly as severe and dysfunctional.

These observations complicate our understanding of personality disorders. A wide range of biological explanations may be necessary to account for the impressive diversity of symptoms associated with the various personality disorders. At the present time, the biological mechanisms underlying personality disorders are largely unknown, or the evidence for them is scanty. I will review for you what is currently known about the biological bases of personality disorders.

personality disorder: a psychological disorder characterized by a consistent, abnormal pattern of behavior that is used over a long period of time by the affected individual

Table 15.3

DSM-IV Symptoms Associated with Each of the 10 Personality Disorders

Personality Disorder	Symptoms
Schizoid	Does not desire or enjoy close relationships, little interest in sexual activities with another, shows emotional detachment, flattened affect
Schizotypal	Discomfort with close relationships, has odd beliefs or magical thinking, inappropriate affect; behavior or appearance is odd
Paranoid	Distrust and suspiciousness of others, preoccupied with doubts about trustworthiness of others, reluctant to confide in others
Antisocial	Engages in unlawful behavior, deceitfulness, impulsivity, aggressive acts, disregard for safety of others, irresponsibility, lack of remorse
Borderline	Fear of abandonment, unstable and intense relationships, moody, unstable self-image, suicidal gestures, impulsivity, temper tantrums
Histrionic	Needs to be center of attention, inappropriately sexually provocative, shallow displays of emotion, theatrical, suggestible
Narcissistic	Has grandiose sense of self-importance, needs constant admiration, takes advantage of others, lacks empathy, is arrogant and haughty
Avoidant	Avoids social or work settings where negative criticism possible, has fear of being ridiculed or rejected, views self as inept/unattractive
Dependent	Has excessive need to be taken care of, needs advice to make decision, afraid to express disagreement, clinging behavior, takes no initiative
Obsessive-Compulsive	Preoccupied with orderliness, details, rules; rigid, miserly, works to exclusion of leisure activities, cannot discard useless items

Schizoid, Schizotypal, and Paranoid Personality Disorders

The three most severe personality disorders—the schizoid, schizotypal, and paranoid disorders—are considered **schizophrenia spectrum disorders** because they appear to be genetically related to schizophrenia and share many of the same symptoms and biological markers of schizophrenia, including abnormal smooth pursuit eye movements (Davis et al., 1991; Thaker et al., 1996). These three personality disorders are more likely to occur in biological relatives of schizophrenics. Approximately 15% of the close relatives of schizophrenics have a schizophrenia spectrum disorder. This means that any genetic model of schizophrenia must also account for the expression of these less severe disorders. Most authorities assume that several different genes are responsible for the expression of schizophrenia and related spectrum personality disorders. Furthermore, authorities believe that these genes are influenced by the environment, producing full-blown schizophrenia in some individuals and less severe symptoms in some of their blood relatives (Straube & Oades, 1992).

Schizoid Personality Disorder

Like schizophrenic individuals, individuals with **schizoid personality disorder** experience social detachment and flat affect—two negative symptoms of schizophrenia. They also exhibit a number of the biological markers for schizophrenia, including right ear advantage in dichotic listening, lower hearing thresholds in the

schizophrenia spectrum disorders: personality disorders that are genetically related to schizophrenia and share many of the same symptoms and biological markers of that disorder

schizoid personality disorder: a personality disorder characterized by social detachment and flat affect

right ear, and overactivation of the left hemisphere. On the other hand, those with schizoid personality disorder do not have disordered thoughts or show any of the psychotic symptoms of schizophrenia. Because of this disorder's close relationship with schizophrenia, a number of authors have suggested that dopamine dysregulation might be involved. A recent gene analysis has demonstrated a strong association between an abnormal form of a gene that regulates D_2 receptors and schizoid behavior (Blum et al., 1997).

Schizotypal Personality Disorder

Of all the schizophrenia spectrum disorders, **schizotypal personality disorder** is most like schizophrenia, and it is the personality disorder that is most closely linked genetically to schizophrenia (Nigg & Goldsmith, 1994). People with schizotypal personality disorder have many symptoms that resemble schizophrenia, but their symptoms are less severe. In addition, they show other characteristics of schizophrenia, which gives us a hint of the biological processes that underlie both schizophrenia and schizotypal personality disorder. For example, schizotypal individuals show abnormal orienting responses and impaired attention, as schizophrenics do (Raine et al., 1997; Roitman et al., 1997). In addition, like individuals with schizophrenia, individuals with schizotypal personality disorder have higher cortisol levels and heightened cortisol release, compared to normal controls and participants with other personality disorders (Walker, Walder, & Reynolds, 2001). In fact, the most severe psychotic-like, schizotypal symptoms are best treated with neuroleptics.

schizotypal personality disorder: a personality disorder characterized by eccentric behavior, avoidance of close relationships, and thought distortions

Paranoid Personality Disorder

The symptoms of **paranoid personality disorder** often bear a remarkable resemblance to the paranoid delusions of schizophrenia. However, delusions are not well organized or clearly formed in paranoid personality disorder. The individual with this disorder is distrustful and suspicious of others, which interferes with the formation of enduring social relationships. Very little research concerned with the biological basis of this disorder has been conducted. A recent report presented the results of PET imaging of the brain of a male patient diagnosed with a paranoid personality disorder (Salmon et al., 1996). Using a radioligand specific for dopamine, Salmon and his colleagues demonstrated reduced dopamine function in the prefrontal lobes of the man with paranoid personality disorder. This reduced prefrontal function is similar to that observed in schizophrenic patients.

paranoid personality disorder: a personality disorder characterized by paranoid ideation that is not well organized

Antisocial and Borderline Personality Disorders

Many investigators agree that antisocial and borderline personality disorders are closely related, if not different sides of the same disorder. They have common symptoms, share the same risk factors, and show a limited response to treatment (Holden, Pakula, & Mooney, 1997; Paris, 1996). In addition, both disorders are characterized by impulsive aggression: toward others in those with antisocial disorder, toward the self in those with borderline disorder. Recall from Chapter 12 that serotonin mediates impulsive aggressive behavior, which suggests that serotonin function may be impaired in these two personality disorders (Kavoussi et al., 1997; Holden et al., 1997). Other authors believe that dysfunctions of neuropeptide Y, beta-endorphin, or insulin may underlie these disorders (Holden et al., 1997). The main difference between the two disorders is that antisocial personality disorder is more prevalent in men and borderline personality disorder is more prevalent in women (Paris, 1996).

Antisocial Personality Disorder

People with **antisocial personality disorder** are often referred to as psychopaths or sociopaths because their social interactions with others are pathological. According to the *DSM-IV*, persons with this disorder will exhibit: (1) criminal behavior,

antisocial personality disorder: a personality disorder characterized by pathological social interactions with others, in which the disturbed individual acts impulsively and exploits others for his or her own gain, showing no remorse often conning or lying to other people to get what they want; (2) impulsivity, especially impulsive aggressive behavior; (3) disregard for the safety or well-being of others; and (4) a lack of remorse for mistreating or taking advantage of others. Any biological explanation must attempt to account for these symptoms and the lack of anxiety that accompanies the expression of these symptoms.

Antisocial behavior appears to be the product of genetic and environmental influences. Because antisocial personality disorder seems to run in families, one way to study the genetic influence would be to analyze the genes of families who transmit the disorder to their offspring and to identify structural variations in those genes. Goldman and his colleagues (1996) have identified amino acid substitutions in the genes of one family with several antisocial relatives and have ascertained that these genetic variants are associated with a number of abnormal dopamine and serotonin receptors. However, genetic studies are complicated by the fact that antisocial personality is often accompanied by alcoholism and other drug addictions, as well as criminal behavior, all of which can produce or encourage the expression of antisocial characteristics (Kendler, Davis, & Kessler, 1997; Moeller & Dougherty, 2001; Morgenstern et al., 1997).

Individuals with antisocial personality disorder also show less inhibition of motor, or somatic nervous system, responses, thereby exhibiting impulsive behaviors. This impulsiveness has been attributed to reduced cortical inhibition. This means that the psychopathic individual is more likely to respond to environmental stimuli with motor responses rather than to stop to think about the consequences, which is mediated by cortical inhibition. Inhibition of impulsive behavior appears to be regulated by serotonin in the brain (Zuckerman, 1995). Studies with rats have demonstrated that lesions of the serotonin system produce unrestrained, impulsive behaviors (Figure 15.16), such as impulsive mice-killing and an inability to suppress punished behaviors (Soubrie, 1986; Valzelli et al., 1981). There is some indirect evidence that serotonin activity is lower than normal in the brains of psychopaths: Their brains contain reduced levels of serotonin metabolites such as 5-hydroxyindolacetic acid (5-HIAA) (Kavoussi, Armstead, & Coccaro, 1997; Soderstrom, Blennow, Manhem, & Forsman, 2001).

Treatment of this disorder, whether with psychotherapy or prescribed drugs, has not been terribly successful. The only symptoms that seem to respond to drugs are impulsive and violent behavior (Fava, 1997; Mulder, 1996). These drugs include antidepressants and atypical neuroleptics that enhance serotonin activity in the brain. Unfortunately, no drug treatment studies have been conducted with control subjects receiving placebos, so the evidence for the benefits of drug treatment is limited.

Borderline Personality Disorder

Mood, self-image, interpersonal relationships, and self-control are all impaired in **borderline personality disorder,** making it difficult to pinpoint a single biological mechanism that can explain this complicated disorder. Emil Coccaro and Richard Kavoussi (1991) have identified three clusters of symptoms that appear to have underlying biological bases: (1) affective instability, (2) transient psychotic symptoms, and (3) impulsive aggression and other impulsive behaviors. Affective instability, which reflects the abnormal mood fluctuations in borderline patients, may be due to dysfunction of the brain's adrenergic and cholinergic systems. As in schizophrenia, the transient psychotic symptoms of borderline personality disorder can most likely be attributed to abnormal dopamine pathways. And, as we discussed in Chapter 12, impulsive aggressive behaviors appear to be related to altered serotonin activity in the brain.

Depressive symptoms are a common feature of borderline personality disorder. However, there is a good deal of evidence that the depressive symptoms of borderline personality disorder are not produced by the same brain mechanism that underlies the symptoms of major depressive disorder. For example, borderline patients with depressive symptoms do not show suppression in response to a dexamethasone suppression test (DST), as patients with major depression often do (De la Fuente & Mendlewicz, 1996). (Refer back to Chapter 14 for a discussion of the DST chal-

borderline personality disorder: a personality disorder characterized by disturbances in mood, self-image, interpersonal relationships, and self-control

lenge.) Although we talked about the roles of serotonin and norepinephrine in depression, we did not talk about the role of acetylcholine. Research by Steinberg and his colleagues (1997), employing a double-blind, placebo-controlled physostigmine challenge paradigm, demonstrated that acetylcholine is indeed involved in the regulation of mood in borderline personality disorder.

One common symptom of borderline personality disorder that has been researched extensively by neuroscientists is self-injurious behavior, including self-mutilation. Dopamine, serotonin, and opiate neurotransmitter systems appear to be involved in self-injury (Winchel & Stanley, 1991; Kavoussi, Armstead, & Coccaro, 1997; Villalba & Harrington, 2001). There are three lines of evidence that suggest that reduced serotonin function might underlie impulsive, self-injurious behavior in borderline personality disorder. First, borderline patients who have attempted to harm or mutilate themselves have lowered levels of 5-HIAA, which is a product of serotonin metabolism (Asberg et al., 1987). Second, individuals with borderline personality disorder have a reduced response to fenfluramine, a drug that causes serotonin to be released in the brain (Coccaro et al., 1991). Third, monoamine oxidase inhibitors and selective serotonin reuptake inhibitors, which increase serotonin activity in the brain, have been used with some success to treat borderline patients (Gitlin, 1993) (see the *Case Study*).

Literally hundreds of papers have been published on the remaining personality disorders defined in the *DSM-IV*. But very few investigators have addressed possible biological mechanisms associated with these disorders. Some disorders, such as the dependent personality disorder, have a strong association with major depression, and others have a strong association with drug and alcohol use or anxiety disorders (Skodol et al., 1996b; Koranger, 1996; Siever & Davis, 1991). These types of associations give us a hint of the neurotransmitter systems that might be involved. However, the comorbidity [*co-* = together, *-morbidity* = occurrence of disease, Greek] among these disorders and others that we've already examined is significant, which makes simple biological explanations impossible (Ronningstam, 1996; Skodol et al., 1996a, b).

Recap 15.4: Personality Disorders

A (a)_____ disorder is characterized by a consistent, abnormal pattern of behavior that is used over a long period of time. The three most severe personality disorders are the (b)_____ _____ disorders, which include schizoid personality disorder, schizotypal personality, and paranoid personality disorder. People with (c)_____ personality disorder experience two negative symptoms of schizophrenia (social detachment and flat affect). (d)_____ personality disorder shares many of the symptoms of schizophrenia and has close genetic links with schizophrenia. In (e)_____ personality disorder, the paranoid symptoms resemble closely the paranoid delusions seen in schizophrenia, although these delusions are not well-organized in people with paranoid personality disorder. (f)_____ personality disorder and (g)_____ personality disorder have common symptoms characterized by impulsive aggression, share the same risk factors, and show a limited response to treatment. People with (h)_____ personality disorder will lie and con to get what they want, have impulsive aggressive behavior, and a lack of remorse for mistreating others. Antidepressants and other drugs that increase (i)_____ levels can be used to treat impulsive and violent behavior associated with antisocial personality disorder. (j)_____ personality disorder is characterized by impairments in mood, self-image, interpersonal relationships, and self-control and depressive symptoms. Drugs that increase (k)_____ activity in the brain are used to treat borderline personality disorder.

Borderline Personality Disorder

Late one Saturday evening, I received a bizarre phone call from an undergraduate student named Erin. It was around midnight when she called, a highly unusual and inappropriate time to phone one's professor. In a subdued voice, Erin told me that she had just slit her wrists and was sitting in a bathtub of warm water. I grabbed a notepad and scribbled a message to my husband to get the cell phone and call campus security. While my husband dialed the campus security office, I kept Erin on the phone, chatting about her evening and the events that led to her slitting her wrists. I also confirmed that the address listed in the campus directory was her apartment and that she was indeed in her apartment. Erin and I continued to talk until the security officers arrived at her apartment about 10 minutes later. As we chatted, I was struck by the realization that Erin seemed remarkably talkative and upbeat for a person who had just slit her wrists.

Early the next morning, I called the campus infirmary to find out how Erin was doing. A nurse assured me that Erin was doing well and that she was never in any real danger because her cuts were all superficial. Indeed, Erin was released from the infirmary later that day and was in my classroom bright and early on Monday morning.

Liz, the student who shared Erin's apartment, came to my office Monday afternoon and introduced herself to me. She came to talk to me about Erin and wanted to know if Erin could be forced to get counseling. When I replied that only Erin could make the decision to seek counseling, Liz burst into tears and said that she didn't think she could take much more of living with Erin. Liz then launched into a description of Erin's misbehaviors.

The two women met at a fraternity party at the end of the previous year. They found they had a lot in common and became fast friends. But even before Erin and Liz found an apartment together, Liz began to have doubts about her friendship with Erin. For example, Erin told her a number of intimate secrets that made Liz feel uncomfortable. In addition, Erin also drank too much and did foolish things when she got drunk, like buy drinks for total strangers at a bar or go home with strange men.

When they began to share an apartment, Erin wanted to go out every night, but Liz preferred to stay home most

nights and study or watch television. Often Erin threw a temper tantrum if Liz wouldn't go out, forcing Liz to go. On nights when Erin did go out by herself, she invariably would bring a total stranger home to sleep with her, often older men who weren't students. Liz complained that she didn't feel comfortable with these strange men in the house, but Erin replied that Liz was just jealous that she was getting laid and Liz was not.

On a number of occasions, Liz told Erin that she was going to move out of the apartment at the end of the semester, and each time Erin would fly into a rage or stage a suicide attempt. That past Saturday night, Liz and Erin were both at an off-campus party when Liz made a comment to Erin that Erin had drunk far too much. Erin responded with an angry, sarcastic remark that Liz wouldn't have to worry about her anymore after Liz moved out in December. At that point, Liz walked away and asked another friend if she could spend the night at her place. She had no idea about Erin's actions later that night until Sunday afternoon when Erin proudly waved her bandaged arms in Liz's face.

Erin's behavior exemplifies many of the classical symptoms of borderline personality disorder. Erin was a person who rushed into intense relationships with others, relationships that faded almost as quickly as they formed. She was very moody and tended to react to adverse situations, especially if they hinted at criticism or abandonment, with anger. In addition, her behavior was impulsive. Her drinking was out of control, and she displayed very risky sexual behavior. When feeling upset or rejected, she resorted to self-injury.

I thanked Liz for her concern for Erin and suggested that she offer to go with Erin for counseling, as a first step to getting help for her friend. After the next class, I invited Erin to my office and asked her how she was feeling. I told her how worried she made me on Saturday night and explained that calling me was inappropriate. We discussed who might have been a more appropriate person to call and put together a list of people who could help her in the future. Before she left my office, I tactfully recommended that she talk to a professional counselor who could help her sort out her "issues."

Chapter Summary

Psychoses

▶ Psychoses are severe mental disorders in which thinking is disturbed and the affected individual is not well oriented for person, time, and place. Dementia is a

disorder that involves cognitive impairment and poor judgment.

▶ Schizophrenia is one of many different psychotic disorders. Other psychotic syndromes can be produced by infections, toxins, malnutrition, brain tumors, stimulant drugs, and traumatic injuries to the brain.

▶ Toxic psychoses are reversible psychoses produced by bacterial infections, which induce symptoms of restlessness, loss of orientation for time and place, hallucinations, inattention, and perceptual distortions.

▶ Reversible psychoses are also produced by viral encephalitis (a brain inflammation caused by a virus) and meningitis (an inflammation of the meninges caused by an infection.

▶ Abuse of stimulants, such as amphetamine, cocaine, and PCP, can also produce reversible psychoses.

▶ An irreversible psychotic state called dementia pugilistica is observed in some boxers who have suffered repeated blows to the head.

Schizophrenia

▶ The symptoms associated with schizophrenia can be classified into two categories, positive symptoms (behaviors observed in addition to normal behaviors, such as hallucinations, disturbed thinking, or delusions) or negative symptoms (diminished functioning, such as blunted mood, apathy, poor judgment).

▶ Although the cause of schizophrenia is not known, a number of hypotheses have been advanced to explain the development of the disorder, including the dopamine hypothesis, the NMDA receptor hypofunction hypothesis, the cannabinoid hypothesis, and the diathesis–stress model.

▶ Of these, the dopamine hypothesis, which emphasizes an imbalance in dopamine activity in the brain, has received the most widespread attention. The dopamine hypothesis of schizophrenia is based on the observation that drugs used to treat schizophrenia are dopamine antagonists called neuroleptics. One particular type of dopamine receptor, called the D_2 receptor, is associated with schizophrenia.

▶ According to the modified dopamine hypothesis of schizophrenia, dopamine activity is diminished in the prefrontal cortex and is increased in the subcortical brain regions.

▶ According to the NMDA receptor hypofunction hypothesis, a decrease in the activity of NMDA receptors is associated with schizophrenia.

▶ The diasthesis–stress model of schizophrenia proposes that stress causes the release of cortisol from the adrenal cortex, which produces a massive increase in dopamine in the mesolimbic dopamine system of schizophrenic individuals.

▶ Imaging studies have revealed a number of structural abnormalities associated with schizophrenia, including enlarged ventricles and reductions in the size of the hippocampus, prefrontal cortex, and thalamus.

▶ The social and cognitive deficits of schizophrenia have been associated with damage to the dorsolateral prefrontal cortex, which is one of the last brain areas to mature.

▶ Functional abnormalities observed in schizophrenic individuals are called biological markers, because they are presumed to be evidence of an underlying biological problem. These functional abnormalities include irregular smooth pursuit eye movements and disturbances in attention and information processing. Schizophrenic individuals perform poorly on the Wisconsin Card Sorting Test, the Continuous Performance Test (Identical Pairs Version), and the Trail-Making Test.

▶ Investigators are studying a number of chromosomes for a possible gene locus for schizophrenia, although most researchers in the field believe that environmental factors, such as prenatal exposure to a virus, can also contribute to the development of schizophrenia. The genetic model that has found the most acceptance in explaining the inheritance of schizophrenia is the multifactorial model, which proposes that a combination of genetic and environmental factors produce schizophrenia.

Mood Disorders

▶ Major depressive disorder is a mood disorder characterized by lethargy, sad affect, diminished interest in activities, cognitive disturbances, and eating and sleeping abnormalities.

▶ A number of biological explanations of major depressive disorders have also been proposed. The most widely accepted explanation for the development of depression is the monoamine hypothesis, which is based on the observation that drugs that increase the availability of serotonin, norepinephrine, and dopamine relieve symptoms of depression. Antidepressants increase the availability of monoamines in the synapse, but depressive symptoms continue for two or more weeks after drug administration has begun.

▶ Increased levels of the neurotransmitter, acetylcholine, have been associated with major depressive disorder.

▶ Hormonal abnormalities associated with major depressive disorder include higher than normal levels of cortisol 9 as indicated by the dexamethasone suppression test), deficiencies in thyroid activity (as indicated by the thyrotropin-releasing hormone stimulation test), low levels of estrogen (associated menopause, childbirth, and the premenstrual phase of the menstrual cycle), and melatonin dysfunction associated with sleep abnormalities and phase advancement of the circadian rhythm.

▶ Treatment for major depressive disorder includes SSRIs, MAO inhibitors, tricyclic antidepressants, GABA agonists, CRH antagonists, acetylcholine antagonists, and substance P antagonists, as well as electroconvulsive therapy and transcranial magnetic stimulation.

▶ Bipolar disorder is characterized by the presence of depressed symptoms for a period of time and symptoms of mania (high excitability, elevated mood and self-esteem) at other times. Bipolar disorder can present with psychotic symptoms, and treatment for this disorder can include drugs to control manic, depressive, and/or psychotic symptoms.

▶ Abnormalities of serotonin, norepinephrine, and dopamine are associated with bipolar disorder.

▶ Treatment for bipolar disorder includes lithium, antidepressant medication, antipsychotic medication, and anticonvulsant medication.

Personality Disorders

▶ A personality disorder is characterized by a consistent, abnormal pattern of behavior that is used over a long period of time.

▶ The *DSM-IV* identifies ten different personality disorders.

▶ The three most severe personality disorders are the schizophrenia spectrum disorders, which include schizoid personality disorder, schizotypal personality, and paranoid personality disorder. Schizoid, schizotypal, and paranoid personality disorders share a number of biological markers with schizophrenia.

▶ People with schizoid personality disorder experience two negative symptoms of schizophrenia (social detachment and flat affect). Schizotypal personality disorder

shares many of the symptoms of schizophrenia and has close genetic links with schizophrenia. In paranoid personality disorder, the paranoid symptoms resemble closely the paranoid delusions seen in schizophrenia, although these delusions are not well-organized in people with paranoid personality disorder.

▶ Antisocial personality disorder and borderline personality disorder have common symptoms characterized by impulsive aggression, share the same risk factors, and show a limited response to treatment.

▶ People with antisocial personality disorder will lie and con to get what they want, have impulsive aggressive behavior, and a lack of remorse for mistreating others. Antidepressants and other drugs that raise serotonin levels can be used to treat impulsive and violent behavior associated with antisocial personality disorder.

▶ Borderline personality disorder is characterized by impairments in mood, self-image, interpersonal relationships, and self-control and depressive symptoms. Drugs that increase serotonin activity in the brain are used to treat borderline personality disorder.

▶ Relatively little research has been conducted on the biological underpinnings of personality disorders.

Key Terms

antisocial personality
 disorder (p. 471)
biological marker (p. 457)
bipolar disorder (p. 468)
borderline personality
 disorder (p. 472)
cannabinoid hypothesis of
 schizophrenia (p. 452)
concordant (p. 453)
dementia (p. 445)
dementia pugilistica (p. 446)
diathesis–stress model of
 schizophrenia (p. 452)
dichorionic (p. 460)
discordant (p. 453)
dopamine hypothesis of
 schizophrenia (p. 448)
electroconvulsive therapy (p. 467)
5-hydroxyindolacetic acid
 (5-HIAA) (p. 464)

gating hypothesis of
 schizophrenia (p. 458)
hallucination (p. 456)
hypothyroid (p. 465)
major depressive disorder (p. 462)
MAO inhibitor (p. 463)
monoamine hypothesis of
 depression (p. 463)
monochorionic (p. 460)
multifactorial model (p. 460)
negative symptoms of
 schizophrenia (p. 447)
neuroleptics (p. 448)
NMDA receptor hypofunction
 hypothesis (p. 451)
paranoid personality
 disorder (p. 471)
personality disorder (p. 469)
phase advancement (p. 466)

positive symptoms of
 schizophrenia (p. 447)
psychosis (p. 444)
schizoid personality
 disorder (p. 470)
schizophrenia (p. 447)
schizophrenia spectrum
 disorders (p. 470)
schizotypal personality
 disorder (p. 471)
smooth pursuit eye
 movements (p. 458)
thyrotropin-releasing hormone stimulation test (p. 465)
toxic psychosis (p. 445)
transcranial magnetic
 stimulation (p. 467)
tricyclic antidepressant (p. 463)
viral encephalitis (p. 445)

Questions for Thought

1. Can early childhood experiences affect future brain function?
2. What is the evidence that supports a multifactorial explanation for schizophrenia?
3. Why are schizophrenia and bipolar disorder often hard to differentiate?
4. How do hallucinations occur?

Questions for Review

1. Identify the numerous hypotheses that have been proposed to explain schizophrenia.

2. What neurotransmitters and hormones have been implicated in the development of major depressive disorder?

3. What characteristics do schizophrenia spectrum disorders share with schizophrenia?

4. How are antisocial and borderline personality disorders alike? How are they different?

Suggested Readings

Andreasen, N. C. (1997). Linking mind and brain in the study of mental illnesses: A project for a scientific psychopathology. *Science, 275,* 1586–1593.

Den Boer, J. A., Westenberg, H. G. M., & van Praag, H. M. (1995). *Advances in the neurobiology of schizophrenia.* New York: John Wiley & Sons.

Knutson, B., Wolkowitz, O. M., Cole, S. W., & Chan, T. (1998). Selective alternation of personality and social behavior by serotonergic intervention. *American Journal of Psychiatry, 155,* 373–379.

Silk, K. R. (1998). *Biology of personality disorders.* Washington, DC: American Psychiatric Press.

Walker, E. F., & Diforio, D. (1997). Schizophrenia: A neural diathesis–stress model. *Psychological Review, 104,* 667–685.

Watson, S. J. (1996). *Biology of schizophrenia and affective disease.* Washington, DC: American Psychiatric Press.

Web Resources

For a chapter tutorial quiz, direct links to the Internet sites listed below and other features, visit the book-specific website at **www.wadsworth.com/product/ 0155074865**. You may also connect directly to the following annotated websites:

http://faculty.washington.edu/chudler/schiz.html
For more information about schizophrenia, its causes, and its effects on the brain visit this site.

http://www.nimh.nih.gov/publicat/ depressionmenu.cfm
This site from the National Institute of Mental Health provides links to more information about major depressive disorder and bipolar disorder.

http://mentalhelp.net/poc/center_index.php?id=8
Learn the basics about personality disorders and then explore a vast amount of detailed links to information about symptoms and treatments.

http://www.psych.org/public_info/ect~1.cfm
Learn more about Electroconvulsive Therapy (ECT) on this site from the American Psychiatric Association.

For additional readings and information, check out InfoTrac College Edition at **http://www.infotrac-college.com/wadsworth**. Choose a search term yourself or enter the following search terms: dementia, electroconvulsive therapy, major depressive disorder, personality disorder, psychoses, schizophrenia, and Wisconsin card sorting test.

CD-ROM: Exploring Biological Psychology

Major Depressive Disorder
    Video: Barbara 1
    Video: Barbara 2
Bipolar Disorder
    Video: Mary 1
    Video: Mary 2
    Video: Mary 3

Schizophrenia
    Video: Common Symptoms of Schizophrenia
    Video: Etta 1
    Video: Etta 2
Interactive Recaps
Chapter 15 Quiz
Connect to the Interactive Biological Psychology Glossary

16

Developmental Disorders and Brain Damage

In the last semester of her senior year of college, Krista was having a fun time. She had planned her last semester so that her course load was light and the courses easy in order that she had plenty of time to party. Krista figured that it was her last semester with her friends before they went off into the "real world," and she wanted to enjoy every last moment with them. Every night she went out with friends to bars on the "strip." There, she would dance the night away, drinking six or more beers a night, go home at closing, and sleep until her first class at 12:30. She was proud of the way she had planned the semester and was pleased that it was going so well.

Many mornings Krista woke up feeling nauseous. Sometimes she even vomited because she felt so ill. But she chalked it up to a good hangover, sipped on a cola, and felt better after a while. Because her menstrual cycles were irregular, Krista never worried when her periods were late. In fact, that semester, Krista didn't have one period all semester, but that didn't worry her a bit. Often, when she ran track, she didn't have a period throughout the track season. However, she wasn't running track that year. It was her last semester of her senior year, and she didn't want to be bothered with track.

About a week before graduation, while she was studying for finals, Krista felt a distinct thrust in her abdomen, as if her intestines had just moved violently. Then there was another. Then it stopped. When the bumping in her abdomen started up a few days later, she went to the college infirmary to find out what was wrong. The physician very quickly reached a diagnosis: Krista was pregnant.

At the time she was nearly 5 months pregnant, although it didn't show. Krista thought she'd gotten a bit of a beer belly. After talking with her parents and her boyfriend, she decided to keep the baby. She had a full-term pregnancy, but her new son was unusually small at birth. He also had abnormal facial features, including abnormally small eyes, a cleft palate, and a broad, flat nose. As her son grew older, he was hyperactive and behaved impulsively, showing little self-control. Neuropsychological testing confirmed that he had *fetal alcohol syndrome*.

Krista drank heavily during the first 5 months of her pregnancy, causing irreparable harm to the developing brain of her son. To understand how this would happen, you need to learn about brain development. In this chapter, we will examine how the brain develops. We will also examine how physical and chemical insults to the developing brain affect brain development and subsequent behavior. In addition, we will look at the effects of brain damage that are incurred during childhood or adulthood. Let's begin with a discussion of the stages of brain development. ●

Brain Development

The **embryo** begins as a single fertilized egg that rapidly divides and redivides until a ball of cells, called a *blastocyst*, is formed. The blastocyst is a hollow, fluid-filled ball that contains two types of cells: 1) *trophoblast cells*, which will become the placenta; and 2) *inner-cell-mass cells*, also known as *embryonic stem cells*, which will differentiate into different types of cells (liver, heart, bone, brain, and so forth) to form the individual. This ball of cells grows and folds in on itself, forming a groove called the *neural tube* (Figure 16.1). Neurons develop along the borders of this neural tube, and they migrate to their final position in the nervous system with the help of radioglial cells that direct the movement of the neurons to their final destination. Each neuron has a final destination, and the glial cells help move it to that destination.

Thus, the first two stages of brain development are *cell proliferation* and *cell migration* (Figure 16.2). **Cell proliferation** is the first stage and begins 4 weeks after fertilization of the egg by sperm. During this stage, neurons are formed at a rate of about *250,000 cells per minute*. You can imagine that anything that disrupts this stage can lead to disastrous effects on brain development.

Cell migration, the second stage of brain development, begins about 6 weeks after fertilization. This is an important stage during which neurons move from the boundary of the neural tube to their final position in the nervous system. Each neuron is born with a given address, and it migrates to that address under the direction of glial cells and protein signals that act as signposts for the migrating neuron (Curran & D'Arcangelo, 1998). Neurons that are born first migrate to positions close to the neural tube. Later-developing neurons migrate past the earlier-born cells to reach their final destinations (Anderson et al., 1997). Thus, the brain develops from the inner layers out, with the cerebral cortex developing last. It is extremely important that each neuron reaches its

embryo: a developing organism that grows from a fertilized ovum
cell proliferation: the first stage of brain development in which neurons are formed along the neural tube at a rate of about 250,000 per minute
cell migration: the second stage of brain development in which neurons migrate from the neural tube to their final position in the nervous system

Figure 16.1 Stages of embryonic development

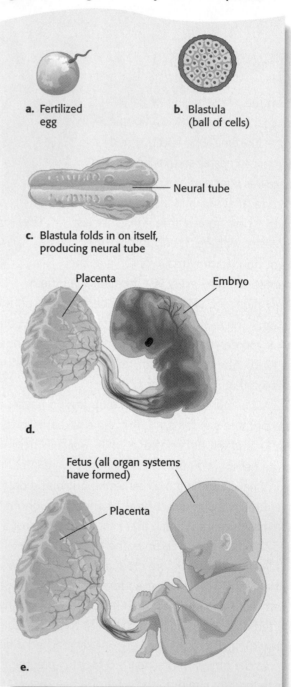

a. Fertilized egg

b. Blastula (ball of cells)

Neural tube

c. Blastula folds in on itself, producing neural tube

Placenta

Embryo

d.

Fetus (all organ systems have formed)

Placenta

e.

final destination because a neuron can function only if it is where it should be. Any insult that interferes with migration of neurons during this critical period will disrupt brain function after birth.

At 8 weeks after conception, all of the organs of the embryo have formed, including the brain. At this point, the embryo becomes a **fetus.** Most gross developmental abnormalities occur during the embryonic stage, and the chances of miscarriage are higher during the embryonic stage. The main task of the fetus is to grow. Bones grow, and organs do, too. Growth of the brain during the fetal stage is due to the growth of dendrites and axons. Although some neurons develop long after birth, neuron proliferation takes place almost exclusively in the embryonic stage.

Figure 16.2 Stages of brain development

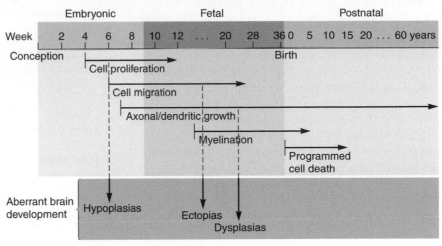

The third stage of brain development is **cell differentiation.** During this stage, which begins 7 to 8 weeks following fertilization, immature neurons begin to change shape to attain their final mature form. That is, during this stage, pyramidal cells begin to look like pyramids, and stellate cells begin to look like stars, and so forth.

The fourth stage, the **stage of axonal and dendritic growth,** is a continuation of the third stage of brain development. During this fourth stage, neurons begin to sprout processes that become dendrites and axons (Figure 16.2). This stage begins about 8 to 10 weeks after conception and continues long after birth. With the help of glial cells and special signaling proteins called *neurotrophins,* axons and dendrites grow in length and form synaptic connections with other neuronal processes. Rita Levi-Montalcini (1965, 1966) first identified **nerve growth factor (NGF),** a protein that promotes the survival of specific neurons in the peripheral and central nervous system during development and maturation. She received a Nobel Prize in 1986 for that discovery.

Throughout life, synaptic connections continue to be made in the human brain. As axons mature, they grow in diameter and become *myelinated.* At birth, most sensory axons are myelinated. Motor pathways, particularly the corticospinal tract (part of the pyramidal system, which coordinates fine motor control, as you learned in Chapter 6), and axons in the frontal and temporal lobes are not completely myelinated until late childhood or adolescence (Paus et al., 1999). This means that some motor and language functions are not fully mature until the teenage years.

Cell death occurs during the fifth and last stage of brain development. This programmed cell death of unwanted neurons is referred to as **apoptosis,** and it appears to be regulated by glutamate (Ikonomidou et al., 1999). Some authors estimate that nearly 50% of neurons present at birth die within the next 12 years (Raff et al., 1993). In addition, about 50% of the synapses present in the brain at age 2 disappear by the time the individual is 16 years old. There is no denying that we are born with many more neurons than we actually need. For example, we are born with the ability to produce all phonemes in any human language, but as we develop and learn to speak our native tongue, we lose the ability to produce the phonemes of other languages due to the death of neurons in our cortex. In order for a neuron to survive, it must make appropriate pre- and postsynaptic connections. An individual's experiences are able to modify brain development because neurons that make inappropriate connections with other neurons are eliminated. During the first 12 to 13 years of life, we lose the neurons that we do not use through programmed cell death.

fetus: a stage of development in which all of the organs have developed and are present in the body

cell differentiation: the third stage of brain development in which immature neurons begin to change shape to attain their mature adult form

stage of axonal and dendritic growth: the fourth stage of brain development in which neurons sprout processes that become axons and dendrites

nerve growth factor (NGF): a protein that promotes the survival of specific neurons in the peripheral and central nervous systems during development and maturation, stimulating the regrowth of axons and sprouting of nearby axons and dendrites

apoptosis: programmed death of unwanted neurons

Damage to the Developing Brain

Damage to the developing brain can be caused by chemical or physical insults, disease, malnutrition, or genetic errors. Insults at particular developmental stages (proliferation, migration, differentiation) will result in different types of abnormalities (Berger-Sweeney & Hohmann, 1997). For example, insults occurring during the cell proliferation stage will produce *hypoplasia*, in which fewer cells are found in a given region of the brain [*hypo-* = less than normal, Greek] (Figure 16.3). In contrast, an insult that interferes with cell migration may produce *ectopsia*, in which neurons do not migrate to their normal positions in the brain [*ecto-* = outside, Greek]. When an ectopsia is present, one or more areas of the brain will contain disorganized clusters of different types of neurons. Insults that occur during the cell differentiation stage will produce *dysplasia*, in which neurons retain immature shapes or grow abnormal dendrites and axons [*dys-* = bad, Greek] (Figure 16.3).

Chemical Insults

Chemical insults can be produced by chemical agents such as poisons or toxins to which the mother is exposed. For example, chronic ingestion of alcohol, cocaine, or benzodiazepines during the pregnancy causes permanent damage to the central nervous system of the developing embryo. Babies born to mothers who regularly consumed benzodiazepines (such as Valium) during the pregnancy have abnormalities of the central and peripheral nervous systems, with extensive damage to the cranial nerves (Laegreid, Olegard, Walstrom, & Conradi, 1989). As a result of the cranial nerve damage, these babies have sullen, expressionless faces. The brains of these babies are smaller than normal, and autopsy of one brain revealed disturbed migration of neurons throughout the brain. Cocaine use by the mother can impair the development of her embryo's brain, but the damage is subtle. Children who were exposed to cocaine during fetal development have trouble concentrating for long periods of time and blocking out distracting stimuli (Kosofsky, 1998; Lester, LaGrasse, & Seifer, 1998).

Fetal alcohol syndrome occurs in embryos whose mothers drink excessively during their pregnancy. The damage to the developing brain produced by alcohol causes long-term behavioral and cognitive problems in the offspring. Although alcohol interferes with all stages of brain development, the stage of cell migration appears to be most affected by alcohol consumption by the mother (Clarren, Alvord, Sumi, Streissguth, & Smith, 1978; Guerri, 1998; Lewis, 1985; Miller, 1993). Recall that, during the stage of migration, neurons move from their birthplace along the walls of the neural tube to their final destination in the nervous system. Alcohol causes the glial cells to lose control of the migration process. Neurons migrate in a haphazard fashion, often never reaching their correct address. This is best seen in the cerebral cortex of children with fetal alcohol syndrome. Whereas the cortex of a healthy child has distinct layers of neurons, the cerebral cortex of a child with fetal alcohol syndrome has neurons from many different cell lines (for example, pyramidal, stellate, granular cells) mixed together. (That is, ectopsia is observed.) Autopsies of infants with fetal alcohol syndrome who died indicate that neurons often migrate right through the external surface of the cortex. Abnormal development of the cerebral cortex, the hippocampus, and the cerebellum is believed to produce the many behavioral and cognitive deficits, including mental retardation, attention and memory deficits, and hyperactivity, seen in children with

Figure 16.3 Effects of damage to the developing brain

a. Hypoplasia

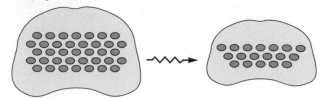

Exposed to insult during cell proliferation stage

b. Ectopsia

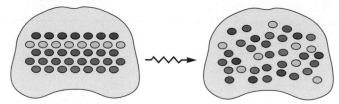

Exposed to insult during cell migration stage

c. Dysplasia

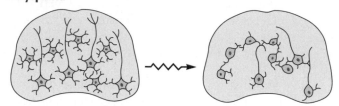

Exposed to insult during cell differentiation stage

fetal alcohol syndrome: a disorder, characterized by behavioral and cognitive deficits, that results from exposure of an embryo to alcohol during the early stages of brain development

this disorder (Guerri, 1998; Olson, Feldman, Streissguth, Sampson, & Bookstein, 1998; Sood et al, 2001).

Physical Insults

Physical damage to the developing brain will also alter its structure and function. Trauma, such as an automobile accident, that the mother experiences will often damage the embryo's brain. The extent of the damage depends on the circumstances of the accident and the stage of brain development at the time of the accident. For example, a motor disorder known as **cerebral palsy** results from any number of causes, including premature rupture of the fetal sac that holds the baby (Ernest, 1998). Blood coagulation problems that cause blood clots to form in the blood vessels of the placenta and the brain of the fetus are also associated with the development of cerebral palsy (Kraus & Acheen, 1999). Any infection or inflammation in the uterus can predispose the fetus to cerebral palsy, as can interruption of the oxygen supply to the brain (Nelson & Grether, 1999).

cerebral palsy: a motor disorder caused by damage to the developing brain

Exposure to *radiation* will damage the developing brain, producing mental retardation and other behavioral abnormalities. Fetuses are exposed to radiation when their mothers receive radiation for treatment of cancer or during nuclear accidents, such as radiation leaks from nuclear power plants. Embryos exposed to radiation during the explosion of atomic bombs over Nagasaki and Hiroshima in Japan during World War II showed variable amounts of brain damage as a result. The embryos most affected by the radiation were the ones whose brains were in the cell migration stage of brain development. Radiation halted the migration of neurons in the brains of these embryos, producing profound mental retardation.

Disease and Malnutrition

The health of a pregnant woman undeniably affects the development of her fetus's nervous system. A woman who is diabetic or has a thyroid condition must carefully monitor her hormone levels because hyperglycemia or abnormal thyroid hormone levels can affect the growth of the fetus. Infectious diseases caused by bacteria and viruses can also damage brain development. A baby born to a pregnant woman who is infected with *syphilis* can be born with a number of nervous system disorders, such as deafness and absence of the vestibular system (Brun, 1972; Wendel, 1988). Viral infections, like *rubella* (also known as German measles) and chicken pox, which the pregnant woman transmits to her unborn fetus, result in blindness, deafness, neuromuscular disorders, and autism in the offspring (Chess, 1977; Chess & Fernandez, 1980). Recall from Chapter 9 that autism is associated with abnormal development of the hindbrain. MRI studies of individuals who were exposed to rubella before birth indicate that these individuals have smaller brains, with significantly reduced gray matter in the cerebral cortex and enlarged lateral ventricles (Lim, Beal, Harvey, Myers, Lane, Sullivan, Faustman, & Pfefferbaum, 1995).

Maternal malnutrition can harm brain growth and development and produce long-term intellectual deficits in children (Galler et al., 1984; Rosso, 1987). Depending on when the malnutrition occurs, its effect on brain development is variable. Malnutrition that occurs early in embryonic life, during the stage of cell proliferation, will produce abnormalities in the shape and form of the brain. Later in brain development, malnutrition can interfere with cell migration, differentiation of neurons, myelination of axons, and the development of synapses (Morgane et al., 1993). For many pregnant women in developing countries, malnutrition continues throughout the pregnancy and into the infant's early years, producing permanent deficits that affect cognitive and intellectual function (Brown & Pollitt, 1996).

Genetic Abnormalities

Over three dozen genetic abnormalities can interfere with brain development, leading to impairment of the cerebrum (Cooper, Bloom, & Roth, 1996). In Chapter 2, you learned about **fragile X syndrome** and **Down's syndrome**, which both

fragile X syndrome: a disorder, characterized by mental retardation, that is associated with a genetic variation on the X chromosome

Down's syndrome: a disorder, characterized by mental retardation, that is associated with the presence of three chromosomes for chromosome 21

produce mental retardation. Fragile X syndrome is produced by a genetic variation on the X chromosome, which causes the chromosome to have long, fragile arms. Down's syndrome is produced by the presence of three chromosomes, instead of paired chromosomes, for chromosome 21. In both disorders, the chromosomal abnormality contributes to faulty development of the brain, particularly the cerebrum, which contributes to impairment of cognition.

For most other forms of developmental abnormalities affecting the brain, the specific genetic variant that produced the abnormality is unknown. For example, researchers are searching for the gene responsible for **holoprosencephaly,** a developmental brain disorder that affects 1 in every 10,000 children and is believed to cause thousands of miscarriages each year (Muenke et al., 2000). Individuals with holoprosencephaly have only one cerebral hemisphere, due to a genetic variation that stopped their brains from dividing into left and right hemispheres early in brain development (Barkovich, Simon, Clegg, Kinsman & Hahn, 2002). This disorder causes a variety of disabilities, including motor problems, seizures, inability to speak or eat solid foods, and facial defects, such as a misshapen head, eyes pushed together, or a single eye centered in the face (Figure 16.4).

Chromosomes can also have subtle effects on the brain that cannot be detected under a microscope. That is, some developmental disorders caused by genetic variants produce behavioral problems that have not been associated with specific brain damage. For example, males are more susceptible to developmental disorders that affect language and social functions, such as autism, learning disabilities, and hyperactivity. Recall that women normally have two X chromosomes, one inherited from each parent, whereas men have one X and one Y chromosome (the X chromosome being inherited from the mother and the Y from the father). Recent research with girls with Turner's syndrome, who have one X chromosome only (see Chapter 12), revealed that girls who inherited the X chromosome from their fathers have better social skills than girls who inherited their mother's X chromosome (McGuffin & Scourfield, 1997). In fact, girls who inherited their mother's X chromosome have severe behavioral difficulties, such as offensive or disruptive behavior (Figure 16.5). Skuse and his colleagues (1997) concluded that a gene associated with social functioning is switched off on the *mother's* X chromosome. That is, the gene is active only if it is inherited from the father. Because all males receive their X chromosomes from their mothers, they are more likely to have deficient social skills and are more susceptible to developmental disorders that affect social functioning.

When considering the effects of genetics on brain development, we must not forget that the environment plays in important role in behavioral development. Nurturing, environmental stimulation, and other external experiences can interact with existing neural processes to improve or worsen the behavioral disturbance that is associated with a specific genetic variant.

Hydrocephalus

Some types of brain damage are associated with more than one of the factors that we have already discussed, such as genetics, disease, and trauma or physical insults. For example, **hydrocephalus** is a disorder that has many causes. Infants with hydrocephalus have enlarged heads due to blockage of the ventricles of the brain. Recall from Chapter 4 that the ventricles provide for circulation of cerebrospinal fluid from the lateral ventricles in the cerebrum through the third ventricles in the diencephalon to the aqueduct of Sylvius in the midbrain and the fourth ventricle in the hindbrain and on down the central canal of the spinal cord. If this canal system becomes blocked for any reason, cerebrospinal fluid cannot flow down this pathway and builds up in the brain. In the infant, the sutures between the bones of the skull have not hardened, which means that pressure inside the brain can force the bones of the skull to separate, permitting the head to swell. This is exactly what happens in hydrocephalus. The ventricles become blocked, and fluid pressure within the ventricles causes the head to swell.

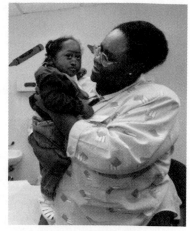

Figure 16.4 A child with holoprosencephaly

holoprosencephaly: a developmental disorder in which only one cerebral hemisphere develops

hydrocephalus: a disorder, caused by any number of insults to the brain, in which the flow of cerebrospinal fluid becomes blocked, and fluid pressure within the ventricles increases

Figure 16.5 Genetics of Turner's syndrome
Individuals with Turner's syndrome have only one sex chromosome (X), which can come from the mother (a) or the father (c). Individuals with Turner's who inherit the X chromosome from their fathers have much better social skills than those individuals with Turner's who inherit the X chromosome from their mothers.

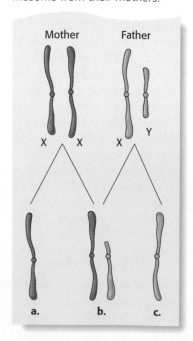

Many cases of hydrocephalus are associated with an X-linked recessive gene. This gene causes blockage of the narrowest part of the ventricular system, the *aqueduct of Sylvius*. However, an aberrant autosomal chromosome can also produce blockage of the aqueduct of Sylvius in rare cases (Hamada et al., 1999). Some infectious diseases, such as tuberculosis, can also cause hydrocephalus (Ozates et al., 2000). In addition, brain tumors and other forms of cancer, like leukemia, are associated with blockage of cerebrospinal fluid (Fisher & Chiello, 2000). Brain injury due to trauma can also result in hydrocephalus (Guyot & Michael, 2000). Injured brain tissue swells, which compresses the ventricles, preventing the flow of cerebrospinal fluid.

Although the infant's brain swells in response to a blockage in one of the ventricles, pressure does build up inside the infant's brain, producing brain damage. Over time, a child with hydrocephalus will often suffer a decline in intellectual, sensory, and motor functioning. For many individuals, hydrocephalus is treated with a *shunt*, or tube, that allows blocked cerebrospinal fluid to flow from the blockage in the brain directly into a vein. The shunt prevents the build-up of pressure within the brain and allows the brain to function normally.

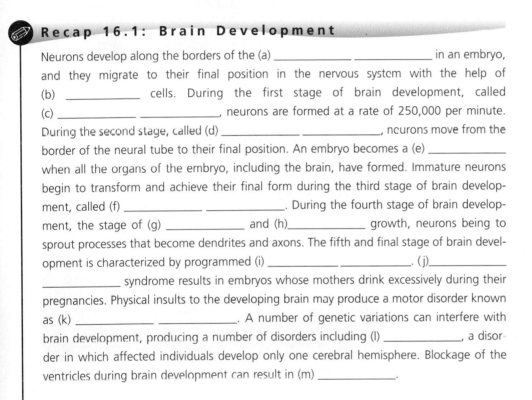

Recap 16.1: Brain Development

Neurons develop along the borders of the (a) _____ _____ in an embryo, and they migrate to their final position in the nervous system with the help of (b) _____ cells. During the first stage of brain development, called (c) _____ _____, neurons are formed at a rate of 250,000 per minute. During the second stage, called (d) _____ _____, neurons move from the border of the neural tube to their final position. An embryo becomes a (e) _____ when all the organs of the embryo, including the brain, have formed. Immature neurons begin to transform and achieve their final form during the third stage of brain development, called (f) _____ _____. During the fourth stage of brain development, the stage of (g) _____ and (h)_____ growth, neurons being to sprout processes that become dendrites and axons. The fifth and final stage of brain development is characterized by programmed (i) _____ _____. (j)_____ _____ syndrome results in embryos whose mothers drink excessively during their pregnancies. Physical insults to the developing brain may produce a motor disorder known as (k) _____ _____. A number of genetic variations can interfere with brain development, producing a number of disorders including (l) _____, a disorder in which affected individuals develop only one cerebral hemisphere. Blockage of the ventricles during brain development can result in (m) _____.

Brain Damage

Brain damage can occur during the *prenatal stage*, the *perinatal stage*, or the *postnatal stage*. The prenatal stage is the period before birth [*pre-* = before; *-natal* = birth, Latin]. We discussed the various causes of prenatal brain damage in the previous section. In general, prenatal brain damage interferes with brain development, altering cell proliferation, migration, or maturation, which affects brain function later in life. *Perinatal* refers to the period surrounding the time of birth [*peri-* = around, Latin], and *postnatal* refers to the period of time after birth [*post* – after, Latin].

Perinatal brain damage is most often caused by *anoxia*, or lack of oxygen [*a-* = without; *-oxia* = referring to oxygen, Greek], that the infant experiences due to a difficult birth or the umbilical cord being wrapped around its neck. Perinatal asphyxia results in a cessation of cerebral function due to lack of oxygen. If the infant is deprived of oxygen for more than a few seconds, neurons die, resulting in permanent brain damage. About 25% of all cases of cerebral palsy are associated with interruption of the supply of oxygen to the fetus's brain at birth (Nelson & Grether, 1999; Suvanand et al., 1997). Trauma at birth can also cause brain damage. For example, neonates can suffer a fractured skull during the delivery process when the mother's vagina is misshapen or inadequate to allow passage of the infant. A baby born with a fractured skull may appear lifeless, unresponsive to stimuli, and lack normal reflexes, such as the sucking reflex.

Brain Damage Produced by Trauma

Postnatal brain damage can be caused by trauma or disease. Head trauma can be classified into three categories, in order of increasing severity: 1) *concussions*, 2) *contusions*, and 3) *lacerations*. A **concussion** is caused by a blow to the head that bruises the brain (Figure 16.6). The bruising causes tiny blood vessels, or capillaries, in the brain to rupture, which compromises blood supply to the neurons supported by those capillaries. As you learned in Chapter 10 when we discussed comas, if the head slams against a solid object, bruising can take place at two points in the brain: at the point of impact (called the *coup*) where the head hits the object *and* on the opposite side of the head (the *contrecoup*) due to recoil of the brain from the first impact.

Three grades of concussion have been distinguished (Kelly & Rosenberg, 1997). A *Grade 1 concussion* is characterized by confusion that lasts for less than 15 minutes, with no loss of consciousness. A *Grade 2 concussion* is characterized by confusion that lasts for more than 15 minutes, with no loss of consciousness. A *Grade 3 concussion* is characterized by any loss of consciousness that lasts for a few seconds to several minutes. Upon regaining consciousness, the individual will be confused and will often not recall the circumstances of the trauma.

A **contusion** refers to head trauma in which the head is jarred with such force that the brain becomes shifted in the skull and is badly bruised (Figure 16.7). Unconsciousness following a contusion may last for minutes or months. Brain contusions may be complicated by bleeding and by increased pressure within the brain due to bleeding, which kills neurons, and produces lasting behavioral or cognitive dysfunction.

Cerebral laceration is caused by tearing of the brain, particularly the outer surface of the brain (Figure 16.6). Objects, such as bullets, that penetrate the skull will enter the brain and rip through brain tissue, unraveling neural connections and causing massive bleeding, or *hemorrhage*. If the skull is fractured, pieces of the skull

Figure 16.6 Concussion, contusion, and cerebral laceration
(a) Head trauma following an impact injury. (b) cerebral laceration.

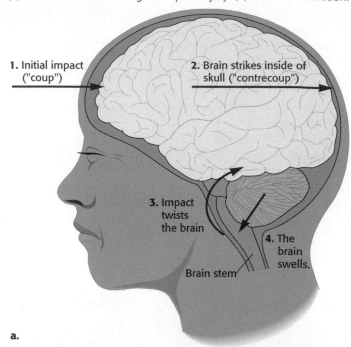

1. Initial impact ("coup")
2. Brain strikes inside of skull ("contrecoup")
3. Impact twists the brain
4. The brain swells.
Brain stem

a.

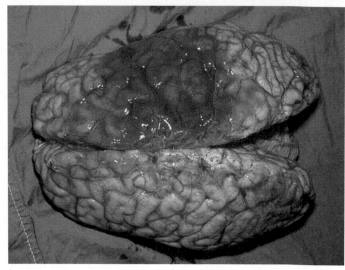

b.

concussion: head trauma that is caused by a blow to the head that bruises the brain

contusion: head trauma in which the head is jarred with such force that the brain becomes shifted in the skull and is badly bruised

cerebral laceration: head trauma caused by tearing of the outer surface of the brain

may be depressed into the brain and produce laceration of brain tissue. In addition to hemorrhage, which deprives neurons of oxygen and needed nutrients, the blood that leaks into the brain tissue can form blood clots, or *hematomas*. These hematomas can be deadly because they increase pressure within the brain, which disrupts neuronal function. Individuals who suffer head trauma that results in cerebral laceration will typically be unconscious for hours or months following the injury. Survival and functional outcome depend on the location and extent of the damage. Damage to the brain stem has the worst prognosis in terms of survival and return to a conscious state, as you learned in Chapter 10.

Boxers who sustain repeated blows to the head can suffer multiple concussions and contusions. Numerous sites of pinpoint bleeding can be identified in the brains of some boxers. This pinpoint bleeding, called **petechial hemorrhage,** is found throughout the brain and is associated with abnormal cognitive and motor function, including memory loss, reduced reaction time to stimuli, and tremor. For some boxers, the brain damage sustained is so severe that they develop a debilitating disorder called **dementia pugilistica,** (Erlanger, Kutner, Barth, & Barnes, 1999) which is characterized by loss of orientation for time and place, delusions, abnormal affect, and cognitive disturbance, as you learned in Chapter 15. Muhammad Ali, a world champion boxer in the 1960s and 1970s, shows many of the effects of repeated head trauma that he sustained during his boxing career, including motor dysfunctions, memory loss, and abnormal affect.

Any abrupt head movement that causes the brain to slam against the skull can produce a traumatic injury to the brain. The meninges provide a protective cushion around the brain, but a rapid change in acceleration can override this protective mechanism and cause brain damage. A recent case report (Kettaneh, Biousse, & Bousser, 2000) describes brain damage in several young adults who rode the same roller-coaster rides repeatedly. Certain roller-coaster rides produce sudden flexion and extension of the head and neck, which can result in brain hemorrhage due to torn arteries, hematomas, or leakage of cerebrospinal fluid into the brain.

petechial hemorrhage: pinpoint bleeding associated with cerebral laceration

dementia pugilistica: an irreversible psychotic state caused by brain trauma that results from repeated blows to the head

Brain Damage Caused by Disease

A number of infectious and noninfectious diseases can cause brain damage. *Infectious diseases* are those that are caused by microorganisms, such as bacteria or viruses. *Noninfectious diseases* are those that are not caused by infectious microorganisms, such as cancer or heart disease. We will examine both classes of brain damage in this section.

Infectious Disease

Meningitis In general, bacteria cannot cross the blood–brain barrier and, thus, cannot directly produce brain damage. **Meningitis,** an infection of the meninges that is produced by bacteria, produces swelling and inflammation of the meninges. As the meninges swell, they put pressure on the brain and spinal cord, killing neurons, as you learned in Chapter 2. Sometimes meningitis will result in temporary disorientation for time and place, impaired memory and confusion, and hallucinations. In addition, some individuals have residual motor and cognitive difficulties following a bout of meningitis, and some die as a result of the damage to the central nervous system caused by the illness.

meningitis: an infection of the meninges produced by bacteria

Syphilis The sexually transmitted disease **syphilis** is an infection produced by a spirochete bacterium. In the tertiary or final stage of syphilis, the infection gets into the brain, particularly in the frontal lobes, causing extensive cognitive and emotional dysfunction. A psychotic disorder known as **general paresis** can be the end result of syphilis. General paresis is a degenerative condition produced by the bacterial spirochete that causes syphilis. It is practically nonexistent in Western society today, although cases abound in less developed parts of the world where medical care is not readily available. As syphilis progresses, the rapidly multiplying spirochetes destroy brain tissue. Damage to the frontal lobes is evident as the

syphilis: a sexually transmitted bacterial infection that can interfere with brain development in the fetus
general paresis: a psychotic disorder caused by an untreated syphilis infection

syphilitic patient exhibits rude or socially unacceptable behavior, become inattentive and careless about his or her personal appearance, and eventually develops symptoms of dementia and psychosis, including thought disorder, confusion, delusions, hallucinations, and inappropriate affect (Fujimoto et al., 2001; Kohler, Pickholtz, Ballas, 2000; Kodama et al., 2000).

Encephalitis Some viruses, due to their minute size, can pass through the blood–brain barrier to infect the brain (Chapter 2). **Viral encephalitis** is caused by a virus that is transmitted by mosquitoes. As the virus invades the neurons, swelling of the brain ensues, killing neurons and disrupting brain function, particularly cerebral function. Nearly 50% of all people infected by this virus will die, and most others will show residual behavioral or cognitive deficits if they recover.

AIDS-Related Dementia A direct infection of the brain by the *human immunodeficiency virus* (HIV) results in **AIDS-related dementia.** AIDS-related dementia is frequently observed in individuals who have been infected with the human immunodeficiency virus and who have symptoms of full-blown acquired immune deficiency syndrome, or AIDS. The HIV virus produces both atrophy of the cerebral cortex and lesions in white matter underlying the cortex (Adams & Ferraro, 1997). Approximately 35% of all AIDS patients will ultimately undergo personality changes and show signs of dementia. Aberrant social behavior (including carelessness in personal habits), apathy, confusion, emotional blunting, and cognitive difficulty are common symptoms in patients with end-stage AIDS. These symptoms are likely the result of brain damage caused by HIV or opportunistic infections by bacteria, fungi, protozoa, or other viruses, which invade the brains of individuals with compromised immune systems (Figure 16.7).

Creutzfeldt-Jakob Dementia A progressive but fortunately very rare dementia, **Creutzfeldt-Jakob dementia** is associated with an infectious process. This disorder produces a rapid decline in motor and mental functioning over a period of months. Intellectual deterioration advances quickly, producing dementia, and the patient usually dies within 1 or 2 years (Buchwald et al., 1996). The cause of Creutzfeldt-Jakob dementia is believed to be a prion, which is a simple protein that causes a form of brain damage known as *spongiosis*, in which the brain loses its normal appearance and looks like a sponge, with tiny empty spaces called *vacuoles* (Prusiner & DeArmond, 1994). Prions are normally found throughout the body, particularly in the brain, although no one knows what they do. And prions come in two forms, depending on how the protein is folded. If folded one way, prions are benign; if folded the other way, prions cause brain deterioration (Figure 16.8) (DebBurman, Raymond, Caughey, & Lindquist, 1997). Recently an upsurge in Creutzfeldt-Jakob cases has been associated with "mad cow disease," which is caused by eating the meat of cows infected with the "bad" form of the prion (Glatzel & Aguzzi, 2001; Prusiner, 1997; Roberts & James, 1997).

Noninfectious Disease

Cardiovascular Disease The two leading causes of death in adults in the United States today are **cardiovascular disease** and *cancer*, and both can produce brain damage. Cardiovascular disease refers to disorders of the heart and blood vessels. For example, a typical American diet results in fatty deposits accumulating along the inner walls of major blood vessels, producing **atherosclerosis.** These deposits narrow the internal diameter of the blood vessels, which can increase blood pressure (Figure 16.9). As the diameters of arteries are reduced, blood flow to the brain is reduced, and neurons receive less oxygen and nutrients than normal, impairing

Figure 16.7 Brain damage with AIDS

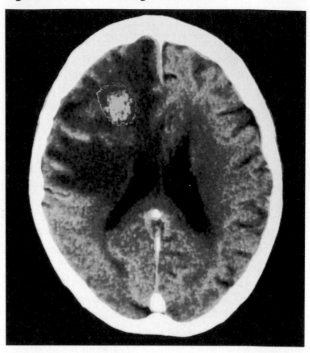

viral encephalitis: an infection of the brain caused by a virus that passes through the blood–brain barrier

Figure 16.8 Two forms of prions
Prions are harmless when found in their normal form (top). In the infectious form of the prion (bottom), the backbone of the protein is stretched out and forms pleated sheets.

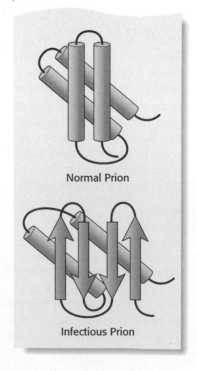

Normal Prion

Infectious Prion

Figure 16.9 Effects of atherosclerosis
One common site for fatty blockage is the bifurcation of the carotid artery, the major artery that carries blood to the brain. At this bifurcation, the artery splits into the internal and external carotid arteries. In the images on the right, you can see the accumulation of fatty matter in the artery and the resultant narrowing of the diameter of the artery.

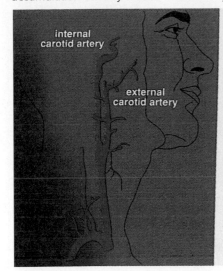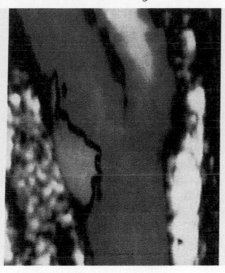

cognitive function (Loeb & Meyer, 1996). Over time, the fatty deposits become mineralized and harden, which reduces the elasticity of the walls of arteries and other blood vessels. Elasticity of blood vessel walls is necessary in order that the blood vessels expand or shrink in diameter to compensate for changes in blood pressure. With increased blood pressure, the hardened arteries cannot expand and are apt to burst. This is exactly what happens when a person has a stroke, or **cerebrovascular accident:** An artery in the brain bursts due to increased blood pressure, and blood rushes out of the artery and into the extracellular spaces in the brain (Morris, 1996).

Strokes produce brain damage in several ways (Hedenemos, 1997). **Ischemic strokes** result from clogged arteries in the brain, which decrease blood flow. When blood flow to neurons is disrupted, neurons are deprived of oxygen and nutrients, and they die (Figure 16.10). **Hemorrhagic strokes** occur when blood vessels rupture, permitting blood to pool in extracellular spaces in the brain. The hemorrhage produced by the stroke can increase the *intracranial pressure*, or the pressure within the skull [*intra-* = inside; *-cranium* = skull]. This, too, will kill neurons. The blood that escapes from the burst artery can produce a hematoma, or clot, which can also increase *intracranial pressure* to fatal levels. The neurons that die as a result of the stroke release *glutamate* into the extracellular space, which overstimulates and kills nearby neurons (Choi, 1992). These neurons, in turn, release excess glutamate, killing their neighbors. Thus, a vicious cycle begins that results in the death of many neurons. The resultant brain damage can produce symptoms of dementia, including confusion, delusions, and cognitive dysfunction, especially when the stroke occurs in the frontal or temporal lobe.

Cancer Cancer is a disease that is characterized by the uncontrolled growth of abnormal tissue called *tumors*. As you learned in Chapter 2, tumors can occur in the brain. These tumors usually consist of abnormal glial cells that are rapidly multiplying, or they are metastatic in nature, which means that they are derived from cancer cells elsewhere in the body (Figure 16.11). As tumors grow in the brain, they put pressure on nearby neurons, interfering with their function and eventually killing them. The result of this damage depends on the location and size of the tumor. For example, a tumor in the motor cortex will interfere with motor function, and one in Broca's area will interfere with the patient's speech. The *Case Study* describes the case of a very gentle man who developed a tumor in his temporal lobe.

AIDS-related dementia: a cognitive disorder produced by direct infection of the brain by the human immuno-deficiency virus

Creutzfeldt-Jakob dementia: a progressive dementia that is associated with a prion infection

cardiovascular disease: disorders of the heart and blood vessels

atherosclerosis: a disorder in which the inner walls of major blood vessels become coated with fatty deposits that harden at a later date

cerebrovascular accident: a stroke in which blood flow to brain structures is interrupted

ischemic stroke: a stroke that results from clogged arteries in the brain, decreasing blood flow

hemorrhagic stroke: a stroke that results from a ruptured blood vessel, in which blood pools in extracellular spaces in the brain

cancer: a disease characterized by the uncontrolled growth of abnormal tissue called tumors

Figure 16.10 SPECT scan of brain following stroke

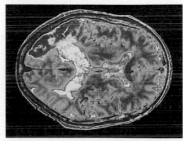

A Tumor in the Limbic System

Conrad was a kind, gentle 54-year-old man, beloved by members of his family and the congregation of his church, where he was a deacon. A farmer his whole life, Conrad worked from dawn to dusk every day of the year. Only when his sons grew old enough to run the farm did he take a much-needed vacation with his wife, Betty, to visit distant family members in another part of the country. He returned from the vacation rested and eager to return to work.

Shortly after he returned to work, Conrad's behavior began to change. Betty noticed that he cursed under his breath a lot. This was unusual behavior for her husband, ordinarily a calm, respectful man who never swore or used bad language. Conrad began to have angry outbursts that resembled temper tantrums when he was frustrated or something went wrong. One day, a grandchild left the door to the chicken house open, and dozens of hens flew into a nearby field. Conrad's reaction was quite uncharacteristic. He picked up a small tree branch and swatted the child across the legs and back, yelling and swearing angrily. When reproached by his son and daughter-in-law for hitting his grandchild, Conrad turned his anger and aggression on them.

Betty and her children became increasingly disturbed by Conrad's behavior. One morning, Betty accidentally dropped a frying pan on the floor of the kitchen. Conrad responded by pitching his empty juice glass at the back of her head. The glass bounced off Betty's head and broke on

the floor at her feet. Tears welled up in Betty's eyes, and she began to weep. Conrad remained seated at the table, filled with remorse.

Betty told him quietly that she was going to leave him if he didn't go for help. She told him that he was not acting like himself and that he needed help. Being an old farmer, Conrad resisted the idea of seeing a psychologist and made an appointment with his long-time doctor instead. Betty went with her husband to see the doctor and described for him Conrad's abnormally angry and aggressive behaviors.

Because Conrad did not have a history of domestic violence or any other type of violent behavior, the doctor ordered a brain scan (an MRI) to see if something was wrong inside his head. Ordinarily, a person does not develop impulsive violent behavior overnight, and the doctor was worried by Conrad's symptoms. As the doctor suspected, the MRI scan revealed a rather large tumor located deep in Conrad's temporal lobe.

Conrad and Betty then met with a neurosurgeon to plan for the removal of the tumor. The surgery was performed shortly after that, and a tumor that stretched from his medial temporal lobe to his third ventricle was removed. Conrad required skilled nursing care for nearly two months following his neurosurgery, but he eventually was able to return home and help his sons out with the work on the farm. His angry, violent behavior disappeared with the removal of his brain tumor.

Alcoholism Other medical problems can also interfere with metabolism or blood flow and cause brain damage. Alcoholism, for example, can produce brain damage via several routes. Alcohol is a toxin that can directly kill neurons by interfering with protein synthesis (Tewari & Noble, 1971). In addition, malnutrition produced by the alcoholism can result in brain damage (Charness, 1993). Recall from Chapter 10 that **Korsakoff's syndrome,** caused by damage to the temporal lobes, is associated with malnutrition, particularly a deficiency in thiamine (a B vitamin), in alcoholics. People who drink heavily also suffer from liver disease. As liver function becomes progressively more compromised due to alcoholism, ammonia builds up in the blood, producing a condition known as *ammonemia* [*ammon-* = ammonia; *-emia* = in the blood]. Ammonemia is associated with brain damage, too, because the high levels of ammonia in the blood kill neurons. High levels of ammonia are associated with lesions in the cerebrum that produce

Korsakoff's syndrome: a cognitive disorder involving retrograde and anterograde amnesia, caused by a thiamine deficiency in alcoholics

Figure 16.11 Glioma and metastic brain tumor
(a) Brain metastasis of breast cancer. (b) Glioma.

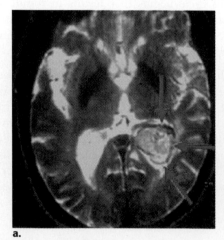
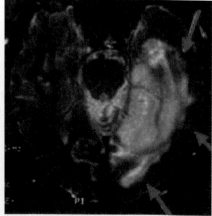

a.

b.

symptoms of dementia (Banciu et al., 1982). Alcohol can also produce high blood pressure, contractile spasms of cerebral blood vessels, and strokes in heavy drinkers (Altura, Altura, & Gebrewold, 1983). Brain damage associated with alcoholism includes gross atrophy of the cerebellar and cerebral cortex, especially the frontal lobes, which results in cognitive dysfunction, including memory loss for recent events and confusion (Smith, 1997).

Although *alcohol-induced dementia* may be a reversible condition that is caused by short-term alcohol overintoxication, most forms of alcohol-induced dementia are not treatable because of extensive brain damage. These include *hepatic encephalopathy*, *Wernicke-Korsakoff's syndrome*, and *alcoholic pellagra*. The term **hepatic encephalopathy** refers to a brain disorder associated with liver function or, more correctly in the case of alcoholics, liver dysfunction. Because over 95% of alcohol consumed is metabolized by the liver, this organ suffers the brunt of long-term alcohol abuse, and all alcoholics eventually develop liver damage, especially cirrhosis of the liver, which interferes with liver function.

Korsakoff's syndrome is characterized by a combination of memory disturbances involving anterograde and retrograde amnesia. Alcoholic patients usually develop *Wernicke's disease* before they show signs of Korsakoff's syndrome. That means an alcoholic person can have Wernicke's without Korsakoff's or have **Wernicke-Korsakoff's syndrome** if the symptoms of both are present. Symptoms of Wernicke's disease include confusion, loss of orientation for time and place, ataxia, and apathy. Cognitive impairment involves difficulty with problem solving, abstract thinking, and planning (Joyce et al., 1994).

Poor nutrition, especially a deficiency of thiamine, has been implicated as the cause of Wernicke-Korsakoff's syndrome (Leong, Oliva, & Butterworth, 1996). Many chronic alcoholics do not eat well but, instead, consume a good deal of their calories as alcohol. Alcohol also interferes with the absorption of B vitamins. A deficiency of thiamine, or vitamin B_1, interferes with the brain's ability to break down glucose and can cause brain damage, which produces the symptoms of Wernicke-Korsakoff's (Figure 16.12). The MRI technique is capable of distinguishing alcoholic dementia due to the neurotoxic effects of alcohol from nutritional encephalopathy. Nutritional deficiencies have been associated with damage to the thalamus and structures surrounding the third ventricle, whereas the toxic effects of alcohol produce widespread shrinkage of the cerebrum (Emsley et al., 1996; Charness, 1993).

Treatment with thiamine will lead to improvement in about 20% of patients diagnosed with Wernicke-Korsakoff's syndrome. Most, however, will never recover from this debilitating disorder.

Other nutritional deficiencies associated with long-term alcoholism are deficiencies of niacin (another B vitamin) and tryptophan, the precursor of serotonin. **Alcoholic pellagra** is a condition caused by a diet deficient in niacin and protein. Pellagra affects the skin, blood, and gastrointestinal system, but its major effects are on the cerebrum, where it produces symptoms of dementia. People with alcoholic pellagra are often confused and psychotic, with accompanying symptoms of apathy, restlessness, depression, insomnia, and impaired memory.

hepatic encephalopathy: a brain disorder associated with liver dysfunction

Wernicke-Korsakoff's syndrome: a cognitive disorder observed in long-term alcoholics, characterized by memory and cognitive disturbance, confusion, loss of orientation for time and place, ataxia, and apathy

alcoholic pellagra: a disorder that affects the skin, blood, and gastrointestinal system and produces dementia, associated with deficiencies of niacin and protein caused by alcoholism

Figure 16.12 PET image of brain damage in a chronic alcoholic

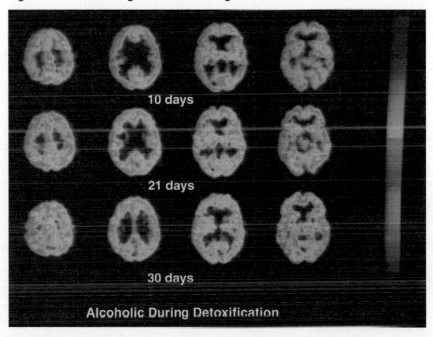

10 days

21 days

30 days

Alcoholic During Detoxification

Brain damage can occur during the (a) _____ stage (before birth), (b) _____ stage (at birth), or (c) _____ stage (after birth). Head trauma can be classified into three categories: (d) _____ (least severe), (e)_____ or (f)_____ (most severe). Boxers who sustain repeated blows to the head can develop pinpoint bleeding in the brain, called (g)_____ _____, or, in more severe cases, (h) _____ _____, characterized by cognitive and emotional disturbances. Infectious diseases caused by bacteria or viruses can produce a number of disorders that cause brain damage, including (i) _____ (bacterial infection of the protective covering on the brain), (j) _____ _____ (associated with syphilis), (k) _____ (viral infection of the brain), (l) _____ _____ dementia (caused by human immunodeficiency virus), and (m) _____-_____ dementia (associated with a simple protein called a prion, which is neither a bacterium nor virus). Two noninfectious diseases, (n) _____ disease (disorders of the heart and blood vessels) and (o) _____ (characterized by uncontrolled growth of tumors), can produce brain damage. When fatty deposits bind to the inside of blood vessels, producing (p) _____, blood flow to the brain is disrupted. Two types of stroke can produce brain damage, (q) _____ strokes (caused by clogged blood vessels, reducing blood flow) and (r) _____ strokes (when blood vessels in the brain rupture, producing a cerebrovascular accident). Neurons that die as a result of stroke release (s) _____, which kills nearby neurons. Alcoholism can produce brain damage in several ways: through (t) _____ (which produces Korsakoff's syndrome and pellagra), through (u)_____ disease (which causes ammonia to build up in the blood, resulting in ammonemia), and through its effect on the cardiovascular system (including high blood pressure or stroke).

Recovery from Brain Damage

Neurons that are destroyed by damage to the brain typically are not replaced by other neurons, although new neurons can be produced and repair damaged brain regions (Lowenstein & Parent, 1999). In the peripheral nervous system, neurons can (and do) regenerate. Thus, injury to the peripheral nervous system produces temporary dysfunction, whereas injury to the brain can be long-lasting and devastating. However, people with brain damage often regain some function. In this section, we will examine the processes that promote recovery from brain damage.

Age and Recovery from Brain Damage

The age at which brain damage occurs can directly influence recovery from brain damage. At the beginning of this chapter, you learned that brain development takes place in stages and that disruption of any of these stages could permanently affect brain development and function. However, there is a good deal of evidence that recovery from brain damage is optimal if the damage occurs before the maturation of the nervous system (Armand & Kably, 1993). Some of the earliest experiments on the effects of infant brain damage were conducted by Mary Kennard, who studied recovery of motor function following brain damage in infant monkeys (Kennard, 1939). Kennard's observation that behavioral function develops normally when brain damage occurs in infancy is known as the **Kennard effect** (Finger & Wolf, 1988).

Since Kennard's early studies, investigators have discovered that recovery or sparing of behavioral function appears to be associated with a *critical period* in brain

Kennard effect: the observation that behavioral function develops normally when brain damage occurs in infancy

development. For example, Bryan Kolb and Robbin Gibb (1991) performed bilateral frontal lobe lesions on newborn rats, rats that were 10 days old, and adult rats. Compared to newborn and adult lesioned rats, rats that were lesioned at 10 days of age showed the most recovery from brain damage. Thus, the neurons in the frontal lobes of 10-day-old rats were at their optimal stage of development (the stage of dendritic and axonal growth) for recovery from brain damage. Armand and Kably (1993) studied the effects of motor cortex damage on grasping and reaching behaviors in kittens. These investigators demonstrated that the critical period for the recovery of grasping skills occurs sometime between the age of 23 and 30 days in kittens, whereas the critical period for the recovery of reaching skills occurs sometime between the age of 45 and 60 days. Different brain areas mature at different times, which means that the extent of recovery observed following brain damage depends on the *location* and the *timing* of the damage.

Structural Versus Functional Recovery

My dog, Brutus, loved to chase cars. One day, a driver didn't see the furry little demon lunging for his front tire, and he accidentally ran over Brutus's left hind leg. The leg was badly fractured and didn't heal well, which necessitated its amputation. At first, Brutus had a very difficult time walking about on three legs. But, within a few weeks, he was running as fast as he was before the amputation and chasing cars once again.

Brutus lost a leg, but he recovered function. He was able to walk and run almost as well after the loss of the leg as before. His recovery was not due to recovered structure because he didn't grow a new leg. His recovery was due to the fact that he learned to compensate for the missing leg.

Recovering from brain damage is very much like learning to walk on three legs after the fourth has been amputated. For most individuals, the structures lost by brain damage are not replaced, and the structures that remain must compensate for the missing structures. That is, a great deal of recovery from brain damage is due to functional recovery and not structural recovery. However, this does not mean that structural recovery does not take place. Let's look at the various forms of structural changes that take place following brain damage.

Structural Recovery

In Chapter 9 we discussed examples of *plasticity* in the brain, particularly in the cerebral cortex. For example, you learned that highly trained musicians devote large areas of their cerebral cortex to processing music, compared to nonmusicians. PET studies of individuals with brain damage indicate that their brains are capable of changing, too. People who sustain damage to the left cerebral hemisphere, for example, tend to use the right hemisphere to process language more than healthy controls do. This is especially true for individuals who suffered left hemispheric injury before the age of 5 years: These individuals use the right hemisphere almost exclusively to process language (Muller et al., 1999).

Studies of individuals between the ages of 2 months and 20 years who have undergone surgical removal of a cerebral hemisphere, called a **hemispherectomy,** also reveal the amazing plasticity of the brain (Vining et al., 1997). For over 30 years, neurosurgeons have performed hemispherectomies to treat people with progressively severe seizures who do not respond to medication. The entire cortex on one side of the brain is removed, along with underlying white matter. Following the surgery, patients can usually walk and run, and some have gone on to run marathons. Younger children show the least impairment following surgery because their brains can more easily compensate for the missing hemisphere. Removal of the left hemisphere does not interfere with the development of speech and language in children under 4 years of age.

How do these structural changes take place? Six mechanisms of structural recovery from brain damage have been identified: 1) *regrowth of neurons,* 2) *waste*

hemispherectomy: surgical removal of a cerebral hemisphere

Repair of Brain Damage with Neural Stem Cells

Research with rats and mice has led to major break-throughs in our ability to stimulate repair following damaged to the central nervous system. Stem cells derived from the hippocampus of mice have been implanted into the brains of rats, producing significant improvements in function following brain damage. For example, Helen Hodges and her colleagues at the Institute of Psychiatry at Kings College London reduced blood flow in the brains of rats by blocking four arteries, which damaged the hippocampus and impaired cognitive function in rats, interfering with their ability to learn new information (Hodges, Sowinski, et al., 2000). Implantation of mouse stem cells into the fore-brains of these rats produced an increase in the number of CA1 neurons in the hippocampus, neurons that plan an important role in long-term potentiation (Chapter 9), and improvements in the rats' cognitive function.

When axons of cholinergic neurons (that is, neurons that release acetylcholine, as you learned in Chapter 3) were destroyed by excitotoxins injected into the hippocampus, memory deficits were observed in rats learning spatial information. These memory deficits were reversed after mouse hippocampal stem cells were implanted into the rats' forebrain (Sinden et al., 2000). Stem cell implants also reversed cognitive impairments caused by normal aging processes in rats (Hodges, Veizovic, et al., 2000). Old (22-month-old) rats showed improved ability to remember the location of an underwater platform in a water maze test after receiving a hippocampal stem cell transplant, compared to age-matched rats that did not receive a trans-plant. In addition, when the middle cerebral artery (a common site for strokes in people) of a rat is blocked, specific sensory and motor deficits are produced, depending on the hemisphere affected. Implantation of hippocampal stem cells into the forebrain leads to an improvement in motor and sensory function in rats (Sinden et al., 2000).

Thus, hippocampal stem cell implants appear to be able to repair many different types of brain injuries, producing improvements in cognitive, sensory, and motor function. However, these stem cells cannot reverse damage in all areas of the brain. For example, hippocampal stem cells do not reverse lesions to the nigrostratal dopamine pathway, which produce symptoms of Parkinson's disease in rats. Another line of mouse stem cells (not hippocampal stem cells) has been shown to repair spinal cord injuries in rats. These stem cells differentiate into neurons, oligoden-odrocytes, and astroglial cells in the area of the spinal cord lesion, producing improvements in gait and reflexes (McDonald et al., 1999).

These lines of research open the possibility that damage to the brain and spinal cord in humans may be reversed by stem cell implants. A number of stem cell lines will need to be developed from different brain areas in order to treat the many disorders arising from brain damage. In time, stem cells may be used to treat cognitive problems associated with stroke, normal aging, and Alzheimer's disease, degenerative disorders like Parkinson's and ALS, and spinal cord and traumatic brain injuries.

---

product removal, 3) *regrowth of axons*, 4) *collateral sprouting of axons*, 5) *dendritic branching*, and 6) *denervation hypersensitivity*. These mechanisms cannot account for all the recovery that is observed following injury to the brain, and other mechanisms will undoubtedly be discovered in the near future. Let's examine these six mechanisms.

Regrowth of Neurons

Although brain damage cannot be reversed, the brain has the potential to produce new neurons and repair damaged areas (Kempermann & Gage, 1999; Lowenstein & Parent, 1999). Progenitor cells, or stem cells, that are capable of producing new neurons are found in the human brain. The newly formed neurons migrate to the injured area, differentiate, and are incorporated into the nervous tissue (Figure 16.13). These stem cells can differentiate into various types of glial cells, as well as neurons, depending on the growth factors present (Palmer et al., 1997). *For Further Thought* describes the treatment of brain damage in rats with neural stem cells. Increased **neurogenesis** in the hippocampus has been observed following seizures, stroke, or injection of a toxin. New drugs are currently being tested that promote the growth of neurons in the brain. These drugs might eventually be used to treat progressive degenerative disorders like Parkinson's disease, Alzheimer's disorder, and multiple sclerosis.

neurogenesis: growth of neurons

Figure 16.13 Repair of the brain
After injury to a site in the brain, precursor stem cells may migrate to the site, and inactive (dormant) progenitor cells at the site may differentiate into neurons and glia.

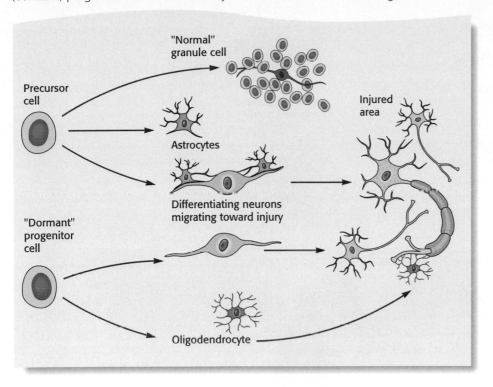

Waste Product Removal

Damage to the brain results in dead neurons, an excess of extracellular glutamate, white blood cells, and other toxins in the area of damage. It takes glial cells days or weeks to clear all this debris away from the site. As the debris is removed, neurons in the area regain their function. Thus, the removal of waste products from the damaged site will enhance brain function. This phenomenon is seen in many individuals recovering from a stroke, for example. At first, the stroke victim may be unable to speak, and movement on one side of the body (contralateral to the site of brain damage) may be absent. However, within a few weeks, speech will slowly return, as will motor function to the impaired side. This improvement in function is *not* due to the regrowth of neurons, rather it is due to the removal of substances that were interfering with neuronal function.

Regrowth of Axons

In Chapter 2 you learned that regrowth of axons is not common in the central nervous system due to the collapse of oligodendrocytes associated with the affected axons. But, there is evidence that some axons can and do regrow after damage to that axon. A damaged axon releases *nerve growth factor*, which stimulates the regrowth of the axon and promotes sprouting of nearby axons and dendrites (Figure 16.14). However, although an axon may regrow and reach its target, lasting sensory or motor deficits may be evident (Freed, Medinaceli, & Wyatt, 1985).

Collateral Sprouting of Axons

Sometimes, following brain damage, neurons come to assume the work of the dead neurons. For example, following removal of a tumor from the motor cortex, the affected individual will show impaired motor function related to the position of the tumor on the precentral gyrus. Over time, that individual might show improved motor function in the affected area. This improvement is due to changes in

Figure 16.14 Regrowth of axons and collateral sprouting
(a) Regrowth of axon. (b) Collateral sprouting in the presence of NGF.

a.   **b.**

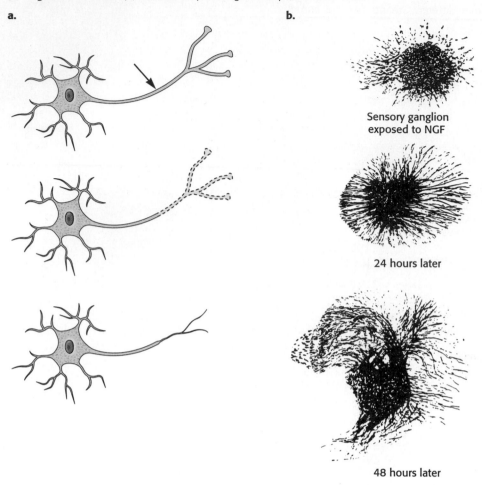

neurons near the damaged site in the brain. These intact neurons near the site of damage produce sprouts on their axons that grow and branch off the main axon. The terminal buttons of these collateral sprouts form synapses with neurons that formerly received input from the dead neurons. Thus, the collateral sprouts come to fill in for the missing axons from the dead neurons and provide stimulation to the postsynaptic neurons originally innervated by the dead neurons. Reorganization of the somatosensory cortex following amputation or damage to a limb, which you learned about in Chapter 8, is most likely due to the sprouting of neuronal processes in the cortex (Florence, Taub, & Kaas, 1998).

Dendritic Branching

Dendrites also respond to brain damage with increased branching or **arborization.** Rats that received frontal lobe lesions when they were 10 days old were observed to recover almost completely from the severe behavioral deficits produced by this brain damage (Kolb & Gibb, 1991). Examination of brain tissues of these recovered animals revealed a striking increase in dendritic arborization compared to control rats that received no lesions. An increase in dendritic arborization does occur in adults, too, but is most dramatic in young animals. Kolb and Gibb (1991) have suggested that age-related differences in dendritic arborization may explain the *Kennard effect*, the observation that young animals recover from brain damage more completely than adults.

arborization: increased branching of dendrites

Denervation Hypersensitivity

When neurons die, their postsynaptic neurons lose their input from the dead cells. That is, the postsynaptic cells become *denervated* due to the death of their presynaptic neurons. This loss of innervation means that the postsynaptic neurons fire less than before. However, over a period of a few weeks, **denervation hypersensitivity** develops in the postsynaptic neurons, which causes the denervated neuron to become supersensitive to excitatory messages from the remaining presynaptic neurons and to fire vigorously to input that previously was below threshold. Thus, just a little bit of stimulation makes these postsynaptic neurons excited and produces action potentials in them.

Denervation hypersensitivity may explain recovery from *spinal shock*. Recall from Chapter 6 that spinal shock results from damage to the spinal cord and is characterized by a total loss of reflexes below the point of injury following spinal cord injury. Several weeks following the injury, reflexes return. In fact, reflexes can be extremely vigorous, producing *hyperreflexia*, or exaggerated reflexes. This recovery of reflexes is thought to be due to denervation hypersensitivity. Motor neurons in the spinal cord become oversensitive to input from sensory neurons due to the loss of input from the brain because of spinal cord damage. Therefore, when a tiny amount of sensory stimulation reaches the hypersensitive cells, they fire vigorously, producing a strong reflexive movement.

> **denervation hypersensitivity:** the heightened responsiveness of a denervated postsynaptic neuron to excitatory messages from remaining presynaptic neurons

Surgical and Medical Treatment of Brain Damage

Throughout this book, we have examined treatments for various brain disorders. Most treatments attempt to compensate for neurotransmitter or hormonal dysfunctions that produce neurological or behavioral problems. For example, in Chapter 15 we considered pharmacological treatments for schizophrenia, and in Chapter 3 we considered various treatments for depression. Surgical interventions for brain disease or brain damage take one of two forms: *removing damaged tissue or transplanting healthy tissue*. In Chapter 13, you learned about the surgical removal or lesioning of brain tissue in individuals with damage to the temporal lobe that impaired amygdaloid function.

Transplantation of brain tissue is not generally feasible because neurons do not spontaneously make connections with newly transplanted neurons. Thus, a surgeon cannot take an amygdala from one person and implant it into the brain of another, as is done with kidney transplants. The transplanted amygdala would not function and would ultimately be rejected and destroyed by glial cells. However, transplants consisting of donor cells from the substantia nigra of fetuses have been used successfully to treat symptoms of Parkinson's disease, as you learned in Chapter 6. Fetal brain tissue is not rejected by the host brain, and it readily adapts to the demands of its new environment.

More recently, exciting research with **embryonic stem cells** suggests that brain transplants may become a common surgical intervention for brain damage in the future. Embryonic stem cells have the capacity to transform into any type of human tissue, as you learned earlier in this chapter. Under the right conditions, these stem cells have transformed themselves into glial cells that form myelin in myelin-deficient rats (Schiff et al., 2002). Research with human neural stem cells has demonstrated that these cells, when injected into the brains of baby mice, differentiated into the cell type of the surrounding neurons and became functional. When injected into mice with a defective gene that prevents granule cells from developing in the cerebellum, these human stem cells migrated to the appropriate layer of the cerebellum and differentiated into normal mouse granule cells (Sikorski & Peters, 1998). This research opens the possibility that, in the near future, functional grafts of embryonic stem cells in the central nervous system may be used to repair damaged tissue and correct defects.

> **embryonic stem cells:** another name for inner-cell-mass cells, cells capable of differentiating into many cell lines

The observation that behavioral function recovers and develops normally when brain damage occurs in infancy is known as the (a)_____ effect. Most recovery from brain damage is due to (b)_____ recovery, rather than (c)_____ recovery. However, structural recovery can occur by means of six mechanisms: (1) (d)_____ of neurons (neurogenesis in the hippocampus, for example), (2) (e)_____ _____ removal (clearing away debris and toxins from damage site), (3) regrowth of (f)_____ (stimulated by nerve growth factor), (4) (g)_____ _____ of axons (formation of synapses with neurons that formerly received input from dead neurons), (5) dendritic (h)_____ (increased arborization of dendrites following brain damage in younger individuals), and (6) (i)_____ _____ (increased response to remaining presynaptic neurons). Surgical interventions for brain damage include (j)_____ of damaged tissue and (k)_____ of healthy tissue. Although mature brain tissue cannot be successfully transplanted, research has revealed that transplants consisting of donor cells from human fetuses or embryonic (l)_____ _____ can be used to repair brain damage.

Aging of the Brain

A recent study of *centenarians* (that is, people who are 100 years of age or older) revealed some very depressing information about the minds of the very elderly: *All* of them showed signs of cognitive decline, including memory deficits (Blansjaar et al., 2000). This decline is related to the signs of aging that have been observed in the human brain. Let's examine the changes that take place in the brain as we age.

Changes in the Normal Aging Brain

The most obvious change in the aging brain is the reduction in intracellular and extracellular fluid (Metcalfe, 1998; Chang, Ernst, Poland, & Jenden, 1996). This loss of fluid is associated with an increase in the concentration of protein in the aging brain. In addition, there is a loss of myelin with aging (La Rue, 1992). This loss of myelin leads to a decrease in the volume of white matter in the brain. As a result of atrophy of white matter, the sulci (the grooves or fissures between the gyri on the surface of the cerebrum, which you learned about in Chapter 4) get wider, and the ventricles get larger with increasing age (Figure 16.15). These changes are greater in men than in women, and men's brains show greater shrinkage with age than women's (Metcalfe, 1998).

In addition to the loss of myelin, neurons themselves die at a rate of approximately 100,000 per day. This normal loss of neurons does not appear to affect function until very late in life. Although cell loss occurs in all parts of the brain, neuronal death associated with aging is concentrated in the *cerebellum* and the *substantia nigra*. By the ninth decade of life, nearly 40% of the

Figure 16.15 The aging brain
The aged monkey brain shows significant loss of white matter (but no loss of gray matter).

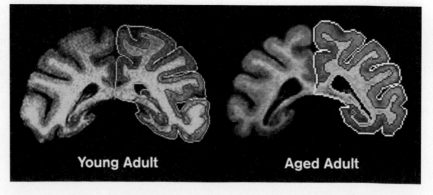

Young Adult   Aged Adult

neurons of the *locus coeruleus* have died, which means less *norepinephrine* is available for cognitive tasks requiring vigilance and arousal (Woodruff-Pak, 1999, 1997).

In the cerebral cortex, dendrites shrink to little stubs in some neurons, inactivating the neurons. Up to 20% of the neurons in the frontal lobe are lost by age 70, with the greatest loss occurring in the dorsolateral prefrontal cortex (Woodruff-Pak, 1999). PET imaging studies reveal reduced activity in the prefrontal cortex in the elderly during facial recognition and word retrieval tasks (Parkin & Walter, 1992). Changes in the hippocampus appear to affect NMDA receptors in the CA1 region, which are important in long-term potentiation and the formation of new long-term memories (McEwen, 1992, 1999). Atrophy of this region of the hippocampus is greater in elderly men than in elderly women. In addition to neuronal loss in the hippocampus, neurofibrillary tangles and extracellular plaques accumulate there, too (de Leon et al., 1995).

When neurons die, their axons degenerate, triggering the release of nerve growth factor. Nerve growth factor stimulates surviving neurons to sprout branches to compensate for the death of nearby neurons. Dendritic trees in the brains of 70-year-olds are significantly more extensive than those in the brains of 50-year-olds. However, dendritic trees stop growing after the age of 70, which means the aging brain loses its ability to compensate for the loss of neurons (Metcalfe, 1998).

One factor that leads to the death of neurons is the accumulation of insoluble pigments in the brains of elderly people. These pigments generally fall into two groups: a dark brain coloration caused by **neuromelanin** and a yellow, fatty substance associated with **lipofuscin**. Death of neurons in the substantia nigra has been attributed to an accumulation of neuromelanin in the substantia nigra. Lipofuscin accumulates in oligodendrocytes and astroglia and is associated with demyelination and loss of white matter in the cerebrum (Shannon, Wherrett, & Nag, 1997).

The changes in the brain that accompany normal aging are responsible for the many behavioral changes observed in the elderly, including *disturbed sleep, increased anxiety, decreased motor activity,* and *declining mental function.* Declines in serotonin function affect sleep, appetite, mood, aggression, and control of impulses (Meltzer et al., 1998; Woodruff-Pak, 1999). Decreases in dopamine impair motor function, and decreases in norepinephrine impair mental function. In addition, degeneration of neurons that produce acetylcholine is associated with learning and memory deficits (Muir, 1997).

neuromelanin: a dark-staining insoluble pigment that accumulates in the brains of elderly individuals and destroys neurons

lipofuscin: a yellow, insoluble fatty substance that accumulates in the brains of elderly individuals and destroys neurons

senile dementia: a progressive cognitive disorder that occurs in patients over 65 years of age

nucleus basalis: a forebrain structure that supplies acetylcholine to the cerebrum and hippocampus

vascular dementia: a form of senile dementia related to cardiovascular disease, particularly hardening of the arteries or stroke

Brain Disorders Associated with Aging

Senile dementia is a progressive cognitive disorder that occurs in patients over 65 years of age. It is characterized by memory dysfunction, disorientation for time and place, and other cognitive deficits. These cognitive disturbances are associated with significantly reduced levels of acetylcholine in the cerebral cortex and hippocampus, which are due to the massive loss of neurons in the **nucleus basalis** (or *basal nucleus*), a forebrain structure that supplies acetylcholine to the cerebrum and hippocampus (Figure 16.16) (Coyle, Price, & DeLong, 1983; Whitehouse, Price, Struble, Clark, Coyle, & DeLong, 1982). Cardiovascular disease related to hardening of the arteries or stroke can produce a form of senile dementia called **vascular dementia**. Senile dementia also occurs in elderly individuals who suffer from any of a number of degenerative brain disorders, including *Alzheimer's disease, Pick's disease,* and *Parkinson's disease.* Let's compare the brain anomalies associated with each of these disorders.

Figure 16.16 Acetylcholine pathways from the nucleus basalis (basal nucleus)

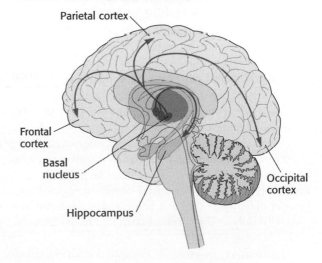

Alzheimer's Disease

The most common senile dementia is **Alzheimer's disease,** which accounts for over half of all dementia cases (Jellinger, 1996). Today, approximately four million people in the United States are afflicted with Alzheimer's disease, and that number is expected to triple in the next 50 years (Geldmacher & Whitehouse, 1997). People with Alzheimer's disease show many of the symptoms of psychosis, particularly as the disease progresses. Prevalent symptoms include memory and related cognitive deficits, disorientation for time and place, inappropriate emotional responses, agitation, hallucinations, and sometimes hostility and paranoia, with a progressive decline in all intellectual and physical functions that leads to death. Although the senile form of Alzheimer's disease is more common, Alzheimer's can occur in middle age. In fact, Dr. Alois Alzheimer, the physician-scientist for whom the disease is named, first described these symptoms in a 51-year-old woman (Alzheimer, 1907).

The exact cause of Alzheimer's disease is still being debated. Numerous abnormalities have been noted in the brains of those afflicted with this devastating condition. As we discussed in Chapter 10, acetylcholine and glutamate levels in the brains of Alzheimer's patients are significantly lower than normal, which could account for their memory and motor deficits. Structural abnormalities include: 1) symmetrical atrophy of the brain and enlarged lateral ventricles due to the loss of neurons in the frontal and temporal lobes; 2) extensive structural damage in the hippocampus; 3) microscopic **neurofibrillary tangles;** and 4) **neuritic** or **amyloid plaques** (de Leon et al., 1995).

MRI, PET, and CT imaging techniques have demonstrated bilateral atrophy of the hippocampus and enlarged ventricles in the brains of Alzheimer's patients (Figure 16.17). First described by Dr. Alzheimer nearly 100 years ago, *neurofibrillary tangles* are twisted masses of protein located in the cytoplasm of neurons. These tangles are especially prevalent in the hippocampus and surrounding temporal lobe regions. Interestingly, neurofibrillary tangles are also found in the brains of boxers with dementia pugilistica (Stern, 1991). Neuritic plaques are enormous (larger than the largest neurons) masses of extracellular beta-amyloid protein and swollen neuronal processes usually found in the hippocampus and frontal cortex (Figure 16.18).

A number of proteins are associated with the development of Alzheimer's disorder (Lovestopne & McLoughlin, 2002). The most common forms of Alzheimer's disorder are associated with an abnormal variant of the apolioprotein E gene (called E4) that directs the manufacture of *ApoE* protein in neurons (Roses & Saunders, 1997). Other proteins implicated in the development of Alzheimer's are *beta-amyloid peptide* and *tau-protein* (Ermekova et al., 1998). Beta-amyloid is responsible for the formation of the neuritic plaques seen in the extracellular spaces of the brains of Alzheimer's patients, and tau-protein accumulates within the neuron to produce neurofibrillary tangles.

The abnormal E4 allele of the apolipoprotein E gene produces a form of ApoE protein that doesn't bind well with tau-protein, causing neurofibrillary tangles to develop (Peskind, 1996). Neurofibrillary tangles, a hallmark of Alzheimer's disease, are rarely seen in the cerebral cortex in normal aging brains. Nearly all brains of people older than 90 have some evidence of neurofibrillary tangles, but they are observed only in the cerebral cortex of individuals with Alzheimer's disease (LaRue, 1992; Morris, 1997).

Head injury in youth is associated with the development of Alzheimer's disease in later years. Head trauma is also related to the appearance of the aberrant E4 gene (Roses & Saunders, 1997; Schmidt, et al., 2001). It may be that head injury pro-

Figure 16.17 MRI scan of enlarged ventricles in Alzheimer's patient

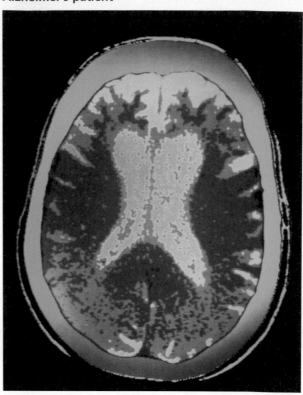

Alzheimer's disease: the most common form of senile dementia, whose symptoms include memory and related cognitive deficits, with a progressive decline in all intellectual and physical functions that leads to death

neurofibrillary tangles: twisted masses of protein located in the cytoplasm of neurons seen in brains of persons with Alzheimer's disease not normally in normal brains

neuritic plaques: another name for amyloid plaques

amyloid plaques: a sign of neuronal degeneration, consisting of amyloid protein, glial cells, white blood cells, and degenerating axons and dendrites

motes the expression of the abnormal E4 gene, which in turn directs the production of the defective form of ApoE protein that doesn't bind with tau-protein. When this protein is produced, tau-protein forms neurofibrillary tangles that ultimately destroy the host neuron. Recall that neurofibrillary tangles are also found in the neurons of boxers with dementia pugilistica. These tangles are most likely the result of E4 expression following head trauma in these boxers (Schmidt et al., 2001).

Amyloid plaques, consisting of amyloid protein, glial cells, white blood cells, and degenerating axons and dendrites, are a sign of neuronal degeneration observed in normal and disordered brains. Unlike neurofibrillary tangles, they are seen in the cerebral cortex initially. The amyloid protein has an unstable structure that, in Alzheimer's disease, adopts beta-sheet structures (beta-amyloid) similar to prions (Welch & Gambetti, 1998). Recall from Chapter 2 that prions produce massive brain damage leading to death. Similarly, the beta-structures of amyloid produce insoluble masses of protein that cause the brain damage and consequent cognitive impairment associated with Alzheimer's disease.

Mutations of the gene that codes for tau-protein are believed to cause deadly tangles with neurons in several other dementias (Spillantini et al., 1998). These hereditary dementias are characterized by intracellular tangles and cell loss in the frontal and temporal lobes, with associated Parkinson's symptoms. All are linked to chromosome 17. The mutated form of tau-protein produces neurofibrillary tangles within neurons, which ultimately result in neurodegeneration. The massive degeneration of neurons in the frontal and temporal lobes leads to symptoms of dementia, psychosis, aphasia, and Parkinson's disease.

Figure 16.18 Extracellular plaques and intracellular neurofibrillary tangles in Alzheimer's disease.

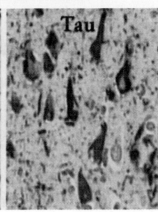

Parkinson's Disease

Dementia is also common in persons with **Parkinson's disease.** In the later stages of Parkinson's, more than 65% will show signs of dementia (Geldmacher & Whitehouse, 1997; Morris, 1996). Bradyphrenia, or a slowing of thinking, is a common complaint in Parkinson's and is one of the earliest signs of dementia. **Parkinson's dementia** is progressively debilitating, ultimately leaving the victim unable to understand or store new information, follow directions, or change behavior to meet the demands of the situation.

Most people who develop Parkinson's dementia have abnormal structures, called **Lewy's bodies,** located in the cytoplasm of their neurons. Lewy's bodies have filaments that radiate from a central core, producing a fuzzy contour when observed under the microscope (Forno, Eng, & Selkoe, 1989). The role that Lewy's bodies play in the development of Parkinson's dementia is unknown. They may be a byproduct, rather than a cause, of the neural degeneration associated with Parkinson's disease.

Pick's Disease

A rare disorder that results in dementia is **Pick's disease.** Usually developing in middle age, Pick's disease has symptoms that resemble those of Alzheimer's disease, although memory and cognitive impairments are not obvious until late in the progression of the disease. Early symptoms in Pick's disease include speech impairment or mutism, emotional blunting, marked personality change, and aberrant social behavior, indicating frontal lobe involvement. Other forms of speech impairment that are observed in Pick's disease include perseveration, or stereotyped repeating of words or phrases, which is related to temporal lobe dysfunction. Language disturbance can be present in Pick's patients for up to 2 years before other cognitive and behavioral impairments are evident (Kertesz & Munoz, 1997).

Parkinson's disease: a movement disorder caused by destruction of dopamine-producing cells in the substantia nigra, with symptoms of tremor, loss of balance, and rigidity of limbs

Parkinson's dementia: a progressively debilitating form of dementia that is associated with Parkinson's disease

Lewy's bodies: abnormal structures found in the cytoplasm of neurons in people who suffer from Parkinson's dementia

Pick's disease: a rare dementia that begins in middle age, producing symptoms that resemble those of Alzheimer's disease late in the progression of the illness

Research has demonstrated that Pick's disease is associated with neuronal atrophy and loss of 40–50% of the synapses in the outer layers of the frontal and temporal cortex (Brun & Passant, 1996). Imaging with CT, SPECT, and MRI can be useful in confirming the diagnosis (Figure 16.19). Under the microscope, we can see abnormal structures, or *cytoplasmic inclusions*, inside the neurons of patients with Pick's disease (Jellinger, 1996). In Pick's disease, the abnormal structures are called **Pick's bodies.** Pick's bodies are chemically similar to the neurofibrillary tangles observed in Alzheimer's disease, although they have different ultrastructures (Ulrich et al., 1987). Pick's bodies

Figure 16.19 Frontal lobe involvement in Pick's disease.

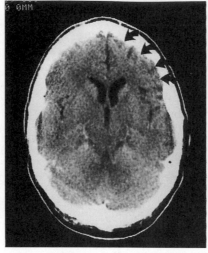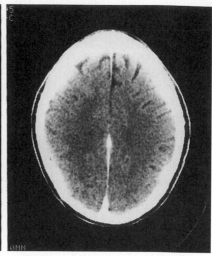

Pick's bodies:

cytoplasmic inclusions found in the neurons of individuals with Pick's disease

also have a different appearance from Lewy's bodies, which are found inside neurons of some people who have Parkinson's dementia. Pick's bodies are composed of random filaments with a smooth contour, whereas Lewy's bodies have a fuzzy contour (Forno, Eng, & Selkoe, 1989). At this point, you might feel a bit overwhelmed at trying to sort out these various forms of dementia. Consider the task of a physician or neuropsychologist whose job it is to diagnose a dementia disorder. The clinician will use clinical signs and symptoms, as well as biopsies, blood analyses, and neuroimaging techniques to reach a diagnosis. One way to differentiate among these disorders is on the basis of signs of motor disturbance (Geldmaster & Whitehouse, 1997). Those dementias that are not accompanied by prominent motor signs include Alzheimer's and Pick's disease. Dementias that are accompanied by severe movement impairment include Parkinson's dementia and vascular dementias. Table 16.1 summarizes the differences among these various forms of irreversible dementias.

Table 16.1

Forms of Senile Dementia

Disorder	Signs of Motor Disturbance	Brain Anomalies	Cytoplasmic Inclusions
Alzheimer's disease	no	amyloid plaques in hippocampus and frontal lobe; atrophy of hippocampus; cell loss in temporal and frontal lobes	neurofibrillary tangles
Parkinson's dementia	yes	abnormalities of basal ganglia; cell loss in temporal and frontal lobes	Lewy's bodies
Pick's disease	no	neuronal atrophy and loss of up to 50% of synapses in frontal and temporal cortex	Pick's bodies
vascular dementia	yes	abnormalities associated with stroke, cardiovascular disease	none

Clinical Diagnosis of Senile Brain Disorders

Brain biopsies, postmortem examinations, and neuroimaging techniques have led investigators to conclude that all dementias are associated to some extent with: (1) atrophy of neurons; (2) synapse loss; (3) gliosis (an abnormal accumulation of glial cells, discussed in Chapter 2); (4) microvacuolation (the formation of tiny spaces, or vacuoles, in brain tissue); or (5) inclusions, or abnormal structures, in the cytoplasm of neurons and glia (Brun & Passant, 1996; Jellinger, 1996). Each type of senile dementia that we've examined thus far has been associated with specific brain anomalies.

For example, neuronal atrophy and structural changes in the hippocampus predominate in Alzheimer's disease, whereas neuronal atrophy and structural changes are limited to the frontal and temporal lobes in Pick's disease. These differences have been confirmed in postmortem examination of brains (Shaw &Alvord, 1997) and in imaging studies using MRI (deLeon et al., 1995; Matthews, Candy, & Bryan, 1992), PET (Friedland et al., 1993; Matthews et al., 1992), and SPECT (Bonte et al., 1990; Mathews et al., 1992; Osimani et al., 1994; Risberg, 1987). Even EEG recordings can differentiate among Alzheimer's, Parkinson's dementia, and cerebrovascular dementias (Rosen, 1997).

Although we can confidently differentiate among different forms of dementia on the basis of the symptoms and brain damage observed, the connection between these brain abnormalities and the production of dementia is not understood at present. For example, investigators cannot yet explain how cytoplasmic inclusions or vacuoles inside neurons interfere with the functioning of the cells and produce symptoms of dementia. Obviously these abnormalities have disastrous effects on thinking, memory, emotions, and movement.

Recap 16.4: Aging of the Brain

Numerous changes occur in the brain as a result of normal aging: a reduction in intracellular and extracellular (a)_____, a loss of (b)_____ (which results in atrophy of white matter), increase in the size of the (c)_____, and shrinkage in the (d)_____ of the brain. Cell death associated with normal aging is concentrated in the (e)_____ and (f)_____ _____. (g)_____ in the cerebral cortex shrink to little stubs during normal aging, resulting in cognitive and perceptual deficits. However, (h)_____ _____ increases to compensate for the death of nearby neurons in older adults, although this branching fails to occur after the age of 70. (i)_____ _____ is a progressive cognitive disorder that occurs in people over 65 years of age. The most common form of senile dementia is (j) _____ disease, which is characterized by numerous abnormalities in the brain, including loss of neurons in the frontal and temporal lobes and extensive damage to the hippocampus, due to neurofibrillary tangles and amyloid plaques. Neurofibrillary tangles result from the accumulation of two proteins, (k)_____-protein and (l) _____ protein, in neurons. (m)_____ disease can also produce senile dementia, which is associated with abnormal structures called Lewy's bodies in the cytoplasm of neurons. (n) _____ disease can also produce the cognitive impairments of senile dementia, although language disturbances develop first, before signs of dementia are evident.

Assessing Brain Damage

The best way to assess brain damage is at autopsy, when the brain is examined for gross abnormalities and then sectioned into slices for microscopic examination. Only then can a diagnostician be really certain of the cause and extent of the brain damage. However, an autopsy is not useful or convenient for a person who wants to know about the source of his or her disability while still alive. For a living patient, two types of tests allow a clinician to diagnose the cause of a behavioral or cognitive impairment: (1) brain-imaging and recording techniques and (2) neuropsychological testing.

Brain-Imaging and Recording Techniques

Brain-imaging techniques can give the clinician important information about the presence or absence of brain damage and brain disease. For example, although CT scans are not accurate in diagnosing Alzheimer's disease, MRI studies have indicated that temporal atrophy is associated with Alzheimer's disease, with the hippocampus being significantly reduced in size (Kesslak, Nalcioglu, & Cotman, 1991; Mathews, Candy, & Bryan, 1992; O'Brien et al., 1997; Rapoport, 1995). PET studies have revealed a typical pattern of impairment for Alzheimer's disease, with reduced glucose metabolic rates in the association cortex in the *temporal* and *parietal lobes* with preservation of primary visual and sensorimotor cortex, basal ganglia, and cerebellum (Figure 16.20). Other dementias typically have more global reduction in glucose metabolic rate, including the *frontal lobes* (Friedland et al., 1993; Herholz, 1995).

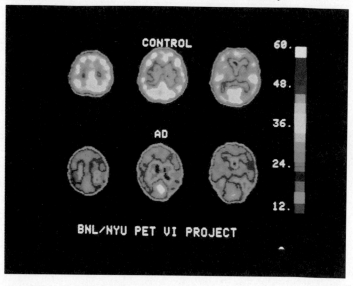

Figure 16.20 PET scans of brains of Alzheimer's patients and controls
Blue indicates areas of extremely low levels of activity.

Statistical studies of EEG recordings of large numbers of healthy people ranging in age from 6 to 90 years have provided a set of normative data for clinicians to use when evaluating individuals with brain injuries. People with brain impairments, such as dementia or learning disabilities, show abnormal EEG values compared to healthy people (John, Prichep, Fridman, & Eaton, 1988). The patterns of abnormal values are distinct for different disorders, which makes this technique useful for diagnosis of brain disorders in children and adults. For example, EEG studies can differentiate among healthy controls and individuals with mild cognitive dysfunction, dementia, schizophrenia, alcoholism, depression, and bipolar disorder. Evoked-potential recordings are useful for diagnosing sensory or perceptual disorders, as well as nerve conduction disorders, such as multiple sclerosis (Fuhr & Kappos, 2001).

Neuropsychological Testing

Brain-injured patients are routinely referred to clinical neuropsychologists for assessment of function. Clinical neuropsychologists are trained to evaluate the skills and abilities of a patient and to relate these to brain function. When assessing a patient, a clinical neuropsychologist has a number of tests available for evaluating different types of abilities. Although it would be convenient and easy if one test could be used to evaluate brain damage, no such test exists to date. Instead, a clinical neuropsychologist will use a group of different tests, called a **test battery**, to test for brain damage.

A typical neuropsychological evaluation may take 2 to 3 hours, although patients with cognitive deficits may require over 6 hours to complete a test battery. A basic test battery will test a wide variety of functions, including attention, visual perception, visual reasoning, memory and learning, verbal functions, academic skills, concept formation, self-regulation, motor ability, and emotional status. However, there are special test protocols for particular disabilities. For example, patients with seizures will also be evaluated with 24-hour EEG monitoring, in addition to the basic test battery. A test for patients with multiple sclerosis is usually limited in duration (less than 2 hours) because these patients fatigue quickly.

A number of ready-made, commercially available neuropsychological test batteries are available, including the *Halstead-Reitan* and *Luria-Nebraska* test batteries.

test battery: a group of tests that measures facets of behavior

These batteries test for a wide variety of function and indicate the strengths, as well as the weaknesses, of the patient. Of the test batteries that are available, the Halstead-Reitan has received the most study and is the most thoroughly validated (Jarvis & Barth, 1997). Originally, in 1947, Halstead put together a battery of 27 tests of cerebral function, and he eventually reduced this battery to 10 measures, which he called the *Halstead Impairment Index*. Reitan further modified Halstead's battery by eliminating some measures. The end result is the *Halstead-Reitan Neuropsychological Test Battery*, which today consists of eight tests that measure problem solving, judgment, memory, abstract reasoning, concept formation, mental efficiency, verbal and nonverbal auditory discrimination, attention, and motor coordination. A special test to screen for aphasia is added, as is a measure of sensory perception, in which tactile, auditory, and visual modalities are tested.

Most neuropsychologists supplement commercial neuropsychological test batteries with additional tests, depending on the patient's needs. An intelligence test may be given, as well a personality inventory, such as the Minnesota Multiphasic Personality Inventory (MMPI). Other memory tests or measures of language ability may be used to get a fuller picture of the patient's impairment. After scoring the tests, the clinical neuropsychologist will look at the pattern of scores to assess the patient's strengths and weaknesses. This information is used to determine the prognosis for the brain-injured individual, as well as to plan his or her treatment and rehabilitation.

Recap 16.5: Assessing Brain Damage

The best way to access brain damage is at (a)_____ _____. For a living patient, a clinician can diagnose the cause of a behavioral or cognitive impairment using (b)_____ or (c)_____ techniques or by neuropsychological testing. (d)_____ and (e)_____ scans can be used to diagnose Alzheimer's disease. (f)_____ studies can also differentiate between healthy individuals and those with mild cognitive dysfunction, dementia, or other disorders. A neuropsychologist uses a group of different tests, known as a (g)_____ _____, to test for brain damage. The best known neuropsychological test batteries are the (h)_____-_____ and (i)_____-_____ test batteries, which test problem solving, judgment, memory, abstract reasoning, concept formation, perceptual discrimination, attention, and motor coordination.

In Conclusion

Thus, we conclude our discussion of the biological foundations of behavior. By now, I hope you have gained an appreciation of all the research that has been conducted on the brain and behavior. In this chapter, we looked at how research has enabled us to identify, treat, and prevent brain damage. We reviewed the stages of brain development and various disorders associated with damage to the developing brain. We also examined the behavioral dysfunctions that result from infectious and noninfectious disease. Finally, we considered the aging brain and changes associated with normal aging and those associated with senile dementias.

Throughout this book, I have related known brain functions to pathological states. We started out by looking at the structure and function of neurons. Then we considered the function of brain structures and groups of neurons. In every instance, I introduced disorders related to dysfunction of the nervous system.

Dysfunctions provide us with a lot of insight into normal brain functioning. Think about the case of Phineas Gage, the man who was injured by a metal rod that accidentally pierced his frontal lobe during a workplace accident. Or consider H. M., who underwent bilateral surgical destruction of the hippocampus to control his epileptic seizures. In both cases, we learned quite a lot about the workings of the brain, based on the behavioral dysfunctions that were evident following damage to particular neurons in the central nervous system.

In this book, we have considered the wide range of human behaviors and experience. We examined the role of the nervous system in movement, sensation, and perception. Next we reviewed research concerning memory, attention, learning, and consciousness. Behaviors associated with motivational states, such as sleep, temperature regulation, eating, drinking, and sex, were discussed. We concluded our study of the brain and behavior with a focus on emotion, stress, and psychopathology. In every chapter, we moved from a discussion of the normal to a discussion of the abnormal. Although the last chapter focused almost entirely on brain damage and dysfunction, every chapter in this textbook presented behavioral disorders associated with known neurochemical or brain pathology.

Dealing with brain damage is one of the most daunting challenges that science has yet to meet. Maybe some of you will join us in this endeavor. We still have a long way to go before we thoroughly understand the workings of the brain and how it initiates, organizes, and controls behavior.

Chapter Summary

Brain Development

▶ Neurons develop along the borders of the neural tube in an embryo, and they migrate to their final position in the nervous system with the help of radioglial cells.

▶ Brain development occurs in five stages: cell proliferation, cell migration, cell differentiation, axonal and dendritic growth, and programmed cell death. During the first stage of brain development, called cell proliferation, neurons are formed at a rate of 250,000 per minute. During the second stage, called cell migration, neuron move from the border of the neural tube to their final position. Immature neurons begin to transform and achieve their final form during the third stage of brain development, called cell differentiation. During the fourth stage of brain development, the stage of axonal and dendritic growth, neurons begin to sprout processes that become dendrites and axons. The fifth and final stage of brain development is characterized by programmed cell death.

▶ Chemical and physical insults, disease, malnutrition, and genetic variations can interfere with brain development and cause permanent brain damage. Fetal alcohol syndrome results in embryos whose mothers drink excessively during their pregnancies. Physical insults to the developing brain may produce a motor disorder known as cerebral palsy. A number of genetic variations can interfere with brain development, producing a number of disorders including holoproencephaly, a disorder in which affected individuals develop only one cerebral hemisphere. Blockage of the ventricles during brain development can result in hydrocephalus.

Brain Damage

▶ Brain damage can occur during the prenatal stage (before birth), perinatal stage (at birth), or postnatal stage (after birth).

▶ Perinatal damage occurs as a result of anoxia and trauma, whereas postnatal damage can be caused by trauma or disease.

▶ Head trauma can be classified into three categories: concussion (least severe), contusion, or laceration (most severe). Boxers who sustain repeated blows to the head can develop pinpoint bleeding in the brain (called petechial hemorrhage) or, in more severe cases, dementia pugilistica, characterized by cognitive and emotional disturbances.

▶ Infectious diseases caused by bacteria or viruses can produce a number of disorders that cause brain damage, including meningitis (bacterial infection of the protective covering on the brain), general paresis (associated with syphilis), encephalitis (viral infection of the brain), AIDS-related dementia (caused by the human immunodeficiency virus), and Creutzfeldt-Jakob dementia (associated with a simple protein called a prion, which is neither a bacterium nor virus).

▶ Two noninfectious diseases, cardiovascular disease (disorders of the heart and blood vessels) and cancer (characterized by uncontrolled growth of tumors), can produce brain damage.

- When fatty deposits bind to the inside of blood vessels, producing atherosclerosis, blood flow to the brain is disrupted. Two types of stroke can produce brain damage, ischemic strokes (caused by clogged blood vessels, reducing blood flow) and hemorrhagic strokes (when blood vessels in the brain rupture, producing a cerebrovascular accident). Neurons that die as a result of a stroke release glutamate, which kills nearby neurons.

- Alcoholism can produce brain damage in several ways: through malnutrition (which produces Korsakoff's syndrome and pellagra), through liver disease (which causes ammonia to build up in the blood, resulting in ammonemia), and through its effect on the cardiovascular system (including high blood pressure or stroke).

Recovery from Brain Damage

- Recovery from brain damage can be structural or functional in nature, with best recovery associated with damage that occurs early in life. The observation that behavioral function recovers and develops normally when brain damage occurs in infancy is known as the Kennard effect.

- Most recovery from brain damage is due to functional recovery, rather than structural recovery.

- Structural recovery can occur by means of six mechanisms: 1) regrowth of neurons (neurogenesis in the hippocampus, for example), 2) waste product removal (clearing away debris and toxins from damage site), 3) regrowth of axons (stimulated by nerve growth factor), 4) collateral sprouting of axons (formation of synapses with neurons that formerly received input from dead neurons), and 5) dendritic branching (increased arborization of dendrites following brain damage in younger individuals), and 6) denervation hypersensitivity (increased response to remaining presynpatic neurons).

- Medical treatments for brain damage attempt to correct hormonal or neurotransmitter dysfunctions. Surgical interventions for brain damage include removal of damaged tissue and transplantation of healthy tissue. Although mature brain tissue cannot be successfully transplanted, research has revealed that transplants consisting of donor cells from human fetuses or embryonic stem cells can be used to repair brain damage.

Aging of the Brain

- Normal aging of the brain is accompanied by a reduction in intracellular and extracellular fluid in the brain, a loss of myelin, atrophy of white matter, shrinkage of dendrites, the accumulation of insoluble pigments, and neuronal death, which all contribute to the sleep, mood, and cognitive disturbances observed in the elderly.

- Cell death associated with normal aging is concentrated in the cerebellum and substantia nigra.

- Dendritic branching increases to compensate for the death of nearby neurons in older adults, although this branching fails to occur after the age of 70.

- Senile dementia is a progressive cognitive disorder that occurs in people over 65 years of age.

- The most common form of senile dementia is Alzheimer's disease, which is characterized by numerous abnormalities in the brain, including loss of neurons in the frontal and temporal lobes and extensive damage to the hippocampus, due to neurofibrillary tangles and amyloid plaques. Neurobrillary tangles result from the accumulation of two proteins, tau-protein and ApoE protein, in neurons.

- Parkinson's disease can also produce senile dementia, which is associated with abnormal structures called Lewy's bodies in the cytoplasm of neurons.

- Pick's disease can also produce the cognitive impairments of senile dementia, although language disturbances develop first, before signs of dementia are evident.

Assessing Brain Damage

- The best way to assess brain damage is at postmortem autopsy. For a living patient, the extent and prognosis for recovery from brain damage can be assessed using brain imaging, EEG recording, and neuropsychological testing.

- MRI and PET scans can be used to diagnose Alzheimer's disease. EEG studies can differentiate between healthy individuals and those with mild cognitive dysfunction, dementia, or other disorders.

- A neuropsychologist uses a group of different tests, known as a test battery, to test for brain damage. The best known neuropsychological test batteries are the Halstead-Reitan and the Luria-Nebraska test batteries, which test problem-solving judgment, memory, abstract reasoning, concept formation, perceptual discrimination, attention, and motor coordination.

Key Terms

AIDS-related dementia (p. 489)
alcoholic pellagra (p. 491)
Alzheimer's disease (p. 500)
amyloid plaques (p. 500)
apoptosis (p. 481)

arborization (p. 496)
atherosclerosis (p. 488)
cancer (p. 489)
cardiovascular disease (p. 488)
cell differentiation (p. 481)

cell migration (p. 480)
cell proliferation (p. 480)
cerebral laceration (p. 486)
cerebral palsy (p. 483)
cerebrovascular accident (p. 488)

concussion (p. 486)
contusion (p. 486)
Creutzfeldt-Jakob
  dementia (p. 488)
dementia pugilistica (p. 486)
denervation hypersensitivity (p. 497)
Down's syndrome (p. 483)
embryo (p. 480)
embryonic stem cells (p. 497)
fetal alcohol syndrome (p. 482)
fetus (p. 481)
fragile X syndrome (p. 483)
general paresis (p. 487)
hemispherectomy (p. 493)
hemorrhagic strokes (p. 488)

hepatic encephalopathy (p. 491)
holoprosencephaly (p. 484)
hydrocephalus (p. 484)
ischemic strokes (p. 489)
Kennard effect (p. 492)
Korsakoff's syndrome (p. 490)
Lewy's bodies (p. 501)
lipofuscin (p. 499)
meningitis (p. 487)
nerve growth factor
  (NGF) (p. 481)
neuritic plaques (p. 500)
neurofibrillary tangles (p. 500)
neurogenesis (p. 494)
neuromelanin (p. 499)

nucleus basalis (p. 499)
Parkinson's dementia (p. 501)
Parkinson's disease (p. 501)
petechial hemorrhage (p. 487)
Pick's bodies (p. 501)
Pick's disease (p. 501)
senile dementia (p. 499)
stage of axonal and dendritic
  growth (p. 481)
syphilis (p. 487)
test battery (p. 504)
vascular dementia (p. 499)
viral encephalitis (p. 488)
Wernicke-Korsakoff's
  syndrome (p. 491)

Questions for Thought

1. What would be the effect of a chemical insult that interfered with cell proliferation? What would be the effect of the same insult that interfered with cell migration? What about its effect on cell differentiation?

2. Identify the prenatal and postnatal effects of alcoholism.

3. What sort of abilities do neuropsychological test batteries assess? How are these abilities related to specific brain structures?

Questions for Review

1. What are the five stages of brain development?

2. Describe the effects of prenatal exposure to radiation, rubella, malnutrition, and trauma on the developing brain.

3. What is the difference between a concussion, a contusion, and a cerebral laceration?

4. Identify the six mechanisms of structural recovery from brain damage.

5. Contrast the changes in the normal aging brain with those in the brain of a person with dementia.

Suggested Readings

Berger-Sweeney, J., & Hohmann, C. F. (1997). Behavioral consequences of abnormal cortical development: Insights into developmental disabilities. *Behavioural Brain Research, 86,* 121–142.

Brown, J. L., & Pollitt, E. (1996). Malnutrition, poverty, and intellectual development. *Scientific American, 274,* 38–43.

Charness, M. E. (1993). Brain lesions in alcoholics. *Alcoholism: Clinical and Experimental Research, 17,* 2–11.

Lezak, M. D. (1995). *Neuropsychological assessment.* New York: Oxford University Press.

Muir, J. L. (1997). Acetylcholine, aging, and Alzheimer's disease. *Pharmacology, biochemistry, and behavior, 56,* 687–696.

Paus, T., Zijdenbos, A., Worsley, K., Collins, D. L., Blumenthal, J., Giedd, J. N., Rapoport, J. L., & Evans, A. C. (1999). Structural maturation of neural pathways in children and adolescents: In vivo study. *Science, 283,* 1908–1911.

Van Bogaert, P., Wikler, D., Damhaut, P., Szliwowski, H. B., & Goldman, S. (1998). Regional changes in glucose metabolism during brain development from the age of 6 years. *Neuroimage, 8,* 62–68.

Web Resources

For a chapter tutorial quiz, direct links to the Internet sites listed below and other features, visit the book-specific website at **www.wadsworth.com/product/ 0155074865**. You may also connect directly to the following annotated websites:

http://www.nih.gov/news/stemcell/scireport.htm
This site from the National Institute of Health outlines the opportunities and challenges of stem cell research and applications.

http://www.asbah.org
To learn more about how hydrocephalus affects the body and brain visit this informative site.

http://www.sfn.org/content/Publications/ BrainBriefings/knocking.html
Do blows or jolts to the head during contact sports affect mental functioning?

http://pedsccm.wustl.edu/All-Net/english/ neurpage/trauma/head-1.htm
This site, which concentrates on pediatric head trauma, highlights the mechanisms of injury as well as treatment and therapy including a video showing the removal of a subdural hematoma.

For additional readings and information, check out InfoTrac College Edition at **http://www.infotrac-college.com/wadsworth**. Choose a search term yourself or enter the following search terms: brain damage, concussion, fetal alcohol syndrome, and meningitis.

CD-ROM: Exploring Biological Psychology

Video: Child with Autism
Video: Brains on Ice
Interactive Recaps

Chapter 16 Quiz
Connect to the Interactive Biological Psychology Glossary

Glossary

ablation: removal of a part of the brain [*ab-* = away; *-latus* = to carry, Latin]

absence seizures: a type of seizure disorder characterized by an inability to focus on the subject at hand

absolute refractory period: a period of time following an action potential during which no stimulus can initiate another action potential

acamprosate: a drug that antagonizes the effect of glutamate and reduces craving in addicts

accommodation: the process by which the lens changes shape in order to focus light

acetylcholine: the first neurotransmitter to be discovered, binds with nicotinic and muscarinic receptors

acetylcholinesterase: an extracellular enzyme that deactivates acetylcholine

achromatopsia: a visual disorder associated with damage to AV4 in which the affected individual cannot see color [*a-* = without; *-chroma-* = color; *-opsia* = vision, Greek]

actin: thin filaments found in muscle fibers

action potential: the voltage change recorded across the cell membrane in an excited neuron

activation-synthesis hypothesis: an explanation of how dreams arise, based on the processing and interpretation of sensory information by the cerebral cortex

active theory of sleep: an explanation of sleep that proposes that the brain is normally active and that sleep arises from a wave of depression that spreads across the cerebrum

acupuncture: an ancient method for treating pain by inserting thin needles into the skin at specially designated points

acute stressor: a stressor that occurs infrequently and for a limited period of time

adaptation: a decrease in the firing of a receptor to repeated stimulation

addiction: a disorder in which the affected person loses control over intake of a particular substance and demonstrates psychological and physical dependence

adoption studies: a type of genetic analysis that compares the rates of occurrence of a disorder in adoptive parents with the rates of occurrence of the disorder in biological parents

adrenal steroids: hormones produced by the cortex of the adrenal gland

adrenergic beta-blockers: drugs that block norepinephrine and epinephrine receptors, thereby decreasing norepinephrine activity in the brain, and that are used to treat some anxiety disorders

adrenocorticotropic hormone (ACTH): a hormone released by the paraventricular nucleus that stimulates the adrenal cortex to produce glucocorticoids [*adreno-* = adrenal gland; *-cortico* = cortex; *-tropic* = to change, Greek]

adrenogenital syndrome: a disorder in which embryos are exposed to high levels of androgens in the uterus, which masculinizes the female embryo

advanced-sleep-phase syndrome: a disorder in which affected individuals feel tired several hours earlier than their normal sleep time

A-fiber: a myelinated axon that has a large diameter

ageusia: an inability to taste [*a-* = without; *-geusi* = to taste, Greek]

agonist: a chemical that binds with and activates a receptor

agraphia: a writing disorder in which affected individuals cannot form letters, have spelling errors, or have difficulty spacing letters and words [*a-* = without; *-graphia* = to write, Latin]

AIDS-related dementia: a cognitive disorder produced by direct infection of the brain by the human immunodeficiency virus

akathisia: an extrapyramidal side effect that involves feelings of restlessness and a need to keep moving [*akathisia* = inability to sit down, Latin]

akinetic mutism: a disorder in which the affected individual is unable to make orienting responses, due to damage to the reticular formation [*a-* = without; *-kine* = movement; *mut-* = no speech, Greek]

akinetopsia: a visual disorder associated with damage to BV5 in which the affected individual cannot perceive movement or moving objects [*a-* = without; *-kine-* = movement; *-opsia* = vision, Greek]

alcoholic pellagra: a disorder that affects the skin, blood, and gastrointestinal system and produces dementia; associated with deficiencies of niacin and protein caused by alcoholism

allodynia: an abnormal pain response to a normally nonpainful stimulus that is observed in individuals who have suffered tissue and nerve damage

all-or-none law: a rule that the action potential always goes all the way to completion if threshold stimulation has been reached and an action potential is initiated

allostasis: a concept that explains non-homeostatic cues that initiate eating and drinking

alpha adrenergic receptor: a receptor that, when stimulated by norepinephrine, increases CRH release and activates the stress response of the HPA axis

alpha-2 adrenergic receptor: an autoreceptor on the presynaptic terminals of neurons that release norepinephrine, controlling the release of norepinephrine

alpha motor neurons: large motor neurons that innervate extrafusal muscle fibers

alpha waves: desynchronized brain waves observed during periods of relaxed wakefulness that occur at a frequency of 8–12 Hz

Alzheimer's disease: the most common form of senile dementia, whose symptoms include memory and related cognitive deficits, with a progressive decline in all intellectual and physical functions that leads to death

ambulatory: able to walk [*ambulare* = to walk, Latin]

amenorrhea: the absence of menstrual cycles [*a-* = without; *-menorrhea* = menstruation]

American Sign Language: a standard system of hand gestures used by deaf individuals to communicate

amino acid: a chemical compound that contain an amino group and an acid (COOH)

ammonemia: a condition in which ammonia builds up in the blood due to liver dysfunction caused by alcoholism and other disorders [*ammon-* = ammonia; *-emia* = in the blood]

amnesia: loss of declarative memory [*a-* = without; *-mnes-* = memory, Greek]

AMPA receptors: a type of glutamate receptor, associated with long-term potentiation, that binds readily with glutamate, producing depolarization of the neuron

amplitude: the height of a wave from its lowest to highest points

ampulla: swelling at the end of a semicircular canal where hair cells are located

amusia: an impairment in music perception [*a-* = without; *-musia* = music, Latin]

amygdala: an almond-shaped structure located in the medial temporal lobe that is implicated in the experience of negative emotions

amyloid plaques: a sign of neuronal degeneration, consisting of amyloid protein, glial cells, white blood cells, and degenerating axons and dendrites

amyotrophic lateral sclerosis (ALS): a progressive disorder caused by degeneration of motor neurons in the spinal cord and brain

analgesia: an absence of pain [*a-* = without; *-algesia* = pain, Greek]

anandamide: a recently discovered neurotransmitter that binds with cannabinoid receptors

androgen insensitivity syndrome: a disorder in which the affected individual is insensitive to all androgens, including testosterone

androgens: male sex hormones, including testosterone [*andro-* = man; *-genos* = to create, Greek]

anencephalic: a condition in which the individual has no cerebrum [*a-* = without; *-encephal-* = brain, cerebrum, Greek]

anesthetized: under the influence of drugs that eliminate sensation [*an-* = without; *aisthesis* = feeling, Greek]

angiotensin I: an inactive hormone that floats in the blood, precursor to angiotensin II

angiotensin II: a hormone activated when renin binds with angiotensin I, which causes constriction of blood vessels and stimulates drinking behavior

angular gyrus: an area of the cortex located at the junction of the temporal, parietal, and occipital lobes that integrates visual, auditory, and somatosensory information

annulospiral receptor: a receptor that fires when stretched

anomia: a language disorder in which the affected individual cannot name familiar objects [*a-* = without; *-nom-* = name, Latin]

anorexia nervosa: an eating disorder in which the individual restricts food intake and loses significant body weight [*an-* = without; *-orex-* = appetite]

anorexia nervosa–bulimic subtype: a form of anorexia nervosa in which the affected individual engages in bingeing and purging, in addition to bouts of food restriction

anosmia: an inability to smell odors [*a-* = without; *-osmi* = smell, Greek]

antagonists: muscles that produce opposite movements around a joint

anterior: toward the front [*ante* = before, Latin]

anterior cingulate cortex: an area of the prefrontal cortex that appears to be part of the central executive system that coordinates working memory, especially attentional processes

anterior commissure: tract that connects neurons in the left and right hippocampus and amygdala

anterior hypothalamus: area of the hypothalamus that participates in temperature and water intake regulation

anterograde amnesia: global amnesia, an inability to form new declarative memories

anterograde tracing: tracing from the soma to the endplates of the axon [*antero-* = forward]

anticholinesterase: a drug that blocks the action of acetylcholinesterase

antidiuretic hormone: a hormone produced by the pituitary gland that inhibits the production of urine, also known as vasopressin

antisocial personality disorder: a personality disorder characterized by pathological social interactions with others, in which the disturbed individual acts impulsively and exploits others for his or her own gain, showing no remorse

anvil: the second ossicle in the middle ear, which receives vibrations from the hammer and relays them to the stirrup

anxiety disorders: disorders characterized by uncontrolled bouts of fear or overactivation of the fear system

anxiogenic: anxiety-producing [*anxio-* = anxiety; *-genic* = to create, Greek]

anxiolytic: anxiety-reducing [*anxio* = anxiety; *-lysis* = to cut, Greek]

aphagia: a failure or refusal to eat [*a-* = without; *-phag-* = to eat, Greek]

ApoE: a protein, called apolipoprotein E, found in neurons

apoptosis: programmed death of unwanted neurons

apperceptive agnosia: a form of visual agnosia in which the affected individual cannot recognize even the simplest shapes and forms

apraxia: a disorder caused by cerebral damage in which a person cannot organize movements into a productive sequence and can no longer perform previously familiar movements with the hands [*a-* = without; *-praxis* = action, Greek]

aqueduct of Sylvius: ventricle located in the midbrain

aqueous humor: watery substance located behind the cornea

arachnoid: middle weblike layer of the meninges [*arachne* = spider, Greek]

arborization: increased branching of dendrites [*arbor-* = tree, Latin]

arcuate fasciculus: the bundle of axons that connects Broca's and Wernicke's areas

area 46: an area in the prefrontal cortex that appears to play a role in switching attention between two or more tasks

area V1: the primary visual cortex located in the occipital lobe, also known as the striate cortex or Brodmann's area 17

arginine-vasopressin: a hormone produced by the paraventricular nucleus that regulates salt and water balance and increases ACTH release when working with CRH

ascending reticular activation system: reticular formation, a diffuse system of axons extending from the hindbrain to the thalamus that activates attentional systems in the cerebrum

Asperger's syndrome: a form of autism in which the affected individual is high functioning, with excellent language skills and evidence of metacognition

astrocytes: astroglia, star-shaped glial cells [*astro-* = star, Greek]

ataxia: an inability to walk in a coordinated fashion [*a-* = without; *-taxi* = to move, Greek]

atherosclerosis: a disorder in which the inner walls of major blood vessels become coated with fatty deposits that harden at a later date

ATP adenosine triphosphate: the principal fuel of the cell

atrophy: deterioration of tissue [*a-* = without; *-trephein* = nourishment, Greek]

attention: a state of being alert or orienting to a specific stimulus or processing information in working memory

attention deficit/hyperactivity disorder: an attentional disorder that impairs the ability of affected individuals to hold information in working memory while they retrieve other information

attention for action: a type of attentional process in which the executive system directs various components of working memory

atypical depression: a mood disorder characterized by fatigue, lethargy, sleeping more than normal, and overeating

auditory nerve: cranial nerve VIII, which carries information from the inner ear to the brain

auditory "What" stream: an auditory pathway that begins in the rostral part of the primary auditory cortex and ends in the ventrolateral prefrontal cortex

auditory "Where" stream: an auditory pathway that originates in the caudal area of the primary auditory cortex and ends in the dorsolateral prefrontal cortex

autism: an attentional disorder characterized by a severe impairment of cognitive and social skills

autonomic nervous system: a division of the peripheral nervous system, controls smooth muscles

autoradiography: a labeling technique using a radioactive tag that traces the pathway of chemicals in the brain [*autos* = self; *graphos* = to write or record, Greek]

autoreceptor: a receptor found on the terminal buttons of some neurons that binds with neurotransmitters released from their own axon [*auto-* = self, Greek]

axon: a single, long process that conducts information away from the cell body of the neuron

axonal propagation: the movement of the action potential down an axon

axon hillock: a thickened area on the soma that gives rise to the axon

B-cell: a white blood cell that is part of the immune system and functions by targeting specific microorganisms using antibodies

Babinsky reflex: positive when a touch to the ball of the foot causes the toes to fan; negative when a touch to the bottom of the foot causes the toes to curl

Ballint's syndrome: a visual disorder in which the affected individual has difficulty locating and reaching for objects in the environment

baroreceptors: receptors located in large veins that monitor blood pressure

basal ganglia: a group of subcortical nuclei that sends and receives information about movement to and from the cerebrum

basal metabolism: the minimum amount of energy expended while a person is at rest

basilar membrane: the thin, flexible membrane in the cochlea that supports the hair cells

bed nucleus of the stria terminalis: a forebrain structure that relays information from the limbic system to the paraventricular nucleus

behavioral genetics: a discipline that studies the genetic basis of behavior and attempts to apply this knowledge to the treatment of behavioral disorders

behavioral neuroscience: a field of neuroscience in which brain function is manipulated and the effect on behavior measured cognitive neuroscience: a field of neuroscience in which cognitive events are manipulated in order to observe the effect on brain functioning

Bell-Magendie law: the rule that motor nerves exit from the ventral horns of the spinal cord and sensory nerves enter the dorsal horns

benzodiazepines: minor tranquilizers that stimulate GABA activity and produce a feeling of calm

beta-adrenergic receptor: a receptor that, when stimulated by norepinephrine, inhibits CRH release and suppresses the stress response of the HPA axis

beta-amyloid peptide: a protein found in neurons that is responsible for the formation of amyloid plaques

beta waves: fast, irregular brain waves associated with states of excitation that occur at a frequency of 13–50 Hz

bilateral: on both sides [*bis-* = twice; *lateralis* = side, Latin]

biological clock: a mechanism controlled by the suprachiasmic nucleus that regulates sleep–wake cycles

biological markers: abnormalities shared by members of a particular subpopulation that are presumed to be evidence of an underlying biological problem

biological psychology: a discipline that involves the study of brain mechanisms underlying behavior

bipolar disorder: a mood disorder in which the affected individual will show symptoms of depression at some times and symptoms of mania at others

bipolar neuron: a neuron with two processes [*bi-* = two, Latin]

blastocyst: a hollow, fluid-filled ball that results from division and redivision of the fertilized egg

blindness: a disorder in which a person is unable to see and recognize objects visually

blindsight: a phenomenon in which a person cannot see an object but will reach accurately toward the object

blobs: specialized areas in HV1 that receive information from the parvocellular layers of the lateral geniculate nucleus

bombesin: an amphibian peptide that inhibits eating

borderline personality disorder: a personality disorder characterized by impulsivity and disturbances in mood, self-image, interpersonal relationships, and self-control

bottom-up: research strategies that involve studying the basic levels of brain function in order to understand higher level behavioral functions

brain stem: composed of the hindbrain, midbrain, and diencephalon

Broca's aphasia: a disorder of language production associated with damage to Broca's area, also called verbal aphasia

Broca's area: an area of the inferior frontal cortex associated with the production of speech

Brodmann's classification system: a system of cerebral mapping that divides the cortex into approximately 50 areas, based on their microscopic appearance

brown fat metabolism: a mechanism of nonshivering thermogenesis that involves burning brown fat to produce heat

bulimia nervosa: an eating disorder characterized by binge eating followed by self-induced vomiting or laxative use

busiprone (Buspar): a drug that alters dopamine activity and is used to treat anxiety

C-fibers: thin, unmyelinated axons

c-fos: a protein produced in a neuron following excitation of the neuron

callosotomy: surgical division of the corpus callosum [*callous-* = callosum; *-otomy* = to cut, Latin]

calorie: a unit of heat energy [*calor-* = heat, Latin]

calorigenic hormones: hormones released by the thyroid gland that produce an increase in body temperature [*calori-* = heat; *-genic* = to create]

cancer: a disease state characterized by the uncontrolled growth of abnormal tissue called tumors

cannabinoid hypothesis of schizophrenia: an explanation of schizophrenia that focuses on the role of endogenous cannabinoids in cognitive impairments observed in schizophrenia

cannabinoid receptor: a newly discovered receptor that binds with anandamide and tetrahydrocannabinol

Cannabis sativa: scientific name for marijuana

Cannon-Bard theory of emotion: an explanation of emotion that maintains that a stimulus elicits an emotion, which produces physiological changes

cannula: miniature tube used to carry chemicals into the brain

capsaicin: an ingredient in hot peppers that produces the burning sensation that we associate with spicy foods

cardiocentric: heart-centered [*kardia-*, Greek, or *cardio-*, Latin, = heart; *-centrum* = center, Latin]

cardiovascular disease: disorders of the heart and blood vessels [*cardio-* = heart; *-vascular* = refers to vessels]

cascade theory of reward: an explanation of how serotonin, endorphin, and GABA participate in the release of dopamine in the nucleus accumbens and hippocampus to produce feelings of pleasure or well-being

case study: a method of investigation in which one or more patients are thoroughly examined for behavioral disorders and associated brain abnormalities

cataplexy: episode in which the affected individual loses all muscle tone

cataract: a visual disorder in which the lens becomes opaque and vision is obstructed

catechol-O-methyltransferase (COMT): an intracellular enzyme that deactivates catecholamines

caudate nucleus: a structure in the striatum of the basal ganglia that processes cognitive information

cavernous sinus: a large pool of venous blood at the base of the skull

cell differentiation: the third stage of brain development in which immature neurons begin to change shape to attain their mature adult form

cell membrane: outer surface of any animal cell

cell migration: the second stage of brain development in which neurons migrate from the neural tube to their final position in the nervous system

cell proliferation: the first stage of brain development in which neurons are formed along the neural tube at a rate of about 250,000 per minute

centenarian: a person who is 100 years of age or older [*cent-* = one hundred, Latin]

central canal: channel that runs down the center of the spinal cord that contains cerebrospinal fluid

central nervous system: the nervous system, composed of the brain and spinal cord

central sulcus: a groove that separates the frontal lobe from the parietal lobe

cerebellar cortex: the cerebellum's outermost layer, which contains Purkinje, Golgi, stellate, basket, and granule cells

cerebellar mutism: a condition immediately following cerebellar surgery in which the affected individual cannot speak

cerebellum hindbrain: structure that controls motor coordination and coordinates movement in response to sensory stimuli [*cerebellum* = little cerebrum, Latin]

cerebral cortex: outermost layers of the cerebrum that contain neurons [*cortex* = bark, rind, Greek]

cerebral hemispheres: the two (left and right) halves of the cerebrum [*hemi-* = half, Greek]

cerebral laceration: head trauma caused by tearing of the outer surface of the brain

cerebral palsy: a motor disorder caused by damage to the developing brain

cerebrospinal fluid: a watery fluid found in the ventricles of the brain and in the spinal cord

cerebrovascular accident: a stroke, in which blood flow to brain structures is interrupted

cerebrum: largest structure in the brain, believed to be the seat of consciousness [*cerebrum* = brain, Latin]

cervical: region of the spinal cord located in the neck [*cervix* = neck, Greek]

chemical synapse: a junction between two neurons that communicate using neurotransmitters

chemoreceptors: receptors that respond to chemical stimuli

cholecystokinin: a peptide released from the duodenum that inhibits eating

chorea: involuntary contractions that produce movements of the head, arms, and legs [*chorea* = dance, Latin]

chromatography: a type of chemical analysis that permits the isolation, identification, and measurement of specific chemical substance

chromosome: structure found in the cell nucleus that contain strings of nucleic acids that code for various genes

chronic fatigue syndrome: a disorder characterized by symptoms of weakness, lethargy, tiredness, impaired concentration or memory, sore throat, and/or muscle and joint pain that last for more than 6 months

chronic stressor: a stressor that occurs repeatedly or for prolonged periods of time

circadian rhythm: a sleep–wake cycle that is approximately 24 hours long in most people [*circa* = about; *dies* = day, Latin]

classical conditioning: a form of implicit learning in which a conditioned stimulus is associated with an unconditioned stimulus and comes to produce a conditioned response, also known as Pavlovian conditioning

classical neurotransmitter: a neurotransmitter that binds to a receptor that is attached to a ligand-gated ion channel

Clock gene: a gene in mice that produces their circadian rhythm

clonus: a series of jerks produced in a limb that is stretched following extrapyramidal damage

coccygeal: region of the spinal cord located at the base of the spine [*coccyx* = tail, Greek]

cochlea: a spiral-shaped canal that contains the inner ear [*cochlea* = snail, Latin]

cochlear duct: the scala media, which contains the organ of Corti

cochlear implant: a device that is surgically placed in the brain where it can stimulate the auditory nerve

cochlear nucleus: a group of neurons in the medulla that receives auditory information from the auditory nerve

cognitive neuroscience: a field of neuroscience in which cognitive events are manipulated in order to observe the effect on brain functioning

colliculi: superior and inferior hill-like structures in the midbrain that process visual and auditory information, respectively

coma: a state of unconsciousness in which the eyes remain closed

computational neuroscience: a field that relates the activity of brain cells to the processing of information in the brain, with the aid of computer-generated models of brain circuits

computed tomography (CT): a recording technique that provides a three-dimensional image of the brain as a result of passing a series of X rays through the head at various angles

concordant: sharing a particular trait

concussion: head trauma that is caused by a blow to the head that bruises the brain

conduction: a heat loss mechanism that involves losing heat to the surrounding air or objects in the environment

conduction aphasia: a communication disorder in which affected individuals have good language production and comprehension but cannot repeat what is said to them

cone: a visual receptor that responds best in bright light

congenital adrenal hyperplasia: a disorder that causes androgens to build up in the female body

congestive dysmenorrhea: a condition that occurs premenstrually and is experienced as abdominal pain and tenderness

consciousness: an awareness of one's self, one's surroundings, and one's behavior

consolidation: a process in which memories are transferred from short-term memory to long-term memory

contrecoup: in a head injury, the point on the opposite side of the head from the point of impact

control subjects: participants in a study who do not receive the treatment under investigation

contusion: head trauma in which the head is jarred with such force that the brain becomes shifted in the skull and is badly bruised

cornea: transparent covering on the front of the eye that aids in focusing light as it enters the eye

corpus callosum: large tract that connects neurons in the left and right cerebral hemispheres

corpus luteum: a yellowish structure in the ovary, which was formerly a ruptured follicle, that produces progesterone [*corpus-* = body; *-luteum* = yellow, Latin]

cortex: the outermost surface of the brain [*cortex* = bark, rind, Greek]

corticosterone: a glucocorticoid produced by rats

corticostriatal system: pathway that projects from the cerebral cortex to the

basal ganglia, which is involved in the formation of nondeclarative memories

corticotropic-releasing hormone (CRH): a hormone released by the paraventricular nucleus that stimulates the release of ACTH from the anterior pituitary gland

cortisol: a glucocorticoid produced by humans

counterirritation: a method for treating pain that uses a brief irritating stimulus to counteract ongoing pain

coup: the point of impact in a head injury

cranial nerves: 12 pairs of nerves that enter and exit the brain through holes in the skull

craniosacral: arising from the brain and sacral region of the spinal cord

craniotomy: an incision in the skull [*crani-* = skull; *-otomy* = to cut, Latin]

Creutzfeldt-Jakob dementia: a progressive dementia that is associated with a prion infection

crista: a structure in the ampulla that contains the vestibular hair cell receptors

crossed extensor reflex: extension of a limb in response to a noxious stimulus applied to the contralateral limb [*contra-* = opposite; *-lateral* = side, Latin]

crossover: a type of experimental procedure in which all subjects receive the treatment under study at some time during the experiment and receive the control condition (or placebo) at another time during the experiment

cryoprobe: a probe that is inserted into the brain to cool specific regions [*krumos* = cold, Greek]

curare: a nicotinic antagonist that produces paralysis

cycle: one complete wave

cytoarchitectonic typing: the process of classifying areas of the cerebral cortex based on their microscopic appearance

cytochrome oxidase: an enzyme in a special stain that reveals the presence of blob and interblob regions in area V1

cytoplasm: fluid found within a cell [*cyto-* = cell, hollow vessel; *-plasm* = plasma, Greek]

cytoplasmic inclusions: abnormal structures found in the cytoplasm of neurons

cytotoxic: having a destructive effect on cells [*cyto-* = cell; *-toxic* = poisonous, Latin]

dark adaptation: a process in which the photopigments become unbleached in the dark, which allows the receptor to become sensitive to light again

deafness: a condition in which an individual cannot perceive auditory stimuli

decibel: unit used to measure loudness

declarative memory: explicit memory, or the conscious retention of facts and events

delayed-sleep-phase syndrome: a disorder in which affected individuals do not feel tired until many hours after normal sleep time and awaken much later than normal

delta waves: large synchronized brain waves with a frequency of 0.5–2.5 Hz that are observed in deeper stages of sleep

dementia: a disorder that involves an impairment of memory, thinking, and emotional function

dementia praecox: the term that Emil Kraepelin introduced to refer to the disorder known as schizophrenia

dementia pugilistica: an irreversible psychotic state caused by brain trauma that results from repeated blows to the head [*pugilist* = boxer, Latin]

dendrite: multibranched neuronal process that receives messages from other neurons

dendritic spines: tiny projections on dendrites that contain special proteins that process signals from other neurons

denervation hypersensitivity: the heightened responsiveness of a denervated postsynaptic neuron to excitatory messages from remaining presynaptic neurons

depersonalization: a state in which affected individuals feel as if they are outside their own body

depolarization: a state in which a neuron loses its negative charge [*de-* = from, Latin]

dermatome: body region innervated by one spinal nerve [*derma-* = skin; *-tomo* = slice, Latin]

desipramine: a drug that blocks the reuptake of norepinephrine and is an effective antidepressant

desynchronized brain waves: rapid, irregular brain waves that are observed during conscious states

dexamethasone: a form of synthetic glucocorticoid that inhibits the release of CRH and ACTH

dexamethasone suppression test: a test that assesses the ability of the HPA axis to regulate glucocorticoid release, which can be used to diagnose depression

diabetes mellitus: another name for Type I diabetes [*mell-* = honey; *itus-* = urine]

diathesis–stress model: a theoretical model that proposes that people who are predisposed to develop schizophrenia have a biological weakness that makes them vulnerable to the effects of stress

dichorionic: having two separate placentas [*di-* = two; *chorion* = placenta, Greek]

dichromat: an individual with two functional cone types who has impaired color vision [*di-* = two, Greek]

diencephalon: forebrain area that contains the thalamus and hypothalamus [*di-* = two; *-encephalon* = brain, Greek]

dihydrotestosterone: the androgen that converts the embryonic external genitalia into the penis and scrotum

discordant: twins who do not share a particular trait

disequilibrium: a loss of balance

dishabituation: an orienting response in a habituated individual to a new or different stimulus

dissociative state: a disorder in which the affected individual experiences altered sensory perceptions, memory loss, and distortion of time perception and identity

distal stimulus: object in the visual field

dizygotic twins: fraternal twins, twins that developed from two fertilized eggs [*di-* = two; *-zygote* = fertilized egg, Greek]

DNA: deoxyribonucleic acid, the type of nucleic acid found in chromosomes

dopamine: a monoamine neurotransmitter that is a precursor of norepinephine and epinephrine

dopamine hypothesis of schizophrenia: the leading biological explanation of schizophrenia that focuses on the role of dopamine in the development and maintenance of schizophrenia

dorsal: toward the back [*dorsum* = back, Latin]

dorsal stream: a visual pathway that is involved in detecting motion and the location of objects in the visual field; the "Where" system

dorsolateral corticospinal tract: group of axons that carries messages from the primary motor cortex to motor neurons in the spinal cord [*cortico-* = from the cortex; *-spinal* = to the spinal cord]

dorsolateral prefrontal cortex: a region of the prefrontal cortex that processes auditory "Where" information; it's also implicated in the development of schizophrenia as it reaches functional maturity in late adolescence

double blind study: an experiment in which neither the participant nor the experimenter knows if the participant is getting the experimental treatment

double dissociation: a type of experiment in which two groups of subjects receive lesions in different regions of the brain and are tested on two different behavioral tasks following recovery

down-regulation: a reduction in the number of receptor sites available for an overabundant neurochemical in the brain

Down's syndrome: a disorder, characterized by mental retardation, that is associated with the presence of three chromosomes for chromosome 21

drive: a condition that motivates an individual to perform a particular behavior or set of behaviors

dualism: a theory that the body and the mind are two separate entities [*dualis, duo* = two, Latin]

duodenum: the first segment of the small intestine connected directly to the stomach

dura mater: tough outer layer of the meninges [*dura* = hard, Latin]

dysarthria: a disorder in which affected individuals cannot control the rate, volume, or rhythm of their speech

dysgeusia: a disagreeable taste in the mouth due to infection, medication, tumors, or chemotherapy

dysmenorrhea: a condition in which a woman experiences painful menstruation

dysplasia: a developmental brain disorder in which neurons retain immature shapes or grow abnormal dendrites and axons, due to an insult during the cell differentiation stage [*dys-* = bad, Greek]

E4: an aberrant allele of the ApoE gene that directs the production of a destructive form of ApoE, which causes neurofibrillary tangles associated with Alzheimer's disease to develop

eardrum: the tympanic membrane, which is stretched across the end of the ear canal

-ectomy: a suffix that refers to a surgery in which body tissue is removed

ectopsia: a developmental brain disorder in which neurons do not migrate to their normal positions in the brain, due to an insult during the cell migration stage [*ecto-* = outside, Greek]

ectotherms: animals that have an external source of heat [*ecto-* = outside; *-therm* = heat, Greek]

electrical synapse: a gap junction between two neurons across which ions pass

electroconvulsive therapy: a procedure, used to treat profoundly depressed patients, in which a high-voltage electrical current is passed through a patient's brain, producing a seizure

electrode: electrical conducting medium

electroencephalography: a recording technique that measures the electrical activity of the brain [*en* + *kephalos* = in the head, brain; *graphos* = to record or write, Greek]

embryo: a developing organism that grows from a fertilized ovum

embryonic stem cells: another name for inner-cell-mass cells, cells capable of differentiating into many cell lines

emotion: a cognitive experience accompanied by an affective reaction and characteristic physiological response

encephalocentric: brain-centered [*en* + *kephalos* = in the head, Greek; *centrum* = center, Latin]

endogenous opiates: neurotransmitters that bind with opiate receptors

endorphins: endogenous opiate neurotransmitters that inhibit pain messages

endotherms: animals that have an internal source of heat [*endo-* = inside; *-therm* = heat, Greek]

endplate: chemically sensitive region on the muscle fiber that responds to acetylcholine

epinephrine: a neurohormone, also known as adrenaline, that is released by the adrenal gland and activates the sympathetic nervous system

episodic memory: memory for events in one's own life

esophageal fistula: an opening in the esophagus that leads directly to the outside of the neck

estrogen: a gonadal hormone produced by the ovaries

estrus: a time period during which a nonhuman female is sexually receptive

eustachian tube: a canal that runs from the middle ear to the throat

evaporation: a heat loss mechanism that involves turning a liquid into a gas

event-related potential: measured change in brain activity following the presentation of a stimulus

evoked potential: a type of event-related potential, or a change in recorded brain activity as measured by EEG, produced in response to a specific stimulus

evolutionary theory of sleep: an explanation of sleep that proposed that all animals sleep to conserve energy during times when it is dangerous or not necessary for them to be awake

excitatory postsynaptic potential: a small increase (~ +.5 mV) in the charge across a postsynaptic membrane

excitotoxin: a chemical that destroys cell bodies of neurons by overexciting them

exhibitionism: a paraphilia in which the affected individual gets sexual gratification from exposing his or her genitals to others, especially strangers

explicit learning: a change in behavior that has taken place with conscious awareness

expressive aphasia: disorders of language production [*a-* = without; *-phanas* = to speak, Greek]

extension: a movement that straightens a limb

external auditory meatus: the ear canal or opening in the temporal bone, leading to the eardrum

external genitalia: include the penis and scrotum in the male, and the clitoris and labia majora and minora in the female

extracellular: outside the cell [*extra-* = outside, Latin]

extracellular compartment: all water found outside the cells of the body

extrafusal fibers: long muscle fibers that run the entire length of the muscle [*extra-* = outside; *-fusa* = spindle, Latin]

extralemniscal pathway: the somatosensory pathway that relays information about pain and temperature to the brain

extralemniscal system: the somatosensory pathway that bypasses the medial lemniscus to reach the secondary somatosensory cortex [*extra-* = outside, Latin]

extrapyramidal motor system: the motor system that coordinates gross postural adjustments and arises from the cerebral cortex, basal ganglia, cerebellum, and reticular formation

facial nerve: cranial nerve VII, which controls the muscles of facial expression

failure of extinction: continuing to respond to a stimulus long after the stimulus (conditioned stimulus) and the stressor (unconditioned stimulus) have been paired

family studies: a type of genetic analysis that examines the rate of occurrence of a disorder within affected families

fatigue disorders: a cluster of disorders characterized by lethargy, loss of drive, and an increase in vegetative disorders such as sleeping and eating

fear conditioning: a process in which an individual learns to fear a neutral stimulus that has been paired with a fear-inducing stimulus

fenfluramine: a drug that reduces food intake by stimulating the satiety

fetal alcohol syndrome: a disorder, characterized by behavioral and cognitive deficits, that results from exposure of an embryo to alcohol during the early stages of brain development

fetus: a stage of development in which all of the organs have developed and are present in the body

fever: an increase in core body temperature above its normal level

fibromyalgia: a disorder characterized by fatigue, headaches, and numbness accompanied by widespread bone and muscle pain

fight-or-flight response: Walter Cannon's term for negative emotional reactions

5-hydroxindolacetic acid (5-HIAA): a serotonin metabolite used to estimate the levels of serotonin activity in the central nervous system

flashback: the emergence of vivid memories that causes a past event to be experienced as happening all over again

flexion: a movement that bends a limb

follicle-stimulating hormone (FSH): a gonadotrophic hormone that stimulates the maturation of immature egg and sperm

forebrain: the largest part of the brain, contains the cerebrum, basal ganglia, limbic system, thalamus, and hypothalamus

fourth ventricle: ventricle located in the hindbrain

fovea: a tiny dimple in the center of the retina where cones are concentrated [*fovea* = cup, Latin]

fragile X syndrome: a disorder, characterized by mental retardation, that is associated with a genetic variation on the X chromosome

frequency: the number of waves that occurs in a specified period of time, usually a second

frequency theory: a theory that proposes that vibrations of incoming sounds are translated into frequencies of action potentials

frontal lobe: most anterior lobe of the cerebrum, which contains the motor cortex and other centers of executive function

frontal lobe syndrome: a disorder caused by damage to the prefrontal cortex, characterized by impairment in attention and in organizing and planning tasks

fugue state: a disturbance in identity function in which affected persons do not know their own identity and have no memory of their past

functionalism: William James's explanation of behavior that identifies the survival benefit of a specific behavior to a particular species

functional magnetic resonance imaging (fMRI): a recording technique that is based on MRI technology and permits localization of accumulation of oxygenated hemoglobin in the brain, which is associated with brain activity

G protein-linked receptor: a protein embedded in a cell membrane that binds with a specific neurotransmitter, which activates G protein inside the neuron

galanin: a brain peptide that stimulates fat consumption

gamma-aminobutyric acid (GABA): a neurotransmitter that is the most abundant inhibitory neurotransmitter in the brain

gamma motor neurons: small motor neurons that innervate intrafusal muscle fibers

ganglia: (ganglion, singular) clusters of soma of neurons found in the peripheral nervous system

ganglion cells: cells on the retina whose axons form the optic nerve

gap junctions: special electrical connections between cells

gate-control theory of pain: a theory proposed by Melzack and Wall to explain how reactions to pain can be modified by inhibitory processes in the brain stem and A-fibers

gating hypothesis of schizophrenia: an explanation of schizophrenia that proposes that the filtering process that controls the relay of information to the cortex is faulty in schizophrenic people

general paresis: a psychotic disorder caused by an untreated syphilis infection

generalized anxiety disorder: a syndrome characterized by excessive apprehension about unknown future events

generalized seizure: a seizure disorder characterized by convulsions with bouts of clonus, followed by a period of unconsciousness

generator potential: a graded potential produced in a receptor when the receptor is stimulated by an appropriate stimulus

genetics: the study of the inheritance of genes

genome: the complete collection of genes that is encoded in a cell's chromosomes

genotype: the genes that a person possesses

glaucoma: a condition in which the intraocular pressure increases, producing damage to the optic nerve

glia: supporting cell in the nervous system

gliosis: the accumulation of glial cells

globus pallidus: a group of neurons that is part of the basal ganglia and receives information from the striatum

glomeruli: special structures in the olfactory bulb that each process information about one kind of odor

glucagon: a hormone produced by the pancreas that inhibits eating

glucocorticoid: a steroid hormone derived from the cortex of the adrenal gland

glucose: a simple sugar that is metabolized by neurons and other cells

glucostatic theory: a theory that postulates that glucose levels control food intake

glutamate: a neurotransmitter that is the most abundant excitatory neurotransmitter in the brain.

glycogen: a complex sugar stored in the liver that is broken down into glucose

glycogenesis: the manufacture of glycogen [*glyco-* = glycogen; *-genesis* = to create]

glycogenolysis: the breakdown of glycogen [*glyco-* = glycogen; *-lysis-* = to cut]

goal neglect: a disorder in which the affected individual disregards instructions and ignores requirements of a task, although the person can explain the instructions or rules

Golgi tendon: organs stretch receptors located in tendons

gonadal hormone: hormone produced by the male or female gonads

gonadotrophic hormones: hormones secreted by the pituitary gland that alter the function of the gonads [*gonado-* = gonad; *-trophic* = to change]

gonadotropin-releasing hormone: a hormone released by the hypothalamus, that signals the anterior pituitary to release follicle-stimulating hormone

Grade 1 concussion: a concussion characterized by confusion that lasts for less than 15 minutes, with no loss of consciousness

Grade 2 concussion: a concussion characterized by confusion that lasts for more than 15 minutes, with no loss of consciousness

Grade 3 concussion: a concussion characterized by any loss of consciousness that lasts from a few seconds to several minutes

grammar: rules that specify how morphemes are to be combined

grand mal seizure: a seizure disorder characterized by convulsions with bouts of clonus followed by unconsciousness

guevedoces: a disorder caused by a recessive gene that produces a deficiency of 5-alpha-reductase, which prevents the conversion of testosterone to dihydrotestosterone

gyrus: raised area in the surface of the cerebrum [*gyrus* = raised, Greek]

habituation: a decrease in response of the nervous system to a repeated stimulus, such as a chronic stressor

hair cells: specialized receptors in the auditory system, located in the cochlea

hallucination: an abnormal perceptual experience that occurs in the absence of external stimuli

Halstead-Reitan Neuropsychological Test Battery: a neuropsychological test battery that consists of eight tests that allow a neuropsychologist to assess the extent of brain damage

hammer: the first ossicle in the middle ear, which receives vibrations from the eardrum and relays them to the anvil

Hebb synapse: an increase in the synaptic strength between two neurons produced by repeated simultaneous firing of the two neurons

hedonic homeostatic dysregulation: a model that explains how an addiction develops, based on alterations in the reward pathway

hemianopia: a disorder in which a brain-damaged individual cannot see the visual field contralateral to the damaged side of the cerebrum [*hemi-* = half; *-a-* = without; *-opia* = vision, Latin]

hemispherectomy: surgical removal of a cerebral hemisphere [*hemispher-* = hemisphere; *-ectomy* = to remove]

hemorrhagic stroke: a stroke that results from a ruptured blood vessel, in which blood pools in extracellular spaces in the brain

hepatic encephalopathy: a brain disorder associated with liver dysfunction

Hertz: a unit of frequency (1 Hertz = 1 cycle/second)

high performance liquid chromatography (HPLC): a type of chromatography that is widely used in neuroscience research because of its great sensitivity

hindbrain: the part of the brain immediately superior to the spinal cord, consists of the medulla, pons, and cerebellum; also known as the rhombencephalon

hippocampus: structure in the limbic system associated with emotions and consolidation of memories

holism: a theory that the brain works as a whole to produce behavior [*holos* = whole, Greek]

holoprosencephaly: a developmental disorder in which only one cerebral hemisphere develops [*holo-* = whole; *-prosencephalon* = forebrain, Greek]

homeostasis: an internal mechanism that maintains certain biological variables at a constant level [*homeo-* = same; *-stasis* = stand, Greek]

homeothermic: animals that maintain a constant core body temperature [*homeo-* = same; *-therm* = heat, Greek]

homovanillic acid: the end product of dopamine metabolism that is used as a measure of dopamine availability

homunculi: little man [*homo-* = man; *-unculi* = diminutive form, Latin]

hormone: a chemical released by a gland

horseradish peroxidase labeling: a histochemical technique used to trace specific pathways in the brain

hot flash: a sudden increase in core body temperature that happens spontaneously in menopausal women

HPA axis: the connection between the hypothalamus, pituitary gland, and adrenal gland

human immunodeficiency virus (HIV): the virus believed to cause AIDS

Huntington's disease: a genetic disorder, linked to chromosome 4, which increases glutamate activity in the striatum, producing tics and uncontrollable muscle contractions

hydrocephalus: a disorder, caused by any number of insults to the brain, in which the flow of cerebrospinal fluid becomes blocked and fluid pressure within the ventricles increases [*hydro-* = water; *-cephalus* = brain, Greek]

hypercomplex cells: neurons in KV1 that respond best to stimuli with a particular length or width in a particular orientation

hyperekplexia: a familial startle disease, a disorder characterized by an overreactive orienting response

hyperglycemia: having higher than normal levels of glucose in the blood, caused by the underproduction of insulin [*hyper-* = greater than normal; *-glyc-* = sugar; *-emia* = in the blood]

hyperinsulinemia: having higher than normal levels of insulin in the blood [*hyper-* = more than normal; *insulin-* = insulin; *-emia* = in the blood]

hyperopia: farsightedness, in which a person cannot bring near objects into focus

hyperphagia: overeating [*hyper-* = more than normal; *-phagi* = to eat]

hyperpolarization: a state in which a neuron becomes more negatively charged than normal [*hyper-* = more, Greek]

hyperreflexia: a state in which reflexes are extremely reactive and exaggerated [*hyper-* = more than normal; *-reflexia* = reflexes, Greek]

hypertonic saline: a salt solution with a greater-than-normal concentration [*hyper-* = more than normal; *-tonic* = concentration]

hypertonic urea: a solution of urea and water that has greater-than-normal concentration [*hyper-* = more than normal; *-tonic* = concentration]

hypoglycemia: having lower than normal levels of glucose in the blood, caused by the overproduction of insulin [*hypo-* = less than normal; *-glyc-* = sugar; *-emia* = in the blood]

hypogonadism: a disorder in which a man has reduced levels of testosterone [*hypo-* = less than normal; *-gonad* = gonad]

hypokalemia: the depletion of potassium levels in the blood [*hypo-* = less than normal; *-kalium* = potassium; *-emia* = in the blood]

hypoplasia: a developmental brain disorder in which fewer cells are found in a given region of the brain, due to an insult during the cell proliferation stage [*hypo-* = less than normal, Greek]

hypothalamus: a structure in the diencephalon that controls the pituitary gland and regulates motivated behaviors [*hypo-* = below; *-thalamus* = thalamus, Greek]

hypothermia: decreased body temperature [*hypo-* = less than normal; *-thermia* = temperature]

hypothesis: proposal, supposition [*hypothesis* = proposal, Greek]

hypothyroid: a condition caused by a deficiency in thyroid activity [*hypo-* = less than normal]

hypovolemic thirst: thirst that is produced when fluid in the extracellular compartment becomes reduced in volume [*hypo-* = less than normal; *vol-* = volume; *emic* = in the blood]

ibotenic acid: an excitotoxin that destroys cell bodies of neurons

imipramine: a drug that blocks the reuptake of catecholamines and is used to treat anxiety disorders

immunocytochemistry: a technique that uses immune system reactions to trace brain activity from one neuron to the next [*immuno-* = relating to immune system; *-cyto* = cell, Greek]

implicit learning: the acquisition of behaviors for which we have no conscious awareness

incus: the anvil, or second of the three ossicles in the middle ear

inferior: lower, below [*inferos* = lower, Latin]

inferior colliculus: a midbrain structure that receives and processes auditory information [*colliculus* = little hill, Latin]

inferior parietal cortex: cortical area believed to process "What" somatosensory information

infertility: a condition in which a woman cannot conceive and become pregnant

infundibulum: the thin, stalklike structure between the hypothalamus and the pituitary gland

inhibitory postsynaptic potential: a small decrease (~ −.5 mV) in the charge across a postsynaptic membrane

inner ear: the innermost part of the ear, consisting of the cochlea

inner-cell-mass cells: cells in the blastocyst that differentiate into different cell types

insomnia: a disorder in which the affected individual has difficulty falling asleep or staying asleep [*in-* = without; *-somn* = sleep, Latin]

institutional animal care and use committee (IACUC): a committee, composed of scientists and nonscientists, that approves all experimentation with nonhuman animals at a particular institution

insula: area of the frontal lobe superior to the Sylvian fissure where the primary taste cortex is located

insulin: a pancreatic hormone that produces satiation

interblobs: nonbloblike regions in area V1 that receive information from the magnocellular layers of the lateral geniculate nucleus

intermittent explosive disorder: a disorder characterized by episodes of uncontrolled, aggressive outbursts that result in assaults causing personal injury or property damage

internal genitalia: include the vas deferens, epididymis, and the prostate gland in the male, and the vagina, uterus, and fallopian tubes in the female

interneuron: an intrinsic neuron that receives information from one neuron and passes it on to another

interoception: the sense that arises from one's internal organs [*intero-* = internal, Latin]

intersexed: a condition in which a person has an atypical reproductive anatomy

interstitial cell–stimulating hormone: a gonadotrophic hormone that stimulates the release of testosterone

interstripe regions: regions of area V2 that receive their information from both the blob and interblob regions of area V1 and transmit this information to area V3

intracellular: inside the cell [*intra-* = inside, Latin]

intracellular compartment: all water located inside cells of the body

intrafusal fibers: muscle fibers located inside muscle spindles [*intra-* = inside; *-fusa* = spindle, Latin]

intralaminar nucleus: a nucleus of the thalamus that controls the transmission of information from the hindbrain to the cerebrum

in vitro: in cultured cells on a lab bench [*in* = in; *vitro* = glass, Latin]

in vivo: in a living body [*in* = in; *vivus* = living, Latin]

ion: an electrically charged molecule

ion channel: special pores in the cell membrane that permit passage of ions into and out of the cell

ionotropic receptor: a receptor that directly opens an ion channel

ipsilateral: on the same side [*ipsa-* = same, Latin]

iris: the circular, colored structure in the front of the eye that regulates the diameter of the pupil

ischemic stroke: a stroke that results from clogged arteries in the brain, decreasing blood flow

isometric contraction: contraction of a muscle that is fixed in length, causing an increase in muscle tone [*iso-* = same; *-metric* = length, Greek]

isotonic contraction: shortening of a muscle that causes movement of a body part [*iso-* = same; *-tonic* = tone, Greek]

James-Lange theory of emotion: an explanation of emotion that maintains that the physiological response to a stimulus produces an emotion

jargon aphasia: a language disorder in which the affected individual speaks fluently with perfect grammar although the content is nonsensical

jet lag: a disturbance of the sleep–wake cycle caused by taking a long flight that crosses several time zones

K-complexes: large changes in voltage in EEG records observed only in Stage II sleep

Kennard effect: the observation that behavioral function develops normally when brain damage occurs in infancy

kinesthesia: the ability to sense movement [*kine-* = to move; *-ethesia* = to sense, Greek]

Klein-Levin syndrome: a rare obesity disorder associated with extremely high levels of testosterone

Kluver-Bucy syndrome: a disorder caused by bilateral damage to the anterior temporal lobe that is characterized by a loss of fear, a lack of emotional responsiveness, inappropriate sexual behavior, and indiscriminate mouthing of inedible items

knockout model: a technique in which a single gene is eliminated to determine its role in a particular behavior

knockout mutants: offspring of animals that possess the knockout gene

Korsakoff's syndrome: a cognitive disorder involving retrograde and anterograde amnesia, caused by a thiamine deficiency in alcoholics

L-dopa: a drug, used to treat Parkinson's disease, which crosses the blood–brain

barrier and is converted to dopamine in the brain

labyrinth system: another name for the vestibular system

lamina terminalis: the most anterior region of the hypothalamus, which is involved in the initiation of drinking

language: a formalized system of symbolic representations that we use to communicate ideas, questions, and commands

lateral: toward the side [*lateralis* = side, Latin]

lateral geniculate nucleus (LGN): a nucleus in the thalamus that receives information directly from ganglion cells in the retina and relays it on the visual cortex

lateral hemiretina: the half of the retina is nearest the side of the head [*laterall* = side, Latin]

lateral hypothalamus: an area of the hypothalamus responsible for the initiation of allostatic eating

lateral inhibition: a process in which neurons (such as horizontal cells) inhibit neighboring neurons

lateral ventricle: ventricle located in the telencephalon

law of equipotentiality: Lashley's finding that the entire cortex is capable of learning and memory

law of mass action: Lashley's finding that the amount of brain damage determines the extent of the behavioral deficit observed

learned helplessness: decreased motor activity and decreased avoidance in response to exposure to an inescapable stressor

lemniscal pathway: the somatosensory pathway that relays information about pressure and stretching to the brain

lens: a yellowish, transparent structure located inside the eyeball that focuses light on the retina

leptin: a hormone secreted by fat cells that suppresses food intake

lesioning: destroying or disrupting the function of a specific brain structure

Lewy's bodies: abnormal structures found in the cytoplasm of neurons in people who suffer from Parkinson's dementia

libido: sex drive

ligand: a chemical that binds to receptors on neurons

ligand-gated channel: ion channels that have a special protein attached that binds with a neurotransmitter or other chemical

ligand-gated ion channel receptor: a protein on the cell membrane that is

attached to a ligand-gated channel and binds with a specific neurotransmitter

limbic system: the two brain circuits that regulate emotions

linkage analysis: a type of genetic analysis that studies whether a gene associated with a biological marker is linked to the gene responsible for the disorder

lipofuscin: a yellow, insoluble fatty substance that accumulates in the brains of elderly individuals and destroys neurons

lipogenic: storing or creating fat [*lipo-* = fat; *-genic* = to create]

lipostatic theory: a theory that postulates that we eat to maintain an optimum level of body fat

liver: an organ in the digestive system that produces and stores glycogen and may play a role in the regulation of short-term food intake

localization: a theory that specific structures in the brain control specific behaviors [*localis* = place, Latin]

locked-in syndrome: a disorder in which the person's motor system is detached from conscious control, although the person is fully conscious and aware

locus coeruleus: hindbrain structure that produces norepinephrine and regulates arousal

long-term memory: a memory system in which large amounts of information are stored indefinitely

long-term potentiation: an increase in the readiness of a postsynaptic neuron to fire following repeated stimulation by the presynaptic neuron

lordosis: a position assumed by the receptive female animal, in which her hindquarters are raised to permit intromission of the penis into the vagina

loss of psychic self-activation: a disorder characterized by mental and motor inactivity except when the individual is stimulated by an environmental demand

loudness: a psychological phenomenon that corresponds to amplitude of sound waves

loudness difference: difference in the intensity of the sound reaching each ear

lumbar: region of the spinal cord located in the lower back

Luria-Nebraska Neuropsychological Test Battery: a neuropsychological test battery that allows a neuropsychologist to assess the extent of brain damage

luteinizing hormone (LH): a gonadotrophic hormone that initiates ovulation and stimulates the development of the corpus luteum

macronutrients: nutrients that we need to eat in large quantities [*macro-* = large, Greek]

macrophage: a blood cell that is part of the immune system and destroys invading microorganisms in a nonspecific way

macula: sensitive region in the utricle and saccule of the vestibular system that contains the hair cell receptors

macula lutea: yellowish spot in the center of the retina that contains the fovea [*macula* = spot; *lutea* = yellow, Latin]

macular degeneration: a disorder in which cones in the macula lutea die, causing blindness

magnetoencephalography: a recording technique that measures magnetic fields generated by the brain [*en* + *kephalos* = in the head, brain; *graphos* = to record or write, Greek]

magnocellular layers: two bottom layers of the lateral geniculate nucleus that process information about form, spatial relations, and motion

major depressive disorder: a mood disorder characterized by lethargy, sad affect, diminished interest in all activities, cognitive disturbances, and eating and sleeping abnormalities

malleus: hammer, or the first of three ossicles, which is adjacent to the eardrum

manic-depressive disorder: an older term for bipolar disorder

MAO inhibitor: an antidepressant medication that inhibits the enzyme that breaks down monoamines, thereby increasing their availability at the synapse

mechanoreceptors: receptors that respond to mechanical stimulation, such as pulling, stretching, or vibrating

medial: toward the midline [*medius* = middle, Latin]

medial forebrain bundle: a bundle of neurons that courses through the center of the forebrain, which is associated with positive emotion

medial geniculate nucleus: a thalamic nucleus that receives auditory information from the midbrain and sends it to the auditory cortex in the temporal lobe

medial preoptic area: an area of the hypothalamus that appears to regulate the expression of male sexual behavior

medulla hindbrain: structure that controls life-support functions

melancholia: an older term for depression first suggested by Hippocrates [*melan-* = black; *chole-* = bile, Greek]

melatonin: a hormone that signals information about the environmental light/dark cycle to the rest of the brain

memory impairment: a symptom associated with a number of disorders, including stress-related disorders, in which memory storage or retrieval is disrupted

Meniere's disease: a disorder characterized by symptoms of vestibular dysfunction, including dizziness and unsteadiness

meninges: protective covering for the central nervous system

menopause: a period in a woman's life following the cessation of the production of sex hormones

menstruation: a process in the human female body in which the uterus sheds its lining, producing a bloody discharge, when estrogen and progesterone levels fall

mesencephalon: midbrain [*mes-* = mid; *-encephalon* = brain, Greek]

mesocortical dopamine pathway: a dopamine pathway that runs from the midbrain to the cerebral cortex [*meso-* = mid]

mesolimbic dopamine pathway: a dopamine pathway associated with positive emotions that extends from the ventral tegmentum in the midbrain to the limbic system [*meso-* = mid]

mesoprefrontal cortex: an area of the prefrontal cortex near the midline that is affected by chronic stress

metabotropic receptor: receptor that activates second messengers

metacognition: an awareness of one's own mental processes

metastasis: the movement of tumor cells from their site of origin to another site in the body [*meta-* = to change; *-stasis* = place, Greek]

microdialysis: an in vivo technique that permits sampling of brain chemicals [*mikros* = small; *dialysis* = separation, Greek]

microelectrode: tiny electrode used to measure the electrical activity of individual neurons [*mikros* = small, Greek]

microglia: tiny glial cells [*mikros* = small, Greek]

micronutrients: nutrients that we need to eat in minuscule quantities [*mikros* = small, Greek]

microspectrophotometer: a device that measures the wavelengths of light that are absorbed by the visual receptors

midbrain: the mesencephalon, consists of the tectum, the tegmentum, and a ventral region that contains the reticular formation

middle ear: the part of the ear that contains the eardrum, three ossicles, and the eustachian tube

midget ganglion cells: small or parvocellular ganglion cells in the retina that receive their information from cones

mitochondrion: organelle that produces ATP, the energy source for the cell

monism: a theory that the mind is not separable from the body [*mono* = single, Greek]

monoamine: a chemical compound that contains one amino group [*mono-* = one, Latin]

monoamine hypothesis of depression: the most widely accepted explanation of depression, which proposes that depression occurs when the availability or activity of one or more monoamines is reduced

monoamine oxidase (MAO): an intracellular enzyme that deactivates monoamines

monochorionic: sharing the same placenta [*mono-* = one; *chorion* = placenta, Greek]

monochromat: an individual who possesses only one functional cone type and sees only black and white and grays [*mono-* = one]

monocular: pertaining to one eye [*mono-* = one; *-oculo* = eye, Latin]

monogenic model: a model that proposes that a single gene produces a particular trait [*mono-* = one; *-genic* = gene]

monopolar neuron: a neuron with only one process [*mono-* = one, Latin]

monozygotic twins: identical twins, or twins that develop from the same fertilized egg [*mono-* = one; *-zygote* = fertilized egg, Greek]

morphemes: meaningful units of sound

motor cortex: located in the precentral gyrus, directs fine motor coordination

motor neuron: a neuron in the central nervous that stimulates muscle contractions

motor pool: the total aggregate of all motor neurons that controls one muscle

Müllerian ducts: the precursors of the female internal genitalia

Müllerian inhibiting substance: a hormone produced by the testes that inhibits the development of the Müllerian ducts

multiple personality disorder: a disturbance in identity function in which the affected person can have a number of different personae, some of whom are unaware of the other personae

multipolar neuron: a neuron with many processes [*multi-* = many, Latin]

muscarine: a muscarinic agonist, binds with G protein-linked acetylcholine receptor

muscarinic receptor: a protein-linked receptor that binds with both muscarine and acetylcholine

muscle fiber: a long, thin muscle cell

muscle spindles: composed of several intrafusal fibers that are joined to a nuclear bag containing an annulospiral receptor

muscle tone: the vigor of a muscular contraction

muscular dystrophy: a disorder characterized by wasting of the muscle fibers, which causes muscular weakness

myasthenia gravis: a disorder characterized by progressive loss of acetylcholine receptors in the neuromuscular junction

myelin: a fatty material that forms a sheath around axons

myopia: nearsightedness, in which an individual cannot see far objects clearly

myosin: thick filaments found in muscle fibers

narcolepsy: a disorder characterized by seizure-like attacks in which the affected individual loses all muscle tone and falls asleep [*narco-* = sleep; *-lepsy* = fit or seizure, Greek]

nasal hemiretina: the half of the retina nearest the nose [*hemi-* = half, Latin]

natural selection: Darwin's theory that proposes that specific traits selectively develop because animals that survive pass them on to their offspring

necrotic: dead [*nekrosis* = death, Greek]

negative afterimage: a perceptual illusion produced by fatigue of neurons in the visual system

negative emotion: an emotion accompanied by feelings of anxiety, depression, or hostility, which makes us avoid the eliciting stimulus

negative reinforcement: a stimulus whose removal increases the likelihood of the behavior that precedes its removal

negative resting potential: the electrical charge across the cell membrane when a neuron is at rest

negative symptoms of schizophrenia: those behaviors observed in schizophrenic individuals who demonstrate diminished functioning

nerve: bundle of axons in the peripheral nervous system

nerve growth factor (NGF): a protein that promotes the survival of specific neurons in the peripheral and central nervous systems during development and maturation, stimulating the regrowth of axons and sprouting of nearby axons and dendrites

nervous system: one of the body's major systems, composed of neurons and glia

neural tube: a groove formed in the developing embryo, along which neurons develop

neuritic plaques: another name for amyloid plaques

neurofibrillary tangles: twisted masses of protein located in the cytoplasm of neurons seen in brains of persons with Alzheimer's disease but not normally in normal brains

neurogenesis: growth of neurons [*-genesis* = to create]

neurohormone: a chemical released into the bloodstream that travels to target neurons

neuroleptics: dopamine antagonists used to treat schizophrenia

neuromelanin: a dark-staining insoluble pigment that accumulates in the brains of elderly individuals and destroys neurons

neuromodulator: a neurotransmitter that binds with a G protein-linked receptor

neuromuscular junction: synapse between the axon of the motor neuron and a muscle fiber

neuron: a specialized cell that is the fundamental unit of the nervous system [*neuron* = nerve, sinew, Greek]

neuropeptide Y: a brain peptide that stimulates the intake of carbohydrates

neuropsychology: the study of higher functions and their disorders following brain injury or disease

neuroscience: a multidisciplinary approach to studying the brain

neurotoxins: chemicals that target and destroy specific neurons or impair their function [*neuro-* = neuron; *-toxin* = poison]

neurotransmitters: chemicals released by neurons to signal neurons and other cells

neurotrophins: special signaling proteins that direct the growth and organization of the nervous system

nicotine: a nicotinic agonist, binds with acetylcholine ligand-gated ion channels

nicotinic receptor: a ligand-gated ion channel receptor that binds with both nicotine and acetylcholine

nightmare: a dream loaded with negative emotional content

night terror: a phenomenon that occurs during non-REM sleep in which the affected individual awaken from deep sleep frightened and showing signs of autonomic arousal

nitric oxide: an atypical neurotransmitter that readily diffuses across the cell membrane of a neuron

NMDA receptors: a type of glutamate receptor, associated with long-term potentiation, that is typically blocked with magnesium

nocturnal animals: animals that are active at night and sleep during the day

NMDA receptor hypofunction hypothesis: one explanation of schizophrenia that focuses on the role of underactive NMDA (glutamate) receptors in the development of schizophrenia

nocturnal enuresis: bed-wetting, which occurs in non-REM sleep

nodes of Ranvier: breaks in the myelin sheath

nominal aphasia: another name for anomia

nondeclarative memory: implicit memory, or nonconscious memory for learned behaviors

nonopiate transmitters: a second class of neurotransmitters that inhibit pain messages

nonseasonal breeders: animals that mate throughout the year, regardless of season

nonshivering thermogenesis: the production of heat by processes other than shivering [*thermo-* = heat; *-genesis* = to create, Greek]

norepinephrine: a monoamine neurotransmitter that plays a role in mood, drive reduction, sleep, arousal, cognition, and emotions

nuclei: clusters of soma of neurons found in the central nervous system

nucleus cell: structure that contains genetic information in the form of chromosomes

nucleus: cluster of neuronal soma (cell bodies) in the central nervous system

nucleus accumbens: a forebrain nucleus where dopamine is released, producing pleasurable feelings

nucleus basalis: a forebrain structure that supplies acetylcholine to the cerebrum and hippocampus

nucleus of the solitary tract: a nucleus in the medulla that receives information from the gut and other receptors by way of cranial nerves VII, IX, and X

nystagmus: oscillation of the eyes following stimulation of the vestibular system

obesity: a disorder in which the individual's body weight is 20% above the normal weight for height

ob gene: a defective gene found in genetically obese mice

obsessive-compulsive disorder: an anxiety disorder characterized by repetitive thoughts and ritualized behaviors that are performed repeatedly

occipital lobe: most posterior lobe of the cerebrum that processes visual information

oculovestibular reflexes: automatic eye movements made to compensate for movements of the head [*oculo-* = eye]

olfaction: the sense of smell

olfactory bulb: brain structure that receives olfactory information directly from the receptors and processes this information before relaying it on to the cerebral cortex

olfactory cortex: the area in the temporal lobe that processes information from the olfactory bulb

olfactory nerve: cranial nerve I, which carries information about odors from the nose to the brain

olfactory receptors: neurons that respond to chemicals associated with odors

oligodendrocytes: glial cells, located in the central nervous system, that have a flattened shape that enables them to wrap around axons of neurons

omnivores: animals that eat a variety of foods [*omni-* = everything; *-vore* = to eat or devour, Latin]

ophthalmoscope: an instrument used to view the interior of the eyeball

opiates: drugs that are derived naturally or synthetically from opium, such as morphine, heroin, codeine, and demerol

opioid receptors: receptors on the cell membranes of neurons that bind with endogenous opiates and opiate drugs

opioids: chemicals (neurotransmitters or synthetic drugs) that bind with opioid receptors

opponent-process theory: a theory of color vision, which proposes that three pairs of opposing colors (red-green, yellow-blue, black-white) code for color in the nervous system

optic chiasm: the structure formed by the merging of the left and right optic nerves

optic disk: the blind spot on the retina where the axons that form the optic nerve exit the retina

optic nerve: cranial nerve II, which carries information about vision from the eye to the brain

optic tract: the axons that emerge from the optic chiasm and enter the brain

orbitofrontal prefrontal cortex: an area of the frontal lobe directly behind the eyeball socket in the skull where the secondary olfactory cortex is located

orbitoprefrontal cortex: an area of the prefrontal cortex near the eye sockets that is affected by chronic stress

orexin: a class of peptides that stimulates food intake and also appears to play a role in producing narcolepsy [*orex-* = appetite, Greek]

organelle: specialized structure within a cell [*organelle* = little organ, Latin]

organ of Corti: a structure located in the scala media that consists of the basilar membrane, hair cells, and tectorial membrane

orienting response: the focusing of receptors on a novel or important stimulus

osmoreceptors: special receptors in the anterior hypothalamus that monitor intracellular concentration

osmotic thirst: thirst that occurs when the concentration of the intracellular compartment becomes greater than normal

ossicle: tiny bone in the middle ear [*os-* = bone; *-icle* = diminutive form]

-otomy: a suffix that refers to a surgery in which a cut is made through body tissues

outer ear: the outermost part of the ear, consisting of the pinna and auditory canal

oval window: the opening to the inner ear covered by a thin membrane that vibrates in response to vibrations by the stapes bone

ovarian cycle: the rhythmic fluctuations in the release of ovarian hormones

ovary: female gonad

ovulation: a process in which the mature ovum bursts out of the ovarian follicle and is available for fertilization

ovum: egg produced by the ovary

oxytocin: a hormone produced by the paraventricular nucleus that regulates lactation and childbirth and is released in response to specific stressors; it also appears to regulate sexual and social behaviors in male and female animals

paired-image subtraction method: an analytical method used in functional brain imaging in which an image obtained while a subject is engaged in a control task is subtracted from an image obtained while the same subject performs a behavior of interest, producing an image that indicates the brain areas uniquely activated by the behavior of interest

pallidotomy: a surgical procedure used to treat Parkinson's disease, involving surgical cuts through the globus pallidus of the basal ganglia [*pallid-* = globus pallidus; *-otomy* = to cut]

panic disorder: a disorder characterized by bouts of intense fear or terror that are unpredictable and appear to occur out of the blue

papillae: little bumps that cover the tongue

parabiotic rats: rats joined surgically that share the same blood supply

paradoxical sleep: another name for REM sleep derived from the observation that the brain appears very active while skeletal muscles are very inactive

paranoid personality disorder: a personality disorder characterized by paranoid ideation that is not well organized

paraphasia: a language disorder that involves the substitution of one phoneme for another, or one word for another

paraphilia: deviant sexual behavior

paraplegia: a disorder involving loss of motor function to the lower limbs [*para-* = beside, on the side; *-plegia* = to strike, Greek]

parasol ganglion cells: large or magnocellular ganglion cells in the retina that receive their information from rods

parasympathetic nervous system: a division of the autonomic nervous system, concerned with energy conservation

paraventricular nucleus: a cluster of neurons in the hypothalamus that organizes behavior, including eating, to respond to changes in internal body states

Parkinson's dementia: a progressively debilitating form of dementia that is associated with Parkinson's disease

Parkinson's disease: a movement disorder caused by destruction of dopamine-producing cells in the substantia nigra, with symptoms of tremor, loss of balance, and rigidity of limbs

parietal lobe: region of the cerebrum, located immediately posterior to the frontal lobe, that processes somatic information relayed from the body [*soma* = body, Latin]

parvocellular layers: four top layers of the lateral geniculate nucleus that process information about color, form, and detail

passive theory of sleep: an explanation of sleep that proposes that the brain is a passive organ and requires stimulation to remain active

pedophilia: a paraphilia in which the affected individual is sexually aroused by children and desires sexual contact with them

peptide: a short chain of amino acids

perception: a process that involves the interpretation of information that comes from the receptors

periaqueductal: gray area in the midbrain that contains neurons that release neurotransmitters that inhibit the transmission of pain messages in the substantia gelatinosa

periaqueductal gray region: a region in the brain stem, located next to the acqueduct of Sylvius, that is associated with the expression of negative emotions

perinatal: occurring around the time of birth [*peri-* = around; *-natal* = birth, Latin]

peripheral nervous system: all nervous tissue located outside the brain and spinal cord

periventricular gray region: a region of the hypothalamus located next to the third ventricle, which is associated with the expression of negative emotions [*peri-* = around]

permanent vegetative state: a nonconscious state in which the affected individual's eyes are open, but behavior is reflexive and primitive

personality disorder: a psychological disorder characterized by a consistent, abnormal pattern of behavior that is used over a long period of time by the affected individual

petechial hemorrhage: pinpoint bleeding associated with cerebral laceration

petit mal epilepsy: a seizure disorder in which the affected individual has absence seizures and cannot focus attention on the subject at hand

PGO spikes: simultaneous electrical activity measured in the pons, lateral geniculate nucleus, and the occipital lobe during REM sleep

phantom limb pain: a type of chronic pain in which an individual who has had a limb amputated continues to feel pain in the missing limb

phase advancement: the shift of hormonal and other physiological functions several hours forward in time

phase difference: difference in the pattern of peaks and troughs striking the two ears

phenotype: the expression of a gene, in which an observable characteristic associated with the gene is present

phenylthiocarbamide (PTC): a substance that produces a bitter taste in people who have inherited the ability to taste this chemical

pheromones: chemical signals that regulate sexual and social behaviors in some species

phobia: intense fear generated by specific stimuli

phonemes: the basic units of spoken language

photon: discrete packet of light energy

photopigments: chemicals that absorb photons entering the eye

phrenology: study of the skull to understand the mind [*phren-* = mind; *-ology* = study of, Greek]

physical dependence: a state characterized by severe physical withdrawal symptoms when an individual abstains from taking an abused substance

physiological psychology: a discipline that involves the study of brain mechanisms underlying behavior

pia mater: innermost layer of the meninges

pica: the eating of nonnutritive substances

Pick's bodies: cytoplasmic inclusions found in the neurons of individuals with Pick's disease

Pick's disease: a rare dementia that begins in middle age, producing symptoms that resemble those of Alzheimer's disease late in the progression of the illness

piloerection: an insulation response in which the hairs covering the body are pulled into an erect position, which allows air to become trapped between the hairs [*pilo-* = hair; *-erection* = to stand, Greek]

pineal gland: an unpaired brain structure that releases melatonin

pinna: outer, fleshy part of ear that collects sound waves

piriform cortex: an area of the ventral temporal lobe where part of the primary olfactory cortex is located

pituitary gland: a structure connected to the hypothalamus by a stalk, that regulates the activity of other major glands in the body; master gland located below the ventral surface of the brain, which receives commands from the hypothalamus

placebo: an inactive compound that looks just like the test drug

place theory of pitch perception: a theory that proposes that different regions of the basilar membrane are particularly sensitive to certain frequencies

plexiform layer: the outermost layer of the cerebral cortex, which contains no neuronal soma

polygenic model: a model that proposes that a disorder is caused by several genes [*poly-* = many; *-genic* = gene]

polysynaptic reflex: a reflex involving a sensory neuron, a motor neuron, and one or more interneurons [*poly-* = many; *-synaptic* = referring to the synapse, Greek]

pons: hindbrain structure that relays information from the spinal cord and medulla to the higher brain structures [*pons* = bridge, Latin]

positive emotion: an emotion that makes a person feel better and draws the person toward the eliciting stimulus

positive reinforcement: a stimulus that increases the likelihood of the behavior that precedes it

positive symptoms of schizophrenia: those behaviors, such as hallucinations and delusions, observed in individuals with schizophrenia that most people typically do not exhibit

positron emission tomography (PET): a recording technique that is used to localize the source of positrons emitted from radioactive isotopes in the brain, which is associated with brain activity

postcentral gyrus: the gyrus immediately posterior to the central sulcus, also known as the somatosensory cortex [*post-* = after, Latin]

posterior: toward the back, behind [*posterus* = coming after, Latin]

posterior commissure: tract that links neurons in the right and left diencephalon and mesencephalon

posterior parietal cortex: cortical area believed to process "Where" somatosensory information

postmortem: occurring after death [*post-* = after; *-mort* = death, Latin]

postnatal: occurring after birth [*post-* = after; *-natal* = birth, Latin]

postrotational vertigo: dizziness that follows a spinning motion of the body

postsynaptic inhibition: inhibition that takes place in the postsynaptic dendrite following the release of an inhibitory neurotransmitter from a presynaptic axon

postsynaptic neuron: the neuron receiving communication across a synapse [*post-* = after, Latin]

post-traumatic stress disorder: a disorder, caused by exposure to one or more traumatic events, which is characterized by recurrent distressing memories of the event and feeling as if the traumatic event were recurring

potassium: a positively charged ion that is found in high concentrations in the inside of neurons

potentiation: a phenomenon in which one taste stimulus causes a receptor to respond more intensely to another stimulus

prandial drinking: drinking that occurs when eating food

precentral gyrus: the gyrus immediately anterior to the central sulcus, also known as the motor cortex [*pre-* = before, Latin]

prefrontal cortex: most anterior region of the frontal lobe, composed of three divisions: dorsolateral, medial, orbitofrontal

premenstrual period: the 3–7 days just before menstruation, when estrogen and progesterone levels are very low

prenatal: occurring before birth [*pre-* = before; *-natal* = birth, Latin]

preoptic area: a region of the anterior hypothalamus that regulates heat loss and production

presbyopia: a condition found in older people in which the lens loses its ability to accommodate [*presby-* = old; *-opi* = eyes, Greek]

presynaptic inhibition: inhibition at axoaxonic synapses that occurs when the presynaptic axon releases inhibitory neurotransmitters that block the release of neurotransmitters from the postsynaptic axon

presynaptic neuron: the neuron sending a message across a synapse [*pre-* = before, Latin]

primary amenorrhea: a condition in which the menstrual cycle fails to begin

primary auditory cortex: an area of the temporal cortex that receives information directly from the medial geniculate nucleus of the thalamus

primary drinking: drinking that occurs in response to osmotic or hypovolemic thirst

primary motor cortex: the precentral gyrus, which sends impulses involving fine motor control to motor neurons

primary olfactory cortex: the region of the cerebral cortex, located in both the frontal and temporal lobes, that receives olfactory information from the olfactory lobe

primary somatosensory cortex: the postcentral gyrus in the parietal lobe, which processes sensory information from the skin and muscles

primary taste cortex: an area of the frontal lobe just anterior to the temporal lobe that receives information about taste stimuli from the thalamus

primary tastes: pure sweet, sour, salty, or bitter tastes

priming: an improvement in the ability to recognize particular stimuli following previous exposure to them

primordial gonads: the undifferentiated gonads found in the developing embryo

progesterone: a gonadal hormone produced by the ovaries that prepares the female body for pregnancy [*pro-* = for; *-gest* = gestation or pregnancy, Latin]

proprioception: the ability to know where a body part is in space

prosencephalon: forebrain [*pro-* = for; *-encephalon* = brain, Greek]

prosopagnosia: a form of visual agnosia in which affected individuals cannot recognize faces of people familiar to them [*proso-* = face, Latin]

proximal stimulus: the visual image that stimulates the visual receptors

psychogenic amnesia: a memory disorder associated with stress of psychological trauma in which episodic memories cannot be retrieved [*psycho-* = mind; *-genic* = source, Greek]

psychological dependence: craving or discomfort experienced when a substance is not available for consumption

psychoneuroimmunology: a field of study that examines the interactions among the nervous system, endocrine system, immune system, and behavior

psychosis: a severe mental disorder in which thinking is disturbed and the affected individual is not well oriented for person, time, and place

puberty: a physical change that involves sexual maturation and occurs in nonseasonal breeders

pupil: the hole in the center of the iris through which light passes to stimulate receptors in the retina

pure alexia: a form of visual agnosia associated with damage to the left inferior temporal lobe in which affected individuals can identify individual letters but cannot put letters together to read them as a whole word [*a-* = without; *-lex* = to read, Latin]

putamen: a nucleus in the striatum of the basal ganglia that relays motor information

pyloric sphincter: a muscular constriction between the stomach and the duodenum

pyramidal cells: neurons shaped like pyramids that are located in the cerebral cortex

pyramidal motor system: the motor system that arises from the primary motor cortex in the frontal lobe and directs fine motor control of skeletal muscles

quadriplegia: disability involving impairment of motor and sensory functions in all four limbs [*quadr-* = four; *plegi-* = to strike, Greek]

quiet sleep: slow-wave sleep

radial glia: glial cells that have long appendages that radiate out from the soma and direct the development of the nervous system

radioligands: chemicals tagged with a radioactive element that bind with specific receptors

raphe nuclei: hindbrain structures that produce serotonin

raphe system: a hindbrain area that produces serotonin and regulates sleep behavior

receptor: a specialized sensory cell that responds to a specific stimulus

reflex: a rapid, automatic set of muscle contractions made in response to a particular stimulus

receptive aphasia: a disturbance in language comprehension

receptivity: the willingness of a nonhuman female to accept a male for mating purposes

receptor potential: an excitatory or generator potential that occurs when a receptor is stimulated

reciprocal innervation: the inhibition of antagonist muscles by motor neurons of contracting muscles

recording: a method of studying the brain that enables investigators to pinpoint active brain regions

reflecting tapetum: a reflective lining, found behind the retina at the back of the eyeball in many animals, that enhances night vision

relative refractory period: a period of time following an action potential during which an action potential can be initiated only by a stronger-than-normal stimulus

REM rebound: an increase in REM sleep observed in individuals who have been deprived of REM sleep

REM sleep: a sleep stage in which desynchronized brain waves predominate and the sleeping individual's eyeballs move rapidly in a jerky fashion under closed eyelids

REM sleep behavior disorder: a disorder characterized by normal skeletal muscle tone during REM sleep and motor activity associated with dream content

renin: a hormone produced by the kidneys that becomes activated by hypovolemic thirst

reproductive behavior: behavior that produces offspring and nurtures them until they are able to live on their own

restorative theory of sleep: an explanation of sleep that proposes that sleep is a state during which waste products are removed from the brain and neurotransmitters are restored

restrained eater: a person who controls his or her eating very rigorously

restricting anorexia: a form of anorexia nervosa that is characterized by severe reduction of food intake, which leads to an emaciated appearance

reticular formation: a group of neurons located in the brain stem that alerts the forebrain to important stimuli

reticular thalamic nucleus: a nucleus in the thalamus that blocks access of sensory information to the cerebrum and limbic system

retina: a flat, multilayered tissue at the back of the eyes that contains the visual receptors

retinitis pigmentosa: a genetic disorder that first destroys rods but eventually spreads to the cones, causing total blindness

retinohypothalamic tract: a band of axons that connects the retina with the suprachiasmatic nucleus, relaying information about the presence of light in the environment

retrograde amnesia: a loss of declarative memory from some point in time backward

retrograde tracing: tracing from the axonal endplates to the soma [*retro-* = backward]

reversed sleep–wake cycle: a disorder in which the affected individual remains asleep during the day and is awake at night

reward deficiency disorder: a disorder characterized by decreased activity of neurons in the nucleus accumbens and hippocampus, which produces dysphoria and cravings for substances that increase dopamine activity

rhodopsin: the photopigment found in rods

rhombencephalon: hindbrain

ribosomes: special cellular structures that direct the production of protein in the cell

rigor mortis: stiffened state of the body's muscles at death [*rigere* = stiff; *mortis* = dead, Latin]

RNA: ribonucleic acid, the type of nucleic acid found in ribosomes

rod: a visual receptor that responds best in dim light

rubella: a viral infection, known as German measles, that can interfere with development of the nervous system of an embryo or fetus

saccule: a vestibular structure that signals information about the position of the head with respect to gravity

sacral: region of the spinal cord located in the pelvic girdle [*sacrum* = pelvis, Greek]

saltatory conduction: the jumping of an action potential along a myelinated axon [*salta-* = to jump, Latin]

satiety: an unconscious physiological process that stops eating

scala media: the middle chamber of the cochlea that contains the hair cells [*media* = middle, Latin]

scala tympani: the tympanic canal in the cochlea that receives vibrations from the scala vestibuli

scala vestibuli: the vestibular canal in the cochlea that receives vibrations from the oval window

Schachter-Singer theory of emotion: an explanation of emotion that maintains that to experience an emotion, an individual needs to experience physiological arousal *and* has to attribute the arousal to an appropriate stimulus

schedule-induced hyperphagia: overeating that occurs when an individual is on a schedule waiting for a non-food reward

schedule-induced polydipsia: over-drinking that occurs when an individual is on a schedule waiting for a nonfluid reward

schizoid personality disorder: a personality disorder characterized by social detachment and flat affect

schizophrenia: a psychotic disorder of unknown origin that is characterized by the disorganization of associations, producing disconnected thoughts, words, and emotions

schizophrenia spectrum disorders: personality disorders that are genetically related to schizophrenia and share many of the same symptoms and biological markers of that disorder

schizotypal personality disorder: a personality disorder characterized by eccentric behavior, avoidance of close relationships, and thought distortions

Schwann cells: glial cells, located in the peripheral nervous system, that have a flattened shape that enables them to wrap around axons of neurons

sclera: tough, white outer coating of the eyeball [*scleros* = hard, Greek]

scotoma: a blind spot in a part of the visual field

seasonal affective disorder: a mood dysfunction or depressive disorder that occurs most commonly in the winter

seasonal breeders: animals that mate only during a particular time of the year

secondary amenorrhea: a condition in which menstrual cycles cease prematurely

secondary auditory cortex: cortical areas lateral and superior to the primary auditory cortex in the temporal lobe that process complex sounds

secondary drinking: nonhomeostatic drinking that occurs in the absence of thirst

secondary olfactory cortex: an area involved in the identification of odors that is located in the orbitofrontal prefrontal cortex

secondary somatosensory cortex: the area of the parietal lobe posterior to the postcentral gyrus, which receives information from the primary somatosensory cortex for "What" and "Where" processing

second messenger: a chemical activated when a neurotransmitter binds with a G protein-linked receptor, which alters a neuron's function

segregation analysis: a type of genetic analysis that examines whether the pattern of inheritance of a disorder in a family agrees with an expected pattern of inheritance

seizure: epileptic episodes in which abnormal electrical activity is detected in the brain, producing inattentiveness (petit mal seizures) or unconsciousness (grand mal seizures)

selective attention: the process by which brain systems select stimuli for processing

semantic memory: memory for general knowledge

semicircular canals: vestibular structures that respond to changes in head movement

semipermeable: allowing some, but not all, substances to cross the cell membrane

senile dementia: a progressive cognitive disorder that occurs in patients over 65 years of age

sensitization: an enhanced response observed when a chronically stressed individual is presented with a new or different stressor (stress effect); a progressive increase in the effect of a drug with repeated administration (addiction)

sensory neuron: a neuron that responds to stimuli in the periphery and sends information about the stimuli to the central nervous system

sensory system: a network of neurons that form a pathway from the receptor to the cerebrum

septum: structure in the limbic system associated with positive emotions

serotonin: a monoamine neurotransmitter that plays a role in sleep, vigilance, mood, appetite, and repetitive movements

serotonin specific reuptake inhibitors (SSRIs): a class of drugs that increases serotonin activity in the brain by interfering with the reuptake of serotonin into the presynaptic neuron

set point: an optimal level set by the hypothalamus for each of several physiological factors, including body temperature and body weight

sexual behavior: behavior in which animals engage to bring ova and sperm together

sexual differentiation: the process by which we become biological males or females

sham feeding: eating that occurs with an esophageal fistula, in which food that is swallowed spills out of the esophagus onto the floor before reaching the stomach

sham-operated control: a participant that undergoes surgery, like the experimental subject, but does not receive the experimental manipulation

shivering thermogenesis: the production of heat by shivering [*thermo-* = heat; *-genesis* = to create, Greek]

short-term memory: a memory system in which limited amounts of information are stored briefly

sildenafil: a drug (better known by its brand name, Viagra) that is currently considered the most effective treatment for erectile dysfunction disorders

simple cells: neurons in NV1 that respond best to a line or edge in a particular orientation

single photon emission computed tomography (SPECT): a recording technique that is an extension of the CT technique and is used to localize the highest concentrations of photon-emitting isotopes in the brain, which are associated with brain activity

6-hydroxydopamine: a neurotoxin that destroys dopamine-containing neurons

skeletal muscle: muscle that is attached to bones and cartilage of skeleton

sleep apnea: a disorder in which breathing is temporarily suspended during sleep [*a-* = without; *-pnea* = breath, Greek]

sleep cycle: a complete cycle from Stage I sleep down to Stage IV sleep and back to Stage I that lasts approximately 90 minutes

sleep spindles: bursts of brain waves with a frequency of 7–14 Hz that are most prevalent in Stage II sleep

slow-wave sleep: stages of sleep that exhibit large, slow brain waves

smooth pursuit eye movements: the movements that the eyes make when following a moving target

sodium: a positively charged ion that is found in high concentrations on the outside of neurons

sodium-potassium pump: a membrane protein that pumps sodium ions out of the neuron and pumps potassium back in

soma: cell body [*soma* = body, Greek]

somatic nervous system: a division of the peripheral nervous system that controls skeletal muscles

somatosensory: bodily sensation [*soma-* = body, Greek; *-sensus* = sensation, Latin]

somatosensory receptors: receptors in the skin, muscles, joints, and tendons

somatosensory system: the sensory system that relays information about the body to the brain

somnambulism: sleepwalking associated with non-REM sleep [*somn-* = sleep; *-ambulare* = walk, Latin]

spasmodic dysmenorrhea: a condition that begins at the onset of menstruation and is characterized by severe cramping and abdominal pain

spasticity: a disorder that is produced by clonus and rigidity, which interferes with smooth movement of a limb

spatial summation: addition of input from many different presynaptic neurons

species-specific defense reactions: characteristic responses made by an animal of a particular species when confronted with a threatening or frightening stimulus

specific hunger: a deprivation state in which the affected individual lacks a specific nutrient in the diet

spina bifida: a disorder in which the bony spinal column fails to close, leaving the spinal cord exposed [*spina* = spine; *bifida* = divided, Latin]

spinal nerves: nerves that enter and exit the spinal cord between bones of the spinal column

spinal shock: condition seen immediately following damage to the spinal cord in which no spinal reflexes can be elicited

split-brain patients: individuals who have undergone a callosotomy

spongiosis: a form of brain damage in which the brain loses its normal appearance and looks like a sponge

stage of axonal and dendritic growth: the fourth stage of brain development in which neurons sprout processes that become axons and dendrites

Stage I sleep: the lightest stage of sleep, characterized by desynchronized theta waves

Stage II sleep: the stage of sleep characterized by desynchronized brain waves, sleep spindles, and K-complexes

Stage III sleep: the stage of sleep characterized by less than 50% synchronized delta waves

Stage IV sleep: the deepest stage of sleep, characterized by more than 50% synchronized delta waves

stapes: the stirrup, or last of the three ossicles, which vibrates against the oval window

stellate cells: star-shaped neurons in the cerebral cortex [*stella* = star, Latin]

stereochemical theory of odor: a theory that proposes that each odorant is a chemical substance that has a particular shape that fits into a specific receptor site

stereotaxic: allowing measurement in three directions [*stereos* = solid, three-dimensional; *tassein* = arrangement, Greek]

stereotaxic instrument: an apparatus that allows investigators to locate subcortical brain structures with great precision

stimulation: a method of studying the brain that involves causing a part of the brain to become active

stimuli: objects or events that excite a sensory neuron or receptor

stress: a negative experience accompanied by characteristic emotional, behavioral, biochemical, and physiological responses

stress-induced analgesia: an absence of pain produced when a stressor stimulates the release of opioid neurotransmitters

stressor: a person, object, place, or event that disrupts homeostasis in the nervous system

stretch reflex: contraction of a muscle in response to stretching of the annulospiral receptors in that muscle

striate cortex: another name for the primary visual cortex, or area V1, in the occipital lobe

striatum: part of the basal ganglia that is composed of the caudate nucleus, putamen, and the nucleus accumbens

stirrup: the third ossicle in the middle ear, which receives vibrations from the anvil and transmits them to the oval window

stuttering: a disturbance of speech production characterized by disfluency, abnormal timing, and uncontrolled repetition of phonemes

subcortical: located below the cortex [*sub-* = under; *cortex* = bark or rind, Greek]

subcutaneous fat: fat located directly beneath the skin [*sub-* = under; *-cutaneous* = skin]

subfornical organ: a region of the hypothalamus that stimulates drinking

substance P: a neurotransmitter used by pain receptors to signal the presence of tissue damage and pain

substantia gelatinosa: a region in the dorsal horn of the spinal cord and medulla where the transmission of pain messages to the cerebrum can be inhibited

substantia nigra: a cluster of cells in the basal ganglia that produces dopamine

sudden infant death syndrome (SIDS): a disorder associated with sleep apnea in which a seemingly healthy baby is placed in a crib to sleep and is found dead sometime later

sulcus: grooves or fissures in the surface of the cerebrum [*sulcus* = fissure, Latin]

superficial blood vessels: blood vessels located in the skin

superior: upper, above [*superos* = upper, Latin]

superior colliculus: a midbrain structure that receives visual information and processes the location of objects in the environment [*colliculus* = little hill, Latin]

superior olive: hindbrain structure that processes auditory information before sending it on to the midbrain

superior temporal gyrus: part of the secondary auditory cortex that is involved in the perception of speech sounds in humans

suprachiasmic nucleus: a nucleus of the hypothalamus that controls the biological clock

Sylvian fissure: the lateral sulcus that separates the temporal lobe from the rest of the cerebrum

sympathetic ganglia: a chain of ganglia (clusters of neurons) that organizes activity of the sympathetic nervous system

sympathetic nervous system: a division of the autonomic nervous system, producing fight-or-flight responses

synapse: a junction between two neurons [*synapse* = gap, Greek]

synaptic cleft: the narrow space between two communicating neurons

synchronized brain waves: large, slow, regular waves associated with deep sleep

synchronous oscillations: firing patterns of 40 action potentials per second that occur in several neurons at the same time

syphilis: a sexually transmitted bacterial infection that can interfere with brain development in the fetus

T-cell: a white blood cell that is part of the immune system and functions by targeting specific intruders inside cells

tactile agnosia: a somatosensory disorder in which the affected individual cannot recognize objects through touch, associated with damage to the inferior parietal cortex

taste buds: tiny structures that contain taste receptors

taste receptors: specialized cells that respond to chemicals dissolved in water

tau-protein: a protein, found in neurons, whose mutated form produces neurofibrillary tangles

tectorial membrane: a stiff membrane located on top of the hair cells [*tectum* = roof, Latin]

tectum: the dorsal area of the midbrain [*tectum* = roof, Latin]

tegmentum: an area of the reticular formation that is associated with the production of orienting responses

telencephalon: forebrain area that contains the basal ganglia, limbic system structures, and the cerebrum

temporal lobe: most inferior lobe of the cerebrum, which processes auditory, smell, and taste information and contains the hippocampus and amygdala

temporal lobe seizures: epileptic seizures caused by damage to the temporal lobes, which produce aggressive behaviors with little or no provocation

temporal summation: addition of input from one presynaptic neuron over a brief period of time

terminal buttons: button-shaped endings on axons where neurotransmitters are stored

test battery: a group of tests that measures facets of behavior

testis: male gonad (plural: testes)

testosterone: a hormone produced by the male gonads or testes

thalamocortical system: a neural pathway between the thalamus and the cerebral cortex, which plays a role in determining our conscious experience

thalamotomy: a surgical procedure used to treat Parkinson's disease, involving surgical cuts through the ventral thalamus [*thalam-* = thalamus; *-otomy* = to cut]

thalamus: structure in the diencephalon that relays information from the brain stem to the cerebrum

thermocautery: to cut away tissue using heat [*thermos* = hot; *kauterion* = to cut, Greek]

thermostatic theory: a theory that postulates that core body temperature drives eating behavior, causing us to eat when core body temperature is lower than normal and to stop eating when core body temperature is elevated

theta waves: slow, irregular brain waves associated with Stage I sleep that occur at a rate of 3–7 Hz

thick stripes: regions of area V2 that receive their information from the interblob regions of area V1 and transmit this information to area V5

thin stripes: regions of area V2 that receive their information from the blob regions of area V1 and transmit this information to area V4

third ventricle: ventricle located in the diencephalon

thoracic: region of the spinal cord located in the chest [*thorax* = chest, Greek]

thoracolumbar: from the thoracic and lumbar areas of the spinal cord

thyroid gland: a butterfly-shaped gland located in the neck that controls the body's metabolic rate

thyrotropin-releasing hormone stimulation test: a test used to study the response of the thyroid gland when thyrotropin-releasing hormone is administered

thyroxin: a thyroid hormone

tic: a brief, involuntary contraction of specific skeletal muscles produced by damage to the basal ganglia

tolerance: a progressive decrease in the effect of a drug with repeated administration

tomography: an imaging technique that involves passing X rays through the brain at various angles to generate a three-dimensional image [*tomos* = slice; *graphos* = to write or record, Greek]

top-down: research strategies that involve studying higher level cognitive function in order to draw conclusions about brain functions at the cellular level

topographical organization: organization of receptive fields in the cerebral cortex, in which specific areas of the cortex receive information from specific regions of the body [*topos* = place, region; *graphos* = to write or record, Greek]

toxic psychosis: a psychotic disorder caused by bacteria that produce powerful toxins

tract: bundle of axons in the central nervous system

transcranial magnetic stimulation: a noninvasive treatment for depression that involves directly stimulating neurons in the cerebral cortex

transcutaneous electrical nerve stimulation (TENS): a form of counterirritation that involves sending a tiny current to the skin to stimulate receptors in the area of the injury to induce analgesia

transducer: something that can convert one form of energy to another

transient flaccid paralysis: complete loss of muscle tone, with paralysis, seen immediately after damage to the pyramidal motor system

trichromat: an individual with three functional cone types who has normal color vision [*tri-* = three]

trichromatic color theory: a theory of color vision that proposes that only three different receptors are needed to see all shades of all colors; also known as Young-Helmholtz color theory

tricyclic antidepressant: a medication that increases norepinephrine availability at the synapse

trigeminal nerve: cranial nerve V, which carries sensory information from the mouth and face and controls facial muscles of mastication

trophoblast cells: cells in the blastocyst that will become the placenta

true hermaphrodite: an individual born with both ovarian and testicular tissue

tumor: abnormal tissue composed of cells that are showing uncontrolled division and growth

tunnel vision: a loss of peripheral vision caused by destruction of rods

Turner's syndrome: a syndrome in which affected individuals have chromosomal designation of 45, XO, which results in the development of female internal and external genitalia and sterile ovaries

tympanic membrane: eardrum

twin studies: a type of genetic analysis that compares the rates of occurrence of a disorder in identical versus fraternal twins

Type 1 diabetes: a disorder in which the affected individual does not produce adequate amounts of insulin

Type 2 diabetes: a disorder due to chronic hyperinsulinemia in which the affected individual produces insulin but does not respond to it

unisynaptic reflex: a reflex that involves only one sensory and one motor neuron and one synapse [*uni-* = one; *-synaptic* = referring to the synapse, Greek]

Urbach-Wiethe disease: a rare disorder caused by bilateral damage to the amygdala that is characterized by markedly impaired declarative memory for emotionally arousing events

uterus: female organ in which the fertilized egg implants and the embryo develops

utricle: a vestibular structure that signals information about the position of the head with respect to gravity

vacuoles: tiny empty spaces seen in spongiosis of the brain

vagus nerve: cranial nerve X, which carries sensory information from the upper abdomen, chest, and neck to the brain and carries motor information from the brain to smooth muscles in those areas of the body

vascular dementia: a form of senile dementia related to cardiovascular disease, particularly hardening of the arteries or stroke

vascular theory of emotion: an explanation of emotion that maintains that warming the brain produces negative emotions and cooling the brain produces positive emotions

vasopressin: another name for antidiuretic hormone

ventral: toward the belly [*ventrum* = belly, Latin]

ventral posterior medial nucleus: a group of neurons in the thalamus that processes taste information

ventral stream: a visual pathway that is concerned with processing information about color and form; the "What" system

ventricle: a cavity in the brain that contains cerebrospinal fluid [*ventriculus* = belly, Latin]

ventrolateral prefrontal cortex: an area of the prefrontal cortex that processes visual and auditory "What" information

ventromedial corticospinal tract: pathway from the primary motor cortex and supplementary motor cortex that synapses with neurons in the extrapyramidal motor system

ventromedial nucleus of the hypothalamus (VMH): a nucleus of the hypothalamus that transmits information about the state of the body to the paraventricular nucleus, inhibiting eating

vertigo: dizziness

vesicle: a tiny sac in which neurotransmitters are stored [*vesicle* = small bladder, Latin]

vestibular system: the sensory system that responds to changes in head movement and to gravity

vestibulospinal tract: bundle of axons that goes from the vestibular nucleus in the medulla to the spinal cord

viral encephalitis: an infection of the brain caused by a virus that passes through the blood–brain barrier

visual agnosia: a visual disorder caused by damage to the inferior temporal lobe in which the affected individual cannot recognize familiar objects in the visual field [*a-* = without; *-gnosia* = knowledge, Latin]

visual extinction: a visual disorder associated with unilateral damage to the posterior parietal cortex in which the affected individual will ignore an object located in the visual field contralateral to the damaged site

visual field: that part of the environment from which visual receptors receive information

visual receptors: rods and cones, which are excited by photons

visual spatial attention: a type of selective attention used when a person is looking for objects in a particular location

visual "What" system: the ventral stream, which processes information about color and form, that begins with the cone receptors and ends in the inferior temporal lobe

visual "Where" system: the dorsal stream, which processes information about movement and location of objects, that begins with the rod receptors and ends in the posterior parietal lobe

volley principle: a theory that proposes hair cells in the cochlea work together to produce a series of action potentials that duplicate the frequency of the sound

voltage clamp technique: an in vitro technique used to study the activity of voltage-gated ion channels

vomeronasal organ: a structure located in the floor of the nasal cavity that contains receptors for the accessory olfactory system

voyeurism: a paraphilia in which the affected individual gets sexual gratification from surreptitiously watching others disrobe or engage in sexual behavior

wavelength: the distance between two corresponding parts of a wave

Wernicke-Korsakoff's syndrome: a cognitive disorder observed in long-term alcoholics, characterized by memory and cognitive disturbance, confusion, loss orientation for time and place, ataxia, and apathy

Wernicke's area: an area in the superior temporal gyrus associated with language comprehension

"What" system: the visual pathway concerned with processing color and form

"Where" system: the visual pathway concerned with detecting motion and the location of objects in the visual field

withdrawal: severe physical symptoms, such as tremors, seizures, hallucinations or nausea, associated with abstinence from an abused substance

withdrawal reflex: flexion of a limb in response to a painful or noxious stimulus

Wolffian ducts: the precursors of the male internal genitalia

word deafness: a form of receptive aphasia in which affected individuals cannot understand spoken words although they can read, write, and talk normally

working memory: a series of operations carried out at different sites in the cerebral cortex

Y chromosome: the tiny sex chromosome that directs the development of the testes

yohimbine: a drug that blocks the alpha-2 adrenergic receptor and produces an increase in the release of norepinephrine

Young-Helmholtz color theory: a theory of color vision that proposes that only three different receptors are needed to see all shades of all colors; also known as Trichromatic Color Theory

zeitgeber: anything, such as light or an alarm clock, that resets the biological clock [*Zeit-* = time, *-Geber* = giver, German]

Answers to Section Recaps

Chapter 1

Recap: 1.1   The History of Brain Research
a. encephalocentric; b. holism; c. localization; d. motor cortex; e. Karl Lashley's; f. dualism; g. monism

Recap: 1.2   Studying the Brain and Behavior
a. neuroscience; b. bottom-up; c. top-down; d. biopsychology; e. neuropsychology; f. top-down; g. bottom-up

Recap: 1.3   Biological Explanations of Behavior
a. natural selection; b. functionalism; c. genetic; d. nervous

Chapter 2

Recap: 2.1   The Organization of the Nervous System
a. central; b. peripheral; c. somatic; d. autonomic; e. sympathetic; f. parasympathetic; g. neurons; h. glia

Recap: 2.2   Neurons and Glial Cells
a. nucleus; b. ribosomes; c. mitochondria; d. axon; e. sensory; f. glia; g. astrocytes; h. microglia; i. dead; j. radioglia; k. Schwann cells; l. multiple sclerosis; m. brain; n. gap junctions; o. immune

Recap: 2.3   Synapses
a. neurons; b. chemical; c. electrical; d. unidirectional; e. bidirectional; f. positive; g. negative

Recap: 2.4   Transmitting Information Within a Neuron
a. voltage; b. potassium; c. positive; d. action; e. spatial; f. temporal; g. excitatory; h. inhibitory

Chapter 3

Recap: 3.1   Opening Ion Channels
a. ion; b. axon; c. release; d. ligand-gated; e. presynaptic inhibition; f. autoreceptors

Recap: 3.2   Types of Receptors
a. acetylcholine; b. nicotinic; c. muscarinic; d. cyclic AMP; e. growth; f. hormone

Recap: 3.3   Neurotransmitters
a. neuromodulator; b. bloodstream; c. epinephrine; d. amino acids; e. peptides; f. monoamines; g. nitric-oxide

Recap: 3.4   The Role of Neurotransmitters in Human Behavior
a. acetylcholine; b. atropine; c. long-term; d. GABA; e. alcohol; f. pain; g. satiety; h. endogenous; i. opioid; j. LSD; k. ecstasy; l. norepinephrine; m. dopamine; n. schizophrenia; o. cognition; p. marijuana; q. nitric oxide

Recap: 3.5   Removing Neurotransmitters from the Synapse
a. synapse; b. acetylcholine; c. serotonin; d. norepinephrine; e. cocaine; f. depression; g. SSRIs

Chapter 4

Recap: 4.1   An Overview of the Central Nervous System
a. meninges; b. dura; c. arachnoid; d. pia; e. cerebrospinal; f. meningitis; g. thoracic; h. sacral; i. spina bifida

Recap: 4.2   The Brain Stem
a. pons; b. cerebellum; c. medulla; d. spinal cord; e. alcohol; f. tegmentum; g. superior; h. inferior; i. reticular; j. prosencephalon; k. telencephalon; l. diencephalon; m. thalamus; n. pituitary

Recap: 4.3   The Telencephalon
a. hippocampus; b. amygdala; c. basal ganglia; d. cerebrum; e. cortex; f. anterior; g. posterior; h. frontal; i. parietal; j. occipital; k. temporal

Recap: 4.4   The Ventricles
a. ventricles; b. lateral; c. third; d. fourth; e. central

Recap: 4.5   The Distribution of Neurotransmitters in the Brain
a. norepinephrine; b. dopamine; c. serotonin; d. interneurons; e. glutamate; f. nicotinic; g. forebrain; h. cannabinoid

Recap: 4.6   The Peripheral Nervous System
a. 31; b. 12; c. olfactory; d. optic; e. trigeminal; f. facial; g. auditory; h. vagus; i. cervical; j. thoracic; k. lumbar; l. sacral; m. coccygeal; n. dermatome; o. thoracic; p. lumbar; q. brain; r. sacral

Chapter 5

Recap: 5.1   Brain Lesions and Brain Stimulation
a. lesioning; b. ablation; c. suctioning; d. stereotaxic; e. stereotaxic; f. electrode; g. neurotoxins; h. stimulation; i. transcranial magnetic

Recap: 5.2
a. electrical; b. evoked; c. microelectrodes; d. vitro; e. in vivo; f. ion; g. magnetoencephalography; h. images; i. single photon; j. neurotransmitter; k. blood; l. microdialysis

Recap: 5.3
a. autoradiography; b. retrograde; c. histological; d. excitation; e. chromatography

Recap: 5.4   Genetic Studies of Behavior
a. genotype; b. phenotype; c. family; d. twin; e. biological; f. monogenic; g. polygenic; h. multifactorial; i. gene

Recap: 5.5   Experimental Design
a. case; b. control; c. double blind; d. crossover; e. sham-operated; f. double dissociation

Chapter 6

Recap: 6.1   Muscle Structure and Function
a. fiber; b. acetylcholine; c. myosin; d. neuromuscular; e. motor unit; f. skeletal; g. red; h. white; i. smooth; j. flexion; k. extension; l. isotonic; m. isometric

Recap: 6.2   Spinal Control of Movement
a. reflexes; b. flexion; c. extrafusal; d. intrafusal; e. intrafusal; f. annulospiral; g. reciprocal innervation; h. Golgi tendon; i. motor neuron; j. crossed extensor; k. stretch

Recap: 6.3 Control of Movement by the Brain
a. pyramidal; b. extrapyramidal; c. primary motor;
d. pyramidal; e. extrapyramidal; f. cerebral; g. cerebellum; h. basal ganglia; i. nuclei; j. striatum

Recap: 6.4 Movement Disorders
a. movement; b. muscles; c. motor; d. quadriplegia;
e. paraplegia; f. transient flaccid; g. extrapyramidal;
h. basal ganglia; i. Parkinson's; j. L-dopa; k. cerebellum

Chapter 7
Recap: 7.1 Sensory Stimuli and Receptors
a. receptors; b. chemoreceptors; c. mechanoreceptors;
d. waves; e. wavelength; f. frequency; g. amplitude;
h. generator; i. transducers; j. adaptation; k. sensory

Recap: 7.2 The Visual System
a. photons; b. rods; c. cones; d. amacrine; e. ganglion;
f. photopigments; g. optic; h. nasal; i. lateral geniculate;
j. Trichromatic Color; k. opponent-process; l. astigmatism; m. glaucoma; n. presbyopia; o. cataracts; p. retinitis pigmentosa

Recap: 7.3 The Auditory System
a. hair; b. hertz; c. decibels; d. pinna; e. auditory meatus;
f. eardrum; g. ossicles; h. eustachian; i. cochlea;
j. vestibuli; k. tympani; l. media; m. basilar; n. auditory;
o. superior; p. inferior; q. medial; r. loudness; s. phase;
t. place; u. frequency; v. hearing aids; w. cochlear implants

Recap: 7.4 The Somatosensory System
a. muscles; b. joints; c. kinesthesia; d. interoception;
e. skin; f. pacinian; g. free; h. Ruffini's i. Krause;
j. stretch; k. lemniscal; l. extralemniscal; m. parietal

Recap: 7.5 The Olfactory System
a. odorants; b. olfactory; c. glomeruli; d. temporal;
e. prefrontal; f. pheromones; g. vomeronasal; h. anosmia; i. deficits

Recap: 7.6 The Taste System
a. sweet; b. sour; c. salty; d. bitter; e. umami; f. potentiation; g. taste buds; h. facial; i. glossopharyngeal; j. vagus;
k. solitary tract; l. frontal; m. ageusia; n. dysgeusia

Recap: 7.7 The Vestibular System
a. hair cells; b. saccule; c. semicircular; d. auditory;
e. nystagmus; f. motion sickness; g. Meniere's; h. vertigo

Chapter 8
Recap: 8.1 The Cerebrum's Role in Perception
a. bones; b. cytoarchitectonic; c. Brodmann's; d. cortex;
e. white matter; f. stellate; g. pyramidal

Recap: 8.2 Visual Processing
a. lateral geniculate; b. visual; c. ventral; d. dorsal;
e. parvocellular; f. magnocellular; g. color; h. temporal
cortex; i. parietal lobe; j. binding; k. blindsight; l. achromatopsia; m. akinetopsia; n. inferior; o. posterior

Recap: 8.3 Auditory Processing
a. temporal; b. ventrolateral; c. dorsolateral; d. pure
tones; e. phonemes; f. morphemes; g. expressive;
h. anomia; i. Wernicke's; j. paraphasia; k. conduction;
l. dysarthia; m. Broca's; n. Wernicke's; o. right; p. right;
q. left; r. left; s. amusia

Recap: 8.4 Somatosensory Processing
a. parietal; b. secondary; c. inferior; d. tactile agnosia;
e. posterior; f. phantom limb; g. gate-control; h. periaqueductal; i. periventricular; j. endorphins; l. P;
m. counterirritation; n. acupuncture; o. transcutaneous
electrical nerve

Recap: 8.5 Olfactory and Taste Processing
a. piriform; b. frontal; c. orbito-frontal; d. odor;
e. insula

Chapter 9
Recap: 9.1 The Frontal Lobe's Role in Cognition
a. frontal lobe; prefrontal; c. premotor; d. dorsolateral;
e. orbitofrontal

Recap: 9.2 Biological Basis of Memory
a. short-term; b. long-term; c. consolidation; d. working; e. working; f. anterior cingulated; g. declarative;
h. nondeclarative; i. hippocampus; j. hippocampus;
k. episodic; l. semantic; m. amygdala; n. epinephrine;
o. cortisol; p. acetylcholine; q. nondeclarative; r. amnesia; s. apraxia; t. Alzheimer's

Recap: 9.3 Biological Basis of Attention
a. event-related potential; b. primary; c. late; d. orienting; e. habituation; f. reticular; g. selective; h. attention
for action; i. action; j. anterior; k. vigilance; l. petit mal;
m. attention deficit hyperactivity; n. akinetic mutism;
o. autism; p. hyperekplexia

Recap: 9.4 Biological Basis of Learning
a. learning; b. explicit; c. implicit; d. synaptic; e. long-
term potentiation; f. glutamate; g. implicit; h. serotonin

Chapter 10
Recap: 10.1 Consciousness
a. consciousness; b. metacognition; c. amnesia; d. frontal
lobe; e. Asperger's; f. akinetic mutism; g. psychic self-
activation; h. coma; i. vegetative; j. locked-in; k. corpus
callosum; l. left

Recap: 10.2 Sleep
a. synchronous oscillations; b. synchronized; c. desynchronized; d. beta; e. alpha; f. I; g. II; h. IV; i. III;
j. sleep cycle; k. REM; l. REM; m. REM rebound

Recap: 10.3 Brain Mechanisms of Sleep and
Consciousness
a. reticular formation; b. raphe; c. norepinephrine;
d. suprachiasmic; e. melatonin; f. thalamocortical;
g. acetylcholine

Recap: 10.4 The Function of Sleep
a. passive; b. active; c. restorative; d. evolutionary;
e. REM; f. activation-synthesis; g. REM; h. non-REM

Recap: 10.5 Sleep Disorders
a. insomnia; b. induce; c. narcolepsy; d. sleep-apnea;
e. somnambulism; f. REM sleep behavior; g. nocturnal
enuresis; h. REM; i. non-REM; j. advanced; k. delayed

Chapter 11
Recap: 11.1 Regulation of Body Temperature
a. endotherms; b. homeothermic; c. shivering;

d. nonshivering; e. metabolism; f. hypothalamus;
g. calorigenic; h. Brown; i. evaporation; j. constrict;
k. piloerection; l. preoptic area; m. fever; n. calories

Recap: 11.2   Regulation of Food Intake
a. homeostasis; b. allostasis; c. macronutrients;
d. micronutrients; e. lateral; f. aphagia; g. paraventricular; h. stimulate; i. stimulate; j. vagus; k. adrenal; l. ventromedial; m. reduce; n. duodenum; o. cholecystokinin;
p. bombesin; q. glucagon; r. insulin; s. leptin; t. liver

Recap: 11.3   Eating Disorders
a. overeating; b. obesity; c. hyperinsulinemia; d. Type 2;
e. hypoglycemia; f. hypothalamus; g. hyperglycemia;
h. thyroid; i. leptin; j. bulimia; k. restricting anorexia;
l. anorexia nervosa–bulimic subtype; m. pica

Recap: 11.4   Regulation of Water Intake
a. intracellular; b. extracellular; c. osmotic; d. antidiuretic; e. hypovolemic; f. baroreceptors; g. renin;
h. angiotensin; i. angiotensin; j. primary; k. secondary;
l. prandial; m. schedule-induced polydipsia

Chapter 12
Recap: 12.1   Sexual Differentiation
a. sexual differentiation; b. X; c. X; d. Y; e. testes;
f. testosterone; g. Müllerian inhibiting substance;
h. Turner's; i. Klinefelter's; j. androgen insensitivity;
k. adrenogenital; l. corpus; m. interstitial; n. androgens

Recap: 12.2   Hormonal Regulation of Female Sexual
Behavior
a. gonadal; b. gonadotrophic; c. follicle-stimulating;
d. luteinizing; e. ovulation; f. progesterone; g. sexual
receptivity; h. amenorrhea; i. infertility; j. dysmenorrhea

Recap: 12.3   Hormonal Regulation of Male Sexual
Behavior
a. seasonal; b. nonseasonal; c. pituitary; d. sperm;
e. testosterone; f. puberty; g. FSH; h. ICSH; i. medial
preoptic; j. dopamine; k. serotonin

Recap: 12.4   Deviant Sexual Behavior
a. paraphilia; b. voyeurism; c. exhibitionism;
d. pedophilia; e. antiandrogen

Recap: 12.5   Comparing the Regulation of Male and
Female Sexual Behavior
a. estrogen; b. testosterone; c. dopamine; d. estrogen;
e. serotonin; f. oxytocin; g. orgasm; h. oxytocin

Chapter 13
Recap: 13.1   Emotion
a. emotion; b. sympathetic; c. positive; d. negative;
e. James-Lange; f. Cannon-Bard; g. Schachter-Singer;
h. vascular; i. cooling; j. increases

Recap: 13.2   Emotional Pathways in the Central
Nervous System
a. locus coeruleus; b. Papez; c. Yakolev's; d. limbic system; e. positive; f. negative; g. medial forebrain;
h. gray

Recap: 13.3   Negative Emotions
a. amygdala; b. Kluver-Bucy; c. Urbach-Wiethe;
d. aggression; e. temporal; f. low; g. high; h. fear;

i. endorphin; j. aggressive; k. anxiety; l. norepinephrine;
m. serotonin

Recap: 13.4   Positive Emotions
a. medial forebrain; b. rewarding; c. dopamine;
d. endorphins; e. reward deficiency

Recap: 13.5   Addiction
a. dopamine; b. D2; c. psychological; d. physical;
e. hedonic homeostatic dysregulation; f. preoccupation-
anticipation; g. binge-intoxication; h. withdrawal-
negative affect; i. preoccupation-anticipation; j.
binge-intoxication; k. withdrawal-negative; l. glutamate;
m. dopamine; n. serotonin; o. endorphin

Chapter 14
Recap: 14.1   Defining Stress
a. stressors; b. stress; c. paraventricular; d. solitary tract;
e. tegmentum; f. reticular; g. periaqueductal gray;
h. bed

Recap: 14.2   The Response to Acute Stress
a. acute; b. increased; c. suppressing; d. immune; e. norepinephrine; f. epinephrine; g. corticotropic releasing
hormone; h. adrenocorticotropic; i. cortisol; j. increase;
k. HPA; l. positive; m. negative; n. suppresses;
o. increases; p. terminated

Recap: 14.3   The Response to Chronic Stress
a. chronic; b. habituation; c. decrease; d. increase;
e. negative; f. hippocampus; g. glutamate; h. mesoprefrontal; i. orbitoprefrontal; j. dopamine; k. habituation;
l. sensitization; m. fear conditioning; n. failure;
o. extinction; p. learned helplessness; q. seizures;
r. memory impairment

Recap: 14.4   Disorders Associated with Stress
a. post-traumatic stress; b. major depressive; c. fatigue;
d. post-traumatic stress; e. flashbacks; f. norepinephrine;
g. norepinephrine; h. antidepressant; i. major depressive; j. cortisol; k. fatigue; l. chronic fatigue; m. seasonal
affective; n. fibromyalgia

Chapter 15
Recap: 15.1   Psychoses
a. psychoses; b. dementia; c. toxic; d. viral encephalitis;
e. meningitis; f. reversible; g. dementia pugilistica

Recap: 15.2   Schizophrenia
a. positive; b. negative; c. neuroleptics; d. D2; e. modified dopamine; f. NMDA receptor hypofunction;
g. diasthesis-stress; h. ventricles; i. hippocampus; j. prefrontal; k. dorsolateral; l. biological; m. smooth pursuit;
n. attention; o. information; p. poorly; q. multifactorial

Recap: 15.3   Mood Disorders
a. major depressive; b. monoamine; c. antidepressants;
d. acetylcholine; e. dexamethasone; f. thyroid; g. estrogen; h. melatonin; i. antidepressant; j. electroconvulsive;
k. transcranial magnetic; l. bipolar disorder; m. serotonin; n. norepinephrine; o. dopamine; p. lithium;
q. antidepressant; r. antipsychotic; s. anticonvulsant

Recap: 15.4   Personality Disorders
a. personality; b. schizophrenia spectrum; c. schizoid;

d. schizotypal; e. paranoid; f. antisocial; g. borderline;
h. antisocial; i. serotonin; j. borderline; k. serotonin

Chapter 16

Recap: 16.1   Brain Development
a. neural tube; b. radioglial; c. cell proliferation; d. cell
migration; e. fetus; f. cell differentiation; g. axonal;
h. dendritic; i. cell death; j. fetal alcohol; k. cerebral
palsy; l. holoproencephaly; m. hydrocephalus

Recap: 16.2   Brain Damage
a. prenatal; b. perinatal; c. postnatal; d. concussion;
e. contusion; f. laceration; g. petechial hemorrhage;
h. dementia pugilistica; i. meningitis; j. general paresis;
k. encephalitis; l. AIDS-related; m. Creutzfeldt-Jakob;
n. cardiovascular; o. cancer; p. atherosclerosis;
q. ischemic; r. hemorrhagic; s. glutamate; t. malnutrition; u. liver

Recap: 16.3   Recovery from Brain Damage
a. Kennard; b. functional; c. structural; d. regrowth;
e. waste product; f. axons; g. collateral sprouting;
h. branching; i. denervation hypersensitivity; j. removal;
k. transplantation; l. stem cells

Recap: 16.4   Aging of the Brain
a. fluid; b. myelin; c. ventricles; d. size; e. cerebellum;
f. substantia-nigra; g. dendrites; h. dendritic branching;
i. senile dementia; j. Alzheimer's; k. tau; l. ApoE;
m. Parkinson's; n. Pick's

Recap: 16.5   Assessing Brain Damage
a. postmortem autopsy; b. imaging; c. recording;
d. MRI; e. PET; f. EEC; g. test battery; h. Halstead-
Reitan; i. Luria-Nebraska

REFERENCES

Aartsen, E. J., Gallee, M. P., Snethlage, R. A., & Van Geel, A. N. (1994). Squamous cell carcinoma of the vagina in a male pseudohermaphrodite with 5alpha-reductase deficiency. *Int J Gynecol Cancer, 4,* 283–287.

Abe, T., Ayabe, M., Fujimoto, H., Imaizumi, T., Miura, Y., Nishimura, Y., & Shoji, H. (2001). Neurosyphilis showing transient global amnesia-like attacks and magnetic resonance imaging abnormalities mainly in the limbic system. *Intern Med, 40,* 439–442.

Abercrombie, E. D., & Jacobs, B. L. (1987). Single-unit response of noradrenergic neurons in the locus coeruleus of freely moving cats. I. Acutely presented stressful and non-stressful stimuli. *Journal of Neuroscience, 7,* 2837–2843.

Abercrombie, E. D., & Zigmond, M. J. (1995). Modification of central catecholiminergic systems by stress and injury. In F. E. Bloom & D. J. Kupfer (Eds.), *Psychopharmacology: The fourth generation.* New York: Raven Press.

Adams, D. B., Gold, A. R., & Burt, A. D. (1978). Rise in female-initiated sexual activity at ovulation and its suppression by oral contraceptives. *New England Journal of Medicine, 299*(21), 1145–1150.

Adams, M. A., & Ferraro, F. R. (1997). Acquired immunodeficiency syndrome dementia complex. *Journal of Clinical Psychology, 53*(7), 767–778.

Adolphs, R., Cahill, L., Schul, R., & Babinsky, R. (1997). Impaired declarative memory for emotional material following bilateral amygdala damage in humans. *Learning & Memory, 4*(3), 291–300.

Adolphs, R., Tranel, D., Damasio, H., & Damasio, A. (1994). Impaired recognition of emotion in facial expressions following bilateral damage to the human amygdala. *Nature, 372*(6507), 669–672.

Agarwal, S. K., Cohen, L., Henninger, E. M., Lloyd, C., Marshall, G. D. Jr., & Morris, G. J. (1998). Cytokine dysregulation associated with exam stress in healthy medical students. *Brain Behav Immun, 12,* 297–307.

Ager, J., Covington, C., Delaney-Black, V., Janisse, J., Martier, S., Nordstrom-Klee, B., Sokol, R. J., Sood, B., & Templin, T. (2001). Prenatal alcohol exposure and childhood behavior at age 6 to 7 years: I. Dose-response effect. *Pediatrics, 108,* E34.

Aggleton, J. P. (1992). *The amygdala: Neurobiological aspects of emotion, memory, and mental dysfunction.* New York: Wiley-Liss.

Aghajanian, G. K. (1995). Electrophysiology of serotonin receptor subtypes and signal transduction pathways. In F. E. Bloom, & D. J. Kupfer (Eds.), *Psychopharmacology: The fourth generation of progress.* New York: Raven Press.

Aghajanian, G. K., Alreja, M., & Nestler, E. J. (1999). Molecular control of locus coeruleus neurotransmission. *Biol Psychiatry, 46,* 1131–1139.

Agmo, A. (1999). Sexual motivation—an inquiry into events determining the occurrence of sexual behavior. *Behavior Brain Research, 105,* 129–150.

Agre, P., Frokiaer, J., Knepper, M. A., Kwon, T. H., Marples, & D., Nielsen, S. (2002). Aquaporins in the kidney: From molecules to medicine. *Physiol Rev, 82,* 205–244.

Aguzzi, A., & Glatzel, M. (2001). The shifting biology of prions. *Brain Res Brain Res Rev, 36,* 241–248.

Ahmed, S. H., & Koob, G. F. (1998). Transition from moderate to excessive drug intake: Change in hedonic set point. *Science, 282*(5387), 298–300.

Aiharam, Y., Akano, F., Hasegawa, H., Ishiwata, T., Otokawaa, M., Yasumatsu, M., & Yazawa, T. (2001). The role of preoptic area and anterior hypothalamus and median raphe nucleus on thermoregulatory system in freely moving rats. *Neurosci Lett, 306,* 126–128.

Akerstedt, T. (1985). Shifted sleep hours. *Annual Clinical Research, 17*(5), 273–279.

Akil, H., & Morano, M. I. (1996). The biology of stress: From periphery to brain. In S. J. Watson (Ed.), *Biology of schizophrenia and affective disease.* Washington, DC: American Psychiatric Press.

Al-Agha, A. E., Batch, J. A., & Thomsett, M. J. (2001). The child of uncertain sex: 17 years of experience. *J Paediatr Child Health, 37,* 348–351.

Al-Agha, A. E., Thomsett, M. J., & Batch, J, A. (2001). The child of uncertain sex: 17 years of experience. *Paediatric Child Health, 37,* 348–351.

Alarcon, G. S., Bradley, L. A., & McKendree-Smith, N. L. (2000). Pain complaints in patients with fibromyalgia versus chronic fatigue syndrome. *Curr Rev Pain, 4,* 148–157.

Alavi, A., Cloud, B., Ding, X. S., Freenberg, J., Groossman, M., Libon, D. J., Morrison, D., & Reivich, M. (2001). Progressive peripheral agraphia. *Neurocase, 7,* 339–349.

Alda, M. (2001). Genetic factors and treatment of mood disorders. *Bipolar Disord, 3,* 318–324.

Alexander, M. P. (2001). Chronic akinetic mutism after mesencephalic-diencephalic infarction: Remediated with dopaminergic medications. *Neurorehabil Neural Repair, 15,* 151–156.

Ali, M., Jha, S. K., Kaur, S., & Mallick, B. N. (1999). Role of GABA—A receptor in the preoptic area in the regulation of sleep–wakefulness and rapid eye movement sleep. *Neuroscience Research, 33,* 245–250.

Allen, L. S., Hines, M., Shryne, J. E., & Gorski, R. A. (1989). Two sexually dimorphic cell groups in the human brain. *Journal of Neuroscience, 9*(2), 497–506.

Allen, L. S., Richey, M. F., Chai, Y. M., & Gorski, R. A. (1991). Sex differences in the corpus callosum of the living human being. *Journal of Neuroscience, 11*(4), 933–942.

Altura, B. M., Altura, B. T., & Gebrewold, A. (1983). Alcohol-induced spasms of cerebral blood vessels: Relation to cerebrovascular accidents and sudden death. *Science, 220*(4594), 331–333.

Alzheimer, A. (1907). Uber eine eigenartige Erkangkung der Hirnrinde. *Allgemeine Zeitschr Psychiatr Psychisch-Gerichtliche Medizin, 64,* 146–148. (English translation: *Archives of Neurology,* 1967, 21, 109–110.)

American Psychiatric Association. (1994). *Diagnostic and statistical manual of mental disorders* (4th ed.) Washington, DC: American Psychiatric Association.

Amoore, J. E. (1971). Stereochemical and vibrational theories of odour. *Nature, 233*(5317), 270–271.

Amoore, J. E. (1974). Evidence for the chemical olfactory code in man. *Annals of the New York Academy of Sciences, 237,* 137–143.

Amoore, J. E. (1977). Specific anosmia and the concept of primary odors. *Chemical Senses, 2,* 267–281.

Ampollini, R., Brambilla, F., Delsignore, R., Gerra, G., Giusti, F., Laviola, G., Macchia, T., Raggi, M. A., & Zaimovic, A. (2001). Experimentally induced aggressive behavior in subjects with 3, 4-methylenedioxy-methamphetamine ("Ecstasy") use history: Psychobiological correlates. *J Subst Abuse, 13,* 471–491.

Anand, B. K., & Brobeck, J. R. (1951). Hypothalamic control of food intake in rats and cats. *Yale Journal of Biology and Medicine, 24,* 123–140.

Anderson, C., Ebers, G., Rice, G., & Risch, N. (1999). Male homosexuality: Absence of linkage to microsatellite markers at Xq28. *Science, 284,* 665–667.

Anderson, J. P., & Harris, J. P. (2001). Impact of Meniere's disease on quality of life. *Otolaryngology Neurotology, 22,* 888–894.

Anderson, J., & Wirz-Justice, A. (1991). Biological rhythms in the pathophysiology and treatment of affective disorders. In R. Horton & C. Katona (Eds.), *Biological aspects of affective disorders.* London: Academic Press.

Anderson, S. A., Eisenstat, D. D., Shi, L., & Rubenstein, J. L. (1997). Interneuron migration from basal forebrain to neocortex: Dependence on Dlx genes. *Science, 278*(5337), 402–406.

Andersson, B., Ekman, L., Gale, C. C., & Sundsten, J. W. (1963). Control of thyrotrophic hormone (TSH) secretion by the "heat loss center." *Acta Physiologica Scandinavica, 59,* 12–33.

Andreasen, N., Gottfries, J., Vanmechelen, E., Vanderstichele, H., Davidson, P., Blennow, K., Rosengren, L., & Blennow, K. (2001). Evaluation of CSF biomarkers for axonal and neuronal degeneration, gliosis, and beta-amyloid metabolism in Alzheimer's disease. *Journal of Neurology, Neurosurgery, and Psychiatry, 71,* 557–558.

Andreasen, N., Nasrallah, H. A., Dunn, V., Olson, S. C., Grove, W. M., Ehrhardt, J. C., Coffman, J. A., & Crossett, J. H. (1986). Structural abnormalities in the frontal system in schizophrenia: A magnetic resonance imaging study. *Archives of General Psychiatry, 43*(2), 136–144.

Andreasen, N. C. (1988). Brain imaging: Applications in psychiatry. *Science, 239,* 1381–1388.

Andreasen, N. C., Arndt, S., Swayze, V., Cizaldo, T., Flaum, M., O'Leary, D., Ehrhardt, J. C., & Yuh, W. T. C. (1994). Thalamic abnormalities in schizophrenia visualized through magnetic resonance image averaging. *Science, 266,* 294–298.

Anonymous. The genetics of homosexuality. *The Journal of NIH Research, 4,* 54.

Antelman, S. M., & Szechtman, H. (1975). Tail pinch induces eating in sated rats which appears to depend on nigrostriatal dopamine. Science, 189(4204), 731–733.

Antoch, M. P., Song, E. J., Chang, A. M., Vitaterna, M. H., Zhao, Y., Wilsbacher, L. D., Sangoram, A. M., King, D. P., Pinto, L. H., & Takahashi, J. S. (1997). Functional identification of the mouse circadian Clock gene by transgenic BAC rescue. *Cell, 89,* 655–667.

Arango, V., Underwood, M. D., & Mann, J. J. (1992). Alterations in monoamine receptors in the brain of suicide victims. *Journal of Clinical Psychopharmacology, 12*(2 Suppl), 8S–12S.

Arendt, J. (1988). Melatonin. *Clinical Endocrinology, 29*(2), 205–229.

Argyropoulos, S. V., & Nutt, D. J. (2000). Substance P antagonists: Novel agents in the treatment of depression. *Expert Opin Investig Drugs, 9,* 1871–1875.

Argiolas, A. (1999). Neuropeptides and sexual behavior. *Neuroscience Biobehavioral Review, 23*(8), 1127–1142.

Armand, J., & Kably, B. (1993). Critical timing of sensorimotor cortex lesions for the recovery of motor skills in the developing cat. *Experimental Brain Research, 93*(1), 73–88.

Arnold, S. E., Bordelon, Y. Gur, R. E., Gurevich, E. V., Joyce, J. N., & Shapiro, R. M. (1997). Mesolimbic dopamine D$_3$ receptors and use of antipsychotics in patients with schizophrenia: A postmortem study. *Arch Gen Psychiatry, 54,* 225–232.

Arpa, J., deAndres, I., Rodriguez, A. A., & Padrino, C. (1994). Insomnia secondary to vascular pontine tegmental lesions: Role of the superior central raphe nucleus. *Neurologia, 9*(9), 433–444.

Asberg, M. (1997). Neurotransmitters and suicidal behavior: The evidence from cerebrospinal fluid studies. In D. M. Stoff, J. Mann, et al. (Eds.), *The neurobiology of suicide: From the bench to the clinic.* New York: New York Academy of Sciences.

Asberg, M., Traskman, L., & Thoren, P. (1976). 5-HIAA in the cerebrospinal fluid: A biochemical suicide predictor? *Archives of General Psychiatry, 33*(10), 1193–1197.

Aserinsky, E., & Kleitman, N. (1953). Regularly occurring periods of eye motility, and concomitant phenomena, during sleep. *Science, 188,* 273–274.

Asherson, P., Mant, R., Williams, N., Cardno, A., Jones, L., Murphy, K., Collier, D. A., Nanko, S., Craddock, N., Morris, S., Muir, W., Blackwood, B., McGuffin, P., & Owen, M. J. (1998). A study of chromosome 4p markers and dopamine D5 receptor gene in schizophrenia and bipolar disorder. *Molecular Psychiatry, 3,* 310–320.

Ashtari, M., Bilder, R. M., Goldman, R. S., Knuth, K. H., Lieberman, J. A., Strous, R. D., & Szeszko, P. R. (2002). Neuropsychological correlates of hippocampal volumes in patients experiencing a first episode of schizophrenia. *Am J Psychiatry, 159,* 217–226.

Assal, G., Bogousslavsky, J., Ghika, J., Ghika-Schmid, F., Maeder, P., Scherer, K., Uske, A., Vuadens, P., & Vuilleumier, P. (1997). Bihippocampal damage with emotional dysfunction: impaired auditory recognition of fear. *Eur Neurol, 38,* 276–283.

Asthana, S., Raffaele, K. C., Greig, N. H., Schapiro, M. B., Blackman, M. R., & Soncrant, T. T. (1999). Neuroendocrine responses to intravenous infusion of physostigmine in patients with Alzheimer disease. *Alzheimer Disease and Associated Disorders, 13,* 102–108.

Aston-Jones, G., Chiang, C., & Alexinsky, T. (1991). Discharge of noradrenergic locus coeruleus neurons in behaving rats and monkeys suggests a role in vigilance. *Progress in Brain Research, 85,* 47–75.

Aujard, Y., Crivello, F., De Schonen, S., Mazoyer, B., Reutter, B., & Tzourio-Mazoyer, N. (2002). Neural correlates of woman face processing by 2-month-old infants. *Neuroimage, 15,* 454–461.

Axel, R. (1995). The molecular logic of smell. *Scientific American, 273*(4), 154–159.

Aye, P., Cazaugade, M., Dessalles, P. H., Labadens, P., Masson, F., Mokni, T., Senjean, P., Schmitt ,V., & Thicoipe M. (2001). Epidemiology of severe brain injuries: A prospective population-based study. *J Trauma, 51,* 481–489.

Azmitia, E. C., & Whitaker-Azmitia, P. M. (1995). Anatomy, cell biology, and plasticity of the serotonergic system. In F. E. Bloom & D. J. Kupfer (Eds.), *Psychopharmacology: The fourth generation of progress.* New York: Raven Press.

Babinski, J. (1914). Contribution a l'etude des troubles mentaux dans l'hemisplegic organique cerebrale (anosognosie). *Revue Neurologique, 27,* 845–848.

Baby, S., Nguyen, M., Raffa, R. B., & Tran, D. (1999). Substance P antagonists: The next breakthrough in treating depression? *J Clin Pharm Ther, 24,* 461–469.

Bachevalier, J., Brickson, M., Hagger, C., & Mishkin, M. (1990). Age and sex differences in the effects of selective temporal lobe lesions on the formation of visual discrimination habits in rhesus monkeys *(Macca mulata). Behavioral Neuroscience, 104,* 885–889.

Bachevalier, J., Hagger, C., & Bercu, B. (1989). Gender differences in visual habit formation in 3-month-old rhesus monkeys. *Developmental Psychobiology, 22,* 585–599.

Badan, M., Lazeyras, F., Ptak, R., Schnider, A., Valenza, N., & Zimine, I. (2001). Dissociated active and passive tactile shape recognition: A case study of pure tactile apraxia. *Brain, 124,* 2287–2298.

Baddeley, A. D., & Hitch, G. J. (2000). Development of working memory: Should the Pascual-Leone and the Baddeley and Hitch models be merged? *Journal of Experimental Child Psychology, 77,* 128–137.

Baddeley, A. D., & Warrington, E. K. (1973). Memory coding and amnesia. *Neuropsychologia, 11*(2), 159–165.

Baez, J., Cai, L. Q., DeFillo-Ricart, M., Herrera, C. Imperato-McGinley, J., Katz, M. D., Shackleton, C. H., & Zhu, Y. S. (1996). 5 alpha-reductase-2 gene mutations in the Dominican Republic. *J Clin Endocrinol Metab, 81*, 1730–1735.

Baghdoyan, H. A., Rodrigo-Angulo, M. L., McCarley, R. W., & Hobson, J. A. (1984). Site-specific enhancement and suppression of desynchronized sleep signs following cholinergic stimulation of three brainstem regions. *Brain Research, 306*(1–2), 39–52.

Bagshaw, C. R. (1993). *Muscle contraction.* London: Chapman & Hall.

Bailey, J. M., & Pillard, R. C. (1991). A genetic study of male sexual orientation. *Archives of General Psychiatry, 48*, 1089–1096.

Bajic, D., Proudfit, H., Valentino R. J., & Van Bockstaele, E. J. (2001). Topographic architecture of stress-related pathways targeting the noradrenergic locus coeruleus. *Physiol Behav, 73*, 273–283.

Bakshi, V. P., Shelton, S. E., & Kalin, N. H. (2000). Neurobiological correlates of defensive behaviors. *Prog Brain Res, 122*, 105–115.

Baldessarini, R. J., & Tarazi, F. I. (1996). Brain dopamine receptors: A primer on their current status, basic and clinical. *Harvard Review of Psychiatry, 3*, 301–325.

Bale, T. L., Davis, A. M., Auger, A. P., Dorsa, D. M., & McCarthy, M. M. (2001). CNS region-specific oxytocin receptor expression: Importance in regulation of anxiety and sex behavior. *Journal of Neuroscience, 21*, 2546–2552.

Ballas, C., Kohler, C. G., & Pickholtz, J. (2000). Neurosyphilis presenting as schizophrenialike psychosis. *Neuropsychiatry Neuropsychol Behav Neurol, 13*, 297–302.

Ballenger, J. C. (1995). Benzodiazepines. In A. F. Schatzberg & C. B. Nemeroff (Eds.), *The American Psychiatric Press textbook of psychopharmacology.* Washington, DC: American Psychiatric Press.

Ballenger, J. C. (2001). Overview of different pharmacotherapies for attaining remission in generalized anxiety disorder. *J Clin Psychiatry, 62*, 11–19.

Banciu, T., Weidenfeld, H., Wilham, V., Berinde, L., David, P., Sgavirdea, C., & Ocica, I. (1982). The hepatic component in alcoholic encephalopathy. *Med Interne, 20*, 67–71.

Bankiewicz, K. S., Eberling, J. L., Kohutnicka, M., Jagust, W., Pivirotto, P., Bringas, J., Cunningham, J.,

Budinger, T. F., & Harvey-White, J. (2000). Convection-enhanced delivery of AAV vector in parkinsonian monkeys; in vivo detection of gene expression and restoration of dopaminergic function using pro-drug approach. *Experimental Neurology, 164*(1), 2–14.

Baranowska, B., Wasilewska-Dziubinska, E., Radzikowska, M., Plonowski, A., & Roguski, K. (1997). Neuropeptide Y, galanin, and leptin release in obese women and in women with anorexia nervosa. *Metabolism, 46*(12), 1384–1389.

Barber, J., & Mayer, D. (1977). Evaluation of the efficacy and neural mechanism of a hypnotic analgesia procedure in experimental and clinical dental pain. *Pain, 4*(1), 41–48.

Bard, P. (1934). Emotion: I. The neurohumoral basis of emotional reactions. In C. Murchison (Ed.), *Handbook of general experimental psychology.* Worcester, MA: Clark University Press.

Bargmann, W., & Scharrer, E. (1951). The site of origin of the hormones of the posterior pituitary. *American Scientist, 39*, 255–259.

Barinaga, M. (1991). Is homosexuality biological? *Science, 253*, 956–957.

Barinaga, M. (1992). Sex on the brain. *Science, 257*, 619–621.

Barinaga, M. (1995). Dendrites shed their dull image. *Science, 268*, 200–201.

Barinaga, M. (1998). New lead to brain neuron regeneration. *Science, 282*, 1018–1019.

Barinaga, M. (2001). Neurobiology. How cannabinoids work in the brain. *Science, 291*, 2530–2531.

Barker, E. L., & Blakely, R. D. (1996). Identification of a single amino acid, phenylalanine 586, that is responsible for high affinity interactions of tricyclic antidepressants with the human serotonin transporter. *Molecular Pharmacology, 50*(4), 957–965.

Barkley, R. A. (1997). Attention-deficit/hyperactivity disorder, self-regulation, and time: Toward a more comprehensive theory. *Journal of Development and Behavioral Pediatrics, 18*(4), 271–279.

Barkovich, A. J., Simon, E. M. Clegg, N. J., Kinsman, S. L., & Hahn, J. S. (2002). Analysis of the cerebral cortex in holoprosencephaly with attention to the sylvian fissures. *AJNR Am J Neuroradiol, 23*, 143–150.

Barnard, E. A. (1995). The molecular biology of GABA$_A$ receptors and their structural determinants. In G. Biggio, E. Sanna, & E Costa, (Eds.), *GABA$_A$ receptors and anxiety: From neurobiology to treatment.* New York: Raven Press.

Barnard, N. D., & Kaufman, S. R. (1997). Animal research is wasteful

and misleading. *Scientific American, 276*, 80–82.

Barnes, T. R., Crawford, T. J., Cuthbert, I., Gibbins, H., Hutton, S. G., Joyce, E. M., & Kennard, C. (2001). Short and long term effects of antipsychotic medication on smooth pursuit eye tracking in schizophrenia. *Psychopharmacology, 157*, 284–292.

Barondes, S. H. (1993). *Molecules and mental illness.* New York: Scientific American Library.

Bartoshuk, L. M., & Beauchamp, G. K. (1994). Chemical senses. *Annual Review of Psychology, 45*, 419–449.

Bartoshuk, L. M., Duffy, V. B., Miller, I. J. (1994). PTC/PROP tasting: Anatomy, psychophysics, and sex effects. *Physiology & Behavior, 56*, 1165–1171.

Bastian, A. J., Mink, J. W., Kaufman, B. A., & Thach, W. T. (1998). Posterior vermal split syndrome. *Annals of Neurology, 44*, 601–610.

Bastian, A. J., & Thach, W. T. (1995). Cerebellar outflow lesions: A comparison of movement deficits resulting from lesions at the level of the cerebellum and thalamus. *Annals of Neurology, 38*, 881–892.

Bates, E., Dick, F., Dronkers, N., Gernsbacher, M. A., Utman, J. A., & Wulfeck, B. (2001). Language deficits, localization, and grammar: Evidence for a distributive model of language breakdown in aphasic patients and neurologically intact individuals. *Psychol Rev, 108*, 759–788.

Bauer, M., Berghofer, A., & Muller-Oerlinghausen, B. (2002). Bipolar disorder. *Lancet, 359*, 241–247.

Baum, A. (1990). Stress, intrusive imagery, and chronic distress. *Health Psychology, 9*, 653–675.

Baum, A., Cohen, L., & Hall, M. (1993). Control and intrusive memories as possible determinants of chronic stress. *Psychosomatic Medicine, 55*, 274–286.

Baum, M. J., Carroll, R. S., Erskine, M. S., & Tobet, S. A. (1985). Neuroendocrine response to estrogen and sexual orientation. *Science, 230*, 960–961.

Baumgarten, H. G., & Grozdanovic, Z. (1998). Role of serotonin in obsessive-compulsive disorder. *British Journal of Psychiatry–Supplement 35*, 13–20.

Bayati, A. L., Coutinho, S. V., Mayer, E. A., McRoberts, J. A., Miller, J. C., Plotsky, P. M., Sablad, M., & Zhou, H. (2002). Neonatal maternal separation alters stress-induced responses to viscerosomatic nociceptive stimuli in rat. *Am J Physiol Gastrointest Liver Physiol, 282*, G307–316

Beebe, K. L., Marshall, R. D., Oldham, M., & Zaninelli, R. (2001). Efficacy and safety of paroxetine treatment for chronic PTSD: A fixed-dose, placebo-controlled study. *Am J Psychiatry, 158,* 1982–1988.

Bell, J., Brady, K. T., Davidson, J., Farfel, G., Hegel, M. T., Londborg, P., Maddock, R., Pearlstein, T., & Rothbaum, B. (2001). Efficacy of sertraline in preventing relapse of posttraumatic stress disorder: Results of a 28-week double-blind, placebo-controlled study. *Am J Psychiatry, 158,* 1974–1981.

Belliveau, J. W., Kennedy, D. N., McKinstry, R. C., Buchbinder, B. R., Weisskoff, R. M., Cohen, M. S., Vevea, J. M., Brady, T. J., & Rosen, B. R. (1991). Functional mapping of the human visual cortex by magnetic resonance imaging. *Science, 254,* 716–719.

Bellugi, U., Hickok, G., Klima, E. S. (2001). Sign language in the brain. *Scientific American, 284,* 58–65.

Bellugi, U., Poizner, H., & Klima, E. S. (1983). Brain organization for language: Clues from sign aphasia. *Human Neurobiology, 2*(3), 155–70.

Benson, R. R., Cosgrove, G. R., Cole, A. J., Jiang, H., LeSueur, L. L., Buchbinder, B. R., Rosen, B. R., & Caviness, V. S. (1996). Functional MRI localization of language in a 9-year-old child. *Canadian Journal of Neurological Science, 23,* 213–219.

Berenbaum, S. A., & Hines, M. (1992). Early androgens are related to childhood sex-typed toy preferences. *Psychological Science, 3*(3), 203–206.

Berger-Sweeney, J., & Hohmann, C. F. (1997). Behavioral consequences of abnormal cortical development: Insights into development disabilities. *Behavioral Brain Research, 86*(2), 121–142.

Bergman, H., Chertkow, H., Wolfson, C., Stern, J., Rush, C., Whitehead, V., & Dixon, R. (1997). HM-PAO (CERETEC) SPECT brain scanning in the diagnosis of Alzheimer's disease. *Journal of the American Geriatric Society, 45,* 15–20.

Berkhout, J., Walter, D. O., & Adey, W. R. (1969). Alterations of the human electroencephalogram induced by stressful verbal activity. *Electroencephalography & Clinical Neurophysiology, 27*(5), 457–469.

Berkovitch, M., Copeliovitch, L., Tauber, C., Vaknin, Z., & Lahat, E. (1998). Hereditary insensitvity to pain with anhidrosis. *Pediatric Neurology, 19*(3), 227–229.

Berman, J. R., Adhikari, S. P., & Goldstein, I. (2000). Anatomy and physiology of female sexual function and dysfunction: Classification, evaluation and treatment options. *European Urology, 38*(1), 20–29.

Berman, K. F., Ostrem, J. L., Randolph, C., Gold, J., Goldberg, T. E., Coppola, R., Carson, R. E., Herscovitch, P., & Weinberger, D. R. (1995).

Physiological activation of a cortical network during performance of the Wisconsin Card Sorting Test: A positron emission tomography study. *Neuropsychologia, 33,* 1027–1046.

Berman, K. F., Torrey, E. F., Daniel, D. G., & Weinberger, D. R. (1992). Regional cerebral blood flow in monozygotic twins discordant and concordant for schizophrenia. *Archives of General Psychiatry, 49*(12), 927–934.

Berman, K. F., Zec, R. F., & Weinberger, D. R. (1986). Physiologic dysfunction of dorsolateral prefrontal cortex in schizophrenia. II. Role of neuroleptic treatment, attention, and mental effort. *Archives of General Psychiatry, 43*(2), 126–135.

Berman, R. M., Krystal, J. H., & Charney, D. S. (1996). Mechanism of action of antidepressants: Monoamine hypotheses and beyond. In S. J. Watson (Ed.), *Biology of schizophrenia and affective disease.* Washington, DC: American Psychiatric Press.

Berninger, B., & Poo, M. (1999). Exciting neurotrophins. *Nature, 401,* 862–863.

Berns, G. S., Cohen, J. D., & Mintun, M. A. (1997). Brain regions responsive to novelty in the absence of awareness. *Science, 276*(5316), 1272–1275.

Berrettini, W. H., Vuoristo, J., Ferraro, T. N., Buono, R. J., Wildenauer, D., & Ala-Kokko, L. (1998). Human G(olf) gene polymorphisms and vulnerability to bipolar disorder. *Psychiatric Genetics, 8*(4), 235–238.

Berry, M., Carlisle, J., & Hunter, A. (1996). Peripheral nerve explants grafted into the vitreous body of the eye promote the regeneration of retinal ganglion cell axons severed in the optic nerve. *Journal of Neurocytology, 25*(2), 147–170.

Bertollo, D. N., Cowen, M. A., & Levy, A. V. (1996). Hypometabolism in olfactory cortical projection areas of male patients with schizophrenia: An initial positron emission tomography study. *Psychiatry Research, 60*(2–3), 113–116.

Betarbet, R., Sherer, T. B., MacKenzie, G., Garcia-Osuna, M., Panov, A. V., & Greenamyre, J. T. (2000). Chronic systemic pesticide exposure reproduces features of Parkinson's disease. *Nature Neuroscience, 3,* 1301–1306.

Betke, K. (1991). New hearing threshold measurements for pure tones under free-field listening conditions. *Journal of Acoustic Soc Am, 89*(5), 2400–2403.

Bever, T. G., & Chiarello, R. G. (1974). Cerebral dominance in musicians and nonmusicians. *Science, 185*(150), 537–539.

Binder, J. R., Rao, S. M., Hammeke, T. A., Frost, J. A., Bandettini, P. A., &

Hyde, J. S. (1994). Effects of stimulus rate on signal response during functional magnetic resonance imaging of auditory cortex. *Brain Research: Cognitive Brain Research, 2*(1), 31–38.

Bito, L., Davson, H., Levin, E., Murray, M., & Snider, N. (1966). The concentration of free amino acids and other electrolytes in cerebrospinal fluid, in vivo dialysates of brain, and blood plasma of dog. *Journal of Neurochemistry, 13,* 1057–1067.

Bjorkum, A. A., Greene, R. W., McCarley, R. W., Porkka-Heiskanen, T., Strecker, R. E., & Thakkar, M. (1997). Adenosine: A mediator of the sleep-inducing effects of prolonged wakefulness. *Science, 276,* 1265–1267.

Black, S. E., Gao, F., Kohler, S., Moscovitch, M., Nadel, L., Priselac, S., & Rosenbaum, R. S. (2000). Remote spatial memory in an amnesic person with extensive bilateral hippocampal lesions. *Nat Neurosci, 3,* 1044–1048.

Blake-Mortimer, J., Gore-Felton, C., Kimerling, R., Turner-Cobb, J. M., & Spiegel, D. (1999). Improving the quality and quantity of life among patients with cancer: A review of the effectiveness of group psychotherapy. *European Journal of Cancer, 35,* 1581–1586.

Blansjaar, B. A., Thomassen, R., & Van Schaick, H. W. (2000). Prevalence of dementia in centenarians. *International Journal of Geriatric Psychiatry, 15*(3), 219–225.

Blanton, S. H., Heckenlively, J. R., & Cottingham, A. W. (1991). Linkage mapping of autosomal dominant retinitis pigmentosa (RP1) to the pericentric region of human chromosome 8. *Genomics, 11,* 857–869.

Blennow, K., Forsman, A., Manhem, A., & Soderstrom, H. (2001). CSF studies in violent offenders: I.5-HIAA as a negative and HVA as a positive predictor of psychopathy. *J Neural Transm, 108,* 869–878.

Bles, W., Bos, J. E., de Graaf, B., Groen, E., & Wertheim, A. H. (1998). Motion sickness: Only one provocative conflict? *Brain Research Bulletin, 47*(5), 481–487.

Bliss, T. V., & Lomo, T. (1973). Long-lasting potentiation of synaptic transmission in the dentate area of the anaesthezied rabbit following stimulation of the perforant path. *Journal of Physiology, 232*(2), 331–356.

Blokland, A. (1996). Acetylcholine: A neurotransmitter for learning and memory? *Brain Research Reviews, 21,* 285–300.

Bloom, K. K., & Kraft, W. A. (1998). Paranoia—an unusual presentation of hydrocephalus. *American Journal of Physical Medicine Rehabilitation, 77,* 157–159.

Blum, D., Torch, S., Lambeng, N., Nissou, M., Benabid, A. L., Sadoul, R., & Verna, J. M. (2001). Molecular pathways involved in the neurotoxicity of 6-OHDA, dopamine and MPTP: Contribution to the apoptotic theory in Parkinson's disease. *Progress in Neurobiology, 65,* 135–172.

Blum, K., Braverman, E. R., Chen, T. J., Comings, D. E., Holder, J. M., Lubar, J. F., Lubar, J. O., Miller, D., & Monastra, V. J. (2000). Reward deficiency syndrome: A biogenetic model for the diagnosis and treatment of impulsive, addictive, and compulsive behaviors. *J Psychoactive Drugs, 32,* 1–112.

Blum, K., Braverman, E. R., Wu, S., Cull, J. G., Chen, T. J., Gill, J., Wood, R., Eisenberg, A., Sherman, M., Davis, K. R., Matthews, D., Fischer, L., Schnautz, N., Walsh, W., Pontius, A. A., Zedar, M., Kaats, G., & Comings, D. E. (1997). Association of polymorphisms of dopamine D_2 receptor (DRD2), and dopamine transporter (DAT1) genes with schizoid/avoidant behaviors (SAB). *Molecular Psychiatry, 2,* 239–246.

Blum, K., Cull, J. G., Braverman, E. R., & Comings, D. E. (1996). Reward deficiency syndrome. *American Scientist, 84,* 132–145.

Blum, K., Sheridan, P., Chen, T., Wood, R., Braverman, E., Cull, J., & Comings, D. (1997). The dopamine D_2 receptor gene locus in reward deficiency syndrome: Meta-analysis. In K. Blum & E. Noble (Eds.), *Handbook of psychiatric genetics.* Boca Raton, FL: CRC Press.

Blumberg, M. S., Deaver, K., & Kirby, R. F. (1999). Leptin disinhibits nonshivering thermogenesis in infants after maternal separation. *Am J Physiol, 276,* R606–610.

Blundell, J. E. (1979). Hunger, appetite, and satiety-constructs in search of identities. In M. Turner (Ed.), *Proceedings of the British Nutrition Foundation.* London: Applied Sciences Publications.

Blundell, J. E. (1981). Bio-grammar of feeding: Pharmacological manipulations and their interpretations. In S. J. Cooper (Ed.), *Theory in psychopharmacology.* London: Academic Press.

Blundell, J. E. (1984). Serotonin and appetite. *Neuropharmacology, 23,* (12B), 1537–1551.

Blundell, J. E., Latham, C. J., & Lesham, M. B. (1976). Differences between the anorexic actions of amphetamine and fenfluramine—possible effects on hunger and satiety. *Journal of Pharmacology, 28*(6), 471–477.

Bogerts, B., & Falkai, P. (1995). Post mortem brain abnormalities in schiz-

ophrenia. In C. L. Shriqui & H. A. Nasrallah (Eds.), *Contemporary issues in the treatment of schizophrenia.* Washington, DC: American Psychiatric Press.

Bogerts, B., Falkai, P., Haupts, M., Greve, B., Ernst, S., Tapernon-Franz, U., & Heinzmann, U. (1990). Postmortem volume measurements of limbic system and basal ganglia structures in chronic schizophrenics. Initial results from a new brain collection. *Schizophrenia Research, 3*(5–6), 295–301.

Bogerts, B., Meertz, E., & Schoenfeldt-Bausch, R. (1985). Basal ganglia and limbic system pathology in schizophrenia: A morphometric study of brain volume and shrinkage. *Archives of General Psychiatry, 42*(8), 784–791.

Bohme, G. A., Bon, C., Stutzmann, J. M., Doble, A., & Blanchard, J. C. (1991). Possible involvement of nitric oxide in long-term potentiation. *European Journal of Pharmacology, 199*(3), 379–381.

Bolles, R. C. (1970). Species-specific defense reactions and avoidance learning. *Psychological Review, 77*(1), 32–48.

Bonte, F. J., Hom, J., Tintner, R., & Weiner, M. F. (1990). Single photon tomography in Alzheimer's disease and the dementias. *Seminar of Nuclear Medicine, 20*(4), 342–352.

Born, J., Hansen, K., Marshall, L., Molle, M., & Fehm, H. L. (1999). Timing the end of nocturnal sleep. *Nature, 397,* 29–30.

Bornstein, W. S. (1940). Cortical representation of taste in man and monkey: II. The localization of the cortical taste area in man and a method of measuring impairment of taste in man. *Yale Journal of Biology and Medicine, 13,* 133–156.

Botting, J. H., & Morrison, A. R. (1997). Animal research is vital to medicine. *Scientific American, 276,* 83–85.

Boucher, R., & Bryden, M. P. (1997). Laterality effects in the processing of melody and timbre. *Neuropsychologia, 35*(11), 1467–1473.

Boyer, P. (2000). Do anxiety and depression have a common pathophysiological mechanism? *Acta Psychiatr Scand Suppl, 406,* 24–29.

Boynton, R. M. (1979). *Human color vision.* New York: Holt, Rinehart and Winston.

Boyton, R. M., & Dolensky, S. (1979). On knowing books by their colors. *Perceptual & Motor Skills, 48*(2), 479–488.

Bracha, H. S., Davis, J. O., & Phelps, J. A. (1995). Prenatal development of monozygotic twins and concordance for schizophrenia. *Schizophrenia Bulletin 21,* 357–366.

Bradley, L. A., McKendree-Smith, N. L., & Alarcon, G. S. (2000). Pain complaints in patients with fibromyalgia versus chronic fatigue syndrome. *Curr Rev Pain, 4,* 148–157.

Brain, R. (1961). *Speech disorders.* London: Butterworth.

Bray, N., Chadwick, A., French, S. J., Gray, J. A., Hodges, H., Patel, S., Rashid, T. P., & Veizovic, T. (2000). Conditionally immortal neuroepithelial stem cell grafts reverse age-associated memory impairments in rats. *Neuroscience, 101,* 945–955.

Brecknell, J. E., & Fawcett, J. W. (1996). Axonal regeneration. *Biological Review of the Cambridge Philosophical Society, 71*(2), 227–255.

Breedlove, S. M. (1994). Sexual differentiation of the human nervous system. *Annual Review of Psychology, 45,* 389–418.

Breier, A., Buchanan, R., Elkashef, A., Munson, R. C., Kirkpatrick, B., & Gellad, F. (1992). Brain morphology and schizophrenia. A magnetic resonance imaging study of limbic, prefrontal cortex, and caudate structures. *Archives of General Psychiatry, 49*(12), 921–926.

Breiter, H. C., & Rosen, B. R. (1999). Functional magnetic resonance imaging of brain reward circuitry in the human. *Annals of the New York Academy of Sciences, 29*(877), 523–547.

Bremer, F. (1935). Cerveau isole and physiologie du sommeil. *Compt Rendus de la Societe de Biologie, 118,* 1235–1242.

Bremner, J. D., Innis, R. B., Ng, C. K., & Staib, L. H. (1997). Positron emission tomography measurement of cerebral metabolic correlates of yohimbine administration in combat-related posttraumatic stress disorder. *Archives of General Psychiatry, 54,* 246–254.

Bremner, J. D., Krystal, J. H., Southwick, S. M., & Charney, D. S. (1996). Noradrenergic mechanisms in stress and anxiety: I. Preclinical studies. *Synapse, 23*(1), 28–38.

Bremner, J. D., Southwick, S. M., Johnson, D. R., & Yehuda, R. (1993). Childhood physical abuse and combat-related posttraumatic stress disorder in Vietnam veterans. *American Journal of Psychiatry, 150,* 235–239.

Bremner, J. D., Southwick, S. M., & Charney, D. S. (1999). The neurobiology of posttraumatic stress disorder: An integration of animal and human research. In P. A. Saigh & J. D. Bremner (Eds.), *Posttraumatic stress disorder: A comprehensive text.* Needham Heights, MA: Allyn and Bacon.

Brewer, J. B., Zhao, Z., Desmond, J. E., Glover, G. H., & Gabrieli, J. D.

(1998). Making memories: Brain activity that predicts how well visual experience will be remembered. *Science, 281*(5380), 1185–1187.

Britton, D. R., Koob, G. F., Rivier, J., & Vale, W. (1982). Intraventricular corticotropin-releasing factor enhances behavioral effects of novelty. *Life Sciences, 31*(4), 363–367.

Brobeck, J. R. (1955). Neural regulation of food intake. *Annals of the New York Academy of Sciences, 63*, 44–55.

Brown, A. S., Dingemans, A., Gispen-de Wied, C. C., Hoek, H. W., Hulshoff Pol, H. E., Kahn, R. S., Pereira Ramos, L. M., Schnack, H. G., Susser, E., & van Haren, N. E. (2000). Prenatal exposure to famine and brain morphology in schizophrenia. *Am J Psychiatry, 157*, 1170–1172.

Brown, A. S., Gorman, J. M., Hoek, H. W., Labovitz, D., Lin, S., & Neugebauer, R. (1996). Schizophrenia after prenatal famine: Further evidence. *Arch Gen Psychiatry, 53*, 25–31.

Brown, C. S., Kent, T. A., Bryant, S. G., & Gevedon, R. M.(1989). Blood platelet uptake of serotonin in episodic aggression. *Psychiatry Research, 27*, 5–12.

Brown, J. L., & Pollitt, E. (1996). Malnutrition, poverty and intellectual development. *Scientific American, 274*(2), 38–43.

Brun, A. (1972). Perinatal encephalopathies caused by maternal diseases during pregnancy. *European Neurology, 7*(4), 201–220.

Brun, A., & Passant, U. (1996). Frontal lobe degeneration of non-Alzheimer type. Structural characteristics, diagnostic criteria and relation to other frontotemporal dementias. *Acta Neurology Scandinavia, Supplement, 168*, 28–30.

Buchalter, E. N., Lantz, M. S., & American Association for Geriatric Psychiatry. (2001). Posttraumatic stress: Helping older adults cope with tragedy. *Geriatrics, 56*, 35–36.

Buchwald, E., & Vorstrup, S. (1996). Creutzfeldt-Jakob disease—A human prion disease. *Nordic Medicine, 111*(6), 180–183.

Buckner, R. L., Corbetta, M., Schatz, J., Raichle, M. E., & Petersen, S. E. (1996). Preserved speech abilities and compensation following prefrontal damage. *Proceedings of the National Academy of Sciences, USA, 93*(3), 1249–1253.

Buffenstein, R., Poppitt, S. D., McDevitt, R. M., & Prentice, A. M. (1995). Food intake and the menstrual cycle: A retrospective analysis, with implications for appetite research. *Physiological Behavior, 58*(6), 1067–1077.

Burgess, N., Maguire, E. A., & Spiers, H. J. (2001). Hippocampal amnesia. *Neurocase, 7*, 357–382.

Burnet, P. W., & Harrison, P. J. (2000). Substance P (NK1) receptors in the cingulate cortex in unipolar and bipolar mood disorder and schizophrenia. *Biological Psychiatry, 47*, 80–83.

Burns, R. S., Chiueh, C. C., Markey, S. P., Ebert, M. H., Jacobowitz, D. M., & Kopin, I. J. (1983). A primate model of parkinsonism: Selective destruction of dopaminergic neurons in the pars compacta of the substantia nigra by N-methyl-4-phenyl-1,2,3,6-tetrahydropyridine. *Proceedings of the National Academy of Sciences, 80*, 4546–4550.

Burt, J. M., & Spray, D. C. (1988). Single channel events and gating behavior of the cardiac gap junction channel. *Proceedings of the National Academy of Sciences, USA, 85*, 3431–3434.

Burton, M. J., Rolls, E. T., & Mora, F. (1976). Effects of hunger on the responses of neurons in the lateral hypothalamus to the sight and taste of food. *Experimental Neurology, 51*(3), 668–677.

Butler, R. J. (2001). Combination therapy for nocturnal enuresis. *Scand J Urol Nephrol, 35*, 364–369.

Butters, N., Delis, D. C., & Lucas, J. A. (1995). Clinical assessment of memory disorders in amnesia and dementia. *Annual Review of Psychology, 46*, 493–523.

Buuck, R. J., Tharp, G. D., & Brumbaugh, J. A. (1976). Effects of chronic exercise on the ultrastructure of the adrenocortical cells in the rat. *Cell Tissue Research,168*, 261–270.

Bylsama, F. W., Moberg, P. J., Doty, R. L., & Brandt, J. (1997). Odor identification in Huntington's disease patients and asymptomatic gene carriers. *Journal of Neuropsychiatry and Clinical Neuroscience, 9*(4), 598–600.

Byne, William. (1994). The biological evidence challenged. *Scientific American, 270*, 51–55.

Cahill, L., Haier, R. J., Fallon, J., Alkire, M. T., Tang, C., Keator, D., Wu, J., & McGaugh, J. L. (1996). Amygdala activity at encoding correlated with long-term, free recall of emotional information. *Proceedings of the National Academy of Sciences, USA, 93*(15), 8016–8021.

Cahill, L., Prins, B., Weber, M., & McGaugh, J. L. (1994). Beta-adrenergic activation and memory for emotional events. *Nature, 371*(6499), 702–704.

Cai, L. Q., Zhu, Y. S., Katz, M. D., Herrera, C., Baez, J., DeFillo-Ricart, M., Shackleton, C. H., Imperato-McGinley, J. (1996). 5 alpha-reductase-2 gene mutations in the Dominican Republic. *J Clin Endocrinol Metab, 81*(5), 1730–1735.

Calogero, A. E., Gallucci, W. T., Chrousos, G. P., & Gold, P. W. (1988). Interaction between GABAergic neurotransmission and rat hypothalamic corticotropin-releasing hormone secretion in vitro. *Brain Research, 463*(1), 28–36.

Calvert, G. A., Bullmore, E. T., Brammer, M. J., Campbell, R., Williams, S. C., McGuire, P. K., Woodruff, P. W., Iverson, S. D., & David, A. S. (1997). Activation of auditory cortex during silent lipreading. *Science, 276*(5312), 593–596.

Campbell, S. S., Dawson, D., & Anderson, M. W. (1993). Alleviation of sleep maintenance insomnia with timed exposure to bright light. *Journal of the American Geriatric Society, 41*(8), 829–836.

Campbell, S. S., & Murphy, P. J. (1998). Extraocular circadian phototransduction in humans. *Science, 279*(5349), 396–399.

Campeau, S., & Davis, M. (1990). Reversible neural inactivation by cooling in anesthetized and freely behaving rats. *Journal of Neuroscience Methods, 32*, 25–35.

Cannon, W. B. (1912). An explanation of hunger. *American Journal of Physiology, 29*, 441–454.

Cannon, W. B. (1927). The James-Lange theory of emotions: A critical examination and an alternative theory. *American Journal of Psychology, 39*, 106–124.

Cannon, W. B. (1929). Hunger and thirst. In C. Murchison (Ed.), *The foundations of experimental psychology*. Worcester, MA: Clark University Press.

Cantor, J. M., Binik, Y. M., & Pfaus, J. G. (1999). Chronic fluoxetine inhibits sexual behavior in the male rat: Reversal with oxytocin. *Psychopharmacology,144*, 355–362.

Caramazza, A., & Hillis, A. E. (1991). Lexical organization of nouns and verbs in the brain. *Nature, 349*(6312), 788–790.

Cardinali, D. P. (1981). Melatonin: A pineal modulatory signal affecting pituatary function. *Prognosis of Clinical Biological Research, 74*, 179–198.

Carmichael, M. S., Warburton, V. L., Dixen, J., & Davidson, J. M. (1994). Relationships among cardiovascular, muscular, and oxytocin responses during human sexual activity. *Archives of Sexual Behavior, 23*(1), 59–79.

Carpenter, D. O. (2001). Effects of metals on the nervous system of humans and animals. *Int J Occup Med Environ Health, 14*, 209–218.

Carpenter, P. A., Just, M. A., & Shell, P. (1990). What one intelligence test measures: A theoretical account of the processing in the Raven Progressive Matrices Test. *Psychological Review, 97,* 404–431.

Carretie, L., Martin-Loeches, M., Hinojosa, J. A., & Mercado F. (2001). Emotion and attention interaction studied through event-related potentials. *J Cogn Neurosci, 13,* 1109–1128.

Carroll, D., Fairman, F., Leijon, G., McQuay, H. J., Moore, R. A., & Tramer, M. (2001). Transcutaneous electrical nerve stimulation (TENS) for chronic pain (Cochrane Review). *Cochrane Database Syst Rev, 3,* CD003222.

Carter, C. S. Neuroendocrine perspectives on social attachment and love. *Psychoneuroendocrinology, 23,* 779–818.

Carter, C. S., Braver, T. S., Barch, D. M., Botvinick, M. M., Noll, D., & Cohen, J. D. (1998). Anterior cingulate cortex, error detection, and the online monitoring of performance. *Science, 280*(5364), 747–749.

Caselli, R. J. (1991). Bilateral impairment of somesthetically mediated object recognition in humans. *Mayo Clinic Proceedings, 66*(4), 357–364.

Casper, R. C. (1996). Carbohydrate metabolism and its regulatory hormones in anorexia nervosa. *Psychiatry Research, 62*(1), 85–96.

Casper, R. C. (1998). Recognizing eating disorders in women. *Psychopharmacology Bulletin, 34,* 267–269.

Cave, C. B., & Squire, L.R. (1992). Intact and long-lasting repetition priming in amnesia. *Journal of Experimental Psychology: Learning, Memory, & Cognition, 18*(3), 509–520.

Cen, X., Lu, L., & Wang, X. (2001). Noradrenaline in the bed nucleus of the stria terminalis is critical for stress-induced reactivation of morphine-conditioned place preference in rats. *Eur J Pharmacol, 432,* 153–161.

Cerezo, M. A., & Frias, D. (1994). Emotional and cognitive adjustment in abused children. *Child Abuse and Neglect, 18*(11), 923–932.

Cermak, L. S., Talbot, N., Chandler, K., & Wolbarst, L. R. (1985). The perceptual priming phenomenon in amnesia. *Neuropsycholgia, 23*(5), 615–622.

Chadwick, A., French, S. J., Gray, J. A., Hodges, H., Kershaw, T. R., Mora, A., Nelson, A., Patel, S., Rashid, T., Sinden, J. D., Sowinski, P., Veizovic, T., Virley, D., & Watson, W.P. (2000). Functional reconstruction of the hippocampus: Fetal versus conditionally immortal neuroepithelial stem cell grafts. *Novartis Found Symp, 231,* 53–65.

Chang, L., Ernst, T., Poland, R. E., & Jenden, D. J. (1996). In vivo proton magnetic resonance spectroscopy of the normal aging human brain. *Life Science, 58,* 2049–2056.

Changeux, J-P. (1993, November). Chemical signaling in the brain. *Scientific American,* 58–62.

Channon, S., Charman, T., Crawford, S., Heap, J., & Rios, P. (2001). Real-life type problem-solving in Asperger's syndrome. *J Autism Dev Disord, 31,* 461–469.

Chapman, P. F., Atkins, C. M., Allen, M. T., Haley, J. E., & Steinmetz, J. E. (1992). Inhibition of nitric oxide synthesis impairs two different forms of learning. *Neuroreport, 3*(7), 567–570.

Charles, T., & Swash, M. (2001). Amyotrophic lateral sclerosis: Current understanding. *Journal of Neuroscience Nursing, 33,* 245–253.

Charness, M. E. (1993). Brain lesions in alcoholics. *Alcohol Clinical Experimental Research, 17*(1), 2–11.

Charness, N. (1998). Ergonomics and aging: The role of interactions. *Student Health Technology Information, 48,* 62–73.

Charney, D. S., Bremner, J. D., & Redmond, D. E. (1995). Noradrenergic neural substrates for anxiety and fear. In F. E. Bloom & D. J. Kupfer (Eds.), *Psychopharmacology: The fourth generation.* New York: Raven Press.

Charney, D. S., Deutch, A. Y., Southwick, S. M., & Krystal, J. H. (1995). Neural circuits and mechanisms of post-traumatic stress disorder. In M. J. Friedman & D. S. Charney (Eds.), *Neurobiological and clinical consequences of stress: From normal adaptation to post-traumatic stress disorder.* Philadelphia: Lippincott Williams & Wilkins.

Charney, D. S., Woods, S. W., Nagy, L. M., Southwick, S. M., Krystal, J. H., & Heninger, G. R. (1990). Noradrenergic function in panic disorder. *Journal of Clinical Psychiatry, 51* (Suppl A), 5–11.

Chemelli, R. M., Willie, J. T., Sinton, C. M., Elmquist, J. K., Scammell, T., Lee, C., Richardson, J. A., Williams, S. C., Xiong, Y., Kisanuki, Y., Fitch, T. E., Nakazato, M., Hammer, R. E., Saper, C. B., & Yanagisawa, M. (1999). Narcolepsy in orexin knockout mice: Molecular genetics of sleep regulation. *Cell, 98*(4), 437–451.

Chen, J. P., Parades, W., Lowinson, J. H., & Gardner, E. L. (1991). Strain-specific facilitation of dopamine efflux by delta 9-tetrahydrocannabinol in the nucleus accumbens of rat: An in vivo microdialysis study. *Neuroscience Letters, 129*(1), 136–180.

Cheney, D. L., & Seyfarth, R. M. (1990). The representation of social relations by monkeys. *Cognition, 37*(1–2), 167–196.

Chertin, B., & Farkas, A. (2001). Feminizing genitoplasty in patients with 46XX congenital adrenal hyperplasia. *J Pediatr Endocrinol Metab, 14,* 713–722.

Chess, S. (1977). Follow-up report on autism in congenital rubella. *Journal of Autism and Child Schizophrenia, 7*(1), 69–81.

Chess, S., & Fernandez, P. (1980). Neurologic damage and behavior disorder in rubella children. *American Annals of the Deaf, 125*(8), 998–1001.

Chicural, M. (2001). Mutant gene speeds up the human clock. *Science, 291,* 226–227.

Choi, D.W. (1992). Excitoxic cell death. *Journal of Neurobiology, 23*(9), 1261–1276.

Choi, D. W., Gottlieb, D. I., Liu, S., Liu X. Z., McDonald, J. W., Mickey, S. K., & Turetsky, D. (1999). Transplanted embryonic stem cells survive, differentiate and promote recovery in injured rat spinal cord. *Nat Med, 5,* 1410–1412.

Ciaranello, R. D. (1992). Brain development: Pervasive development disorders and infantile autism. *New Directions in Mental Health Service, 54,* 9–17.

Ciaranello, R. D. (1996). Linkage and molecular genetics of infantile autism. In S. J. Watson (Ed.), *Biology of schizophrenia and affective disease.* Washington, DC: American Psychiatric Press.

Civardi, C., Cantello, R., Asselman, P., Rothwell, J. C. (2001). Transcranial magnetic stimulation can be used to test connections to primary motor areas from frontal and medial cortex in humans. *Neuroimage, 14,* 1444–1453.

Clark, A. S., & Goldman-Rakic, P. (1989). Gonadal hormones influence the emergence of cortical function in nonhuman primates. *Behavioral Neuroscience, 103,* 1287–1295.

Clark, J. M., Clark, A. J., Bartle, A., & Winn, P. (1991). The regulation of feeding and drinking in rats with lesions of the lateral hypothalamus made by N-methyl-D-aspartate. *Neuroscience, 45*(3), 631–640.

Clarke, J. M. (1994). Brain structure and function. In D. W. Zaidel (Ed.), *Neuropsychology* (pp. 1–28). San Diego, CA: Academic Press.

Clarren, S. K., Alvord, E. C., Sumi, S. M., Streissguth, A. P., & Smith, D. W. (1978). Brain malformations related to prenatal exposure to ethanol. *Journal of Pediatrics, 92,* 64–67.

Clayton, E. C., & Williams, C. L. (2000). Adrenergic activation of the nucleus tractus solitarius potentiates amygdala norepinephrine release and enhances retention performance in emotionally arousing and spatial memory tasks. *Behavioural Brain Research, 112,* 151–158.

Cleare, A. J., Heap, E., Miell, J., Malhi, G. S., Miell, J., O'Keane, V.,

Sookdeo, S., & Young L. (2001). Hypothalamo-pituitary-adrenal axis dysfunction in chronic fatigue syndrome, and the effects of low-dose hydrocortisone therapy. *J Clin Endocrinol Metab, 86*, 3545–3554.

Coccaro, E. F., & Kavoussi, R. J. (1991). Biological and pharmacological aspects of borderline personality disorder. *Hospital Community Psychiatry, 42*(10), 1029–1033.

Coccaro, E. F., Kavoussi, R. J., Hauger, R. L., Cooper, T. B., & Ferris, C. F. (1998). Cerebrospinal fluid vasopressin levels: Correlates with aggression and serotonin function in personality-disordered subjects. *Archives of General Psychiatry, 55*, 708–714.

Cockerill, I. M., & Riddington, M. E. (1996). Exercise dependence and associated disorders: A review. *Counseling Quarterly Journal, 9*, 119–129.

Cohen, D. (1968). Magnetoencephalography: Evidence of magnetic field produced by alpha-rhythm current. *Science, 161*, 784–786.

Cohen, D., Cuffin, B. N., Yunokuchi, K., Maniewski, R., Purcell, C., Cosgrove, G. R., Ives, J., Kennedy, J. G., & Schomer, D. L. (1990). MEG versus EEG localization test using implanted sources in the human brain. *Annals of Neurology, 28*, 811–817.

Cohen, S., Tyrrell, D. A., & Smith, A. P. (1991). Psychological stress and susceptibility to the common cold. *New England Journal of Medicine, 325*, 606–612.

Cole, S. W., Kemeny, M. E., Miller, G. E., Taylor, S. E., & Visscher, B. R. (1997). Social relationships and immune processes in HIV seropositive gay and bisexual men. *Ann Behav Med, 19*, 139–151.

Cole, V. A. (1995). Different uses of chromatic signals in patients with congenital and acquired colour vision deficiencies. *Ophthalmic Physiological Optometry, 15*(5), 399–402.

Collins, D. L., Baum, A., Singer, J. E. (1983). Coping with chronic stress at Three Mile Island: Psychological and biochemical evidence. *Health Psychology, 2*, 149–166.

Collins, M. P., Lorenz, J. M., Jetton, J. R., & Paneth, N. (2001). Hypocapnia and other ventilation-related risk factors for cerebral palsy in low birth weight infants. *Pediatric Research, 50*, 712–719.

Comer, R. J. (1996). *Fundamentals of abnormal psychology*. New York: W. H. Freeman.

Connor, B., Kozlowski, D. A., Schallert, T., Tillerson, J. L., Davidson, B. L., & Bohn, M. C. (1999). Differential effects of glial cell line-derived neurotrophic factor (GDNF) in the striatum and substantia nigra of the aged Parkinsonian rat. *Gene Therapy, 6*, 1936–1951.

Conti, L., Sipione, S., Magrassi, L., Bonfanti, L., Rigamonti, D., Pettirossi, V., Peschanski, M., Haddad, B., Pelicci, P., Milanesi, G., Pelicci, G., & Cattaneo, E. (2001). Shc signaling in differentiating neural progenitor cells. *Nature Neuroscience, 4*, 579–586.

Cooper, J. R., Bloom, F. E., & Roth, R. H. (1996). *The biochemical basis of neuropharmacology* (7th ed.). New York: Oxford University Press.

Cooper, S. J., & Higgs, S. (1994). Neuropharmacology of appetite and taste preferences. In C. R. Legg & D. A. Booth (Eds.), *Appetite: Neural and behavioural bases*. New York: Oxford University Press.

Coppen, A. J. (1968). Depressed state and indolealkylamines. *Advanced Pharmacology, 6*, 283–291.

Corballis, M. C. (1994). Can commissurotomized subjects compare digits between the visual fields? *Neuropsychologia, 32*(12), 1475–1486.

Corballis, M. C. (1995). Visual integration in the split brain. *Neuropsychologia, 33*(8), 937–959.

Corbetta, M., Miezin, F. M., Shulman, G. L., & Petersen, S. E. (1991). Selective attention modulates extrastriate visual regions in humans during visual feature discrimination and recognition. *Ciba Foundation Symposium*, 165–180.

Corina, D. P., Vaid, J., & Bellugi, U. (1992). The linguistic basis of left hemisphere specialization. *Science, 255*(5049), 1258–1260.

Cotman, C. W., Kahle, J. S., Miller, S. E., Ulas, J., Bridges, R. J., & Paul, S. M. (1995). Amino acids. In F. E. Bloom & D. Kupfer (Eds.), *Psychopharmacology: The fourth generation of progress*. New York: Raven Press.

Coull, J. T. (1998). Neural correlates of attention and arousal: Insights from electrophysiology, functional neuroimaging and psychopharmacology. *Prog Neurobiology, 55*(4), 343–361.

Courtney, S. M. (1996). Object and spatial visual working memory activate separate neural systems in human cortex. *Cerebral Cortex, 6*(1), 39–49.

Courtney, S. M., Petit, L., Maisog, J. M., Ungerleider, L. G., & Haxby, J. V. (1998). An area specialized for spatial working memory in human frontal cortex. *Science, 279*, 1347–1351.

Courtney, S. M., Ungerleider, L. G., Keil, K., & Haxby, J. V. (1996). Object and spatial visual working memory activate separate neural systems in human cortex. *Cerebral Cortex, 6*, 39–49.

Coutinho, S. V., Plotsky, P. M., Sablad, M., Miller, J. C., Zhou, H., Bayati, A. I., McRoberts, J. A., & Mayer, E. A. (2002). Neonatal maternal separation alters stress-induced responses to viscerosomatic nociceptive stimuli in rat. *Am J Physiol Gastrointest Liver Physiol, 282*, G307–G316.

Cowan, W. M. (1979). The development of the brain. *Scientific American, 241*(3), 113–133.

Cowey, A., Hodinott-Hill, I., & Weiskrantz, L. (2002). Prime-sight in a blindsight subject. *Nat Neurosci, 5*, 101–102.

Coyle, J. T., Price, D. L., & Delong, M. R. (1983). Alzheimer's disease: A disorder of cortical cholinergic innervation. *Science, 219*(4589), 1184–1190.

Craig, A. D., Reiman, E. M., Evans, A., & Bushnell, M. C. (1996). Functional imaging of an illusion of pain. *Nature, 384*, 258–260.

Craig, J. C., & Rollman, G. B. (1999). Somethesis. *Annual Review of Psychology, 50*, 305–331.

Craig, K. J., Brown, K. J., & Baum, A. (1995). Environmental factors in the etiology of anxiety. In F. E. Bloom & D. J. Kupfer (Eds.), *Psychopharmacology: The fourth generation*. New York: Raven Press.

Craven, C. (2001). Pineal germinoma and psychosis. *J Am Acad Child Adolesc Psychiatry, 40*, 6.

Crawley, J. N. (1999). Behavioral phenotyping of transgenic and knockout mice: Experimental design and evaluation of general health, sensory functions, motor abilities, and specific behavioral tests. *Brain Research, 835*(1), 18–26.

Crease, R. P. (1991). Images of conflict: MEG vs. EEG. *Science, 253*, 374–375.

Creed, R. S., Denny-Brown, D., Eccles, J. C., Liddell, E. G. T., & Sherrington, C. S. (1932). *Reflex activity of the spinal cord*. Oxford: Clarendon Press.

Creed, R. S., Denny-Brown, D., Eccles, J. C., Liddell, E. G. T., & Sherrington, C. S. (1972). *Reflex activity of the spinal cord*. Oxford: Clarendon Press.

Crick, F. (1966). *Of molecules and men*. Seattle: University of Washington Press.

Crick, F. (1984). Function of the thalamic reticular complex: The searchlight hypothesis. *Proceedings of the National Academy Science, USA, 81*(14), 4586–4590.

Crick, F. (1988). *What mad pursuit*. New York: Basic Books.

Crick, F. (1994). *The astonishing hypothesis: The scientific search for the soul*. New York: Charles Scribner's Sons.

Crow, T. J. (1980). Positive and negative schizophrenia symptoms and the role of dopamine. II. *British Journal of Psychiatry, 137*, 383–386.

Csibra, G., Davis, G., Spratling, M. W., & Johnson, M. H. (2000). Gamma oscillations and object processing in the infant brain. *Science, 290,* 1582–1585.

Cullinan, W. E., Herman, J. P., Helmreich, D. L., & Watson, S. J. (1995). A neuroanatomy of stress. In M. J. Friedman, & D. S. Charney (Eds.), *Neurobiological and clinical consequences of stress: From normal adaptation to post-traumatic stress disorder.* Philadelphia: Lippincott Williams & Wilkins.

Curran, T., & D'Arcangelo, G. (1998). Role of reelin in the control of brain development. *Brain Res Brain Res Rev, 26,* 285–294.

Curtis, C., Lebow, B., Lake, D., Katsanis, J., & Iacono, W. (1999). Acoustic startle reflex in schizophrenia patients and their first-degree relatives: Evidence of normal emotional modulation. *Psychophysiology, 36*(4), 469–475.

Cutler, W. B., Preti, G., Krieger, A., & Huggins, G. R. (1986). Human axillary secretions influence women's menstrual cycles: The role of donor extract from men. *Hormones & Behavior, 20,* 463–473.

Czeisler, C. A., Duffy, J. F., Shanahan, T. L., Brown, E. N., Mitchell, J. F., Rimmer, D. W., Ronda, J. M., Silva, E. J., Allan, J. S., Emens, J. S., Dijk, D. J., & Kronauer, R. E. (1999). Stability, precision, and near-25-hour period of the human circadian pacemaker. *Science, 284*(5423), 2177–2181.

Czoty, P. W., Justice, J. B., & Howell, L. L. (2000). Cocaine-induced changes in extracellular dopamine determined by microdialysis in awake squirrel monkeys. *Psychopharmacology, 148*(3), 299–306.

Dai, J., Van Der Vliet, J., Swaab, D. F., & Buijs, R. M. (1998). Postmortem anterograde tracing of intrahypothalamic projections of the human dorsomedial nucleus of the hypothalamus. *Journal of Computational Neurology, 401*(1), 16–33.

Dallos, P., & Evans, B. N. (1995). High-frequency motility of outer hair cells and the cochlear amplifier. *Science, 267*(5206), 2006–2009.

Damasio, A. R. (1985). Disorders of simple visual processing: Agnosias, achromatopsia, Balint's syndrome, and related difficulties of orientation and construction. In M. M. Mesulam (Ed.), *Principles of behavioral neurology.* Philadelphia: Davis.

Damasio, A. R. (1989). Time-locked multiregional retroactivation: A systems-level proposal for the neural substrates of recall and recognition. *Cognition, 33*(1–2), 25–62.

Damasio, A. R. (1995a). Consciousness. Knowing how, knowing where. *Nature, 375,* 106–107.

Damasio, A. R. (1995b). On some functions of the human prefrontal cortex. *Annals of the New York Academy of Sciences, 769,* 241–251.

Damasio, A. R. (1999). How the brain creates the mind. *Scientific American, 281*(6), 112–117.

Damasio, A. R., & Van Hoesen, G. W. (1983). In K. M. Heilman & P. Satz (Eds.), *Neuropsychology of human emotion.* New York: Guilford.

Daneman, M., & Carpenter, P. A. (1980). Individual differences in working memory and reading. *Journal of Verbal Learning & Verbal Behavior, 19,* 450–466.

Daneman, M., & Merikle, P. M. (1996). Working memory and language comprehension: A meta-analysis. *Psychonomic Bulletin & Review, 3,* 422–433.

Danker-Hopfe, H., Roczen, K., & Lowenstein-Wagner, U. (1995). Regulation of food intake during the menstrual cycle. *Anthropologischer Anzeiger, 53*(3), 231–238.

Daum, I., Schugens, M. M., Ackerman, H., Lutzenberger, W., Dichgans, J., & Birbaumer, N. (1993). Classical conditioning after cerebellar lesions in humans. *Behavioral Neuroscience, 107*(5), 748–756.

Davidson, L. M., & Baum, A. (1986). Chronic stress and posttraumatic stress disorders. *Journal of Consulting & Clinical Psychology, 54,* 303–308.

Davidson, L. M., Fleming, R., & Baum, A. (1987). Chronic stress, catecholamines, and sleep disturbance at Three Mile Island. *Journal of Human Stress, 13,* 75–83.

Davidson, R. J. (1992). Anterior cerebral asymmetry and the nature of emotion. (1992). *Brain Cognition, 20*(1), 125–151.

Davidson, J. R. (2001). Pharmacotherapy of generalized anxiety disorder. *Journal of Clinical Psychiatry, 62*(Suppl 11), 46–50.

Davidson, R. J., Kalin, N. H., Kelley, A. E., & Shelton, S. E. (2001). The primate amygdala mediates acute fear but not the behavioral and physiological components of anxious temperament. *J Neurosci, 21,* 2067–2074.

Davis, H. P., Rosensweig, M. R., Becker, L. A., & Sather, K. J. (1988). Biological psychology's relationships to psychology and neuroscience. *American Psychologist, 43,* 359–371.

Davis, J. O., & Phelps, J. A. (1995). Twins with schizophrenia: Genes or germs? *Schizophr Bull, 21,* 13–18.

Davis, J. O., Phelps, J. A., & Bracha, H. S. (1995). Prenatal development of monozygotic twins and concordance for schizophrenia. *Schizophrenia Bulletin, 21,* 357–366.

Davis, K. L., Kahn, R. S., Ko, G., & Davidson, M. (1991). Dopamine in schizophrenia: A review and reconceptualization. *American Journal of Psychiatry, 148*(11), 1474–1486.

Davis, M. (1992). The role of the amygdala in fear and anxiety. *Annual Review of Neuroscience, 15,* 353–375.

Davis, S. (2000). Testosterone and sexual desire in women. *Journal of Sex Education & Therapy, 25,* 25–32.

Deakin, J. F. (1998). The role of serotonin in panic, anxiety, and depression. *International Clinical Psychopharmacology, 13*(S4), 1–5.

DeArmond, S. J., & Prusiner, S. B. (1995). Prion protein transgenes and the neuropathology in prion diseases. *Brain Pathology, 5*(1), 77–89.

DebBurman, S., Raymond, G., Caughey, B., & Lindquist, S. (1997). Chaperone-supervised conversion of prion protein to its protease-resistant form. *Proceedings of the National Academy of Sciences, USA, 94*(25), 13938–13943.

DeCastro, J. M., & Balagura, S. (1975). Ontogeny of meal patterning in rats and its recapitulation during recovery from lateral hypothalamic lesions. *Journal of Comparative & Physiological Psychology, 89*(7), 791–802.

Decker, M. W., Brioni, J. D., Bannon, A. W., & Arneric, S. P. (1995). Diversity of neuronal nicotinic acetylcholine receptors: Lessons from behavior and implications for CNS therapeutics. *Life Sciences, 56,* 545–570.

De Fuise, E., Dulac, O., Hernandez, M. T., Lortie, A., Lassonde, M., Lussier, F., Jambaque, I. I., & Sauerwein, H. C. (2002). Deficits in executive functions and motor coordination in children with frontal lobe epilepsy. *Neuropsychologia, 40,* 384–400.

Degueldre, C., Franck, G., Franco, G., & Salmon, E. (1996). Frontal lobe dementia presenting as personality disorder. *Acta neurol. beig, 96,* 130–134.

DeJong, F. H., Muntjewerff, J. W., Louwerse, A. L., & van de Poll, N. E. (1988). Sexual behavior and sexual orientation of the female rat after hormonal treatment during various stages of development. *Hormonal Behavior, 22*(1), 100–115.

DeLacoste, M. C., Adesanya, T., & Woodward, D. J. (1990). Measures of gender differences in the human brain and their relationship to brain weight. *Biological Psychiatry, 28*(11), 931–942.

DeLacoste-Utamsing, C., & Holloway, R. L. (1982). Sexual dimorphism in the human corpus callosum. *Science, 216*(4553), 1431–1432.

Delacour, J. (1995). An introduction to the biology of consciousness. *Neuropsychologia, 33*(9), 1061–1074.

De la Fuente, J. M., & Mendlewicz, J. (1996). TRH stimulation and dexamethasone suppression in borderline personality disorder. *Biological Psychiatry, 40*(5), 412–418.

de Leon, M. J., Convit, A., DeSanti, S., Golomb, J., Tarshish, C., Rusinek,

H., Bobinski, M., Ince, C., Miller, D. C., & Wisniewski, H. M. (1995). The hippocampus in aging and Alzheimer's disease. *Neuroimaging Clinic of North America, 5*(1), 1–17.

Deligeoroglou, E. (2000). Dysmenorrhea. *Annals of the New York Academy of Sciences, 900*, 237–1244.

DeLisi, L. E., Dauphinais, I. D., & Gershon, E. S. (1988). Perinatal complications and reduced size of brain limbic structures in familial schizophrenia. *Schizophrenic Bulletin, 14*(2), 185–191.

Delville, Y., DeVries, G. J., Schwartz, W. J., & Ferris, C. F. (1998). Flankmarking behavior and the neural distribution of vasopressin innervation in golden hamsters with suprachiasmatic lesions. *Behavioral Neuroscience, 112*(6), 1486–1501.

Dement, W., & Kleitman, N. (1957). The relation of eye movements during sleep to dream activity: An objective method for the study of dreaming. *Journal of Experimental Psychology, 53*, 339–346.

Demonet, J. F., Celsis, P., Nespoulous, J. L., Viallard, G., Marc-Vergnes, J. P., & Rascol, A. (1992). Cerebral blood flow correlates of word monitoring in sentences: Influence of semantic incoherence. A SPECT study in normals. *Neuropsychologia, 30*(1), 1–11.

Den Boer, J. A., & Westenberg, H. G. M. (1995). Atypical antipsychotics in schizophrenia: A review of recent developments. In J. A. Den Boer, H. G. M. Westenberg, & H. M. van Praag (Eds.), *Advances in the neurobiology of schizophrenia.* New York: John Wiley & Sons.

Denny-Brown, D., Meyers, J. S., & Horenstein, S. (1952). The parietal lobe and behavior. *Research Publications-Associations for Research in Nervous and Mental Disease, 36*, 35–117.

Denny-Brown, D., & Pennybacker, J. B. (1938). Fibrillation and fasciculation in voluntary muscle. *Brain, 61*, 311–334.

De Renzi, E. (2000). Disorders of visual recognition. *Semin Neurol, 20*, 479–485.

Derrick, B. E., & Martinez, J. L. (1996). Associative, bidirectional modifications at the hippocampal mossy fibre-CA3 synapse. *Nature, 381*(6581), 429–434.

Desfontaines, B., Pillon, B., Deweer, B., Dubois, B., & Laplane (1996). The mental and cognitive syndrome of patients with focal lesions of basal ganglia: Preliminary results. In C. Ohye & M. Kimura (Eds.), *The basal ganglia.* New York: Plenum Press.

Desimone, R., & Duncan, J. (1995). Neural mechanisms of selective visual

attention. *Annual Review of Neuroscience, 18*, 193–222.

De Souza, E. B., & Grigoriadis, D. E. (1995). Corticotropin-releasing factor: Physiology, pharmacology, and role in central nervous system and immune disorders. In F. E. Bloom & D. J. Kupfer (Eds.), *Psychopharmacology: The fourth generation.* New York: Raven Press.

D'Esposito, M., Aguirre, G. K., Zarahn, E., Ballard, D., Shin, R. K., & Lease, J. (1998). Functional MRI studies of spatial and nonspatial working memory. *Brain Research: Cognitive Brain Research, 7*(1), 1–13.

D'Esposito, M., Ballard, D., Aguirre, G. K., & Zarahn, E. (1998). Human prefrontal cortex is not specific for working memory: A functional MRI study. *Neuroimage, 8*(3), 274–282.

D'Esposito, M., Detre, J. A., Aguirre, G. K., Stallcup, M., Alsop, D. C., Tippet, L. J., & Farah, M. J. (1997). A functional MRI study of mental image generation. *Neuropsychologia, 35*(5), 725–730.

D'Esposito, M., & Druzgal, T. J. (2001). A neural network reflecting decisions about human faces. *Neuron, 32*, 947–955.

D'Esposito, M., & Postle, B. R. (1999). The dependence of span and delayed-response performance on prefrontal cortex. *Neuropsychologia, 37*(11), 1303–1315.

Deutch, A. Y., & Young, C. D. (1995). A model of the stress-induced activation of prefrontal cortical dopamine systems: Coping and the development of post-traumatic stress disorder. In M. J. Friedman & D. S. Charney (Eds.), *Neurobiological and clinical consequences of stress: From normal adaptation to post-traumatic stress disorder.* Philadelphia: Lippincott Williams & Wilkins.

Devane, W. A., Dysarz, F. A., Johnson, M. R., Melvin L. S., & A. C. Howlett. (1988). Determination and characterization of a cannabinoid receptor in rat brain. *Molecular Pharmacology, 34*(5), 605–613.

Devane, W. A., Hanus, L., Breuer, A., Pertwee, R. G., Stevenson, L. A., Griffin, G., Gibson, D., Mandelbaum, A., Etinger A., & Mechoulam, R. (1992). Isolation and structure of a brain constituent that binds to the cannabinoid receptor. *Science, 258*(5090), 1946–1949.

Dewsbury, D. A. (1991). Psychobiology. *American Psychologist, 46*, 198–205.

Diamond, M. C. (1991). Environmental influences on the young brain. In K. R. Gibson & A. C. Petersen (Eds.), *Brain maturation and cognitive development: Comparative and cross-cultural perspectives.* Hawthorne, NY: Aldine de Gruyter.

Di Cara, L., & Miller, N. E. (1968). Instrumental learning of systolic blood pressure responses by curarized rats: Dissociation of cardiac and vascular changes. *Psychosomatic Medicine, 30*(5, Pt. 1), 489–494.

Di Girolamo, S., Picciotti, P., Sergi, B., D'Ecclesia, A., & Di Nardo, W. (2001). Postural control and glycerol test in Meniere's disease. *Acta Otolaryngologia, 121*, 813–817.

Di Lazzaro, V., Oliviero, A., Profice, P., Meglio, M., Cioni, B., Tonali, P., & Rothwell, J. C. (2001). Descending spinal cord volleys evoked by transcranial magnetic and electrical stimulation of the motor cortex leg area in conscious humans. *Journal of Physiology, 537*, 1047–1058.

Di Pellegrino, G., & Wise, S. P. (1991). A neurophysiological comparison of three distinct regions of the primate frontal lobe. *Brain, 114*(2), 951–978.

Di Pellegrino, G., & Wise, S. P. (1993). Visuospatial versus visuomotor activity in the premotor and prefrontal cortex of a primate. *Journal of Neuroscience, 13*, 1227–1243.

Doi, T., Jackman, A., Liu, M., Seeley, R. J., Shen, L., Tso, P., Woods, S. C., & Zheng, S. (2001). Intestinal satiety protein apolipoprotein AIV is synthesized and regulated in rat hypothalamus. *Am J Physiol Regul Integr Comp Physiol, 280*, R1382–R1387.

Domino, E. F. (1998). Tobacco smoking and nicotine neuropsychopharmacology: Some future research directions. *Neuropsychopharmacology, 18*, 456–468.

Donovick, P. J., & Burright, R. G. (1992). Lead poisoning, toxocariasis, and pica: Links to neurobehavioral disorders. In R. L. Isaacson & K. F. Jensen (Eds.), *The vulnerable brain and environmental risks: Vol. 1: Malnutrition and hazard assessment. Vol. 2: Toxins in food.* New York: Plenum Press.

Dorian, B., Garfinkel, P., Brown, G., Shore, A., Gladman, D., & Keystone, E. (1982). Aberrations in lymphocyte subpopulations and function during psychological stress. *Clinical Experimental Immunology, 50*(1), 132–138.

Doty, R. L. (1997). Studies of human olfaction from the University of Pennsylvania Smell and Taste Center. *Chemical Senses, 22*, 565–586.

Doty, R. L., Applebaum, S., Zusho, H., & Settle, R. G. (1985). Sex differences in odor identification ability: A cross-cultural analysis. *Neuropsychologia, 23*(5), 667–672.

Doty, R. L., Ford, M., Preti, G., & Huggins, G. R. (1975). Changes in the intensity and pleasantness of human vaginal odors during the menstrual cycle. *Science, 190*, 1316–1318.

Doty, R. L., Perl, D. P., Steele, J. C., Chen, K. M., Pierce, J. D., Jr, Reyes, P., & Kurland, L. T. (1991). Olfactory dysfunction in three neurodegenerative diseases. *Geriatrics, 46*(Suppl 1), 47–51.

Doty, R. L., Steele, J. C., Chen, K. M., Pierce, J. D., Reyes, P., & Kurland, L. T. (1991). Odor identification deficit of the parkinsonism-dementia complex of Guam: Equivalence to that of Alzheimer's and idiopathic Parkinson's disease. *Neurology, 41*(5), 77–80.

Dougherty, D. M., & Moeller, F. G. (2001). Antisocial personality disorder, alcohol, and aggression. *Alcohol Res Health, 25*, 5–11.

Doyle, T. G., Berridge, K. C., & Gosnell, B. A. (1993). Morphine enhances hedonic taste palatability in rats. *Pharmacological Biochemical Behavior, 46*(3), 745–749.

Dressler, D., & Potter, H. (1991). *Discovering enzymes.* New York: Scientific American Library.

Druzgal, T. J., & D'Esposito, M. (2001). Activity in fusiform face area modulated as a function of working memory load. *Brain Research & Cognitive Brain Research, 10*, 355–364.

Duhamel, J. R., Colby, C. L., & Goldberg, M. E. (1998). Ventral intraparietal area of the macaque: Congruent visual and somatic response properties. *Journal of Neurophysiology, 79*(1), 126–136.

Duman, R. S. (1995). Regulation of intracellular signal transduction and gene expression by stress. In M. J. Friedman, D. S. Charney, & A. Y. Deutch, *Neurobiological and clinical consequences of stress: From normal adaptation to post-traumatic stress disorder.* Philadelphia: Lippincott Williams & Wilkins.

Duman, R. S., Heninger, G. R., & Nestler, E. J. (1994). Molecular psychiatry: Adaptation of receptor-coupled signal transduction pathways underlying stress- and drug-induced neural plasticity. *Journal of Nervous Mental Disorders, 182*(12), 692–700.

Duman, R. S., & Nestler, E. J. (1995). Signal transduction pathways for catecholamine receptors. In F. E. Bloom & D. J. Kupfer (Eds.), *Psychopharmacology: The fourth generation of progress.* New York: Raven Press.

Duncan, J. (1984). Selective attention and the organization of visual information. *Journal of Experimental Psychological Genetics, 113*(4), 501–517.

Duncan, J. (1995). Attention, intelligence, and the frontal lobes. In M. S. Gazzaniga (Ed.), *The cognitive neurosciences.* Cambridge, MA: MIT Press.

Duty, S., Henry, B., Crossman, A. R., & Brotchie, J. M. (1996). Speculations on the molecular mechanisms underlying dopamine agonist-induced dyskinesias in Parkinsonism. In C. Ohye

& M. Kimura (Eds.), *The basal ganglia V.* New York: Plenum Press.

Dyr, W., McBride, W. J., Lumeng, L., Li, T. K., & Murphy, J. M. (1993). Effects of D_1 and D_2 dopamine receptor agents on ethanol consumption in the high-alcohol-drinking (HAD) line of rats. *Alcohol, 10*(3), 207–212.

Eastman, C. L., Stewart, K. T., Mahoney, M. P., Liu, L., & Fogg, L. F. (1994). Dark goggles and bright light improve circadian rhythm adaptation to night-shift work. *Sleep, 17*(6), 535–543.

Eberhardt, N. L., Michael, D. J., & Levine, J. A. 1999. Role of nonexercise activity thermogenesis in resistance to fat gain in humans. *Science, 283*, 212–214.

Eckhorn, R., Bauer, R., Jordan, W., Brosch, M., Kruse, W., Munk, M., & Reitboeck, H. J. (1988). Coherent oscillations: A mechanism of feature linking in the visual cortex? Multiple electrode and correlation analyses in the cat. *Biological Cybernetics, 60*(2), 121–130.

Edmonds, B., Gibb, A. J., & Colquhoun, D. (1995). Mechanisms of activation of muscle nicotinic acetylcholine receptors and the time course of endplate currents. *Annual Review of Physiology, 57*, 469–493.

Ehlert, F. J., Roeske, W. R., & Yamamura, H. I. (1995). Molecular biology, pharmacology, and brain distribution of subtypes of the muscarinic receptor. In F. E. Bloom & D. J. Kupfer (Eds.), *Psychopharmacology: The fourth generation of progress.* New York: Raven Press.

Ehman, G. K., Albert, D. J., & Jamieson, J. L. (1971). Injections into the duodenum and the induction of satiety in the rat. *Canadian Journal of Psychology, 25*(2), 147–166.

Ehrhardt, A. A., Epstein, R., & Money, J. (1968). Fetal androgens and female gender identity in the early-treated adrenogenital syndrome. *Johns Hopkins Medical Journal, 122*, 160–167.

Ehrhardt, A. A., & Meyer-Bahlburg, H. F. (1981). Effects of prenatal sex hormones on gender-related behavior. *Science, 211*, 1312–1318.

Ekman, P. (1992). Are there basic emotions? *Psychological Review, 99*(3), 550–553.

Elbert, T., Pantev, C., Wienbruch, C., Rockstroh, B., & Taub, E. (1995). Increased cortical representation of the fingers of the left hand in string players. *Science, 270*(5234), 305–307.

El-Deiry, A., & McCabe, B. F. (1990). Temporal lobe tumor manifested by localized dysgeusia. *Annual Otol Rhinol Laryngology, 99*(7), 586–587.

Elliott, M. A., & Muller, H. J. (2000). Evidence for 40-Hz oscillatory short-

term visual memory revealed by human reaction-time measurements. *Journal of Experimental Psychology: Learning, Memory, & Cognition, 26*, 703–718.

Emrich, H. M., Giuffrida, A., Lewweke, F. M., Piomelli, D., & Wurster, U. (1999). Elevated endogenous cannabinoids in schizophrenia. *Neuroreport, 10*, 1665–1669.

Emrich, H. M., Leweke, F. M., & Schneider, U. (1997). Towards a cannabinoid hypothesis of schizophrenia: Cognitive impairments due to dysregulation of the endogenous cannabinoid system. *Pharmacology, Biochemistry, and Behavior, 56*, 803–807.

Emsley, R., Smith, R., Roberts, M., Kapnias, S., Pieters, H., & Maritz, S. (1996). Magnetic resonance imaging in alcoholic Korsakoff's syndrome: Evidence for an association with alcoholic dementia. *Alcohol, 31*(5), 479–486.

Engleman, E. A., McBride, W. J., Wilber, A. A., Shaikh, S. R., Eha, R. D., Lumeng, L., Li, T. K., & Murphy, J. M. (2000). Reverse microdialysis of a dopamine uptake inhibitor in the nucleus accumbens of alcohol-preferring rats: Effects on dialysate dopamine levels and ethanol intake. *Alcohol Clinical Experimental Research, 24*(6), 795–801.

Epstein, R., & Kanwisher, N. (1998). A cortical representation of the local visual environment. *Nature, 392*, 598–601.

Erlanger, D. M., Kutner, K. C., Barth, J. T., & Barnes, R. (1999). Neuropsychology of sports-related head injury: Dementia pugilistica to post concussion syndrome. *Clin Neuropsychol, 13*, 193–209.

Ermekova, K. S., Chang, A., Zambrano, N., de Candia, P., Russo, T., & Sudol, M. (1998). Proteins implicated in Alzheimer disease: The role of FE65, a new adapter which binds to beta-amyloid precursor protein. *Advanced Experimental Medical Biology, 446*, 161–180.

Ernest, J. M. (1998). Neonatal consequences of preterm PROM. *Clinical Obstetrics Gynecology, 41*(4), 827–831.

Etgen, A. M., Chu, H. P., Fiber, J. M., Karkanias, G. B., & Morales, J. M. (1999). Hormonal integration of neurochemical and sensory signals governing female reproductive behavior. *Behavioral Brain Research, 105*(1), 93–103.

Evans, D. L., O'Reardon, J. P., & Szuba, M. P. (2000). Physiological effects of electroconvulsive therapy and transcranial magnetic stimulation in major depression. *Depress Anxiety, 12*, 170–177.

Evans, W. J., Cui, L, & Starr, A. (1995). Olfactory event-related potentials in normal human subjects: Effects of age and gender. *Electroencephalography and Clinical Neurophysiology, 95*(4), 293–301.

Everitt, B. J., & Robbins, T. W. (1997). Central cholinergic systems and cognition. *Annual Review of Psychology, 48*, 649–684.

Fakhrai, H., Dorigo, O., Shawler, D. L., Lin, H., Mercola, D., Black, K. L., Royston, I., & Sobol, R. E. (1996). Eradication of established intracranial rat gliomas by transforming growth factor beta antisense gene therapy. *Proceedings of the National Academy of Sciences, 93*, 2909–2914.

Falk, J. L. (1961). Production of polydipsia in normal rats by an intermittent food schedule. *Science, 26*, 35–36.

Falk, J. L. (1971). The nature and determinants of adjunctive behavior. *Physiology & Behavior, 6*, 577–588.

Falk, J. L. (1977). The origin and functions of adjunctive behavior. *Animal Learning & Behavior, 5*, 325–335.

Fanselow, M. S. (1994). Neural organization of the defensive behavior system responsible for fear. *Psychonomic Bulletin & Review, 1*(4), 429–438.

Fanselow, M. S., DeCola, J. P., De Oca, B. M., & Landeira-Fernandez, J. (1995). Ventral and dorsolateral regions of the midbrain periaqueductal gray (PAG) control different stages of defensive behavior: Dorsolateral PAG lesions enhance the defensive freezing produced by massed and immediate shock. *Aggressive Behavior, 21*(1), 63–77.

Farah, M. J. (1994). Neuropsychological inference with an interactive brain: A critique of the "locality" assumption. *Behavioral & Brain Sciences, 17*, 43–104.

Farkas, A., & Chertin, B. (2001). Feminizing genitoplasty in patients with 46XX congenital adrenal hyperplasia. *J Pediatr Endocrinol Metab, 14*, 713–722.

Farrah, M. J. (1994). Neuropsychological inference with an interactive brain: A critique of the "locality" assumption. *Behavioral and Brain Sciences, 17*, 43–104.

Faurion, A., Cerf, B., LeBihan, D., Pillias, A. M., & Youseman. (1998). MRI study of taste cortical areas in humans. *Annals of the New York Academy of Sciences, 855*.

Fausto-Sterling, A. (1992). *Myths of gender: Biological theories about women and men.* New York: Basic Books.

Fausto-Sterling, A. (1999). Is gender essential? In M. Rottnek (Ed.), *Sissies and tomboys: Gender nonconformity and homosexual childhood.* New York: New York University Press.

Fausto-Sterling, A., & Balaban, E. (1993). Genetics and male sexual orientation. *Science, 261*, 1257–1258.

Fava, M. (1997). Psychopharmacologic treatment of pathologic aggression. *Psychiatric Clinic North America, 20*(2), 427–451.

Federoff, I. C., Stoner, S. A., Andersen, A. E., Doty, R. L., & Rolls, B. J. (1995). Olfactory dysfunction in anorexia and bulimia nervosa. *International Journal of Eating Disorders, 18*, 71–77.

Felder, C. C., Porter, A. C., Skillman, T. L., Zhang, L., Bymaster, F. P., Nathanson, N. M., Hamilton, S. E., Gomeza, J., Wess, J., & McKinzie, D. L. (2001). Elucidating the role of muscarinic receptors in psychosis. *Life Sciences, 68*, 2605–2613.

Fendt, M., & Fanselow, M. S. (1999). The neuroanatomical and neurochemical basis of conditioned fear. *Neuroscience & Biobehavioral Reviews, 23*(5), 743–760.

Ferini-Strambi. L., & Zucconi, M. (2000). REM sleep behavior disorder. *Clinical Neurophysiology, 111*(2), 136–140.

Fernandez, G., Effern, A., Grunwald, T., Pezer, N., Lehnertz, L., Duemplemann, M., Van Roost, D., & Elger, C. E. (1999). Real-time tracking of memory formation in the human rhinal cortex and hippocampus. *Science, 285*(5433), 1582–1585.

Fernstrom, J. D. (1987). Food-induced changes in brain serotonin synthesis: Is there a relationship to appetite for specific macronutrients? *Appetite, 3*, 162–182.

Ferrari, G., Cusella-De Angelis, G., Coletta, M., Paolucci, E., Stornaiuolo, A., Cossu, G., & Mavilio, F. (1998). Muscle regeneration by bone marrow-derived myogenic progenitors. *Science, 279*, 1528–1530.

Ferrie, C. D., Robinson, R. O., Giannakodimos, S., & Panayiotopoulos, C. P. (1994). Video-game epilepsy. *Lancet, 344*(8938), 1710–1711.

Ferrier, D. (1876). Experiments on the brains of monkeys. *Philosophical Transactions of the Royal Society, 165*, 433–488.

Ferrier, D. (1886). *The functions of the brain.* New York: G. P. Putnam & Sons.

Figiel, G. S., Epstein, C., McDonald, W. M., Amazon-Leece, J., Figiel, L., Saldivia, A., & Glover, S. (1998). The use of rapid-rate transcranial magnetic stimulation (rTMS) in refractory depressed patients. *Journal of Neuropsychiatry & Clinical Neuroscience, 10*(1), 20–25.

Finger, S. (1994). History of neuropsychology. In D. W. Zaidel (Ed.), *Neuropsychology* (pp. 1–28). San Diego, CA: Academic Press.

Fiorentino, M. R. (1973). *Reflex testing methods for evaluating C. N. S. development.* Springfield, IL: Charles C Thomas.

Fischbach, G. D. (1992). Mind and brain. *Scientific American, 267*, 48–57.

Fischer, K. M. (1997). Etiology of (CAG)n triplet repeat neurodegenerative diseases such as Huntington's disease is connected to stimulation of glutamate receptors. *Medical Hypotheses, 48*, 393–398.

Fisher, P. G., & Chiello, C. (2000). Meningeal leukemia with cerebrospinal fluid block. *Medical Pediatric Oncology, 34*(4), 281–283.

Fishman, S. (1988). *A bomb in the brain.* New York: Charles Scribner's Sons.

Fitzsimons, J. T. (1998). Angiotensin, thirst, and sodium appetite. *Physiol Rev, 78*, 583–686.

Flechtner, K. M., Mackert, A., Mahlberg, R., & Steinacher, B. (2001). Basic parameters of saccadic eye movements—differences between unmedicated schizophrenia and affective disorder patients. *Eur Arch Psychiatry Clin Neurosci, 251*, 205–210.

Flor, H., Elbert, T., Mahlnickel, W., Pantev, C., Wienbruch, C., & Taub, E. (1998). Cortical reorganization and phantom phenomena in congenital and traumatic upper-extremity amputees. *Experimental Brain Research, 119*(2), 205–212.

Florence, S. L., Taub, H. B., & Kaas, J. H. (1998). Large-scale sprouting of cortical connections after peripheral injury in adult macaque monkeys. *Science, 282*(5391), 1117–1121.

Follett, K. A. (2000). The surgical treatment of Parkinson's disease. *Annual Review of Medicine, 51*, 135–147.

Folstein, S. E. (1989). *Huntington's disease.* Baltimore: Johns Hopkins University Press.

Foote, S. L., & Aston-Jones, G. S. (1995). Pharmacology and physiology of central noradrenergic systems. In F. E. Bloom & D. J. Kupfer (Eds.), *Psychopharmacology: The fourth generation of progress.* New York: Raven Press.

Forno, L. S., Eng, L. F., & Selkoe, D. J. (1989). Pick bodies in the locus ceruleus. *Acta Neuropathology of Berlin, 79*(1), 10–17.

Forster, R. E., & Ferguson, T. B. (1952). Relationship between hypothalamic temperature and thermoregulatory effectors in the unanesthetized cat. *American Journal of Physiology, 169*, 255–269.

Foulkes, D. (1993). Symposium: Normal and abnormal REM sleep regulation: Dreaming and REM sleep. *Journal of Sleep Research, 2*(4), 199–202.

Foundation for Biomedical Research. (1988). *The use of animals in biomedical* research and testing. Washington, DC: Foundation for Biomedical Research.

Fowler, J. S., Volkow, N. D., Wang, G. J., Pappas, N., Logan, J., MacGregor, R., Alexoff, D., Shea, C., Schlyer, D. Wolf, A. P., Warner, D., Zezulkova, I., & Cilento, R. (1996). Inhibition of monoamine oxidase B in the brains of smokers. *Nature, 379,* 733–736.

Fox, P. T., Ingham, R. J., Ingham, J. C., & Hirsch, T. B. (1996). A PET study of the neural systems of stuttering. *Nature, 382*(6587), 158–162.

Freed, W. J., de Medinaceli, L., & Wyatt, R. J. (1985). Promoting functional plasticity in the damaged nervous system. *Science, 227*(4694), 1544–1552.

Freedman, D. J., Miller, E. K., Poggio T., & Risenhuber M.(2001). Categorical representation of visual stimuli in the primate prefrontal cortex. *Science, 291,* 312–316.

French, S. J., Grigoryan, G., Hodges, H., Patel, S., Sinden, J. D., & Stroemer, P. (2000). Functional repair with neural stem cells. *Novartis Found Symp, 231,* 270–283.

Fridge, E., & Mechoulam, R. (2001). A hunger for cannabinoids. *Nature, 410,* 763–765.

Friedland, R. P., Koss, E., Lerner, A., Hedera, P., Ellis, W., Dronkers, N., Ober, B. A., & Jagust, W. J. (1993). Functional imaging, the frontal lobes, and dementia. *Dementia, 4,* 192–203.

Friedman, M. (1967). "Brown fat" as a source of heat production in the newborn. *Midwife Health Visit, 3*(2), 75–76.

Friedman, M. I., & Tordoff, M. G. (1986). Fatty acid oxidation and glucose utilization interact to control food intake in rats. *American Journal of Physiology, 251*(2), 840–845.

Friedman-Hill, S. R., Robertson, L. C., & Treisman, A. (1995). Parietal contributions to visual feature binding: Evidence from a patient with bilateral lesions. *Science, 269*(5225), 853–855.

Frith, U. (1993). Autism. *Scientific American, 268*(6), 108–114.

Frohlich, J., Ogawa, S., Morgan, M., Burton, L., & Pfaff, D. (1999). Hormones, genes, and the structure of sexual arousal. *Behavioral Brain Research, 105*(1), 5–27.

Fuhr, P., & Kappos, L. (2001). Evoked potentials for evaluation of multiple sclerosis. *Clin Neurophysiol, 112,* 2185–2189.

Fujimoto, H., Imaizumi, T., Nishimura, Y., Miura, Y., Ayabe, M., Shoji, H., & Abe, T. (2001). Neurosyphilis showing transient global amnesia-like attacks and magnetic resonance imaging abnormalities mainly in the limbic system. *Internal Medicine, 40,* 439–442.

Fukada, Y., Kashino, M., Katori, H., Mizobuchi, A., & Nakakoshi, S. (2001). Disorder in sequential speech perception: A case study on pure word deafness. *Brain Lang, 76,* 119–129.

Fulton, S., Woodside, B., & Shizgal, P. (2000). Modulation of brain reward circuitry by leptin. *Science, 287*(5450), 125–128.

Furey, M. L., Pietrini, P., & Haxby, J. V. (2000). Cholinergic enhancement and increased selectivity of perceptual processing during working memory. *Science, 290,* 2315–2319.

Gabrieli, J. D. (1998). Cognitive neuroscience of human memory. *Annual Review of Psychology, 49,* 87–115.

Gajewski, A., & Hensch, S. A. (1999). Ginkgo biloba and memory for a maze. *Psychological Report, 84,* 481–484.

Galaburda, A. M., LeMay, M., Kemper, T. L., & Geschwind, N. (1978). Right–left asymmetrics in the brain. *Science, 199*(4331), 852–856.

Galea, L. A., & Kimura, D. (1993). Sex differences in route-learning. *Personality & Individual Differences, 14*(1), 53–65.

Galler, J. R., Ramsey, F., & Solimano, G. (1984). The influence of early malnutrition on subsequent behavioral development. III. Learning disabilities as a sequel to malnutrition. *Pediatric Research, 18,* 309–313.

Gallo, V., & Chittajallu, R. (2001). Neuroscience. Unwrapping glial cells from the synapse: What lies inside? *Science, 292,* 872–873.

Gallup, G. G., & Suarez, S. D. (1991). Social responding to mirrors in rhesus monkeys (*Macaca mulatta*): Effects of temporary mirror removal. *Journal of Comparative Psychology, 105*(4), 376–379.

Galow, G., Jacobit, G., Kieslich, M., Lorenz, R., & Marquardt, G. (2001). Neurological and mental outcome after severe head injury in childhood: A long-term follow-up of 318 children. *Disabil Rehabil, 23,* 665–669.

Garfinkel, P. E., Lin, E., Goering, P., Spegg, C., Goldbloom, D. S., Kennedy, S., Kaplan, A. S., & Woodside, D. B. (1995). *American Journal of Psychiatry, 152*(7), 1052–1058.

Garrett, B. E., & Griffiths, R. R. (1997). The role of dopamine in the behavioral effects of caffeine in animals and humans. *Pharmacology, Biochemistry, and Behavior, 57,* 533–541.

Garthwaite, J., & Boulton, C. L. (1995). Nitric oxide signalling in the central nervous system. *Annual Review of Physiology, 57,* 683–706.

Gazzaniga, M. S. (1989). Organization of the human brain. *Science, 245,* 947–952.

Gazzaniga, M. S., Bogen, J. E., & Sperry, R. W. (1962). Some functional effects of sectioning the cerebral commissures in man. *Proceedings of the National Academy of Sciences, 48,* 1765–1769.

Gazzaniga, M. S., Bogen, J. E., & Sperry, R. W. (1965). Observations on visual perception after disconnection of the cerebral hemispheres in man. *Brain, 88*(2), 221–236.

Gazzaniga, M. S., Bogen, J. E., & Sperry, R. W. (1992). Some functional effects of sectioning the cerebral commissures in man. In *Frontiers in cognitive neuroscience.* Cambridge, MA: The MIT Press.

Gazzaniga, M. S., & LeDoux, J. E. (1978). *The integrated mind.* New York: Plenum Press.

Geary, N. (1998). Glucagon and the control of meal size. In G. P. Smith (Ed.), *Satiation: From gut to brain.* New York: Oxford University Press.

Geary, N., Asarian, L., & Langhans, W. (1997). The satiating potency of hepatic portal glucagon in rats is not affected by [corrected] insulin or insulin antibodies. *Physiological Behavior, 61*(2), 199–208.

Geisler, C. D. (1993). A realizable cochlear model using feedback from motile outer hair cells. *Hearing Research, 68*(2), 253–262.

Geldmacher, D. S., & Whitehouse, P. J. (1997). Differential diagnosis of Alzheimer's disease. *Neurology, 48* (Suppl 6), S2–S9.

George, M. S., Wassermann, E. M., & Post, R. M. (1996). Transcranial magnetic stimulation: A neuropsychiatric tool for the 21st century. *Journal of Neuropsychiatry Clinical Neuroscience, 1996, 8,* 373–382.

Gerra, G., Zaimovic, A., Ampollini, R., Giusti, F., Delsignore, R., Raggi, M. A., Laviola, G., Macchia, T., & Brambilla, F. (2001). Experimentally induced aggressive behavior in subjects with 3,4-methylenedioxymethamphetamine ("Ecstasy") use history: Psychobiological correlates. *Journal of Substance Abuse, 13,* 471–491.

Gershon, E. S., & Rieder, R. O. (1992). Major disorders of mind and brain. *Scientific American, 267*(3), 126–133.

Geschwind, N., & Galaburda, A. M. (1985). Cerebral lateralization. Biological mechanisms, associations, and pathology: I. A hypothesis and a program for research. *Archives of Neurology, 42*(5), 428–459.

Geschwind, N., & Levitsky, W. (1968). Human brain: Left–right asymmetrics in temporal speech region. *Science, 161*(837), 186–187.

Gessa, G. L. (1996). Dysthymia and depressive disorders: Dopamine hypothesis. *European Psychiatry, 11*(3), 123–127.

Gevins, A. S., Morgan, N. H., Bressler, S. L., Cutillo, B. A., White, R. M, Illes, J., Greer, D. S., Doyle, J. C., & Zeitlin, G. M. (1987). Human neuro-electric patterns predict performance accuracy. *Science, 235,* 580–585.

Ghaemi, S. N., & Goodwin, F. K. (1999). Use of atypical antipsychotic agents in bipolar and schizoaffective disorders: Review of the empirical literature. *Journal of Clinical Psychopharmacology, 19*(4), 354–361.

Ghika-Schmid, F., Ghika, J., Vuilleumier, P., Assal, G., Vuadens, P., Scherer, K., Maeder, P., Uske, A., & Bogous-slavsky, J. (1997). Bihippocampal damage with emotional dysfunction: Impaired auditory recognition of fear. *European Neurology, 38,* 276–283.

Gianotti, G. (1972). Emotional behavior and hemispheric side of lesion. *Cortex, 8,* 41–55.

Gibbs, A. C., & Wilson, J. F. (1999). Sex differences in route learning by children. *Perceptual Motor Skills, 88*(2), 590–594.

Gibbs, J., Young, R. C., & Smith, G. P. (1973). Cholecystokinin decreases food intake in rats. *Journal of Comparative Physiological Psychology, 84*(3), 488–495.

Gill, T. J., Smith, G. J., Wissler, R. W., & Kunz, H. W. (1989). The rat as an experimental animal. *Science, 245,* 269–276.

Gillberg, C. (1995). Endogenous opioids and opiate antagonists in autism: Brief review of empirical findings and implications for clinicians. *Developmental Medical Child Neurology, 37*(3), 239–245.

Gingras, J. R., Harber, V., Field, C. J., & McCargar, L. J. (2000). Metabolic assessment of female chronic dieters with either normal or low resting energy expenditures. *American Journal of Clinical Nutrition, 71*(6), 1413–1420.

Gitlin, M. J. (1993). Pharmacotherapy of personality disorders: Conceptual framework and clinical strategies. *Journal of Clinical Psychopharmacology, 13*(5), 343–353.

Glatzel, M., & Aguzzi, A. (2001). The shifting biology of prions. *Brain Res Brain Res Rev, 36,* 241–248.

Glavin, G. B., Tanaka, M., Tsuda, A., Kohno, Y., Hoaki, Y., & Nagasaki, N. (1983). Regional rat brain noradrenaline turnover in response to restraint stress. *Pharmacology, Biochemistry, and Behavior, 19,* 287–290.

Glennon, R. A., & Dukat, M. (1995). Serotonin receptor subtypes. In F. E. Bloom & D. J. Kupfer (Eds.), *Psychopharmacology: The fourth generation of progress.* New York: Raven Press.

Gloor, P. (1992). Role of the amygdala in temporal lobe epilepsy. In J. P.

Aggleton (Ed.), *The amygdala: Neurobiological aspects of emotion, memory, and mental dysfunction.* New York: Wiley-Liss.

Gloor, P., Olivier, A., Quesney, L., Andermann, F., & Horowitz, S. (1982). The role of the limbic system in experiential phenomena of temporal lobe epilepsy. *Annals of Neurology, 12*(2), 129–144.

Gold, P. E., & McCarty, R. C. (1995). Stress regulation of memory processes: Role of peripheral catecholamines and glucose. In M. J. Freidman & D. S. Charney (Eds.), *Neurobiology and clinical consequences of stress: From normal adaptation to post-traumatic stress disorder.* Philadelphia, PA: Lippincott Williams & Wilkins.

Gold, P. W. (1998). Lack of attention from loss of time. *Science, 281,* 1149–1151.

Goldberg, E. (2001). *The executive brain: Frontal lobes and the civilized mind.* New York: Oxford University Press.

Goldberg, H. L., & Finnerty, R. J. (1979). The comparative efficacy of buspirone and diazepam in the treatment of anxiety. *American Journal of Psychiatry, 136*(9), 1184–1187.

Goldman, D. (1996). The search for genetic alleles contributing to self-destructive and aggressive behaviors. In D. Stoff & R. Cairns (Eds.), *Aggression and violence: Genetic, neurobiological, and biosocial perspectives.* Mahwah, NJ: Lawrence Erlbaum Associates.

Goldman, P. S., & Alexander, G. E. (1977). Maturation of prefrontal cortex in the monkey revealed by local reversible cryogenic depression. *Nature, 267*(5612), 613–615.

Goldman-Rakic, P. S. (1987). Motor control function of the prefrontal cortex. *Ciba Foundation Symposium, 132,* 187–200.

Goldsmith, S. G., Gurevich, E. V., & Joyce, J. N. (1997). Limbic circuits and monoamine receptors: Dissecting the effects of antipsychotics from disease processes. *J Psychiatr Res, 31,* 197–217.

Goldstein, G. W., & Betz, A. L. (1986). The blood–brain barrier. *Scientific American, 255,* 74–83.

Goldstein, K. (1948). *Language and language disturbances.* New York: Grune & Stratton.

Golombek, D. A., Pevet, P., & Cardinali, D. P. (1996). Melatonin effects on behavior: Possible mediation by the central GABAergic system. *Neuroscientific Biobehavioral Review, 20*(3), 403–412.

Goodale, M. A., & Milner, A. D. (1992). Separate visual pathways for perception and action. *Trends in Neuroscience, 15*(1), 20–25.

Goodglass, H. (1993). *Understanding aphasia.* San Diego: Academic Press.

Gonzalez-Heydrich, J., & Peroutka, S. J. (1990). Serotonin receptor and reuptake sites: Pharmacologic significance. *Journal of Clinical Psychiatry, 51,* 5–12.

Gordon, N. (1996). Speech, language, and the cerebellum. *European Journal of Disorders Commun, 31*(4), 359–367.

Gorski, R. A., Gordon, J. H., Shryne, J. E., & Southam, A. M. (1978). Evidence for a morphological sex difference within the medial preoptic area of the rat brain. *Brain Research, 48,* 333–346.

Gorski, R. A., Harlan, R. E., Jacobson, C. D., Shryne, J. E., & Southam, A. M. (1980). Evidence of the existence of a sexually dimorphic nucleus in the preoptic area of the rat. *Journal of Comparative Neurology, 193*(2), 529–539.

Gotter, A. L., & Reppert, S. M. (2001). Analysis of human Per4. *Brain Res Mol Brain Res, 92,* 19–26.

Gottesmann, C. (1999). Neurophysiological support of consciousness during waking and sleep. *Prognosis Neurobiology, 59*(5), 469–508.

Gottfries, C. G. (1988). Dementia: Classification and aspects of treatment. *Psychopharmacology, 5,* 187–195.

Gould, E., & McEwen, B. S. (1993). Neuronal birth and death. *Current Opinion in Neurobiology, 3*(5), 676–682.

Grace, G. M., & Hudson, A. J. (2000). Misidentification syndromes related to face specific area in the fusiform gyrus. *J Neurol Neurosurg Psychiatry, 69,* 645–648.

Graeberg, M. B., Kreutzberg, G. W., & Streit, W. J. (1993). Microglia. *Glia, 7,* special issue no. 1.

Graf, W. D., Marin-Garcia, J., Gao, H. G., Pizzo, S., Naviaux, R. K., Markusic, D., Barshop, B. A, Courchesne, E., & Haas, R. H. (2000). Autism associated with the mitochondrial DNA G8363A transfer RNA(Lys) mutation. *Journal of Child Neurology, 15,* 357–361.

Grasby, P., Malizia, A., & Bench, C. (1996). Psychopharmacology—*in vivo* neurochemistry and pharmacology. *British Medical Bulletin, 52,* 513–526.

Gray, C. M., Koenig, P., Engel, A. K., & Singer, W. (1989). Oscillatory responses in cat visual cortex exhibit inter-columnar synchronization which reflects global stimulus properties. *Nature, 338*(6213), 334–337.

Gray, C. M., & Singer, W. (1989). Stimulus-specific neuronal oscillations in orientation columns of cat visual cortex. *Proceedings of the National Academy of Sciences, USA, 86*(5), 1698–1702.

Gray, J. A., Young, A. M., & Joseph, M. H. (1997). Dopamine's role. *Science, 278*(5343), 1548–1549.

Graziano, M. S., Cooke, D. F., & Taylor, C. S. (2000). Coding the location of the arm by sight. *Science, 290,* 1782–1786.

Graziottin, A. (2000). Libido: The biological scenario. *Maturitas, 34*(S1), 9–16.

Greenberg, D. (1998). Fats and satiety: The role of the small intestine. *Appetite, 31*(2), 229.

Green, L., Fein, D., Modahl, C., Feinstein, C., Waterhouse, L., & Morris, M. (2001). Oxytocin and autistic disorder: Alterations in peptide forms. *Biological Psychiatry, 50,* 609–613.

Greene, R. (2001). Circuit analysis of NMDAR hypofunction in the hippocampus, in vitro, and psychosis of schizophrenia. *Hippocampus, 11,* 569–577.

Gregg, T. R., & Siegel, A. (2001). Brain structures and neurotransmitters regulating aggression in cats: Implications for human aggression. *Prog Neuropsychopharmacol Biol. Psychiatry, 25,* 91–140.

Gresch, P. J., Sved, A. F., Zigmond, M. J., & Finley, J. M. (1995). Local influence of endogenous norephinephrine on extracellular dopamine in rat medial prefrontal cortex. *Journal of Neurochemistry, 65*(1), 111–116.

Griffin, D. R. (1992). *Animal minds.* Chicago: University of Chicago Press.

Groethuysen, U. C., Robinson, D. B., Haylett, C. H., Estes, H. R., & Johnson, A. M. (1957). Depth electrographic recording of a seizure during a structured interview. *Psychosomatic Medicine, 19,* 353–362.

Gron, G., Wunderlich, A. P., Spitzer, M., Tomczak, R., & Riepe, M. W. (2000). Brain activation during human navigation: Gender-different neural networks as substrate of performance. *Natural Neuroscience, 3*(4), 404–408.

Gross, S. S., & Wolin, M. S. (1995). Nitric oxide: Pathophysiological mechanisms. *Annual Review of Physiology, 57,* 737–769.

Grossman, M., Libon, D. J., Ding, X. S., Cloud, B., Jaggi, J., Morrison, D., Greenberg, J., Alavi, A., & Reivich, M. (2001). Progressive peripheral agraphia. *Neurocase, 7,* 339–349.

Grossman, S. P. (1967). *A textbook of physiological psychology.* New York: John Wiley.

Gruber, R. P., Stone, G. C., & Reed, D. R. (1967). *International Journal of Neuropharmacology, 6,* 187–190.

Guerri, C. (1998). Neuroanatomical and neurophysiological mechanisms involved in central nervous system dysfunctions induced by prenatal alcohol exposures. *Alcohol Clinical Experimental Research, 22*(2), 304–312.

Guilleminault, C., Heinzer, R., Mignot, E., & Black, J. (1998). Investigations into the neurologic basis of narcolepsy. *Neurology, 50*(2), 8–15.

Guo, S. W., & Reed, D. R. (2001). The genetics of phenylthiocarbamide perception. *Annals of Human Biology, 28,* 111–142.

Gur, R. C., & Gur, R. E. (1991). The impact of neuroimaging on human neuropsychology. In R. G. Lister & H. J. Weingartner (Eds.), *Perspectives on cognitive neuroscience* (pp. 417–435). New York: Oxford University Press.

Gur, R. C., Mozley, L. H., Mozley, P. D., Resnick, S. M., Karp, J. S., Alavi, A., Arnold. S. E., & Gur, R. E. (1995). Sex differences in regional cerebral glucose metabolism during a resting state. *Science, 267,* 528–531.

Gur, R. E., & Gur, R. C. (1990). Gender differences in regional cerebral blood flow. *Schizophrenia Bulletin, 16*(2), 247–254.

Gur, R. E., Kohler, C., Lisanby, S. H., & Swanson, C. L. (1998). Psychosis secondary to brain tumor. *Semin Clin Neuropsychiatry, 3,* 12–22.

Gurevich, E. V., & Joyce, J. N. (1997). Alterations in the cortical serotonergic system in schizophrenia: A postmortem study. *Biol Psychiatry, 42,* 529–545.

Gurevich, E. V., & Joyce, J. N. (1999a). D_3 receptors and the actions of neuroleptics in the ventral striatopallidal system of schizophrenics. *Ann NY Acad Sci, 29,* 595–613.

Gurevich, E. V., & Joyce, J. N. (1999b). Distribution of dopamine D_3 receptor expressing neurons in the human forebrain: Comparison with D_2 receptor expressing neurons. *Neuropsychopharmacology, 20,* 60–80.

Gurvits, T. V., Lasko, N. B., Schacter, S. C., Kuhne, A. A., Orr, S. P., & Pitman, R. K. (1993). Neurological status of Vietnam veterans with chronic posttraumatic stress disorder. *Journal of Neuropsychiatry and Clinical Neuroscience, 5*(2), 183–188.

Guyot, L. L., & Michael, D. B. (2000). Post-traumatic hydrocephalus. *Neurology Research, 22*(1), 25–28.

Hadders-Algra, M. (2001). Early brain damage and the development of motor behavior in children: Clues for therapeutic intervention? *Neural Plasticity, 8,* 31–49.

Hademenos, G. J. (1997). The biophysics of stroke. *American Scientist, 85,* 226–235.

Hagger, C., Bachevalier, J., & Bercu, B. (1987). Sexual dimorphism in the development of habit formation: Effects of perinatal steroidal gonadal hormones. *Neuroscience, 22*(Suppl. S520).

Hainsworth, F. R., & Epstein, A. N. (1966). Severe impairment of heat-induced saliva-spreading in rats recovered from lateral hypothalamus lesions. *Science, 153*(741), 1255–1257.

Hajek, T., & Hoschl, C. (2001). Hippocampal damage mediated by corticosteroids—A neuropsychiatric research challenge. *Eur Arch Psychiatry Clin Neurosci, 251,* II81–88.

Halgren, E. (1992). Emotional neurophysiology of the amygdala within the context of human cognition. In J. P. Aggleton (Ed.), *The amygdala: Neurobiological aspects of emotion, memory, and mental dysfunction.* New York: Wiley-Liss.

Halgren, E., Walter, R. D., Cherlow, D. G., & Crandell, P. H. (1978). Mental phenomena evoked by electrical stimulation of the human hippocampal formation and amygdala. *Brain, 101*(1), 83–117.

Hall, R. D., Bloom, F. E., & Olds, J. (1977). Neuronal and neurochemical substrates of reinforcement. *Neuroscience Research Program Bulletin, 15*(2), 131–314.

Halmi, K. A. (1995). Current concepts and definitions. In G. I. Szmukler, C. Dare, et al. (Eds.), *Handbook of eating disorders: Theory, treatment, and research.* New York: John Wiley.

Hamada, H., Watanabe, H., Sugimoto, M., Yasuoka, M., Yamada, M., Yamada, M., & Kubo, T. (1999). Autosomal recessive hydrocephalus due to congenital stenosis of the aqueduct of Sylvius. *Prenatal Diagnosis, 19*(11), 1067–1069.

Hamer, D. H., Hu, S., Magnuson, V. L., Hu, N., & Pattatucci, A. M. (1993). A linkage between DNA markers on the X chromosome and male sexual orientation. *Science, 261,* 321–327.

Hamer, Dean H., & LeVay, Simon. 1994. Evidence for a biological influence in male homosexuality. *Scientific American,* 44–49.

Hamilton, S., Khan, F. A., Manalo, M., Norris, K. C., & Rothenberg, S. J. (2001). Neonatal lead poisoning from maternal pica behavior during pregnancy. *J. Natl. Med. Assoc. 93,* 317–319.

Hamann, S. B., Ely, T. D., Grafton, S. T., & Kilts, C. D. (1999). Amygdala activity related to enhanced memory for pleasant and aversive stimuli. *Natural Neuroscience, 2*(3), 289–293.

Hammond, C. (1996). Glial cells. In C. Hammond (Ed.), *Cellular and molecular neurobiology* (pp. 47–59). San Diego: Academic Press.

Hanna, M. G., & Bhatia, K. P. (1997). Movement disorders and mitochondrial dysfunction. *Current Opinion in Neurobiology, 10*(4), 351–356.

Hari, R., & Lounasmaa, O. V. (1989). Recording and interpretation of cerebral magnetic fields. *Science, 244,* 432–436.

Harrington, C. J., & Villalba, R. (2000). Repetitive self-injurious behavior: A neuropsychiatric perspective and review of pharmacologic treatments. *Semin Clin Neurosychiatry, 5,* 215–226.

Hasegawa, I, Fukushima, T., Ihara, T., & Miyashita, Y. (1998). Callosal window between prefrontal cortices: Cognitive interaction to retrieve long-term memory. *Science, 281*(5378), 814–818.

Hasselmo, M. E. (1995). Neuromodulation and cortical function: Modeling the physiological basis of behavior. *Behavioural Brain Research, 67,* 1–27.

Hasselmo, M. E. (1999). Neuromodulation: Acetylcholine and memory consolidation. *Trends in Cognitive Science, 3*(9), 351–359.

Hassler, M. (2000). Music medicine. A neurobiological approach. *Neuroendocrinol Lett, 21,* 101–106.

Hawkins, R. D., Abrams, T. W., Carew, T. J., & Kandel, E. R. (1983). A cellular mechanism of classical conditioning in aplysia: Activity-dependent amplification of pre-synaptic facilitation. *Science, 219*(4583), 400–405.

Hawranko, A. A., & Smith, D. J. (1999). Stress reduces morphine's antinociceptive potency: Dependence upon spinal cholecystokinin processes. *Brain Research, 10,* 251–257.

Haxby, J. V., Ungerleider, L. G., Clark, V. P., Schouten, J. L., Hoffman, E. A., & Martin, A. (1999). The effect of face inversion on activity in human neural systems for face and object perception. *Neuron, 22,* 189–199.

Haxby, J. V., Ungerleider, L. G., Horwitz, B., Maisog, J. M., Rapoport, S. I., & Grady, C. L. (1996). Face encoding and recognition in the human brain. *Proceedings of the National Academy of Sciences, 93,* 922–927.

Healy, D. (1998). Commentary: Meta-analysis of trials comparing antidepressants with active placebos. *British Journal of Psychiatry, 172,* 232–234.

Heath, R. G., & Mickle, W. A. (1960). Evaluation of seven years' experience with depth electrode studies in human patients. In E. Ramey & D. O'Doherty (Eds.), *Electrical studies on the unanesthetized brain.* New York: Hoeber.

Hebb, D. O. (1949). *The organization of behavior.* New York: Wiley.

Heinrichs, R. W. (1993). Schizophrenia and the brain: Conditions for a neuropsychology of madness. *American Psychologist, 48*(3), 221–233.

Heller, W. (1994). Cognitive and emotional organization of the brain: Influences on the creation and perception of art. In D. W. Zaidel (Ed.), *Neuropsychology.* San Diego: Academic Press.

Heller, W., Miller, G. A., & Nitschke, J. B. (1998). Lateralization in emotion and emotional disorders. *Current Directions in Psychological Science, 1,* 26–32.

Heninger, G. R. (1995). Indolamines: The role of serotonin in clinical disorders. In F. E. Bloom & D. J. Kupfer (Eds.), *Psychopharmacology: The fourth generation of progress.* New York: Raven Press.

Henneman, E. (1957). Relation between size of neurons and their susceptibility to discharge. *Science, 126,* 1345–1347.

Herholz, K. (1995). FDG PET and differential diagnosis of dementia. *Alzheimer Disease and Associated Disorders, 9*(1), 6–16.

Herkenham, M., Groen, B., Lynn, A., De Costa, B., & Richfield, E. (1991). Neuronal localization of cannabinoid receptors and second messengers in mutant mouse cerebellum. *Brain Research, 552*(2), 301–310.

Herkenham, M., Lynn, A. B., Johnson, M. R., Melvin, L. S., de Costa, B. R., & Rice, K. C. (1991). Characterization and localization of cannabinoid receptors in rat brain: A quantitative in vitro autoradiographic study. *Journal of Neuroscience, 11,* 563–583.

Herkenham, M., Lynn, A., Little, M., Johnson, M., Melvin, L., de Costa, B., & Rice, K. (1990). Cannabinoid receptor localization in brain. *Proceedings of the National Academy of Sciences, 87*(5), 1932–1936.

Herman, B. H., & Panksepp, J. (1978). Effects of morphine and naloxone on separation distress and approach attachment: Evidence for opiate mediation of social affect. *Pharmacological Biochemical Behavior, 9*(2), 213–220.

Herrmann, D. (1998). *Helen Keller: A life.* New York: Alfred A. Knopf.

Hernandez, L., & Hoebel, B. G. (1990). Feeding enhances dopamine turnover in the prefrontal cortex. *Brain Research Bulletin, 25,* 975–979.

Hernandez, M. T., Sauerwein, H. C., Jambaque, I., De Guise, E., Lussier, F., Lortie, A., Dulac, O., & Lassonde, M. (2002). Deficits in executive functions and motor coordination in children with frontal lobe epilepsy. *Neuropsychologia, 40,* 384–400.

Hernandez-Tristan, R., Arevalo, C., & Canals, S. (1999). Effect of prenatal uterine position on male and female rats' sexual behavior. *Physiological Behavior, 67*(3), 401–408.

Hetherington, A. W., & Ranson, S. W. (1940). Hypothalamic lesions and adiposity in the rat. *Anatomical Record, 78,* 149–172.

Hier, D. B. (1979). A genetic explanation for no sex difference in spatial ability among Eskimos. *Perceptual Motor Skills, 48*(2), 593–594.

Hillis, A. E., Mordkoff, J. T., & Caramazza, A. (1999). Mechanisms of spatial attention revealed by hemispatial neglect. *Cortex, 35*(3), 433–442.

Hiort, O. (2000). Neonatal endocrinology of abnormal male sexual differentiation: Molecular aspects. *Hormone Research, 53*(S1), 38–41.

Hiort, O., & Holterhus, P. M. (2000). The molecular basis of male sexual differentiation. *European Journal of Endocrinology, 142*(2), 101–110.

Hirata, Y., Kuriki, S., & Pantev, C. (1999). Musicians with absolute pitch show distinct neural activities in the auditory cortex. *Neuroreport, 10*(6), 999–1002.

Hiscock, M., Inch, R., Hawryluk, J., Lyon, P. J., & Perachio, N. (1999). Is there a sex difference in human laterality? III. An exhaustive survey of tactile laterality studies from six neuropsychology journals. *Journal of Clinical Experimental Neuropsychology, 21*(2), 17–28.

Hodges, H., Sowinski, P., Virley, D., Nelson, A., Kershaw, T. R., Watson, W. P., Veizovic, T., Patel, S., Mora, A., Rashid, T., French, S. J., Chadwick, A., Gray, J. A., & Sinden, J. D. (2000). Functional reconstruction of the hippocampus: Fetal versus conditionally immortal neuroepithelial stem cell grafts. *Novartis Foundation Symposium, 231,* 53–65.

Hodges, H., Veizovic, T., Bray, N., French, S. J., Rashid, T. P., Chadwick, A., Patel, S., & Gray, J. A. (2001). Conditionally immortal neuroepithelial stem cell grafts reverse age-associated memory impairments in rats. *Neuroscience, 101,* 945–955.

Hodgkin, A. L., & Huxley, A. F. (1952). A quantitative description of membrane current and its application to conduction and excitation in nerve. *Journal of Physiology, 117,* 500–544.

Hofmann, S., Bezold, R., Jaksch, M., Kaufhold, P., Obermaier-Kusser, B., & Gerbitz, K. D. (1997). Analysis of the mitochondrial DNA from patients with Wolfram (DIDMOAD) syndrome. *Molecular Cell Biochemistry, 174*(1–2), 209–213.

Hokfelt, T., Pernow, B., & Wahren, J. (2001). Substance P: A pioneer amongst neuropeptides. *J Intern Med, 249,* 27–40.

Hokfelt, T. G. M., Castel, M-N., Morino, P., Zhang, X., & Dagerlind, A. (1995). General overview of neuropeptides. In F. E. Bloom & D. J. Kupfer(Eds.), *Psychopharmacology: The fourth generation of progress.* New York: Raven Press.

Holden, R. J., Pakula, I. S., & Mooney, P. A. (1997). A neuroimmunological model of antisocial and borderline personality disorders. *Human Psychopharmacology Clinical & Experimental, 12,* 291–308.

Holden, R. J., Pakula, I. S., & Mooney, P. A. (1998). An immunological model connecting the pathogenesis of stress, depression, and carcinoma. *Medical Hypotheses, 51*(4), 309–314.

Hollister, J. M., Laing, P., Mednick, S. A. (1996). Rhesus incompatibility as a risk factor for schizophrenia in male adults. *Arch Gen Psychiatry, 53,* 19–24.

Horgan, J. (1994). Can science explain consciousness? *Scientific American, 271*(1), 88–94.

Horger, B. A., & Roth, R. H. (1995). Stress and central amino acid systems. In M. J. Friedman, D. S. Charney, & A. Y. Deutch (Eds.), *Neurobiological and clinical consequences of stress: From normal adaptation to post-traumatic stress disorder.* Philadelphia, PA: Lippincott Williams & Wilkins.

Horger, B. A., & Roth, R. H. (1996). The role of mesoprefrontal dopamine neurons in stress. *Critical Review of Neurobiology, 10*(3–4), 395–418.

Horn, G. (1963). The response of single units in the striate cortex of unrestrained cats to photic and soma-esthetic stimuli. *Journal of Physiology, 165,* 80–81.

Horton, J. C., & Hubel, D. H. (1981). Regular patchy distribution of cytochrome oxidase staining in primary visual cortex of macaque monkey. *Nature, 292*(5825), 762–764.

Horvitz, J. C., Stewart, T., & Jacobs, B. L. (1997). Burst activity of ventral tegmental dopamine neurons is elicited by sensory stimuli in the awake cat. *Brain Research, 759*(2), 251–258.

Hoschl, C., & Hajek, T. (2001). Hippocampal damage mediated by corticosteroids—a neuropsychiatric research challenge. *Eur Arch Psychiatry Clin Neurosci, 251*(Suppl 2), II81–II88.

Houpt, K. A. (1982). Gastrointestinal factors in hunger and satiety. *Neuroscience Biobehavioral Review, 6*(2), 145–164.

Hsieh, J. C., Stahle-Baeckdahl, M., Haeermark, O., & Stone-Elander, S. (1996). Traumatic nociceptive pain activates the hypothalamus and the periaqueductal gray. *Pain, 61*(2), 303–314.

Hu, S., Pattatucci, A. M., Patterson, C., Li, L., Fulker, D. W., Cherny, S. S., Kruglyak, L., & Hamer, D. H. (1995). Linkage between sexual orientation and chromosome Xq28 in males but not in females. *Nature Genetics, 11,* 248–256.

Hubel, D. H., & Wiesel, T. N. (1962). Receptive fields, binocular interaction and functional architecture in the cat's visual cortex. *Journal of Physiology, 160,* 106–154.

Hudson, A. J., & Grace, G. M. (2000). Misidentification syndromes related to face specific area in the fusiform gyrus. *Journal of Neurology, Neurosurgery, & Psychiatry, 69,* 645–648.

Hughes, A. (1975). A quantitative analysis of the cat retinal ganglion cell topography. *Journal of Comparative Neurology, 163*(1), 107–128.

Hull, E. M., Lorrain, D. S., Du, J., Matuszewich, L., Lumley, L. A., Putnam, S. K., & Moses, J. (1999). Hormone–neurotransmitter interactions in the control of sexual behavior. *Behavioral Brain Research, 105*(1), 105–116.

Hulshoff Pol, H. E., Hoek, H. W., Susser, E., Brown, A. S., Dingemans, A., Schnack, H. G., van Haren, N. E., Pereira Ramos L. M., Gispen-de Wied, C. C., & Kahn, R. S. (2000). Prenatal exposure to famine and brain morphology in schizophrenia. *American Journal of Psychiatry, 157,* 1170–1172.

Humphreys, G. W., Donnelly, N., & Riddoch, M. J. (1993). Expression is computed separately from facial identity, and it is computed separately from moving and static faces: Neuropsychological evidence. *Neuropsychologia, 31,* 173–181.

Hutton, S. B., Crawford, T. J., Gibbins, H., Cuthbert, I., Barnes, T. R., Kennard, C., & Joyce, E. M. (2001). Short and long term effects of antipsychotic medication on smooth pursuit eye tracking in schizophrenia. *Psychopharmacology, 157,* 284–291.

Hwang, I. P., & Olson, R. J.(2001). Patient satisfaction after uneventful cataract surgery with implantation of a silicone or acrylic foldable intraocular lens. Comparative study. *Journal of Cataract Refractory Surgery, 27,* 1607–1610.

Iacoboni, M., Koski, L., & Mazziotta, J. C. (2002). Deconstructing apraxia: Understanding disorders of intentional movement after stroke. *Curr Opin Neurol, 15,* 71–77.

Ignarro, L. J., Buga, G. M., Wood, K. S., Byrnes, R. E., & Chaudhuri, G. (1987). Endothelium-derived relaxing factor produced and released from artery and vein is nitric oxide. *Proceedings of the National Academy of Sciences, 84,* 9265–9269.

Iino, M., Goto, K., Kakegawa, W., Okado, H., Sudo, M., Ishiuchi, S., Miwa, A., Takayasu, Y., Saito, I., Tsuzuki, K., & Ozawa, S. (2001). Glia-synapse interaction through Ca2+-permeable AMPA receptors in Bergmann glia. *Science, 292,* 926–929.

Ikonomidou, C., Bosch, F., Miksa, M., Bittigau, P., Vockler, J., Dikranian, K., Tenkova, T., Stefovska, V., Turski, L., & Olney, J. (1999). Blockade of NMDA receptors and apoptotic neurodegeneration in the developing brain. *Science, 283*(5398), 70–74.

Imperato-McGinley, J., Guerrero, L., Gautier, T., & Peterson, R. E. (1974). Steroid 5 alpha-reductase deficiency in man: An inherited form of male pseudohermaphroditism. *Science, 186,* 1213–1215.

Ingvar, M., Ghatan, P. H., Wirsen-Muerling, A., Risberg, J., Von Heijne, G., Stone-Elander, S., & Ingvar, D. H. (1998). Alcohol activates the cerebral reward system in man. *Journal of the Study of Alcohol, 59*(3), 258–269.

Insel, T. R. (1992). Oxytocin—a neuropeptide for affiliation: Evidence from behavioral, receptor autoradiographic, and comparative studies. *Psychoneuroendocrinology, 17,* 3–35.

Ishiwata, T., Hasegawa, H., Yasumatsu, M., Akano, F., Yazawa, T., Otokawa, M., & Aihara, Y. (2001). The role of preoptic area and anterior hypothalamus and median raphe nucleus on thermoregulatory system in freely moving rats. *Neuroscience Letters, 306,* 126–128.

Islam, F., Jha, S. K., & Mallick, B. N. (2001). GABA exerts opposite influence on warm and cold sensitive neurons in medial preoptic area in rats. *J Neurobiol, 48,* 291–300.

Jaber, M., Robinson, S. W., Missale, C., & Caron, M. G. (1996). Dopamine receptors and brain function. *Neuropharmacology, 35*(11), 1503–1519.

Jackson, M. B., & Yakel, J. L. (1995). The 5-HT3 receptor channel. *Annual Review of Physiology, 57,* 447–468.

Jacobs, B. L. (1994). Serotonin, motor activity, and depression-related disorders. *American Scientist, 82,* 456–463.

Jacobs, B. L., & Fornal, C. A. (1995). Serotonin and behavior. In F. E. Bloom & D. J. Kupfer (Eds.), *Psychopharmacology: The fourth generation of progress.* New York: Raven Press.

Jacobs, B. L., & Fornal, C. A. (1997). Serotonin and motor activity. *Current Opinion in Neurobiology, 7,* 820–825.

Jacobs, B. L., & Fornal, C. A. (1999). Activity of serotonergic neurons in behaving animals. *Neuropsychopharmacology, 21*(2 Suppl), 9S–15S.

James, L. E., & MacKay, D. G. (2001). H.M., word knowledge, and aging: Support for a new theory of long-term retrograde amnesia. *Psychol Sci, 12,* 485–492.

James, W. (1890). *The principles of psychology.* New York: Holt.

Janowsky, D. S., el-Yousef, M. K., Davis, J. M., & Sekerke, H. J. (1977). A cholinergic-adrenergic hypothesis of mania and depression. *Lancet, 2*(7778), 632–635.

Janowsky, D. S., Halbreich, U., & Rausch, J. (1996). Association among ovarian hormones, other hormones, emotional disorders, and neurotransmitters. In M. F. Jensvold & U. Halbreich (Eds.), *Psychopharmacology and women: Sex, gender, and hormones.* Washington, DC: American Psychiatric Press.

Janzer, R. C., & Raff, M. C. (1987). Astrocytes induce blood–brain barrier properties in endothelial cells. *Nature, 325,* 253–257.

Jarvis, P. E., & Barth, J. T. (1997). *The Halstead-Reitan Neuropsychological Battery: A guide to interpretation and clinical applications.* Odessa, FL: Psychological Assessment Resources.

Jellinger, K. A. (1996). Structural basis of dementia in neurodegenerative disorders. *Journal of Neural Transmission, 47,* 1–29.

Jellinger, K. A. (2001). The pathology of Parkinson's disease. *Advances in Neurology, 86,* 55–72.

Jensen, A. M., & Chiu, S-Y. (1993). Astrocyte networks. In S. Murphy (Ed.), *Astrocytes: Pharmacology and function* (pp. 309–330). San Diego: Academic Press.

Jensen, N., & Kristensen G. (2001). Frequency of nightly wetting and the efficiency of alarm treatment of nocturnal enuresis. *Scand J Urol Nephrol, 35,* 357–363.

Jentsch, J., Redmond, D., Elsworth, J., Taylor, J., Youngren, K., & Roth, R. (1997). Enduring cognitive deficits and cortical dopamine dysfunction in monkeys after long-term administration of phencyclidine. *Science, 277*(5328), 953–955.

Jeste, D. V., & Lohr, J. B. (1989). Hippocampal pathologic findings in schizophrenia. A morphometric study. *Archives of General Psychiatry, 46,* 1019–1024.

Jha, S. K., Islam, F., & Mallick, B. N. (2001). GABA exerts opposite influence on warm and cold sensitive neurons in medial preoptic area in rats. *Journal of Neurobiology, 48,* 291–300.

Jiang, Y., Haxby, J. V., Martin, A., Ungerleider, L. G., & Parasuraman, R. (2000). Complementary neural mechanisms for tracking items in human working memory. *Science, 287*(5453), 643–646.

John, E. R., Prichep, L. Fridman, J., & Easton, P. (1988). Neurometrics: Computer-assisted differential diagnosis of brain functions. *Science, 239*(4836), 162–169.

Johnson, B. A., & Ait-Daoud, N. (1999). Medications to treat alcoholism. *Alcohol Res Health, 23,* 99–106.

Jones, A. K., Friston, K., & Frackowiak, R. S. (1992). Localization of responses to pain in human cerebral cortex. *Science, 255*(5041), 215–216.

Jones, R. D., & Tranel, D. (2001). Severe developmental prosopagnosia in a child with superior intellect. *Journal of Clinical Experimental Neuropsychology, 23,* 265–273.

Jonides, J., Smith, E. E., Koeppe, R. A., & Awh, E. (1993). Spatial working memory in humans as revealed by PET. *Nature, 363,* 623–625.

Jordan, B. D. (2000). Chronic traumatic brain injury associated with boxing. *Semin Neurol, 20,* 179–185.

Josselyn, S. A., Miller, R., & Beninger, R. J. (1997). Behavioral effects of clozapine and dopamine receptor subtypes. *Neuroscience and Biobehavioral Reviews, 21,* 531–558.

Jouvet, M. (1999). Sleep and serotonin: An unfinished story. *Neuropsychopharmacology, 21*(2 Suppl), 24S–27S.

Jouvet, M., & Michel, F. (1958). Recherches sur l'activite electrique cerebrale au cours du sommeil. *Comptes Rendus de la Societe de Biologie, 152,* 1167–1170.

Joyce, E. M., Rio, D. E., Ruttimann, U. E., Rohrbaugh, J. W., Martin, P. R., Rawlings, R. R., & Eckardt, M. J. (1994). Decreased cingulate and precuneate glucose utilization in alcoholic Korsakoff's syndrome. *Psychiatry Research, 54,* 225–239.

Joyce, J. N., & Gurevich E. V. (1999, June 29). D$_3$ receptors and the actions of neuroleptics in the ventral striatopallidal system of schizophrenics. Ann N Y Acad Sci, 877, 595–613.

Kaas, J. H., & Hackett, T. A. (1999). "What" and "where" processing in the auditory cortex. *Nat Neuroscience, 2*(12), 1045–1047.

Kakuma, T., Kojima, T., Matsushima, E., Ibayashi, S., Ohkura, T., & Okubo, Y. (2001). Relationship between exploratory eye movements and clinical course in schizophrenic patients. *Eur Arch Psychiatry Clin Neurosci, 251,* 211–216.

Kalin, N. H. (1993). The neurobiology of fear. *Scientific American, 268*(5), 94–101.

Kalin, N. H., & Shelton, S. E. (1989). Defensive behaviors in infant rhesus monkeys: Environmental cues and neurochemical regulation. *Science, 243*(4899), 1718–1721.

Kalin, N. H., Shelton, S. E., Davidson, R. J., & Kelley, A. E. (2001). The primate amygdala mediates acute fear but not the behavioral and physiological components of anxious temperament. *Journal of Neuroscience, 21,* 2067–2074.

Kalogeris, T. J., Liu, M., Thomson, A. B., & Tso, P. (2001). The role of apolipoprotein A-IV in the regulation of food intake. *Annu Rev Nutr, 21,* 231–254.

Kalogeris, T. J., Liu, M., & Tso, P. (1999). The role of apolipoprotein A-IV in food intake regulation. *J Nutr, 129,* 1503–1506.

Kanarek, R. B., & Hirsch, E. (1977). Dietary-induced overeating in experimental animals. *Federation Proceedings, 36,* 154–158.

Kandel, E. R., & Hawkins, R. D. (1992). The biological basis of learning and individuality. *Scientific American, 267*(3), 78–86.

Kanosue, K., Zhang, Y. H., Yanase-Fujiwara, M., & Hosono, T. (1994). Hypothalamic network for thermoregulatory shivering. *American Journal of Physiology, 267*(1), 275–282.

Kapur, S., & Mann, J. (1992). Role of the dopaminergic system in depression. *Biological Psychiatry, 32*(1), 1–17.

Kapur, S., & Mann, J. J. (1993). Antidepressant action and the neurobiologic effects of ECT: Human studies. In C. E. Coffey (Ed.), *The clinical science of electroconvulsive therapy.* Washington, DC: American Psychiatric Press.

Kastner, S., DeWeerd, P., Desimone, R., & Ungerleider, L. G. (1998). Mechanisms of directed attention in the human extrastriate cortex as revealed by functional MRI. *Science, 282*(5386), 108–111.

Katayama, Y., DeWitt, D. S., Becker, D. P., & Hayes, R. L. (1984). Behavioral evidence for a cholinoceptive pontine inhibitory area: Descending control of a spinal motor output and sensory input. *Brain Research, 296*(2), 241–262.

Kato, T. (2001). Molecular genetics of bipolar disorder. *Neuroscience Research, 40,* 105–113.

Katz, J. L., Newman, A. H., & Izenwasser, S. (1997). Relations between heterogenieity of dopamine transporter binding and function and the behavioral pharmacology of cocaine. *Pharmacology, Biochemistry, and Behavior, 57,* 505–512.

Katzman, D. K., Lambe, E. K., Mikulis, D. J., Ridgley, J. N., Goldbloom, D. S., & Zipursky, R. B. (1996). Cerebral gray matter and white matter volume deficits in adolescent girls with anorexia nervosa. *Journal of Pediatrics, 129*(6), 794–803.

Katzman, D. K., Zipursky, R. B., Lambe, E. K., & Mikulis, D. J. (1997). A longitudinal magnetic resonance imaging study of brain changes in adolescents with anorexia nervosa. *Arch Pediatric Adolescent Medicine, 151*(8), 793–797.

Kavanau, J. L. (1997). Memory, sleep, and the evolution of mechanisms of synaptic efficacy maintenance. *Neuroscience, 79*(1), 7–44.

Kavoussi, R., Armstead, P., & Coccaro, E. (1997). The neurobiology of impulsive aggression. *Psychiatric Clinics of North America, 20*(2), 395–403.

Kaye, W., Gendall, K., & Stober, M. (1998). Serotonin neuronal function and selective serotonin reuptake inhibitor treatment in anorexia and bulimia nervosa. *Biological Psychiatry, 44*(9), 825–838.

Kaye, W. H. (1997). Anorexia nervosa, obsessional behavior, and serotonin. *Psychopharmacology Bulletin, 33*(3), 335–344.

Kaye, W. H., Klump, K. L., Frank, G. K., & Strober, M. (2000). Anorexia and bulimia nervosa. *Annual Review of Medicine, 51*, 299–313.

Kebabian, J. W., & Neumeyer, J. L. (1994). *The RBI handbook of receptor classification*. Natick, MA : Research Biochemicals International.

Keller, H. (1954). *The story of my life*. Garden City, NY: Doubleday.

Kelly, J. P., & Rosenberg, J. H. (1997). Diagnosis and management of concussion in sports. *Neurology, 48*(3), 575–580.

Kempermann, G., & Gage, F. (1999). New nerve cells for the adult brain. *Scientific American, 280*(5), 48–53.

Kendler, K.S., Davis, C. G., & Kessler, R. C. (1997). The familial aggregation of common psychiatric and substance use disorders in the National Comorbidity Survey: A family history study. *British Journal of Psychiatry, 170*, 541–548.

Kennard, M. A. (1939). Alterations in response to visual stimuli following lesions of frontal lobe in monkeys. *Archives of Neurology and Psychiatry, 41*, 1153–1165.

Kennedy, J. L., Basile, V. S., & Macciardi, F. M. (1998). Chromosome 4 Workshop Summary: Sixth World Congress on Psychiatric Genetics, Bonn, Germany, October 6–10, 1998. *American Journal of Medical Genetics, 88*, 224–228.

Kerrison, J. B., Howell, N., Miller, N. R., Hirst, L. & Green, W. R. (1995). Leber hereditary optic neuropathy: Electron microscopy and molecular genetic analysis of a case. *Ophthalmology, 10*, 1509–1516.

Kertesz, A., & Munoz, D. (1997). Primary progressive aphasia. *Clinical Neuroscience, 4*(2), 95–102.

Kesslak, J. P., Nalcioglu, O., & Cotman, C. W. (1991). Quantification of magnetic resonance scans for hippocampal and parahippocampal atrophy in Alzheimer's disease. *Neurology, 41*(1), 51–54.

Kettaneh, A., Biousse, V., & Bousser, M. (2000). Neurological complications after roller coaster rides: An emerging new risk? *Presse Medicine, 29*(4), 175–180.

Keynes, R. D., & Aidley, D. J. (1991). *Nerve & muscle* Cambridge: Cambridge University Press.

Kiecolt–Glaser, J. K., Glaser, R., Shuttleworth, E. C., Dyer, C. S., Ogrocki, P., & Speicher, C. E. (1987). Chronic stress and immunity in family caregivers of Alzheimer's disease victims. *Psychosomatic Medicine, 49*(5), 523–535.

Kiess, W., Siebler, T., Englaro, P., Kratzsch, J., Deutscher, J., Meyer, K., Gallaher, B., & Blum, W. F. (1998). Leptin as a metabolic regulator during fetal and neonatal life and in childhood and adolescence. *Journal of Pediatric Endocrinological Metabolism, 11*(4), 483–496.

Kimura, D. (1992). Sex differences in the brain. *Scientific American, 267*, 118–125.

Kinnamon, S. C. (1988). Taste transduction: A diversity of mechanisms. *Trends in Neuroscience, 11*(11), 491–496.

Kinomura, S., Larsson, J., Gulyas, B., & Roland, P. E. (1996). Activation by attention of the human reticular formation and thalamic intralaminar nuclei. *Science, 271*(5248), 512–515.

Kirkcaldie, M., Pridmore, S., & Pascual-Leone, A. (1997). Transcranial magnetic stimulation as therapy for depression and other disorders. *Australian and New Zealand Journal of Psychiatry, 31*(2), 264–272.

Kirkham, T. C., Perez, S., & Gibbs, J. (1995). Prefeeding potentiates anorectic actions of neuromedin B and gastrin releasing peptide. *Physiology and Behavior, 58*(6), 1175–1179.

Klaiber, E., Broverman, D., Vogel, W., & Kobayashi, Y. (1979). Estrogen therapy for severe persistent depressions in women. *Archives of General Psychiatry, 36*(5), 550–554.

Kluver, H., & Bucy, P. C. (1937). "Psychic blindness" and other symptoms following bilateral temporal lobe lobectomy in rhesus monkeys. *American Journal of Psychology, 119*, 352–353.

Koch, C. (2001). A mind for consciousness. *Scientific American, 285*(1), 36–37.

Koch, C., Zador, A., & Brown, T. H. (1992). Dendritic spines: Convergence of theory and experiment. *Science, 256*, 973–974.

Kodama, K., Komatsu, N., Kumakiri, C., Noda, S., Okada, S., Sato, T., & Yamanouchi, N. (2000.) Relationship between MRI findings and prognosis for patients with general paresis. *J Neuropsychiatry Clin Neurosci, 12*, 246–250.

Kojima, Y., Hayashi, Y., Asai, N., Maruyama, T., Sasaki, S., & Kohri, K. (1998). Detection of the sex-determining region of the Y chromosome in 46,XX true hermaphroditism. *Urology International, 60*(4), 235–238.

Kolb, B., & Gibb, R. (1991). Sparing of function after neonatal frontal lesions correlates with increased cortical dendritic branching: A possible mechanism of the Kennard effect. *Behavioral Brain Research, 43*(1), 51–56.

Koning, C., & Magill-Evans, J. (2001). Social and language skills in adolescent boys with Asperger syndrome. *Autism, 5*, 23–36.

Koob, G. F., & Bloom, F. E. (1988). Cellular and molecular mechanisms of drug dependence. *Science, 242*, 715–723.

Koob, G. F., & LeMoal, M. (1997). Drug abuse: Hedonic homeostatic dysregulation. *Science, 278*(5335), 52–58.

Kordower, J. H., Emborg, M. E., Bloch, J., Ma, S. Y., Chu, Y., Leventhal, L., McBride, J., Chen, E. Y., Palfi, S., Roitberg, B. Z., Brown, W. D., Holden, J. E., Pyzalski, R., Taylor, M. D., Carvey, P., Ling, Z., Trono, D., Hantraye, P., Deglon, N., & Aebischer, P. (2000). Neurodegeneration prevented by lentiviral vector delivery of GDNF in primate models of Parkinson's disease. *Science, 290*, 767–773.

Koski, L., Iacoboni, M., & Mazziotta, J. C. (2002). Deconstructing apraxia: Understanding disorders of intentional movement after stroke. *Current Opinion in Neurology, 15*, 71–77.

Kosofsky, B. E. (1998). Cocaine-induced alternations in neuro-development. *Seminar of Speech Language, 19*(2), 109–121.

Kovelman, J. A., & Scheibel, A. B. (1984). A neurohistological correlate of schizophrenia. *Biological Psychiatry, 19*(12), 1601–1621.

Krahl, W., & Kuhnle, U. (2002). The impact of culture on sex assignment and gender development in intersex couples. *Perspect Biol Med, 45*, 85–103.

Kraly, F. S. (1978). Abdominal vagotomy inhibits osmotically induced drinking in the rat. *Journal of Comparative Psychology, 92*(6), 999–1013.

Kraly, F. S., Carty, W. J., & Smith, G. P. (1978). Effect of pregastric food stimuli on meal size and intermeal interval in the rat. *Physiology and Behavior, 20*, 779–784.

Kramer, M. S., Cutler, N., Feighner, J., Shrivastava, R., Carman, J., Sramek, J. J., et al. (1998). Distinct mechanism for antidepressant activity by blockade of central substance P receptors. *Science, 281*, 1640–1645.

Kratz, C. M., & Levitsky, D. A. (1979). Responses to protein dilution in the adult female rat. *Physiology Behavior, 23*(4), 709–715.

Kraus, F. T., & Acheen, V. I. (1999). Fetal thrombotic vasculopathy in the placenta: Cerebral thrombi and infarcts, coagulopathies, and cerebral palsy. *Human Pathology, 30*(7), 759–769.

Kreis, R., Ross, B. D., Farrow, N. A., & Ackerman, Z. (1992). Metabolic disorders of the brain in chronic hepatic encephalopathy detected with H-1 MR spectroscopy. *Radiology, 182,* 19–27.

Kreitzer, A. C., & Regehr, W. G. (2001). Cerebellar depolarization-induced suppression of inhibition is mediated by endogenous cannabinoids. *Journal of Neuroscience, 21,* RC174.

Krukoff, T. L., & Shan, J. (2001). Intracerebroventricular adrenomedullin stimulates the hypothalamic-pituitary-adrenal axis, the sympathetic nervous system and production of hypothalamic nitric oxide. *J. Neuroendocrinol, 13,* 975–984.

Krupa, D. J., Thompson, J. K., & Thompson, R. F. (1993). Localization of a memory trace in the mammalian brain. *Science, 260*(5110), 989–991.

Krystal, J. H., Bennett, A. L., Bremner, J. D., Southwick, S. M., & Charney, D. S. (1995). Toward a cognitive neuroscience of dissociation and altered memory functions in post-traumatic stress disorder. In *Neurobiological and clinical consequences of stress: From normal adaptation to post-traumatic stress disorder.* Philadelphia: Lippincott Williams & Wilkins.

Kuhnle, U., & Krahl, W. (2002). The impact of culture on sex assignment and gender development in intersex patients. *Perspectives in Biological Medicine, 45,* 85–103.

Kupfermann, I. (1964). Eating behavior induced by sounds. *Nature, 201,* 324–325.

LaBar, K. S., Gatenby, J. C., Gore, J. C., LeDoux, J. E., & Phelps, E. A. (1998). Human amygdala activation during conditioned fear acquisition and extinction: A mixed-trial fMRI study. *Neuron, 20,* 937–945.

Labows, J. N., & Wysocki, C. J. (1984). Individual differences in odor perception. *Perfume Flavorist, 9,* 21–26.

Lack, L. C., Mercer, J. D., & Wright, H. (1996). Circadian rhythms of early morning awakening insomniacs. *Journal of Sleep Research, 5*(4), 211–219.

Laegreid, L., Olegard, R., Walstrom, J., & Conradi, N. (1989). Teratogenic effects of benzodiazepine use during pregnancy. *Journal of Pediatrics, 114*(1), 126–131.

Lai, C. W., & Trimble, M. R. (1997). Stress and epilepsy. *Journal of Epilepsy, 10*(4), 177–186.

Lai, Y. Y., & Siegel, J. M. (1988). Medullary regions mediating atonia. *Journal of Neuroscience, 8*(12), 4790–4796.

Lallemand, F., Soubrie, P. H., & De Witte, P. H. (2001). Effects of CB1 cannabinoid receptor blockade on ethanol preference after chronic ethanol administration. *Alcohol,*

Clinical and Experimental Research, 25, 1317–1323.

Lambe, E. K. (1999). Dyslexia, gender, and brain imaging. *Neuropsychologia, 37*(5), 521–536.

Lambe, E. K., Katzman, D. K., Mikulis, D. J., Kennedy, S. H., & Zipursky, R. B. (1997). Cerebral gray matter volume deficits after weight recovery from anorexia nervosa. *Arch General Psychiatry, 54*(6), 537–542.

Laming, P. R., Kimelberg, H., Robinson, S., Salm, A., Hawrylak, N., Muller, C., Roots, B., & Ng, K. (2000). Neuronal–glial interactions and behaviour. *Neuroscience and Biobehavioral Review, 24,* 295–340

Lane, P., & Gross, S. S. (1999). Cell signalling by nitric oxide. *Seminars in Nephrology, 19,* 215–229.

Lane, R. D., Reiman, E. M., Bradley, M. M., Lang, P. J., Ahern, G. L., Davidson, R. J., & Schwartz, G. E. (1997). Neuroanatomical correlates of pleasant and unpleasant emotion. *Neuropsychologia, 35*(11), 1437–1444.

Lane, R. D., Sechrest, L., Reidel, R., Weldon, V., Kaszniak, A., & Schwartz, G. E. (1996). Impaired verbal and nonverbal emotion recognition in alexithymia. *Psychosomatic Medicine, 58*(3), 203–210.

Lange, C. G., & James, W. (1922). *The emotions.* New York: Hafner.

Lantz, M. S., & Buchalter, E. N. (2001). Posttraumatic stress. Helping older adults cope with tragedy. *Geriatrics, 56,* 35–36.

Lappin, J. S., & Craft, W. D. (2000). Foundations of spatial vision: From retinal images to perceived shapes. *Psychology Review, 107*(1), 6–38.

Larson, M. C., Gunnar, M. R., & Hertsgaard, L. (1991). The effects of morning naps, car trips, and maternal separation on adrenocortical activity in human infants. *Child Development, 62*(2), 362–372.

LaRue, A. (1992). *Aging and neuropsychological assessment.* New York: Oxford University Press.

Laruelle, M., & Huang, Y. (2001). Vulnerability of positron emission tomography radiotracers to endogenous competition. New insights. *Quarterly Journal of Nuclear Medicine, 45,* 124–138.

Lashley, K. S. (1929). *Brain mechanisms and intelligence: A quantitative study of injuries to the brain.* Chicago: University of Chicago Press.

Lassen, N. A., Ingvar, D. H., & Skinhoj, E. (1978). Brain function and blood flow. *Scientific American, 239,* 62–71.

Laudenslager, M. L. (1976). Proportional hypothalamic control of behavioral thermoregulation in the squirrel monkey. *Physiological Behavior, 17*(3), 383–390.

Laurent, G. (1999). A systems perspective on early olfactory coding. *Science, 286*(5440), 723–728.

Lawes, I. N. C. (1988). The central connections of area postrema define the paraventricular system involved in antinoxious behaviors. In J. Kucharczyk, D. Stewart, & A. Miller (Eds.), *Nausea and vomiting: Recent research and clinical advances.* Boca Raton, FL: CRC Press.

Lawless, M. R., & McElderry, D. H. (2001). Nocturnal enuresis: Current concepts. *Pediatr, 22,* (22), 339–407.

Leckman, J. F., Pauls, D. L., & Cohen, D. J. (1995). Tic disorders. In F. E. Bloom & D. J. Kupfer (Eds.), *Psychopharmacology: The fourth generation of progress.* New York: Raven Press.

LeDoux, J. E. (1992). Emotion and the amygdala. In J. P. Aggleton (Ed.), *The amygdala: Neurobiological aspects of emotion, memory, and mental dysfunction.* New York: Wiley-Liss.

LeDoux, J. E. (1994). Emotion, memory, and the brain. *Scientific American, 270*(6), 50–57.

LeDoux, J. E. (1995). Emotion: Clues from the brain. *Annual Review of Psychology, 46,* 209–235.

Lee, V. M., Newell, K. L., Schmmidt, M. L., Trojanowski, J. Q., & Zhukareva, V. (2001). *Acta Neuropathol, 101,* 518–524.

Leenders, K. L., Maguire, P. R., Missimer, J., Nienhusmeier, M., Roelcke, U., Schultz, W., & Thut, G. (1997). Activation of the human brain by monetary reward. *NeuroReport, 8,* 1225–1228.

Leibowitz, S. F. (1995). Brain peptides and obesity: Pharmacologic treatment. *Obesity Research, 3*(4), 573–589.

Leibowitz, S. F. (1998). Differential functions of hypothalamic galanin cell grows in the regulation of eating and body weight. *Annals of the New York Academy of Sciences, 21,* 206–220.

Leibowitz, S. F., Akabayashi, A., Alexander, J. T., & Wang, J. (1998). Gonadal steroids and hypothalamic galanin and neuropeptide Y: Role in eating behavior and body weight control in female rats. *Endocrinology, 139*(4), 1771–1780.

Lenox, R. H., & Manji, H. K. (2001). Lithium. In A. F. Schatzberg & C. B. Nemeroff (Eds.), *Essentials of clinical psychopharmacology.* Washington, DC: American Psychiatric Association.

Leonard, B. E. (1997). Neurotransmitters in depression: Noradrenaline and serotonin and their interactions. *Journal of Clinical Psychopharmacology, 17*(S1), 1.

Leonard, B. E. (2001). Stress, norepinephrine and depression. *Journal of Psychiatry and Neuroscience, 26,* S11–S16.

Leone, P., McPhee, S. W., Janson, C. G., Davidson, B. L., Freese, A., & During, M. J. (2000). Multi-site partitioned delivery of human tyrosine hydroxylase gene with phenotypic recovery in Parkinsonian rats. *Neuroreport, 11*(6), 1145–1151.

Leong, D. K., Oliva, L.. & Butterworth, R. F. (1996). Quantitative autoradiography using selective radioligands for central and peripheral-type benzodiazepine receptors in experimental Wernicke's encephalopathy: Implications for positron emission tomography imaging. *Alcoholism: Clinical and Experimental Research, 20*, 601–605.

Lepkovsky, S., Bortfield, P., Dimick, M. K., Feldman, S. E., Furuta, F., Sharon, I. M., & Park, R. (1971). Role of upper intestines in the regulation of food intake in parabiotic rats with their intestines "crossed" surgically. *Israeli Journal of Medical Science, 7*(5), 639–646.

Lepkovsky, S., Dimick, M. K., Furuta, F., Feldman, S. E., & Park, R. (1975). Stomach and upper intestine of the rat in the regulation of food intake. *Journal of Nutrition, 105*, 1491–1499.

Lerman, C., Caporaso, N. E., Audrain, J., Main, D., Bowman, E. D., Lockshin, B., Boyd, N. R., & Shields, P. G. (1999). Evidence suggesting the role of specific genetic factors in cigarette smoking. *Health Psychology, 18*(1), 14–20.

Lescaudron, L., Fulop, Z., Sutton, R. L., Geller, H. M., & Stein, D. G. (2001). Behavioral and morphological consequences of primary astrocytes transplanted into the rat cortex immediately after nucleus basalis ibotenic lesion. *International Journal of Neuroscience, 106*, 63–85.

Leshner, A. I. (1997). Drug abuse and addiction treatment research: The next generation. *Archives of General Psychiatry, 54*(8), 691–694.

Lester, B., LaGasse, L., & Seifer, R. (1998). Cocaine exposure and children: The meaning of subtle effects. *Science, 282*(5389), 633–634.

Leung, P. M., Rogers, Q. R., & Harper, A. E. (1968). Effect of amino acid imbalance on dietary choice in the rat. *Journal of Nutrition, 95*(3), 483–492.

LeVay, S. (1991). A difference in hypothalamic structure between heterosexual and homosexual men. *Science, 253*(5023), 1034–1037.

Levesque, M. F., Taylor, S., Rogers, R., Le, M. T., & Swope, D. (1999). Subthalamic stimulation in Parkinson's disease. *Stereotactic Functional Neurosurgery, 72*(2–4), 170–173.

Levi-Montalcini, R. (1965). Morphological and metabolic effects of the nerve growth factor. *Archives of Biology (Liege), 76*, 387–417.

Levi-Montalcini, R. (1966). The nerve growth factor: Its mode of action on sensory and sympathetic nerve cells. *Harvey Lectures, 60*, 217–259.

Levi-Montalcini, R. (1987). The nerve growth factor 35 years later. *Science, 237*(4819), 1154–1162.

Levin, E. D., & Simon, B. B. (1998). Nicotinic acetylcholine involvement in cognitive function in animals. *Psychopharmacology, 138*, 217–230.

Levine, D. N., Mani, R. B., & Calvanio, R. (1988). Pure agraphia and Gerstmann's syndrome as a visuospatial-language dissociation: An experiment case study. *Brain & Language, 35*(1), 172–196.

Levitan, I. B., & Kaczmarek, L. K. (1997). *The neuron.* New York: Oxford University Press.

Leweke, F. M., Giuffrida, A., Wurster, U., Emrich, H. M., & Piomelli, D. (1999). Elevated endogenous cannabinoids in schizophrenia. *Neuroreport, 10*, 1665–1669.

Lewis, M. E. (1999). Crossing the blood–brain barrier to central nervous system gene therapy. *Clinical Genetics, 56*, 10–13.

Lewis, P. D. (1985). Neuropathological effects of alcohol on the developing nervous system. *Alcohol, 20*(2), 195–200.

Libet, B. (1993). The neural time factor in conscious and unconscious events. *Ciba Foundation Symposium, 174*, 123–146.

Liebowitz, M. R., Gorman, J., Fyer, A., Levitt, M., Levy, G., Dillon, D., Appleby, I., Anderson, S., Palij, M., & Davies, S. O. (1984). Biological accompaniments of lactate-induced panic. *Psychopharmacology Bulletin, 20*(1), 43–44.

Liegeois-Chauvel, C., Peretez, I., Babai, M., Laguitton, V., & Chauvel, P. (1998). Contribution of different cortical areas in the temporal lobes to music processing. *Brain, 121*(10), 1853–1867.

Lim, K., Beal, D., Harvey, R., Myers, T., Lane, B., Sullivan, E., Faustman, W., & Pfefferbaum, A. (1995). Brain dysmorphology in adults with congenital rubella plus schizophrenialike symptoms. *Biological Psychiatry, 37*(11), 764–776.

Lin, L. Faraco, J., Li, R., Kadotani, H., Rogers, W., Lin, X., Qiu, X., de Jong, P. J., Nishino, S., & Mignot, E. (1999). The sleep disorder canine narcolepsy is caused by a mutation in the hypocretin (orexin) receptor 2 gene. *Cell, 98*(3), 365–376.

Lin, S. P., & Susser, E. S. (1992). Schizophrenia after prenatal exposure to the Dutch Hunger Winter of 1944–1945. *Arch Gen Psychiatry, 49*, 983–988.

Lindvall, O., Brundin, P., Widner, H., Rehncrona, S., Gustavii, B., Frackowiak, R., Leenders, K. L., Sawle, G., Rothwell, J. C., & Marsden, C. D. (1990). Grafts of fetal dopamine neurons survive and improve motor function in Parkinson's disease. *Science, 247*(4942), 574–577.

Linnoila, M., de Jong, J., & Virkkunen, M. (1989). Family history of alcoholism in violent offenders and impulsive fire setters. *Archives of General Psychiatry, 46*(7), 613–616.

Lisanby, S. H., Kohler, C., Swanson, C. L., & Gur, R. E. (1998). Psychosis secondary to brain tumor. *Seminars in Clinical Neuropsychiatry, 3*, 12–22.

Little, J. W., Ditunno, J. F., Stiens, S. A., & Harris, R. M. (1999). Incomplete spinal cord injury: Neuronal mechanisms of motor recovery and hyperreflexia. *Archives of Physical and Medical Rehabilitation, 80*, 587–599.

Liu, M., Doi, T., Shen, L., Woods, S. C., Seeley, R. J., Zheng, S., Jackman, A., & Tso, P. (2001). Intestinal satiety protein apolipoprotein A IV is synthesized and regulated in rat hypothalamus. *Am J Physiol Regul Integr Comp Physiol, 280*, R1382–R1387.

Livingstone, M. S., & Hubel, D. H. (1982). Thalamic inputs to cytochrome oxidase-rich regions in monkey visual cortex. *Proceedings of the National Academy of Sciences, USA, 79*(19), 6098–7101.

Livingstone, M. S., & Hubel, D. H. (1988). Segregation of form, color, movement, and depth: Anatomy, physiology, and perception. *Science, 240*(4853), 740–749.

Lockwood, A. H., Yap, E. W. H., Rhoades, H. M., & Wong, W-H. (1991). Cerebral blood flow and glucose metabolism in patients with liver disease and minimal encephalopathy. *Journal of Cerebral Blood Flow and Metabolism, 11*, 331–336.

Lockwood, A. H., Yap, E. W. H., & Wong, W-H. (1991). Cerebral ammonia metabolism in patients with severe liver disease and minimal hepatic encephalopathy. *Journal of Cerebral Blood Flow and Metabolism, 11*, 337–341.

Loeb, C., & Meyer, J. (1996). Vascular dementia: Still a debatable entity? *Journal of Neurological Science, 143*(1–2), 31–40.

Loefberg, C., Agren, H., Harro, J., & Oreland, L. (1998). Cholecystokinin in CSF from depressed patients: Possible relations to severity of depression and suicidal behaviour. *European Neuropsychopharmacology, 8*, 153–157.

Lohr, J. B., & Jeste, D. V. (1986). Cerebellar pathology in schizophrenia? A neurometric study. *Biological Psychiatry, 21*(10), 865–875.

LoPiccolo, P. (1996). "Something snapped." *Technology Review, 99*(7), 52–63.

Lord, T., & Kasprzak, M. (1989). Identification of self through olfaction. *Perceptual & Motor Skills, 69,* 219–224.

Lovestone, S., & McLoughlin, D. M. (2002). Protein aggregates and dementia: Is there a common toxicity? *J Neurol Neurosurg Psychiatry , 72,* 152–161.

Lovett, D., & Booth, D. A. (1970). Four effects of exogenous insulin on food intake. *Quarterly Journal of Experimental Psychology, 22*(3), 406–419.

Lowenstein, D. H., & Parent, J. M. (1999). Brain, heal thyself. *Science, 283,* 1126–1127.

Lu, M. L., & Yeh, I. J. (2001). Onset of psychosis after cerebellum pathology: A case report. *Gen Hosp Psychiatry, 23,* 41–42.

Luddens, H., Korpi, E. R., & Seeburg, P. H. (1995). GABA$_A$/benzodiazepine receptor heterogeneity: Neurophysiological implications. *Neuropharmacology, 34,* 245–254.

Ludvig, N., Nguyen, M. C., Botero, J. M., Tang, H. M., Scalia, F., Scharf, B. A., & Kral, J. G. (2000). Delivering drugs, via microdialysis, into the environment of extracellularly recorded in hippocampal neurons in behaving primates. *Brain Research Protocol, 5*(1), 75–84.

Luria, A. R. (1973) *The working brain.* London: Penguin.

Lustig, R. H. (1994). Sex hormone modulation of neural development in vitro. *Hormones & Behavior, 28,* 383–395.

MacLean, P. D. (1990). *The triune brain in evolution : Role in paleocerebral functions.* New York : Plenum Press.

MacLusky, N. J., & Naftolin, F. (1981). Sexual differentiation of the central nervous system. *Science, 211,* 1294–1303.

MacPherson, R. D. (2000). The pharmacological basis of contemporary pain management. *Pharmacol Ther, 88,* 163–185.

Madhusree, M. (1997, February). Trends in animal research. *Scientific American,* 86–93.

Maguire, E. A., Frith, C. D., Burgess, N, Donnett, J. G., & O'Keefe, J. (1998). Knowing where things are: Parahippocampal involvement in encoding object relations in virtual large-scale space. *Journal of Cognitive Neuroscience, 10*(1), 61–76.

Mahlberg, R., Steinacher, B., Mackert, A., & Flechtner, K. M. (2001). Basic parameters of saccadic eye movements—differences between unmedicated schizophrenia and affective disorder patients. *Eur Arch Psychiatry Clin Neurosci, 251,* 205–210.

Maier, S. F., & Watkins, L. R. (1998). Cytokines for psychologists: Implications of bidirectional immune-to-brain communication for understanding behavior, mood, and cognition. *Psychological Review, 105*(1), 83–107.

Maier, S. F., Watkins, L. R., & Fleshner, M. (1994). Psychoneurimmunology: The interface between behavior, brain, and immunity. *American Psychologist, 49*(12), 1004–1017.

Majewska, M. D. (1996). Sex differences in brain morphology and pharmacodynamics. In M. F. Jensvold & U. Halbreich (Eds.), *Psychopharmacology and women: Sex, gender, and hormones.* Washington, DC: American Psychiatric Press.

Malenka, R. C., & Nicoll, R. A. (1999). Long-term potentiation—A decade of progess? *Science, 285*(5435), 1870–1874.

Malizia, A. L., Coupland, N. J., & Nutt, D. J. (1995). Benzodiazepine receptor function in anxiety disorders. *Advances in Biochemical Psychopharmacology, 48,* 115–133.

Malizia, A. L., & Richardson, M. P. (1995). Benzodiazepine receptors and positron emission tomography: Ten years of experience. A new beginning. *Journal of Psychopharmacology, 9,* 355–368.

Mallot, H. A. (2000). *Computational vision: Information processing in perception and visual behavior.* Cambridge, MA: MIT Press.

Manber, R., & Armitage, R. (1999). Sex, steroids, and sleep: A review. *Sleep, 22*(5), 540–555.

Maneuf, Y. P., & Brotchie, J. M. (1997). Paradoxical action of the cannabinoid WIN 55, 212-2 in stimulated and basal cyclic AMP accumulation in rat globus pallidus slices. *Br Journal of Pharmacology, 120*(8), 1397–1398.

Maneuf, Y. P., Nash, J. E., Crossman, A. R., & Brotchie, J. M. (1996). Activation of the cannabinoid receptor by delta 9-tetrahydrocannabinol reduces gamma-aminobutyric acid uptake in the globus pallidus. *European Journal of Pharmacology, 308,* 161–164.

Mann, J. J., Arango, V., & Underwood, M. D. (1990). Serotonin and suicidal behavior. *Annals of the New York Academy of Sciences, 600,* 476–484.

Maranto, Gina. (1984). The mind within the brain. *Discover, 5*(5), 35–43.

Marder, S. R., & VanPutten, T. (1995). Antipsychotic medications. In A. F. Schatzberg & C. B. Nemeroff (Eds.), *The American Psychiatric Press textbook of psychopharmacology.* Washington, DC: American Psychiatric Press.

Margarit, E., Coll, M. D., Oliva, R., Gomez, D., Soler, A., & Ballesta, F. (2000). SRY gene transferred to the long arm of the X chromosome in a Y-positive XX true hermaphrodite. *American Journal of Medical Genetics, 90,* 25–28.

Marin, C., Jimenez, A., Bonastre, M., Chase, T. N., & Tolosa, E. (2000). Non-NMDA receptor-mediated mechanisms are involved in levodopa-induced motor response alterations in Parkinsonian rats. *Synapse, 36*(4), 267–274.

Marin, D. B., Davis, K. L., & Speranza, A. J. (1995). Cognitive enhancers. In A. F. Schatzberg & C. B. Nemeroff, (Eds.), *The American Psychiatric Press textbook of psychopharmacology.* Washington, DC: American Psychiatric Press.

Marin, P., & Arver, S. (1998). Androgens and abdominal obesity. *Baillieres Clinical Endocrinological Metabolism, 12*(3), 441–451.

Mark, V. H., & Ervin, F. R. (1975). *Violence and the brain.* New York: Harper & Row.

Markowitsch, H. J. (1995). Which brain regions are critically involved in the retrieval of old episodic memory? *Brain Research Review, 21*(2), 117–127.

Markowitsch, H. J., Calabrese, P., Fink, G. R., Durwen, H. F., Kessler, J., Harting, C., Konig, M., Mirzaian, E. B., Heiss, W. D., Heuser, L., & Gehlen, W. (1997). Impaired episodic memory retrieval in a case of probable psychogenic amnesia. *Psychiatric Review, 74*(2), 119–126.

Markowitsch, H. J., Calabrese, P., Wurker, M., Durwen, H. F., Kessler, J., Babinsky, R., Brechtelsbauer, D., Heuser, L., & Gehlen, W. (1994). The amygdala's contribution to memory—A study on two patients with Urbach-Wiethe disease. *NeuroReport, 5*(11), 1349–1352.

Marshall, G. D., Agarwal, S. K., Lloyd, C., Cohen, L., Henninger, E. M., & Morris, G. J. (1998). Cytokine dysregulation associated with exam stress in healthy medical students. *Brain Behav Immun, 12,* 297–307.

Marshall, J. F., Richardson, J. S., & Teitelbaum, P. (1974). Nigrostriatal bundle damage and the lateral hypothalamic syndrome. *Journal of Comparative Physiological Psychology, 87*(5), 808–30.

Marshall, R. D., Beebe, K. L., Oldham, M., & Zaninelli, R. (2001). Efficacy and safety of paroxetine treatment for chronic PTSD: A fixed-dose, placebo-controlled study. *American Journal of Psychiatry, 158,* 1982–1988.

Martin, B. R. (1995). Marijuana. In F. E. Bloom & D. J. Kupfer (Eds.), *Psychopharmacology: The fourth generation of progress.* New York: Raven Press.

Martinez, J. L., & Derrick, B. E. (1996). Long-term potentiation and learning. *Annual Review of Psychology, 47,* 173–203.

Masson, F., Thicoipe, M., Aye, P., Mokni, T., Senjean, P., Schmitt, V., Dessalles, P. H., Cazaugade, M., & Labadens, P. (2001). Epidemiology of severe brain injuries: A prospective population-based study. *Journal of Trauma, 51*, 481–489.

Matheson, A. J., Darlington, C. L., & Smith, P. F. (1999). Further evidence for age-related deficits in human postural function. *Journal of Vestibular Research, 9*(4), 261–264.

Mathews, V. P., Candy, E. R., & Bryan, R. N. (1992). Imaging of neurodegenerative diseases. *Current Opinion in Radiology, 4*, 89–94.

Matsuda, L. A. (1997). Molecular aspects of cannabinoid receptors. *Critical Reviews in Neurobiology, 11*, 143–166.

Matthies, M., Silvestrini M., Troisi, E., Cupini, L. M., & Caltagirone, C. (1997). Transcranial doppler assessment of cerebral flow velocity during perception and recognition of melodies. *Journal of Neurological Science, 149*(1), 57–61.

Mauri, M. C., Rudelli, R., Somaschini, E., Roncoroni, L., Papa, R., Mantero, M., Longhini, M., & Penati, G. (1996). Neurobiological and psychopharmacological basis in the therapy of bulimia and anorexia. *Prog Neuropsychopharmacological Biological Psychiatry, 20*(2), 207–240.

Mayer, D. J. (1975). Pain inhibition by electrical brain stimulation comparison to morphine. *Neuroscience Research Progress Bulletin, 13*, 94–99.

Mayer, J. (1953). Glucostatic mechanisms of regulation of food intake. *New England Journal of Medicine, 249*, 13–16.

Maynert, E. W., & Levi, R. (1964). Stress-induced release of brain norepinephrine and its inhibition by drugs. *J. Pharmacol. Exp. Ther., 143*, 90–97.

McBride, W. J., Chernet, E., Dyr, W., Lumeng, L., & Li, T. K. (1993). Densities of dopamine D_2 receptors are reduced in CNS regions of alcohol-preferring P rats. *Alcohol, 10*(5), 387–390.

McCance, R. A., Widdowson, E. M. (1977). Fat. *Pediatric Research, 11*(10), 1081–1083.

McCann, U. D., Szabo, Z., Scheffel, U., Dannals, R. F., & Ricaurte, G. A. (1998). Positron emission tomographic evidence of toxic effect of MDMA ("Ecstasy") on brain serotonin neurons in human beings. *Lancet, 352*, 1433–1437.

McCarley, R. W., & Hoffman, E. (1981). REM sleep dreams and the activation-synthesis hypothesis. *American Journal of Psychiatry, 138*(7), 904–912.

McCarthy, M. M., Davis, A. M., & Mong, J. A. (1997). Excitatory neurotransmission and sexual differentia-

tion of the brain. *Brain Research Bulletin, 44*(4), 487–495.

McClelland, J. L., McNaughton, B. L., & O'Reilly, R. C. (1995). Why there are complementary learning systems in the hippocampus and neocortex: Insights from the successes and failures of connectionist models of learning and memory. *Psychological Review, 102*(3), 419–457.

McClintock, M. K. (1971). Menstrual synchrony and suppression. *Nature, 229*(5282), 244–245.

McCloskey, M., Rapp, B., Yantis, S., & Rubin, G. (1995). A developmental deficit in localizing objects from vision. *Psychological Science, 6*(2), 112–117.

McCormick, C. M., & Witelson, S. F. (1991). A cognitive profile of homosexual men compared to heterosexual men and women. *Psychoneuroendocrinology, 16*, 459–473.

McCormick, C. M., & Witelson, S. F. (1994). Functional cerebral asymmetry and sexual orientation in men and women. *Behavioral Neuroscience, 108*, 525–531.

McCormick, C. M., Witelson, S. F., & Kingstone, E. (1990). Left-handedness in homosexual men and women: Neuroendocrine implications. *Psychoneuroendocrinology, 15*, 69–76.

McDonald, J. W., Liu, X. Z., Qu, Y., Liu, S., Mickey, S. K., Turetsky, D., Gottlieb, D. I., & Choi, D. W. (1999). Transplanted embryonic stem cells survive, differentiate and promote recovery in injured rat spinal cord. *Nature Medicine, 5*, 1410–1412.

McEwen, B. S. (1992). Re-examination of the glucocorticoid hypothesis of stress and aging. *Prognoses in Brain Research, 93*, 365–381.

McEwen, B. S. (1995a). Adrenal steroid actions on brain: Dissecting the fine line between protection and damage. In M. J. Freidman & D. S. Charney (Eds.), *Neurobiological and clinical consequences of stress: From normal adaptation to post-traumatic stress disorder*. Philadelphia, PA: Lippencott Williams & Wilkins.

McEwen, B. S. (1995b). Stressful experience, brain, and emotions: Developmental, genetic, and hormonal influences. In M. S. Gazzaniga (Ed.), *The cognitive neurosciences*. Cambridge, MA: MIT Press.

McEwen, B. S. (1995c). Neuroendocrine interactions. In F. E. Bloom & D. J. Kupfer (Eds.), *Psychopharmacology: The fourth generation*. New York: Raven Press.

McEwen, B. S. (1999). Stress and the aging hippocampus. *Front Neuroendocrinology, 20*(1), 49–70.

McEwen, B. S., Spencer, R. L., & Sakai, R. R. (1993). Adrenal steroid actions upon the brain: Versatile hormones

with good and bad effects. In J. Schulkin (Ed.), *Hormonally induced changes in mind and brain*. New York: Academic Press.

McFadden, D., & Pasanen, E. G. (1999). Spontaneous otoacoustic emissions in heterosexuals, homosexuals, and bisexuals. *Journal of the Acoustical Society of America, 105*, 2403–2413.

McGaugh, J. L. (2000). Memory: A century of consolidation. *Science, 287*(5451), 248–251.

McGehee, D. S., & Role, L. W. (1995). Physiological diversity of nicotinic acetylcholine receptors expressed by vertebrate neurons. *Annual Review of Physiology, 57*, 521–546.

McGlone, M. J. (1978). Sex differences in functional brain asymmetry after damage to the left and right hemisphere. *Dissertation Abstracts International, 38*(9), 4471.

McGue, M., & Gottesman, J. I. (1989). Genetic linkage in schizophrenia: perspectives from genetic epidemiology. *Schizophrenic Bulletin, 15*(3), 453–464.

McGuffin, P., & Scourfield, J. (1997). Human genetics: A father's imprint on his daughter's thinking. *Nature, 387*(6634), 652–653.

McKeever, P. E. (1993). Human astrocytic neoplasms. In S. Murphy (Ed.), *Astrocytes: Pharmacology and function* (pp. 399–436). San Diego: Academic Press.

McLusky, N. J., & Naftolin, F. (1981). Sexual differentiation of the central nervous system. *Science, 211*(4488), 1294–1302.

Mednick, S. A., Parnas, J., & Schulsinger, F. (1987). The Copenhagen High-Risk Project, 1962–86. *Schizophrenic Bulletin, 13*(3), 485–495.

Mei, N. (1994). Role of digestive afferents in food intake regulation. In C. R. Legg & D. A. Booth (Eds.), *Appetite: Neural and behavioural bases*. New York: Oxford University Press.

Melis, M. R., & Argiolas, A. (1995). Dopamine and sexual behavior. *Neuroscience Biobehavioral Review, 19*(1), 19–38.

Melman, A., & Christ, G. J. (2001). Integrative erectile biology. The effects of age and disease on gap junctions and ion channels and their potential value to the treatment of erectile dysfunction. *Urological Clinics of North America, 28*, 217–231.

Meltzer, C., Smith, G., DeKosky, S., Pollock, B., Mathis, C., Moore, R., Kupfer, D., & Reynolds, C. (1988). Serotonin in aging, late-life depression, and Alzheimer's disease: The emerging role of functional imaging. *Neuropsychopharmacology, 21*(2), 321–322.

Melzack, R. & Wall, P. D. (1965). Pain mechanisms: A new theory. *Science, 150*(699), 971–979.

Melzack, R., & Wall, P. D. (1994). Pain mechanisms: A new theory. In A. Steptoe & J. Wardle (Eds.), *Psychological processes and health: A reader.* Cambridge: Cambridge University Press.

Mendez, M. F. (2001). Visualspatial deficits with preserved reading ability in a patient with posterior cortical atrophy. *Cortex, 37,* 535–543.

Mercer, M. E., & Holder, M. D. (1997). Food cravings, endogenous opioid peptides, and food intake: A review. *Appetite, 29,* 325–352.

Merzenich, M. (1998). Long-term change of mind. *Science, 282*(5391), 1062–1063.

Merzenich, M. M., Kaas, J. H., & Roth, G. L. (1976). Auditory cortex in the grey squirrel: Tonotopic organization and architectonic fields. *Journal of Comparative Neurology, 166*(4), 387–401.

Meschler, J. P., Howlett, A. C., & Madras, B. K. (2001). Cannabinoid receptor agonist and antagonist effects on motor function in normal and 1-methyl-4-phenyl-1,2,5,6-tetrahydropyridine (MPTP)-treated non-human primates. *Psychopharmacology, 156,* 79–85.

Mesholam, R. I., Moberg, P. J., Mahr, R. N., & Doty, R. L. (1998). Olfaction in neurodegenerative disease: A meta-analysis of olfactory functioning in Alzheimer's and Parkinson's diseases. *Archive of Neurology, 55*(1), 84–90.

Mesulam, M-M. (1995). Structure and function of cholinergic pathways in the cerebral cortex, limbic system, basal ganglia, and thalamus of the human brain. In F. E. Bloom & D. J. Kupfer (Eds.), *Psychopharmacology: The fourth generation of progress.* New York: Raven Press.

Metcalfe, J. (1998). *The brain: Degeneration, damage, and disorder.* New York: Springer.

Meyerson, B. J. (1968). Female copulatory behaviour in male and adrogenized female rats after oestrogen-amine depletor treatment. *Nature, 217,* 683–684.

Michelson, D., Licinio, J., & Gold, P. (1995). Mediation of the stress response by the hypothalamic-pituitary-adrenal axis. In M. J. Friedman & D. S. Charney (Eds.), *Neurobiological and clinical consequences of stress: From normal adaptation to post-traumatic stress disorder.* Philadelphia: Lippincott Williams & Wilkins.

Mignard, M., & Malpeli, J. G. (1991). Paths of information flow through visual cortex. *Science, 251*(4998), 1249–1251.

Mihic, S. J., Sanna, E., Whiting, P. J., & Harris, R. A. (1995). Pharmacology of recombinant GABA_A receptors. In G. Biggio, E. Sanna, & E. Costa (Eds.), *GABA_A receptors and anxiety: From neurobiology to treatment.* New York: Raven Press.

Miller, B., & McGown, A. (1997). Bereavement: Theoretical perspectives and adaptation. Canberra, Australia. *Am J Hosp Palliat Care, 14,* 156–177.

Miller, E. K., Erickson, C. A., & Desimone, R. (1996). Neural mechanisms of visual working memory in prefrontal cortex of the macaque. *Journal of Neuroscience, 16*(16), 5154–5167.

Miller, E. K., Li, L., & Desimone, R. (1991). A neural mechanism for working and recognition memory in inferior temporal cortex. *Science, 254*(5036), 1377–1379.

Miller, G. A. (1956). The magic number seven, plus or minus two: Some limits on our capacity for processing information. *Psychological Review, 63,* 81–97.

Miller, M., Epstein, R., Sugar, J., Pinchoff, B., Sugar, A., Gammon, J., Mittelman, D., Dennis, R., & Israel, J. (1984). Anterior segment anomalies associated with the fetal alcohol syndrome. *Journal of Pediatric Ophthalmology Strabismus, 21*(1), 8–18.

Miller, M. W. (1993). Migration of cortical neurons is altered by gestational exposure to ethanol. *Alcohol Clinical Experimental Research, 17*(2), 304–314.

Milner, A. D. (1995). Cerebral correlates of visual awareness. *Neuropsychologia, 33*(9), 1117–1130.

Milner, B. (1966). Amnesia following operation on the temporal lobes. In C. W. M. Whitty & O. L. Zangwill (Eds.), *Amnesia.* London: Butterworth.

Milner, B. (1971). Interhemispheric *differences* in the localization of psychological processes in man. *Brain Medicine Bulletin, 27*(3), 272–277.

Mirra, S. S. (1997). Alzheimer's disease and other dementias: Neuropathological considerations. In L. L. Heston (Ed.), *Alzheimer's disease and similar conditions.* Washington, DC: American Psychiatric Press.

Mishkin, M., & Ungerleider, L. G. (1982). Contribution of striate inputs to the visualspatial functions of parieto-preoccipital cortex in monkeys. *Behavioral Brain Research, 6*(1), 57–77.

Mitchell, P. B., & Malhi, G. S. (2002). The expanding pharmacopoeia for bipolar disorder. *Annual Review of Medicine, 53,* 173–188.

Moberg, P. J., Agrin, R., Gur, R. E., Turetsky, B. I., & Doty, R. L. (1999). Olfactory dysfunction in schizophrenia: A qualitative and quantitative review. *Neuropsychopharmacology, 21*(3), 325–340.

Moberg, P. J., & Doty, R. L. (1997). Olfactory function in Huntington's disease patients and at-risk offspring. *International Journal of Neuroscience, 89*(1–2), 133–139.

Moberg, P. J., Doty, R. L., Turetsky, B. I., Arnold, S. E., Mahr, R. N., Gur, R. C., Bilker, W., & Gur, R. E. (1997). Olfactory identification deficits in schizophrenia: Correlation with duration of illness. *American Journal of Psychiatry, 154*(7), 1016–1018.

Moeller, F. G., & Dougherty, D. M. (2001). Antisocial personality disorder, alcohol, and aggression. *Alcohol Res Health, 25,* 5–11.

Montine, T. J., Powers, J. M., Vogel, F. S., & Radtke, R. A. (1995). Alpers' syndrome presenting with seizures and multiple stroke-like episodes in a 17-year-old male. *Clinical Neuropathology, 14*(6), 322–326.

Moore, P. S., & Broome, C. V. (1994). Cerebrospinal meningitis epidemics. *Scientific American, 271,* 38–45.

Morgane, P., Austin-LaFrance, R., Bronzino, J., Tonkiss, J., Diaz-Cintra, S., Cintra, L., Kemper, T., & Galler, J. (1993). Prenatal malnutrition and development of the brain. *Neuroscience Biobehavioral Review, 17*(1), 91–128.

Morgenstern, J., Langenbucher, J., Labouvie, E., & Miller, K. (1997). The comorbidity of alcoholism and personality disorders in a clinical population: Prevalence rates and relation to alcohol typology variables. *Journal of Abnormal Psychology, 106*(1), 74–84.

Morilak, D. A. (1997). Brain adrenergic receptors. In K. Blum & E. P. Noble (Eds.), *Handbook of psychiatric genetics.* Boca Raton: CRC Press.

Morris, J. C. (1996). Classification of dementia and Alzheimer's disease. *Acta Neurology Scandinavia, 165,* 41–50.

Morris, J. C. (1997). Clinical dementia rating: A reliable and valid diagnostic and staging measure for dementia of the Alzheimer type. *International Psychologeriatric, 9*(1), 173–176.

Morris, M. E., Viswanathan, N., Kuhlman, S., Davis, F. C., & Weitz, C. J. (1998). A screen for genes induced in the suprachiasmatic nucleus by light. *Science, 279*(5356), 1544–1547.

Morris, N. M., Udry, J. R., Khan-Dawood, F., & Dawood, M. Y. (1987). Marital sex frequency and midcycle female testosterone. *Archives of Sex Behavior, 16*(1), 27–37.

Morrison, A. R. (2001). Personal reflections on the "animal-rights" phenomenon. *Perspectives in Biological Medicine, 44*(1):62–75.

Moruzzi, G., & Magoun, H. W. (1949). Brain stem reticular formation and activation of the EEG. *Electroencephalography and Clinical Neurophysiology, 1,* 455–473.

Muir, J. L. (1997). Acetylcholine, aging, and Alzheimer's disease. *Pharmacology & Biochemical Behavior, 56*(4), 587–596.

Mukhametov, L. M. (1985). Unihemispheric slow wave sleep in the brain of dolphins and seals. In S. Inoue & A. A. Borbely (Eds.), *Endogenous sleep substances and sleep regulation.* Tokyo: Japanese Scientific Societies Press.

Mukhametov, L. M. (1988). The absence of paradoxical sleep in dolphins. In W. P. Koella, F. Obal, H. Schulz, and P. Visser (Eds.), *Sleep '86.* New York: Gustav Fischer Verlag.

Muller, R., Behen, M., Rothermel, R., Muzik, O., Chakraborty, P., & Chugani, H. (1999). Brain organization for language in children, adolescents, and adults with left hemisphere lesion: A PET study. *Prognoses in Neuropsychopharmacology & Biological Psychiatry, 23*(4), 657–668.

Muller-Oerlinghausen, B., Berghofer, A., & Bauer, M.. (2002). Bipolar disorder. *Lancet, 359,* 241–247.

Munro, J. F., Seaton, D. A., & Duncan, L. J. (1966). Treatment of refractory obesity with fenfluramine. *British Medical Journal, 2*(514), 624–625.

Musen, G., & Squire, L. R. (1992). Nonverbal priming in amnesia. *Memory and Cognition, 20*(4), 441–448.

Nakanishi, S. (1992). Molecular diversity of glutamate receptors and implications for brain function. *Science, 258,* 597–603.

Nakao, M., Nomura, S., Shimosawa, T., Fujita, T., & Kuboki, T. (2000). Blood pressure biofeedback treatment of white-coat hypertension. *Journal of Psychosomatic Research, 48,* 161–169.

Narabayashi, H. (1996). Does stereotactic treatment for Parkinson's disease slow the progression of the disease? *Advanced Neurology, 69,* 557–562.

Nathan, K. I., Musselman, D. L., Schatzberg, A. F., & Nemeroff, C. B. (1995). Biology of mood disorders. In A. F. Schatzberg & C. B. Nemeroff (Eds.), *The American Psychiatric Press textbook of psychopharmacology.* Washington, DC: American Psychiatric Press.

Nathanson, M. H. (1937). The central action of beta-aminopropylbenzene (benzedrine). *Journal of the American Medical Association 108,* 528–531.

Naya, Y., Yoshida, M., & Miyashita, Y. (2001). Backward spreading of memory-retrieval signal in the primate temporal cortex. *Science, 291,* 661–664.

Needleman, H. L., Riess, J. A., Tobin, M. J., Biesecker, G. E., & Greenhouse, J. B. (1996). Bone lead levels and delinquent behavior. *Journal of the American Medical Association, 275,* 363–369.

Neely, J. G. (2001). Clinical experience with a surgical approach to hydrops. *Annals of the New York Academy of Sciences, 942,* 322–327.

Nehra, A. (2000). Treatment of endocrinologic male sexual dysfunction. *Mayo Clinic Proceedings, 75*(S), 40–45.

Neitz, M., & Neitz, J. (2000). Molecular genetics of color vision and color vision defects. *Archives of Ophthalmology, 118,* 691–700.

Nelson, K. B., & Grether, J. K. (1999). Causes of cerebral palsy. *Current Opinions in Pediatrics, 11*(6), 487–491.

Nelson, R. J., Kriegsfeld, L. J., Dawson, V. L., & Dawson, T. M. (1997). Effects of nitric oxide on neuroendocrine function and behavior. *Frontiers in Neuroendocrinology, 18,* 463–491.

Neophytou, S. I., Graham, M., Williams, J., Aspley, S., Marsden, C. A., & Beckett, S. R. G. (2000). Strain differences to the effects of aversive frequency ultrasound on behaviour and brain topography of c-*fos* expression in the rat. *Brain Research, 854,* 158–164.

Nestler, E. J., & Aghajanian, G. K. (1997). Molecular and cellular basis of addiction. *Science, 278*(5335), 58–63.

Nestler, E. J., Alreja, M., & Aghajanian, G. K. (1999). Molecular control of locus coeruleus neurotransmission. *Biological Psychiatry, 46,* 1131–1139.

Neville, H. J., Bavelier, D., Corina, D., Rauschecker, J., Karni, A., Lalvani, A., Braun, A., Clark, V., Jezzard, P., & Turner, R. (1998). Cerebral organization for language in deaf and hearing subjects: Biological constraints and effects of experience. *Proceedings of the National Academy of Sciences, 95,* 922–929.

Ng, G. Y. K., George, S. R., & O'Dowd, B. F. (1997). Studies on dopamine receptors and role in drug addiction. In K. Blum & E. P. Noble (Eds.), *Handbook of psychiatric genetics.* Boca Raton, FL: CRC Press.

Nicholson, L. F. B., & Faull, R. L. (1996). GABA-A receptor subunit subtypes in the human putamen and globus pallidus in Huntington's disease. In C. Ohye & M. Kimura (Eds.), *The basal ganglia V.* New York: Plenum Press.

Nicolela, M. T., Drance, S. M., Broadway, D. C., Chauhan, B. C., McCormick, T. A., & LeBlanc, R. P. (2001). Agreement among clinicians in the recognition of patterns of optic disk damage in glaucoma. *American Journal of Ophthalmology, 132,* 836–844.

Nielsen, S., Frokiaer, J., Marples, D., Kwon, T. H., Agre, P., & Knepper, M. A. (2002). Aquaporins in the kidney: From molecules to medicine. *Physiological Review, 82,* 205–244.

Nigg, J. T., & Goldsmith, H. H. (1994). Genetics of personality disorders: Perspectives from personality and psychopathology research. *Psychology Bulletin, 115*(3), 346–380.

Nisenbaum, L. K., Zigmond, M. J., Sved, A. F., & Abercrombie, E. D. (1991). Prior exposure to chronic stress results in enhanced synthesis and release of hippocampal norepinephrine in response to a novel stressor. *Journal of Neuroscience, 11*(5), 1478–1484.

Nishino, S., Mignot, E., & Dement, W. C. (2001). Sedative-hypnotics. In A. F. Schatzberg & C. B. Nemeroff (Eds.), *Essentials of clinical psychopharmacology.* Washington, DC: American Psychiatric Association.

Norris, S. L., Lee, C., Burshteyn, D., & Cea-Aravena, J. (2001). The effects of Performance Enhancement Training on hypertension, human attention, stress, and brain wave patterns: A case study. *Journal of Neurotherapy, 4,* 29–44.

Novy, M. J., & Resko, J. A. (1981). *Fetal endocrinology.* New York: Academic Press.

Nowell, P. D., Buysse, D. J., Morin, C. M., Reynolds, C. F., & Kupfer, D. J. (1998). Effective treatments for selected sleep disorders. In P. E. Nathan & J. M. Gorman (Eds.), *A guide to treatments that work.* New York: Oxford University Press.

Nussbaum, E. (2000). A question of gender. *Discover, 21*(1), 92–99.

Nutt, D. (1998). Substance-P antagonists: A new treatment for depression? *Lancet, 352,* 1644–1646.

Obayashi, S., Matsushima, E., Okubo, Y., Ohkura, T., Kojima, T., & Kakuma, T. (2001). Relationship between exploratory eye movements and clinical course in schizophrenic patients. *Eur Arch Psychiatry Clin Neurosci, 251,* 211–216.

O'Brien, J. T., Desmond, P., Ames, D., Schweitzer, I., Chiu, E., & Tress, B. (1997). Temporal lobe magnetic resonance imaging can differentiate Alzheimer's disease from normal ageing, depression, vascular dementia and other causes of cognitive impairment. *Psychological Medicine, 27,* 1267–1275.

O'Dell, T. J., Hawkins, R. D., Kandel, E. R., & Arancio, O. (1991). Tests of the roles of two diffusible substances in long-term potentiation: Evidence for nitric oxide as a possible early retrograde messenger. *Proceedings of the National Academy of Sciences, 88,* 11285–11289.

Ogawa, S., Lee, T. M., Kay, A. R., & Tank, D. W. (1990). Brain magnetic resonance imaging with contrast dependent on brain oxygenation. *Proceedings of the National Academy of Sciences, 87,* 9868–9872.

Ohno-Shosaku, T., Maejima, T., & Kano, M. (2001). Endogenous cannabinoids mediate retrograde signals from depolarized postsynaptic neurons to presynaptic terminals. *Neuron, 29,* 729–738.

Olds, J., & Milner, P. (1954). Positive reinforcement produced by electrical stimulation of the septal area and other regions of rat brain. *Journal of Comparative and Physiological Psychology, 47,* 419–427.

Olds, M. E., & Olds, J. (1969). Effects of anxiety-relieving drugs on unit discharges in hippocampus, reticular midbrain, and pre-optic area in the freely moving rat. *International Journal of Neuropharmacology, 8*(2), 87–103.

Oliet, S. H., Piet, R., & Poulain, D. A. (2001). Control of glutamate clearance and synaptic efficacy by glial coverage of neurons. *Science, 292,* 923–926.

Olney, J. W., & Farber, N. B. (1995). NMDA antagonists as neurotherapeutic drugs, psychotogens, neurotoxins, and research tools for studying schizophrenia. *Neuropsychopharmacology, 13*(4), 335–345.

Olson, E. J., Boeve, B. F., & Silber, M. H. (2000). Rapid eye movement sleep behaviour disorder: Demographic, clinical and laboratory findings in 93 cases. *Brain, 123*(2), 331–339.

Olson, H. C., Feldman, J. J., Streissguth, A. P., Sampson, P. D., & Bookstein, F. L. (1988). Neuropsychological deficits in adolescents with fetal alcohol syndrome: Clinical findings. *Alcohol Clinical & Experimental Research, 22*(9), 1998–2012.

Olson, L. (2000). Biomedicine. Combating Parkinson's disease—step three. *Science, 290,* 721–724.

Onishi, H., Kawanishi, C., Iwasawa, T., Osaka, H., Hanihara, T., Inoue, K., Yamada, Y., & Kosaka, K. (1997). Depressive disorder due to mitochondrial transfer RNALeu(UUR) mutation. *Biological Psychiatry, 41*(11), 1137–1139.

Oren, D. A., & Terman, M. (1998). Tweaking the human circadian clock with light. *Science, 279*(5349), 333–334.

Ortiz, J., Fitzgerald, L. W., Lane, S., Terwilliger, R., & Nestler, E. J. (1996). Biochemical adaptations in the mesolimbic dopamine system in response to repeated stress. *Neuropsychopharmacology, 14*(6), 443–452.

Ortony, A., & Turner, T. J. (1990). What's basic about basic emotions? *Psychological Review, 97,* 315–331.

Osimani, A., Ichise, M., Chung, D., Pogue, J., & Freedman, M. (1994). SPECT for differential diagnosis of dementia and correlation of rCBF with cognitive impairment. *Canadian Journal of Neurological Sciences, 21*(2), 104–111.

Ossowska, K., Lorenc-Koci, E., Konieczny, J., & Wolfarth, S. (1998). The role of striatal glutamate receptors in models of Parkinson's disease. *Amino Acids, 14*(1–3), 11–15.

Overman, W. H., Bachevalier, J., Schuhmann, E., & Ryan, P. (1996). Cognitive gender differences in very young children parallels biologically based cognitive gender differences in monkeys. *Behavioral Neuroscience, 110,* 673–684.

Ozates, M., Kemaloglu, S., Gurkan, F., Ozkan, U., Hosoglu, S., & Simsek, M. (2000). CT of the brain in tuberculous meningitis: A review of 289 patients. *Acta of Radiology, 41*(1), 13–17.

Packard, M. G., & McGaugh, J. L. (1992). Double dissociation of fornix and caudate nucleus lesions on acquisition of two water maze tasks: Further evidence for multiple memory systems. *Behavioral Neuroscience, 106*(3), 439–446.

Palmblad, J., Petrini, B., Wasserman, J., & Akerstedt, T. (1979). Lympocyte and granulocyte reactions during sleep deprivation. *Psychosomatic Medicine, 41*(4), 273–278.

Palmer, R. M., & Ferrige, A. G. (1987). Nitric oxide release accounts for biological activity of endothelium-derived relaxing factor. *Nature, 327,* 524–526.

Palmer, R. M., Ferrige, A. G., & Moncada, S. (1987). Nitric oxide release accounts for the biological activity of endothelium-derived relaxing factor. *Nature, 327,* 524–526.

Palmer, S. E. (1999). *Vision science: Photons to phenomenology.* Cambridge, MA: MIT Press.

Palmer, T. D., Takahashi, J., & Gage, F. H. (1997). The adult rat hippocampus contains primordial neural stem cells. *Molecular Cell Neuroscience, 8*(6), 389–404.

Panksepp, J. (1975). Feeding in response to repeated protamine zinc insulin injections. *Physiology & Behavior, 14*(4), 487–493.

Panksepp, J. (1989). The neurobiology of emotions: Of animal brains and human feelings. In H. Wagner & A. Manstead (Eds.), *Handbook of social psychophysiology.* New York: John Wiley & Sons.

Panksepp, J. (1992). A critical role for "affective neuroscience" in resolving what is basic about basic emotions. *Psychological Review, 99*(3), 554–560.

Panksepp, J., & Ritter, M. (1975). Mathematical analysis of energy regulatory patterns of normal and diabetic rats. *Journal of Comparative Physiological Psychology, 89*(9), 1019–1028.

Pant, K. C., Rogers, Q. R., & Harper, A. E. (1972). Food selection studies of rats fed tryptophan-imbalanced diets with or without niacin. *Journal of Nutrition, 102*(1), 131–142.

Pantev, C., Oostenveld, R., Engelien, A., Ross, B., Roberts, L. E., & Hoke, M. (1998). Increased auditory cortical representation in musicians. *Nature, 392*(6678), 811–814.

Papa, S. M., & Chase, T. N. (1996). Levodopa-induced dyskinesias improved by a glutamate antagonist in Parkinsonian monkeys. *Annals of Neurology, 39*(5), 574–578.

Papez, J. W. (1937). A proposed mechanism of emotion. *Archives of Neurology and Psychiatry, 38,* 725–743.

Pare, D., & Llinas, R. (1995). Conscious and pre-conscious processes as seen from the standpoint of sleep–waking cycle neurophysiology. *Neuropsychologia, 33*(9), 1155–1168.

Paris, J. (1996). Antisocial personality disorder: A biopsychology model. *Canadian Journal of Psychiatry, 41*(2), 75–80.

Parkin, A. J., & Walter, B. M. (1992). Recollective experience, normal aging, and frontal dysfunction. *Psychology & Aging, 7*(2), 290–298.

Parry, B. L., & Newton, R. P. (2001). Chronobiological basis of female-specific mood disorders. *Neuropsychopharmacology, 25*(5 Suppl), S102–S108.

Pascual-Leone, A., & Torres, F. (1993). Plasticity of the sensorimotor cortex representation of the reading finger in Braille readers. *Brain, 116*(1), 39–52.

Pasternak, G. W., Goodman, R., & Snyder, S. H. (1975). An endogenous morphine-like factor in mammalian brain. *Life Science, 16*(12), 1765–1769.

Paul, S. M. (1995). GABA and glycine. In F. E. Bloom & D. J. Kupfer (Eds.), *Psychopharmacology: The fourth generation of progress.* New York: Raven Press.

Paul, S. M., & Skolnick, P. (1982). Comparative neuropharmacology of antianxiety drugs. *Pharmacology, Biochemistry, & Behavior, 17*(Suppl 1), 37–41.

Paus, T., Zijdenbos, A., Worsley, K., Collins, D., Blumenthal, J., Giedd, J., Rapoport, J., & Evans, A. (1999). Structural maturation of neural pathways in children and adolescents: In vivo study. *Science, 283*(5409), 1908–1911.

Pederson, C. L., Wolske, M., Peoples, L. L., & West, M. O. (1997). Firing rate dependent effect of cocaine on single neurons of the rat lateral striatum. *Brain Research, 760,* 261–265.

Pellizzari, R., Rossetto, O., Schiavo, G., & Montecucco, C. (1999). Tetanus and botulinum neurotoxins: Mechanism of action and therapeutic uses. *Philosophical Transactions, Royal Society of London. Series B. Biological Sciences, 354,* 259–268.

Penfield, W. (1975). *The mystery of the mind.* Princeton, NJ: Princeton University Press.

Penfield, W. (1977). *No man alone: A neurosurgeon's life.* Boston: Little, Brown.

Penfield, W., & Baldwin, M. (1952). Temporal lobe seizures and the technic of subtotal temporal lobectomy. *Annals of Surgery, 136,* 625–634.

Penfield, W., & Roberts, L. (1959). *Speech and brain mechanisms.* Princeton, NJ: Princeton University Press.

Pert, C. B., & Snyder, S. H. (1973). The opiate receptor: Demonstration in the nervous tissue. *Science, 173,* 1011–1014.

Peskind, E. R. (1996). Neurobiology of Alzheimer's disease. *Journal of Clinical Psychiatry, 57*(Suppl 1), 5–8.

Petersen, S. E., Fox, P. T., Posner, M. I., Mintun, M., & Raichle, M. E. (1988). Positron emission tomographic studies of the cortical anatomy of single-word processing. *Nature, 331,* 585–589.

Petty, F. (1995). GABA and mood disorders: A brief review and hypothesis. *Journal of Affective Disorders, 34*(4), 275–281.

Petty, F., Kramer, G., Wilson, L., & Chae, Y. L. (1993). Learned helplessness and in vivo hippocampal norepinephrine release. *Pharmacological Biochemical Behavior, 46*(1), 231–235.

Petty, F., Trivedi, M., Fulton, M., & Rush, A. (1995). Benzodiazepines as antidepressants: Does GABA play a role in depression? *Biological Psychiatry, 38*(9), 578–591.

Platt, D., Frohlich, J., & Morgan, M. Hormonal and genetic influences on arousal-sexual and otherwise. *Trends in Neuroscience, 25,* 45–50.

Pfrieger, F. W., & Barres, B. A. (1997). Synaptic efficacy enhanced by glial cells in vitro. *Science, 277,* 1684–1687.

Phelps, E. A., O'Connor, K. J., Gatenby, J. C., Gore, J. C., Grillon, C., & Davis, M. (2001). Activation of the left amygdala to a cognitive representation of fear. *Nature Neuroscience, 4,* 437–441.

Pinel, J. P., Assanand, S., & Lehman, D. R. (2000). Hunger, eating, and ill health. *American Psychologist, 55,* 1105–1116.

Pines, M. (1973). *The brain changers.* New York: Harcourt Brace Jovanovich.

Placidi, G. P., Oquendo, M. A., Malone, K. M., Huang, Y. Y., Ellis, S. P., & Mann, J. J. (2001). Aggressivity, suicide attempts, and depression: Relationship to cerebrospinal fluid monoamine metabolite levels. *Biological Psychiatry, 50,* 783–791.

Plaitakis, A., & Shashidharan, P. (1995). Amyotrophic lateral sclerosis, glutamate, and oxidative stress. In F. E. Bloom & D. J. Kupfer (Eds.), *Psychopharmacology: The fourth generation of progress.* New York: Raven Press.

Pliszka, S. R., McCracken, J. T., & Maas, J. W. (1996). Catecholamines in attention-deficit hyperactivity disorder: Current perspectives. *Journal of American Academy of Child Adolescent Psychiatry, 35*(3), 264–272.

Ploghaus, A., Tracey, I., Gati, J. S., Clare, S., Menon, R. S., Matthews, P. M., Rawlins, J., & Nicholas, P. (1999). Dissociating pain from its anticipation in the human brain. *Science, 284*(5422), 1979–1981.

Plomin, R. (1995). Molecular genetics and psychology. *Current Directions in Psychological Science, 4,* 114–117.

Pohl, R., Yeragani, V. K., Balon, R., Rainey, J. M., Lycaki, H., Ortiz, A., Berchou, R., & Weinberg, P. (1988). Isoproterenol-induced panic attacks. *Biological Psychiatry, 24*(8), 891–902.

Poizner, H., Klima, E. S., & Bellugi, U. (1987). *What the hands reveal about the brain.* Cambridge, MA: MIT Press.

Polivy, J., & Herman, C. P. (1976). Effects of alcohol on eating behavior: Influences of mood and perceived intoxication. *Journal of Abnormal Psychology, 85,* 601–606.

Popper, K. R., & Eccles, J. C. (1977). *The self and its brain.* New York: Springer International.

Porsolt, R. D. (1993). Serotonin: Neurotransmitter "a la mode." *Pharmacopsychiatry, 26,* 20–24.

Posner, M. I. (1993). Seeing the mind. *Science, 262*(5134), 673–674.

Posner, M. I. (1994). Attention: The mechanisms of consciousness. *Proceedings of the National Academy of Sciences, 91,* 7398–7403.

Posner, M. I., Petersen, S. E., Fox, P. T., & Raichle, M. E. (1988). Localization of cognitive operations in the human brain. *Science, 240*(4859), 1627–1631.

Post, R., Kimbrell, T., McCann, U., Dunn, R., Osuch, E., Speer, A., & Weiss, S. (1999). Repetitive transcranial magnetic stimulation as a neuropsychiatric tool: Present status and future potential. *Journal of ECT, 15*(1), 39–59.

Prange, T., Garbay-Jaureguiberry, C., Roques, B., & Anteunis, M. (1974).

High field 1H NMR studies: Influence of the cis-trans isomerism on the N-acetyl-4-hydroxy proline ring conformation. *Biochemical & Biophysical Research Communications, 61*(1), 104–109.

Prasad, A. S. (2001). Recognition of zinc-deficiency syndrome. *Nutrition, 17,* 67–69.

Prescott, C. A., Aggen, S. H., & Kendler, K. S. (1999). Sex differences in the sources of genetic liability to alcohol abuse and dependence in a population-based sample of U.S. twins. *Alcohol Clinical Experimental Research, 23*(7), 1136–1144.

Preti, G., Cutler, W. B., Garcia, C. R., Huggins, G. R., & Lawley, H. J. (1986). Human axillary secretions influence women's menstrual cycles: The role of donor extract of females. *Hormonal Behavior, 20*(4), 474–482.

Pridmore, S. (1999). Rapid transcranial magnetic stimulation and normalization of the dexamethasone suppression test. *Psychiatry Clinical Neuroscience, 53*(1), 33–37.

Pritchard, T. C., Macaluso, D. A., & Eslinger, P. J. (1999). Taste perception in patients with insular cortex lesions. *Behavioral Neuroscience, 113*(4), 663–671.

Probst, T. (1998). The sensory conflict concept for the generation of nausea. *Journal of Psychophysiology, 12*(1), 34–49.

Probst, T., & Schmidt, U. (1998). The sensory conflict concept for the generation of nausea. *Journal of Psychophysiology, 12*(Suppl 1), 34–49.

Provins, K.A. (1997). Handedness and speech: A critical reappraisal of the role of genetic and environmental factors in the cerebral lateralization of function. *Psychological Review, 104*(3), 554–571.

Prusiner, S. B. (1997). Prion diseases and the BSE crisis. *Science, 278*(5336), 245–251.

Prusiner, S. B., & DeArmond, S. J. (1994). Prion diseases and neurodegeneration. *Annual Review of Neuroscience, 17,* 311–39.

Pycock, C. J., Kerwin, R. W., & Carter, C. J. (1980). Effect of lesion of cortical dopamine terminals on subcortical dopamine receptors in rats. *Nature, 286,* 74–76.

Quintana, J., & Fuster, J. M. (1992). Mnemonic and predictive functions of cortical neurons in a memory task. *Neuroreport, 3*(8), 721–724.

Quintana, J., & Fuster, J. M. (1999). From perception to action: Temporal integrative functions of prefrontal and parietal neurons. *Cerebral Cortex, 9,* 213–221.

Racagni, G., Tinelli, D., Bianchi, E., Brunello, N., & Perez, J. (1991).

cAMP-dependent binding proteins and endogenous phosphorylation after antidepressant treatment. In M. Sandler & A. Coppen (Eds.), *5-hydroxytryptamine in psychiatry: A spectrum of ideas*. New York: Oxford University Press.

Raff, M., Barres, B., Burne, J., Coles, H., Ishizaki, Y., & Jacobson, M. (1993). Programmed cell death and the control of cell survival: Lessons from the nervous system. *Science, 262*(5134), 695–700.

Ragozzino, M. E. (2000). The contribution of cholinergic and dopaminergic afferents in the rat prefrontal cortex to learning, memory, and attention. *Psychobiology, 28*(2), 238–247.

Raichle, M. E. (1994a). Images of the mind: Studies with modern imaging techniques. *Annual Review of Psychology, 45*, 333–356.

Raichle, M. E. (1994b). Visualizing the mind. *Scientific American, 270*, 58–64.

Raine, A., Benishay, D., Lencz, T., & Scarpa, A. (1997). Abnormal orienting in schizotypal personality disorder. *Schizophrenia Bulletin, 23*(1), 75–82.

Rainville, P., Duncan, G. H., Price, D. D., Carrier, B., & Bushnell, M. C. (1997). Pain affect encoded in human anterior cingulate, but not somatosensory cortex. *Science, 277*(5328), 968–971.

Rajendra, S., Lynch, J. W., Pierce, K. D., French, C. R., Barry, P. H., & Schofield, P. R. (1994). Startle disease mutations reduce the agonist sensitivity of the human inhibitory glycine receptor. *Journal of Biological Chemistry, 269*(29), 18739–18742.

Ramachandran, V. S., Rogers-Ranachandran, D., & Stewart, M. (1992). Perceptual correlates of massive cortical reorganization. *Science, 258*(5085), 1159–1160.

Ramey, E. R., & O'Doherty, D. (1960). *Electrical studies on the unanesthetized brain*. New York: Hoeber.

Ramirez, O. A., Nordholm, A. F., Gellerman, D., Thompson, J. K., & Thompson, R. F. (1997). The conditioned eyeblink response: A role for the GABA-B receptor? *Pharmacology, Biochemistry, & Behavior, 58*, 127–132.

Ramon y Cajal, S. (1933). *Histology*. Baltimore: William Wood.

Ramsay, D. J., & Thrasher, T. N. (1990). Thirst and water balance. In E. M. Stricker (Ed.), *Neurobiology of food and fluid intake*. New York: Plenum Press.

Ramsay, D. J., & Thrasher, T. N. (1991). Regulation of fluid intake in dogs following water deprivation. *Brain Research Bulletin, 27*(3–4), 495–499.

Rao, S. C., Rainer, G., & Miller, E. K. (1997). Integration of what and where in the primate prefrontal cortex. *Science, 276*(5313), 821–824.

Rapoport, J. L. (1991). Recent advances in obsessive-compulsive disorder. *Neuropsychopharmacology, 5*, 1–10.

Rapoport, S. I. (1995). Anatomic and functional brain imaging in Alzheimer's disease. In F. E. Bloom & D. J. Kupfer (Eds.), *Psychopharmacology: The fourth generation*. New York: Raven Press.

Rauschecker, J. P., & Shannon, R. V. (2002). Sending sound to the brain. *Science, 295*, 1025–1029.

Rauschecker, J. P., Tian, B., & Hauser, M. (1995). Processing of complex sounds in the macaque nonprimary auditory cortex. *Science, 268*(5207), 111–114.

Ray, W. J., & Cole, H. W. (1985). EEG activity during cognitive processing: Influence of attentional factors. *International Journal of Psychophysiology, 3*(1), 43–48.

Reed, C. L., & Caselli, R. J. (1994). The nature of tactile agnosia: A case study. *Neuropsychologia, 32*(5), 527–539.

Reed, C. L., Caselli, R. J., & Farah, M. J. (1996). Tactile agnosia: Underlying impairment and implications for normal tactile object recognition. *Brain, 119*(3), 875–888.

Reid, P. D., & Pridmore, S. (1999). Dexamethasone suppression test reversal in rapid transcranial magnetic stimulation-treated depression. *Australian and New Zealand Journal of Psychiatry, 33*(2), 264–267.

Reiner, P. B., & Fibiger, H. C. (1995). Functional heterogeneity of central cholinergic systems. In F. E. Bloom & D. J. Kupfer (Eds.), *Psychopharmacology: The fourth generation of progress*. New York: Raven Press.

Reiner, W. G., Gearhart, J. P., & Jeffs, R. (1999). Psychosexual dysfunction in males with genital anomalies: Late adolescence, Tanner Stages IV to VI. *Journal of the American Academy of Child & Adolescent Psychiatry, 38*(7), 865–872.

Reppert, S. M. (1997). Melatonin receptors: Molecular biology of a new family of G protein-coupled receptors. *Journal of Biological Rhythms, 12*(6), 528–531.

Reppert, S. M., Weaver, D. R., Rivkees, S. A., & Stopa, E. G. (1988). Putative melatonin receptors in a human biological clock. *Science, 242*(4875), 78–81.

Ressler, K. J., & Nemeroff, C. B. (1999). Role of norepinephrine in the pathophysiology and treatment of mood disorders. *Biological Psychiatry, 46*, 1219–1233.

Reuter, G., & Zenner, H. P. (1990). Active radial and transverse motile responses of outer hair cells in the organ of Corti. *Hearing Research, 43*(2–3), 219–230.

Reynolds, C. F., Buysse, D. J., & Kupfer, D. J. (1995). Sleep disorders. In F. E. Bloom & D. J. Kupfer (Eds.), *Psychopharmacology: The fourth generation of progress*. New York: Raven Press.

Rice, G., Anderson, C., Risch, N., & Ebers, G. (1999). Male homosexuality: Absence of linkage to microsatellite markers at Xq28. *Science, 284*, 665–667.

Richter, C. P. (1955). Experimental production of cycles in behavior and physiology in animals. *Acta Medica Scandinavica, 152*(Suppl 307), 36–37.

Ricker, J. H., & Zafonte, R. D. (2000). Functional neuroimaging and quantitative electroencephalography in adult traumatic head injury: Clinical applications and interpretive cautions. *Journal of Head Trauma Rehabilitation, 15*, 859–868.

Riedel, W. (1976). Warm receptors in the dorsal abdominal wall of the rabbit. *Pflugers Archives, 361*(2), 205–206.

Riley, A., & Riley, E. (2000). Controlled studies on women presenting with sexual drive disorder: I. Endocrine status. *Journal of Sex Marital Therapy, 26*(3), 269–283.

Rioult-Pedotti, M. S., Friedman, D., & Donoghue, J. P. (2000). Learning-induced LTP in neocortex. *Science, 290*, 533–536.

Risberg, J. (1987). Frontal lobe degeneration of non-Alzheimer type. III. Region cerebral flow. *Archives of General Psychiatry, 6*(3), 225–233.

Rissman, E. F. (1995). An alternative animal model for the study of female sexual behavior. *Current Directions in Psychological Science, 4*(1), 6–10.

Rivier, C., & Vale, W. (1984). Corticotropin-releasing factor (CRF) acts centrally to inhibit growth hormone secretion in the rat. *Endocrinology, 114*(6), 2409–2411.

Robbins, T. W., & Everitt, B. J. (1995). Central norepinephrine neurons and behavior. In F. E. Bloom & D. J. Kupfer (Eds.), *Psychopharmacology: The fourth generation of progress*. New York: Raven Press.

Roberts, A. J., McDonald, J. S., Heyser, C. J., Kieffer, B. L., Matthes, H. W., Koob, G. F., & Gold, L. H. (2000). Mu-opioid receptor knockout mice do not self-administer alcohol. *Journal of Pharmacological Experimental Therapy, 293*(3), 1002–1008.

Roberts, G. W., & James, S. (1996). Prion diseases: Transmission from mad cows? *Current Biology, 6*(10), 1247–1249.

Robinson, B. E. (1997). Guideline for initial evaluation of the patient with memory loss. *Geriatrics, 52*, 30–39.

Rodieck, R. W. (1998). *The first steps in seeing*. Sunderland, MA: Sinauer Associates.

Rodier, P. M. (2000). The early origins of autism. *Scientific American, 282*(2), 56–63.

Rodier, S., Cornblatt, B., Bergman, A., Obuchowski, M., Mitropoulou, V., Keefe, R., Silverman, J., & Siever, L. (1997). Attentional functioning in schizotypal personality disorder. *American Journal of Psychiatry, 154*(5), 655–660.

Roitman, S. E., Keefe, R. S., Harvey, P. D., Siever, L. J., & Mohs, R. C. (1997). Attentional and eye tracking deficits correlate with negative symptoms in schizophrenia. *Schizophrenia Research, 26*(2–3), 139–146.

Rolls, B. J., Rowe, E. A., & Rolls, E. T. (1982). How sensory properties of foods affect human feeding behavior. *Physiology & Behavior, 29*(3), 409–417.

Rolls, E. T. (1992). Neurophysiology and functions of the primate amygdala. In J. P. Aggleton (Ed.), *The amygdala: Neurobiological aspects of emotion, memory, and mental dysfunction*. New York: Wiley-Liss.

Rolls, E. T. (1994). Neural processing related to feeding in primates. In C. R. Legg & D. A. Booth (Eds.), *Appetite: Neural and behavioural bases*. New York: Oxford University Press.

Rolls, E. T. (2000). The representation of umami taste in the taste cortex. *Journal of Nutrition, 130*(4), 960–965.

Rolls, E. T., Burton, M. J., & Mora, F. (1980). Neurophysiological analysis of brain-stimulation reward in the monkey. *Brain Research, 194*(2), 339–357.

Rolls, E. T., Murzi, E., Yaxley, S., Thorpe, S. J., Simpson, S. J. (1986). Sensory-specific satiety: Food-specific reduction in responsiveness of ventral forebrain neurons after feeding in the monkey. *Brain Research, 368*(1), 79–86.

Rolls, E. T., & Rolls, B. J. (1982). Brain mechanisms involving feeding. In L. M. Barker (Ed.), *Psychobiology of human food selection*. Westport, CT: AVI Publishing.

Romanski, L. M., Tian, B., Fritz, J., Mishkin, M., Goldman-Rakic, P. S., & Rauschecker, J. P. (1999). Dual streams of auditory afferents target multiple domains in the primate prefrontal cortex. *Nature Neuroscience, 2*(12), 1131–1136.

Roof, R. L., Duvdevani, R., & Stein, D. G. (1993). Gender influences outcome of brain injury: Progesterone plays a protective role. *Brain Research, 607*(1–2), 333–336.

Rosadini, G., & Rossi, G. F. (1967). On the suggested cerebral dominance for consciousness. *Brain, 90*(1), 101–112.

Rosen, I. (1997). Electroencephalography as a diagnostic tool in dementia. *Dementia and Geriatric Cognitive Disorders, 8*(2), 110–116.

Rosenthal, D. (1970). *Genetic theory and abnormal behavior*. New York: McGraw-Hill.

Rosenzweig, M. R. (1996). Aspects of the search for neural mechanisms of memory. *Annual Review of Psychology, 47*, 1–32.

Roses, A. D., & Saunders, A. M. (1997). Apolipoprotein E genotyping as a diagnostic adjunct for Alzheimer's disease. *International Psychogeriatrics, 9*(1), 277–288.

Rosler, A., & Witztum, E. (1998). Treatment of men with paraphilia with a long-acting analogue of gonadotropin-releasing hormone. *New England Journal of Medicine, 338*(7), 416–422.

Rosler, A., & Witztum, E. (2000). Pharmacotherapy of paraphilias in the next millennium. *Behavioral Science Law, 18*(1), 43–56.

Rosler, K. M. (2001). Transcranial magnetic brain stimulation: A tool to investigate central motor pathways. *News in Physiological Science, 16*, 297–302.

Rossi, G. S., & Rosadini, G (1967). Experimental analysis of cerebral dominance in man. In C. Millikan & F. L. Darley (Eds.), *Brain mechanisms underlying speech and language*. New York: Grune & Stratton.

Rosso, P. (1987). Regulation of food intake during pregnancy and lactation. *Annals of the New York Academy of Sciences, 499*, 191–196.

Roy, A., DeWong, J., & Linnoila, M. (1989). Cerebrospinal fluid monoamine metabolites and suicidal behavior in depressed patients: A 5-year follow-up study. *Archives of General Psychiatry, 46*(7), 609–612.

Roy, E. A., & Square, P. A. (1994). Neuropsychology of movement sequencing disorders and apraxia. In D. W. Zaidel (Ed.), *Neuropsychology*. San Diego, CA: Academic Press.

Rugg, M. D. (1995). Memory and consciousness: A selective review of issues and data. *Neuropsychologia, 33*(9), 1131–1141.

Rugg, M. D. (1998). Convergent approaches to electrophysiological and hemodynamic investigations of memory. *Human Brain Mapping, 6*(5–6), 394–398.

Ruggiero, D. A., Underwood, M. D., Mann, J. J., Anwar, M., & Arando, V. (2000). The human nucleus of the solitary tract: Visceral pathways revealed with an "in vitro" post-mortem tracing method. *Journal of the Autonomic Nervous System, 79*(2–3), 181–190.

Russek, M. (1981). Current status of the hepatostatic theory of food intake control. *Appetite, 2*(2), 137–143.

Russell, M. B., Diamant, M., & Norby, S. (1997). Genetic heterogeneity of migraine with and without aura in Danes cannot be explained by mutation in mtDNA nucleotide pair 11084. *Acta Neurol Scand, 96*(3), 171–173.

Russell, M. J. (1976). Human olfactory communication. *Nature, 260*(5551), 520–522.

Sacks, Oliver. (1984). *A leg to stand on*. New York: Harper & Row.

Sacks, O. L. (1985). *The Man Who Mistook His Wife for a Hat*. New York: Simon & Schuster.

Sagar, H. J., Cohen, N. J., Corkin, S., & Growdon, J. H. (1985). Dissociations among processes in remote memory. *Annals of the New York Academy of Sciences, 444*, 533–535.

Sagar, S. M., Sharp, F. R., & Curran, T. (1988, June 3). Expression of c-*fos* protein in brain: Metabolic mapping at the cellular level. *Science*, 1328–1331.

Saint-Cyr, J. A., Taylor, A. E., & Lang, A. E. (1988). Procedural learning and neostriatal dysfunction in man. *Brain, 111*(4), 941–959.

Sakurai, T., Amemiya, A., Ishii, M., Matsuzaki, I., Chemelli, R. M., Tanaka, H., Williams, S. C., Richardson, J. A., Kozlowski, G. P., Wilson, S., Arch, J. R., Buckingham, R. E., Haynes, A. C., Carr, S. A., Annan, R. S., McNulty, D. E., Liu, W. S., Terrett, J. A., Elshourbagy, N. A., Bergsma, D. J., & Yanagisawa, M. (1998). Orexins and orexin receptors: A family of hypothalamic neuropeptides and G protein-coupled receptors that regulate feeding behavior. *Cell, 92*, 573–585.

Salmon, E., Degueldre, C., Franco, G., & Franck, G. (1996). Frontal lobe dementia presenting as personality disorder. *Acta Neurol Belg, 96*, 130–134.

Santorelli, F. M., Tanji, K., Sano, M., Shanske, S., El-Shahawi, M., Kranz-Eble, P., DiMauro, S. & DeVivo, D. C. (1997). Maternally inherited encephalopathy associated with a single-base insertion in the mitochondrial tRNA Trp gene. *Annual Neurology (6AE), 42*(2), 256–260.

Saper, C. B. (1998). Neurobiological basis of fever. *Annual New York Academic Sciences, 856*, 90–94.

Sapolsky, R. M. (1996). Stress, glucocorticoids and damage to the nervous system: The current state of confusion. *The International Journal on the Biology of Stress, 1*, 1–19.

Sapolsky, R. M. (1997). Induced modulation of endocrine history: A partial review. *Stress, 2*(1), 1–12.

Sarrel, P. M. (2000). Effects of hormone replacement therapy on sexual psychophysiology and behavior in post-menopause. *Journal of Women's Gender Based Medicine, 9*(S1), 25–32.

Sarter, M., Berntson, G. G., & Cacioppo, J. T. (1996). Brain imaging and cognitive neuroscience: Toward strong inference in attributing function to structure. *American Psychologist, 51,* 13–21.

Sarter, M., & Bruno, J. P. (1997a). Dopamine role. *Science, 278*(5343), 1549–1550.

Sarter, M., & Bruno, J. P. (1997b). Trans-synaptic stimulation of cortical acetylcholine and enhancement of attentional functions: A rational approach for the development of cognition enhancers. *Behavioral Brain Research, 83*(1–2), 7–14.

Satinoff, E., Valentino, D., & Teitelbaum, P. (1976). Thermoregulatory cold-defense deficits in rats with preoptic/anterior hypothalamic lesions. *Brain Research Bulletin, 1*(6), 553–565.

Satterfield, J. M., Monahan, J., Seligman, M. E. (1997). Law school performance predicted by explanatory style. *Behavioral Science Law, 15*(1), 95–105.

Savoy R. L. (2001). History and future directions of human brain mapping and functional neuroimaging. *Acta Psychologica, 107,* 9–42.

Scalzitti, J. M., & Hensler, J. G. (1997). Serotonin receptors: Role in psychiatry. In K. Blum & E. P. (Eds.), *Handbook of psychiatric genetics.* Boca Raton, FL: CRC Press.

Schacter, D. L., & Buckner, R. L. (1998). Priming and the brain. *Neuron, 20*(2), 185–195.

Schacter, D. L., Savage, C. R., Alpert, N. M., Rauch, S. L., & Albert, M. S. (1996). The role of hippocampus and frontal cortex in age-related memory changes: A PET study. *Neuroreport, 7*(6), 1165–1169.

Schachter, S., & Rodin, J. (1974). *Obese humans and rats.* Potomac, MD: Lawrence Erlbaum.

Schachter, S., & Singer, J. E. (1962). Cognitive, social, and physiological determinants of emotional state. *Psychological Review, 69,* 379–399.

Schaeffer, M. A., & Baum, A. (1984). Adrenal cortical response to stress at Three Mile Island. *Psychosomatic Medicine, 46,* 227–237.

Schaffer, L., Schaffer, C., & Caretto, J. (1999). The use of primidone in the treatment of refractory bipolar disorder. *Annals of Clinical Psychiatry, 11*(2), 61–66.

Schendel, D. E. (2001). Infection in pregnancy and cerebral palsy. *Journal of the American Medical Women's Association, 56,* 105–108.

Schibler, U., Ripperger, J. A., & Brown, S. A. (2000). Circadian rhythms. Chronobiology-reducing time. *Science, 293,* 437–438.

Schiff, R., Rosenbluth, J., Dou, W. K., Liang, W. L., & Moon, D. (2002). Distribution and morphology of transgenic mouse oligodendroglial-lineage cells following transplantation into normal and myelin-deficient rat CNS. *Journal of Comparative Neurology, 446,* 46–57.

Schildkraut, J. J. (1965). The catecholamine hypothesis of affective disorders: A review of supporting evidence. *American Journal of Psychiatry, 122,* 509–522.

Schlaug, G., Knorr, U., & Sietz, R. (1994). Inter-subject variability of cerebral activations in acquiring a motor skill: A study with positron emission tomography. *Experimental Brain Research, 98*(3), 523–534.

Schleidt, M., Hold, B., & Attili, G. (1981). A cross-cultural study on the attitude towards personal odors. *Journal of Chemical Ecology, 7,* 19–31.

Schmidt, M. L., Zhukareva, V., Newell, K. L., Lee, V. M., & Trojanowski, J. Q. (2001). Tau isoform profile and phosphorylation state in dementia pugilistica recapitulate Alzheimer's disease. *Acta Neuropathologica, 101,* 518–524.

Schmidt, W. J., & Kretschmer, B. D. (1997). Behavioural pharmacology of glutamate receptors in the basal ganglia. *Neuroscience and Biobehavioral Reviews, 21,* 381–392.

Schnitzer, J. J., & Donahoe, P. K. (2001). Surgical treatment of congenital adrenal hyperplasia. *Endocrinology Metabolic Clinics of North America, 30,* 137–154.

Scholander, P. F., Hock, R., Walters, F., Johnson, F., & Irving, L. (1950). Heat regulation in some arctic and tropical mammals and birds. *Biological Bulletin, 99,* 237–258.

Schulkin, J., McEwen, B. S., & Gold, P. W. (1994). Allostasis, amygdala, and anticipatory angst. *Neuroscience Biobehavioral Review, 18*(3), 385–396.

Schultz, W., Dayan, P., & Montague, P. R. (1997). A neural substrate of prediction and reward. *Science, 275*(5306), 1593–1599.

Schuman, E. M., & Madison, D. V. (1991). A requirement for the intercellular messenger nitric oxide in long-term potentiation. *Science, 254,* 1503–1506.

Schuppert, M., Munte, T. F., Wieringa, B. M., & Altenmuller, E. (2000). Receptive amusia: Evidence for cross-hemispheric neural networks underlying music processing strategies. *Brain, 123*(3), 546–559.

Schwarz, R. D., Callahan, M. J., Coughenour, L. L., Dickerson, M. R. Kinsora, J. J., Lipinski, W. J., Raby, C. A., Spencer, C. J., & Tecle, H. (1999). Milameline (CI-979/RU35926): A muscarinic receptor agonist with cognition-activating properties: Biochemical and in vivo characterization. *Journal Pharmacol Exp Ther., 291,* 812–822.

Scott, T. R., Giza, B. K., & Yan, J. (1999). Gustatory neural coding in the cortex of the alert cynomolus macaque. *Journal of Neurophysiology, 81*(1), 60–71.

Scott, T. R., & Plata-Salaman, C. R. (1999). Taste in the monkey cortex. *Physiology & Behavior, 67*(4), 489–511.

Seeman, P. (1995). Dopamine receptors: Clinical correlates. In F. E. Bloom & D. J. Kupfer (Eds.), *Psychopharmacology: The fourth generation of progress.* New York: Raven Press.

Seeman, P., Guan, H., Nobrega, J., Jiwa, D., Markstein, R., Balk, J., Picetti, R., Borrelli, E., & Van Tol, H. (1997). Dopamine D_2-like sites in schizophrenia, but not in Alzheimer's, Huntington's, or control brains, for [3H] benzquinoline. *Synapse, 25*(2), 137–146.

Seeman, P., Guan, H., & Van Tol, H. (1993). Dopamine D4 receptors elevated in schizophrenia. *Nature, 365*(6445), 441–445.

Segovia, S., Guillamon, A., del Cerro, M. C., Ortega, E., Perez-Laso, C., Rodriguez-Zafra, M., & Beyer, C. (1999). The development of brain sex differences: A multisignaling process. *Behavioral Brain Research, 105*(1), 69–80.

Seifritz, E. (2001). Contribution of sleep physiology to depressive pathophysiology. *Neuropsychopharmacology, 25*(5 Suppl), S85–S88.

Sejnowski, T. J., Koch, C., & Churchland, P. S. (1988). Computational neuroscience. *Science, 241,* 1299–1306.

Seligman, M. E., & Maier, S. F. (1967). Failure to escape traumatic shock. *Journal of Experimental Psychology, 74*(1), 1–9.

Sell, L. A., Morris, J., Bearn, J., Frackowiak, R. S., Friston, K. J., & Dolan, R. J. (1999). *European Journal of Neuroscience, 11*(3), 1042–1048.

Settipane, G. A. (1987). The restaurant syndromes. *New England Reg Allergy Proceedings, 8,* 39–46.

Shadmehr, R., & Holcomb, H. H. (1997). Neural correlates of motor memory consolidation. *Science, 277*(5327), 821–825.

Shallice, T., & Warrington, E. K. (1970). Independent functioning of verbal memory stores: A neuropsychological study. *Q Journal of Experimental Psychology, 22*(2), 261–273.

Shannon, P., Wherrett, J., & Nag, S. (1997). A rare form of adult onset leukodystrophy: Orthochromatic leukodystophy with pigmented glia. *Canadian Journal of Neurological Sciences, 24*(2), 146–150.

Shaw, C. M., & Alvord, E. C. (1997). Neuropathology of the limbic system. *Neuroimaging Clinics of North America*, 7, 101–142.

Shaywitz, B. A., Shaywitz, S. E., Pugh, K. R., Constable, R. T., Skudlarski, P., Fulbright, R. K., Bronen, R. A., Fletcher, J. M., Shankweiler, D. P., & Katz, L. (1995). Sex differences in the functional organization of the brain for language. *Nature*, 373(6515), 607–609.

Sheinberg, D. L., & Logothetis, N. K. (2001). Noticing familiar objects in real world scenes: The role of temporal cortical neurons in natural vision. *Journal of Neuroscience*, 21, 1340–1350.

Sheline, Y. I., Wang, P. W., Gado, M. H., Csernansky, J. G., & Vannier, M. W. (1996). Hippocampal atrophy in recurrent major depression. *Proceedings of the National Academy of Sciences, USA*, 93(9), 3908–3913.

Shelton, R. C., Karson, C. N., Doran, A. R., Pickar, D., Bigelow, L. B., & Weinberger, D. R. (1988). Cerebral structural pathology in schizophrenia: Evidence for a selective prefrontal cortical defect. *American Journal of Psychiatry*, 145, 154–163.

Shen, Y., Muramatsu, S. L., Ikeguchi, K., Fujimoto, K. I., Fan, D. S., Ogawa, M., Mizukami, H., Urabe, M., Kume, A., Nagatsu, I., Urano, F., Suzuki, T., Ichinose, H., Nagatsu, T., Monahan, J., Nakano, I., & Ozawa, K. (2000). Triple transduction with adeno-associated virus vectors expressing tyrosine hydroxylase, aromatic-L-amino-acid decarboxylase, and GTP cyclohydrolase I for gene therapy of Parkinson's disease. *Human Gene Therapy*, 11(11), 1509–1519.

Sherrington, C. S., & Grunbaum, A. S. F. (1901). An address on localization in "motor" cerebral cortex. *British Medical Journal*, 2, 1857–1859.

Sherrington, C. S., & Grunbaum, A. S. F. (1902). A discussion on the motor cortex as exemplified in the anthropoid apes. *British Medical Journal*, 2, 784–785.

Shiang, R., Ryan, S. G., Zhu, Y. Z., Hahn, A. F., O'Connell, P., & Wasmuth, J. J. (1993). Mutations in the alpha 1 subunit of the inhibitory glycine receptor cause the dominant neurologic disorder, hyperekplexia. *Natural Genetics*, 5(4), 351–358.

Shifren, J. L., Braunstein, G. D., Simon, J. A., Casson, P. R., Buster, J. E., Redmond, G. P., Burki, R. E., Ginsburg, E. S., Rosen, R. C., Leiblum, S. R., Caramelli, K. E., & Mazer, N. A. (2000). Transdermal testosterone treatment in women with impaired sexual function after oöphorectomy. *New England Journal of Medicine*, 343(10), 682–688.

Shih, C. C., Chen, K. J-S., & Gallaher, T. K. (1995). Molecular biology of serotonin receptors. In F. E. Bloom & D. J. Kupfer (Eds.), *Psychopharmacology: The fourth generation of progress*. New York: Raven Press.

Shimizu, E., Tang, Y. P., Rampon, C., & Tsien, J. Z. (2000). NMDA receptor-dependent synaptic reinforcement as a crucial process for memory consolidation. *Science*, 290, 1170–1174.

Shinoda, H., Marini, A. M., Cosi, C., & Schwartz, J. P. (1989). Brain region and gene specificity of neuropeptide gene expression in cultured astrocytes. *Science*, 245, 415–420.

Shouse, M. N., Staba, R. J., Saquib, S. F., & Farber, P. R. (2000). Monoamines and sleep: Microdialysis findings in pons and amygdala. *Brain Research*, 860(1–2), 181–190.

Shuman, E. M., & Madison, D. V. (1991). A requirement for the intercellular messenger nitric oxide in long-term potentiation. *Science*, 254(5037), 1503–1506.

Siegel, J. M. (2000). Narcolepsy. *Scientific American*, 282, 76–81.

Siegel, S. (1979). The role of conditioning in drug tolerance and addiction. In J. D. Keehn (Ed.), *Psychopathology in animals: Research and clinical implications*. San Diego, CA: Academic Press.

Siegel, S., Baptista, M., Kim, J., McDonald, R., & Weise-Kelly, L. (2000). Pavlovian psychopharmacology: The associative basis of tolerance. *Experimental & Clinical Psychopharmacology*, 8(3), 276–293.

Siever, L. J., & Davis, K. L. (1985). Overview: Toward a dysregulation hypothesis of depression. *American Journal of Psychiatry*, 142(9), 1017–1031.

Siever, L. J., & Davis, K. L. (1991). A psychobiological perspective on the personality disorders. *American Journal of Psychiatry*, 148(12), 1647–1658.

Sigvardsson, S., Bohman, M., & Cloninger, C. R. (1996). Replication of the Stockholm Adoption Study of alcoholism: Confirmatory cross-fostering analysis. *Archives of General Psychiatry*, 53, 681–687.

Sikorski, R., & Peters, R. (1998). Brain transplants? *Science*, 282(5397), 2213.

Silbersweig, D. A., Stern, E., Frith, C., Cahill, C., Holmes, A., Grootoonk, S., Seaward, J., McKenna, P., Chua, S. E., & Schnorr, L. (1995). A functional neuroanatomy of hallucinations in schizophrenia. *Nature*, 378, 176–179.

Sillito, A. M., Jones, H. E., Gerstein, G. L., & West, D. C. (1994). Feature-linked synchronization of thalamic relay cell firing induced by feedback from the visual cortex. *Nature*, 369(6480), 479–482.

Silverstone, J. T., Cooper, R. M., & Begg, R. R. (1970). A comparative trial of fenfluramine and diethylpropion in obesity. *British Journal of Clinical Practice*, 24(10), 423–425.

Silverstone, T. (1993). Mood, food and 5-HT. *International Clinical Psychopharmacology*, 8, 91–94.

Simansky, K. J. (1996). Serotonergic control of the organization of feeding and satiety. *Behavioral Brain Research*, 73(1–2), 37–42.

Simansky, K. J. (1998). Serotonin and the structure of satiation. In G. P. Smith (Ed.), *Satiation: From gut to brain*. New York: Oxford University Press.

Sinclair, A. H., Berta, P., Palmer, M. S., Hawkins, J. R., Griffiths, B. L., Smith, M. J., Foster, J. W., Frischauf, A. M., Lovell-Badge, R., & Goodfellow, P. N. (1990). A gene from the human sex-determining region encodes a protein with homology to a conserved DNA-binding motif. *Nature*, 346(6281), 240–244.

Sinden, J. D., Stroemer, P., Grigoryan, G., Patel, S., French, S. J., & Hodges, H. (2000). Functional repair with neural stem cells. *Novartis Foundation Symposium*, 231, 270–283.

Singareddy, R. K., & Balon, R. (2001). Sleep and suicide in psychiatric patients. *Annals of Clinical Psychiatry*, 13, 93–101.

Singer, W. (1993). Synchronization of cortical activity and its putative role in information processing and learning. *Annual Review of Physiology*, 55, 349–374.

Singer, W., & Gray, C. M. (1995). Visual feature integration and the temporal correlation hypothesis. *Annual Review of Neuroscience*, 18, 555–586.

Sivian, L. S., & White, S. D. (1933). On minimal audible sound fields. *Journal of the Acoustical Society of America*, 4, 288–321.

Skodol, A. E., Gallagher, P. E., & Oldham, J. M. (1996). Excessive dependency and depression. Is the relationship specific? *Journal of Nervous Mental Disorders*, 184(3), 165–171.

Skodol, A. E., & Oldham, J. M. (1996). Phenomenology, differential diagnosis, and comorbidity of the impulsive-compulsive spectrum of disorders. In A. E. Oldham & E. Hollander (Eds.), *Impulsivity and Compulsivity*. Washington, DC: American Psychiatric Press.

Skolnick, P., & Paul, S. M. (1982). Buspirone: Chemistry, pharmacology, and behavior. *Journal of Clinical Psychiatry*, 43(12), 40–44.

Skosnik, P. D., Spatz-Glenn, L., & Park, S. (2001). Cannabis use is associated with schizotypy and attentional disinhibition. *Schizophrenia Research*, 48, 83–92.

Skuse, D., James, R., Bishop, D., Coppin, B., Dalton, P., Amodt-Leeper, G., Bacarese-Hamilton, M., Creswell, C., McGurk, R., & Jacobs, P. (1997). Evidence from Turner's syndrome of an imprinted X-linked locus affecting cognitive functions. *Nature, 387*(6634), 705–708.

Slob, A. K., Bax, C. M., Hop, W. C., & Rowland, D. L. (1996). Sexual arousability and the menstrual cycle. *Psychoneuroendocrinology, 21*(6), 545–558.

Sloman, S. A., Hayman, C. G., Ohta, N., & Law, J. (1988). Forgetting in primed fragment completion. *Journal of Experimental Psychology: Learning, Memory, & Cognition, 14*(2), 223–239.

Smith, E. E., & Jonides, J. (1998). Neuroimaging analysis of human working memory. *Proc Natl Acad Sci USA, 95*(20), 12061–12068.

Smith, E. E., & Jonides, J. (1999). Storage and executive processes in the frontal lobes. *Science, 283*(5408), 1657–1661.

Smith, E. E., Jonides, J., & Koeppe, R. A. (1996). Dissociating verbal and spatial working memory using PET. *Cerebral Cortex, 6*(1), 11–20.

Smith, G. P. (1995). Pavlov and appetite. *Int Physiol Behav Sci, 30,* 169–174.

Smith, G. P. (1996). The direct and indirect controls of meal size. *Neuroscience Biobehavioral Review, 20,* 41–46.

Smith, G. P. (1998). *Satiation: From gut to brain.* New York: Oxford University Press.

Smith, G. P., & Gibbs, J. (1992). Role of CCK in satiety and appetite control. *Clinical Neuropharmacology, 15*(1), 476.

Smith, G. P., & Gibbs, J. (1998). The satiating effects of cholecystokinin and bombesin-like peptides. In G. Smith (Eds.), *Satiation: From gut to brain.* New York: Oxford University Press.

Smith, J. W. (1997). Neurological disorders in alcoholism. In A. M. Gurnack (Ed.), *Older adults' misuse of alcohol, medicines, and other drugs: Research and practice issues.* New York: Springer.

Smith, M. E., & Oscar-Berman, M. (1990). Repetition priming of words and pseudowords in divided attention and in amnesia. *Journal of Experimental Psychology: Learning, Memory, & Cognition, 16*(6), 1033–1042.

Smith, R. S., Doty, R. L., Burlingame, G. K., & McKeown, D. A. (1993). Smell and taste function in the visually impaired. *Perceptual Psychophysiology, 54*(5), 649–655.

Snyder, S. H. (1980). Brain peptides as neurotransmitters. *Science, 209,* 976–983.

Sobel, N., Prabhakaran, V., Desmond, J. E., Glover, G. H., Goode, R. L. Sullivan, E. V., & Gabrieli, J. D. (1998). Sniffing and smelling: Separate subsystems in the human olfactory cortex. *Nature, 392*(6673), 282–286.

Soderstrom, H., Blennow, K., Manhem, A., & Forsman, A. (2001). CSF studies in violent offenders. I. 5-HIAA as a negative and HVA as a positive predictor of psychopathy. *J Neural Transm, 108,* 869–878.

Soetens, E., Casaer, S., D'Hooge, R., & Hueting, J. E. (1995). Effect of amphetamine on long-term retention of verbal material. *Psychopharmacology, 119*(2), 155–162.

Sokoloff, L. (1981). Relationships among local functional activity, energy metabolism, and blood flow in the central nervous system. *Fed Proc, 40*(8), 2311–2316.

Sood, B., Delaney-Black, V., Covington, C., Nordstrom-Klee, B., Ager, J., Templin, T., Janisse, J., Martier, S., & Sokol, R. J. (2001). Prenatal alcohol exposure and childhood behavior at age 6 to 7 years: I. Dose-response effect. *Pediatrics, 108,* E34.

Soubrie, P. (1986). Reconciling the role of central serotonin neurons in human and animal behavior. *Behavioral & Brain Sciences, 9,* 319–335.

Soubrie, P., Martin, P., el Mestikawy, S., Thiebot, M., Simon, P., & Hamon, M. (1986). The lesion of serotonergic neurons does not prevent antidepressant-induced reversal of escape failures produced by inescapable shocks in rats. *Pharmacological & Biochemical Behavior, 25*(1), 1–6.

Southwick, S. M., Yehuda, R., & Morgan, C. A. (1995). Clinical studies of neurotransmitter alterations in post-traumatic stress disorder. In M. J. Friedman & D. S. Charney (Eds.), *Neurobiological and clinical consequences of stress: From normal adaptation to post-traumatic stress disorder.* Philadelphia, PA: Lippincott Williams & Wilkins.

Spector, R., & Johanson, C. E. (1989). The mammalian choroid plexus. *Scientific American, 261,* 68–74.

Sperry, R. W., Gazzaniga, M. S., & Bogen, J. E. (1969). In P. J. Vinken & G. W. Bruyn (Eds.), *Handbook of Clinical Neurology.* Amsterdam: North-Holland.

Spiegel, D. (1996). Cancer and depression. *British Journal of Psychiatry, 30,* 109–116.

Spiegel, E. A., Wycis, H. T., Baird, H. W., & Szekely, E. G. (1960). Physiopathologic observations on the basal ganglia. In E. Ramey & D. O'Doherty (Eds.), *Electrical studies on the unanesthetized brain.* New York: Hoeber.

Spiegel, E. A., Wycis, H. T., Marks, M., & Lee, A. J. (1966). Stereotaxic apparatus for operations on the human brain. *Science, 106,* 349–350.

Spiers, H. J,. Maguire, E. A., & Burgess, N. (2001). Hippocampal amnesia. *Neurocase, 7,* 357–382.

Spillane, J. D. (1981). *The doctrine of the nerves.* London: Oxford University Press.

Spillantini, M., Crowther, R., Kamphorst, W., Heutink, P., & van Sweiten, J. (1998). Tau pathology in two Dutch families with mutations in the microtubule-binding region of tau. *American Journal of Pathology, 153*(5), 1359–1363.

Sprague, J. M., Chambers, W. W., & Stellar, E. (1961). Attentive, affective, and adaptive behavior in the cat. *Science, 133,* 165–173.

Spring, P. J., & Spies, J. M. (2001) Myasthenia gravis: Options and timing of immunomodulatory treatment. *BioDrugs, 15,* 173–183.

Squire, L. R., Knowlton, B., & Musen, G. (1993). The structure and organization of memory. *Annual Review of Psychology, 44,* 453–495.

Squires, R. F. (1997). How a poliovirus might cause schizophrenia: A commentary on Eagles' hypothesis. *Neurochemical Research, 22,* 647–656.

Stanilla, J. K., de Leon, J., & Simpson, G. M. (1997). Clozapine withdrawal resulting in delirium with psychosis: A report of three cases. *Journal of Clinical Psychiatry, 58*(6), 252–255.

Stanilla, J. K., & Simpson, G. M. (1996). Drugs to treat extrapyramidal side effects. In A. F. Schatzberg & C. B. Nemeroff (Eds.), *The American Psychiatric Press textbook of psychopharmacology.* Washington, DC: American Psychiatric Press.

Stanilla, J. K., & Simpson, G. M. (2001). Treatment of extrapyramidal side effects. In A. F. Schatzberg & C. B. Nemeroff (Eds.), *Essentials of clinical psychopharmacology.* Washington, DC: American Psychiatric Association.

Stanley, M., & Mann, J. (1983). Increased serotonin-2 binding sites in frontal cortex of suicide victims. *Lancet, 1*(8318), 214–216.

Starkman, M. N., Giordani, B., Gebarski, S. S., Berent, S., Schork, M. A., & Schteingart, D. E. (1999). Decrease in cortisol reverses human hippocampal atrophy following treatment of Cushing's disease. *Biological Psychiatry, 46*(12), 1595–1602.

Starr, M. S. (1995). Antiparkinsonian actions of glutamate antagonists-alone and with L-DOPA: A review of evidence and suggestions for possible mechanisms. *Journal of Neural Transmission, Parkinson's Disease Dementia Sect, 10,* 141–185.

Steckler, T., & Holsboer, F. (1999). Corticotropin-releasing hormone receptor subtypes and emotion. *Biological Psychiatry, 46,* 1480–1508.

Steele, James. (1998). Cerebral asymmetry, cognitive laterality and human evolution. *Cahiers de psychologie cognitive/current psychology of cognition, 17*(6), 1202–1214.

Stehling, M. K., Turner, R., & Mansfield, P. (1991). Echo-planar imaging: Magnetic resonance imaging in a fraction of a second. *Science, 254*, 43–50.

Stein, M. B., & Uhde, T. W. (1995). Biology of anxiety disorders. In A. F. Schatzberg & C. B. Nemeroff (Eds.), *The American Psychiatric Press textbook of psychopharmacology*. Washington, DC: American Psychiatric Press.

Steinberg, B. J., Trestman, R., Mitropoulou, V., Serby, M., Silverman, J., Coccaro, E., Weston, S., de Vegvar, M., & Siever, L. J. (1997). Depressive response to physostigmine challenge in borderline personality disorder patients. *Neuropsychopharmacology, 17*, 264–273.

Steiner, J. E. (1977). Facial expressions of the neonate infant indicating the hedonics of food-related chemical stimuli. In J. M. Weiffenbach (Ed.), *Taste and development: The genesis of sweet preference*. Bethesda, MD: U.S. National Institutes of Health.

Steinmetz, M. A., & Constantinidis, C. (1995). Neurophysiological evidence for a role of posterior parietal cortex in redirecting visual attention. *Cerebral Cortex, 5*(5), 448–456.

Stellar, E. (1954). The physiology of motivation. *Psychological Review, 61*, 5–22.

Steriade, M., McCormick, D. A., & Sejnowski, T. J. (1993). Thalamocortical oscillations in the sleeping and aroused brain. *Science, 262*, 679–685.

Stern, M. B. (1991). Head trauma as a risk factor for Parkinson's disease. *Movement Disorders, 6*(2), 95–97.

Stevens, J. R. (1959). Emotional activation of the electroencephalogram in patients with convulsive disorders. *Journal of Nervous and Mental Disorders, 128*, 339–351.

Stewart, J., & Kolb, B. (1988). The effects of neonatal gonadectomy and prenatal stress on cortical thickness and asymmetry in rats. *Behavioral Neural Biology, 49*(3), 344–360.

Stewart, T. D. (1958). Stone age skull surgery: A general review, with emphasis on the New World. *Smithsonian Report for 1957*, 1958, 469–491.

Stocker, S. D., Stricker, E. M., & Sved, A. F. (2001). Acute hypertension inhibits thirst stimulated by ANG II, hyperosmolality, or hypovolemia in rats. *Am J Physiol Regul Integr Comp Physiol, 280*, R214–R224.

Stores, G. (1981). Memory impairment in children with epilepsy. *Acta Neurologica Scandinavica, 64*(S89), 21–27.

Stores, G., & Lwin, R. (1981). A study of factors associated with the occurrence of generalized seizure discharge in children with epilepsy using the Oxford Medilog System for ambulatory monitoring. In M. Dam, L. Gram, & K. Penry (Eds.), *Advances in epileptology*. New York: Raven Press.

Stornetta, R. L., Hawelu-Johnson, C. L., Guyenet, P. G., & Lynch, K. R. (1988). Astrocytes synthesize angiotensinogen in brain. *Science, 242*, 1444–1446.

Stout, S. C., Kilts, C. D., & Nemeroff, C. B. (1995). Neuropeptides and stress: Preclinical findings and implications for pathophysiology. In M. J. Friedman, D. S. Charney, & A. Y. Deutch (Eds.), *Neurobiological and clinical consequences of stress: From normal adaptation to post-traumatic stress disorder*. Philadelphia, PA: Lippincott Williams & Wilkins.

Straube, E. R., & Oades, R. D. (1992). *Schizophrenia: Empirical research and findings*. San Diego, CA: Academic Press.

Streit, W. J., & Kincaid-Colton, C. A. (1995, November). The brain's immune system. *Scientific American*, 54–61.

Stricker, E. M. (1966). Extracellular fluid volume and thirst. *American Journal of Physiology, 211*(1), 232–238.

Strittmatter, W. J., & Roses, A. D. (1996). Apolipoprotein E and Alzheimer's disease. *Annual Review of Neuroscience, 19*, 53–77.

Strubbe, J. H., & Steffens, A. B. (1975). Rapid insulin release after ingestion of a meal in the unanesthetized rat. *American Journal of Physiology, 229*(4), 1019–1022.

Stuss, D. T., & Benson, D. F. (1984). Neuropsychological studies of the frontal lobes. *Psychological Bulletin, 95*(1), 3–28.

Suddath, R. L., Christison, G. W., Torrey, E. F., Casanova, M. F., & Weinberger, D. R. (1990). Anatomical abnormalities in the brains of monozygotic twins discordant for schizophrenia. *New England Journal of Medicine, 322*(12), 789–794.

Sugawara, J., Namura, I., & Hishikawa, Y. (1997). Alcoholism and cerebral damage: Findings by SPECT and MRI. *Nippon Rinsho (KIM), 55*, 406–415.

Sule, S., & Madugu, H. N. (2001). Pica in pregnant women in Zaria, Nigeria. *Nigerian Journal of Medicine, 10*, 25–27.

Sullivan, J. M. (2000). Cellular and molecular mechanisms underlying learning and memory impairments produced by cannabinoids. *Learning & Memory, 7*, 132–139.

Sullivan, L. S., Heckenlively, J. R., & Bowne, S. J. (1999). Mutations in a novel retina-specific gene cause autosomal dominant retinitis pigmentosa *Nature Genetics, 22*, 255–259.

Sullivan, M. A., & Rudnik-Levin, F. (2001). Attention deficit/hyperactivity disorder and substance abuse. Diagnostic and therapeutic considerations. *Annals of the New York Academy of Sciences, 931*, 251–270.

Sun, H., & Nathans, J. (2001). ABCR, the ATP-binding cassette transporter responsible for Stargardt macular dystrophy, is an efficient target of all-trans-retinal-mediated photooxidative damage in vitro. Implications for retinal disease. *Journal of Biological Chemistry, 276*, 11766–11774.

Suomalainen, A. (1997). Mitochondrial DNA and disease. *Ann Med (AMD), 29*(3), 235–246.

Susser, E. S., & Lin, S. P. (1992). Schizophrenia after prenatal exposure to the Dutch Hunger Winter of 1944–1945. *Archives of General Psychiatry, 49*, 983–988.

Susser, E., Neugebauer, R., Hoek, H. W., Brown, A. S., Lin, S., Labovitz, D., & Gorman, J. M. (1996). Schizophrenia after prenatal famine. Further evidence. *Arch Gen Psychiatry, 53*, 25–31.

Sutton, R. E., Koob, G. F., LeMoal, M., Rivier, J., & Vale, W. (1982). Corticotropin releasing factor produces behavioral activation in rats. *Nature, 297*(5864), 331–333.

Suvanand, S., Kapoor, S., Reddaiah, V., Singh, U., & Sundaram, K. (1997). Risk factors for cerebral palsy. *Indian Journal of Pediatrics, 64*(5), 677–685.

Swaab, D. F., & Hofman, M. A. (1990). An enlarged suprachiasmatic nucleus in homosexual men. *Brain Research, 537*, 141–148.

Swanson, L. W. (1987). The hypothalamus. In A. Bjorklund, T. Hokfelt, & L. W. Swanson (Eds.), *Handbook of chemical neuroanatomy: Vol. 5. Integrated systems of the CNS*. New York: Elsevier.

Swazey, J. P. (1969). *Reflexes and motor integration: Sherrington's concept of integrative action*. Cambridge, MA: Harvard University Press.

Swinburn, B., & Ravussin, E. (1993). Energy balance or fat balance? *American Journal of Clinical Nutrition, 57*(5), 766–770.

Swindells, S., McConnell, J., McComb, R., & Gendelman, H. (1995). Utility of cerebral proton magnetic resonance spectroscopy in differential diagnosis of HIV-related dementia. *Journal of Neurovirology, 1*(3–4), 268–274.

Szeszko, P. R., Strous, R. D., Goldman, R. S., Ashtari, M., Knuth, K. H., Lieberman, J. A., & Bilder, R. M. (2002). Neuropsychological correlates of hippocampal volumes in patients experiencing a first episode of schizophrenia. *American Journal of Psychiatry, 159,* 217–226.

Szuba, M. P., O'Reardon, J. P., & Evans, D. L. (2000). Physiological effects of electroconvulsive therapy and transcranial magnetic stimulation in major depression. *Depression and Anxiety, 12,* 170–177.

Takahashi, J. S. (1999). Narcolepsy genes wake up the sleep field. *Science, 285*(5436), 2076–2077.

Takami, S., Getchell, M. L., Chen, Y., Monti-Bloch, L., Berliner, D. L., Stensaas, L. J., & Getchell, T. V. (1993). Vomeronasal epithelial cells of the adult human express neuron-specific molecules. *Neuroreport, 4*(4), 375–378.

Talbot, J. D., Marrett, S., Evans, A. C., & Meyer, E. (1991). Multiple representations of pain in human cerebral cortex. *Science, 251*(4999), 1355–1358.

Tallon-Baudry, C., Bertrand, O., Delpuech, C., & Pernier, J. (1996).Stimulus specificity of phase-locked and non-phase-locked 40 Hz visual responses in human. *Journal of Neuroscience, 16,* 4240–4249.

Tamminga, C. A. (1996). Images in neuroscience: Neuroimaging, XI. *American Journal of Psychiatry, 153,* 973.

Tanaka, M., Kohno, Y., Nakawaga, R., Ida, Y., Takeda, S., Nagasaki, N., & Noda, Y. (1983). Regional characteristics of stress-induced increases in brain noradrenaline release in rats. *Pharmacology, Biochemistry, & Behavior, 19,* 543–547.

Tanda, G., Pontieri, F. E., Frau, R., & Di Chiara, G. (1997). Contribution of blockade of the noradrenaline carrier to the increase of extracellular dopamine in the rat prefrontal cortex by amphetamine and cocaine. *European Journal of Neuroscience, 9*(10), 2077–2085.

Taylor, D. P., Riblet, L. A., Stanton, H. C., Eison, A. S., Eison, M. S., & Temple, D.L. (1982). Dopamine and antianxiety activity. *Pharmacology & Biochemical Behavior, 17*(S1), 25–35.

Teas, D. C. (1989). Auditory physiology: Present trends. *Annual Review of Psychology, 40,* 405–429.

Teasdale, G., & Jennett, B. (1974). Assessment of coma and impaired consciousness: A practical scale. *Lancet, 2*(7872), 81–84.

Temple, D. L., Yevich, J. P., & New, J. S. (1982). Buspirone: Chemical profile of a new class of anxioselective agents. *Journal of Clinical Psychiatry, 43*(12), 4–9.

Terenius, L., & Wahlstrom, A. (1975). Search for an endogenous ligand for the opiate receptor. *Acta Physiol Scand, 94*(1), 74–81.

Tewari, S., & Noble, E. (1971). Ethanol and brain protein synthesis. *Brain Research, 26*(2), 469–474.

Thach, W. T. (1998). A role for the cerebellum in learning movement coordination. *Neurobiology: Learning & Memory, 70*(1–2), 177–188.

Thaker, G., Ross, D., Buchanan, R., Moran, M., Lahti, A., Kim, C., & Medoff, D. (1996). Does pursuit abnormality in schizophrenia represent a deficit in the predictive mechanism. *Psychiatry Research, 59*(3), 221–237.

Tharp, G. D. (1975). The role of glucocorticoids in exercise. *Medical Science Sports, 7,* 6–11.

Tharp, G. D., & Barnes, M. W. (1990). Reduction of saliva immunoglobulin levels by swim training. *Eur J Appl Physiol Occup Physiol, 60,* 61–64.

Thase, M. E., & Howland, R. H. (1995). Biological processes in depression: An updated review and integration. In E. E. Beckham & W. R. Leber (Eds.), *Handbook of depression* (2nd ed.). New York: Guilford Press.

Thompson, J. L., Manore, M. M., & Thomas, J. R. (1996). Effects of diet and diet-plus-exercise programs on resting metabolic rate: A meta-analysis. *International Journal of Sports Nutrition, 6*(1), 41–61.

Thompson, L. (1992). Fetal transplants show promise. *Science, 257,* 868–870.

Thompson, R. F. (1986). The neurobiology of learning and memory. *Science, 233*(4767), 941–947.

Thornhill, J., & Halvorson, I. (1994). Activation of shivering and non-shivering thermogenesis by electrical stimulation of the lateral and medial preoptic areas. *Brain Research, 656*(2), 367–374.

Thorpe, S. J., & Fabre-Thorpe, M. (2001). Seeking categories in the brain. *Science, 291,* 260–263.

Thut, G., Halsband, U., Roelcke, U., Nienhusmeier, M., Missimer, J., Maguire, R. P., Regard, M., Landis, T., & Leenders, K. L. (1997). Intermanual transfer of training: Blood flow correlates in the human brain. *Behavioral Brain Research, 89*(1–2), 129–134.

Tian, B., Reser, D., Durham, A., Kustov, A., & Rauschecker, J. P. (2001). Functional specialization in rhesus monkey auditory cortex. *Science, 292,* 290–293.

Tillerson, J. L., Cohen, A. D., Philhower, J., Miller, G. W., Zigmond, M. J., & Schallert, T. (2001). Forced limb-use effects on the behavioral and neurochemical effects of 6-hydroxydopamine. *Journal of Neuroscience, 21,* 4427–4435.

Tjian, R. (1995, February). Molecular machines that control genes. *Scientific American,* 55–61.

Tollefson, G. D. (1996). Selective serotonin reuptake inhibitors. In A. F. Schatzberg & C. B. Nemeroff (Eds.), *The American Psychiatric Press textbook of psychopharmacology.* Washington, DC: American Psychiatric Press.

Tononi, G., & Edelman, G. M. (1998). Consciousness and the integration of information in the brain. *Advanced Neurology, 77,* 245–279.

Travis, J. (1994). Glia: The brain's other cells. *Science, 266,* 970–972.

Trestman, R., Keefe, R., Mitropoulou, V., Harvey, P., deVegvar, M., Lees-Roitman, S., Davidson, M., Aronson, A., Silverman, J., & Siever, L. (1995). Cognitive function and biological correlates of cognitive performance in schizotypal personality disorder. *Psychiatry Research, 59*(1–2), 127–136.

Trottier, Y., & Mandel, J. L. (2001). Biomedicine. Huntingtin-profit and loss. *Science, 293,* 445–446.

Tso, P., Liu, M., & Kalogeris, T. J. (1999). The role of apolipoprotein A-IV in food intake regulation. *Journal of Nutrition, 129,* 1503–1506.

Tso, P., Liu, M., Kalogeris, T. J., & Thomson, A. B. (2001). The role of apolipoprotein A-IV in the regulation of food intake. *Annual Review of Nutrition, 21,* 231–254.

Tuiten, A., Van Honk, J., Koppeschaar, H., Bernaards, C., Thijssen, J., & Verbaten, R. (2000). Time course of effects of testosterone administration on sexual arousal in women. *Archives of General Psychiatry, 57*(2), 149–153.

Tulving, E. (1989). Knowing and remembering the past. *American Scientist, 77,* 361–367.

Tulving, E. (1992). Memory systems and the brain. *Clinical Neuropharmacology, 15*(1), 327–328.

Tuomanen, E. (1993, February). Breaching the blood–brain barrier. *Scientific American,* 80–84.

Turner, T. J., & Ortony, A. (1992). Basic emotions: Can conflicting criteria converge? *Psychological Review, 99*(3), 566–571.

Ullian, E. M., Sapperstein, S. K., Christopherson, K. S., & Barres, B. A. (2001). Control of synapse number by glia. *Science, 291,* 657–661.

Ulrich, J., Haugh, M., Anderton, B., Probst, A., Lautenschlager, C., & His, B. (1987). Alzheimer dementia and Pick's disease: Neurofibrillary tangles and Pick bodies are associated with identical phosphorylated neurofilament epitopes. *Acta Neuropathologica, 73,* 240–246.

Uncini, A., Lodi, R., DiMuzio, A., Silvestri, G., Servidei, S., Lugaresi, A., Iotti, S., Zaniol, P., & Barbiroli, B. (1995). Abnormal brain and muscle energy metabolism shown by 31P-MRS in familial hemiplegic migraine. *Journal of Neurological Science, 129*(2), 214–222.

Ungerstedt, U. (1973). Selective lesions of central catecholamine pathways: application in functional studies. *Neuroscience Research, 5,* 73–96.

Usher, M., Cohen, J. D., Servan-Schreiber, D., Rajkowski, J., & Aston-Jones, G. (1999). The role of locus coeruleus in the regulation of cognitive performance. *Science, 283*(5401), 549–554.

Valenstein, E. S. (1973). History of brain stimulation: Investigations into the physiology of motivation. In E. S. Valenstein (Ed.), *Brain stimulation and motivation.* Glenview, IL: Scott, Foresman.

Valenstein, E. S. (1986). *Great and desperate cures.* New York: Basic Books.

Valentino, R. J., & Aston-Jones, G. S. (1995). Physiological and anatomical determinants of locus coeruleus discharge. In F. E. Bloom & D. J. Kupfer (Eds.), *Psychopharmacology: The fourth generation of progress.* New York: Raven Press.

Valentino, R. J., Foote, S. L., & Aston-Jones, G. (1983). Corticotropin-releasing factor activates noradrenergic neurons of the locus coeruleus. *Brain Research, 270*(2), 363–367.

Valenza, N., Ptak, R., Zimine, I., Badan, M., Lazeyras, F., & Schnider, A. (2001). Dissociated active and passive tactile shape recognition: A case study of pure tactile apraxia. *Brain, 124*(Pt 11), 2287–2298.

Valzelli, L., Bernasconi, S., & Garattini, S. (1981). P-Chlorophenylalanine-induced muricidal aggression in male and female laboratory rats. *Neuropsychobiology, 7*(6), 315–320.

Van Bockstaele, E. J., Menko, A. S., & Drolet, G. (2001). Neuroadaptive responses in brainstem noradrenergic nuclei following chronic morphine exposure. *Molecular Neurobiology, 23,* 155–171.

Van Brockhoven, C., & Verheyen, G. (1999). Report of the chromosome 18 workshop. *American Journal of Medical Genetics, 88,* 263–270.

Van de Poll, N. E., Taminiau, M. S., Endert, E., & Louwerse, A. L. (1988). Gonadal steroid influence upon sexual and aggressive behavior of female rats. *International Journal of Neuroscience, 41*(3–4), 271–286.

Van de Poll, N. E., van Zanten, S., & de Jong, F. H. (1986). Effects of testosterone, estrogen, and dihydrotestosterone upon aggressive and sexual behavior of female rats. *Hormonal Behavior, 20*(4), 418–431.

Vanderhorst, V. G., Terasawa, E., Ralston, H. J., & Holstege, G. (2000). Monosynaptic projections from the lateral periaqueductal gray to the nucleus retroambiguous in the rhesus monkey: Implications for vocalization and reproductive behavior. *Journal of Comparative Neurology, 424,* 251–268.

VanderWeele, D. A. (1998). Insulin as a satiating signal. In G. P. Smith (Ed.), *Satiation: From gut to brain.* New York: Oxford University Press.

VanderWeele, D. A., & Novin, D. (1981). On hepatic involvement in the short-term regulation of food ingestion. *Appetite, 2*(2), 153–156.

Van Essen, D. C., Anderson, C. H., & Felleman, D. J. (1992). Information processing in the primate visual system: An integrated systems perspective. *Science, 255*(5043), 419–423.

Van Furth, W. R., van Emst, M. G., & van Ree, J. M. (1995). Opioids and sexual behavior of male rats: Involvement of the medial preoptic area. *Behavioral Neuroscience, 109*(1), 123–134.

Van Furth, W., Wolterink, G., & van Ree, J. M. (1995). Regulation of masculine sexual behavior: Involvement of brain opioids and dopamine. *Brain Research Reviews, 21,* 162–184.

Van Stegeren, A. H., Everaerd, W., Cahill, L., McGaugh, J. L., & Gooren, L. J. (1998). Memory for emotional events: Differential effects of centrally versus peripherally acting beta-blocking agents. *Psychopharmacology, 138*(3–4), 305–310.

Verheul, R., van den Brink, W., & Geerlings, P. (1999). A three-pathway psychobiological model of craving for alcohol. *Alcohol and Alcoholism, 34,* 197–222.

Verney, E. B. (1947). The antidiuretic hormone and the factors that determine its release. *Proceedings of the Royal Society, B135,* 25–106.

Viguera, A. C., & Rothschild, A. J. (1996). Depression: Clinical features and pathogenesis. In K. I. Shulman & M. Tohen (Eds.), *Mood disorders across the life span.* New York: Wiley-Liss.

Villalba, R., & Harrington, C. J. (2000). Repetitive self-injurious behavior: A neuropsychiatric perspective and review of pharmacologic treatments. *Seminars in Clinical Neuropsychiatry, 5,* 215–226.

Vining, E., Freeman, J., Pillas, D., Uematsu, S., Carson, B., Brandt, J., Boatman, D., Pulsifer, M., & Zuckerberg, A. (1997). Why would you remove half a brain? The outcome of 58 children after hemispherectomy—The Johns Hopkins experience: 1968–1996. *Pediatrics, 100*(2), 163–171.

Volkow, N. D., Brodie, J. D., Wolf, A. P., Gomez-Mont, F., Cancro, R., Van Gelder, P., Russell, J. A., & Overall, J. (1986). Brain organization in schizophrenia. *Journal of Cerebral Blood Flow Metabolism, 6*(4), 441–446.

Volkow, N. D., Fowler, J. S., & Wang, G. J. (1999). Imaging studies on the role of dopamine in cocaine reinforcement and addiction in humans. *Journal of Psychopharmacology, 13*(4), 337–345.

Volkow, N. D., Fowler, J. S., Wang, G. J., Hitzemann, R., Logan, J., Schlyer, D. J., Dewey, S. L., & Wolf, A. P. (1993). Decreased dopamine D_2 receptor availability is associated with reduced frontal metabolism in cocaine abusers. *Synapse, 14,* 169–177.

Volkow, N. D., Wang, G. J., Fowler, J. S., Logan, J., Gatley, S. J., Gifford, A., Hitzemann, R., Ding, Y. S., & Pappas, N. (1999). Prediction of reinforcing responses to psychostimulants in humans by brain dopamine D_2 receptor levels. *American Journal of Psychiatry, 156*(9), 1440–1443.

Wagner, J. J., & Chavkin, C. I. (1995). Neuropharmacology of endogenous opioid peptides. In F. E. Bloom & D. J. Kupfer (Eds.), *Psychopharmacology: The fourth generation of progress.* New York: Raven Press.

Wahlestedt, C. (1998). Reward for persistence in substance P research. *Science, 281,* 1624–1625.

Walker, E. F., & Diforio, D. (1997). Schizophrenia: A neural diathesis-stress model. *Psychology Review, 104*(4), 667–685.

Walker, E. F., Savoie, T., & Davis, D. (1994). Neuromotor precursors of schizophrenia. *Schizophrenia Bulletin, 20*(3), 441–451.

Walker, E. F., Walder, D. J., & Reynolds, F. (2001). Developmental changes in cortisol secretion in normal and at-risk youth. *Development & Psychopathology, 13,* 721–732.

Walsh, B. T., & Devlin, M. J. (1995). Pharmacotherapy of bulimia nervosa and binge eating disorder. *Addictive Behaviors, 20*(6), 757–764.

Walters, D. E., DuBois, G. E., & Kellogg, M. S. (1993). Design of sweet and bitter tastants. In S. A. Simon & S. D. Roper (Eds.), *Mechanisms of taste transduction.* Boca Raton, FL: CRC Press.

Wang, J., Akabayashi, A., Yu, H. J., Dourmashkin, J., Alexander, J. T., Silva, I., Lighter, L., & Liebowitz, S. F. (1998). Hypothalamic galanin: Control by signals of fat metabolism. *Brain Research, 804*(1), 7–20.

Wang, X., Cen, X., & Lu, L. (2001). Noradrenaline in the bed nucleus of the stria terminalis is critical for stress-induced reactivation of morphine-conditioned place preference in rats. *Eur J Pharmacology, 432,* 153–161.

Wardle, J. (1990). Overeating: A regulatory behaviour in restrained eaters. *Appetite, 14*(2), 133–136.

Warrington, E. K., & Shallice, T. (1969). The selective impairment of auditory verbal short-term memory. *Brain, 92*(4), 885–896.

Warshaw, D. M., McBride, W. J., & Work, S. S. (1987). Corkscrew-like shortening in single smooth muscle cells. *Science, 236,* 1457–1459.

Waterhouse, L., Fein, D., & Modahl, C. (1996). Neurofunctional mechanisms in autism. *Psychological Review, 103*(3), 457–489.

Watkins, L. R., & Mayer, D. J. (1982). Organization of endogenous opiate and nonopiate pain control systems. *Science, 216*(4551), 1185–1192.

Weekes, N. Y. (1994). Sex differences in the brain. In D. W. Zaidel (Ed.), *Neuropsychology.* San Diego, CA: Academic Press.

Wei, L.-N., & Loh, H. H. (1997). Molecular biology of opioid receptors and associated proteins. In K. Blum & E. P. Noble (Eds.), *Handbook of psychiatric genetics.* Boca Raton, FL: CRC Press.

Weinberger, D. R. (1987). Implications of normal brain development for the pathogenesis of schizophrenia. *Archives of General Psychiatry, 44*(7), 660–669.

Weinberger, D. R., Berman, K. F., & Zec, R. F. (1986). Physiologic dysfunction of dorsolateral prefrontal cortex in schizophrenia. I. Regional cerebral blood flow evidence. *Archives of General Psychiatry, 43*(2), 114–124.

Weiner, W. J., & Lang, A. E. (1995). *Behavioral neurology of movement disorders.* New York: Raven Press.

Weisenfeld-Hallin, Z., Aldskogius, H., Grant, G., Hao, J.-X., Hokfelt, T., & Xu, X.-J. (1997). Central inhibitory dysfunctions: Mechanisms and clinical implications. *Behavioral and Brain Sciences, 20,* 420–425.

Weiskrantz, L., Cowey, A., & Hodinott-Hill, I. (2002). Prime-sight in a blindsight subject. *Nature Neuroscience, 5,* 101–102.

Welch, I., Saunders, K., & Read, N. W. (1985). Effect of ileal and intravenous infusions of fat emulsions on feeding and satiety in human volunteers. *Gastroenterology, 89*(6), 1293–1297.

Welch, W. J., & Gambetti, P. (1998). Chaperoning brain diseases. *Nature, 392*(6671), 23–24.

Wendel, G. D. (1988). Gestational and congenital syphilis. *Clinical Perinatology, 15*(2), 287–303.

Wever, E. G. (1970). *Theory of hearing.* New York: Wiley.

Wheless, J. W., Willmore, L. J., Breier, J. I., Kataki, Mi, Smith, J. R., King, D. W., Meador, K. J., Park, Y. D., Loring, D. W., Clifton, G. L, Baumgartner, J., Thomas, A. B., Constantinou, J. E., & Papanicolaou, A. C. (1999). A comparison of magnetoencephalography, MRI, and -EEG in patients evaluated for epilepsy surgery. *Epilepsia, 40,* 931–941.

Whitaker, H. A., & Kahn, H. J. (1994). Brain and language. In D. W. Zaidel (Ed.), *Neuropsychology.* San Diego, CA: Academic Press.

White, P. C. (2001). Congenital adrenal hyperplasias. *Best Practice and Research in Clinical Endocrinology, 15,* 17–41.

Whitehouse, P. J., Price, D. L., Struble, R. G., Clark, A. W., Coyle, J. T., & Delong, M. R. (1982). Alzheimer's disease and senile dementia: Loss of neurons in the basal forebrain. *Science, 215,* 1237–1239.

Wickelgren, I. (1996). For the cortex, neuron loss may be less than thought. *Science, 273*(5271), 48–50.

Wickelgren, I. (1997). Getting the brain's attention. *Science, 278*(5335), 35–37.

Wickelgren, I. (1998a). Teaching the brain to take drugs. *Science, 280*(5372), 2045–2046.

Wickelgren, I. (1998b). The cerebellum: The brain's engine of agility. *Science, 281*(5383), 1588–1590.

Wilcox, R. E., & Gonzales, R. A. (1995). Introduction to neurotransmitters, receptors, signal transduction, and second messengers. In A. F. Schatzberg & C. B. Nemeroff (Eds.), *The American Psychiatric Press textbook of psychopharmacology.* Washington, DC: American Psychiatric Press.

Wilson, F. A., O'Scalaidhe, S. P., & Goldman-Rakic, P. S. (1993). Dissociation of object and spatial processing domains in primate prefrontal cortex. *Science, 260,* 1955–1958.

Wilson, F. A., O'Scalaidhe, S. P., & Goldman-Rakic, P. S. (1994). Functional synergism between putative gamma-aminobutyrate-containing neurons and pyramidal neurons in prefrontal cortex. *Proc Natl Acad Sci USA, 91*(9), 4009–4013.

Wilson, F. A., & Rolls, E. T. (1990). Learning and memory is reflected in the responses of reinforcement-related neurons in the primate basal forebrain. *Journal of Neuroscience, 10*(4), 1254–1267.

Wilson, G. T., & Fairburn, C. G. (1993). Cognitive treatments for eating disorders. *Journal of Consult Clinical Psychology, 61*(2), 261–269.

Wilson, G. T., & Fairburn, C. G. (1999). Treatments for eating disorders. In P. E. Nathan & J. M. Gorman (Eds.), *A guide to treatments that work.* New York: Oxford University Press.

Wilson, J. F. (1991). Teaching physiological psychology versus teaching biological psychology: Is there a difference? *Teaching of Psychology, 18,* 43–45.

Wilson, J. F., & Cantor, M. B. (1986). Noise-induced eating in rats facilitated by prior tail pinch experience. *Physiology and Behavior, 37,* 523–526.

Wilson, J. F., & Cantor, M. B. (1987). An animal model of excessive eating: Schedule-induced hyperphagia in food-satiated rats. *Journal of the Experimental Analysis of Behavior, 47*(3), 335–346.

Wilson, R. I., & Nicoll, R. A. (2001). Endogenous cannabinoids mediate retrograde signalling at hippocampal synapses. *Nature, 410,* 588–592.

Wilson, V. J., Boyle, R., Fukushima, K., Rose, P. K., Shinoda, Y., Sugiuchi, Y., & Uchino, Y. (1995). The vestibulocollic reflex. *Journal of Vestibular Research, 5*(3), 147–170.

Winchel, R. M., & Stanley, M. (1991). Self-injurious behavior: A review of the behavior and biology of self-mutilation. *American Journal of Psychiatry, 148*(3), 306–317.

Winn, P. (1995). The lateral hypothalamus and motivated behavior: An old syndrome reassessed and a new perspective gained. *Current Directions in Psychological Science, 4*(6), 182–187.

Winn, P., Tarbuck, A., & Dunnett, S. B. (1984). Ibotenic acid lesions of the lateral hypothalamus: Comparison with the electrolytic lesion syndrome. *Neuroscience, 12*(1), 225–240.

Wirz-Justice, A. (1995). Biological rhythms in mood disorders. In F. E. Bloom & D. J. Kupfer (Eds.), *Psychopharmacology: The fourth generation.* New York: Raven Press.

Wise, R. A., & Rompre, P. P. (1989). Brain dopamine and reward. *Annual Review of Psychology, 40,* 191–225.

Wong, K. L., Bruch, R. C., & Farbman, A. I. (1991). Amitriptyline-mediated inhibition of neurite outgrowth from chick embryonic cerebral explants involves a reduction in adenylate cyclase activity. *Journal of Neurochemistry, 57*(4), 1223–1230.

Woodruff-Pak, D. S. (1997). *The neuropsychology of aging.* Malden, MA: Blackwell Publishers.

Woodruff-Pak, D. S. (1999). Theories of neuropsychology and aging. In V. L. Bengtson & K. W. Schaie (Eds.), *Handbook of theories of aging.* New York: Springer.

Woodward, E. (1970). Clinical experience with fenfluramine in the United States. In E. Costa & S. Garattini (Eds.), *Amphetamines and related compounds.* New York: Raven.

Woodward, S., & Freedman, R. R. (1994). The thermoregulatory effects of menopausal hot flashes on sleep. *Sleep, 17*(6), 497–501.

Wu, J. C., & Bunney, W. E. (1990). The biological basis of an antidepressant response to sleep deprivation and relapse: Review and hypothesis.

American Journal of Psychiatry, 147(1), 14–21.

Wysocki, C. J., & Meredith, M. (1987). *The vomeronasal system.* New York: Wiley.

Yakovlev, P. I. (1948). Motility, behavior, and the brain: Stereodynamic organization and neural coordinates in behavior. *Journal of Nervous and Mental Disease, 107,* 313–335.

Yasuno, F., Nishikawa, T., Tokunaga, H., Yoshiyama, K., Nakagawa, Y., Ikejiri, Y., Oku, N., Hashikawa, K., Tanabe, H., Shinozaki, K., Sugita, Y., Nishimura, T., & Takeda, M. (2000). The neural basis of perceptual and conceptual word priming—A PET study. *Cortex, 36*(1), 59–69.

Yehuda, R. (1997). Sensitization of the hypothalamic-pituitary-adrenal axis in posttraumatic stress disorder. *Annals of the New York Academy of Sciences, 821,* 57–75.

Yin, T. H., & Tsai, C.T. (1973). Effects of glucose on feeding in relation to routes of entry in rats. *Journal of Comparative & Physiological Psychology, 85*(2), 258–264.

Yoshihara, Y., Nagao, H., & Mori, K. (2001). Neurobiology. Sniffing out odors with multiple dendrites. *Science, 291,* 835–837.

Young, S. N. (1996). Behavioral effects of dietary neurotransmitter precursors: Basic and clinical aspects. *Neuroscience and Biobehavioral Reviews, 20,* 313–323.

Young, W. G., & Deutsch, J. A. (1981). The construction, surgical implantation, and use of gastric catheters and a pyloric cuff. *Journal of Neuroscientific Methods, 3*(4), 377–384.

Yousem, D. M., Maldjian, J. A., Siddiqi, F., Hummel, T., Alsop, D. C., Geckle, R. J., Bilker, W. B., & Doty, R. L. (1999). Gender effects on odor-stimulated functional magnetic resonance imaging. *Brain Research, 818,* 480–487.

Yurek, D. M., & Fletcher-Turner, A. (2001). Differential expression of GDNF, BDNF, and NT-3 in the aging nigrostriatal system following a neurotoxic lesion. *Brain Research, 891,* 228–235.

Yuste, R., Peinado, A., & Katz, L. C. (1992). Neuronal domains in developing neocortex. *Science, 257,* 665.

Zajonc, R. B., Murphy, S. T., & Inglehart, M. (1989). Feeling and facial efference: Implications of the theory of emotion. *Psychology Review, 96*(3), 395–416.

Zalla, T., Koeschlin, E., Pietrini, P., Basso, G., Aquino, P., & Sirigu, A. (2000). Differential amygdala responses to winning and losing: A functional magnetic resonance imaging study in humans. *European Journal of Neuroscience, 12*(5), 1764–1770.

Zatorre, R. J., Evans, A. C., Meyer, E., & Gjedde, A. (1992). Lateralization of phonetic and pitch discrimination in speech processing. *Science, 256*(5058), 846–849.

Zeigler, H. P. (1994). Brainstem orosensorimotor mechanisms and the neural control of ingestive behavior. In C. R. Legg & D. A. Booth (Eds.) *Appetite: Neural and behavioural bases.* New York: Oxford University Press.

Zeki, S. (1992). The visual image in mind and brain. *Scientific American, 267*(3), 68–76.

Zeki, S., & Marini, L. (1998). Three cortical stages of colour processing in the human brain. *Brain, 121*(9), 1669–1685.

Zhang, Y. H., Yanase-Fujiwara, M., Hosono, T., & Kanosue, K. (1995). Warm and cold signals from the preoptic area: Which contribute more to the control of shivering in rats? *Journal of Physiology, 485*(1), 195–202.

Zigmond, M. J., Finlay, J. M., & Sved, A. F. (1995). Neurochemical studies of central noradrenergic responses to acute and chronic stress: Implications for normal and abnormal behavior. In M. J. Friedman, D. S. Charney, & A. Y. Deutch (Eds.), *Neurobiological and clinical consequences of stress: From normal adaptation to post-traumatic stress disorder.* Philadelphia, PA: Lippincott Williams & Wilkins.

Zironi, I., Iacovelli, P., Aicardi, G., Liu, P., & Bilkey, D. K. (2001). Prefrontal cortex lesions augment the location-related firing properties of area TE/perirhinal cortex neurons in a working memory task. *Cerebral Cortex, 11,* 1093–1100.

Zola-Morgan, S. (1995). Localization of brain function: The legacy of Franz Joseph Gall. *Annual Review of Neuroscience, 18,* 359–383.

Zola-Morgan, S., & Squire, L. R. (1990). The primate hippocampal formation: Evidence for a time-limited role in memory storage. *Science, 250*(4978), 288–290.

Zola-Morgan, S., Squire, L. R., & Amaral, D. G. (1986). Human amnesia and the medical temporal region: Enduring memory impairment following a bilateral lesion limited to field CA1 of the hippocampus. *Journal of Neuroscience, 6*(10), 2950–2967.

Zuckerman, M. (1995). Good and bad humors: Biochemical bases of personality and its disorders. *Psychological Science, 6*(6), 325–332.

Zwanzger, P., Baghai, T. C., Schuele, C., Strohle, A., Padberg, F., Kathmann, N., Schwarz, M., Moller, H. J., & Rupprecht, R. (2001). Vigabatrin decreases cholecystokinin-tetrapeptide (CCK-4) induced panic in healthy volunteers. *Neuropsychopharmacology, 25,* 699–703.

Credits

This page constitutes an extension of the copyright page. We have made every effort to trace the ownership of all copyrighted material and to secure permission from copyright holders. In the event of any question arising as to the use of any material, we will be pleased to make the necessary corrections in future printings. Thanks are due to the following authors, publishers, and agents for permission to use the material indicated.

Chapter 1: 7: Fig. 1.3 from Fig. 1 from "History of Neuropsychology," by S. Finger. In D. W. Zaidel (Ed.) *Neuropsychology*, p. 5. Copyright 1994 Academic Press. Reprinted by permission. **8:** Fig. 1.6 from "Ferrier's Findings on the Monkey Brain," by J. D. Spillane. In *The Doctrine of the Nerves*, Fig. 161, p. 390. Copyright © John D. Spillane 1981. Used by permission of Oxford University Press. **10:** Fig. 1.9 from *Brain Mechanisms and Intelligence*, by K. S. Lashley, 1929. Copyright © 1929 The University of Chicago Press. Reprinted by permission.

Chapter 2: 34: Fig. 2.10 from "Neuroglica Cells" from Legado Cajal. Copyright 1933 Instituto Cajal. Reprinted by permission.

Chapter 5: 122: Fig. 5.3 from *Stereotaxic and Radiosurgery*, Lars Leksell, 1991. Courtesy of Charles C Thomas, Publisher, Ltd., Springfield, Illinois.

Chapter 8: 225: Fig. 8.7 from "The Rey-Osterreich Complex Figure," by McCloskey et al., 1995, *Psychological Science*, 6, Fig. 1, p. 113. Copyright © 1995 American Psychological Society. Reprinted by permission. **241:** Fig. 8.14 reprinted with permission from "Reorganization of the Primary Somatosensory Cortex Following Amputation of an Arm," by M. Merzenich, 1998, *Science*, 282, p. 1063. Illus. K. Sutliff. Copyright © 1998 American Association for the Advancement of Science.

Chapter 9: 250: Fig. 9.1 figure first published in "(This is not a) Genius Test," *Esquire*, 132, 1999, pp. 150–153. Reprinted courtesy of Esquire and the Hearst Corporation. 257: Fig. 9.6 reprinted with permission from "Phases of Memory Consolidation," by J. L. McGaugh, 2000, *Science*, 287, p. 249. Copyright © 2000 American Association for the Advancement of Science. **268:** Fig. 9.15 from Fisch and Spehlmann, *EEG Primer*, Third Edition. 272: Fig. 9.17 from "Biological Basis Learning and Individuality," by Kandel and Hawkins, 1992, *Scientific American*, 9, pp. 81 and

83. Figure © Ian Worpole. Reprinted with permission. **273:** Fig. 9.19 from "The Biological Basis of Learning and Individuality," by Kandel and Hawkins, *Scientific American*, 9, 1992. Copyright © Patricia Wynne. Used with permission.

Chapter 10: 294: Fig. 10.10 reprinted with permission from "Spike Activity in the Raphe Associated with Various States of Consciousness," by Jacobs, 1994, *American Scientist*, 82, p. 460. Copyright © 1994 American Scientist/Linda Hoff.

Chapter 11: 333: Table 11.5 reprinted with permission of MetLife. This information is not intended to be a substitute for professional medical advice and should not be regarded as an endorsement or approval of any product or service.

Chapter 16: 495: Fig. 16.14 reprinted with permission from "Intrinsic Repair Potential of the Brain," by Lowenstein and Parent, 1999, *Science*, 283, p. 1127. Copyright © 1999 American Association for the Advancement of Science. **496:** Fig. 16.15 from "The Nerve Growth Factor 35 Years Later," by Levi-Montalcini, 1987, *Science*, 237, p. 1154. Copyright © 1986 The Nobel Foundation. Used with permission of The Nobel Foundation.

Photo Credits

Chapter 1: CO-1: © H. Morgan / Science Source/Photo Researchers, Inc.; **Figure 1.1:** © Kevin and Betty Collins/Visuals Unlimited; **Figure 1.4:** © Musee de l'Homme; **Figure 1.10:** © Wellcome Dept. of Cognitive Neurology/Science Photo Library/ Science Source/Photo Researchers, Inc.; **Figure 1.12 (left):** Courtesy of the Foundation for Biomedical Research; **Figure 1.12 (right):** © Science Source/Photo Researchers, Inc.

Chapter 2: CO-2: © Oliver Meckes/Ottawa/Science Source/Photo Researchers, Inc.; **Figure 2.4 (top):** © Lester V. Bergman/CORBIS; Figure 2.4 (bottom): © Valeric Lindgren/Visuals Unlimited; **Figure 2.14:** © PACHA/CORBIS; **Figure 2.17:** © 1999 Roseman/Custom Medical Stock Photo, Inc.; **Figure 2.19:** © Eye of Science/Photo Researchers, Inc.

Chapter 3: CO-3: © Ghislain & Marie David de Lossy/Image Bank/Getty Images.

Chapter 4: CO-4: © Simon Fraser/ Royal Victoria Infirmary, Newcastle Upon Tyne/SPL/Photo Researchers, Inc.; **Figure 4.4:** Courtesy of Dr. Cathy Pederson; **Figure 4.13:** © SIU/Visuals

Unlimited, Inc.; **Figure 4.20:** © Wally McNamee/CORBIS.

Chapter 5: CO-5: © Roger Ressmeyer/ CORBIS; **p. 123 (left):** © CC Studio/ Science Photo Library/Photo Researchers, Inc.; **p. 123 (right):** © James King-Holmes/Science Photo Library/Photo Researchers, Inc.; **Figure 5.5:** Courtesy of Josephine Wilson; **Figure 5.6:** Courtesy of Josephine Wilson; **Figure 5.7:** © 1990 Science Photo Library/Custom Medical Stock Photo, Inc.; **Figure 5.8:** © Burt Glinn/Magnum; **Figure 5.9:** James King-Holmes/Photo Researchers, Inc.; **Figure 5.10:** Reprinted with permission from "Brain Imaging: Applications in Psychiatry" by Nancy C. Andreasen, *Science*, Vol. 239, p.1384. Copyright 1988, American Association for the Advancement of Science; **Figure 5.11:** *Scientific American*, 4/94 p. 62. Reprinted with permission of Professor Marcus Raichle, Washington University, St. Louis; **Figure 5.12:** © UMRD/ Visuals Unlimited; **Figure 5.13:** Reprinted by permission from *Nature*, vol.379, 1996 Macmillan Magazines Ltd.; **Figure 5.14:** *Le Journal Canadien des Sciences Neurologiques*, vol 23, no. 3, 8/96; **Figure 5.16 (top):** APF/ Corbis ID# FT0072007; **Figure 5.16 (bottom):** © Eastcott/Momatiuk/Photo Researchers, Inc.

Chapter 6: CO-6: © Robbie Jack/CORBIS; **Figure 6.1 (left & right):** © Ray Ellis/PhotoResearchers, Inc.; **Figure 6.8:** © Will and Deni McIntyre/PhotoResearchers, Inc.; **Figure 6.15:** Courtesy of Robert E. Schmidt, Washington University; **Figure 6.16 (top)** © AFP/ CORBIS; **Figure 6.16 (left):** © AP/Wide World Photos; **Figure 6.16 (right):** © Reuters New-Media Inc./CORBIS.

Chapter 7: CO-7: ©Scott T. Baxter/ PhotoDisc/Getty Images; **Figure 7.1:** © CORBIS; **Figure 7.8:** © Stanford Eye Clinic/Photo Researchers, Inc.; **Figure 7.21:** Courtesy, Jacob Steiner.

Chapter 8: CO-8: © H. Mark Weidman; **Figure 8.6:** McCloskey et al, *Psychological Science*, vol 6., no. 2, March 1995; **Figure 8.09:** © Copyright 1998 National Academy of Sciences, U.S.A.; **Figure 8.10:** Reprinted by permission from *Nature*, vol.283, 1996 Macmillan Magazines Ltd.; **Figure 8.15:** Reprinted from D.M. Yousem et al., *Brain Research* 818 (1999) 480–487. with permission from Elsevier Science; **Figure 8.17:** Courtesy, Jacob Steiner.

Name Index

Folstein, S. E., 160
Foote, S. L., 77, 419
Ford, M., 197
Fornal, C. A., 76, 155
Forno, L. S., 501, 502
Forsman, A., 472
Forster, R. E., 314
Foulkes, D., 300
Fowler, J. S., 18, 398, 401, 402
Fox, M. J., 165, 166
Fox, P. T., 227, 231, 266
Frackowiak, R. S., 239
Freed, W. J., 495
Freedman, D. J., 219
Freedman, R. R., 316
Freud, S., 299
Frias, D., 429
Fridman, J., 504
Friedland, R. P., 503, 504
Friedman, D., 271
Friedman, M. I., 311, 331
Friedman-Hill, S. R., 220
Friston, K., 239
Frith, U., 269
Fritsch, G., 8
Fritz, J., 225
Frohlich, J., 363, 372
Frokiaer, J., 342
Fuhr, P., 504
Fujimoto, H., 488
Fukushima, K., 206
Fukushima, T., 257
Fulton, M., 464
Fulton, S., 323, 331
Furchgott, R. F., 80
Furey, M. L., 259
Fuster, J. M., 256

G
Gabrieli, J. D., 241, 259
Gage, F., 494
Gage, P., 282, 506
Gajewski, A., 258
Galaburda, A. M., 231, 357
Gale, C. C., 311
Galea, L. A., 359
Galen, 6
Gall, F., 7
Gallaher, T. K., 76
Galler, J. R., 483
Gallo, V., 38
Gallup, G. G., 280
Gambetti, P., 501
Garfinkel, P., 416
Garfinkel, P. E., 337
Garthwaite, J., 79
Gazzaniga, M. S., 104, 286
Geary, N., 331
Gebrewold, A., 491
Geerlings, P., 402
Geisler, C. D., 189
Geldmacher, D. S., 500, 501, 502
Gellad, F., 453
George, M. S., 125, 467
George, S. R., 77, 78
Gerra, G., 390
Gershon, E. S., 445
Gerstein, G. L., 98
Geschwind, N., 231, 357
Gessa, G. L., 463, 464
Gevins, A. S., 126
Ghaemi, S. N., 468
Ghika-Schmid, F., 388
Gianotti, G., 385
Gibb, A. J., 70
Gibb, R., 493, 496
Gibbs, A. C., 359

Gibbs, J., 330
Gill, T. J., 16
Gillberg, C., 270
Gingras, J. R., 316
Gitlin, M. J., 473
Giza, B. K., 242
Gladman, D., 416
Glatzel, M., 488
Glavin, G. B., 414
Glennon, R. A., 76
Gloor, P., 389, 450
Glover, G. H., 241
Gold, A. R., 363, 364
Gold, J., 455
Gold, L. H., 137
Gold, P., 410, 416
Gold, P. E., 258, 428, 430
Gold, P. W., 268, 318
Goldberg, E., 10
Goldberg, H. L., 395
Goldberg, M. E., 235
Goldberg, T. E., 455
Goldman, D., 472
Goldman, P. S., 456
Goldman-Rakic, P. S., 13, 14, 225, 252, 253, 254, 356
Goldsmith, H. H., 471
Goldstein, G. W., 37
Goldstein, K., 385
Golgi, C., 27
Golombek, D. A., 295, 296
Gonzalez, R. A., 63, 65
Gonzalez-Heydrich, J., 464
Goodale, M. A., 216, 220
Goode, R. L., 241
Goodglass, H., 226
Goodman, R., 75
Goodwin, F. K., 468
Gordon, N., 229, 269
Gorman, J. M., 455
Gorski, R. A., 357
Gosnell, B. A., 323
Gottesman, J. I., 460
Gottesmann, C., 300
Gottfries, C. G., 445
Gould, E., 33
Grace, G. M., 219
Graeberg, M. B., 35
Graf, W. D., 29
Grasby, P., 129
Gray, C. M., 221, 288
Gray, J. A., 398
Graziano, M. S., 235
Graziottin, A., 366
Green, L., 372
Greenamyre, T., 166
Greenberg, D., 329
Greene, R., 451
Greenhouse, J. B., 18
Gregg, T. R., 390
Grether, J. K., 483, 486
Griffin, D. R., 280
Grigoriadis, D. E., 417, 418, 435, 436
Groethuysen, U. C., 430
Gron, G., 359
Gross, S. S., 79
Grossman, M., 230
Grossman, S. P., 320
Grozdanovic, Z., 396
Gruber, R. P., 258
Grunbaum, A. S., 157
Guan, H., 448
Guerri, C., 482, 483
Guilleminault, C., 301
Gulyas, B., 297
Gunnar, M. R., 411

Guo, S. W., 203
Gur, R. C., 10, 359
Gur, R. E., 10, 359, 446
Gurevich, E., 448, 449
Gurvits, T. V., 425
Guyenet, P. G., 38
Guyot, L. L., 485

H
Hackett, T. A., 225
Hadders-Algra, M., 164
Hagger, C., 15
Hahn, J. S., 484
Hainsworth, F. R., 312
Hajek, T., 425
Halbreich, U., 365
Halgren, E., 388, 389, 450
Hall, M., 422
Hall, R. D., 397
Halmi, K. A., 330, 338
Halvorson, I., 313
Hamada, H., 485
Hamann, S. B., 258
Hamer, D. H., 358
Hamilton, S., 340
Hammond, C., 33, 34, 36, 104
Hanna, M. G., 29
Hansen, K., 294
Hanus, L., 78
Harber, V., 316
Hari, R., 128
Harper, A. E., 340
Harrington, C. J., 473
Harris, J. P., 207
Harris, R. A., 73
Harris, R. M., 162
Harrison, P. J., 74
Harro, J., 91
Harvey, R., 483
Hasegawa, I., 257
Hasselmo, M. E., 258
Hauser, M., 225, 226
Hawelu-Johnson, C. L., 38
Hawkins, R. D., 271, 272, 273, 274
Hawranko, A. A., 74
Haxby, J. V., 129, 219, 254, 259
Hayes, R. L., 297
Healy, D., 82
Hebb, D. O., 252, 273
Heinrichs, R. W., 447, 461
Heller, W., 385, 386
Helmholtz, H. von, 184, 191
Helmreich, D. L., 410
Heninger, G. R., 76
Henneman, E., 148
Henry, B., 167
Hensch, S. A., 258
Hensler, J. G., 76
Herholz, K., 504
Hering, E., 185
Herkenham, M., 452
Herman, B. H., 270
Herman, C. P., 336
Herman, J. P., 410
Hernandez, L., 132
Hernandez, M. T., 256
Hernandez-Tristan, R., 356
Herscovitch, P., 455
Hertsgaard, L., 411
Hertz, H., 175
Hetherington, A. W., 327
Heyser, C. J., 137
Hier, D. B., 357
Higgs, S., 323, 327
Hillis, A. E., 227, 266
Hines, M., 355

Hiort, O., 352
Hippocrates, 5, 462
Hirata, Y., 233
Hirsch, E., 337
Hiscock, M., 357
Hishikawa, Y., 33
Hitch, G. J., 252
Hitzig, E., 8
Hobson, J. A., 297
Hock, R., 313
Hodges, H., 494
Hodgkin, A. L., 44
Hodinott-Hill, I., 221
Hoebel, B., 132
Hoek, H. W., 455
Hoffman, E. A., 219
Hoffman, J. A., 299
Hofman, M. A., 358
Hofmann, S., 29
Hohmann, C. F., 482
Hoke, M., 233
Hokfelt, T., 464
Hokfelt, T. G. M., 74
Holcomb, H. H., 259
Hold, B., 197
Holden, R. J., 471
Holder, M. D., 74
Hollister, J. M., 455
Holloway, R. L., 357
Holsboer, F., 65
Holstege, G., 133
Holterhus, P. M., 352
Horenstein, S., 385
Horgan, J., 304
Horger, B. A., 425, 427, 430
Horn, G., 265
Horton, J. C., 218
Horvitz, J. C., 269
Hoschl, C., 425
Houpt, K. A., 329
Howland, R. H., 462, 466, 468
Howlett, A. C., 78
Hsieh, J. C., 239
Hu, N., 358
Hu, S., 358
Huang, Y., 130
Huang Ti, 4
Hua T'o, 4
Hubel, D. H., 216, 218, 219
Hudson, A. J., 219
Huggins, G. R., 197
Hughes, A., 75
Hull, E. M., 368, 369, 372
Hulshoff, H. E., 455
Hunter, A., 36
Hutton, S. B., 458
Huxley, A. F., 44
Hwang, I. P., 186

I
Ignarro, L. J., 79
Ihara, T., 257
Iino, M., 38
Ikonomidou, C., 481
Imperato-McGinley, J., 353
Inglehart, M., 382
Ingvar, M., 401
Insel, T. R., 372
Irving, L., 313
Ishiwata, T., 313
Islam, F., 313

J
Jaber, M., 77, 78
Jackson, M. B., 76
Jacobs, B. L., 76, 153, 155, 293, 414

Masson, F., 283
Matheson, A. J., 207
Mathews, V. P., 503, 504
Matsuda, L. A., 79
Matthes, H. W., 137
Matthies, M., 233
Mauri, M. C., 338
Mavilio, F., 161
Mayer, D. J., 236, 238, 239, 322
Maynert, E. W., 414
McBride, W. J., 149, 402
McCabe, B. F., 204
McCance, R. A., 311
McCann, U. D., 76
McCargar, L. J., 316
McCarley, R. W., 297, 299
McCarthy, M. M., 356, 372
McCarty, R. C., 258, 428, 430
McClelland, J. L., 257
McClintock, M. K., 200
McCloskey, M., 223
McCormick, C. M., 359
McCormick, D. A., 160, 288, 297
McCormick, T. A., 186
McCracken, J. T., 269
McDevitt, R. M., 326
McDonald, J. S., 137
McDonald, J. W., 494
McDonald, R., 404
McElderry, D. H., 303
McEwen, B. S., 33, 318, 325, 421, 425, 426, 427, 429, 430, 499
McFadden, D., 359
McGaugh, J. L., 140, 258
McGehee, D. S., 70
McGlone, M. J., 357
McGue, M., 460
McGuffin, P., 484
McKeever, P. E., 39
McKeown, D. A., 197
McLoughlin, D. M., 500
McNaughton, B. L., 257
Mednick, S. A., 455
Mei, N., 324
Melis, M. R., 368
Melman, A., 369
Meltzer, C., 499
Melvin, L. S., 78
Melzack, R., 236
Mendel, G., 136-137
Mendez, M. F., 223
Mendlewicz, J., 472
Mercer, M. E., 74
Meredith, M., 199
Merikle, P., 253
Merzenich, M. M., 233, 235
Meschler, J. P., 79
Mesholam, R. I., 201
Mesulam, M-M., 70
Metcalfe, J., 498, 499
Meyer, J., 489
Meyer-Bahlburg, H. F., 355
Meyers, J. S., 385
Michael, D. B., 485
Michel, F., 290
Michelson, D., 410, 416, 417, 418, 419, 421, 424, 425, 434, 435, 436
Mignard, M., 215
Mignot, E., 301
Mihic, S. J., 73
Mikulis, D. J., 339, 340
Miller, B., 416
Miller, E. K., 219, 220, 221, 254
Miller, G. A., 252, 385
Miller, I. J., 203

Miller, M. W., 482
Miller, N. E., 25
Milner, A. D., 216, 219, 220, 221, 222, 223
Milner, B., 252, 257
Milner, P., 100, 397
Mink, J. W., 168
Mintun, M. A., 227, 299
Mishkin, M., 225
Missale, C., 77, 78
Mitchell, P. B., 468
Miyashita, Y., 257
Moberg, P. J., 201
Modahl, C., 270, 372
Moeller, F. G., 472
Molle, M., 294
Monahan, J., 429
Moncada, S., 79
Money, J., 355
Mong, J. A., 356
Montague, P. R., 269
Montecucco, C., 70
Montine, T. J., 29
Mooney, P. A., 471
Moore, P. S., 91
Mora, F., 321
Morano, M. I., 412, 414, 417, 419, 421, 426, 431, 435, 465
Mordkoff, J. T., 266
Morgan, C. A., 432
Morgan, M., 363, 372
Morgane, P., 483
Morgenstern, J., 472
Mori, K., 198
Morilak, D. A., 77
Morin, C. M., 301
Morino, P., 74
Morris, J. C., 489, 500, 501
Morris, M. E., 296, 372
Morris, N. M., 364
Morrison, A. R., 15
Moruzzi, G., 293
Muir, J. L., 499
Mukhametov, L. M., 291
Muller, H. J., 221
Muller, R., 231, 493
Muller-Oerlinghausen, B., 468
Munoz, D., 501
Munro, J. F., 327
Munson, R. C., 453
Munte, T. F., 233
Murad, F., 80
Murphy, P. J., 295
Murphy, S. T., 382
Murray, M., 131
Murzi, E., 321
Musen, G., 252, 261
Myers, T., 483

N
Naftolin, F., 351, 357, 358
Nag, S., 499
Nagao, H., 198
Nakanishi, S., 72
Nakao, M., 25
Nalcioglu, O., 504
Namura, I., 33
Narabayashi, H., 167
Narby, S., 29
Nathan, K. I., 416, 465, 468
Nathans, J., 186
Nathanson, M. H., 327
Naya, Y., 257
Needleman, H. L., 18
Neely, J. G., 207
Nehra, A., 369
Neitz, J., 184

Neitz, M., 184
Nelson, K. B., 483, 486
Nelson, R. J., 79
Nemeroff, C. B., 463
Neophytou, S. I., 134
Nestler, E. J., 403, 417
Neugebauer, R., 455
Neumeyer, J. L., 65
Neville, H., 229, 230, 231
Newton, R. P., 466
Ng, G. Y. K., 77, 78
Nguyen, M., 464
Nicholson, L. F. B., 165
Nicolela, M. T., 186
Nicoll, R. A., 107, 271
Nielsen, S., 342
Nigg, J. T., 471
Nisenbaum, L. K., 423
Nishino, S., 301
Nitschke, J. B., 385
Noble, E., 490
Norris, S. L., 25
Novin, D., 332
Novy, M. J., 351
Nowell, P. D., 301
Nussbaum, E., 353
Nutt, D. J., 396, 464, 465

O
Oades, R. D., 457, 458, 459, 460, 470
Obayashi, S., 458
O'Brien, J. T., 504
O'Dell, T. J., 272
O'Doherty, D., 125
O'Dowd, B. F., 77, 78
Ogawa, S., 130, 372
Ohno-Shosaku, T., 107
Oldham, M., 435
Olds, J., 100, 397
Olds, M. E., 397
Olegard, R., 482
Oliet, S. H., 38
Oliva, L., 491
Olney, J. W., 451, 456, 458
Olson, E. J., 302
Olson, H. C., 483
Olson, L., 168
Olson, R. J., 186
Onishi, H., 29
Oostenveld, R., 233
O'Reardon, J. P., 467
O'Reilly, R. C., 257
Oreland, L., 91
Oren, D. A., 304
Ortiz, J., 401
Ortony, A., 379
O'Scalaidhe, S. P., 253
Oscar-Berman, M., 261
Osimani, A., 503
Ossowska, K., 167
Ostrem, J. L., 455
Overman, W. H., 13, 14
Ozates, M., 485

P
Packard, M. G., 140
Pakula, I. S., 471
Palmblad, J., 416
Palmer, R. M., 79
Palmer, S. E., 216
Palmer, T. D., 494
Panksepp, J., 270, 334, 378, 386
Pant, K. C., 340
Pantev, C., 233, 235
Paolucci, E., 161
Papa, S. M., 167

Papez, J. W., 384
Pare, D., 290, 296
Parent, J. M., 492, 494
Paris, J., 471
Park, S., 452
Parkin, A. J., 499
Parry, B. L., 466
Pasanen, E. G., 359
Pascual-Leone, A., 235, 467
Passant, U., 502, 503
Pasternak, G. W., 75
Pattatucci, A. M., 358
Paul, S. M., 72, 73, 106, 395
Pauls, D. L., 164
Paus, T., 481
Pavlov, I., 259, 298, 328
Pederson, C. L., 126
Peinado, A., 42
Pellizzari, R., 70
Penfield, W., 5, 10, 227
Pennybacker, J. B., 148
Peoples, L. L., 126
Pernier, J., 221
Pernow, B., 464
Peroutka, S. J., 464
Pert, C., 75
Pertwee, R. G., 78
Peskind, E. R., 500
Peters, R., 497
Petersen, S. E., 227, 229, 266
Petrini, B., 416
Petty, F., 429, 464, 467
Pevet, P., 295, 296
Pfaff, D., 363, 372
Pfaus, J. G., 372
Pfefferbaum, A., 483
Pfrieger, F. W., 34, 38
Phelps, E. A., 388
Phelps, J. A., 455, 461
Pickar, D., 453
Piet, R., 38
Pietrini, P., 259
Pillard, R. C., 358
Pillon, B., 281
Pinel, J. P., 17
Placidi, G. P., 77
Plaitakis, A., 162
Plata-Salaman, C. R., 242
Plato, 5, 11
Pliszka, S. R., 269
Ploghaus, A., 239
Plomin, R., 28
Poggio, T., 219
Pohl, R., 394
Poizner, H., 231
Poland, R. E., 498
Polivy, J., 336
Pollitt, E., 483
Poo, M., 65
Popper, K., 11
Poppitt, S. D., 326
Porkka-Heiskanen, T., 295
Porsolt, R. D., 76
Posner, M. I., 227, 251, 254, 256, 266
Post, R. M., 125, 467
Postle, B. R., 256
Poulain, D. A., 38
Prabhakaran, V., 241
Prange, T., 468
Prasad, A. S., 340
Prentice, A. M., 326
Prescott, C. A., 136
Preti, G., 197, 200
Price, D. D., 239
Price, D. J., 62, 499
Prichep, L., 504

Subject Index

cell membrane, 27
cell migration, 480–481
cell proliferation, 480
cells
  parts of, 28
  types of, 30
centenarians, 498
central canal, 105
central deafness, 193
central executive system, 255–256
central nervous system, 24,
  90–93, 115
    eating behavior and, 320–324,
      326–328
    emotional pathways in,
      384–387
    protection of, 90–91
    spinal cord and, 91–93
    stress and, 411–415
    See also brain
central sulcus, 102
cerebellar cortex, 159
cerebellum, 96
  alcohol impairment of, 96, 99
  effects of damage to, 168, 229
  extrapyramidal motor system
    and, 158–159
  nondeclarative memory and,
    259
  organization of, 159
  structure of, 98
cerebral cortex, 101–102
  emotions and, 385–386
cerebral hemispheres, 102,
  103–104, 385–386
cerebral laceration, 486–487
cerebral palsy, 164, 483
cerebrospinal fluid, 90, 104
cerebrovascular accident, 489
cerebrum, 98, 101–104
  anatomical views of, 101, 102
  hemispheres of, 102, 103–104
  lobes of, 102, 103
  perceptual processes and,
    214–215, 243–244
cervical region, 92
C–fibers, 195, 234
c–fos, 134, 412
chemical stimuli, 174
chemical substances
  acetylcholine receptors and,
    70–71
  agonist vs. antagonist, 66
  brain studies using, 133–135,
    142
  glutamate receptors and, 72
  See also drugs
chemical synapses, 40–41
chemoreceptors, 174, 194
Chinese medicine, 4, 5
cholecystokinin (CCK), 67, 74,
  330
cholinergic hypothesis of depression, 464
choreas, 164
choroid plexus, 90, 104
chromatography, 134
chromosomes, 28
chronic fatigue syndrome, 436
chronic stress, 422–431, 438
  behavior and, 426, 427–430
  brain and, 425–427
  failure of extinction and, 429
  fear conditioning and,
    428–429
  habituation and, 423–424,
    427–428

HPA axis and, 424–425, 426
learned helplessness and, 429,
  430
locus coeruleus and, 423–424,
  426
memory impairment and, 430
seizures and, 429–430
sensitization and, 423–424,
  428
chronic stressor, 422
ciliary muscles, 178
circadian rhythm, 294
  resetting of, 295, 296
  sleep disorders associated
    with, 303–304
classical conditioning
  bed–wetting treatments and,
    303
  implicit learning and,
    273–274
  nondeclarative memory and,
    259–260
classical neurotransmitters, 59, 66
clinical neuropsychologists, 13
cloacal exstrophy, 349
Clock gene, 296
clonidine, 77
clonus, 164
Clostridium bacterium, 70
cocaine, 82
coccygeal region, 92
cochlea, 189
cochlear duct, 189
cochlear implants, 192
cochlear nucleus, 190
codeine, 75
cognitive behavioral therapy, 301
cognitive–evaluative dimension of
  pain, 239
cognitive neuroscience, 12
cognitive processes, 248–277
  attention, 263–270
  explicit learning, 271–273
  frontal lobe and, 250–251,
    275
  implicit learning, 273–274
  memory, 252–263
cognitive stressors, 414–415
cold–blooded animals, 310
color blindness, 184
color perception, 218
color vision, 184–185
coma, 97, 283
communication, intracellular, 42
complex cells, 219
complex sounds, 225–226
comprehension of speech, 226
computational neuroscience, 13
computed tomography (CT)
  scans, 127, 128, 504
  See also brain–imaging studies
concentration gradient, 44
concordance rate, 136
concordant twins, 453
concurrent discrimination, 13–15
concussion, 486
conditioned fear, 259–260
conditioned response (CR), 259
conditioned stimulus (CS), 259
conduction, 312
conduction aphasia, 228–229
conductive hearing loss, 191, 193
cones, 179–180, 184
congenital adrenal hyperplasia,
  354
congestive dysmenorrhea, 365
consciousness, 280–287, 305

brain mechanisms of,
  292–298, 305
characteristics of, 280
disorders of, 281–284
electrophysiology of, 287–288
research on, 285–286
sleep and, 287–304
consolidation, 252
Continuous Performance Test,
  268, 459
control subjects, 139
contusion, 486
cornea, 178, 185
corpus callosum, 102, 285, 357
corpus luteum, 362
cortex, 7
corticosterone, 417
corticostriatal system, 259
corticotropic releasing hormone
  (CRH), 417–421, 435–436
cortisol, 258, 417
counterirritation, 238
cranial nerves, 32, 108, 109–110
craniosacral system, 113
craniotomy, 4
Creutzfeldt–Jakob dementia, 488
cribiform plate, 198
cristae, 205
critical period, 492–493
crossbridges, 147
crossed extensor reflex, 154–155,
  156
crossover procedure, 139
cryoprobe, 122
CT scans. See computed tomography (CT) scans
cupola, 205
curare, 70, 71
cycles, 174
cycles per second, 174
cyclic GMP, 79
cyclic guanine monophosphate
  (cGMP), 369
cytoarchitectonic typing, 214
cytochrome oxidase, 218
cytoplasm, 27
cytoplasmic inclusions, 502
cytoskeleton, 29
cytotoxic effect, 425

dark adaptation, 180
deafness, 191–193
decibels (dB), 175, 188
declarative memory, 256–259
decussation, 157
defecation reflex, 155
defensive reactions, 388, 392
delayed–sleep–phase syndrome,
  303
delta waves, 288
dementia, 445
dementia praecox, 447
dementia pugilistica, 446, 487
demerol, 75
dendrites, 29–30
dendritic branching, 496
dendritic spines, 29
dendrodendritic synapse, 40, 41
denervation hypersensitivity, 497
dependence, 400
dependent personality disorder,
  470
depersonalization, 284
depolarization, 44–45
depression, 398
  biological explanations of,
    462–463

drugs for treating, 82–83
hormonal explanations of,
  465–466
major depressive disorder,
  435–436
neurotransmitter–based explanations of, 463–465
treatment of, 82–83, 467
depth perception, 220
dermatomes, 111, 112
desipramine, 83, 396
destructive surgical treatments,
  167
desynchronized brain waves, 288
deviant sexual behavior, 371, 374
dexamethasone, 421
dexamethasone suppression test
  (DST), 421, 472
dextroamphetamine, 269
diabetes, 186–187
diabetes mellitus, 335
Diagnostic and Statistical Manual of
  Mental Disorders (DSM–IV),
  393, 432, 444, 447, 462, 470
diathesis–stress model of schizophrenia, 452
dichorionic monozygotic twins,
  460–461
dichromats, 184
diencephalon, 97, 98–99
diet
  macronutrients and, 318–319
  micronutrients and, 319
  serotonin and, 69
  See also food intake
digestive tract, 328
dihydrotestosterone, 351–352
discordant twins, 453
disease
  brain damage caused by,
    487–490
  brain development and, 483
disequilibrium, 168
dishabituation, 265
disorders
  aggressive, 392–393
  aging brain, 499–503
  anxiety, 393–396
  attentional, 267–270
  auditory, 191–193
  bipolar, 468–469
  consciousness, 281–284
  depressive, 462–467
  eating, 332–340
  memory, 261–262
  mood, 462–469
  movement, 161–169, 170
  olfactory, 200–201
  personality, 469–474
  positive emotion, 398–399
  psychotic, 444–446
  schizophrenia, 446–461
  sexual, 365–366, 369–370
  sleep, 300–304
  somatosensory, 196
  stress–related, 431–437
  taste, 203–204
  temperature regulation,
    315–316
  vestibular, 206–207
  visual, 185–187, 221–224
dissociative states, 284
distal stimulus, 178
Diving Bell and the Butterfly, The
  (Bauby), 284
dizygotic twins, 136
dizziness, 207

jargon aphasia, 228
jet lag, 303
joints, 149

Kallman's syndrome, 200
Kanizsa square, 221
K–complexes, 288
Kennard effect, 492, 496
kidneys, 342
kinesthesia, 194
Klein–Levin syndrome, 335
Klinefelter's syndrome, 352
Kluver–Bucy syndrome, 388
knockout model, 137
knockout mutants, 137
Korsakoff's syndrome, 490, 491
Krause endbulbs, 194, 195

L cones, 184
labioscrotal swellings, 351
labyrinth system, 204
language, 226
    brain–imaging studies of,
        229–231
    lateralization of functions for,
        231–232
    See also speech processing
lateral coordinate, 121
lateral geniculate nucleus (LGN),
    182, 216, 217
lateral hemiretina, 182
lateral hypothalamus, 320, 322
lateral inhibition, 181
lateralization of language
    functions, 231–232
lateral preoptic area, 313, 342
lateral sulcus, 102
lateral ventricles, 104
Law of Equipotentiality, 10
Law of Mass Action, 10
L–dopa, 167
learned helplessness, 429, 430
learning, 271–274, 276
    explicit, 271–273
    implicit, 271, 273–274
left–brain consciousness, 285
lemniscal pathway, 195–196
lens, 178, 183, 186
leptin, 323, 331, 336
lesioning, 120–124, 141
    early studies with, 120–121
    lateral hypothalamus,
        320–321
    subcortical, 121–124
Lewy's bodies, 501, 502
libido, 366
ligand–gated ion channel, 57, 61
ligand–gated ion channel
    receptors, 62
ligands, 57
light
    biological clock and, 295–296
    characteristics of, 174, 175
limbic system, 100, 384–385, 414
linkage analysis, 136
lipofuscin, 499
lipogenic substances, 335
lipostatic theory, 323
Lissauer's tract, 195
lithium, 468
liver, 331–332
LM cones, 184
localization of sound, 190–191
localization theory, 7
local neurons, 31
locked–in syndrome, 283–284
locus coeruleus, 105

emotions and, 384
sleep and consciousness and,
    293–294
stress response and, 413–414,
    417, 419, 423–424
long–term memory, 252, 256–261
    declarative memory, 256–259
    disorders of, 256–257,
        261–262
    nondeclarative memory, 256,
        259–261
long–term potentiation (LTP),
    271–273
long–wavelength light, 174
lordosis, 363, 364
loss of psychic self–activation,
    281–282
loudness, 175, 188
loudness difference, 191
Lou Gehrig's disease, 162
LSD (drug), 76
lumbar region, 92
luteinizing hormone (LH),
    361–362
lyrics, 232

M cones, 184
macronutrients, 318–319
macrophages, 35, 416
macula, 205
macula lutea, 186
macular degeneration, 186
magnetic resonance imaging
    (MRI), 130
    anorexia studies, 339–340
    brain damage studies, 504
    schizophrenia studies, 453
    stress studies, 425
    See also brain–imaging studies
magnetoencephalography
    (MEG), 127–128
magnocellular layers, 216
major depressive disorder,
    462–467
    biological explanations of,
        462–463, 465
    DSM–IV criteria for, 462
    hormonal explanations of,
        465–466
    neurotransmitter–based
        explanations of, 463–465
    stress and, 435–436
    treatment of, 467
male sexual behavior, 366–370
    disorders of, 369–370
    mating behavior and, 366–368
    regulation of, 368–369,
        371–372, 374
malleus, 189
malnutrition
    brain damage caused by, 491
    brain development and, 483
mania, 398
manic–depressive disorder. *See*
    bipolar disorder
MAO inhibitors, 82, 463
marijuana, 79, 400, 401
mating, 361
MDMA (drug), 76
mechanical stimuli, 174
mechanoreceptors, 174, 194
medial coordinate, 121
medial forebrain bundle, 386, 397
medial geniculate nucleus, 190
medial lemniscus, 195–196
medial prefrontal cortex, 250
medial preoptic area, 313, 368

medications
    anticholinergic, 167
    antidepressant, 82–83, 238,
        434–435, 467
    dopaminergic, 167
    experimental testing of, 139
    pain, 238
    sleep, 301
    See also drugs
medulla, 94–95
MEG imaging technique,
    127–128
Meissner's corpuscles, 194
melatonin, 295, 296
melatonin dysfunction, 466
melody, 232
memory, 252–263, 275
    declarative, 256–259
    disorders of, 261–262
    episodic, 257–258
    long–term, 252, 256–261
    nondeclarative, 259–261
    semantic, 257–258
    short–term, 252
    stress and, 430
    working, 252–256
memory impairment, 430
Meniere's disease, 207
meninges, 90, 91
meningitis, 91, 445, 487
menopausal dysregulation,
    315–316
menopause, 316, 365
menstruation, 362
mental retardation, 28
Merkel's disks, 194
mesencephalon, 94, 96–97
mesocortical system, 106
mesolimbic dopamine pathway,
    397
mesolimbic system, 106
mesoprefrontal cortex, 427
metabotropic receptors, 65
metacognition, 280
metastatic tumors, 39
methyl–phenyl–tetrahydropyridene
    (MPTP), 165–166
Metropolitan Life Insurance
    Company, height and weight
    charts, 333
microdialysis, 131–132, 412
microelectrodes, 126–127
microglia, 34, 38
micronutrients, 318, 319
microspectrophotometer, 184
microvilli, 176, 203
midbrain, 93, 94, 95, 96–97
middle ear, 188–189
middle ear deafness, 191
middle temporal cortex, 220
mind, location of, 10–11
    See also brain
minerals, 319
Minnesota Multiphasic Personality
    Inventory (MMPI), 505
mitochondria, 29
modified dopamine hypothesis of
    schizophrenia, 450
modulatory neuron, 274
monism, 11
monoamine hypothesis of
    depression, 463
monoamine neurotransmitters,
    68, 75–78
    depression and, 463
    dopamine, 77–78
    norepinephrine, 77

reuptake of, 82–83
    serotonin, 76
monoamine oxidase (MAO), 82
monochorionic monozygotic
    twins, 460–461
monochromats, 184
monocular information, 217
monogenic model, 136–137
monopolar neurons, 31
monosodium glutamate (MSG),
    72
monozygotic twins, 136
mood disorders, 462–469,
    475–476
    bipolar disorder, 468–469
    major depressive disorder,
        462–467
morphemes, 226
morphine, 75, 323
motion perception, 219–220
motion sickness, 206
motivated behaviors, 308–347
    eating disorders and, 332–340
    food intake and, 318–332
    temperature regulation and,
        310–317
    water intake and, 340–344
motivational–affective dimension
    of pain, 239
motor cortex, 103, 157, 250
    pyramidal motor system and,
        157–158
    topographical organization
        of, 9
motor neurons, 31
    alpha and gamma, 151
    damage to, 162
motor pool, 162
motor system
    extrapyramidal, 157, 158–161
    pyramidal, 157–158
motor units, 148
movement, 144–171
    basal ganglia and, 160–161,
        164–168
    brain and, 157–161, 169–170
    cerebellum and, 158–159, 168
    disorders of, 161–169, 170
    extrapyramidal motor system
        and, 157, 158–161, 164
    motor neurons and, 151, 162
    muscle structure/function
        and, 147–150, 169
    pyramidal motor system and,
        157–158, 163
    reflexes and, 151–156
    spinal control of, 150–156,
        169
MRI. *See* magnetic resonance
    imaging
Mullerian ducts, 351
Mullerian inhibiting substance,
    351
multifactorial model, 137, 460
multiple personality disorder, 284
multiple sclerosis, 36
multipolar neurons, 31
mu–opioid receptor, 137
muscarine, 71
muscarinic receptors, 62–63, 65,
    70, 71, 107
muscle fibers, 147
muscle filaments, 147, 148
muscles, 147–150
    contraction of, 147–148,
        149–150
    damage to, 161–162

skeletal, 24, 148–150
smooth, 25, 108, 149
striated, 24, 108
structure and function of, 147–150, 169
types of, 148–149
muscle spindles, 152
muscle tone, 148
muscular dystrophy, 161
music perception, 232–233
myasthenia gravis, 161
myelin, 31, 35–36
myelinated axons, 36, 48–49, 481
myopia, 186
myosin, 147

naloxone, 323
narcissistic personality disorder, 470
narcolepsy, 291, 301–302
narcotics, 75
nasal hemiretina, 182
natural selection, 16–17
nearsightedness, 186
negative afterimage, 185
negative emotions, 378–379, 387–396, 405–406
amygdala and, 387–389
disorders associated with, 392–396
fear and anxiety, 391–392, 393–396
rage and aggression, 389–391, 392–393
negative feedback loop, 361, 419, 424–425
negative reinforcer, 403
negative resting potential, 43
negative symptoms of schizophrenia, 447
neospinothalamic tract, 195
nerve deafness, 192
nerve growth factor (NGF), 481, 495
nerves, 92
cranial, 108, 109–110
spinal, 108, 110–112
nervous system, 24–27, 51, 88–117
central, 24, 90–93
peripheral, 24–27, 108–115
scar tissue in, 35
See also brain
neural tube, 35, 480
neuritic plaques, 500
neuroanatomists, 297
neuroblastoma, 114
neurofibrillary tangles, 500–501
neurogenesis, 494
neurohormones, 67
neuroleptics, 448
neuromedin, 330
neuromelanin, 499
neuromodulators, 66
neuromuscular junction, 147, 148
neuronal stem cells, 198, 494
neuronavigation, 123
Neuron Doctrine, 27
neurons, 12, 27, 51
action potential of, 45–49
classification of, 31–32
depolarization of, 44–45
function of, 40–50, 51–52
information transmission in, 42–49
integrative action of, 154
neurotransmitter associations with, 108

nourishment provided for, 34
regrowth of, 494–495
resting potential of, 42–46
role of glial cells in, 33–39
special features of, 32–33
structure of, 27–31
thermosensitive, 313–314
neuropeptides, 74, 323–324
neuropeptide Y, 323, 336
neuropsychological testing, 504–505
neuropsychology, 13
neuroscience, 12
neurotoxins, 46, 123, 320
neurotransmitters, 29, 56, 66–84
acetylcholine, 61, 62, 69–71
addictive behavior and, 401–402
aggressive behavior and, 390–391
amino acids, 71–73
anandamide, 78–79
antidepressants and, 82–83
brain distribution of, 105–108
classical, 59, 66
classifying, 67–68
depression and, 463–465
eating behavior and, 323, 324, 329–331
families of, 67
human behavior and, 69–80
monoamine, 75–78
neurons associated with, 108
nitric oxide, 79–80
nonopiate, 237
peptide, 74–75
receptors associated with, 65
removing from the synapse, 80–84, 85
storage and release of, 59
neurotrophins, 481
new mammalian brain, 98
nicotine, 62, 71, 401
nicotinic receptors, 62, 63, 70, 71, 107
night blindness, 186
nightmare, 303
night terror, 303
nigrostriatal system, 106
nitric oxide, 68, 79–80, 272, 369
NMDA receptor hypofunction hypothesis, 451
NMDA receptors, 72, 271–272, 451
nocturnal animals, 299
nocturnal enuresis, 302–303
nodes of Ranvier, 35
nominal aphasia, 227
nondeclarative memory, 256, 259–261
nondestructive surgical treatments, 167
nongated ion channels, 57, 61
nonhomeostatic drinking, 343–344
noninfectious diseases, 488–490
non–NMDA receptors, 72
nonopiate analgesics, 238
nonopiate transmitters, 237
nonseasonal breeders, 366, 368
nonshivering thermogenesis, 311
norepinephrine, 68, 77
ADHD and, 269
aggressive behavior and, 390, 393
arousal from sleep and, 293–294

brain pathways for, 105, 106
chronic stress and, 423–424
depression and, 463
dissociative states and, 284
drugs associated with, 77
nuclear bag, 152
nucleic acids, 28
nucleus (nuclei)
cell, 28
neuronal cluster, 32, 92, 99
nucleus accumbens, 132, 160, 384, 397
nucleus basalis, 499
nucleus of the solitary tract
eating behavior and, 324, 327
internal stressors and, 412, 413
taste system and, 203
vestibular system and, 206
nutrients, 318–319
nystagmus, 206

obesity, 327
behavioral factors and, 336–337
genetic factors and, 336
hormonal factors and, 334–336
producing in the laboratory, 337
ob gene, 336
object identification, 254, 255
object location, 220
object recognition, 220
object reversal, 13–14
obsessive–compulsive disorder, 394–395, 470
occipital lobe, 102, 103, 183
oculovestibular reflexes, 206
odorants, 197
odors, 175, 197
offset of eating, 326–332
central offset mechanisms, 327–328
peripheral offset mechanisms, 328–332
old mammalian brain, 98
olfaction, 197
olfactory bulb, 198, 384–385
olfactory cortex, 198
olfactory epithelium, 197
olfactory mucosa, 197
olfactory nerve, 109, 198
olfactory processing, 241, 245
olfactory receptors, 175
olfactory system, 197–201, 209
accessory, 199–200
anatomy and function of, 197–199
disorders of, 200–201
nature of odors and, 197
pathway to the brain in, 198–199
oligodendrocytes, 34, 35–36
omnivores, 318
onset of eating, 320–326
central onset mechanisms, 320–324
peripheral onset mechanisms, 324–326
ophthalmoscope, 179
opiates, 75, 238
opioid receptors, 74–75
opioids, 368
opium, 75
Opponent–Process Theory, 184–185

optic axis, 179
optic chiasm, 182
optic disk, 182
optic nerve, 109, 182
optic tract, 182
oral contraceptives, 363
orbitofrontal cortex, 321, 322
orbitofrontal prefrontal cortex, 241, 250
orexins, 302, 323–324
organelles, 27–28
organic disorders, 444
organizational effects, 351
orienting response, 154, 264–265
osmoreceptors, 342
osmotic thirst, 341–342
ossicles, 189
outer ear, 188
outer ear deafness, 191
outer hair cells, 189, 190
ova, 360
oval window, 189
ovarian cycle, 361, 363
ovarian hormones, 325–326, 335
ovaries, 350–351
ovulation, 362, 364
oxytocin, 372, 419

Pacinian corpuscles, 194
pain, 236–240
cortical processing of, 239–240
Gate–Control Theory of, 236–237
treatments for, 237–239
painful stressors, 413
pain receptors, 6, 196
paired–image subtraction method, 129
paleospinothalamic tract, 195
pallidotomy, 167
panic disorder, 394
Papez circuit, 384
papillae, 203
parabiotic rats, 329, 330
paradoxical sleep, 290
parahippocampal place area, 219
paralysis
spinal cord injury and, 162–163
transient flaccid, 163
paranoid personality disorder, 470, 471
paraphasia, 228
paraphilia, 371
paraplegia, 162
parasympathetic nervous system, 25, 108, 113–114
distribution of, 113
effects of, 26, 114
paraventricular nucleus
homeostatic regulation and, 321, 322
stress response and, 411, 412, 417–418, 419
paraventricular system, 321–322
parenting behavior, 360
parietal lobe, 102, 103
Parkinson's dementia, 501, 502
Parkinson's disease, 165–168, 501
cause of, 165–166
symptoms of, 165
treatment for, 167–168
parvocellular layers, 216
passive theory of sleep, 293, 298
Pavlovian conditioning, 259–260
pedophilia, 371

wavelength, 174
waves, 174–175
    light, 174
    sound, 175, 187–188
weight regulation
    activity and, 317
    food intake and, 316–317
Wernicke–Korsakoff's syndrome,
    491
Wernicke's area, 228, 229–230,
    254
"What" system

for auditory processing, 225
for somatosensory processing,
    235
for visual processing, 216,
    218–219
"Where" system
for auditory processing, 225
for somatosensory processing,
    235
for visual processing, 216,
    219–220
white matter, 31

Wisconsin Card Sorting (WCS)
    Test, 454, 455
withdrawal reflex, 151
withdrawal symptoms, 400, 401
Wolffian ducts, 351
word deafness, 228
working memory, 252–256
    central executive system and,
        255–256
    intelligence and, 253
    object identification and, 254,
        255

spatial location and, 254, 255
verbal information and,
    254–255

Yakovlev circuit, 384
Y chromosome, 350
yohimbine, 77, 284, 432–434
Young–Helmholtz Theory, 184

zeitgeber, 295